HITCHCOCK'S CLASSICS. THE BEST OF OBSESSION, FEAR, AND MURDER.

All the finest qualities movies have to offer. Eleven Alfred Hitchcock classics, each a rare cinematic masterpiece of mystery, thrills and romance. And they're all ready for you, exclusively on MCA Home Video.

Don't keep yourself in suspense any longer. See your favorite video dealer and make these Hitchcock greats a part of your permanent collection. Take Hitchcock home. If you dare.

D1596768

MCA HOME VIDEO

70 Universal City Plaza
Universal City, CA 91608

Preface

The Video Tape & Disc Guide to Home Entertainment, 6th Edition, is designed to provide home viewers with detailed information on more than 7,000 video programs available to them. Most of the titles included herein are easily available from your local video retailer; if he doesn't have them in stock, he may be able to special order them. Other tapes described in this *Guide* are more generally available directly by mail order from the program sources listed.

Special features included in this edition are the Closed-Captioned Index, Cast Index and Video Index. The Closed-Captioned Index is a complete, up-to-date listing of all videocassettes and discs which have been closed-captioned for the hearing impaired. The Cast Index is designed to help you locate the video performances of more than 280 favorite stars and directors. The Videodisc Index is a guide to programs available on both the laser optical (LV) and capacitance electronic disc (CED) formats.

This publication has been compiled from catalogs, supplementary lists and additional information provided by the video program sources. The wholesalers or distributors do not pay to have their programs listed, nor does the publisher pay them for information about their titles. The publisher is not responsible for any program changes, withdrawals, or additions, or for the listing of any unauthorized distribution of any title.

Our editorial staff has sought to provide you, the home video viewer, with the most comprehensive, up-to-date, useful guide to home video available.

Table of Contents

Acknowledgements

This guide is an original work compiled by the staff of The National Video Clearinghouse, Inc. Those who have contributed to its creation include: George Hatch, Chairman of the Board; Harvey Seslowsky, President; Robert M. Reed, Vice President; Liz Doris, Editor; David J. Weiner, Director of Information and Data Services; Gregory P. Fagan, Mary S. Bean and Robin Ames, Editorial Coordinators; Jeffrey M. Kerwin and Christine LaMarca, Editorial Assistants; Arnold Menis, Director of Marketing; Barbara Levine, Assistant Sales Manager; Christine Schmidt, Sales Coordinator; Costas Mendonis, Graphic Designer; Meg Plastino and Debbie Freiberg, Editorial Secretaries.

Use Guide

The Video Tape & Disc Guide to Home Entertainment, 6th Edition, is divided into six major sections: (1) Program Listings; (2) Subject Category Index; (3) Videodisc Index; (4) Closed Captioned Index; (5) Cast Index; and (6) Video Program Sources Index. A description of each section is given below.

(1) PROGRAM LISTINGS

The main body of this book consists of more than 7,000 program listings. Each entry may contain up to 19 different pieces of information, most of which is supplied by the distributor, or "video program source." Standard film and video reference materials are utilized to obtain pertinent information when not supplied by the distributor. Full explanations of the information included are given below; consult the Key for illustrated examples.

ALPHABETIZATION

Each program is listed alphabetically. "A," "an" and "the" and their foreign counterparts are not considered in alphabetization.

RELEASE DATE

"Release date" is defined as the year in which the film or program was initially made available for public viewing.

SUBJECT CATEGORY

Each title has been assigned a specific subject heading, i.e.,"Comedy," "Music Video," etc. This descriptive category will identify the contents of the program. In some entries, a second category has also been assigned.

ACCESSION NUMBER

Each title is assigned an accession number. The number is simply an identifying code for the publisher and has no other meaning.

RUNNING TIMES

The running time of a program is listed as "88 mins." When edited or different versions of a program are available, they are listed separately with the appropriate running times.

COLOR AND BLACK AND WHITE

Each title listing indicates whether the program is available in color (C) or black and white (B/W).

FORMAT AVAILABILITY

Each entry includes the video formats available for that particular program. The most common home video formats are Beta and VHS, although others are listed, when available. Laser optical videodisc (LV) and capacitance electronic disc (CED) availabilities are also included.

TELEVISION STANDARDS

All programs listed in this *Guide* are available on the U.S. television standard (NTSC).

PROGRAMS FOR THE HEARING IMPAIRED

When a program has been captioned or signed for the hearing impaired, the entry includes the notation "Open Captioned," "Closed Captioned" or "Signed" below the accession number.

CAST/STARS/HOSTS/GUESTS

The major stars or other members of the cast of dramatic television programs or movies are listed. In some instances, the director is listed as well. For instructional, talk show and documentary programs, the host, narrator or instructor is given, when known.

SERIES: NUMBER OF PROGRAMS

The number of programs in a generic series is listed as "11 pgms." The individual titles of each program within the series are listed in the sequence in which they are given by the distributor. When the distributor will make programs available either as a series or individually, the individual programs may also be listed in the main text.

PROGRAM DESCRIPTION

The narrative program descriptions are designed to briefly identify the major plot, subject, or theme of the program.

AWARDS

The major awards and the year of the award are listed in each entry. Unless there is an obvious abbreviation for well-known awards, the awards are spelled out. Nominations are normally not listed.

ANCILLARY MATERIALS

Brochures, study guides, and other printed and audio materials are occasionally available from the distributor to aid in the use of the program. This is noted by the phrase "AM Available."

AUDIENCE RATING

For theatrical films, the standard Motion Picture Association of America ratings are listed according to the MPAA Classification and Rating Program.

FOREIGN LANGUAGE

Virtually all titles found in this publication are available in English. Some foreign films have retained their original foreign language soundtrack; other English-language films have been dubbed into foreign languages. The availability of a foreign language version is indicated according to the following codes:

EL	English	JA	Japanese
AF	Afrikaans	LA	Latin
AB	Arabic	LI	Lithuanian
BE	Belgian	NE	Nepalese
CH	Chinese	NO	Norwegian
CZ	Czech	PO	Polish
DA	Danish	PR	Portuguese
DU	Dutch	RU	Russian
EG	Egyptian	SE	Serbo-Croatian
FI	Finnish	SP	Spanish
FL	Flemish	SA	Swahili
FR	French	SW	Swedish
GE	German	TH	Thai
GR	Greek	TU	Turkish
HE	Hebrew	WE	Welsh
IT	Italian		

When EL is not given along with a foreign language code, the program is not available in English.

SILENT/DUBBED/SUBTITLES

Silent films or those with dubbing or different language soundtracks are noted in the program descriptions. Similarly, a program with subtitles is so indicated at the end of the program description.

ORIGINAL PRODUCER

The original producer (studio, company, and/or individual person) is listed in each entry. When the actual producer cannot be determined, but the country of origin (other than the U.S.) is known, that information will be listed.

VIDEO PROGRAM SOURCES

The video program source, also known as the wholesaler or distributor, appears to the right of the original producer in the listing. More than one source will be listed when the program is legitimately available from more than one wholesaler. This normally occurs when the program is in the public domain, or when it is available from one source on cassette and from another on disc. When multiple sources are listed, the format and acquisition availabilities apply to the first source. Most of the alternate sources will make the program available in Beta and VHS formats; special notations for those companies offering videodisc formats will be found in the Video Program Sources Index at the back of this book.

ACQUISITION AVAILABILITY

Video programs may be acquired in several ways. Full explanations of the information included are given; consult the Key for illustrated examples.

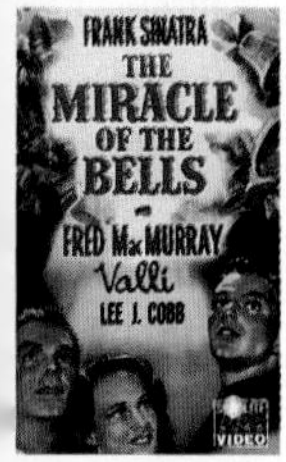

A VALUE BONANZA

Spotlite Home Video brings you an exciting bonanza of great prices...great values...and great titles!

You get the finest film classics at outstanding prices...

classics that should be in every video library!

You'll delight at the incredible values you'll get

when you cash in on the fantastic value bonanza...

only from Spotlite Home Video.

P.O.P HOTLINE—(213) 306-4040 x212

SPOTLITE VIDEO

A DIVISION OF REPUBLIC PICTURES CORP. 12636 Beatrice St. P.O. Box 66930 Los Angeles, CA 90066-0930 (213) 306-4040

(2) SUBJECT CATEGORY INDEX

Each title in *The Video Tape & Disc Guide to Home Entertainment, 6th Edition* has been assigned a subject category. A complete list of all subjects and titles within them appears after the Program Listings. When a program is assigned two different subjects, that title is indexed under both. This index is designed to help the reader quickly locate programs in his area of interest, be it drama, gardening, football or any of 400 other subjects.

(3) VIDEODISC INDEX

The Videodisc Index is a compilation of all programs available on LV and CED videodisc formats at the time of publication. Titles are listed alphabetically under the Laser Optical Videodisc and Capacitance Electronic Disc headings. For complete information on each title, see entries in the Program Listings.

(4) CLOSED CAPTIONED INDEX

The Closed Captioned Index is a listing of cassettes and discs which are closed captioned. Full information on each title can be found in the Program Listings.

(5) CAST INDEX

We have compiled videographies of selected performers and directors. This cast listing is by no means complete, since it would be impossible to list every performer in every movie available on video; however, more than 280 entertainers have been included.

(6)VIDEO PROGRAM SOURCES INDEX

The full corporate name, address and telephone number(s) for each video program source whose entries appear in *The Guide* are listed alphabetically in the Video Program Sources Index at the back of this book. Contact the individual program sources for further information about their titles.

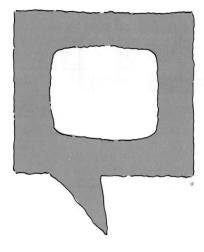

New Releases

As we go to press, several companies listed in this *Guide* have announced the release of new programs. All titles listed below are available on Beta and VHS videocassettes only, unless otherwise noted. A notation for closed-captioned titles *(cc)* appears where applicable.

ALL AMERICAN VIDEO
The Dirty Seven
Invaders of the Lost Gold
Ninja vs. the Shaolin
School of Death

AMERICAN SPORTS NETWORK
1984 Mr. & Mrs. America Bodybuilding Championships
1985 Mr. & Mrs. America Bodybuilding Championships
1982 Mr. Olympia Bodybuilding Championships
1983 Mr. Olympia Bodybuilding Championships
1984 Mr. Olympia Bodybuilding Championships
1985 Mr. Olympia Bodybuilding Championships
1985 National Bodybuilding Championships

CBS/FOX VIDEO
The Compleat Al
Faerie Tale Theatre:
The Dancing Princesses *(cc)*
The Princess Who Had Never Laughed *(cc)*
The House on Skull Mountain *(cc)*
Hush ... Hush, Sweet Charlotte *(cc)*
The Legend of Hell House *(cc)*
1918 *(cc)*
Porky's Revenge

CHILDREN'S VIDEO LIBRARY
Bible Stories—Tales From the Old Testament
It's Your Birthday Party! with Rainbow Brite and Friends

CONTINENTAL VIDEO
Cathy's Curse
Cinema Kid Volume I
Cinema Kid Volume II
Deadly Rivals
Female Trouble
Johnny Cash—Live in London
Women of Iron

FAMILY HOME ENTERTAINMENT
G.I Joe: Cobra's Creatures
G.I Joe: Cobra Stops the World
G.I Joe: Countdown for Zartran
G.I Joe: Red Rocket's Glare
G.I Joe: Satellite Down
The Transformers: Divide and Conquer
The Transformers: Fire in the Sky
The Transformers: Roll for It
The Transformers: S.O.S. Dinobots
The Transformers: Transport to Oblivion
The Raft Adventures of Huck and Jim
Witch's Night Out

KEY VIDEO
Finders Keepers
Hot Dog ... The Movie!
The Night They Raided Minsky's
What Do You Say to a Naked Lady?
The World of Henry Orient

MAGNUM ENTERTAINMENT
Bummer
Dr. Jekyll's Dungeon of Death
Dr. Tarr's Torture Dungeon
The Legend of Sleepy Hollow
The Night After Halloween
Poor White Trash II
The Reincarnate
The Rogue
Score
Speeding Up Time

MGM/UA HOME VIDEO
The Aviator
Baby Love
Equus
Grace Quigley
Knute Rockne—All American
Mrs. Soffel

MONTEREY HOME VIDEO
And Hope to Die
Creation of the Humanoids
The Day and the Hour

MOVIE BUFF VIDEO
Becky Sharp
The Black Raven
Dreams That Money Can Buy
Escapade
Ghidrah, The 3-Headed Monster
The Great Flamarion
Johnny One-Eye
The Powers Girl
Time of Your Life

MPI HOME VIDEO INC.
Cinemagic
A Man Named Lombardi
Roger Corman: Hollywood's Wild Angel
Secret Agent # 2

NEW WORLD VIDEO
Certain Fury *(B,V,LV)*
Fraternity Vacation *(B,V,LV)(cc)*
Peacekillers
Night Patrol *(cc)*
The Shadow of Chikara *(B,V,LV)*
The Spirit of West Point
Trap on Cougar Mountain *(B,V,LV)*

NFL FILMS VIDEO
Glory Days of Yesteryear: The Baltimore Colts
The Legacy Begins: Miami Dolphins
The Purple Power Years: The Minnesota Vikings
A Winning Tradition: The Cleveland Browns
Years of Glory ... Years of Pain
Years to Remember: The New York Giants

PARAMOUNT HOME VIDEO
Autumn Portrait *(B,V,LV)*
Water's Path *(B,V,LV)*
Western Light *(B,V,LV)*
Winter *(B,V,LV)*

PRISM
Death Target
Goldie and Kids
The Killing Machine
Legend of Eight Samurai
Texas Detour

RCA/COLUMBIA PICTURES HOME VIDEO
Aesop's Fables
Bob Marley–Legend
Carmen
Go-Go's Wild at the Greek
It Came From Beneath the Sea
Mad Dogs and Englishmen
A Passage to India *(cc)*
The Return of the Vampire
Rush–Through the Camera Eye
Scorpions–World Wide Live
The Secret of the Sword *(cc)*
The Slugger's Wife *(cc)*
13 Ghosts
Torture Garden
Zombies of Mora Tau

REPUBLIC PICTURES HOME VIDEO
Betty Boop Special Collector's Edition II
Julius Caesar
The Little Rascals Comedy Classics Volume II

SONY CORPORATION OF AMERICA
Fugitive Samurai
Voltron, Defender of the Universe: Planet Doom

SPOTLITE VIDEO
Four Faces West
Good Sam
The Little Rascals Volume I
Magic Town
The Miracle of the Bells
Showdown at Boot Hill

THORN EMI/HBO VIDEO
Amadeus
Beach Blanket Bingo
Braingames
Detroit 9000
Polyester
Ready Steady Go, Volume 3
Samson et Dalila
Swan Lake

UNICORN VIDEO
Beyond the Living Dead
Dead for a Dollar
The Killer Elephants
Magnum Killers
A Place in Hell
Someone Behind the Door
Your Show of Shows, Vols. III & IV

UNITED HOME VIDEO
Aladdin and his Magic Lamp
The Asphyx
Asylum of Satan
Blood Cult
Crypt of the Living Dead
King Solomon's Treasure
Manson

U.S.A. HOME VIDEO
The Ambush Murders
The Bellboy
The Blue Knight
Cinderfella
The Disappearance of Aimee
Jerry Lewis Live
Language Plus Presents Survival Spanish
The Triangle Factory Fire Scandal

VCL HOME VIDEO
Legend of the Werewolf

VESTRON VIDEO
Final Justice
The Honeymoon Killers
The Instructor
Jennifer
Scream and Scream Again

VIDEO ARTS INTERNATIONAL
Anna Russell: The First Farewell Concert
Black Tights
The Glory of Spain
Medea
Renata Scotto: Prima Donna in Recital
Toscanini: The Maestro/Hymn of the Nations

WARNER HOME VIDEO
AC/DC: Let There Be Rock
Huey Lewis and the News: The Heart of Rock & Roll
Police Academy 2: Their First Assignment
Steelyard Blues
Up the Academy
Which Way to the Front

WIZARD VIDEO
Famous T & A
Fraulein Devil
Revenge in the House of Usher
Space Vampires
Tormentor
Virgin Among the Living Dead

Key

This sample entry will assist the reader in interpreting the individual Program Listings. For a complete explanation of each code, please see the USE GUIDE.

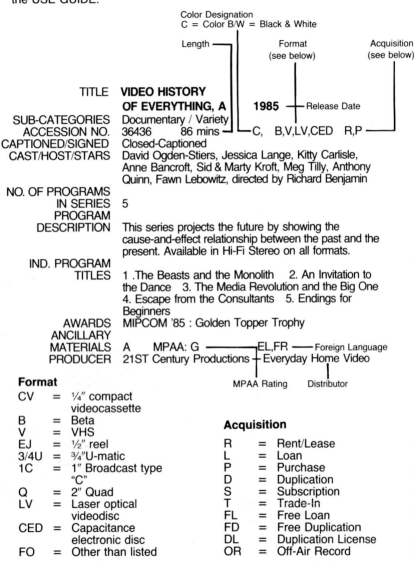

Color Designation
C = Color B/W = Black & White

Length — Format (see below) — Acquisition (see below)

TITLE	**VIDEO HISTORY OF EVERYTHING, A** **1985** — Release Date
SUB-CATEGORIES	Documentary / Variety
ACCESSION NO.	36436 86 mins C, B,V,LV,CED R,P
CAPTIONED/SIGNED	Closed-Captioned
CAST/HOST/STARS	David Ogden-Stiers, Jessica Lange, Kitty Carlisle, Anne Bancroft, Sid & Marty Kroft, Meg Tilly, Anthony Quinn, Fawn Lebowitz, directed by Richard Benjamin
NO. OF PROGRAMS IN SERIES	5
PROGRAM DESCRIPTION	This series projects the future by showing the cause-and-effect relationship between the past and the present. Available in Hi-Fi Stereo on all formats.
IND. PROGRAM TITLES	1 .The Beasts and the Monolith 2. An Invitation to the Dance 3. The Media Revolution and the Big One 4. Escape from the Consultants 5. Endings for Beginners
AWARDS	MIPCOM '85 : Golden Topper Trophy
ANCILLARY MATERIALS	A MPAA: G EL,FR — Foreign Language
PRODUCER	21ST Century Productions Everyday Home Video

MPAA Rating — Distributor

Format

CV	=	¼″ compact videocassette
B	=	Beta
V	=	VHS
EJ	=	½″ reel
3/4U	=	¾″U-matic
1C	=	1″ Broadcast type "C"
Q	=	2″ Quad
LV	=	Laser optical videodisc
CED	=	Capacitance electronic disc
FO	=	Other than listed

Acquisition

R	=	Rent/Lease
L	=	Loan
P	=	Purchase
D	=	Duplication
S	=	Subscription
T	=	Trade-In
FL	=	Free Loan
FD	=	Free Duplication
DL	=	Duplication License
OR	=	Off-Air Record

PLACE
¢ 22
STAMP
HERE

The National Video
Clearinghouse, Inc.

100 Lafayette Drive
Syosset, N.Y. 11791

For Information On New Publications

from

The National Video Clearinghouse Inc.

Fill out and send the coupon below (please print)

Name ____________________

Address ____________________

City ____________ State ____________ Zip ____________

We welcome your comments on *The Video Tape & Disc Guide To Home Entertainment®, Sixth Edition.*

____

____

____

Where did you purchase this book? ____________________

Did you receive this book as a gift? yes ____ no ____

What type VCR do you own? VHS ____ Beta ____ 8mm ____ other ____

What is your favorite brand of blank tape? ____________________

A

A, B & C **1968**
Drama
79896 52 mins C B, V P
Patrick McGoohan, Katherine Kath, Colin Gordon
Number two attempts to find out why the Prisoner resigned from his previous profession by drugging The Prisoner to enter his dreams.
Patrick McGoohan — *MPI Home Video*

A Mi Las Mujeres N, Fu, N, Fa **1980**
Comedy
64499 90 mins C B, V P
This musical comedy features the well-known Spanish and Latin American singer Peret. English title: "I Don't Care for Women."
SP
Jose Antonio Cascales Guijarro — *Media Home Entertainment*

A Nos Amours **1984**
Drama
80787 99 mins C B, V P
Sandrine Bonnaire, Maurice Pialat, Evelyne Ker, Maurice Pialat
A young girl is having casual affairs while searching for the love and attention she was denied at home. With English subtitles.
MPAA:R
Triumph Films — *RCA/Columbia Pictures Home Video*

Aaron Loves Angela **1975**
Drama
81432 99 mins C B, V P
Irene Cara, Moses Gunn, Kevin Hooks, Robert Hooks, Jose Feliciano, directed by Gordon Parks, Jr.
A Puerto Rican girl falls in love with a black boy amidst the harsh realities of the Harlem ghetto. Available in VHS and Beta Hi-Fi.
MPAA:R
Columbia Pictures — *RCA/Columbia Pictures Home Video*

Abba **1980**
Music-Performance
48539 60 mins C LV P
Abba
Popular Swedish rock band gives a visual concert performance which includes their hits "Waterloo" and "Dancin' Queen."
Unknown — *MCA Home Video*

Abba **1983**
Music-Performance
66008 60 mins C B, V P
The internationally-famous group performs "Knowing Me, Knowing You," "Take a Chance on Me," "The Name of the Game," "Dancing Queen" and other hits.
Polar Music International — *Monterey Home Video*

Abba, Again **1983**
Music-Performance
76797 30 mins C B, V P
The popular rock group performs such hits as "Supertrooper" and "When All Is Said And Done" in this taped concert.
Polar Music International — *Monterey Home Video*

Abba in Concert **1979**
Music-Performance
64832 ? mins C LV P
This concert combines sequences from an American tour and London's Wembley Arena in 1979. Features songs such as "I Have a Dream," "Gimme! Gimme! Gimme!," "Summer Night," and "Dancing Queen." In stereo.
Curt Edman — *Pioneer Video Imports*

Abbott and Costello Cartoon Carnival #1 **1966**
Cartoons
59932 60 mins C B, V P
Animated
Animated Abbott and Costello involved in a series of comic mishaps. Cartoons include: "Cherokee Choo Choo," "Pinocchio's Double Trouble," "Son of Kong," "Teenie Weenie Genie," "Indestructible Space Suit," "Bouncing Rubber Man," "Germ Squirm," "Marauding Mummy," and "Wizardland."
Hanna Barbera — *United Home Video*

Abbott and Costello in Hollywood **1945**
Comedy
58292 83 mins B/W B, V P
Bud Abbott, Lou Costello, Frances Rafferty, Warner Anderson, Lucille Ball
Bud and Lou appear as a barber and porter of a high class tonsorial parlor in Hollywood.
MGM — *MGM/UA Home Video*

Abbott and Costello Meet Captain Kidd **1952**
Comedy
00384 70 mins C B, V P
Abbott and Costello, Charles Laughton
With Captain Kidd on their trail, Abbott and Costello follow up on a treasure map.
Warner Brothers — *United Home Video*

Abbott and Costello Meet Dr. Jekyll and Mr. Hyde **1952**
Comedy/Horror
65204 77 mins B/W B, V P
Bud Abbott, Lou Costello, Boris Karloff, Helen Westcott
Abbott and Costello take on evil Dr. Jekyll, who has transformed himself into Mr. Hyde, and is terrorizing London.
Universal — *MCA Home Video*

Abbott and Costello Meet Frankenstein **1948**
Comedy
47680 83 mins B/W B, V P
Bud Abbott, Lou Costello, Lon Chaney Jr., Bela Lugosi
Chick and Wilbur, two unsuspecting baggage clerks, deliver a crate containing the last remains of Dracula and Frankstein's monster.
Universal — *MCA Home Video*

ABC—Mantrap **1983**
Music-Performance
65461 ? mins C B, V P
A music video that follows "Mantrap" on a path that leads from obscurity to international stardom. Includes many of their top hits: "Look of Love," "All of My Heart," and "Poison Arrow." In stereo VHS and Beta Hi-Fi.
Michael Hamlyn — *RCA/Columbia Pictures Home Video; RCA VideoDiscs*

Abduction **1975**
Drama
65373 100 mins C B, V P
Leif Erickson, Dorothy Malone, Judith-Marie Berigan
"Abduction" is the explicit and straight-forward account of Patricia Prescott's transformation from distraught captive to knowing participant. Based on the novel by Harrison James.
MPAA:R
Kent E Carroll — *Media Home Entertainment*

Abductors, The **1971**
Adventure
63084 90 mins C B, V P
Ginger
Sexy Ginger infiltrates a ring of kidnappers by offering her body as bait.
Abductors Productions — *Monterey Home Video*

Abdulla the Great **1956**
Adventure
57344 89 mins C B, V, FO P
Gregory Ratoff, Kay Kendall, Sydney Chaplin
A dissolute Middle-East monarch falls for a model, who spurns him for an army officer critical of the King.
Gregory Ratoff — *Video Yesteryear*

Abe Lincoln: Freedom Fighter **198?**
Drama/Biographical
65723 53 mins C B, V P
Allen Williams, Andrew Prine, Brock Peters
A turning point in the young life of Abe Lincoln, the 16th President of the United States, is re-created in this moving historical drama.
James L Conway — *United Home Video*

Abe Lincoln in Illinois **1939**
Drama
00260 110 mins B/W B, V, 3/4U P
Raymond Massey, Gene Lockhart, Ruth Gordon
Massey portrays a very human backwoods lawyer involved with his two loves—Ann Rutledge and Mary Todd.
RKO; Max Gordon — *Nostalgia Merchant*

Abominable Dr. Phibes, The **1971**
Horror
64897 90 mins C B, V P
Vincent Price
An evil genius decides that the surgical team that let his wife die shall each perish by a different biblical plague.
American International Pictures — *Vestron Video*

Abraham Lincoln **1930**
Drama
11218 93 mins B/W B, V P, T
Walter Huston, Una Merkel, Henry B. Walthall, directed by D. W. Griffith
D.W. Griffith's first talking movie takes Lincoln from his birth through his assassination. This restored version includes the original slavery sequences which were thought lost. Musical score included.
United Artists — *Blackhawk Films; Hal Roach Studios; Video Yesteryear; Sheik Video; Cable Films; Budget Video; Discount Video Tapes; Classic Video Cinema Collector's Club; Kartes Productions*

Absence of Malice **1981**
Drama
59602 116 mins C B, V, LV P
Paul Newman, Sally Field, Melinda Dillon, Bob Balaban, directed by Sydney Pollack
A private citizen suddenly reads that he is the subject of a criminal investigation when an investigative reporter writes a story that was purposely leaked. A drama about the responsibility of the press.
MPAA:PG
Columbia — *RCA/Columbia Pictures Home Video; RCA VideoDiscs*

 (For explanation of codes, see USE GUIDE and KEY)

Absent-Minded Professor, The 1961
Comedy
55567 97 mins B/W B, V, LV R, P
Fred MacMurray, Keenan Wynn, Tommy Kirk, Ed Wynn, Leon Ames, Nancy Olson, directed by Robert Stevenson
A professor accidentally invents a substance known as flubber which causes cars to fly and people to leap great heights. The invention, however, leads to complications of all kinds.
Walt Disney — *Walt Disney Home Video; RCA VideoDiscs*

Academy Award Winners Animated Short Films 1984
Film/Cartoons
77179 60 mins C B, V, CED P
Animated
This is a collection of six short films that includes Jimmy Picker's "Sunday in New York," "The Hole," "Munro" and "Closed Mondays."
Academy Award '84: Best Short Subject (Picker).
Videoline Inc — *Vestron Video*

Accident 1967
Drama
63340 100 mins C B, V R, P
Dirk Bogarde, Michael York, Stanley Baker, Jacqueline Sassard
A tangled web of guilt, remorse, humor and thwarted sexuality is unravelled against the background of the English countryside in this story of an Oxford love triangle.
Royal Avenue Chelsea Productions Ltd — *THORN EMI/HBO Video*

Accident, The 1983
Drama
78400 104 mins C B, V P
Terence Kelly, Fiona Reid, Frank Perry
A hockey game turns into a nightmare when the roof over the arena collapses under the weight of too much ice and snow.
Independent — *Trans World Entertainment*

Across the Great Divide 1976
Adventure
63382 102 mins C B, V P
Robert Logan, George "Buck" Flower, Heather Rattray
Two orphans must cross the rugged snow-covered Rocky Mountains in 1876 in order to claim their inheritance—a 400-acre plot of land in Salem, Oregon.
MPAA:G
Pacific International Enterprises — *Media Home Entertainment*

Act, The 1982
Comedy
73033 90 mins C B, V P
Jill St. John, Eddie Albert
This is a satire about political double dealing.
MPAA:R
Film Ventures — *Vestron Video*

Act of Aggression 1973
Drama
80118 100 mins C B, V P
Jean Louis Trintignant, Catherine Deneuve, Claude Brasseur
When a Parisian man finds his wife and daughter murdered at a summer resort, he takes the law into his own hands.
MPAA:R
Joseph Green Pictures — *King of Video*

Adam 1983
Drama
81255 100 mins C B, V P
Daniel J. Travanti, Jobeth Williams, Martha Scott, Richard Masur, directed by Michael Tuchner
This is the true story of John and Reve Walsh's search for their six-year-old son Adam who was kidnapped from a large department store.
Alan Landsburg Productions — *U.S.A. Home Video*

Adam Had Four Sons 1941
Drama
76023 81 mins B/W B, V P
Ingrid Bergman, Warner Baxter, Susan Hayward, Fay Wray, and Robert Shaw
An intense drama of love, jealousy, and hatred; a governess to a man'sfour sons sees them growing up.
Robert Sherwood — *RCA/Columbia Pictures Home Video*

Adam's Rib 1949
Comedy
44647 101 mins B/W B, V P
Katherine Hepburn, Spencer Tracy, Tom Ewell, Judy Holliday, directed by George Cukor
A husband and wife lawyer team clash when the wife defends a woman on trial for shooting her spouse. The other half of the team (the husband) is the prosecutor.
MGM — *MGM/UA Home Video*

Adultress, The 1977
Drama
80723 88 mins C B, V P
Tyne Daly, Eric Braeden, Gregory Morton
When a husband and wife cannot satisfy their desire to have a family, they hire a young man to help them.
MPAA:R
Cinema Overseas Ltd. — *Active Home Video*

Adventure Called Menudo, An 1982
Musical
69540 90 mins C B, V P
Xavier, Miguel, Johnny, Ricky and Charlie (the members of Menudo) sing 14 songs in this story of their misadventures, which begin with a flight in a balloon. In Spanish.
SP
Embassy Communications — *Embassy Home Entertainment*

Adventures in Paradise 1982
Documentary/Sports-Water
77452 79 mins C B, V P
Champion surfers Mike Ho, Chris Lassen, and Bobby Owens go on a worldwide search for the perfect wave. Available in Beta Hi Fi and VHS Stereo.
Scott Dittrich Films — *Monterey Home Video*

Adventures in Space with Scott McCloud Volume 2 196?
Cartoons
80718 60 mins C B, V P
Animated
A collection of three episodes from the series: In "Red Alert" Scott and Taurus become blinded by an atomic blast, in "The Day the Earth Went Dark" Scott's crew attempts to ward off an atomic reactor explosion, and in "The Queen of the Three Suns" Taurus and Captain O'Hara are captured by Queen Nila.
Unknown — *All Seasons Entertainment*

Adventures in Space with Scott McCloud: Volume 3 196?
Cartoons
80722 60 mins C B, V P
Animated
Law enforcer Scott McCloud fights off intergalactic injustice in this collection of three animated adventures.
Unknown — *All Seasons Entertainment*

Adventures of Babar, The 197?
Fantasy
70366 60 mins C B, V R, P
In this French TV production, actors wear puppet-like costumes that recreate the illustrations of this popular childrens book. Several Babar adventures are included on the tape.
Tel Hechete — *Video City Productions*

Adventures of Black Beauty Vol. I, The 1972
Adventure/Cartoons
75891 60 mins C B, V P
Animated
This program is the first volume containing "The Fugitive" and "Pit Pony" from the animated story of Black Beauty.
LWI Productions; Tablot Television — *Sony Corporation of America*

Adventures of Black Beauty Vol. 2, The 1972
Adventure/Cartoons
75893 60 mins C B, V P
Animated
This program is the second volume containing "A Member of the Family" from the animated story of Black Beauty.
LWI Productions; Tablot Television — *Sony Corporation of America*

Adventures of Black Beauty Vol. 3, The 1972
Adventure/Cartoons
75894 60 mins C B, V P
Animated
This program is the third volume containing "Mission of Mercy" and "Out of the Night" from the animated story of Black Beauty.
LWI Productions; Tablot Television — *Sony Corporation of America*

Adventures of Buckaroo Banzai, The 1984
Science fiction/Fantasy
80047 100 mins C B, V, LV, CED P
Peter Weller, Ellen Barkin, Jeff Goldblum, Christopher Lloyd, John Lithgow, directed by W.D. Richter
Neurosurgeon/physicist Buckaroo Banzai travels through the eighth dimension to battle with Dr. Emilie Lizardo and his lectoids for control of the overthruster.
MPAA:PG
Twentieth Century Fox — *Vestron Video*

Adventures of Buster the Bear, The 1978
Cartoons
53142 52 mins C B, V P
Animated
Joe the Otter doesn't want to share the fish in the stream with Buster, until Grandfather Bullfrog shows him that sharing makes life fun.
EL, SP
Ziv Intl — *Family Home Entertainment*

Adventures of Captain Future Volume 1, The 1980
Science fiction/Cartoons
53159 54 mins C B, V P
Animated
Captain Future and his crew use a time machine to go back a million years into the past to save a planet. They encounter strange prehistoric creatures.
EL, SP
Ziv Intl — *Family Home Entertainment*

Adventures of Captain Future Volume 2, The **1980**
Science fiction/Cartoons
53160 54 mins C B, V P
Animated
Captain Future and his crew save an entire planet from destruction by solving the problem of finding a safe energy source.
EL, SP
Ziv Intl — *Family Home Entertainment*

Adventures of Captain Fabian **1951**
Adventure
80030 100 mins B/W B, V P
Errol Flynn, Vincent Price, Agnes Moorehead, Micheline Prelle.
When the captain of the "China Sea" learns that a beautiful woman has been falsely imprisoned, he comes to her rescue.
Republic Pictures — *Republic Pictures Home Video*

Adventures of Captain Marvel **1941**
Adventure/Serials
07334 240 mins B/W B, V, 3/4U P
Tom Tyler, Frank Coghlan Jr., Louise Currie
A serial about the adventures of Captain Marvel in his fight against crime. In twelve episodes.
Republic — *Video Connection; Republic Pictures Home Video*

Adventures of Curley and His Gang, The **1947**
Comedy
66112 54 mins C B, V P
Larry Olsen
The children's favorite teacher is replaced.
Hal Roach — *Unicorn Video*

Adventures of Droopy, The **1955**
Cartoons
81052 53 mins C B, V P
Animated, directed by Tex Avery
This is a collection of seven classic cartoons featuring that sad-eyed bloodhound Droopy including: "Domb-Hounded," "Wags to Riches," "Champ Champ" and "Deputy Droopy."
MGM — *MGM/UA Home Video*

Adventures of Eliza Fraser, The **1976**
Comedy
80820 114 mins C B, V, LV P
Susannah York, Trevor Howard, Leon Lissek, Abigail, Noel Ferrier, Carole Skinner
A young shipwrecked couple move from bawdy pleasures to cannibalism after their tropical island's aborigines capture them.
Hexagon Productions — *New World Video*

Adventures of Ellery Queen, The **1951**
Mystery/Crime-Drama
47487 25 mins B/W B, V, FO P
Richard Hart, Sono Osato, Kurt Katch
The first television portrayal of Ellery Queen featured Richard Hart as the famed detective. In this episode, Ellery solves the murder of a carnival acrobat.
Dumont — *Video Yesteryear*

Adventures of Felix the Cat, The **1960**
Cartoons
65482 56 mins C B, V P
Animated
In this episode of light-hearted episodes, Felix is joined by a whole array of amazing characters—the devious and evil Professor, the absent-minded Poindexter, and the Strongman Rock Bottom.
Joseph Oriolo — *Media Home Entertainment*

Adventures of Frontier Fremont, The **1975**
Adventure
35366 95 mins C B, V P
Dan Haggerty, Denver Pyle
A rough and tumble story of a man who makes the wilderness his home and the animals his friends.
Sunn Classic — *United Home Video*

Adventures of Grizzly Adams at Beaver Dam, The **198?**
Adventure
65759 60 mins C B, V P
Dan Haggerty
Fearing that a dam will flood his valley, Grizzly tries desperately to convince a misplaced family of beavers to build their dam elsewhere.
Charles E Sellier Jr — *United Home Video*

Adventures of Huckleberry Finn, The **1939**
Adventure
52744 89 mins B/W B, V P
Mickey Rooney, Lynne Carver, Rex Ingram, William Frawley
Mark Twain's immortal classic about a boy who runs away down the Mississippi on a raft, accompanied by a runaway slave, is the basis of this film.
MGM — *MGM/UA Home Video; VidAmerica*

Adventures of Huckleberry Finn, The **1978**
Adventure
75616 97 mins C B, V, CED P
Forrest Tucker, Larry Storch
The classic adventure by Mark Twain of a Missouri boy and a runaway slave.
Sunn Classic Productions — *Children's Video Library*

Adventures of Huckleberry Finn, The **1984**
Cartoons
80395 48 mins C B, V P
Animated
An animated version of the Mark Twain classic novel about the friendship between a young boy and a runaway slave.
Unknown — *Embassy Home Entertainment*

Adventures of Little Lulu and Tubby Volume 1, The **1978**
Cartoons
53135 50 mins C B, V P
Animated
In "Good Luck Guard," Lulu tries to join Tubby's club for boys. In "The Endurance Test," Lulu gets back at Tubby when they go on an all-day hike, without any food for Tubby.
EL, SP
Ziv Intl — *Family Home Entertainment*

Adventures of Little Lulu and Tubby Volume 2, The **1978**
Cartoons
53136 50 mins C B, V P
Animated
In "Save the Prisoners," Lulu helps Tubby escape from the dreaded Westside gang. In "Little Fireman," Lulu fools all the boys and becomes the first one on the block to ride in a real fire truck.
EL, SP
Ziv Intl — *Family Home Entertainment*

Adventures of Mighty Mouse-Volumes IV & V, The **194?**
Cartoons
29125 60 mins C B, V P
Animated
Paul Terry's Mighty Mouse character is featured in two cartoon collections, both available individually. Volume IV runs 90 minutes.
EL, SP
Viacom International — *CBS/Fox Video*

Adventures of Ozzie and Harriet, The **1966**
Comedy
38994 57 mins C B, V, FO P
Ozzie, Harriet, David and Ricky Nelson
2 pgms
Two episodes from the long-running television series: "Wally the Author" and "The Sheik of Araby." Commercials are included; they are in black and white.
ABC — *Video Yesteryear*

Adventures of Ozzie and Harriet, The **1964**
Comedy/Television
57346 55 mins C B, V, FO P
Ozzie, Harriet, David and Ricky Nelson
Two complete episodes of the long-running situation comedy: "Ricky's Horse," where Ricky finds himself the proud owner of a horse after a financial "discussion" between Ozzie and Harriet, and "Ozzie the Babysitter," where Ozzie's in big trouble after damaging a slot car set belonging to the nine-year-old he's babysitting. Black and white commercials included.
ABC — *Video Yesteryear; Discount Video Tapes*

Adventures of Ozzie and Harriet I, The **195?**
Comedy
45022 120 mins B/W B, V, 3/4U P
Ozzie, Harriet, David and Ricky Nelson
Four of the classic shows from 1953, 1955, 1958, and 1964, complete with commercials.
ABC — *Shokus Video*

Adventures of Ozzie and Harriet II, The **1980**
Comedy
54041 120 mins B/W B, V, 3/4U P
Ozzie, Harriet, David and Ricky Nelson
Four more episodes from the classic TV series starring America's favorite family. Featured are shows from 1953—Ozzie has a problem when he orders two new chairs; 1955—fishing trip for Ozzie and Thorny turns into disaster; 1957—Ozzie's craving for tutti-fruity ice cream gets totally out of hand; 1964—Rick's fraternity must hide their sexy housemother from the dean. All shows contain original commercials.
ABC — *Shokus Video*

Adventures of Ozzie and Harriet III, The **195?**
Comedy
58831 120 mins B/W B, V, 3/4U P
Ozzie, Harriet, David and Ricky Nelson
Four episodes of the classic series: In "The Party" (1953), Dave and Ricky are miffed because their friend didn't invite them to his party; in "A Matter of Inches" (1954), Ozzie promises Dave $50 as soon as Dave passes him in height; in "The Road Race" (1957), Ozzie bets Ricky that an old car can withstand more than a souped-up hot rod; and, in "Little

 (For explanation of codes, see USE GUIDE and KEY)

Handprints in the Sidewalk" (1961), a cement slab causes problems for Ozzie.
ABC — *Shokus Video*

Adventures of Ozzie and Harriet IV, The **196?**
Comedy
62688 120 mins B/W B, V, 3/4U P
Ozzie, Harriet, David and Ricky Nelson
Four episodes from this popular TV series: "David's Birthday" (1953), "Ball of Tinfoil" (1955), "David Becomes a Football Coach" (1958) and " An Honor for Oz" (1966). The final show is in color. Original commercials included.
ABC — *Shokus Video*

Adventures of Ozzie and Harriet V **1955**
Comedy
76013 120 mins B/W B, V, 3/4U P
Four fun filled episodes of the adventures of Ozzie and Harriet.
ABC — *Shokus Video*

Adventures of Reddy the Fox, The **1978**
Cartoons
53143 52 mins C B, V P
Animated
While Granny Fox is away, Reddy the Fox gets into all kinds of trouble, until, much to his relief, Granny returns to set everything right.
EL, SP
Ziv Intl — *Family Home Entertainment*

Adventures of Robin Hood, The **1938**
Adventure
58832 102 mins C B, V, LV P
Errol Flynn, Basil Rathbone, Claude Rains, Olivia de Havilland, Alan Hale
Errol Flynn stars as the rebel outlaw who outwits Sir Guy of Gisbourne and Prince John and saves the throne for the absent King Richard. Academy Awards '38: Interior Decoration; Film Editing; Original Score (Erich Wolfgang Korngold). EL, SP
United Artists — *CBS/Fox Video; RCA VideoDiscs*

Adventures of Sherlock Holmes' Smarter Brother, The **1978**
Comedy
29126 91 mins C B, V P
Gene Wilder, Madeline Kahn, Marty Feldman, Dom DeLuise
The unknown brother of the famous Sherlock Holmes takes on some of his brother's more disposable excess cases and makes some hilarious moves.
MPAA:PG
20th Century Fox — *CBS/Fox Video*

Adventures of Sinbad the Sailor, The **1975**
Cartoons/Adventure
53138 87 mins C B, V P
Animated
Sinbad receives a map to a treasure island where fabulous stores of jewels are hidden, and, in his search, falls in love with the King's daughter.
Ziv Intl — *Family Home Entertainment*

Adventures of Superman, The **194?**
Cartoons
53799 55 mins C B, V, FO P
Animated
Seven cartoons from 1942 and 1943 are included in this package: "Underground World," "Terror on the Midway," "Volcano," "Destruction Inc.," "Secret Agent," "Billion Dollar Limited," and "Showdown." Some black and white.
Paramount; Max Fleischer — *Video Yesteryear*

Adventures of Tarzan, The **1921**
Adventure/Serials
11390 153 mins B/W B, V, FO P
Elmo Lincoln
The screen's first Tarzan in an exciting jungle thriller. Silent.
Artclass — *Video Yesteryear; Classic Video Cinema Collector's Club*

Adventures of the Flying Cadets **1944**
War-Drama
54163 169 mins B/W B, V P
Johnny Downs, Regis Toomey
An early war adventure serial in thirteen complete chapters.
Universal — *Video Connection; Video Yesteryear*

Adventures of the Masked Phantom, The **1938**
Adventure
78092 56 mins B/W B, V, FO P
Monte Rawlins, Betty Burgess, Larry Mason, Sonny Lamont
This film presents the exciting adventures of the Masked Phantom.
Monogram — *Video Yesteryear*

Adventures of the Wilderness Family, The **1976**
Adventure
47749 100 mins C B, V, LV P
Robert F. Logan, Susan Damente Shaw

The story of a modern-day pioneer family who becomes bored with the troubles of city life and head for life in the wilderness.
MPAA:G
Arthur R Dubs — *Media Home Entertainment*

Adventures of Tom Sawyer, The 1973
Adventure
81441 76 mins C B, V P
Jane Wyatt, Buddy Ebsen, Vic Morrow, John McGiver, Josh Albee, Jeff Tyler
Tom Sawyer is a mischievous Missouri boy who gets into all kinds of trouble in this adaptation of the Mark Twain book. Available in VHS and Beta Hi-Fi.
Universal TV — *MCA Home Video*

Adventures of Tom Sawyer, The 1938
Adventure
52736 77 mins C B, V, CED P
Tommy Kelly, Jackie Moran, Ann Gillis, Walter Brennan, May Robson, Victor Jory
Mark Twain's classic about a Missouri boy whose adventures range from tricking the neighborhood into whitewashing the fence for him to running away on a raft to become a pirate.
United Artists; David O. Selznick — *CBS/Fox Video*

Adventures of Topper, The 1953
Comedy
78360 120 mins B/W B, V P
Leo G. Carroll, Anne Jeffreys, Bob Sterling, Lee Patrick
When a bank president purchases a house, he inherits the three ghosts who lived there before him. Four episodes from the long-running TV series.
Loveton Schubert Productions — *U.S.A. Home Video*

Adventures of Ultraman, The 1981
Cartoons/Adventure
58541 90 mins C B, V P
Animated
The adventures of Ultraman, a futuristic hero from a distant plant.
EL, SP
Tsuburaya Productions — *Family Home Entertainment*

Aerobic Dancing 1982
Physical fitness
63167 56 mins C B, V P
Jacki Sorensen
Aerobic dancing, a blend of dancing and jogging, is demonstrated on this workout tape by its creator, Jacki Sorensen. She performs a complete exercise session at three activity levels: walking, jogging and running. VHS is in stereo, with music on one track and instructions on the other.
Feeling Fine Productions; Jacki Sorensen's Aerobic Dancing Inc — *MCA Home Video*

Aerobic Dancing—Encore 1983
Physical fitness/Dance
65205 57 mins C B, V P
Jacki Sorensen
A blending of dancing and jogging into a complete workout. The program is choreographed to strengthen the heart and lungs while firming up the entire body.
Priscilla Ulene — *MCA Home Video*

Aerobic Self-Defense 1984
Physical fitness/Martial arts
72890 60 mins C B, V P
A "How to" program that combines aerobics and the martial arts.
NTA — *Republic Pictures Home Video*

Aerobicise: The Beautiful Workout 1981
Physical fitness
58875 113 mins C B, V, LV R, P
Aerobic dancing to original music, produced by Ron Harris, fashion photographer. An erotic exercise program.
Ron Harris — *Paramount Home Video; RCA VideoDiscs*

Aerobicise: The Beginning Workout 1982
Physical fitness
63427 96 mins C B, V, LV R, P
This is a basic, simple exercise regimen for the uninitiated aerobiciser.
Ron Harris — *Paramount Home Video; RCA VideoDiscs*

Aerobicise: The Ultimate Workout 1983
Physical fitness
66032 100 mins C B, V, LV R, P
The last installment of Paramount's Aerobicise trilogy is the most advanced, designed for those in excellent shape. In stereo.
Ron Harris — *Paramount Home Video*

Aesop and His Friends 1982
Fairy tales/Cartoons
58577 50 mins C B, V P
A collection of Aesop's most beloved fables: "The Fox and the Crow," "The Lion and the Mouse," "The Grasshopper and the Ant," "The City Mouse and the Country Mouse," plus "The Snowman's Dilemma" and "The Owl and the

(For explanation of codes, see USE GUIDE and KEY)

Pussycat" as told by Cyril Ritchard. Others included as well.
McGraw Hill — *Mastervision*

Affair 1975
Drama
76641 81 mins C B, V P
Lucretia Love, Paola Senatore, Mauro Parenti
A determined wife tries to win back the love of her husband who is having affairs with her best friend as well as his secretary.
Italy — *Trans World Entertainment*

Affair of the Pink Pearl, The 1984
Mystery
80447 60 mins C B, V P
James Warwick, Francesca Annis
The husband and wife private investigation team of Tommy and Tuppence must find the culprit who stole a valuable pink pearl within twenty four hours. Based on the Agatha Christie story.
London Weekend Television — *Pacific Arts Video*

Affairs of Annabel 1938
Comedy
29491 68 mins B/W B, V P, T
Lucille Ball, Jack Oakie, Ruth Donnelly
The first of the popular series of Annabel pictures Lucy made in the late 30's. This appealing adolescent is zoomed to movie stardom by her press agent's stunts. A behind-the-scenes satire on Hollywood, stars, and agents.
RKO, Lou Lusty Republic — *Blackhawk Films; RKO HomeVideo*

Africa Screams 1949
Comedy
00386 79 mins B/W B, V P
Abbott and Costello
Abbott and Costello go on an African safari in possession of a secret map. Then the trouble begins.
United Artists — *Electric Video; Budget Video; Sheik Video; Media Home Entertainment; VCII; King of Video; Video Connection; Video Yesteryear; Discount Video Tapes; Nostalgia Merchant; Classic Video Cinema Collector's Club; Vestron Video (disc only); Kartes Productions*

Africa Texas Style 1967
Adventure
80031 109 mins C B, V P
Hugh O'Brien, John Mills, Nigel Green, Tom Nardini
An East African rancher hires an American cowboy and his Navajo sidekick to help run his wild game ranch.
Paramount; Ivan Tors — *Republic Pictures Home Video*

African Queen, The 1951
Adventure
08471 105 mins C B, V, LV P
Humphrey Bogart, Katharine Hepburn, Robert Morley, Theodore Bikel, directed by John Huston
In the Congo during World War I, a spinster persuades a dissolute captain to try to destroy a German gunboat.
Academy Awards '51: Best Actor (Bogart). EL, SP
United Artists; Horizon Romulus Prod — *CBS/Fox Video; RCA VideoDiscs*

After Mein Kampf 1942
World War II/Propaganda
52321 40 mins B/W B, V P
British propaganda film which blends German cartoons and contemporary footage to illustrate the rise of Hitler and the Third Reich.
British — *Prism; International Historic Films*

After Mein Kampf (The Story of Adolf Hitler) 1940
Documentary/World War II
69575 43 mins B/W B, V, FO P
This combination of newsreel footage and recreations presents the life story of Hitler, made by the British as a propaganda move during the early months of World War II.
British Lion — *Video Yesteryear; Discount Video Tapes*

After the Fall of New York 1985
Science fiction
80928 95 mins C B, V P
Michael Sopkiw, Valentine Monnier, Roman Geer, George Eastman
The sole survivors of a nuclear war to New York City seeking the final fertile femme fatale on Earth.
MPAA:R
Almi Pictures — *Vestron Video*

After the Fox 1966
Comedy
72894 103 mins C B, V P
Peter Sellers, Victor Mature
A con artist disguises himself as a film director in order to steal gold from Rome.
Delegate Productions — *CBS/Fox Video*

After the Rehearsal 1984
Drama
77377 72 mins C B, V P
Erland Josephson, Ingrid Thulin, Lena Olin, directed by Ingmar Bergman

Three actors reveal their hearts and souls on an empty stage after the rehearsal of a Strindberg play. Swedish with English subtitles.
MPAA:R SW
Triumph Films — *RCA/Columbia Pictures Home Video*

Aftermath **1985**
Science fiction
80323 96 mins C B, V P
Steve Barkett, Larry Latham
Three astronauts who return to Earth are shocked to discover that the planet has been ravaged by a nuclear war.
Independent — *Prism*

Against A Crooked Sky **1975**
Drama
79315 89 mins C B, V P
Richard Boone, Stewart Peterson, Clint Richie, directed by Earl Bellamy
A young boy and an elderly trapper set out to find his sister who was captured by the Indians.
MPAA:G
Cinema Shares — *Vestron Video*

Against All Odds **1984**
Drama
Closed Captioned
70185 122 mins C B, V, CED P
Jeff Bridges, Rachel Ward, James Woods, Alex Karras, directed by Taylor Hackford
An ex-football player travels to Mexico in search of his friend's girl. When he finds her, things become complicated as they fall passionately in love. In Beta Hi-Fi Stereo and VHS Hi-Fi Dolby Stereo.
Columbia Pictures — *RCA/Columbia Pictures Home Video*

Against All Odds **1969**
Adventure
76830 93 mins C B, V P
Christopher Lee, Richard Greene, Shirley Eaton
Fu Manchu plans to murder several world leaders by using beautiful slave girls saturated with poisonous venom that will instantly kill any man who kisses them.
Commonwealth — *Republic Pictures Home Video*

Agatha **1979**
Mystery
47391 98 mins C B, V R, P
Dustin Hoffman, Vanessa Redgrave, Timothy Dalton, Helen Morse, Tony Britton, Timothy West, Celia Gregory
Agatha Christie mysteriously disappears when faced with a failing marriage. Numerous people turn out to search the British countryside for some sign of her.
MPAA:PG
Warner Bros — *Warner Home Video*

Agency **1981**
Drama
62778 94 mins C B, V, CED P
Robert Mitchum, Lee Majors, Valerie Perrine
An advertising agency attempts to manipulate public behavior and opinion through the use of subliminal advertising.
MPAA:R
Jensen Farley Pictures — *Vestron Video*

Aida **1981**
Opera
59878 210 mins C LV P
Verdi's tragic opera performed live at the Arena Di Verona. In stereo.
Covent Garden Video — *Pioneer Artists*

Aida **1984**
Opera
80055 150 mins C B, V R, P
Maria Chiara, Nicola Martinucci
A performance of Giuseppe Verdi's opera taped at the Arena di Verona in Italy.
Radiotelevision Italiana — *THORN EMI/HBO Video*

Air Force **1943**
War-Drama
65064 124 mins B/W CED P
John Garfield, Gig Young, Arthur Kennedy, directed by Howard Hawks
This film about the early days of World War II follows the exploits of the crew of a Flying Fortress bomber as they see action at Pearl Harbor, Manila and the Coral Sea.
Warner Bros — *RCA VideoDiscs*

Air Supply Live in Hawaii **1982**
Music-Performance
76024 60 mins C B, V P
This concert features Air Supply's biggest hits, including "Lost in Love," "The One That You Love" and "Event the Nights Are Better."
Danny O'Donovan — *RCA/Columbia Pictures Home Video*

Airplane! **1980**
Comedy
54667 88 mins C B, V, LV R, P
Kareem Abdul-Jabbar, Lloyd Bridges, Peter Graves, Ethel Merman, Robert Hays, Jimmie Walker, directed by Jim Abrahams
A comical twist to disaster films. First the passengers on a flight to Chicago are poisoned by their fish dinners. Then the plane must be landed by a shell-shocked veteran who has a drinking problem.
MPAA:PG
Paramount, Howard W Koch — *Paramount Home Video; RCA VideoDiscs*

 (For explanation of codes, see USE GUIDE and KEY)

Airplane II: The Sequel 1982
Comedy
64505 84 mins C B, V, LV R, P
Robert Hays, Julie Hagerty, Lloyd Bridges, Raymond Burr, Peter Graves, William Shatner
There's a mad bomber aboard the first lunar shuttle in this loony sequel to "Airplane," which spoofs the familiar cliches of disaster movies.
MPAA:PG
Paramount — *Paramount Home Video; RCA VideoDiscs*

Airport 1970
Drama
53395 137 mins C B, V P
Dean Martin, Burt Lancaster, Jean Seberg, Jacqueline Bisset, George Kennedy, Helen Hayes, Van Heflin, Maureen Stapleton
The first of the "Airport" movies is based on Arthur Hailey's novel about a snow storm, a mired plane, and an aircraft in dire distress after a bomb explodes on it.
Academy Award '70: Best Supporting Actress (Hayes). MPAA:G
Universal; Ross Hunter — *MCA Home Video; RCA VideoDiscs*

Al Ponerse el Sol 197?
Romance
49746 90 mins C B, V P
Serena Hercan
The plot revolves around the relationships between women auditioning for a Madrid stage show, and the men who will choose them.
SP
Independent — *Media Home Entertainment*

Aladdin and the Wonderful Lamp 1982
Cartoons/Adventure
59668 65 mins C B, V P
Animated
Aladdin must use his magical lamp to defeat the wicked wizard and own the most valuable treasures in the land.
Toei Company — *Media Home Entertainment*

Alamo, The 1960
Western
31660 161 mins C B, V, CED P
John Wayne, Richard Widmark, Laurence Harvey, Frankie Avalon, directed by John Ford
An historical account of the men who came to the aid of Texas in its fight for freedom against the Mexican army.
Academy Awards '60: Best Sound Recording.
EL, SP
United Artists — *CBS/Fox Video*

Albino 197?
Mystery/Drama
53943 85 mins C B, V P
Christopher Lee, Trevor Howard, Sibyle Danning, Horst Frank
An albino, played by Horst Frank, stalks the street in search of his female victim.
MPAA:R
Jurgen Goslar — *Media Home Entertainment*

Alchemy—Live Dire Straits 1984
Music-Performance
79266 95 mins C B, V P
The exciting progressive rock sounds of Dire Straits are captured live in concert.
Polygram Music Video — *Music Media*

Aldrich Family, The 1950
Comedy
42973 27 mins B/W B, V, FO P
Jackie Kelk, House Jameson, Lois Wilson, Robert Casey
Upset because he hasn't received an invitation to a costume party, Henry decides to go as the rear end of a horse.
NBC — *Video Yesteryear*

Alexander Nevsky 1938
Drama
08701 107 mins B/W B, V, 3/4U P
Nikolai Cherkasson, N.P. Okholopkov, Al Abrikossov, directed by Sergei Eisenstein
A story of the invasion of Russia in 1241 by the Teutonic Knights, "Alexander Nevsky" emerges as more than a film spectacle. Dubbed in English.
Russian — *International Historic Films; Discount Video Tapes; Sheik Video; Video Yesteryear; Budget Video; Western Film & Video Inc; Classic Video Cinema Collector's Club; Kartes Productions*

Alexander the Great 1955
Biographical
80626 135 mins C B, V P
Richard Burton, Fredric March, Claire Bloom, Harry Andrews, Peter Cushing, directed by Robert Rossen
This is the life story of Alexander the Great who conquered the world before the age of thirty three.
Rossen Films; United Artists — *MGM/UA Home Video*

Algiers 1938
Drama
01786 96 mins B/W B, V P
Charles Boyer, Hedy Lamarr, Sigrid Gurie, Gene Lockhart, directed by John Cromwell
Spoiled rich girl falls under romantic spell of Pepe Le Moko, the Casbah's most notorious citizen.
U A; Walter Wanger — *Budget Video; Movie Buff Video; Cable Films; VCII; Video Connection; Video Yesteryear; Western Film &*

Video Inc; Discount Video Tapes; Kartes Productions; Classic Video Cinema Collector's Club

---

Ali: Skill, Brains and Guts 1975
Boxing
07874 90 mins C B, V P
Muhammad Ali
From teenage Golden Glove to Heavyweight champion, Ali tells his own story with highlights of over twenty-five fights.
Big Fights Inc — *VidAmerica*

Alibaba's Revenge 1984
Cartoons
70582 53 mins C B, V P
Animated, voice of Jim Backus, directed by H. Shidar
The efforts of Al Huck, his rodent side-kick, and a goofy genie combine to overthrow the tyrannical king of Alibaba. The Alibaban peasants (all cats) revolt behind Huck's leadership in response to unfair food and luxury taxes.
ATA Trading Corporation — *MPI Home Video*

Alice Adams 1935
Drama
45103 99 mins B/W B, V P, T
Katharine Hepburn, Fred MacMurray
Girl from small, midwestern town falls in love with a man from the upper level of society and tries to fit in.
Pandro S Berman — *Blackhawk Films; Nostalgia Merchant*

Alice Cooper and Friends 1978
Music-Performance
12044 50 mins C B, V P
Alice Cooper, The Tubes, Nazareth, Sha-Na-Na
A rock extravaganza, taped at the Anaheim Stadium in California in the summer of 1978, featuring the exotic stylings of Alice Cooper.
Drew Cummings — *Media Home Entertainment*

Alice Cooper: Welcome to My Nightmare 1975
Music
65134 66 mins C B, V R, P
Alice Cooper, Vincent Price
An elaborate video version of the "Welcome to My Nightmare" record album, featuring such ghoulish tunes as "Department of Youth," "Ballad of Dwight Frye" and "Cold Ethyl."
Alive Enterprises — *Warner Home Video*

Alice Doesn't Live Here Anymore 1975
Drama/Comedy
52706 113 mins C B, V R, P
Ellen Burstyn, Kris Kristofferson, Diane Ladd, Jodi Foster, Harvey Keitel, directed by Martin Scorcese
A young woman's husband dies suddenly, leaving her to care for their eleven-year-old son. She heads toward Monterey, California, where she was once a singer, but gets delayed in Phoenix where she falls for a rancher.
MPAA:PG
Warner Bros; David Suskind; Audrey Maas — *Warner Home Video; RCA VideoDiscs*

Alice Goodbody 1976
Comedy
66288 83 mins C B, V P
Sharon Kelly, Daniel Kauffman, Keith McConnell
A sex spoof of a lonely girl's misadventures in Hollywood.
MPAA:R
Tom Scheuer — *Media Home Entertainment*

Alice in Wonderland 1951
Fantasy/Cartoons
53794 75 mins C CED P
Animated
Disney's version of Lewis Carroll's fable about a girl who falls into a hole and ends up in Wonderland with the Mad Hatter, the Cheshire Cat, and the Queen of Hearts.
Walt Disney — *RCA VideoDiscs*

Alice in Wonderland 1977
Satire
55212 76 mins C B, V P
Kristine DeBell
Adult version of the classic tale starring Playboy cover girl Kristine DeBell.
MPAA:R EL, SP
General National Enterprises — *Media Home Entertainment*

Alice in Wonderland 1982
Musical/Fantasy
63841 81 mins C B, V P
Annie Enneking, Solvieg Olsen, Wendy Lehr, Jason McLean, Gary Briggle, Elizabeth Fink
All of Lewis Carroll's beloved characters come alive in this musical adaptation of his classic tale, performed by the Children's Theatre Company and School. VHS in stereo.
Television Theater Company — *MCA Home Video*

Alice Sweet Alice 1976
Suspense
29498 112 mins C B, V P
Brooke Shields, Linda Miller, Paula Sheppard
A spine-chilling story of macabre murders: who and why is this masked person butchering their victims?

Allied Artists — *Spotlite Video; King of Video; Sound Video Unlimited; Budget Video; World Video Pictures; Discount Video Tapes*

Alice Through the Looking Glass **1966**
Adventure
70679 72 mins C B, V P
Judi Rolin, Ricardo Montalban, Nanette Fabray, Robert Coote, Agnes Moorehead, Jack Palance, Jimmy Durante, The Smothers Brothers, Roy Castle, Richard Denning, directed by Alan Handley
Based on Lewis Carroll's classic adventure, this show follows the further adventures of young Alice. After a chess piece comes to life, it convinces Alice that excitement and adventure lie through the looking glass.
NBC; Alan Handley; Bob Wynn — *Embassy Home Entertainment*

Alice's Adventures in Wonderland **1972**
Comedy
03697 96 mins C B, V P
Peter Sellers, Dudley Moore, Fiona Fullerton
An updated film version of the delightful novel by Lewis Carroll.
Rainbow Adventure Films; Joseph Shaftel — *United Home Video*

Alice's Adventures in Wonderland **1973**
Fantasy
69614 100 mins C B, V P
Peter Sellers, Sir Ralph Richardson, Dudley Moore, Michael Horndern, Spike Mulligan
This adaptation of Lewis Carroll's classic tale features an all-star cast.
Josef Shaftel — *Children's Video Library*

Alice's Restaurant **1969**
Comedy/Drama
65333 111 mins C B, V, CED P
Arlo Guthrie
A young folk singer has difficulties with the police, the draft board and a Massachusetts community of flower children.
MPAA:R
United Artists — *CBS/Fox Video*

Alien **1979**
Science fiction
44930 116 mins C B, V, LV, CED P
Tom Skerritt, Sigourney Weaver, Veronica Cartwright
Seven astronauts on a routine mission encounter an awesome galactic horror.
MPAA:R
20th Century Fox — *CBS/Fox Video*

Alien Dead **1982**
Horror
81076 87 mins C B, V P
Buster Crabbe, Linda Lewis
The victims of a bizarre meteor crash reincarnate as flesh-eating ghouls anxious for a new supply of human food.
MPAA:R
Cannon Films — *Academy Home Entertainment*

Alien Factor, The **1978**
Science fiction
69803 82 mins C B, V P
John Leifert, Tom Griffiths, Mary Mertens
A spaceship crashes in the countryside, and a small town is jolted out of its sleepy state by havoc wreaked by a host of grotesque extraterrestrial monsters.
MPAA:PG
Don Dohler — *United Home Video*

Aliens from Spaceship Earth **1977**
Science fiction
33805 107 mins C B, V R, P
Donovan, Lynda Day George
Are strange, celestial forces invading our universe? If they are, is man prepared to defend his planet against threatening aliens of unknown strength?
International TF Productions — *Video Gems*

Alison's Birthday **1983**
Horror
70048 99 mins C B, V P
A teenage girl learns that some of her family and friends are Satan worshipers at a terrifying birthday party.
David Hannay — *VidAmerica*

All About Eve **1950**
Drama
29127 138 mins B/W B, V P
Bette Davis, Anne Baxter, Gary Merrill, Celeste Holme, George Sanders, Marilyn Monroe, directed by Joseph L. Mankiewicz
An aspiring young actress ingratiates herself with a prominent group of theatre people, but passion to perform and jealousy consume her as she viciously betrays her colleagues in her struggle for success.
Academy Awards '50: Best Picture; Best Supporting Actor (Sanders); Best Direction (Mankiewicz); Best Screenplay (Mankiewicz).
20th Century Fox — *CBS/Fox Video*

All in a Night's Work **1961**
Mystery
16136 94 mins C B, V P
Dean Martin, Shirley MacLaine, Cliff Robertson
The founder of a one-man publishing empire is found dead with a smile on his face.

EL, SP
Paramount; Hal Wallis Prod — *CBS/Fox Video*

All Mine to Give **1956**
Drama
10400 102 mins C B, V P
Glynis Johns, Cameron Mitchell
Saga of a family of eight who braved frontier hardships, epidemics, and death in the Wisconsin wilderness a century ago.
RKO — *United Home Video*

All Night Long **1981**
Comedy
59682 100 mins C B, V P
Gene Hackman, Barbra Streisand, Dianne Ladd, Dennis Quaid
A man who is passed over for a promotion begins his comic liberation and joins the drifters, weirdos and thieves of the night at his new job.
MPAA:R
Universal — *MCA Home Video*

All of Me **1984**
Comedy
80329 93 mins C B, V R, P
Steve Martin, Lily Tomlin, Victoria Tennant, Selma Diamond, Richard Libertine, directed by Carl Reiner
A lawyer inherits the soul of a dead woman by accident and it winds up taking over the right side of his body.
MPAA:PG
Universal — *THORN EMI/HBO Video*

All Quiet on the Western Front **1930**
Drama
55556 103 mins B/W B, V P
Lew Ayres, Louis Wolheim, John Wray
A dramatization of Erich Maria Remarque's novel about a young German soldier facing the horrors of World War I.
Universal — *MCA Home Video*

All Quiet on the Western Front **1979**
Drama
55528 150 mins C B, V P
Richard Thomas, Ernest Borgnine, Donald Pleasance, Patricia Neal
A sensitive German youth plunges excitedly into World War I and discovers its terror and degradation. Based on the novel by Erich Maria Remarque.
Norman Rosemont Prods; Marble Arch Prods — *CBS/Fox Video*

All Screwed Up **1974**
Film-Avant-garde
37406 104 mins C B, V P
Luigi Diberti, Lina Polito, directed by Lina Wertmuller
The story of a group of young immigrants in Milan—where everything is in its place—but nothing is in order.
New Line Cinema — *CBS/Fox Video*

All-Star Batting Tips **1975**
Baseball
33844 28 mins C B, V P
Tony Kubek, Mickey Mantle, Stan Musial, Pete Rose, Willie Mays, Harmon Killebrew
Tony Kubek moderates an All-Star panel as they discuss their philosophies on hitting and teach the six essential steps necessary to become a better hitter.
Major League Baseball — *Major League Baseball Productions*

All Star Cartoon Parade **19??**
Cartoons
66470 54 mins C B, V P
Animated
A collection of popular vintage cartoons, starring such favorites as Little Lulu, Casper the Friendly Ghost, Betty Boop and Raggedy Ann and Andy.
Famous Studios — *Republic Pictures Home Video*

All-Star Catching and Base Stealing Tips **1975**
Baseball
35533 28 mins C B, V P
Johnny Bench, Thurman Munson, Carlton Fisk, Steve Yeager, Del Crandall
The fine points of catching and the art of stealing bases are the featured topics on this program. Game-action footage of today's stars is presented in an easy-to-understand manner.
Major League Baseball — *Major League Baseball Productions*

All-Star Game, 1967 **1967**
Baseball
49550 30 mins C B, V P
Tony Perez' 15th inning home run off Catfish Hunter gives the National League a 2-1 victory in the longest All-Star game ever played. Young Mets' pitcher Tom Seaver gets credit for the victory.
Winik Films — *Major League Baseball Productions*

All-Star Game, 1970: What Makes an All-Star **1970**
Baseball
45030 30 mins C B, V P
The National League wins its eighth straight midsummer classic, 5-4, in 12 innings. Pete Rose barrels into American League catcher Ray Fosse at home plate to score the winning run on Jim Hickman's single.

W and W Prods — *Major League Baseball Productions*

All-Star Game, 1971: Home Run Heroes 1971
Baseball
33843 26 mins C B, V P
Some or the great home run sluggers of the past are paid tribute, including Babe Ruth, Hank Greenberg, Mel Ott, and Mickey Mantle. The game itself produces six home runs, one of them a mammoth blast by Oakland's Reggie Jackson, and the American League goes on to a 6-4 victory.
W and W Productions — *Major League Baseball Productions*

All-Star Game, 1972: Years of Tradition, Night of Pride 1972
Baseball
33841 26 mins C B, V P
Highlights from the first All-Star Game in 1933 to the present ones are shown prior to the National League's 10-inning, 4-3 victory at Atlanta Stadium. Hank Aaron thrills the home-team crowd with a dramatic home run.
W and W Prods — *Major League Baseball Productions*

All-Star Game, 1973: A New Generation of Stars 1973
Baseball
33840 26 mins C B, V P
The great Willie Mays plays in his last All-Star Game, while the up-and-coming stars such as Bobby Bonds and Johnny Bench lead the National League to victory.
W and W Productions — *Major League Baseball Productions*

All-Star Game, 1974: Mid-Summer Magic 1974
Baseball
33839 26 mins C B, V P
Write-in candidate Steve Garvey leads the National League to its third straight victory at Pittsburgh's Three Rivers Stadium. A sequence of ironic dream game performances by All-Stars throughout the years is included.
W and W Productions — *Major League Baseball Productions*

All-Star Game, 1975: All-Star Fever 1975
Baseball
33838 28 mins C B, V P
National League home runs by Steve Garvey and Jimmy Wynn give them an early lead. Carl Yastrzemski's homer ties the game for the American leaguers. The Nationals score three times in the ninth inning with Bill Madlock's single the key hit in a 6-3 victory at County Stadium in Milwaukee.
Major League Baseball — *Major League Baseball Productions*

All-Star Game, 1976: Champions of Pride 1976
Baseball
33837 28 mins C B, V P
The National League celebrates its 100th anniversary with another victory over the American League. Unusual viewpoints are featured, including Randy Jones' sinkerball, the many motions of Luis Tiant, the aggressive play of Pete Rose and Mickey Rivers, and the zany antics of Tigers' pitcher, "The Bird," Mark Fidrych.
Major League Baseball — *Major League Baseball Productions*

All-Star Game, 1977: The Man Behind the Mask 1977
Baseball
33836 29 mins C B, V P
This program highlights the game and the individual stars of the National League's 7-5 victory over the American League, while featuring the work of home plate umpire Bill Kunkel, from his pre-game preparation to the final out.
Major League Baseball — *Major League Baseball Productions*

All-Star Game, 1978: What Makes an All-Star 1978
Baseball
33835 26 mins C B, V P
Los Angeles Dodger first baseman Steve Garvey collects two hits, two RBI's, and the game's MVP award as the National League defeats the American League 7-3 in San Diego. "Mr. Cub," Ernie Banks, comments from the stands along with the youngsters who won the "Pitch, Hit, and Run" competition.
Major League Baseball — *Major League Baseball Productions*

All-Star Game, 1979: Inches and Jinxes 1979
Baseball
45029 30 mins C B, V P
The National League is victorious again. A 7-6 win in Seattle's Kingdome is highlighted by Lee Mazzili's home run and Dave Parker's throw to home plate to nail Brian Downing, a potentially important run for the American League. Ron Guidry walks Mazzili to force in the winning run.
Major League Baseball — *Major League Baseball Productions*

All-Star Game, 1980: Heroes to Remember 1980
Baseball
49549 30 mins C B, V P
Cubs' relief pitcher Bruce Sutter wins the game's MVP award, as he nails down yet another victory for the National League in the Midsummer's Classic.
Major League Baseball — *Major League Baseball Productions*

All-Star Game, 1981 1981
Baseball
59376 30 mins C B, V P
In the first baseball game played since the great strike, Gary Carter of the Expos captures the MVP award by crashing two home runs in leading the National League to still another victory over the American League, at Cleveland's Municipal Stadium.
Major League Baseball Prods — *Major League Baseball Productions*

All-Star Game, 1982 1982
Baseball
64658 30 mins C B, V P
American and National League All-Star Players
The National League wins again. Cincinnati Reds' shortstop Dave Concepcion homers and is named MVP of this All-Star Game at Montreal. Montreal's own Steve Rogers is the winning pitcher, and Boston's Dennis Eckersley takes the 4-1 loss for manager Billy Martin's American League squad. Detroit catcher Lance Parrish stars in defeat, throwing out three NL runners attempting to steal bases.
Major League Baseball — *Major League Baseball Productions*

All-Star Game, '84: Something Special 1984
Baseball
81130 25 mins C B, V P
Here are highlights from the 1984 mid summer classic where the National League triumphad over the American League once again.
Major League Baseball — *Major League Baseball Productions*

All-Star Pitching Tips 1975
Baseball
33845 28 mins C B, V P
Whitey Ford, Tom Seaver, Claude Osteen, Bert Blyleven, Catfish Hunter, Mike Marshall, Nolan Ryan
The basics of pitching are explained by host and Hall of Famer Whitey Ford, along with helpful hints from many major league pitching stars.
Major League Baseball — *Major League Baseball Productions*

All-Star Game, 1983: Golden Memories 1983
Baseball
81129 25 mins C B, V P
The American League wins the All-Star Game for the first time in twelve years by a score of 13 to 3. Fred Lynn hits the first grand slam home run in the fifty-year history of the game.
Major League Baseball — *Major League Baseball Productions*

All That Jazz 1979
Musical-Drama
48515 120 mins C B, V, LV, CED P
Roy Scheider, Jessica Lange, Ann Reinking, Ben Vereen, John Lithgow, directed by Bob Fosse
A show business personality is so obsessed by his career that it takes a heart attack to bring him down to earth. Along the way, the tensions, sweat, and tears that go into the making of a Broadway show are exposed.
Academy Awards '79: Best Film Editing, Best Art Direction, Best Costume Design, Best Song Adaptation Score MPAA:R
Twentieth Century Fox — *CBS/Fox Video*

All the Best from Russia 1977
Dance/Variety
58564 58 mins C B, V P
An inside look at the Russian Winter Arts Festival which includes performances by the Bolshoi Ballet, the Don Cossack dancers and the American Folk Ensemble.
Canadian — *Mastervision*

All the Marbles 1981
Comedy
59365 113 mins C B, V, CED R
Peter Falk, Burt Young
A manager of two beautiful lady wrestlers has dreams of going to the top.
MPAA:R
MGM — *MGM/UA Home Video*

All the President's Men 1976
Drama
38939 135 mins C B, V R, P
Robert Redford, Dustin Hoffman, Jason Robards, directed by Alan J. Pakula
The investigation into the Watergate break-in by Washington Post reporters Bob Woodward and Carl Bernstein is dramatized in this powerful film.
MPAA:PG
Warner Bros — *Warner Home Video; RCA VideoDiscs*

All the Right Moves 1983
Drama
Closed Captioned
65752 90 mins C B, V, CED P

(For explanation of codes, see USE GUIDE and KEY)

Tom Cruise, Lea Thompson, Craig T. Nelson
A young man attempts to move up in the world and out of the dying mill town where he grew up.
MPAA:R
20th Century Fox — *CBS/Fox Video*

All the Way Boys 1973
Adventure/Comedy
80042 105 mins C B, V P
Bud Spencer, Terence Hill
Two adventurers crash-land a plane in the Amazon jungles to find riches and danger.
MPAA:PG
Joseph E. Levine; Italo Zingarelli — *Embassy Home Entertainment*

All You Need Is Cash 1978
Comedy/Music
65335 70 mins C B, V P
Eric Idle, Neil Innes, Rikki Fataar, Dan Ayleroyd, Gilda Radner, John Belushi, George Harrison, directed by Eric Idle
"The Rutles" star in this parody of The Beatles' legend, from the early days of the "Pre-Fab Four" in Liverpool to their worldwide success.
Lorne Michaels — *Pacific Arts Video*

Allegheny Uprising 1939
Western
10074 81 mins B/W B, V P, T
John Wayne, Claire Trevor, George Sanders, Brian Donlevy, Chill Wills
Set in 1759, man clashes with military commander in order to stop sale of firearms to Indians.
RKO — *Blackhawk Films; Nostalgia Merchant*

Alley Cat 1984
Martial arts
73042 82 mins C B, V P
Karin Mani
A woman fights back against a street gang that attacked her.
MPAA:R
Film Ventures — *Vestron Video*

Almost Perfect Affair, An 1979
Comedy/Romance
81117 92 mins C B, V R, P
Keith Carradine, Monica Vitti, Raf Vallone, Christian deSica, directed by Michael Ritchie
An American Filmmaker falls in love with the wife of an Italian producer during the Cannes Film Festival.
MPAA:PG
Paramount; Terry Carr — *Paramount Home Video*

Almost Royal Family, The 1984
Drama
80806 52 mins C B, V P
Sarah Jessica Parker, John Femia
All kinds of problems arise when a family inherits an island on the St. Lawrence River embargoed by the United States and Canada.
Scholastic Productions Inc. — *Scholastic Lorimar*

Aloha, Bobby and Rose 1974
Drama
77521 90 mins C B, V P
Paul LeMat, Dianne Hull, Robert Carradine, Tim McIntire, directed by Floyd Mutrux
A mechanic and his girlfriend become accidentally involved in an attempted robbery and murder.
MPAA:PG
Columbia Pictures — *Media Home Entertainment*

Alone in the Dark 1982
Horror
65063 92 mins C CED P
Jack Palance, Donald Pleasance, Martin Landau
The inmates of an insane asylum escape during a power blackout and terrorize an isolated family.
MPAA:R
New Line Cinema — *RCA VideoDiscs*

Alone in the Dark 1982
Horror
68262 92 mins C B, V P
Jack Palance, Donald Pleasance, Martin Landau
Three patients from a mental hospital decide that they must kill their doctor. They get this chance when there is a city-wide blackout.
MPAA:R
Robert Shaye; New Line Cinema — *RCA/Columbia Pictures Home Video*

Along Came Jones 1945
Western/Comedy
73974 93 mins B/W B, V P
Gary Cooper, Loretta Young, Dan Duryea, William Demarest
A cowboy is the victim of mistaken identity as the good guys and the bad guys pursue him.
United Artists — *Key Video*

Alpha Incident, The 1977
Drama/Science fiction
65366 86 mins C B, V P
Ralph Meeker, Stafford Morgan, John Goff, Carol Irene Newell
A frightening doomsday drama about an alien organism with the potential to destroy all living things.
MPAA:PG
Bill Rebane — *Media Home Entertainment*

Alpine Ski School 1984
Sports-Winter
73704 76 mins C B, V P
This program shows you everything you'll need to know about skiing before hitting the slope. When you buy the videocassette, you get a tote bag as a bonus.
AM Available
Special Projects International Inc — *Embassy Home Entertainment*

Altered States 1980
Science fiction/Drama
58215 103 mins C B, V, LV R, P
William Hurt, Blair Brown, directed by Ken Russell
A research scientist experimenting with altered states of consciousness discovers horrors in the secret landscapes of the mind. Based on the novel by Paddy Chayefsky.
MPAA:R
Warner Bros — *Warner Home Video; RCA VideoDiscs*

Alternative, The 1976
Drama
80130 90 mins C B, V P
Wendy Hughes, Peter Adams, Mary Mackie
An unmarried pregnant magazine editor is caught in a tug of war between the baby's father and her lover.
Grundy Organization — *King of Video*

Alvarez Kelly 1966
Western
44786 116 mins C B, V P
William Holden, Richard Widmark, Janice Rule
Holden and Widmark employ some two-fisted action amidst the Civil War setting.
Sol C Siegel — *RCA/Columbia Pictures Home Video*

Alvin Purple 1973
Comedy
81253 97 mins C B, V, LV P
Graeme Blundell, George Whaley, Elli Maclure, Jacki Weaver
This film chronicles the adventures of Alvin Purple, a man who is constantly being pursued by throngs of sexually insatiable women.
MPAA:R
Hexagon Productions — *New World Video*

Alvin Rides Again 1974
Comedy
80662 89 mins C B, V P
Graeme Blundell, Alan Finney, Brionny Behets, Frank Thring, Jeff Ashby
The sexually insatiable Alvin Purple is asked to impersonate an American gangster who was accidentally killed.
Hexagon Productions — *New World Video*

Always Ready 1985
Documentary/History-US
70685 45 mins C B, V P
Narrated by Ken Howard, directed by Fred Warshofsky
Part of the "In Defense of Freedom" series, this program traces the history of the U.S. Coast Guard.
A.B. Marian — *MPI Home Video*

Am I Normal? 1979
Adolescence/Sexuality
63878 24 mins C B, V P
Focusing on three fictional characters, this program presents the facts about male sexual development, while raising important questions about masculinity, identity and peer pressure.
Copperfield Films — *MGM/UA Home Video*

Amante Para Dos 1981
Drama
47858 95 mins C B, V P
Alberto Olmedo, Tato Bores, Maria Casan
Mauricio is a serious man and loves his wife, but his weakness is Monica, his lover. Alberto, another married man, is also Monica's lover, until both men decide that she is dangerous. In Spanish.
SP
Nicolas Carreras; Luis Repetto — *Media Home Entertainment*

Amarcord 1974
Comedy
54798 124 mins C B, V R, P
Magall Noel, Bruno Zanin, Pupella Maggio, Armando Brancia, directed by Federico Fellini
The life of a small Italian coastal town in the 1930's is recalled by a director with a superstar's access to the resources of the Italian film industry.
Academy Awards '74: Best Foreign Film.
MPAA:R
Warner Bros, New World Pictures — *Warner Home Video*

Amateur, The 1982
Adventure
62776 112 mins C B, V, CED P
John Savage, Christopher Plummer, Marthe Keller, Arthur Hill
A computer technologist dives into a plot of international intrigue when he investigates the death of his girlfriend, murdered by terrorists.
MPAA:R
20th Century Fox — *CBS/Fox Video*

Amazing Apes, The 1977
Animals/Documentary
29128 93 mins C B, V R, P
This feature reveals never-before-known facts about these fascinating primates through

absorbing highlights such as monkey worship, life-style of snow monkeys in Japan, and studies of gorillas and chimps in the wild.
Bill Burrud Productions — *Walt Disney Home Video*

Amazing Dobermans, The **1976**
Adventure
47818 96 mins C B, V, 3/4U P
Fred Astaire, Barbara Eden, James Franciscus
The owner of five trained dogs assists an undercover agent in foiling a small-time criminal's gambling and extortion racket.
MPAA:G
Golden Films — *Media Home Entertainment; Nostalgia Merchant*

Amazing Howard Hughes, The **1977**
Biographical/Drama
63341 119 mins C B, V R, P
Tommy Lee Jones, Ed Flanders, James Hampton, Tovah Feldshuh, Lee Purcell
This film reveals the full story of the legendary millionaire's life and career, from daring test pilot to inventor to Hollywood film producer to death as a paranoiac in isolation.
Roger Gimbel Productions; EMI Television Programmes — *THORN EMI/HBO Video*

Amazing Spider-Man, The **1982**
Cartoons/Adventure
59038 100 mins C B, V P
A collection of Spider-Man's most exciting adventures.
Marvel Comics Group — *MCA Home Video*

Amazing Spider-Man, The **1977**
Adventure
59334 94 mins C B, V, CED P
Nicholas Hammond, David White
Spider-Man's unique powers are put to the test when he comes to the rescue of the government by preventing an evil scientist from blackmailing the government.
Charles Fries Prods — *CBS/Fox Video*

Amazing World of Psychic Phenomena, The **1977**
Occult sciences
45039 91 mins C B, V P
Hosted and narrated by Raymond Burr
A look at the mysteries of parapsychology.
Sunn Classic — *VidAmerica*

Ambassador's Boots, The **1985**
Mystery/Drama
70661 60 mins C B, V P
James Warwick, Francesca Annis
In this chapter of the "Partners in Crime" series, the Beresfords aid the American Ambassador to England in answering some curious queries regarding the handling of his luggage.
Unknown — *Pacific Arts Video*

Ambrose Bierce: The Man and the Snake/The Return **1978**
Literature-American/Mystery
58733 60 mins C B, V P
A pair of stories by American author Ambrose Bierce.
Independent — *Mastervision*

America at the Movies **1976**
Film-History/Documentary
44776 116 mins C B, V P
John Wayne, Orson Welles, Peter Sellers, James Dean, Gene Hackman, Burt Lancaster, Julie Harris, Deborah Kerr, Al Pacino, Robert De Niro
Scenes from over eighty of the finest American motion pictures tell the story of American movies and give a portrait of America as it has been seen on screen for half a century. Scenes from "The Birth of a Nation," "Citizen Kane," "Dr. Strangelove," "East of Eden," "The French Connection," and "From Here to Eternity," are among the many included. Some black and white scenes.
American Film Institute — *RCA/Columbia Pictures Home Video*

America Between the Great Wars **1978**
History-US/Documentary
10153 60 mins B/W B, V P, T
Covers celebrations and tragedies from the roaring twenties. Includes the century of Progress Exposition in Chicago, the Prohibition era, Hindenburg disaster, and off-screen activities of Charlie Chaplin.
Blackhawk — *Blackhawk Films*

America Live in Central Park **1981**
Music-Performance
59876 53 mins C LV P
Conceptual sequences combine with stirring performances as the folk-rock group America offers this concert of hits including "Tin Man," "Ventura Highway," "Horse with No Name." In stereo.
Peter Clifton — *Pioneer Artists*

America/The Fall of Babylon **1924**
Film-History
50636 56 mins B/W B, V P, T
Neil Hamilton, Lionel Barrymore, Constance Tallmadge, Elmer Clifton, Alfred Paget
A double feature containing abridged versions of these two motion pictures. In "America", a

Boston patriot and the daughter of an aristocratic Virginia Tory fall in love during the Revolutionary War. "The Fall of Babylon" is one of the stories in D.W. Griffith's "Intolerance." Silent.
D W Griffith — *Blackhawk Films*

American Alcoholic, The/Reading, Writing and Reefer **1981**
Drug abuse/Alcoholism
52609 102 mins C CED P
Two important contemporary issues—alcoholism and marijuana abuse—are explored in two enlightening documentaries.
NBC — *RCA VideoDiscs*

American Caesar **1985**
Biographical/World War II
81450 300 mins C B, V P
Hosted by John Huston
This documentary examines the life and military career of General Douglas MacArthur.
John McGreevey; Ian McLeod — *Embassy Home Entertainment*

American Dream **1981**
Drama
80422 90 mins C B, V P
Stephen Macht, Karen Carlson, John Karlen, Andrea Smith, John McIntire
A mid western family leaves the suburbs and move into a Chicago inner city neighborhood.
Mace Neufield Productions — *Unicorn Video*

American Dreamer **1984**
Comedy/Adventure
Closed Captioned
81171 105 mins C B, V P
Jobeth Williams, Tom Conti, Giancarlo Giannini, Coral Browne, directed by Rick Rosenthal
A housewife wins a trip to Paris as a prize from entering a mystery writing contest. Silly from a blow on the head, she begins living the fictional life of her favorite literary adventures. Hi-Fi Stereo for both formats.
MPAA:PG
CBS Theatrical Films — *CBS/Fox Video*

American Empire **1942**
Western
10921 82 mins B/W B, V P
Preston Foster, Richard Dix, Frances Gifford, Leo Carrillo, directed by William McGann
Partners building cattle empire in Texas have trouble between themselves with Mexican rustlers.
United Artists; Harry Sherman Prods — *Discount Video Tapes; Video Yesteryear; Cable Films*

American Friend **1982**
Drama
72178 127 mins C B, V P
Dennis Hopper, Bruce Ganz
Reverence is paid to Hitchcock and Fuller in this gripping thriller.
Wim Wenders — *Pacific Arts Video*

American Gigolo **1979**
Drama
48507 117 mins C B, V, LV R, P
Richard Gere, Lauren Hutton
A professional lover becomes involved with the wife of a California state senator, then is framed for murder.
MPAA:R
Jerry Bruckheimer — *Paramount Home Video; RCA VideoDiscs*

American Graffiti **1973**
Comedy
11565 112 mins C B, V, LV P
Richard Dreyfuss, Ronny Howard, Cindy Williams, Mackenzie Phillips, Wolfman Jack, directed by George Lucas
A look at one hectic night in the life of a group of high school friends just before they go off to college, jobs, or the army.
MPAA:PG
Universal; Francis Ford Coppola — *MCA Home Video; RCA VideoDiscs*

American History: America Grows Up (1850-1900's) **1982**
History-US
58572 50 mins C B, V P
America's growth from a nation of farms and villages to one of the leading industrial nations of the world from 1850 to 1900 is discussed.
McGraw Hill — *Mastervision*

American History: Americans Courageous (1600-Today) **1982**
History-US
58566 50 mins C B, V P
Two films featuring tales of courage: "The Gloucesterman," a filmed celebration of the townsfolk of the historic Massachusetts village who go down to the sea in ships, and "Not for Ourselves Alone," a 200 year history of America's Armed Forces.
WGBH Boston — *Mastervision*

American History: Colonial America (1500's-1600's) **1982**
History-US
58567 50 mins C B, V P

(For explanation of codes, see USE GUIDE and KEY)

A look at the days when France, Spain, and England were fighting for the riches of the New World.
McGraw Hill — *Mastervision*

American History: Gathering Strength (1840-1914) **1982**
History-US
58571 50 mins C B, V P
The differences between the old immigrants from northern Europe and the new wave of settlers from the counties of eastern and southern Europe are discussed.
McGraw Hill — *Mastervision*

American History: Opening the West (1860-1900) **1982**
History-US
58570 50 mins C B, V P
Lincoln's efforts to reunite the nation after the bloody fratricide of the Civil War and begin the epic westward expansion are discussed.
McGraw Hill — *Mastervision*

American History: Roots of Democracy (1700's) **1982**
History-US
58568 50 mins C B, V P
This program portrays the relationship between foreign trade and domestic activity which led to the rebellion against English restraints and the American Revolution.
McGraw Hill — *Mastervision*

American History: The Game of Monopoly (1870-1914) **1982**
History-US
58573 50 mins C B, V P
This program examines the rise to wealth and power of the industrial titans under the leadership of such men as Morgan, Carnegie, Rockefeller, and Vanderbilt.
McGraw Hill — *Mastervision*

American History: Two Great Crusades (1930-1945) **1982**
History-US/World War II
58575 50 mins C B, V P
The New Deal and the Second World War are the focus of this look at the U.S.'s two modern crises.
McGraw Hill — *Mastervision*

American History: War Between the States (1800's) **1982**
History-US
58569 50 mins C B, V P
This program analyzes the institution of slavery and shows how it came to divide our country.
McGraw Hill — *Mastervision*

American History: Warring and Roaring (1914-1929) **1982**
History-US/World War I
58574 50 mins C B, V P
This program examines the U.S. involvement in World War I and the spirited 1920's, which ended with the stock market crash of '29.
McGraw Hill — *Mastervision*

American Hot Wax **1978**
Comedy
64781 91 mins C CED P
Chuck Berry, Jerry Lee Lewis, Tim McIntire, Laraine Newman
1950's rock 'n' roll is revived in this tribute to pioneering disk jockey Alan Freed.
MPAA:R
Paramount — *RCA VideoDiscs*

American in Paris, An **1951**
Musical
39092 113 mins C B, V, LV, CED P
Gene Kelly, Leslie Caron, Oscar Levant, directed by Vincente Minnelli
Gene Kelly plays an ex-G.I. artist living in Paris, who is torn between his love for a dancer, Leslie Caron, and his artistic mentor, Nina Foch. George Gershwin score includes a 15-minute ballet based on "An American in Paris." Winner of seven Academy Awards, including Best Picture.
Academy Awards '51: Best Picture; Best Story and Screenplay; Best Musical Scoring.
MGM — *MGM/UA Home Video*

American Nightmare **1983**
Drama
64231 85 mins C B, V P
Lawrence Day, Lora Stanley, Lenore Zann
A young man searches for his missing sister against a background of pornography, drug peddling and prostitution in the slums of a city.
Independent — *Media Home Entertainment*

American Werewolf in London, An **1981**
Horror
58629 95 mins C B, V, LV P
David Naughton, Griffin Dunne, Jenny Agutter, Frank Oz, Brian Glover, directed by John Landis

Special effects highlight this telling of the werewolf story, as two young Americans backpacking in northern England are attacked by a werewolf.
MPAA:R
Universal; George Folsey Jr — *MCA Home Video; RCA VideoDiscs*

Americana 1983
Drama
65603 90 mins C B, V P
David Carradine, Barbara Hershey
The gripping drama captures the pain and determination of a Vietnam veteran struggling to rebuild his life.
MPAA:PG
David Carradine — *Vestron Video*

Americano, The 1955
Adventure
80032 85 mins C B, V P
Glenn Ford, Frank Lovejoy, Abbe Lane, Cesar Romero, directed by William Castle
A cowboy travelling to Brazil with a shipment of Brahma bulls discovers the rancher he's delivering them to has been murdered.
RKO; Robert Stillman Productions — *Republic Pictures Home Video*

Americano, The/Variety 192?
Adventure
10119 54 mins B/W B, V P, T
Douglas Fairbanks, directed by John Emerson
"The Americano" (1917) features Douglas Fairbanks, Sr. saving a revolt-ridden Caribbean country. "Variety" portrays the Flying Artinellis, a trapeze act hampered by jealous love. Both films are abridged.
Fine Arts Triangle; Unknown — *Blackhawk Films*

America's Team: The Dallas Cowboys 1975-79 1982
Football
63164 120 mins C B, V, FO P
Dallas Cowboys
A compilation of individual Dallas Cowboys team highlight films from the second half of the 1970's.
NFL Films — *NFL Films Video*

Americathon 1979
Comedy
80888 85 mins C B, V P
John Ritter, Nancy Morgan, Harvey Korman, Peter Riegart, Fred Willard, Meat Loaf, directed by Neal Isreal
It is the year 1998 and the United States is almost bankrupt, so the President decides to stage a telethon to keep the country from going broke. The soundtrack features music by The Beach Boys and Elvis Costello.
MPAA:PG
Lorimar Productions — *Karl/Lorimar Home Video*

Amin: The Rise and Fall 1982
Drama/Biographical
69677 101 mins C B, V R, P
This is a dramatization of Idi Amin's 8-year reign of terror in Uganda, which resulted in the deaths of a half million people and the near ruin of a nation.
Sharad Patel — *THORN EMI/HBO Video*

Amityville Horror, The 1979
Horror
53505 117 mins C B, V R, P
James Brolin, Margot Kidder, Rod Steiger, Don Stroud, Murray Hamilton
The tale of the Lutz family and their supernatural experiences in their Long Island home, once the scene of a mass murder.
MPAA:R
American International Pictures — *Warner Home Video; RCA VideoDiscs; Vestron Video (disc only)*

Amityville 3D 1983
Horror
65473 98 mins C B, V, CED P
Tony Roberts, Tess Harper
The infamous Amityville house is once again the centerpiece of terror.
MPAA:R
Stephen F Kesten — *Vestron Video*

Amityville II: The Possession 1982
Horror
60438 110 mins C B, V, LV, CED P
Burt Young, Andrew Prine, Moses Gunn, Rutanya Alda
This prequel to "The Amityville Horror" tells the story of how the house became possessed by demonic forces.
MPAA:R
Dino DeLaurentiis — *Embassy Home Entertainment*

Among the Cinders 1983
Drama
81252 103 mins C B, V, LV P
Paul O'Shea, Derek Hardwick, Rebecca Gibney, Yvonne Lawley, Amanda Jones
A sixteen-year-old New Zealand boy runs away to his grandfather's farm to forget about his friend's accidental death. At the farm, he meets an older woman and compromises his virtue.
Pacific Films — *New World Video*

Amos 'n' Andy Comedy Classics 195?
Comedy
80465 70 mins B/W B, V P
Three complete and uncut episodes from the popular TV series of the early 1950's are featured on this tape with original commercials included.
CBS — *Spotlite Video*

Amsterdam Connection 197?
Martial arts/Adventure
47705 90 mins C B, V P
Chen Shing, Jason Pai Piu, Kid Sherrif
A film company acts as a cover for prostitution and drug smuggling, with the girls acting as international couriers.
KK Wong — *Master Arts Video*

Amsterdam Kill, The 1978
Adventure
64574 93 mins C B, V P
Robert Mitchum, Richard Egan, Keye Luke, Leslie Nielsen, Bradford Dillman
An ex-agent of the U.S. Drug Enforcement Agency is hired to hunt down the kingpin of a narcotics syndicate.
MPAA:R
Columbia — *RCA/Columbia Pictures Home Video*

Amy 1981
Drama
53795 100 mins C B, V R, P
Jenny Agutter, Barry Newman, Kathleen Nolan, Margaret O'Brien, Nanette Fabray, Chris Robinson, Lou Fant, directed by Vincent McEveety
Set in the early 1900's, the story follows the experiences of a woman after she leaves her well-to-do husband to teach at a school for the deaf and blind.
MPAA:G
Walt Disney Productions — *Walt Disney Home Video*

Anarchy, U.S.A. 1966
Propaganda
69574 78 mins B/W B, V, FO P
A blatantly propagandistic film which offers the premise that the Civil Rights Movement in America is part of a worldwide scheme organized by Soviet Communists to enslave mankind.
Independent — *Video Yesteryear*

Anchors Aweigh 1985
Documentary/History-US
70682 45 mins C B, V P
Narrated by Ken Howard, directed by Fred Warshofsky
Part of the "In Defense of Freedom" series, this program looks at the history of the United States Navy.
A.B. Marian — *MPI Home Video*

And God Created Woman 1957
Drama
58894 93 mins C B, V, LV, CED P
Brigitte Bardot, Curt Jurgens, Jean-Louis Trintignant, Christian Marquand
An eighteen-year-old is given a home by a local family with three handsome young sons.
Raoul J Levy — *Vestron Video; Time Life Video*

And If I'm Elected 1984
Satire
79704 53 mins C B, V P
The Smothers Brothers satirize famous presidential television commercials.
Trans World Entertainment — *Trans World Entertainment*

...And Justice for All 1979
Drama
52750 120 mins C B, V P
Al Pacino, Jack Warden, John Forsythe, Lee Strasberg, directed by Norman Jewison
A young lawyer battles not only one-on-one injustice in the courts, but the whole system as well.
MPAA:R
Norman Jewison; Patrick Palmer — *RCA/Columbia Pictures Home Video; RCA VideoDiscs*

And Nothing But the Truth 1984
Drama
80213 90 mins C B, V P
Glenda Jackson, Jon Finch, Kenneth Colley, James Donnelly
A multinational corporation is out to ruin the investigative TV report team trying to do a story on the company.
Castle Hill Productions — *Monterey Home Video*

And Now for Something Completely Different 1972
Comedy
47782 89 mins C B, V P
John Cleese, Michael Palin, Eric Idle, Graham Chapman, Terry Gilliam, Terry Jones
A compilation of skits from BBC-TV's "Monty Python's Flying Circus" featuring Monty Python's own weird, hilarious brand of humor.
Patricia Casey — *RCA/Columbia Pictures Home Video*

And Now the Screaming Starts 1973
Horror
54913 87 mins C B, V, 3/4U P
Peter Cushing, Herbert Lom, Patrick Magee, Ian Ogilvy, Stephanie Beacham, Geoffrey Whitehead, Guy Rolfe, directed by Roy Ward Baker
The young bride-to-be of the lord of a British manor house is greeted by bloody faces at the window, a severed hand, and five corpses.
MPAA:R
Cinerama Releasing — *Nostalgia Merchant*

And the Ship Sails On 1984
Drama
80371 130 mins C B, V P
Freddie Jones, Barbara Jefford, Janet Suzman, Peter Cellier, directed by Federico Fellini
A group of devoted opera lovers take a luxury cruise to pay their respects to a recently deceased opera diva. With English subtitles and Available in Beta Hi-Fi.
MPAA:PG IT
Triumph Films — *RCA/Columbia Pictures Home Video*

And Then There Were None 1945
Mystery
11602 97 mins B/W B, V P
Louis Hayward, Barry Fitzgerald, Walter Huston
Based on Agatha Christie's play about ten people invited to an island who are murdered one by one.
20th Century Fox — *United Home Video*

Anderson Tapes, The 1971
Suspense
21279 98 mins C B, V P
Sean Connery, Dyan Cannon, Martin Balsam, directed by Sidney Lumet
The story of an epic million-dollar robbery of a luxury apartment house. Based on the novel by Lawrence Sanders.
MPAA:PG
Columbia — *RCA/Columbia Pictures Home Video*

Android 1982
Science fiction
76019 80 mins C B, V P
Klaus Kinski, Don Opper, Brie Howard
A classic saga of men versus machines combining science fiction, suspense and cloned romance.
MPAA:PG
Mary Ann Fisher — *Media Home Entertainment*

Andromeda Strain, The 1971
Science fiction
58213 131 mins C B, V P
Arthur Hill, David Wayne, James Olson, Kate Reid, Paula Kelly, directed by Robert Wise
A satellite falls back to earth carrying a deadly bacteria which must be identified in time to save the population from extermination.
MPAA:G
Universal; Robert Wise — *MCA Home Video*

Andy Warhol's Dracula 1975
Horror
56928 106 mins C B, V R, P
Joe Dallesandro, Udo Kler, Arno Juergling, directed by Paul Morrissey
Sex and camp humor, as well as a large dose of blood, highlight this tale of the gardener who beds the young ladies and finally does Dracula in.
MPAA:R
Bryanston Pictures — *Video Gems*

Andy Warhol's Frankenstein 1975
Horror
56929 95 mins C B, V R, P
Joe Dallesandro, Monique Van Vooren, Udo Kler, directed by Paul Morrissey
One of the most outrageous versions of Frankenstein, featuring plenty of gore and sex.
MPAA:R
Bryanston Pictures — *Video Gems*

Angel 1975
Cartoons/Adventure
56747 48 mins C B, V P
Animated
An animated adventure laced with fantasy, magic, and music which tells the story of an independent girl and her travel companions, a lovable dog and a talking cat. Available in English and Spanish versions.
EL, SP
ZIV International — *Media Home Entertainment*

Angel 1984
Drama
65744 94 mins C B, V R, P
Donna Wilkes, Cliff Gorman, Susan Tyrell, Dick Shawn
A 15-year old honor student attends an expensive Los Angeles private school during the daytime and by night becomes Angel, a streetwise prostitute making a living amid the slime and sleaze of Hollywood Boulevard.
MPAA:R
Roy Watts; Donald P Borchers — *THORN EMI/HBO Video*

Angel and the Badman 1947
Western
00282 100 mins C B, V, 3/4U P
John Wayne, Gail Russell, Irene Rich

Notorious badman is humanized by the love of a young Quaker girl.
Republic — *Nostalgia Merchant; Sheik Video; Discount Video Tapes; Prism; Video Dimensions; Cable Films; VCII; Video Connection; Video Yesteryear; Media Home Entertainment; Budget Video; Cinema Concepts; Western Film & Video Inc; Spotlite Video; Kartes Productions; Classic Video Cinema Collector's Club; Republic Pictures Home Video*

Angel of H.E.A.T. 1982
Adventure
62862 90 mins C B, V, LV, CED P
Marilyn Chambers
A female super-agent is on a mission to save the world from total destruction.
MPAA:R
Myrl A. Schreibman; Hal Kant — *Vestron Video*

Angel on My Shoulder 1980
Fantasy
64982 96 mins C B, V, CED P
Peter Strauss, Richard Kiley, Barbara Hershey, Janis Paige
In this remake of the 1946 classic, a small-time hood wrongfully executed for murder comes back as an incorruptible district attorney, with a little help from the devil.
Mace Neufeld Productions — *Embassy Home Entertainment*

Angela 1977
Drama
65430 91 mins C B, V P
Sophia Loren, Steve Railsback, John Huston
An extraordinary love story which transpires between a mother and son who after a twenty-three year separation meet again, unaware that they are related.
20th Century Fox — *Embassy Home Entertainment*

Angelo My Love 1983
Drama
66350 91 mins C B, V P
Robert Duvall wrote this compassionate tale of New York's gypsy community, following the adventures of 12-year-old Angelo Evans, the streetwise son of a fortune teller.
MPAA:R
Cinecom International — *RCA/Columbia Pictures Home Video*

Angels Die Hard 1984
Adventure
80462 86 mins C B, V, LV P
William Smith
A marauding gang of bikers confronts a mob of angry townspeople in a series of brutal attacks, beatings and other incidents.
MPAA:R
New World Pictures — *New World Video*

Angels with Dirty Faces 1938
Drama
66076 97 mins B/W B, V, CED P
James Cagney, Pat O'Brien, Humphrey Bogart, Ann Sheridan, George Bancroft, Dead End Kids
A classic in which two young hoodlums grow up-one to the priesthood and one to prison. The priest then tries to keep a group of young toughs from idolizing the famed gangster and following in his footsteps.
Warner Bros — *CBS/Fox Video*

AngKor: Cambodia Express 1984
Drama
81165 96 mins C B, V P
Robert Walker, Christopher George
An American journalist travels back to Vietnam to search for his long lost love.
Monarex Hollywood Corp. — *Vestron Video*

Animal Crackers 1930
Comedy
14018 98 mins B/W B, V P
Marx Brothers, Lillian Roth, Margaret Dumont, directed by Victor Neerman
One of the funniest Marx Brothers films, "Animal Crackers" is a screen classic. Complete with the Harry Ruby music score—including Groucho's "Hooray for Captain Spaulding."
Paramount — *MCA Home Video; RCA VideoDiscs*

Animal Farm 1955
Satire
53287 73 mins C B, V, FO P
Animated, directed by John Halas and Joy Batchelor
An animated version of George Orwell's classic political satire about a barnyard full of animals who parallel the growth of totalitarian dictatorships.
Louis de Rochemont; Halas and Batchelor — *Video Yesteryear; Sheik Video; Video Connection; Budget Video; Cable Films; Western Film & Video Inc; Discount Video Tapes; Phoenix Films & Video*

Animal House 1978
Comedy
11567 109 mins C B, V, LV P
John Belushi, Tim Matheson, John Verna, Donald Sutherland, Thomas Hulce, directed by John Landis
Every college tradition from fraternity rush week to the homecoming pageant, is irreverently and relentlessly mocked in this wild comedy.
MPAA:R

Universal; Matty Simmons; Ivan Reitman — *MCA Home Video; RCA VideoDiscs*

Animal Quiz #1 1984
Animals
65638 60 mins C B, V R, P
This series is an invitation to children and their parents to test their animal expertise. This volume features "Looney Gooney," a look at the comical aerodynamics of the Gooney bird of Midway Island; the dragon-like lizards of Indonesia in "Komodo Dragons"; and the San Diego Zoo's collection of animal infants in "Zoo Babies."
Walt Disney — *Walt Disney Home Video*

Animal Quiz #2 1984
Animals
65639 60 mins C B, V R, P
This volume takes viewers to the arid state of Chihuahua, Mexico, for a glimpse of the "Mexican Grizzly", an oasis-like watering hole in Africa for "Kenya's Spring of Life"; and the frigid, desolate realm of the Emperor penguin in "Adventure Antarctica."
Walt Disney — *Walt Disney Home Video*

Animal Quiz #3 1984
Animals
65640 60 mins C B, V R, P
The third volume provides insights to "The Strange Creatures of the Galapagos," and traces the training and breeding of racehorses in "Thoroughbred" and the monkeyshines performed by "The Apes of Gibraltar."
Walt Disney — *Walt Disney Home Video*

Animal Quiz #4 1984
Animals
72799 84 mins C B, V P
Viewers are shown the creatures of the Sonoran desert, visit the famed Masai warriors of Africa and participate in a Pacific shark watch.
Walt Disney Productions — *Walt Disney Home Video*

Animal Quiz #5 1984
Animals
72800 84 mins C B, V P
Viewers witness unique structures built by animals, visit the Mexican desert where jaguars roam and observe the crocodile population of the Nile.
Walt Disney Productions — *Walt Disney Home Video*

Animal Quiz #6 1984
Animals
72801 84 mins C B, V P
The big cats of South Africa are filmed in their habitat, as are Japan's snow monkeys.
Walt Disney Productions — *Walt Disney Home Video*

Animal Quiz #7 1985
Animals
80357 83 mins C B, V R, P
Here's a chance to test your knowledge about the jungle jaguar, the brown bears of Alaska, and New Zealand sheep dogs.
Walt Disney Productions — *Walt Disney Home Video*

Animal Quiz #8 1985
Animals
80358 83 mins C B, V R, P
This volume visits the Yagua Indian tribe and looks at the various animals who inhabit a Kenyan game reserve.
Walt Disney Productions — *Walt Disney Home Video*

Animal Quiz #9 1985
Animals
80359 83 mins C B, V R, P
In this volume, find out about the elephants of Thailand, Kenya's pink flamingos, and a colony of fur seals on the Pribilof Islands.
Walt Disney Productions — *Walt Disney Home Video*

Animals Are Beautiful People 1974
Wildlife/Documentary
58216 92 mins C B, V R, P
Narrated by Paddy O'Byrne, directed by Jamie Uys
A profile of the African wilderness that captures the unique mood of the animal community.
MPAA:G
Mimosa Films — *Warner Home Video*

Animalympics 1980
Cartoons
47378 78 mins C B, V R, P
Voices of Gilda Radner, Billy Crystal, Harry Shearer, Michael Fremer
In this animated feature, animals from all over the world gather for the first Animal Olympics—and the fur really flies.
Lisberger Studios Film — *Warner Home Video*

Animation in the 1930's 193?
Cartoons
11288 57 mins B/W B, V, FO P
Animated
A collection of nine cartoons from the studios of Warner Brothers and Max Fleischer, including "Crosby, Columbo and Vallee," "Three's a Crowd," "Hollywood Capers," "Songs You Like to Sing—Margie," "Grampy's Indoor Outing," "Betty in Blunderland," "Let's Sing with

Popeye," "Happy You and Me," and "Sinkin' in the Bathtub."
Warner Bros; Max Fleischer — *Video Yesteryear*

Animation Wonderland **1975**
Cartoons
58587 75 mins C B, V R, P
Animated
A collection of delightful animated shorts for children.
Peabody Award: Best Children's Entertainment.
MPAA:G
John Wilson — *Video Gems*

Ann Vickers **1933**
Drama
76842 76 mins B/W B, V P
Irene Dunne, Walter Huston, Bruce Cabot, Conrad Nagel
A dashing young army captain wins over the heart of a dedicated social worker.
RKO; Pandro S. Berman — *RKO HomeVideo*

Anna Christie **1930**
Drama
80210 90 mins B/W B, V P
Greta Garbo, Marie Dressler, Charles Bickford, George F. Marion, directed by Clarance Brown
An adaptation of the classic Eugene O'Neill play about a prostitute who fights her past for the man she loves.
MGM — *MGM/UA Home Video*

Anna to the Infinite Power **1984**
Drama
65466 ? mins C B, V P
Dina Merrill, Martha Byrne, Mark Patton
Based on the book of the same name, this powerful drama follows a young girl who desperately seeks to unravel the mystery of her life. In Beta Hi-Fi.
Bruce Graham; Blue Marble Company Films — *RCA/Columbia Pictures Home Video*

Annabel Takes a Tour/Maids Night Out **1938**
Comedy
76844 131 mins B/W B, V P
Lucille Ball, Jack Oakie, Ruth Donnelly, Joan Fontaine, Allan Lane, Hedda Hopper
A delightful comedy double feature: In "Annabel Takes a Tour" a fading movie star falls in love with a writer while on a tour to boost her career, and in "Maids Night Out" a heiress and a millionare fall in love.
RKO — *RKO HomeVideo*

Anne of Green Gables **1934**
Drama
76843 79 mins B/W B, V P
Anne Shirley, Tom Brown, O.P. Heggie
A lonely couple have their hands full when they adopt a little girl whose background causes them problems.
RKO; Kenneth McGowan — *RKO HomeVideo*

Anne of the Thousand Days **1969**
Biographical/Drama
77211 145 mins C B, V P
Richard Burton, Genevieve Bujold, Irene Pappas, Anthony Quayle, directed by Charles Jarrott
England's Henry VIII separates from Queen Katherine to pursue a romance with feisty Anne Boleyn.
MPAA:R
Hal B. Wallis; Universal Pictures — *MCA Home Video*

Annie **1982**
Musical
63437 130 mins C B, V, LV P
Aileen Quinn, Carol Burnett, Albert Finney, Bernadette Peters, Ann Reinking, Tim Curry, directed by John Huston
Based on the hit Broadway musical, this is the story of America's favorite orphan, a plucky, red-haired girl who dreams of a life outside her dingy orphanage.
MPAA:PG
Columbia; Ray Stark — *RCA/Columbia Pictures Home Video; RCA VideoDiscs*

Annie Hall **1977**
Comedy
13322 94 mins C B, V, LV P
Woody Allen, Diane Keaton, Paul Simon, Carol Kane, directed by Woody Allen
Autobiographical love story with incisive Allenisms on romance, relationships, fame, and other topics.
Academy Awards '77: Best Picture; Best Actress (Keaton); Best Direction (Allen); Best Screenplay (Allen, Brickman). MPAA:PG
United Artists; Jack Rollins; Charles H Joffe — *CBS/Fox Video; RCA VideoDiscs*

Annie Oakley **1935**
Drama
66335 90 mins B/W B, V, 3/4U P
Barbara Stanwyck, Preston Foster, Melvyn Douglas, directed by George Stevens
A biographical drama based on the life and legend of sharpshooter Annie Oakley and her on-off relationship with Wild Bill Hickok.
RKO — *Nostalgia Merchant*

Another Country **1984**
Drama
79698 90 mins C B, V P
Rupert Everett, Colin Firth, Michael Jenn, Robert Addie, Rupert Wainwright

Two English boarding school friends wind up as spies for the Soviet Union.
Goldcrest Films — *Embassy Home Entertainment*

Another Time, Another Place 1983
War-Drama
80760 101 mins C B, V P
Phyllis Logan, Giovanni Mauriello, Gian Luca Favilla, Paul Young, Tom Watson, directed by Michael Radford
A bored young Scottish housewife falls in love with an Italian prisoner-of-war who works on her farm during World War II.
MPAA:R
Samuel Goldwyn Co. — *Embassy Home Entertainment*

Antarctica 1984
Adventure
76930 112 mins C B, V P
Ken Jakakura, Masako Natsume, Keiko Oginome
A group of scientists leave a pack of fifteen huskies chained to posts on a frozen glacier in the Antarctic.
TLC Films — *CBS/Fox Video*

Antony and Cleopatra 1973
Drama
81443 150 mins C B, V P
Charlton Heston, Hildegarde Neff, Fernando Rey, Eric Porter, directed by Charlton Heston
This is an adaptation of the Shakespeare play that centers on the torrid romance between Mark Antony and Cleopatra.
MPAA:PG
Peter Snell — *Embassy Home Entertainment*

Ants 1977
Suspense
77208 88 mins C B, V P
Lynda Day George, Myrna Loy, Robert Foxworth, Suzanne Sommers
An army of killer ants are terrorizing the guests of a posh summer resort.
Alan Landsburg Productions — *U.S.A. Home Video*

Any Which Way You Can 1980
Comedy
58217 116 mins C B, V, LV R, P
Clint Eastwood, Sondra Locke, Ruth Gordon
This sequel to "Every Which Way But Loose" finds brawler Philo Beddoe and Clyde the orangutan facing a big bout with big bucks at stake.
MPAA:PG
Warner Bros — *Warner Home Video; RCA VideoDiscs*

Apache 1954
Western
55583 91 mins C CED P
Burt Lancaster, John Mc Intire, Jean Peters
The chronicle of a bitter battle between the Indians and the U.S. cavalry in the struggle for the west.
EL, SP
United Artists — *CBS/Fox Video*

Apando, El 198?
Drama
77351 85 mins C B, V P
Salvador Sanchez, Manuel Ojeda
A group of prisoners are sentenced to the world's worst prison.
SP
Foreign — *Unicorn Video*

Apartment, The 1960
Comedy-Drama
58948 125 mins B/W CED P
Jack Lemmon, Shirley MacLaine, Fred MacMurray, Ray Walston, Edie Adams, directed by Billy Wilder
A lonely, ambitious clerk rents out his apartment to philandering executives and finds that one of them is after his own girl.
Academy Awards '60: Best Picture; Best Director; Best Screenplay (Wilder, I.A.L. Diamond).
United Artists — *RCA VideoDiscs*

Aphrodite 1983
Drama
65360 89 mins C B, V P
Valerie Kaprisky
A steamy drama based on Pierre Louy's masterpiece of erotic literature.
Adolphe Viezzi — *Vestron Video*

Apocalypse Now 1979
Drama
58493 139 mins C B, V, LV R, P
Marlon Brando, Martin Sheen, Robert Duvall, Fredric Forrest, Sam Bottoms, Dennis Hopper, directed by Francis Ford Coppola
Coppola's epic set during the Vietnam War, concerning one officer's trip through the jungle to locate and eliminate a megalomaniac officer whose methods have become "unsound."
Academy Awards '79: Best Cinematography; Best Sound. MPAA:R
United Artists; Francis Ford Coppola — *Paramount Home Video; RCA VideoDiscs*

Apple Dumpling Gang, The 1975
Comedy
44299 100 mins C B, V R, P

Bill Bixby, Susan Clark, Don Knotts, Tim Conway, David Wayne, Slim Pickens, Harry Morgan
Three frisky kids strike it rich and trigger the wildest bank robbery in the gold-mad West.
MPAA:G
Walt Disney — *Walt Disney Home Video; RCA VideoDiscs*

Apple Dumpling Gang, The 1975
Comedy/Western
70672 100 mins C B, V R, P
Bill Bixby, Susan Clark, Don Knotts, Tim Conway
Slapstick shenanigans abound in cops and robbers comedy set in California's gold rush. Everyone gets beaten at their own game on their way to an explosive climax.
MPAA:G
Walt Disney Productions — *Walt Disney Home Video*

Apple Dumpling Gang Rides Again, The 1979
Comedy/Western
55570 88 mins C B, V R, P
Tim Conway, Don Knotts, Tim Matheson, Kenneth Mars, Harry Morgan, Jack Elam, directed by Vincent McEveety
Two lovable hombres terrorize the West in their bungling attempt to go straight.
Walt Disney — *Walt Disney Home Video*

Apprenticeship of Duddy Kravitz, The 1974
Comedy-Drama
59859 121 mins C B, V R, P
Richard Dreyfuss, Randy Quaid, Denholm Elliot, Jack Warden, Micheline Lanctot, Joe Silver, directed by Ted Kotcheff
A young Jewish man in Montreal circa 1948 is driven by an insatiable need to be a "somebody."
MPAA:PG
Paramount — *Paramount Home Video*

April Wine 1981
Music-Performance
58467 67 mins C B, V R, P
The hard-rock group, April Wine, performs hits from their Capitol LP's.
EMI Music — *THORN EMI/HBO Video; Pioneer Artists*

Aquaman 1967
Cartoons/Fantasy
81087 60 mins C B, V R, P
Animated
Here is a collection of eight animated adventures featuring that mighty superhero, Aquaman.
Filmation — *Warner Home Video*

Arch of Triumph 1948
Drama
64537 120 mins B/W B, V P
Ingrid Bergman, Charles Boyer, Charles Laughton, directed by Lewis Milestone
An Austrian refugee searches for the Gestapo agent who tortured him and killed his friends.
United Artists; Enterprise — *Republic Pictures Home Video*

Archie 1978
Cartoons
69624 60 mins C B, V R, P
Animated
Three separate cartoons feature the escapades of Archie, Jughead, Veronica, Betty, Reggie, Mr. Weatherbee and the rest of the gang from Riverdale High.
Filmation — *THORN EMI/HBO Video*

Archie, Volume II 1978
Cartoons
65745 23 mins C B, V R, P
Animated
Archie and the "Gang" carry on with their hilarious pranks, while Mr. Weatherbee loses his glasses and thinks Hot Dog is the Commodore of a ship.
Filmation — *THORN EMI/HBO Video*

Archie, Volume 3 1984
Cartoons
78392 60 mins C B, V R, P
Animated
Here's the third installment of the animated escapades of Archie Andrews and all of his friends at Riverdale High.
Filmation Studios — *THORN EMI/HBO Video*

Archie, Cassette #4 1968
Cartoons
81183 60 mins C B, V R, P
Animated
Archie and the rest of the Riverdale High gang are back to cause more comic commotion in this collection of three episodes from the series.
Filmation — *THORN EMI/HBO Video*

Are You in the House Alone? 1978
Suspense
65664 100 mins C B, V P
Blythe Danner, Kathleen Beller, Tony Bill, Scott Colomby
A high school coed becomes the target of a terror campaign.
Charles Fries — *Worldvision Home Video*

Far Frontier, The 1948
Western
70572 60 mins B/W B, V P
Roy Rogers, Andy Divine

Roy saves the day by thwarting a band of no-good niks who are smugglingthemselves across the border in soy bean oil cans.
Republic — *Captain Bijou*

Argentinisima I 1972
Music
47860 115 mins C B, V P
Inspired by the verses of famed singers like Mercedes Sosa and Atahualpa Yupanqui, various singers and groups relate the tales of the different regions and music from past and present Argentina. In Spanish.
SP
Luis Repetto — *Media Home Entertainment*

Arizona Days 1937
Western
08791 56 mins B/W B, V P
Tex Ritter, Eleanor Stewart
Cowboys join a minstrel group and rescue the show when a group of toughs try to break it up.
Grand National — *United Home Video; Video Connection; Video Yesteryear; Discount Video Tapes*

Arizona Raiders 1965
Western
11603 88 mins C B, V P
Audie Murphy, Buster Crabbe
Arizona rangers hunt down killers who have been terrorizing the territory.
Columbia; Grant Whytock — *United Home Video; Video Connection*

Armed Forces Workout 1984
Physical fitness
72536 75 mins C B, V, CED P
A U.S. Marine Corps drill instructor instructs a program of daily exercises designed to strengthen one's body and attitude toward working-out.
K Tel International Inc — *Vestron Video*

A.R.M.S. Concert, The 1983
Music-Performance
76642 60 mins C B, V P
Jeff Beck, Eric Clapton, Bill Wyman
An ensemble of rock-n-roll stars from Eric Clapton to Bill Wyman perform in this live benefit concert.
Glyn Johns — *Music Media*

Arnold 1973
Comedy
79673 95 mins C B, V P
Stella Stevens, Roddy McDowell, Farley Granger, Victor Buono, Bernard Fox
When a group of heirs get together to watch a videotaped reading of a dead man's will, they start to disappear one by one.
MPAA:PG
Bing Crosby Productions — *Lightning Video*

Arnold Schwarzenegger: Mr. Olympia (The Comeback) 1982
Sports-Minor/Physical fitness
59566 50 mins C B, V P
Hosted by Arnold Schwarzenegger
A filmed record of the seventh annual body-building contest for the World Title, comprised of former Mr. Universe winners.
Aspac Prods — *Mastervision*

Around the World in 80 Days 1956
Adventure
65322 178 mins C B, V P
David Niven, Shirley MacLaine, Frank Sinatra, Marlene Dietrich, Robert Newton, Cantinflas
An unflappable Victorian Era Englishman wagers that he can circumnavigate the earth in four-score days, which sends him on a spectacular journey. In VHS stereo and Beta Hi-fi.
MPAA:G
Michael Todd — *Warner Home Video*

Around the World in 80 Days 1972
Cartoons
78904 60 mins C B, V P
Animated
An animated adaptation of the Jules Verne novel about a man who bets 20,000 pounds that he can go around the globe in eighty days via balloon, elephant, ship and railroad.
Air Programs International — *Prism*

Around the World in 80 Days 1984
Cartoons
79879 80 mins C B, V P
Animated
Phineas Fogg and Passepartout set out to travel around the world in a balloon within a timespan of eighty days.
API — *Active Home Video*

Around the World Under the Sea 1965
Adventure
79209 111 mins C B, V P
David McCallum, Shirley Eaton, Gary Merill, Keenan Wynn, Brian Kelly
A group of scientists race against time to plant earthquake detectors along the ocean floor.
Ivan Tors — *MGM/UA Home Video*

Arrangement, The 1969
Drama
81491 126 mins C B, V R, P

Kirk Douglas, Faye Dunaway, Deborah Kerr, Richard Boone, directeed by Elia Kazan
A veteran advertising executive sets out to search for the meaning of life as he attempts to patch up his "arrangements" with his wife, his mistress and his father.
MPAA:R
Warner Bros; Elia Kazan — *Warner Home Video*

Arrival, The 1968
Drama
79894 52 mins C B, V P
Patrick McGoohan, Virginia Maskell, Guy Doleman
This pilot episode of "The Prisoner" series explains how Number 6 wound up in The Village.
Patrick McGoohan — *MPI Home Video*

Arsenic and Old Lace 1944
Comedy/Mystery
64459 158 mins B/W B, V P
Cary Grant, Josephine Hull, Jean Adair, Raymond Massey, Jack Carson, John Ridgely, James Gleason, Peter Lorre, directed by Frank Capra
Grant plays Mortimer Brester, an easygoing drama critic, who discovers that his gentle maiden aunts derive pleasure from poisoning gentlemencallers and burying them in the cellar.
Warner Bros — *CBS/Fox Video; RCA VideoDiscs*

Art and Science of Making Movies, The 1957
Filmmaking/Film-History
80750 58 mins B/W B, V P
Here are three fascinating documentaries on films and filmmaking: "Origins of the Motion Picture" (1956) traces the evolution of moving pictures; "Film Editing—Interpretation and Values" shows the editing of a "Gunsmoke" sequence; while "The Soundman" (1949) examines the evolution of sound in the movies.
U.S. Navy; et al — *Video Yesteryear*

Arthur 1981
Comedy
58218 97 mins C B, V, LV R, P
Dudley Moore, Liza Minnelli, John Gielgud, Geraldine Fitzgerald, directed by Steve Gordon
A billionaire stands to lose everything unless he gives up the woman he loves. Music by Burt Bacharach.
MPAA:PG
Orion Pictures — *Warner Home Video; RCA VideoDiscs*

Arthur and the Square Knights of the Round Table 1984
Cartoons
79338 80 mins C B, V P
Animated
A tongue in cheek approach is used in this animated retelling of the legends of King Arthur and Camelot.
Wrightswood Entertainment; API — *Active Home Video*

Arthur Godfrey Show, The 1955
Variety
12848 29 mins B/W B, V, FO P
Arthur Godfrey, Tony Martin, Jack E. Leonard, Carmel DeQuinn
Godfrey's ukelele solo in "Ain't She Sweet" and Jack E. Leonard's rock version of "Sittin' on Top of the World" highlight this program.
CBS — *Video Yesteryear*

Artur Rubinstein 1981
Music-Performance
57252 78 mins B/W B, V P
Artur Rubinstein, Gregor Piatigorsky, Jascha Heifetz
Rare footage never before seen showcases this great violinist in his home and in the recording studio. Rubinstein is featured in two solo spots and in a trio with cellist Gregor Piatigorsky and violinist Jascha Heifetz.
Kultur — *Kultur*

As You Like It 1936
Comedy
11393 96 mins B/W B, V, FO P
Elisabeth Bergner, Laurence Olivier, Henry Ainley
A Duke's banished daughter poses as a man in this Shakespearian comedy.
Inter Allied — *Video Yesteryear; Blackhawk Films; Sheik Video; Cable Films; Video Connection; Budget Video; Western Film & Video Inc; Discount Video Tapes; Classic Video Cinema Collector's Club*

Asesinos, Los 196?
Western
77356 95 mins C B, V P
Nick Adams, Pedro Armendariz
Two rival bandits battle each other for control of a lawless town.
SP
Foreign — *Unicorn Video*

Asesinos, Los 1968
Western
80492 95 mins C B, V P
Nick Adams, Regina Torne, Pedro Armendariz, Elsa Cardenas

Two rival bandits arrive in a lawless town and fight for control. Dialogue in Spanish.
SP
Spanish — *Unicorn Video*

Ashford and Simpson 1982
Music-Performance
63351 75 mins C B, V R, P
Nick Ashford, Valerie Simpson
This well-known duo perform their greatest hits live in concert, including "Ain't No Mountain High Enough," "Ain't Nothing Like the Real Thing" and "Let's Go Get Stoned."
EMI Music — *THORN EMI/HBO Video; Pioneer Artists; RCA VideoDiscs*

Ashford and Simpson 1984
Music-Performance
75912 21 mins C B, V P
This program presents the popular 60's group Ashford and Simpson performing their best songs.
Capital Records Inc — *Sony Corporation of America*

Asi No Hay Cama Que Aguante 1980
Comedy
47856 95 mins C B, V P
Chico Novarro, Patricia Dal
Horacio and Claudio pretend to have money to win the friendship of Marcela and Silvana, who appear to be wealthy. In Spanish.
SP
Nicolas Carreras; Luis Repetto — *Media Home Entertainment*

Asia in Asia 1983
Music-Performance
72217 60 mins C B, V P
Fusion rock group Asia plays a concert at Budokan, Japan.
Independent — *Vestron Video*

Assasination 197?
Adventure
81042 93 mins C B, V P
Jesper Langberg
A police detective heads a relentless hunt for the assassin gunning for a leading European politician.
Foreign — *Trans World Entertainment*

Assassin, The 1979
Martial arts
64906 86 mins C B, V P
Sonny Chiba
An athletic karate fighter poses as an underworld figure and infiltrates the largest gang in Japan where he is hired as a hit man.
Toei Company — *CBS/Fox Video; Unicorn Video*

Assault 1970
Drama
59827 89 mins C B, V P
Suzy Kendall, Lesley-Anne Down, Frank Finlay
Violent sex murders in a girl's school have the police baffled. The school's pretty art teacher offers to act as bait in order to catch the murderer.
George H Brown — *Embassy Home Entertainment*

Assault on Agathon 197?
Adventure
59349 95 mins C B, V R, P
Nina Van Pallandt, Marianne Faithful
An "executed" W.W. II guerilla leader returns to lead a revolution.
MPAA:PG
Heritage Enterprises — *Video Gems*

Assault on Precinct 13 1979
Horror
42910 91 mins C B, V P
This movie from the producers of "Halloween" takes a frightening look at the destruction of law and order.
EL, SP
Irwin Yablans — *Media Home Entertainment*

Asterix the Gaul 1985
Cartoons
76816 67 mins C B, V R, P
Animated
Asterix the Gaul and his sidekick Obelix take on an inept legion of Roman warriors when they try to take over Asterix's Gallic territory.
Productions Dargaud Films — *Walt Disney Home Video*

Astro Zombies, The 1970
Horror
05526 83 mins C B, V P
John Carradine, Wendell Corey
Human transplants go berserk and threaten the safety of a city.
MPAA:PG
Ram Ltd — *Wizard Video*

Asylum 1972
Horror
54912 100 mins C B, V, 3/4U P
Peter Cushing, Herbert Lom, Britt Ekland, Barbara Parkins, Patrick Magee, Barry Morse, directed by Roy Ward Baker
A search of an eerie insane asylum for its former director, now a raving maniac, leads a young psychiatrist on a tour of terror. His interviews with inmates reveal their case histories in flashback—all weird, horrible, or murderous.

MPAA:PG
Cinerama Releasing — *Nostalgia Merchant*

At Gunpoint 1955
Drama
65687 81 mins C B, V P
Fred MacMurray, Dorothy Malone
A store owner becomes the town hero when, by accident, he shoots and kills a bank robber.
Allied Artists — *Republic Pictures Home Video*

At Sword's Point 1952
Adventure
00295 81 mins C B, V, 3/4U P
Cornel Wilde, Maureen O'Hara
Adventure tale based on "The Three Musketeers."
RKO — *Nostalgia Merchant*

At the Circus 1939
Comedy
59360 87 mins B/W B, V P
The Marx Brothers, Margaret Dumont, Kenny Baker, Florence Rice, Eve Arden, Nat Pendleton, Fritz Feld
The Marx Brothers, as circus performers, cause their usual comic insanity. Groucho sings, "Lydia the Tattooed Lady."
MGM — *MGM/UA Home Video*

At the Earth's Core 1976
Science fiction
65135 90 mins C B, V R, P
Doug McClure, Peter Cushing, Caroline Munro
A Victorian scientist invents a giant burrowing machine, which he and his crew use to dig deeply into the Earth. To their surprise, they discover a lost world of subhuman creatures and prehistoric monsters.
MPAA:PG
American International — *Warner Home Video*

At War with the Army 1950
Comedy
39009 93 mins B/W B, V P
Dean Martin, Jerry Lewis, Polly Bergen
Martin and Lewis' first starring appearance, as soldiers getting mixed up in all kinds of wild situations at their army base.
Paramount — *Prism; Electric Video; Sheik Video; Cable Films; Video Connection; Video Yesteryear; Discount Video Tapes*

Atalante, L' 1934
Film-Avant-garde
06225 82 mins B/W B, V P
Dita Parlo, Jean Daste, Michel Simon, directed by Jean Vigo
A bride on her honeymoon becomes bored and starts flirting with other men. French with English subtitles.
FR
J L Nounez; Gaumont — *Budget Video; Sheik Video; Video Yesteryear; Western Film & Video Inc; Discount Video Tapes*

Atlanta Braves: Team Highlights 1984
Baseball
81132 30 mins C B, V P
Hank Aaron, Dale Murphy, Bob Horner, Chris Chambliss 4 pgms
This series highlights the many shining moments from the Atlanta Braves' past seasons.
1.1966: Here Come The Braves 2.1982: Coming To America 3.1983: The A Team 4.1984: Ready To Rebound
Major League Baseball — *Major League Baseball Productions*

Atlantic City 1981
Drama
53930 104 mins C B, V, LV R, P
Burt Lancaster, Susan Sarandon, Kate Reid, Michel Piccoli, Hollis Mc Laren, directed by Louis Malle
A smalltime, aging mafia hood falls in love with a clam bar waitress, and they share the spoils of a big score against the backdrop of a changing Atlantic City.
MPAA:R
Dennis Heroux; Cine Neighbor; Selta Films — *Paramount Home Video; RCA VideoDiscs*

Atoll K 1951
Comedy
05436 82 mins B/W B, V, 3/4U P, T
Stan Laurel, Oliver Hardy, Suzy Delair
Laurel and Hardy inherit an island and turn it into a Utopia, but their peace is disturbed when uranium is discovered.
Exploitation Films; Franco-London Films — *Video Yesteryear; Discount Video Tapes; Sheik Video; Vestron Video (disc only)*

Atom Age Vampire 1961
Horror
65198 71 mins B/W B, V P
Alberto Lupo, Susanne Loret, Sergio Fantoni
A mad scientist falls in love with a woman who has been disfigured in an auto crash. To remove her scars, he treats her with a formula derived from the glands of freshly killed women. English dubbed.
Lion Film; Topaz Film Corp — *Video Yesteryear*

Atom Ant 196?
Cartoons
47686 53 mins C B, V P
Animated
Eight episodes in which the ant with atomic strength battles Ferocious Flea and Karate Ant.

Hanna Barbera — *Worldvision Home Video*

Atomic Cafe, The **1982**
Documentary/Satire
64210 92 mins C B, V R, P
A chillingly humorous compilation of newsreels and government films of the 1940's and 1950's that show America's preoccupation with the A-Bomb. Some sequences are in black and white.
Archives Project Inc — *THORN EMI/HBO Video*

Ator the Fighting Eagle **1983**
Adventure/Fantasy
69392 98 mins C B, V R, P
Miles O'Keeffe
According to legend, Ator, son of Thorn, must put an end to the tragic Dynasty of the Spiders.
MPAA:PG
Comworld Pictures — *THORN EMI/HBO Video*

Attack and Reprisal **1946**
World War II
78972 55 mins C B, V P
Two short films about the Japanese attack on Pearl Harbor and the bombing of Hiroshima.
Maljack Productions — *MPI Home Video*

Attack Force Z **1984**
Adventure
74107 84 mins C B, V P
Mel Gibson, John Philip Law, John Waters
An elite volunteer corps, Force Z, is given the dangerous mission of finding a defected Japanese government official who was lost in a plane crash somewhere in the South Pacific.
Lee Robinson — *VCL Home Video*

Attack of the Killer Tomatoes **1977**
Comedy
42912 87 mins C B, V P
In this low-budget spoof, tomatoes suddenly turn savage and begin attacking people. Many familiar cliches of the science fiction genre are parodied and a few musical numbers are included.
MPAA:PG EL, SP
Four Square Productions — *Media Home Entertainment*

Attack of the Robots **1966**
Comedy
66133 88 mins B/W B, V, FO P
Eddie Constantine, Fernando Rey
A spy spoof about individuals being turned into robots.
American Intl Pictures — *Video Yesteryear*

Attack of the Super Monsters **1984**
Cartoons/Adventure
78958 85 mins C B, V P
Animated
A group of prehistoric monsters are developing dastardly plots below the earth to ruin the human race.
Independent — *Trans World Entertainment*

Attack!—The Battle of New Britain **1944**
World War II
53654 45 mins B/W B, V, 3/4U P
Frank Capra supervised production on this film, which provides a record of the attacks on Arawa and Cape Gouster on New Britain.
Unknown — *International Historic Films; Spotlite Video*

Attic, The **1980**
Drama
79335 92 mins C B, V P
Carrie Snodgrass, Ray Milland
A young woman isolates herself from the world by hiding away in her parent's attic.
MPAA:R
Raymond M. Dryden; Phillip Randall — *Monterey Home Video*

Audience with Mel Brooks, An **1984**
Comedy
75490 60 mins C B, V P
Mell Brooks, Anne Bancroft
Mel Brooks puts on a number of sketches, sings and tells jokes in this live comedy concert appearance.
Prism — *Prism*

Auditions **1973**
Comedy
60436 82 mins C B, V P
Real, bizarre, erotic and outrageously funny auditions for X-rated stardom.
MPAA:R
Charles Band Productions — *Wizard Video*

Audrey Rose **1977**
Horror
72464 113 mins C B, V P
Marsha Mason, Anthony Hopkins, John Beck
The parents of a young girl are traumatized when a man tells them his dead daughter lives on inside her.
MPAA:PG
United Artists — *MGM/UA Home Video*

Auntie Mame **1958**
Comedy
47620 161 mins C B, V R, P

Rosalind Russell, Patrick Knowles, Roger Smith, Peggy Cass
A young boy is brought up by his only surviving relative—flamboyant and eccentric Auntie Mame. Part of the "A Night at the Movies" series, this tape simulates a 1958 movie evening, with a Road Runner cartoon, "Hook, Line and Stinker," a newsreel and coming attractions for "No Time for Sergeants" and "Chase a Crooked Shadow."
Warner Bros — *Warner Home Video*

Australia Now 1984
Music-Performance/Documentary
81192 60 mins C B, V P
Little River Band, Inxs, Men at Work, Midnight Oil, Split Enz, Moving Pictures
This documentary takes a look at the people and the music from the lands down under, Australia and New Zealand.
Pom Oliver; Peter Clifton — *Music Media*

Author! Author! 1982
Comedy
63391 100 mins C B, V, CED P
Al Pacino, Tuesday Weld, Dyan Cannon, Alan King, directed by Arthur Hill
Al Pacino portrays a struggling playwright whose wife leaves him with their son and four children from her previous marriage. Pacino becomes involved with the leading lady of his new Broadway play, but she is more concerned with the social scene than with his children.
MPAA:PG
20th Century Fox — *CBS/Fox Video*

Autobiography of Miss Jane Pittman, The 1974
Drama
52333 110 mins C B, V P
Cecily Tyson, Odetta, Joseph Tremice
This program, based on the novel by Ernest J. Gaines, tells the story of a courageous black woman whose life spans from the Civil War to the Civil Rights movement in the 1960's.
Tomorrow Entertainment — *Prism; RCA VideoDiscs*

Autumn Born 1979
Drama
60411 76 mins C B, V P
Dorothy Stratten
A young heiress is abducted by her guardian and imprisoned while she's taught to obey his will.
MPAA:R
North American Pictures Ltd — *Monterey Home Video*

Avalanche 1978
Suspense
65072 91 mins C B, V, CED P
Rock Hudson, Mia Farrow, Robert Forster, Rick Moses
Vacationers at a new winter ski resort are at the mercy of a monster avalanche which leaves a path of terror and destruction in its wake.
New World Pictures — *Embassy Home Entertainment*

Avant Garde and Experimental Film Program No. 1 193?
Film-Avant-garde
11290 55 mins B/W B, V, FO P
A collection of five avant-garde films: "Un Chien Andulou," by Luis Bunuel and Salvadore Dali; "Rain," by Joris Ivens and Mannus Franken; "Umberfall," by Erno Marzner; "Hearts of Age," directed by and starring Orson Welles; and "Ballet Mecanique," by Fernand Leger.
Unknown — *Video Yesteryear*

Avant-Garde #2 192?
Film-Avant-garde
58266 42 mins B/W B, V, FO P
Three avant-garde films: "Symphonie Diagonale" (1921, Germany), by Viking Eggeling, a Dada-ist; "L'Etoile de Mer" (1928, France), directed by Man Ray, an early surrealist; and, "Entr'acte" (1924, France), directed by Rene Clair, pure cinematic imagery.
Germany; France — *Video Yesteryear*

Avengers, The 196?
Adventure
54135 50 mins B/W B, V P
Diana Rigg, Patrick Macnee
This program contains an episode entitled "Dial a Deadly Number" from this classic TV series.
Associated British Corp — *Video Dimensions; Video Yesteryear*

Avenging Angel 1985
Drama
80818 94 mins C B, V, LV P
Betsy Russell, Rory Calhoun, Susan Tyrell, Ossie Davis, Barry Pearl, Ross Hagen
Law student Molly "Angel" Stewart is back out on the streets again to retaliate against the men who killed the policeman who saved her from a life of prostitution.
MPAA:R
New World Pictures — *New World Video*

Avenging Conscience, The 1914
Film-History
11388 78 mins B/W B, V, FO P
Henry B. Walthall, Blanche Sweet, directed by D.W. Griffith
An early eerie horror film, based on tales of Edgar Allen Poe. D.W. Griffith's first large-scale feature. Silent.

Biograph — *Video Yesteryear; Sheik Video; Classic Video Cinema Collector's Club*

Average White Band Shine 1984
Music-Performance
79893 30 mins C B, V P
The popular soul band plays their greatest hits in this taped concert from their European tour.
Independent — *VCL Home Video*

Aviation Volume I 197?
Aeronautics
10151 60 mins B/W B, V P, T
Newsreels highlight aviation history from Wright Brothers through evolution of the helicopter. Includes de Pinedo's death, the Graf Zeppelin, Lindberg's trans-Atlantic flight, and Pan American Clippers.
Unknown — *Blackhawk Films*

Awakening, The 1980
Horror
52717 102 mins C B, V R, P
Charlton Heston, Susannah York, Stephanie Zimbalist
An archeologist discovers the tomb of a murderous queen, but upon opening the coffin, the mummy's spirit is transferred to his baby daughter, born at that instant.
MPAA:R
Orion Pictures — *Warner Home Video*

Ay Jalisco No Te Rajes! 197?
Drama
52792 90 mins C B, V P
Rodolfo De Anda, Angel Garasa, Sonia Infante
General Carvajal forbids Salvador Perez Gomez to woo his daughter. Salvador kills him and must flee from the general's sons. One year later he finds the daughter in a convent, and she professes her love for him. In Spanish.
SP
Gonzalo Elvira — *Media Home Entertainment*

B

B.C. Rock 1984
Fantasy/Cartoons
80923 82 mins C B, V P
Animated
A cave man learns how to defend himself and has some prehistoric fun with a tribe of female amazons.
MPAA:R
Almi Pictures — *Vestron Video*

Babes in Arms 1939
Musical
80858 91 mins B/W B, V P
Judy Garland, Mickey Rooney, Charles Winninger, Guy Kibbee, June Preisser, directed by Busby Berkeley
The children of several vaudeville performers team up to put on a show to raise money for their financially impoverished parents. The Rodgers and Hart score features "Where or When" and "I Cried For You."
MGM; Arthur Freed — *MGM/UA Home Video*

Babes in Toyland 1961
Musical
63124 119 mins C B, V R, P
Annette Funicello, Ray Bolger, Tommy Sands, Ed Wynn, Tommy Kirk
A lavish production of Victor Herbert's timeless operetta, with Toyland being menaced by the evil Barnaby and his Bogeymen.
Walt Disney Productions — *Walt Disney Home Video*

Baby, The 1972
Suspense
01648 85 mins C B, V P, T
Anjanette Comer, Ruth Roman, Marianna Hill, directed by Ted Post
Bizarre story of a social worker attempting to free a retarted man-child from over-protection of his mother and sisters. Murder follows.
Scotia Intl Films — *King of Video*

Baby Doll 1956
Drama
81492 115 mins B/W B, V R, P
Eli Wallach, Carroll Baker, Karl Malden, Mildred Dunnock, directed by Elia Kazan
When a slow-witted Mississippian is frustrated by his nubile child bride, he becomes an arsonist and burns down his competitor's cotton gin. However, the competitor has a surprise in store for the couple.
Warner Bros; Newtown Prods — *Warner Home Video*

Baby Dynamics 1985
Childbirth/Physical fitness
81456 36 mins C B, V P
2 pgms
Linda Westin, the co-founder of the Baby Dynamics program demonstrates an exercise regiment that aids in developing young children's motor skills and coordination.
Sheri Singer — *Embassy Home Entertainment*

Baby, the Rain Must Fall 1964
Drama
66351 100 mins B/W B, V P
Steve McQueen, Lee Remick, Don Murray, directed by Robert Mulligan

A rootless drifter, paroled from prison, returns home to his wife and daughter, but his outbursts of violence make the reunion difficult.
Columbia; Alan Pakula — *RCA/Columbia Pictures Home Video*

Babylon Story from "Intolerance," The **1916**
Drama
58645 25 mins C B, V, FO P
Constance Talmadge, Alfred Paget, directed by D. W. Griffith
A condensation of the Babylon sequence from Griffith's epic, "Intolerance." The story concerns the simple mountain girl befriended by Belshazzar, King of Babylonia, who tries to warn the city of its impending doom. Silent with music score, tinted color.
D W Griffith — *Video Yesteryear*

Bachelor and the Bobby Soxer, The **1947**
Comedy
44814 95 mins B/W B, V P, T
Cary Grant, Myrna Loy, Shirley Temple, Rudy Vallee
A playboy is brought before Judge Myrna for disturbing the peace and sentenced to court her teenage sister.
Academy Awards 1947: Best Original Screenplay (Sidney Sheldon).
Dore Schary — *Blackhawk Films; Nostalgia Merchant*

Bachelor Bait **1934**
Comedy
44985 75 mins B/W B, V P, T
Stuart Erwin, Rochelle Hudson, Pert Kelton, Skeets Gallagher
A marriage license clerk who's tired of just handing out licenses opens a matrimonial service for men.
Pandro S Berman — *Blackhawk Films*

Bachelor Mother **1939**
Comedy
10037 82 mins B/W B, V P, T
Ginger Rogers, David Niven, Charles Coburn
Single salesgirl causes scandal when she finds abandoned baby.
RKO; B G DeSylva — *Blackhawk Films; Nostalgia Merchant*

Bachelor Party **1984**
Comedy
Closed Captioned
76928 105 mins C B, V P
Tom Hanks, Tawny Kitaen, George Grizzard, Adrian Zmed, directed by Neal Israel
When a young couple plans to marry, her parents and his friends do all that they can to prevent it.
20th Century Fox — *CBS/Fox Video*

Back Among the Best/NFL '83 **1984**
Football
72940 46 mins C B, V, FO P
San Francisco 49'ers
Highlights from the San Francisco 49'ers 1983 season and "NFL 83."
NFL Films — *NFL Films Video*

Back from Eternity **1956**
Drama
11608 97 mins B/W B, V P
Robert Ryan, Rod Steiger
Eleven survivors of a plane crash are stranded in a headhunter region of South America's jungle.
Universal; John Farrow — *United Home Video*

Back (Rehabilitation and Injury) **1978**
Physical fitness
52760 30 mins C B, V P
Hosted by Ann Dugan
Back strengthening exercises to help overcome weaknesses, relieve pain, and condition muscles and tissue to prevent further stress. Part of the "Rehabilitation and Injury" series.
Health 'N Action — *RCA/Columbia Pictures Home Video*

Back Roads **1981**
Comedy-Drama
53939 94 mins C B, V, CED P
Sally Field, Tommy Lee Jones, David Keith, directed by Martin Ritt
A Southern hooker meets a down-on-his-luck boxer and both head out for the better life in California.
MPAA:R
Ronald Sheldo — *CBS/Fox Video*

Back Street **1961**
Drama
70555 107 mins C B, V P
Susan Hayward, John Gavin, Vera Miles, directed by David Miller
The forbidden affair between a married man and a beautiful fashion designer carrys on through many anxious years to a tragic end. This lavish third film version of the Fanny Hurst novel features Hi-Fi Mono sound in all formats.
Universal — *MCA Home Video*

Back to Bataan **1945**
War-Drama
10073 95 mins B/W B, V P, T
John Wayne, Anthony Quinn
Colonel forms guerrilla army to raid Japanese and to help Americans landing on Leyte.

RKO; Robert Fellows — *Blackhawk Films; Nostalgia Merchant*

Backstage at the Kirov 198?
Dance
72179 80 mins C B, V P
A unique look at the Russian Kirov ballet company mixed with a profile of Leningrad.
Dr Armand Hammer — *Pacific Arts Video*

Bad 1977
Comedy
80763 105 mins C B, V P
Carroll Baker, Perry King, Susan Tyrell, Stefania Cassini, Mary Boylon
A suburban housewife runs a side business of providing hit women to perform other people's dirty deeds.
MPAA:X
New World Films — *Embassy Home Entertainment*

Bad Boys 1983
Drama
69039 123 mins C B, V, CED R, P
Sean Penn
Two young hoodlums who hate each other are sent to a Juvenile Hall together and end up in the same dorm. Backed into a corner by their mutual hatred and the escalating peer pressure, the two are pushed over the brink into a final and shattering fight-to-the-death.
Robert Solo — *THORN EMI/HBO Video*

B.A.D. Cats 1980
Suspense/Drama
81125 74 mins C B, V P
Asher Brauner, Michelle Pfeiffer, Vic Morrow, Jimmie Walker, Steve Hanks, La Wanda Page
Two members of a police burglary auto detail chase after a group of car thieves who are planning a million-dollar gold heist.
Aaron Spelling and Douglas S. Cramer — *Karl/Lorimar Home Video*

Bad Manners 1984
Comedy
79709 85 mins C B, V R, P
Martin Mull, Karen Black
A group of orphans attempt to rescue a young boy adopted by a wealthy family.
MPAA:R
New World Pictures — *THORN EMI/HBO Video*

Bad News Bears, The 1976
Comedy
38606 102 mins C B, V, LV R, P
Walter Matthau, Tatum O'Neal, Vic Morrow, Joyce Van Patten, Jackie Earle Haley
Family comedy about a misfit little league team who gets whipped into shape by their sloppy, beer-drinking coach (Walter Matthau).
MPAA:PG
Paramount — *Paramount Home Video; RCA VideoDiscs*

Bad News Bears in Breaking Training, The 1977
Comedy
10984 97 mins C B, V R, P
William Devane, Clifton James
With a chance to play the Houston Toros for a shot at the Japanese champs, the Bears devise a way to get to Texas to play at the famed Astrodome.
MPAA:PG
Paramount; Leonard Goldberg — *Paramount Home Video; RCA VideoDiscs*

Badlands 1974
Drama
51988 95 mins C B, V, LV R, P
Martin Sheen, Sissy Spacek, Warren Oates
A garbage man from South Dakota falls in love with a 15-year-old girl. He doesn't hesitate to kill anyone who tries to interfere with their romance.
MPAA:PG
Warner Bros — *Warner Home Video*

Badman's Territory 1946
Western
81029 97 mins B/W B, V P
Randolph Scott, Gabby Hayes, Steve Brodie
A straight-shooting marshal has to deal with such notorious outlaws as the James and Dalton boys in a territory outside of government control.
RKO — *RKO HomeVideo*

Baer vs. Louis/Louis vs. Schmeling 193?
Boxing
60056 54 mins B/W B, V P, T
Max Baer, Joe Louis
Joe Louis meets ex-champ Max Baer at Yankee Stadium on September 24, 1935. On June 19, 1936 Joe Louis fights with Max Schmeling at Yankee Stadium.
Unknown — *Blackhawk Films*

Baffled 1972
Suspense/Drama
59341 96 mins C CED P
Leonard Nimoy, Susan Hampshire, Vera Miles
A story of the supernatural, blending drama and suspense with comic undertones.
ATV — *CBS/Fox Video*

Bakery, The/The Grocery Clerk **1921**
Comedy
63994 55 mins B/W B, V P, T
Larry Semon, Oliver Hardy, Lucille Carlisle, directed by Larry Semon
A package of shorts featuring crazy comedian Larry Semon, getting tangled up in mayhem and molasses. Silent with piano score.
Vitagraph — *Blackhawk Films*

Bal, Le **1984**
Musical
74207 112 mins C B, V R, P
This movie captures a 50-year span of contemporary history through the music and dance of periods from the 1930s through 1983.
French Academy Awards '83: Best Picture; Best Director (Scola); Best Music Score.
Giorgio Silvagni — *Warner Home Video*

Ball of Fire **1942**
Comedy
81477 111 mins B/W B, V, LV P
Gary Cooper, Barbara Stanwyck, Dana Andrews, Gene Krupa, directed by Howard Hawks
A professor of semantics gets more than he can handle when he consults a stripper for his study of slang in the English language.
Sameul Goldwyn — *Embassy Home Entertainment*

Ballad in Blue **1966**
Drama
79326 88 mins B/W B, V P
Ray Charles, Tom Bell, Mary Peach, Dawn Addams, directed by Paul Henried
The pianist befriends a blind British boy and his mother and guides them through the trials and tribulations of everyday life. In Beta Hi-Fi and VHS Stereo.
Alexander Salkind — *U.S.A. Home Video*

Ballad of Gregorio Cortez, The **1983**
Drama
64990 99 mins C B, V P
Edward James Olmos
Based on one of the most famous manhunts in Texas history, this is the story of a Mexican cowhand who killed a Texas sheriff in self-defense and tried to elude the law, all because of a misunderstanding of the Spanish language.
EL, JA
Moctesuma Esparza Productions — *Embassy Home Entertainment*

Ballerina: Karen Kain **1980**
Dance
58562 58 mins C B, V P
A profile of the dancer about whom Nureyev has said "in her the star quality is unmistakable." Includes scenes from "Carmen," "Romeo and Juliet," and "Cappelia."
MasterVision — *Mastervision*

Ballerina: Lynn Seymour **1980**
Dance
58563 58 mins C B, V P
Rudolph Nureyev
Prima ballerina Lynn Seymour is seen dancing with some of the world's leading male stars. Scenes from "Romeo and Juliet" and "The Two Pigeons" are included.
MasterVision — *Mastervision*

Balloonatic, The/One Week **192?**
Comedy
60051 48 mins B/W B, V P, T
Buster Keaton, Phyllis Haver, Sybil Seely
"The Balloonatic" (1923) features Keaton in several misadventures. In "One Week" (1920) Buster and his new bride, Sybil, receive a new home as a wedding gift—the kind you have to assemble yourself. Silent.
Buster Keaton Prods; Metro — *Blackhawk Films*

Baltimore Bullet, The **1980**
Adventure
55533 103 mins C B, V, CED P
James Coburn, Omar Sharif, Bruce Boxleitner, Ronee Blakely, Jack O'Halloran
Two men make their living traveling through the country as pool hustlers, bilking would-be pool sharks. Features ten of the greatest pool players in the world.
MPAA:PG
Avco Embassy; John Brascia — *Embassy Home Entertainment*

Baltimore Orioles: Team Highlights **1984**
Baseball
81134 30 mins C B, V P
Jim Palmer, Earl Weaver, Rick Dempsey, Eddie Murray, Ken Singleton, Benny Ayala 4 pgms
Here are highlights from the Baltimore Orioles four successful early eighties seasons.
1.1981: Oriole Magic 2.1982: Something Magic Happened 3.1983: O's What A Feeling 4.1984: A Winning Tradition
Major League Baseball — *Major League Baseball Productions*

Bamboo Saucer **1967**
Science fiction
80181 103 mins C B, V P
Dab Duryea, John Ericson
Two groups of Russian and American scientists race to find a U.F.O. in Red China
NTA — *Republic Pictures Home Video*

Banana Splits & Friends, The 197?
Cartoons
66279 60 mins C B, V P
Four large furry creatures, the Banana Splits, perform their slapstick antics and present cartoons.
Hanna Barbera — *Worldvision Home Video*

Bananas 1971
Comedy
58484 82 mins C B, V P
Woody Allen, Louise Lasser, Carlos Montalban, Howard Cosell, Sylvester Stallone, directed by Woody Allen
A frustrated product tester from New York runs off to South America, where he volunteers his support to the revolutionary force of a shaky Latin-American dictatorship and winds up the leader.
MPAA:PG
United Artists; Rollins Jaffe; Jack Grossberg — *CBS/Fox Video; RCA VideoDiscs*

Band Reunion, The 1984
Music-Performance
78369 87 mins C B, V P
The Band is together again performing their greatest hits at a concert taped in Vancouver, Canada.
Jack McAndrew — *Music Media*

Bandits, The 1973
Western
47667 83 mins C B, V P
Robert Conrad, Jan Michael Vincent, Roy Jenson
Three cowboys team up with a band of Mexican outlaws to fight a Mexican traitor.
Lone Star Pictures — *Unicorn Video*

Bandolero 1968
Adventure
65412 106 mins C CED P
James Stewart, Raquel Welch, Dean Martin, George Kennedy, Will Geer, Andrew Prine
In Texas, two fugitive brothers run into trouble with their Mexican counterparts.
20th Century Fox — *CBS/Fox Video*

Band Wagon, The 1953
Musical
59136 112 mins C B, V P
Fred Astaire, Cyd Charisse, Oscar Levant, Nanette Fabray, Jack Buchanan, directed by Vincente Minnelli
A Hollywood song-and-dance man finds trouble when he is persuaded to star in a Broadway musical. Songs by Howard Dietz and Arthur Schwartz include "That's Entertainment," and "Dancing in the Dark."
MGM;Arthur Freed — *MGM/UA Home Video*

Bang the Drum Slowly 1973
Drama
59390 97 mins C B, V, LV R, P
Robert DeNiro, Michael Moriarty, Vincent Gardenia, Phil Foster, Ann Wedgeworth, Heather MacRae, Selma Diamond
The story of a major league catcher who suffers from a fatal illness, and his friendship with a quiet, senstive teammate.
NY Film Critics Awards '73: Best Supporting Actor (DeNiro). MPAA:PG
Paramount — *Paramount Home Video*

Bank Dick, The 1940
Adventure/Comedy
69030 73 mins B/W B, V P
W.C. Fields, Cora Witherspoon, Una Richard Purcell, Jack Norton
A man accidentally trips a bank robber and finds himself a guard. A classic W.C. Fields film.
Universal — *MCA Home Video*

Bank on the Stars 1954
Game show
42980 30 mins B/W B, V, FO P
Bill Cullen
Contestants watch an action scene from a newly released movie and then answer questions based on what they've seen. Scenes on this show are from "Apache," "Johnny Dark," "Mr. Hulot's Holiday," and "The Caine Mutiny."
NBC — *Video Yesteryear*

Barabbas 1961
Drama
64239 144 mins C B, V P
Anthony Quinn, Silvana Mangano, Arthur Kennedy, Jack Palance
Barabbas, a thief and murderer, is freed by Pontius Pilate in place of Jesus, but he is haunted by this event for the rest of his life.
Columbia; Dino de Laurentiis — *RCA/Columbia Pictures Home Video*

Barbarella 1968
Fantasy
38615 98 mins C B, V, LV R, P
Jane Fonda, John Phillip Law, David Hemmings, directed by Roger Vadim
Based on the popular French sci-fi comic strip drawn by Jean-Claude Forest, this popular film stars Jane Fonda as a sexually emancipated space woman who vanquishes evil robots and monsters and rewards the many men she meets in her travels.
MPAA:PG
Paramount — *Paramount Home Video; RCA VideoDiscs*

(For explanation of codes, see USE GUIDE and KEY)

Barbarosa 1982
Western
63398 90 mins C B, V, CED P
Willie Nelson, Gilbert Roland, Gary Busey
Nelson stars as an aging, legendary outlaw whose Mexican in-laws never succeed in killing. He takes in a naive farmboy and teaches him his survival skills to continue the legend.
MPAA:PG
ITC Entertainment — *CBS/Fox Video*

Barber Shop, The 1933
Comedy
59401 21 mins B/W B, V P, T
W.C. Fields, Elise Cavanna, Harry Watson, Dagmar Oakland, Frank Yaconelli
Fields portrays the bumbling, carefree barber Cornelius O'Hare, purveyor of village gossip and solver of problems. Havoc begins when a gangster enters the shop and demands that Cornelius change his appearance.
Paramount — *Blackhawk Films*

Barcelona Kill, The 197?
Suspense
73147 86 mins C B, V P
Linda Hayden, John Austin, Simon Andrew, Maximo Valverde
When a journalist and her boyfriend get in too deep with the Barcelona mob, their troubles begin.
Michael Klinger Production — *VCL Home Video*

Barefoot Contessa, The 1954
Drama
55584 128 mins C CED P
Ava Gardner, Humphrey Bogart, Edmond O'Brien
The story, told in flashback, of a girl's rise to stardom and the loneliness she finds at the top.
Academy Awards '54: Best Supporting Actor (O'Brien).
United Artists — *CBS/Fox Video*

Barefoot in the Park 1967
Comedy
54675 105 mins C B, V, LV R, P
Robert Redford, Jane Fonda, Charles Boyer, Mildred Natwick, directed by Gene Saks
A newly wedded bride tries to get her husband to loosen up and be as free spirited as she is.
Paramount, Hal Wallis — *Paramount Home Video; RCA VideoDiscs*

Barkleys, The 1972
Cartoons
80146 44 mins C B, V P
Animated
Canine cabdriver Arnie Barkley gets into hot water with his family over his outrageous opinions in this collection of two episodes from the series.
De Patie Freleng — *Trans World Entertainment*

Barkleys—Volume 3, The 1972
Cartoons
81045 44 mins C B, V P
Animated
That opinionated canine cabdriver Arnie Barkley winds up in the dog house again in this collection of two episodes from the series.
De Patie Freleng — *Trans World Entertainment*

Barkleys—Volume 2, The 1972
Cartoons
76947 53 mins C B, V P
Animated
That opinionated canine Arnie Barkley foams off at the mouth about women's liberation and young children in these two episodes from the series.
DePatie-Freleng Enterprises — *Trans World Entertainment*

Barnaby and Me 1977
Comedy
70647 90 mins C B, V P
Sid Caesar, Juliet Mills, Sally Boyden
Australian star Barnaby the Koala Bear joins an international con-man in this romantic adventure. The mob is chasing the con-man when he meets and falls for a lovely young woman and her daughter.
Transatlantic Entprs. — *Academy Home Entertainment*

Barney Oldfield's Race for a Life/Super-Hooper-Dyne Lizzies 19??
Comedy-Drama
60057 42 mins B/W B, V P, T
Barney Oldfield, Mack Sennett, Mabel Normand, Ford Sterling, Billy Bevan, Andy Clyde
In the first of two shorts on this tape from 1913, Barney chases a villain who has abducted a lovely girl. In the second film from 1925, radio-controlled Model-T Fords co-star with comic Billy Bevan.
Mack Sennett; Pathe — *Blackhawk Films*

Baron and the Kid, The 1984
Drama
81556 100 mins C B, V P
Johnny Cash, Darren McGavin, June Carter Cash, Richard Roundtree, directed by Gary Nelson
A pool shark finds out that his opponent at a charity exhibition game is his long-lost son. Based upon Johnny Cash's song. Available in VHS and Beta Hi-Fi.
Telecom Entertainment — *Playhouse Video*

Baron Muenchhausen 19??
Comedy-Drama
65643 120 mins C B, V R, P
Kaethe Kaack, Hermann Speelmanns, Leo Slezak, directed by Josef von Baky
The German film studio UFA celebrated its 25th anniversary with the lavish version of the Baron Muenchhausen legends, starring a cast of top-name German performers of the period. Filmed in Agfacolor and stereophonic sound; available in English subtitled or dubbed versions.
GE
UFA — *Video City Productions*

Barry Gibb: Now Voyager 1984
Music-Performance/Music video
70558 79 mins C B, V P
Barry Gibb, Michael Hordern
The prominent Mr. Gibb dives headlong into the conceptual video world with this unified production of nine songs. His exotic and musical travels with singers and dancers feature stereo sound on all formats.
Polygram Musicvideo — *MCA Home Video*

Barry Lyndon 1975
Drama
68232 184 mins C B, V R, P
Ryan O'Neal, Marisa Berenson
Ryan O'Neal stars as an Irish scoundrel and gentleman in this film.
MPAA:PG
Warner Brothers — *Warner Home Video*

Barry Manilow Live at the Greek 1982
Music-Performance
72445 75 mins C LV P
Pop star Barry Manilow thrills his audience in this live performance at the Greek Theater.
Marty Pasetta; Barry Manilow — *Pioneer Video Imports*

Barry McKenzie Holds His Own 1975
Comedy
77013 93 mins C B, V P
Barry Humphries, Barry Crocker, Donald Pleasence, directed by Bruce Beresford
When a young man's aunt is mistaken for the Queen of England, two emissaries of Count Plasma of Transylvania kidnap her to use as a Plasma tourist attraction.
Satori Entertainment — *VidAmerica*

Baseball: Fun and Games 1980
Baseball
29231 60 mins C B, V P
Features great baseball trivia quizzes and gives you another chance to see the close plays and make the calls.
Major League Baseball Productions — *VidAmerica; RCA VideoDiscs*

Baseball: The Now Career 1975
Baseball
33830 26 mins C B, V P
Chuck Connors, Nolan Ryan, Johnny Bench, Tug McGraw
Television star Chuck Connors, a former ballplayer, helps tell the story of the road to the major leagues, along with several of the game's stars.
Major League Baseball — *Major League Baseball Productions*

Baseball's Hall of Fame 1981
Baseball
51658 60 mins C B, V, CED P
Hosted by Donald Sutherland
The most glorious moments in baseball history are relived through speeches and footage of some of baseball's greatest players, such as oldtimers Babe Ruth, Mel Ott, Ted Williams, and Bob Feller, and newer inductees such as Al Kaline, Mickey Mantle, Duke Snider, and Warren Spahn.
Major League Baseball — *VidAmerica*

Basic Art By Video I: Painting 1984
Painting
76968 120 mins C B, V P
Instructor Charles Haddock teaches the basic techniques of painting.
Charles Haddock — *Mastervision*

Basic Art By Video II: Drawing & Design 1984
Drawing
76969 120 mins C B, V P
Instructor Charles Haddock teaches the basic skills needed for drawing.
Charles Haddock — *Mastervision*

Basic Art By Video III: Color 1984
Painting
76970 120 mins C B, V P
Instructor Charles Haddock demonstrates the color techniques used by painters from the Renaissance through modern times.
Charles Haddock — *Mastervision*

Basic English for Hispanics by Video 1985
Languages-Instruction
76965 90 mins C B, V P
An introductory course for Hispanics that teaches the basics of the English language.
L Productions; Mastervision — *Mastervision*

(For explanation of codes, see USE GUIDE and KEY)

Basic English Grammar by Video 1983
Languages-Instruction
74489 90 mins C B, V P
This tape is designed to teach the basic fundamentals of English grammar.
Mastervision — *Mastervision*

Basic French by Video 1983
Languages-Instruction
74488 90 mins C B, V P
This tape is designed to teach basic conversational French.
Mastervision Inc — *Mastervision*

Basic Italian by Video 1983
Languages-Instruction
66205 90 mins C B, V P
A basic, working vocabulary of Italian is taught in this program.
Mastervision — *Mastervision*

Basic Spanish by Video 1983
Languages-Instruction
66204 90 mins C B, V P
This program is designed to provide the viewer with a working vocabulary of Spanish.
Mastervision — *Mastervision*

Basket Case 1982
Horror
63891 89 mins C B, V P
Kevin Van Hentenryck, Terri Susan Smith, Beverly Bonner
A pair of Siamese twins, one deformed and one normal, set out to avenge their surgical separation.
Edgar levins — *Media Home Entertainment*

Basketball with Gail Goodrich 1982
Basketball
60439 30 mins C B, V P
Gail Goodrich
Two pros take the viewer through basic shooting, free throws, jump shots, jumps from the dribble and shots close to the basket. For novice and advanced player alike.
MPAA:G
Unknown — *Embassy Home Entertainment*

Batman 1967
Cartoons/Fantasy
81088 60 mins C B, V R, P
Animated
The caped crusader and his faithful sidekick Robin battle crime in Gotham City in this collection of eight animated adventures.
Filmation — *Warner Home Video*

Battle at Elderbush Gulch, The/The Musketeers of Pig Alley 1914
Drama/Film-History
62871 33 mins B/W B, V P, T
Lillian Gish, Mae Marsh, Harry Carey, directed by D.W. Griffith
Two classic D.W. Griffith two-reelers from 1914 and 1912 respectively are contained on this tape.
Biograph — *Blackhawk Films*

Battle Beneath the Earth 1968
Science fiction
75540 112 mins C B, V P
Kerwin Mathews, Peter Arne
American scientists discover a Chinese plot to invade the U.S. via a series of underground tunnels.
MGM — *MGM/UA Home Video*

Battle Beyond the Stars 1980
Science fiction
66100 103 mins C B, V, CED P
Richard Thomas, Robert Vaughn, George Peppard
A variety of extraordinary aliens set out on an intergalactic mission.
MPAA:PG
Orion Pictures — *Vestron Video*

Battle Cry 1955
War-Drama
47617 170 mins C B, V R, P
Van Heflin, Aldo Ray, Mona Freeman, Tab Hunter, Dorothy Malone, Anne Francis
A group of U.S. Marines train, romance, and enter battle in World War II. Part of the "A Night at the Movies" series, this tape simulates a 1955 movie evening, with a cartoon, "Speedy Gonzales," a newsreel and coming attractions for "Mr. Roberts" and "East of Eden."
Warner Bros — *Warner Home Video*

Battle for the Falklands 1984
Great Britain/Documentary
75925 110 mins C B, V R, P
This program documents the complete account of the dramatic battle for the Falklands.
Thorn — *THORN EMI/HBO Video*

Battle for the Planet of the Apes 1973
Science fiction
81544 96 mins C B, V P
Roddy McDowall, Lew Ayres, John Huston, Paul Williams, directed by J. Lee Thompson
A tribe of human atomic bomb mutations are out to make life miserable for the peaceful ape tribe in the year 2670 A.D.
MPAA:G
20th Century Fox — *Playhouse Video*

Battle Hell 1956
War-Drama
80938 112 mins B/W B, V P
Richard Todd, Akim Tamiroff, Keye Luke
This film tells the true story of how a British ship was attacked by the Chinese Peoples Liberation Army on the Yangtze River in 1949.
Distributors Corp. of America — *VidAmerica*

Battle of Austerlitz 1960
Drama
79192 180 mins C B, V P
Orson Welles, Rossaro Brazzi, Jack Palance, Claudia Cardinale, Vittorio de Sica
An account of how Napoleon became Emperor after winning a series of battles is presented in this dramatization.
MPAA:PG
Michael Salkind; Alexander Salkind — *U.S.A. Home Video*

Battle of China, The 1944
Documentary/World War II
44993 67 mins B/W B, V P
Directed by Frank Capra
A look at the people, culture, and industry of China, and Japan's total commitment to conquer the country during World War II, through authentic newsreel footage.
US War Department — *MPI Home Video; Budget Video; Western Film & Video Inc; Discount Video Tapes*

Battle of El Alamein, The 1971
War-Drama
59354 92 mins C B, V R, P
George Hilton, Michael Rennie
The world's mightiest tank armadas, the U.S. vs. Rommel's forces, battle for desert supremacy.
MPAA:G
Heritage Enterprises — *Video Gems*

Battle of El Alamein, The 1971
War-Drama
80791 92 mins C B, V R, P
Michael Rennie, George Hilton, Ira Furstemberg, Frederick Stafford
The control of North Africa is at stake when General Montgomery's 8th Army and General Rommel's Afrika Korps lock horns for one of World War II's most intense battles.
Plaza Pictures — *Video Gems*

Battle of Neretva 1970
Drama
65459 112 mins C B, V P
Yul Brynner, Curt Jurgens, Orson Welles
Yugoslav partisans are facing German and Italian troops and local Chetniks as they battle for freedom.
American International — *Republic Pictures Home Video*

Battle of Russia, The 1944
Documentary/World War II
44994 83 mins B/W B, V P
Directed by Frank Capra
Hitler's forces are victorious in Moscow and Leningrad but are thoroughly defeated at the battle of Stalingrad. Authentic newsreel footage.
US War Department — *Budget Video; Blackhawk Films; Western Film & Video Inc; MPI Home Video; Discount Video Tapes*

Battle of the Bulge, The 1965
War-Drama
73012 141 mins C B, V P
Henry Fonda, Robert Shaw, Robert Ryan, Dana Andrews, Pier Angeli
A recreation of the famous offensive by Nazi Panzer troops on the Belgian front during 1944-45, an assault that could have changed the course of World War Two.
Sidney Harmon; Warner Bros — *Warner Home Video*

Battle of the Commandos 1971
War-Drama
81420 94 mins C B, V P
Jack Palance, Curt Jurgens, Thomas Hunter, Robert Hunter
A tough Army colonel leads a group of convicts on a dangerous mission to destroy a German built cannon before it's used against the Allied Forces.
Commonwealth United — *Republic Pictures Home Video*

Battle of the Last Panzer, The 1980
War-Drama
77393 90 mins C B, V P
Guy Madison, Stan Cooper
A beautiful French girl and a German commander swap excess passion while trapped behind Allied lines during World War II.
MPAA:R
Prodimex; Hispaner Film — *Wizard Video*

Battle Shock 1956
Mystery/Drama
76831 88 mins C B, V P
Ralph Meeker, Janice Rule, Paul Henried
A painter on a honeymoon with his wife in Mexico is accused of murdering a cantina waitress.
Republic Pictures — *Republic Pictures Home Video*

Battlestar Galactica 1978
Science fiction
14066 125 mins C B, V, LV, CED P
Lorne Greene, Richard Hatch, Dirk Benedict, Ray Milland, directed by Richard A Colla

(For explanation of codes, see USE GUIDE and KEY)

A spaceship tries a desperate attempt to reach the ancient planet called Earth. Spectacular special effects. A movie made for television.
MPAA:PG
Glen Larson — *MCA Home Video*

Battling Beauties **1984**
Boxing
79880 60 mins C B, V P
A group of women compete in no holds barred boxing and mud wrestling matches.
Bert Rhine — *Active Home Video*

Batty World of Baseball, The **1982**
Baseball
59381 ? mins C B, V P
A humorous look at the personalities who make the game interesting: managers like John McGraw, Leo Durocher, Casey Stengel, and Billy Martin, and a rarely-seen side of Babe Ruth.
Major League Baseball Prods — *RCA/Columbia Pictures Home Video*

B.C. The First Thanksgiving **1984**
Cartoons/Holidays
78349 25 mins C B, V P
Animated
The caveman B.C. and his friends are trying to find a turkey to flavor their rock soup in this animated featurette.
King Features — *Embassy Home Entertainment*

Be My Valentine, Charlie Brown/Is This Goodbye, Charlie Brown **1983**
Cartoons
76847 50 mins C B, V P
Animated
Here are two Peanuts specials: In "Be My Valentine, Charlie Brown," Charlie waits by his mailbox hoping for a valentine and in "Is This Goodbye, Charlie Brown," Linus and Lucy are moving because of their father's job transfer to another city.
Lee Mendelson; Bill Melendez — *Snoopy's Home Video Library*

Beach Boys: An American Band, The **1985**
Documentary/Music-Performance
80684 103 mins C B, V P
Brian Wilson, Carl Wilson, Dennis Wilson, Mike Love, Al Jardine, Bruce Johnson, directed by Malcolm Leo
This film takes an in-depth look at the lives and music of the Beach Boys with a soundtrack that features over forty of their songs.
MPAA:PG13
High Ridge Productions — *Vestron Video*

Beach Girls, The **1982**
Comedy
64030 91 mins C B, V, LV R, P
Debra Blee, Val Kline, Jeana Tomasina
Three voluptuous coeds intend to re-educate a bookish young man and the owner of a beach house.
MPAA:R
Crown International Pictures — *Paramount Home Video; RCA VideoDiscs*

Beach House **1982**
Comedy
66187 89 mins C B, V R, P
Adolescents frolic on the beach, get inebriated and listen to rock 'n' roll.
Unknown — *THORN EMI/HBO Video*

Beach Party **1963**
Comedy/Musical
64892 101 mins C CED P
Frankie Avalon, Annette Funicello, Bob Cummings
A scientist studying the mating habits of teenagers intrudes on a group of surfers, beach bums and motorcyclists.
American International Pictures — *Warner Home Video; Vestron Video (disc only)*

Beany & Cecil, Volume VII **196?**
Cartoons
Closed Captioned
77372 60 mins C B, V P
Animated
Join Beany, Cecil and Captain Huffenpuff as they board the Leakin' Lena for seven animated adventures.
Bob Clampett — *RCA/Columbia Pictures Home Video*

Beany and Cecil Volume 8 **196?**
Cartoons
Closed Captioned
81435 45 mins C B, V P
Animated, directed by Bob Clampett
Beany and Cecil along with Captain Huffenpuff board the Leakin' Lena to battle an assortment of bad guys in this collection of six episodes from the series.
Bob Clampett — *RCA/Columbia Pictures Home Video*

Beany & Cecil, Volume III **196?**
Cartoons
76035 60 mins C B, V P
Animated
There's lots of fun and adventure in this third volume of cartoons featuring Beany, Cecil the

Sea Sick Sea Serpent, Dishonest John, Captain Huffenpuff, and all their friends.
Bob Clampett — *RCA/Columbia Pictures Home Video*

Beany and Cecil, Volume Four **196?**
Cartoons
Closed Captioned
72922 60 mins C B, V P
Animated
More classic cartoon adventures with Beany and Cecil including: "Beany and the Boo Birds," and "The Rat Race for Space."
Bob Clampett — *RCA/Columbia Pictures Home Video*

Beany and Cecil Volume VI **196?**
Cartoons
Closed Captioned
78878 45 mins C B, V P
Animated
Beany, his friend the sea serpent Cecil, and the commander of the Leakin' Lena, Captain Huffenpuff sail around the world to battle Dishonest John in this fifth volume of animated adventures. In Beta Hi-Fi.
Bob Clampett — *RCA/Columbia Pictures Home Video*

Beany & Cecil Volume VI **196?**
Cartoons
Closed Captioned
80379 60 mins C B, V P
Animated
Beany, Cecil and Captain Huffenpuff team up once again to battle Dishonest John in this new collection of six episodes from the series.
Bob Clampett — *RCA/Columbia Pictures Home Video*

Beany & Cecil, Volumes 1 & 2 **196?**
Cartoons
66345 60 mins C B, V P
The lovable characters of the little boy Beany and his loyal companion, Cecil the Sea Sick Sea Serpent are featured in 14 classic cartoons. In Beta Hi-Fi.
Bob Clampett; ABC — *RCA/Columbia Pictures Home Video; RCA VideoDiscs*

Bear Island **1980**
Adventure
77358 102 mins C B, V P
Donald Sutherland, Richard Widmark, Barbara Parkins, Vanessa Redgrave, Christopher Lee, Lloyd Bridges
A group of secret agents disguising themselves as U.N. weather researchers, converge upon Bear Island in search of a Nazi U-Boat.
MPAA:PG
Taft International Pictures — *Media Home Entertainment*

Bear Who Slept Through Christmas, The **1983**
Christmas
65161 60 mins C B, V P
Animated, voices of Tommy Smothers, Arte Johnson, Barbara Feldon, Kelly Lange
As Christmas approaches, all the bears are getting ready to go to sleep for the winter, except Ted E. Bear, who wants to see just what Christmas is.
Dimenmark International — *Family Home Entertainment*

Bears and I, The **1975**
Adventure
56874 88 mins C CED P
Patrick Wayne, Chief Dan George, Andrew Duggan, Michael Ansara
A young war veteran in search of himself heads for the wilderness, befriends a trio of orphaned bears, and helps an Indian tribe in their struggle to retain their rights.
MPAA:G
Walt Disney — *RCA VideoDiscs*

Beast, The **1975**
Horror
58555 82 mins C B, V P
Edward Connell, Barbara Hewitt
Two teenagers are menaced by a gigantic mutant ape after discovering a devil-worshipping cult.
MPAA:PG
Tonlyn; Jack Harris — *Wizard Video*

Beast Must Die, The **1975**
Horror
55563 93 mins C B, V, 3/4U P
Peter Cushing, Calvin Lockhart
A millionaire sportsman invites a group of men and women connected with bizarre deaths or the eating of human flesh to spend the cycle of a full moon at his isolated lodge.
MPAA:PG
Cinerama Releasing; Max Rosenberg — *Nostalgia Merchant*

Beast of I.R.S. Volume I, The **1984**
Music video
72864 40 mins C B, V P
Some of I.R.S. artists' best video clips are featured. The Alarm and the Go-Go's are included.
International Record Syndicate Video — *I.R.S. Video*

Beast Within, The 1982
Horror
64568 98 mins C B, V, CED P
Ronny Cox, Bibi Besch, Paul Clemens, Don Gordon
A young woman is raped by an unseen creature in a Mississippi swamp. Seventeen years later, her son begins to act strangely, forcing a return to the rape scene. In stereo.
MPAA:R
MGM/UA — *MGM/UA Home Video*

Beastmaster, The 1982
Adventure
68239 119 mins C B, V, CED P
Marc Singer, Tanya Roberts, and Rip Torn
This adventure film is set in a wild and primitive world. The Beastmaster is involved in a life and death struggle with overwhelming forces of evil. In stereo.
MPAA:PG
MGM/UA — *MGM/UA Home Video*

Beasts 1983
Adventure/Drama
80892 92 mins C B, V P
Tom Babson, Kathy Christopher, Vern Potter
A young couple's plans for a romantic weekend in the Rockies are slightly changed when the pair are savagely attacked by wild beasts.
American National Enterprises — *Prism*

Beat Goes On, The 1981
Football
51168 23 mins C B, V, FO R, P
Houston Oilers
Coach Bum Phillips predicted 1980 would be the year that his team 'broke down the door' to the Super Bowl. Instead, at season's end, he was shown the door. However, when Oiler stars such as Ken Stabler and Earl Campbell were good, there were few better.
NFL Films — *NFL Films Video*

Beat of the Live Drum, The 1985
Music video/Music-Performance
80881 75 mins C B, V P
Rick Springfield
Guitarist/singer/songwriter Rick Springfield performs such hits as "Jessie's Girl", "Affair of the Heart" and "Love Somebody" in this concert taped in Tuscon, Arizona. This tape also features three conceptual music videos from his "Tao" LP.
Z Street Films; Famous Dog Productions — *RCA/Columbia Pictures Home Video*

Beat Street 1984
Musical
70151 106 mins C B, V P
This quasi-documentary about break dancing features the music of Ruben Blades, Afrika Bambaata and the Soul Sonic Force, and Grand Master Melle Mel and the Furious Five.
MPAA:PG
Harry Belafonte; David Picker;
Orion — *Vestron Video*

Beatlemania—The Movie 1983
Music-Performance
65445 60 mins C B, V P
This program pictorially and musically reflects the tumultuous events of the 60's, featuring 30 of the greatest songs of John Lennon and Paul McCartney. In stereo VHS and Beta Hi-Fi. Not the Beatles, but an incredible simulation.
Edie and Ely Landau — *U.S.A. Home Video*

Beauty and the Beast 1984
Fairy tales
Closed Captioned
73851 60 mins C B, V, LV, CED P
Susan Sarandon, Klaus Kinski, directed by Roger Vadim
From "Faerie Tale Theatre" comes the story of a Beauty who befriends a Beast and learns a lesson about physical ugliness.
Gaylord Productions; Platypus Productions — *CBS/Fox Video*

Because of the Cats 1975
Horror
70600 90 mins C B, V P
Bryan Marshall, Alexandra Stewart, Sylvia Kristel, Sebastian Graham Jones, directed by Fons Rademakers
A police inspector uncovers an evil cult within his seaside village while investigating a bizarre rape/burglary.
American Transcontinental Pictures — *Prism*

Becket 1964
Drama
51574 148 mins C B, V P
Richard Burton, Peter O'Toole, John Gielgud
A drama dealing with 12th century friendship between Becket and the King of England, Becket's appointment as Archbishop of Canterbury, and the furor which arises when he takes his position too seriously.
Academy Awards '64: Best Screenplay (Edward Anhalt).
Paramount; Hal Wallis — *MPI Home Video; United Home Video*

Bedazzled 1968
Comedy
58951 107 mins C B, V P
Dudley Moore, Peter Cook, Eleanor Bron, Michael Bates, Raquel Welch, directed by Stanley Donen

A short-order cook is saved from suicide by a man who offers him seven wishes in exchange for his soul.
EL, SP
20th Century Fox — *CBS/Fox Video*

Bedford Incident, The **1965**
Adventure
44787 102 mins B/W B, V P
Richard Widmark, Sidney Poitier, James MacArthur, Martin Balsam, Wally Cox
The U.S.S. Bedford discovers an unidentified submarine in North Atlantic waters. The Bedford's commander drives his crew to the point of nerve-taut exhaustion when they find themselves the center of a fateful controversy.
James B Harris, Richard Widmark,
Columbia — *RCA/Columbia Pictures Home Video*

Bedlam **1945**
Horror
00317 79 mins B/W B, V, 3/4U P
Boris Karloff, Anna Lee, Richard Fraser
Horror melodrama of a seventeenth century insane asylum and a sane female reformer.
RKO — *Nostalgia Merchant*

Bedtime for Bonzo **1951**
Comedy
56872 83 mins B/W B, V P
Ronald Reagan, Diána Lynn, Walter Slezak, Jesse White, Bonzo the Chimp, directed by Fred deCordova
A professor adopts a chimp to prove that environment determines a child's future, disproving the Dean's theory that his children-to-be might inherit criminal tendencies because his father was a crook.
Universal — *MCA Home Video*

Bees, The **1978**
Drama
53506 93 mins C B, V R, P
John Saxon, John Carradine, Angel Tompkins
A strain of bees have ransacked South America and are threatening the rest of the world.
MPAA:PG
New World; Bee One Panorama Films — *Warner Home Video*

Before I Hang **1940**
Horror/Mystery
78965 60 mins B/W B, V P
Boris Karloff, Evelyn Keyes, Bruce Bennett, Edward Van Sloan
When a doctor invents a youth serum from the blood of a murderer, he'll stop at nothing to keep his secret. In Beta Hi-Fi.
Columbia Pictures — *RCA/Columbia Pictures Home Video*

Beguiled, The **1970**
War-Drama
64797 109 mins C B, V P
Clint Eastwood, Geraldine Page, Elizabeth Hartman, directed by Donald Siegel
A wounded Union soldier is taken in by the women at a girl's school in the South. He manages to seduce both a student and a teacher, and jealousy and revenge ensue.
MPAA:R
Universal — *MCA Home Video*

Behind Your Radio Dial **1948**
Mass media/Documentary
12844 45 mins B/W B, V, FO P
An early TV show which gives the viewer an entertaining glimpse of NBC radio and many of its stars.
NBC — *Video Yesteryear*

Behold a Pale Horse **1964**
Drama
66015 118 mins B/W B, V P
Gregory Peck, Anthony Quinn, Omar Sharif, Mildred Dunnock, directed by Fred Zinneman
A post-Spanish Civil War tale concerning an ideological battle between a guerilla leader and a cruel police captain.
Columbia — *RCA/Columbia Pictures Home Video*

Being, The **1983**
Horror
73022 82 mins C B, V R, P
Ruth Buzzi, Martin Landau, Jose Ferrer
People in Idaho are terrorized by a freak who became abnormal after radiation was disposed in the local dump.
William Osco — *THORN EMI/HBO Video*

Being There **1979**
Comedy
54838 126 mins C B, V, CED P
Peter Sellers, Shirley MacLaine, Melvyn Douglas, directed by Hal Ashby
A feeble-minded gardener whose entire knowledge of life comes from watching television is sent out into the real world when his employer dies. Equipped with his prize possession, his remote control unit, the gardener encounters a series of hilarious events.
Academy Awards '79: Best Supporting Actor (Douglas). MPAA:PG
Lorimar Prods, Andrew Braunsberg Prod — *CBS/Fox Video*

Bela Lugosi Meets a Brooklyn Gorilla **1952**
Comedy/Horror
73551 74 mins B/W B, V P
Bela Lugosi, Duke Mitchell, Sammy Petrillo

 (For explanation of codes, see USE GUIDE and KEY)

Two men who look like Dean Martin and Jerry Lewis get lost in the jungle where they meet a mad scientist.
Jack Broder Prods — *Admit One Video*

Belafonte Presents Fincho 1975
Africa/Documentary
58580 79 mins C B, V P
Hosted by Harry Belafonte, directed by Sarn Zebba
A docudrama shot in Nigeria concerning the problems a jungle village faces when suddenly brought into the 20th Century.
Rohauer Films — *Mastervision*

Belfast Assassin, The 1984
Drama
80326 130 mins C B, V P
Derek Thompson, Ray Lonnen
A British anti-terrorist agent goes undercover to find an IRA assassin who shot a British cabinet minister.
Independent — *Prism*

Bell, Book and Candle 1959
Comedy
35378 103 mins C B, V P
James Stewart, Kim Novak, Jack Lemmon, Elsa Lanchester, Ernie Kovacs, Hermione Gingold
A young witch makes up her mind to refrain from using her powers. When an interesting man moves into her building, she forgets her decision and enchants him with a love spell.
Columbia — *RCA/Columbia Pictures Home Video*

Bell Jar, The 1979
Drama
65474 113 mins C B, V P
Marilyn Hasset, Julie Harris, Barbara Barrie, Anne Bancroft
Based on poet Sylvia Plath's acclaimed semi-autobiographical novel, this is the story of a young woman who becomes the victim of mental illness.
MPAA:R
Avco Embassy — *Vestron Video*

Belle Starr Story, The 197?
Western
70369 90 mins C B, V R, P
Elsa Martinelli, Robert Wood, directed by Lina Wertmuller
This film follows the career of Belle Starr and her rise to infantry in the Wild West.
Foreign — *Video City Productions*

Belles of St. Trinian's, The 1953
Comedy
66020 86 mins B/W B, V R, P
Alastair Sim
Alastair Sim is superb in a dual role as the prim headmistress of a private girls school and her slick bookmaker brother.
Lauder Gillist Productions — *THORN EMI/HBO Video*

Bells, The 1926
Drama
69563 92 mins B/W B, V, FO P
Lionel Barrymore, Boris Karloff
The Burgomeister of an Alsatian village kills a wealthy merchant and steals his money. The murderer experiences pangs of guilt which are accentuated when a traveling mesmerist comes to town who claims to be able to discern a person's darkest secrets. Silent with music score.
Independent — *Video Yesteryear*

Bells Are Ringing 1960
Musical/Comedy
58294 126 mins C B, V, CED P
Judy Holliday, Dean Martin, Fred Clark, Eddie Foy Jr., Jean Stapleton, directed by Vincente Minnelli
A girl who works for a telephone answering service can't help but take an interest in the lives of the clients, especially a playwright with an inferiority complex. Based on Adolph Green and Betty Comden's Broadway musical.
MGM — *MGM/UA Home Video*

Bells of St. Mary's, The 1945
Drama
47989 126 mins B/W B, V P
Bing Crosby, Ingrid Bergman, Henry Travers, directed by Leo McCarey
An easy-going priest finds himself in a subtle battle of wits with the Sister Superior over how the children of St. Mary's school should be raised. Songs include the title tune and "Aren't You Glad You're You?"
Academy Awards '45: Best Sound. NY Film Critics Award '45: Best Female Performance (Bergman).
RKO — *Republic Pictures Home Video*

Belly Dancing—You Can Do It! 1982
Dance
47678 ? mins C LV P
Four lovely belly dancers teach the basic moves of this ancient art, from basic belidi to the use of veils and zills. An interactive disc which runs 60 minutes when played through.
Asselin Productions — *Optical Programming Associates*

Below the Belt 1980
Drama
63330 92 mins C B, V R, P
Regina Baff, Mildred Burke, John C. Becher

A street-smart woman from New York City becomes part of the blue-collar "circus" of lady wrestling.
MPAA:R
Aberdeen/RLF/Tom-Mi Productions — *THORN EMI/HBO Video*

Belstone Fox, The 1973
Adventure
59828 103 mins C B, V P
Eric Porter, Rachel Roberts, Jeremy Kemp
An orphaned fox goes into hiding, and is hunted by the hound he has befriended and his former owner.
Julian Wintle — *Embassy Home Entertainment*

Ben Hur 1959
Drama
44648 217 mins C B, V, CED P
Charlton Heston, Jack Hawkins, Stephen Boyd, Hugh Griffith, Sam Jaffe, directed by William Wyler
Jewish nobleman Ben Hur struggles against Roman tyranny in first-century Palestine. Winner of ten Academy Awards.
Academy Awards '59: Best Picture; Best Actor (Heston); Best Supporting Actor (Griffith); Best Director (Wyler).
MGM — *MGM/UA Home Video*

Ben Turpin Rides Again 1923
Comedy
42948 45 mins B/W B, V, FO P
Ben Turpin 3 pgms
Ben Turpin, the cross-eyed wonder, stars in three shorts by Mack Sennett.
1. The Daredevil 2. Yukon Jake 3. The Eyes Have It
Mack Sennett — *Video Yesteryear*

Beneath the Planet of the Apes 1970
Science fiction
Closed Captioned
81541 95 mins C B, V P
Charlton Heston, James Franciscus, Kim Hunter, Maurice Evans, Victor Buono, directed by Ted Post
An astronaut discovers an underground society of mutated aliens when he is sent to New York to find a fellow astronaut believed to be lost in the rubble of an atomic blast.
MPAA:G
Apjac Productions, 20th Century Fox — *Playhouse Video*

Beneath the Twelve Mile Reef 1953
Adventure
75934 102 mins C B, V R, P
Robert Wagner, Terry Moore, Gilbert Roland, Peter Graves, directed by Robert Webb
This movie presents the story of murderous competition for the rich but dangerous sponge beds between the divers of Tarpon.
20th Century Fox — *Video Gems; Discount Video Tapes*

Benji 1973
Comedy-Drama
49626 87 mins C B, V P
Benji, Peter Brek, Christopher Connelly, Patsy Garrett, Deborah Walley, Cynthia Smith, directed by Joe Camp
In the loveable pooch's first feature-length movie, he falls in love with a female named Tiffany, and saves Paul and Cindy from the danger of sinister intruders.
MPAA:G
Mulberry Square Prods; Joe Camp — *Vestron Video; CBS/Fox Video (disc only)*

Benji Takes a Dive at Marineland/Benji at Work 1982
Animals
72230 60 mins C B, V P
Television's Adam Rich goes to Marineland with Wonder-dog Benji, and chronicles the canine's busy work schedule.
Carolyn Camp — *Children's Video Library*

Benji's Very Own Christmas Story 1983
Fantasy/Christmas
69532 60 mins C B, V P
Benji and his friends go on a magic trip and meet Kris Kringle and learn how Christmas is celebrated around the world. Also included: "The Phenomenon of Benji," a documentary about Benji's odyssey from the animal shelter to international stardom.
Mulberry Square Productions — *Children's Video Library*

Berenstain Bears' Comic Valentine, The 1982
Cartoons
65418 25 mins C B, V P
Animated
The whole Berenstain Bear family gets in on the fun when Brother Bear receives a mysterious Valentine from Miss Honey Bear, a secret admirer; but can he keep his mind on the upcoming Valentine's Day Championship Hockey Game against the Beartown Bullies?
Buzz Potamkin — *Embassy Home Entertainment*

Berenstain Bears' Easter Surprise, The 1981
Cartoons
65437 25 mins C B, V P
Animated
Boss Bunny, who usually controls the seasons, has quit, Poppa Bear's vainglorious effort to

construct his own Easter egg machine is a failure; and Brother Bear anxiously awaits his "Extra Special" Easter Surprise.
Buzz Potamkin — *Embassy Home Entertainment*

Berenstain Bears Meet Big Paw, The 1980
Cartoons
78352 25 mins C B, V P
Animated
Brother and Sister Bear meet up with the monster Big Paw and find out he is not a beast at all.
Buzz Potamkin — *Embassy Home Entertainment*

Berenstain Bears Play Ball, The 1983
Cartoons
74081 25 mins C B, V P
Animated
In this animated feature, Papa Bear learns a valuable lesson about winning and losing.
Buzz Potamkin — *Embassy Home Entertainment*

Bergonzi Hand, The 1970
Drama
78096 62 mins C B, V, FO P
Keith Mitchell, Gordon Jackson, Martin Miller
A drama about two scoundrels of the world of art who are astonished when an immigrant admits to painting a forged "Bergonzi."
ABC — *Video Yesteryear*

Berkshires and Hudsons of the Boston & Albany/Railroading in the Northeast 195?
Trains
62870 30 mins B/W B, V P, T
Railroad buffs will enjoy these scenes of classic steam locomotives from the New Haven, New York Central, Central Vermont, Delaware & Hudson and B & A lines.
J W Deely; E R Blanchard — *Blackhawk Films*

Berlin Alexanderplatz 1980
Drama
66463 920 mins C B, V P
Gunter Lamprecht, Hanna Schygulla, Barbara Sukowa, directed by Rainer Werner Fassbinder
Fassbinder's 15 1/2-hour epic, originally produced for German television, follows the life, death and resurrection of Franz Biberkof, a former transit worker who has just finished a lengthy prison term. With the Berlin of the 1920's as a backdrop, Fassbinder has contrived a melodramatic parable with Biblical overtones.
Teleculture Films; Peter Martheshmeimer — *MGM/UA Home Video*

Berlin Express 1948
War-Drama
00306 86 mins B/W B, V, 3/4U P
Robert Ryan, Merle Oberon, Paul Lukas
Battle of wits between the Allies and Nazi fanatics seeking to keep Germans disunited.
RKO — *Nostalgia Merchant*

Bermuda Triangle, The 1979
Documentary/Speculation
29227 94 mins C B, V P
Brad Campbell
One of the world's great mysteries, still unsolved in our time. The facts are that in the last 300 years more than 700 boats and planes and thousands of people have vanished without a trace in the area we call "The Bermuda Triangle."
MPAA:G
Sunn Classic Pictures — *VidAmerica*

Bernadette Peters in Concert 1981
Music-Performance
55561 47 mins C LV P
Bernadette Peters, directed by John Blanchard
This two-sided stereo disc presents Bernadette Peters' live performance, recorded at the 3,000 seat Jubilee Auditorium in Edmonton, Canada.
Doug Holtby; Nicholas Wry — *MCA Home Video*

Best Chest in the West 1984
Variety
79686 60 mins C B, V P
Dick Shawn, Pat McCormick, Carol Wayne, Avery Schreiber
A group of celebrity judges decide which of a dozen California girls is the most endowed
Bert Rhine — *Active Home Video*

Best Defense 1984
Comedy
80397 94 mins C B, V, LV, CED P
Dudley Moore, Eddie Murphy, Kate Capshaw, Helen Shaver, directed by Willard Huyck
A U.S. Army tank operator is sent to Kuwait to test a new state-of-the- art tank in a combat situation.
MPAA:R
Gloria Katz; Paramount Pictures — *Paramount Home Video*

Best Friends **1982**
Comedy
66121 108 mins C B, V, LV, CED R, P
Goldie Hawn, Burt Reynolds, Jessica Tandy, Barnard Hughes, Audra Lindley, Keenan Wynn, Ron Silver, directed by Norman Jewison
A team of screenwriters decide to marry after years of living and working together.
MPAA:PG
Warner Bros — *Warner Home Video*

Best Little Whorehouse in Texas, The **1982**
Musical/Comedy
63168 111 mins C B, V, LV, CED P
Dolly Parton, Burt Reynolds, Dom De Luise, Charles Durning, Jim Nabors, Lois Nettleton, directed by Colin Higgins
Dolly Parton is the buxom owner of The Chicken Ranch, a house of ill-repute that may be closed down unless Sheriff Burt Reynolds can think of a way out. Based on the long-running Broadway musical.
MPAA:R
Universal — *MCA Home Video*

Best of Amos 'n Andy Vol. 1, The **195?**
Comedy
44851 100 mins B/W B, V, 3/4U P
Alvin Childress, Spencer Williams
Four classic television shows are contained in this volume. They include "Young Girls," "The Rare Coin," "The Turkey Dinner," and "The Secretary."
CBS — *Nostalgia Merchant*

Best of Benny Hill, The **1981**
Comedy
58457 104 mins C B, V R, P
Benny Hill
Humorous sketches featuring the off-beat comedy of this British funnyman.
Thames Video — *THORN EMI/HBO Video*

Best of the Benny Hill Show, Vol. 5, The **1985**
Comedy
80814 97 mins C B, V R, P
Here is another volume of madcap comedy from British funnyman Benny Hill. Available in VHS and Beta Hi Fi.
Thames Video — *THORN EMI/HBO Video*

Best of Betty Boop, Volume I, The **193?**
Cartoons
64836 90 mins C B, V P
Animated, voice of Mae Questal
Sweet Betty Boop sashays through eleven of her classic cartoon adventures in this collection of original shorts. Mastered from the original negatives.
Max Fleischer; Paramount — *Republic Pictures Home Video*

Best of Betty Boop Volume II **19??**
Cartoons
66471 85 mins C B, V P
Animated
Another collection of original cartoons starring the "Boop-Oop-a-Doop" girl, assisted by Bimbo and Koko the Clown. These black-and-white cartoons have been recolored for this release.
Max Fleischer — *Republic Pictures Home Video*

Best of Blondie, The **1981**
Music-Performance
58880 60 mins C B, V P
Deborah Harry, Jimmy Destri, Chris Stein, Nigel Harrison, Frank Infante, Clem Burke
Original footage from the group's early days combines with promotional videos to present fifteen Blondie hits linked with film shot in New York locations. Songs include: "Rapture," "The Tide is High," "Heart of Glass," "Call Me" and others.
Chrysalis Records — *Chrysalis Visual Programming; Pacific Arts Video*

Best of Broadway, "The Philadelphia Story," The **1958**
Drama
12847 55 mins B/W B, V, FO P
Dorothy McGuire, John Payne, Richard Carlson, Herbert Marshall, Mary Astor, Charles Winninger, Dick Moran
A superb dramatization of the Philip Barry play.
CBS — *Video Yesteryear*

Best of Everything Goes, The **1983**
Comedy/Game show
70731 56 mins C B, V P
Jaye P. Morgan, The Unknown Comic, Pat McCormick, Dick Shawn, Miss Miller, Kip Addotta
Incorrect answers to the queries of adult humorists results in the contestants removing their clothing.
Playboy Cable Network — *Active Home Video*

Best of Heckle and Jeckle and Friends, The **19??**
Cartoons
69609 60 mins C B, V P
Animated
This cartoon collection features such memorable characters as Heckle and Jeckle, Deputy Dawg, Sad Cat, Possible Possum and Sidney, the baby elephant.

Terrytoons — *Children's Video Library*

Best of Heckle and Jeckle—Volumes IV & V, The 194?
Cartoons
29130 90 mins C B, V P
Animated
Terrytoons' characters Heckle and Jeckle are featured in two programs, both available individually.
EL, SP
Viacom International — *CBS/Fox Video*

Best of Little Lulu 19??
Cartoons
65688 60 mins C B, V P
Animated
Mischief-prone Little Lulu returns in this special collection of cartoon adventures.
Paramount — *Republic Pictures Home Video*

Best of Little Rascals, The 193?
Comedy
79878 103 mins B/W B, V P
A collection of six classic "Our Gang" two reelers featuring everyone's favorite rascals Spanky, Alfalfa, Stymie and Buckwheat.
Hal Roach — *Republic Pictures Home Video*

Best of Marvel Comics, The 1982
Fantasy/Cartoons
62878 112 mins C B, V P
Animated
Five episodes featuring Marvel Comics favorites: Spiderman, Mr. Fantastic, Invisible Girl, Spiderwoman and The Thing. Titles are "The Great Magini," "The Mole Men," "The Menace Magneto," "Calamity on Campus" and "Diamond Dust."
Marvel Comics — *MCA Home Video*

Best of Mary Hartman, Mary Hartman, Volume II, The 1976
Comedy
76908 70 mins C B, V, LV P
Louise Lasser, Greg Mullavey, Mary Kay Place, Dody Goodman, Debralee Scott
The town of Fernwood, Ohio is jumping with excitement as everyone's trying to guess the identity of the Fernwood Flasher.
Jerry Adler; Lou Gallo — *Embassy Home Entertainment*

Best of Popeye, The 1983
Cartoons
65109 56 mins C B, V, CED P
Animated
Eight classic Popeye cartoons are included in this compilation.
MGM/UA Home Entertainment Group; Max Fleischer — *MGM/UA Home Video*

Best of Sex and Violence, The 1981
Movie and TV trailers
47756 78 mins C B, V P
Narrated by John Carradine, directed by Ken Dixon
A collection of trailers, or coming attractions, from films which feature blood, sexploitation, soft porn, bizarre comedy, bike flicks, blacksploitation, Kung fu, etc.
S and V Prods; Charles Band — *Wizard Video*

Best of 60 Minutes, The 1984
History-Modern/Television
Closed Captioned
65754 60 mins C B, V, CED P
Mike Wallace, Morley Safer, Harry Reasoner, Ed Bradley, Andy Rooney
Included in this program are 4 of the most gripping segments ever shown on this long running news series.
Don Hewitt; CBS News — *CBS/Fox Video*

Best of 60 Minutes Volume 2, The 1985
History-Modern/Television
Closed Captioned
77466 60 mins C B, V P
Mike Wallace, Morley Safer, Harry Reasoner, Ed Bradley, Andy Rooney, Dan Rather
A collection of five hard hitting stories from those intrepid investigative reporters of television's longest running news magazine.
Don Hewitt; CBS News — *CBS/Fox Video*

Best of Terrytoons, The 1983
Cartoons
69530 60 mins C B, V, CED P
Animated
This is a compilation of cartoons featuring Mighty Mouse, Heckle and Jeckle, Deputy Dawg, Gandy Goose, Dinky Duck, Terry Bears and Little Roquefort.
Terrytoons — *Children's Video Library*

Best of the Benny Hill Show, Vol. II, The 1981
Comedy
63346 115 mins C B, V R, P
Benny Hill
Another compilation of humorous sketches from "The Benny Hill Show."
Thames Video — *THORN EMI/HBO Video*

Best of the Benny Hill Show, Vol. III, The **1983**
Comedy
65092 110 mins C B, V R, P
Benny Hill
British funnyman Benny Hill mugs and jokes his way through a new collection of comedy sketches from his popular television series.
Thames Video — *THORN EMI/HBO Video*

Best of the Benny Hill Show, Volume 4, The **1984**
Comedy
78391 95 mins C B, V R, P
Here's another collection of zany sketches from British funnyman Benny Hill.
Thames Television — *THORN EMI/HBO Video*

Best of the Big Bands, The **1980**
Music
38962 80 mins B/W B, V, FO P
Artie Shaw, Benny Goodman, Gene Krupa, Ray Eberle, Jimmy Dorsey, Harry James, Frank Sinatra, Tommy Dorsey, Count Basie
A compilation of big band film excerpts. Highlights include Harry James and Frank Sinatra performing "Saturday Night (1944), the Benny Goodman Trio with Gene Krupa and Teddy Wilson, and Jimmy Dorsey's Orchestra with Bob Eberly and Helen O'Connell.
United Artists et al — *Video Yesteryear*

Best of the Big Laff-Off, The **1983**
Comedy-Performance
65546 60 mins C B, V P
Featuring top comics delivering their most hilarious routines, emphasis is from waistlines to punchlines. It's the best, funniest and fastest-moving segments of "The Big Laff-Off". Premiers Eddie Murphy and Robin Williams.
Chuck Braverman — *Karl/Lorimar Home Video*

Best of the Kenny Everett Video Show, The **1981**
Comedy
59705 104 mins C B, V R, P
Kenny Everett
Great scenes from the popular British late-night TV show combining new wave rock music, outrageous dancing and innovative video special effects.
David Mallett — *THORN EMI/HBO Video*

Best of the New York Erotic Film Festival Parts I & II **197?**
Film
64841 210 mins C B, V P
Two cassette collections of prize-winning and specially selected films presented at the annual New York Erotic Film Festival.
Various — *HarmonyVision*

Best of the WWF, Vol. I, The **1985**
Sports
81391 90 mins C B, V P
Hulk Hogan, Gorilla Monsoon, Big John Studd, Jimmy Superfly, Snuka, Wendy Richter
This anthology features many great wrestling matches including Wendy Richter's bout against the Fabulous Moolah and Bruno Sanmartino versus Larry Zybysko.
Evart Enterprises — *Coliseum Video*

Best of Upstairs Downstairs, The **1971**
Drama
79711 50 mins C B, V R, P
Jean Marsh, Lesley Anne Down, David Longton, Simon Williams, Angela Baddeley
The foibles of London's Bellamy Family and their servants at the turn of the century are chronicled in these fourteen untitled programs.
London Weekend Television — *THORN EMI/HBO Video*

Best of W.C. Fields, The **193?**
Comedy
80464 58 mins B/W B, V P
W.C. Fields, Elsie Cavenna
Three of W.C. Field's Mack Sennett shorts are presented in their complete, uncut form.
Mack Sennett — *Spotlite Video*

Best Years of Our Lives, The **1946**
Drama
80946 170 mins B/W B, V, LV P
Frederic March, Harold Russell, Myrna Loy, Dana Andrews, Virginia Mayo, Hoagy Carmichael, directed by William Wyler
Three World War II veterans return to the homefront attempting to pick up the threads of their lives.
Academy Awards '46: Best Picture?Best Director (Wyler)?Best Actor (March)?Best Supporting Actor (Russell).
Samuel Goldwyn — *Embassy Home Entertainment*

Bete Humaine, La **1938**
Film-Avant-garde
06223 90 mins B/W B, V P
Jean Gabin, Simone Simon, directed by Jean Renoir
Son of drunkard finds his own abstinence from drink is no escape from self-hate and sadness. French; English subtitles.
FR

France — *Budget Video; Sheik Video; Cable Films; Video Yesteryear; Discount Video Tapes*

Bethune **1977**
Biographical/Drama
78955 88 mins C B, V P
Donald Sutherland, Kate Nelligan, directed by Eric Till
The life story of a Canadian doctor who started a practice in Communist China.
Robert Allen — *Trans World Entertainment*

Betrayal **1983**
Drama
65490 95 mins C B, V, CED P
Ben Kingsley, Patricia Hodge, Jeremy Irons
An unusual drama, beginning at the end of a seven-year adulterous affair and finally ending at the start of the betrayal of a husband by his wife and his best friend.
MPAA:R
20th Century Fox International Classics — *CBS/Fox Video*

Betsy, The **1978**
Drama
65753 125 mins C B, V, CED P
Laurence Olivier, Kathleen Beller, Robert Duvall, Lesley-Anne Down, Tommy Lee Jones, Katherine Ross, Jane Alexander
A story of romance, money, power and mystery centering around the wealthy Hardeman family and their automobile manufacturing business.
MPAA:R
Harold Robbins International Productions — *CBS/Fox Video*

Betsy Lee's Ghost Town Jamboree, Volume 1 **1981**
Music-Performance/Comedy
70712 60 mins C B, V P
Ruth Buzzi, Stubby Kaye, music by Gene Casey, Jan Casey, Suzanne Buhrer
Betsy inherits and moves into an authentic ghost town with her country band, then discovers that there are friendly spirits. This tape incorporates two programs.
Century Video Corp. — *Kid Time Video*

Bette Midler: Art or Bust **1984**
Music-Performance/Comedy
77410 82 mins C B, V P
Bette Midler
The outrageous Bette Midler performs in the concert taped at the University of Minnesota in Minneapolis.
HBO — *Vestron Video*

Bette Midler Show, The **1976**
Music-Performance
65419 84 mins C B, V, LV, CED P
Bette Midler, accompanied by the Harlettes, jokes, dances and belts out a medley of songs ranging from the Andrew Sisters' "Boogie Woogie Bugle Boy" to "Friends."
Home Box Office — *Embassy Home Entertainment*

Better Late Than Never **1983**
Comedy
70248 95 mins C B, V P
Art Carney, David Niven
A precocious 10-year-old heiress must choose between a struggling photographer and an aging cabaret singer, one who will be her grandfather. The film is set on the French Riviera. Niven's last film.
MPAA:PG
Galaxy — *Key Video*

Better Team, A **1980**
Football
50080 24 mins C B, V, FO R, P
Seattle Seahawks
Highlights of the 1979 Seattle Seahawks' football season.
NFL Films — *NFL Films Video*

Betty Boop Classics **19??**
Cartoons
65689 60 mins C B, V P
Animated
A compilation of Betty Boop and her cartoon pals most fun-filled escapades.
Paramount — *Republic Pictures Home Video*

Betty Boop Special Collectors Edition **193?**
Cartoons
65740 60 mins B/W B, V P
Animated, directed by Max Fleischer
Betty Boop returns in this collection of vintage cartoons, presented in their original black-and-white form, with appearances by jazz stars Louis Armstrong, Cab Calloway and Don Redman.
Paramount; Max Fleischer — *Republic Pictures Home Video*

Between Friends **1983**
Drama
72225 105 mins C B, V P
Elizabeth Taylor, Carol Burnett
Two women help each other through the traumatic period following their respective divorces.
Robert Cooper Films — *Vestron Video*

Between the Lines **1977**
Comedy
59871 101 mins C B, V, CED P
John Heard, Lindsay Crouse, Jeff Goldblum, Jill Eikenberry, Stephen Collins, Lewis J. Stadlen,

Michael J. Pollard, Marilu Henner, directed by Joan Micklin Silver
A comic exploration of the rapidly changing world of a group of friends working together on a small alternative newspaper.
MPAA:R
Raphael D Silver; Midwest Film Productions — *Vestron Video*

Between Wars 1974
Drama
77015 97 mins C B, V P
Corin Redgrave
A young doctor in Australia's Medical Corps encounters conflict when he tries to introduce Freud's principles into his work.
Satori Entertainment — *VidAmerica*

Beulah Show, The 1952
Comedy
39001 51 mins B/W B, V, FO P
Louise Beavers, Ruby Dandridge, Ernest Whitman, Arthur Q. Bryan 2 pgms
Lovable housemaid Beulah outwits her employers as usual in these episodes from the early 1950's TV series: "Marriage on the Rocks" and "Imagination."
ABC — *Video Yesteryear*

Beyond and Back 1978
Documentary/Speculation
48265 93 mins C B, V P
Narrated by Brad Crandall
The supposed reincarnation experiences of a dozen people are explored in this documentary.
Sunn Classic — *United Home Video*

Beyond Death's Door 1979
Death/Speculation
60350 106 mins C B, V P
Tom Hallick, Howard Platt, Jo Ann Harris, Melinda Naud
A documentary look at people who have seen death but lived to tell about it.
MPAA:PG
Stan Siegel; Sunn Pictures — *United Home Video*

Beyond Evil 1980
Horror
65111 98 mins C B, V P
John Saxon, Lynda Day George, Michael Dante, Mario Milano
A newlywed couple moves into an old mansion despite rumors that the house is haunted. The wife becomes possessed by the vengeful spirit of a woman murdered 200 years earlier, and a reign of terror begins.
MPAA:R
David Baughn; Herb Freed — *Media Home Entertainment*

Beyond Fear 1975
Drama
15720 92 mins C B, V P
Michael Boquet
Explores moral implications of a man forced to aid a gang in robbery while they hold his wife and son captive.
France — *Prism; Cinema Concepts*

Beyond Reason 1982
Drama
81190 88 mins C B, V P
Telly Savalas, Laura Johnson, Diana Muldaur, Marvin Laird, directed by Telly Savalas
A psychologist uses unorthodox methods, treating the criminally insane with dignity and respect.
Howard W. Koch — *Media Home Entertainment*

Beyond Reasonable Doubt 1984
Drama/Mystery
65396 117 mins C B, V P
David Hemmings, John Hargreaves
A chilling true life murder mystery which shatters the peaceful quiet of a small New Zealand town and eventually divides a country.
Satori Entertainment Corporation — *VidAmerica*

Beyond the Door 1975
Horror
47853 97 mins C B, V P
Juliet Mills, Richard Johnson
A San Francisco woman finds herself pregnant with a demonic child.
MPAA:R
Avido Assonnitis — *Media Home Entertainment*

Beyond the Door II 1979
Horror
69303 90 mins C B, V P
John Steiner, Daria Nicolodi, David Colin Jr., Ivan Rassimov
A family is tormented by supernatural revenge.
MPAA:R
Film Ventures — *Media Home Entertainment*

Beyond the Limit 1983
Drama
65398 103 mins C B, V R, P
Michael Caine, Richard Gere
The story of an intense and darkly ominous love triangle which takes place in the South American coastal city of Corrientes. Based on Graham Greene's novel "The Honorary Consul."
MPAA:R
Norma Heyman — *Paramount Home Video*

Beyond the Valley of the Dolls 1970
Drama
56458 109 mins C B, V P
Edy Williams, Dolly Reed, directed by Russ Meyer
Russ Meyer's story of an all-girl rock combo and their search for Hollywood stardom.
MPAA:X
Twentieth Century Fox — *CBS/Fox Video*

Bible, The 1966
Drama
34287 155 mins C B, V P
Richard Harris, Stephen Boyd, George C. Scott, directed by John Huston
The book of Genesis is dramatized, including the stories of Adam and Eve, Cain and Abel, and Noah and the Flood.
EL, SP
Twentieth Century Fox, Dino DeLaurentiis — *CBS/Fox Video*

Big Bad Mama 1974
Drama
54805 83 mins C B, V R, P
Angie Dickinson, William Shatner, Tom Skerritt, Susan Sennett, Robie Lee, Noble Willingham, directed by Steve Carver
A tough, intelligent, pistol-packing mother moves her two teenage daughters out of poverty-stricken Texas in 1932. They become bank robbers.
MPAA:R
New World Pictures; Roger Corman — *Warner Home Video; RCA VideoDiscs*

Big Bands at Disneyland 1984
Music-Performance
77536 60 mins C B, V R, P
Peter Marshall, Lionel Hampton, Woody Herman, Cab Calloway 3 pgms
The swinging big band sounds of Lionel Hampton, Woody Herman, and Cab Calloway are captured in these three concerts taped at Disneyland. Available in VHS Stereo and Beta Hi-Fi.
Walt Disney Productions — *Walt Disney Home Video*

Big Bird Cage 1972
Drama
54801 88 mins C B, V R, P
Pam Grier, Sid Haig, Anitra Ford, Candice Roman, Teda Bracci, Carol Speed, Karen McKevic, directed by Jack Hill.
Several females living out prison terms in a rural jail decide to defy their homosexual guards and plan an escape. They are aided by revolutionaries led by a Brooklynese expatriate and his lover. Two of the girls survive the escape massacre.
MPAA:R
New World Pictures — *Warner Home Video*

Big Blue Marble 1981
Adventure
59304 105 mins C CED P
Two segments from the award-winning children's series of the same name: "My Seventeenth Summer" (1978), an adventure story that crackles with intrigue and suspense while imparting a lesson in understanding people of different origins; and "Flying for Fun," which examines everything from a frisbee championship to the flight of a sailplane (1981).
EL, JA
Blue Marble Co — *RCA VideoDiscs*

Big Boss II 197?
Martial arts
70745 90 mins C B, V P
Dragon Lee, Jacky Chang
The Big Boss returns in this thrilling, spilling kung-fu caper.
Mogul Communications, Inc. — *All American Video*

Big Brawl, The 1980
Martial arts
78622 95 mins C B, V P
Jackie Chan, Jose Ferrer, Mako, Rosalind Chao
A Chicago gangster recruits a martial arts expert to fight in a free-for-all match in Texas.
MPAA:R
Warner Bros; Golden Harvest — *Warner Home Video*

Big Breakdowns—Hollywood Bloopers of the 1930's, The 193?
Outtakes and bloopers
47468 27 mins B/W B, V, FO P
Joan Blondell, Humphrey Bogart, James Cagney, Bette Davis, Errol Flynn, John Garfield, Leslie Howard, Boris Karloff, Dick Powell, Edward G. Robinson
Leftover shots, gag scenes, flubs and goofs from Warner Brothers films of the late 30's, featuring nearly every contract player on the lot.
Warner Bros — *Video Yesteryear*

Big Bus, The 1976
Comedy/Adventure
60217 88 mins C B, V R, P
Joseph Bologna, Stockard Channing, Ned Beatty, Ruth Gordon, Larry Hagman
The wild adventures of the world's first nuclear-powered bus as it makes its maiden voyage from New York to Denver.
MPAA:PG
Fred Freeman; Lawrence J. Cohen — *Paramount Home Video*

Big Chill, The 1983
Comedy-Drama
72930 108 mins C B, V, CED P
Tom Berenger, Glenn Close, Jeff Goldblum, William Hurt, Kevin Kline, Mary Kay Place, Meg Tilly, Jobeth Williams, directed by Lawrence Kasdan
A group of college graduates from the 1960's reunite at the funeral of a friend.
MPAA:R
Michael Shambers — *RCA/Columbia Pictures Home Video*

Big Country Live 1984
Music-Performance
72889 75 mins C B, V P
Big Country
This is a concert taped in Scotland on New Year's Eve 1984. Big Country performs "Wonderland" "Fields of Fire" and "In a Big Country."
Aubrey Powell — *Music Media*

Big Fights, Vol. 1—Muhammad Ali's Greatest Fights, The 1980
Boxing
56878 90 mins C CED P
Thrilling moments from the career of Muhammad Ali, including bouts with Sonny Liston, Archie Moore, Floyd Patterson, Ken Norton, Joe Frazier, and Leon Spinks.
ABC — *RCA VideoDiscs*

Big Fights, Vol. 2—Heavyweight Champions' Greatest Fights, The 1981
Boxing
59017 89 mins C CED P
Muhammad Ali, Jack Johnson, Jack Dempsey, Gene Tunney, Joe Louis, Rocky Marciano, Floyd Patterson
All of the heavyweight greats are seen in this collection of boxing's greatest heavyweight matches. Contains rare early footage. Some black and white footage.
ABC — *RCA VideoDiscs*

Big Fights, Vol. 3—Sugar Ray Robinson's Greatest Fights, The 1982
Boxing
60377 90 mins C CED P
The career of boxer Sugar Ray Robinson is examined in this program, which highlights his greatest title matches.
ABC — *RCA VideoDiscs*

Big Game America 1968
Football
50086 51 mins C B, V, FO R, P
Pro football's fascinating first fifty years. Don Meredith wired for sound in his last game as a Cowboy is also included.
NFL Films — *NFL Films Video*

Big Heat, The 1963
Drama
13227 90 mins B/W B, V P
Glenn Ford, Lee Marvin, Gloria Grahame, Jocelyn Brando, Alexander Scourby, directed by Fritz Lang
A detective's wife is killed in an explosion meant for him, as he pursues his quest to trap a nest of criminals.
Columbia; Robert Arthur — *RCA/Columbia Pictures Home Video*

Big Jake 1971
Drama
65496 90 mins C CED P
John Wayne, Richard Boone, Maureen O'Hara, Patrick Wayne, Chris Mitchum, Bobby Vinton
An elderly Texas cattleman swings into action when his grandson is kidnapped.
Batjac; Cinema Center — *CBS/Fox Video*

Big Mo 1973
Biographical/Drama
76770 110 mins C B, V P
Bernie Casey, Bo Svenson, Stephanie Edwards, Janet MacLahlan
This is the true story of the friendship that developed between Cincinnati Royals basketball stars Maurice Stokes and Jack Twyman after a strange paralysis hits Stokes.
MPAA:G
National General — *Vestron Video*

Big Red 1962
Drama
65637 89 mins C B, V R, P
Walter Pidgeon, Gilles Payant
Set amid the spectacular beauty of Canada's Quebec Province, an orphan boy protects a dog which later saves him from a mountain lion.
Buena Vista — *Walt Disney Home Video*

Big Red One, The 1980
War-Drama
52742 113 mins C B, V, CED P
Lee Marvin, Robert Carradine, directed by Sam Fuller
Fuller's semi-autobiographical account of the U.S. Army's famous First Infantry Division in World War II, the "Big Red One." A rifle squad composed of four very young men cut a fiery path of conquest from the landing in North Africa to the liberation of the concentration camp at Falkenau, Czechoslovakia.
MPAA:PG
Lorimar Prods — *CBS/Fox Video*

 (For explanation of codes, see USE GUIDE and KEY)

Big Score, The 1983
Drama
79309 88 mins C B, V P
Fred Williamson, John Saxon, Richard Roundtree, Nancy Wilson, EdLauter, Ron Dean
When a policeman is dismissed from the Chicago Police Department he goes after the men who stole money from a drug bust.
MPAA:R
Almi Pictures — *Vestron Video*

Big Sky, The 1952
Western
81028 122 mins B/W B, V P
Kirk Douglas, Dewey Martin, Arthur Hunnicutt, directed by Howard Hawks
It's 1830, and a rowdy band of furtrappers embark upon a back breaking expedition up the uncharted Missouri River.
RKO — *RKO HomeVideo*

Big Sleep, The 1946
Suspense
59303 114 mins B/W B, V P
Humphrey Bogart, Lauren Bacall, Martha Vickers, Elisha Cook Jr, Dorothy Malone, directed by Howard Hawks
Bogie protrays private eye Philip Marlowe, hired to protect a young woman from her own indiscretions, and falls in love with her older sister.
Warner Bros — *CBS/Fox Video; RCA VideoDiscs*

Big Steal, The 1949
Adventure
33901 72 mins B/W B, V P
Robert Mitchum, William Bendix, Jane Greer, Ramon Novarro
An Army officer recovers a missing payroll and captures the thieves after a tumultuous chase through Mexico.
RKO — *Nostalgia Merchant*

Big Surprise, The 1956
Game show
42979 30 mins B/W B, V, FO P
Mike Wallace, Errol Flynn
This $100,000 prize quiz extravaganza was NBC's answer to the "$64,000 Question." Mike Wallace hosts as Errol Flynn wins $30,000 answering questions on ships and the sea.
NBC — *Video Yesteryear*

Big Time, The 1960
Comedy
12839 51 mins B/W B, V, FO P
George Burns, Jack Benny, Eddie Cantor, George Jessell, Bobby Darin, The Kingston Trio, Jeff Alexander
A live TV variety show featuring well-done comedy, singing, and dancing.
Unknown — *Video Yesteryear*

Big Trees, The 1952
Drama
66509 89 mins C B, V P
Kirk Douglas, Patrice Wymore, Eve Miller, Alan Hale Jr., Edgar Buchanan
A ruthless lumberman attempts a takeover of the California Redwood Timberlands that are owned by a group of peaceful homesteaders.
Warner Bros — *Hal Roach Studios; Discount Video Tapes; Video Gems*

Big Wednesday 1978
Drama
81085 120 mins C B, V R, P
Jan Michael-Vincent, Gary Busey, William Katt, Lee Purcell, Patti D'Arbanville, directed by John Millius
Three California surfers from the early sixties get back together after the Vietnam war to reminisce about the good old days. Available in VHS and Beta Hi-Fi Stereo.
MPAA:PG
Warner Bros. — *Warner Home Video*

Big Foot and Wild Boy 1978
Adventure
76909 48 mins C B, V P
Ray Young, Joseph Butcher
A collection of two episodes from the series: In "The Secret Invasion" the Lorcan monsters vow to get revenge on Big Foot and in "Space Prisoner" Bigfoot and wildboy must save a friend from an evil space criminal.
Sid and Marty Krofft — *Embassy Home Entertainment*

Bikini Beach 1964
Musical
65068 100 mins C B, V P
Annette Funicello, Frankie Avalon, Martha Hyer, Harvey Lembeck, Don Rickles, Stevie Wonder
The surfing teenagers at Bikini Beach and a visitor, British recording star The Potato Bug, join forces to keep their beach from being turned into a retirement community. Songs include "Bikini Drag," "Love's a Secret Weapon" and "Because You're You."
Alta Vista Productions; American International — *Embassy Home Entertainment*

Bilitis 1977
Drama
50729 95 mins C B, V P
Patti D'Arbanville, Bernard Giraudeau, Mona Kristensen, directed by David Hamilton
A young girl from a private girls' school is initiated into the pleasures of sex and the unexpected demands of love.
MPAA:R

Topar; Sylvio Tabet; Jacques Nahum — *Media Home Entertainment*

Bill **1981**
Drama
73532 97 mins C B, V R, P
Mickey Rooney, Dennis Quaid
The true story of Bill Sackler, a mentally retarded adult who was released from a mental institution after 44 years. Available in Beta Hi-Fi and VHS stereo.
Emmy Awards '82: Best Actor (Mickey Rooney); Best Story.
Alan Landsburg — *U.S.A. Home Video*

Bill Cosby's Picturepages—Volume 3 **1985**
Children/Language arts
70773 55 mins C B, V R, P
Bill Cosby
Cosby teaches "basic concepts" to kiddies. In this volume, he uses colorful pictures and patter to help children learn mathematics preparedness in his own unique way.
AM Available
Walt Disney Productions — *Walt Disney Home Video*

Bill Cosby's Picturepages—Volume 2 **1985**
Language arts
76821 55 mins C B, V R, P
Bill Cosby combines humor with solid instructional material to teach basic concepts to pre-schoolers.
Walt Disney Productions — *Walt Disney Home Video*

Bill Cosby's Picturepages—Volume I **1985**
Language arts
76817 55 mins C B, V R, P
Bill Cosby teaches lessons that describe and demonstrate shapes, senses, and sizes for toddlers.
Walt Disney Productions — *Walt Disney Home Video*

Bill Watrous **1983**
Music-Performance
76672 24 mins C B, V P
This program presents the jazz trombonist Bill Watrous performing with his Refuge West Band.
Dig it Recordings — *Sony Corporation of America*

Bill Wyman **1983**
Music-Performance
64930 11 mins C B, V P
Bill Wyman of the Rolling Stones performs three songs solo on this Video 45: "Si Si (Je Suis Un Rock Star)," "A New Fashion" and "Come Back Suzanne."
Ripple Records — *Sony Corporation of America*

Billion Dollar Hobo, The **1978**
Comedy
58707 96 mins C B, V, CED P
Tim Conway, Will Geer, Eric Weston, Sydney Lassick
Tim Conway stars as a poor, unsuspecting heir of a multimillion dollar fortune, who must duplicate his benefactor's experience as a hobo during the Depression in order to collect his inheritance.
MPAA:G
Samuel Goldwyn Home Entertainment — *CBS/Fox Video*

Billy Connolly—Bites Yer Bum **1981**
Comedy-Performance
66039 105 mins C B, V P
A live recording of the Scottish Funnyman, capturing his earthy humor in stories and songs.
Chrysalis Group Ltd — *Chrysalis Visual Programming*

Billy Crystal: A Comic's Line **1983**
Comedy-Performance
80519 59 mins C B, V, LV P
Billy Crystal
Comedian Billy Crystal performs a one-man show, highlighting spoofs, of rock videos and other stand-up comics. In stereo.
Crystal/R.J.M.B. Productions — *Paramount Home Video*

Billy Jack **1971**
Drama
52705 112 mins C B, V R, P
Tom Laughlin, Delores Taylor, Clark Howat
A half-breed ex-Green Beret stands between a redneck town and a Freedom School for runaways located on an Arizona Indian Reservation.
MPAA:PG
Warner Bros; National Student Film Corp — *Warner Home Video; RCA VideoDiscs*

Billy Joel: Live from Long Island **1983**
Music-Performance
65413 80 mins C B, V, LV, CED P
A recording of Billy Joel's dynamic New Year's Eve performance at Nassau Coliseum. Classic tunes showcased include "Piano Man," "Allentown," "You May Be Right," and "Still Rock and Roll to Me." In VHS stereo and Beta Hi-Fi.

CBS Fox — *CBS/Fox Video*

Billy Liar 1963
Comedy-Drama
66188 94 mins B/W B, V R, P
Tom Courtenay, Julie Christie
A young Englishman dreams of escaping from his working class family and dead-end job.
Continental — *THORN EMI/HBO Video*

Billy: Portrait of a Street Kid 1977
Drama
77153 96 mins C B, V P
Le Var Burton, Tina Andrews, Ossie Davis, Michael Constantine
A ghetto youngster tries to better himself through education but complications arise when his girlfriend becomes pregnant.
Mark Carliner Productions — *Worldvision Home Video*

Billy Squier 1982
Music-Performance
63350 60 mins C B, V R, P
Billy Squier
Billy Squier performs some of his best songs live in concert, including "In the Dark," "Rich Kids" and "My Kinda Lover."
EMI Music — *THORN EMI/HBO Video; Pioneer Artists*

Billy the Kid Versus Dracula 1966
Horror/Western
69568 73 mins C B, V, FO P
John Carradine, Chuck Courtney
Dracula travels to the Old West, anxious to "put the bite" on a pretty lady ranchowner. Her fiance, the legendary outlaw Billy the Kid, steps in to save his girl from becoming a vampire herself.
Avco Embassy — *Video Yesteryear*

Bimini Code 1984
Adventure
80896 95 mins C B, V P
Vickie Benson, Krista Richardson
Two female adventurers accept a dangerous mission where they wind up on Bimini Island in a showdown with the mysterious Madame X.
American National Enterprises — *Prism*

Bing Crosby Show, The 1963
Variety
38990 57 mins B/W B, V, FO P
Bing Crosby, Bob Hope, Edie Adams, the Pete Fountain Quintet, the Smothers Brothers
A Bing Crosby special, with music from Bing and Pete Fountain's group, and comedy sketches by Bing and Bob and the Smothers Brothers. Commercials included.
NBC — *Video Yesteryear*

Bingo Long Traveling All-Stars & Motor Kings, The 1976
Comedy
64796 111 mins C B, V P
Billy Dee Williams, James Earl Jones, Richard Pryor, directed by John Badham
Set during the Depression of 1939, this film follows the comedic adventures of a lively group of black ball players who have defected from the old Negro National League. The All-Stars travel the country challenging local white teams.
MPAA:PG
Universal — *MCA Home Video*

Bird of Paradise 1932
Romance
51611 80 mins B/W B, V P
Joel McCrea, Dolores Del Rio, Lon Chaney Jr.
An exotic South Seas romance in which an adventurer falls in love with a native girl.
RKO — *Budget Video; Cable Films; Video Connection; Discount Video Tapes; Movie Buff Video; Classic Video Cinema Collector's Club; Kartes Productions*

Bird with the Crystal Plumage, The 1970
Mystery
51575 98 mins C B, V P
Tony Musante, Susy Kendall, Eva Renzi
An alleged murderer is cleared when the woman believed to be his next victim is revealed to be a psychopathic murderer.
MPAA:PG
UMC; Salvatore Argento — *United Home Video*

Birdman & Galaxy Trio 197?
Cartoons
66280 60 mins C B, V P
Animated
Birdman, a former secret agent, is bestowed with powerful wings.
Hanna Barbera — *Worldvision Home Video*

Birdman of Alcatraz, The 1961
Drama
59342 148 mins B/W CED P
Burt Lancaster, Karl Malden, Thelma Ritter, Edmond O'Brien, Neville Brand, Telly Savalas, directed by John Frankenheimer
An imprisoned murderer makes a name for himself as an ornithologist.
United Artists — *RCA VideoDiscs*

Birds, The 1963
Horror
45001 120 mins C B, V P
Rod Taylor, Tippi Hedren, Jessica Tandy, directed by Alfred Hitchcock

A small shore town north of San Francisco is attacked by thousands of birds of varying shapes, sizes, and colors.
Universal — *MCA Home Video; RCA VideoDiscs*

Birds of Paradise 1984
Drama
80119 90 mins C B, V P
Three attractive women who inherit a yacht travel to the Florida Keys to find romance.
MPAA:R
Playboy Video — *King of Video*

Birds of Prey 1972
Drama
70603 81 mins C B, V P
David Janssen, Ralph Meeker, Elayne Heilveil
This action film pits a WWII army pilot against a group of kidnapping thieves in an airborne chopper chase.
Tomorrow Entertainment — *Prism*

Birdy 1984
Drama
Closed Captioned
80879 120 mins C B, V P
Matthew Modine, Nicholas Cage, John Harkins, Sandy Baron, Karen Young, directed by Alan Parker
This film chronicles the friendship of two young men from their youth in Philadelphia, to their participation in the Vietnam War. One of the characters enters a psychological bird land upon their return, straining their relationship. Peter Gabriel's soundtrack enjoys Beta and VHS Stereo Hi-Fi reproduction.
MPAA:R
Tri Star Pictures — *RCA/Columbia Pictures Home Video*

Birth of a Legend, The 1984
Theater
76011 25 mins B/W B, V P, T
Mary Pickford, Douglas Fairbanks Sr.
A documentary showing the on and off antics of Miss Pickford and Mr. Fairbanks when they reigned as the King and Queen of the movies in 1926.
Matty Kemp; Mary Pickford Company — *Blackhawk Films*

Birth of a Nation, The 1915
Film-History/War-Drama
47465 175 mins B/W B, V, FO P
Lillian Gish, Henry B. Walthall, Mae Marsh, directed by D. W. Griffith
The Civil War-era classic by D. W. Griffith, presented here from the most complete print of the film known to exist.
Epoch — *Video Yesteryear*

Birth of a Nation 1915
Film-History
57204 158 mins B/W B, V P, T
Lillian Gish, Henry B. Walthall, Mae Marsh, Wallace Reid, directed by D.W. Griffith
A special tinted and musically scored print of D.W. Griffith's milestone classic recalling the Civil War and Reconstruction.
Epoch — *Blackhawk Films; Glenn Video Vistas; Discount Video Tapes; Cinema Concepts; Classic Video Cinema Collector's Club; Kartes Productions*

Bishop's Wife, The 1948
Fantasy
78642 109 mins B/W B, V P
Cary Grant, Loretta Young, David Niven, Monty Wooley, Elsa Lanchester
An angel comes down to earth to help a young bishop, his wife and his parishioners.
RKO; Samuel Goldwyn Productions — *Embassy Home Entertainment*

Bitch, The 1978
Drama
63337 90 mins C B, V R, P
Joan Collins
This continuation of "The Stud" tells of the erotic adventures of a beautiful divorcee playing sex games for high stakes on the international playgrounds of high society.
MPAA:R
Brent Walker Film Productions — *THORN EMI/HBO Video*

Bite the Bullet 1975
Western
76025 131 mins C B, V P
Gene Hackman, James Coburn, Candice Bergen, Jan-Michael Vincent
This exciting action-adventure featuring an all-star cast tells of a grueling 700-mile horse race in the rugged west of the early 1900's.
MPAA:PG
Richard Brooks — *RCA/Columbia Pictures Home Video*

Black and Tan/St. Louis Blues 1929
Musical
60048 36 mins B/W B, V P, T
Duke Ellington and his Cotton Club Orchestra, Fredi Washington, Bessie Smith, the Hall Johnson Choir
Two early jazz two-reelers are combined on this tape: "Black and Tan" is the first film appearance of Duke Ellington's Orchestra, featuring Cootie Williams and Johnny Hodges. "St. Louis Blues" is the only surviving film made by legendary blues singer Bessie Smith. She is backed by the Hall Johnson Choir, members of the Fletcher Henderson band directed by James P. Johnson and dancer Jimmy Mordecai.

RKO; Dudley Murphy — *Blackhawk Films*

Black Arrow 1984
Adventure
77537 93 mins C B, V R, P
Oliver Reed, Benedict Taylor, Georgia Slowe, Stephan Chase
An exiled bowman returns to England to avenge the injustices of a villainous nobleman.
Walt Disney Productions — *Walt Disney Home Video*

Black Beauty 1978
Cartoons
47687 49 mins C B, V P
Animated
The tale of a sweet-tempered horse sold into the slavery of a harsh master.
Hanna Barbera — *Worldvision Home Video*

Black Beauty/Courage of Black Beauty 19??
Adventure
59151 145 mins C B, V, 3/4U P
Mona Freeman, Johnny Crawford
Two feature-length films based on Anna Sewell's novel about the love of a child for a black stallion comprise this cassette. "Black Beauty" was first released in 1946; "Courage of Black Beauty" in 1957.
20th Century Fox — *Nostalgia Merchant*

Black Belt Jones 1974
Martial arts
78623 87 mins C B, V P
Jim Kelly, Gloria Hendry, Scatman Crothers
A martial arts expert fights the mob to save a school of self defense in Los Angeles' Watts district.
MPAA:R
Warner Bros; Golden Harvest — *Warner Home Video*

Black Belt Karate I 1982
Martial arts
59571 60 mins C B, V P
Hosted by Jay T. Will
An introduction to the basic philosophy and moves of this Oriental self-defense system.
Professional Karate Assn — *Mastervision*

Black Belt Karate II 1982
Martial arts
59572 60 mins C B, V P
Hosted by Jay T. Will
Jay T. Will takes the aficionado up the ladder and sets the athletic stage for the student's next upward move to karate expertise.
Professional Karate Assn — *Mastervision*

Black Belt Karate III 1981
Martial arts
59573 60 mins C B, V P
Hosted by Jay T. Will
This program takes the practitioner into the rarefied atmosphere of the highest karate plane.
Professional Karate Assn — *Mastervision*

Black Bird, The 1975
Comedy
62814 98 mins C B, V P
George Segal, Stephane Audran, Lionel Stander, Lee Patrick
In this satiric "sequel" to "The Maltese Falcon," detective Sam Spade, Jr. searches for the mysterious black falcon statuette that caused his father such trouble.
MPAA:PG
Columbia — *RCA/Columbia Pictures Home Video*

Black Box Affair, The 1966
Mystery/Drama
80715 95 mins C B, V P
Craig Hill, Teresa Gimpera, Luis Martin, George Rigaud
An American secret agent must find a black box lost in a B-52 plane crash befoe it falls into the wrong hands.
Silvio Battistini — *All Seasons Entertainment*

Black Cat, The/The Raven 193?
Horror
63842 126 mins B/W B, V P
Boris Karloff, Bela Lugosi, Jacqueline Wells, John Carradine, Irene Ware, Lester Matthews
Both parts of this double feature star Boris Karloff and Bela Lugosi in leading roles. "The Black Cat" (1934, 65 minutes) features an architect who preserves the corpses of young girls and a doctor who plays chess in an attempt to keep a new bride from becoming a sacrifice to Satan. In "The Raven" (1935, 61 minutes), an insane plastic surgeon who is obsessed by the works of Edgar Allan Poe creates an elaborate torture chamber.
Universal — *MCA Home Video*

Black Emanuelle 1976
Drama
60584 121 mins C B, V P
Karin Schubert, Angelo Infanti, Don Powell
Emanuelle travels to Africa on an assignment, but work turns to play as she becomes a willing partner.
Independent — *CBS/Fox Video*

Black Fury 1935
Drama
73975 95 mins B/W B, V P
Paul Muni, Barton MacLane, Henry O'Neill, directed by Michael Curtiz

A coal miner tries to shed light on the poor working conditions that exist in the mines.
Warner Bros — *Key Video*

Black Hand, The **1976**
Drama
77256 90 mins C B, V P
Lionel Stander, Mike Placido
An unemployed Italian immigrant becomes drawn into a web of murder and betrayal after he is attacked by an Irish gang.
Stiletto Productions — *Magnum Entertainment*

Black Hole, The **1979**
Science fiction
44297 97 mins C B, V, LV R, P
Maximilian Schell, Anthony Perkins, Ernest Borgnine, Yvette Mimieux
This is your basic mad scientist movie, with Maximilian Schell as a man determined to acquire the secrets of the universe by plunging into a black hole. In preparation for his journey he has manufactured an army of robots to assist him such as his body guard robot, Maximilian.
MPAA:G
Walt Disney — *Walt Disney Home Video; RCA VideoDiscs*

Black Jack **1950**
Drama
66363 112 mins B/W B, V P
George Sanders, Agnes Moorhead, Herbert Marshall, Patricia Roc, directed by Julien Duvivier
A Riviera socialite pretends to be an undercover agent, but she is actually a dope smuggler. Also known as "Captain Black Jack."
United Artists; Walter Gould — *Movie Buff Video; U.S.A. Home Video*

Black Like Me **1964**
Drama
45049 110 mins B/W B, V P
Roscoe Lee Browne, James Whitmore, Clifton James, Dan Priest
This movie is based on the true story of a white writer who chemically changes the color of his skin and travels through the South experiencing the humiliation and terror of the black man.
Continental, Alan Enterprises — *United Home Video; Continental Video*

Black Magic **1949**
Adventure
45148 105 mins B/W B, V, 3/4U P
Orson Welles, Akim Tamiroff, Nancy Guild
Cogliostro the magician becomes involved in a plot to supply a double for Marie Antoinette.
Edward Small; United Artists — *Nostalgia Merchant*

Black Magic Terror **1979**
Horror/Suspense
70571 85 mins C B, V P
Suzanna, W.D. Mochtar, Alan Nuary, directed by L. Sudjio
That old queen of black magic has got everybody under her spell. Troublestarts when she turns her back on one of her subjects.
World Northal — *Twilight Video*

Black Marble, The **1979**
Crime-Drama
56454 110 mins C B, V, CED P
Paula Prentiss, Harry Dean Stanton, Robert Foxworth
A beautiful policewoman is paired with a policeman who drinks too much, is divorced, and is ready to retire. Surrounded by urban craziness and corruptness, they eventually fall in love. Based on the Joseph Wambaugh novel.
MPAA:PG
Avco Embassy, Frank Capra Jr — *Embassy Home Entertainment*

Black Narcissus **1947**
Drama
50914 101 mins C B, V P
Deborah Kerr, Jean Simmons, Flora Robson, Sabu, David Farrar
A group of Anglican nuns attempting to found a hospital and school in the Himalayas confront native distrust and their own human frailties.
Universal — *VidAmerica*

Black Orpheus **1959**
Drama
52741 98 mins C B, V, CED P
Breno Mello, Marpessa Dawn, Lourdes De Oliveira, directed by Marcel Camus
The legend of Orpheus and Eurydice unfolds against the colorful background of the carnival in Rio de Janeiro. In the black section of the city, Orpheus is a street-car conductor and Eurydice a country girl fleeing from a man sworn to kill her. Dubbed in English.
Cannes Film Festival '59: Grand Prize Winner; Academy Awards '59: Best Foreign Language Film.
France; Brazil; Lopert Pictures — *CBS/Fox Video*

Black Pirate, The **1926**
Adventure
47460 122 mins B/W B, V, FO P
Douglas Fairbanks, Donald Crisp, Billie Dove
A shipwrecked mariner vows revenge on the pirates who destroyed his father's ship. Quintessential Fairbanks, this film features astounding athletic feats and exciting swordplay. Originally filmed in Technicolor, this print is in black and white. Silent film with music score.

Elton Corp; Douglas Fairbanks — *Video Yesteryear; Discount Video Tapes; Classic Video Cinema Collector's Club; See Hear Industries*

Black Planet, The **1983**
Cartoons
65707 78 mins C B, V P
Animated
The distant planet of Terre Verte is rapidly running out of energy. To keep the remaining fuel, warhawks Senator Calhoun and General McNab think their part of the Planet should blow up the other part. Will the whole planet be destroyed?
Paul Williams — *Embassy Home Entertainment*

Black Room, The **1935**
Horror/Mystery
78964 70 mins B/W B, V P
Boris Karloff, Marian Marsh, Robert Allen, Katherine De Mille, directed by Roy William Neill
As an evil count lures victims into his castle of terror, the count's twin brother returns to fulfill an ancient prophecy. In Beta Hi-Fi.
Columbia Pictures — *RCA/Columbia Pictures Home Video*

Black Room, The **1982**
Horror
76774 90 mins C B, V P
Couples are lured to a mysterious mansion where a brother and his sister promise to satisfy their sexual desires.
MPAA:R
Butler/Cronin Productions — *Vestron Video*

Black Sabbath Live **1984**
Music-Performance
76645 60 mins C B, V P
Heavy metal superstar, Ozzy Osbourne, as a member of Black Sabbath, performs such hits as "War Pigs," "Never Say Die" and "Paranoid."
VCL — *VCL Home Video*

Black Six, The **1974**
Drama
79324 91 mins C B, V P
Gene Washington, Carl Eller, Lem Barney, Mercury Morris, Joe Greene, directed by Matt Cimber
Six black Vietnam veterans are out to avenge the white gang who killed one of the black men's brother.
MPAA:R
Cinemation Industries — *Unicorn Video*

Black Stallion Returns, The **1983**
Adventure/Drama
69375 103 mins C B, V, LV, CED P
Kelly Reno, Teri Garr
This sequel to "The Black Stallion" follows the adventures of young Alec as he travels to North Africa to search for his beautiful horse, which was stolen by an Arab chieftain.
MPAA:PG
Zoetrope — *CBS/Fox Video; RCA VideoDiscs*

Black Stallion, The **1979**
Adventure
47058 120 mins C B, V, LV P
Kelly Reno, Mickey Rooney, Teri Garr, Clarence Muse, directed by Carroll Ballard
A young boy and a wild Arabian Stallion are the only survivors of a shipwreck, and they develop a deep affection for each other. Music by Carmine Coppola.
MPAA:PG
United Artists, Francis Coppola — *CBS/Fox Video; RCA VideoDiscs*

Black Sunday **1977**
Drama
64451 143 mins C B, V R, P
Robert Shaw, Bruce Dern, Marthe Keller, Fritz Weaver, Steven Keats
An Arab terrorist group plots to kidnap the Goodyear blimp and load it with explosives with the intent for it to explode over a Miami Super Bowl game to assassinate the U.S. president and to kill all the fans.
MPAA:R
Paramount — *Paramount Home Video; RCA VideoDiscs*

Black Sunday: Highlights of Super Bowl XVII **1984**
Football
72934 46 mins C B, V, FO P
Highlights from SuperBowl XVIII include playoffs for each of the nine teams that qualified; also included in the program is "NFL 83" a summary of the NFL 1983 Season.
NFL Films — *NFL Films Video*

Black Tower, The **1950**
Mystery
78110 54 mins B/W B, V, FO P
Peter Cookson, Warren Williams, Anne Gwynn, Charles Calvert
An interesting murder mystery telling the story of an impoverished medical student who needs money desperately.
PRC — *Video Yesteryear*

Blackbeard's Ghost **1967**
Comedy
59810 107 mins C B, V R, P

Peter Ustinov, Dean Jones, Suzanne Pleshette, Elsa Lanchester, Richard Deacon
The famed 18th-century pirate's spirit returns to play havoc in a modern-day college town.
Walt Disney Productions — *Walt Disney Home Video*

Blackenstein 1974
Horror
03562 87 mins C B, V P
A doctor restores a man's arms and legs, but a jealous assistant causes the man to turn into a monster who starts attacking people.
MPAA:R
Prestige Pictures Releasing Corp — *Media Home Entertainment*

Blacksmith, The/Cops 1922
Comedy
60052 38 mins B/W B, V P, T
Buster Keaton, Virginia Fox
"The Blacksmith" is a burlesque of Longfellow's famous poem "The Village Blacksmith." In "Cops" Buster tries a new business venture to win his girl's hand. Chaos ensues. Silent.
Comique Film Company — *Blackhawk Films*

Blacksmith, The/The Balloonatic 192?
Comedy
56909 57 mins B/W B, V, FO P
Buster Keaton, Virginia Fox, Phyllis Haver
Two Buster Keaton shorts: "The Blacksmith (1922) features Buster as the local blacksmith's apprentice who suddenly finds himself in charge. "The Balloonatic" (1923) presents Buster trapped in a runaway hot air balloon. Both films include music score.
First National — *Video Yesteryear*

Blackstar 1981
Cartoons/Adventure
66006 60 mins C B, V P
Animated
Blackstar fights the forces of evil in three animated adventures.
Filmation — *Family Home Entertainment*

Blackstar Volume III 1981
Cartoons
73368 60 mins C B, V P
Animated
John Blackstar and his friends take on the evil overlord in three adventures: "The Mermaid of Serpent Sea," "Lightning City of the Clouds" and "The Airwhales of Anchar."
Filmation Associates — *Family Home Entertainment*

Blackstar, Volume 2 1981
Cartoons/Adventure
69805 60 mins C B, V P
Animated
John Blackstar and his friends on the planet Sagar continue their never-ending battle against the cruel and ruthless Overlord in three animated adventures.
Filmation — *Family Home Entertainment*

Blackstone on Tour 1984
Magic
78659 60 mins C B, V P
Here are highlights from magician Harry Blackstone's cross country tour.
RKO — *RKO HomeVideo*

Blacula 1972
Horror
81481 92 mins C B, V R, P
William Marshall, Thalmus Rasulala, Denise Nicholas, Vonetta Mcgee
The African Prince Mamuwalde is stalking the streets of Los Angeles trying to satisfy his insationable desire for blood.
MPAA:PG
American International Pictures — *THORN EMI/HBO Video*

Blade 1972
Crime-Drama
59351 79 mins C B, V R, P
Steve Landesburg, John Schuck, Kathryn Walker
An honest cop challenges a dirty cover-up in killer-stalked New York.
MPAA:PG
Heritage Enterprises — *Video Gems*

Blade Master 1984
Adventure
78342 92 mins C B, V P
Miles O'Keefe, Lisa Foster
Ator, The Blade Master leads a small band of men to the castle of knowledge to obtain the ultimate weapon.
MPAA:PG
Chris Trainor — *Media Home Entertainment*

Blade of the Ripper 1984
Horror
80469 90 mins C B, V P
George Hilton, Edwige Fenech
A madman armed with a razor slashes his way through the lovelies of the international jet set.
Regal Video — *Regal Video*

Blade Runner 1982
Science fiction
60437 122 mins C B, V, LV, CED P
Harrison Ford, Rutger Hauer, Sean Young, Darryl Hannah, M. Emmet Walsh, Joanna Cassidy, directed by Ridley Scott

 (For explanation of codes, see USE GUIDE and KEY)

A hard-boiled ex-cop (known as Blade Runner) is forced out of retirement for an extremely dangerous mission. He must track down and kill a group of genetically manufactured beings impersonating humans.
MPAA:R
Ladd Co; Sir Run Run Shaw; Warner Bros — *Embassy Home Entertainment*

Blake of Scotland Yard **1936**
Drama/Serials
10931 70 mins B/W B, V P
Ralph Byrd, Lloyd Hughes, directed by Robert Hill
Feature film version of this exciting serial, with Blake up again a villain who has constructed a murderous death ray.
Victory — *Discount Video Tapes; Video Connection; Video Yesteryear*

Blame It on Rio **1984**
Comedy
72908 90 mins C B, V P
Michael Caine, Joseph Bologna, Demi Moore, Michelle Johnson
A middle-aged man has a fling with his best friend's daughter while on a vacation in Rio de Janeiro.
MPAA:R
Sherwood Productions — *Vestron Video*

Blasphemer, The **1921**
Drama/Religion
78116 89 mins B/W B, V, FO P
A well-crafted, engrossing drama about misfortune that befalls someone who disobeys one of the sacred Commandments. Silent music score.
Religious Film Association — *Video Yesteryear*

Blazing Saddles **1974**
Comedy
38945 90 mins C B, V, LV R, P
Cleavon Little, Harvey Korman, Madeleine Kahn, Gene Wilder, Mel Brooks, directed by Mel Brooks
A wild, wacky spoof by Mel Brooks of every cliche in the western film genre, telling the story of a black sheriff who is sent to clean up a frontier town, with unpredictable results.
MPAA:R
Warner Bros — *Warner Home Video; RCA VideoDiscs*

Bless the Beasts & Children **1971**
Drama
81210 109 mins C B, V P
Bill Mumy, Barry Robins, Miles Chapin, Darel Glaser, Bob Kramer, directed by Stanley Kramer
A group of six teenaged boys at a summer camp attempt to save a herd of buffalo from slaughter at a national preserve.
MPAA:R
Columbia, Stanley Kramer — *RCA/Columbia Pictures Home Video*

Blind Date **1984**
Mystery
77218 100 mins C B, V P
Joseph Bottoms, Kirstie Alley
A blind man agrees to have a visual computer implanted in his brain in order to help the police track down a psychopathic killer.
MPAA:R
Wescom Productions — *Lightning Video*

Blind Fist of Bruce **197?**
Martial arts/Adventure
47696 92 mins C B, V P
Bruce Li
A rich, idle young man learns the techniques of Kung Fu from a former warrior.
Luk Suie Yee — *Master Arts Video*

Blind Husbands **1919**
Drama
11391 98 mins B/W B, V, FO P
Erich von Stroheim, directed by Erich von Stroheim
An Austrian officer is attracted to the pretty wife of a dull surgeon. This film was considered shocking at the time of its release.
Universal — *Video Yesteryear; Sheik Video; Classic Video Cinema Collector's Club*

Blind Rage **1983**
Martial arts
73363 81 mins C B, V P
Fred Williamson
When the United States Government transports fifteen million dollars to Manilla, five blind Kung fu masters want a piece of the action.
MPAA:R
MGM; Cannon Films — *MGM/UA Home Video*

Blob, The **1958**
Science fiction
52611 83 mins C B, V R, P
Steve McQueen, Aneta Corseaut, Olin Howlin, Earl Rowe
McQueen's first starring role in this science fiction thriller about a small town's fight against a slimy invader from space.
Paramount; Jack Harris — *Video Gems*

Blockheads **1938**
Comedy
33909 55 mins B/W B, V, 3/4U P
Stan Laurel, Oliver Hardy, Billie Gilbert, Patricia Ellis, James Finlayson
Stan is a famous WWI soldier who stays on the battleground for eighteen years after the war had ended, since nobody told him it was over.

Old friend Ollie finds him later at an old soldiers' home, and brings him to his house to live.
Hal Roach, MGM — *Nostalgia Merchant; Blackhawk Films*

Blockheads **1938**
Comedy
63984 75 mins B/W B, V P, T
Stan Laurel, Oliver Hardy, Billy Gilbert, Patricia Ellis, Jimmy Finlayson
Twenty years after the end of World War I, soldier Stan is found, still in his foxhole, and brought back to America, where he moves in with old pal Ollie. This tape also includes a 1934 Charley Chase short, "I'll Take Vanilla."
Hal Roach; MGM — *Blackhawk Films*

Blondie—Eat to the Beat **1980**
Music-Performance
54690 60 mins C B, V R, P
Blondie
This program features the multi-million seller platinum album, "Eat to the Beat," taped on location and in a studio. The program contains twelve songs, including the hit singles "Dreaming" and "The Hardest Part."
Warner Bros — *Warner Home Video; RCA VideoDiscs*

Blondie Live **1983**
Music video
75015 55 mins C B, V P
This tape features the group Blondie's last concert. Among the tunes performed are "Heart of Glass," "Call Me" and "Rapture."
MCA Home Video — *MCA Home Video*

Blood and Black Lace **1965**
Horror
79224 90 mins C B, V P
Cameron Mitchell, Eva Bartok, Mary Arden
A police inspector must solve a series of grisly murders at a fashion salon.
Allied Artists — *Media Home Entertainment*

Blood and Sand **1922**
Drama/Romance
58613 80 mins B/W B, V, 3/4U R, P
Rudolph Valentino, Nita Naldi, Lila Lee, Walter Long
Classic film based on Vincente Blasco Ibanez's novel about the tragic rise and fall of a matador, and the women in his life. (Silent).
Paramount — *Cable Films; Sheik Video; Video Connection; Blackhawk Films; Western Film & Video Inc; Classic Video Cinema Collector's Club*

Blood and Sand/Son of the Sheik **1926**
Film-History
50637 56 mins B/W B, V P, T
Rudolph Valentino, Lila Lee, Vilma Banky
A double feature containing two abridged versions of these motion pictures. In "Blood and Sand," an idolized matador meets another woman just before his wedding. In "Son of the Sheik," a man believes he has been betrayed by a dancing girl, and he abucts her to seek revenge. Silent.
Famous Players Lasky Corp; United Artists — *Blackhawk Films*

Blood Beach **1981**
Horror
59047 92 mins C B, V P
David Huffman, Marianna Hill, John Saxon, Burt Young
A group of teenagers is devoured by menacing sand which keeps people from getting to the water.
MPAA:R
Shaw Beckerman Productions — *Media Home Entertainment*

Blood Couple **1973**
Horror
80798 83 mins C B, V R, P
Duanne Jones, Marlene Clark
A newlywed vampire couple pursue their favorite nocturnal pastime-blood sucking.
MPAA:R
Karl Munson — *Video Gems*

Blood Feud **1979**
Drama
65004 112 mins C B, V P
Sophia Loren, Marcello Mastroianni, Giancarlo Giannini, directed by Lina Wertmuller
Set in Italy preceding Europe's entry into WWII, a young widow is in mourning over the brutal murder of her husband by the Sicilian Mafia. A rivalry between two men in her life ensues.
ITC Entertainment — *CBS/Fox Video*

Blood for a Silver Dollar **1966**
Western
78118 98 mins C B, V, FO P
Montgomery Wood, Evelyn Stewart
An action-filled western, telling an ambitious tale of murder, revenge and romance.
Italio-France Co-productions — *Video Yesteryear*

Blood Legacy **1973**
Horror
58549 77 mins C B, V R, P
John Carradine, John Russel, Faith Domergue
Four heirs must survive a night in a lonely country estate. Also titled "Legacy of Blood."
MPAA:R
ASW Films Inc — *Video Gems*

(For explanation of codes, see USE GUIDE and KEY)

Blood Lust **198?**
Horror
80127 90 mins C B, V P
Dr. Jekyll returns to London to wreak havoc upon the human race.
Independent — *King of Video*

Blood Mania **1970**
Horror
79758 90 mins C B, V P
Peter Carpenter, Maria de Arogon
A retired surgeon's daughter decides to murder her father to collect her inheritance prematurely.
MPAA:R
Crown International — *United Home Video*

Blood of a Poet **1930**
Film-Avant-garde
08688 55 mins B/W B, V P
Jean Cocteau, directed by Jean Cocteau
A realistic documentary composed of unreal happenings. Built around the central character of a poet who "lives what he creates'. French with English subtitles.
FR
France — *Budget Video; Video Yesteryear; Sheik Video; Discount Video Tapes; Classic Video Cinema Collector's Club; Texture Films*

Blood of Dracula's Castle **1969**
Horror
60347 84 mins C B, V P
John Carradine, Paula Raymond, Alex D'Arcy
Young lovers move into an inherited castle, only to find it occupied by immovable vampires.
Al Adamson — *United Home Video*

Blood on the Moon **1948**
Western
00288 88 mins B/W B, V, 3/4U P
Robert Mitchum, Robert Preston, Walter Brennan
Well-acted film about a cowboy's involvement in a friend's underhanded schemes who mends his ways to aid a girl.
United Artists — *Nostalgia Merchant*

Blood on the Sun **1945**
Suspense
01794 98 mins B/W B, V P
James Cagney, Sylvia Sydney, Robert Armstrong, directed by Frank Lloyd
Politics, violence, and intrigue are combined in this story of Japan's plans for Pearl Harbor and world conquest.
United Artists — *Budget Video; Sheik Video; Video Yesteryear; Discount Video Tapes; Video Dimensions; Kartes Productions; See Hear Industries*

Blood on the Sun **1975**
Martial arts/Adventure
59070 81 mins C B, V R, P
Martial arts action highlights this tale of adventure.
Dandrea Releasing Corp — *Video Gems*

Blood Simple **1985**
Suspense/Mystery
81198 96 mins C B, V P
John Getz, M. Emmet Walsh, Dan Hedaya, Frances McDormand, directed by Joel Coen
A jealous husband hires a sleazy private eye to murder his adulterous wife and her lover. Plot twists around, though, and everybody gets into trouble. Available in VHS and Beta Hi-Fi.
MPAA:R
River Road Productions — *MCA Home Video*

Blood Voyage **1977**
Horror
81398 80 mins C B, V P
Jonathon Lippe, Laurie Rose, Midori, Mara Modair
A crewman aboard a pleasure yacht must find out who is killing off his passengers one by one. Available in VHS Stereo and Beta Hi-Fi.
MPAA:R
Gene Levy — *Monterey Home Video*

Bloodbeat **198?**
Horror
81047 84 mins C B, V P
Helen Benton, Terry Brown, Claudia Peyton
A supernatural being terrorizes a family as they gather at their country home to celebrate Christmas.
Trans World Entertainment — *Trans World Entertainment*

Bloodbrothers **1978**
Drama
52702 116 mins C B, V R, P
Richard Gere, Paul Sorvino, Tony LoBianco, Marilu Henner, directed by Richard Mulligan
An Italian New York family battle with each other in this story of emotional problems, and a son who wants to break out of his family existence.
MPAA:R
Warner Bros; Stephen Friedman — *Warner Home Video*

Bloodsuckers **1985**
Horror
70249 90 mins C B, V P
Patrick Macnee, Peter Cushing, Patrick Mower
Three friends search for a professor who has been abducted by a blood drinking cult. They rescue him from the lips of the coven's leader.
VCL Communications — *VCL Home Video*

Bloodsucking Freaks **1975**
Horror/Comedy
65380 89 mins C B, V P
This outrageous comedic bloodbath has developed a tremendous cult following, second only to the "Rocky Horror Picture Show."
MPAA:R
Joel Reed — *Vestron Video*

Bloody Brood, The **1959**
Drama
66364 80 mins B/W B, V P
Peter Falk, Barbara Lord, Jack Betts
A young man, searching for his brother's murderer, encounters a group of beatniks who kill for thrills.
Key Films — *Movie Buff Video*

Bloody Fight, The **197?**
Martial arts/Adventure
47704 89 mins C B, V P
Alan Tang, Yu In Yin, Tan Chin
Two young people learn the cost of courage and the high price of justice when they avenge a murderer.
Chiang Chung Pin — *Master Arts Video*

Bloody Fist **197?**
Martial arts/Adventure
47700 90 mins C B, V P
An exciting story set in China with outstanding martial arts scenes.
Independent — *Master Arts Video*

Bloody Mama **1970**
Drama
64896 90 mins C B, V, CED P
Shelley Winters, Robert DeNiro, Don Stroud, Pat Hingle, Bruce Dern, Diane Varsi
The story of the infamous Barker Gang, led by the bloodthirsty and sex-crazed Ma Barker.
MPAA:R
American International Pictures — *Vestron Video*

Bloopers from Star Trek and Laugh-In **1966**
Outtakes and bloopers
43022 26 mins C B, V, FO P
William Shatner, Leonard Nimoy, Bill Cosby, Milton Berle, Jonathan Winters, Orson Welles, Dick Martin, Dan Rowan
Some well-known faces are seen and heard cracking up in this compilation of hilarious goofs, flubbed lines, and kidding around in the NBC studios.
NBC — *Video Yesteryear*

Blow Out **1981**
Suspense
51992 107 mins C B, V R, P
John Travolta, Nancy Allen, John Lithgow, Dennis Franz, directed by Brian De Palma
When a prominent senator is killed in a car crash, a sound effects engineer becomes involved in political intrigue when he tries to expose a conspiracy with the evidence he has gathered.
MPAA:R
Filmways Pictures — *Warner Home Video; RCA VideoDiscs; Vestron Video (disc only)*

Blow-Up **1966**
Drama
54101 110 mins C B, V P
David Hemmings, Vanessa Redgrave, Sarah Miles, directed by Michelangelo Antonioni
A young London photographer takes some pictures of a couple in the park. After blowing the pictures up he discovers what looks like a murder involving the couple.
Carlo Ponti — *MGM/UA Home Video*

Blue Canadian Rockies **1952**
Western
60050 58 mins B/W B, V P, T
Gene Autry, Pat Buttram
Gene's employer sends him to Canada to discourage his daughter from marrying a fortune hunter. The daughter has turned the place into a dude ranch and wild game preserve. When Gene arrives, he encounters some mysterious killings.
BLA — *Blackhawk Films*

Blue Collar **1978**
Drama
47412 114 mins C B, V P
Richard Pryor, Harvey Keitel, Yaphet Kotto, directed by Paul Schrader
An auto assembly line worker, tired of the poverty of his life, hatches a plan to rob his own union.
MPAA:R
Universal — *MCA Home Video*

Blue Country **1978**
Comedy
76026 104 mins C B, V P
Brigitte Fossey, Jacques Serres
A joyful romantic comedy about a pair of free souls who leave their stagnant lives behind to seek out a more idyllic existence. This movie is subtitled in English.
MPAA:PG FR
Alain Poire — *RCA/Columbia Pictures Home Video*

Blue Fin **1978**
Adventure
70681 93 mins C B, V P
Hardy Kruger, Greg Rowe, directed by Carl Schultz

When their tuna boat is shipwrecked, and the crew disabled, a young boy and his father learn lessons of love and courage as the son tries to save the ship.
South Australian Film Corporation/Hal McElroy — *Embassy Home Entertainment*

Blue Fire Lady **1978**
Drama
65289 96 mins C B, V P
Cathryn Harrison, Mark Holden, Peter Cummins
This is the heartwarming story of a young girl and her obsession for horses.
Antony I Ginnane — *Media Home Entertainment*

Blue Hawaii **1962**
Musical
08385 101 mins C B, V, LV P
Elvis Presley, Angela Lansbury, Joan Blackman, Roland Winters
Soldier, returning to Hawaiian home, takes job with tourist agency against parents' wishes.
EL, SP
Paramount; Hal Wallis — *CBS/Fox Video; RCA VideoDiscs*

Blue Lagoon, The **1980**
Drama
58434 105 mins C B, V P
Brooke Shields, Christopher Atkins, Leo McKern, William Daniels, directed by Randal Kleiser
Two beautiful teenagers marooned on a desert isle discover love without the restraints of society.
MPAA:R
Columbia; Randal Kleiser — *RCA/Columbia Pictures Home Video; RCA VideoDiscs*

Blue Max, The **1966**
Drama
29133 155 mins C B, V P
George Peppard, James Mason, Ursula Andress
During World War II a young German, fresh out of aviation training school, competes for the coveted "Blue Max" flying award with other members of a squadron of seasoned flyers of the aristocratic set. Based on a novel by Jack D. Hunter.
EL, SP
20th Century Fox — *CBS/Fox Video*

Blue Skies Again **1983**
Comedy
69312 91 mins C B, V R, P
Robyn Barto, Harry Hamlin, Mimi Rogers, Kenneth McMillan, Dana Elcar
A spunky young woman determined to play major league baseball locks horns with the chauvinistic owner and the gruff manager of her favorite team. In Beta Hi-Fi and stereo VHS.
MPAA:PG
Lantana Productions — *Warner Home Video*

Blue Steel **1934**
Western
08827 55 mins B/W B V, 3/4U P
John Wayne
Typical John Wayne excitement as he rides into danger and violence.
Monogram — *Sony Corporation of America; Video Connection; Video Dimensions; Sheik Video; Discount Video Tapes; Cable Films; Nostalgia Merchant; Spotlite Video; Kartes Productions*

Blue Sunshine **1977**
Horror
72909 94 mins C B, V P
A certain brand of L.S.D. called Blue Sunshine starts to make its victims go insane.
MPAA:R
Excel Video — *Vestron Video*

Blue Thunder **1983**
Adventure
65314 110 mins C B, V P
Roy Scheider, Daniel Stern, Malcolm McDowell, Candy Clark, Warren Oates
Roy Scheider is the police helicopter pilot who is chosen to test an experimental high-tech chopper that can see through walls, record a whisper and level a city block. In VHS stereo and Beta Hi-Fi.
MPAA:R
Gordon Carroll — *RCA/Columbia Pictures Home Video; RCA VideoDiscs*

Bluebeard **1972**
Drama
65446 128 mins C B, V P
Raquel Welch, Richard Burton, Joey Heatherton, Virna Lisi, Sybil Danning
An American dancer, married to an Australian aristocrat, discovers the frozen bodies of seven women in his refrigerated vault, and fights for her survival.
MPAA:R
Alexander Salkind — *U.S.A. Home Video*

Blues Alive **1983**
Music-Performance
64780 91 mins C B, V P
Albert King, Junior Wells and Buddy Guy join John Mayall in a concert celebration of their blues roots. Also appearing are ex-Rolling Stone Mick Taylor and Fleetwood Mac's John McVie.
Monarch Entertainment — *RCA/Columbia Pictures Home Video; RCA VideoDiscs*

Blues Brothers, The **1980**
Musical/Comedy
48608 133 mins C B, V, LV P

John Belushi, Dan Aykroyd, James Brown, Cab Calloway, Ray Charles, Aretha Franklin, Carrie Fisher, directed by John Landis
As an excuse to run rampant on the city of Chicago, Jake and Elwood Blues attempt to raise $5,000 for their childhood parish by putting their old band back together.
MPAA:R
Universal, Robert K Weiss — *MCA Home Video; RCA VideoDiscs*

Blues 1 **1983**
Music-Performance
65224 58 mins C B, V P
Linda Hopkins, B.B.King, Leatta Galloway, Ernie Andrews, Eddie "Cleanhead" Vinson, Vi Reed, "Pee Wee" Crayton
Brock Peters is the host of this historic journey to "the roots" of the Blues. In Beta Hi-Fi and VHS stereo.
Skylark Savoy Productions Ltd — *Video Gems*

Blume in Love **1973**
Comedy/Drama
58219 115 mins C B, V R, P
George Segal, Susan Anspach, Kris Kristofferson, Shelley Winters, Marsha Mason, directed by Paul Mazursky
An ironic comedy/drama about a man now hopelessly in love with his ex-wife who divorced him for cheating on her while they were married.
MPAA:R
Warner Bros — *Warner Home Video*

Boarding School **1983**
Comedy
72222 100 mins C B, V P
Nastassia Kinski
A group of restless young women hatch a plan to turn their spare time into money.
MPAA:R
Atlantic Releasing — *Vestron Video*

Boat, The **1982**
War-Drama
63432 150 mins C B, V P
Jurgen Prochnow, Herbert Gronemeyer
"The Boat" (original title: "Das Boot") is a World War II drama about a German submarine and its crew on patrol in the North Atlantic and their fight for survival. Stereo soundtrack, dubbed in English.
MPAA:PG
Gunter Rohrback; Bavaria Atelier — *RCA/Columbia Pictures Home Video; RCA VideoDiscs*

Boatniks, The **1970**
Comedy
65635 99 mins C B, V R, P
Robert Morse, Stefanie Powers, Phil Silvers, Norman Fell, Wally Cox, Don Ameche
An accident-prone Coast Guard ensign finds himself in charge of the "Times Square" of waterways: Newport Harbor. Adding to his already "titanic" problems is a gang of ocean-going jewel thieves who won't give up the ship!
Ron Miller — *Walt Disney Home Video*

Bob & Carol & Ted & Alice **1969**
Comedy
47435 104 mins C B, V P
Natalie Wood, Robert Culp, Dyan Cannon, Elliot Gould, directed by Paul Mazursky
Two California couples, influenced by a group sensitivity session, decide to loosen their sexual inhibitions and try wife-swapping.
MPAA:R
Columbia — *RCA/Columbia Pictures Home Video*

Bob & Ray, Jane, Laraine & Gilda **1983**
Comedy
66284 75 mins C B, V P
Bob & Ray, Jane Curtin, Laraine Newman, Gilda Radner, Willie Nelson, Leon Russell
The whimsical world of Bob & Ray is transferred to video.
Jean Doumanian; Lorne Michaels — *Pacific Arts Video*

Bob Hope Chevy Show **1956**
Variety
22234 52 mins B/W B, V, FO P
Bob Hope, Lucille Ball, Desi Arnaz, James Cagney
The first program of this series from the 1956 season, featuring comedy, music and a takeoff on "I Love Lucy."
NBC — *Video Yesteryear*

Bob Hope Chevy Show I, The **1957**
Comedy/Variety
64827 120 mins B/W B, V, 3/4U P
Bob Hope, Joan Davis, Julie London, Perry Como, Rosemary Clooney, Lana Turner, Wally Cox
Two complete programs that were originally telecast on November 11, 1956 and March 10, 1957. Bob and his guest do spoofs of "Playhouse 90" and the Elvis Presley craze; Julie London, Perry Como and Rosemary Clooney sing their current hits. All original commercials are included.
NBC — *Shokus Video*

Bob Hope Chevy Show II, The **1957**
Comedy/Variety
64828 120 mins B/W B, V, 3/4U P

Bob Hope, Eddie Fisher, Betty Grable, Harry James, Rowen and Martin, Frank Sinatra, Natalie Wood, Janis Paige
Bob Hope and a stellar array of guest stars present songs and comedy routines in these two complete programs, originally telecast on January 25, 1957 and April 5, 1957. All original commercials are included.
NBC — *Shokus Video*

Bob Le Flambeur **1955**
Drama
65464 106 mins B/W B, V P
Roger Duchesne, Isabel Corey, Daniel Cauchy
The story of a compulsive gambler who decides to take a final fling by robbing the casino at Deauville. Subtitled in English. In stereo VHS and Beta Hi-Fi.
FR
Jean Pierre Melville — *RCA/Columbia Pictures Home Video; Video Dimensions*

Bob Marley and the Wailers **1983**
Music-Performance
77070 60 mins C B, V R, P
This is one of Bob Marley's last live concerts taped at the County Bowl in Santa Barbara, California.
Avalon Productions — *THORN EMI/HBO Video*

Bob Marley and the Wailers Live from the Santa Barbara Bowl **1980**
Music-Performance
59880 59 mins C LV P
Reggae king Bob Marley, accompanied by a 12-piece band performs his hits in this stereo presentation filmed during his last complete U.S. tour in the Fall of 1979. Songs include "I Shot the Sheriff," "Jamming," and "Africa Unite." Also includes a personal interview.
Avalon Attractions — *Pioneer Artists*

Bob Welch and Friends **1982**
Music-Performance
47805 81 mins C CED P
This stereo concert features the one-time member of Fleetwood Mac, joined by members of Fleetwood Mac, drummer Carmine Appice, and Ann Wilson of Heart. Songs include "Gold Dust Woman," "Rattlesnake Shake," and "Sentimental Lady."
RCA — *RCA VideoDiscs*

Bobby Darin and Friends **1961**
Variety
56932 52 mins B/W B, V, FO P
Bobby Darin, Bob Hope, Joanie Summers
Bobby sings several of his hits, followed by Hope's monologue which centers around the Kennedy Inauguration, finally joined by Joanie for a soft shoe—"Won't You Come Home Bill Bailey."
Unknown — *Video Yesteryear*

Bobby Deerfield **1977**
Drama
58220 123 mins C B, V R, P
Al Pacino, Marthe Keller, Anny Duperey, Romolo Valli, directed by Sydney Pollack
A cold-blooded Grand Prix driver comes face to face with death each time he races, but finally learns the meaning of life when he falls in love with a critically ill woman.
MPAA:PG
Columbia Pictures; Warner Bros — *Warner Home Video*

Bobby Jo and the Outlaw **1976**
Drama/Adventure
64895 89 mins C B, V, CED P
Lynda Carter, Marjoe Gortner
A woman who wants to be a country singer and a man who emulates Billy the Kid are fugitives from the law.
MPAA:R
American International Pictures; Mark L. Lester — *Vestron Video*

Bobby Raccoon **1985**
Cartoons/Adventure
70360 60 mins C B, V P
Animated
Bobby learns to trust and respect his friendly neighborhood forest critters in this program. The masked mammal's adventures can be enjoyed in stereo on all formats.
Filmation — *Family Home Entertainment*

Bobby Vinton **1984**
Music-Performance
75285 60 mins C B, V P
This tape features singer Bobby Vinton performing some greatest hits at the Sands Hotel in Las Vegas. In Beta Hi-Fi stereo and VHS Dolby stereo.
RKO Home Video — *RKO HomeVideo*

Bobo, The **1967**
Comedy
58221 105 mins C B, V R, P
Peter Sellers, Britt Ekland, Rossano Brazzi, Adolfo Celi
A third-rate matador has three days to woo and win a legendary beauty.
Gina Productions; Warner Bros — *Warner Home Video*

Body and Soul **1947**
Drama
47991 104 mins B/W B, V P

John Garfield, Lilli Palmer, Hazel Brooks, Anne Revere, William Conrad, Canada Lee, directed by Robert Rossen
A young boxer fights his way unscrupulously to the top.
United Artists — *Republic Pictures Home Video*

Body and Soul **1981**
Drama
68240 109 mins C B, V, CED P
Leon Isaac Kennedy, Jayne Kennedy, Peter Lawford, Muhammad Ali
A hard hitting film about a boxer who loses his perspective in the world of fame, fast cars and women.
MPAA:R
Cannon Films — *MGM/UA Home Video*

Body by Jake **1984**
Physical fitness
78893 55 mins C B, V P
Jake Steinfield
The man who keeps Hollywood celebrities looking good with his "Smokin' Workout" brings his secrets to home video.
Marie Cantin — *MCA Home Video*

Body Double **1984**
Drama/Suspense
Closed Captioned
70560 114 mins C B, V P
Craig Wasson, Melanie Griffith, directed by Brian De Palma
A voyeuristic unemployed actor peeps on a neighbor's nightly disrobing and sees more than he wants to. A grisly murder leads him into an obsessive guest through the world of pornographic film-making. In Hi-Fi Stereo on all formats.
MPAA:R
Columbia Pictures — *RCA/Columbia Pictures Home Video*

Body Heat **1981**
Suspense/Drama
51993 113 mins C B, V, LV R, P
William Hurt, Kathleen Turner, Richard Crenna, Ted Danson
Two people involved in a steamy love affair plot to kill the woman's husband in this atmospheric melodrama.
MPAA:R
Ladd Company — *Warner Home Video; RCA VideoDiscs*

Body Rock **1984**
Musical-Drama
77164 93 mins C B, V P
Lorenzo Lamas, Vicki Frederick, Ray Sharkey, Carole Ita White
A Brooklyn breakdancer deserts his buddies to work at a chic Manhattan nightclub.
MPAA:PG13
New World Pictures — *THORN EMI/HBO Video*

Body Snatcher, The **1945**
Horror
00315 77 mins B/W B, V, 3/4U P
Boris Karloff, Bela Lugosi
Based on R.L. Stevenson's novel about a grave robber who supplies corpses to research scientists.
RKO — *Nostalgia Merchant*

Bodyguard, The **197?**
Adventure/Martial arts
59045 89 mins C B, V P
Sonny Chiba, Aaron Banks, Bill Louie, Judy Lee
The "yellow mafia" and New York's big crime families face off in this martial arts extravaganza.
MPAA:R
Terry Levene — *Media Home Entertainment*

Bogie: The Last Hero **1980**
Biographical/Drama
79327 99 mins C B, V P
Kevin O'Connor, Kathryn Harrold, Ann Wedgeworth, Drew Barrymore, directed by Vincent Sherman
How Bogie coped with trying to balance out his image as a tough guy on the screen and his gentle off screen image is the subject of this biopic. In Beta Hi-Fi and VHS Stereo.
Charles Fries Productions — *U.S.A. Home Video*

Boheme, La **1982**
Opera
60575 116 mins C B, V P
The Royal Opera, Ileana Cortrubas, Neil Shicoff, Marilyn Zschau, Thomas Allen, Gwynne Howell
Puccini's opera about the lives and loves of four 19th century Parisian Bohemians performed at the Covent Garden Opera House on February 16, 1982. Includes libretto. In stereo.
Covent Garden — *THORN EMI/HBO Video; Pioneer Artists*

Bohemian Girl, The **1936**
Musical/Comedy
47139 74 mins B/W B, V, 3/4U P
Stan Laurel, Oliver Hardy, Mae Busch, Darla Hood, Jacqueline Wells, Thelma Todd, Jimmy Finlayson
The last of Laurel and Hardy's comic operettas finds them as guardians of a young orphan, whom no one realizes is actually a kidnapped princess.
Hal Roach; MGM — *Nostalgia Merchant*

Boiling Point **1932**
Western
14206 67 mins B/W B, V P
Hoot Gibson
Lawman proves once again that justice always triumphs.
Allied Artists — *United Home Video; Discount Video Tapes; Video Connection*

Bold Caballero, The **1936**
Adventure
56599 69 mins B/W B, V P
Robert Livingston, Heather Angel
Rebel chieftain Zorro overthrows oppressive Spanish rule in the days of early California.
Republic — *Video Dimensions; Video Connection; Nostalgia Merchant; Discount Video Tapes*

Bolero **1982**
Drama
63970 173 mins C B, V, CED P
James Caan, Geraldine Chaplin, Robert Hossein, Nicole Garcia, Jacques Villeret, directed by Claude Lelouch
Beginning in 1936, this international epic traces the lives of four families across three continents and five decades, highlighting the music and dance that is central to their lives.
Films 13; TF1 Films — *Vestron Video*

Bolero **1984**
Romance/Drama
79186 106 mins C B, V P
Bo Derek, George Kennedy, Andrew Occhipinti, Ana Obregon, directed by John Derek
A young college graduate sets off on a worldwide quest to lose her virginity.
MPAA:X
Bo Derek; The Cannon Group — *U.S.A. Home Video*

Bolo **197?**
Martial arts/Adventure
47698 90 mins C B, V P
Yang Sze
The authorities pardon two tough prison inmates, setting the scene for revenge.
Star Film Company — *Master Arts Video*

Bolshoi Ballet **1967**
Dance
57255 90 mins C B, V P
Raissa Struhkova, Maya Samokhvalova, Vladimir Vasiliev, Ekaterina Maximova, Natalie Bessmertnova, The Bolshoi Ballet and Bolshoi Symphony
The world-famous dancers of the Bolshoi Ballet are featured in excerpts from eight works, including Ravel's "Bolers" and "La Valse," Prokofiev's "Stone Flower," music by Paganini and Rachmaninoff and"Bolshoi Ballet '67."
Kultur — *Kultur*

Bon Voyage, Charlie Brown **1980**
Comedy/Cartoons
48508 76 mins C B, V, LV R, P
Animated
The comic strip group from "Peanuts" become exchange students in Europe, led by Charlie Brown, Linus, Peppermint Patty, Marcie, and the irrepressible beagle, Snoopy.
MPAA:G
Lee Mendelson, Bill Melendez — *Paramount Home Video*

Bongo Man **1980**
Musical-Drama
70716 89 mins C B, V P
Jimmy Cliff
A reggae star brings some hope of peace, love and unity to his troubled homeland, Jamaica.
New World Pictures — *VCL Home Video*

Bonnie and Clyde **1967**
Drama
44588 105 mins C B, V, LV R, P
Warren Beatty, Faye Dunaway, Michael J. Pollard, Gene Hackman, Estelle Parsons, directed by Arthur Penn
The story of the two infamous bank robbers, Clyde Barrow and Bonnie Parker, who spent their days adrift in the Southwest during the depression era.
Academy Awards '67: Best Supporting Actress (Parsons).
Warner Bros — *Warner Home Video; RCA VideoDiscs*

Bonnie's Kids **1975**
Drama
76658 107 mins C B, V P
Tiffany Bolling, Robin Mattson, Scott Brady, Alex Rocco
A story about two sisters who become involved in murder, sex and stolen money.
MPAA:R
General Film Corp — *Monterey Home Video*

Boogey Man, The **1980**
Horror
52864 86 mins C B, V P
John Carradine, Suzanna Love, Ron James
A horrifying story of a brother and sister and the power of a broken mirror. The sister views the reflection of her brother murdering their mother's lover in a hallway mirror. The memory haunts the sister twenty years later.
MPAA:R EL, SP
Jerry Gross Organization — *Wizard Video; Vestron Video (disc only)*

Boom in the Moon 1945
Comedy
81258 83 mins B/W B, V P
Buster Keaton, Angel Grassa, Virginia Serret
An American GI is set adrift in the Atlantic Ocean at the end of World War II. When the ship runs aground, the soldier thinks that he's landed in Japan but it is actually Mexico. Available in VHS Stereo and Beta Hi-Fi.
Alexander Salkind — *U.S.A. Home Video*

Boots and Saddles 1937
Western
11383 54 mins B/W B, V, FO P
Gene Autry, Judith Allen, Smiley Burnette
A young English lord wants to sell the ranch he has inherited but Gene Autry is determined to make him a real Westerner.
Republic — *Video Yesteryear; Blackhawk Films; Video Connection; Budget Video; Discount Video Tapes; Nostalgia Merchant*

Border, The 1982
Drama
59681 107 mins C B, V, LV P
Jack Nicholson, Harvey Keitel, Valerie Perrine, Warren Oates, directed by Tony Richardson
A border guard faces corruption and violence within his department and tests his own sense of decency when the infant of a poor Mexican girl is kidnapped.
MPAA:R
Universal — *MCA Home Video*

Border Romance 1930
Western
38982 58 mins B/W B, V, FO P
Don Terry, Armide, Marjorie Kane
Three Americans have their horses stolen by bandits while riding through Mexico. Trouble with the Rurales follows in this early sound western.
Tiffany — *Video Yesteryear*

Borderline 1980
Drama
65005 106 mins C B, V P
Charles Bronson, A. Wilford Brimley, Bruno Kirby, Benito Morales, Ed Harris
This contemporary human action drama depicts the plight of illegal Mexican aliens.
MPAA:PG
ITC Entertainment — *CBS/Fox Video*

Born Again 1978
Biographical/Drama
78643 110 mins C B, V P
Dean Jones, Anne Francis, Dana Andrews, directed by Irving Rapper
This is the filmed adaptation of Charles Colson's biography of why he became a born again Christian.
Avco Embassy — *Embassy Home Entertainment*

Born Free 1966
Adventure
21280 95 mins C B, V P
Virginia McKenna, Bill Travers
A game warden in Kenya and his wife raise three orphan lion cubs. When the last cub is old enough they try to return her to the wild.
Academy Awards '66: Best Song.
Columbia — *RCA/Columbia Pictures Home Video; RCA VideoDiscs*

Born Losers 1967
Drama
66098 103 mins C B, V, CED P
Tom Laughlin
The original "Billy Jack" film in which the Indian martial arts expert takes on a group of incorrigible bikers.
American International Pictures — *Vestron Video*

Born to Kill 1947
Mystery
57127 92 mins B/W B, V P
Lawrence Tierney, Claire Trevor, Walter Slezak
A ruthless killer marries a girl for her money.
RKO — *King of Video*

Born Yesterday 1950
Comedy
21281 103 mins B/W B, V P
Judy Holliday, Broderick Crawford, William Holden, directed by George Cukor
A wealthy racketeer hires a writer to instruct his girl friend in etiquette. Based on the Broadway play.
Academy Awards '51: Best Actress (Holliday).
Columbia — *RCA/Columbia Pictures Home Video*

Borneo 1937
Documentary/Africa
65197 76 mins B/W B, V P
Martin Johnson, Osa Johnson, narrated by Lowell Thomas and Lew Lehr
Explorer and naturalist Martin Johnson investigates the many unusual sights and inhabitants of Borneo in this pioneering documentary.
Osa Johnson; 20th Century Fox — *Video Yesteryear*

Boss' Son, The 1979
Drama
72223 97 mins C B, V P
Rita Moreno, James Darren
A coming of age tale, as a young man tries to implement his dreams in the real world.
Boss Son Productions — *Vestron Video*

 (For explanation of codes, see USE GUIDE and KEY)

Boston and Maine—Its Fitchburg Division and Hoosac Tunnel in Steam Days 195?
Trains
64825 11 mins B/W B, V P, T
This vintage film shows steam locomotive activity on many parts of the B&M Fitchburg Division, which stretches west from Boston to Troy and Mechanicsville, N.Y.
J W Dealey; E R Blanchard — *Blackhawk Films*

Boston Strangler, The 1968
Suspense
08437 116 mins C B, V P
Tony Curtis, Henry Fonda, George Kennedy, Murray Hamilton, Sally Kellerman, directed by Richard Fleisher
Based on Gerold Frank's factual book about the killer who terrorized Boston for about a year and a half.
SP
20th Century Fox — *CBS/Fox Video*

Bostonians, The 1984
Drama
77181 120 mins C B, V, LV, CED P
Christopher Reeve, Vanessa Redgrave, Linda Hunt, directed by James Ivory
A faith healer's daughter is forced to choose between the affections of a militant suffragette and a young lawyer in 19th Century Boston.
MPAA:PG
Almi Pictures — *Vestron Video*

Bottoms Up '81 1981
Variety
55547 75 mins C B, V R, P
A screen recreation of this long-running comedy revue, combining slapstick, satire, beautiful showgirls, and lavish musical numbers. Taped on location at Harrah's Lake Tahoe.
Breck Wall Prods — *Paramount Home Video*

Boum, La 1983
Comedy
65699 90 mins C B, V P
Sophie Marceau, Claude Brasseur, Brigitte Fossey
A teenager adjusting to the changes brought about by a move to a new home is compounded by her parents, who are having marital problems.
Alain Poire — *RCA/Columbia Pictures Home Video*

Bourgeois Gentilhomme, Le 1958
Comedy
59371 97 mins C B, V, FO P
Translated "The Would-Be Gentleman." A comedy-ballet in five acts in prose, performed by the Comedie Francais. Subtitled in English.
FR
France — *Video Yesteryear*

Bowery at Midnight 1942
Mystery
73542 60 mins B/W B, V P
Bela Lugosi
A college professor becomes a killer at night, turning criminalsinto zombies who commit crimes for the professor's benefit.
Monogram — *Admit One Video; Discount Video Tapes*

Boxcar Bertha 1972
Drama
66096 89 mins C B, V, CED P
Barbara Hershey, David Carradine, directed by Martin Scorcese
Scorcese's vivid portrayal of the South during the 1930's Depression.
MPAA:R
American International Pictures — *Vestron Video*

Boxcar Willie in Concert 1983
Music-Performance
73566 60 mins C B, V P
Boxcar Willie performs his story songs of freight-hopping and hoboing in this concert tape at the Hammersmith Odeon in 1983.
Videoform — *Prism*

Boxing's Greatest Champions 1980
Boxing
29230 59 mins B/W B, V P
Hosted by Curt Gowdy, Barney Ross, Rocky Marciano, Archie Moore, Sugar Ray Robinson, Joe Louis
Presented are "the greatest" in each division, as selected by the Boxing Writers Association. Match your boxing knowledge against the Boxing Writers.
Big Fights Inc — *VidAmerica*

Boy and His Dog, A 1976
Science fiction
42909 87 mins C B, V P
Don Johnson, Susanne Benton, Jason Robards
This is a movie adaptation of Harlan Ellison's novella about a misogynistic society in the post World War IV civilizaton of 2024.
EL, SP
Alvy Moore — *Media Home Entertainment*

Boy, Did I Get a Wrong Number! 1966
Comedy
81550 100 mins C B, V P

Bob Hope, Phyllis Diller, Marjorie Lord, Elke Sommer, directed by George Marshall
A real estate agent gets more than he bargained for when he accidentally dials a wrong number. Available in VHS and Beta Hi-Fi.
United Artists — *Playhouse Video*

Boy in the Plastic Bubble, The **1976**
Drama
80296 100 mins C B, V P
John Travolta, Robert Reed, Glynnis O'Connor, Diana Hyland, Ralph Bellamy
A young man born with immunity deficiencies grows up in a specially controlled plastic environment.
Aaron Spelling; Leonard Goldberg — *Prism*

Boy Named Charlie Brown, A **1969**
Cartoons
Closed Captioned
78885 80 mins C B, V P
Animated, music by Vince Guaraldi and Rod McKuen
Charlie Brown enters the National Spelling Bee in New York and makes the final rounds with one other contestant.
Cinema Center Films — *Playhouse Video*

Boy of Two Worlds **1970**
Adventure
59358 103 mins C B, V R, P
Jimmy Sternman
Because he is of a lineage foreign to his late father's town, a boy is exiled to the life of a junior Robinson Crusoe.
MPAA:G
GG Communications — *Video Gems*

Boy Who Left Home to Find Out About the Shivers, The **1981**
Fairy tales
73145 60 mins C B, V, CED P
Peter MacNicol, Christopher Lee, Vincent Price, directed by Graeme Clifford
From "Faerie Tale Theatre" comes the story of a young man, played by Peter MacNicol, who had no fear.
Shelley Duvall — *CBS/Fox Video*

Boy with the Green Hair, The **1948**
Drama
59061 82 mins C B, V P
Pat O'Brien, Robert Ryan, Barbara Hale, Dean Stockwell, directed by Joseph Losey
When he hears that his parents were killed in an air raid, a boy's hair turns green.
RKO — *King of Video*

Boys from Brazil, The **1978**
Drama
44935 123 mins C B, V, LV P
Gregory Peck, James Mason, Sir Laurence Olivier
Incredible plot of human cloning when children formed from Hitler's likeness are used to implement a neo-Nazi takeover.
MPAA:R
20th Century Fox — *CBS/Fox Video; RCA VideoDiscs*

Boys from Brooklyn, The **1952**
Comedy
53432 60 mins B/W B, V, FO P
Bela Lugosi, Duke Mitchell, Sammy Petrillo
Two comedians that bear a striking resemblance to Dean Martin and Jerry Lewis get mixed up with a mad scientist and crazed gorillas in Africa.
Jack Broder — *Video Yesteryear; Discount Video Tapes; See Hear Industries*

Boys in Company C, The **1977**
War-Drama
47786 125 mins C B, V P
Stan Shaw, Andrew Stevens, James Canning, Michael Lembeck, Craig Wasson
A frank, hard-hitting drama about five young men involved in the Vietnam War.
MPAA:R
Andre Morgan — *RCA/Columbia Pictures Home Video*

Boys in the Band, The **1970**
Drama
54102 120 mins C B, V, CED P
Frederick Combs, Cliff Gorman, Lawrence Luckinbill, Kenneth Nelson, Leonard Frey, directed by William Friedkin
Mart Crawley adapts his own award-winning play concerning the lives of a group of homosexuals. While playing a parlor game where each is to call out the one he loves, they learn a lot about themselves and their way of life.
MPAA:R
National General, Cinema Center Films — *CBS/Fox Video*

Boys of Summer, The **1983**
Baseball
66002 90 mins C B, V, CED P
Duke Snider, Roy Campanella, Carl Erskine, Preacher Roe
Based on Roger Kahn's best-selling book, this program tells the story of the 1947-57 Brooklyn Dodgers.
Video Corporation of America; Thorn EMI Video Programming — *VidAmerica*

Bozo the Clown Volume I 196?
Cartoons
47659 59 mins C B, V P
Animated
Animated adventures of Bozo the clown.
EL, SP
Larry Harmon — *Unicorn Video*

Bozo the Clown Volume 2 196?
Cartoons
47660 59 mins C B, V P
Animated
The further animated adventures of Bozo the clown
EL, SP
Larry Harmon — *Unicorn Video*

Bozo the Clown Volume 3 196?
Cartoons
47661 59 mins C B, V P
Animated
Bozo the clown stars in the these animated tales.
EL, SP
Larry Harmon — *Unicorn Video*

Bozo the Clown Volume 4 196?
Cartoons
47662 59 mins C B, V P
Animated
More fun with animated Bozo the Clown.
EL, SP
Larry Harmon — *Unicorn Video*

Brady's Escape 1984
War-Drama
75670 90 mins C B, V P
An American World War II pilot is shot down in the Hungarian countryside and befriended by Hungarian Csikos (cowboys).
Satori Entertainment Corp — *VidAmerica*

Brain, The 1965
Horror
81402 83 mins B/W B, V P
Anne Heywood, Peter Van Eyck, Bernard Lee
A scientist finds himself being manipulated by the dead man's brain he's trying to keep alive. Available in VHS Stereo and Beta Hi-Fi.
Raymond Stross Prods. — *Monterey Home Video*

Brain From Planet Arous, The 1957
Science fiction
73546 70 mins B/W B, V P
Robert Fuller, John Agar
An evil brain from the Planet Arous possesses a scientist's body intending to conquer the world.
Howco Films — *Admit One Video*

Brain That Wouldn't Die, The 1963
Science fiction/Horror
65136 70 mins B/W B, V R, P
Herb Evers, Virginia Leith, Adele Lamont
A brilliant surgeon keeps the decapitated head of his fiancee alive after an auto accident while he searches for a suitable body to transplant the head onto.
American International — *Warner Home Video*

Brainwaves 1982
Science fiction
66042 83 mins C B, V P
Suzanna Love, Tony Curtis, Kier Dullea
A young woman is treated by a noted neuroscientist with a mysterious form of treatment, "the Clavins Process."
MPAA:R
Ulli Lommel — *Embassy Home Entertainment*

Brainstorm 1983
Science fiction
66456 106 mins C B, V, CED P
Natalie Wood, Christopher Walken, Cliff Robertson, Louise Fletcher, directed by Douglas Trumbull
A scientist invents a device that can record dreams and allow other people to experience them. Stereo VHS and CED.
MPAA:PG
MGM UA Entertainment Co — *MGM/UA Home Video*

Brainwash 1984
Drama
76020 98 mins C B, V P
Yvette Mimieux, Christopher Allport, John Considine
Yvette Mimieux stars in a shocking and dramatic commentary on the capitalistic system, and the lengths to which people will go to acquire wealth and power.
MPAA:R
Gary L Mehlman — *Media Home Entertainment*

Brannigan 1975
Suspense/Crime-Drama
58829 111 mins C CED P
John Wayne, John Vernon, Mel Ferrer, Daniel Pilon, James Booth, Richard Attenborough
The Duke travels across the Atlantic to arrest a racketeer who has fled the States rather than face a grand jury indictment.
MPAA:PG
United Artists — *CBS/Fox Video*

Breach of Promise 1941
Comedy-Drama
66365 70 mins B/W B, V P
Clive Brook, Judy Campbell, C.V. France

A girl snares the man she wants by serving him with a breach of promise suit.
British Mercury; MGM — *Movie Buff Video*

Breaker, Breaker! 1977
Drama/Martial arts
63371 86 mins C B, V P
Chuck Norris, George Murdock
A convoy of angry truck drivers launch an assault on the corrupt and sadistic locals of a small Texas town.
MPAA:R
American International — *Embassy Home Entertainment*

Breaker Morant 1980
Drama
58496 107 mins C B, V P
Edward Woodward, Jack Thompson, John Waters, Bryan Brown, directed by Bruce Beresford
In 1901 South Africa, three Australian soldiers are put on trial for avenging the murder of a comrade.
MPAA:PG
Matt Carroll; South Australian Film Corp — *RCA/Columbia Pictures Home Video; Embassy Home Entertainment (disc only)*

Breakfast at Tiffany's 1961
Comedy
38587 114 mins C B, V, LV R, P
Audrey Hepburn, George Peppard, Patricia Neal, directed by Blake Edwards
Truman Capote's story of an eccentric New York City playgirl and her shaky romance with a young writer. Music by Henry Mancini.
Academy Awards '61: Best Song ("Moon River").
Paramount — *Paramount Home Video; RCA VideoDiscs*

Breakfast Club, The 1985
Comedy-Drama
Closed Captioned
81436 92 mins C B, V P
Ally Sheedy, Molly Ringwald, Judd Nelson, Emilio Estavez, Anthony Michael Hall, directed by John Hughes
Five students at a Chicago suburban high school bare their souls to each other and wind up becoming friends while spending a Saturday detention together.
MPAA:R
Universal; A&M Films — *MCA Home Video*

Breakfast in Hollywood 1946
Comedy
11224 93 mins B/W B, V, FO P
Tom Breneman, Bonita Granville, Eddie Ryan, Beulah Bondi, Billie Burke, Zasu Pitts, Hedda Hopper, Spike Jones and His Slickers
A movie about the popular morning radio show of the 1940's hosted by Tom Breneman—a coast-to-coast coffee klatch.
United Artists — *Video Yesteryear; Movie Buff Video*

Breakheart Pass 1976
Western
64936 92 mins C CED P
Charles Bronson, Ben Johnson, Richard Crenna, Jill Ireland, Charles Durning, Archie Moore
A governor, his female companion, a band of cavalrymen and a mysterious man travel on a train through the mountains of Idaho in 1870. The mystery man turns out to be a murderer.
MPAA:PG
United Artists — *CBS/Fox Video*

Breakin' 1984
Film/Dance
78045 87 mins C B, V, CED P
This program presents the movie about the dance phenomenon break dancing along with the hit songs that accompany the film.
Allen DeBevoise; David Zito — *MGM/UA Home Video*

Breaking Away 1979
Comedy
37410 100 mins C B, V, CED P
Dennis Christopher, Dennis Quaid, Daniel Stern, Jackie Earle Haley
A comedy about a high school graduate's addiction to bicycle racing whose dreams are tested against the realities of a crucial race. Shot on location at Indiana University.
Academy Awards '79: Best Original Screenplay.
MPAA:PG
20th Century Fox — *CBS/Fox Video*

Breaking Glass 1980
Musical
54674 104 mins C B, V R, P
Hazel O'Connor, Phil Daniels, Jon Fich, Jonathan Pryce, directed by Brian Gibson
A "New Wave" musical that gives an insight into the punk record business and at the same time tells of the rags-to-riches life of a punk rock star.
Paramount — *Paramount Home Video*

Breaking the Ice 1938
Musical
42954 79 mins B/W B, V, FO P
Bobby Breen, Charles Ruggles, Dolores Costello, Billy Gilbert
An improbable mixture of Mennonites and a big city ice skating show. Musical numbers abound with backing by Victor Young and his Orchestra.
RKO; Sol Lesser — *Video Yesteryear; Discount Video Tapes*

 (For explanation of codes, see USE GUIDE and KEY)

Breaking with the Mighty Poppalots **1984**
Dance
70150 60 mins C B, V P
The break dance group The Mighty Poppalots teach all aspects of break dancing from moon walks to windmills in this instructional program.
Adler Enterprises — *Vestron Video*

Breakout **1975**
Drama
21282 96 mins C B, V P
Charles Bronson, Jill Ireland, Robert Duvall, John Huston
The wife of a man imprisoned in Mexico hires a Texas bush pilot to help her husband escape.
MPAA:PG
Columbia — *RCA/Columbia Pictures Home Video; RCA VideoDiscs*

Breakthrough **1979**
War-Drama
65666 96 mins C B, V P
Richard Burton, Robert Mitchum, Rod Steiger, Michael Parks, Curt Jurgens
German and American officers join forces to assassinate Hitler.
Wolf C Hartwig; Hubert Lukowski — *Worldvision Home Video*

Breathless **1959**
Drama
55801 89 mins B/W B, V P
Jean-Paul Belmondo, Jean Seberg, directed by Jean-Luc Godard
Godard's first feature catapulted him to the vanguard of the French new-wave with this story of a carefree crook who has an affair with an American, with tragic results. English subtitled.
FR
Films Around the World — *Movie Buff Video; Festival Films; Discount Video Tapes*

Breathless **1983**
Drama
65340 105 mins C B, V, LV P
Richard Gere, Valerie Kaprisky
Richard Gere is a car thief turned cop killer, who has a torrid love affair with a French student studying in Los Angeles as the police slowly close in. This is a remake of Jean-Luc Godard's 1960 classic.
MPAA:R
Jean Luc Godard — *Vestron Video; RCA VideoDiscs*

Brewster McCloud **1970**
Comedy
79211 101 mins C B, V P
Bud Cort, Sally Kellerman, Shelley Duvall, Michael Murphy, directed by Robert Altman
A killer is on the loose in Houston and the likely suspect is a young man who lives in the Astrodome where he is building giant wings.
MPAA:R
MGM — *MGM/UA Home Video*

Brewster's Millions **1945**
Comedy
70741 79 mins B/W B, V P
Dennis O'Keefe, June Havoc, Eddie Anderson, Helen Walker, directed by Allan Dwan
If Brewster, an ex-GI, can spend a million dollars in one year, he will inherit a substantially greater fortune.
United Artists — *Nostalgia Merchant*

Brian's Song **1971**
Drama
Closed Captioned
44788 73 mins C B, V P
James Caan, Billy Dee Williams, Jack Warden, Shelley Fabares, Judy Pace
The story of the unique relationship between Gale Sayers, the Chicago Bears' star running back, and his teammate Brian Piccolo. The friendship between the Bears' first interracial roommates ended suddenly when Brian Piccolo lost his life to cancer.
MPAA:G
Paul Junger Witt, CPT — *RCA/Columbia Pictures Home Video; RCA VideoDiscs*

Bride of Frankenstein **1935**
Horror
70156 75 mins B/W B, V P
Boris Karloff, Elsa Lanchester, Ernest Thesiger O.P. Heggie, directed by James Whale
When an evil doctor meets a lonely Frankenstein, he decides to build him a mate in this horror classic.
Universal Pictures — *MCA Home Video*

Bride of the Monster **1956**
Horror
57347 70 mins B/W B, V, FO P
Bela Lugosi, Tor Johnson, Loretta King, Tony McCoy
Lugosi stars as a mad doctor trying to create a race of giants.
Banner Prods; Edward Wood Jr — *Video Yesteryear; Budget Video; Classic Video Cinema Collector's Club*

Bride Walks Out, The **1936**
Comedy
80238 81 mins B/W B, V P
Barbara Stanwyck, Gene Raymond, Robert Young, Ned Sparts, Willie Best
A rich woman learns how to adjust to living on her husband's poor salary.
RKO — *RKO HomeVideo*

Brides Wore Blood, The **1984**
Horror
80474 86 mins C B, V P
Four prospective brides are mysteriously murdered, but one is brought back to life and becomes a vampire's mate.
Regal Video — *Regal Video*

Bridge of San Luis Rey, The **1944**
Drama
81221 89 mins B/W B, V, LV P
Lynn Bari, Francis Lederer, Louis Calhern
A priest investigates the famous bridge collapse in Lima Peru that left five people dead. Based upon the novel by Thorton Wilder.
United Artists — *New World Video*

Bridge on the River Kwai, The **1957**
Drama
13232 161 mins C B, V, LV P
William Holden, Alec Guinness, Sessue Hayakawa, James Donald, directed by David Lean
A British Colonel is forced to labor in building a bridge for the enemy during World War II, and Holden is assigned to destroy it.
Academy Awards '57: Best Picture; Best Actor (Guinness); Best Director (Lean).
Columbia; Sam Spiegel — *RCA/Columbia Pictures Home Video; RCA VideoDiscs*

Bridge Too Far, A **1977**
War-Drama
47144 175 mins C B, V, CED P
James Caan, Michael Caine, Sean Connery, Elliot Gould, Gene Hackman, Laurence Olivier, Ryan O'Neal, Robert Redford, Liv Ullmann, Dirk Bogarde, directed by Richard Attenborough
A meticulous recreation of one of the most disastrous battles of World War II, the Allied defeat at Arnhem in 1944. Misinformation, adverse conditions, and overconfidence combined to prevent the Allies from capturing six bridges that connected Holland to the German border.
MPAA:PG
United Artists; Joseph E. Levine — *CBS/Fox Video*

Brigadoon **1954**
Musical
53349 108 mins C B, V, LV, CED P
Gene Kelly, Van Johnson, Cyd Charisse, directed by Vincente Minnelli
The story of a magical, 18th century Scottish village which awakens once every 100 years, highlighted by Lerner and Loewe's score. Songs include: "Heather on the Hill," "Almost Like Being in Love," "I'll Go Home with Bonnie Jean," "Wedding Dance."
MGM; Arthur Freed — *MGM/UA Home Video*

Brighton Strangler, The **1945**
Mystery
73696 67 mins B/W B, V P
John Loder, June Duprez
An actor who plays a murderer takes his part too seriously.
RKO — *RKO HomeVideo*

Brighton Strangler, The/Before Dawn **1945**
Mystery
80427 128 mins B/W B, V P
John Loder, June Duprez, Miles Mander, Stuart Oland, Dorothy Wilson
A mystery double feature: In "The Brighton Strangler," an actor takes his part too seriously as he murders Londoners at night and in "Before Dawn" a brilliant scientist turns to a life of murderous crime.
RKO — *RKO HomeVideo*

Brighty of the Grand Canyon **1967**
Drama/Adventure
79341 92 mins C B, V P
Joseph Cotten, Pat Conway, Dick Foran, Karl Swenson
Ths spunky donkey Brighty roams across the Grand Canyon in search of adventure.
Feature Film Corp of America — *Active Home Video*

Brimstone and Treacle **1982**
Drama
68243 85 mins C B, V, CED P
Sting, Denholm Elliot, Joan Plowright, Suzanna Hamilton, directed by Richard Loncraine
A mysterious man charms his way into the lives of a middle-aged couple whose pretty daughter has been paralyzed since a car accident. In stereo.
MPAA:R
Namara Films — *MGM/UA Home Video*

Brink of Life **1957**
Drama
65201 82 mins B/W B, V P
Eva Dahlbeck, Ingrid Thulin, Bibi Andersson, Max Von Sydow, directed by Ingmar Bergman
Three pregnant women in a hospital maternity ward await their respective births with mixed feelings. Swedish dialogue with English subtitles
SW
Svenskfilmindustri — *Video Yesteryear*

Britannia Hospital **1982**
Comedy
69625 111 mins C B, V R, P
Malcolm McDowell, Leonard Rossiter, Graham Crowden, Jean Plowright

(For explanation of codes, see USE GUIDE and KEY)

This is a portrait of a hospital at its most chaotic: the staff threatens to strike, demonstrators surround the hospital, a nosey BBC reporter pursues an anxious professor, and the eagerly-anticipated royal visit degenerates into a total shambles.
MPAA:R
Independent — *THORN EMI/HBO Video*

Broadway Danny Rose **1984**
Comedy
72224 85 mins B/W B, V, LV, CED P
Woody Allen, Mia Farrow
Second rate booking agent Woody Allen has a paternal relationship with his third-rate acts in this funny-poignant film.
MPAA:PG
Orion — *Vestron Video*

Broadway Highlights **1936**
Nightclub
56911 40 mins B/W B, V, FO P
Narrated by Ted Husing, Milton Berle, George Jessel, Babe Ruth, Jack Dempsey, Ed Wynn, Fannie Brice, Burns and Allen, Jimmy Durante, Ed Sullivan
Four different tours through the nightlife of New York City in the 1930's, with visits to restaurants, nightclubs, and theaters.
Unknown — *Video Yesteryear; Discount Video Tapes*

Broken Strings **1940**
Drama
11225 50 mins B/W B, V, FO P
Clarence Muse, Sybil Lewis, William Washington, Stymie Beard
An all-black feature in which a concert violinist must come to terms with himself after an auto accident limits the use of his left hand.
International Roadshows — *Video Yesteryear; Video Connection; Discount Video Tapes*

Bronco Billy **1980**
Comedy
58222 118 mins C B, V R, P
Clint Eastwood, Sondra Locke, directed by Clint Eastwood
A Wild West Show entrepreneur leads his ragged troupe from one improbable adventure to the next.
MPAA:PG
Warner Bros — *Warner Home Video; RCA VideoDiscs*

Bronson Lee, Champion **1978**
Adventure/Martial arts
66127 81 mins C B, V R, P
Kung-fu and karate highlight this action adventure.
MPAA:PG
Unknown — *Warner Home Video*

Brood, The **1979**
Drama/Horror
65420 92 mins C B, V P
A man, whose wife is in a mental hospital seemingly unable to get better, finds himself somehow involved in a series of murders, but neither the doctors nor the police will help him.
MPAA:R
New World — *Embassy Home Entertainment*

Brother, Can You Spare a Dime? **1975**
History-US/Documentary
35381 103 mins C B, V P
A compilation of documentary film footage from the 1930's—Hollywood in its heyday, Dillinger vs. the G-men, bread liners, and other memorabilia.
Sandy Lieberson, David Puttnam — *United Home Video*

Brother from Another Planet, The **1984**
Science fiction/Adventure
Closed Captioned
80728 109 mins C B, V P
Joe Morton, Dee Dee Bridgewater, Ren Woods, Steve James, Maggie Renzi, directed by John Sayles
An alien slave escapes captivity from his native planet and winds up in Harlem where he's pursued by two alien bounty hunters. Available in VHS and Beta Hi-Fi stereo.
A-Train Films — *Key Video*

Brother Sun, Sister Moon **1973**
Drama
60329 122 mins C B, V R, P
Graham Faulkner, Judi Bowker, Alec Guinness, Leigh Lawson, Kenneth Cranham, Lee Montague, Valentina Cortese
The life of Francis of Assisi. Musical score by Donovan.
MPAA:PG
Paramount — *Paramount Home Video*

Brotherhood of Death **1976**
Drama
77237 85 mins C B, V P
Roy Jefferson, Larry Jones, Mike Bass
Three black Vietnam veterans return to their southern hometown to get even with the Klansmen who slaughtered all of the townspeople.
MPAA:R
Cinema Shares International — *MPI Home Video*

Brothers Lionheart, The **1985**
Adventure
77300 120 mins C B, V P
The Lion brothers fight for life, love and liberty during the Middle Ages.
Olle Nordemar — *Pacific Arts Video*

Brothers O'Toole, The **1973**
Comedy/Western
80660 94 mins C B, V P
John Astin, Steve Carlson, Pat Carroll, Hans Conried, Lee Meriwether
This film depicts the misadventures of a pair of slick drifters who, by chance, ride into a broken-down mining town in the 1890's.
Gold Key Entertainment — *United Home Video*

Brubaker **1980**
Drama
56900 131 mins C B, V, CED P
Robert Redford, Jane Alexander
Drama about a reform warden who risks his life to replace brutality and corruption with humanity and integrity in a state prison farm.
MPAA:R
Twentieth Century Fox, Ron Silverman — *CBS/Fox Video*

Bruce Jenner Workout, The **1984**
Physical fitness
79687 80 mins C B, V P
Bruce and Linda Jenner describe their physical fitness regimen that the whole family can do.
AHV Productions — *Active Home Video*

Bruce Lee Fights Back from the Grave **1976**
Martial arts
63892 97 mins C B, V P
Bruce Lee, Deborah Chaplin, Anthony Bronson
Bruce Lee returns from the grave to fight the Black Angel of Death and to wreak vengeance on the evil ones who brought about his untimely demise.
MPAA:R
Bert Lenzi — *Media Home Entertainment*

Bruce Lee The Man/The Myth **1984**
Biographical/Martial arts
77221 90 mins C B, V P
A dramatization of the life and times of martial arts master Bruce Lee.
Cinema Shares International — *Lightning Video*

Bruce Le's Greatest Revenge **1980**
Adventure/Martial arts
56922 94 mins C B, V R, P
Kung-fu action and martial arts fighting highlight this film, in which a martial arts student gets involved in a clash between Chinese and a discriminatory European Club.
MPAA:R
Fourseas Film Company — *Video Gems*

Bruce Li in New Guinea **1980**
Adventure/Martial arts
56924 98 mins C B, V R, P
Bruce Li
The tribe of a remote island worships the legendary Snake Pearl. Two masters of Kung-fu visit the isle and discover they must defend the daughter of the murdered chief against a cruel wizard.
MPAA:PG
Fourseas Film Company — *Video Gems*

Brute Man, The **1946**
Drama
73539 62 mins B/W B, V P
Rondo Hattan, Tom Neal, Jane Adams
After a young man is disfigured by his school mates, he goes out on a trail of revenge later in life.
PRC — *Admit One Video*

Bryan Adams, Reckless **1984**
Music video
77247 30 mins C B, V P
Directed by Steve Barron
A conceptual music video EP featuring guitarist/vocalist Bryan Adams playing five songs from his "Reckless" album.
Simon Fields; Limelight — *A & M Video; RCA/Columbia Pictures Home Video*

Buck and the Preacher **197?**
Comedy-Drama/Western
64576 102 mins C B, V P
Sidney Poitier, Harry Belafonte, Ruby Dee, Cameron Mitchell, Denny Miller, directed by Sidney Poitier
A trail guide and a conman join forces to help a wagon train of former slaves who are seeking to homestead out West.
MPAA:PG
Columbia — *RCA/Columbia Pictures Home Video*

Buck Privates **1941**
Comedy
69031 84 mins B/W B, V P
Bud Abbott, Lou Costello, Lee Norman, Alan Curtis, The Andrews Sisters
Abbott and Costello star as two dim-witted tie salesmen, running from the law, who become buck privates during World War II.
Universal — *MCA Home Video*

 (For explanation of codes, see USE GUIDE and KEY)

Buck Rogers Conquers the Universe 1939
Science fiction
29134 91 mins B/W B, V P
Buster Crabbe, Constance Moore, Jackie Moran
The story of Buck Rogers, written by Phil Nolan in 1928, was the first science fiction story done in the modern super-hero space idiom. Many of the "inventions" seen in this movie have actually come into existence—spaceships, ray guns (lasers), anti-gravity belts—as a testament to Nolan's almost psychic farsightedness.
Viacom International — *CBS/Fox Video*

Buck Rogers in the 25th Century 1979
Science fiction
48628 90 mins C B, V, LV P
Gil Gerard, Pamela Hensley, Erin Gray, Henry Silva
An American astronaut, preserved in space for 500 years, is brought back to life by a passing Draconian flagship. Outer space adventures begin when he is accused of being a spy from Earth. Based on the classic movie serial.
MPAA:PG
Universal — *MCA Home Video*

Buck Rogers: Planet Outlaws 1938
Science fiction
08630 70 mins B/W B, V, 3/4U P
Buster Crabbe, Constance Moore, Jackie Moran
Drama of the world as it might exist in the 25th century. Compiled from the "Buck Rogers" serial.
Universal — *Video Yesteryear*

Buddy Buddy 1981
Comedy
59845 96 mins C B, V, CED P
Jack Lemmon, Walter Matthau, directed by Billy Wilder
A professional hitman's well-ordered arrangement to knock off a state's witness keeps being interrupted by the suicide attempts of a man in the next hotel room.
MPAA:R
MGM — *MGM/UA Home Video*

Buddy Hackett: Live and Uncensored 1984
Comedy-Performance
66610 72 mins C B, V P
Buddy Hackett
Comedian Buddy Hackett lets loose in a no-holds-barred recording of his nightclub show.
USA — *U.S.A. Home Video*

Buddy System, The 1983
Drama
Closed Captioned
76042 110 mins C B, V P
Richard Dreyfuss, Susan Sarandon, Jean Stapleton
A tale of contemporary love and the modern myths that outline the boundaries between lovers and friends.
MPAA:PG
Alain Chammas — *Key Video*

Budo 1981
Martial arts/Documentary
70607 75 mins C B, V P
This program explores the Eastern techniques of Kendo, karate, akido, and judo while it discusses the history of Oriental philosophical and theological thought.
Prism Entertainment — *Prism*

Buffalo Bill and the Indians 1976
Western
76044 135 mins C B, V P
Paul Newman, Geraldine Chaplin, Joel Grey, Will Sampson
A story about the rough-and-tumble days of Wild Bill Hickok's traveling Wild West Show.
MPAA:PG
David Susskind — *Key Video*

Bug 1975
Horror/Science fiction
60215 100 mins C B, V R, P
Bradford Dillman, Joanna Miles
The city of Riverside is threatened with destruction after a massive earth tremor unleashes a super-race of mega-cockroaches.
MPAA:PG
William Castle — *Paramount Home Video*

Bugs Bunny/Road Runner Movie, The 1979
Comedy/Cartoons
38948 90 mins C B, V R, P
Animated
A compilation of classic Warner Brothers cartoons, starring Bugs Bunny, Daffy Duck, Elmer Fudd, the Road Runner, Wile E. Coyote, Porky Pig, and Pepe Le Pew, including some all-new animated sequences.
MPAA:G
Warner Bros — *Warner Home Video; RCA VideoDiscs*

Bugs Bunny's 3rd Movie: 1,001 Rabbit Tales 1982
Cartoons
60560 74 mins C B, V R, P
Animated, voices by Mel Blanc

A compilation of old and new classic cartoons featuring Bugs, Daffy, Sylvester, Porky, Elmer, Tweety, Speedy Gonzalez and Yosemite Sam.
MPAA:G
Warner Bros — *Warner Home Video*

Bugs Bunny's Wacky Adventures **1957**
Cartoons
81571 59 mins C B, V P
Animated, voice of Mel Blanc
Here is a collection of that rascally rabbit's classic cartoons featuring "Ali Baba Bunny", "Hare Do" and "Duck! Rabbit! Duck!".
Warner Bros. — *Warner Home Video*

Bugsy Malone **1976**
Musical
58709 94 mins C B, V, LV R, P
Jodie Foster, Scott Baio, directed by Alan Parker
An all-children's cast highlights this spoof of '30's gangster movies. Songs by Paul Williams.
MPAA:G
Paramount; Alan Marshall — *Paramount Home Video*

Building Blocks of Life, The **1982**
Biology/Science
59561 61 mins C B, V P
A no-nonsense look at the basic unit of life, the cell, of which 60 trillion are required to constitute the human body.
McGraw Hill — *Mastervision*

Bulldog Drummond Escapes **1937**
Mystery
08764 67 mins B/W B, V, 3/4U P
Ray Milland, Heather Angel, Reginald Denny, Sir Guy Standing
Drummond, aided by his side-kick and valet, rescues a beautiful girl from spies. He then falls in love with her.
Paramount — *Video Yesteryear*

Bulldog Drummond's Bride **1939**
Mystery
80736 69 mins B/W B, V P
John Howard, Heather Angel, H. B. Warner, E. E. Clive, Reginald Denny
Ace detective Bulldog Drummond has to interrupt his honeymoon in order to pursue a gang of bank robbers across France and England.
Paramount — *Hal Roach Studios; Discount Video Tapes*

Bullfighter and the Lady **1950**
Drama
76825 87 mins B/W B, V P
Robert Stack, Gilbert Roland, Katy Jurado
An American comes to Mexico to learn the fine art of bullfighting from a matador to impress a beautiful woman.
Republic Pictures — *Republic Pictures Home Video*

Bullfighters, The **1945**
Comedy
81549 61 mins B/W B, V P
Stan Laurel, Oliver Hardy, Margo Wood, Richard Lane, directed by Mal St. Clair
Stan and Ollie are in hot pursuit of a dangerous criminal which leads them to Mexico where Stan winds up in a bull ring. Available in VHS and Beta Hi-Fi.
20th Century Fox — *Playhouse Video*

Bullitt **1968**
Drama
44589 105 mins C B, V R, P
Steve McQueen, Robert Vaughn, Jacqueline Bisset, Don Gordon, Robert Duvall, directed by Peter Yates
A detective lieutenant has an assignment to keep a star witness out of danger for 48 hours. He senses that something is fishy about the setup and before the night is out has a murder on his hands. Based on the novel "Mute Witness" by Robert L. Pike.
MPAA:PG
Warner Bros — *Warner Home Video; RCA VideoDiscs*

Bullpen **1974**
Baseball
33834 22 mins C B, V P
Joe Page, Jim Konstanty, Roy Face, Hoyt Wilhelm, Ron Perranoski, Tug McGraw
This program about baseball's relief pitchers goes behind the scenes into the relievers' home away from home, the bullpen. Some of the best "firemen" of the past and present are seen in action. Some black and white sequences.
W and W Productions — *Major League Baseball Productions*

Bulls Eye Archery **1985**
Sports
81601 50 mins C B, V P
Olympic Coach Dwight Nygurst demonstrates basic archery fundamentals.
Morris Video — *Morris Video*

Bullshot Crummond **1984**
Satire
78664 90 mins C B, V P
The Low Moan Spectacular comedy troupe performs this satire that trashes oldtime adventure serials.

RKO — *RKO HomeVideo*

Bullwhip 1958
Western
80843 80 mins C B, V P
Guy Madison, Rhonda Fleming, James Griffith, Peter Adams
A man falsely accused of murder saves himself from the hangman's noose by agreeing to a shotgun wedding.
Allied Artists — *Republic Pictures Home Video*

Bullwinkle & Rocky and Friends, Volume I 1960
Cartoons
64709 95 mins C CED P
Animated
A collection of cartoon segments featuring all the "Rocky and His Friends" characters, including Rocket J. Squirrel, Bullwinkle Moose, Boris Badenov, Natasha, Dudley Doright, Mr. Peabody and Sherman.
Filmtel; Jay Ward — *RCA VideoDiscs*

Bunco 1983
Drama
80887 60 mins C B, V P
Tom Selleck, Robert Urien, Donna Mills, Will Geer, Arte Johnson, Alan Feinstein
Two policemen working for the Los Angeles Police Department's Bunco Squad discover a college for con artists complete with tape-recorded lessons and on the job training.
Lorimar Productions — *Karl/Lorimar Home Video*

Bundle of Joy 1956
Comedy
11643 98 mins C B, V P
Debbie Reynolds, Eddie Fisher
Salesgirl, who saves an infant from falling off the steps of a foundling home, is mistaken for the child's mother.
Universal; Edmund Grainger — *United Home Video*

Bunnicula—The Vampire Rabbit 1982
Cartoons
80641 23 mins C B, V P
Animated
Strange things happen to a family after they adopt an abandoned bunny so their dog and cat team up to prove that their furry friend is a vampire in disguise.
Ruby-Spears Prods. — *Worldvision Home Video*

Burn! 1970
Drama
76045 113 mins C B, V P
Marlon Brando, Evarist Marquez, Renato Salvatori
An Italian-made saga about the rise of a people from slavery to freedom.
United Artists — *Key Video*

Burning, The 1982
Horror
59694 90 mins C B, V R, P
Brian Matthews, Leah Ayres
A story of macabre revenge set in the dark woods of a seemingly innocent summer camp.
MPAA:R
Harvey Weinstein — *THORN EMI/HBO Video*

Burnt Offerings 1976
Horror
78632 116 mins C B, V P
Oliver Reed, Karen Black, Bette Davis, Burgess Meredith, directed by Don Curtis
A family rents a house for the summer and they become affected by evil forces that possess the house.
MPAA:PG
United Artists — *MGM/UA Home Video*

Bury Me an Angel 1971
Drama
80663 85 mins C B, V, LV P
Dixie Peabody, Terry Mace, Clyde Ventura, Dan Haggerty
A female biker sets out to seek revenge against the men who killed her brother.
New World Pictures — *New World Video*

Bus Is Coming, The 1972
Drama/Romance
66242 95 mins C B, V R, P
A love story entwined with the problems of blacks in a small town.
William Thompson Productions — *Video City Productions*

Bus Stop 1956
Comedy
08460 96 mins C B, V, CED P
Marilyn Monroe, Arthur O'Connell, Hope Lange, Don Murray, Hans Conried, directed by Joshua Logan
A motley collection of travelers arrive at some truths about themselves while snowbound at an Arizona bus stop. Based on William Inge's play.
20th Century Fox — *CBS/Fox Video*

Bushido Blade, The 1980
Adventure/Suspense
59697 92 mins C B, V R, P
Richard Boone, James Earl Jones, Frank Converse
An action-packed samurai thriller of adventure and betrayal set in medieval Japan.

Arthur Rankin Jr — *THORN EMI/HBO Video*

Buster and Billie **1974**
Drama
81431 100 mins C B, V P
Jan-Michael Vincent, Joan Goodfellow, Clifton James, Pamela Sue Martin, directed by Daniel Petrie
Tragedy ensues when a popular high school student falls in love with the class tramp in rural Georgia in 1948. Available in VHS and Beta Hi-Fi.
MPAA:R
Columbia Pictures — *RCA/Columbia Pictures Home Video*

Buster Keaton Rides Again/The Railrodder **1965**
Comedy/Documentary
65229 81 mins C B, V, FO P
Buster Keaton
"The Railrodder" is a silent comedy short that returns Buster Keaton to the type of slapstick he made famous in his legendary 20's films. "Buster Keaton Rides Again" (in black-and-white) is a documentary-style look at Keaton filmed during the making of "The Railrodder." Besides scenes of Keaton at work, there is also a capsule rundown of his career.
National Film Board of Canada — *Video Yesteryear*

Buster Keaton: The Great Stone Face **1968**
Documentary/Comedy
17236 60 mins B/W B, V P
Narrated by Henry Morgan
This program from the Rohauer Collection contains footage of Buster Keaton in "Fatty at Coney Island," "Cops," "Ballonatics," "Day Dreams," and "The General."
Funnyman Inc — *Mastervision*

Bustin' Loose **1981**
Comedy
58211 94 mins C B, V, LV P
Richard Pryor, Cicely Tyson, Robert Christian, George Coe, Bill Quinn, directed by Oz Scott
A fast-talking con man reluctantly shepherds a busload of misplaced kids and their keeper cross-country.
MPAA:R
Universal; Richard Pryor; Michael Glick — *MCA Home Video*

Bustling Narrow Gauge/White Pass and Yukon/Rio Grande Southern/Trestles of Ophir **1951**
Trains
77362 56 mins B/W B, V P, T
This collection of four short films fondly recalls classic trains such as the San Juan and the White Pass.
Woodrow Gorman — *Blackhawk Films*

Butch Cassidy and the Sundance Kid **1969**
Adventure
09093 110 mins C B, V, LV P
Paul Newman, Robert Redford, Katharine Ross
A couple of legendary outlaws at the turn of the century take it on the lam with a beautiful, willing ex-school teacher.
Academy Awards '69: Best Song (Raindrops Keep Falling on My Head). MPAA:PG EL, SP
20th Century Fox — *CBS/Fox Video*

Butler's Dilemma, The **1943**
Comedy
63620 75 mins B/W B, V, FO P
Richard Hearne, Francis Sullivan, Hermione Gingold, Ian Fleming
A jewel thief and a playboy both clain the identity of a butler who never existed, with humorous results.
British National — *Video Yesteryear*

Butterflies Are Free **1972**
Comedy-Drama
13234 109 mins C B, V P
Goldie Hawn, Edward Albert, Eileen Heckart, Michael Glaser, directed by Milton Katselas
An actress helps a blind man gain independence from his over protective mother.
Academy Awards '72: Best Supporting Actress (Heckart). MPAA:PG
Columbia; MJ Frankovich — *RCA/Columbia Pictures Home Video*

Butterfly **1982**
Drama
59658 105 mins C B, V, LV, CED P
Pia Zadora, Stacy Keach, Orson Welles, Edward Albert, James Franciscus, Lois Nettleton, Stuart Whitman
James M. Cain's novel about an amoral young woman who uses her beauty and sensual appetite to manipulate the men in her life, including her father. Set in Nevada of the 1930's, father and daughter are drawn into a daring and forbidden love affair by their lust and desperation.
Golden Globe Awards '82: Newcomer of the Year (Zadora). MPAA:R
Analysis Films — *Vestron Video*

Butterfly Ball, The **1976**
Musical/Fantasy
80269 85 mins C B, V P
Twiggy, Ian Gillian, David Coverdale, narrated by Vincent Price.

This retelling of the 19th century classic combines the music of Roger Glover, live action and animation by Halas and Batchelor for a unique film experience.
Tony Klinger — *VCL Home Video*

By Design 1982
Comedy
63329 90 mins C B, V R, P
Patty Duke Astin, Sara Botsford
Two women who live together want to have a baby, so they embark on a search for the perfect stud.
MPAA:R
Atlantic Releasing Corp; Beryl Fox and Werner Aellen — *THORN EMI/HBO Video*

Bye, Bye, Birdie 1963
Musical
21283 112 mins C B, V P
Dick Van Dyke, Janet Leigh, Ann-Margret, Paul Lynde, Bobby Rydell, Trudi Ames, directed by George Sidney
The film version of the Broadway musical in which a rock and roll idol is drafted. Songs include "Put on a Happy Face."
Columbia — *RCA/Columbia Pictures Home Video*

Bye Bye Brazil 1979
Drama
53507 100 mins C B, V R, P
Jose Wilker, Betty Faria, Fabio Junior, directed by Carlos Diegues
A changing Brazil is seen through the eyes of four wandering minstrels, gypsy actors exploring the exotic and picturesque north.
Lucy Barreto; Brazil — *Warner Home Video*

C

Cabaret 1972
Musical-Drama
55207 119 mins C B, V, CED P
Liza Minnelli, Joel Grey, Michael York, directed by Bob Fosse
In early 1930's Berlin, singer Sally Bowles shares her English lover with a homosexual German baron. Songs include "Money, Money, Money," "Wilkommen," and "Mein Herr."
Academy Awards '72: Best Actress (Minnelli); Best Supporting Actor (Grey); Best Director (Fosse); Best Cinematography; Best Editing.
MPAA:PG
ABC Pictures; Allied Artists — *CBS/Fox Video*

Cabinet of Dr. Caligari 1919
Film-Avant-garde
06215 52 mins B/W B, V P
Conrad Veidt, Werner Krauss, directed by Robert Wiene
Silent classic in surrealistic style about a somnambulist under spell of mad doctor. New sound track and music.
Decla Bioscop — *Budget Video; International Historic Films; Discount Video Tapes; Video Yesteryear; Sheik Video; Western Film & Video Inc; Classic Video Cinema Collector's Club*

Cabo Blanco 1981
Drama
66599 87 mins C B, V P
Charles Bronson, Jason Robards, Dominque Sanda
A remake of "Casablanca," set in a South American village in the years just after World War II.
MPAA:R
Paul Joseph; Lance Hool — *Media Home Entertainment*

Cactus Flower 1969
Comedy
59604 103 mins C B, V P
Walter Matthau, Goldie Hawn, Ingrid Bergman, directed by Gene Saks
A middle-aged bachelor dentist gets involved with a kookie mistress and his prim and proper receptionist.
Academy Awards '69: Best Supporting Actress (Hawn). MPAA:PG
Columbia — *RCA/Columbia Pictures Home Video*

Caddie 1981
Drama
63338 107 mins C B, V R, P
Helen Morse, Jack Thompson
This is the story of a woman who leaves her unfaithful husband to face hardship and romance on her own in 1930's Australia.
Anthony Buckley Productions — *THORN EMI/HBO Video*

Caddyshack 1980
Comedy
54808 99 mins C B, V, LV R, P
Chevy Chase, Rodney Dangerfield, Ted Knight, Michael O'Keefe, Bill Murray, directed by Harold Ramis
This comic spoof takes place at Bushwood Country Club, where a young caddy is bucking to win the club's college scholarship. Within this context we meet an obnoxious club president, a playboy who is too laid back to keep his score, a vulgar, loud, extremely rich, but hated man, and a gopher-hunting groundskeeper.
MPAA:R
Warner Bros — *Warner Home Video; RCA VideoDiscs*

Caesar and Cleopatra 1945
Comedy
79106 135 mins C B, V P
Claude Rains, Vivien Leigh, Stewart Granger, Flora Robson
A filmed adaptation of the classic George Bernard Shaw play.
Rank/Gabriel Pascal — *VidAmerica*

Caesar's Hour 1956
Comedy/Variety
52460 52 mins B/W B, V, FO P
Sid Caesar, Carl Reiner, Howard Morris, Nanette Fabray
This episode of Sid Caesar's famous series is the last show of the 1956 season. Nanette Fabray plays Sid Caesar's long-suffering wife in one of several featured sketches.
NBC — *Video Yesteryear*

Caesar's Hour 1954
Television/Comedy
63624 59 mins B/W B, V, FO P
Sid Caesar, Howard Morris, Carl Reiner
First telecast on October 25, 1954, this is the fourth show of the comedy-variety series. Slapstick sketches, dance, and a circus act are featured, and original commercials for Speidel, Glenn Miller Records, and others are included.
NBC — *Video Yesteryear*

Caesar's Hour 1957
Comedy/Variety
78098 45 mins B/W B, V, FO P
Sid Caesar, Carl Reiner, Howard Morris, Janet Blair, Shirl Conway, Pat Carroll, Hugh Downs
A comedy show from Sid Caesar's variety series that was the replacement for "Your Show of Shows."
NBC — *Video Yesteryear*

Cage aux Folles, La 1979
Comedy
55585 91 mins C B, V, LV P
Ugo Tognazzi, Michel Serrault
A situation comedy about a club in St. Tropez notorious for putting on a drag show featuring men dressed as women, focusing on the manager of the club and the club's headliner who share an apartment.
MPAA:R
United Artists — *CBS/Fox Video; RCA VideoDiscs*

Cage Aux Folles II, La 1980
Comedy
58844 100 mins C B, V, CED P
Ugo Tognazzi, Michel Serrault, Marcel Bozzuffi, Michel Galabru, directed by Edouard Molinaro
The sequel to the highly successful "La Cage aux Folles." Albin sets out to prove to his companion that he still has sex appeal.
United Artists; Da Ma Produzione — *CBS/Fox Video*

Caged Fury 1980
Drama/Adventure
79389 90 mins C B, V P
Bernie William, Taafee O'Connell, Jeniffer Lane
American P.O.W's being held captive in Southeast Asia are brainwashed into becoming walking time bombs.
MPAA:R
Emily Blas — *World Premiere*

Caged Women 1984
Drama
73038 97 mins C B, V P
An undercover journalist enters a women's prison.
MPAA:R
Motion Picture Marketing — *Vestron Video*

Cahill: United States Marshal 1973
Western
74208 103 mins C B, V R, P
John Wayne, Gary Grimes, George Kennedy
The "Duke" stars as a marshal who comes to the aid of his sons who are mixed up with a gang of outlaws.
MPAA:PG
Michael Wayne; Batjac Productions — *Warner Home Video*

Caine Mutiny, The 1954
Drama
Closed Captioned
77240 125 mins C B, V P
Humphrey Bogart, Jose Ferrer, Van Johnson, Fred Mac Murray, directed by Edward Dmytryk
A group of naval officers revolt against a Captain they consider mentally unfit.
Columbia; Stanley Kramer — *RCA/Columbia Pictures Home Video*

Cain's Cutthroats 1971
Western
80827 87 mins C B, V R, P
Scott Brady, John Carradine, Robert Dix
A former Confederate army captain and a bounty hunting preacher team up to settle the score with the soldiers who gang raped his wife and murdered his son.
MPAA:R
Fanfare Productions — *Video Gems*

Cal 1984
Drama
77266 104 mins C B, V P
Helen Mirren, John Lynch, Donal McCann, Kitty Gibson, directed by Pat O'Connor

 (For explanation of codes, see USE GUIDE and KEY)

A 19-year-old IRA activist falls in love with a widowed Protestant librarian. The music is by Dire Straits guitarist Mark Knopfler.
Cannes Film Festival '84: Best Actress (Mirren). MPAA:R
Warner Bros.; Goldcrest — *Warner Home Video*

Caledonian Dreams **1982**
Photography/Music
60577 46 mins C LV P
Directed by Shoji Otake
This sequel to "Oriental Dreams" follows the intimate escapades of three beautiful women as they explore the exotic lifestyle of the South Seas. Music by Norio Maeda and Windbreakers. Stereo.
Japanese — *Pioneer Video Imports*

California Angels: Team Highlights **1982**
Baseball
81135 30 mins C B, V P
Bob Boone, Reggie Jackson, Fred Lynn, Bobby Grich 3 pgms
This series chronicles the first twenty-one years of the California Angels.
1.1961-1971: The First Ten Years 2.1981: In The Groove For '82 3.1982: Something To Prove
Major League Baseball — *Major League Baseball Productions*

California Dreaming **1979**
Drama
80701 93 mins C B, V P
Dennis Christopher, Tanya Roberts, Glynnis O'Connor, John Calvin, Seymour Cassel
A young man heads west to California where he meets up with a beach groupie and a surfer who teach him something about life and love.
MPAA:R
American International Pictures — *Vestron Video*

California Girls **1984**
Comedy
70225 83 mins C B, V P
Al Music, Mary McKinley, Alicia Allen, Lantz Douglas, Barbara Parks
A radio station stages an outrageous contest, and three sexy ladies prove to be tough competition. Soundtrack features music by The Police, Kool & the Gang, Blondie, Queen and 10cc.
William Webb; Monica Webb — *VCL Home Video*

California Gold Rush **1981**
Adventure
65760 100 mins C B, V P
Robert Hays, John Dehner, Ken Curtis
In 1849, a young aspiring writer in search of adventure arrives in Sutter's Fort and takes on a job at the local sawmill. When gold is found, Sutter's Fort is soon overrun with fortune hunters whose greed, violence and corruption threaten to tear apart the peaceful community.
James L Conway — *United Home Video*

California Suite **1978**
Comedy
47023 103 mins C B, V, LV P
Alan Alda, Michael Caine, Bill Cosby, Jane Fonda, Walter Matthau, Richard Pryor, Maggie Smith
This Neil Simon comedy has four different story lines, all set in the Beverly Hills Hotel.
Academy Award '78: Best Supporting Actress (Smith). MPAA:PG
Columbia; Ray Stark — *RCA/Columbia Pictures Home Video; RCA VideoDiscs*

Caligula **1980**
Drama
65475 143 mins C B, V P
Malcolm McDowell, Sir John Gielgud, Peter O'Toole
Impeccably faithful to the historical events of Caligula's Rome, this program also captures in detail the decadence and debauchery that marked his reign. Explicit sex and violence.
Bob Guccione; Franco Rossellini — *Vestron Video*

Caligula **1980**
Drama
65476 105 mins C B, V, LV, CED P
Malcolm McDowell, Sir John Gielgud, Peter O'Toole
A slightly edited version, with some of the sexually explicit scenes toned down.
MPAA:R
Bob Guccione; Franco Rossellini — *Vestron Video*

Call of the Canyon **1942**
Western
44987 71 mins B/W B, V P, T
Gene Autry, Smiley Burnette
A crooked agent for a local meat packer won't pay a fair price, so Gene goes off to talk to the head man to set him straight.
Republic — *Blackhawk Films; Video Connection*

Call of the Wild **1972**
Adventure
47389 105 mins C B, V R, P
Charlton Heston, Michele Mercier, George Eastman
Jack London's famous story about a man whose survival depends upon his knowledge of

the Alaskan wilderness comes to life in this film version.
MPAA:PG
Intercontinental Releasing Corp — *Warner Home Video*

Call of the Wild 1983
Adventure/Cartoons
81169 68 mins C B, V P
Animated
This is an adaptation of the Jack London story about a dog's trek across the Alaskan tundra.
Northstar Productions — *Vestron Video*

Call Out the Marines 1942
Comedy/Adventure
73692 67 mins B/W B, V P
Victor McLaglen, Binnie Barnes, Paul Kelly, Edmund Lowe
A group of army buddies re-enlist to break up a spy ring.
RKO — *RKO HomeVideo*

Call to Glory 1984
Drama
81106 120 mins C B, V R, P
Craig T. Nelson, Cindy Pickett, Gabriel Damon, Keenan Wynn, Elisabeth Shue, G.D. Spradlin
This is the premier episode of the series about the turbulent times faced by an Air Force pilot and his family during the Cuban Missile Crisis.
Tisch/Avnet Productions; Paramount TV — *Paramount Home Video*

Camel Boy, The 1984
Adventure
76779 78 mins C B, V P
Animated
This is the true story of a young Arabian boy who befriends a camel and their treacherous trek across the desert.
Yorum Gross Films — *Vestron Video*

Camelot 1967
Musical
58223 150 mins C B, V, LV R, P
Richard Harris, Vanessa Redgrave, Daivd Hemmings, directed by Joshua Logan
The long-running Broadway musical about King Arthur, Guinevere, and Lancelot. Score by Lerner and Loewe includes "If Ever I Would Leave You," "How to Handle a Woman" and "Camelot."
Warner Bros — *Warner Home Video*

Camouflage 194?
World War II
11227 20 mins C B, V, FO P
Animated
A training film by the Walt Disney studios for the Armed Forces, in which Yehudi the Chameleon teaches camouflage to young Air Corps fliers. Contains some condemning attitudes towards Japan.
Walt Disney Productions — *Video Yesteryear*

Campus Corpse, The 1977
Horror
76767 92 mins C B, V P
Charles Martin Smith
A young man discovers evil doings when he pledges to a college fraternity.
The Miraleste Company — *Vestron Video*

Can I Do It...Till I Need Glasses? 1980
Comedy
56740 72 mins C B, V P
Robin Williams, Roger Behr, Debra Klose, Moose Carlson, Walter Olkewicz
This suggestive comedy features outrageous, risque humor, and stars TV's "Mork," Robin Williams.
Mike Callie — *Media Home Entertainment*

Can She Bake a Cherry Pie? 1983
Comedy-Drama
72448 118 mins C B, V P
Karen Black, Michael Emil, Michael Margotta, Frances Fisher, Martin Frydberg
This critically acclaimed film concerns the doubts involved when two people contemplate getting married. The official U.S. selection at the 1983 Cannes Festival.
International Rainbow Pictures; Jagfilm Productions — *Monterey Home Video*

Canadian Capers... Cartoons Volume I 19??
Cartoons/Christmas
65231 61 mins C B, V, FO P
Animated
A collection of innovative animated shorts produced by the National Film Board of Canada. Titles include: "The Great Toy Robbery," "The Animal Movie," "The Story of Christmas," "The Energy Carol," "The Bear's Christmas," "Carrousel" and "TV Sale."
National Film Board of Canada — *Video Yesteryear*

Canadian Capers... Cartoons Volume II 19??
Cartoons
65232 58 mins C B, V, FO P
Animated
A second collection of thought-provoking cartoons from the National Film Board of Canada, including "Spinnolio," "Doodle Film," "Hot Stuff," "The Cruise," "The Specialists" and "No Apple for Johnny."
National Film Board of Canada — *Video Yesteryear*

Candid Candid Camera 1983
Comedy
66106 55 mins C B, V, CED P
Allen Funt
A compilation of funny, sexy escapades compiled especially for home video.
Allen Funt — *Vestron Video*

Candidate, The 1972
Satire
44590 105 mins C B, V R, P
Robert Redford, Peter Boyle, Don Porter, Allen Garfield, Karen Carlson, Melvyn Douglas, directed by Michael Ritchie
A true to life look at politics and political campaigning. A young, idealistic lawyer is talked into trying for the Senate seat and learns the truth about running for office.
Academy Awards '72: Best Story and Screenplay (Larner). MPAA:PG
Warner Bros — *Warner Home Video; RCA VideoDiscs*

Candleshoe 1977
Adventure/Comedy
56875 101 mins C CED P
Jodie Foster, David Niven, Helen Hayes
A street-wise tomboy poses as a long-lost granddaughter to help a villain steal a fortune on the estate, Candleshoe.
MPAA:G
Ron Miller, Walt Disney — *RCA VideoDiscs*

Candleshoe 1978
Comedy/Adventure
77530 101 mins C B, V R, P
Helen Hayes, David Niven, Jodie Foster
A Los Angeles street kid poses an an English matron's long lost granddaughter in order to steal a fortune hidden in her country estate, Candleshoe.
MPAA:G
Walt Disney Productions — *Walt Disney Home Video*

Candy-Candy 1981
Cartoons
53157 60 mins C B, V P
Animated
This animated program for children is designed in soap opera fashion.
Ziv Intl — *Family Home Entertainment*

Candy Tangerine Man, The 197?
Drama
80423 88 mins C B, V P
John Daniels, Tom Hankerson, Eli Haines, Marva Farmer
A respectable businessman leads a double life as a loving father and as Los Angeles most powerful pimp.
Matt Cimber — *Unicorn Video*

Canned Heat Boogie Assault 1983
Music-Performance
65212 60 mins C B, V P
America's premier boogie band comes to life in their very first rock video. In Beta Hi-Fi and stereo VHS.
Full Circle Productions — *Monterey Home Video*

Cannery Row 1982
Comedy-Drama
59846 120 mins C B, V, CED P
Nick Nolte, Debra Winger, directed by David S. Ward
Steinbeck's tale of down-and-outers who struggle to survive in a seedy part of town is brought to life in this screen adaptation.
MPAA:PG
MGM — *MGM/UA Home Video*

Cannon Ball, The/The Eyes Have It 192?
Comedy
58599 41 mins B/W B, V P, T
Chester Conklin, Keystone Cops, Ben Turpin, Georgia O'Dell, Helen Gilmore, Jack Lipson
Chester Conklin stars in "The Cannon Ball" (1915), as an explosives expert in the Boom Powder Factory. "The Eyes Have It" (1928), stars Ben Turpin involved in another misunderstanding with wifey and mother-in-law. Silent.
Mack Sennett — *Blackhawk Films*

Cannonball 1976
Adventure
51989 93 mins C B, V R, P
David Carradine, Bill McKinney, Veronica Hamel, Gerrit Graham, Robert Carradine
A variety of ruthless and determined people compete for the $100,000 grand prize in an illicit cross-country auto race.
MPAA:PG
New World Pictures — *Warner Home Video*

Cannonball Run, The 1981
Comedy
58895 95 mins C B, V, LV, CED P
Burt Reynolds, Farrah Fawcett, Roger Moore, Dom DeLuise, Dean Martin, Sammy Davis Jr, Jack Elam, Adrienne Barbeau, Peter Fonda
Reynolds and sidekick Dom DeLuise disguise themselves as paramedics in order to foil the cops while they compete in the cross-country Cannonball race.
MPAA:PG
20th Century Fox — *Vestron Video*

Cannonball Run II 1984
Comedy
78621 109 mins C B, V, LV P
Burt Reynolds, Dom DeLuise, Jamie Farr, Marilu Henner, Shirley MacLaine, direct by Hal Needham
A group of race car drivers are after a one million dollar prize in a no holds barred cross country car race.
MPAA:PG
Warner Bros; Golden Harvest — *Warner Home Video*

Can't Stop the Music 1980
Musical
58456 120 mins C B, V R, P
Valerie Perrine, Bruce Jenner, Steve Guttenberg, Paul Sand, The Village People, directed by Nancy Walker
A retired model invites friends from Greenwich Village to a party to help the career of her roommate, an aspiring disco composer.
MPAA:PG
Allan Carr; Associated Film Distributors — *THORN EMI/HBO Video*

Cantinflas 1984
Cartoons
74077 60 mins C B, V P
Animated
The delightful cartoon character Cantinflas takes you on a trip through history to meet King Tut, Daniel Boone, Madame Curie and many other famous people.
Diamexsa — *Family Home Entertainment*

Cantinflas, Volume II: Galaxies and Gomes 1984
Cartoons
78373 60 mins C B, V P
Animated
Cantinflas takes a tour of the galaxy in an alien's space scooter and learns all about sports in his return visit to Earth.
Family Entertainment — *Family Home Entertainment*

Cantonen Iron Kung Fu 197?
Martial arts/Adventure
47706 90 mins C B, V P
Liang Jia Ren
The ten tigers of Quon Tung perfect martial arts skills known as Cantonen Iron Kung Fu.
Jing Kno Jung — *Master Arts Video; World Video Enterprises*

Capricorn One 1978
Science fiction
45059 123 mins C B, V, LV, CED P
Elliot Gould, James Brolin, Brenda Vaccaro
The whole world is watching America's first manned space flight to Mars. But before the countdown ends, three astronauts are plunged into a battle for survival in an incredible cover-up conspiracy.
MPAA:R
Warner Brothers — *CBS/Fox Video*

Captain Apache 1972
Western
12028 95 mins C B, V P
Lee Van Cleef, Carroll Baker, Stuart Whitman
An Apache is assigned by Union intelligence to investigate an Indian commissioner's murder.
Philip Yordan; Official Films — *King of Video; Prism*

Captain Blood 1935
Adventure
60427 99 mins B/W B, V, CED P
Errol Flynn, Olivia DeHavilland, Basil Rathbone, J. Carrol Naish, Guy Kibbee, Lionel Atwill
An exciting adaptation of the Sabatini adventure story of a pirate and his swashbuckling exploits.
Warner Bros — *CBS/Fox Video; RCA VideoDiscs*

Captain Caution 1940
Adventure
64373 84 mins B/W B, V, 3/4U P
Victor Mature, Louise Platt, Bruce Cabot, Alan Ladd
During the War of 1812, a young girl takes over her late father's ship and does battle with the British.
Hal Roach — *Nostalgia Merchant*

Captain Future in Space 197?
Cartoons/Science fiction
56748 54 mins C B, V P
Animated
The outer-space adventures of Captain Future and his crew aboard the spaceship Comet, fighting evil and making the universe safe for mankind. Available in English and Spanish versions.
EL, SP
ZIV International — *Media Home Entertainment*

Captain Harlock 1980
Science fiction/Cartoons
53158 60 mins C B, V P
Animated
Captain Harlock, the space pirate, is left alone to protect Earth from invasion by an evil alien planet.
Ziv Intl — *Family Home Entertainment*

Captain Harlock 1981
Cartoons/Adventure
69811 60 mins C B, V P
Animated

(For explanation of codes, see USE GUIDE and KEY)

The stardate is 2977, and Earth is in grave danger of being attacked by a mysterious alien force. Only one man—the famous freedom fighter, Captain Harlock—can save the planet from total destruction.
Ziv International — *Family Home Entertainment*

Captain Kangaroo and His Friends **1985**
Variety
81073 60 mins C B, V P
Bob Keeshan, Mr. Greenjeans, Joan Rivers, Phil Donahue, Dolly Parton
Join Captain Kangaroo and his special guests as they participate in many enjoyable adventures.
Jim Hirschfeld — *MPI Home Video*

Captain Kangaroo and His Friends **1985**
Children
70593 60 mins C B, V P
Bob Keeshan, Phil Donahue, Joan Rivers, Dolly Parton
Composed of short clips from the Captain's library of shows, this program introduces the young viewer to many of the Kangaroo guy's buddies.
Enclyclopedia Britannica Educational Corporation — *MPI Home Video*

Captain Kangaroo and the Right Thing to Do **1985**
Children
70594 60 mins C B, V P
Bob Keeshan
Composed of short clips from the Captain's library of shows, this program offers advice for life to youngsters.
Encyclopedia Britannica Educational Corporation — *MPI Home Video*

Captain Kangaroo's Baby Animal Album **1985**
Children
70591 60 mins C B, V P
Bob Keeshan
Composed of short clips from the Captain's library of shows, this program features segments designed to inform young humans about baby critters.
Encyclopedia Britannica Educational Corporation — *MPI Home Video*

Captain Kangaroo's Favorite Stories **1985**
Fairy tales
76924 58 mins C B, V P
Bob Keeshan, Lumpy Brannum, Gus Allegretti
Captain Kangaroo reads from his favorite children's stories.
Jim Hirschfeld — *MPI Home Video*

Captain Kronos: Vampire Hunter **1974**
Horror/Science fiction
60216 91 mins C B, V R, P
Horst Janson, John Carson, Caroline Munro
Captain Kronos sets out to capture a vampire before more beautiful young girls fall prey to his curse.
MPAA:R
Albert Fennell — *Paramount Home Video*

Captain Scarlet Vs. The Mysterons **1980**
Science fiction
77422 90 mins C B, V P
Animated
When Captain Scarlet's expeditionary team mistakenly fires upon an extraterrestrial military complex, the humorless aliens retaliate by setting out to destroy the world.
ITC Entertainment — *Family Home Entertainment*

Captain Scarlett **1953**
Adventure
80033 75 mins C B, V P
Richard Greene, Leonora Amar, Isobel del Puerto, Nedrick Young
A nobleman and his friend take on French Royalists who demand loyalty payments from poor French citizens.
United Artists; Howard Dimsdale — *Republic Pictures Home Video; World Video Pictures; Video Gems; Hal Roach Studios; Discount Video Tapes*

Captains Courageous **1937**
Drama
53407 116 mins B/W B, V P
Spencer Tracy, Lionel Barrymore, Freddie Bartholemew, Mickey Rooney, Melvyn Douglas, Charley Grapewin, John Carradine
A spoiled rich boy falls off a cruise liner and lives for a while among fisher folk who teach him about life. Based on the Rudyard Kipling novel.
Academy Award '37: Best Actor (Tracy).
MGM; Louis D Lighton — *MGM/UA Home Video*

Captain's Paradise, The **1954**
Comedy
66019 89 mins B/W B, V R, P
Alec Guinness, Yvonne de Carlo
The amiable Captain of the Golden Fleece marries two women.
London Films — *THORN EMI/HBO Video*

Car Wash **1976**
Comedy
53392 97 mins C B, V P

Franklyn Ajaye, Sully Boyar, Richard Brestoff, George Carlin, Richard Pryor, Ivan Dixon, Antonio Fargas
A day in the lives of the people involved in a car wash operation including the pot-smoking owner's son and a cab driver looking for a missing passenger.
MPAA:PG
Universal; Art Linson and Gary Stromberg — *MCA Home Video*

Carbon Copy **1981**
Comedy
59333 92 mins C B, V, LV, CED P
George Segal, Susan St. James, Jack Warden, Paul Winfield, Dick Martin, Vicky Dawson, Tom Poston, directed by Michael Schultz
A business executive faces the arrival of his heretofore unknown son who happens to be black.
MPAA:PG
Carter De Haven; Stanley Shapiro — *Embassy Home Entertainment*

Care Bears Battle the Freeze Machine, The **1984**
Fantasy
Closed Captioned
66615 60 mins C B, V P
Animated
The Care Bears' adventure with the Freeze Machine leads off this tape wich also includes two read-a-long Care Bears stories, "The Witch Down the Street" and "Sweet Dreams for Sally."
CPG Products Corp — *Family Home Entertainment*

Care Bears in the Land Without Feeling, The **1983**
Cartoons
69809 60 mins C B, V P
Animated
The Care Bears attempt to save a little boy named Kevin from the icy spell of Professor Coldheart and turn the Land Without Feeling into a land of friendship and love.
CPG Products Corp — *Family Home Entertainment*

Care Bears Movie, The **1985**
Cartoons
80692 90 mins C B, V P
Animated, voices of Mickey Rooney and Georgia Engel
The Care Bears leave their cloud home in care-a-lot to try and teach earthlings how to share their feelings of love and caring for each other.
MPAA:G
Samuel Goldwyn — *Vestron Video*

Carefree **1938**
Musical
00272 83 mins B/W B, V, 3/4U P
Fred Astaire, Ginger Rogers
Dizzy radio singer falls for her psychiatrist in this classic musical with an Irving Berlin score.
RKO; Pandro S Berman — *Nostalgia Merchant*

Caring for Your Newborn **1985**
Infants
81535 55 mins C B, V P
Dr. Avner Kauffman and Frank Beaman answer the most often asked questions concerning newborn children.
Maljack Productions — *MPI Home Video*

Caring for Your Newborn with Dr. Benjamin Spock **1980**
Infants
44953 111 mins C B, V P
In this program Dr. Benjamin Spock gives advice and guidance on baby care. He demonstrates with clear visual presentations everything from bathing the baby to treating early disorders and discomforts.
Gregory Jackson — *VidAmerica; RCA VideoDiscs*

Carlin at Carnegie **1983**
Comedy-Performance
65216 60 mins C B, V, CED P
It's George Carlin at his funniest, with his classic routine of the "Seven Words You Can Never Say on Television."
Brenda Carlin — *Vestron Video*

Carlin on Campus **1984**
Comedy-Performance
80115 59 mins C B, V, LV, CED P
George Carlin performs his classic routines and new material in this concert filmed at UCLA's Wadsworth Theater.
Carlin Productions — *Vestron Video*

Carmen **1983**
Drama
79223 99 mins C B, V P
Antonio Gades, Laura Del Sol, Paco De Lucia, Cristina Hoyos, directed by Carlos Saura
A choreographer casting a dance production of "Carmen" falls in love with his leading lady and winds up acting out the Bizet opera in real life. In Spanish with English Subtitles.
MPAA:R SP
Orion Classics — *Media Home Entertainment*

Carnal Knowledge **1971**
Drama
08369 96 mins C B, V, LV, CED P

Jack Nicholson, Candice Bergen, Art Garfunkel, Ann-Margret, Rita Moreno, directed by Mike Nichols
This adult satire takes a look at two young men from their college days in the 1940's and follows them into the seventies, exploring the way they treat their women.
MPAA:R EL, JA
Avco Embassy; Mike Nichols Production — *Embassy Home Entertainment; RCA VideoDiscs*

Carnival Rock **1957**
Musical-Drama
73544 80 mins B/W B, V P
Directed by Roger Carman
This early rock movie was one of Roger Corman's earliest and features music by Bob Luman?David Houston and the Blockbusters
Howco Films — *Admit One Video*

Carnival Story **1954**
Drama
75933 94 mins C B, V R, P
Anne Baxter, Steve Cochran, Lye Bettger, George Nader
The story of a German girl who joins an American-owned carnival in Germany.
RKO — *Video Gems; Discount Video Tapes*

Carnivores, The **1983**
Documentary/Animals
63668 90 mins C B, V R, P
The flesh-eaters of the animal kingdom—bears, lions, tigers, and others—and their survival instincts are the focus of this nature documentary.
Bill Burrud Productions — *Walt Disney Home Video*

Carny **1980**
Drama
56755 102 mins C B, V, CED P
Gary Busey, Robbie Robertson, Jodie Foster, directed by Robert Kaylor
A carnival "bozo" and the carnival "patchman" both fall in love with a young runaway in this drama set in a traveling carnival.
MPAA:R
Robbie Robertson, Lorimar, Jonathan Taplin — *CBS/Fox Video*

Carol Burnett Show: Bloopers and Outtakes, The **1977**
Comedy/Outtakes and bloopers
47489 92 mins B/W B, V, FO P
Carol Burnett, Dick Van Dyke, Tim Conway, Steve Lawrence, Eydie Gorme, Harvey Korman, Don Crichton
A collection of flubs, missed lines, malfunctioning props and other goofs from "The Carol Burnett Show," featuring the whole cast cracking up over their mistakes.
CBS — *Video Yesteryear*

Carpathian Eagle, The **1981**
Horror/Mystery
77441 60 mins C B, V P
Suzzane Danielle, Sian Phillips, Pierce Brosnan, Anthony Valentine, directed by Francis Megahy
The police are baffled by a bizzare series of murders where the victims' hearts are ripped out.
Hammer House of Horror — *Thriller Video*

Carpenters, Yesterday Once More, The **1985**
Music video
77248 60 mins C B, V P
Richard Carpenter, Karen Carpenter
This is a retrospective look at the musical career of The Carpenters.
A & M Video — *A & M Video; RCA/Columbia Pictures Home Video*

Carrie **1976**
Horror
55590 98 mins C B, V, LV, CED P
Sissy Spacek, Piper Laurie, John Travolta, William Katt, Amy Irving, directed by Brian de Palma
A withdrawn teenager lives in a ramshackle house with her religious fanatic mother. On the night of the senior prom, Carrie gets revenge on all who have hurt her, through her special powers. Based on the novel by Stephen King.
MPAA:R
United Artists — *CBS/Fox Video; RCA VideoDiscs*

Carrott Gets Rowdie **1984**
Comedy-Performance
66358 60 mins C B, V P
Popular English comedian Jasper Carrott comments upon the differences between British and American people in this concert taped in Tampa Bay, Florida.
Pacific Arts — *Pacific Arts Video*

Carry On Behind **1975**
Comedy
59829 95 mins C B, V P
Kenneth Williams, Elke Sommer, Joan Sims
The "Carry On" crew head for an archeological dig and find themselves sharing the site with a holiday caravan.
Peter Rogers — *Embassy Home Entertainment*

Carry On Cleo **1965**
Satire/Comedy
66026 91 mins C B, V R, P

Sidney James, Amanda Barrie, Kenneth Williams, Kenneth Connor, Jim Dale, Charles Hawtrey, Joan Sims
A saucy spoof of Shakespeare's "Antony and Cleopatra" in the inimitable "Carry On" style.
Governor Films — *THORN EMI/HBO Video*

Carry On Nurse **1958**
Comedy
43012 86 mins B/W B, V, FO P
Shirley Eaton, Kenneth Connor
The men's ward in a British hospital declares war on their nurses and the rest of the hospital. English slapstick. The first of the "Carry On" series.
Governor Films; British — *Video Yesteryear*

Cars: 1984-1985—Live, The **1985**
Music-Performance
81160 60 mins C B, V, LV, CED P
Ric Ocasek, Elliot Easton, Greg Hawkes, David Robinson, Ben Orr
The Cars perform such hits as "You Might Think," "Drive" and "Hello Again" in this concert video. Hi-Fi stereo sound in both formats.
FF Productions — *Vestron Video*

Carson City Kid **1940**
Western
14375 54 mins B/W B, V P
Roy Rogers, Dale Evans
Roy sings and fights his way to justice and love.
Republic — *Video Connection; Nostalgia Merchant; Discount Video Tapes*

Carthage in Flames **1960**
Drama
70374 90 mins C B, V R, P
Anne Heywood, Jose Suarez, Pierre Brasseur
This tape shows the destruction of Carthage in a blood and guts battle for domination of the known world. A tender love story comes with this colorful epic.
Columbia — *Video City Productions*

Cartoon Carnival Volume I **194?**
Cartoons
64837 90 mins C B, V P
Animated
A collection of ten original Max Fleischer cartoons, featuring Little Lulu and others, plus two "Bouncing Ball" sing-alongs. Mastered from the original negatives.
Max Fleischer; Paramount — *Republic Pictures Home Video*

Cartoon Carnival Volume II **194?**
Cartoons
64838 90 mins C B, V P
Animated
Another package of ten Max Fleischer cartoons, featuring Casper and several "Bouncing Ball" sing-alongs. Mastered from the original negatives.
Max Fleischer; Paramount — *Republic Pictures Home Video*

Cartoon Cavalcade **1935**
Cartoons
77365 23 mins C B, V P, T
Animated
Here are three classic cartoons from Burt Gillette and UB Iwerkes: "Molly Moo Cow and the Indians," "The Three Bears," and "Molly Moo Cow and Rip Van Winkle."
RKO Radio Pictures — *Blackhawk Films*

Cartoon Classics in Color #1 **1934**
Cartoons
78088 60 mins C B, V, FO P
Animated
Eight cartoon classics filled with color, movement and lots of fun comprise this tape: "Little Black Sambo," "Jack Frost," "Sinbad the Sailor," "Simple Simon," "Ali Baba," Molly Moo Cow and the Butterflies," "The Toonerville Trolley," and "Somewhere in Dreamland."
RKO; Van Beuren — *Video Yesteryear*

Cartoon Classics in Color #2 **194?**
Cartoons
78119 60 mins C B, V, FO P
Animated
Eight fun and exciting, animated cartoons featuring some of cartoon favorites: Daffy Duck in "Yankee Doodle Duffy," Porky Pig in "Ali Baba Bound" and Bugs Bunny in "Falling Hare."
Warner Bros; Max Fleischer — *Video Yesteryear*

Cartoon Classics of the 1930's **193?**
Cartoons
03591 58 mins C B, V P
Animated
Eight cartoon classics of the 1930's including "Felix the Cat," "Daffy and the Dinosaur," and "Bold King Cole."
Ub Iwerks; Warner Bros; Fleischer — *Media Home Entertainment*

Cartoon Classics Volume One: Chip 'n' Dale Featuring Donald Duck 194?
Cartoons
66055 45 mins C B, V, LV, CED R, P
Animated
Six cartoon shorts: "Chip 'n' Dale," "Three for Breakfast," "Winter Storage," "Up a Tree," "Out on a Limb," "Out of Scale," and "Corn Chips."
Walt Disney Productions — *Walt Disney Home Video*

Cartoon Classics Volume Two: Pluto 194?
Cartoons
66056 45 mins C B, V, LV, CED R, P
Animated
Six Pluto shorts: "Pluto's Fledgling," "The Pointer," "Private Pluto," "The Legend of Coyote Rock," "Bone Trouble," "Camp Dog," and "In Dutch."
Walt Disney Productions — *Walt Disney Home Video*

Cartoon Classics Volume Three: Disney's Scary Tales 194?
Cartoons
66177 55 mins C B, V, LV, CED R, P
Animated
Seven "chilling" Disney cartoon treasures including "The Haunted House," "Pluto's Judgement Day," and "The Skeleton Dance," the first of the Silly Symphonies (1929).
Walt Disney Productions — *Walt Disney Home Video*

Cartoon Classics Volume Four: Sport Goofy 194?
Cartoons
66178 50 mins C B, V, LV, CED R, P
Animated
Goofy comically demonstrates how to play tennis, gymnastics, baseball and hockey.
Walt Disney Productions — *Walt Disney Home Video*

Cartoon Classics Volume 5: Disney's Best of 1931-1948 19??
Cartoons
69319 48 mins C B, V, LV R, P
Animated
This collection of six animated short subjects that won or were nominated for Academy Awards from 1931 to 1948 includes "The Ugly Duckling" (1939); "Mickey's Orphans" (black and white; 1931); "Flowers and Trees" (1932); "Truant Officer Donald" (1941); "The Country Cousin" (1936); and "Mickey and the Seal" (1948).
Academy Awards: Cartoon Short Subject Winner '39 ("The Ugly Duckling"); Cartoon Short Subject Winner '31-'32 ("Flowers and Trees"); Cartoon Short Subject Winner '36 ("The Country Cousin").
Walt Disney — *Walt Disney Home Video*

Cartoon Classics Volume 7: More of Disney's Best: 1932-1946 19??
Cartoons
66314 50 mins C B, V R, P
Animated
An assortment of six classic shorts, all of which were Oscar nominees or winners, including "The Three Little Pigs" (1933), "The Brave Little Tailor" (1938) and "The Old Mill" (1937), which was the first cartoon to use Disney's multiplane camera.
Academy Awards '33 and '37: Best Cartoon.
Walt Disney Productions — *Walt Disney Home Video*

Cartoon Classics Volume 8: Sport Goofy's Vacation 1983
Cartoons
66315 41 mins C B, V R, P
Animated
Goofy takes a break from his athletic endeavors to relax on a variety of disastrous vacations.
Walt Disney Productions — *Walt Disney Home Video*

Cartoon Classics Volume 9: Donald Duck's First 50 Years 1983
Cartoons
66316 45 mins C B, V R, P
Animated
Half a century of great Donald Duck cartoons are featured, starting with Donald's first appearance in the 1934 short, "The Wise Little Hen." Other cartoons highlight his first meeting with Daisy Duck and the introduction of his nephews, Huey, Dewey and Louie.
Walt Disney Productions — *Walt Disney Home Video*

Cartoon Classics Volume 10: Mickey's Crazy Careers 1983
Cartoons
66317 46 mins C B, V R, P
Animated
Mickey Mouse shows off some of the unusual occupations he has tried through the years in this collection of vintage cartoons which includes "Clock Cleaners," "Magician Mickey" and "The Mail Pilot." Several are in black-and-white.

Walt Disney Productions — *Walt Disney Home Video*

Cartoon Classics Volume II: Continuing Adventures of Chip 'N' Dale Featuring Donald Duck **194?**
Cartoons
76810 50 mins C B, V R, P
Animated
Those impish chipmunks Chip 'N' Dale are out to make loads of trouble for Donald Duck in this collection of seven cartoons.
Walt Disney Productions — *Walt Disney Home Video*

Cartoon Classics Volume 12: Disney's Tall Tales **1942**
Cartoons
76811 50 mins C B, V R, P
Animated
A collection of six classic tales such as "Casey at the Bat" and "The Big Bad Wolf" told in the inimitable Disney style.
Walt Disney Productions — *Walt Disney Home Video*

Cartoon Collection I **194?**
Cartoons
33686 115 mins C B, V, 3/4U P
Bugs Bunny, Daffy Duck, Betty Boop, Popeye, Donald Duck, Casper the Friendly Ghost
A collection of sixteen classic cartoons from the thirties, forties and fifties. Included are Bugs Bunny in, "All This and Rabbit Stew," Daffy Duck in, "Scrap Happy Daffy," Popeye in "Eugene the Jeep," and "Poop Deck Pappy," and Betty Boop in "Minnie the Moocher." Some in black and white.
Warner Bros; Max Fleischer; Walt Disney — *Shokus Video*

Cartoon Collection II: Warner Brothers Cartoons **194?**
Cartoons
33687 115 mins C B, V, 3/4U P
Animated
A collection of sixteen favorite Warner Brothers cartoons from the forties and fifties including Bugs Bunny in "Fresh Hare," and "Falling Hare," Daffy Duck in "The Daffy Commando," and Daffy's Southern Exposure," and Porky Pig in "Notes to You," and "Porky's Midnight Matinee."
Warner Bros — *Shokus Video*

Cartoon Collection III: Vintage Warner Bros. Cartoons **194?**
Cartoons
66458 115 mins B/W B, V, 3/4U P
Animated
Another package of 16 Warner Bros. cartoons from the 1930's and 40's, featuring Bugs Bunny, Daffy Duck and Porky Pig. Titles include "Coal Black and de Sebben Dwarfs," "Calling Dr. Porky," "Tom Turkey and Daffy" and "Daffy Doc."
Warner Bros — *Shokus Video*

Cartoon Collection IV: Early Animation **193?**
Cartoons
76012 110 mins B/W B, V, 3/4U P
Animated
Sixteen golden classics from the depression era, all in their original fully-animated form in glorious black and white.
Max Fleischer et al — *Shokus Video*

Cartoon Magic **19??**
Cartoons
65223 55 mins C B, V P
Animated
This first package of vintage cartoons from the MGM vaults contains eight popular favorites: "The Captain and the Kids" (1938), "Blue Danube" (1939), "The Unwelcome Guest" (1945), "Screwball Squirrel" (1944), "The Lonesome Stranger" (1940), "The Captain's Christmas" (1938), "Barney Bear" (1939) and "King-Sized Canary" (1947).
MGM — *MGM/UA Home Video*

Cartoon Parade No. 1 **194?**
Cartoons
07345 120 mins C B, V, 3/4U P
Animated
A collection of cartoons starring Bugs Bunny, Daffy Duck, Porky Pig, Popeye, Superman, and more.
Warner Bros — *Nostalgia Merchant*

Cartoon Parade No. 2 **194?**
Cartoons
44857 117 mins C B, V, 3/4U P
Animated
Laugh with some of your favorite cartoon characters. Included are Bugs Bunny in "Wabbit Who Came to Supper," Popeye in "Popeye Meets Ali Baba," Superman in "Terror on the Midway," Little Lulu in "Bored of Education," and many more.
Warner Bros — *Nostalgia Merchant*

Cartoon Parade No. 3 **194?**
Cartoons
44858 110 mins C B, V, 3/4U P
Animated
A collection of cartoon classics including "Falling Hare" with Bugs Bunny, "Cheese Burglar" staring Herman and Katnip, "Somewhere in Dreamland," "Robin Hood Makes Good," and others.

Warner Bros — *Nostalgia Merchant*

Cartoon Parade No. 4 194?
Cartoons
47141 120 mins C B, V, 3/4U P
Another collection of popular cartoons from the 30's and 40's, featuring Max Fleischer's Bouncing Ball, Little Lulu, Superman, Bugs Bunny, and Porky Pig. Some cartoons are in black and white.
Warner Bros et al — *Nostalgia Merchant*

Cartoonies 193?
Cartoons
79876 50 mins C B, V P
Animated
A collection of Max Fleischer's best loved cartoons including Betty Boop, Gabby, Casper, and Little Lulu.
Fleischer Studios; Paramount — *Republic Pictures Home Video*

Cas du Dr. Laurent, Le 1957
Drama
69562 88 mins B/W B, V, FO P
Jean Gabin
A country doctor in a small French town tries to introduce methods of natural childbirth to the native women, but meets opposition from the superstitious townspeople.
France — *Video Yesteryear*

Casa Flora 197?
Comedy
52795 106 mins C B, V P
Maximo Valverde, Antonio Garisa, Rafael Alonso
When the funeral of an important bullfighter is held in a small Andalusian town, the president of the Bullfighting Club decides to use every lodging possible, including those in a hotel of questionable reputation. In Spanish.
SP
Moviola Films — *Media Home Entertainment*

Casablanca 1943
Drama
13316 102 mins B/W B, V, LV P
Humphrey Bogart, Ingrid Bergman, directed by Michael Curtiz
Classic story of an American expatriot who involves himself in romance and espionage in North Africa during World War II.
Academy Awards '43: Best Picture; Best Screenplay; Best Direction (Curtiz). EL, SP
Warner Bros; Hal Wallis — *CBS/Fox Video; RCA VideoDiscs*

Case of Libel, A 1983
Drama
73531 90 mins C B, V P
Daniel J. Travanti, Edward Asner
This movie documents the true story of lawyer Louis Nizer's account of the libel suit Quentin Reynolds brought against Westbrook Pegler. Available in Beta hi-fi and VHS stereo.
Showtime — *U.S.A. Home Video*

Casey's Shadow 1978
Comedy-Drama
63443 116 mins C B, V P
Walter Matthau, Alexis Smith, Robert Webber, Murray Hamilton
The eight-year-old son of an impoverished horse trainer raises a quarter horse and enters it in the world's richest horse race.
MPAA:PG
Columbia; Ray Stark — *RCA/Columbia Pictures Home Video*

Casino Gambling 1983
Gambling
65644 50 mins C B, V R, P
Jerry Reed has challenged Binion's Horseshoe Casino in Las Vegas to 44 consecutive days of playing their dice table. Jerry explains the most effective ways known to combat the adverse odds encountered when casino gaming.
Jerry Reed — *Video City Productions*

Casper and the Angels 1979
Cartoons
47688 55 mins C B, V P
Animated
Five episodes in which the world's friendliest ghost teams up with the Angels—Mini and Maxi—the first policewomen in outer space.
Hanna Barbera — *Worldvision Home Video*

Casper and the Angels II 1979
Cartoons
69292 55 mins C B, V P
Animated
Five more exciting adventures of Casper the friendly ghost, Mini, and Maxi.
Hanna-Barbera — *Worldvision Home Video*

Casper and the Angels Vol III 1979
Cartoons
77158 55 mins C B, V P
Animated
Casper along with two space patrol women Minnie and Maxie blast off for another series of intergalactic adventures.
Hanna-Barbera — *Worldvision Home Video*

Cass 1978
Drama
77006 76 mins C B, V P
A disenchanted filmmaker returns home to Australia to experiment with alternative lifestyles.

Don Harley — *VidAmerica*

Castaway Cowboy, The **1974**
Adventure
72792 91 mins C B, V P
James Garner, Robert Culp
A shanghaied cowboy becomes partners with a widow when she turns her Hawaiian potato farm into a cattle ranch.
Walt Disney Productions — *Walt Disney Home Video*

Castle of Evil **1966**
Horror
70202 81 mins C B, V P
Scott Brady, Virginia Mayo, Hugh Marlowe
A group of heirs gather on a deserted isle to hear the reading of a will. One by one, they fall victim to mysterious "accidents."
World Entertainment — *Republic Pictures Home Video*

Castle of the Walking Dead **1984**
Horror
80471 89 mins C B, V P
Christopher Lee
A reincarnated vampire kidnaps young women to use as sacrifices in his quest for immortality.
Regal Video — *Regal Video*

Cat and Mouse **1978**
Mystery
39015 107 mins C B, V P
Michele Morgan, Serge Reggiani, Jean-Pierre Aumont, directed by Claude Lelouch
A very unorthodox police inspector is assigned to investigate a millionaire's mysterious death. Who done it? French dialogue with English subtitles.
MPAA:PG FR
Quartet Films — *RCA/Columbia Pictures Home Video*

Cat and the Canary, The **1978**
Mystery
58959 96 mins C B, V P
Carol Lynley, Olivia Hussey, Daniel Masey, Honor Blackman, Wilfred Hyde White
A stormy night, a gloomy mansion, and a mysterious will combine to create an atmosphere for murder.
Grenadier Films Ltd — *RCA/Columbia Pictures Home Video*

Cat and the Canary, The **1927**
Mystery
57348 99 mins B/W B, V, FO P
Laura La Plante, Creighton Hale, Tully Marshall, Gertrude Astor
One of the great silent ghost stories, about the ghost of a madman that wanders nightly through the corridors of an old house.
Universal — *Video Yesteryear; Sheik Video; Budget Video; Classic Video Cinema Collector's Club; Glenn Video Vistas*

Cat Ballou **1965**
Western
13237 96 mins C B, V P
Jane Fonda, Lee Marvin, Michael Callan, Dwayne Hickman, Nat King Cole, Stubby Kaye
School teacher and cattle rustler stage a train robbery.
Academy Awards '65: Best Actor (Marvin).
Columbia; Harold Hecht — *RCA/Columbia Pictures Home Video; RCA VideoDiscs*

Cat from Outer Space, The **1978**
Comedy
69317 103 mins C B, V R, P
Ken Berry, Sandy Duncan, Harry Morgan, Roddy McDowall, McLean Stevenson
An extraterrestrial cat named Jake crashlands his spaceship on Earth and leads a group of people on endless escapades.
MPAA:G
Buena Vista; Walt Disney Prods — *Walt Disney Home Video*

Cat on a Hot Tin Roof **1958**
Drama
53409 108 mins C B, V, LV, CED P
Paul Newman, Burl Ives, Elizabeth Taylor, Jack Carson, directed by Richard Brooks
Tennessee Williams' play about deception destroying a patriarchal Southern family.
MGM; Lawrence Weingarten — *MGM/UA Home Video*

Cat on a Hot Tin Roof **1984**
Drama
80683 148 mins C B, V, LV, CED P
Jessica Lange, Tommy Lee Jones, Rip Torn, directed by Jack Hofsiss
An adaptation of the Tennessee Williams play wherein a young couple face difficulties over the husband's uncertain sexuality.
International TV Group — *Vestron Video*

Cat People **1942**
Horror
00311 73 mins B/W B, V, 3/4U P
Simone Simon, Kent Smith, Tom Conway
Young bride believes she's the victim of a curse that can change her into a deadly panther.
RKO — *Nostalgia Merchant; King of Video*

Cat People 1982
Horror
47679 118 mins C B, V, LV, CED P
Nastassia Kinski, Malcolm McDowell, John Heard, Annette O'Toole, directed by Paul Schrader
A beautiful young woman learns that she has inherited a feline characteristic, making a relationship with a man impossible.
MPAA:R
Universal — *MCA Home Video*

Cat Women of the Moon 1953
Science fiction
33479 65 mins B/W B, V P
Sonny Tufts, Marie Windsor, Victor Jory
Scientists land on the moon and encounter an Amazon-like force of female chauvinists.
Astor Pictures — *Mossman Williams Productions; Nostalgia Merchant*

Catamount Killing, The 197?
Suspense
70391 82 mins C B, V P
Horst Bucholz, Ann Wedgeworth
The story of a small town bank manager and his lover. They decide to rob the bank and run for greener pastures only to find their escape befuddled at every turn.
MPAA:PG
Manfred Durnick — *VidAmerica*

Catch a Rising Star's 10th Anniversary 1983
Variety
80380 66 mins C B, V P
Pat Benatar, Billy Crystal, Gabe Kaplan, Joe Piscopo, Robin Williams
Some of the biggest names in comedy and music got together to celebrate the tenth anniversary of this New York night club.
Rising Star Video Pictures Ltd — *RCA/Columbia Pictures Home Video*

Catch Me a Spy 1971
Suspense/Drama
80298 94 mins C B, V P
Kirk Douglas, Tom Courtenay, Trevor Howard, Marlene Jobert
A foreign agent attempts to lure an innocent man into becomming part of a swap for an imprisioned Russian spy.
Ludgate Films; Capitole Films — *Prism*

Catch-22 1970
Satire
38930 121 mins C B, V, LV R, P
Alan Arkin, Martin Balsam, Art Garfunkel, Jon Voight, directed by Mike Nichols
An adaptation of Joseph Heller's black comedy about a group of fliers in the Mediterranean during World War II; biting anti-war satire.
MPAA:R
Paramount — *Paramount Home Video; RCA VideoDiscs*

Catherine and Co. 1976
Comedy
55259 91 mins C B, V P
A lonely, penniless girl arrives in Paris and "opens shop" on the streets of Paris. As business booms, she takes a cue from the big corporations and sells stock in herself.
MPAA:R
Warner Bros — *VidAmerica*

Catherine The Great 1934
Drama
08694 93 mins B/W B, V, 3/4U P
Douglas Fairbanks, Jr., Elisabeth Bergner, Flora Robson, directed Paul Czinner
Historical costume drama based on the life of Catherine of Russia. Her rise to power as Empress of Russia.
UA — *VCII; Sheik Video; Cable Films; Video Yesteryear; Budget Video; Discount Video Tapes; Classic Video Cinema Collector's Club*

Catherine the Great 1934
Drama
81457 93 mins B/W B, V, LV P
Douglas Fairbanks Jr., Elizabeth Bergner
This is the story of how the Russian czarina's life was ruined through a rigidly planned marriage.
Alexander Korda — *Embassy Home Entertainment*

Catholic Hour, The 1960
Drama/Biographical
80756 30 mins B/W B, V P
Edward Cullen, Arthur Gary
A dramatized version of the life story of Thomas Frederick Price who co-founded the Maryknoll Missionaries in the early 1900's.
The National Council of Catholic Men — *Video Yesteryear*

Catholics 1973
Drama
65438 86 mins C B, V P
Martin Sheen, Trevor Howard
A sensitive exploration of contemporary mores and changing attitudes within the Roman Catholic church. Based on Brian Moore's short novel.
Glazier Productions — *U.S.A. Home Video*

Caught 1949
Drama
77478 90 mins B/W B, V P
James Mason, Barbara Bel Geddes, Robert Ryan, directed by Max Ophuls

An unhappily married woman falls in love with the struggling physician she works for.
MGM — *Republic Pictures Home Video*

Cauldron of Blood **1968**
Horror
70201 101 mins C B, V P
Boris Karloff, Viveca Lindfors, Jean Pierre Aumont
A blind sculptor uses human skeletons as the framework of his popular art pieces.
Robert D. Weinbach Prods — *Republic Pictures Home Video*

Cavalcade of Stars **1951**
Variety
11270 55 mins B/W B, V, FO P
Jackie Gleason, Art Carney, Georgia Gibbs, The June Taylor Dancers, Arthur Lee Simpson
"The Great One" clowns and sings with support from Carney in comedy sketches. Simpson sings, "Back in Donegal," and Gibbs performs "I Can't Give You Anything But Love," in this comedy-variety hour.
DuMont — *Video Yesteryear*

Cavaleur, Le (Practice Makes Perfect) **198?**
Comedy
76036 90 mins C B, V P
jean Rochfort
A light hearted comedy about a philandering concert pianist features Jean Rochfort with Nicole Aarcia, Annie Girardot, Lila Kedrova and Catherine Leprince as some of the women in his life.
EL, FR
Georges Dancigers; Alexandre Mnouchkine — *RCA/Columbia Pictures Home Video*

Cavalier, The **198?**
Martial arts
73959 90 mins C B, V P
Tang Wei, Loon Fei, Yeh Yuen, Tseng Tsao
A Chinese cavalier faces love, danger and intrigue in this martial arts film.
Independent — *Unicorn Video*

Caveman **1981**
Comedy
58823 92 mins C B, V, CED P
Ringo Starr, Barbara Bach, John Matuszak, Dennis Quaid, Jack Gilford, Shelley Long
A group of cavemen banished from different tribes band together to form a tribe called "The Misfits."
MPAA:PG
United Artists; Lawrence Turman; David Foster — *CBS/Fox Video*

CBS/Fox Guide to Complete Dog Care, The **1983**
Pets
65411 60 mins C B, V, CED P
A guide to home pet care from feeding to grooming.
CBS Fox — *CBS/Fox Video*

CBS/FOX Guide to Home Videography, The **1983**
Video
65007 45 mins C B, V P
This original home video production follows the adventures of a fictitious character who owns a new video camera. Five easy to follow segments include camera movement, framing and composition, lighting and sound planning and production and advanced techniques.
CBS/FOX Video — *CBS/Fox Video*

C.C. and Company **1970**
Drama
76906 91 mins C B, V P
Joe Namath, Ann-Margret, William Smith, Jennifer Billingsley
A young man who joins a rowdy motorcycle gang becomes the enemy in the camp because he does not adhere to their rules.
MPAA:PG
Rogallan Productions; Avco Embassy — *Embassy Home Entertainment*

Celebration, A **1981**
Music-Performance
65213 60 mins C B, V P
Glen Campbell, Kris Kristofferson, Tanya Tucker, Roger Miller
A star-studded tribute in memory of a musical legend—Dorsey Burnett. Available in Beta Hi-fi and stereo VHS.
DID Productions — *Monterey Home Video*

Centerfold **1980**
Photography
57453 60 mins C B, V P
The side of the centerfold model we never see—in the dressing room preparing for a shooting session. Model Martha Thomsen talks candidly about her conflicts with men, how she felt posing nude for the first time, and her years growing up "plain."
At Home Video — *VidAmerica*

Centerfold Girls, The **197?**
Suspense
59043 93 mins C B, V P
Andrew Prine, Tiffany Bolling
A deranged man is determined to kill the voluptuous young women who have posed nude for a centerfold.
MPAA:R
Charles Stroud — *Media Home Entertainment*

Century of Progress Exposition, The/New York World's Fair 1939-40 193?
Documentary
60055 19 mins B/W B, V P, T
Fox Movietone newsreels of Chicago's Century of Progress Exposition of 1933-34 and the most impressive exhibits of the New York World's Fair of 1939-1940 are combined on this tape.
Blackhawk Movietone
Compilation — *Blackhawk Films*

Chain Gang Killings, The 1985
Adventure
77401 99 mins C B, V P
Ian Yule, Ken Gampu
A pair of shackled prisoners, one black the other white, escape from a truck transporting them to prison.
Clive Harding — *VCL Home Video*

Chain Reaction, The 1980
Suspense
78353 87 mins C B, V P
Steve Bisley, Ross Thompson
When a nuclear scientist is exposed to radiation after an accident at an atomic power plant, he must escape to warn the public of the danger.
David Elfick — *Embassy Home Entertainment*

Chained for Life 1951
Drama/Exploitation
55816 81 mins B/W B, V P
Daisy Hilton, Violet Hilton
Daisy and Violet Hilton, the real life siamese twins, star in this old-fashioned "freak" show. When a gigolo deserts one twin on their wedding night, the other twin shoots him dead. The twins go on trial and the judge asks the viewer to hand down the verdict.
Unknown — *Festival Films; Admit One Video*

Chained Heat 1983
Drama
65341 97 mins C B, V P
Linda Blair, Stella Stevens, Sybil Danning
A startling and explicit saga exposing the vicious reality of life for women behind bars.
MPAA:R
Billy Fine — *Vestron Video*

Challenge, The 1938
Drama/Adventure
57349 77 mins B/W B, V, FO P
Luis Trenker, Robert Douglas
This classic mountaineering film features incredible avalanche scenes, as it follow the courageous party of explorers who conquered the Matterhorn.
England — *Video Yesteryear; Movie Buff Video*

Challenge, The 1982
Adventure
60425 108 mins C B, V, CED P
Scott Glenn, Toshiro Mifune
A contemporary action spectacle which combines modern swordplay with the mysticism and fantasy of ancient Samurai legends.
MPAA:R
CBS Theatrical Production — *CBS/Fox Video*

Challenge to Be Free 1974
Adventure
63379 90 mins C B, V P
Mike Mazurki, Jimmy Kane
This is the legend of a man named Trapper, who struggles across 1,000 miles of frozen wilderness while being pursued by 12 men and 100 dogs.
MPAA:G
Pacific International Enterprises — *Media Home Entertainment*

Chamber of Fear 197?
Horror
79325 88 mins C B, V P
Boris Karloff, Isela Vega, Julissa and Carlos East
A madman inhabits a castle where he practices mental torture on innocent victims.
Luis Enrique Vergara — *Unicorn Video*

Chamber of Horrors 1940
Horror
72949 80 mins B/W B, V P
Leslie Banks, Lilli Palmer
A family is brought together at an English castle to claim a fortune left by an aristocrat. But there's one catch—there are seven keys that could open the vault with the fortune.
Monogram — *United Home Video*

Champ, The 1979
Drama
44650 121 mins C B, V, LV, CED P
Jon Voight, Faye Dunaway, Ricky Schroder, Jack Warden, directed by Franco Zeffirelli
An ex-fighter with a weakness for gambling and drinking is forced to return to the ring in an attempt to keep the custody of his son. A remake of the 1931 classic.
MPAA:PG
MGM — *MGM/UA Home Video*

Champagne for Caesar 1950
Comedy
65156 90 mins B/W B, V P
Ronald Colman, Celeste Holm, Vincent Price, Art Linkletter, directed by Richard Whorf
A self-proclaimed genius on every subject goes on a TV quiz show and proceeds to win everything in sight. The program's sponsor, in

desperation, hires a femme fatale to distract the contestant before the final program.
Universal — *United Home Video*

Champion 1949
Drama
64542 99 mins B/W B, V P
Kirk Douglas, Arthur Kennedy, Marilyn Maxwell, Ruth Roman
An ambitious prizefighter alienates the people who helped him on the way to the top.
United Artists — *Republic Pictures Home Video*

Champions, The 1983
Drama
Closed Captioned
64987 90 mins C B, V P
John Hurt, Ben Johnson, Edward Woodward
This is the story of two championsa courageous, cancer-stricken British jockey and the horse he rode to victory in the Grand National, who came back from a severe, near-fatal injury.
Unknown — *Embassy Home Entertainment*

Champions 1984
Drama
72877 113 mins C B, V, LV P
John Hurt
The true story of Bob Champion, who overcame cancer to win England's Grand National, a top horse racing event.
Peter Shaw — *Embassy Home Entertainment*

Champions of the AFC East 1982
Football
47711 23 mins C B, V, FO P
Team highlights of the 1981 Miami Dolphins, who won the AFC Eastern Division with a strong defense.
NFL Films — *NFL Films Video*

Championship Training 1985
Physical fitness
70541 60 mins C B, V P
Brad Lackey
Brad Lackey shows the balanced physical and mental training that brought him the World Motorcross Champion title.
Bookshelf — *Bookshelf Video*

Chandu on the Magic Island 1940
Mystery/Adventure
53357 67 mins B/W B, V, FO P
Bela Lugosi, Maria Alba, Clark Kimball Young
Chandu the Magician takes his powers of the occult to the mysterious lost island of Lemuri to battle the evil cult of Ubasti.
United Artists; Sol Lesser — *Video Yesteryear; Sheik Video*

Chanel Solitaire 1981
Drama
72906 124 mins C B, V P
Karen Black, Marie-France Pisier, Rutger Hauer
The biography of Gabrielle "Coco" Chanel, as portrayed by Marie-France Pisier, follows her career as a fabulous dress designer.
MPAA:R
George Kaczender — *Media Home Entertainment*

Change of Habit 1969
Drama/Comedy
55555 93 mins C B, V P
Elvis Presley, Mary Tyler Moore, Barbara McNair
Three novitiates undertake to learn about the world before becoming full-fledged nuns. While working at a ghetto clinic a young doctor forms a strong, affectionate relationship with one of them.
MPAA:G
Universal; Joe Connelly — *MCA Home Video*

Change of Mind 1968
Adventure/Fantasy
70581 52 mins C B, V P
Patrick McGoohan, Angela Brown, John Sharpe, directed by Joseph Serf
In this thirteenth episode of "The Prisoner" TV series, Number 2 uses drugs and ultra-sonic waves to break the Prisoner's resolve.
Associated TV Corp. — *MPI Home Video*

Change of Seasons, A 1980
Romance/Comedy
55456 102 mins C B, V, CED P
Shirley MacLaine, Bo Derek, Anthony Hopkins, Michael Brandon, Mary Beth Hurt
A sophisticated comedy that looks at contemporary relationships and values. The wife of a college professor learns of her husband's affair with a seductive student and decides to have a fling with a younger man. The situation reaches absurdity when the couples decide to vacation together.
MPAA:R
Twentieth Century Fox — *CBS/Fox Video*

Changeling, The 1980
Horror
44918 114 mins C B, V, LV, CED P
George C. Scott, Trish Van Devere, John Russell
A music teacher moves into an old house and discovers that a young boy's ghostly spirit is her housemate.
MPAA:R

Associated Film Distribution — *Vestron Video*

Chaplin: A Character Is Born/Keaton: The Great Stone Face **197?**
Comedy/Film-History
64842 90 mins C B, V P
Narrated by Keenan Wynn and Red Buttons
Wynn narrates "A Character Is Born," with scenes from "Little Champ," "The Pawnshop," "The Rink" and "The Immigrant." Buttons presents "The Great Stone Face" featuring scenes from "Cops," "The Playhouse" "The Boat" and "The General."
SL Film Productions — *HarmonyVision*

Chaplin Mutuals, Volume I **1917**
Comedy
10076 60 mins B/W B, V P, T
Charlie Chaplin, Edna Purviance, John Rand, Eric Campbell, James T. Kelley
Package includes Chaplin's "The Immigrant," "The Count," and Easy Street." Silent.
Mutual — *Blackhawk Films*

Chaplin Mutuals, Volume II **1917**
Comedy
10080 60 mins B/W B, V P, T
Charlie Chaplin, Edna Purviance, Eric Campbell, Albert Austin, Henry Bergman, John Rand
Package includes Chaplins "The Pawnshop" (1916), "The Adventurer" (1917), and "One A.M." (1916).
Mutual — *Blackhawk Films*

Chaplin Mutuals, Volume III **1916**
Comedy
10084 60 mins B/W B, V P, T
Charlie Chaplin, Edna Purviance, Eric Campbell, Albert Austin
Package includes Chaplin's "The Cure" (1916), "The Floorwalker" (1916), and "The Vagabond."
Mutual — *Blackhawk Films*

Chaplin Mutuals, Volume IV **1916**
Comedy
10088 60 mins B/W B, V P, T
Charlie Chaplin, Edna Purviance, Eric Campbell, Lloyd Bacon, Albert Austin, James T. Kelly
Package includes Chaplin's, "Behind the Screen," "The Fireman" (1916), and "The Rink" (1916).
Mutual — *Blackhawk Films*

Chaplin Revue, The **1958**
Comedy
08395 119 mins B/W B, V P
Charlie Chaplin
The "Revue," put together by Chaplin in 1958, consists of three of his best shorts: "A Dog's Life" (1918), "Shoulder Arms" (1918), and "The Pilgrim" (1922).
rbc Films — *CBS/Fox Video; Playhouse Video*

Chapter Two **1979**
Romance
Closed Captioned
44789 120 mins C B, V, LV P
James Caan, Marsha Mason, Valerie Harper, Joseph Bologna
A shy mystery writer and widower wins the heart of a young divorcee. The memory of his deceased wife nearly ruins their new marriage.
MPAA:PG
Ray Stark — *RCA/Columbia Pictures Home Video*

Charade **1963**
Mystery/Comedy
58212 113 mins C B, V P
Cary Grant, Audrey Hepburn, Walter Matthau, James Coburn, George Kennedy, directed by Stanley Donen
After her husband is murdered, a young wife finds herself on the run from crooks and double agents who want 250,000 dollars her husband stole during World War II. Filmed on location in Paris. Music by Henry Mancini.
Film Daily Poll 10 Best Pictures of the Year '63.
Universal; Stanley Donen — *MCA Home Video*

Charge of the Light Brigade, The **1936**
Drama
64783 115 mins B/W B, V, CED P
Olivia De Havilland, Errol Flynn, David Niven, Nigel Bruce, directed by Michael Curtiz
An army officer deliberately starts the Balaclava charge to even an old score with Surat Khan, who's on the other side.
Warner; Hal B. Wallis; Sam Bischoff — *CBS/Fox Video; RCA VideoDiscs*

Charge of the Model T's **1979**
Comedy
69553 94 mins C B, V P
Louis Nye, John David Carson, Herb Edelman, Carol Bagdasarian, Arte Johnson
Set during World War I, this comedy is about a German spy who tries to infiltrate the U.S. army.
MPAA:G
Jim McCullough — *Embassy Home Entertainment*

Chariots of Fire **1981**
Drama
47788 123 mins C B, V, LV R, P
Ben Cross, Ian Charleson, Nigel Havers, Nick Farrell, John Gielgud, Alice Krige, Nigel

Davenport, Ian Holm, Patrick Magee, Cheryl Campbell, Lindsay Anderson
Motivation and the will to win are poignantly and dramatically portrayed in this story of two British track athletes striving to win major events at the 1924 Paris Olympics.
Academy Awards '81: Best Picture. MPAA:PG
Enigma Productions; David Puttnam — *Warner Home Video; RCA VideoDiscs*

Chariots of the Gods 1973
Documentary/Speculation
14643 98 mins C B, V P
Directed by Dr. Harold Reinl
The possibility of extraterrestrial visitors inhabiting Earth many years ago is examined.
MPAA:G
Sun International Productions — *United Home Video*

Charley Varrick 1973
Drama
68257 111 mins C B, V P
Walter Matthau, Joe Don Baker, Felicia Farr
A crop dusting pilot robs a bank only to find that the bank belongs to the Mafia.
MPAA:PG
Universal — *MCA Home Video*

Charlie and the Talking Buzzard 1979
Adventure
75629 70 mins C B, V P
Charlie and his dog uncover a secret plot to destroy the biggest business in town.
Unknown — *Trans World Entertainment*

Charlie Brown Christmas, A 1965
Cartoons
79264 25 mins C B, V P
Animated
Disillusioned by the commercialization of the holiday season, Charlie Brown sets out to find the true meaning of Christmas.
Lee Mendelson—Bill Melendez Productions — *Snoopy's Home Video Library*

Charlie Brown Festival, A 1981
Cartoons
56889 120 mins C CED P
Animated
Four complete stores featuring Charlie Brown, trying to cope with Peppermint Patty, a losing baseball team, the Junior Olympics, and his love for the little red-haired girl.
United Features Syndicate — *RCA VideoDiscs*

Charlie Brown Festival Vol. II, A 1981
Cartoons
59019 102 mins C CED P
Four animated adventures featuring the Peanuts gang: "Be My Valentine, Charlie Brown," "It's the Easter Beagle, Charlie Brown," "He's Your Dog, Charlie Brown," and, "Life is a Circus, Charlie Brown."
United Features Syndicate — *RCA VideoDiscs*

Charlie Brown Festival Vol. III, A 1982
Cartoons
47803 102 mins C CED P
Animated
The Peanuts Gang are featured in this compilation containing "It Was a Short Summer Charlie Brown" (1969); "It's the Great Pumpkin Charlie Brown" (1966); "You're Not Elected Charlie Brown" (1972); and "A Charlie Brown Thanksgiving" (1973).
United Features Syndicate — *RCA VideoDiscs*

Charlie Brown Festival Vol. IV, A 1983
Cartoons
64327 102 mins C CED P
Animated
Snoopy is a super detective, Lucy is after Schroeder and Charlie Brown is facing a player walk-out in this collection of Peanuts favorites.
United Features Syndicate — *RCA VideoDiscs*

Charlie Brown's All Stars 1966
Cartoons
75610 30 mins C B, V P
Animated
The team is ready to give up after losing 999 games when Charlie Brown gets an offer to have the team sponsored in a real league.
Lee Mendelson Bill Melendez Productions — *Snoopy's Home Video Library*

Charlie Chan and the Curse of the Dragon Queen 1981
Satire/Comedy
66060 97 mins C B, V P
Peter Ustinov, Lee Grant, Angie Dickinson, Richard Hatch, Brian Kieth, Roddy McDowall.
The famed Oriental sleuth confronts his old enemy the Dragon Queen, and reveals the true identity of a killer.
MPAA:PG
American Cinema — *Media Home Entertainment*

Charlie Chaplin: The Funniest Man in the World 1981
Documentary/Comedy
58561 93 mins B/W B, V P
Charlie Chaplin, Fatty Arbuckle, Mabel Normand, Ben Turpin, Stan Laurel, narrated by Douglas Fairbanks Jr.

 (For explanation of codes, see USE GUIDE and KEY)

A profile of Chaplin, from his youth in England through his vaudeville days in America to his triumph in Hollywood.
Vernon Becker; Mel May — *Mastervision*

Charlie Chaplin's Keystone Comedies 1914
Comedy
58655 59 mins B/W B, V, FO P
Charlie Chaplin, Mabel Normand, Mack Swain
Six one-reelers which Chaplin filmed in 1914, his first movie-making year: "Making a Living," Chaplin's first, in which he plays a villain; "Kid Auto Races," in which Charlie now sports baggy pants, bowler hat and cane; "A Busy Day," featuring Charlie in drag; "Mabel's Married Life;" "Laughing Gas;" and "The New Janitor." Silent with musical score.
Sennett; Keystone — *Video Yesteryear*

Charlie Daniels Band: The Saratoga Concert, The 1982
Music-Performance
59133 75 mins C B, V, LV, CED P
The Charlie Daniels Band performs live in concert at Saratoga Springs, New York, September 4, 1981. The program also includes two "conceptualized" songs filmed in North Carolina and narrated by Charlie Daniels. Songs include: "In America," "The Devil Went Down to Georgia," "South's Gonna Do It Again."
Richard Namm — *CBS/Fox Video*

Charlotte's Web 1972
Musical/Cartoons
38607 94 mins C B, V, LV R, P
Animated, voices of Debbie Reynolds, Agnes Moorehead, Paul Lynde, Henry Gibson
E.B. White's famous story of Wilbur the pig and his friendship with Charlotte the spider, transformed into a cartoon musical for the whole family.
MPAA:G
Paramount — *Paramount Home Video; RCA VideoDiscs*

Charmkins, The 1983
Cartoons
80973 60 mins C B, V P
Animated, voices of Ben Vereen, Sally Struthers, Aileen Quinn
Here are the animated adventures of Lady Slipper and her friends in Charm World where they battle the evil Dragonweed.
Sunbow Prods; Marvel Prods. — *Family Home Entertainment*

Chase, The 1946
Drama
66366 86 mins B/W B, V P
Robert Cummings, Michele Morgan, Peter Lorre, Steve Cochran
A World War II veteran finds a wealthy man's wallet on the street. When he returns it, he becomes involved in a web of intrigue.
United Artists — *Movie Buff Video*

Chattanooga Choo Choo 1984
Comedy
80649 102 mins C B, V R, P
Barbara Eden, Joe Namath, George Kennedy, Melissa Sue Anderson, directed by Bruce Bilson
A football team owner must restore the Chattanooga Choo Choo and make a twenty-four hour run from Chattanooga to New York in order to collect one-million dollars left to him in a will.
MPAA:PG
April Fools Prods. — *THORN EMI/HBO Video*

Chatterbox 1976
Comedy
66099 73 mins C B, V, CED P
Candice Rialson
A young starlet has a very conversant anatomy.
Bruce Cohn Curtis — *Vestron Video*

Chatterer the Squirrel 1983
Cartoons
65655 60 mins C B, V P
Animated
Chatterer the Squirrel learns a much-needed lesson in humility in "The Big Boast," and in "Captive Chatterer," the farmer's son tries to make a house pet out of Chatterer, but a new home and plenty of food are no substitute for freedom!
Ziv International — *Family Home Entertainment*

Cheaper to Keep Her 1980
Comedy-Drama
68222 92 mins C B, V P
Mac Davis, Tovah Feldshuh, Jack Gilford, Rose Marie
Upon leaving his wife, Bill Dekker (Mac Davis) begins a new job working for a feminist attorney who has him investigating husbands of clients, who happen to be in the same predicament that he is in.
MPAA:R
American Cinema — *Media Home Entertainment*

Cheaters 1984
Theater/Drama
78660 103 mins C B, V P
Peggy Cass, Jack Kruschen
Two middle class couples are having affairs with each other's spouses and complications arise when their respective children decide to marry each other.
Showtime — *RKO HomeVideo*

Check and Double Check 1930
Comedy
11226 75 mins B/W B, V, FO P
Freeman Gosden and Charles Correll (Amos 'n' Andy), Duke Ellington and His Orchestra
Radio's original Amos 'n' Andy help solve a lover's triangle in this film version of the popular radio series. Duke Ellington's band plays "Old Man Blues" and "Three Little Words."
RKO — *Video Yesteryear; Discount Video Tapes; Video Connection; Budget Video; Western Film & Video Inc; Kartes Productions; See Hear Industries*

Checkmate 1968
Suspense/Fantasy
77417 52 mins C B, V P
Patrick McGoohan, Ronald Radd, Peter Wyngarde, directed by Don Chaffey
The Prisoner participates in an unusual chess game in the Village. An episode from "The Prisoner" series.
ITC Productions — *MPI Home Video*

Cheech and Chong's Next Movie 1980
Comedy
48629 99 mins C B, V, LV P
Cheech Marin, Tommy Chong, Evelyn Guerrero
A pair of messed-up bumblers adventure into a welfare office, massage parlor, nightclub, and flying saucer, while always living in fear of the cops.
MPAA:R
Universal — *MCA Home Video*

Cheech & Chong's Nice Dreams 1981
Comedy
60344 97 mins C B, V, LV P
Richard "Cheech" Marin, Tommy Chong, Evelyn Guerrero, Stacy Keach
The spaced-out duo are selling their own "specially mixed" ice cream to make cash and realize their dreams.
MPAA:R
Columbia — *RCA/Columbia Pictures Home Video; RCA VideoDiscs*

Cheerleaders, The 1973
Comedy
59081 84 mins C B, V P
The locker room hi-jinks of rival football teams and a squad of uninhibited cheerleaders mix and match in this racy comedy.
MPAA:R
Paul Glickler; Richard Lerner — *HarmonyVision*

Cheerleaders' Wild Weekend 1985
Comedy
77413 87 mins C B, V P
Jason Williams, Kristine DeBell
A group of cheerleaders plot to escape from their kidnapper, a disgruntled former football star.
MPAA:R
Fountain Productions — *Vestron Video*

Cheers for Miss Bishop 1941
Drama
63622 95 mins B/W B, V, FO P
Martha Scott, William Gargan, Edmund Gwenn, Sterling Holloway, Rosemary DeCamp
This is the story of a young girl who graduates from a new college and stays on to teach English for over 50 years.
United Artists — *Video Yesteryear; Kartes Productions*

Cherry Hill High 1976
Comedy
62783 86 mins C B, V P
Carrie Olsen, Nina Carson, Lynn Hastings, Gloria Upson, Stephanie Lawlor
Five high school coeds decide to have a contest to see which of them can lose her virginity first.
MPAA:R
Cannon Films — *MCA Home Video*

Cheryl Ladd—Fascinated 1982
Music-Performance
66018 50 mins C B, V R, P
The ex-Angel performs "Just Like Old Times," "I Love How You Love Me," "Cold as Ice" and more.
EMI Music — *THORN EMI/HBO Video*

Chesty Anderson U.S. Navy 1976
Comedy
47672 90 mins C B, V P
Shari Eubank, Dorri Thompson, Rosanne Katon, Marcie Barkin, Scotman Crothers, Frank Campanella, Fred Willard
The comic adventures of a W.A.V.E.S. unit populated by well-endowed ladies.
Unknown — *Unicorn Video; World Video Pictures*

Chevy Show, The 1957
Variety
38993 43 mins B/W B, V, FO P
Pat Boone, Shirley MacLaine, Gisele MacKenzie, George Gobel, Jeff Donnell
Pat Boone sings "Love Letters in the Sand" and does a comedy routine with George Gobel. Gisele MacKenzie vocalizes, and Shirley MacLaine is featured in a dance routine in this TV special originally shown on June 7, 1957.
NBC — *Video Yesteryear*

(For explanation of codes, see USE GUIDE and KEY)

Cheyenne Rides Again 1938
Western
11261 60 mins B/W B, V, FO P
Tom Tyler, Lucille Browne, Jimmy Fox
Cheyenne poses as an outlaw to hunt a gang of rustlers.
Victory — *Video Yesteryear; Video Connection*

Chicago Bears 1984 Team Highlights 1985
Football
70544 70 mins C B, V, FO P
Like their '84 Cubby cousins, the Chicagoans awoke from hibernation to win their division in a "Fight to the Finish." The tape features 47-minutes of highlights from the entire NFL's '84 season as well.
NFL Films — *NFL Films Video*

Chicago Cubs: Team Highlights 1984
Baseball
81136 30 mins C B, V P
Dave Kingman, Mel Hall, Ryne Sandberg, Ron Cey, Leon Durnham, Jody Davis 6 pgms
The Chicago Cubs' meteoric rise from the National League baseball to division champions is chronicled in this series.
1.1978: We Love The Cubs 2.1979: Summer of '79 3.1980: Summer of '80 4.1981: Summer of '81 5.1982: Summer of '82 6.1984: Cubs Win
Major League Baseball — *Major League Baseball Productions*

Chicago White Sox: Team Highlights 1984
Baseball
81137 30 mins C B, V P
Carlton Fisk, Steve Trout, Greg Luzinski, Tom Seaver, Harold Baines 4 pgms
This series describes how the Chicago White Sox clinched the American League western division title by "winning ugly" in 1983.
1.1981: On The Beginning 2.1982: One Step Closer 3.1983: Winning Ugly 4.1984; Chicago White Sox '84
Major League Baseball — *Major League Baseball Productions*

Chick Corea & Gary Burton Live in Tokyo 1985
Music-Performance
70663 60 mins C B, V P
Chick Corea, Gary Burton
The talents of this Grammy award-winning duo thrill the audience at Yuhbin Chokin Hall in Tokyo. This tape of their performance includes favorites like "La Fiesta," "Senor Mouse," and "Children's Songs" all in Hi-Fi sound.
Pacific Arts Music Video — *Pacific Arts Video*

Chick Corea/Gary Burton Live in Tokyo 1981
Music-Performance
64829 58 mins C LV P
The music of pianist/composer Corea and vibraphonist Burton is captured in a live performance. Features Corea compositions such as "La Fiesta," "Senior Mouse" and "Children's Songs." In stereo.
Chick Corea; Gary Burton — *Pioneer Artists*

Chicken Chronicles, The 1977
Comedy
80775 94 mins C B, V P
Phil Silvers, Ed Lauter, Steve Guttenberg, Lisa Reeves, Meridith Baer
The rich high school students of Beverly Hills bring the sixties and their teen years to a close by experimenting with sex and drugs.
MPAA:PG
AVCO Embassy — *Embassy Home Entertainment*

Chicken Ranch 1983
Documentary
65381 84 mins C B, V P
This documentary focuses on the women who work at and the men who frequent "The Chicken Ranch," the country's best-known legal brothel.
MPAA:R
Nick Broomfield — *Vestron Video*

Child Bride of Short Creek 1981
Drama
80299 100 mins C B, V P
Diane Lane, Conrad Bain, Christopher Atkins, Kiel Martin, Helen Hunt
Two young people are trapped in a town where the government is out to stop the community's practice of polygamy.
Lawrence Schriller Productions — *Prism*

Childbirth Preparation 1985
Physical fitness
70540 60 mins C B, V P
Jack La Lanne, Elaine La Lanne
This informative video describes the operation of all different parts of the woman's body during childbirth, and offers a series of exercises to prepare mothers for labor.
Bookshelf — *Bookshelf Video*

Children, The 1980
Mystery/Suspense
65609 93 mins C B, V P
A New England town is unprepared after a school bus passes through a mysterious yellow cloud and the children are transformed to terrifying, powerful menaces.
MPAA:R

World Northal — *Vestron Video*

Children of Sanchez 1979
Drama
76659 103 mins C B, V P
Anthony Quinn, Dolores Del Rio, Katy Jurado, Lupita Ferrer
A story of one man's attempts to provide for his family with very little except faith and love.
MPAA:R
Paul Bartlett Films — *Monterey Home Video*

Children of the Corn 1984
Horror
74089 93 mins C B, V, LV, CED P
This is another spine-tingling horror epic from that master of horror, Stephen King. This one is set in a small town in Nebraska where the local children worship the corn by making adult sacrifices.
MPAA:R
Donald P. Borchers; Terrence Kirby — *Embassy Home Entertainment*

Children of the Full Moon 1984
Horror
80478 60 mins C B, V P
Christopher Cazenove, Celia Gregory, Diana Dors, Jacof Witken, Robert Urquhart
A young couple find themselves lost in a forest that is the home of a family of werewolves. In Beta Hi-Fi and VHS stereo.
Hammer Films — *Thriller Video*

Children of Theatre Street, The 1977
Documentary/Dance
81568 100 mins C B, V P
Narrated by Princess Grace of Monaco
This is a behind-the-scenes look at the students who attend the Kirov Ballet School in Leningrad, Russia.
Earle Mack Films — *Kultur*

Children's Heroes of the Bible—David and Moses 19??
Cartoons
72944 46 mins C B, V P
The animated history of David and Moses from the Old Testament is brought to life in this family program.
MPAA:G
VCI — *United Home Video*

Children's Songs and Stories with the Muppets 1985
Variety
Closed Captioned
80746 56 mins C B, V P
Kermit the Frog, Scooter, Twiggy, Julie Andrews, Charles Aznavour, Brooke Shields, Judy Collins
The Muppets and their special guests perform unique renditions of well loved childrens songs.
Henson Associates — *Playhouse Video*

Chimes of Big Ben, The 1968
Drama
79895 52 mins C B, V P
Patrick McGoohan, Nadia Gray, Leo McKern
The Prisoner and a new arrival to the Village attempt an escape.
Patrick McGoohan — *MPI Home Video*

China Syndrome, The 1979
Drama
Closed Captioned
44784 122 mins C B, V, LV P
Jack Lemmon, Michael Douglas, Jane Fonda
A television news reporter and cameraman try to make public a dangerous incident which they stumbled upon at a nuclear power plant. The integrity of a nuclear engineer makes him a murder target.
MPAA:PG
Michael Douglas — *RCA/Columbia Pictures Home Video; RCA VideoDiscs*

Chinatown 1974
Mystery
38592 131 mins C B, V, LV R, P
Jack Nicholson, Faye Dunaway, John Huston, Diane Ladd, directed by Roman Polanski
A complex tangled mystery involving Jack Nicholson as a private detective working on a seemingly routine case that mushrooms into more than he bargained for.
Academy Awards '74: Best Original Screenplay (Robert Towne). MPAA:R
Paramount — *Paramount Home Video; RCA VideoDiscs*

Chinese Connection, The 1973
Adventure/Martial arts
55831 107 mins C B, V P
Bruce Lee, James Tien, Robert Baker
Revenge is the motive as Lee sets out to catch the men who murdered the revered teacher of his martial arts school.
MPAA:R
National General Pictures — *CBS/Fox Video; Video City Productions; Master Arts Video; Spotlite Video*

Chinese Connection II 1984
Martial arts
66490 96 mins C B, V P
Bruce Li
Bruce Li journeys to Shanghai to honor his brother's dying wish—he must re-establish the Ching Wing Wu Martial Arts School. When Bruce finds that the school has been taken over

by Miyamoto, a Japanese karate master, a fight to the death ensues.
Trans World Entertainment — *Trans World Entertainment*

Chinese Gods **1980**
Folklore/China
44341 90 mins C B, V R, P
Animated
This program is an animated story of Chinese mythology. It explains the battles and rivalries occurring circa 1000 B.C. in the period of the Shang Dynasty. Cruel King Cheo's troops defeated the troops of the Marquis Hsi-pa in a huge war. After an evil flying serpent tries but fails to kill him, the Marquis, Chiang, wins a series of battles, and his rival, Cheo, eventually burns himself to death.
MPAA:G
Four Seas Films — *Video Gems*

Chinese Web, The **1978**
Adventure
66069 95 mins C B, V P
Nicholas Hammond
A Spider-man adventure in which Spidey becomes entwined in international intrigue.
Danchuk Productions — *CBS/Fox Video*

Chino **1975**
Western
47384 97 mins C B, V R, P
Charles Bronson, Jill Ireland, directed by John Sturges
A half-breed horse trainer with an independent streak "adopts" a runaway fifteen-year-old boy.
MPAA:PG
Intercontinental Releasing Corp — *Warner Home Video*

Chisum **1970**
Western
51962 111 mins C B, V R, P
John Wayne, Forrest Tucker, Geoffrey Deuel
A cattle baron meets Billy the Kid and together they fight the corrupt town government.
MPAA:G
Warner Bros — *Warner Home Video*

Chitty Chitty Bang Bang **1968**
Musical/Fantasy
58483 142 mins C B, V, CED P
Dick Van Dyke, Sally Ann Howes, Lionel Jeffries, directed by Ken Hughes
An eccentric inventor spruces up an old car and, in fantasy, takes his children to a land where the evil rulers have forbidden children.
MPAA:G EL, SP
United Artists; Albert R Broccoli — *CBS/Fox Video*

Choose Me **1984**
Drama/Romance
77357 106 mins C B, V P
Genevieve Bujold, Keith Carradine, Lesley Ann Warren, Rae Dawn Chong, directed by Alan Rudolph
A neurotic radio psychologist becomes involved in a menage a trois with a drifter and a nightclub owner. Teddy Pendergrass sings the title song.
MPAA:R
Island Alive — *Media Home Entertainment*

Chosen, The **1981**
Drama
65404 107 mins C B, V P
Rod Steiger, Robby Benson, Barry Miller
This is the story of two young Jewish men whose friendship survives the deep conflicts arising from having been raised in two different worlds. Based on Chaim Potok's acclaimed novel.
MPAA:PG
Edie and Ely Landau — *CBS/Fox Video*

Christiane F **1982**
Drama
78343 120 mins C B, V P
Natja Brunkhorst, Thomas Haustein
A true story about a fourteen year old girl who becomes a junkie and a prostitute in Berlin's Zoo Station. David Bowie makes a guest appearance in the film and sings "Heroes".
MPAA:R
Bernd Eichinger; Hans Weth — *Media Home Entertainment*

Christina **1974**
Suspense/Drama
70583 95 mins C B, V P
Barbara Parkins, Peter Haskell, directed by Paul Krasny
An unemployed and lonely man meets a beautiful woman who offers him $25,000 to marry him. She then vanishes. Obsessed and in love, he searches for clues that lead him through haunted mansions and other evil locations.
MPAA:PG
New World Pictures — *MPI Home Video*

Christine **1984**
Suspense
76034 110 mins C B, V P
Keith Gordon, John Stockwell, Alexandra Paul, Robert Prosley, Harry Dean Stanton, directed by John Carpenter
Christine is a sleek red and white 1958 Plymouth Fury that seduces a teenage boy and demands his complete and unquestioned devotion. Anyone who gets in her way becomes a victim of Christine's wrath. Based on the Stephen King novel.
MPAA:R

Richard Kobritz — *RCA/Columbia Pictures Home Video*

Christine McVie Concert, The **1984**
Music-Performance
72535 60 mins C B, V, CED P
Concert footage is intermixed with state-of-the-art videos of Fleetwood Mac's Christine McVie, who is enjoying a successful solo venture.
Time Life Multimedia — *Vestron Video*

Christmas Carol, A **1951**
Drama
11659 86 mins B/W B, V P
Alastair Sim, Kathleen Harrison
Dickens' classic story of how a miserly old man is brought to change on Christmas Eve.
United Artists; Renown Pictures — *United Home Video*

Christmas Lilies of the Field **1979**
Drama
78969 98 mins C B, V P
Billy Dee Williams, Maria Schell, Fay Hauser, Judith Piquet, directed by Ralph Nelson
An ex-soldier volunteers his skills as a carpenter to help a church build an orphange for nine children.
Rainbow Productions; Osmond Television — *MPI Home Video*

Christmas on Grandfather's Farm **1959**
Christmas
00831 14 mins C B, V P, T
An old-fashioned Christmas celebration at Grandma and Grandpa's big farmhouse reveals what the holiday celebration was like in the 1890's.
Coronet Films — *Blackhawk Films*

Christmas Raccoons, The **1984**
Cartoons/Christmas
73706 30 mins C B, V P
Animated, narrated by Rich Little
The Raccoons have their very own special animated Christmas story to tell, and with a purchase of this videocassette a wand is included.
AM Available
Kevin Gillis — *Embassy Home Entertainment*

Christmas Story, A **1983**
Comedy
79206 95 mins C B, V P
Peter Billingsley, Darren McGavin, Melinda Dillon, directed by Bob Clark
An adaptation of the Jean Shepherd story about a little boy's efforts to own a Red Ryder air rifle.
MPAA:PG
MGM/UA Entertainment — *MGM/UA Home Video*

Christmas Tree, A/Puss-In-Boots **198?**
Cartoons
78900 60 mins C B, V P
Animated
An animated double feature: In "A Christmas Tree," two young children return a stolen Christmas tree from an evil giant, and in "Puss-In-Boots," a magical cat helps his master woo a princess.
Rankin-Bass Productions — *Prism*

Christmas Tree, The **1969**
Drama
45054 110 mins C B, V P
William Holden, Virna Lisi, Andre Bourvil, Brook Fuller
When the son of an extremely wealthy businessman contracts radiation poisoning and is given only a few months to live, his father devotes his entire life to the boy's happiness.
MPAA:G
Alan Enterprises — *United Home Video*

Christopher Strong **1933**
Drama
76841 77 mins B/W B, V P
Katherine Hepburn, Billie Burke, Colin Clive, Helen Chandler, directed by Dorothy Arzner
A daredevil aviatrix falls in love with a married British statesman who also has a family.
RKO; David O. Selznick — *RKO HomeVideo*

Chu Chu and the Philly Flash **1981**
Comedy
58824 102 mins C B, V, CED P
Alan Arkin, Carol Burnett, Jack Warden, Danny Aiello, Ruth Buzzi, Lou Jacobi
A has-been baseball player and a lame dance teacher meet while hustling the same corner; he sells hot watches, she's a one-man band. A briefcase full of government secrets soon involves them with the feds, the mob, and a motley collection of back-alley bums.
MPAA:PG
United Artists; Lawrence Turman; David Foster — *CBS/Fox Video*

Chuck Berry Live at The Roxy **1982**
Music-Performance
73564 60 mins C B, V P
Chuck Berry, Tina Turner
This is a performance of Chuck taped in 1982 where he performs all his hits and duets with Tina Turner.
Jack Malstead; C D Haifly — *Prism*

(For explanation of codes, see USE GUIDE and KEY)

Chuck's Choice Cuts 1982
Variety
73541 120 mins C B, V P
Chuck the security guard hosts this wild melange of crazy shorts, vintage TV show segments and musical clips.
Admit One — *Admit One Video*

C.H.U.D. 1984
Science fiction
76648 90 mins C B, V P
John Heard, Daniel Stern, Christopher Curry, Kim Griest
This program is based on a true New York Times story about life in the tunnels and caverns under the city and the exposure of a possible U.S. government plan to store wastes in these underground passages.
Andrew Bonime — *Media Home Entertainment*

Chump at Oxford, A 1940
Comedy
47140 63 mins B/W B, V, 3/4U P
Stan Laurel, Oliver Hardy, James Finlayson, Wilfrid Lucas, Peter Cushing, Charlie Hall
Street cleaners Laurel and Hardy foil a bank robbery and receive an all-expenses-paid education at Oxford as their reward.
Hal Roach — *Nostalgia Merchant; Blackhawk Films*

Chump at Oxford, A 1940
Comedy
63986 83 mins B/W B, V P, T
Stan Laurel, Oliver Hardy, Jimmy Finlayson, Wilfred Lucas, Peter Cushing
As a reward for foiling a bank robbery, Stan and Ollie receive a free education at Oxford University. This tape also includes a Charley Chase short, "The Tabasco Kid," made in 1932.
Hal Roach; MGM — *Blackhawk Films*

Churchill and the Generals 1981
Biographical/World War II
81080 180 mins C B, V P
Timothy West, Joseph Cotten, Arthur Hill, Eric Porter, Richard Dysart, narrated by Eric Sevareid
This is the true story of how Winston Churchill led England away from the bleak Dunkirk battle and rallied the Allied generals to a D-Day victory. Based upon Churchill's memoirs.
BBC — *Prism*

Cincinnati Kid, The 1965
Drama
60591 104 mins C B, V, CED P
Steve McQueen, Edward G. Robinson, Ann-Margret, Tuesday Weld, Karl Malden, Joan Blondell
A young New Orleans gambler is determined to take the expert crown away from an old dapper man known as the King of Stud Poker.
MGM — *MGM/UA Home Video*

Cincinnati Reds: Team Highlights 1984
Baseball
81138 30 mins C B, V P
Pete Rose, Dave Concepcion, Johnny Bench, Dan Driessen, George Foster, Dave Parker
6 pgms
The sagas of "The Big Red Machine" and Pete Rose's return to the Reds as player/manager are chronicled in this series.
1.1979: 25 Men 2.1980: A Good Year 3.1981: Baseball's Real Winners 4.1982: Building For '83 5.1983: A New Beginning 6.1984: The Hustle's Back
Major League Baseball — *Major League Baseball Productions*

Cinderella 1984
Fairy tales
Closed Captioned
73575 60 mins C B, V, CED P
Jennifer Beals, Jean Stapleton, Matthew Broderick, Eve Arden
From the "Faerie Tale Theatre" comes the story of a girl who gets even with her three stepsisters and ends up going to the ball to meet the man of her dreams.
Gaylord Productions; Platypus Productions — *CBS/Fox Video*

Cinderella Seahawks/NFL '83, The 1984
Football
72941 46 mins C B, V, FO P
Seattle Seahawks
Highlights from the 1983 season of the Seattle Seahawks and "NFL 1983."
NFL Films — *NFL Films Video*

Circle of Iron 1978
Adventure
37419 102 mins C B, V P
Jeff Cooper, David Carradine, Roddy McDowall, Eli Wallach, Christopher Lee
Plenty of action and martial arts combat abound in this story of one man's eternal quest for truth.
MPAA:R
New World — *Embassy Home Entertainment*

Circus, The/Day's Pleasure, A 1928
Comedy
81552 105 mins B/W B, V P
Charlie Chaplin, Merna Kennedy, Allan Garcia, Harry Crocher, directed by Charlie Chaplin
A comedy double feature: In "The Circus" Chaplin falls in love with a circus owner's equestrian stepdaughter and nothing seems to

go right for a man and his family when they seek "A Day's Pleasure."
Academy Awards '27/'28: Special Achievement Award: (Chaplin).
RBC Films — *Playhouse Video*

Circus World **1964**
Drama
16808 137 mins C B, V P
John Wayne, Rita Hayworth
American circus owner in Europe searches for aerialist he loved 15 years before and whose daughter he has reared.
Paramount; Samuel Bronston — *United Home Video*

Citizen Kane **1941**
Drama
00255 120 mins B/W B, V, 3/4U P
Orson Welles, Joseph Cotton, Agnes Moorehead
Citizen Kane is the story of a powerful newspaper publisher, told by those who thought they knew him best.
Academy Awards '41: Best Original Screenplay; N.Y. Film Critics Award '41: Best Motion Picture
RKO — *Nostalgia Merchant; VidAmerica; King of Video; RCA VideoDiscs*

Citizen Soldiers **1985**
Documentary/History-US
70686 45 mins C B, V P
Narrated by Ken Howard, directed by Fred Warshofsky
Part of the "In Defense of Freedom" series, this program traces the history of the United States Army.
A.B. Marian — *MPI Home Video*

City Heat **1984**
Comedy
Closed Captioned
80955 98 mins C B, V, LV P
Clint Eastwood, Burt Reynolds, Jane Alexander, Irene Cara, Madeline Kahn, Richard Roundtree, directed by Richard Benjamin
A tough cop and a wisecracking private eye team up to find out who murdered the detective's partner in Kansas City during the 1930's. Available in VHS and Beta Hi-Fi.
MPAA:PG
Malapso Company; Deliverance Prods — *Warner Home Video*

City Lights **1931**
Comedy
08420 81 mins B/W B, V P
Charlie Chaplin, Virginia Cherrill, Harry Myers, Henry Bergman, Jean Harlow, directed by Charlie Chaplin.
The story is of a tramp (Chaplin) who, by a series of lucky accidents, is able to restore the sight of a blind flowergirl.
United Artists — *CBS/Fox Video; RCA VideoDiscs; Playhouse Video*

City of Gold/Drylanders **19??**
Documentary/Canada
65233 92 mins B/W B, V, FO P
This tape combines two riveting Canadian documentaries: "City of Gold" (1957), which is about the Klondike Gold Rush of the 1890's, and "Drylanders" (1962), the story of a city family's attempt to live on a lonely Sakatchewan farm.
National Film Board of Canada — *Video Yesteryear*

City's Edge, The **1983**
Drama
81507 86 mins C B, V P
A young man becomes involved with the mysterious residents of a boarding house on the edge of the ocean.
Australia Film Office — *MGM/UA Home Video*

Clan of the Cave Bear, The **1985**
Fantasy/Drama
80036 120 mins C B, V P
Daryl Hannah, James Remar, Pamela Reed, John Doolittle, directed by Michael Chapman.
Producers Sales Organization — *Embassy Home Entertainment*

Clarence Darrow **1974**
Drama/Biographical
56888 90 mins C CED P
Henry Fonda
Henry Fonda's tour-de-force, one-man show portraying the controversial trial lawyer who defended over one hundred accused murderers, including Leopold and Loeb, and made history in the Scopes Monkey Trial.
Dome Prods — *RCA VideoDiscs*

Clash by Night **1952**
Drama
11661 105 mins B/W B, V P
Barbara Stanwyck, Paul Douglas, Marilyn Monroe
Lonely woman marries fishing boat captain and falls in love with his best friend.
RKO; Jerry Wald; Norman Krasna; Harriet Parsons — *United Home Video*

Clash of the Titans **1981**
Adventure
58702 118 mins C B, V, LV, CED P
Laurence Olivier, Maggie Smith, Claire Bloom, Ursula Andress, Burgess Meredith
Special effects highlight this telling of ancient Greek mythology and Nordic legends.
MPAA:PG

(For explanation of codes, see USE GUIDE and KEY)

MGM — *MGM/UA Home Video*

Class 1983
Comedy
65361 98 mins C B, V, LV P
Jacqueline Bisset, Rob Lowe, Andrew McCarthy, Cliff Robertson
A rich and funny farce, this is the outrageous story of a young prep school student whose torrid new love turns out to be his roommate's mother.
MPAA:R
Martin Ransohoff — *Vestron Video*

Class of Miss MacMichael, The 1979
Comedy-Drama
Closed Captioned
81174 95 mins C B, V P
Glenda Jackson, Oliver Reed, Michael Murphy, Rosalind Cash
A headstrong teacher tries to get through to her students at a London school for delinquents. Hi-Fi sound available for both formats.
MPAA:R
Brut Pictures — *Movie Buff Video*

Class of 1984 1982
Drama
66092 93 mins C B, V, LV, CED P
Perry King, Roddy McDowall, Timothy Van Patten
An explosive portrait of a school gang on the loose. A confrontation between the humanity of the past and a darkly violent future.
MPAA:R
United Film — *Vestron Video*

Classic Comedy Video Sampler 1949
Comedy
76918 78 mins B/W B, V P
Bud Abbott, Lou Costello, Moe Howard
This is a collection of classic comedy shorts featuring Amos and Andy, The Three Stooges, and Abbott and Costello.
Max Fleischer, et al — *United Home Video*

Classic Performances 1984
Music-Performance
79712 150 mins C B, V R, P
Maria Chiara, Kirite Kanawa 3 pgms
Three of the greatest operas and ballets are now available in one package.
1. Messiah 2.Aida 3.Die Fledermaus
Metropolitan Opera et al — *THORN EMI/HBO Video*

Claude Bolling: Concerto for Classic Guitar and Jazz Piano 1982
Music-Performance
47810 ? mins C LV P
Pianist George Shearing appears with guitarist Angel Romero, drummer Shelly Manne, and bassist Brian Torff in this definitive performance of Bolling's piece. In stereo.
Unknown — *Pioneer Artists*

Claws 1977
Adventure
80789 100 mins C B, V R, P
Leon Ames, Jason Evers, Anthony Caruso, Glenn Sipes, Carla Layton
A woodsman, a game commissioner and an Indian band together to stop a grizzly bear who is killing residents of a small Alaskan town.
MPAA:PG
Alaska Pictures — *Video Gems*

Clay Pigeon, The 1949
Drama
73693 63 mins B/W B, V P
Bill Williams, Barbara Hale, Richard Loo, directed by Richard Fleischer
A veteran wrongly accused of treason goes after the man who set him up.
RKO — *RKO HomeVideo*

Clean Slate (Coup de Torchon) 1981
Comedy-Drama
81442 128 mins C B, V P
Philippe Noiret, Isabelle Huppert, Jean-Pierre Marielle, Stephane Audran, directed by Bertrand Tavernier
An easy-going police officer has a sudden change of heart when he starts killing off residents of a small French West African village in 1938. Available in French with English subtitles or dubbed into English.
FR
Adolphe Viezzi — *Embassy Home Entertainment*

Cleopatra 1963
Drama
08431 246 mins C B, V, CED P
Elizabeth Taylor, Richard Burton, Rex Harrison, Pamela Brown, directed by Joseph L. Mankiewicz
After the death of Julius Caesar, Cleopatra, Queen of Egypt, becomes infatuated with Mark Antony. In stereo.
Academy Awards '63: Best Cinematography.
20th Century Fox; Walter Wanger — *CBS/Fox Video*

Clergyman's Daughter, The 1984
Mystery
80450 60 mins C B, V P
James Warwick, Francesca Annis
A clergyman's daughter calls upon detectives Tommy and Tuppence to investigate some murders at the family's country house. Based on the Agatha Christie story.
London Weekend Television — *Pacific Arts Video*

Cleveland Indians: Team Highlights 1984
Baseball
81139 30 mins C B, V P
Julio Franco, Bert Blyleven, Andre Thornton, Pat Tabler 5 pgms
This series highlights the Cleveland Indians' best moments from their past seasons.
1.1978: Good Vibrations 2.1981:A Baseball Tradition 3.1982: 50 Years at Municipal Stadium 4.1983: Building An Indian Uprising 5.1984: It's A Whole New Ballgame
Major League Baseball — *Major League Baseball Productions*

Cliffhangers, Comebacks, and Character 1982
Football
47714 23 mins C B, V, FO P
Team highlights of the 1981 San Diego Chargers, who had the most prolific offense in NFL history.
NFL Films — *NFL Films Video*

Clinic, The 1983
Comedy
77016 95 mins C B, V P
Chris Haywood, Simon Burke, Gerda Nicolson
A humorous look at an average day in a VD clinic.
Film House; Generation Films — *VidAmerica*

Cloak and Dagger 1984
Suspense/Adventure
Closed Captioned
80074 101 mins C B, V P
Dabney Coleman, Henry Thomas, Michael Murphy, directed by Richard Franklin
A young boy depends upon his imaginary friend to help him out when some agents are after his video game. Available in Beta Hi-Fi Stereo and VHS Dolby B Stereo.
MPAA:PG
Allan Carr; Universal — *MCA Home Video*

Clockwork Orange, A 1971
Science fiction
54118 137 mins C B, V, LV R, P
Malcolm McDowell, Patrick Magee, Adrienne Corri, directed by Stanley Kubrick
The head of a gang of punks is imprisoned for rape. When he is released he finds the world to be even more violent, especially when he is brutally beaten by his old adversaries. Based on the novel by Anthony Burgess.
MPAA:R
Warner Bros, Stanley Kubrick — *Warner Home Video; RCA VideoDiscs*

Clones of Bruce Lee, The 1980
Adventure/Martial arts
50731 87 mins C B, V P
Dragon Lee, Bruce Le, Bruce Lai, Bruce Thai, directed by Joseph Kong
A Kung-Fu fan's delight, as gallant warriors fr the Far East battle to reign supreme over th land of exotic self-defense.
MPAA:R
Newport Releasing — *Media Home Entertainment*

Close Encounters of the Third Kind (The Special Edition) 1980
Science fiction
Closed Captioned
54107 152 mins C B, V, LV P
Richard Dreyfuss, Teri Garr, Melinda Dillon, Francois Truffaut, directed by Steven Spielberg
A middle class American couple, who have had encounters of the first and second kinds, sighting UFO's and finding physical evidence of them, are determined to have the third encounter—actual contact with the occupants. In this special edition, which contains about 15 extra minutes, the man does go inside the UFO and makes contact.
MPAA:PG
Columbia Pictures — *RCA/Columbia Pictures Home Video; RCA VideoDiscs*

Closely Watched Trains 1966
Drama
72927 89 mins C B, V P
A young man who works in a train station during World War Two is going through his rites of passage. This film is subtitled.
CZ
Filmove Studio Barrandov — *RCA/Columbia Pictures Home Video*

Cloud Dancer 1980
Drama
66630 108 mins C B, V P
David Carradine, Jennifer O'Neill, Joseph Bottoms, directed by Barry Brown
A champion acrobatic trapeze flier selfishly pursues his career to the exclusion of those who care about him.
MPAA:PG
Blossom Pictures; Melvin Simon Productions — *Prism*

Clouds Over Europe **1939**
Mystery
81458 82 mins B/W B, V, LV P
Laurence Olivier, Valerie Hobson, Ralph Richardson, directed by Tim Whelan
A test pilot and a man from Scotland Yard team up to find out why new bomber planes are disappearing.
Alexander Korda — *Embassy Home Entertainment*

Clown, The **1952**
Comedy-Drama
58870 91 mins B/W B, V P
Red Skelton, Jane Greer, Tim Considine, Steve Forrest
A derelict ex-comedian, after several attempts at a comeback, faces his last chance in a make-or-break situation.
MGM — *MGM/UA Home Video*

Clown Murders, The **1983**
Suspense
76939 94 mins C B, V P
John Candy, Al Waxman, Susan Keller, Laurence Dane
Deadly consequences result from a Halloween kidnapping.
Magnum International Prods. — *Trans World Entertainment*

Clowns, The **1971**
Drama
03560 90 mins C B, V P
Directed by Federico Fellini
Directed by Federico Fellini, this movie recreates some of the most famous clown acts in circus history, presents the two major types of clowns, and suggests that the world is peopled with clowns.
Universal — *Media Home Entertainment; Discount Video Tapes*

Club, The **1981**
Drama
81564 93 mins C B, V P
Jack Thompson, Graham Kennedy, Frank Wilson, Alan Cassell, directed by Bruce Beresford
A soccer team coach has a difficult task in store for him; as he must inspire his losing team to capture the league trophy.
MPAA:PG
New South Wales Film Corp. — *Academy Home Entertainment*

Club Med **1983**
Comedy
80726 60 mins C B, V P
Alan Thicke, Jim Carrey, Jean-Claude Killy, Rita Coolidge, Ronnie Hawkins
A shy young comic and his wild and crazy companion set out to take the ski slopes by storm on a vacation they'll never forget.
MPAA:PG
Damian Lee; David Mitchell — *Active Home Video*

Coach **1978**
Comedy
63893 100 mins C B, V P
Cathy Lee Crosby, Michael Biehn, Keenan Wynn, Sidney Wicks
A female coach is hired to make a losing high school boys' basketball team into a championship one.
MPAA:G
Mark Tenser — *Media Home Entertainment*

Coal Miner's Daughter **1980**
Drama
45104 125 mins C B, V, LV P
Sissy Spacek, Tommy Lee Jones
The rags-to-riches story of how Loretta Lynn became "the queen of country music."
Academy Awards '80: Best Actress (Spacek).
MPAA:PG
Universal, Bernard Schwartz — *MCA Home Video; RCA VideoDiscs*

Coast to Coast **1980**
Comedy-Drama
54673 95 mins C B, V, LV R, P
Dyan Cannon, Robert Blake, Quinn Redeker, Michael Lerner, Maxine Stuart, Bill Lucking, directed by Joseph Sargent
A woman whose playboy husband is trying to have her judged insane rather than grant her the divorce she wants escapes from an East Coast hospital and hitches a ride with a trucker. The action centers on their cross-country trip, during which they are pursued by a detective (hired by the husband) and a finance company thug who is trying to repossess the trucker's vehicle.
MPAA:PG
Paramount — *Paramount Home Video*

Cocaine Cowboys **1979**
Drama
42913 90 mins C B, V P
Jack Palance
This modern day thriller tells the story of a rock and roll band smuggling cocaine to help their expenses and, in doing so, run afoul of the mob.
MPAA:R
International Harmony Films — *Media Home Entertainment*

Cocaine Fiends **1937**
Drama/Exploitation
03854 74 mins B/W B, V P
Lois January, Noel Madison, directed by W.A. Conner

A camp classic from the 1930's warning of the evils of cocaine. A brother and sister are led to the depths of degradation upon trying cocaine; heroin addiction, prostitution, and suicide are the inevitable results.
New Line Cinema — *Media Home Entertainment; Budget Video; Video Dimensions; Discount Video Tapes*

Cockeyed Cavaliers 1934
Comedy
44809 70 mins B/W B, V P, T
Wheeler and Woolsey, Dorothy Lee, Thelma Todd
Wheeler and Woolsey are stockaded for stealing the Duke's horses and carriage. To escape jail they swap clothes with some drunken royalty.
RKO — *Blackhawk Films*

Cockfighter 1974
Drama
74082 84 mins C B, V P
Warren Oates
This is the story of a man so obsessed with cockfighting he loses his money, possessions and lover because of it.
MPAA:R
Roger Corman — *Embassy Home Entertainment*

C.O.D. 1983
Comedy
80688 96 mins C B, V P
Corinne Alphen, Carol Davis
Two comedy advertising executives must create an exciting ad campaign for the Beaver Bra Company.
MPAA:PG
Lone Star Pictures International — *Vestron Video*

Coke Time with Eddie Fisher and The Perry Como Show 1955
Variety
42981 26 mins B/W B, V, FO P
Eddie Fisher, Perry Como
Here are highlights of two shows from the early evening live TV era before the news conquered all, when prime time TV had 15-minute programs included. Relaxed singing by both Como and Fisher.
NBC, CBS — *Video Yesteryear*

Cold Feet 1984
Comedy-Drama
80136 96 mins C B, V P
Griffin Dunne, Blanche Baker, Mark Cronogue
A television director tired of his wife leaves her for a lab researcher.
MPAA:PG
Cinecom International Films — *CBS/Fox Video*

Cold River 1981
Drama
65406 94 mins C B, V, CED P
An experienced Adirondacks guide takes his two children on an extended trip through the Adirondacks. For the children, it's a fantasy vacation until their father succumbs to a heart attack in the chilly mountains. "Cold River" is a journey of survival, and an exploration of human relationships.
MPAA:PG
Fred G Sullivan — *CBS/Fox Video*

Cold Room, The 1984
Mystery/Suspense
76862 95 mins C B, V P
George Segal, Renee Soutenjijk, Amanda Pays, Warran Clarke, Anthony Higgins
A teenaged girl on vacation with her father in East Berlin discovers the horrors hidden in an antiquated hotel room.
Mark Forstater; Bob Weis — *Media Home Entertainment*

Colditz Story, The 1955
War-Drama
63343 93 mins B/W B, V R, P
John Mills, Eriç Portman, Lionel Jeffries, Bryan Forbes, Ian Carmichael
Prisoners of war from the Allied countries join together in an attempt to escape from Colditz, a castle-prison deep within the Third Reich, reputed to be escape-proof.
British Lion; Ivan Foxwell — *THORN EMI/HBO Video*

Colgate Comedy Hour 1954
Variety
11271 54 mins B/W B, V, FO P
Spike Jones and His City Slickers, Nat King Cole, Bobby Van, Paul Gilbert, Senor Wences
Comedy, music, and a dash of sports give an indication of what the general public enjoyed on television during the early 1950's.
NBC — *Video Yesteryear*

Colgate Comedy Hour, The 1951
Comedy/Variety
47496 60 mins B/W B, V, FO P
Spike Jones and the City Slickers, Gale Robbins, Dave Garroway, Mike Wallace
Spike Jones' first appearance on this series features his band playing many of their hits: "Laura," "Be My Love," "Glow-Worm," "Chloe" and "Cocktails for Two."
NBC — *Video Yesteryear*

Colgate Comedy Hour, The 1955
Comedy/Variety
47494 29 mins B/W B, V, FO P
Dean Martin, Jerry Lewis, Margaret Dumont
This partial show features several songs and sketches by Dean and Jerry.
NBC — *Video Yesteryear*

Colgate Comedy Hour, The 1952
Comedy/Variety
78102 60 mins B/W B, V, FO P
Ray Bolger, Rise Stevens, Betty Kean, Roger De Koven
A classic TV Christmas program featuring music, dance and comedy.
NBC — *Video Yesteryear*

Colgate Comedy Hour I, The 1951
Variety
79238 60 mins B/W B, V, 3/4U P
Bud Abbott, Lou Costello, Vera Zorina, Joe Kirk, Bobby Barber
A series of comic complications arise as Abbott and Costello take a cruise to Paris.
NBC — *Shokus Video*

Colgate Comedy Hour, The 1952
Variety
79239 60 mins C B, V, 3/4U P
Keefe Braselle, Sonja Henie, Bud Abbott, Lou Costello
Abbott and Costello take a tour of a movie studio's prop department and meet up with the Creature From The Black Lagoon, plus Sonja Henie ice skates in this vintage 1952 kinescope.
NBC — *Shokus Video*

Colgate Comedy Hour, III, The 1951
Comedy
77188 60 mins B/W B, V P
Bud Abbott, Lou Costello, Lon Chaney Jr
Abbott and Costello wander into Lon Chaney Jr's haunted mansion and perform a comic opera "Don Juan Costello" in this Kinescope that includes the original commercials.
NBC — *Shokus Video*

Colgate Comedy Hour, IV, The 1951
Comedy
77189 60 mins B/W B, V P
Bud Abbott, Lou Costello, Charles Laughton
Bud and Lou head off to New York to make an appearance at the premiere of their latest movie.
NBC — *Shokus Video*

Colgate Comedy Hour: "Let's Face It," The 1954
Musical
47497 60 mins B/W B, V, FO P
Bert Lahr, Vivian Blaine, Gene Nelson, Betty Furness
A TV adaptation of Cole Porter's 1941 Broadway musical.
NBC — *Video Yesteryear*

Colgate Comedy Hour (The Eddie Cantor Show) 1952
Variety
42964 60 mins B/W B, V, FO P
Eddie Cantor, Kirk Douglas, Robert Clary
Aired January 20, 1952, this program stars Eddie Cantor singing and in comedy routines such as "Cantor Goes to College" and "The Detective Story," with Eddie playing the lead.
NBC — *Video Yesteryear*

Colgate Comedy Hour (The Tony Martin Show) 1951
Variety
42963 53 mins B/W B, V, FO P
Tony Martin, Celeste Holm, Fred Allen
This program, aired April 15, 1951 over NBC, features singing and comedy routines including "One Long Pan," a mystery sketch with Fred Allen as the Chinese sleuth.
NBC — *Video Yesteryear*

Colgate Comedy Hour with Martin and Lewis, The 1955
Variety
59089 29 mins B/W B, V, FO P
Dean Martin, Jerry Lewis, Margaret Dumont
Dean and Jerry in a classroom sketch, Dean croons "Sweet Kentucky Babe," and Dean teaches Jerry how to meet girls and handle ruffians on the beach.
NBC — *Video Yesteryear*

Collector, The 1965
Drama
13245 119 mins C B, V P
Terence Stamp, Samantha Eggar, Maurice Dallimore, directed by William Wyler
Lonely clerk kidnaps a girl and locks her in the cellar hoping she will fall in love with him. Filmdoms Famous Five '65: Best Actress (Eggar); Outstanding Director (Wyler).
Columbia — *RCA/Columbia Pictures Home Video; RCA VideoDiscs*

Collectors Item: The Left Fist of David 1960
Mystery
38999 27 mins B/W B, V, FO P
Vincent Price, Peter Lorre

The pilot program for a TV series that was never produced, featuring Price and Lorre as a pair of art dealers who become embroiled in mysterious doings.
CBS — *Video Yesteryear*

College 1927
Comedy
10093 60 mins B/W B, V P, T
Buster Keaton, A. Cornwall, directed by James W. Horne
Keaton graduates valedictorian from high school, tries out for every sport in college, and works as a soda jerk. Musical score by John Muri.
United Artists — *Blackhawk Films; Video Dimensions; Sheik Video; Video Yesteryear; Classic Video Cinema Collector's Club*

Color Adventures of Superman, The 194?
Cartoons
57350 52 mins C B, V, FO P
Animated
Seven cartoon adventures of the Man of Steel, as animated by the Fleischer Studio; produced between 1941 and 1943. Titles include "Superman," "The Mechanical Monsters," "The Magnetic Telescope," "The Japoteurs," "The Bulleteers," "Jungle Drums," and "The Mummy Strikes."
Max Fleischer — *Video Yesteryear*

Color Them Tough 1981
Football
51169 23 mins C B, V, FO R, P
New York Jets
1980 never materialized for the Jets the way they, their fans, and the experts had expected. Key injuries, offensive problems, and defensive inconsistency provided the problems. Still, they did manage to score upsets over strong clubs like Houston, Miami, and Atlanta.
NFL Films — *NFL Films Video*

Colorado 1940
Western
64390 54 mins B/W B, V, 3/4U P
Roy Rogers, Gabby Hayes
Roy and Gabby bring law and order to the untamed Colorado Territory.
Republic — *Nostalgia Merchant; Discount Video Tapes*

Columbia Pictures Cartoons Volume I: Mr. Magoo 1980
Comedy/Cartoons
44848 40 mins C B, V P
Animated
The famous near-sighted old codger is seen in five of his adventures: "Barefoot Flatfoot," "Bungled Bungalow," "Bwana Magoo," "Destination Magoo," and "Madcap Magoo."
UPA — *RCA/Columbia Pictures Home Video*

Columbia Pictures Cartoons Volume II: Mr. Magoo 1980
Comedy/Cartoons
44849 40 mins C B, V P
Animated
Mr. Magoo, through the voice of Jim Backus, entertains in his near-sighted fashion in: "Magoo Beats the Heat," "Magoo Breaks Par," "Magoo Goes Overboard," "Magoo Goes West," and "Magoo Saves the Bank."
UPA — *RCA/Columbia Pictures Home Video*

Columbia Pictures Cartoons Volume III: Gerald McBoing-Boing 1980
Cartoons
44850 30 mins C B, V P
Animated
This is a compilation of four Gerald McBoing-Boing cartoons: "Gerald McBoing-Boing," "Gerald McBoing-Boing on the Planet Moon," "Gerald McBoing-Boing's Symphony," and "How Now Boing-Boing."
UPA — *RCA/Columbia Pictures Home Video*

Columbia Pictures Cartoons Volume IV: UPA Classics 1980
Cartoons
44839 40 mins C B, V P
Animated
A collection of five favorite cartoons from UPA: "Christopher Crumpet's Playmate," "The Emperor's New Clothes," "The Jay Walker," "The Man on the Flying Trapeze," and "The Tell Tale Heart."
UPA — *RCA/Columbia Pictures Home Video*

Columbia Pictures Cartoons Volume V: Mr. Magoo 1983
Comedy/Cartoons
63444 60 mins C B, V P
Animated
Eight more misadventures with the near-sighted Mr. Magoo: "Stage Door Magoo," "Magoo's Glorious July 4th," "Sloppy Jalopy," "Magoo's Homecoming," "Trouble Indemnity," "Fuddy Duddy Buddy," "Magoo's Masquerade" and "Magoo Saves the Bank."
UPA — *RCA/Columbia Pictures Home Video*

Columbia Pictures Cartoons, Volume VI 19??
Cartoons
66013 60 mins C B, V P
Animated

Eight classic cartoons: "Pete Hothead," "Unicorn in the Garden," "Family Circus," "Ballet-Oop," "Christopher Crumpet," "Popcorn Story," "The Rise of Duton Lang," and "Four Wheels, No Breaks."
Columbia — *RCA/Columbia Pictures Home Video*

Columbia Pictures Cartoons, Volume VII **196?**
Comedy
68265 60 mins C B, V P
Animated, voice of Jim Backus
Eight more amusing adventures of Mr. Magoo.
UPA — *RCA/Columbia Pictures Home Video*

Coma **1978**
Suspense
44641 113 mins C B, V, LV, CED P
Genevieve Bujold, Michael Douglas, Elizabeth Ashley, Rip Torn, Richard Widmark, Lois Chiles, Harry Rhodes, directed by Michael Crichton
A young doctor at Boston hospital finds that patients, one of which is her best friend, suffer irreparable brain damage when supposed minor operations are performed. All these operations take place in the same operating room. Based on the novel by Robin Cook.
MPAA:PG
MGM — *MGM/UA Home Video*

Comancheros, The **1961**
Western
64903 108 mins C B, V, CED P
John Wayne, Stuart Whitman, Nehemiah Persoff
Wayne, a Texas Ranger, penetrates the ranks of the Comancheros, an outlaw gang supplying guns and liquor to the dreaded Comanches.
20th Century Fox — *CBS/Fox Video*

Come Back Champions/NFL '83 **1984**
Football
72936 46 mins C B, V, FO P
Detroit Lions
Highlights from the Detroit Lions' 1983 season and "NFL 83."
NFL Films — *NFL Films Video*

Come Back to the 5 and Dime Jimmy Dean, Jimmy Dean **1982**
Drama
60559 109 mins C B, V, CED P
Sandy Dennis, Cher, Karen Black, Sudie Bond, directed by Robert Altman
In 1975, the workers and customers of a small town 5 and Dime are celebrating the 20th anniversary of the death of James Dean. A complex look into the past begins when a woman announces that her son is the product of a one-night stand with the late actor twenty years ago.
Cinecom Intl — *Embassy Home Entertainment*

Come On, Cowboys **1937**
Western
64419 54 mins B/W B, V, 3/4U P
Bob Livingston, Ray Corrigan
The Three Mesquiteers rescue an old circus friend from certain death.
Republic — *Nostalgia Merchant; Discount Video Tapes*

Comeback **1983**
Drama/Music
65659 105 mins C B, V P
Eric Burdon
This is the story of a disillusioned rock star who gives up his life in the fast lane and tries to go back to his roots... and to himself.
TeleCulture Inc — *MGM/UA Home Video*

Comedy and Kid Stuff I **1952**
Comedy
33688 120 mins C B, V, 3/4U P
A collection of four light-hearted shows from the 50's including single episodes from "The Burns and Allen Show," and "I Married Joan," "Winky Dink," with host Jack Barry, and "Carson's Cellar," starring a twenty-five year old Johnny Carson and the late Jack Bailey.
CBS et al — *Shokus Video*

Comedy and Kid Stuff II **195?**
Comedy
33689 120 mins C B, V, 3/4U P
Four episodes from popular TV shows of the 1950's; "The Burns and Allen 1951 Christmas Show," "The Abbott and Costello Show," featuring the "Who's on First" routine and the retired actor's home, "Howdy Doody," and "The Lucy Show." Some black and white.
CBS et al — *Shokus Video*

Comedy and Kid Stuff III **1959**
Comedy
77193 120 mins B/W B, V P
Jack Benny, Art Linkletter, Andy Devine, Bob Hope, Senor Wences
A collection of three comedies from the 50's: Jack Benny clowns around with Bob Hope on "The Jack Benny Hour", Art Linkletter talks to kids on "House Party" and Andy Devine hosts a childrens show, "Andy's Gang."
CBS et al — *Shokus Video*

Comedy Classics of Mack Sennett and Hal Roach, The **1915**
Comedy
78103 51 mins B/W B, V, FO P

This program presents three comedy silent films: "Love, Loot and Crash"; "Looking for Trouble"; and "A Desperate Scoundrel."
Mack Sennett; Hal Roach — *Video Yesteryear*

Comedy Tonight **1977**
Comedy-Performance
59307 76 mins C B, V, CED P
Hosted by David Steinberg, Andy Kaufman, Robin Williams, Gallagher, Ed Bluestone, Richard Libertini, McIntyre Dixon
Los Angeles' "Improv" club is the scene for this night of stand-up comedy. Andy Kaufman performs his infamous Tony Clifton routine. Robin Williams reveals his X-rated side, and Gallagher offers his "Sledge-O-Matic" routine.
Home Box Office — *Vestron Video*

Comes a Horseman **1978**
Western
58954 119 mins C B, V P
James Caan, Jane Fonda, Jason Robards, Richard Farnsworth, Jim Davis, Mark Harmon, directed by Alan J. Pakula
A cattle baron, attempting to gobble up all the land in his territory, must contend with a woman who has the courage to stand up to him.
MPAA:PG
United Artists — *CBS/Fox Video*

Comfort and Joy **1984**
Comedy
77213 93 mins C B, V P
Bill Paterson, Eleanor David, C.P. Grogan, directed by Bill Forsyth
A Scottish disc jockey is forced to reevaluate his life when his kleptomaniac girlfriend walks out on him. The music is by Dire Straits guitarist Mark Knopfler.
MPAA:PG
Davina Belling; Clive Parsons — *MCA Home Video*

Comic Book Kids, The **1982**
Musical/Fantasy
64950 90 mins C B, V R, P
Joseph Campanella, Mike Darnell, Robyn Finn, Jim Engelhardt, Fay De Witt
Two youngsters enjoy visiting their friend's comic strip studio, since they have the power to project themselves into the cartoon stories.
MPAA:G
Century Video — *Video Gems*

Comic Book Kids, The **1985**
Children/Education
70573 60 mins C B, V P
Joseph Campanella, Mike Darnell, Robyn Finn, Jim Englehardt 13 pgms
The two adventurous youngsters of these videos step from reality to the comic book world with the aid of their magic belts. In the fantasy world, they learn a positive winning attitude from frustrated wizards and singing dragons.
Century Video Corp. — *Kid Time Video*

Comic Book Kids 2, The **1981**
Adventure/Comedy
70710 60 mins C B, V P
Joe Campanella, Mike Darnell, Robyn Finn, Jim Engelhardt, music by Jeffrey Rockwell, directed by Gene Weed
This time the magic belted youngsters enter the worlds of "Bigfoot Bluff," and the "Time Tables."
Skylark Prods. Ltd. — *Kid Time Video*

Coming Attractions #1—The Super Stars **1975**
Movie and TV trailers
42953 31 mins C B, V, FO P
This program in partial color is a collection of movie trailers from 12 all-time hits, starring some of Hollywood's biggest stars. Titles include "Presenting Lily Mars" with Judy Garland, "The Singing Kid" with Al Jolson, "Funny Lady" with Barbra Strisand, and others dating back to 1930.
MGM et al — *Video Yesteryear*

Coming Home **1978**
Drama
16051 127 mins C B, V, LV P
Jane Fonda, Jon Voight, Bruce Dern, directed by Hal Ashby.
Fonda falls in love with paraplegic Voight while her husband is overseas. A look at the effect of the Vietnam War on people.
Academy Awards '78: Best Actor (Voight), Best Actress (Fonda). MPAA:R
Jerome Hellman — *CBS/Fox Video; RCA VideoDiscs*

Coming Next Week: Those Great Movie Trailers **1984**
Movie and TV trailers
73547 120 mins C B, V P
Here are two hours of the movie previews from the 30's to the 80's covering all film genres. Some trailers are in black and white.
Admit One — *Admit One Video*

Coming of Age: The Story of the Dallas Cowboys 1970-74 **1982**
Football
63163 120 mins C B, V, FO P
Dallas Cowboys
A compilation of individual Dallas Cowboys team highlight films from the first half of the 1970's.
NFL Films — *NFL Films Video*

Coming Out Alive 197?
Drama
75623 73 mins C B, V P
A woman tries to rescue her kidnapped son from his estranged father who is involved in an assassination plot.
Export CBC — *Trans World Entertainment*

Coming Soon 1983
Movie and TV trailers
69029 55 mins C B, V P
Narrated by Jamie Lee Curtis
This program features over 50 excerpts from the "previews of coming attractions" of the most famous and infamous of the horror films.
Universal — *MCA Home Video*

Commandos 1972
War-Drama
59355 100 mins C B, V R, P
Lee Van Cleef, Jack Kelly
A 48-hour odyssey of courage lays the groundwork for Rommel's eventual defeat in Africa.
MPAA:PG
Heritage Enterprises — *Video Gems*

Commitment to Excellence/NFL '82 1983
Football
66223 45 mins C B, V, FO P
Highlights of the L.A. Raiders' 1982-83 season plus an overview of the whole NFL season.
NFL Films — *NFL Films Video*

Committee, The 1968
Satire/Comedy
66028 88 mins C B, V P
Howard Hesseman, Barbara Bosson, Peter Bonerz, Gary Goodrow, Carl Gottlieb
A comedy film of the seminal comedy troupe "The Committee," specialists in short, punchy satire.
Allen Myerson; Del Jack — *Pacific Arts Video*

Company of Wolves, The 1985
Horror/Fantasy
81162 95 mins C B, V P
Angela Lansbury, David Warner, Tusse Silberg, Sarah Patterson, Brian Glover, directed by Neil Jordan
A young girl on the threshold of womanhood dreams of a medieval fantasy world inhabited by wolves and werewolves.
MPAA:R
ITC Entertainment; Palace Productions — *Vestron Video*

Competition, The 1980
Drama
58480 125 mins C B, V P
Richard Dreyfuss, Amy Irving, Lee Remick, directed by Joel Oliansky
Two virtuoso pianists meet at an international competition and fall in love—something their careers have taught them to avoid.
MPAA:PG
Columbia — *RCA/Columbia Pictures Home Video*

Compleat Beatles, The 1982
Music
47738 120 mins C B, V, LV, CED P
The Beatles, George Martin, Brian Epstein, Billy Preston, Milt Oken, Bruce Johnston, Roger McGuinn, Mike McCartney, Mick Jagger
Music interviews, film clips, animation and live performances make up this "rockumentary" on the Beatles. New interviews are featured, as well as vintage film clips and studio footage. The first U.S press conference, legendary Hamburg footage, and an in-depth interview with George Martin are highlights.
Delilah Films — *MGM/UA Home Video*

Computability 1984
Electronic data processing
74075 60 mins C B, V P
This program, hosted by Steve Allen and Jayne Meadows, is the complete guide to computer software. It was developed to help viewers understand how their needs might best be served by current computer software.
Karl Home Video — *Karl/Lorimar Home Video*

Computer Wizard 1977
Comedy
70222 91 mins C B, V P
Henry Darrow, Kate Woodville, Guy Madison, Marc Gilpin
An 8-year-old boy with a genius I.Q. builds a powerful electronic device. His intentions are good, but the invention disrupts the entire town and lands him in big trouble.
MPAA:G
William H White; Torga Brown — *VCL Home Video*

Compututor 1984
Electronic data processing
78644 90 mins C B, V P
This series of twelve untitled programs instructs in the usage of micro computer operation and technology.
Embassy Home Entertainment — *Embassy Home Entertainment*

Con Artists, The 1980
Crime-Drama
69585 86 mins C B, V P
Anthony Quinn, Adriano Celentano
A con man recently sprung from prison and his protege set up a sting operation in Italy.

Unknown — *VidAmerica*

Conan the Barbarian 1982
Adventure
47848 115 mins C B, V, LV, CED P
Arnold Schwarzenegger, James Earl Jones, Max von Sydow, directed by John Milius
Conan sets out to avenge the murder of his parents and retrieve the sword bequeathed him by his father.
MPAA:R
Universal — *MCA Home Video*

Conan the Destroyer 1984
Adventure/Fantasy
Closed Captioned
78891 101 mins C B, V, LV P
Arnold Schwarzenegger, Grace Jones, Wilt Chamberlain, Sarah Douglas, directed by Richard Fleischer
Conan is manipulated by Queen Tamaris into searching for a treasure in return for bringing Conan's love Valeria back to life.
MPAA:PG
Raffaella De Laurentis; Universal Pictures — *MCA Home Video*

Concert For Bangladesh, The 1972
Music-Performance
75926 90 mins C B, V R, P
George Harrison, Bob Dylan, Ringo Starr, Billy Preston, Eric Clapton, Ravi Shankar, Kalus Voorman
This program presents the concert held in 1971 for the benefit of the needy.
Thorn — *THORN EMI/HBO Video*

Concrete Jungle, The 1982
Drama
64242 106 mins C B, V P
Tracy Bregman, Jill St. John, Barbara Luna
After being set up by her boyfriend, a woman is sent to a correctional facility for drug smuggling.
MPAA:R
Columbia; Billy Fine — *RCA/Columbia Pictures Home Video*

Condemned to Live 1935
Mystery
66367 68 mins B/W B, V P
Ralph Morgan, Maxine Doyle, Mischa Auer
Terror and murder enter a small, peaceful town when a mysterious stranger arrives.
Chesterfield — *Movie Buff Video*

Condorman 1981
Comedy
58623 90 mins C B, V R, P
Michael Crawford, Oliver Reed, Barbara Carrera, James Hampton, Jean-Pierre Kalfon, directed by Charles Jarrott
Woody Wilkins, an inventive comic book writer, adopts the identity of his own character, Condorman, in order to help a beautiful Russian spy defect.
MPAA:PG
Walt Disney Productions — *Walt Disney Home Video*

Confessional, The 1980
Suspense/Horror
80287 108 mins C B, V P
Anthony Sharp, Susan Pehaligon, Stephanie Beacham, Norman Eshley
A mad priest unleashes a monster from his confessional to wreak havoc upon the world.
MPAA:R
Lone Star Pictures — *Prism*

Confessions of a Police Captain 1972
Drama
80389 104 mins C B, V P
Martin Balsam, Franco Nero, Marilu Tolo
A police captain is trying to wipe out the corruption that is infecting his city.
MPAA:PG
Bruno Turchetto; Mario Montanari — *Embassy Home Entertainment*

Confessions of a Young American Housewife 1978
Drama
59675 85 mins C B, V P
Jennifer Wells, Rebecca Brooke, Chris Jordan
A recent divorcee moves in with two younger couples and experiences sexual liberation.
MPAA:R
Joe Sarno — *Media Home Entertainment*

Conformist, The 1971
Drama
60330 115 mins C B, V R, P
Jean-Louis Trintignant, Stefania Sandrelli, Dominique Sanda, Pierre Clementi, directed by Bernardo Bertolucci
Repressing his homosexual drives, Marcello Clerici strives for an "acceptable" life as a member of the Italian Fascist Secret Service, and middle-class would-be wife-chaser, until an odd series of events make him a willing murderer.
MPAA:R
Paramount — *Paramount Home Video*

Conqueror, The 1956
Adventure
65120 111 mins C B, V P
John Wayne, Susan Hayward, William Conrad, Agnes Moorehead, directed by Dick Powell

 (For explanation of codes, see USE GUIDE and KEY)

John Wayne stars as Genghis Khan in this tale of the warlord's early life and involvement with the kidnapped daughter of a powerful enemy.
Universal; Howard Hughes; RKO — *MCA Home Video*

Conquest **1983**
Fantasy/Adventure
77361 92 mins C B, V P
George Rivero, Andrea Occhipinti, Violeta Cela
Two valiant warriors team up to destroy an evil sorceress who controls a planet's life-giving sun.
MPAA:R
Giovanni Di Clemente — *Media Home Entertainment*

Conquest of the Planet of the Apes **1972**
Science fiction
81543 87 mins C B, V P
Roddy McDowell, Don Murray, Ricardo Montalban, Hari Rhodes, directed by J. Lee Thompson
The apes turn the tables on the human Earth population when they lead a revolt against their cruel masters.
MPAA:PG
Apjac Productions; 20th Century Fox — *Playhouse Video*

Conrack **1974**
Biographical/Drama
Closed Captioned
81555 111 mins C B, V P
Jon Voight, Paul Winfield, Madge Sinclair, Hume Cronyn, directed by Martin Ritt
This is the true story of how Pat Conroy tried to teach a group of ignorant black children in a dilapidated schoolhouse in South Carolina. Available in VHS and Beta Hi-Fi.
MPAA:PG
20th Century Fox — *Playhouse Video*

Constructing Stud Walls **1984**
Home improvement
Closed Captioned
77259 30 mins C B, V P
Carpenter George Giangrante demonstrates the proper procedures for constructing a stud wall.
You Can Do It Videos — *You Can Do It Videos*

Contempt **1964**
Drama
65428 102 mins C B, V P
Brigitte Bardot, Jack Palance, Fritz Lang
A struggling playwright accepts a writing offer from a crude, manipulative American producer to please his wife. When the producer is attracted to the wife, she thinks her husband is trying to push her into an affair.
Avco Embassy — *Embassy Home Entertainment*

Contes D'Hoffman, Les **1984**
Music-Performance
80816 135 mins C B, V R, P
Placido Domingo, Ileana Cotrubas, Agnes Baltsa
A performance of the Offenbach opera where in a poet tells of his rivals thwarting of his last three romantic encounters. Available in VHS and Beta Hi Fi.
John Schlesinger — *THORN EMI/HBO Video*

Continental Divide **1981**
Comedy/Romance
59036 103 mins C B, V, LV, CED P
John Belushi, Blair Brown, Allen Goorwitz, directed by Michael Apted
A hard-nosed political columnist takes off for the Colorado Rockies on an "easy assignment"—interviewing a reclusive arnithologist he eventually falls in love with.
MPAA:PG
Universal — *MCA Home Video*

Conversation, The **1974**
Drama
58494 113 mins C B, V, LV R, P
Gene Hackman, John Cazale, Frederick Forrest, Cindy Williams, Robert Duvall, directed by Francis Ford Coppola
A professional eavesdropper's conscience interferes with his job when he fears that he might be acting as an accomplice to murder.
MPAA:PG
Paramount; Francis Ford Coppola — *Paramount Home Video*

Convoy **1978**
Adventure
73018 106 mins C B, V R, P
Kris Kristofferson, Ali McGraw, Ernest Borgnine
A trucker is out to form an indestructible truck convoy to Mexico.The film was inspired by the song "Convoy" by C. W. Mc Call.
MPAA:R
Robert M Sherman — *THORN EMI/HBO Video*

Coogan's Bluff **1968**
Drama
47413 100 mins C B, V P
Clint Eastwood, Lee J. Cobb, Tisha Sterling, Don Stroud, Betty Field
An Arizona deputy sheriff travels to New York in order to extradite an escaped murderer.
MPAA:PG
Universal — *MCA Home Video*

Cooking for Compliments 1984
Cookery
70570 72 mins C B, V P
Lee Gerovitz, Steve Cassarino
Two professional chefs show viewers a lively approach to meal preparation on this tape. They offer recipes for ten dinners, four breakfasts, side dishes, and even make table setting suggestions. Bound recipe cards are included.
AM Available
Television Communications Network — *Clever Cleaver Productions*

Cool Cats: 25 Years of Rock 'n' Roll Style 1983
Music/Documentary
66457 90 mins C B, V P
The effect of rock music on contemporary style and mores is the subject of this "rockumentary" which features performance clips and interviews by thirty-four rock trendsetters, including Elvis, The Beatles, Culture Club, David Bowie and many others.
Delilah Films; Stephanie Bennett — *MGM/UA Home Video*

Cool Hand Luke 1967
Drama
58224 126 mins C B, V, LV R, P
Paul Newman, George Kennedy, J. D. Cannon, Strother Martin, Jo Van Fleet, directed by Stuart Rosenberg
A man sentenced to sweat out a term on a prison farm refuses to compromise with authority.
Warner Bros; Jalem Productions — *Warner Home Video*

Cool World, The 1963
Documentary/Drama
63628 107 mins B/W B, V, FO P
This docudrama, set on the streets of Harlem, focuses on a 15-year-old black youth whose one ambition in life is to own a gun and lead his gang.
Frederick Wiseman — *Video Yesteryear*

Copacabana 1947
Musical/Comedy
64543 91 mins B/W B, V P
Groucho Marx, Carmen Miranda, Steve Cochran, Gloria Jean, Andy Russell
A quick-thinking theatrical agent books a nightclub singer into two shows at the same time, which leads to the expected complications.
United Artists — *Republic Pictures Home Video*

Coppelia with Fernando Bujones 1982
Dance
47406 110 mins C B, V P
Fernando Bujones
Mr. Bujones, the featured dancer of Barishnikov's American Ballet Theater, plays Franz, the young lover. Recorded with the Ballets de San Juan.
Kultur — *Kultur*

Copperhead 1984
Horror
79759 90 mins C B, V P
Jack Renner, Gretta Ratliff, David Fritts, Cheryl Nickerson
A group of copperhead snakes attack a family who possess a stolen Incangold necklace.
MPAA:R
Independent — *United Home Video*

Cornered 1945
Suspense
81024 102 mins B/W B, V P
Dick Powell, Walter Slezak, Micheline Cheirel, Luther Adler, directed by Edward Dmytryk
When a Canadian airman is released from a German prison camp he pursues a Nazi war criminal to Buenos Aires to avenge the death of his wife and child.
RKO — *RKO HomeVideo*

Corpse Vanishes, The 1942
Mystery
16158 64 mins B/W B, V P
Bela Lugosi
Scientist experiments with various potions and turns himself into an ape.
Prime TV — *VidAmerica; Kartes Productions*

Corrupt 1984
Crime-Drama
72183 99 mins C B, V R, P
Harvey Keitel
A policeman becomes involved in illegal activities in order to catch a murderer.
MPAA:PG
Elda Ferri — *THORN EMI/HBO Video*

Corrupt Ones, The 1967
Adventure
76905 87 mins C B, V P
Robert Stack, Elke Sommer, Nancy Kwan, Christian Marguand
Everyone's after a photographer who has a medallion that will lead to buried treasure in Red China.
Warner Bros. — *Embassy Home Entertainment*

Corsican Brothers, The 1984
Comedy/Adventure
77217 91 mins C B, V P
Richard "Cheech" Marin, Tommy Chong
The Corsican Brothers join forces to battle against an evil French Baron.

MPAA:PG
Orion Pictures — *Lightning Video*

Corsican Brothers, The **1942**
Adventure
55352 111 mins B/W B, V, 3/4U P
Douglas Fairbanks Jr, Akim Tamiroff, Ruth Warrick, J. Carrol Naish
Alexandre Dumas' classic about siamese twins who, although separated, remain spiritually tied through various adventures.
Edward Small; United Artists — *Nostalgia Merchant*

Cosmic Monsters **1958**
Science fiction
49902 75 mins B/W B, V P
Forrest Tucker, Gaby Andre, Alec Mango, Hugh Latimer
Alien beings in flying saucers terrorize a countryside with giant insects and other strange things from outer space.
DCA — *United Home Video; Mossman Williams Productions*

Cosmos: The Championship Years 1977-1980 **1981**
Soccer
51086 115 mins C B, V R, P
New York Cosmos
Highlights of the past four seasons of New York Cosmos soccer, featuring Pele, Giorgio Chinaglia, Franz Beckenbauer, and championship moments, are included in this program.
Cosmos Soccer Club — *Warner Home Video*

Cotton Club, The **1984**
Musical-Drama
80426 121 mins C B, V P
Diane Lane, Richard Gere, Gregory Hines, Lonette McKee, directed by Francis Ford Coppola
A musician playing at The Cotton Club falls in love with gangster Dutch Schultz's girlfriend. Songs featured include "Crazy Rhythm," "Am I Blue," "Cotton Club Stomp," "Jitter Bug" and "I'll Wind."
MPAA:R
Robert Evans; Orion Pictures — *Embassy Home Entertainment*

Count Basie Live at the Hollywood Palladium **1984**
Music-Performance
79874 60 mins C B, V P
One of the Count's last concerts taped at the Hollywood Palladium. Songs performed include "Shiny Stockings," "Splanky" and "Big Stuff."
VCL Home Video — *VCL Home Video*

Count Dracula **1971**
Horror
70199 90 mins C B, V P
Christopher Lee, Herbert Lom, Klans Kinski
A "new" version of the Dracula legend, based closely on the original novel by Bram Stoker.
Independent — *Republic Pictures Home Video*

Count of Monte Cristo, The **1980**
Cartoons
66578 52 mins C B, V P
Animated
An animated version of the classic Alexander Dumas story of a swordsman who seeks revenge on the men who wrongly imprisoned him.
Hanna-Barbera Productions — *Worldvision Home Video*

Count of Monte Cristo, The **1934**
Adventure
55349 114 mins B/W B, V, 3/4U P
Robert Donat, Elissa Landi, Louis Calhern, directed by Rowland V. Lee
Alexandre Dumas' classic about Edmon Dantes who, after years in prison, escapes and avenges himself on those who framed him.
Edward Small; Reliance; United Artists — *Nostalgia Merchant; Blackhawk Films*

Count of Monte Cristo, The **1975**
Drama/Adventure
56892 120 mins C B, V P
Richard Chamberlain, Kate Nelligan, Donald Pleasence, Alessio Orano, Tony Curtis, Louis Jourdan, Trevor Howard
The Alexandre Dumas classic with the swashbuckling Edmond Dantes and the villainous Mondego.
Norman Rosemont Productions, ITC — *CBS/Fox Video; RCA VideoDiscs*

Count, The/The Adventurer **1917**
Comedy
58657 52 mins B/W B, V, FO P
Charlie Chaplin, Eric Campbell, Edna Purviance, Frank Coleman, directed by Charlie Chaplin
Two Chaplin two-reelers: "The Count (The Phoney Nobleman)" (1916), in which Charlie impersonates a count at the home of Miss Moneybags, and "The Adventurer" (1917), Chaplin's final film for Mutual, in which he plays an escaped convict with the law relentlessly on his trail. Silent with musical score.
Mutual — *Video Yesteryear*

Count Yorga, Vampire 1970
Horror
81180 90 mins C B, V R, P
Robert Quarry, Roger Perry, Michael Murphy, Michael MacBrady
The vampire Count Yorga conducts a seance to conjure up the spirit of a young girl's recently deceased mother. Things get weird at his mansion. Available in VHS Stereo and Beta Hi-Fi.
MPAA:PG
American International Pictures — *THORN EMI/HBO Video*

Countdown 1968
Science fiction
65356 102 mins C B, V P
James Caan, Robert Duvall, Michael Murphy, Ted Knight, Joanna Moore, Barbara Baxley, Charles Aidman
Robert Altman directed this thrilling adventure about the first moon mission and its toll on the astronauts and their families.
Warner Brothers — *Warner Home Video*

Countdown to World War II 194?
World War II
10154 59 mins B/W B, V P, T
Newsreels cover rise of Hitler and Mussolini.
Unknown — *Blackhawk Films*

Country 1984
Drama
76851 109 mins C B, V R, P
Jessica Lange, Sam Shepard, Wilford Brimley, Matt Clark, directed by Richard Pearce
A farm family's life starts to unravel when the government attempts to foreclose on their land.
MPAA:PG
Far West Productions; Pangaea Corporation Productions — *Touchstone Home Video*

Country Gentlemen 1936
Comedy
46347 54 mins B/W B, V, FO P
Ole Olsen, Chic Johnson, Joyce Compton, Lila Lee
Olsen and Johnson play fast-talking conmen who sell shares in a worthless oil field to a bunch of World War I veterans.
Republic — *Video Yesteryear; Discount Video Tapes; See Hear Industries*

Country Girl, The 1982
Drama
63344 137 mins C B, V R, P
Dick Van Dyke, Faye Dunaway, Ken Howard
An aging, alcoholic actor, desperate for a comeback, blames his fiercely loving wife for his downfall.
Group W Productions — *THORN EMI/HBO Video*

Country Girl, The 1954
Drama
64506 104 mins B/W B, V R, P
Bing Crosby, Grace Kelly, William Holden, Gene Reynolds, directed by George Seaton
The wife of an alcoholic actor is unfairly blamed for his sodden condition. Based on the play by Clifford Odets
Academy Awards '54: Best Actress (Kelly); Best Screenplay (George Seaton).
Paramount — *Paramount Home Video; RCA VideoDiscs*

Country Lovers, City Lovers 1972
Drama
78635 121 mins C B, V P
Here are two adaptations of short stories by South African novelist Nadine Gordimer about interracial love.
Profile Productions — *MGM/UA Home Video*

Country Music with the Muppets 1985
Variety/Music-Performance
Closed Captioned
81547 55 mins C B, V P
Rowlf, Kermit the Frog, Fozzie Bear, Johnny Cash, Roy Clark, Crystal Gayle, Roger Miller
Join Rowlf as he plays some of his favorite country music videos in this collection of highlights from "The Muppet Show".
Henson Associates — *Playhouse Video*

Country Style USA and Community Jamboree 1959
Variety
38996 30 mins B/W B, V, FO P
Roy Acuff, the Smoky Mountain Boys, Ferlin Husky, Carl Smith, Patsy Cline 2 pgms
Two 15-minute syndicated programs produced in Nashville featuring a number of popular country performers from the Grand Ole Opry.
Army Recruiting, National Guard Recruiting — *Video Yesteryear*

Country-Western All-Stars 1956
Music-Performance/Variety
47479 52 mins B/W B, V, FO P
Carl Smith, Jim Reeves, Faron Young, Hank Snow, Minnie Pearl, Tex Ritter, The Sons of the Pioneers
A live country-western variety show broadcast from the Ryman Auditorium in Nashville.
WSM Nashville — *Video Yesteryear*

 (For explanation of codes, see USE GUIDE and KEY)

Countryman 1983
Drama/Adventure
65371 103 mins C B, V P
Countryman, Hiram Keller, Kristine St. Clair
Countryman is no ordinary man. He is a man of the sea, a man of knowledgde, in effortless harmony with everything that lives and breathes.
MPAA:R
Chris Blackwell — *Media Home Entertainment*

Courage of Rin Tin Tin, The 1983
Adventure
79336 90 mins C B, V P
James Brown, Lee Aaker
Rusty and his faithful dog Rin Tin Tin help the cavalry soldiers of Fort Apache keep law and order in a small Arizona town.
Screen Gems — *Monterey Home Video*

Courageous Dr. Christian, The 1940
Drama
47458 66 mins B/W B, V, FO P
Jean Hersholt, Dorothy Lovett, Tom Neal
Dr. Christian is faced with an epidemic of meningitis among the inhabitants of a shanty town.
RKO — *Video Yesteryear; Discount Video Tapes*

Court Jester, The 1956
Comedy
65399 101 mins C B, V R, P
D. Norman Panama, Melvin Frank, Danny Kaye, Glynis Johns, Basil Rathbone, Angela Lansbury
A 12th century court jester in England becomes involved with a desperate band of outlaws who are attempting to overthrow the king.
Paramount — *Paramount Home Video*

Court Jester, The 1956
Comedy
79182 101 mins C B, V R, P
Danny Kaye, Glynis Johns, Basil Rathbone, Angela Lansbury, directed by Norman Panama and Melvin Frank
A former circus clown teams up with a band of outlaws who attempt to get rid of a tyrant king and replace him with the real king.
Paramount — *Paramount Home Video*

Cousin, Cousine 1976
Drama/Comedy
52745 95 mins C B, V, CED P
Marie-Christine Barrault, Marie-France Pisier, Victor Lanoux, Guy Marchand, directed by Jean-Charles Tacchella
Distant cousins who meet at a round of family parties, funerals, and weddings fall in love with each other, but their relationship soon becomes more than platonic.
France; Libra Films — *CBS/Fox Video*

Cousteau—Diving for Roman Plunder 1978
Oceanography
47392 59 mins C B, V R, P
Jacques Cousteau and the crew of the Calypso embark upon an underwater search for ancient Roman artifacts.
Cousteau Society — *Warner Home Video*

Cousteau—The Nile 1979
Travel/Documentary
47388 116 mins C B, V R, P
Jacques Cousteau
A double-length episode of the "Cousteau Odyssey" series, taking the viewer on a spectacular journey down the Earth's longest river to reveal the fabled past and challenging present of the Nile River.
Cousteau Society — *Warner Home Video*

Covergirl 1983
Drama
65746 98 mins C B, V R, P
Jeff Conaway, Irena Ferris, Cathie Shirriff
Covergirl tells the story of one girl's meteoric rise to become a superstar model. The heartaches and struggles involved in the climb to success are also depicted.
MPAA:R
Claude Heroux — *THORN EMI/HBO Video*

Cow Town 1950
Western
66307 70 mins B/W B, V P, T
Gene Autry, Gail Davis, Jock Mahoney
A range war results when ranchers begin fencing in their land to prevent cattle rustling.
Columbia — *Blackhawk Films*

Cowboy Previews # 1 194?
Movie and TV trailers/Western
64416 60 mins B/W B, V, 3/4U P
A collection of theatrical trailers from over thirty-five "B" westerns. Titles include "Riders in the Sky," "King of the Bullwhip," "Utah Wagon Train," "Trail of Robin Hood," "Sioux City Sue" and many others.
Republic et al — *Nostalgia Merchant*

Cowboys, The 1972
Western
74209 128 mins C B, V R, P
John Wayne, Roscoe Lee Browne, Bruce Dern
Wayne stars as a cattle rancher who is forced to hire eleven schoolboys to help him drive his cattle 400 miles to market.
MPAA:PG
Mark Rydell — *Warner Home Video*

Cowboys from Texas 1939
Western
64402 54 mins B/W B, V, 3/4U P
Bob Livingston, Raymond Hatton, Duncan Renaldo, Carole Landis
The Three Mesquiteers bring about a peaceful settlement to a fight between cattlemen and homesteaders.
Republic — *Nostalgia Merchant*

Crack Shadow Boxers 197?
Martial arts/Adventure
47699 91 mins C B, V P
Ku Feng, Chou Li Lung
Through a series of misadventures, Wu Lung and Chu San battle to protect the inhabitants of a small village from the onslaught of relentless bandits.
United Enterprises Ltd — *Master Arts Video*

Crackers 1984
Comedy
74090 92 mins C B, V, LV, CED P
Donald Sutherland, Jock Warden, Sean Penn
This is the off beat story of two bumbling thieves who round up a gang of equally inept neighbors and go on the wildest crime spree you have ever seen.
MPAA:PG
Universal — *MCA Home Video*

Cracking Up 1983
Comedy
66323 90 mins C B, V P
Jerry Lewis, Herb Edelman, Foster Brooks, Milton Berle, Sammy Davis Jr., directed by Jerry Lewis
Jerry Lewis stars as an accident-prone misfit whose mishaps on the road to recovery create chaos for everyone he meets.
MPAA:PG
Warner Bros — *Warner Home Video*

Crackler, The 1984
Mystery
80446 60 mins C B, V P
James Warwick, Francesca Annis
During the 20's, a husband and wife private investigation team set out to find a gang of forgers operating in high society circles. Based on a story by Agatha Christie.
London Weekend Television — *Pacific Arts Video*

Craig Claiborne's New York Times Video Cookbook 1985
Cookery
81488 120 mins C B, V R, P
"The New York Times" food editor Craig Claiborne prepares twenty of his most requested recipes and gives expert cooking advice in this program.
NYT Productions — *Warner Home Video*

Crash of Flight 401, The 1982
Drama
75459 101 mins C B, V P
William Shatner, Adrienne Barbeau, Lloyd Bridges
This jetliner story is based on an incident that occurred during a landing at Miami's airport.
King Features — *U.S.A. Home Video*

Crater Lake Monster, The 1977
Horror
59655 85 mins C B, V P
Richard Cardella, Glenn Roberts, Mark Siegel, Bob Hyman
A meteor crashes into a mountain lake causing it to warm up. The dormant egg of a prehistoric creature lying at the bottom is incubated, and the newborn creature heads for land.
MPAA:PG
William R Stromberg — *United Home Video*

Crawling Eye, The 1958
Science fiction/Horror
44349 87 mins B/W B, V, 3/4U P
Forrest Tucker, Laurence Payne, Janet Munro, Jennifer Jayne
Hidden in a radioactive fog, the crawling eye decapitates its victims and returns these humans to Earth to threaten mankind. Includes previews of coming attractions from classic science fiction films.
VCC Films — *Nostalgia Merchant*

Crawling Hand, The 1963
Horror/Science fiction
59348 89 mins B/W B, V R, P
Alan Hale, Rod Lauren
An astronaut's hand takes off without him, on an unearthly spree of stranglings.
Medallion — *Video Gems*

Crazed 1982
Horror
78399 88 mins C B, V P
Laslo Papas, Belle Mitchell, Beverly Ross
A psychopath keeps a dead girl's body in a boarding house and kills all intruders to keep his secret.
Independent — *Trans World Entertainment*

Crazy Mama 1975
Drama
65074 81 mins C B, V, CED P
Cloris Leachman, Stuart Whitman, Ann Southern, Jim Backus
A band of female outlaws turn to crime on the way to Arkansas to repossess the family farm that was sold during the Depression.

MPAA:PG
New World Pictures — *Embassy Home Entertainment*

Creative Camera, The **1982**
Photography
63424 60 mins C LV P
This interactive videodisc is a primer of single lens reflex photography offering a practical and detailed introduction to SLR photographic techniques.
Valley Isle Productions; Jac Holzman — *Pioneer Video Imports*

Creature from Black Lake **1976**
Horror
80666 95 mins C B, V P
Jack Elan, Dub Taylor, Dennis Fimple, John David
Two anthropology students from Chicago travel to the Louisiana swamps searching for the creature from Black Lake.
MPAA:PG
Jim McCullough Prods. — *Lightning Video*

Creature from the Haunted Sea **1960**
Satire
56914 76 mins B/W B, V, FO P
Antony Carbone, Betsy Jones-Moreland
A monster movie satire set in Cuba shortly after the revolution and centering around an elaborate plan to loot the Treasury and put the blame on a strange sea monster.
Roger Corman — *Video Yesteryear*

Creeping Flesh, The **1972**
Horror
62808 89 mins C B, V P
Peter Cushing, Christopher Lee, Lorna Heilbron
A scientist decides he can cure evil by injecting his patients with a serum derived from the blood of evil humans. The plan backfires.
MPAA:PG
Columbia — *RCA/Columbia Pictures Home Video*

Creeping Terror **1964**
Horror
59653 81 mins B/W B, V P
Vic Savage, Shannon O'Neal, William Thourlby
A spaceship discovered in the Rocky Mountains contains a creeping monster that devours its human victims while computing their metabolism and sending the information to the mother craft somewhere in space.
A J Nelson — *United Home Video*

Creepshow **1982**
Horror
60561 120 mins C B, V, CED R, P
Hal Holbrook, Adrienne Barbeau, Viveca Lindfors, E.G. Marshall, Stephen King, Leslie Nielsen, Carrie Nye, Fritz Weaver, Ted Danson, directed by George A. Romero
Stephen King's tribute to E.C. Comics, those pulp horror comic books that delight in the grizzly, the grotesque and morbid humor.
MPAA:R
Warner Bros — *Warner Home Video*

Cricket, The **1983**
Drama
80037 90 mins C B, V P
Clio Goldsmith, Virna Lisi, Anthony Franciosa, Renato Saluatori
The sparks fly when a woman and her seventeen year old daughter become rivals for the affections of the same man.
IT
Ibrahim Moussa; Samuel Goldwyn — *Embassy Home Entertainment*

Cricket on the Hearth, The **1923**
Drama/Christmas
66353 68 mins B/W B, V P
Paul Gerson, Virginia Brown Faire, Paul Moore, Joan Standing
An adaptation of Charles Dickens' short story about the life of a mail carrier and his bride, who find the symbol of good luck, a cricket on the hearth, when they enter their new home. Silent with organ score.
Paul Gerson Pictures; Selznick Releasing — *Blackhawk Films*

Cries and Whispers **1972**
Drama
54802 94 mins C B, V R, P
Harriet Andersson, Ingrid Thulin, Liv Ullman, Kary Sylway, Erland Josephson, directed by Ingmar Bergman
A Bergman production that dramatizes states of mind. It is the story of the lives of three sisters, all in their thirties. The middle sister is dying of cancer and the other two, along with a peasant woman, take care of her.
MPAA:R
New World Pictures — *Warner Home Video*

Crimes of Passion **1984**
Drama
Closed Captioned
80459 101 mins C B, V, LV P
Kathleen Turner, Anthony Perkins, directed by Ken Russell
A prostitute becomes the object of a disturbed priest's erotic fantasies. Music score by Rick Wakeman.
New World Pictures — *New World Video*

(For explanation of codes, see USE GUIDE and KEY)

Criminal Code, The **1931**
Drama
78879 98 mins B/W B, V P
Walter Huston, Boris Karloff, Constance Cummings, directed by Howard Hawks
A young man is jailed for killing a man in self defense and his life worsens at the hands of a sadistic prison warden. In Beta Hi-Fi.
Harry Cohn; Columbia Pictures — *RCA/Columbia Pictures Home Video*

Crimson **1985**
Horror
81035 90 mins C B, V P
Paul Nash, Sylvia Solar
A criminal goes on a bloody rampage when he receives a Brain transplant.
MPAA:R
Empire Entertainment — *Wizard Video*

Crisis at Central High **1980**
Drama
80673 120 mins C B, V P
Joanne Woodward, Charles Durning, William Ross, Henderson Forsythe, directed by Lamont Johnson
This is a dramatic recreation of the events that lead up to the integration of Central High in Little Rock, Arkansas in 1957.
Time Life TV — *Lightning Video*

Crocodile **1981**
Horror
65510 95 mins C B, V R, P
Nat Puvanai, Tany Tim, directed by Herman Cohen
Nature strikes with unbelievable fury, creating the largest and most savage crocodile on earth. No experts can kill this monster animal that is too huge and powerful to trap. Soon the giant crocodile attacks a beach town, killing and devouring dozens of people.
MPAA:R
Dick Randall; Robert Chan — *THORN EMI/HBO Video*

Crosby, Stills & Nash: Daylight Again **1983**
Music-Performance
64792 108 mins C B, V, LV, CED P
Directed by Tom Trbovich
This video concert taped in November 1982 at the New Universal Amphitheater in Los Angeles represents the group's first tour since 1977. Includes such songs as "Just a Song Before I Go," "Chicago," "Suite: Judy Blue Eyes," and from the recent "Daylight Again" album, "Wasted on the Way." In stereo.
Universal Pay TV; Neal Marshall — *MCA Home Video*

Cross Country **1983**
Crime-Drama/Suspense
65421 95 mins C B, V P
Richard Beymer, Nina Axelrod, Michael Ironside
Action revolves around the brutal murder of a call girl with initial suspicion falling on a TV advertising director involved with the woman. The story twists and turns from the suspect to the investigating detective.
MPAA:R
Pieter Kroonenburg — *Embassy Home Entertainment*

Cross Creek **1983**
Adventure/Biographical
69678 120 mins C B, V, CED R, P
Mary Steenburgen, Rip Torn
This film is based on the life of Marjorie Kinnan Rawlings who, after 10 years as a frustrated reporter/writer, moved to the remote and untamed Everglades, where she received the inspiration to write numerous bestsellers.
Universal — *THORN EMI/HBO Video*

Cross of Iron **1976**
War-Drama
47815 120 mins C B, V, 3/4U P
James Coburn, Maximilian Schell, James Mason, David Warner, Senta Berger, directed by Sam Peckinpah
During World War II, two antagonistic German officers clash over personal ideals as well as strategy in combatting the relentless Russian attack.
MPAA:R
ITC Entertainment — *Nostalgia Merchant; Media Home Entertainment*

Crossbar **1980**
Handicapped
52428 30 mins C B, V P
John Ireland, Brent Carver, Kate Reid
Aaron Kornylo is determined to reach Olympic qualifications in the high jump despite having only one leg. Inspired by a true story, this program dramatically shows how far determination and work can take a person.
AM Available
Canadian Broadcasting — *Trans World Entertainment*

Crossfire **1947**
Drama
64368 86 mins B/W B, V, 3/4U P
Robert Young, Robert Mitchum, Robert Ryan, Gloria Grahame, Paul Kelly, directed by Edward Dmytryk
A Jewish hotel guest is murdered and three soldiers are suspected of the crime, one of whom is violently anti-Semitic. The first Hollywood film that explored racial bigotry.
RKO — *Nostalgia Merchant*

Crowded Paradise **1956**
Drama
66368 94 mins B/W B, V P
Hume Cronyn, Nancy Kelly, Mario Alcalde, Frank Silvera
A Puerto Rican auto mechanic encounters discrimination when he looks for a job in New York City.
Tudor Pictures — *Movie Buff Video*

Crucible of Terror **1972**
Horror
58548 95 mins C B, V R, P
Mike Raven, Mary Maude, James Bolam
A mad sculptor covers beautiful models with hot wax, then imprisons them in a mold of bronze.
Scotia Barber — *Video Gems*

Cruel Sea, The **1953**
War-Drama
58459 121 mins B/W B, V R, P
Jack Hawkins, Stanley Baker, Denholm Elliott
The story of a Royal Navy corvette on convoy duty in the Atlantic.
Ealing Studios — *THORN EMI/HBO Video*

Cruise Into Terror **1978**
Suspense/Drama
80300 100 mins C B, V P
Ray Milland, Hugh O'Brian, John Forsythe, Christopher George, Stella Stevens
A sarcophagus brought aboard a pleasure cruise ship unleashes an evil force which starts to slowly kill off the ship's passengers.
Aaron Spelling Productions — *Prism*

Cruise Missile **1978**
Suspense
60415 100 mins C B, V P
Peter Graves, Curt Jurgens, Michael Dante
A unique task force is on a mission to keep the world from nuclear holocaust.
Noble Production — *Monterey Home Video*

Cruising **1980**
Drama
56753 102 mins C B, V, CED P
Al Pacino, Paul Sorvino, Karen Allen, directed by William Friedkin
A bizarre murder-mystery set in the homosexual nightlife scene of New York's West Village. Music by Jack Nitzsche.
MPAA:R
Jerry Weintraub, Lorimar — *CBS/Fox Video*

Crusaders Live!, The **1984**
Music-Performance
80851 52 mins C B, V P
Joe Sample, Wilton Felder, Stix Hooper
The infectious jazz-fusion sounds of the Crusaders are captured in this taped concert. Available in VHS and Beta Hi Fi.
MCA Home Video — *MCA Home Video*

Cry For Love, A **1981**
Drama
80633 98 mins C B, V P
Susan Blakely, Powers Boothe, Gene Barry, Lainie Kazan, Charles Siebert, Herb Edelman
A divorced woman hiding her amphetamine addiction begins a near tragic romance with an alcoholic. Adapted from Jill Robinson's "Bed/Time/Story". Available in Beta Hi-Fi and VHS Stereo.
Charles Fries Prods.; Alan Sacks Prods. — *U.S.A. Home Video*

Cry of the Black Wolves **197?**
Adventure
79342 90 mins C B, V P
Ron Ely, Catherine Conti
A trapper wrongly accused of murder saves the life of a bounty hunter hired to capture him.
Cinema Shares International — *Active Home Video*

Cry of the Innocent **1980**
Adventure
74108 93 mins C B, V P
Rod Taylor, Joanna Pettet, Nigel Davenport
An action-packed thriller about a Vietnam veteran who is out to find a group of Irish terrorists that killed his family.
Michael O'Herlihy — *VCL Home Video*

Cry Panic **1974**
Mystery/Drama
80301 74 mins C B, V P
John Forsythe, Anne Francis, Earl Holliman, Ralph Meeker
A man is thrown into a strange series of events after accidentally running down a man on a highway.
Spelling/Goldberg Productions — *Prism*

Crystal Gayle in Concert **1984**
Music-Performance
66495 60 mins C B, V P
Crystal Gayle
A live concert by country singer Crystal Gayle, taped at Hamilton Place, Canada.
Prism — *Prism*

Cuando Tu No Estas **197?**
Drama
49743 90 mins C B, V P
Maria Jose Alfonso, Ricardo Lucia, Margaret Peters, Jose Martin
A young man leaves his provincial town, looking for success in the city. He becomes familiar with the works of a female journalist, and she does

likewise with his. Finally they meet, and love runs its course. In Spanish.
SP
Independent — *Media Home Entertainment*

Cucaracha, La **1934**
Musical-Drama
12832 21 mins C B, V, FO P
Steffi Duna
A lavish production filled with Mexican songs and dances. The first three-strip, live-action Technicolor film ever made.
Academy Awards '34: Best Comedy Short Subject.
RKO — *Video Yesteryear*

Cuchillo ("Knife") **1984**
Adventure
72960 90 mins C B, V P
Cuchillo is the weapon of the Apaches which they use to fight the white man in this violent tale of revenge and murder.
SP
Foreign — *Unicorn Video*

Cuckoo Clock That Wouldn't Cuckoo, The **1958**
Fairy tales/Cartoons
00666 12 mins C B, V P, T
Animated
An animated fable of a clockmaker who tries to get the cuckoo in the royal cuckoo clock to break his silence.
Coronet Films — *Blackhawk Films; Coronet Films*

Cujo **1983**
Horror
66324 94 mins C B, V, LV, CED P
Dee Wallace, Daniel Hugh-Kelly, Danny Pintauro, Ed Lauter, Christopher Stone
A rabid dog goes berserk and attacks a mother and her child who are trapped inside a broken-down car. Based on the Stephen King bestseller.
MPAA:R
Warner Bros — *Warner Home Video*

Culture Club: Kiss Across the Ocean **1984**
Music-Performance
72188 60 mins C B, V P
America's favorite drag queen, Boy George, leads his pop group Culture Club through a string of hits performed live at the Hammersmith Odeon in London.
Tessa Watts and Richard Branston — *CBS/Fox Video*

Curious George **1982**
Cartoons
75892 30 mins C B, V P
3 pgms
This program is a three-volume animated series of adventures of the monkey Curious George.
LWI Productions; Tablot Television — *Sony Corporation of America*

Curley and His Gang in the Haunted Mansion **1947**
Comedy/Mystery
66111 54 mins C B, V P
Larry Olsen
An eccentric scientist gets involved in a haunted mansion mystery.
Hal Roach — *Unicorn Video*

Currier & Ives Christmas, A **1983**
Christmas
66309 90 mins C B, V P
A video music Christmas album that sets the classic American art of Currier & Ives and other early lithographers to a continuous background of favorite Christmas music.
NTA — *Republic Pictures Home Video*

Curse of King Tut's Tomb, The **1980**
Drama/Suspense
70565 98 mins C B, V P
Robin Ellis, Harry Andrews, Eva Marie Saint, Raymond Burr, Wendy Heller, directed by Philip Leacock
It's 1922 and archeologists have opened Tutankhamens tomb. The curse of the Boy King seems unleashed as tragic events bring the adventurers uncommon gloom.
Stromberg-Kerby Prods. in assoc. with CPT and H.T.V. West — *RCA/Columbia Pictures Home Video*

Curse of the Cat People **1944**
Fantasy
44802 70 mins B/W B, V, 3/4U P
Simone Simon, Kent Smith, Jane Randolph, directed by Robert Wise
A young sensitive girl is guided by the vision of her dead mother.
RKO — *Nostalgia Merchant*

Curse of the Pink Panther, The **1983**
Comedy
72465 110 mins C B, V P
Ted Wass, David Niven, Robert Wagner, Herbert Lom, Capucine, Harvey Korman, directed by Blake Edwards
Ted Wass stars as Clifton Sleigh, an inept New York City detective, assigned to find the missing Inspector Clouseau. The plot is complicated by

an assortment of gangsters and aristocrats who cross paths with the detective.
MPAA:PG
Tital Productions & United Artists Corporation — *MGM/UA Home Video*

Curtains **1983**
Horror
65351 90 mins C B, V P
John Vernon, Samantha Eggar
A director has a clash of wills with a film star that spells "Curtains" for a group of aspiring actresses.
MPAA:R
Peter and Richard Simpson — *Vestron Video*

Custodio de Senoras **1979**
Suspense
47857 100 mins C B, V P
Augusto Larreta, Carlos Rotundo
Monica is threatened by death by a grudging boyfriend. George, the detective, becomes Monica's protector. In Spanish.
SP
Nicolas Carreras; Luis Repetto — *Media Home Entertainment*

Cut Above, A **1980**
Football
45130 24 mins C B, V, FO R, P
Pittsburgh Steelers
Highlights of the 1979 Pittsburgh Steelers World Championship season
NFL Films — *NFL Films Video*

Cut Above/NFL '83, A **1984**
Football
72942 46 mins C B, V, FO P
Washington Redskins
Highlights from the Washington Redskins' 1983 season and "NFL 83."
NFL Films — *NFL Films Video*

Cutter's Way **1981**
Mystery/Drama
63109 105 mins C B, V, CED P
Jeff Bridges, John Heard, Lisa Eichhorn, directed by Ivan Passer
Two friends, one an embittered Vietnam veteran, become involved in a puzzling murder. Originally titled "Cutter and Bone."
MPAA:R
United Artists — *MGM/UA Home Video*

Cyrano **1974**
Cartoons
79241 48 mins C B, V P
Animated, voice of Jose Ferrer
An animated version of the classic story of a physically unattractive man who uses an attractive man to express his feelings to the woman he loves.
Hanna-Barbera Productions — *Worldvision Home Video*

Cyrano de Bergerac **1946**
Drama
39008 112 mins B/W B, V P
Jose Ferrer, Mala Powers, William Prince, Elena Verdugo, Morris Carnovsky, directed by Michael Gordon
The classic film version of the story of Cyrano, the tragic wit renowned for his nose, but longing of the love of a beautiful lady, Roxanne. Based on Edmond Rostand's play of 17th century Paris.
Academy Awards '50: Best Actor (Ferrer)
United Artists, Stanley Kramer — *Prism; Republic Pictures Home Video; Electric Video; Video Yesteryear; Cable Films; Video Connection; Budget Video; Discount Video Tapes; Classic Video Cinema Collector's Club*

D

Daddy Long Legs **1982**
Fantasy
72231 60 mins C B, V P
Animated
Jean Webster's story about an orphaned girl who is sent to school by an anonymous benefactor is animated for the first time.
Bunker Jenkins — *Children's Video Library*

Daffy Duck: The Nuttiness Continues... **1956**
Cartoons
81572 59 mins C B, V P
Animated, voice of Mel Blanc
Daffy Duck runs amuck in this collection of cartoon classics that include "Beanstalk Bunny", "Deduce You Say", "Dripalong Daffy" and "The Scarlet Pumpernickel".
Warner Bros. — *Warner Home Video*

Daffy Duck's Movie: Fantastic Island **1983**
Comedy/Cartoons
65323 78 mins C B, V, LV, CED P
Animated
A compilation of classic Warner Brothers cartoons, starring Daffy Duck, Speedy Gonzales, Bugs Bunny, Porky Pig, Sylvester, Tweety, Pepe Le Pew, Pirate Sam, Granny, Foghorn Leghorn and the Tasmanian Devil.
MPAA:G
Warner Brothers — *Warner Home Video*

Daggers 8 1980
Martial arts
76935 90 mins C B, V P
The Kung Fu masters are back battling their opponents with deadly daggers.
Foreign — *Trans World Entertainment*

Dagora, the Space Monster 1965
Science fiction/Horror
69570 80 mins C B, V, FO P
Yosuke Natsuki, Yoko Fujiyama
A giant, slimy, pulsating mass from space lands on Earth and begins eating everything in sight. Scientists join together in a massive effort to destroy the creature.
Toho — *Video Yesteryear*

Dain Curse, The 1978
Mystery/Suspense
64972 118 mins C B, V P
James Coburn, Jason Miller, Jean Simmons, Beatrice Straight
In 1928, private eye Hamilton Nash must recover stolen diamonds, solve a millionaire's suicide, avoid being murdered, and end an insane family curse. Based on the novel by Dashiell Hammett.
Martin Poll Productions — *Embassy Home Entertainment*

Dakota 1945
Western
00284 82 mins B/W B, V P
John Wayne, Vera Ralston, Walter Brennan
Brawling saga with Wayne battling land grabbers in Dakota.
Republic — *Republic Pictures Home Video*

Dakota Incident 1956
Western
74484 88 mins C B, V P
Dale Robertson, Ward Bond
This is the story of a group of people brought together by a stagecoach ride across the dangerous Cheyenne territory.
Republic — *Republic Pictures Home Video*

Dallas Cowboys 1984 Team Highlights 1985
Football
70545 70 mins C B, V, FO P
The Cowboys proved that you don't need to make the playoffs to have a "Silver Season" in '84. This tape features 47-minutes of highlights from the entire NFL's '84 season as well.
NFL Films — *NFL Films Video*

Dam Busters, The 1955
War-Drama
63353 119 mins B/W B, V R, P
Michael Redgrave, Richard Todd
In 1942 London, a scientist develops a plan to destroy the great Moehne and Eder dams in Germany.
ABPC; Richard Clark — *THORN EMI/HBO Video*

Dames 1934
Musical
73981 95 mins B/W B, V P
Dick Powell, Joan Blondell, Ruby Keeler, ZaSu Pitts, Guy Kibbee, directed by Ray Enright
A fanatical puritanistic millionaire tries to stop the opening of a Broadway show. Songs from this movie include "I Only Have Eyes for You" and choreography by Busby Berkeley.
Warner Bros — *Key Video*

Damien—Omen II 1978
Horror
45106 110 mins C B, V, CED P
William Holden, Lee Grant, Lew Ayres, Robert Foxworth, Sylvia Sidney, directed by Don Taylor
This sequel to "The Omen" is about a young boy, possessed with mysterious demonic powers, who kills those people he comes in contact with.
MPAA:R EL, SP
20th Century Fox, Harvey Bernard — *CBS/Fox Video*

Damien: The Leper Priest 1980
Biographical/Drama
81261 96 mins C B, V P
Ken Howard, Mike Farrell, Wilfred Hyde-White, William Daniels, David Ogden Stiers
This is the true story of Father Damien, a Roman Catholic priest who devoted his life to helping Hawaiian lepers on Molokai island. Available in VHS stereo and Beta Hi-Fi.
Tomorrow Entertainment — *U.S.A. Home Video*

Damn Yankees 1958
Musical
74202 110 mins C B, V R, P
Gwen Verdon, Ray Walston, Tab Hunter
This musical feature is adapted from the Broadway hit about a baseball fan who makes a pact with the devil.
George Abbott; Stanley Donen — *Warner Home Video*

Damnation Alley 1977
Science fiction/Drama
70698 87 mins C B, V P
George Peppard, Jan-Michael Vincent, Paul Winfield, Dominique Sanda, Jackie Earle Haley, directed by Jack Smigth
A warrior, an artist and a biker set off in search of civilization after armageddon. Hi-Fi stereo sound in both formats.
MPAA:PG

 (For explanation of codes, see USE GUIDE and KEY)

20th Century Fox — *Key Video*

Damned, The 1969
Drama
58225 150 mins C B, V R, P
Dirk Bogarde, Ingrid Thulin, Helmut Griem, Charlotte Rampling, directed by Luchino Visconti
Visconti's study of a family's disintegration in greed, lust, and the madness of pre-war Germany. English language version.
MPAA:R
Warner Bros — *Warner Home Video*

Damsel in Distress, A 1937
Musical
63992 101 mins B/W B, V P, T
Fred Astaire, Joan Fontaine, George Burns, Gracie Allen, Ray Noble, directed by George Stevens
Fred falls for an upper-class British girl, whose family wants her to have nothing to do with him. George and Ira Gershwin's memorable songs include "A Foggy Day," "Nice Work If You Can Get It," "Stiff Upper Lip" and "Put Me to the Test."
RKO — *Blackhawk Films; Nostalgia Merchant*

Dance of the Dead 1968
Adventure/Fantasy
76921 50 mins C B, V P
Patrick McGoohan
The members of the village use a succession of women in an attempt to break The Prisoner's will. An episode from "The Prisoner" TV series.
ITC — *MPI Home Video*

Danger Lights 1930
Drama
44992 73 mins B/W B, V P, T
Jean Arthur, Loius Wohleim
This movie depicts the railroads and the railroad men's dedication to the tenet of giving the best possible care to each other and their trains.
RKO — *Blackhawk Films; Sheik Video; Kartes Productions*

Danger Mouse, Cassette #1 1984
Cartoons
78394 60 mins C B, V R, P
Animated
Danger Mouse must save the world from the evil Baron Greenback in this first volume of episodes from the animated series.
Independent — *THORN EMI/HBO Video*

Danger Mouse Cassette #2 1983
Cartoons
80335 60 mins C B, V R, P
Animated
In this volume, Danger Mouse and his sidekick Penfold solve the mystery of the disappearing bagpipes and the evil Baron Greenback causes Danger Mouse to lose his memory.
Thames Television — *THORN EMI/HBO Video*

Danger Mouse, Cassette # 3 1983
Cartoons
80651 60 mins C B, V R, P
Animated
Danger Mouse and his faithful sidekick Penfold return to battle evil-doers in this collection of four animated adventures.
Cosgrove Hall Productions — *THORN EMI/HBO Video*

Danger on Wheels 1939
Drama
66369 61 mins B/W B, V P
Richard Arlen, Andy Devine
A hotshot race car driver faces tragedy on and off the track.
Universal — *Movie Buff Video*

Dangermouse, Cassette #4 1984
Cartoons
81484 60 mins C B, V R, P
Animated
Dangermouse and his faithfull sidekick Penfold find themselves in trouble again in this collection of four episodes from the series.
Cosgreave Hall Productions — *THORN EMI/HBO Video*

Dangerous Company 1982
Drama
70254 98 mins C B, V P
Beau Bridges, Karen Carlson, Jan Sterling, Carlos Brown, Ralph Macchio.
Based on the success story of Ray Johnson, who survives childhood adversity and 27 years of crime and imprisonment to become a wealthy businessman and a respected member of his community.
Dangerous Co. in assoc. with CBS Entertainment — *U.S.A. Home Video*

Dangerous Holiday 1937
Adventure
12811 54 mins B/W B, V, FO P
Hedda Hopper, Franklin Pangborn, Guinn Williams, Jack La Rue
A young violin prodigy would rather be just "one of the boys." He runs away from his greedy relatives but begins to hang out with a gang of kidnappers.
Republic — *Video Yesteryear*

Dangerous Mission 1954
Mystery
33900 75 mins B/W B, V P
Victor Mature, Piper Laurie, Vincent Price, William Bendix
A New York girl witnesses a gangland murder and flees to the Midwest, pursued by killers and the police.
RKO;Irwin Allen — *Nostalgia Merchant*

Dangerous Summer, A 1982
Suspense
73148 100 mins C B, V P
James Mason, Tom Skeritt
James Mason is sent to Australia to investigate a murderous insurance fraud.
McElroy & McElroy Prods — *VCL Home Video*

Danguard Ace 1982
Cartoons/Science fiction
63119 100 mins C B, V P
Animated
A heroic young fighter pilot seeks the aid of Danguard Ace, mighty robot, to combat the evil forces of Komisar Krel.
Toei Animation; MK Company; Jim Terry Production Services — *Family Home Entertainment*

Daniel 1983
Drama
66410 130 mins C B, V R, P
Timothy Hutton, Amanda Plummer, Mandy Patinkin, Lindsay Crouse
The children of a couple who were executed for espionage suffer many agonizing trials as they grow to maturity with the constant reminder of their parents' treasonous activities. Based on E.L. Doctorow's "The Book of Daniel."
MPAA:R
Paramount — *Paramount Home Video*

Daniel Boone 1936
Western
65228 77 mins B/W B, V P
George O'Brien, Heather Angel, John Carradine
Daniel Boone guides a party of settlers from North Carolina to the fertile valleys of Kentucky, facing Indians, food shortages and bad weather along the way.
RKO — *Hal Roach Studios; Blackhawk Films; Video Connection; Budget Video; Discount Video Tapes; See Hear Industries*

Danny 1979
Drama
76800 90 mins C B, V P
Rebecca Page, Janet Zarish, Gloria Maddox, George Luce
A young girl begins to mature when a mysterious benefactor gives her a pony.
MPAA:G
Wombat Prods — *Monterey Home Video*

Danny Boy 1946
Comedy-Drama
12864 67 mins B/W B, V, FO P
A returning war dog has difficulty adjusting to normal life. Things get worse for him and his young master when Danny Boy is assumed to be dangerous.
PRC — *Video Yesteryear; Sheik Video*

Danny Boy 1984
Drama
77243 92 mins C B, V P
Stephen Rea, Honor Heffernan
A young saxophone player who witnesses a murder embarks on a path to find the killer.
MPAA:R
Triumph Films — *RCA/Columbia Pictures Home Video*

Danspak II 1984
Music-Performance
76667 30 mins C B, V P
Six different New York groups combining night-life scenes, dance routines, humor and much more. The groups include: The Jim Carroll Band, The Lenny Kaye Connection, Strange Party, Michael Musto and the Must, Go Ohgami, Jason Harvey.
Co Directions Inc — *Sony Corporation of America*

Danton 1982
Biographical
72921 136 mins C B, V P
Gerard Depardieu
An historical period film about the leader of the French Revolution, Georges Danton. This film is in French with subtitles.
MPAA:PG FR
Les Films Du Losange Maragret Menegoz — *RCA/Columbia Pictures Home Video*

Darby O'Gill and the Little People 1959
Fantasy
53796 93 mins C B, V R, P
Albert Sharpe, Janet Munro, Sean Connery, Estelle Winwood, directed by Robert Stevenson
Set in Ireland, a roguish old story teller tumbles into a well and visits the land of leprechauns, who give him three wishes in order to rearrange his life.
Walt Disney — *Walt Disney Home Video*

Daring Game 1968
Adventure
80034 100 mins C B, V P
Lloyd Bridges, Brock Peters, Michael Ansara, Joan Blackman, directed by Laslo Benedek

A group of scuba divers attempt to rescue a woman's husband and daughter from an island dictatorship.
Paramount; Ivan Tors — *Republic Pictures Home Video*

Dark, The 1979
Horror
47317 92 mins C B, V P
William Devane, Cathy Lee Crosby, Richard Jaeckel, Keenan Wynn, Vivian Blaine
A supernatural beast commits a string of gruesome murders.
MPAA:R
Dick Clark; Film Ventures International — *Media Home Entertainment*

Dark Command 1940
Western
66310 95 mins B/W B, V P
John Wayne, Walter Pidgeon, Claire Trevor, Roy Rogers, Marjorie Main
The story of Quantrell's Raiders, who patrolled Kansas territory during the Civil War, in search of wrongdoers.
Republic — *Republic Pictures Home Video*

Dark Crystal, The 1982
Fantasy/Adventure
69390 93 mins C B, V, CED R, P
Directed by Jim Henson
Jen and Kira, two of the last surviving Gelflings, attempt to return a crystal shard (discovered with the help of a sorceress) to the castle where the Dark Crystal lies, guarded by the cruel and evil Skeksis.
MPAA:PG
ITC Entertainment; Jim Henson and Gary Kurtz — *THORN EMI/HBO Video*

Dark Forces 1983
Mystery/Suspense
81092 96 mins C B, V P
Robert Powell, David Hemmings, Broderick Crawford
Things get weird for a Senator when an enigmatic stranger comes to visit him.
MPAA:PG
Antony I. Ginnane — *Media Home Entertainment*

Dark Mirror, The 1946
Mystery
76832 85 mins B/W B, V P
Olivia de Havilland, Lew Ayres, Thomas Mitchell, Garry Owen
A psychologist and a detective must determine which twin sister murdered a prominent physician.
Nunnally Johnson — *Republic Pictures Home Video*

Dark Passage 1947
Drama/Mystery
73967 107 mins B/W B, V P
Humphrey Bogart, Lauren Bacall, Agnes Moorehead, Bruce Bennett, Tom D'Andrea
A convict escapes from San Quentin to prove he was framed for the murder of his wife, aided by a women who believes his story.
Warner Bros — *Key Video*

Dark Places 1973
Horror
65426 91 mins C B, V P
Joan Collins, Christopher Lee, Robert Hardy
Masquerading as a hospital administrator, a former mental patient inherits the ruined mansion of a man who had killed his wife and children and died insane. As he lives in the house, the spirit of its former owner seems to overcome him, and the bizarre crime is repeated.
MPAA:PG
Cinerama — *Embassy Home Entertainment*

Dark Room, The 1984
Suspense/Drama
80491 90 mins C B, V P
A disturbed young man becomes obsessed with his father's voluptuous mistress and longs to possess her.
VCL Communications — *VCL Home Video*

Dark Star—The Special Edition 1974
Science fiction
66029 91 mins C B, V P
Dan O'Brian, Brian Narelle, directed by John Carpenter
A scoutship is entrusted with clearing a path in space for a Colony's ships.
MPAA:G
John Carpenter; Bryanston Pictures — *United Home Video*

Dark Victory 1939
Drama
64707 106 mins B/W CED P
Bette Davis, George Brent, Geraldine Fitzgerald, Humphrey Bogart, Ronald Reagan
Bette Davis portrays a young heiress who discovers she is dying from a brain condition. She attempts to pack a lifetime into a few months.
Warner Bros — *Key Video; RCA VideoDiscs*

Dark Waters 1944
Drama
81222 93 mins B/W B, V, LV P
Merle Oberan, Franchat Tone, Thomas Mitchell, directed by Andre de Toth
A woman is convinced that someone is trying to drive her insane when she returns to her mansion after a sailing disaster.

United Artists — *New World Video*

Darling **1965**
Drama
64991 122 mins B/W B, V P
Julie Christie, Laurence Harvey, Dirk Bogarde
A young model, searching for love in the world of the jet set, leaves her husband and manages to reach the top of European society by marrying a prince. She learns that life at the top can be very empty.
Academy Awards '65: Best Actress (Christie).
Avco-Embassy — *Embassy Home Entertainment*

Daryl Hall & John Oates—Rock 'n Soul Live **1983**
Music-Performance
66349 50 mins C B, V P
Taped during their 1983 "H20" tour, Daryl Hall and John Oates perform a program of hits including "She's Gone," "Family Man" and "Maneater." Stereo VHS and Beta Hi-Fi.
RCA — *RCA/Columbia Pictures Home Video*

Daryl Hall and John Oates Video Collection: 7 Big Ones **1984**
Music video
80367 30 mins C B, V P
A collection of conceptual music videos from those masters of blue eyed soul, Daryl Hall and John Oates. Available in VHS Hi-Fi Dolby Stereo and Beta Hi-Fi Stereo.
RCA Video Productions — *RCA/Columbia Pictures Home Video*

Dastardly & Muttley **196?**
Cartoons
66274 53 mins C B, V P
Animated
The villainous commanders of the Vulture Squardon will stop at nothing in their diabolical, do-anything flying machines.
Hanna Barbera — *Worldvision Home Video*

Dave Mason in Concert **1984**
Music-Performance
77231 60 mins C B, V P
The guitarist performs such hits as "We Just Disagree" and "Feeling' Alright" in this taped concert.
Neal Marshall — *Monterey Home Video*

Dave Mason Live at Perkins Palace **1982**
Music-Performance
47811 ? mins C LV P
The veteran rock singer/guitarist performs "We Just Disagree," "Every Woman," "Let It Go," "Feelin' Alright," "Take It to the Limit" and other hits. In stereo.
Unknown — *Pioneer Artists*

David Bowie **1983**
Music-Performance
75902 14 mins C B, V P
This program presents David Bowie at his best performing "Let's Dance," "China Girl" and "Modern Love."
EMI America Records — *Sony Corporation of America*

David Bowie—Serious Moonlight **1984**
Music-Performance
65683 90 mins C B, V P
Drawing from all phases of his career, Bowie performs 19 songs that have made him rock's most enigmatic and commanding performer. Included are "Space Oddity," "Young Americans," "Let's Dance," and "China Girl."
Anthony Eaton — *Music Media*

David Copperfield **1983**
Cartoons
77177 72 mins C B, V, CED P
Animated
An animated adaptation of the Dickens classic about a young boy growing up in 19th century England.
Burbank Films — *Vestron Video*

David Copperfield **1935**
Drama
81499 132 mins B/W B, V P
Lionel Barrymore, W.C. Fields, Freddie Bartholomew, Maureen O'Sullivan, Basil Rathbone, Lewis Stone, directed by George Cukor
This is an adaptation of the Charles Dickens novel about David Copperfield who undergoes a great deal of struggles and hardship in Victorian England.
MGM — *MGM/UA Home Video*

David Steinberg in Concert **1984**
Comedy-Performance
78661 60 mins C B, V P
Comedian David Steinberg performs some of his best routines in this concert taped in Toronto.
Nordic Productions; Global Television Network — *RKO HomeVideo*

Davy Crockett and the River Pirates **1956**
Adventure
55566 81 mins C LV R, P
Fess Parker, Buddy Ebsen, Jeff York
The King of the Wild Frontier meets up with Mike Fink, the King of the Ohio River, and the two engage in a furious keelboat race, and then

unite to track down a group of thieves masquerading as Indians and threatening the peace.
Walt Disney — *Walt Disney Home Video*

Davy Crockett, King of the Wild Frontier **1955**
Western/Adventure
77528 89 mins C B, V R, P
Fess Parker, Buddy Ebsen, Hans Conried, Ray Whiteside, Pat Hogan
This film chronicles the life and adventures of Davy Crockett from his days as an Indian fighter, to his gallant death in defense of the Alamo.
Walt Disney Productions — *Walt Disney Home Video*

Davy Crockett on the Mississippi **1973**
Cartoons
66582 47 mins C B, V P
Animated
The animated adventures of the American folk hero during his days as a frontiersman along the Mississippi River.
Hanna-Barbera — *Worldvision Home Video*

Dawn! **1983**
Biographical/Drama
77012 114 mins C B, V P
Bronwyn Mac Kay-Payne, Tom Richards
This is the true story of Dawn Fraser, the Olympic champion swimmer who really was an unfulfilled woman who fought for her happiness.
Satori Entertainment — *VidAmerica*

Dawn of the Dead **1978**
Horror
69627 126 mins C B, V R, P
Directed by George Romero
Flesh-eating zombies run amok in a shopping mall.
MPAA:R
Richard P Rubinstein — *THORN EMI/HBO Video*

Dawn of the Mummy **1982**
Horror
64213 93 mins C B, V R, P
From the depths of a pharaoh's tomb, a mummy awakes to kill the tomb's desecrators—four beautiful American models.
Frank Agarna; Harmony Gold Productions — *THORN EMI/HBO Video*

Dawn Patrol, The **1938**
Drama/World War I
70696 103 mins B/W B, V P
Errol Flynn, David Niven, Basil Rathbone, directed by Edmund Goulding
The brave fighters of WW I's air war face their deaths each time they fly. This film focuses on the effects of that pressure on three British airmen. Hi-Fi sound on both formats.
United Artists; Warner Bros. — *Key Video*

Dawn Rider **1935**
Western
51635 60 mins B/W B, V P
John Wayne, Marion Burns, Yakima Canutt
Love and gunfights in the action-filled old American West.
Monogram — *Sony Corporation of America; Spotlite Video; Discount Video Tapes*

Dawn Rider/Frontier Horizon **1938**
Western
81018 114 mins B/W B, V P
John Wayne, Jennifer Jones, Marion Burns
This is a double feature of two of John Wayne's earliest western films.
Republic Pictures — *Spotlite Video*

Day After, The **1983**
Drama/Nuclear warfare
65387 126 mins C B, V, LV, CED P
A powerful drama which graphically depicts the nuclear bombing of a midwestern city and its aftereffects on the survivors.
ABC Circle Films — *Embassy Home Entertainment*

Day at Disneyland, A **1982**
Travel
47411 39 mins C B, V P
A colorful souvenir of the attractions at Disneyland. Highlights include a ride down Main Street, a visit to Sleeping Beauty's castle and trips through Adventureland, Frontierland, Fantasyland and Tomorrowland.
Walt Disney Prods — *Walt Disney Home Video*

Day at the Races, A **1937**
Comedy
53938 109 mins B/W B, V, LV, CED P
Marx Brothers, Allan Jones, Maureen O'Sullivan
The Marx Brothers help a girl who owns a sanitorium and a race horse.
MGM — *MGM/UA Home Video*

Day for Night **1973**
Drama
58226 116 mins C B, V R, P
Jacqueline Bisset, Jean-Pierre Aumont, directed by Francois Truffaut
An affectionate look at the profession of moviemaking—its craft, its character, and the personalities that interact against the performances commanded by the camera. English language version.

Academy Awards '73: Best Foreign Language Film. MPAA:PG
Les Films Du Carrosse — *Warner Home Video*

Day of Frustration—Season of Triumph **1984**
Football
72938 46 mins C B, V, FO P
Miami Dolphins
Highlights from the Miami Dolphins' 1983 season and "NFL 83."
NFL Films — *NFL Films Video*

Day of Judgement **1981**
Horror
80332 101 mins C B, V R, P
A mysterious stranger arrives in a town to slaughter those people who violate the Ten Commandments.
E.O. Corporation — *THORN EMI/HBO Video*

Day of the Animals **1977**
Horror
47316 97 mins C B, V P
Christopher George, Leslie Nielsen, Lynda Day George, Richard Jaeckel, Michael Ansara, Ruth Roman
Animals begin attacking human beings when the earth's ozone layer is depleted to a critical level.
MPAA:PG
Edward Montoro; Film Ventures International — *Media Home Entertainment*

Day of the Cobra, The **1984**
Adventure
80271 95 mins C B, V P
Franco Nero, Sybil Danning, Mario Maranzana, Licinia Lentini
A corrupt narcotics bureau official hires an ex-cop to find a heroin kingpin on the back streets of Genoa, Italy.
Turi Vasile — *Media Home Entertainment*

Day of the Dolphin, The **1973**
Adventure
08370 104 mins C B, V, CED P
George C. Scott, Trish Van Devere, Paul Sorvino, Fritz Weaver, directed by Mike Nichols
Research scientist, after successfully working out a means of teaching dolphins to talk, finds his animals kidnapped.
MPAA:PG
Avco Embassy — *Embassy Home Entertainment*

Day of the Dolphins/NFL '82 **1983**
Football
66220 45 mins C B, V, FO P
Highlights of the 1982-83 season for the Miami Dolphins combined with an overview of the whole NFL season.
NFL Films — *NFL Films Video*

Day of the Jackal, The **1973**
Suspense
60590 142 mins C B, V P
Edward Fox, Alan Badel, Tony Britton, Derek Jacobi, Cyril Cusack, Olga Georges-Picot, directed by Fred Zinnemann
Frederick Forsyth's best-selling novel of political intrigue concerning a suave British assassin hired to kill DeGaulle is the basis of this film.
MPAA:PG
Universal — *MCA Home Video*

Day of the Locust **1975**
Drama
66035 140 mins C B, V R, P
Donald Sutherland, Karen Black, Burgess Meredith, William Atherton, Geraldine Page, directed by John Schlesinger
Nathaniel West's novel concerning the dark side of 1930's Hollywood is brought to life in this film.
MPAA:R
Paramount; Jerome Hellman — *Paramount Home Video*

Day of the Triffids **1963**
Science fiction
01658 94 mins C B, V P
Howard Keel, Janet Scott, Nicole Maurey, directed by Steve Sekely
Giant pea-pods drop to earth and become man-eating plants. A professor finally discovers a way to destroy them.
Allied Artists — *Media Home Entertainment; King of Video; Budget Video*

Day the Bookies Wept, The **1939**
Comedy
29470 50 mins B/W B, V P, T
Betty Grable, Joe Penner, Tom Kennedy, Richard Lane
A cab driver who loves pigeons is tricked into buying an old nag who loves alcohol and entering him in the big race.
RKO, Robert Sisk — *Blackhawk Films*

Day the Earth Caught Fire, The **1962**
Science fiction
58461 100 mins B/W B, V R, P
Janet Munro, Edward Judd, Leo McKern
World powers unite to save the earth after faulty nuclear tests.
Val Guest — *THORN EMI/HBO Video*

 (For explanation of codes, see USE GUIDE and KEY)

Day the Earth Stood Still, The 1951
Science fiction
08433 92 mins B/W B, V P
Michael Rennie, Patricia Neal, Hugh Marlowe, Bobby Gray
An emissary from another planet lands on Earth on a mission of peace and is brutally shot down by Washington, D.C. policemen.
EL, SP
20th Century Fox — *CBS/Fox Video*

Day the Loving Stopped, The 1982
Romance
75458 96 mins C B, V P
Dennis Weaver, Valerie Harper
A couple goes through a difficult break-up.
King Features — *U.S.A. Home Video*

Day Time Ended, The 197?
Science fiction
42916 80 mins C B, V P
Chris Mitchum, Jim Davis, Dorothy Malone
A pair of glowing UFO's streaking across the sky and an alien mechanical device with long menacing appendages are only two of the bizarre phenomena in a house that is slipping into different dimensions.
Wayne Schmidt; Steve Neil; Paul Gentry — *Media Home Entertainment*

Daydreamer, The 1966
Fantasy/Fairy tales
64974 98 mins C B, V P
Paul O'Keefe, Ray Bolger, Jack Gilford, Margaret Hamilton, voices of Tallulah Bankhead, Boris Karloff, Burl Ives, Terry Thomas
Young Hans Christian Andersen falls asleep and dreams some of his most famous fairy tales"The Little Mermaid," "The Emperor's New Clothes," and "Thumbelina." Live action is combined with animation and highlighted with songs.
Avco-Embassy — *Embassy Home Entertainment*

Days of Heaven 1978
Drama
38593 95 mins C B, V, LV R, P
Richard Gere, Brooke Adams, Sam Shepard, directed by Terence Malick
Critically acclaimed story of a drifter (Gere) who becomes involved in the lives of a Texas sharecropper family. Story and screenplay by Terence Malick.
MPAA:PG
Paramount — *Paramount Home Video; RCA VideoDiscs*

Days of Wine and Roses 1962
Drama
63451 134 mins B/W B, V R, P
Jack Lemmon, Lee Remick, Charles Bickford, Jack Klugman, directed by Blake Edwards
A harrowing tale of an alcoholic advertising man who gradually drags his wife down with him into a life of booze. Part of the 'A Night at the Movies" series, this tape simulates a 1962 movie evening, with a Bugs Bunny cartoon, "Martian Through Georgia," a newsreel and coming attractions for "Gypsy" and "Rome Adventure."
Academy Awards '62: Best Song ("Days of Wine and Roses").
Warner Bros — *Warner Home Video*

Days of Wine and Roses, The 1958
Drama
65014 89 mins B/W B, V P
Cliff Robertson, Piper Laurie, directed by John Frankenheimer
The original "Playhouse 90" television version of J.P. Miller's story about a young couple whose social drinking becomes total dependence.
CBS — *MGM/UA Home Video*

Dazzledancin 1984
Dance
65611 60 mins C B, V P
The dance spectacle of the 80's gives an inside look at the raw, acrobatic finesse of the most energetic breakdancers, spinners, and poplockers.
Four Star International — *U.S.A. Home Video*

D.C. Cab 1984
Comedy
Closed Captioned
65516 100 mins C B, V, LV, CED P
Mr. T., Adam Baldwin, Charlie Barnett, Irene Cara, Anne De Salvo, Max Gail, Gloria Gifford, Gary Busey
A rag-tag Washington D.C. cab company is the setting for a young man who brings pride and esteem to a group of society's outcasts. Closed captioned in VHS and Beta only. In stereo VHS and Beta Hi-Fi.
MPAA:R
Universal — *MCA Home Video*

Dead and Buried 1981
Horror
64875 95 mins C B, V, CED P
James Farentino
A sheriff is bewildered and bewitched by the perpetrator of a series of strange murders in his town.
MPAA:R

Ronald Shusett; Robert Bentruss — *Vestron Video*

Dead Don't Die, The **1975**
Adventure
79248 74 mins C B, V P
George Hamilton, Ray Milland, Linda Cristal, Ralph Meeker, directed by Curtis Harrington
When a young man tries to prove his brother was wrongly executed for murder, he encountes a man who wants to rule the world with an army of zombies.
Douglas S. Cramer Company — *Worldvision Home Video*

Dead Don't Die, The **1975**
Suspense
80487 90 mins C B, V P
George Hamilton, Ray Milland, Linda Cristal, Ralph Meeker, Joan Blondell
A sailor is drawn into the world of the living dead while trying to prove that his brother was wrongly executed for murder.
Douglas C Cramer — *Worldvision Home Video*

Dead Easy **1984**
Mystery/Suspense
76662 92 mins C B, V P
Scott Burgess
A cop and two street characters team-up to run a scam and, in the process, cross a hoodlum who turns every one of his allies on them.
Unknown — *VCL Home Video*

Dead End Street **1983**
Drama
76938 86 mins C B, V P
Anat Atzman, Yehoram Gaon
A young prostitute attempts to save herself from a life of self-destruction.
Foreign — *Trans World Entertainment*

Dead Men Don't Wear Plaid **1982**
Comedy
62779 91 mins B/W B, V, LV P
Steve Martin, Rachel Ward, Reni Santoni, Carl Reiner, directed by Carl Reiner
A private detective encounters a bizarre assortment of suspects while trying to find out the truth about a scientist's death. This black-and-white film is ingeniously interspliced with clips from old Warner Brothers films, featuring Humphrey Bogart, Bette Davis, Alan Ladd, Burt Lancaster, Ava Gardner, Barbara Stanwyck, Ray Milland and others.
MPAA:PG
Universal — *MCA Home Video*

Dead of Night **1945**
Suspense
47302 102 mins B/W B, V R, P
Sir Michael Redgrave, Sally Ann Howes, Basil Radford, Naunton Wayne, Mervyn Johns, Roland Culver
This suspense classic, set in a remote country house, follows a small group of people as they find their worst nightmares becoming reality.
Universal International — *THORN EMI/HBO Video*

Dead Wrong **1983**
Adventure
76863 93 mins C B, V P
Britt Ekland, Winston Rekert, Jackson Davies
An undercover agent falls in love with the drug smuggler she's supposed to bring to justice.
Len Kowalewich — *Media Home Entertainment*

Dead Zone, The **1983**
Suspense
Closed Captioned
65615 103 mins C B, V, LV, CED R, P
Christopher Walken, Brooke Adams, Tom Skerritt, Martin Sheen
A man gains extraordinary psychic powers following a near-fatal accident. He is forced to decide between seeking absolute seclusion in order to escape his frightening visions, or using his "gift" to save mankind from impending evil.
MPAA:R
Debra Hill — *Paramount Home Video*

Deadline **1981**
Suspense
79170 94 mins C B, V P
Barry Newman, Trisha Noble, Bill Kerr
A journalist must find out the truth behind a minor earthquake in Australia.
Hanna-Barbera/PTY Limited — *Worldvision Home Video*

Deadly and the Beautiful, The **1974**
Adventure
59673 82 mins C B, V P
Nancy Kwan, Ross Hagen
Dr. Tsu sends her "deadly but beautiful" task force to kidnap the world's prime male athletes for use in her private business enterprise.
MPAA:PG
Ross Hagen — *Media Home Entertainment*

Deadly Blessing **1981**
Horror
60440 104 mins C B, V, CED P
Ernest Borgnine, Maren Jensen, Jeff East, Lisa Hartman, Lois Nettleton
Imminent danger and relentless psychological terror highlight this frightening story of a young woman who marries a member of a bizarre religious sect.
MPAA:R

Polygram — *Embassy Home Entertainment*

Deadly Encounter 1982
Adventure
81415 90 mins C B, V P
Larry Hagman, Susan Anspach
A helicopter pilot is surprised when his ex-girlfriend comes to visit him in Mexico. She asks him to help her find a black book that her deceased husband kept information that could put many people behind bars.
Paul Cameron, Robert Boris — *VCL Home Video*

Deadly Eyes 1983
Horror
69311 87 mins C B, V R, P
Sam Groom, Sara Botsford, Scatman Crothers
A genetically altered urban colony of super-rats seeks a new source of food—man.
MPAA:R
Golden Harvest — *Warner Home Video*

Deadly Force 1983
Suspense
64970 95 mins C B, V, CED P
Wings Hauser
An ex-cop turned private detective stalks a killer in Los Angeles who has left an "X" carved in the forehead of each of his 17 victims.
MPAA:R
Sandy Howard/Hemdale — *Embassy Home Entertainment*

Deadly Game, The 1982
Drama/Suspense
60441 108 mins C B, V P
George Segal, Robert Morley
A reunion at a remote hotel leads to an ordeal of psychological terror and murderous intrigue.
Unknown — *Embassy Home Entertainment*

Deadly Games 1980
Horror
63082 94 mins C B, V P
Sam Groom, JoAnn Harris, Steve Railsback, Dick Butkus, June Lockhart
A mysterious strangler terrorizes young women seemingly at random.
Great Plains Entertainment Corp — *Monterey Home Video*

Deadly Intruder, The 1984
Horror
77167 86 mins C B, V R, P
A quiet vacation spot is being terrorized by an escapee from a mental institution.
Independent — *THORN EMI/HBO Video*

Deadly Thief 1984
Drama
73559 90 mins C B, V P
Rex Harrison, John Saxon, Sylvia Miles
A retired jewel thief comes out of retirement to challenge his protege to steal the world's most precious gem as the prize.
Unknown — *Prism*

Deadly Vengance 1981
Mystery
70734 84 mins C B, V P
Grace Jones, Alan Marlowe, Arthur Roberts
The mob killed Jones' boyfriend and she mounts a vengeful offensive against the crime syndicate's bigwigs.
Unknown — *Active Home Video*

Dead Men Walk 1943
Horror
76917 65 mins B/W B, V P
A deadman returns from the netherworld to haunt the man who murdered him.
Sigmund Newfeld — *United Home Video*

Deal of the Century 1983
Comedy
69799 99 mins C B, V, LV, CED R, P
Chevy Chase, Sigourney Weaver, Gregory Hines, directed by William Friedkin
A first-rate hustler and his cohorts sell second-rate weapons to third-world nations, but their latest deal threatens to blow up in their faces—literally. In stereo on all formats.
MPAA:PG
Warner Bros. — *Warner Home Video*

Dealers in Death 1984
Documentary
77235 60 mins B/W B, V P
Narrated by Broderick Crawford
This documentary looks at the gangsters who have left their impact on American history such as Al Capone and John Dillinger.
John McNaughton — *MPI Home Video*

Dear Detective 1979
Crime-Drama
64998 92 mins C B, V P
Brenda Vaccaro
A woman head of police homicide takes on the most challenging case of her career.
Viacom Enterprises — *U.S.A. Home Video*

Dear Diary 1981
Adolescence/Sexuality
63877 25 mins C B, V P
Focusing on three fictional characters, this program presents facts about female sexuality and physical development, and addresses the

issues of self-image, peer pressure, and pressure to date.
Copperfield Films — *MGM/UA Home Video*

Death at Love House **1975**
Mystery
80302 74 mins C B, V P
Robert Wagner, Kate Jackson, Sylvia Sydney, Joan Blondell, John Carradine
A screen writer and his wife are hired to write the life story of a silent movie queen.
Spelling/Goldberg Productions — *Prism*

Death Cruise **1974**
Drama/Mystery
70728 74 mins C B, V P
Kate Jackson, Celeste Holm, Tom Bosley, Edward Albert, Polly Bergen, Michael Constantine, Richard Long
The winners of a free cruise find that there was one catch, a fatal one.
Aaron Spelling — *Active Home Video*

Death Driver **1978**
Drama
78388 93 mins C B, V R, P
Earl Owenbsy, Mike Allen
In order for a stuntman to make a comeback, he attempts to do a stunt that had ended his career ten years before.
Independent — *THORN EMI/HBO Video*

Death Duel of Mantis **1984**
Martial arts
72958 90 mins C B, V P
A martial arts film featuring Chin Yin Fei.
Foreign — *Unicorn Video*

Death Force **198?**
Drama
80126 90 mins C B, V P
Jayne Kennedy, Leon Issac Kennedy
When a Vietnam veteran comes to New York City, he becomes a hitman for the Mafia.
MPAA:R
Independent — *King of Video*

Death Game **1976**
Drama
80188 91 mins C B, V P
Sondra Lucke, Colleen Camp, Seymour Cassel
When a man lets two girls into his house to make a phone call the pair lead the man through 48 hours of sheer terror.
MPAA:R
First American Films — *United Home Video*

Death Games **1982**
Suspense
72532 78 mins C B, V P
Two young men shooting a documentary about an influential music promoter ask too many wrong questions, causing the powers-that-be to want them out of the picture for good.
Williams and Gardiner — *VidAmerica*

Death Hunt **1981**
Adventure
58851 98 mins C B, V, LV, CED P
Charles Bronson, Lee Marvin, Ed Lauter, Andrew Stevens, Carl Weathers, Angie Dickinson
A man unjustly accused of murder pits his knowledge of the wilderness against the superior numbers of his pursuers.
MPAA:R
20th Century Fox — *CBS/Fox Video*

Death in Venice **1971**
Drama
58227 127 mins C B, V R, P
Dirk Bogarde, Mark Burns, Bjorn Andresen, directed by Luchino Visconti
Thomas Mann's novel about a man obsessed by ideal beauty is brought to life in this film.
Cannes Film Festival '71: Grand Prize Winner.
MPAA:PG
Alta Cinematograjica — *Warner Home Video*

Death Journey **1976**
Adventure
47669 mins C B, V P
Fred Williamson, D'Urville Martin
Fred Williamson portrays Jesse Crowder, a man-for-hire hired by the New York D.A. to escort a key witness cross-country.
MPAA:R
Po Boy Productions — *Unicorn Video*

Death Kiss **1977**
Drama
80281 90 mins C B, V P
Larry Daniels, Dorothy Moore
When a man hires a psychopath to murder his wife, a strange series of events starts to happen that foils his plot.
MPAA:R
Joseph Brenner Associates — *Prism*

Death Kiss, The **1933**
Mystery
08757 75 mins B/W B, V P
Bela Lugosi, David Manners, Adrienne Ames
Eerie doings at a major Hollywood film studio where a sinister killer does away with his victims while a cast-of-thousands movie spectacular is under production.
World Wide; KBS Prod — *Movie Buff Video; Cable Films; Discount Video Tapes*

Death Machines **1976**
Suspense/Martial arts
51117 90 mins C B, V P
Ron Marchini, Michael Chong, Joshua Johnson
One man dares to defy three martial arts experts, trained to carry the deadly plans of organized crime.
MPAA:R
Crown International — *United Home Video*

Death of a Centerfold **1981**
Drama
75535 96 mins C B, V P
Jamie Lee Curtis, Bruce Weitz, Robert Reed, Mitch Ryan, Bibi Besch
A drama based on the life of Dorothy Stratten.
Larry Wilcox Productions — *MGM/UA Home Video*

Death on the Nile **1978**
Mystery
58455 135 mins C B, V, CED R, P
Peter Ustinov, Jane Birkin, Lois Chiles, Bette Davis, Mia Farrow, David Niven, Olivia Hussey, Angela Lansbury, Jack Warden, Maggie Smith
Agatha Christie's fictional detective, Hercule Poiret, is called upon to discover who killed an heiress aboard a steamer cruising down the Nile.
MPAA:PG
EMI; Paramount — *THORN EMI/HBO Video*

Death Race 2000 **1975**
Drama
54800 80 mins C B, V R, P
David Carradine, Simone Griffeth, Sylvester Stallone, directed by Paul Bartel
Five racing car contenders challenge the national champion of a cross country race in which drivers score points by killing pedestrians. Based on the 1956 story by Ib Melchior.
MPAA:R
New World Pictures; Roger Corman — *Warner Home Video*

Death Rage **1977**
Suspense
44913 92 mins C B, V P
Yul Brynner, Martin Balsam
A hitman comes out of retirement to handle the toughest assignment he has ever faced: search for and kill the man who murdered his brother. But he is trapped by a Mafia doublecross, with himself as the real target.
MPAA:R
S. J. International — *United Home Video*

Death Rides the Plains **1944**
Western
11269 53 mins B/W B, V, FO P
Bob Livingston, Fuzzy St. John, Nica Doret, Ray Bennet
A man lures prospective buyers to his ranch, kills them, and steals their money.
PRC — *Video Yesteryear*

Death Sentence **1974**
Suspense/Drama
80303 74 mins C B, V P
Cloris Leachman, Laurence Luckinbill, Nick Nolte, William Schallert
When a woman juror on a murder case finds out that the wrong man is on trial, she is stalked by the real killer.
Spelling/Goldberg Productions — *Prism*

Death Sport **1978**
Adventure
52703 83 mins C B, V R, P
David Carradine, Claudia Jennings, Richard Lynch
A popular game of the future involves gladiators willing to lose their lives against lethal motorcyclists.
MPAA:R
New World; Roger Corman — *Warner Home Video*

Death Squad **1973**
Drama
80304 74 mins C B, V P
Robert Forster, Melvyn Douglas, Michelle Phillips, Claude Akins
A police commissioner hires an ex-cop to find a group of vigilante cops who are behind a series of gangland style executions.
Spelling/Goldberg Productions — *Prism*

Death Stalk **1974**
Adventure
59353 90 mins C B, V R, P
Vince Edwards, Vic Morrow, Anjanette Comer, Robert Webber, Carol Lynley
Two couples' dream holiday turns into a hostage nightmare.
Heritage Enterprises — *Video Gems*

Death Valley **1981**
Drama
59678 90 mins C B, V P
Paul LeMat, Catherine Hicks, Peter Billingsley
A trio sets out to drive through Death Valley, a trip which soon becomes a nightmare of danger and insanity.
MPAA:R
Universal — *MCA Home Video*

Death Valley Days **1965**
Western
78358 60 mins B/W B, V P
Clint Eastwood, hosted by Ronald Reagan and Robert Taylor

Two episodes from the long-running Western anthology television series are contained on this tape.
Madison Productions — *U.S.A. Home Video*

Death Valley Days, Volume II **196?**
Western
79328 75 mins C B, V P
Jim Davis, Forrest Tucker, Tom Skerritt, Robert Blake, James Caan
A second volume of two episodes from the series that features stories about the old west. In Beta Hi-Fi and VHS Stereo.
Madison Productions — *U.S.A. Home Video*

Death Watch **1979**
Drama
72881 117 mins C B, V, LV P
Harvey Keitel, Romy Schneider, Max Von Sydow
A television director implants a video camera in a man's brain to film a documentary on a dying woman without her knowledge.
MPAA:R
Planfilms; Selta Films — *Embassy Home Entertainment*

Death Wish **1974**
Drama
38594 93 mins C B, V, LV R, P
Charles Bronson, Vincent Gardenia, William Redfield, Hope Lange, directed by Michael Winner
Charles Bronson turns vigilante after his wife and daughter are violently attacked and raped by a gang of hoodlums. He stalks the streets of New York seeking revenge on other muggers, pimps, and crooks. Music by Herbie Hancock.
MPAA:R
Paramount — *Paramount Home Video; RCA VideoDiscs*

Death Wish II **1982**
Adventure
60337 89 mins C B, V R, P
Charles Bronson, Jill Ireland, Vincent Gardenia, Anthony Franciosa, directed by Michael Winner
Bronson recreates the role of Paul Kersey, an architect who takes the law into his own hands when his family is victimized once again.
MPAA:R
City Films — *Warner Home Video; Vestron Video (disc only)*

Deathcheaters **1976**
Adventure
77004 96 mins C B, V P
The Australian Secret Service offers two stuntmen a top secret mission in the Phillipines.
MPAA:G
Brian Trenchard Smith — *VidAmerica*

DeathStalker **1984**
Fantasy
80048 80 mins C B, V, CED P
Richard Hill, Barbi Benton, Richard Brooker, Vicrot Bo, Lana Clarkson
Deathstalker sets his sights on seizing the evil wizard Munkar's magic amulet so he can take over Munkan's castle.
MPAA:R
Palo Alto Productions — *Vestron Video*

Deathtrap **1982**
Suspense
60336 116 mins C B, V R, P
Michael Caine, Christopher Reeve, Dyan Cannon, directed by Sidney Lumet
Ira Levin's Broadway smash concerning a creatively blocked playwright of mysteries, his ailing rich wife and a former student who has written a surefire hit worth killing for.
MPAA:PG
Warner Bros — *Warner Home Video*

Decade of the Waltons, A **1985**
Drama
80890 120 mins C B, V P
Richard Thomas, Ellen Corby, Will Geer, Michael Learned, Ralph Waite, narrated by Earl Hamner
"The Waltons" creator Earl Hamner narrates this retrospective program which features poignant highlights from the series.
Lorimar Productions — *Karl/Lorimar Home Video*

Decameron Nights **1953**
Drama
75932 87 mins B/W B, V R, P
Louis Jourdan, Joan Fontaine, Binnie Barnes, Joan Collins
A trio of tales about a beautiful young wife of an older man who is pursued by a tempestuous lover.
RKO — *Hal Roach Studios; Video Gems; Discount Video Tapes*

Decline of Western Civilization, The **1981**
Documentary/Music-Performance
81193 100 mins C B, V P
X, Circle Jerks, Black Flag, Fear, Germs, Catholic Discipline, directed by Penelope Spheeris
This documentary examines the L.A. hard core punk scene.
Penelope Spheeris — *Music Media*

Deep, The **1977**
Suspense
21284 123 mins C B, V P
Nick Nolte, Jacqueline Bisset, Robert Shaw
An underwater search for a shipwreck. Based on the novel by Peter Benchley.

Columbia — *RCA/Columbia Pictures Home Video; RCA VideoDiscs*

Deep in the Heart **1984**
Drama
73023 99 mins C B, V R, P
Karen Young, Clayton Day
When a young woman gets raped at gunpoint on a second date she takes the law into her own hands. This film is based upon a true story.
MPAA:R
Tony Garrett and David Streit — *THORN EMI/HBO Video*

Deep Red: Hatchet Murders **1982**
Horror/Suspense
63358 100 mins C B, V R, P
David Hemmings, Daria Nicolodi
A composer reads a book on the occult that relates to the brutal murder of his neighbor. He goes to visit the book's author and discovers that she has been horribly murdered as well.
Rizzoli Films — *THORN EMI/HBO Video*

Deep Six, The **1958**
War-Drama
29800 110 mins C B, V P
Alan Ladd, William Bendix, James Whitmore, Keenan Wynn, Efrem Zimbalist Jr., Joey Bishop
A World War II drama that examines the conflict between pacifism and loyalty to country in wartime. A staunch Quaker is called to active duty as a lieutenant in the U.S. Navy. His pacifism puts him into disfavor with shipmates.
Warner Bros — *United Home Video*

Deer Hunter, The **1978**
Drama
31585 183 mins C B, V, LV P
Robert DeNiro, Christopher Walken, John Savage, Meryl Streep, directed by Michael Cimino
Three buddies from a Pennsylvania steel town go to Viet Nam and learn that war is a human roulette game. The town, their loves, and their lives will never be the same.
Academy Awards '78: Best Picture; Best Director (Cimino). MPAA:R
Universal — *MCA Home Video; RCA VideoDiscs*

Deerslayer, The **1978**
Drama
45052 98 mins C B, V P
Steve Forrest, Ned Romero, John Anderson, Joan Prather
Based on the classic novel by James Fenimore Cooper, this movie about the intrepid frontiersman Hawkeye and his Indian companion Chingachgook who set out to rescue a beautiful Indian maiden and must fight bands of hostile Indians and Frenchmen along the way.
Schick Sunn Classic — *United Home Video; Lucerne Films*

Defenders, The **1980**
Football
45123 30 mins C B, V, FO R, P
Narrated by John Facenda
A look at how defensive styles, players, and coaches have evolved into today's hard-hitting offensive stoppers.
NFL Films — *NFL Films Video*

Defiance **1979**
Drama
64362 101 mins C B, V, CED P
Jan-Michael Vincent, Art Carney, Theresa Saldona
A former merchant seaman moves into a tenement in a bad area of New York City. When a local street gang begins terrorizing the neighborhood, he decides to take a stand.
MPAA:PG
American International — *Vestron Video*

Defiant Ones, The **1958**
Drama
65006 97 mins B/W B, V, CED P
Tony Curtis, Sidney Poitier, Theodore Bikel, Cara Williams, directed by Stanley Kramer
This symbolic story about racism revolves around two prisoners in a chain gang in the rural south who escape. Their societal conditioning to distrust and dislike each other dissolves as they face each constant peril together.
United Artists; Stanley Kramer — *CBS/Fox Video*

Degas, Erte and Chagall **1977**
Arts/Painting
58565 60 mins C B, V P
"Degas in New Orleans" is a dramatization of the pictures painted when he visited this city. "Erte" is a profile of French designer Romain de Tirtoff. The last film features Marc Chagall giving viewers an inside look at his paint-on-glass technique.
Gary L. Goldman; Chuck Olin — *Mastervision*

Delinquent Daughters **1944**
Drama
47637 71 mins B/W B, V, FO P
June Carlson, Fifi Dorsay, Teala Loring
After a high school girl commits suicide, a cop and a reporter try to find out why so many kids are getting into trouble.
PRC Pictures; American Prods Inc — *Video Yesteryear*

Delinquent Schoolgirls 1984
Drama/Exploitation
81166 89 mins C B, V P
Michael Pataki, Bob Minos, Stephen Stucker
Three escapees from an asylum get more than they bargained for when they visit a Female Correctional Institute to fulfill their sexual fantasies.
MPAA:R
Rainbow Distributors — *Vestron Video*

Deliverance 1972
Drama
38943 105 mins C B, V, LV R, P
Jon Voight, Burt Reynolds, Ned Beatty, John Boorman
A superb action film about four men who go riding down a wild river for a weekend that turns into a disaster. Based on James Dickey's novel.
MPAA:R
Warner Bros — *Warner Home Video; RCA VideoDiscs*

Delusion 1984
Drama
72878 93 mins C B, V P
Joseph Cotten
A young woman comes to a house to nurse an elderly man only to have a fling with his sixteen year old grandson.
MPAA:R
Unknown — *Embassy Home Entertainment*

Demented 1980
Horror
59662 92 mins C B, V P
Sally Elyse, Bruce Gilchrist
A beautiful and talented woman is brutally gang-raped by four men but her revenge is sweet and deadly as she entices each to bed and murders them.
MPAA:R
Arthur Jeffreys; Mike Smith — *Media Home Entertainment*

Dementia 13 1963
Horror
11315 75 mins B/W B, V, FO P
William Campbell, Luana Anders, Bart Patton, written and directed by Francis Ford Coppola
A woman drives her husband to a heart attack as her family clings strangely to the memory of a sister who drowned years ago.
American Intl; Roger Corman — *Video Yesteryear; Budget Video; Video Dimensions; Cable Films; King of Video; Discount Video Tapes; World Video Pictures*

Demon, The 1981
Horror
51120 94 mins C B, V P
Cameron Mitchell, Jennifer Holmes
A small town may be doomed to extinction, courtesy of a monster's thirst for the blood of its inhabitants.
MPAA:R
Hollard Productions — *United Home Video*

Demon, The 1981
Horror
63355 94 mins C B, V R, P
Jennifer Holmes, Cameron Mitchell
A demon-like maniac terrorizes the well-to-do Parker family's country residence.
Gold Key Entertainment — *THORN EMI/HBO Video*

Demon Lover, The 1975
Horror
47665 87 mins C B, V P
A young girl is the victim of psychic attack from a demonologist.
MPAA:R
Donald G Jackson; Jerry Younkins — *Unicorn Video*

Demon Rage 1982
Horror
64843 98 mins C B, V P
Britt Ekland, Lana Wood, John Carradine
A neglected housewife drifts under the spell of a phantom lover.
MPAA:R
MPM — *HarmonyVision*

Demon Seed 1977
Science fiction/Horror
73362 97 mins C B, V P
Julie Christie, Fritz Weaver
When a scientist and his wife separate so he can work on his computer, the computer takes over the house and impregnates the wife.
MPAA:R
MGM — *MGM/UA Home Video*

Demoniac 1979
Horror
77396 87 mins C B, V P
A depraved religious fanatic subjects a group of demon worshipers to gruesome rites of exorcism.
MPAA:R
Foreign — *Wizard Video*

Demonoid 1981
Horror
63386 85 mins C B, V P
Samantha Eggar, Stuart Whitman, Roy Cameron Jenson
The discovery of an ancient temple of Satan worship drastically changes the lives of a young couple when the husband become possessed by the Demonoid.
MPAA:R

Zach Motion Pictures; Panorama Films — *Media Home Entertainment*

Demons, The 198?
Horror
73957 90 mins C B, V P
Anne Libert, Britt Nichols, Doris Thomas, Karen Field
A woman accused of being a witch vows a curse of death upon her accusers.
Independent — *Unicorn Video*

Dentist, The 1932
Comedy
59402 22 mins B/W B, V P, T
W.C. Fields, Elise Cavanna, Babe Kane, Bud Jamison, Zedna Farley
Fields treats several oddball patients in his office.
Paramount — *Blackhawk Films; Festival Films*

Denver Broncos 1984 Team Highlights 1985
Football
70546 70 mins C B, V, FO P
The Broncos crisp no-bucking-around style of play led them to a 13-3 record as they went about "The Winning of the West," the NFL's toughest division. This tape features 47-minutes of highlights from the entire NFL's '84 season as well.
NFL Films — *NFL Films Video*

Derek and Clive Get the Horn 1978
Comedy
59931 90 mins C B, V P
Peter Cook, Dudley Moore
England's favorite comedy team in a four-letter funfest.
Peter Cook — *Pacific Arts Video*

Dernier Combat, Le (The Last Battle) 1984
Drama
70564 93 mins B/W B, V P
Pierre Jolivet, Fritz Wepper, Jean Reno, Jean Bouise, Christiane Kruger, directed Luc Besson
This dialogueless, stark film about life after a devastating war marks the directorial debut of Besson. The characters wander through the rubble, staking claims to turf and forming new relationships with other survivors. In stereo on all formats.
MPAA:R
Triumph Films — *RCA/Columbia Pictures Home Video*

Desde el Abismo 19??
Drama
66415 115 mins C B, V P
Thelma Biral, Alberto Argibay, Olga Zubarry
After the birth of her son, a young mother takes to drink while in the throes of post-partum depression.
SP
Spanish — *Media Home Entertainment*

Desert Fox, The 1951
War-Drama
08436 87 mins B/W B, V P
James Mason, Sir Cedric Hardwicke, Jessica Tandy, directed by Henry Hathaway
Personal and political sides of Field Marshal Rommel are featured.
EL, SP
20th Century Fox; Nunnaly Johnson — *CBS/Fox Video*

Desert of the Tartars, The 1982
Adventure
74083 140 mins C B, V, CED P
This is the story of a young soldier who dreams of war and discovers that the real battle for him is with time.
MPAA:PG
Buz Potamkin; Hal Hoffer — *Embassy Home Entertainment*

Desert Trail 1935
Western
08828 57 mins B/W B, V, 3/4U P
John Wayne
John Wayne stars as a rough-and-tough cowboy in this action-packed Western adventure.
Monogram — *Sony Corporation of America; Spotlite Video; Discount Video Tapes; Video Dimensions; Cable Films; Video Connection; Nostalgia Merchant; Kartes Productions*

Despair 1979
Drama
66128 120 mins C B, V R, P
Dirk Bogarde, Andrea Ferreal, directed by Rainer Werner Fassbinder
A chilling and comic study of a victimized factory owner's descent into madness, set against the backdrop of Nazi Germany.
New Line Cinema — *Warner Home Video*

Desperate Women 1978
Western/Comedy
81260 98 mins C B, V P
Dan Haggerty, Susan Saint-James, Ronee Blakley, Ann Dusenberry, directed by Earl Bellamy
A hired gun rescues three female convicts from a stranded prison wagon in the desert. Problems arise when they are chased across the desert by an outlaw gang.
Lorimar Prods. — *U.S.A. Home Video*

Desperately Seeking Susan 1985
Comedy/Adventure
81479 104 mins C B, V R, P
Rosanna Arquette, Madonna, Aidan Quinn, Robert Joy, Steven Wright, directed by Susan Seidelman
A bored New Jersey housewife's life starts to get exciting when a case of mistaken identity ensues after she answers a personal ad placed by a mysterious woman's boyfriend.
MPAA:PG13
Orion Pictures — *THORN EMI/HBO Video*

Destination Moon 1950
Science fiction
49899 91 mins C B, V, 3/4U P
Warner Anderson, Tom Powers, Dick Wesson, Erin O'Brien Moore
This story of man's first lunar voyage contains Chesley Bonstell's astronomical artwork and a famous Woody Woodpecker cartoon. Includes previews of coming attractions from classic science fiction films.
Academy Award '50: Special Effects.
George Pal — *Nostalgia Merchant*

Destination Moonbase Alpha 1975
Science fiction
64904 93 mins C B, V P
Martin Landau, Barbara Bain
In the 21st century, an explosion has destroyed half the moon, causing it to break away from the earth's orbit. The moon is cast far away, but the 311 people manning Alpha, a research station on the moon, must continue their search for other life forms in outer space.
ITC Entertainment — *CBS/Fox Video*

Detective, The 1968
Mystery
34286 114 mins C B, V P
Frank Sinatra, Lee Remick
A beaufiful woman requests the services of a detective in order to discover her husband's killer.
SP
Twentieth Century Fox — *CBS/Fox Video*

Detour 1946
Crime-Drama
11672 69 mins B/W B, V P
Tom Neal, Ann Savage
New York piano player hitchhikes west to be with singer in California. He encounters murder along the way.
Producers Releasing Corp — *Video Yesteryear; Western Film & Video Inc; Festival Films; Classic Video Cinema Collector's Club; Kartes Productions*

Detour 1981
Football
50649 24 mins C B, V, FO R, P
Seattle Seahawks
When the passing combination of Jim Zorn to Steve Largent led the young expansion team to a winning record in 1979, Seahawks fans had high hopes for the 1980 season. Instead, it turned out to be a year coach Jack Patera and his young team would rather forget.
NFL Films — *NFL Films Video*

Deutsche Wochen-Schau, Die (Nazi Newsreel) 194?
World War II/Propaganda
52466 50 mins B/W B, V, FO P
This wartime propaganda film shows the power of the Nazi war machine, and the way that people on the home front helped to produce planes, tanks, and troops that conquered all obstacles in their path. Original German narration, no subtitles.
GE
Germany — *Video Yesteryear*

Devil and Daniel Mouse, The 1978
Fantasy
54692 30 mins C B, V R, P
Animated
A young songstress, Jan Mouse, sells her soul to the Devil in exchange for fame, fortune, and old records. Features John Sebastian's original songs.
Nelvana Prods Ltd — *Warner Home Video*

Devil and Max Devlin, The 1981
Comedy/Fantasy
58624 95 mins C B, V R, P
Elliott Gould, Bill Cosby, Susan Anspach, Adam Rich, Julie Budd, directed by Steven Hilliard Stern
The recently deceased Max Devlin strikes a bargain with the devil—he will be restored to life if he can convince three mortals to sell their souls. Music by Marvin Hamlisch.
MPAA:PG
Walt Disney Productions — *Walt Disney Home Video*

Devil and Miss Jones, The 1941
Comedy
65738 90 mins B/W B, V P
Jean Arthur, Robert Cummings
A rich department store owner poses as an employee in order to learn about impending labor trouble.
RKO — *Republic Pictures Home Video*

Devil at 4 O'Clock, The 1961
Drama
65189 126 mins B/W B, V P

Spencer Tracy, Frank Sinatra, Kerwin Mathews, Jean-Pierre Aumont, directed by Mervyn LeRoy
An alcoholic missionary and three convicts work to save a colony of leper children from a South Seas volcano.
Columbia — *RCA/Columbia Pictures Home Video*

Devil Bat, The **1941**
Horror
66370 70 mins B/W B, V P
Bela Lugosi, Dave O'Brien, Suzanne Kaaren
A crazed madman trains a swarm of monstrous blood-sucking bats to attack whenever they smell perfume.
Producers Releasing Corp — *Movie Buff Video; Discount Video Tapes*

Devil Dog: The Hound of Hell **1978**
Horror
80668 95 mins C B, V P
Richard Crenna, Yvette Mimieux, Kim Richards, Victor Jory, directed by Curtis Harrington
A family has trouble with man's best friend when they adopt a dog who is the son of the "Hound of Hell".
Zeitman-Landers-Roberts Prods. — *Lightning Video*

Devil Girl from Mars **1955**
Science fiction
49898 76 mins B/W B, V, 3/4U P
Patricia Laffan, Hazel Court, Hugh McDermott, Adrienne Corri
A female creature from Mars and her very large robot terrorize the English countryside where they land. The robot is capable of causing mass incineration.
Danzigers — *Nostalgia Merchant; Mossman Williams Productions*

Devil Thumbs a Ride, The **1947**
Drama
73697 63 mins B/W B, V P
Ted North, Lawrence Tierney, Nan Leslie
A traveller picks up a hitchhiker not knowing he's wanted for murder.
RKO — *RKO HomeVideo*

Devil Thumbs a Ride/Having Wonderful Crime **1947**
Mystery
79320 132 mins B/W B, V P
Lawrence Tierney, Pat O'Brien, George Murphy, Carole Landis
A mystery double feature: in ""Devil," a ruthless killer hitches a ride from a travelling salesman and in ""Having..." a criminal lawyer investigates the disappearance of a magician.
RKO — *RKO HomeVideo*

Devil Times Five **1982**
Horror
47751 87 mins C B, V P
Gene Evans, Sorrel Booke, Shelly Morrison
To take revenge for being incarcerated in a mental hospital, five children methodically murder the adults who befriend them.
MPAA:R
Dylan Jones; Michael Blowitz — *Media Home Entertainment*

Devils, The **1971**
Drama
53508 108 mins C B, V R, P
Vanessa Redgrave, Oliver Reed, directed by Ken Russell
In 1631 France, a young priest is accused of commerce with the devil and of sexually abusing a convent. Based on Aldous Huxley's "The Devils of Loudun."
MPAA:X
Warner Bros; Robert H. Solo; Ken Russell — *Warner Home Video*

Devil's Daughter, The **1939**
Horror
11229 60 mins B/W B, V, FO P
Nina Mae McKinney, Jack Carter, Ida James, Hamtree Harrington
A sister's hatred and voodoo ceremonies play an important part in this all-black drama.
Unknown — *Video Yesteryear; Sheik Video*

Devil's Eye **1960**
Comedy-Drama
65627 90 mins B/W B, V P
Bibi Anderson, Jarl Kulle, directed by Ingmar Bergman
The devil dispatches Don Juan to tempt and seduce a young virgin bride-to-be.
Janus Films — *Embassy Home Entertainment*

Devil's Rain **1975**
Horror
35368 85 mins C B, V P
Ernest Borgnine, Ida Lupino, William Shatner, Eddie Albert, Keenan Wynn
This gruesomely horrifying film relates the rituals and practices of devil worship, possession, and satanism.
MPAA:PG
Sandy Howard — *United Home Video*

Devils Triangle, The **1978**
Documentary
81058 59 mins C B, V P
Narrated by Vincent Price
This documentary examines the unexplained incidents which have occurred in the Bermuda Triangle.
Richard Winer Productions — *MGM/UA Home Video*

Devil's Undead, The 1975
Suspense
65451 90 mins C B, V P
Christopher Lee, Peter Cushing
When a Scottish orphanage is besieged by a rash of cold blooded murders, the police are summoned to investigate. Their relentless search to determine the truth leads to a climax as shocking as it is terrifying.
MPAA:PG
Charlemagne Inc — *Monterey Home Video*

Devil's Wedding Night, The 1973
Horror
79761 85 mins C B, V P
Mark Damon, Sara Bay
An archaeologist and his twin brother fight over a ring that lures Virgins into Count Dracula's Transylvanian castle.
MPAA:R
Dimension Pictures — *United Home Video*

Devo 1983
Music-Performance
75919 54 mins C B, V P
This program presents a combination of videos from the group Devo.
Devovision — *Sony Corporation of America*

Devo: The Men Who Make the Music 1979
Music-Performance
42905 55 mins C B, V R, P
New Wave rock group Devo perform robot-like interpretations from their first album, "Q—Are We Not Men? A—We Are Devo." Electronic music tinged thematically with de-evolution processes.
Chuck Statler — *Warner Home Video*

Devonsville Terror, The 1983
Horror
64985 97 mins C B, V P
Suzanna Love, Robert Walker, Donald Pleasance
Strange things begin to happen when a new school teacher arrives in Devonsville, a town which has a history of torture, murder and witchcraft. The hysterical townspeople begin a 20th century witch hunt.
Unknown — *Embassy Home Entertainment*

Dial "M" for Murder 1954
Suspense
47616 123 mins C B, V R, P
Ray Milland, Grace Kelly, Robert Cummings, John Williams, directed by Alfred Hitchcock
An unfaithful husband plots to murder his wife for her money. Part of the "A Night at the Movies" series, this tape simulates a 1954 movie evening, with a Daffy Duck cartoon, "My Little Duckaroo," a newsreel and coming attractions for "Them" and "A Star Is Born."
Warner Bros — *Warner Home Video; RCA VideoDiscs*

Diamonds Are Forever 1971
Adventure
59302 120 mins C B, V, LV, CED P
Sean Connery, Jill St. John, Charles Gray
Connery's last outing as James Bond finds him taking a lighter approach to the spy business, highlighted by spectacular stunt work and special effects.
United Artists — *CBS/Fox Video; RCA VideoDiscs*

Diana Ross in Concert 1982
Music-Performance
63439 90 mins C B, V P
Diana Ross
Diana Ross performs her greatest hits live at Caesar's Palace, including "Baby Love," "Ain't No Mountain High Enough," "Love Hangover," and "Reach Out and Touch."
Diana Ross Enterprises — *RCA/Columbia Pictures Home Video; RCA VideoDiscs*

Diary of a Mad Housewife 1970
Comedy-Drama
47414 94 mins C B, V P
Carrie Snodgress, Richard Benjamin, Frank Langella
Despairing of her miserable family life, a housewife has an affair with a writer, only to find him to be more selfish and egotistical than her husband.
MPAA:R
Universal — *MCA Home Video*

Diary of a Rebel 1984
Adventure
80472 89 mins C B, V P
John Ireland, Francisco Rabal
A fictional account of the rise of Cuban rebel leader Che Guevara.
Regal Video — *Regal Video*

Diary of a Teenage Hitchhiker 1982
Drama
60183 96 mins C B, V R, P
Charlene Tilton, Dick Van Patten
A 17-year-old girl ignores family restrictions and police warnings about a homicidal rapist stalking the area and continues to thumb rides to her job at a beach resort until one night she is picked up for a one-way ride to terror.
Stan Shpetner — *Lightning Video; Time Life Video*

Diary of Anne Frank, The **1959**
Drama
29140 150 mins C B, V, CED P
Millie Perkins, Joseph Schildkraut, Shelley Winters, Richard Beymer, Gusti Huber, Ed Wynn
In June 1945, a liberated Jewish refugee returns to the hidden third floor of an Amsterdam factory where he finds the diary kept by his younger daughter during their years in hiding from the Nazis.
National Board of Review '59: Best Picture; Academy Awards '59: Best Supporting Actress (Winters).
20th Century Fox — *CBS/Fox Video*

Diary of Forbidden Dreams **1976**
Fantasy
79705 94 mins C B, V P
Marcello Mastroianni, Hugh Griffith, Sydne Rome, directed by Roman Polanski
A young girl finds herself drawn into bizarre incidents that cause her to go insane.
MPAA:R
Foreign — *Trans World Entertainment*

Diary of a Young Comic **1979**
Drama
70664 74 mins C B, V P
Stacey Keach, Dom DeLouise, Richard Lewis, Bill Macy, George Jessel, Gary Muledeer, Nina Van Pollandt.
The story of a New York comedian in search of the meaning of lunacy. He finds it in Los Angeles.
Late Nite Prods — *Pacific Arts Video*

Dias de Ilusion **1980**
Suspense
47861 94 mins C B, V P
Andrea Del Boca, Luisina Brando
The fantasy world in which Lucia and her sister live was created for only one reason, and only Lucia's diary has the secret. In Spanish.
SP
Hector Olivera; Luis Repetto — *Media Home Entertainment*

Dick Cavett's Hocus Pocus, It's Magic **1979**
Magic
39079 101 mins C B, V, CED P
Mark Wilson, Harry Blackstone Jr., Slydini, hosted by Dick Cavett
Amateur magician Dick Cavett hosts this tribute to the great magicians, with many of today's master wizards performing their most spectacular tricks and illusions.
MPAA:G
Unknown — *Vestron Video; VERVE Films Inc*

Dick Deadeye **1976**
Adventure
59326 80 mins C B, V P
Animated
From the operas of Gilbert and Sullivan, based on drawings by Ronald Searle, comes the unlikeliest of heroes, Dick Deadeye. Sporting an I.Q. of zero, Dick is hired to wipe out pirates, thieves, and a sorcerer.
Sandy Cobe; David Baugh — *Family Home Entertainment*

Dick Tracy **1937**
Crime-Drama
11689 100 mins B/W B, V P
Ralph Byrd, Smiley Burnett
Dick Tracy faces the fiend, "Spider," and his demented hunchback.
Republic — *United Home Video*

Dick Tracy **1937**
Crime-Drama/Serials
14618 310 mins B/W B, V P
Ralph Byrd, Smiley Burnett
Serial, based on the comic strip character, in fifteen chapters. The first chapter is thirty minutes and each additional chapter is twenty minutes.
Republic — *United Home Video; Video Connection; Video Yesteryear; Discount Video Tapes*

Dick Tracy **1945**
Crime-Drama
58658 62 mins B/W B, V, FO P
Morgan Conway, Anne Jeffreys, Mike Mazurki, Jane Greer, Lyle Latell
The first Dick Tracy feature film, in which Splitface is on the loose, a schoolteacher is murdered, the Mayor is threatened, and a nutty professor uses a crystal ball to give Tracy the clue needed to connect the crimes.
RKO — *Video Yesteryear; Sheik Video; Nostalgia Merchant*

Dick Tracy Double Feature #1 **194?**
Crime-Drama
45053 122 mins B/W B, V P
Ralph Byrd, Lyle Latelle, Morgan Conway, Anne Jeffreys
This video double feature presents two Dick Tracy adventures: "Dick Tracy Detective," "Dick Tracy's Dilemma", a mystery-adventure package starring Chester Gould's popular comic strip hero.
RKO, Gold Key — *United Home Video*

Dick Tracy Double Feature #2 **194?**
Mystery/Adventure
45005 127 mins B/W B, V P

Boris Karloff, Ralph Byrd, Morgan Conway, Anne Jeffreys
Chester Gould's famous comic strip character is personified in: "Dick Tracy Meets Gruesome," "Dick Tracy vs. Cueball;" a double feature videocassette featuring Dick Tracy battling two of his arch enemies.
RKO, Gold Key — *United Home Video*

Dick Tracy Meets Gruesome **1947**
Crime-Drama
58642 66 mins B/W B, V, FO P
Boris Karloff, Ralph Byrd, Lyle Latell
Gruesome and his partner in crime, Melody, stage a bank robbery using the secret formula of Dr. A. Tomic. Tracy has to solve the robbery before word gets out and people rush to withdraw their savings, destroying civilization as we know it.
RKO — *Video Yesteryear; Video Connection; Hal Roach Studios; Western Film & Video Inc; Nostalgia Merchant; Admit One Video*

Dick Tracy Returns **1938**
Crime-Drama
11694 100 mins B/W B, V P
Ralph Byrd, Charles Middleton
Public Enemy Paw Stark and his gang set out on a wave of crime that brings them face to face with Dick Tracy.
Republic — *United Home Video*

Dick Tracy Returns **1938**
Crime-Drama/Serials
14619 310 mins B/W B, V P
Ralph Byrd, Charles Middleton
Serial, based on the comic strip character, in fifteen chapters. The first chapter is thirty minutes and each additional chapter is twenty minutes.
Republic — *United Home Video; Video Connection*

Dick Tracy vs. Crime Inc. **1941**
Crime-Drama/Serials
14620 310 mins B/W B, V P
Ralph Byrd, Ralph Morgan
Serial, based on the comic strip character, in fifteen chapters. The first chapter is thirty minutes and each additional chapter is twenty minutes.
Republic — *United Home Video; Video Connection*

Dick Tracy vs. Crime Inc. **1941**
Crime-Drama
07220 100 mins B/W B, V P
Ralph Byrd, Ralph Morgan
Dick Tracy encounters many difficulties when he tries to track down a criminal who can make himself invisible.
Republic — *United Home Video*

Dick Tracy vs. Cueball **1946**
Mystery
80738 62 mins B/W B, V P
Morgan Conway, Anne Jeffreys
Dick Tracy has his work cut out for him when the evil gangster Cueball appears on the scene. Based upon Chester Gould's comic strip.
RKO — *Hal Roach Studios*

Dick Tracy's Dilemma **1947**
Mystery
80737 60 mins B/W B, V P
Ralph Byrd, Lyle Latelle
The renowned police detective Dick Tracy becomes involved in a nearly unsolvable case. Based upon the Chester Gould comic strip.
RKO — *Hal Roach Studios*

Dick Tracy's G-Men **1939**
Crime-Drama/Serials
14621 310 mins B/W B, V P
Ralph Byrd, Irving Pichel
Serial, based on the comic strip character, in fifteen chapters. The first chapter is thirty minutes and each additional chapter is twenty minutes.
Republic — *United Home Video; Video Connection*

Dick Tracy's G-Men **1939**
Crime-Drama
11692 100 mins B/W B, V P
Ralph Byrd, Jennifer Jones
Tracy and his G-Men must stop international spy, Aarnoff, from stealing America's top secrets.
Republic — *United Home Video*

Die Laughing **1980**
Comedy
52716 108 mins C B, V R, P
Robby Benson, Charles Durning, Bud Cort, Elsa Lanchester
A cab driver unwittingly becomes involved in murder, intrigue, and the kidnapping of a monkey that has memorized a scientific formula that can destroy the world.
MPAA:PG
Orion Pictures — *Warner Home Video*

Die Sister, Die! **1974**
Horror/Suspense
70578 88 mins C B, V P
Jack Ging, Edith Atwater, Kent Smith, directed by Randall Hood
This gothic-mansion-with-a-secret-in-the-basement thriller features a battle between a senile, reclusive sister and her disturbed, tormenting brother.
Randall Hood — *MPI Home Video*

Different Story, A **1978**
Comedy/Romance
76903 107 mins C B, V P
Perry King, Meg Foster, Valerie Curtain, Peter Donat, Richard Bull
Romance develops when a lesbian real estate agent offers a homosexual chauffeur a job with her firm.
MPAA:PG
Alan Belkin; Avco Embassy — *Embassy Home Entertainment*

Digital Dreams **1983**
Music video
77526 70 mins C B, V P
Animated, Bill Wyman, Astrid Wyman, James Coburn
This film presents a surrealistic journey into the life of Rolling Stones bassist Bill Wyman from his electronic childhood to his adult obsession with computers.
Bill and Astrid Wyman — *Music Media*

Dillinger **1973**
Crime-Drama
64894 106 mins C B, V, CED P
Warren Oates, Michelle Phillips, Richard Dreyfuss, Cloris Leachman
The most colorful period of criminality in America is brought to life in this story of John Dillinger, "Baby Face" Nelson and the notorious "Lady in Red."
MPAA:R
American International Pictures — *Vestron Video*

Dinah Shore Show, The **1963**
Variety
12846 59 mins B/W B, V, FO P
Dinah Shore, Steve Allen, Audrey Meadows, Peter Lind Hayes, Mary Healy, Yves Montand
Steve Allen's hilarious man in the street survey highlights this music and comedy show.
NBC — *Video Yesteryear*

Diner **1982**
Comedy-Drama
47777 110 mins C B, V, CED P
Steve Guttenberg, Daniel Stern, Mickey Rourke, Kevin Bacon, directed by Barry Levinson
The bittersweet experiences of a group of Baltimore teenagers growing up, circa 1959.
MPAA:R
MGM — *MGM/UA Home Video*

Dinner at Eight **1933**
Comedy-Drama
77378 110 mins C B, V, LV P
John Barrymore, Lionel Barrymore, Wallace Beery, Madge Evans, Jean Harlow, Billie Burke, Marie Dressler, Phillips Holmes, Jean Hersholt, directed by George Cukor
A social climbing woman and her husband throw a dinner party where each of the guests reveal something about themselves.
MGM; David O. Selznick — *MGM/UA Home Video*

Dinner at the Ritz **1937**
Drama
11392 78 mins B/W B, V, FO P
David Niven, Annabella, Paul Lucas
Daughter of a murdered Parisian banker vows to find his killer with help from her fiance.
20th Century Fox — *Video Yesteryear; Cinema Concepts; Cable Films; Sheik Video; Budget Video; Western Film & Video Inc; Kartes Productions*

Dino **1957**
Drama
77479 96 mins B/W B, V P
Sal Mineo, Brian Keith, Susan Kohner, directed by Thomas Carr
A social worker joins a young woman in helping a seventeen-year-old delinquent to re-enter society.
Allied Artists — *Republic Pictures Home Video*

Dionne Quintuplets **1978**
Biographical/History-Modern
46693 87 mins C B, V, FO P
The true story of five identical girls born in 1934 who were taken from their parents by a court order. This program presents the tragic story of exploitation and publicity that surrounded this family and the hardships they endured as a result.
National Film Board of Canada — *Video Yesteryear; National Film Board of Canada*

Dionne Warwick in Concert **1983**
Music-Performance
75492 120 mins C B, V P
Dionne Warwick
Dionne Warwick's Chicago 1983 concert includes great hits such as "Alfie," "Walk On By," "Do You Know the Way to San Jose" and "Deja Vu."
MusicAmerica Live — *Prism*

Diplomaniacs **1933**
Comedy
65227 62 mins B/W B, V P
Bert Wheeler, Robert Woolsey, Marjorie White, Hugh Herbert
Wheeler and Woolsey, official barbers on an Indian reservation, are sent to the Geneva peace conference to represent the tribe.
RKO — *Blackhawk Films*

Dire Straits 1981
Music-Performance
52709 21 mins C B, V R, P
Dire Straits
The English rock group performs songs from the album "Making Movies" including "Romeo and Juliet," "Tunnel of Love," and "Skateaway."
Mervyn Lloyd — *Warner Home Video*

Dirt Band Tonight, The 1982
Music-Performance
64830 58 mins C B, V P
Filmed at Denver's Rainbow Music Hall, The Dirt Band performs such classics as "Mr. Bojangles," "Rocky Top," "Will the Circle Be Unbroken" and "Make a Little Magic." In stereo.
EMI Music Video — *THORN EMI/HBO Video; Pioneer Artists*

Dirt Gang, The 1971
Drama
81532 89 mins C B, V P
Paul Carr, Michael Pataki, Michael Forest
A motorcycle gang terrorize the members of a film crew on location in the desert.
MPAA:R
Shermart Distributing Co. — *MPI Home Video*

Dirty, Dirty Jokes 1984
Comedy-Performance
79306 60 mins C B, V P
Redd Foxx hosts this program that features up and coming stand-up comics.
Vestron Video — *Vestron Video*

Dirty Dozen, The 1967
War-Drama
39090 149 mins C B, V, CED P
Lee Marvin, Ernest Borgnine, Charles Bronson, Jim Brown, George Kennedy
A tough Army major is assigned to train and command twelve hardened convicts on the suicidal mission into Nazi Germany in 1944.
Academy Awards '67: Best Sound Effects.
MGM — *MGM/UA Home Video*

Dirty Gertie From Harlem U.S.A. 1946
Drama
08889 60 mins B/W B, V, 3/4U P
Gertie LaRue
An all-black cast does a variation on Somerset Maugham's "Rain." Gertie goes to Trinidad to hide out from her jilted boyfriend.
Unknown — *Sheik Video; Video Yesteryear; Discount Video Tapes*

Dirty Harry 1971
Drama
38947 103 mins C B, V, LV R, P
Clint Eastwood, directed by Don Siegel
Clint Eastwood is detective Harry Callahan, who is attempting to track down a psychopathic rooftop killer before a kidnapped girl dies.
MPAA:R
Warner Bros — *Warner Home Video; RCA VideoDiscs*

Dirty Mind of Young Sally, The 1972
Comedy
53147 84 mins C B, V P
Sharon Kelly
Sally's erotic radio program broadcasts from a mobile studio, which must stay one step ahead of the police.
MPAA:R
Valiant Intl Pictures — *Monterey Home Video*

Dirty Tricks 1981
Comedy
65070 91 mins C B, V P
Elliot Gould, Kate Jackson, Arthur Hill, Rich Little, directed by Arthur Hill
A history professor searches for an incriminating letter that was written by George Washington.
MPAA:PG
Filmplan International — *Embassy Home Entertainment*

Disappearance, The 1981
Suspense
65607 80 mins C B, V P
Donald Sutherland, David Hemmings, John Hurt, Christopher Plummer
A hired assassin discovers an ironic link between his new target and his missing wife.
MPAA:R
World Northal — *Vestron Video*

Dishonored Lady 1947
Suspense
66371 85 mins B/W B, V P
Hedy Lamarr, Dennis O'Keefe, William Lundigan, John Loder
A lady art director is accused of murdering her ex-boyfriend and refuses to testify in her own defense.
Mars Films — *Movie Buff Video*

Disney Cartoon Parade, Vol. 1 1981
Cartoons
56877 120 mins C CED P
Animated
Mickey Mouse, Goofy, Minnie, Pluto, Donald, Chip 'n Dale, and Peg-leg Pete star in "On Vacation with Mickey Mouse and Friends," and "The Adventures of Chip 'n Dale."
Walt Disney Productions — *RCA VideoDiscs*

Disney Cartoon Parade, Vol. 2 **1982**
Cartoons
59020 88 mins C CED P
Animated
This Disney compilation includes "At Home with Donald Duck" (1956), a festival of classic cartoons featuring Donald , Mickey, Pluto, and Goofy, and "The Coyote's Lament" (1961), featuring Pluto out West.
Walt Disney Productions — *RCA VideoDiscs*

Disney Cartoon Parade, Vol. 3 **1982**
Cartoons
59641 100 mins C CED P
Animated
Some of Disney's most memorable cartoons: "Kids Is Kids" features the zany antics of Donald Duck and his nephews, as Prof. Ludwig von Drake tries to answer why kids are hard to handle; "Goofy's Salute to Father" follows Goofy's hilarious misadventures from bachelorhood to the altar to bottles and diapers.
Walt Disney Productions — *RCA VideoDiscs*

Disney Cartoon Parade, Vol. 4 **1982**
Cartoons
60389 85 mins C CED P
Animated
This volume contains "Thru the Mirror," "The Sleepwalker," "Donald's Golf Game," "Pluto and Gopher," "Dragon Around, " "The Whalers," "Society Dog Show," "Pluto's Sweater," "Donald Applecore," "The Little Whirlwind," "Donald's Diary" and "Pluto's Blue Note."
Walt Disney Productions — *RCA VideoDiscs*

Disney Cartoon Parade, Vol. 5 **1983**
Cartoons
64328 90 mins C CED P
Animated
This collection includes such Disney favorites as "Goofy Over Sports," "Boat Builders," and "Pluto's Quintuplets," plus many others.
Walt Disney Productions — *RCA VideoDiscs*

Disney Christmas Gift, A **1984**
Cartoons
79178 46 mins C B, V R, P
Animated
A collection of Christmas scenes from such Disney classics as ""Peter Pan," ""The Sword In The Stone," and ""Cinderella."
Walt Disney Productions — *Walt Disney Home Video*

Disney's American Heroes **1982**
Cartoons/Folklore
63190 39 mins C B, V R, P
Animated, the voices of Roy Rogers and the Sons of the Pioneers
Two Disney tall tales of American folk heroes: "Pecos Bill" and "Paul Bunyan."
Walt Disney Productions — *Walt Disney Home Video*

Disney's Halloween Treat **1984**
Cartoons/Holidays
73792 47 mins C B, V R, P
Animated
Scenes from Disney classics, such as "Snow White and the Seven Dwarfs," "Fantasia", "Peter Pan" and "The Sword and the Stone" are tied together with a Halloween theme.
Walt Disney — *Walt Disney Home Video*

Disney's Storybook Classics **1982**
Cartoons
63127 121 mins C B, V R, P
Animated, the voice of Sterling Holloway and the Andrews Sisters
A collection of classic children's fables, featuring: "Little Toot" (1948—excerpted from "Melody Time"), the story of a little harbor tugboat; "Chicken Little" (1943), "The Grasshopper and the Ants" (1934—a Silly Symphony) and "Peter and the Wolf" (1946—excerpted from "Make Mine Music"), a Disneyized version of Prokofiev's famous concert piece.
Walt Disney Productions — *Walt Disney Home Video*

Diva **1982**
Suspense/Romance
60394 123 mins C B, V, CED P
Frederic Andrei, Roland Bertin, Richard Bohringer, Gerard Darmon, Jacques Fabbri, Wilhelmenia Wiggins Fernandez, Dominique Pinon
A young mail courier with a passion for opera manages to tape his idol who has avoided the recording studio. At the same time, a prostitute hides a tape recording in his delivery bag which fingers a local drug kingpin. Bizarre chases and plot twists follow.
Galaxie Films; Greenwich Films — *MGM/UA Home Video*

Divide and Conquer **1943**
World War II/Documentary
50614 60 mins B/W B, V, 3/4U P
Directed by Frank Capra
Hitler's Nazis invade Belgium, Holland, Denmark, and Norway. They take France, and

drive the British into the sea of Dunkirk. Part of the "Why We Fight" series.
US War Department — *Western Film & Video Inc; MPI Home Video*

Divine Madness 1980
Music-Performance
47374 87 mins C B, V R, P
Bette Midler
Bette Midler is captured at her best in a live concert at Pasadena Civic Auditorium.
MPAA:R
The Ladd Company — *Warner Home Video; RCA VideoDiscs*

Divorce His, Divorce Hers 1972
Drama
70713 144 mins C B, V P
Richard Burton, Elizabeth Taylor
The first half of this drama shows the crumbling of a marriage through the husband's eyes. The second half offers the wife's perspective.
John Heyman — *VCL Home Video*

Divorce of Lady X 1938
Drama
07120 92 mins C B, V P
Merle Oberon, Laurence Olivier, directed by Tom Whelan
British debutante, in guise of "Lady X', makes a woman-hating divorce lawyer eat his words through romance and marriage.
United Artists; Alexander Korda;
British — *Unicorn Video; Discount Video Tapes; World Video Pictures; Hal Roach Studios; See Hear Industries*

Dixie: Changing Habits 1983
Drama
80899 96 mins C B, V P
Suzanne Pleshette, Cloris Leachman, Kenneth McMillan, John Considine, Geraldine Fitzgerald
The flamboyant madam of a New Orleans bordello is sent to a convent for ninety days of rehabilitation. Available in VHS Stereo and Beta Hi-Fi.
George Englund Productions — *U.S.A. Home Video*

Dixie Dynamite 1976
Drama
80950 88 mins C B, V P
Warren Oates, Christopher George, Jane Anne Johnstone, Kathy McHaley, R.G. Armstrong
The two daughters of a Georgia moonshiner set out to avenge the murder of their father. The music is performed by Duane Eddy and Dorsey Burnette.
MPAA:PG
Dimension Pictures — *United Home Video; Continental Video*

Dixie Jamboree 1944
Comedy/Musical
57351 69 mins B/W B, V, FO P
Guy Kibbee, Frances Langford, Louise Beavers, Charles Butterworth
A gangster "on the lam" uses an unusual method of escape from St. Louis—the last Mississippi Showboat.
Producers Releasing Corp — *Video Yesteryear; Discount Video Tapes; See Hear Industries*

Dizzy Gillespie 1981
Music-Performance
75895 19 mins C B, V P
This program presents a jazz concert by Dizzy Gillespie featuring his compositions "Be Bop" and "Birks' Works."
Jazz America Ltd — *Sony Corporation of America*

Dizzy Gillespie's Dream Band 1981
Music-Performance
75896 16 mins C B, V P
This program presents a concert by Dizzy Gillespie featuring his songs "Groovin' High" and "Hothouse," played by an all star band of Gillespie alumni.
Jazz American Ltd — *Sony Corporation of America*

Django 1968
Western
81516 90 mins C B, V P
Franco Nero, Loredana Nusciak, Angel Alvarez
Django is a stranger who arrives in a Mexican border town to settle a dispute between a small band of Americans and Mexicans.
MPAA:PG
Sergio Corbucci Prods — *Sagebrush Productions*

Django Shoots First 1974
Western
78117 96 mins C B, V, FO P
Glenn Saxon, Evelyn Stewart, Alberto Lupo
A colorful western with plenty of action and plot twists.
Italy — *Video Yesteryear*

Do Not Forsake Me Oh My Darling 1968
Adventure/Fantasy
76922 50 mins C B, V P
Patrick McGoohan
The Prisoner's mind is needed to find a professor who's developed a process which can transmit the mind and personality of one man into the body of another. An episode from "The Prisoner" TV series.
ITC — *MPI Home Video*

Do They Know It's Christmas? 1984
Music video/Documentary
80364 30 mins C B, V P
Bob Geldof, Sting, Phil Collins, Paul Young, Bono Vox, Simon Le Bon, Boy George
A documentary about how over forty of rock's biggest stars got together to record "Do They Know It's Christmas" plus a music video of the song. Available in VHS and Beta Hi-Fi.
Vestron Music Video — *Vestron Video*

D.O.A. 1949
Suspense
33495 83 mins B/W B, V, FO P
Edmond O'Brien, Pamela Britton, directed by Rudolph Mate
A man is accidentally given a lethal, slow-acting poison. As his time runs out, he frantically seeks to learn who is responsible and why he was poisoned.
United Artists — *Video Yesteryear; Sheik Video; Cable Films; Western Film & Video Inc; United Home Video; Classic Video Cinema Collector's Club; Kartes Productions*

Doctor at Large 1957
Comedy
73793 98 mins C B, V P
Dirk Bogarde, Donald Sinden, Anne Heywood
A doctor blunders his way to his dream of being a surgeon.
J Arthur Rank — *VidAmerica*

Doctor at Sea 1956
Comedy-Drama
73794 93 mins C B, V P
Dirk Bogarde, Brigitte Bardot
To escape his marriage, a doctor signs on a cargo boat as a ship's doctor and becomes involved with a French girl.
J Arthur Rank — *VidAmerica*

Dr. Black, Mr. Hyde 1976
Horror
35383 88 mins C B, V P
Rosalind Cash, Stu Gilliam
Horrifying tale of a black man who can't control himself when drinking the special potion.
MPAA:R
Charles Walker, Manfred Bernhard — *United Home Video*

Dr. Detroit 1983
Comedy
65117 91 mins C B, V, LV, CED P
Dan Aykroyd, Howard Hesseman, Donna Dixon
A meek college professor becomes involved with four beautiful hookers and creates another identity as their flamboyant pimp, Dr. Detroit.
MPAA:R
Universal — *MCA Home Video*

Doctor Doolittle 1967
Musical
08456 144 mins C B, V, CED P
Rex Harrison, Samantha Eggar, Anthony Newley, Richard Attenborough
An adventure about a 19th century English doctor who embarks on linguistic lessons for his animals. Based on Hugh Lofting's stories.
Academy Awards '67: Best Song ("Talk to the Animals"). EL, SP
20th Century Fox; APJAC — *CBS/Fox Video*

Dr. I. Q. 1953
Game show
42971 30 mins B/W B, V, FO P
George Ansbro, Art Fleming, Bob Shepherd, Jimmy McLain
Early television quiz fun abounds as the good doctor, Jimmy McLain, gives away silver dollars for the correct answers to questions like "Who wrote the quote, "To err is human, to forgive divine?"
ABC — *Video Yesteryear*

Doctor in Distress 1963
Comedy
73795 102 mins C B, V P
Dirk Bogarde, Leo McKern, Samantha Eggar
An aging chief surgeon falls in love with a physiotherapist and tries to recapture his youth.
J Arthur Rank — *VidAmerica*

Dr. Jekyll and Mr. Hyde 1920
Horror
48293 65 mins B/W B, V P, T
John Barrymore, Nita Naldi, Brandon Hurst
The first American film version of Robert Louis Stevenson's horror tale about a schizophrenic physician. Silent.
Famous Players Lasky Corp — *Blackhawk Films; Festival Films; Western Film & Video Inc; Discount Video Tapes; Classic Video Cinema Collector's Club; MGM/UA Home Video*

Dr. No 1963
Adventure
58822 111 mins C B, V, LV, CED P
Sean Connery, Ursula Andress, Joseph Wiseman, Jack Lord
James Bond, investigating murders in Jamaica, discovers a nuclear base established to divert the course of rockets projected from Cape Canaveral.
United Artists; Eon Prods — *CBS/Fox Video; RCA VideoDiscs*

Doctor Snuggles 1984
Cartoons
80040 60 mins C B, V P

Animated
Doctor Snuggles pursues the evil Professor Emerald after a strange series of events occurs.
Jim Terry — *Embassy Home Entertainment*

Dr. Strangelove **1964**
Comedy
63962 93 mins B/W B, V P
Peter Sellers, George C. Scott, Sterling Hayden, Keenan Wynn, Slim Pickens, directed by Stanley Kubrick
Peter Sellers plays a triple role in Stanley Kubrick's classic black comedy about a group of war-eager military men and the psychotic genius who is behind a scheme to attack Russia.
Columbia — *RCA/Columbia Pictures Home Video; RCA VideoDiscs*

Dr. Terror's House of Horrors **1965**
Horror
70200 92 mins C B, V P
Christopher Lee, Peter Cushing
Six traveling companions have their fortunes told by a mysterious doctor through the use of Tarot cards.
Hammer — *Republic Pictures Home Video*

Dr. Who and the Daleks **1965**
Science fiction
81181 78 mins C B, V R, P
Peter Cushing, Roy Castle, directed by Gordon Fleming
The time-lord Dr. Who and his three grandchildren accidentally transport themselves to a futuristic planet inhabited by the Daleks, who capture the travelers and hold them captive. Available in VHS and Beta Hi-Fi.
Joe Vegoda — *THORN EMI/HBO Video*

Doctor Zhivago **1965**
Drama
44642 197 mins C B, V, LV, CED P
Omar Sharif, Julie Christie, Geraldine Chaplin, Rod Steiger, Alec Guinness, Tom Courtenay, directed by David Lean
An historical account of the lives of the people who lived through the dark days of the Russian Revolution. Based on the Nobel Prize winning novel by Boris Pasternak.
Academy Awards '65: Best Screenplay From Another Medium (Bolt); Best Costume Design, Color (Dalton); Best Cinematography (Young); Best Art Direction, Color (Box and Marsh).
MGM — *MGM/UA Home Video*

Dodge City **1939**
Western
68229 104 mins C B, V P
Errol Flynn, Olivia De Havilland
Errol Flynn stars as Wade Hutton, the roving cattleman who becomes the sheriff of Dodge City. His job is to run the ruthless outlaw and his gang out of town.
Warner Bros — *CBS/Fox Video*

Dodsworth **1936**
Drama
81467 101 mins B/W B, V, LV P
Walter Huston, David Niven, Paul Lukas, John Payne, Mary Astor, directed by William Wyler
The lives of an American businessman and his wife are drastically changed when they take a tour of Europe. Based upon the Sinclair Lewis novel.
Samuel Goldwyn — *Embassy Home Entertainment*

Dog Day Afternoon **1975**
Comedy-Drama
44591 120 mins C B, V R, P
Al Pacino, John Cazale, Charles Durning, James Broderick, Chris Sarandon, Carol Kane, directed by Sidney Lumet
The true story of a bank robbery that occured on August 22, 1972 in the early morning of a scorching New York summer day. The gunmen turned the robbery into a bizarre event—from the way they handled their hostages, to their demands, to their order for take-out pizza.
Academy Awards '75: Best Original Screenplay (Pierson). MPAA:R
Warner Bros — *Warner Home Video; RCA VideoDiscs*

Dog of Flanders, A **1959**
Drama
81100 96 mins C B, V R, P
David Ladd, Donald Crisp, Theodore Bikel
A young Dutch boy and his grandfather find a badly beaten dog and restore it to health.
20th Century Fox; Robert Radnitz — *Paramount Home Video*

Dogs of Hell **1983**
Horror
81093 90 mins C B, V P
Earl Owensby, Bill Gribble, Jerry Rushing
The sheriff of an idyllic resort community must stop a pack of killer dogs from terrorizing the residents.
MPAA:R
Earl Owensby — *Media Home Entertainment*

Dogs of War, The **1981**
Adventure/Drama
47147 102 mins C B, V, CED P
Christopher Walken, Tom Berenger, Colin Blakely
A group of professional mercenaries are hired to overthrow the dictator of a new West African nation. Based on the novel by Frederick Forsythe.
MPAA:R

 (For explanation of codes, see USE GUIDE and KEY)

United Artists — *CBS/Fox Video*

Doin What the Crowd Does **1973**
Horror
66108 89 mins C B, V P
Robert Walker Jr, Cesar Romero
The tale of the death of Poe's lover Lenore.
MPAA:PG EL, SP
William Herbert — *Unicorn Video*

Dolce Vita, La **1960**
Drama
47990 174 mins B/W B, V P
Morcello Mastroianni, Anita Ekberg, Anouk Aimee, directed by Federico Fellini
A journalist mixes in modern Roman high society and is alternately bewitched and sickened by what he sees.
Riama; Pathe Consortium — *Republic Pictures Home Video*

Doll Face **1946**
Musical
41075 80 mins B/W B, V P
Vivian Blaine, Dennis O'Keefe, Perry Como, Carmen Miranda, Martha Stewart, Reed Madley
This entertaining film includes songs such as "Somebody's Walking in My Dream," "Hubba Hubba," "Here Comes Heaven Again," and "Chico Chico."
20th Century Fox — *Budget Video; Discount Video Tapes; Video Yesteryear; See Hear Industries*

Dollars **1971**
Suspense/Comedy
80784 119 mins C B, V P
Warren Beatty, Goldie Hawn, Gert Frobe, Scott Brady, Robert Webber, directed by Richard Brooks
A bank employee and his dizzy assistant plan to steal its assets while installing a new security system in the bank. Music by Quincy Jones. Available in Beta Hi-Fi.
MPAA:R
Columbia Pictures; M.J. Frankovich — *RCA/Columbia Pictures Home Video*

Doll's House, A **1973**
Drama
66492 98 mins C B, V P
Jane Fonda, Edward Fox, Trevor Howard, David Warner
Jane Fonda plays Nora, a subjugated housewife who breaks free to establish herself as an individual. Based on Henrik Ibsen's classic play.
World Film Services; Tomorrow Entertainment — *Prism*

Doll's House, A **19??**
Drama
66455 89 mins B/W B, V P
Julie Harris, Christopher Plummer, Jason Robards, Hume Cronyn, Eileen Heckart, Richard Thomas
An all-star cast is featured in this original television production of Henrik Ibsen's classic play about an independent woman's quest for freedom in ninettenth-century Norway.
Sonny Fox Productions — *MGM/UA Home Video*

Doll's House, A **1973**
Drama
52389 109 mins C CED P
Jane Fonda, Edward Fox, Trevor Howard
Henrik Ibsen's 1879 play is the basis of this authentic portrayal of nineteenth century society and values.
World Film Services, Tomorrow Entertainment — *RCA VideoDiscs; Learning Corp of America*

Dolly in London **1983**
Music-Performance
69623 50 mins C B, V P
Dolly Parton
Dolly Parton is featured in a video concert from London's Dominion Theatre singing such hits as "9 to 5," "Jolene" and "Here You Come Again," among others. In stereo VHS and Beta Hi-Fi.
Stan Harris; Speckled Bird Inc — *RCA/Columbia Pictures Home Video; RCA VideoDiscs*

Dominique Is Dead **1979**
Drama
66493 95 mins C B, V P
Cliff Robertson, Jean Simmons, Jenny Agutter, Simon Ward, Ron Moody
A woman is driven to suicide by her greedy husband—now someone is trying to drive him mad.
Sword and Sorcery Productions — *Prism*

Domino Principle, The **1977**
Drama/Prisons
46151 97 mins C CED P
Gene Hackman, Candice Bergen, Richard Widmark, Mickey Rooney, Edward Albert, Eli Wallach, directed by Stanley Kramer
Gene Hackman plays a convict plotting to escape from San Quentin prison.
MPAA:G
Stanley Kramer, Avco Embassy — *CBS/Fox Video*

Don Amigo/Stage to Chino **194?**
Western
80429 122 mins B/W B, V P

Duncan Renaldo, Leo Carrillo, George O'Brien
A western double feature: The Cisco Kid and Pancho ride together again in "Don Amigo" and in "Stage to Chino" a postal inspector investigates a gang who robs rival stage lines.
RKO — *RKO HomeVideo*

Don Daredevil Rides Again 1951
Serials
64426 180 mins B/W B, V, 3/4U P
Ken Curtis
Don Daredevil flies into danger in this twelve-episode serial.
Republic — *Nostalgia Merchant*

Don Kirshner's Rock Concert, Vol. 1 1981
Music-Performance
52606 77 mins C CED P
Don Kirshner presents seventeen magnetic performances by Motown superstars Billy Preston, The Commodores, Smokey Robinson, and Bonnie Pointer.
Don Kirshner Prods — *RCA VideoDiscs*

Don Q., Son of Zorro 1925
Adventure
47791 111 mins B/W B, V, 3/4U P
Douglas Fairbanks Sr, Mary Astor
Zorro's son takes up his father's fight against evil and injustice. Silent.
United Artists — *Western Film & Video Inc; Blackhawk Films; Classic Video Cinema Collector's Club; Discount Video Tapes*

Don Quixote 1984
Dance
80815 135 mins C B, V R, P
Mikhail Baryshnikov, Cynthia Harvey
This tape offers a production of the Richard Strauss work, choreographed by Baryshnikov, and performed at the Metropolitan Opera House in New York. Available in VHS and Beta Hi Fi.
Mikhail Baryshnikov — *THORN EMI/HBO Video*

Don Rickles—Buy this Tape, You Hockey Puck 1985
Comedy-Performance
81320 51 mins C B, V P
Don Rickles, Don Adams, Jack Klugman, Michele Lee
Don Rickles performs some of his best stand up and put down routines in this comedy video.
Paul Brownstein — *Lightning Video*

Don Winslow of the Navy 1943
Adventure/Serials
08876 234 mins B/W B, V, 3/4U P
Don Terry, Walter Sands, Ann Nagel
Thirteen episodes centered around the evil Scorpion, who plots to attack the Pacific Coast.
Universal — *Video Connection; Sheik Video; Video Yesteryear; Discount Video Tapes; Nostalgia Merchant*

Dona Flor and Her Two Husbands 1978
Comedy
53509 106 mins C B, V R, P
Sonia Braga, Jose Wilker, Mauro Mendonca, directed by Bruno Baretto
A woman becomes a widow when her philandering husband finally expires from drink, gambling, and women. She remarries, but her new husband is so boringly proper, she begins fantasizing husband number one's return.
New Yorker Films; Brazil — *Warner Home Video*

Donner Pass—The Road to Survival 1984
Drama
69802 98 mins C B, V P
Robert Fuller, Diane McBain, Andrew Prine, John Anderson, Michael Callan
Stranded in a mountain pass during an unexpected snowstorm in 1846, a group of settlers trying to reach California is faced with two choices: starvation or cannibalism. Based on a true episode in American history.
James Simmons — *United Home Video*

Donovan's Reef 1963
Comedy/Romance
64023 109 mins C B, V, LV R, P
John Wayne, Lee Marvin, Elizabeth Allen, Dorothy Lamour
Two ex-Navy buddies are enjoying life on a South Pacific island, where they spend most of their time in the local saloon—until the arrival of a straight-laced Boston woman in search of her father.
Paramount — *Paramount Home Video*

Don's Party 1982
Comedy
65730 91 mins C B, V P
John Hargreaves
This off-beat comedy focuses on a party that is not what anyone expected.
Phillip Adams — *VidAmerica*

Don't Answer the Phone 1980
Horror
47854 94 mins C B, V P
James Westmoreland, Flo Gerrish, Ben Frank
A deeply troubled photographer stalks and attacks the patients of a beautiful psychologist talk show hostess.
MPAA:R
Robert Hammer — *Media Home Entertainment*

Don't Be Afraid of the Dark 1973
Suspense
77207 74 mins C B, V P
Kim Darby, Jim Hutton, Barbara Anderson, William Demarest
Mysterious gnomes terrorize a young couple who have inherited an old house.
Lorimar Productions — *U.S.A. Home Video*

Don't Change My World 1983
Drama
69536 89 mins C B, V P
Roy Tatum, Ben Jones
To preserve the natural beauty of the north woods, a wildlife photographer must fight a villainous land developer and a reckless poacher.
MPAA:G
George P Macrenaris — *Children's Video Library*

Don't Cry, It's Only Thunder 1981
Drama
69622 108 mins C B, V P
Dennis Christopher, Susan Saint James
A young army medic who works in a mortuary in Saigon becomes involved with a group of Vietnamese orphans and a dedicated army doctor.
MPAA:PG
Sanrio Communications — *RCA/Columbia Pictures Home Video*

Don't Go in the House 1980
Horror
59666 90 mins C B, V P
Dan Grimaldi, Robert Osth, Ruth Dardick
A long dormant psychosis is brought to life by the death of a young man's mother.
MPAA:R
Ellen Hammill — *Media Home Entertainment*

Don't Go in the Woods 1981
Suspense/Horror
65217 88 mins C B, V P
Four young campers are being stalked by a crazed killer.
MPAA:R
James Bryan — *Vestron Video*

Don't Look Now 1974
Drama
57280 110 mins C B, V, LV R, P
Donald Sutherland, Julie Christie, Hilary Mason, directed by Nicholas Roeg
Psychic terror in a Gothic setting provides the chilling backdrop in this tale of a couple's search for the ghost of their dead child.
MPAA:R
Paramount — *Paramount Home Video; RCA VideoDiscs*

Don't Open the Door! 1980
Horror
81615 90 mins C B, V P
Susan Bracken, Gene Ross, Jim Harrell
A young woman is terrorized by a killer located inside her house.
MPAA:PG
Cinema Shares International — *Video Gems*

Don't Raise the Bridge, Lower the River 1968
Comedy
21285 99 mins C B, V P
Jerry Lewis, Terry-Thomas
After his wife leaves him, an American with crazy, get-rich-quick schemes turns her ancestral English home into a Chinese discotheque.
Columbia — *RCA/Columbia Pictures Home Video*

Don't Shove/Two Gun Gussie 1919
Comedy
64823 27 mins B/W B, V P, T
Harold Lloyd, Bebe Daniels, Noah Young, Snub Pollard
Two early Harold Lloyd shorts feature the comedian's embryonic comic style as a young fellow impressing his date at a skating rink ("Don't Shove") and a city slicker out West ("Two Gun Gussie"). Silent with piano scores.
Rolin Film; Pathe — *Blackhawk Films*

Doobie Brothers Live, The 1981
Music-Performance
60381 65 mins C CED P
The seminal rock group performs in Santa Barbara, California, for over 20,000 fans. Songs include "Minute by Minute," "Takin It to the Streets," "What a Fool Believes," "Listen to the Music."
Doobro Corp — *RCA VideoDiscs*

Doonesbury Special, A 1978
Cartoons/Satire
69022 30 mins C B, V P
Animated
This animated program features Doonesbury, Zonker, Joanie Caucus, Mike, B.D, Marcus and Jimmy.
Cannes Film Festival: Special Jury Award.
Barry Trudeau; John and Faith Hubley — *Pacific Arts Video*

Door to Door 1984
Comedy
77552 93 mins C B, V P

Ron Leibman, Arliss Howard, Alan Austin, Jane Kaczmarek
Two salesmen travel across the United States selling vacuum cleaners door to door.
MPAA:PG
Shapiro Entertainment — *Media Home Entertainment*

Door with Seven Locks **1940**
Mystery
66372 86 mins B/W B, V P
Leslie Banks, Lilli Palmer, Cathleen Nesbitt
A police inspector uncovers a mad doctor's conspiracy to steal jewels from a young heiress.
Rialto; Pathe — *Movie Buff Video*

Doors: A Tribute to Jim Morrison, The **1981**
Music-Performance
47387 60 mins C B, V R, P
Jim Morrison, Ray Manzarek, Bobby Krieger, John Densmore
Interviews and live performance footage capture the power of this famous rock group and its quixotic leader, Jim Morrison. Songs performed include "Light My Fire" and "The End."
Independent — *Warner Home Video*

Doors, Dance on Fire, The **1985**
Music video/Documentary
77212 65 mins C B, V P
Jim Morrison, John Densmore, Robby Krieger, Ray Manzarek
This is a musical documentary that chronicles the music and wild times of Jim Morrison and The Doors with a new conceptual music video for "L.A. Woman." Available in VHS and Beta Hi Fi Stereo.
MCA Home Video — *MCA Home Video*

Doozer Music **1983**
Music-Performance
65641 16 mins C B, V R, P
An exclusive collection of tuneful highlights from Jim Henson's "Fraggle Rock" series. In stereo VHS and Beta Hi-Fi.
Jim Henson — *MuppetMusic Home Video*

Dorian Gray **1971**
Horror
66311 91 mins C B, V P
Richard Todd, Helmut Berger, Herbert Lom
A modern-day version of the famous tale by Oscar Wilde about an ageless young man whose portrait reflects the ravages of time.
MPAA:R
Towers of London Productions — *Republic Pictures Home Video*

Dorm That Dripped Blood, The **1982**
Horror
65374 84 mins C B, V P
Laura Lopinski, Stephen Sachs, Pamela Holland
Five college students volunteer to close the dorm during their Christmas vacation. In a series of grisly and barbaric incidents, the students begin to disappear. As the terror mounts, the remaining students realize that they are up against a terrifyingly real psychopathic killer.
MPAA:R
Jeffrey Obrow — *Media Home Entertainment*

Dorothy in the Land of Oz **1981**
Cartoons/Fantasy
66180 60 mins C B, V P
Animated, narrated by Sid Ceasar
The further adventures of L. Frank Baum's characters from the "Wizard of Oz."
Muller Rosen Productions — *Family Home Entertainment*

Dos Chicas de Revista **197?**
Drama
49747 90 mins C B, V P
A former film actor now recovering from a mental breakdown and drug addiction comes across a book written about him when he was big-time. He meets the girl who wrote the book and they enjoy a happy relationship. In Spanish.
SP
Independent — *Media Home Entertainment*

Dot and Santa Claus **1979**
Fantasy
65326 73 mins C B, V, CED P
Animated
Dot has lost her kangaroo and through fate, meets Santa Claus who helps her find him in Central Park's zoo.
Yoram Gross — *Playhouse Video*

Dot and the Bunny **1982**
Cartoons
Closed Captioned
65506 79 mins C B, V, CED P
Animated
The adventures of a spunky young red-haired heroine on her quest for a missing baby kangaroo named Joey are followed.
Satori — *Playhouse Video*

Dot and the Kangaroo **1981**
Fantasy
58834 75 mins C B, V, CED P
Animated
Dot, the small daughter of a settler, wanders into the forest and gets lost. She meets a friendly kangaroo who takes her on a fabulous journey.
Satori Prods — *Playhouse Video*

Double Agents 1959
War-Drama/Suspense
69567 81 mins B/W B, V, FO P
Marina Vlady, Robert Hossein
Two double agents are sent on a rendezvous to exchange vital government secrets. Dubbed in English.
French Italo Productions — *Video Yesteryear*

Double Deal 1984
Drama/Suspense
79891 90 mins C B, V P
Louis Jourdan, Angela Punch-McGregor
An unfaithful woman and her lover plot to steal her husband's priceless opal.
Brian Kavanagh; Lynn Baker — *VCL Home Video*

Double Exposure 1982
Suspense
64876 95 mins C B, V, CED P
Michael Callan, James Stacy, Joanna Pettet
A young photographer has violent nightmares which seem to become the next day's headlines.
Michael Callan; Von Deming; William Byron Hillman — *Vestron Video*

Double Life, A 1947
Drama
64536 103 mins B/W B, V P
Ronald Colman, Shelley Winters, Signe Hasso, Edmond O'Brien, directed by George Cukor
A Shakespearean actor becomes obsessed by the role of Othello and begins to duplicate the character's actions.
Academy Awards '47: Best Actor (Colman).
Universal; Garson Kanin — *Republic Pictures Home Video*

Double McGuffin, The 1979
Adventure
75615 100 mins C B, V P
Ernest Borgnine, George Kennedy, Elke Sommer
A group of adventurous youngsters try to avert a plot to assassinate a middle eastern ambassador.
Mulberry Square — *Children's Video Library*

Double McGuffin, The 1979
Comedy
49625 100 mins C B, V P
Ernest Borgnine, George Kennedy, Elke Sommer, Ed "Too Tall" Jones, Lisa Whelchel, directed by Joe Camp
A plot of international intrigue is uncovered when a prime minister and her security guard pay a visit to a small Virginia community.
MPAA:PG
Mulberry Square Prods; Joe Camp — *Vestron Video*

Double Trouble 1967
Musical
80153 92 mins C B, V P
Elvis Presley, Annette Day, John Williams Yvonne Romain
When a rock star falls in love with an English heiress, he winds up involved in an attempted murder.
Metro Goldwyn Mayer — *MGM/UA Home Video*

Doughnuts and Society 1936
Comedy
69558 70 mins B/W B, V, FO P
Louise Fazenda, Maude Eburne, Eddie Nugent, Ann Rutherford, Hedda Hopper, Franklin Pangborn
Two elderly ladies who run a coffee shop suddenly strike it rich and find that life among the bluebloods is not all it's cracked up to be.
Mascot — *Video Yesteryear*

Down Among the Z Men 1952
Comedy
79113 71 mins B/W B, V P
Peter Sellers, Spike Milligan, Harry Secombe, Carole Carr
An enlisted man helps a girl save an atomic formula from spies.
E.J. Fancey Productions — *Pacific Arts Video*

Down Mexico Way 1941
Western
77363 78 mins B/W B, V P, T
Gene Autry, Smiley Burnette, Fay McKenzie, Duncan Renaldo, Champion
Two cowboys come to the aid of a Mexican town whose residents have been hoodwinked by a phony movie company.
Republic Pictures — *Blackhawk Films*

Down On the Farm with Captain Kangaroo and Mr. Green Jeans 1985
Children
70592 60 mins C B, V P
Bob Keeshan
Composed of short clips from the Captains' library of shows, this program features segments that look at farm living, where land stretches out so far and wide.
Encyclopedia Britannica Educational Corporation — *MPI Home Video*

Down to the Sea in Ships 1922
Adventure
66338 83 mins B/W B, V P
Marguerite Courtot, Raymond McKee, Clara Bow
Clara Bow made her movie debut in this drama about the whalers of the 19th-century Massachusetts. Exciting action scenes of an

actual whale hunt are the film's highlight. Silent with music score and original tinted footage.
Whaling Film Corp; Hodkinson Corp — *Blackhawk Films; Darryl L. Sink & Associates; Classic Video Cinema Collector's Club*

Downhill Racer 1969
Drama
48510 102 mins C B, V, LV R, P
Robert Redford, Camilla Sparv, Gene Hackman
An undisciplined American skier conflicts with his coach and new-found love on his way to becoming an Olympic superstar.
MPAA:PG
Richard Gregson — *Paramount Home Video*

Dr. Seuss: The Cat in the Hat/Dr. Seuss on the Loose 1971
Cartoons
Closed Captioned
81510 51 mins C B, V P
Animated
A Dr. Seuss double feature: "The Cat in the Hat" helps two young children fight boredom on a rainy day and "Dr. Seuss on the Loose" features stories about "The Sneetches," "The Zax" and "Green Eggs and Ham." Available in VHS and Beta Hi-Fi Stereo.
DePatie-Freleng Productions — *Playhouse Video*

Dr. Seuss: The Lorax/Hoober Bloob Highway 1975
Cartoons
Closed Captioned
81511 51 mins C B, V P
Animated
Here are two animated adaptations of Dr. Seuss' stories: "The Lorax" is a creature who is trying to stop the greedy Once-ler from destroying the forest, and Mr. Hoober-Bloob is the proprietor of "The Hoober-Bloob Highway" a floating island that sends babies to Earth. Available in VHS and Beta Hi-Fi Stereo.
DePatie-Freleng Productions — *Playhouse Video*

Dracula 1931
Horror
14023 75 mins B/W B, V P
Bela Lugosi, David Manners, directed by Tod Browning
A vampire terrorizes the countryside in its search for human blood. From Bram Stoker's novel, "Horror of Dracula'.
Universal — *MCA Home Video; RCA VideoDiscs*

Dracula 1979
Horror
45046 109 mins C B, V, LV P
Frank Langella, Sir Laurence Olivier
Remake of the classic story of the count who is among the undead and needs human blood for nourishment.
MPAA:R
Universal — *MCA Home Video*

Dracula 1984
Cartoons/Horror
70092 90 mins C B, V P
Animated
The prince of darkness returns looking for blood in this animated adaptation of Bram Stoker's classic novel.
Northstar Productions — *Vestron Video*

Dracula and Son 1976
Horror/Satire
62809 88 mins C B, V R, P
Christopher Lee, Bernard Menez, Marie Breillat
A Dracula spoof, in which the Count fathers a son who prefers girls and football to blood.
MPAA:PG
Quartet Films — *RCA/Columbia Pictures Home Video*

Dracula Sucks 1979
Satire
55217 91 mins C B, V P
Jamie Gillis, Annette Haven, John Holmes
The erotic undertones of the vampire legend are made quite explicit in this version of the Dracula tale.
MPAA:R
MR Productions — *Media Home Entertainment*

Dracula/The Garden of Eden 1928
Film-History
50638 52 mins B/W B, V P, T
Max Schreck, Alexander Granach, Corrine Griffith, Charles Ray, Louise Dressler
The abridged version of the chilling "Nosferatu" is coupled with "The Garden of Eden," in which Tini Le Brun meets her Prince Charming while vacationing with her Baroness friend.
Janus Films; Lewis Milestone — *Blackhawk Films*

Dracula's Dog 1978
Horror
48474 90 mins C B, V P
Michael Pataki, Reggie Nalder, Jose Ferrer
An explosion unearths the tomb of one of Dracula's servants and his dog. The dog puts other dogs under his spell to help the two vampires search for their new master.
MPAA:R
Crown International — *United Home Video*

Dracula's Great Love 1972
Horror
81071 96 mins C B, V P
Paul Naschy, Charo Soriano
The insatiable count is looking for a woman to join his world of darkness.
MPAA:R
International Amusement Corp. — *MPI Home Video*

Dragnet 1954
Adventure
68256 71 mins C B, V P
Jack Webb, Ben Alexander, Richard Boone, Ann Robinson
The Dragnet team tries to solve a mob slaying but has a rough time. Sgt. Joe Friday and Officer Frank Smith figure it out just in time.
Universal — *MCA Home Video*

Dragon Fist, The 1980
Martial arts
81523 90 mins C B, V P
A young man must avenge the death of his father in this martial arts film.
Alpha Film and Video — *All Seasons Entertainment*

Dragon Lee Vs. the Five Brothers 1981
Martial arts
70702 89 mins C B, V P
Dragon Lee
Mr. Lee thwarts an attempted overthrow of the Ching Government with his furiously brutal fighting talents.
master Arts — *Master Arts Video*

Dragon Lives Again, The 198?
Martial arts
64962 90 mins C B, V P
Bruce Leong, Alexander Grand, Jenny
A martial arts adventure that is dedicated to the memory of Bruce Lee.
Dragon Lady Productions — *Unicorn Video*

Dragon Seed 1944
Drama
81500 148 mins B/W B, V P
Katherine Hepburn, Walter Huston, Agnes Moorehead, Akim Tamiroff
The lives of the residents of a small Chinese village are turned upside down when the Japanese invade it.
MGM — *MGM/UA Home Video*

Dragon the Hero, The 1981
Martial arts
69278 80 mins C B, V P
John Liu, Dragon Lee, Tino Wong, Philip Ku, Yang Sze
A crippled gangster kills the winners of fights he stages. Two men seek revenge. Mandarin dialogue, English subtitles.
CH
IFD Films & Arts — *Silverline Video*

Dragonslayer 1981
Fantasy/Adventure
59423 108 mins C B, V, LV R, P
Peter MacNicol, Caitlin Clarke, Ralph Richardson, John Hallam, Albert Salmi
A sorcerer's apprentice suddenly finds himself the only person who can save the kingdom from a horrible, firebreathing dragon.
Academy Awards '81: Best Special Effects.
MPAA:PG
Walt Disney Productions; Paramount; Barwood Robbins Productions — *Paramount Home Video; RCA VideoDiscs*

Dream Called Walt Disney World, A 1981
Documentary
58628 25 mins C B, V R, P
This souvenir of Orlando, Florida's Walt Disney World discusses the creation of the magnificent theme park.
Walt Disney Productions — *Walt Disney Home Video*

Dream No Evil 1975
Horror
80725 93 mins C B, V P
Edmond O'Brien, Brooke Mills, Marc Lawrence, Arthur Franz
A mentally disturbed woman is forced to commit bizarre murders to protect her warped fantasy world.
Daniel Cady; John Hayes — *Active Home Video*

Dream Street 1921
Drama
58646 138 mins B/W B, V, FO P
Carol Dempster, Ralph Graves, Charles Mack, Tyrone Power Sr., directed by D. W. Griffith
A morality tale of London's lower depths. Two brothers, both in love with the same dancing girl, woo her in their own way. Silent with music score.
D W Griffith — *Video Yesteryear*

Dreaming Lips 1937
Drama
13646 70 mins B/W B, V P, T
Raymond Massey, Elizabeth Bergner
Orchestra conductor's wife falls in love with her husband's friend. Tragedy befalls the couple.
United Artists; Max Schach;
British — *Blackhawk Films*

Dreams of Gold **1983**
Sports
72180 60 mins C B, V P
Members of the U.S. Olympic team were filmed during a qualifying competition. A dramatic musical score accompanies and enhances the film.
Bruce Goronsky — *Pacific Arts Video*

Dreams of Gold **1984**
Sports
79110 55 mins C B, V P
A unique visualization of the American Olympic hopefuls competing in events to qualify for the Summer Olympic Games, set to the music of Ken Nordine.
Pacific Arts Video Records — *Pacific Arts Video*

Dreamscape **1984**
Science fiction/Fantasy
79706 99 mins C B, V R, P
Dennis Quaid, Max Von Sydow, Christopher Plummer, Eddie Albert, Kate Capshaw
When a doctor teaches a young psychic how to enter into other people's dreams, somebody else wants to use this psychic for evil purposes.
MPAA:PG13
Zupnick Curtis Enterprises — *THORN EMI/HBO Video*

Dressed to Kill **1946**
Mystery
01753 72 mins B/W B, V, 3/4U R, P
Basil Rathbone, Nigel Bruce, Patricia Morison, directed by Roy William Neill
Sherlock Holmes finds a music box holds the key to plates stolen from the Bank of England.
Universal; Howard Benedict — *Hal Roach Studios; Cable Films; Western Film & Video Inc; Discount Video Tapes; Budget Video; VCII; Classic Video Cinema Collector's Club*

Dressed to Kill **1980**
Suspense
53510 105 mins C B, V R, P
Angie Dickinson, Michael Caine, Nancy Allen, Keith Gordon, Dennis Franz, directed by Brian De Palma
A woman is brutally slashed to death and her son teams up with a prostitute who saw the killer in order to reveal the identity of the attacker.
MPAA:R
George Litto; Samuel Z Arkoff — *Warner Home Video; RCA VideoDiscs; Vestron Video (disc only)*

Dresser, The **1983**
Drama
Closed Captioned
73858 119 mins C B, V, CED P
Albert Finney, Tom Courtenay, Edward Fox, directed by Peter Yates
The film adaptation of the Broadway play about an English actor/manager, his dresser and their theatre company that tours war-torn England during World War II. In Beta Hi-Fi.
MPAA:PG
Peter Yates; Columbia Pictures — *RCA/Columbia Pictures Home Video*

Driller Killer **1974**
Horror
77253 78 mins C B, V P
Jimmy Laine, Carolyn Marz, Bob De Frank, directed by Abel Ferrara
A frustrated artist goes insane and begins to kill off Manhattan residents with a carpenter's drill.
MPAA:R
Mavaron Films — *Magnum Entertainment*

Drive-In Massacre **1974**
Horror
77255 78 mins C B, V P
Jake Barnes, Adam Lawrence
Two police detectives investigate a bizarre series of double murders at the local drive-in.
MPAA:R
Independent — *Magnum Entertainment*

Driver, The **1978**
Adventure
Closed Captioned
80656 131 mins C B, V P
Ryan O'Neal, Bruce Dern, Isabelle Adjani, Ronee Blakely, directed by Walter Hill
A police detective will stop at nothing to catch "The Driver," a man who has the reputation of driving the fastest getaway car around. Available in VHS and Beta Hi-Fi.
MPAA:PG
20th Century Fox — *CBS/Fox Video*

Driver's Seat, The **1975**
Suspense
64971 101 mins C B, V P
Elizabeth Taylor, Ian Bannon, Mona Washbourne
A deranged woman looks for a man to whom she can give herself completely, but when she finds him she demands much more than love.
MPAA:R
Avco Embassy — *Embassy Home Entertainment*

Drowning Pool, The **1975**
Mystery
72917 109 mins C B, V P
Paul Newman, Joanne Woodward, Tony Franciosa
Paul Newman returns as detective Lew Harper to solve another case—the murder of a New Orleans businessman.
MPAA:PG

Warner Bros — *Warner Home Video*

Drum Beat 1954
Western
11701 111 mins C B, V P
Alan Ladd, Charles Bronson, Marisa Pavan
Unarmed Indian fighter sets out to negotiate peace treaty with renegade Indian leader.
Warner Bros — *United Home Video*

Drum Taps 1933
Western
58723 55 mins B/W B, V P
Ken Maynard, Dorothy Dix, Junior Coughlin
Ken saves the day for a young girl who is being pushed off her land by a group of speculators.
Worldwide — *Video Dimensions; Video Yesteryear; Video Connection*

Drums 1938
Adventure
81459 96 mins B/W B, V, LV P
Sabu, Raymond Massey, Valerie Hobson, directed by Zoltan Korda
A native prince helps to save the British army in India from being anihilated by a tyrant.
Alexander Korda — *Embassy Home Entertainment*

Drums in the Deep South 1951
War-Drama
80800 87 mins C B, V R, P
James Craig, Guy Madison, Craig Stevens, Barbara Dayton, Barton Maclare
A rivalry turns ugly as two former West Point roommates wind up on opposite sides when the Civil War breaks out.
RKO — *Videograf*

Drying Up the Streets 1976
Drama
80697 90 mins C B, V P
Len Cariou, Don Francks
The members of a police drug squad are out to terminate the pattern wherein young women are turned to a life of prostitution and drugs.
Movie Store Prods. — *Vestron Video*

DTV—Golden Oldies 1984
Cartoons/Music video
79175 46 mins C B, V R, P
Animated
Animator-director Chuck Brauerman took some of the best Disney animation and recut them to the music of Annette Funicello and others for this collection of music videos.
Walt Disney Productions — *Walt Disney Home Video*

DTV—Love Songs 1985
Music video/Cartoons
77532 45 mins C B, V R, P
Animated, Directed by Chuck Braxerman
All your favorite Disney characters swoon and sway to the music in this collection of love song music videos.
Walt Disney Productions — *Walt Disney Home Video*

DTV—Pop and Rock 1984
Cartoons/Music video
79176 46 mins C B, V R, P
Animated
Classic Disney animation has been recut to the music of the fifties and sixties for this collection of music videos.
Walt Disney Productions — *Walt Disney Home Video*

DTV—Rock, Rhythm and Blues 1984
Cartoons/Music video
79177 46 mins C B, V R, P
Some of Walt Disneys' best animation has been re-edited to the music of Hall and Oates and The Doobie Brothers for this collection of music videos.
Walt Disney Productions — *Walt Disney Home Video*

Mussolini and I 1985
Biographical/Drama
76796 200 mins C B, V P
Bob Hoskins, Anthony Hopkins, Susan Sarandon, Annie Girardot
This is the true story of the struggle of power between Italy's Benito Mussulini and his son-in-law Galeazzo Ciano over who will rule the country.
Rai Radiotelevisione Italiana — *Embassy Home Entertainment*

Duchess and the Dirtwater Fox, The 1976
Comedy/Western
09095 105 mins C B, V P
George Segal, Goldie Hawn
A music-hall girl meets a man on the make.
MPAA:PG EL, SP
20th Century Fox — *CBS/Fox Video*

Duck Soup 1933
Comedy
44810 72 mins B/W B, V P
The Marx Brothers
Groucho becomes a dictator in a mythical land while Chico and Harpo run a peanut stand.
Paramount — *MCA Home Video; RCA VideoDiscs*

Duel **1971**
Suspense
14069 90 mins C B, V P
Dennis Weaver, Lucille Benson, Eddie Firestone, Cary Loftin, directed by Steven Spielberg
The story of a man's desperate attempt to stay alive. What begins as an ordinary business trip becomes a life and death battle for a man who is followed by a menacing psychopath.
Universal — *MCA Home Video*

Duel of the Seven Tigers **1980**
Martial arts
78396 80 mins C B, V P
Cliff Lok, Ka Sa Fa, Chio Chi Ling, Lam Men Wei, Yang Pan Pan, Charlie Chan
Nine of the world's greatest Kung fu and Karate exponents team up in this martial arts spectacular.
Foreign — *Trans World Entertainment*

Duellists, The **1978**
Drama
33714 101 mins C B, V R, P
Keith Carradine, Harvey Keitel, Albert Finney, Edward Fox, Christina Raines, Diana Quick, directed by Ridley Scott
A beautifully photographed picture about the long running feud between two French officers during the Napoleonic wars.
MPAA:PG
Paramount — *Paramount Home Video*

Duke Ellington Story, The **1980**
Music
38965 90 mins C B, V, FO P
Duke Ellington and his Orchestra
Three film appearances by Duke Ellington make up this program: the 1929 Paramount short "Black and Tan" (in black and white), "Duke Ellington in Concert" (Goodyear, 1962), and "Duke in Concert on the Cote D'Azur" (1965). Songs performed include "Kinda Dukish," "Such Sweet Thunder," "La Plus Belle African," and "Cotton Club Stomp."
Paramount et al — *Video Yesteryear*

Duke Is Tops, The **1938**
Musical
51228 80 mins C B, V P
Ralph Cooper, Lena Horne, Basin St. Boys, Rubber Neck Boys, Marie Bryant
In Lena Horne's earliest existing film appearance, she's off to attempt the "big-time," while her boyfriend joins a traveling medicine show.
Unknown — *Movie Buff Video; Video Connection; Discount Video Tapes*

Dumbo **1941**
Cartoons
55564 64 mins C B, V, LV, CED R, P
Animated
The story of an elephant who is ridiculed for his large ears, until he discovers he can fly.
Walt Disney — *Walt Disney Home Video; RCA VideoDiscs*

Dunderklumpen **197?**
Fantasy
40730 85 mins C B, V R, P
Animated
Dunderklumpen is a little creature from the forest who is only two feet tall and sneaks into Carmilla's room and steals her dolls. From then on magical things keep happening.
MPAA:G EL, SP
21st Century — *Video Gems; Vestron Video (disc only)*

Dune **1984**
Science fiction/Fantasy
77451 137 mins C B, V, LV P
Kyle MacLachlan, Francesca Annis, Jose Ferrer, Sting, Max Von Sydow, Sean Young, directed by David Lynch
Controlling the spice of Arrakis permits control of the universe. Paul, the heir of the Atreides family leads the Freemen in a revolt against the evil Harkhonens who have violently seized control of Arrakis, also known as Dune, the desert planet. Adapted from Frank Herbert's popular novel. Music by Brian Eno and Toto. Available in VHS and Beta HiFi stereo.
MPAA:PG13
Universal; Raffaella De Laurentiis — *MCA Home Video*

Dungeonmaster, The **1985**
Fantasy
81153 80 mins C B, V P
Jeffrey Byron, Richard Moll, Leslie Wing
A nice warlord forces a computer operator to participate in a bizzare "Dungeons and Dragons" styled game.
MPAA:PG13
Empire Pictures; Charles Band — *Lightning Video*

Dunwich Horror, The **1970**
Horror
64984 90 mins C B, V P
Sandra Dee, Dean Stockwell, Lloyd Bochner, Ed Begley
The town of Dunwich has a history of weird and evil happenings. When a young man acquires a rare and banned book on the occult, the horror begins again.
American International Pictures — *Embassy Home Entertainment*

(For explanation of codes, see USE GUIDE and KEY)

Duran Duran **1982**
Music-Performance
66027 55 mins C B, V R, P
The hot new-music group performs "Planet Earth," "Rio," "Hungry Like the Wolf," and others.
EMI Music Video — *THORN EMI/HBO Video; RCA VideoDiscs*

Duran Duran **1983**
Music-Performance
75918 10 mins C B, V P
This program presents the popular British band singing their hits "Girls on Film" and "Hungry Like the Wolf."
Tritec Music Limited — *Sony Corporation of America*

Duran Duran: Girls on Film/Hungry Like the Wolf **1982**
Music/Video
66160 11 mins C B, V P
A hot, sexy music video clip featuring the smash new group from England. In stereo.
Capitol; EMI MusicVideo — *Sony Corporation of America*

Dvorak's Slavic Dance **1981**
Music-Performance
60578 72 mins C LV P
Recorded at Dvorak Hall in Prague, Czechoslovakia, this program presents Dvorak's sixteen colorful and rhythmical Slavonian dances. In stereo.
Koichi Takemoto — *Pioneer Video Imports*

D.W. Griffith: An American Genius **1975**
Film-History/Documentary
29495 56 mins C B, V P, T
Narrated by Richard Schickel
A penetrating documentary of a legendary filmmaker, narrated by the renowned film critic Richard Schickel. Excerpted works include early Biographs, "Birth of a Nation," "Way Down East," and "Intolerance."
Unknown — *Blackhawk Films*

Dynamite Chicken **1970**
Musical
15786 75 mins C B, V P
Joan Baez, Richard Pryor, Lenny Bruce, Jimi Hendrix, Sha-Na-Na
Focuses on the attitudes of American youth in the 70's. Includes performances by Joan Baez, Lenny Bruce, B. B. King, and others.
MPAA:R
EYR — *Monterey Home Video*

Dynamite Pass **1950**
Western
64405 61 mins B/W B, V, 3/4U P
Tim Holt, Richard Martin
Disgruntled ranchers attempt to stop the construction of a new road.
RKO — *Nostalgia Merchant*

Dynamo **1980**
Martial arts
81472 81 mins C B, V P
A glamorous advertising executive pursues a kung fu expert to sign a contract with her agency for a kick boxing contest.
MPAA:R
World Northal Corporation — *Embassy Home Entertainment*

Dynasty of Fear **1973**
Suspense
81075 93 mins C B, V P
Joan Collins, Peter Cushing, Ralph Bates, Judy Geeson, directed by Jimmy Sangster
Matters get rather sticky at a British boys' school when the headmaster's wife seduces her husband's assistant. Together they conspire to murder her husband and share his fortune.
MPAA:PG
Hammer Productions — *Academy Home Entertainment*

E

Eagle, The **1925**
Drama
08851 72 mins B/W B, V, 3/4U P
Rudolph Valentino, Vilma Banky, Louise Dresser
Romantic adventure story of a Russian Robin Hood.
United Artists — *Video Yesteryear; Cable Films; Video Connection; Discount Video Tapes; Western Film & Video Inc; Classic Video Cinema Collector's Club*

Eagle Has Landed, The **1977**
War-Drama
45062 123 mins C B, V P
Michael Caine, Donald Sutherland, Robert Duvall
German paratroopers stage a dramatic attempt to kidnap Winston Churchill.
MPAA:PG
Columbia — *CBS/Fox Video*

Eagles Attack at Dawn **1974**
War-Drama
80937 96 mins C B, V P
Rick Jason, Peter Brown, Joseph Shiloal

After escaping from an Arab prison, an Israeli soldier vows to return with a small commando force and kill the sadistic commander of the prison.
MPAA:PG
Yoram Globus — *VidAmerica*

Early Days 1981
Comedy/Drama
60585 67 mins C B, V P
Sir Ralph Richardson
A cantankerous, salty, once-powerful politician now awaits death wandering around the garden rambling on about his life.
Independent — *CBS/Fox Video*

Early Elvis 1956
Music-Performance
58653 56 mins B/W B, V, FO P
Ed Sullivan, Charles Laughton, Elvis Presley
Elvis appears on "Stage Show" with the Tommy and Jimmy Dorsey Orchestra, on the "Steve Allen Show" where he also participates in a comedy sketch, and the "Ed Sullivan Show." Ten songs in all.
CBS et al — *Video Yesteryear*

Early Frost 1984
Mystery
76647 95 mins C B, V P
Diana McLean, Jon Blake, Janet Kingsbury, David Franklin
A suspenseful whodunit, centering around a simple divorce investigation that leads to the discovery of a corpse.
David Hannay; Geoff Brown — *VCL Home Video*

Earth 1930
Drama/Film-History
52343 56 mins B/W B, V, 3/4U P
Semyon Svashenko, Stephan Shkurat, directed by Alexander Dovzhenko
Classic Russian silent film with English subtitles. Problems begin in a Ukranian village when a landowner resists handing over his land for a collective farm.
USSR — *International Historic Films; Sheik Video; Blackhawk Films*

Earth, Wind & Fire in Concert 1982
Music-Performance
66094 60 mins C B, V, CED P
The funky R&B band performs "Sing a Song," "Fantasy," and "Shining Star." (Stereo).
Mike Schultz; Gloria Schultz; Maurice White — *Vestron Video*

Earth, Wind and Fire 1983
Music-Performance
72218 60 mins C B, V P
Using spectacular special effects, Earth, Wind and Fire puts on one of their typically engaging shows.
Independent — *Vestron Video*

Earthling, The 1981
Drama
66093 98 mins C B, V, CED P
William Holden, Ricky Schroder
A tale of two people alone in the Australian wilderness, learning survival and caring.
MPAA:PG
Filmways — *Vestron Video*

Earthquake 1974
Drama
53397 129 mins C B, V P
Charlton Heston, Ava Gardner, George Kennedy, Lorne Greene, Genevieve Bujold, Richard Roundtree, Marjoe Gortner, Barry Sullivan
The effects of a major earthquake in Los Angeles on the lives of an engineer and his spoiled wife, his mistress, his father-in-law and a suspended policeman make up the central theme of this drama.
Academy Award '74: Special Achievement for Visual Effects. MPAA:PG
Universal — *MCA Home Video*

East End Hustle 1976
Drama
76773 86 mins C B, V P
A high-priced call girl rebels against her pimp and sets out to free other prostitutes as well. Also available in an 88-minute unrated version.
MPAA:R
Troma Films — *Vestron Video*

East of Borneo 1931
Drama/Romance
53449 75 mins B/W B, V P
Charles Bickford, Rose Hobart
An idyllic tropical romance.
Universal — *Movie Buff Video; Discount Video Tapes*

East of Eden 1954
Drama
38940 105 mins C B, V R, P
James Dean, Julie Harris, Richard Davalos, Raymond Massey, Jo Van Fleet, directed by Elia Kazan
John Steinbeck's sprawling novel provides the basis for this World War I-era retelling of the Biblical tale of Cain and Abel. James Dean's first starring role.
Warner Bros — *Warner Home Video; RCA VideoDiscs*

(For explanation of codes, see USE GUIDE and KEY)

East of Eden 1980
Drama
65439 240 mins C B, V P
Jane Seymour, Bruce Boxleitner, Timothy Bottoms, Lloyd Bridges
John Steinbeck's sprawling novel of family passions is wholly captured in this adaptation from the popular television mini-series. The 1955 movie version only used a third of the original story.
Viacom International — *U.S.A. Home Video*

East of Elephants Rock 1981
Drama
72879 93 mins C B, V P
John Hurt, Jeremy Kemp, Judi Bowker
In 1948, a young first secretary of the British Embassy returns from leave in England to a tense atmosphere in a Colony in Southeast Asia.
Great Britian — *Embassy Home Entertainment*

Easter Bunny Is Coming to Town, The 1978
Holidays
75618 60 mins C B, V P
Narrated by Fred Astaire
This animated tale is about the Easter Bunny and Easter traditions.
Rankin Bass Productions — *Children's Video Library*

Easy Come, Easy Go 1967
Musical
29768 95 mins C B, V R, P
Elvis Presley, Dodie Marshall, Pat Priest, Pat Harrington
A Navy frogman accidentally locates what he believes to be a vast sunken treasure, only to find it filled with copper coins of little value.
Paramount, Hal Wallis — *Paramount Home Video*

Easy Money 1983
Comedy
Closed Captioned
65385 95 mins C B, V P
Rodney Dangerfield
A basic slob has the chance to inherit millions... if he can give up smoking, drinking and gambling! It's an effort that nearly kills him!
MPAA:R
John Nicolella — *Vestron Video; RCA VideoDiscs*

Easy Rider 1969
Drama
52752 88 mins C B, V, LV P
Peter Fonda, Dennis Hopper, Jack Nicholson
Two young men undertake a motorcycle trip to New Orleans, meeting hippies, rednecks, prostitutes, and drugs along the way.
MPAA:R
Columbia; Pando Co; Raybert Prods — *RCA/Columbia Pictures Home Video; RCA VideoDiscs*

Eat My Dust 1976
Drama
65388 89 mins C B, V P
Ron Howard, Christopher Norris, Warren Kemmerling
The teenage son of a California sheriff steals the best of stock cars from a race track to take the town's heart throb for a joy ride and leads the town on the wildest car chase ever filmed.
MPAA:PG
New World Pictures; Roger Corman Production — *Embassy Home Entertainment*

Eat to Win 1985
Physical fitness
77228 60 mins C B, V P
Judy Landers, Audrey Landers
A video adaptation of the Robert Haas bestseller that details a fourteen day diet plan and a daily aerobic workout.
Bob Giraldi — *Karl/Lorimar Home Video*

Eaten Alive 1976
Horror
73558 90 mins C B, V P
Neville Brand, Mell Ferrer, Stuart Whitman, directed by Tobe Hooper
A resident of the Southern swamps takes an unsuspecting group of tourists into a crocodile death trap.
Unknown — *Prism*

Eating Raoul 1982
Comedy
69377 87 mins C B, V P
Mary Woronov, Paul Bartel
This is the story of a happily married couple who share many interests: good food and wine, entrepreneurial dreams and an aversion to sex.
MPAA:R
Quartet Films — *CBS/Fox Video*

Echoes 1983
Horror
66001 100 mins C B, V P
Mercedes McCambridge, Ruth Roman, Gale Sondergaard
A haunting, erotic thriller journeying into mystic phenomena and reincarnation.
Herbeval — *VidAmerica*

Echoes 1983
Suspense/Drama
80940 90 mins C B, V P
Gale Sondergaard, Mercedes McCambridge, Richard Alferi, Nathalie Nell
A young painter's life slowly comes apart as he is tormented by a past incarnation.

MPAA:R
Herbeval Productions — *VidAmerica*

Ecstasy 1933
Drama
08887 70 mins B/W B, V P
Hedy Lamarr, Jaromir Rogoz, directed by Gustav Machaty
A romantic, erotic story about a young woman married to an older man. This film brought world fame and notoriety to Hedy Lamarr. Original title: Extase.
Universal Elektra Film — *Movie Buff Video*

Ed Sullivan Show, The 1964
Variety
12850 51 mins B/W B, V, FO P
Ed Sullivan, The Moscow State Circus
Ed Sullivan presents "The Moscow State Circus," performing in Minneapolis as part of a cultural exchange program.
Sullivan Prods; Bob Precht — *Video Yesteryear; Discount Video Tapes*

Ed Wynn Show, The 1949
Comedy/Variety
63782 110 mins B/W B, V, 3/4U P
Ed Wynn, guests Mel Torme, Dinah Shore, Virginia O'Brien, Buster Keaton, the Lud Gluskin Orchestra
Three complete kinescopes of Ed Wynn's early variety series, originally telecast October-December 1949. Original Speidel commercials included. Also on this tape is a 20-minute documentary produced by NBC and RCA in color which reviews the history of television and promotes the latest innovation—color TV.
CBS — *Shokus Video*

Ed Wynn Show, The 1949
Variety/Comedy
11274 24 mins B/W B, V, FO P
Ed Wynn, Diana Lynn
A rare piece of entertainment featuring one of television's great clowns in an early example of TV comedy/variety.
CBS — *Video Yesteryear*

Eddie and the Cruisers 1983
Drama
64989 90 mins C B, V, LV, CED P
Tom Berenger, Michael Pare
In the early 1960's, Eddie and the Cruisers had one hit album; years later, a former band member begins a search for the missing tapes of the Cruisers' unreleased second album.
MPAA:PG
Embassy Pictures — *Embassy Home Entertainment*

Eddie Macon's Run 1983
Drama
68252 95 mins C B, V, LV, CED P
Kirk Douglas, John Schneider, Lee Purcell, Leah Ayers
Based on a true story, Eddie Macon has been unjustly jailed in Texas and plans an escape to run to Mexico. He is followed by a tough cop who is determined to catch Eddie so his dignity will not be hurt.
MPAA:PG
Universal — *MCA Home Video*

Eddy Arnold Time 1955
Music/Variety
78101 26 mins B/W B, V, FO P
Eddy Arnold, Betty Johnson, The Gordonaires, Hank Garland, Roy Wiggins
Some fine country music with a barn dance setting highlight this episode of an early country-and-western TV series.
ABC — *Video Yesteryear*

Edgar Kennedy Slow Burn Festival, The 197?
Comedy
65196 59 mins B/W B, V P
Edgar Kennedy, Florence Lake, Dot Farley, Jack Rice, Vivien Oakland, Tiny Sandford
Popular 30's comedian Edgar Kennedy stars in three shorts from his long-running "Average Man" series: "Poisoned Ivory" (1934), "Edgar Hamlet" (1935) and "A Clean Sweep" (1938).
RKO — *Video Yesteryear*

Edge of Fury 198?
Martial arts
80128 90 mins C B, V P
Bruce Li, Andrew Sage, Michael Danna, Tommy Lee
When a businessman is unjustly arrested on a drug charge, it is up to his chauffer to clear the man's name.
German Valder — *King of Video*

Edie in Ciao! Manhattan 1972
Drama
65469 90 mins C B, V P
Edie Sedgwick, Baby Jane Holzer, Roger Vadim, Paul America, Viva
The real-life story of Edie Sedgwick, Warhol superstar and international fashion model, whose life in the fast lane led to ruin.
MPAA:R
David Weisman — *Pacific Arts Video*

Edward and Mrs. Simpson 1980
Drama
59700 260 mins C B, V R, P
Edward Fox, Cynthia Harris

 (For explanation of codes, see USE GUIDE and KEY)

The dramatic reconstruction of the years leading to the abdication of King Edward VII, who gave up the British throne in 1936 so that he could marry American divorcee Wallis Simpson.
Emmy Awards '80: Best Drama.
Andrew Brown; Thames Television — *THORN EMI/HBO Video*

Eiger Sanction, The **1975**
Suspense
59067 125 mins C B, V P
Clint Eastwood, George Kennedy, Vonetta McGee, Jack Cassidy, directed by Clint Eastwood
An art teacher returns to the CIA as an exterminator, and finds himself in a party climbing the Eiger.
MPAA:R
Universal — *MCA Home Video*

---

8 1/2 **1963**
Drama
66102 135 mins B/W B, V P
Marcello Mastroianni, directed by Federico Fellini
Fellini's surreal self-portrait, a cinematic classic.
Academy Awards '63: Best Foreign Film.
Embassy — *Vestron Video*

Eisenstein **1958**
Film-History/Documentary
12805 48 mins B/W B, V, FO P
A well-done biography of Sergei Eisenstein, the famous Russian director. Footage of his early life, first works and masterpieces such as "Potemkin" and "Ivan the Terrible."
Unknown — *Video Yesteryear*

El Cid **1961**
Adventure
16809 187 mins C B, V, CED P
Charlton Heston, sophia Loren, raf Vallone, Hurd Hatfield, Genevieve Page, directed by Anthony Mann
This is the story of El Cid, the legendary eleventh century Christian hero who freed Spain from the Moorish invaders. The music is by Miklos Roza.
Allied Artists; Samuel Bronston — *Lightning Video; United Home Video; Vestron Video (disc only)*

El Dorado **1967**
Western
64509 126 mins C B, V R, P
John Wayne, Robert Mitchum, James Caan, Charlene Holt, Ed Asner, directed by Howard Hawks
A gunfighter rides into the frontier town of El Dorado in order to bring peace between a cattle baron and farmers who are fighting over land rights.

Paramount — *Paramount Home Video; RCA VideoDiscs*

Electric Boogalo, Breakin 2 **1984**
Musical
80853 94 mins C B, V, LV P
Lucinda Dickey, Adolfo "Shabba Doo" Quinones, Michael "Boogaloo Shrimp" Chambers
Break-dancers Kelly, Ozone and Turbo stage a fundraising dance to prevent a greedy real-estate developer from tearing down their community center. Available in VHS and Beta Hi-Fi Dolby Stereo.
MPAA:PG
Cannon Films — *MGM/UA Home Video*

Electric Dreams **1984**
Drama
80360 96 mins C B, V, LV P
Bud Cort, Lenny Von Dohlen, Virginia Madsen, directed by Steve Barron
When a young man buys a computer, it winds up taking over his life. Available in VHS and Beta Hi-Fi.
MPAA:PG
MGM — *MGM/UA Home Video*

Electric Horseman, The **1979**
Drama
29734 120 mins C B, V, LV P
Robert Redford, Jane Fonda, John Saxon
A newspaper woman seeking a story discovers the reason behind a rodeo star's kidnapping of a prized horse. In the process she falls in love with the rodeo star.
MPAA:PG
Columbia, Ray Stark — *MCA Home Video; RCA VideoDiscs*

Electric Light Orchestra Live at Wembly **1978**
Music-Performance
44936 58 mins C B, V, CED P
The ELO perform some of their greatest hits, including "Roll Over Beethoven," "Do Ya," "Living Thing" and "Evil Woman," live from the arena in Wembley, England.
MGM — *CBS/Fox Video*

Electric Light Voyage **1980**
Film-Avant-garde/Video
56741 60 mins C B, V P
Animated
This electronic fantasy featuring computer animation can control and change your moods of elation and tranquility. The animated visuals are in sync with a mesmerizing soundtrack.
Astralvision Productions — *Media Home Entertainment*

Eleni 1984
Drama
79850 120 mins C B, V P
Kate Nelligan, John Malkovich, Linda Hunt, directed by Peter Yates
The true story of author Nicholas Gage's search for the truth about his mother's death.
CBS Theatrical Films — *Embassy Home Entertainment*

Elephant Boy 1937
Adventure
81460 81 mins B/W B, V, LV P
Sabu, Walter Hudd, W.E. Holloway
An Indian boy helps government conservationists locate a herd of elephants in the jungle.
Alexander Korda — *Embassy Home Entertainment*

Elephant Man, The 1980
Drama
55537 123 mins B/W B, V, LV R, P
Anthony Hopkins, John Hurt, Anne Bancroft, directed by David Lynch
The tragic, true-life story of John Merrick, a hideously deformed man who went from freak show to the attraction of London society.
MPAA:PG
Paramount; Jonathan Sanger — *Paramount Home Video; RCA VideoDiscs*

Elephant Parts 1981
Music/Comedy
51226 60 mins C B, V, CED P
A video album by Michael Nesmith, which contains several amusing comedy sketches and original music by Nesmith.
Grammy Awards '81: Video of the Year Award.
Michael Nesmith; Kathryn Nesmith — *Pacific Arts Video; Pioneer Artists*

Elizabeth of Ladymead 1948
Drama
66373 97 mins C B, V P
Anna Neagle, Hugh Williams, Bernard Lee
Four generations of a British family live through their experiences in the Crimean War, Boer War, World War I and World War II.
Imperadio Pictures — *Movie Buff Video*

Ella Fitzgerald in Concert 1980
Music
38964 70 mins B/W B, V, FO P
Ella Fitzgerald, Duke Ellington, Benny Goodman, Jo Stafford, Harry James, Teddy Wilson, Red Norvo
Ella Fitzgerald performs in concert with Duke Ellington in the 1960's, and with Benny Goodman from the "Swing Into Spring" TV specials of 1958-59. Songs include "Street of Dreams," "Lover Man," "Ridin' High," "Satin Doll," and "Summertime." Instrumental performances by Ellington and Goodman are also included.
CBS et al — *Video Yesteryear*

Ellie 1983
Comedy
81163 90 mins C B, V P
Shelley Winters, Sheila Kennedy, Pat Paulsen, George Gobel, Edward Albert
A murderous widow's stepdaughter tries to save her father from being added to the woman's extensive list of dearly departed husbands.
MPAA:R
Rudine-Wittman Productions — *Vestron Video*

Elmer 1976
Drama/Adventure
70694 82 mins C B, V P
Elmer Swanson, Phillip Swanson, directed by Christopher Cain
This film follows the exploits of a temporarily blind youth and a lovable hounddog who meet in the wilderness and together set off in search of civilization.
Film Advisory Board '76: Award of Excellence
MPAA:G
Cinema Shares — *Lightning Video*

Elmer Gantry 1960
Drama
68225 146 mins C B, V, CED P
Burt Lancaster, Jean Simmons, Shirley Jones
Burt Lancaster stars as Elmer Gantry, the charismatic preacher who promises eternal salvation, but in return pursues wealth and power.
United Artists — *CBS/Fox Video*

Elton John 1982
Music-Performance
76670 14 mins C B, V P
This program presents this rock-n-roll Superstar performing his greatest hits.
Sunport Productions Intl Inc — *Sony Corporation of America*

Elton John Live in Central Park 1984
Music-Performance
74109 59 mins C B, V P
The largest concert audience in the U.S. since Woodstock was the setting for a fabulous free concert in New York's Central Park. Among the songs performed are "Your Song," "Goodbye Yellow Brick Road" and "Benny and the Jets."
Danny O'Donovan — *VCL Home Video*

Elton John—Night and Day: The Nighttime Concert 1975
Music-Performance
80691 53 mins C B, V P

Elton John, Davey Johnstone, Dee Murray, Fred Mandel, Nigel Olsson
The outlandish rock superstar performs such hits as "Your Song," "Crocodile Rock" and "I Guess That's Why They Call It the Blues" in this concert taped at London's Wembley Stadium.
John Reid, Mike Mansfield — *Vestron Video*

Elton John: Visions **1982**
Music-Performance
47847 45 mins C B, V, LV, CED P
Elton John performs "Breaking Down Barriers," "Just Like Belgium," "Nobody Wins," "Elton's Song," and other classics.
Al Schoenberger — *Embassy Home Entertainment*

Elusive Corporal, The **1962**
Drama
47648 109 mins B/W B, V, FO P
Jean-Pierre Cassel, Claude Brasseur, O. E. Hasse, directed by Jean Renoir
Set in a P.O.W. camp on the day France surrendered to Germany, the story of the French and Germans, and memories of a France that is no more is told.
France — *Video Yesteryear*

Elvira Madigan **1967**
Romance
63339 90 mins C B, V R, P
Pia Degermark, Thommy Berggren
This film, based on a true incident, chronicles the 19th-century romance between a young officer and a beautiful circus dancer.
MPAA:PG
Atlantic Releasing; Europa Films — *THORN EMI/HBO Video*

Elvis...Aloha from Hawaii **1973**
Music-Performance
38118 60 mins C B, V, FO P
Elvis Presley
Elvis' 1973 Hawaiian concert appearance.
RCA Record Tours — *Video Yesteryear; Media Home Entertainment; Sound Video Unlimited; RCA VideoDiscs*

Elvis—His 1968 Comeback Special **1968**
Music-Performance
64453 76 mins C CED P
Elvis Presley, the Jordanaires
Elvis is showcased in this famous TV special, which sparked his return to live performances. Featured are a medley of Elvis' 50's hits, plus newer tunes including "Guitar Man," "If I Can Dream" and "Let Yourself Go."
NBC — *RCA VideoDiscs*

Elvis on Tour **1972**
Music-Performance/Documentary
63110 93 mins C B, V, CED P
Elvis Presley
A revealing glimpse of Elvis Presley, on stage and off, during a whirlwind concert tour.
MGM — *MGM/UA Home Video*

Elvis—'68 Comeback Special **1968**
Music-Performance
79873 76 mins C B, V P
Elvis Presley
Elvis regained his title as king of rock and roll from his powerful performance on this special originally broadcast in 1968.
Bob Finkel; Steve Binder; NBC — *Media Home Entertainment*

Emanuelle Around the World **1980**
Drama
72954 92 mins C B, V P
Laura Gemser
The further erotic adventures of that insatiable lady Emanuelle.
Jerry Gross — *Wizard Video*

Emanuelle in America **1976**
Drama
58737 95 mins C B, V P
Laura Gemser
Provocative reporter Emanuelle sets out to expose the inner secrets of the Jet Set at play.
MPAA:R
Monarch — *VidAmerica*

Emanuelle in Bangkok **1978**
Drama
55258 94 mins C B, V, CED P
Emanuelle's exotic, erotic experiences in the Far East include the royal masseuse, suspense, and the Asian arts of love.
MPAA:R
Monarch Releasing Corp — *VidAmerica*

Emanuelle the Queen **1975**
Drama
63419 90 mins C B, V P
Laura Gemser
Seeking revenge, Emanuelle plots the murder of her sadistic husband. The lecherous assassin she hires in turn tries to blackmail her, and she challenges him at his own game of deadly seduction.
Othello Films; Andromeda Films — *VidAmerica*

Embryo **1982**
Science fiction
75460 103 mins C B, V P
Rock Hudson, Roddy McDowell, Diane Ladd

(For explanation of codes, see USE GUIDE and KEY)

A scientist develops a growth hormone that allows embryos to become adults in 4 1/2
MPAA:PG
King Features — *U.S.A. Home Video*

Emilienne **1978**
Drama
55257 94 mins C B, V P
An artistic young couple toys with the sexual possibilities that exist outside of, and within, a marriage.
MPAA:X
Gades Films International — *VidAmerica*

Emily **1977**
Drama
63120 87 mins C B, V, CED P
Koo Stark
Returning from her exclusive Swiss finishing school, young Emily is ready for erotic encounters at the hands of her willing "instructors."
Christopher Neame — *MGM/UA Home Video*

Emmanuelle **1974**
Drama
55261 92 mins C B, V P
Sylvia Kristel, Alain Cuny, Marika Green
Filmed in Bangkok, a young, beautiful, and restless woman is introduced to an uninhibited world of sensuality where she experiences her wildest dreams.
MPAA:X
Columbia; Yves Rousset Rouard — *RCA/Columbia Pictures Home Video*

Emmanuelle Black and White **1978**
Drama
77394 95 mins C B, V P
Anthony Gizmond, Mary Longo
The jilted fiance of a plantation owner in the old south begins a depraved quest for revenge against her former lover.
S.E.F.I. — *Wizard Video*

Emmanuelle in the Country **1978**
Drama
77257 90 mins C B, V P
Laura Gemser
Emmanuelle becomes a nurse in an attempt to bring comfort to those in need.
Monarch Releasing Corp. — *Magnum Entertainment*

Emmanuelle, the Joys of a Woman **1976**
Drama
55512 92 mins C B, V, LV R, P
Sylvia Kristel, Umberto Orsini, Frederic Lagache
The amorous exploits of a sensuous, liberated couple take them and their erotic companions to exotic Hong Kong, Bangkok, and Bali.
MPAA:X
Paramount — *Paramount Home Video*

Emmet Otter's Jug-Band Christmas **1977**
Comedy
47349 50 mins C B, V R, P
Emmet Otter and his Ma enter the Frog Town Hollow talent contest and try to beat out a rock group called the Riverbottom Nightmares for the prize money, which will enable them to have a merry Christmas.
Henson Associates — *Muppet Home Video*

Emotions of Life, The **1982**
Psychology/Alcoholism
59564 63 mins C B, V P
This program examines three of the most interesting and critical manifestations of the human psyche: aggression, depression, and addiction.
McGraw Hill — *Mastervision*

Emperor's New Clothes, The **1984**
Fairy tales
Closed Captioned
73572 60 mins C B, V, CED P
Art Carney, Alan Arkin, Dick Shawn
From "Faerie Tale Theatre" comes the story of an emperor and the unusual outfit he gets from his tailor.
Gaylord Productions; Platypus Productions — *CBS/Fox Video*

Empire of the Ants **1977**
Science fiction
80765 89 mins C B, V P
Joan Collins, Robert Lansing, John David Carson, Albert Salmi, Jacqueline Scott
A group of enormous, unfriendly ants stalk a real estate dealer and his prospective buyers when they look at some undeveloped ocean front property.
MPAA:PG
American International Pictures — *Embassy Home Entertainment*

Empire of the Dragon **198?**
Martial arts
64964 90 mins C B, V P
Chen Tien Tse, Chia Kai, Chang Shan
A rip-roaring martial arts adventure.
Dragon Lady Productions — *Unicorn Video*

Empire Strikes Back, The **1980**
Science fiction/Adventure
78890 124 mins C B, V P

 (For explanation of codes, see USE GUIDE and KEY)

Mark Hamill, Carrie Fisher, Harrison Ford, Billy Dee Williams, David Prowse, Kenny Baker, Frank Oz, directed by Irvin Kershner
While the Rebel Alliance hides from Darth Vader on the frozen planet Hoth, Luke Skywalker learns how to be a Jedi knight from Jedi master Yoda. In Beta and VHS Hi-Fi.
MPAA:PG
Gary Kurtz; 20th Century Fox; Lucas Film — *CBS/Fox Video*

Enchanted Forest **1945**
Adventure
81223 77 mins C B, V, LV P
Harry Davenport, Edmund Lowe, Brenda Joyce, directed by Lew Landers
An elderly man teaches a boy about life and the beauty of nature when he gets lost in a forest.
PRC — *New World Video*

Enchanted Island **1958**
Drama
72943 94 mins C B, V P
Jane Powell, Dana Andrews
Based upon Herman Melville's "Typee", Dana Andrews is a whaler who stops on an island to find provisions and ends up falling in love with a cannibal princess.
RKO Radio Pictures — *United Home Video*

Enchanted Studio, The/More from the Enchanted Studio **1907**
Film-History
63982 57 mins B/W B, V P, T
A collection of short films produced by Pathe Freres studios during the early years of this century. Titles include: "Policeman's Little Run," "The Dog and His Various Merits," "A Diabolical Itching," "The Red Spectre," "The Yawner," "Poor Coat," "Wiffles Wins a Beauty Prize," "I Fetch the Bread" and "Down in the Deep." Silent with music score. Some color-tinted sequences.
Pathe Freres — *Blackhawk Films*

Encounter with Disaster **1979**
Disasters
59330 93 mins C B, V P
Using authentic footage from some of the worst and most frightening events of the century, this film explores how tragic events unfold—and how man has prevailed.
MPAA:PG
Charles E Sellier Jr; James Conway — *United Home Video*

Encounter with the Unknown **1975**
Adventure
11704 90 mins C B, V P
Narrated by Rod Serling
Relates three fully documented supernatural events including a death prophesy and a ghost.
Gold Key — *United Home Video*

End, The **1978**
Comedy
44941 100 mins C B, V, CED P
Burt Reynolds, Sally Field, Dom DeLuise, Carl Reiner, Joanne Woodward
Burt Reynolds plays a young man who finds out that he is dying from a rare disease. Deciding not to prolong his suffering, he tries various tried-and-true methods for committing suicide, with little success.
MPAA:R
United Artists — *CBS/Fox Video*

End of St. Petersburg, The **1927**
Film-History
49075 75 mins B/W B, V P
Directed by V. I. Pudovkin
A Russian peasant becomes a scab during a workers' strike in 1914. He is then forced to enlist in the army prior to the revolution. Silent.
Russian — *CBS/Fox Video; Sheik Video; Discount Video Tapes*

End of the World **1977**
Science fiction
33889 88 mins C B, V P
Christopher Lee, Sue Lyon, Lew Ayres, MacDonald Carey
A coffee machine explodes, sending a man flying and screaming through a window and into a neon sign, where he is electrocuted. A haunted priest witnesses this and retreats to a convent where he meets his double and heads for more trouble.
MPAA:PG
Irwin Yablans Company — *Media Home Entertainment*

Endangered Species **1982**
Drama
64570 97 mins C B, V, CED P
Robert Urich, Jobeth Williams, Paul Dooley, Hoyt Axton
A New York cop on vacation in Wyoming becomes involved in a mysterious series of cattle killings.
MPAA:R
MGM/UA — *MGM/UA Home Video*

Endgame **1985**
Science fiction/Fantasy
77360 96 mins C B, V P
Al Oliver, Moira Chen, Jack Davis
Grotesquely deformed survivors of World War III fight their way out of radioactive New York City to seek a better life.
Independent — *Media Home Entertainment*

Endless Love 1981
Drama
58495 115 mins C B, V, LV P
Brooke Shields, Martin Hewitt, Don Murray, Shirley Knight, Beatrice Straight, Richard Kiley
Scott Spencer's novel concerning two teenagers' doomed romance and sexual obsession.
MPAA:R
Universal; Dyson Lovell — *MCA Home Video; RCA VideoDiscs*

Endless Night 1972
Mystery
63356 95 mins C B, V R, P
Hayley Mills, Hywel Bennett
This screen adaptation of an Agatha Christie tale focuses on a young chauffeur who wants to build a dream house, and his chance meeting with an heiress.
British Lion — *THORN EMI/HBO Video*

Endless Summer, The 1966
Documentary/Sports-Water
59928 90 mins C B, V, LV, CED P
Directed by Bruce Brown
Director Bruce Brown follows two young surfers around the world in their search for the perfect wave.
Bruce Brown — *Pacific Arts Video*

Enforcer, The 1976
Crime-Drama
58228 97 mins C B, V R, P
Clint Eastwood, Tyne Daly, Harry Guardino, Brad Dillman
Dirty Harry takes on a vicious terrorist group threatening the city of San Francisco.
MPAA:R
Warner Bros — *Warner Home Video; RCA VideoDiscs*

Enigma 1983
Suspense
69545 101 mins C B, V P
Martin Sheen, Brigitte Fossey, Sam Neill
Trapped behind the Iron Curtain, a double agent tries to find the key to five pending murders by locating a Russian coded microprocessor holding information that would unravel the assassination scheme.
MPAA:PG
Filmcrest International Corp — *Embassy Home Entertainment*

Enigma 1983
Drama/Adventure
66043 101 mins C B, V, LV, CED P
Martin Sheen, directed by Jeannot Szwarc
Five assassins from the Soviet's KGB are sent to the West to eliminate five Soviet dissidents.
MPAA:PG
Ben Arbeid; Peter Shaw — *Embassy Home Entertainment*

Enola Gay 1980
War-Drama
70743 150 mins C B, V P
Patrick Duffy, Billy Crystal, Kim Darby, Gary Frank, Gregory Harrison, Ed Nelson, Robert Walden, directed by D.L. Rich
Based on the best-selling book by Gordon Thomas and Max Gordon Witts, this film tells the story of the airmen aboard the B-29 that dropped the first atomic bomb on Hiroshima.
Viacom in assoc. with The Production Co. — *Prism*

Ensign Pulver 1964
Comedy
73013 104 mins C B, V P
Robert Walker, Walter Matthau, Burl Ives, directed by Joshua Logan
A continuation of the further adventures of the crew of the U.S.S. Reluctant from "Mister Roberts," which was adapted from the Broadway play.
Joshua Logan; Warner Bros — *Warner Home Video*

Enter the Dragon 1973
Adventure/Martial arts
38946 90 mins C B, V, LV R, P
Bruce Lee, John Saxon, Jim Kelly
Martial arts film starring Bruce Lee, with spectacular fighting sequences featuring karate, judo, tai kwan do, tai chi chuan, and hapkido techniques.
MPAA:R EL, SP
Warner Bros — *Warner Home Video; RCA VideoDiscs*

Enter the Ninja 1981
Martial arts/Adventure
60593 101 mins C B, V, CED P
Franco Nero, Susan George
The story of the Ninja warrior's lethal, little-known Art of Invisibility.
MPAA:R
Cannon Films Release — *MGM/UA Home Video*

Entertaining Mr. Sloane 1970
Drama
58886 90 mins C B, V R, P
Beryl Reid, Harry Andrews, Peter McEnery, Alan Webb
Playwright Joe Orton's masterpiece of black comedy concerning a handsome criminal who becomes the guest and love interest of a widow and her brother.
Pathe; Canterbury — *THORN EMI/HBO Video*

(For explanation of codes, see USE GUIDE and KEY)

Entity, The 1982
Horror
69376 119 mins C B, V, CED P
Barbara Hershey
An unseen entity repeatedly torments a woman both physically and mentally.
MPAA:R
20th Century Fox — *CBS/Fox Video*

Entre Nous (Between Us) 1983
Drama
80497 110 mins C B, V P
Isabelle Huppert, Miou-Miou
Two attractive young French mothers find in each other the fulfillment their husbands cannot provide. French dialogue with English subtitles.
MPAA:PG FR
Alexandre Films — *MGM/UA Home Video*

Eraserhead 1977
Film-Avant-garde/Satire
47783 90 mins C B, V P
John Nance, Charlotte Stewart
A cult classic, with special effects that create an eerie, dreamlike world, about a very strange couple and their deformed child.
David Lynch — *RCA/Columbia Pictures Home Video*

Erick Friedman Plays Fritz Kreisler 1982
Music-Performance
59393 60 mins C B, V P
A recital of music composed by famed violinist Fritz Kreisler and performed by American violinist Erick Friedman and pianist Pavel Ostrosky. Selections include: "Tambourin Chinois," "Caprice Viennois," "The Old Refrain," "Song without Words" and "Schon Rosmarin."
Kultur — *Kultur*

Ernani 1984
Music-Performance
77172 135 mins C B, V R, P
Placido Domingo, Mirella Freni, Renato Bruson
A performance of the Verdi opera taped at the Teatro Alla Scala in Italy.
National Video Corporation Limited — *THORN EMI/HBO Video*

Ernie Kovacs: Television's Original Genius 198?
Television/Comedy
66603 86 mins C B, V, LV P
Ernie Kovacs, Edie Adams, Steve Allen, Jack Lemmon, Chevy Chase, hosted by John Barbour
A comedic tribute to one of television's pioneers, humorist Ernie Kovacs. His career is chronicled through clips from his numerous series and specials. Some black-and-white segments.
Simcom — *Vestron Video*

Eroticise 1983
Physical fitness
64336 60 mins C B, V, CED P
Kitten Natividad
Kitten and her entourage guide the viewer into a sensual exercise workout, designed for adults. In stereo.
Pisanti Productions — *Vestron Video*

Errand Boy, The 1961
Comedy
80241 95 mins B/W B, V P
Jerry Lewis, Brian Donlevy, Fritz Feld, directed by Jerry Lewis
A Hollywood studio head hires an errand boy to spy on his employees.
Paramount — *U.S.A. Home Video*

Eruption: St. Helens Explodes 1980
Volcanoes/Documentary
54108 25 mins C B, V P, T
A look at the eruption of Mount St. Helens on May 18, 1980. Station KOIN-TV in Portland, Oregon shot the blast, showing the volcanic peak being torn away. They almost lost a $70,000 remote broadcast truck while shooting.
KOIN Portland — *Blackhawk Films*

Escape 1978
Adventure
77390 100 mins C B, V P
Anthony Steffen, Ajita Wilson
Two women escape from a sadistic penal colony and are pursued by a man who wants them to become his personal sex slaves.
Mark Alabiso — *Wizard Video*

Escape from Alcatraz 1979
Drama
44752 112 mins C B, V, LV R, P
Clint Eastwood, Patrick McGoohan, directed by Don Siegel
A fascinating account of the one and only successful escape from the maximum security prison at Alcatraz by three men who were never heard from again.
MPAA:PG
Paramount, Don Siegel — *Paramount Home Video; RCA VideoDiscs*

Escape from New York 1981
Science fiction/Adventure
65193 99 mins C B, V, LV P
Kurt Russell, Lee Van Cleef, Isaac Hayes, Adrienne Barbeau, Season Hubley, directed by John Carpenter

In 1997, the island of Manhattan has been turned into a maximum security prison inhabited by millions of felons. When the President's plane crashes there, a convicted criminal is sent in to save him.
MPAA:R EL, JA
Avco Embassy — *Embassy Home Entertainment; RCA VideoDiscs*

Escape from the Bronx 1985
Adventure/Science fiction
81188 82 mins C B, V P
Mark Gregory, Henry Silva, Valeria D'Obici, Timothy Brant, Thomas Moore, Andrea Coppola
Invading death squads seek to level the Bronx. Local street gangs cry foul and ally to defeat the uncultured barbarians.
Fabrizio De Angelis — *Media Home Entertainment*

Escape from the Planet of the Apes 1971
Science fiction
81542 97 mins C B, V P
Roddy McDowell, Kim Hunter, Sal Mineo, Ricardo Montalban, William Windom, directed by Don Taylor
Two intelligent apes from the future travel back in time and find themselves in present-day America where they are the targets of a relentless search.
Apjac Productions; 20th Century Fox — *Playhouse Video*

Escapadein Japan 1957
Adventure/Drama
79767 93 mins C B, V P
Cameron Mitchell, Teresa Wright, Jon Provost, Roger Nakagawa
A Japanese and an American boy frantically search the city of Tokyo for their parents.
RKO — *United Home Video*

Escape to Athena 1979
Adventure
57460 102 mins C CED P
Roger Moore, Telly Savalas, David Niven
A group of losers are in a German POW camp on a Greek island digging up Greek art treasures. When they manage to escape, the rumors abound.
MPAA:PG
Associated Film Distributors — *CBS/Fox Video*

Escape to the Sun 1972
Adventure/Suspense
66633 94 mins C B, V P
Laurence Harvey, Josephine Chaplin, John Ireland, Jack Hawkins
A pair of Russian university students plan to flee their homeland so they can be allowed to live and love free from oppression.
MPAA:PG
Transamerican Productions — *Monterey Home Video*

Escape to Witch Mountain 1975
Fantasy
29745 97 mins C B, V, LV R, P
Kim Richards, Ike Eisenmann, Eddie Albert, Ray Milland
Two young orphans with supernatural powers find themselves on the run from a greedy millionaire who wants to exploit their amazing powers for his own gains.
MPAA:G
Walt Disney, Jerome Coutland — *Walt Disney Home Video; RCA VideoDiscs*

Escape 2000 1983
Science fiction
69541 80 mins C B, V P
Steve Railsback, Olivia Hussey, Michael Craig
In a future society where individuality is considered a crime, those who refuse to conform are punished by being hunted down in a jungle.
MPAA:R
Unknown — *Embassy Home Entertainment*

Escort Girls 1974
Drama
80797 77 mins C B, V R, P
David Dixon, Maria O'Brien, Marika Mann, Gil Barber, Helen Christie
The escort girls are a group of actresses, models and secretaries who really know how to show their clients a good time.
Donovan Winter — *Video Gems*

Esposa y Amante 197?
Drama
49744 95 mins C B, V P
Ramiro Oliveros, Ricardo Merino, Victoria Abril, Frika Wallner
While her daughter contemplates suicide, a mother remembers the happy early years of her marriage, followed by the wrongdoings of her husband which caused her to seek comfort in the arms of an old lawyer friend. Her daughter is now suffering for the problems of her marriage. In Spanish.
SP
Independent — *Media Home Entertainment*

Eternally Yours 1939
Comedy
00395 95 mins B/W B, V P
David Niven, Loretta Young, Hugh Herbert, Broderick Crawford
Witty magician's career threatens to break up his marriage.

United Artists; Tay Garnett — *Budget Video; Cable Films; Movie Buff Video; Classic Video Cinema Collector's Club; Kartes Productions*

Eubie! 1982
Musical
59387 100 mins C CED P
Gregory Hines, Maurice Hines, Leslie Dockery, Alaina Reed, Lynnie Godfrey, Mel Johnson Jr., Jeffrey V. Thompson
The popular Broadway musical revue based on the life and songs of Eubie Blake is presented in a video transfer. Some of Eubie's best known songs, performed here by members of the original cast, include "I'm Just Wild About Harry," "Memories of You," "In Honeysuckle Time" and "The Charleston Rag." In stereo.
American Video Productions — *Warner Home Video; Video Tape Network; RCA VideoDiscs*

Europeans, The 1979
Drama
56935 90 mins C B, V P
Lee Remick, Lisa Eichorn, directed by James Ivory
Henry James' satirical novel about two fortune-seeking expatriates and their sober American relations.
MPAA:G
Ismail Merchant — *Vestron Video*

Eurythmics—Sweet Dreams (The Video Album) 1983
Music-Performance
66347 50 mins C B, V P
Directed by Derek Burbidge
Eurythmics' David Stewart and Annie Lennox perform their hits "Sweet Dreams (Are Made of This)" and "Love Is a Stranger" plus twelve other songs in a combination of live concert performances and music videos. In stereo VHS and Beta Hi-Fi.
Jon Roseman — *RCA/Columbia Pictures Home Video; RCA VideoDiscs; Pioneer Artists*

Eve, The 1980
Music-Performance
59872 60 mins C LV P
The Inner Galaxy Orchestra, a contemporary ensemble led by Bingo Miki of the Japanese jazz scene, performs "The Eve," an incredible trip through his audiovisual fantasies. In stereo.
Yutaka Shigenobu — *Pioneer Video Imports*

Evel Knievel 1971
Drama/Biographical
75694 90 mins C B, V P
George Hamilton, Bert Freed, Rod Cameron
The life of stuntman Evel Knievel is depicted in this movie, as portrayed by George Hamilton.
MPAA:PG

Fanfare — *MPI Home Video*

Evening with Liza Minnelli, An 1981
Music-Performance
59626 50 mins C B, V P
Liza Minnelli
Liza is seen performing everything from blues to ballads at this concert recorded at the New Orleans Theater of the Performing Arts. Songs include "Cabaret" and "New York, New York."
Artel Home Video — *CBS/Fox Video*

Evening with Professor Irwin Corey, An 1983
Comedy-Performance
70367 50 mins C B, V R, P
Prof. Irwin Corey
This taped performance features the world's foremost authority and minister of the department of redundancy.
Oaks Productions — *Video City Productions*

Evening with Quentin Crisp, An 1981
Biographical/Theater
58582 90 mins C B, V P
Introduction by John Hurt
Taped during performances of Crisp's one-man show during his first theatrical tour of the U.S., this program presents the "gospel according to Crisp," and features Crisp fielding questions from the audience.
Hillard Elkins — *Family Home Entertainment*

Evening with Ray Charles, An 1981
Music-Performance
58807 40 mins C B, V P
Ray Charles
The living legend, Ray Charles, performs live at the Jubilee Auditorium in Edmunton, Canada, showcasing his many musical moods. Songs include: "Riding Thumb," "Busted," "Georgia on My Mind," "Oh What a Beautiful Morning," "Some Enchanted Evening," "Hit the Road Jack," "I Can't Stop loving You," "Take These Chains from My Heart," "I Can See Clearly Now," "What'd I Say," and "America the Beautiful."
Allarco Prods Ltd; Optical Programming Associates — *MCA Home Video; Optical Programming Associates*

Evening with Robin Williams, An 1983
Comedy-Performance
64501 92 mins C B, V R, P
Robin Williams
Robin Williams explodes all over the screen in this live nightclub performance taped at the Great American Music Hall in San Francisco.

Don Mischer — *Paramount Home Video; RCA VideoDiscs*

Evening with Sir William Martin, An 1981
Comedy
49676 30 mins C B, V P
Bill Martin, Michael Nesmith
A "Mr. Toad" encounters his senile father, who is later transported to another planet. Then a moose hands him a cigarette which instantly transports him to Antarctica. This program probably has to be seen to be believed.
Pacific Arts Video Records — *Pacific Arts Video*

Evening with the Royal Ballet, An 1963
Dance
81203 87 mins C B, V P
Rudolph Nureyev, Margot Fonteyn
Rudolph Nureyev and Margot Fonteyn join with the Royal Ballet to perform excerpts from such favorites as "The Sleeping Beauty" and "Les Sylphides."
British Home Entertainment Ltd. — *MCA Home Video*

Evening with the Royal Ballet, An 197?
Dance
56886 100 mins C CED P
Rudolf Nureyev, Margot Fonteyn
Performances of "La Valse," "Les Sylphides," "Le Corsaire," "Aurora's Wedding," and the last act of "The Sleeping Beauty."
RCA — *RCA VideoDiscs*

Evening with Utopia, An 1983
Music-Performance
60587 85 mins C B, V P
Directed by Joshua White
Utopia, the popular rock group and brainchild of Todd Rundgren, in concert. The 21 songs include "Feet Don't Fail Me Now" and others from the LP "Utopia." Stereo.
Neo Utopian Laboratories Ltd — *MCA Home Video*

Evergreen 1934
Musical
33506 90 mins B/W B, V, FO P
Jessie Matthews, Sonnie Hale, Betty Balfour, Barry Mackey
The daughter of a retired British music hall star is mistaken for her mother and it is thought that she has discovered the secret of eternal youth.
Gaumont British — *Video Yesteryear; Cable Films; Sheik Video; Western Film & Video Inc; Video Dimensions; Classic Video Cinema Collector's Club*

Everly Brothers Reunion Concert 1983
Music-Performance
65658 60 mins C B, V P
After years of bitter separation and crises, the undisputed NO. 1 duo of the golden age of rock 'n' roll join together at London's Royal Albert Hall and perform such megahits as "Bye Bye Love," "Wake Up Little Susie," "All I Have To Do Is Dream," and "Cathy's Clown."
Delilah Films Inc; The Everly Brothers — *MGM/UA Home Video*

Every Girl Should Be Married 1948
Comedy
73686 84 mins B/W B, V P
Cary Grant, Betsy Drake, Diana Lynn
A shopgirl uses her wiles to land herself a bachelor doctor.
RKO — *RKO HomeVideo*

Every Man for Himself and God Against All 1975
Drama
69621 110 mins C B, V P
Bruno S., directed by Werner Herzog
This film tells the story of Kaspar Hauser, a young man who mysteriously appears in a small German town, hardly able to speak, write or even function in the world of 1828. In German with English subtitles.
Cannes Film Festival: Grand Special Jury Prize.
Werner Herzog; Almi — *RCA/Columbia Pictures Home Video*

Every Which Way But Loose 1978
Comedy/Adventure
54119 119 mins C B, V R, P
Clint Eastwood, Sondra Locke, Geoffrey Lewis, Beverly D'Angelo, Ruth Gordon, directed by James Fargo
A beer guzzling, country music-loving truck driver earns a living as a barroom brawler. He and his orangutan travel to Colorado in pursuit of a woman he loves. Behind him are a motorcycle gang and an L.A. cop. All have been victims of his fists.
MPAA:R
Warner Bros — *Warner Home Video; RCA VideoDiscs*

Everyday with Richard Simmons: Family Fitness 1983
Physical fitness
60558 90 mins C B, V P
This exercise regimen includes a 15-minute warm-up, an hour long exercise session, and emphasis on toning the face, stomach, legs, and thighs.
Karl Video Corp — *Karl/Lorimar Home Video*

Everything You Always Wanted to Know About Sex But (Were Afraid to Ask) 1972
Comedy
44942 88 mins C B, V P
Woody Allen, John Carradine, Lou Jacobi, Louise Lasser, Anthony Quayle, Lynn Redgrave, Tony Randall, Burt Reynolds, Gene Wilder, directed by Woody Allen
A series of comical sketches involving sex, such as a timid sperm cell, an oversexed court jester, and a giant disembodied breast.
MPAA:R
United Artists — *CBS/Fox Video; RCA VideoDiscs*

Everything You Always Wanted to Know About Computers But Were Afraid to Ask 1984
Electronic data processing
79208 88 mins C B, V P
John Wood presents in a clear cut fashion everything you need to know to operate a computer.
MGM UA Home Entertainment Group — *MGM/UA Home Video*

Evictors, The 1979
Horror
65218 92 mins C B, V P
Vic Morrow, Michael Parks, Jessica Harper
Three innocent victims are caught up in the horror surrounding an abandoned farmhouse in a small Louisiana town.
MPAA:PG
Charles B Pierce — *Vestron Video*

Evil Dead, The 1979
Horror
69674 126 mins C B, V R, P
Five vacationing college students unwittingly resurrect demons which transform the students into monsters.
New Line Cinema — *THORN EMI/HBO Video*

Evil Mind, The 1935
Drama
08760 81 mins B/W B, V, 3/4U P
Claude Rains, Fay Wray, Jane Baxter
Fraudulent mindreader predicts many disasters that start coming true.
British — *VCII; Video Yesteryear; Cable Films; Video Connection*

Evil That Men Do, The 1984
Drama
Closed Captioned
80375 90 mins C B, V P
Charles Bronson, Rene Enriquez, Jose Ferrer, Theresa Saladana
A hitman comes out of retirement to break up a Central American government's political torture ring. Available in VHS and Beta Hi-Fi.
MPAA:R
Tri-Star Pictures — *RCA/Columbia Pictures Home Video*

Evil Under the Sun 1981
Mystery
63332 102 mins C B, V, CED R, P
Peter Ustinov, Jane Birkin, Maggie Smith, Colin Blakely, Roddy McDowall, Diana Rigg, Sylvia Miles, James Mason
An opulent beach resort is the setting as Hercules Poirot attempts to unravel a murder mystery. Based on the Agatha Christie novel.
MPAA:PG
Universal — *THORN EMI/HBO Video*

Evilspeak 1982
Horror
59629 89 mins C B, V, CED P
Clint Howard, Don Stark, Lou Gravance, Lauren Lester
A bumbling misfit enrolled at a military school is mistreated by the other cadets. He retaliates with satanic power.
MPAA:R
Leisure Investments — *CBS/Fox Video*

Evolutionary Spiral 1983
Music-Performance/Video
76668 45 mins C B, V P
A combination of visual imagery and a musical soundtrack by the group Weather Report.
Earth Sky and Open Sky Productions — *Sony Corporation of America*

Ex-Mrs. Bradford, The 1936
Mystery/Comedy
44854 80 mins B/W B, V, 3/4U P
William Powell, Jean Arthur, James Gleason, Eric Blore, Robert Armstrong, directed by Stephen Roberts
Amateur sleuth Dr. Bradford teams up with his ex-wife Jean Arthur to solve the race track murders. Sophisticated comedy-mystery.
RKO — *Nostalgia Merchant*

Excalibur 1981
Fantasy
58229 140 mins C B, V R, P
Nicol Williamson, Nigel Terry, Helen Mirren, directed by John Boorman
An elegant version of the King Arthur legend focusing on the rise of Christian civilization out of the magic, murder, and chaos of the Dark Ages.
MPAA:R
Orion Pictures — *Warner Home Video; RCA VideoDiscs*

Executioner's Song, The **1982**
Biographical/Drama
77386 157 mins C B, V P
Tommy Lee Jones, Rosanna Arquette, Eli Wallach, Christine Lahti, directed by Lawrence Schiller
An adaptation of the Norman Mailer book about the last nine months of convicted murderer Gary Gilmore's life. Available in Beta Hi Fi and VHS Stereo.
Lawrence Schiller — *U.S.A. Home Video*

Executive Action **1973**
Drama
44753 90 mins C B, V R, P
Burt Lancaster, Robert Ryan, Will Geer, Gilbert Green, John Anderson, directed by David Miller
A recreation of the events that led up to the assassination of JFK. A millionaire pays a professional spy to organize a secret conspiracy; their mission—kill President Kennedy.
MPAA:PG
National General — *Warner Home Video*

Exercise **1983**
Physical fitness
60412 60 mins C B, V P
An adults-only erotic exercise program.
Appaloosa Productions — *Monterey Home Video*

Exercise Now! **1981**
Physical fitness
52766 50 mins C B, V P
An intensive, two-part aerobic exercise program set to popular music and led by professional exercise instructors, complete with a poster detailing each exercise.
AM Available
Karl Video — *Karl/Lorimar Home Video*

Exit the Dragon, Enter the Tiger **1976**
Adventure/Martial arts
37361 84 mins C B, V P
"Exit the Dragon, Enter the Tiger" is a motion picture about the death of karate specialist Bruce Lee.
Dimension — *United Home Video*

Exodus **1960**
Drama
37523 207 mins C B, V P
Paul Newman, Eva Marie Saint, Lee J. Cobb, Sal Mineo, Ralph Richardson, Peter Lawford, Jill Haworth, John Derek, directed by Otto Preminger
Based on the novel by Leon Uris and filmed in Cyprus and Israel, this is the story of an Israeli underground leader who leads a group of Jewish refugees into Israel, and an American nurse who becomes involved with the movement.
Academy Award '60: Best Music Score.
United Artists, Otto Preminger — *CBS/Fox Video*

Exorcist, The **1973**
Suspense
38944 120 mins C B, V, LV R, P
Ellen Burstyn, Linda Blair, Jason Miller, Max Von Sydow, directed by William Friedkin
A harrowing film based on William Peter Blatty's novel of a young girl who is possessed by a demon, raising havoc with her family and the priests who attempt to exorcise her.
MPAA:R EL, SP
Warner Bros — *Warner Home Video; RCA VideoDiscs*

Exorcist II: The Heretic **1977**
Horror
44804 118 mins C B, V R, P
Richard Burton, Linda Blair, Louise Fletcher, Kitty Winn, James Earl Jones, Ned Beatty
A sequel to the 1973 hit "The Exorcist." After four years Blair is still under psychiatric care, suffering from the effects of being possessed by the devil.
MPAA:R
Warner Bros — *Warner Home Video*

Expansion of Life, The **1982**
Biology/Science
59560 58 mins C B, V P
This program deals with the fundamentals of cell division, invertebrates and fish life in the early seas, amphibians and reptiles, and the emergence of man.
McGraw Hill — *Mastervision*

Experience Preferred... But Not Essential **1982**
Comedy
75539 77 mins C B, V P
Produced by David Puttnam
An English schoolgirl gets her first job at a resort where she learns about life.
MPAA:PG
Samuel Montagu & Co Ltd — *MGM/UA Home Video*

Expertos en Pinchazos **1979**
Comedy
47855 100 mins C B, V P
Porcel and Olmedo
Albert and George, experts at giving injections to women, inject a patient with venom by mistake. Now they must find her within 48 hours. In Spanish.
SP
Luis Osvaldo Repetto; Nicolas Carreras — *Media Home Entertainment*

 (For explanation of codes, see USE GUIDE and KEY)

Explosion 1970
Drama
70387 96 mins C B, V P
Don Stroud, Gordon Thompson, Michele Chicione, Richard Conte, directed by Jules Bricken
A distraught and disturbed young man evades the draft after losing a brother in Vietnam. Arriving in Canada, he meets another draft-dodger with whom he embarks on a murderous rampage.
MPAA:R
American International Pictures — *Trans World Entertainment*

Exposed 1983
Suspense
66450 100 mins C B, V, CED P
Nastassia Kinski, Rudolph Nureyev, Harvey Keitel, directed by James Toback
A high fashion model falls in with a terrorist gang, while at the same time, a group of anti-terrorists want to use her for their purposes.
MPAA:R
United Artists — *MGM/UA Home Video*

Exterminator, The 1980
Suspense
63369 101 mins C B, V, CED P
Christopher George, Samantha Eggar
A man seeks vengeance and becomes the target of the police, the CIA and the underworld in this tale of murder and intrigue.
MPAA:R
Avco Embassy; Interstar Productions — *Embassy Home Entertainment*

Exterminator II 1984
Adventure
80499 88 mins C B, V P
Robert Ginty
The Exterminator battles the denizens of New York's underworld after his girlfriend is crippled by the ruthless Mr. X.
MPAA:R
Cannon Films — *MGM/UA Home Video*

Exterminators of the Year 3000 1983
Adventure
80330 101 mins C B, V R, P
Alan Collins, Fred Harris
The Exterminator and his mercenary girlfriend battle with nuclear mutants over the last remaining tanks of purified water on Earth.
MPAA:R
Samuel Goldwyn — *THORN EMI/HBO Video*

Eye for an Eye, An 1981
Adventure
60346 106 mins C B, V, CED P
Chuck Norris, Christopher Lee, Richard Roundtree, Matt Clark
A story of pursuit and revenge with Chuck Norris as an undercover cop pitted against San Francisco's underworld and high society.
MPAA:R EL, JA
Avco Embassy — *Embassy Home Entertainment*

Eye Hears, the Ear Sees, The 1970
Filmmaking
36349 59 mins C B, V, FO P
Norman McLaren
This introduction to Norman McLaren and his work shows how he has created many innovative films which have become classic examples of film art. McLaren discusses and demonstrates some of his techniques, and excerpts from his films are shown.
BBC — *Video Yesteryear; National Film Board of Canada*

Eye of the Needle 1981
Suspense
58848 118 mins C B, V P
Donald Sutherland, Kate Nelligan, directed by Richard Marquand
Ken Follett's novel about a German spy posing as a shipwrecked sailor on a deserted English island during World War II.
MPAA:R
United Artists — *CBS/Fox Video*

Eyeball 1978
Horror
80288 91 mins C B, V P
John Richardson, Martine Brochard
An intrepid policeman must keep an eye out for the madman who is removing eyeballs from his victims.
MPAA:R
Joseph Brenner Associates — *Prism*

Eyes of a Stranger 1980
Horror
58230 82 mins C B, V R, P
Lauren Tewes, John Disanti, Jennifer Jason Leigh, directed by Ken Wiederhorn
A terrifying maniac stalks his female prey by watching their every move.
MPAA:R
Georgetown Productions — *Warner Home Video*

Eyes of Laura Mars 1978
Mystery
Closed Captioned
35377 104 mins C B, V P
Faye Dunaway, Tommy Lee Jones
A photographer (Dunaway) exhibits strange powers—she can foresee a murder before it happens. Title song performed by Barbra Streisand.
MPAA:R

Columbia — *RCA/Columbia Pictures Home Video; RCA VideoDiscs*

Eyes of the Amaryllis, The **1982**
Horror
80926 94 mins C B, V P
Ruth Ford, Marsha Byrne, Guy Boyd
A young girl becomes involved in a mysterious game when she arrives in Nantucket to care for her invalid grandmother.
MPAA:R
Amaryllis Company — *Vestron Video*

Eyes Right **1926**
Comedy-Drama
11387 65 mins B/W B, V, FO P
Francis X. Bushman
An interesting portrayal of life in a military prep school. (Silent.)
Goodwill — *Video Yesteryear*

Eyes, The Mouth, The **1983**
Drama
70194 100 mins C B, V P
Lou Castel, Angela Molina, directed by Marco Bellochio
A young man has an affair with his dead twin brother's fiancee. Happiness eludes them as they are haunted by the dead man's memory. In Beta Hi-Fi.
MPAA:R
Triumph Films — *RCA/Columbia Pictures Home Video*

Eyewitness **1981**
Suspense
47154 102 mins C B, V, CED P
William Hurt, Sigourney Weaver, Christopher Plummer, James Woods, Steven Hill, directed by Peter Yates
The janitor of an office building tells a TV reporter that he knows something about a murder that took place in his building.
MPAA:R
20th Century Fox; Peter Yates — *CBS/Fox Video*

F

Fables of the Green Forest **19??**
Cartoons/Adventure
56750 40 mins C B, V P
Animated
Johnny Chuck, Peter Cottontail, Chatter the Squirrel and other memorable Thorton W. Burgess characters come to life in "Whose Footprint Is That?" and "Johnny's Hibernation." Available in English and Spanish versions.
EL, SP
ZIV International — *Media Home Entertainment*

Fabulous Adventures of Baron Munchausen, The **1979**
Adventure/Cartoons
80689 77 mins C B, V P
Animated
The legendary Baron Munchausen tells the story of his trek to the strange and beautiful land of Trukesban.
Jean Image Productions — *Vestron Video*

Fabulous Dorseys, The **1947**
Musical/Drama
01609 91 mins B/W B, V P
Tommy and Jimmy Dorsey and Orchestras, Janet Blair, Paul Whiteman, Directed by Alfred E. Green
The musical lives of Tommy and Jimmy Dorsey are portrayed in this biographical film. Guest stars include Art Tatum, Charlie Barnet, Ziggy Elman, Bob Eberly and Helen O'Connell.
UA; Charles R Rogers — *Hal Roach Studios; Budget Video; Video Connection; Video Yesteryear; Discount Video Tapes; Nostalgia Merchant; U of Alabama Birmingham; Republic Pictures Home Video; Kartes Productions; See Hear Industries*

Fabulous Fifties, The **19??**
History-US/Documentary
10150 mins B/W B, V P, T
Film covers MacArthur's "Old Soldier's Speech," Eisenhower and Nixon, Korea, Stalin's death, hydrogen bomb testing, Suez Canal crisis, the Cold War, and Castro.
Unknown — *Blackhawk Films*

Fabulous Fleischer Folio, Volume Two, The **193?**
Cartoons
77535 50 mins C B, V R, P
Animated
This new volume features five more classic cartoons from the Fleischer Studios including "Hawaiian Birds," "Greedy Humpty Dumpty," "Snubbed by a Snob," "Base Brawl" and "Somewhere in Dreamland."
Fleischer Studios — *Walt Disney Home Video*

Fabulous Fleischer Folio, Volume One, The **193?**
Cartoons
76813 50 mins C B, V R, P
Animated
This is a collection of six vintage Max Fleischer "Color Classics" from the 1930's.

 (For explanation of codes, see USE GUIDE and KEY)

Max Fleischer Studios — *Walt Disney Home Video*

Fabulous Fred Astaire, The **1958**
Variety
38119 70 mins B/W B, V, FO P
Fred Astaire, Barrie Chase
Contains Fred Astaire's 1958 Emmy Award winning special, "An Evening With Fred Astaire," plus a "Person-to-Person" interview by Edward R. Murrow with Astaire.
NBC — *Video Yesteryear*

Fabulous Funnies **1978**
Cartoons
75493 60 mins C B, V P
The cartoons in this video include Alley Oop, Broomhilda, Nancy and Sluggo and Tumbleweeds.
Unknown — *Prism*

Fabulous Funnies Volume 2 **1984**
Cartoons
70613 60 mins C B, V P
Animated
Many familiar comic strip characters appear in this volume including Nancy and Sluggo, Alley Oop, Broomhilda, and the Captain and the Kids.
Videocraft International Ltd. — *Prism*

Fabulous Joe, The **1974**
Comedy
66113 54 mins C B, V P
Walter Abel
A dog named Joe gets involved in a necklace caper.
Hal Roach — *Unicorn Video*

Face in the Crowd, A **1957**
Drama
81493 126 mins B/W B, V R, P
Andy Griffith, Patricia Neal, Lee Remick, Walter Matthau, Anthony Franciosa, directed by Elia Kazan
A hillbilly entertainer becomes a major success thanks to his television program. Things take a turn for the worse when he starts to believe his own publicity.
Warner Bros; Newtown Prods. — *Warner Home Video*

Faces of Death **1974**
Death/Documentary
65154 88 mins C B, V P
Narrated by Dr. Frances B. Gross
This gruesome documentary looks at death experiences around the world, uncensored film footage offers graphic coverage of autopsies, suicides, executions, and animal slaughter. Not for the squeamish.
Rosilyn T Scott — *MPI Home Video; Gorgon Video*

Faces of Death Part II **1985**
Death/Documentary
70580 84 mins C B, V P
This sequel to "Faces of Death" further explores violent termination of man by man and by nature in a graphic-grisly gala. Not for the squeamish.
Rosilyn T. Scott — *MPI Home Video*

Fade to Black **1980**
Horror/Suspense
63894 100 mins C B, V P
Dennis Christopher, Tim Thomerson, Linda Kerridge
A young man obsessed with movies loses his grip on reality and adopts the personalities of cinematic characters to seek revenge on people who have wronged him.
MPAA:R
Irwin Yablans; Sylvio Tabet — *Media Home Entertainment*

Faerie Tale Theatre **1983**
Fairy tales
Closed Captioned
69320 60 mins C B, V, LV, CED P
Shelley Duvall, Robin Williams, Elliot Gould, Jeff Bridges, Christopher Reeve, Tatum O'Neal et al
17 pgms
"Faerie Tale Theatre," conceived and produced by Shelley Duvall, is a series of hour-long enactments of classic fairy tales featuring many well-known actors and actresses. All programs are available individually.
1.The Tale of the Frog Prince 2.Jack and the Beanstalk 3.Rapuznel 4.Sleeping Beauty 5.Goldilocks and the Three Bears 6.Little Red Riding Hood 7.Hansel and Gretal 8. Rumpelstiltskin 9.Boy Who Left Home to Find Out About the Shivers 10. Pinocchio 11.The Snow Queen 12. The Three Little Pigs 13.The Emperor's New Clothes 14.The Pied Piper of Hamlin 15.Puss 'N Boots 16.Cinderella 17.The Little Mermaid 18.The Dancing Princesses 19.The Princess Who Had Never Laughed.
Shelley Duvall — *CBS/Fox Video*

Fail Safe **1964**
Drama
Closed Captioned
63440 111 mins B/W B, V P
Henry Fonda, Dan O'Herlihy, Walter Matthau, directed by Sidney Lumet
A computer malfunction sets off events that may possibly result in a nuclear war.
Columbia; Max E. Youngstein — *RCA/Columbia Pictures Home Video*

Fairy Tale Classics 1983
Fairy tales
69533 50 mins C B, V, CED P
Animated
This is a compilation of five of the world's best-loved fairy tales: "Cinderella," "The Ugly Duckling," "The Red Shoes," "Ali Baba and the Forty Thieves" and "The Bremen Band."
MPAA:G
Toei Animation Productions — *Children's Video Library*

Fairy Tale Classics: Volume II 19??
Fairy tales
69612 60 mins C B, V P
Animated
This collection of animated fairy tales includes "The Owl and the Pussycat," "The Three Bears," Aesop's fable of "The Tiger King," "Beanstalk Jack," and more.
Viacom International — *Children's Video Library*

Fairy Tales, Volume Two 1977
Fairy tales/Cartoons
73664 55 mins C B, V P
Animated
Five animated versions of fairy tale classics are available in one program: "Snow White," "The Emperor's New Clothes," "The Twelve Months," "The Happy Prince" and "The Three Wishes."
Unknown — *Embassy Home Entertainment*

Fairy Tales, Volume I 1977
Cartoons
72868 55 mins C B, V P
Some of the world's best fairy tales come to life, including "Cinderella" and "Beauty and the Beast."
Unkown — *Embassy Home Entertainment*

Fairytales 1979
Satire
55218 83 mins C B, V P
Don Sparks, Prof. Irwin Corey, Brenda Fogarty
An enchanting musical fantasy for adults. In order to save the kingdom, the prince must produce an heir. The problem is that only the girl in the painting of "Princess Beauty" can "interest" the prince—and she must be found.
MPAA:R
Fairytales Distributing Company — *Media Home Entertainment*

Fake Out 1982
Suspense/Drama
78389 89 mins C B, V R, P
Pia Zadora, Telly Savalas, Desi Arnaz, Jr
A nightclub singer is caught between the mob and the police who want her to testify against her gangland lover.
Matt Cimber — *THORN EMI/HBO Video*

Falcon and the Snowman, The 1985
Suspense
77185 110 mins C B, V, CED P
Sean Penn, Timothy Hutton, Lori Singer, Pat Hingle, directed by John Schlesinger
This is the true story of two childhood friends who become spies and sell American intelligence secrets to the KGB. Pat Metheny and Lyle Mays perform the musical score.
MPAA:R
Orion Pictures — *Vestron Video*

Falcon in Mexico, The 1944
Mystery
64381 70 mins B/W B, V, 3/4U P
Tom Conway, Mona Maris, Nestor Paiva
The manhunt for a dangerous killer leads the Falcon to Mexico.
RKO — *Nostalgia Merchant*

Falcon Takes Over, The/Strange Bargain 1949
Mystery
76839 131 mins B/W B, V P
George Sanders, Ward Bond, Allen Jenkins, Martha Scott, Henry Morgan, Hans Conried
An exciting mystery double feature: In "The Falcon Takes Over," The Falcon becomes involved in a bogus fortunetelling scheme and in "Strange Bargain" an underpaid bookkeeper gets in on an insurance swindle.
RKO — *RKO HomeVideo*

Falcon's Adventure, The/Armored Car Robbery 1950
Mystery
81026 122 mins B/W B, V P
Tom Conway, Madge Meredith, William Talman, Charles McGraw, Adele Jergens
A mystery double feature: The Falcon uncovers a vicious plot to steal a formula for synthetic diamonds in "The Falcon's Adventure," and four participants in an armored car robbery flee after slaying a policeman in "Armored Car Robbery."
RKO — *RKO HomeVideo*

Falcon's Brother, The 1942
Mystery
11299 64 mins B/W B, V, FO P
Tom Conway, George Sanders, Keye Luke, Jane Randolph
Enemy agents intent on killing a South American diplomat are the targets of the Falcon's brother.
RKO — *Nostalgia Merchant*

 (For explanation of codes, see USE GUIDE and KEY)

Fall of the House of Usher, The 1960
Horror
53511 85 mins C B, V R, P
Vincent Price, Myrna Fahey, Mark Damon, directed by Roger Corman
The last of the Usher line is buried alive by her brother and returns to wreak vengeance. Also titled "House of Usher." Based on the story by Edgar Allen Poe.
American Intl; Roger Corman — *Warner Home Video*

Fall of the House of Usher, The 1979
Drama
37362 101 mins C B, V P
Martin Landau, Robert Hays, Charlene Tilton, Ray Walston
Another version of Edgar Allan Poe's classic tale of a family doomed to destruction through insanity.
MPAA:PG
Sunn Classic — *United Home Video; Classic Video Cinema Collector's Club*

Fall of the Roman Empire, The 1964
Drama
16810 153 mins C B, V P
Sophia Loren, Alec Guiness
The licentious son of Marcus Aurelius arranges for his father's murder and takes over as emperor.
Paramount; Samuel Bronston — *United Home Video*

Fallen Idol 1949
Drama
03858 92 mins B/W B, V P
Sir Ralph Richardson, Bobby Henrey, Michele Morgan, directed by Carol Reed
A young boy wrongly believes that a man he idolizes is guilty of murder, so the child tries to influence the police investigation of the crime. Screenplay by Graham Greene from his short story, "The Basement Room."
Selznick; British — *Prism; Budget Video; Cable Films; Western Film & Video Inc; Classic Video Cinema Collector's Club; Movie Buff Video*

Falling for the Stars 1985
Documentary/Filmmaking
70667 58 mins C B, V R, P
Richard Farnsworth, Harvey Perry, Polly Burson, Buddy Ebsen, Robert Duvall, Robert Conrad, Betty Thomas
This film shows both stars and their stunt-doubles talking about the perils involved in movie stunts. Using spectacular clips and insightful commentary, the program steps back from the camera to show familiar camaraderie of the stunt trade.
Walt Disney Productions — *Walt Disney Home Video*

Falling In Love 1984
Drama
Closed Captioned
70760 106 mins C B, V, LV R, P
Robert De Niro, Meryl Streep, Harvey Keitel, Dianne Wiest, George Martin, directed by Ulu Grosbard
Two married New Yorkers unexpectedly fall in love after a coincidental meeting at the Rizzoli Book Store.
MPAA:PG13
Paramount; Marvin Worth — *Paramount Home Video*

Falling in Love Again 1980
Comedy/Romance
64966 103 mins C B, V, CED P
Elliot Gould, Susannah York
A middle-aged dreamer and his realistic wife travel from Los Angeles to their hometown of New York, where the man is filled with nostalgia for his youth.
MPAA:PG
Steven Paul — *Embassy Home Entertainment*

Fallout 1968
Fantasy/Adventure
70688 52 mins C B, V P
Patrick McGoohan, Leo McKern, Alexis Kanner, Kenneth Griffith, directed by Patrick McGoohan
The final suspenseful episode of "The Prisoner" shows Number 6 in his final showdown with Numbers 1 and 2.
Associated TV Corp. — *MPI Home Video*

False Colors 1943
Western
80751 54 mins B/W B, V P
William Boyd, Robert Mitchum, Andy Clyde, Jimmy Rogers
Hopalong Cassidy unmasks a crook posing as a murdered ranch heir. A rare print with Portugese subtitles.
United Artists — *Video Yesteryear*

Falstaff 1983
Opera
72446 140 mins C LV P
Shakespeare's Falstaff is brought to life in this operatic version of the rogue's exploits.
BBC Television; Covert Garden Video Productions Ltd — *THORN EMI/HBO Video; Pioneer Artists*

Fame 1980
Musical-Drama
56751 133 mins C B, V, LV, CED P

Irene Cara, Barry Miller, Paul McCrane, Anne Meara, Joanna Merlin, directed by Alan Parker
Eight talented teenagers from New York's High School of Performing Arts struggle to perfect their skills while aspiring to stardom.
Academy Awards '80: Best Song ("Fame"); Best Original Score (Michael Gore). MPAA:R
MGM — *MGM/UA Home Video*

Fame Is the Spur **1947**
Drama
66374 116 mins B/W B, V P
Michael Redgrave, Rosamund John, Bernard Miles, directed by Roy Boulting
The story of Hamer Radshaw, British politician and socialist, from his youth to his days as an elder statesman.
Two Cities — *Movie Buff Video*

Family, The **1973**
Crime-Drama
72059 94 mins C B, V P
Charles Bronson, Jill Ireland, Telly Savalas, directed by Sergio Sollima
As a hit-man who resists joining the mob, Charles Bronson initiates an all-out war on the syndicate and its boss, played by Telly Savalas.
International Corp; Unidis and Fono Roma — *MPI Home Video*

Family Circus Christmas, A **1979**
Cartoons/Christmas
75468 30 mins C B, V P
Animated
Cartoonist Bil Keane animates the Family Circus at Christmas time.
Cullen Kasden Productions Ltd — *Family Home Entertainment*

Family Circus Easter, A **1980**
Cartoons/Holidays
75470 30 mins C B, V P
Animated
Cartoonist Bil Keane animates an Easter with the Family Circus.
Cullen Kasden Productions Ltd — *Family Home Entertainment*

Family Circus Valentine **1978**
Cartoons
76971 25 mins C B, V P
Animated
The Family Circus Kids learn a lesson in humility after making fun of baby PJ's Valentine's Day card for his parents.
Cullen-Kasdan Productions — *Family Home Entertainment*

Family Entertainment Playhouse, Vol. 2 **1979**
Literature
59644 106 mins C CED P
A compilation of stories for children: "The Ransom of Red Chief," based on O. Henry's famed short story about a banker's son who is kidnapped by bumbling conmen; "Mr. Gimme," about a boy who wants everything; "Shoeshine Girl," where a young girl finds that a first job is more than hard work; "Best Horse," about a strong-willed teenager determined to win a horse race.
Robert McDonald — *RCA VideoDiscs*

Family Game, The **1967**
Game show
80749 29 mins C B, V P
Hosted by Bob Barker
In "The Newlywed Game" fashion, mom and dad return from the isolation booth to guess what their children said about them in their absence.
Chuck Barris — *Video Yesteryear*

Family Life **1972**
Drama
59382 108 mins C B, V P
Sandy Ratcliff, Bill Dean, Grace Cave, directed by Ken Loach
A portrait of a 19-year-old girl in the midst of an identity crisis (Also titled, "Wednesday's Child).
Cinema Five — *RCA/Columbia Pictures Home Video*

Family Plot **1976**
Suspense
11579 120 mins C B, V P
Karen Black, Bruce Dern, Barbara Harris, William Devane, directed by Alfred Hitchcock
Alfred Hitchcock's last film; the search for a missing heir is undertaken by a phony psychic and her private eye boyfriend. Their search ends when they discover that the heir is dead—or is he?
MPAA:PG
Universal — *MCA Home Video*

Famous Generals **1964**
Biographical
78970 60 mins C B, V P
These two short films about the life and military career of George S. Patton are narrated by Ronald Reagan and President Dwight D. Eisenhower.
Maljack Productions — *MPI Home Video*

Famous T and A **1982**
Variety
59765 70 mins C B, V P
Ursula Andress, Brigitte Bardot, Jacqueline Bisset, Sybil Danning, Claudia Jennings,

Nastassia Kinski, Joan Prather, Laurie Walters, Edy Williams
An all-star collection of recognizable personalities who have displayed their celebrity skins for the camera.
Ken Dixon — *Wizard Video*

Fan, The 1981
Suspense
53931 95 mins C B, V, LV R, P
Lauren Bacall, Maureen Stapleton, James Garner, Hector Elizondo, directed by Edward Bianchi
A Broadway star is threatened by a lovestruck fan who feels he has been rejected by his idol.
MPAA:R
Robert Stigwood — *Paramount Home Video*

Fanciulla Del West, La 1983
Music-Performance/Opera
81487 135 mins C B, V R, P
Placido Domingo, Carol Neblett, Silvano Carroli
This is a production of the Puccini opera about the California gold rush performed at London's Royal Opera House in Covent Garden.
National Video Corporation Ltd. — *THORN EMI/HBO Video*

Fandango 1985
Comedy
81084 91 mins C B, V R, P
Judd Nelson, Kevin Costner, Sam Robards, Chuck Bush, Brian Cesak, directed by Kevin Reynolds
Five college roommates take a wild weekend drive across the Texas Badlands for one last fling before graduation. Available in VHS and Beta Hi-Fi Stereo.
MPAA:PG
Warner Bros., Amblin Entertainment — *Warner Home Video*

Fangface 1983
Cartoons
66573 60 mins C B, V P
Animated
The adventures of Fangface, the teenage werewolf, and his crime-fighting friends Biff, Kim and Puggsy are featured on this tape.
Ruby Spears — *Worldvision Home Video*

Fanny 1961
Drama
63450 150 mins C B, V R, P
Leslie Caron, Maurice Chevalier, Charles Boyer, Horst Buchholz
A young girl is left with child by an adventuresome sailor in the picturesque port of Marseilles. Part of the "A Night at the Movies" series, this tape simulates a 1961 movie evening, with a Tweety Pie cartoon, "The Last Hungry Cat," a newsreel and coming attractions for "Splendor in the Grass" and "The Roman Spring of Mrs. Stone."
Warner Bros — *Warner Home Video*

Fanny and Alexander 1983
Drama
64992 197 mins C B, V, LV P
Ewa Froling, Erland Josephson, directed by Ingmar Bergman
Set in a rural Swedish town in 1907, this film tells the story of one year in the lives of the Ekdahl family, focusing on the young children, Fanny and Alexander. In Swedish with English subtitles.
Academy Awards '83: Best Foreign Language Film Best Cinematography, Best Art Direction, Best Costume Design MPAA:R EL, SW
Cinematograph AB — *Embassy Home Entertainment*

Fantasies 1973
Drama
80134 81 mins C B, V P
Bo Derek, Peter Hooten, directed by John Derek
Two unrelated children raised as brother and sister find that their childhood affection changes to passionate love as they grow older.
John Derek — *CBS/Fox Video*

Fantastic Adventures of Unico, The 1984
Cartoons
Closed Captioned
73860 89 mins C B, V P
Animated
This is the animated story of a magical unicorn who can make everyone around him happy. With a purchase of the video cassette comes a Unico School Fun Kit. This program is available in Beta Hi-Fi.
AM Available
Shintaro Tsuji — *RCA/Columbia Pictures Home Video*

Fantastic Animation Festival 1977
Fantasy/Cartoons
05415 91 mins C B, V P
Animated
Fourteen award-winning animated shorts are combined into one feature-length program. Included are 'Closed Mondays," "The Last Cartoon Man," "French Windows," "Moonshadow," and "Cosmic Cartoon."
MPAA:PG
Crest Film Distributors — *Media Home Entertainment*

Fantastic Balloon Voyage, The 198?
Adventure
64949 100 mins C B, V R, P
Hugo Stiglitz, Jeff Cooper

Three men embark on a journey across the equator in a balloon, encountering countless adventures along the way.
MPAA:G
Unknown — *Video Gems*

Fantastic Planet 1973
Science fiction
57352 68 mins C B, V, FO P
Animated, directed by Rene Laloux
Mind-boggling imagery, vivid colors, and music tell the story of the "Revolt of the Oms"—survivors of Earth who are kept as pets.
Cannes Film Festival: Grand Prix.
French; Czech — *Video Yesteryear; Sheik Video; Discount Video Tapes*

Fantastic Voyage 1966
Science fiction
08425 100 mins C B, V P
Stephen Boyd, Edmond O'Brien, Raquel Welch, Arthur Kennedy, Donald Pleasence, Arthur O'Connell
A famous scientist, rescued from behind the Iron Curtain, is so severely wounded by enemy agents that surgery is impossible.
Academy Awards '66: Best Art Direction.
20th Century Fox; Saul David — *CBS/Fox Video*

Fantasy in Blue 197?
Drama
59547 81 mins C B, V P
The search for the solution to a sexual stalemate results in a couple's strange experimentation.
Frederick Fox — *Media Home Entertainment*

Fantasy Island 1976
Drama
80305 100 mins C B, V P
Ricardo Montalban, Bill Bixby, Sandra Dee, Peter Lawford, Carol Lynley
Three people fly out to an island paradise and get to live out their fantasies.
Spelling/Goldberg Productions — *Prism*

Far Cry From Home, A 197?
Drama
81051 87 mins C B, V P
Mary Ann Mcdonald, Richard Monette
A battered wife attempts to escape from her domineering husband before it's too late.
Anne Frank — *Trans World Entertainment*

Far Out Space Nuts, Vol. I 1975
Comedy
80768 48 mins C B, V P
Bob Denver, Chuck McCann
Two NASA ground crewmen accidentally launch a spacecraft propelling themselves into the vastness of outer space.
Sid and Marty Krofft — *Embassy Home Entertainment*

Far Pavilions, The 1984
Romance/Adventure
80331 108 mins C B, V R, P
Ben Cross, Amy Irving, Omar Sharif, Christopher Lee
A British Officer falls in love with an Indian princess during the second Afghan War.
HBO; Goldcrest — *THORN EMI/HBO Video*

Farewell, My Lovely 1975
Mystery
56456 95 mins C CED P
Robert Mitchum, Charlotte Rampling, Sylvia Miles, John Ireland
A remake of the 1944 Raymond Chandler mystery, "Murder, My Sweet," featuring private eye Phillip Marlowe hunting for an ex-convict's lost sweetheart.
MPAA:R
Avco Embassy — *RCA VideoDiscs*

Farewell to Arms, A 1932
Drama
11215 85 mins B/W B, V, FO P
Helen Hayes, Gary Cooper
The original film version of Ernest Hemingway's novel about a tragic love affair between an ambulance driver and a nurse during World War I.
Academy Awards '33: Best Cinematography; Best Sound Recording.
Paramount — *Video Yesteryear; Budget Video; Sheik Video; Cable Films; Video Connection; Discount Video Tapes; Western Film & Video Inc; Cinema Concepts; Classic Video Cinema Collector's Club; Prism; Hal Roach Studios; Kartes Productions*

Farmer's Daughter, The 1947
Comedy
64902 97 mins B/W B, V P
Loretta Young, Joseph Cotten, Ethel Barrymore, Charles Bickford, Rhys Williams, Rose Hobart
Young portrays Katrin Holmstrom, a Swedish farm girl who runs for Congress and captures the heart of a congressman along the way.
Academy Awards '47: Best Actress (Young).
RKO; David O. Selznick — *CBS/Fox Video*

Fast Break 1979
Comedy
64238 107 mins C B, V P
Gabe Kaplan, Harold Sylvester, Randee Heller
A deli clerk who is a compulsive basketball fan talks his way into a college coaching job.
MPAA:PG
Columbia — *RCA/Columbia Pictures Home Video*

 (For explanation of codes, see USE GUIDE and KEY)

Fast Company 1978
Adventure
73540 90 mins C B, V P
William Smith, John Saxon, Claudia Jennings, directed by David Cronenberg
This is the life story of champion race car driver Lonnie Johnson and his women, the money and the sponsors of drag races.
Michael Lebowitz; Peter O'Brian; Courtney Smith — *Admit One Video*

Fast Fists, The 198?
Martial arts
64959 90 mins C B, V P
Jimmy Wang Tu
A martial arts adventure.
Dragon Lady Productions — *Unicorn Video*

Fast Forward 1985
Musical
Closed Captioned
81428 110 mins C B, V P
John Scott Clough, Don Franklin, Tracy Silver, Cindy McGee, directed by Sidney Poitier
A group of eight teenagers learn how to deal with success and failure when they enter a national dance contest in New York City. Available in VHS Dolby Hi-Fi Stereo and Beta Hi-Fi Stereo.
MPAA:PG
Columbia; John Patrick Veitch — *RCA/Columbia Pictures Home Video*

Fast Lane Fever 1982
Drama
80854 94 mins C B, V P
A drag racer challenges a factory worker to a no-holds-barred race. Available in Dolby Hi Fi Stereo for both formats.
MPAA:R
Cannon Films — *MGM/UA Home Video*

Fast Times at Ridgemont High 1982
Comedy
63359 92 mins C B, V, LV, CED P
Sean Penn, Jennifer Jason Leigh, Judge Reinhold, Phoebe Cates, Ray Walston
Based on the bestselling book by Cameron Crowe, this is the story of teenagers' struggles with independence, success, sexuality, money, maturity and school.
MPAA:R
Universal — *MCA Home Video*

Fast Walking 1981
Drama
81068 116 mins C B, V P
James Woods, Kay Lenz, M. Emmet Walsh, Robert Hooks, Tim McIntire
A bigoted prison guard is offered fifty-thousand dollars to help a militant black leader escape from jail. Available in VHS and Beta Hi-Fi.
MPAA:R
Pickman Films; Lorimar Productions — *Key Video*

Fat Albert and the Cosby Kids 1978
Cartoons
69626 60 mins C B, V R, P
Animated, voice of Bill Cosby
In three separate cartoon episodes, Fat Albert and the Cosby Kids learn something important about life, growing up, and the people around them.
Filmation Studios — *THORN EMI/HBO Video*

Fat Albert and the Cosby Kids Cassette #2 1982
Cartoons
65747 23 mins C B, V R, P
Animated
This tape consists of two episodes, with Fat Albert teaching the viewer something important about life, the people around them and growing up.
Filmation — *THORN EMI/HBO Video*

Fat Albert and the Cosby Kids Cassette #3 1984
Cartoons
78393 60 mins C B, V R, P
Animated, voice of Bill Cosby
Fat Albert and the Cosby Kids are back with more cartoon fun and lessons about growing up.
Filmation Studios — *THORN EMI/HBO Video*

Fat Albert and the Cosby Kids, Cassette #4 1978
Cartoons
81182 60 mins C B, V R, P
Animated, voice of Bill Cosby
Fat Albert and the Cosby Kids are back to have some fun and teach everyone some important values in this collection of three episodes from the series. Available in Beta and VHS Hi-Fi.
Filmation — *THORN EMI/HBO Video*

Fatal Games 1984
Suspense
72904 88 mins C B, V P
Young female athletes are mysteriously disappearing at the Falcon Academy of Athletics and a crazed killer is responsible.
Christopher Mankeiwicz — *Media Home Entertainment*

Fatal Glass of Beer, The 1933
Comedy
59403 18 mins B/W B, V P, T

W.C. Fields, Rosemary Theby, George Chandler, Richard Cramer
Field's son returns to his home in the North Woods after serving a jail term.
Paramount — *Blackhawk Films*

Father 1967
Drama
47459 89 mins B/W B, V, FO P
After World War II, a Hungarian youth becomes obsessed with the facts surrounding his father's death at the hands of the enemy. Hungarian dialogue with English subtitles.
Hungarofilm — *Video Yesteryear*

Father Figure 1980
Drama
81155 94 mins C B, V P
Hal Linden, Timothy Hutton, Cassie Yates, Martha Scott, Jeremy Licht
When a divorced man attends his ex-wife's funeral, he discovers that he must take care of his estranged sons.
Finnegan Associates; Time-Life Films — *Lightning Video*

Father Goose 1964
Comedy
64538 116 mins C B, V P
Cary Grant, Leslie Caron, Trevor Howard
During World War II, a plane-spotter stationed on a remote Pacific isle finds himself stuck with a group of French refugee schoolgirls and their teacher.
Universal — *Republic Pictures Home Video*

Father Guido Sarducci Goes to College 1985
Comedy-Performance
70383 60 mins C B, V P
Don Novello
The satirical character of the title is shown performing at a campus concert. The tape also includes footage from the padre's campus tours, and a glimpse into Sarducci's secret Vatican film archives.
Steve Binder — *Vestron Video*

Father's Little Dividend 1951
Comedy
80739 82 mins B/W B, V P
Spencer Tracy, Joan Bennett, Elizabeth Taylor, Don Taylor, directed by Vincette Minnelli
A father fears that his peace and quiet is about to be interrupted when he finds that he'll soon be a grandfather.
MGM — *Hal Roach Studios; Discount Video Tapes*

Fatty and Mabel Adrift/Mabel, Fatty and the Law 1916
Comedy
64824 40 mins C B, V P, T
Fatty Arbuckle, Mabel Normand, Al St. John, Minta Durfee, Teddy the Dog
Fatty and Mabel have problems enjoying their wedded bliss in these two silent shorts, which have a newly recorded orchestral score on the soundtrack.
Triangle Film; Keystone Film — *Blackhawk Films*

Fatty's Tin-Type Tangle/Our Congressman 192?
Comedy
59410 44 mins B/W B, V P, T
Roscoe "Fatty" Arbuckle, Louise Fazenda, Edgar Kennedy, Frank Hayes, The Keystone Cops, Will Rogers, Jimmy Finlayson
In "Fatty's Tin-Type Tangle" (1915), Fatty and Louise are snapped by a traveling tintyper. In "Our congressman" (1924), Will Rogers offers an "expose" of political life.
Mack Sennett; Hal Roach — *Blackhawk Films*

Favorita, La 1952
Music-Performance
12823 80 mins B/W B, V, FO P
Sophia Loren, voices of Palmira Vitali Marini, Gino Sinimberghi, Paolo Silveri, Alfredo Colella
The great Italian opera with Sophia Loren in a supporting role. Narrated in English.
Unknown — *Video Yesteryear*

Favorite Black Exploitation Cartoons 194?
Cartoons/Film-History
66235 60 mins B/W B, V R, P
Animated
Black stereotype cartoons exhibiting the bigotry of the times they were produced.
Warner Bros et al — *Video City Productions*

Favorite Celebrity Cartoons 194?
Comedy/Cartoons
66236 60 mins B/W B, V R, P
Animated
Famous people, events and literature are seen in comic cartoon portrayals.
Warner Bros et al — *Video City Productions*

Favorite Racists Cartoons 194?
Film-History/Cartoons
66234 60 mins B/W B, V R, P
Animated
A compilation of banned racist cartoons.

Warner Bros et al — *Video City Productions*

Fear **1954**
Drama
66375 84 mins B/W B, V P
Ingrid Bergman, directed by Roberto Rossellini
A pitiless study of a woman's gradual disintegration from the daily pressures of life.
Roberto Rossellini — *Movie Buff Video*

Fear **1981**
Horror
77397 87 mins C B, V P
A movie company arrives at an isolated island to make a film and winds up involved in murder, witchcraft, and deadly passion.
Independent — *Wizard Video*

Fear City **1985**
Suspense
81480 93 mins C B, V R, P
Billy Dee Williams, Tom Berenger, Jack Scalia, Melanie Griffith, Rae Dawn Chong, Joe Santos, Rossano Brazzi, directed by Abel Ferrara
Two partners who own a talent agency are after the psychopath who is killing off their prized strippers.
MPAA:R
Zupnick Curties Enterprises — *THORN EMI/HBO Video*

Fear in the Night **1972**
Horror/Suspense
63342 82 mins C B, V R, P
Judy Gesson, Joan Collins, Ralph Bates, Peter Cushing
The young bride of a school master in a boys' prep school becomes convinced that her husband intends to kill her while the school is closed for the holidays.
Hammer Films — *THORN EMI/HBO Video*

Fear No Evil **1980**
Horror
64986 90 mins C B, V, CED P
Stefan Arngrim, Kathleen Rowe McAllen, Elizabeth Hoffman
A teenager who is the human embodiment of the demon Lucifer commits acts of demonic murder and destruction. His powers are challenged by an 18-year-old girl, who is the embodiment of the archangel Gabriel.
MPAA:R
Avco Embassy — *Embassy Home Entertainment*

Fearless Hyena **1979**
Martial arts
81521 97 mins C B, V P
Jackie Chan
A young man uses his martial arts skills to get revenge against the men who murdered his grandfather.
Alpha Film and Video — *All Seasons Entertainment*

Feelin' Up **1976**
Drama
80117 84 mins C B, V P
A young man sells all his possessions to come to New York in search of erotic adventures.
MPAA:R
Troma Productions — *Vestron Video*

Felix in Outer Space **1985**
Cartoons
76861 55 mins C B, V P
Animated
Felix and Poindexter travel through the galaxy to do battle with the evil duo of the Professor and Rock Bottom.
Felix the Cat Productions; Joseph Oriolo — *Media Home Entertainment*

Felix's Magic Bag of Tricks **1984**
Cartoons
72900 60 mins C B, V P
Animated
The professor is after Felix's Magic Bag of Tricks once again in this collection of cartoon favorites.
Felix the Cat Productions; Joe Oriolo — *Media Home Entertainment*

Female Impersonator Pageant, The **1985**
Variety
80821 74 mins C B, V, LV P
Hosted by Ruth Buzzi and Lyle Waggoner
Thirty of America's top female impersonators compete for the coveted title of Female Impersonator of the Year.
New World Video — *New World Video*

Fer-De-Lance **1974**
Suspense
80488 120 mins C B, V P
David Janssen, Hope Lange, Ivan Dixon, Jason Evers
A stricken submarine is trapped at the bottom of the sea, with a nest of deadly snakes crawling through the ship.
Leslie Stevens Productions — *Worldvision Home Video*

Ferry to Hong Kong **1959**
Adventure
59831 103 mins C B, V P
Curt Jurgens, Orson Welles, Sylvia Sims
A world-weary traveler comes aboard the "Fat Annie," a ship skippered by the pompous

Captain Hart. The two men clash, until an act of heroism brings them together.
George Maynard — *Embassy Home Entertainment*

Festival of Funnies, A 1980
Football
50089 48 mins C B, V, FO R, P
The lighter side of pro football. Wacky plays and zany players provide fun and entertainment in a new collection of NFL comedy action. Contains "Sym Funny," "The Jar 'Em and Daze 'Em Circus," "Believe It or Else," and other shorts.
NFL Films — *NFL Films Video; Champions on Film and Video*

Feud of the West 1935
Western
14656 60 mins B/W B, V P
Hoot Gibson
Old West disagreements settled with guns.
Grand National — *United Home Video; Video Connection; Discount Video Tapes*

Ffolkes 1980
Adventure
81201 99 mins C B, V P
Roger Moore, James Mason, Anthony Perkins, David Hedison, Michael Parks, directed by Andrew V. McLaglen
Rufus Excalibur ffolkes is in eccentric underwater expert who is called upon to stop a madman from blowing up an oil rig in the North Sea.
MPAA:PG
Universal; Elliott Kastner — *MCA Home Video*

Fiction Makers, The 1967
Adventure/Suspense
68230 102 mins C B, V P
Roger Moore, Sylvia Sims
Roger Moore stars as Templer, a sophisticated detective who is hired to help Amos Klein. Amos Klein is just an alias for a beautiful novelist who is being threatened by the underworld crime ring.
ATV/ITC — *CBS/Fox Video*

Fiddler on the Roof 1971
Musical
37524 184 mins C B, V, LV P
Topol, Norma Crane, Leonard Frey, Molly Picon, directed by Norman Jewison
This movie, based on the long-running Broadway musical, is the story of a poor Jewish farmer at the turn of the century in a small Ukranian village, his five dowry-less daughters, his lame horse, his wife, and his companionable relationship with God.
Academy Awards '71: Best Cinematography; Best Adaptation and Original Song Score; Best Sound. MPAA:G
United Artists — *CBS/Fox Video; RCA VideoDiscs*

Fiend 1983
Drama/Horror
70597 93 mins C B, V P
Don Liefert, Richard Nelson, Elaine White, George Stover
Longfellow, the small-town music teacher, feeds parasitically on his students to satisfy his supernatural hunger. His neighbor suspects some discord.
Unknown — *Prism*

Fiend Without a Face 19'5
Science fiction
59404 77 mins B/W B, V P, T
Marshall Thompson, Terence Kilburn
A scientist working on materialized thought produces monsters from his own id.
Producers Associates — *Blackhawk Films; Republic Pictures Home Video*

Fiendish Plot of Dr. Fu Manchu, The 1980
Comedy
52718 108 mins C B, V R, P
Peter Sellers, David Tomlinson, Sid Caesar
Peter Sellers' last film concerns Dr. Fu's desperate quest for the necessary ingredients for his secret life-preserving formula.
MPAA:PG
Orion Pictures — *Warner Home Video*

Fiesta 1941
Musical/Comedy
56908 44 mins C B, V, FO P
Anne Ayars, George Negrete, Armida
A girl comes from Mexico City to her father's hacienda where her old boyfriend awaits her return with a proposal of marriage. Full of authentic Mexican dances and music.
Hal Roach — *Video Yesteryear; Discount Video Tapes*

Fifth Avenue Girl 1939
Comedy
79683 83 mins B/W B, V P
Ginger Rogers, Walter Connolly, Tim Holt, James Ellison, directed by Gregory La Cava
An unhappy millionaire takes a poor homeless girl into his care to brighten his life.
RKO — *RKO HomeVideo*

Fifth Floor, The 1980
Mystery/Suspense
69304 90 mins C B, V P
Bo Hopkins, Dianne Hull, Patti D'Arbanville, Mel Ferrer
An alleged suicide victim struggles to prove her innocence and maintain her sanity within the

walls of an asylum. The only way out is to escape.
MPAA:R
Howard Avedis — *Media Home Entertainment*

55 Days at Peking 1963
Drama
16811 150 mins C B, V P
Charlton Heston, Ava Gardner
The Chinese people's resentment against the infiltration of Western ideas erupts into violence against missionaries and foreigners.
Samuel Bronston — *United Home Video*

$50,000 Reward 1925
Western
65226 49 mins B/W B, V P
Ken Maynard, Esther Ralston, Tarzan the Horse
Ken Maynard's first Western finds him being victimized by an unscrupulous banker who wants Ken's land deeds for property on which a new dam is being built.
Davis Distributing — *Blackhawk Films*

50 Years of Baseball Memories 1980
Baseball
33829 30 mins B/W B, V P
Babe Ruth, Lou Gehrig, Tris Speaker, Ty Cobb, Mel Ott, Joe DiMaggio, Warren Spahn, Mickey Mantle
A thrilling and nostalgic look at some of the most outstanding players in baseball history. Scenes of baseball's most memorable moments, dating back to the teens and twenties, are included.
Lou Fonseca — *Major League Baseball Productions*

Fight for Survival 1977
Martial arts
65327 101 mins C B, V P
Shang Kuan Ling-Feng
A young female aspirant of kung fu must recover sacred books that were stolen by disguised kung fu masters.
MPAA:R
Fann Jiann Gong; Lee Lin Lin — *CBS/Fox Video*

Fight for Your Life 1979
Drama
79332 89 mins C B, V P
William Sanderson, Robert Judd, Lela Small
Three criminals who narrowly escape from an accident take a hostage and head for the Canadian border.
Canada — *Monterey Home Video*

Fighter, The 1983
Drama
75454 96 mins C B, V P
Gregory Harrison, Glynnis O'Connor
An out of work millworker decides to become an amateur boxer against his wife's wishes.
King Features — *U.S.A. Home Video*

Fighting Black Kings 1976
Martial arts/Adventure
66129 90 mins C B, V R, P
Martial arts and karate masters appear in this tale of action.
MPAA:PG
Unknown — *Warner Home Video*

Fighting Caravans 1932
Western
11373 80 mins B/W B, V, FO P
Gary Cooper
Great outdoor adventure based on a story by Zane Grey.
Paramount — *Video Yesteryear*

Fighting Life 1980
Martial arts/Adventure
60513 90 mins C B, V P
The tale of two brothers who overcome immense physical and emotional handicaps and become vital members of society. The two stars of the film are both physically handicapped.
Unknown — *Master Arts Video*

Fighting Marines, The 1936
War-Drama
57353 69 mins B/W B, V, FO P
Jason Robards, Grant Withers, Ann Rutherford, Pat O'Malley
The U.S. Marines are trying to establish an airbase on Halfway Island in the Pacific, but are thwarted by the "Tiger Shark," a modern-day pirate. First appeared as a serial.
Mascot — *Video Yesteryear*

Fighting Seabees, The 1944
War-Drama
59092 100 mins B/W B, V P
John Wayne, Susan Hayward, Dennis O'Keefe
A salute to the Navy's construction corps, with the Duke as a tough foreman fighting the Japanese and Navy regulations.
Republic — *Republic Pictures Home Video*

Fille Mal Gardee, La 1981
Dance
59873 210 mins C LV P
Two young lovers must overcome a disapproving mother and differences in class in this performance by the Royal Ballet. In stereo.
Covent Garden Video — *Pioneer Artists*

Film Firsts 1960
Film-History
10155 51 mins B/W B, V P, T

Documentary-style look at early film segments from the "History of the Motion Picture" series. Includes the first attempt at science fiction with Georges Melies' "Trip to the Moon" (1902), and the first cartoon and western.
Killiam — *Blackhawk Films*

Filming the Big Thrills/Filming the Fantastic 193?
Documentary/Disasters
60054 20 mins B/W B, V P, T
"Big Thrills" includes scenes of the 1920's Florida hurricane, 1930's floods of the Mississippi and Ohio rivers, the tragedy of the Hindenburg, and more. "Fantastic" shows giant boys and midget girls, a library of books inside a walnut, a young man wearing a drape of honeybees and more.
20th Century Fox — *Blackhawk Films*

Final Assignment 1982
Suspense/Drama
80045 97 mins C B, V, CED P
Genevieve Bujold, Michael York, Burgess Meredith, Colleen Dewhurst.
A Canadian television reproter agrees to smuggle a dissident Soviet scientist's ill granddaughter out of Russia for treatment.
Persephone Productions — *Vestron Video*

Final Conflict, The 1981
Horror
58846 108 mins C B, V, CED P
Sam Neill, Lisa Harrow, Barnaby Holm, Rossano Brazzi
The third installment in the "Omen" series, concerning Damien, now 32, who has become the head of an international conglomerate.
MPAA:R
20th Century Fox — *CBS/Fox Video*

Final Countdown, The 1980
Drama
64893 92 mins C B, V, CED P
Kirk Douglas, Martin Sheen, Katherine Ross, James Farentino, Charles Durning
A nuclear warship is transported back in time to Pearl Harbor just hours before the fateful bombing that started World War II.
MPAA:PG
Bryna Company; Peter Vincent Douglas — *Vestron Video*

Final Exam 1981
Horror
66050 90 mins C B, V, CED P
Cecile Bagdadi, Joel Rice
A psychotic killer stalks college students during exam week.
MPAA:R
John Chambliss — *Embassy Home Entertainment*

Final Programme, The 1981
Science fiction/Fantasy
63328 85 mins C B, V R, P
Jon Finch, Jenny Runacre, Sterling Hayden, Patrick Magee
In this futuristic story, a man must rescue his sister and the world from their brother who holds a microfilmed plan for global domination, and himself from a bisexual computer programmer who wants to make him father to a new, all-purpose human being.
EMI Films Ltd — *THORN EMI/HBO Video*

Final Terror, The 1984
Horror
76776 90 mins C B, V, CED, LV P
Daryl Hannah, Rachel Ward, Adrian Zmed
A group of campers are stalked by a mad killer stalking the forest looking for innocent victims.
MPAA:R
Samuel Arkoff — *Vestron Video*

Finessing the King 1984
Mystery
80449 60 mins C B, V P
James Warwick, Francesca Annis
Private eyes Tommy and Tuppence follow a mysterious newspaper notice to a masked ball where a murder is about to occur. Based on the Agatha Christie Story.
London Weekend Television — *Pacific Arts Video*

Finian's Rainbow 1968
Musical
74204 141 mins C B, V, LV R, P
Fred Astaire, Petula Clark
This is the story of a leprechaun who is out to resteal a pot of gold taken by an Irishman and his daughter.
MPAA:G
Joseph Landon — *Warner Home Video*

Finnegan Begin Again 1985
Comedy
84182 112 mins C B, V R, P
Mary Tyler Moore, Robert Preston, Sam Waterston, Sylvia Sidney, directed by Joan Micklin Silver
An unusual set of circumstances helps to spark an unlikely romance between a middle-aged widow and a crotchety newspaper man.
HBO — *THORN EMI/HBO Video*

Fiona 1978
Drama
66199 82 mins C B, V P
Fiona Richmond, Victor Spinetti

A ravishing blonde exposes her legendary sexual appetite.
Assay Films Ltd — *U.S.A. Home Video*

Fire and Ice **1983**
Adventure/Fantasy
65463 81 mins C B, V P
Animated, directed by Ralph Bakshi
An animated adventure film that culminates in a tense battle between good and evil, surrounded by the mystical elements of the ancient past. In stereo VHS and Beta Hi-Fi.
MPAA:PG
Ralph Bakshi; Frank Frazetta; Producers Sales Organization — *RCA/Columbia Pictures Home Video*

Fire Over England **1937**
Drama
11232 81 mins B/W B, V, FO P
Flora Robson, Raymond Massey, Laurence Olivier, Vivien Leigh
Spain and Great Britain engage in war while Queen Elizabeth is torn between duty and personal desire.
United Artists, British — *Video Yesteryear; Budget Video; Sheik Video; Cable Films; Discount Video Tapes; Western Film & Video Inc; Kartes Productions*

Firebird 2015 A.D. **1981**
Science fiction
65717 97 mins C B, V P
Darren McGavin, Doug McClure
A tongue-in-cheek adventure involving a 21st century society where automobile use is banned because of extreme oil shortage.
MPAA:PG
Glen Ludlow — *Embassy Home Entertainment*

Firecracker **1971**
Martial arts/Adventure
63086 83 mins C B, V P
Jillian Kessner, Darby Hinton
A female Martial arts expert retaliates against the crooks who murdered her sister.
New World Pictures — *Monterey Home Video*

Firefox **1982**
Adventure
62886 136 mins C B, V, LV, CED R, P
Clint Eastwood, directed by Clint Eastwood
A special agent sneaks into the Soviet Union to steel a top-secret Russian warplane and fly it out of the country. VHS in stereo.
MPAA:PG
Warner Bros — *Warner Home Video*

Firemen's Ball **1968**
Comedy
66014 73 mins C B, V P
Josef Svet, directed by Milos Forman
A comedy about an honorary ball held for a retiring fire chief. Czech dialogue, subtitled in English.
CZ
Barrandov Film Studios — *RCA/Columbia Pictures Home Video*

Firepower **1979**
Drama/Suspense
69381 104 mins C B, V P
Sophia Loren, James Coburn, O.J. Simpson, Christoper F. Bean
A U.S. government agent is sent to the Caribbean to capture an American multimillionaire engaged in illegal activities and bring him to justice.
MPAA:R
Associated Film Distributors — *CBS/Fox Video*

Fires on the Plain **1959**
Drama
51948 105 mins B/W B, V P
Eiji Funakoshi, Osamu Takizawa, Mickey Custis, Asao Suno, directed by Kon Ichikawa
A group of men from the Japanese Army struggle to survive the perils of war in this disturbing drama. One soldier maintains his humanity while those around him resort to any crime. Japanese dialogue, English subtitles.
JA
Japanese — *Budget Video; Discount Video Tapes*

Fireside Theatre: Sergeant Sullivan Speaking **195?**
Comedy-Drama
66120 24 mins B/W B, V P, T
William Bendix, Joan Blondell, William Fawcett, Sarah Selby
From the TV series "Return Engagement," a romance blossoms over the telephone between a youthful widow and a police sergeant.
Procter and Gamble — *Blackhawk Films*

Firesign Theatre Presents Nick Danger in The Case of the Missing Yolk, The **1983**
Comedy
63389 60 mins C B, V, CED P
The Firesign Theatre (Phil Proctor, Phil Austin, Peter Bergman)
Firesign characters Nick Danger and Rocky Rococo are featured in this story of a truly interactive family who live through their television set.
VHD Programs; Pacific Arts Corporation — *Pacific Arts Video*

Firestarter 1984
Horror
70157 115 mins C B, V, LV P
Drew Barrymore, George C. Scott, Heather Locklear, David Keith, directed by Mark Lester
A C.I.A. like organization is after a little girl who has the ability to set anything on fire in this filmed adaptation of Stephen King's bestseller.
MPAA:R
Universal; Dino De Laurentis — *MCA Home Video*

First Aid: The Video Kit 1984
First aid
Closed Captioned
65755 95 mins C B, V P
This program provides the viewer with "eyes-on" experience of basic first aid principles that could make the difference in those crucial seconds when a crisis strikes.
CBS Fox Video — *CBS/Fox Video*

First Aid Video Book, The 1981
First aid
52768 40 mins C B, V P
Several emergencies, such as choking, poisoning, and shock are covered, with instructions on how to handle each emergency quickly.
Karl Video — *Karl/Lorimar Home Video*

First Blood 1982
Drama
64335 96 mins C B, V R, P
Sylvester Stallone, Richard Crenna, Brian Dennehy, Jack Starrett
Stallone portrays a former Green Beret survivor of Vietnam whose nightmares of wartime horrors are triggered by a wrongful arrest.
MPAA:R
Orion Picture — *THORN EMI/HBO Video; RCA VideoDiscs*

First Born 1984
Drama
77446 100 mins C B, V, LV R, P
Terri Garr, Peter Weller, Christopher Collet, directed by Michael Apted
A divorced woman's son tries to save her from her evil cocaine dealing boyfriend.
MPAA:PG13
Paramount Pictures — *Paramount Home Video*

First Deadly Sin, The 1980
Drama
72918 112 mins C B, V P
Frank Sinatra, Faye Dunaway, David Dukes, Brenda Vaccaro
A police lieutenant tracks down a homicidal killer in spite of family troubles which intrude on his work.
MPAA:R
Filmways; Artanis; Cinema Seven — *Warner Home Video*

First Family 1980
Comedy
58231 100 mins C B, V R, P
Bob Newhart, Madeline Kahn, Gilda Radner, Richard Benjamin, directed by Buck Henry
A biting satire of life in the White House for one President and his family.
MPAA:R
Warner Bros — *Warner Home Video*

First Love 1977
Romance
29765 92 mins C B, V R, P
William Katt, Susan Dey, John Heard, Beverly D'Angelo
A story of an idealistic college student who takes love, and especially making love, more seriously than the rest of his peers, including his girlfriend.
MPAA:R
Paramount — *Paramount Home Video*

First Love 1970
Drama
65158 90 mins C B, V P
John Moulder-Brown, Dominique Sanda, Maximilian Schell, Valentina Cortese, directed by Maximilian Schell
In the days before the 1917 Revolution, a young Russian boy meets and becomes infatuated with an impoverished princess. Years later, after war and strife have swept the country, he seeks her out again.
MPAA:R
Franz Seitz Filmproduktion; UMC Pictures — *United Home Video*

First Monday in October 1981
Comedy
58710 99 mins C B, V, LV R, P
Walter Matthau, Jill Clayburgh, Barnard Hughes, James Stephens, directed by Ronald Neame
A comedy concerning the first woman appointed to the Supreme Court and her colleague, a crusty but benign liberal judge.
MPAA:R
Paramount — *Paramount Home Video*

First National Kidisc, The 1981
Variety
57775 ? mins C LV P
Subtitled "1001 Things to Do on a Rainy Day," this one-sided interactive disc may occupy a child's attention up to 40 or 50 hours.
Bruce Seth Green — *Optical Programming Associates*

First Nudie Musical, The 1975
Comedy
12700 93 mins C B, V P
Cindy Williams, Stephan Nathan, Diana Canova, Bruce Kimmel
Producer attempts success by staging a nudie musical in 1930's style.
MPAA:R
Jack Reeves — *Media Home Entertainment; King of Video; Budget Video*

First Spaceship on Venus, The 1964
Science fiction
11717 78 mins C B, V P
Yoko Tani
Eight scientists set out for Venus and find the remains of a civilization far in advance of Earth's.
Crown International — *United Home Video*

First Time, The 1982
Comedy
66023 96 mins C B, V R, P
A comedy about a college student who can't quite succeed with women.
Sam Irvin — *THORN EMI/HBO Video*

First Turn On, The 1983
Adolescence/Exploitation
70691 84 mins C B, V P
Sheila Kennedy, Michael Sanville, Googy Gress, Jenny Johnson, Heide Basset, directed by Michael Hertz and S. Weil
Not to be confused with "The Thomas Edison Story," this film follows the adventures of five young campers who decide to die happy when an avalanche leaves them un-rescueably trapped in a cave. A longer unrated version is available.
MPAA:R
Troma — *Lightning Video*

Fish Hawk 1979
Adventure
72903 95 mins C B, V P
Will Sampson
When an alcoholic Indian, Fish Hawk, meets a young boy in the forest, and they strike up a friendship.
MPAA:G
Edgar J. Scherick; Stanley Chase — *Media Home Entertainment*

Fish that Saved Pittsburgh, The 1979
Comedy
80889 104 mins C B, V P
Jonathan Winters, Stockard Channing, Flip Wilson, Julius Erving, Meadowlark Lemon
A floundering basketball team hires an astrologer to try and change their luck.
MPAA:PG
Lorima Productions — *Karl/Lorimar Home Video*

Fishing U.S.A. 1969
Fishing
59072 105 mins C B, V R, P
R. Vernon "Gadabout" Gaddis
Outdoor scenes from Maine to California, including bass fighting on the line, are featured in this program about fishing in America.
GG Communications — *Video Gems*

Fist 1979
Adventure/Martial arts
59085 84 mins C B, V P
Richard Lawson, Annazette Chase, Dabney Coleman
A street fighter battles his way through the urban jungle seeking personal freedom and revenge.
MPAA:R
Larrabure Kaye — *HarmonyVision*

F.I.S.T. 1978
Drama
53451 145 mins C B, V, CED P
Sylvester Stallone, Rod Steiger, Peter Boyle, Melinda Dillon, Tony Lo Bianco, Kevin Conway, Cassie Yates, directed by Norman Jewison
The story of an idealistic labor union organizer who works his way to the top of the union by accepting mob favors which cost him his integrity.
MPAA:R
United Artists; Norman Jewison — *CBS/Fox Video*

Fist of Fear—Touch of Death 1980
Adventure
52858 90 mins C B, V P
Bruce Lee, Fred Williamson, Lee Van Cleef
The three greatest martial arts masters star in this kung-fu action adventure film. A compilation of clips from Bruce Lee's films.
MPAA:R
Aquarius Releasing — *Wizard Video*

Fist of Vengeance 197?
Martial arts/Adventure
47703 90 mins C B, V P
Shoji Karada, Lu Pi Chen
The East Asia Society hires a Samurai to kill a young Chinese officer.
Sung Kuang Lung — *Master Arts Video*

Fistful of Dollars, A 1967
Western
58825 96 mins C B, V P
Clint Eastwood, Gian Maria Volonte, Marianne Koch, directed by Sergio Leone

An avenging stranger gets involved in a feud between two powerful families.
United Artists; Harry Colombo; George Papi — *CBS/Fox Video; RCA VideoDiscs*

Fists of Fury **1973**
Adventure/Martial arts
55833 102 mins C B, V P
Bruce Lee, Maria Yi
Bruce Lee stars in this violent Kung Fu action adventure in which Lee must defend his honor and break a solemn vow to avoid fighting.
MPAA:R
National General Pictures — *CBS/Fox Video; Video City Productions; Master Arts Video; Discount Video Tapes; Spotlite Video*

Fists of Fury II **1980**
Adventure/Martial arts
44340 90 mins C B, V R, P
Bruce Li, Ho Chung Do, Shum Shim Po
This story centers around character Chen Shan (Bruce Li) and his efforts to survive the Organizations' onslaughts to kill him. He escapes their perilous plots only to return to battle against them after they had killed his mother for her inability to disclose Chen's hiding place. Finally Chen defeats the evil Organization himself.
MPAA:R
Four Seas Films — *Video Gems*

Fitzcarraldo **1982**
Drama
66124 150 mins C B, V R, P
Klaus Kinski, Claudia Cardinale, directed by Werner Herzog
The epic story of a charismatic Irishman's impossible quest to build an opera house in the middle of the Amazon jungles.
Cannes Film Festival '82: Best Director.
MPAA:PG
New World Pictures — *Warner Home Video*

Five Came Back **1939**
Adventure
76837 93 mins B/W B, V P
Lucille Ball, Chester Morris, John Carradine, Wendy Barrie, Kent Taylor, directed by John Farrow
When a plane with twelve passengers crashes in the South American jungle, extenuating circumstances cuts the number of survivors down to five.
RKO — *RKO HomeVideo*

Five Days One Summer **1982**
Romance
66123 108 mins C B, V R, P
Sean Connery, Betsy Brantley, Lambert Wilson, directed by Fred Zinnemann
The story of a haunting and obsessive love affair between a married Scottish doctor and a younger woman.
MPAA:PG
Ladd Company — *Warner Home Video*

Five Mile Creek—Volume 5 **1985**
Adventure
77533 96 mins C B, V R, P
An American woman wants to return home as settlers begin to put down roots in Australia's outback.
Walt Disney Productions — *Walt Disney Home Video*

Five Mile Creek—Volume 6 **1985**
Adventure
70668 96 mins C B, V P
Jack Taylor, Con Madigan, Jay Kerr, Liz Burch, Gus Mercurio, Rod Mullinar, Louise Caire Clark, Michael Caton, Priscilla Weems
This tape features two more episodes from Australia. First, Jack and Con must enter the boxing ring in order to win a contract for their stagecoach line in "The Prize." Then, in "Tricks of the Trade," Kate needs to find a husband so that she can adopt Sam.
Walt Disney Productions — *Walt Disney Home Video*

Five Mile Creek, Volume 1 **1984**
Adventure
72787 94 mins C B, V P
The Australian frontier serves as backscape for this story about a group of American and Australian settlers who make an inspiring drive to establish a stage coach line on the route to Australia's gold fields.
Walt Disney Productions — *Walt Disney Home Video*

Five Mile Creek Volume 2 **1984**
Adventure
72797 111 mins C B, V P
Treacherous busrangers and an aristocratic entourage threaten the pioneer heroes of the Australian frontier.
Walt Disney Productions — *Walt Disney Home Video*

Five Mile Creek—Volume 3 **1984**
Adventure
79226 100 mins C B, V R, P
Rod Mullinar, Jay Kerr, Louise Claire Clark
Two men who are looking to expand their stagecoach line in Australia encounter opposition from a local squatter.
Walt Disney Productions — *Walt Disney Home Video*

Five Mile Creek—Volume 4 **1985**
Drama
20355 111 mins C B, V R, P
A collection of two episodes from the series: Maggie Scott finds her lost husband in "Gold Fever" and a woman in labor arrives at the outpost in "Annie."
AM Available
Walt Disney Productions — *Walt Disney Home Video*

Five Weeks in a Balloon **1962**
Adventure
81512 101 mins C B, V P
Fabian, Peter Lorre, Red Buttons, Sir Cedric Hardwicke, Barbara Eden, directed by Irwin Allen
This is an adaptation of the Jules Verne novel about a British expedition that encounters many adventures on their balloon trek to Africa. Available in VHS and Beta Hi-Fi.
20th Century Fox — *Playhouse Video*

Fixx: Live in the USA, The **1984**
Music-Performance
81202 58 mins C B, V P
New wave rockers The Fixx, perform such hits as "Saved by Zero," "Deeper and Deeper" and "One Thing Leads to Another" in this concert video. Available in Hi-Fi stereo for both formats.
Loading Dock Film and Video — *MCA Home Video*

Flaming Frontiers **1938**
Western/Serials
08872 300 mins B/W B, V, 3/4U P
Johnny Mack Brown, Eleanor Hanson, Ralph Bowman
A frontier scout matches wits against gold mine thieves. In fifteen episodes.
Universal — *Video Connection; Video Yesteryear; Budget Video; Discount Video Tapes*

Flaming Star **1960**
Drama
64931 92 mins C B, V P
Elvis Presley, Dolores del Rio, Barbara Eden, Steve Forrest, John McIntire
Set in 1870's Texas, a mixed Indian and white family is caught in the midst of an Indian uprising. A half-Indian youth must choose which side he is on.
20th Century Fox — *Key Video; CBS/Fox Video (disc only)*

Flamingo Kid, The **1984**
Comedy
76764 100 mins C B, V, CED P
Matt Dillon, Richard Crenna, Hector Elizondo, Jessica Walter, directed by Garry Marshall
A Brooklyn teenager finds out about life and love when he gets a summer job at a fancy beach club on Long Island.
MPAA:PG13
Michael Phillips, Twentieth Century Fox — *Vestron Video*

Flash Gordon **1980**
Science fiction
56870 111 mins C B, V, LV, CED P
Sam J. Jones, Melody Anderson, Topol, Max von Sydow
Dino DeLaurentiis-produced version of the adventures of Flash Gordon in outer space. This time, Flash and Dale Arden are forced by Dr. Zarkov to accompany him on a mission to far-off Mongo, where Ming the Merciless is threatening the destruction of Earth. Music by Queen.
MPAA:PG
Universal, Dino DeLaurentiis — *MCA Home Video*

Flash Gordon—Space Adventure, Vol 1 **1979**
Science fiction/Cartoons
81186 58 mins C B, V P
Animated
Join Flash Gordon, Dale Arden and Dr. Zarkov as they encounter all kinds of adventures while traveling through outer space.
Don Christensen — *Media Home Entertainment*

Flash Gordon—Space Adventure, Vol 2 **1979**
Science fiction/Cartoons
81187 59 mins C B, V P
Animated
Flash Gordon returns to battle with Ming The Merciless in this collection of adventures.
Don Christensen — *Media Home Entertainment*

Flash Gordon Conquers the Universe **1940**
Science fiction/Serials
08629 240 mins B/W B, V P
Buster Crabbe, Carol Hughes, Charles Middleton, Frank Shannon
Ravaging plague strikes the earth and Flash Gordon undertakes to stop it. A serial in twelve chapters.
Universal — *Video Connection; Cable Films; Video Yesteryear; Discount Video Tapes*

Flash Gordon: Rocketship **1936**
Science fiction
13694 75 mins B/W B, V, FO P
Buster Crabbe, Charles Middleton

Flash Gordon saves Earth from a planet that almost collides with it.
Universal — *Video Yesteryear; Sheik Video; Cable Films; Cinema Concepts*

Flashdance **1983**
Musical-Drama
Closed Captioned
65096 96 mins C B, V, LV, CED R, P
Jennifer Beals, Michael Nouri, Belinda Bauer, Lilia Skala
A young female welder dreams of becoming a professional ballet dancer, trying out her original dance routines every night at a local bar. Title song sung by Irene Cara. In stereo.
MPAA:R
Paramount — *Paramount Home Video*

Flashpoint **1984**
Suspense
77163 95 mins C B, V R, P
Treat Williams, Kris Kristofferson, Tess Harper, directed by William Tannen
A pair of Texas border patrolmen discover an abandoned jeep that contains evidence of a conspiracy.
MPAA:R
Tri-Star Pictures — *THORN EMI/HBO Video*

Flashpoint Africa **1984**
Adventure
79890 99 mins C B, V P
Trevor Howard, Gayle Hunnicutt, James Faulkner
When a news team follows a terrorist group's activities it winds up being a power struggle with terrifying consequences.
Barrie Saint Clair — *VCL Home Video*

Flask of Fields, A **193?**
Comedy
58654 61 mins B/W B, V, FO P
W.C. Fields, Babe Kane, Elsie Cavanna, Bud Jamison, Rosemary Theby
Three classic Fields shorts: "The Golf Specialist" (1930), in which J. Effington Bellweather finds himself teaching a lovely young lady how to play the game; "The Fatal Glass of Beer" (1933); and "The Dentist" (1932), in which Fields tackles a room filled with patients.
RKO; Paramount — *Video Yesteryear*

Flat Top **1952**
War-Drama
81421 85 mins C B, V P
Sterling Hayden, Richard Carlson, Keith Larsen, John Bromfield
This is the story of how the Navy fighter pilots were trained aboard "Flat Top" during World War II.
Monogram — *Republic Pictures Home Video*

Flavors of China **1979**
Cookery
38956 119 mins C B, V R, P
Master chef Titus Chan guides the viewer through classic Chinese recipes that can be prepared at home. Chinese cooking utensils are explained, and basic techniques of cooking such as stir frying, steaming, poaching, and deep frying are presented. Contains instructions on such dishes as lemon chicken, beef with oyster sauce, chicken with cashews, sweet and sour pork, and many others.
AM Available
Valley Isle Productions — *Warner Home Video*

Fledermaus, Volume I, Die **1984**
Opera
80052 90 mins C B, V R, P
Kirite Kanawa, Hermann Prey, Charles Aznavour, Benjamin Luxon
Placido Domingo conducts this production of Johann Strauss' opera taped at the Royal Opera House in Covent Garden.
BBC Television; Arts International — *THORN EMI/HBO Video*

Fledermaus Volume II, Die **1984**
Opera
80053 90 mins C B, V R, P
Kirite Kanawa, Hermann Prey, Charles Aznaibur, Benjamin Luxon
Placido Domingo makes his British conducting debut in this production of Johann Strauss' opera taped at the Royal Opera House in Covent Garden.
BBC Television; Arts International — *THORN EMI/HBO Video*

Fleetwood Mac, Documentary and Live Concert **1980**
Music-Performance
54687 60 mins C B, V R, P
Fleetwood Mac
Both interviews with members of Fleetwood Mac and footage from their recent tour are featured in this program. Musical selections include "Sarah," "Sisters of the Moon," "Go Your Own Way," "Angel," and "Tusk."
Warner Bros — *Warner Home Video; RCA VideoDiscs; MCA Home Video (disc only)*

Fleetwood Mac in Concert—Mirage Tour 1982 **1982**
Music-Performance
64240 80 mins C B, V P

Filmed during Fleetwood Mac's 1982 tour, this concert tape features such songs as "Rhiannon," "Gypsy," "Go Your Own Way," and "Songbird." In Dolby stereo.
Marty Callner — *RCA/Columbia Pictures Home Video; RCA VideoDiscs*

Flesh Gordon **1974**
Satire
55213 70 mins C B, V P
Jason Williams, Suzanne Fields
An adult super-spoof of science fiction films. The Earth is thrown into carnal chaos by a mysterious sex ray, and Flesh travels to the planet Porno to save the earth from an evil emperor.
MPAA:X EL, SP
Graffitti Productions Corp — *Media Home Entertainment*

Fleshburn **1984**
Adventure
80273 91 mins C B, V P
An Indian Vietnam War veteran escapes from a mental institution to get revenge on the four psychiatrists who committed him.
MPAA:R
Beth Gage — *Media Home Entertainment*

Flight from Vienna **1958**
Drama
69566 54 mins B/W B, V, FO P
Theodore Bikel, John Bentley, Donald Gray
A high-ranking Hungarian security officer, disenchanted with communism, stages a daring escape from his country. In Vienna, he asks the British for political asylum, but is sent back to Hungary to help a scientist escape.
E J Fancey — *Video Yesteryear*

Flight of Dragons **19??**
Fantasy
69613 98 mins C B, V P
Animated, voices of John Ritter, Victor Buono, James Earl Jones
This animated tale takes place between the Age of Magic and the Age of Science, in a century when dragons ruled the skies.
Rankin Bass — *Children's Video Library*

Flight of the Eagle, The **1982**
Adventure
79339 115 mins C B, V P
Max von Sydow, Goran Stangertz, Clement Harari, Sverre Anker, directed by Jan Troell
A Swedish man and two friends attempt to fly from Sweden to the North Pole in a hydrogen balloon. With English subtitles.
SW
Goran Setterberg — *Active Home Video*

Flight to Mars **1952**
Science fiction
44355 72 mins C B, V, 3/4U P
Cameron Mitchell, Marquerite Chapman, Arthur Franz
An expedition crash lands on the red planet and discovers an advanced underground society. Includes previews of coming attractions from classic science fiction films.
Monogram, Walter Mirisch — *Nostalgia Merchant*

Flights and Flyers **193?**
Documentary/Biographical
50635 30 mins B/W B, V P, T
Three Fox-Movietone newsreels covering stories about famous flyers such as Will Rogers, Amelia Earhart, Howard Hughes, Eddie Rickenbacker, and Wrong Way Corrigan, to name a few.
Blackhawk; Movietone — *Blackhawk Films*

Flights and Flyers: Amelia Earhart **19??**
Documentary/Biographical
50632 11 mins B/W B, V P, T
The flying exploits and heroics of Amelia Earhart are chronicled in this program. The determination of a woman who made both cross-country and trans-Atlantic flights, and vowed to follow her failures with successes, is emphasized.
Blackhawk; Movietone — *Blackhawk Films*

Flim-Flam Man, The **1967**
Comedy
Closed Captioned
81514 104 mins C B, V P
George C. Scott, Michael Sarrazin, Slim Pickens, Sue Lyon, Jack Albertson, Harry Morgan, directed by Irvin Kershner
A con man teams up with an army deserter to teach him the fine art of flim-flamming as they travel through small southern towns.
20th Century Fox — *Playhouse Video*

Flintstones, The **1960**
Cartoons
77156 50 mins C B, V P
Animated, voices of Alan Reed, Mel Blanc, Jean Vander Pyl, Bea Benaderet
The foibles of two Stone Age families The Flintstones and the Rubbles are chronicled in these two episodes of this classic series.
Hanna-Barbera — *Worldvision Home Video*

Flintstones Meet Rockula and Frankenstone, The **1980**
Cartoons
77154 52 mins C B, V P
Animated

Fred, Wilma, Barney and Betty win a trip to Rocksylvania and meet up with Count Rockula and his monster, Frankenstone.
Hanna-Barbera — *Worldvision Home Video*

Flock of Seagulls, A 1983
Music-Performance
76669 13 mins C B, V P
This program presents the British band performing "Wishing (If I Had a Photograph of You)," "Nightmares" and "I Ran."
Zomba Productions Inc — *Sony Corporation of America*

Flood of Fury 1952
Adventure
10034 25 mins B/W B, V P, T
Kirby Grant
Town is flooded by ravaging rain, escaped prisoners rob bank, and Penny and Clipper are kidnapped. Sky King attempts to help. From the TV series "Sky King."
CBS — *Blackhawk Films*

Florida Connection, The 1974
Adventure
47673 90 mins C B, V P
An action thriller set in the Florida Swamps with a collection of villains.
Samuel Hyman — *Unicorn Video*

Flower Angel, The 1980
Cartoons
53664 46 mins C B, V P
Animated
The Flower Angel and her friends, a white kitty and a lovable brown dog, are searching for the Flower of Seven Colors. In their travels they help a lonely old man and his beautiful daughter find the love they have for each other.
EL, SP
Ziv Intl — *Family Home Entertainment*

Flower Out of Place, A 1974
Music
05413 50 mins C B, V P
Concert performances by Johnny Cash, Roy Clark, Linda Ronstadt, and Foster Brooks.
Independent — *Media Home Entertainment*

Fly, The 1958
Science fiction
80732 94 mins C B, V P
Vincent Price, David Hedison, Herbert Marshall, Patricia Owens, directed by Kurt Neumann
During an experiment with atomic energy, a scientist accidentally transforms his atomic structure onto a common housefly. Available in VHS and Beta Hi-Fi Stereo.
20th Century Fox — *Key Video*

Flying Blind 1941
Drama
66376 69 mins B/W B, V P
Richard Arlen, Jean Parker, Marie Wilson
Foreign agents are thwarted in their attempt to steal a vital air defense secret.
Paramount — *Movie Buff Video; Discount Video Tapes*

Flying Deuces, The 1939
Comedy
08577 70 mins B/W B, V P
Stan Laurel, Oliver Hardy, Jean Parker, Reginald Gardner
Laurel and Hardy join the Foreign Legion.
RKO — *Prism; Hal Roach Studios; Kartes Productions; Republic Pictures Home Video; Nostalgia Merchant; United Home Video; VCII; Budget Video; Cable Films; Video Yesteryear; Discount Video Tapes; Sheik Video; Video Connection; Vestron Video; Classic Video Cinema Collector's Club*

Flying Down To Rio 1933
Musical
00268 89 mins B/W B, V, 3/4U P
Fred Astaire, Ginger Rogers
First Astaire-Rogers musical, featuring Vincent Youmans' score, including "The Carioca."
RKO; Merian C Cooper — *Nostalgia Merchant*

Flying Leathernecks 1951
War-Drama
29343 102 mins C B, V, 3/4U P
John Wayne, Robert Ryan, Janis Carter
A tough squadron leader wins the admiration and devotion of his fliers. This memorable World War II film deals with war in human terms.
RKO — *Nostalgia Merchant; VidAmerica*

Flying Tigers 1942
War-Drama
81425 101 mins B/W B, V P
John Wayne, Paul Kelly, John Carroll, Anna Lee
A squadron leader and his pal are both vying for the affections of a pretty nurse while fighting the Japanese during World War II.
Republic Pictures — *Republic Pictures Home Video*

Fog, The 1978
Horror
56460 91 mins C B, V, LV, CED P
Hal Holbrook, Adrienne Barbeau, Jamie Lee Curtis, Janet Leigh, John Houseman, directed by John Carpenter
John Carpenter's contemporary tale of supernatural horror concerns a ghostly fog that reappears to fulfill a curse.
MPAA:R

Avco Embassy, Debra Hill — *Embassy Home Entertainment; RCA VideoDiscs*

Follow Me, Boys! 1966
Comedy
65636 120 mins C B, V R, P
Fred MacMurray, Vera Miles, Lillian Gish, Charles Ruggles, Elliott Reid, Kurt Russell, Luana Patten, Ken Murray
After one year too many on the road with a ramshackle jazz band, a simple man decides to put down roots and enjoy the quiet life—a life that is suddenly just a memory when he volunteers to head a troop of high-spirited youngsters.
Buena Vista — *Walt Disney Home Video*

Follow the Fleet 1936
Musical
01611 110 mins B/W B, V, 3/4U P
Fred Astaire, Ginger Rogers, Randolph Scott, directed by Mark Sandrich
Set to Irving Berlin's score, song and dance man joins Navy with pal and meets two sisters in need of help. Look for Betty Grable, Lucille Ball, and Tony Martin in minor roles.
RKO — *Nostalgia Merchant*

Food of the Gods, The 1976
Horror
80696 88 mins C B, V P
Marjoe Gortner, Pamela Franklin, Ralph Meeker, Ida Lupino, Jon Cypher
A farmer on a secluded island creates a race of giant rats who crave for human flesh, blood, bones, organs and other assorted body parts.
MPAA:PG
American International — *Vestron Video*

Foolin' Around 1980
Comedy/Romance
64978 101 mins C B, V, CED P
Gary Busey, Annette O'Toole, Eddie Albert, Tony Randall, Cloris Leachman
An innocent Oklahoma farm boy arrives at college and falls in love with a beautiful heiress. He will stop at nothing to win her overincluding crashing her lavish wedding ceremony.
MPAA:PG
Columbia — *Embassy Home Entertainment*

Foolin' Around 1980
Comedy
80388 101 mins C B, V P
Gary Busey, Annette O'Toole, Eddie Albert, Tony Randall, Cloris Leachman
A young man falls in love with a college student who is conducting psychological experiments at the University they both attend.
MPAA:PG
Columbia Pictures — *Embassy Home Entertainment*

Foolish Wives 1922
Drama
47821 107 mins B/W B, V P, T
Erich Von Stroheim, Mae Busch, Maud George, Cesare Gravina, directed by Erich Von Stroheim
A reconstruction of Von Stroheim's classic depicting the confused milieu of post-war Europe traced through the actions of a bogus count and his seductive, corrupt ways. This version is as close as possible to the original film.
Universal; Carl Laemmle — *Blackhawk Films*

Football Follies 1980
Football
45125 30 mins C B, V, FO R, P
The original chaos and comedy collection of wild and wacky events that sometimes happen on the one-hundred yard stage.
NFL Films — *NFL Films Video; Champions on Film and Video*

Football Follies/Highlights of Super Bowl V 1980
Football
56790 46 mins C B, V P
A collection of hilarious snafus by the great pro football players, plus highlights of the Cowboys and Colts "Blooper Bowl."
NFL Films — *VidAmerica*

Footlight Frenzy 1984
Satire
78665 110 mins C B, V P
The Law Moan Spectacular comedy troupe are at it again as they perform a benefit play where everything goes wrong.
RKO — *RKO HomeVideo*

Footlight Parade 1933
Musical
73983 104 mins B/W B, V P
Ruby Keeler, James Cagney, Dick Powell, Joan Blondell, directed by Lloyd Bacon
Despite great difficulty a producer manages to get the show on in the Busby Berkeley choreographed musical that features a 20,000 gallon aquacade and the song "By A Waterfall."
Warner Bros — *Key Video*

Footloose 1984
Musical-Drama
75808 106 mins C B, V, LV, CED R, P
Kevin Bacon, Lori Singer, music by Kenny Loggins
A teenage boy tries to bring rock music to a small, religious town.
MPAA:PG
Paramount — *Paramount Home Video*

(For explanation of codes, see USE GUIDE and KEY)

For a Few Dollars More 1967
Western
64705 125 mins C CED P
Clint Eastwood, Lee Van Cleef
A band of cutthroats has a sadistic leader who is pursued by two bounty hunters. When the two offer to help the outlaws crack a stolen safe, the vicious leader is shot. Sequel to "A Fistful of Dollars."
MPAA:PG
United Artists — *CBS/Fox Video; RCA VideoDiscs*

For Ladies Only 1981
Drama
65312 94 mins C B, V P
Gregory Harrison, Lee Grant
Gregory Harrison is a struggling, unemployed actor by day and an exotic male stripper by night.
Viacom International — *U.S.A. Home Video*

For Love of Ivy 1968
Comedy/Drama
47148 102 mins C B, V P
Sidney Poitier, Abbey Lincoln, Beau Bridges, Carroll O'Connor, directed by Daniel Mann
When the black maid of a wealthy family decides to quit, the family tries to find a boyfriend for her so she will stay on. Based on a story by Sidney Poitier.
MPAA:PG
Cinerama Releasing; Palomar — *CBS/Fox Video*

For Pete's Sake 1974
Comedy
44833 90 mins C B, V P
Barbra Streisand, Michael Sarrazin, Estelle Parsons, William Redfield, Molly Picon
Topsy-turvy comedy about a woman who goes to great lengths for her husband.
MPAA:PG
Martin Erlichman, Columbia — *RCA/Columbia Pictures Home Video*

For the Love of Benji 1977
Comedy-Drama
49627 85 mins C B, V, CED P
Benji, Patsy Garrett, Cynthia Smith, Allen Finzat, Ed Nelson, directed by Joe Camp
Benji and his companion Tiffany join their human friends for a Greek vacation. But Benji is kidnapped to be used as a messenger for a secret code. He escapes, and the case is on.
MPAA:G
Mulberry Square Prods; Joe Camp — *Vestron Video*

For the Love of Benji 1983
Animals
75614 85 mins C B, V P
Benji battles an international spy ring.
Mulberry Square Productions — *Children's Video Library*

For the Love of It 1980
Comedy
66616 98 mins C B, V P
Deborah Raffin, Jeff Conaway, Don Rickles, Tom Bosley, Henry Gibson, William Christopher
A young couple steal some top-secret Soviet documents and become the target of bumbling FBI agents.
Charles Fries Productions — *U.S.A. Home Video*

For Your Eyes Only 1981
Adventure
58845 127 mins C B, V, LV, CED P
Roger Moore, Carole Bouquet, Lynn-Holly Johnson
Another James Bond epic, in which 007 is called upon to keep the Soviets from getting hold of the valuable instrument aboard a sunken British spy ship.
MPAA:PG
United Artists — *CBS/Fox Video; MGM/UA Home Video (disc only)*

Forbidden Planet 1956
Science fiction
55210 98 mins C B, V, LV, CED P
Walter Pidgeon, Anne Francis, Leslie Nielsen, directed by Fred McLeod Wilcox
In 2200 A.D., a space cruiser visits the planet Altair Four to uncover the fate of a previous mission of space colonists, and discovers a former civilization.
MGM; Nicholas Nayfack — *MGM/UA Home Video*

Forbidden World 1982
Science fiction/Horror
65715 82 mins C B, V P
Jesse Vint, Dawn Dunlap
The lives of a genetic research team become threatened by the very life form they helped to create: a man-eating organism capable of changing its genetic structure as it grows and matures.
MPAA:R
Roger Corman — *Embassy Home Entertainment*

Forbidden Zone 1980
Film-Avant-garde/Science fiction
66600 75 mins B/W B, V P
Herve Villechaize, Susan Tyrrell, The Kipper Kids, Viva
Frenchy Hercules is flung headlong into the sixth dimension. This kingdom is ruled by the midget, King Fausto and inhabited by dancing frogs, bikini-clad tootsies, robot boxers and

degraded beings of all kinds. Original music by Oingo Boingo.
MPAA:R
Richard Elfman — *Media Home Entertainment*

Force Beyond, The 197?
Speculation/Occult sciences
47314 85 mins C B, V P
Don Elkins, Peter Byrne, Renee Dahinden
This program provides a look at inexplicable phenomena, including psychic investigation, alien encounters, Bigfoot, and the Bermuda Triangle.
Donn Davidson — *Media Home Entertainment*

Force: Five 1981
Adventure
68223 95 mins C B, V P
Joe Lewis, Pam Huntington, Master Bong Soo Han
The daughter of a very powerful man has been taken to Rhee's Island, a retreat for people involved in the cult. The mission is to get her back and ruin Rhee's Island. Only a force of five agents can do this job.
MPAA:R
American Cinema — *Media Home Entertainment*

Force of Evil 1949
Drama
76826 80 mins B/W B, V P
John Garfield, Thomas Gomez, Marie Windsor, directed by Abraham Polonsky
An attorney who works for a mobster tries to break out of the numbers racket.
MGM — *Republic Pictures Home Video*

Force of One, A 1979
Martial arts/Adventure
66062 91 mins C B, V P
Chuck Norris, Bill Wallace, Jennifer O'Neill
A team of undercover narcotics agents is being eliminated mysteriously.
MPAA:PG
Alan Belkin — *Media Home Entertainment*

Force 10 from Navarone 1978
War-Drama
64301 118 mins C B, V R, P
Robert Shaw, Harrison Ford, Barbara Bach, Edward Fox
During World War II, five desperate Allied soldiers and one beautiful woman plot to blow up a dam and destroy an impregnable bridge.
MPAA:PG
Orion Pictures — *Warner Home Video; Vestron Video (disc only)*

Forced Entry 1980
Suspense
59082 92 mins C B, V P
Tanya Roberts, Ron Max, Nancy Allen
A psychopathic killer rapist becomes obsessed with a beautiful woman.
MPAA:R
Jim Sotos — *HarmonyVision*

Forced Landing 1942
Drama
66377 70 mins B/W B, V P
Richard Arlen, Eva Gabor
A scientist's daughter, who fears her father may have been captured by Nazis, seeks the aid of an American flyer.
Paramount — *Movie Buff Video*

Forced Vengeance 1982
Adventure/Martial arts
60568 103 mins C B, V, CED P
Chuck Norris, Mary Louise Weller
The story of a Vietnam vet pitted against the Underworld of the Far East.
MPAA:R
MGM; SLM Entertainment — *MGM/UA Home Video*

Forces of Life, The 1982
Chemistry/Physics
59562 56 mins C B, V P
This program examines the essential properties which make up our physical universe.
McGraw Hill — *Mastervision*

Ford Show, The 1960
Variety
47499 30 mins B/W B, V, FO P
Tennessee Ernie Ford, Keenan Wynn
Country humor with Tennessee Ernie Ford, featuring his hound dog, Ring, and Emmy Lou, the pig.
NBC — *Video Yesteryear*

Ford Star Jubilee: "Together with Music" 1955
Music-Performance
47492 79 mins B/W B, V, FO P
Mary Martin, Noel Coward
A memorable television special—originally broadcast on October 22, 1955—teaming two Broadway luminaries. Mary Martin sings songs from "South Pacific," "Leave It to Me" and other shows. Noel Coward sings his "Mad Dogs and Englishmen" and other tunes, ending with a lengthy duet.
CBS — *Video Yesteryear*

Ford Startime 1960
Drama
69577 50 mins B/W B, V, FO P
Audie Murphy, Thelma Ritter
An original television drama, "The Man" is a psychological study of an unbalanced veteran

who visits the mother of an old army buddy and proves impossible to get rid of.
NBC — *Video Yesteryear*

Foreign Correspondent **1940**
Suspense
81152 120 mins B/W B, V P
Joel McCrea, Laraine Day, Herbert Marshall, George Sanders, Robert Benchley, directed by Alfred Hitchcock
A reporter is sent to Europe during World War II to cover a pacifist conference in London, where he becomes romantically involved with the daughter of the group's founder and he friends an elderly diplomat. When the diplomat is kidnapped, the reporter uncovers a Nazi spy-ring headed by his future father-in-law.
United Artists; Walter Wanger — *Lightning Video*

Foreplay **1975**
Comedy
64879 100 mins C B, V, CED P
Pat Paulsen, Jerry Orbach, Estelle Parsons, Zero Mostel
A trilogy of hilarious comedy segments. Also known as "The President's Women."
Cinema National Corp — *Vestron Video*

Forever Emmanuelle **1982**
Drama
69282 89 mins C B, V P
Annie-Belle, Emmanuelle Arsan, Al Cliver
A sensual young woman finds love and the ultimate erotic experience in the wilds of the South Pacific.
MPAA:R
A-Erre Cinematografica — *Vestron Video*

Formula, The **1980**
Drama
55206 117 mins C B, V, CED P
Marlon Brando, George C. Scott, directed by John G. Avildsen
Steve Shagan's novel about a hard-nosed Los Angeles policeman who, despite numerous attempts on his life, continues to search for the formula that could end America's dependence on foreign oil forever.
MPAA:R
Steve Shagan — *MGM/UA Home Video*

Fort Apache **1948**
Western
00277 125 mins B/W B, V, 3/4U P
John Wayne, Henry Fonda, Shirley Temple
Indian attacks and conflict between men on the Western frontier arise in this film.
RKO; John Ford — *Nostalgia Merchant; King of Video; VidAmerica*

Fort Apache, The Bronx **1981**
Drama
58896 123 mins C B, V, LV, CED P
Paul Newman, Ed Asner, Ken Wahl, Danny Aiello, Rachel Ticotin, Pam Grier, Kathleen Beller, directed by Daniel Petrie
A police drama set in the beleaguered South Bronx of New York City, based on the real-life experiences of two former New York cops who served there.
MPAA:R
Time-Life Films — *Vestron Video; Time Life Video*

Fortune's Fool **1921**
Comedy
11231 60 mins B/W B, V, FO P
Emil Jannings, Daguey Servaes, Reinhold Schunzel, directed by Reinhold Schunzel
A beef king and profiteer marries a younger woman and soon discovers the problems that ambition can cause.
UFA — *Video Yesteryear; Discount Video Tapes*

Forty Carats **1973**
Comedy
63964 110 mins C B, V P
Liv Ullman, Edward Albert, Gene Kelly, Binnie Barnes, Deborah Raffin
A middle-aged, divorced woman falls in love with a young man half her age; in turn, her young daughter marries a widower who is in his forties.
MPAA:PG
Columbia Pictures — *RCA/Columbia Pictures Home Video*

---

48 Hrs. **1982**
Comedy
66034 100 mins C B, V, LV R, P
Nick Nolte, Eddie Murphy
A convict and a detective make an unlikely team trying to solve a crime in San Francisco.
MPAA:R
Paramount — *Paramount Home Video; RCA VideoDiscs*

Forty Ninth Parallel, The **1941**
World War II
75673 90 mins B/W B, V P
Laurence Olivier, Leslie Howard, Eric Portman, Raymond Massey, Glynis Johns
Six Nazi servicemen, seeking to reach neutral American land, are trapped and their U-boat is sunk by Royal Canadian Air Force bombers.
Rank Film Distributors — *VidAmerica*

42nd Street **1933**
Musical
55582 89 mins B/W B, V P

 (For explanation of codes, see USE GUIDE and KEY)

Warner Baxter, Ruby Keeler, Bebe Daniels, Dick Powell, Guy Kibbee, Ginger Rogers, Una Merkel, directed by Lloyd Bacon
A Broadway musical producer has troubles during rehearsal but reaches a successful opening night. Choreography by Busby Berkeley. Songs by Harry Warren and Al Dubin include the title song, "You're Getting to Be a Habit with Me," "Young and Healthy," and "Shuffle Off to Buffalo."
Warner Bros — *CBS/Fox Video; RCA VideoDiscs*

Foul Play **1978**
Comedy
38931 118 mins C B, V, LV R, P
Goldie Hawn, Chevy Chase, Dudley Moore, directed by Colin Higgins
Chevy Chase is a San Francisco detective who becomes involved with Goldie Hawn and a plot to kidnap the Pope in this lighthearted comedy thriller.
MPAA:PG
Paramount — *Paramount Home Video; RCA VideoDiscs*

Fountainhead, The **1949**
Drama
73973 113 mins C B, V P
Gary Cooper, Patricia Neal, Raymond Massey, directed by King Vidor
An idealistic architect clashes with big business over his designs for a housing project. Adapted from Ayn Rand's novel.
Warner Bros — *Key Video*

Four Deuces, The **1975**
Drama
77168 87 mins C B, V P
Jack Palance, Carol Lynley
A gang war is underway between the Chico Hamilton mob and Vic Morano and the Four Deuces during the depression.
Cinema Shares International — *THORN EMI/HBO Video*

Four Feathers, The **1978**
Adventure
47796 95 mins C B, V R, P
Beau Bridges, Jane Seymour, Simon Ward, Harry Andrews
Determined to return the symbols of cowardice-four feathers-to his friends and fiancee, a man courageously saves his friends' lives and regains the love of his lady.
Trident Films Ltd; Norman Rosemont Productions — *THORN EMI/HBO Video*

Four Feathers, The **1939**
Adventure
81461 130 mins C B, V, LV P
John Clements, Ralph Richardson, C. Aubrey Smith, June Duprez, directed by Zoltan Korda
A coward redeems himself when he goes underground to rescue a friend during the Sudan campaign of the late nineteenth century.
Alexander Korda — *Embassy Home Entertainment*

Four for Thrills **1982**
Cartoons/Literature-American
58578 50 mins C B, V P
Narrated by Herschel Bernardi and Harry Belafonte
A quartet of colorful animated, shorts containing Edgar Allen Poe's classic "Masque of the Red Death," Harry Belafonte's presentation of the Hand," the immortal, "Casey at the Bat," and Herschel Bernardi's presentation of "The Hangman."
McGraw Hill — *Mastervision*

Four Friends **1981**
Comedy-Drama
60338 116 mins C B, V R, P
Craig Wasson, Jodi Thelen, Michael Huddleston, Jim Metzler, Reed Birney, directed by Arthur Penn
Set against the turbulence of the 1960's, a young immigrant comes of age, learning of life and love from his friends.
MPAA:R
Filmways Pictures — *Warner Home Video; Vestron Video (disc only)*

Four Horsemen of the Apocalypse, The **1962**
Drama
81498 153 mins C B, V P
Glen Ford, Charles Boyer, Lee J. Cobb, Paul Henried, Yvette Mimieux, directed by Vincente Minnelli
The members of a German family find themselves fighting on opposite sides during World War II.
MGM — *MGM/UA Home Video*

Four Musketeers, The **1973**
Comedy/Adventure
60374 107 mins C CED P
Raquel Welch, Richard Chamberlain, Faye Dunaway, Michael York
A bawdy continuation of the "Three Musketeers" based on the classic Dumas novel.
MPAA:R
Ilya Salkind — *RCA VideoDiscs*

Four Musketeers, The **1974**
Adventure
66617 103 mins C B, V P
Michael York, Oliver Reed, Raquel Welch, Faye Dunaway, Charlton Heston, directed by Richard Lester
This continuation of "The Three Musketeers" finds Athos, Porthos, Aramis and D'Artagnan

continuing their adventures against the evil forces of Cardinal Richelieu.
MPAA:PG
20th Century Fox; Film Trust SA — *U.S.A. Home Video*

Four Rode Out 1969
Western
65209 99 mins C B, V P
Pernell Roberts, Leslie Nielsen
The story of a woman in love with a suspected killer. To save his life, she rides out with his would be captors.
MPAA:R
Sagittarius Productions — *U.S.A. Home Video*

Four Seasons, The 1981
Comedy
58433 107 mins C B, V, LV P
Alan Alda, Carol Burnett, Sandy Dennis, Len Cariou, Jack Weston, Rita Moreno, Bess Armstrong
Three upper-middle-class New York couples share their vacations together, as well as their friendship, their frustrations and their jealousies.
MPAA:PG
Universal; Martin Bregman — *MCA Home Video; RCA VideoDiscs*

Four Seasons, The 1984
Music
66597 45 mins C B, V P
Orchestre National de France, conducted by Lorin Maazel
Vivaldi's famous concert piece is performed with a visual background of travelog scenes of Paris, New York, Moscow and Venice. In stereo.
Curiator Spiritus Company Ltd; Promedifilm; MGM UA — *MGM/UA Home Video*

4th Man, The 1984
Mystery/Suspense
76858 104 mins C B, V P
Jeroen Krabbe, Renee Soutendijk, Thom Hoffman, directed by Paul Verhoeven
A Dutch writer en route to an out of town speaking engagement has a grisly series of visions that foretell his future. With English subtitles.
DU
Bob Houwer — *Media Home Entertainment*

Fourth Wish, The 1975
Drama
80767 107 mins C B, V P
John Meillon, Robert Bettles
When a single father learns that his son is dying, he vows to make his son's last months as fulfilling as possible.
Matt Carroll — *Embassy Home Entertainment*

Fraggle Songs, Volume One 1983
Fantasy/Music
65306 52 mins C B, V, LV, CED R, P
The Fraggles, furry little creatures who come in every color of the rainbow, sing and dance their way into your heart. This program is in stereo on all formats.
Henson Associates — *Muppet Home Video*

Fraidy Cat 1974
Cartoons
75498 45 mins C B, V P
This program includes four animated fantasies for children.
Filmation — *Prism*

Frances 1982
Drama
66021 134 mins C B, V, CED R, P
Jessica Lange, Kim Stanley, Sam Shepherd
The tragic story of Frances Farmer, the beautiful and talented screen actress driven to a mental breakdown by a neurotic, domineering mother.
Universal — *THORN EMI/HBO Video*

Francis Gary Powers: The True Story of the U-Z Spy Incident 1976
Drama
79246 100 mins C B, V P
Lee Majors, Noah Beery Jr., Hehemiah Persoff, Brooke Bundy, Lew Ayres
The true story of how U-2 pilot Francis Gary Powers was shot down over Russia while on an espionage mission.
Charles Fries Productions — *Worldvision Home Video*

Francis Gary Powers: The True Story of the U-2 Spy Incident 1976
Drama
80485 120 mins C B, V P
Lee Majors, Noah Beery Jr, Nehemiah Persoff, Brooke Bundy, directed by Delbert Mann
A dramatization of the true experiences of Gary Powers, a CIA spy pilot whose plane was shot down over the Soviet Union in 1960. His capture, trial and conviction are all portrayed in graphic detail, taken from Power's own reminiscences.
Worldvision Enterprises — *Worldvision Home Video*

Frank Shorter's Run 1984
Running
65690 57 mins C B, V P
America's foremost authority on running, world-class marathoner Frank Shorter gives information and instruction on warm-up racing

and tempo running, injury prevention and treatment.
Paul Rost; Bruce Miller — *Media Home Entertainment*

Franken and Davis at Stockton State **1984**
Comedy-Performance
79109 55 mins C B, V P
Former "Saturday Night Live" writers-stars Al Franken and Tom Davis perform stand-up comedy in this concert taped at Stockton College in New Jersey.
Broadway Video — *Pacific Arts Video*

Franken and Davis Special, The **1984**
Comedy-Performance
66359 60 mins C B, V P
Writer-performers Al Franken and Tom Davis, once featured on "Saturday Night Live," star in this live comedy concert taped in New Jersey
Pacific Arts — *Pacific Arts Video*

Frankenstein **1931**
Horror
14025 71 mins B/W B, V P
Boris Karloff, Mae Clark, Colin Clive, John Boles
An adaptation of the Mary Shelley novel about Dr. Henry Frankenstein, the scientist who creates a terrifying yet strangely sympathetic monster.
Universal — *MCA Home Video; RCA VideoDiscs*

Frankenstein **1984**
Cartoons/Horror
70091 90 mins C B, V P
Animated
This is an animated version of the classic Mary Shelley novel about Dr. Frankenstein and his new creation.
Northstar Productions — *Vestron Video*

Frankenstein **1973**
Horror
77442 130 mins C B, V P
Robert Foxworth, Bo Svenson, Willie Aames, Susan Strasberg
A brilliant scientist unleashes an adaptation of the classic Mary Shelley novel from the remains of the dead.
Dan Curtis Productions — *Thriller Video*

Frankenstein Island **198?**
Mystery
75583 97 mins C B, V P
John Carradine, Andrew Duggan, Cameron Mitchell
Four balloonists get pulled down in a storm and end up on Frankenstein island.
MPAA:PG
Unknown — *Monterey Home Video*

Frankie and Johnnie **1936**
Musical-Drama
59407 68 mins B/W B, V P, T
Helen Morgan, Chester Morris
Based on the song of the same name, Helen Morgan portrays a nightclub floozie who shoots her unfaithful lover.
Republic — *Blackhawk Films*

Frankie Laine Show with Connie Haines **1955**
Variety
12843 50 mins B/W B, V, FO P
Frankie Laine, Connie Haines, the Harry Zimmerman Orchestra
Two TV shows featuring plenty of songs, variety acts, knife throwers, and girl bagpipers.
CBS — *Video Yesteryear*

Frankie Valli: Twentieth Anniversary Concert **1983**
Music-Performance
75497 100 mins C B, V P
Frankie Valli
Frankie Valli's Chicago 1982 concert includes great hits such as "Grease," "My Eyes Adored You," "Sherry," "Walk Like a Man" and "Rag Doll."
MusicAmerica Live — *Prism*

Franklin D. Roosevelt, Declaration of War **1941**
Presidency-US/World War II
59651 9 mins B/W B, V P, T
Franklin D. Roosevelt
This Fox Movietone newsreel captures FDR's declaration of war following the December 7th bombing of Pearl Harbor.
William Fox — *Blackhawk Films*

Frantic **1958**
Drama
12803 92 mins B/W B, V, FO P
Maurice Ronet, Jeanne Moreau
A former commando commits murder of an employer's wife, making it look like suicide. A teenage prank then frames him for murders he did not commit.
Times Films; Irenee Leriche — *Video Yesteryear; Budget Video; Discount Video Tapes*

Freaky Friday **1977**
Comedy/Fantasy
47409 95 mins C B, V R, P
Barbara Harris, Jodie Foster, Patsy Kelly, Dick Van Patten, Ruth Buzzi
A housewife and her teenage daughter inadvertently switch bodies and each then tries to carry on the other's normal routine.

MPAA:G
Walt Disney — *Walt Disney Home Video*

Fred Astaire: Change Partners and Dance **1980**
Musical/Documentary
70184 60 mins C B, V P
Fred Astaire, Leslie Caron, Cyd Charisse, Barrie Chase, narrated by Joanne Woodward
Fred Astaire's post-Ginger Rogers career is the subject of this documentary that features scenes from Fred's films of the '40s and '50s, plus segments from his '60s TV specials. Some sequences are in black and white.
PBS — *RKO HomeVideo*

Fred Astaire: Puttin' on His Top Hat **1980**
Musical/Documentary
70183 60 mins C B, V P
Fred Astaire, Ginger Rogers, Adele Astaire, narrated by Joanne Woodward
Fred Astaire's career in Hollywood from 1933-1939 is the focus of this documentary, with scenes from his RKO films with Ginger Rogers. Some segments are in black and white.
PBS — *RKO HomeVideo*

Freddie Hubbard **1981**
Music-Performance
76663 59 mins C B, V P
A top rate jazz performance by one of the greatest trumpet players of our time, Freddie Hubbard.
Audio Visual Images — *Sony Corporation of America*

Free for All **1968**
Adventure/Fantasy
80417 50 mins C B, V P
Patrick McGoohan, Angelo Muscat, Colin Gordon, Alexis Kanner, Leo McKern, directed by Patrick McGoohan
The Prisoner runs for the position of Number Two in the Village hoping to meet Number One. An episode from the popular TV series.
Associated TV Corp. — *MPI Home Video*

Free to Be... You and Me **1983**
Identity/Children
69534 45 mins C B, V P
Marlo Thomas, Alan Alda, Harry Belafonte, Mel Brooks, Diana Ross, Rosey Grier
This is a joyful celebration of childhood through song, story and poetry—created to let children feel "free to be who they are and who they want to be."
Marlo Thomas; Carole Hart — *Children's Video Library*

Freebie and the Bean **1974**
Comedy
79553 114 mins C B, V R, P
Alan Arkin, James Caan, Loretta Swit, Valerie Harper, directed by Richard Rush
Two San Francisco cops nearly ruin the city in their pursuit of a mobster.
MPAA:R
Richard Rush; Warner Bros. — *Warner Home Video*

Freedom **1981**
Drama
80936 102 mins C B, V P
Jon Blake, Candy Raymond, Jad Capelja, Reg Lye, John Clayton
A young man finds the price of freedom when he tries to escape from Australian society in a silver Porsche.
Matt Carroll — *VidAmerica*

Freedom Force, The **1984**
Adventure/Cartoons
66494 60 mins C B, V P
Animated
The Freedom Force takes on the powers of evil and triumphs over the forces of darkness.
Prism — *Prism*

French Connection, The **1971**
Crime-Drama
08432 102 mins C B, V, LV P
Gene Hackman, Fernando Rey, Roy Scheider, Tony LoBianco, Marcel Bozzuffi
Two N.Y. hard-nosed narcotics detectives stumble onto what turns out to be the biggest narcotics haul to that time.
Academy Awards '71: Best Picture; Best Actor (Hackman); Best Director (William Friedkin).
MPAA:R EL, SP
20th Century Fox; Philip D'Antoni — *CBS/Fox Video*

French Connection II **1975**
Drama
Closed Captioned
80653 118 mins C B, V P
Gene Hackman, Fernando Rey, Bernard Fresson, directed by John Frankenheimer
New York policeman "Popeye" Doyle goes to Marseilles to crack a heroin ring headed by his arch nemesis, Frog One, who he failed to stop in the United States. Available in Beta and VHS Hi-Fi.
MPAA:R
20th Century Fox — *CBS/Fox Video*

French Detective, The **1975**
Suspense
63960 90 mins C B, V P
Lino Ventura, Patrick Dewaere, Victor Lanoux

A cunning detective and an ambitious young politician clash in this story of murder and intrigue. Dubbed in English.
Les Films Ariane; Quartet Films — *RCA/Columbia Pictures Home Video*

French Lieutenant's Woman, The **1981**
Drama
59392 124 mins C B, V, LV P
Meryl Streep, Jeremy Irons, directed by Karel Reisz
John Fowles' best seller which intertwines two love stories, one between two present-day actors and one between the historical characters they portray.
MPAA:R
United Artists — *CBS/Fox Video; MGM/UA Home Video (disc only)*

French Line **1954**
Comedy
10030 102 mins C B, V P, T
Jane Russell, Gilbert Roland, Craig Stevens
Millionairess beauty travels incognito while trying to sort out which men are after her money, and which ones aren't.
RKO; Edmund Graiger — *Blackhawk Films*

French Postcards **1980**
Drama/Romance
81119 91 mins C B, V R, P
Miles Chapin, Blanche Baker, Valerie Quennessen, Debra Winger, Mandy Patinkin, Marie-France Pisier, directed by Willard Huyck
Three American students study all aspects of French culture when they spend their junior year of college at the Institute of French Studies in Paris.
MPAA:PG
Paramount; Gloria Katz — *Paramount Home Video*

French Quarter **1978**
Drama
47404 101 mins C B, V P
Bruce Davison, Virginia Mayo, Lindsay Bloom, Alisha Fontaine, Lance Legault, Ann Michelle
A young girl travels to the French Quarter in New Orleans. Desperate for work, she falls victim to an old woman who practices witchcraft and voodoo. The woman's voodoo causes the young girl to "slip" away. She awakens in the year 1900, under the care of prostitutes.
MPAA:R
Crown Intl Pictures; Dennis Kane — *United Home Video*

French Woman, The **1979**
Drama
55595 97 mins C B, V P
Francois Fabian, Klaus Kinski
A sensuous story of blackmail, murder, and sex involving French cabinet ministers mixing passion and politics.
MPAA:R
Monarch Pictures; Claire Duval — *VidAmerica*

Frenzy **1972**
Suspense
11582 116 mins C B, V P
Jon Finch, Barry Foster, Barbara Leigh-Hunt, Anna Massey, Directed by Alfred Hitchcock
A sex criminal known as The Necktie Murderer is terrorizing London, and Alfred Hitchcock has everyone guessing who the culprit is—including Scotland Yard.
MPAA:R
Universal; Alfred Hitchcock — *MCA Home Video*

Friday the 13th **1980**
Horror
54669 95 mins C B, V, LV R, P
Betsy Palmer, Adrienne King, Harry Crosby, Laurie Bartrarr, Mark Nelsor, directed by Sean S. Cunningham
A New Jersey camp that's been closed for 20 years after a history of "accidental" deaths reopens and the horror begins again. Six would-be counselors arrive to get the place ready. Each are progressively murdered—knifed, speared, and axed.
MPAA:R
Paramount — *Paramount Home Video; RCA VideoDiscs*

Friday the 13th, Part 2 **1981**
Horror
53932 87 mins C B, V, LV P
Amy Steel, John Furey, Adrienne King, Betsy Palmer, directed by Steve Miner
A group of teen camp counselors are gruesomely executed by yet another unknown assailant.
MPAA:R
Steve Miner — *Paramount Home Video; RCA VideoDiscs*

Friday the 13th, Part 3 **1982**
Horror
64021 96 mins C B, V, LV R, P
Dana Kimmell, Paul Krata, Richard Brooker
Yet another group of naive counselors at Camp Crystal Lake fall victim to the maniacal Jason.
MPAA:R
Jason Productions — *Paramount Home Video*

Friday the 13th, The Final Chapter **1984**
Horror
79183 90 mins C B, V P
Kimberly Beck, Ted White, Peter Barton

Jason escapes from the morgue to once again slaughter and annihilate teenagers at a lakeside cottage.
MPAA:R
Paramount — *Paramount Home Video*

Friday the 13th, Part V—A New Beginning **1985**
Horror
Closed Captioned
81509 92 mins C B, V R, P
John Shepherd, Shavar Ross, Richard Young
Jason rises from the dead to slice up the residents of a secluded halfway house.
MPAA:R
PARAMOUNT — *Paramount Home Video*

Friendly Persuasion **1956**
Drama
80140 140 mins C CED P
Gary Cooper, Dorothy McGuire, Anthony Perkins, Marjorie Main, directed by William Wyler
The outbreak of the Civil War disrupts the lives of a Quaker family in southern Indiana.
William Wyler — *CBS/Fox Video*

Frightmare **1983**
Horror
64874 84 mins C B, V P
A great horror star dies, but he refuses to give up his need for adoration and revenge.
MPAA:R
Patrick and Tallie Wright — *Vestron Video*

Frisco Kid, The **1979**
Comedy
58232 119 mins C B, V R, P
Gene Wilder, Harrison Ford, directed by Robert Aldrich
An orthodox rabbi from Poland sets out for the wild west.
MPAA:PG
Warner Bros — *Warner Home Video*

Fritz the Cat **1972**
Comedy
59850 77 mins C B, V R, P
Animated
Ralph Bakshi's animated tale for adults about a cat's adventures as he gets into group sex, college radicalism and other hazards of life in the 60's.
MPAA:X
Steve Krantz — *Warner Home Video*

Frog Prince, The **1971**
Fairy tales
47346 50 mins C B, V, LV R, P
The Muppets
Kermit the Frog narrates the Muppet version of this classic fairy tale. A handsome prince has been turned into a frog by an evil witch's spell, and only the kiss of a beautiful princess can change him back.
RLP Canada/Henson Associates — *Muppet Home Video*

Frogs **1972**
Horror
64839 91 mins C B, V R, P
Ray Milland, Sam Elliott, Joan Van Ark, Adam Roarke, Judy Pace, directed by George McCowan
Amphibians and reptiles on a tropical island take revenge against the family of a wildlife-hating recluse.
MPAA:PG
American International Pictures — *Warner Home Video; Vestron Video (disc only)*

Frolics on Ice **1940**
Comedy
38976 65 mins B/W B, V, FO P
Roscoe Karns, Lynne Roberts, Irene Dare, Edgar Kennedy
Pleasant comedy-musical about a family man saving to buy the barber shop he works at. Irene Dare is featured in several ice skating production numbers.
Hal Roach — *Video Yesteryear*

From Broadway to Hollywood **193?**
Film-History
10157 48 mins B/W B, V P, T
Ed Sullivan, Eddie Cantor, Shirley Temple
Includes highlights from the 30's such as Shirley Temple's "Biggest Little Star of the Thirties" and Lew Lehr's "Cwazy Monkies." Also features Ed Sullivan, Eddie Cantor, Jack Dempsey, and Little Rascals.
Educational et al — *Blackhawk Films*

From D-Day to Victory in Europe **1985**
History-US/World War II
70752 112 mins C B, V P
Written and narrated by Max Hastings
Based on Mr. Hastings best selling novel, this program combines original battlefield fontage with computer graphics for a thorough description of the War's turning point.
Bob Hunter — *MPI Home Video*

From Hell to Victory **1979**
War-Drama
79222 100 mins C B, V P
George Peppard, George Hamilton, Horst Bucholz, Anny Duprey, Sam Wanamaker, Capucine
A group of friends who meet in Paris before World War II vow to return there again to reminisce about old times.
MPAA:PG

New Film Productions — *Media Home Entertainment*

From Russia with Love **1963**
Suspense
53787 118 mins C B, V, LV, CED P
Sean Connery, Robert Shaw, Daniela Bianchi, Lotte Lenya
A Russian spy joins an international crime organization and develops a plan to kill James Bond and steal a coding machine. The second Bond feature.
United Artists; Eon; Harry Saltzman; Albert Broccoli — *CBS/Fox Video; RCA VideoDiscs*

From the Earth to the Moon **1958**
Science fiction
11723 100 mins C B, V P
George Sanders, Joseph Cotton
Jules Verne's thriller in which three men and a woman rocket to the moon.
Warner Bros — *United Home Video*

From the Life of the Marionettes **1980**
Drama
81262 103 mins C B, V P
Robert Atzorn, Christine Bucheggar, Martin Benrath, Rita Russek, directed by Ingmar Bergman
This film follows a rich businessman's descent into madness as he murders and sexually assaults a prostitute that resembles his nagging wife. With English subtitles. Available in VHS Stereo and Beta Hi-Fi.
MPAA:R SW
ITC; Martin Starger — *U.S.A. Home Video*

From the New World **1982**
Music-Performance
47807 ? mins C LV P
Dvorak's "Symphony No. 9 in E minor, Op.95—From the New World" is performed by the Czech Philharmonic Orchestra (stereo).
Unknown — *Pioneer Video Imports*

From Worst to First **1980**
Football
45131 24 mins C B, V, FO R, P
Tampa Bay Buccaneers
Highlights of the 1979 Tampa Bay Buccaneers football season.
NFL Films — *NFL Films Video*

Front, The **1976**
Drama
58961 95 mins C B, V P
Woody Allen, Zero Mostel, Herschel Bernardi, Michael Murphy, Diana Marcovicci, directed by Martin Ritt
A bookmaker becomes a "front" for blacklisted writers during the communist witch hunts of the 1950's.
MPAA:PG
Columbia — *RCA/Columbia Pictures Home Video*

Front Page, The **1931**
Comedy
57760 101 mins B/W B, V P
Adolph Menjou, Pat O'Brien, Edward Everett Horton, directed by Lewis Milestone
The original version of the Hecht-MacArthur play about a battling newspaper reporter and his editor in Chicago.
United Artists — *Budget Video; Discount Video Tapes; Cable Films; Video Connection; Video Yesteryear; Western Film & Video Inc; Classic Video Cinema Collector's Club*

Frontier Horizon **1948**
Western
56601 55 mins B/W B, V, 3/4U R, P
John Wayne, Phyllis Isley (Jennifer Jones), Ray Carrigan
A promoter is swindling ranchers out of land in order to build a dam to flood the land for a reservoir.
Republic — *Spotlite Video; Cable Films*

Frontier Pony Express **1939**
Western
64389 54 mins B/W B, V, 3/4U P
Roy Rogers
Roy and Trigger do their best to help the Pony Express riders who are being attacked by marauding gangs.
Republic — *Nostalgia Merchant; Discount Video Tapes*

Frontier Vengeance **1940**
Western
64420 54 mins B/W B, V, 3/4U P
Don "Red" Barry
A stagecoach driver helps a young girl who is being terrorized by crooks.
Republic — *Nostalgia Merchant*

Fugitive: The Final Episode, The **1967**
Drama
53788 103 mins C B, V P
David Janssen, Barry Morse, Bill Raisch, Diane Baker, Joseph Campanella, Michael Constantine
The final episode of the acclaimed series, aired on August 29, 1967, in which Dr. Richard Kimble meets up with the one-armed man who murdered his wife. This episode was the highest rated program up to that time.
Quinn Martin Prods — *Worldvision Home Video; RCA VideoDiscs*

Fugitive, The (The Taking of Luke McVane) 1915
Western
66134 28 mins B/W B, V, FO P
William S. Hart, Enid Markey
An early silent western in which Hart upholds the cowboy code of honor.
Thomas Ince — *Video Yesteryear*

Full Hearts and Empty Pockets 1963
Drama
63623 88 mins B/W B, V, FO P
Linda Christian, Gino Cervi, Senta Berger
This film follows the happy-go-lucky adventures of a young, handsome, impoverished gentleman on the loose in Rome. Dubbed in English.
Screen Gems — *Video Yesteryear*

Fuller Brush Man, The 1948
Comedy
80786 93 mins B/W B, V P
Red Skelton, Janet Blair, Don McGuire, Adele Jergens, directed by Frank Tashlin
A newly hired Fuller Brush man becomes involved in murder and romance as he tries to win the heart of his girlfriend.
Columbia Pictures — *RCA/Columbia Pictures Home Video*

Fun and Fancy Free 1947
Musical/Comedy
63126 96 mins C B, V R, P
Edgar Bergen, Charlie McCarthy, Jiminy Cricket, Mickey Mouse, Donald Duck, Goofy, the voice of Dinah Shore
This part-animated, part-live-action feature is split into two segments: "Bongo," with Dinah Shore narrating the story of a happy-go-lucky circus bear; and "Mickey and the Beanstalk," a "new" version of an old fairy tale.
Walt Disney Productions — *Walt Disney Home Video*

Fun and Games 1982
Games
47677 ? mins C LV P
Maureen McGovern, Meadowlark Lemon, Bill Murray
An innovative participative program combining fun and learning in a collection of old and new games from around the world: tongue twisters, yo-yo, frisbees, etc. An interactive disc which runs 60 minutes when played through.
Scholastic Productions — *Optical Programming Associates*

Fun Factory/Clown Princes of Hollywood 196?
Comedy
10110 56 mins B/W B, V P, T
Mack Sennett, Charlie Chaplin, Buster Keaton, Charley Chase, Ben Turpin, Stan Laurel
Collection of various slapstick situations including Keystone Cops segments. From the "History of Motion Pictures" series.
Mack Sennett et al — *Blackhawk Films*

Fun in Acapulco 1963
Musical
08382 97 mins C B, V P
Elvis Presley, Ursula Andress, Elsa Cardenas, Paul Lukas
Elvis romances two beauties and acts as a part-time lifeguard and night club entertainer.
EL, SP
Paramount; Hal Wallis — *CBS/Fox Video; RCA VideoDiscs*

Fun with Dick and Jane 1977
Comedy
21286 104 mins C B, V P
George Segal, Jane Fonda, Ed McMahon
An upper-middle class couple turn to armed robbery to support themselves when the husband is fired from his job.
MPAA:PG
Columbia — *RCA/Columbia Pictures Home Video*

Fundamentals of Women's Basketball 1985
Basketball
81599 60 mins C B, V P
2 pgms
Veteran basketball coach Cathy Benedetto demonstrates various offensive and defensive techniques.
1.Defensive Play 2.Offensive Play
Morris Video — *Morris Video*

Funeral for an Assassin 1977
Adventure
52610 92 mins C B, V R, P
Vic Morrow, Peter Van Dissel
A professional assassin seeks revenge for his imprisonment by the government of South Africa, a former client. Planning to kill all of the country's leading politicians, he masquerades as a black man, a cover which is designed to fool the apartheid establishment.
MPAA:PG
Walter Brough; Ivan Hall — *Video Gems*

Funhouse, The 1981
Horror
47415 96 mins C B, V P
Elizabeth Berridge, Shawn Carson, Cooper Huckabee, Largo Woodruff, Sylvia Miles, directed by Tobe Hooper
Four teenagers spend the night at a carnival funhouse and are brutally hacked and maimed by a crazed father and son.
MPAA:R
Universal — *MCA Home Video*

Funny Face **1957**
Musical
77447 103 mins C B, V, LV R, P
Fred Astaire, Audrey Hepburn, Kay Thompson, Suzy Parker, directed by Stanley Donen
A fashion photographer turns a girl working in a bookstore into a high fashion model. The musical score features such Gershwin songs as "Bonjour Paris" and "Funny Face".
Paramount Pictures — *Paramount Home Video*

Funny Farm, The **1982**
Comedy
69675 90 mins C B, V R, P
Miles Chapin, Eileen Brennan, Peter Ackroyd
A group of ambitious young comics strive to make it in the crazy world of comedy at Los Angeles' famous club, The Funny Farm.
Independent — *THORN EMI/HBO Video*

Funny Girl **1968**
Musical-Drama
64237 151 mins C B, V P
Barbra Streisand, Omar Sharif, Walter Pidgeon, Kay Medford, Anne Francis, directed by William Wyler
This films follows the early career of Fanny Brice, her rise to stardom with the Ziegfeld Follies and her stormy romance with Nick Arnstein. The classic songs "People" and "Don't Rain on My Parade" are featured. In stereo.
Academy Awards '68: Best Actress (Streisand).
MPAA:G
Columbia; Ray Stark — *RCA/Columbia Pictures Home Video; RCA VideoDiscs*

Funny Guys and Gals of the Talkies **193?**
Comedy
11285 60 mins B/W B, V, FO P
W.C. Fields, Shirley Temple, Charlotte Greenwood, Groucho Marx, Marlene Dietrich
Four short pictures featuring the comedy stars of the early talking pictures: "The Golf Specialist," "Pardon My Pups," "Girls Will Be Boys," and "Band Rally Radio Show."
Mack Sennett et al — *Video Yesteryear*

Funny Thing Happened on the Way to the Forum, A **1966**
Comedy
47794 99 mins C B, V, LV, CED P
Zero Mostel, Phil Silvers, Jack Gilford, Buster Keaton, directed by Richard Lester
A bawdy Broadway farce set in ancient Rome where a conniving, eager-to-be-free slave sees his way to freedom.
United Artists — *CBS/Fox Video; RCA VideoDiscs*

Funstuff **193?**
Comedy
10042 59 mins B/W B, V P, T
Shirley Temple, Harold Lloyd
Shirley Temple and friends struggle for stardom. Harold Lloyd plays "Non-Stop Kid" and Snub Pollard strives to be an artist.
Educational et al — *Blackhawk Films*

Further Adventures of Super Ted, The **1985**
Cartoons
76809 48 mins C B, V R, P
Animated
Super Ted and Spottyman once again match wits with Texas Pete, Bulk, and Skelton in this new collection of animated adventures.
Siriol Animation Ltd; Mike Young — *Walt Disney Home Video*

Fury, The **1978**
Horror
56903 117 mins C B, V P
Kirk Douglas, John Cassavetes, Carrie Snodgress, Andrew Stevens, Amy Irving, Charles Durning, directed by Brian dePalma
The head of a government institute for psychic research finds that his own son is wanted by terrorists who wish to use his lethal powers.
MPAA:R
Twentieth Century Fox, Frank Yablans — *CBS/Fox Video*

Futureworld **1976**
Science fiction
53512 107 mins C B, V R, P
Peter Fonda, Blythe Danner, Arthur Hill, Yul Brenner, Stu Margolin
In the sequel to "Westworld," two reporters junket to the new "Futureworld," where they support a scheme to clone and control world leaders.
MPAA:PG
American Intl Pictures — *Warner Home Video; Vestron Video (disc only)*

Fuzz **1972**
Adventure/Comedy-Drama
69383 92 mins C B, V, CED P
Burt Reynolds, Tom Skerritt, Yul Brynner, Raquel Welch
Combining fast action and sharp-edged humor, this film portrays the life of a band of police officers trying to keep the streets of Boston safe.
MPAA:PG
United Artists — *CBS/Fox Video*

Fyre **1978**
Drama
55215 90 mins C B, V P
The story of a young beautiful girl who moves from the midwest to Los Angeles unfolds as she

becomes a prostitute and encounters many new experiences.
MPAA:R
Fyre Productions — *Media Home Entertainment*

G

Gas-s-s-s 1970
Comedy
81318 79 mins C B, V P
Cindy Williams, Ben Vereen, Talia Shire, Bud Cort, Elaine Giftes, directed by Roger Corman
When a defense plant in Alaska springs a gas main, everyone over twenty five dies. Those still alive take over the world with humorous results.
MPAA:PG
Roger Corman — *Lightning Video*

Gabriela 1984
Comedy
80632 105 mins C B, V P
Marcello Mastroianni, Sonia Braga, Nelson Xavier, Antonio Cantafora, directed by Bruno Barreto
A hot and sultry romance develops between a Brazilian tavern keeper and the new cook that he's just hired. Music by Antonio Carlos Jobim. With English subtitles.
MPAA:R
United Artists — *MGM/UA Home Video*

Gaiety 1943
Musical
08737 40 mins B/W B, V, 3/4U P
Antonio Moreno, Armida, Anne Ayers
Explores the lighter side of lion hunting.
Hal Roach — *Hal Roach Studios*

Gaiking 1982
Cartoons
64199 100 mins C B, V P
Animated
The mighty flying rubork, Gaiking, becomes earth's strongest and most heroic defense against the cunning Davius.
EL, SP
Toei Animation; Jim Terry Production — *Family Home Entertainment*

Galactica III: Conquest of the Earth 1980
Science fiction
59684 99 mins C B, V P
Lorne Greene, Kent McCord, Barry Van Dyke, Robin Douglas, Robert Reed
In an encounter with Earth, Commander Adama sends Lt. Troy and Lt. Dillon to the U.S. in order to bring the earthlings up to their level of technology.
MPAA:R
Universal — *MCA Home Video*

Galaxina 1981
Science fiction/Comedy
55550 96 mins C B, V, LV P
Dorothy Stratten, Avery Schreiber, Stephen Macht
In the 31st century, a beautiful robot woman capable of human feelings is created. A parody of superspace fantasies.
MPAA:R
Crown International; Marilyn Tenser — *MCA Home Video*

Galaxy Express 1980
Fantasy/Cartoons
65709 94 mins C B, V P
Animated, voices by Booker Bradshaw, Corey Burton
A young boy sets out to find immortality by traveling on The Galaxy Express, an ultra-modern 35th century Ospace train that carries its passengers in search of their dreams.
MPAA:PG
Toei — *Embassy Home Entertainment*

Galaxy Invader, The 1985
Science fiction
77199 90 mins C B, V P
Richard Ruxton, Faye Tilles, Don Liefert
Chaos erupts when an alien explorer crashlands his spacecraft in a backwoods area of the United States.
MPAA:PG
Moviecraft Entertainment — *United Home Video*

Galaxy of Terror 1981
Science fiction/Horror
65719 85 mins C B, V P
Erin Moran, Edward Albert, Ray Walston
The mind's innermost fears become reality when a spaceship rescue mission lands on a dark and barren planet.
MPAA:R
Roger Corman; Marc Siegler — *Embassy Home Entertainment*

Gallagher—Stuck in the 60's 1984
Comedy-Performance
80400 60 mins C B, V, LV, CED P
Comic Gallagher describes what his life was like in the 1960's in this concert performance.
Showtime — *Paramount Home Video*

Gallagher—The Maddest **1984**
Comedy-Performance
80399 60 mins C B, V, LV, CED P
The madcap comedy of Gallagher is captured in this concert.
Showtime — *Paramount Home Video*

Gallery of Horror **1981**
Horror
70648 90 mins C B, V P
Lon Chaney, John Carradine
This "Gallery" features memorable—that is, nightmarish-moments from Messrs. Chaney and Carradine's portfolios of horror.
Transatlantic Entprs. — *Academy Home Entertainment*

Gallipoli **1981**
Drama
59203 111 mins C B, V, LV R, P
Mel Gibson, Mark Lee, directed by Peter Weir
History blends with the destiny of two friends as they become part of a legendary World War I confrontation between Australia and the German Allied Turks.
MPAA:PG
Paramount; Robert Stigwood — *Paramount Home Video*

Galyon **1977**
Adventure
77234 92 mins C B, V P
Stan Brock, Lloyd Nolan, Ina Balin
A soldier of fortune is recruited by an oil tycoon to find his daughter and son-in-law in South America.
MPAA:PG
Ivan Tors — *Monterey Home Video*

Gambler, The **1974**
Drama
59425 111 mins C B, V, LV R, P
James Caan, Lauren Hutton, Paul Sorvino, Burt Young, directed by Karl Reisz
The story of a college professor who is also a compulsive gambler who falls into debt and trouble with the mob.
MPAA:R
Paramount — *Paramount Home Video*

Gambling Samurai, The **1960**
Adventure
76900 93 mins C B, V P
Toshiro Mifune, Michiko Aratama
A roving warrior leads a vengeful quest to restore justice to the village where he was born.
JA
Toho — *Video Action*

Game of Death **1979**
Martial arts/Adventure
59624 100 mins C B, V, CED P
Bruce Lee, Dean Jagger, Colleen Camp
Bruce Lee's final kung fu thriller about a young martial arts movie star who gets involved with the syndicate.
MPAA:R
Galaxy Films — *CBS/Fox Video*

Game Show Program **195?**
Game show
33692 120 mins B/W B, V, 3/4U P
Exciting quiz shows of the 1950s are seen in their entirety: "Do You Trust Your Wife," with Edgar Bergen and Charlie McCarthy, "You Bet Your Life," with Groucho Marx, "The Price Is Right," with Bill Cullen, and "Play Your Hunch," with Merv Griffin.
CBS et al — *Shokus Video*

Game Show Program II **196?**
Game show
33693 120 mins B/W B, V, 3/4U P
A collection of four game show programs including: "People Are Funny," with Art Linkletter, "Take a Good Look," with Ernie Kovacs, "Concentration," with Hugh Downs, and "I've Got a Secret," starring Steve Allen and a celebrity panel.
CBS et al — *Shokus Video*

Game Show Program III **196?**
Game show
33695 120 mins C B, V, 3/4U P
Four favorite game shows of the past twenty years are seen in their entirety: "The Price Is Right," "Truth or Consequences," "The Face Is Familiar," and "PDQ." Some black and white.
NBC et al — *Shokus Video*

Gameplan: The Language and Strategy of Pro Football **1985**
Football
70720 60 mins C B, V P
John Riggins
Based on the book by Riggins and sportswriter Jack Winter, this program uses filmclips and commentary to explain the finer points of football.
Jelly Bean Productions — *Sportsvideo*

Games Girls Play **1975**
Comedy
81399 90 mins C B, V P
Christina Hart, Jane Anthony, Jill Damas, Drina Pavlovic, directed by Jack Arnold
The daughter of an American diplomat organizes a contest at a British boarding school to see which of her classmates can seduce important dignitaries. Available in VHS Stereo and Beta Hi-Fi.

Peter J. Oppenheimer — *Monterey Home Video*

Gandhi **1982**
Drama
65186 188 mins C B, V P
Ben Kingsley, Candice Bergen, Edward Fox, John Gielgud, John Mills, Martin Sheen, directed by Sir Richard Attenborough
A sprawling biography of Mahatma Gandhi, India's man of peace, which follows his life from his simple beginnings as a lawyer in South Africa through his struggle to free India from colonial rule.
Academy Awards '82: Best Picture; Best Actor (Kingsley); Best Director. MPAA:PG
Columbia — *RCA/Columbia Pictures Home Video; RCA VideoDiscs*

Gangbusters **1938**
Mystery/Serials
07381 253 mins B/W B, V, 3/4U R, P
Kent Taylor, Irene Hervey, Robert Armstrong
Men battle crime in the city. A serial based on the popular radio series of the same name. In thirteen episodes.
Universal — *Cable Films; Video Connection; Video Dimensions; Video Yesteryear; Discount Video Tapes*

Gangster Wars, The **1981**
Crime-Drama
47416 121 mins C B, V P
Michael Nouri, Joe Penny
A specially edited-for-video version of the television mini-series, "The Gangster Chronicles." Based on fact, it deals with the growth of organized crime in America from the early days of this century, concentrating on three ghetto kids who grow up to become powerful mobsters.
Universal — *MCA Home Video*

Gangsters **19??**
Crime-Drama
65645 90 mins C B, V R, P
A city is ruled by the mob and nothing can stop their bloody grip except "The Special Squad."
Italian — *Video City Productions*

Garbo Talks **1984**
Comedy
Closed Captioned
70658 104 mins C B, V P
Anne Bancroft, Ron Silver, Carrie Fisher, Catherine Hicks, Steven Hill, Howard DaSilva, Dorothy Loudon, directed by Sidney Lumet
A dying eccentric's last request is to meet the reclusive screenlegend Greta Garbo. Her son goes to extreme and amusing lengths in order to fulfill this wish. Available in Hi-Fi stereo.
MPAA:PG13
MGM/UA — *CBS/Fox Video*

Garden of the Finzi-Continis, The **1971**
Drama
37519 90 mins C B, V R, P
Dominique Sanda, Helmut Berger, Lino Capolicchio, Fabio Testi, directed by Vittorio De Sica
The story of an aristocratic Jewish family living under increasing Fascist opporession in pre-World War II Italy.
MPAA:R
Cinema 5 — *RCA/Columbia Pictures Home Video*

Gardening in the City: I **1982**
Gardening/Plants
59574 60 mins C B, V P
Members of the world-famous New York Botanical Gardens' staff offer an illuminating introduction to plant life.
New York Botanical Gardens — *Mastervision*

Gardening in the City: II **1982**
Gardening/Plants
59575 60 mins C B, V P
The scientists of the New York Botanical Gardens give examples of proper soil and planting conditions and offer lessons in the use of fertilizers and correct pruning methods.
New York Botanical Gardens — *Mastervision*

Gary Numan—The Touring Principal '79 **1980**
Music-Performance
54689 60 mins C B, V R, P
Gary Numan
This program features Gary Numan, the British singer/composer, on his 1979 world tour. Material includes selections from his second album "The Pleasure Principle" including the hit single. "Cars."
Warner Bros — *Warner Home Video*

Gas **1981**
Comedy
58711 94 mins C B, V R, P
Donald Sutherland, Susan Anspach, Sterling Hayden, Peter Aykroyd, Helen Shaver
A gas shortage hits an average American town.
MPAA:R
Paramount; Claude Heroux — *Paramount Home Video*

Gaslight **1944**
Mystery/Drama
80208 114 mins B/W B, V, LV P
Charles Boyer, Ingrid Bergman, Joseph Cotten, Angela Lansbury, Terry Moore, directed by George Cukor

An evil man tries to conjure up ways to drive his wife insane.
Academy Awards '44: Best Actress (Bergman); Best Art Direction, Black and White.
MGM — *MGM/UA Home Video*

Gathering, The **198?**
Drama
78069 94 mins C B, V P
Ed Asner, Maureen Stapleton
A dying man seeks out the wife and family he has alienated for a final Christmas gathering.
Harry R Sherman — *Worldvision Home Video*

Gator **1976**
Adventure
63401 116 mins C B, V P
Burt Reynolds, Jerry Reed, Lauren Hutton, directed by Burt Reynolds
This sequel to "White Lightning" follows the adventures of Gator (Reynolds), who is recruited to gather evidence to convict a corrupt political boss.
MPAA:PG
United Artists — *CBS/Fox Video*

Gauntlet, The **1977**
Crime-Drama/Adventure
58233 111 mins C B, V R, P
Clint Eastwood, Sondra Locke, directed by Clint Eastwood
A cop is ordered to Las Vegas to bring back a key witness for an important trial—but the witness turns out to be a beautiful prostitute being hunted by killers.
MPAA:R
Warner Bros — *Warner Home Video; RCA VideoDiscs*

Gay Divorcee, The **1934**
Musical
00269 107 mins B/W B, V, 3/4U P
Fred Astaire, Ginger Rogers, Edward Everett Horton, Alice Brady, Erik Rhodes, Betty Grable
Fred pursues Ginger to an English seaside resort, where she mistakes him for her hired co-respondent. Songs include "Night and Day," "Don't Let It Bother You" and "Needle in a Haystack."
Academy Awards '34: Best Song (The Continental; Con Conrad and Herb Magidson).
RKO; Pandro S Berman — *Nostalgia Merchant*

Gemini Affair **198?**
Romance
73956 88 mins C B, V P
Marta Kristen, Kathy Kersh, Anne Seymour
Two women go to Hollywood to become rich and famous but end up being very disappointed.
Independent — *Unicorn Video*

General, The **1968**
Adventure/Fantasy
80419 50 mins C B, V P
Patrick McGoohan, Angelo Muscat, Colin Gordon, Alexis Kanner, Leo McKern
The General, a mysterious, unseen figure is introducing a new technique of speed learning to the Villagers.
Associated TV Corp. — *MPI Home Video*

General, The **1927**
Comedy
12429 80 mins B/W B, V P
Buster Keaton, Marion Mack, directed by Buster Keaton, Clyde Bruckman
A Civil War espionage spoof. A Confederate soldier almost wins the war single handedly when he goes behind Northern lines to recover his beloved locomotive. (Silent).
United Artists — *Budget Video; Video Yesteryear; Video Dimensions; Sheik Video; Cable Films; Western Film & Video Inc; Discount Video Tapes; Kartes Productions; Classic Video Cinema Collector's Club; See Hear Industries*

General, The/Slapstick **1926**
Film-History
50639 56 mins B/W B, V P, T
Buster Keaton, Marion Mack, Charlie Murray, Mabel Normand, Fatty Arbuckle, Edgar Kennedy
A double feature composed of abridged versions of the Buster Keaton spoof on Civil War espionage, and a Mack Sennett anthology of slapstick comedy.
United Artists — *Blackhawk Films*

Genesis/Three Sides Live **1982**
Music-Performance
63352 90 mins C B, V R, P
Rock supergroup Genesis performs some of their greatest hits live in concert, including "No Reply at All," "Misunderstanding" and "Behind the Lines."
Rooster Video — *THORN EMI/HBO Video*

Genevieve **1953**
Comedy
59904 86 mins C B, V P
Dianah Sheridan, John Gregson, Kay Kendall, Kenneth More, directed by Henry Cornelius
Two friendly rivals engage in a race on the way back from the Brighton veteran car rally.
Rank — *Embassy Home Entertainment*

Gentle Giant **1967**
Adventure
79877 93 mins C B, V P
Dennis Weaver, Vera Miles, Ralph Meeker, Clint Howard
An orphaned bear is taken in by a boy and his family and grows to be a 750 pound giant.

Ivan Tors Productions — *Republic Pictures Home Video*

Gentleman Jim 1942
Drama
53671 104 mins B/W CED P
Errol Flynn, Alan Hale, Alexis Smith, Jack Carson, Ward Bond, William Frawley, directed by Raoul Walsh
The rise to fame of boxer Jim Corbett, during the 1880's when boxing was outlawed.
Warner Bros; Robert Buckner — *RCA VideoDiscs*

Gentlemen Prefer Blondes 1953
Comedy
08441 91 mins C B, V P
Marilyn Monroe, Jane Russell, Charles Coburn, Elliot Reid, directed by Howard Hawks
Two showgirls land in police court while seeking rich husbands or diamonds.
20th Century Fox — *CBS/Fox Video*

George 1970
Comedy-Drama
80951 87 mins C B, V P
Marshall Thompson, Jack Mullaney, Inge Schoner
A carefree bachelor takes his girlfriend and his 250 pound St. Bernard on a trip to the Swiss Alps where he proves that a dog is not always man's best friend.
MPAA:G
Marshall Thompson — *United Home Video*

George Burns and Gracie Allen Show, The 1952
Comedy
77191 115 mins B/W B, V P
George Burns, Gracie Allen, Bea Benaderet, Fred Clark, Harry Von Zell, Ronnie Burns
This is a collection of four live episodes of the show including the first television appearance of Burns and Allen from 1950.
CBS — *Shokus Video*

George Burns and Gracie Allen Show, The 1951
Comedy
38991 30 mins B/W B, V, FO P
George Burns, Gracie Allen, Harry Von Zell, Bea Benaderet, Fred Clark
A live Christmas show from the first year of the popular series. Gracie gives her unique version of "A Christmas Carol." Originally telecast December 23, 1951.
CBS — *Video Yesteryear*

George Burns in Concert 1982
Comedy-Performance
80239 60 mins C B, V P
George Burns
The ageless comedian reminisces about his long show business career in this concert taped in Ontario.
GBF Productions — *U.S.A. Home Video*

George Burns Show, The 1959
Comedy
58638 30 mins B/W B, V, FO P
George Burns, Harry Von Zell, Larry Keating, Ronnie Burns, Bea Benaderet, Judi Meredith, Lisa Davis, Carol Channing
Carol Channing sues George in this episode, "The Hollywood Television Courtroom." George sings "Please Don't Take Me Home," and Harry steals the show as an announcer forced to drink his sponsors' products. Sponsored by Colgate, Fab and Ajax, with original commercials included.
NBC — *Video Yesteryear*

George Melies, Cinema Magician 1978
Science fiction/Film-History
59405 17 mins C B, V P, T
A look at film pioneer George Melies who originated the use of special effects in cinema. (Some black and white).
Patrick Montgomery — *Blackhawk Films*

George White's Scandals 1945
Musical
13644 95 mins B/W B, V P, T
Joan Davis, Jack Haley, Jane Greer
Musical comedy look at show biz world. Jazz numbers by Gene Krupa and his band.
RKO; George White — *Blackhawk Films*

Geppetto's Music Shop 1982
Fairy tales
64953 90 mins C B, V R, P
Kindly toymaker Geppetto gathers the children of the village in his house to tell them stories, seen in animation, all drawn from the greats of children's literature.
MPAA:G
Century Video — *Video Gems*

Gerry Mulligan 1981
Music-Performance
75897 18 mins C B, V P
This program presents the jazz music of Gerry Mulligan featuring his compositions "K4 Pacific" and "North Atlantic Run."
Jazz America Ltd — *Sony Corporation of America*

Get Crazy 1983
Comedy/Musical
64981 90 mins C B, V, LV, CED P

Malcolm McDowell, Allen Goorwitz, Daniel Stern, Gail Edwards
The owner of the Saturn Theatre is attempting to stage the biggest rock-and-roll concert of all time on New Year's Eve 1983, and everything is going wrong.
Unknown — *Embassy Home Entertainment*

Get Fit, Stay Fit 1978
Physical fitness
42778 60 mins C B, V P
Ann Dugan
This series of three 20-minute programs is intended for all ages interested in total body conditioning.
Health N Action — *RCA/Columbia Pictures Home Video*

Get Happy 193?
Comedy
10043 59 mins B/W B, V P, T
Shirley Temple, Weber and Fields, Bessie Smith
Includes Shirley Temple in "Glad Rags to Riches," Weber and Fields in "Beer is Here," and Bessie Smith in "St. Louis Blues." Also a Flip the Frog Cartoon.
Educational et al — *Blackhawk Films*

Get Out Your Handkerchiefs 1978
Comedy
47372 109 mins C B, V R, P
Gerard Depardieu, Patrick Dewaere, Casole Laure
Two men try to make one woman happy, then lose her to a precocious, 13-year-old boy.
Academy Awards '78: Best Foreign Language Film. MPAA:R
Springmill Productions — *Warner Home Video*

Getaway, The 1972
Adventure
68233 122 mins C B, V R, P
Steve McQueen, Ali MacGraw
Steve McQueen and Ali MacGraw star as husband and wife bank robbers traveling across Texas to get away from a corrupt politician and the state police.
MPAA:PG
Warner Brothers — *Warner Home Video*

Getting It On 1983
Comedy
72226 100 mins C B, V P
A high school student uses his new-found video equipment for voyeuristic activity.
MPAA:R
Cromworld — *Vestron Video*

Getting of Wisdom, The 1980
Drama
52743 100 mins C CED P
Susannah Fowle, directed by Bruce Beresford
An adaptation of the classic Australian novel, about the trials of an extraordinary teenage girl at an exclusive finishing school in turn of the century Melbourne, the heroine—Laura Rambotham—a gifted pianist who struggles to assert her individuality in the stuffy climate of Victorian conformity.
Australia; Southern Cross Films — *CBS/Fox Video*

Getting Straight 1970
Comedy/Satire
70191 124 mins C B, V P
Elliott Gould, Candice Bergen
A former student activist returns to his alma mater as a teacher and tries unsuccessfully to avoid involvement in the student radical movement.
MPAA:R
Columbia Pictures — *RCA/Columbia Pictures Home Video*

Getting Wasted 1980
Comedy
59331 98 mins C B, V P
Brian Kerwin, Stephen Furst, Cooper Huckabee
Set in 1969 at a military academy for troublesome young men, chaos ensues when the cadets meet the hippies.
MPAA:PG
David Buanno — *United Home Video*

Ghastly Ones,The 1965
Horror
79347 81 mins C B, V P
Three couples are invited to a strange island to participate in the reading of a will.
Andy Milligan — *Video Home Library*

Ghidrah the Three Headed Monster 1965
Science fiction
01668 85 mins C B, V P
Yosuke Natsuki, Yuriko Hoshi, Rodan and Mothra, Directed by Inoshiro Honda
When three-headed monster from outer-space threatens world, humans appeal to the friendly Mothra, Rodan, and Godzilla.
Toho Productions — *Prism; Budget Video; Video Connection; VCII; Discount Video Tapes; Video Yesteryear; Admit One Video*

Ghost Dance 1983
Horror
75624 93 mins C B, V P
A sacred Indian burial ground is violated, with grim results.
Looseyard Ltd — *Trans World Entertainment*

Ghost in the Noonday Sun 1974
Comedy
70718 95 mins C B, V P
Peter Sellers, Anthony Franciosa, Spike Milligan, Peter Boyle, Clive Revell, James Villiers, Directed by Peter Medak
A group of silly pirates search for buried treasure under the direction of their zang chief who turns everything into a mess.
Gareth Wigan — *VCL Home Video*

Ghost of Yotsuya, The 1958
Horror
76901 100 mins C B, V P
Shigeru Amachi
A horrifying tale of the supernatural that deals with the psychological torture of the inner mind. With English subtitles.
JA
Toho — *Video Action*

Ghost Patrol 1936
Western
11728 57 mins B/W B, V P
Tim Mc Coy
G-Men of the West ride hard in this action western.
Puritan — *Video Connection; United Home Video*

Ghost Ship 1953
Mystery
77202 69 mins B/W B, V P
Dermot Walsh, Hazel Court
A young couple is tortured by ghostly apparitions when they move into an old yacht with a dubious past.
Lippert Productions — *United Home Video*

Ghost Story 1981
Suspense
47417 110 mins C B, V, LV P
Fred Astaire, Melvyn Douglas, Douglas Fairbanks Jr., John Houseman, Patricia Neal
Four elderly men, members of an informal social club called the Chowder Society, share a terrible secret buried deep in their pasts. Based on the best-selling novel by Peter Straub.
MPAA:R
Universal — *MCA Home Video*

Ghosts of Berkeley Square, The 1947
Comedy
63621 61 mins B/W B, V, FO P
Robert Morley, Felix Aylmer
The ghosts of two retired soldiers of the early 18th century are doomed to haunt their former home, and only a visit from a reigning monarch can free them.
NTA Pictures — *Video Yesteryear*

Ghoul, The 1975
Horror
58282 88 mins C B, V P
Peter Cushing, John Hurt
A group of stranded travellers is reduced in number when they take shelter in the house of a former clergyman.
MPAA:R
J Arthur Rank; Tyburn Studios — *Electric Video; VCL Home Video*

Ghoul, The 1981
Horror
81195 90 mins C B, V P
John Hurt, Peter Cushing, directed by Freddie Francis
A creature of unknown origin that lives off human flesh is looking for some tasty tidbits at an English mansion.
Tyburn Films — *Media Home Entertainment*

Ghoulies 1985
Horror
80694 81 mins C B, V P
Lisa Pelikan, Jack Nance, Scott Thompson, Tamara DeTreaux
A young boy gets more than he bargained for when he inherits his father's house inhabited by evil little creatures, the ghoulies.
MPAA:PG13
Empire Pictures — *Vestron Video*

G. I. Blues 1960
Musical
08386 104 mins C B, V P
Elvis Presley, Juliet Prowse, Robert Ivers, James Douglas
Three G. I.'s form a musical combo while stationed in Germany.
EL, SP
Paramount; Hal Wallis — *CBS/Fox Video; RCA VideoDiscs*

G.I. Joe: A Real American Hero 1983
Cartoons
79204 94 mins C B, V P
Animated
G.I. Joe and his army must fight off Cobra to control a device that reduces people and objects to a molecular level.
Sunbow Productions — *Family Home Entertainment*

G.I. Joe: A Real American Hero, The Revenge of Cobra Vol. 2 1984
Cartoons
76973 99 mins C B, V P
Animated
G.I. Joe's army must destroy COBRA's weather dominator which is pointed at the nation's capitol.

Sunbow Productions — *Family Home Entertainment*

Giant 1956
Drama
Closed Captioned
81490 201 mins C B, V, LV R, P
Elizabeth Taylor, Rock Hudson, James Dean, Carroll Baker, Chill Wills, Jane Withers, Sal Mineo, Mercedes McCambridge, directed by George Stevens
This is the epic saga of a wealthy Texan who marries a strong willed Maryland woman and the problems they have adjusting to life on a ranch. Available in Stereo Hi-Fi for all formats.
Academy Awards '56: Best Director (Stevens)
Warner Bros — *Warner Home Video*

Giant Step, A 1982
Football
47712 23 mins C B, V, FO P
Team highlights of the 1981 New York Giants who posted their first appearance in NFL post-season play in almost 20 years.
NFL Films — *NFL Films Video*

Gideon's Trumpet 1980
Drama
66277 104 mins C B, V P
Henry Fonda, Jose Ferrer, John Houseman, Dean Jagger, Sam Jaffe, Fay Wray
A true story of how one man's fight for justice changed the course of U.S. legal history.
John Houseman — *Worldvision Home Video*

Gidget 1959
Comedy-Drama
81209 95 mins C B, V P
Sandra Dee, James Darren, Cliff Robertson, Mary Laroche, Arthur O'Connell
A plucky teenaged girl discovers romance and wisdom when she becomes a mascot for a group of college boys as they spend the summer surfing at Malibu.
Columbia — *RCA/Columbia Pictures Home Video*

Gidget Goes Hawaiian 1961
Comedy
81430 102 mins C B, V P
Deborah Walley, James Darren, Carl Reiner, Peggy Cass, Michael Callan, Eddie Foy, Jr.
There's trouble in paradise for Gidget when someone starts a nasty rumor about her while she's on vacation in Hawaii. Available in VHS and Beta Hi Fi.
Columbia Pictures — *RCA/Columbia Pictures Home Video*

Gielgud's Chekhov 1 1981
Literature
58557 52 mins C B, V P
Hosted by John Gielgud
Three tales of escape, literal and figurative: "The Fugitive," "Desire for Sleep," and "Rothschild's Violin."
MasterVision — *Mastervision*

Gielgud's Chekhov 2 1981
Literature
58558 52 mins C B, V P
A pair of tales dealing with illicit love: "Volodya" and "The Boarding House."
MasterVision — *Mastervision*

Gielgud's Chekhov 3 1981
Literature
58559 51 mins C B, V P
A pair of works which investigate the inner world of hopes and dreams: "Revenge" and "The Wallet."
MasterVision — *Mastervision*

Gift for Heidi, A 1962
Drama
11731 71 mins C B, V P
Sandy Descher, Van Dyke Parks
An allegorical tale of Heidi and the lessons she learns uponreceiving three carved figures on her birthday. They represent Faith,Hope and Charity and bring her three adventures to teach their meaning.
RKO — *United Home Video*

Gift, The (Le Cadeau) 1982
Drama
69040 105 mins C B, V R, P
The story of 55-year-old Gregoire Dufour, who chooses early retirement with the hope of somehow changing his dull and boring life. Unknown to Gregoire, his co-workers have arranged the ultimate retirement gifta woman.
Michel Zemer — *THORN EMI/HBO Video*

Gigglesnort Hotel 1976
Puppets/Children
80885 45 mins C B, V P
The puppets inhabiting the Gigglesnort Hotel teach kids to cope with the foibles of growing up.
BILL JACKSON — *Karl/Lorimar Home Video*

Gilda 1946
Drama
21287 110 mins B/W B, V P
Rita Hayworth, Glenn Ford, George Macready
A South American gambling casino owner hires a young American as his trusted aide, unaware of his wife's love for the man. Hayworth sings "Put the Blame on Mame."
Columbia — *RCA/Columbia Pictures Home Video; RCA VideoDiscs*

Gilda Live 1980
Comedy
54120 124 mins C B, V R, P
Gilda Radner, "Father" Guido Sarducci, directed by Mike Nichols
A live taping of Gilda Radner's stage show at New York's Winter Garden Theater. Gilda presents many of her "Saturday Night Live" characters, including dimwitted Lisa Loopner, loudmouthed Roseanne Roseannadanna and punk rocker Candy Slice.
MPAA:R
Warner Bros — *Warner Home Video*

Gimme Shelter 1970
Music-Performance
44777 91 mins C B, V P
The Rolling Stones
Something went wrong at the free concert attended by 300,000 people in Altamont, California and this "Woodstock West" became a bitter remembrance in the history of the rock generation.
Cinema 5 — *RCA/Columbia Pictures Home Video; RCA VideoDiscs*

Gin Game, The 1984
Comedy-Drama
75286 82 mins C B, V P
Jessica Tandy, Hume Cronyn
This tape features a performance of the Broadway play about an aging couple who find romance in an old age home. In Beta Hi-Fi stereo and VHS Dolby stereo.
RKO Home Video — *RKO HomeVideo*

Ginger 1970
Adventure
63083 90 mins C B, V P
Ginger
Fabulous super-sleuth Ginger faces the sordid world of prostitution, blackmail and drugs.
Ginger Productions — *Monterey Home Video*

Gino Vannelli 1981
Music-Performance
47375 60 mins C B, V R, P
Gino Vannelli
Gino Vannelli performs his hit songs in concert, including "I Just Wanna Stop," "Living Inside Myself," "Brother to Brother," and others.
Henry Less and Associates — *Warner Home Video*

Girl, a Guy and a Gob, A 1941
Comedy
80237 91 mins B/W B, V P
Lucille Ball, Edmund O'Brien, George Murphy, Franklin Pangborn, Lloyd Corrigan
A secretary and her sailor boyfriend teach her stuffy boss how to enjoy life.
RKO — *RKO HomeVideo*

Girl Groups: The Story of a Sound 1983
Music/Documentary
64941 90 mins C B, V, CED P
The Supremes, The Ronettes, The Shangri-Las, The Marvelettes, The Shirelles
This documentary on the "girl group" sound of the early 60's features rare footage and interviews with many of the original singers, record producers and songwriters of that period. Among the 25 songs performed are "Please Mr. Postman," "Be My Baby," "Chapel of Love," "Boby Love" and "Stop! In the Name of Love."
Delilah Films — *MGM/UA Home Video*

Girl in Every Port, A 1952
Comedy
29486 86 mins B/W B, V P, T
Groucho Marx, William Bendix, Marie Wilson, Don Defore, Gene Lockhart
Navy buddies acquire two race horses and try to conceal them aboard ship.
RKO — *Blackhawk Films*

Girl in Room 2A, The 1976
Horror
80291 90 mins C B, V P
Raf Vallone, Daniela Giordaro
A young woman recently released from prison discovers the family she boarded with has turned their house into a torture chamber.
MPAA:R
Joseph Brenner Associates — *Prism*

Girl Most Likely, The 1957
Comedy
11732 98 mins C B, V P
Jane Powell, Cliff Robertson
Romance-minded girl dreams of marrying wealthy, handsome man. She runs into a problem when she must choose one of three men.
Universal; RKO — *United Home Video*

Girl Who Was Death, The 1968
Adventure/Fantasy
70589 52 mins C B, V P
Patrick McGoohan, Justine Lord, Kenneth Griffith, directed by David Tomblin
Death, a female assassin, stalks the Prisoner. He narrowly escapes trap after craftly trap in this fifteenth episode of "The Prisoner."
Associated TV Corp. — *MPI Home Video*

Girlfriends 1978
Drama
58234 87 mins C B, V R, P
Melanie Mayron, Anita Skinner, Eli Wallach, Christopher Guest, Amy Wright, Viveca Lindfors, directed by Claudia Weill
The bittersweet, true-to-life story of a young woman learning to make it on her own.
MPAA:PG

(For explanation of codes, see USE GUIDE and KEY)

Claudia Weill — *Warner Home Video*

Girls Are for Loving 1973
Adventure
63085 90 mins C B, V P
Ginger
Undercover agent Ginger faces real adventure when she battles it out with her counterpart, a seductive enemy agent.
Loving Productions — *Monterey Home Video*

Girls, Girls, Girls 1962
Musical
08381 106 mins C B, V P
Elvis Presley, Stella Stevens, Laurel Goodwin, Jeremy Slate, Guy Lee
A boy refuses his girlfriend's gift of a boat. He finds he has a rival for her affections and changes his mind.
EL, SP
Paramount; Hal Wallis — *CBS/Fox Video*

Girls Night Out 1983
Suspense/Horror
78386 96 mins C B, V R, P
Hal Holbrook
An ex-cop must stop a killer who is murdering participants of a sorority house scavenger hunt and leaving cryptic clues on the local radio station.
MPAA:R
GK Productions — *THORN EMI/HBO Video*

Girls of Rock & Roll 1984
Variety/Music video
76929 53 mins C B, V P
An intimate look at this country's up and coming female rock musicians with special on stage performances from the ladies.
Playboy Enterprises — *CBS/Fox Video*

Giselle 1979
Dance
55471 77 mins C CED P
Rudolf Nureyev
An international cast highlights this version of Nureyev's greatest success, produced by Stanley Dorfman for television.
Lord Lew Grade; ITC Entertainment; Stanley Dorfman — *RCA VideoDiscs*

Giselle 1983
Dance
80327 135 mins C B, V R, P
Galina Mezentseva, Konstantin Zaklinsky, Gennady Selyutsky
The classic ballet about a peasant girl who becomes a ghost to destroy the man who betrayed her.
Covent Garden Video Productions — *THORN EMI/HBO Video*

Git Along Little Dogies 1937
Western
08789 60 mins B/W B, V, 3/4U P
Gene Autry, Judith Allen, Champion, Smiley Burnette
Gene Autry and banker's daughter at odds.
Republic — *Video Yesteryear; Discount Video Tapes*

Give 'Em Hell, Harry! 1975
Biographical/Drama
47684 103 mins C B, V P
James Whitmore
James Whitmore's one-man show as Harry S Truman at his feisty best.
Theatro Vision — *Worldvision Home Video*

Gizmo! 1977
Documentary/Inventions
47385 77 mins C B, V R, P
A hilarious and affectionate tribute to crackpot inventors everywhere, with footage of dozens of great and not-so-great machines and other creations. Some segments in black-and-white.
Howard Smith — *Warner Home Video*

Gladys Knight & the Pips and Ray Charles in Concert 1978
Music-Performance
33979 75 mins C B, V P
Gladys Knight, Ray Charles
Backed by the ever-present Pips, Gladys Knight sings "Imagination,""Midnight Train to Georgia," and "Heard It Through the Grapevine." Ray Charles performs several numbers after making a surprise appearance. Gladys and Ray finally combine in a magic blend of inspired song.
HBO — *Vestron Video*

Gladys Knight & The Pips and Ray Charles 1982
Music-Performance
72219 78 mins C B, V P
The dynamic combination perform some of their biggest hits including "Imagination" and "Midnight Train to Georgia."
Independent — *Vestron Video*

Glen or Glenda 1953
Drama/Exploitation
08680 70 mins B/W B, V, 3/4U P
Bela Lugosi, Lyle Talbot, Donald Woods, directed by Ed Woods
A documentary advocating transvestism. The director Ed Woods portrays the haunted figure of Glen or Glenda.
Unknown — *Video Yesteryear; Video Dimensions.; Admit One Video*

Glenn Miller—A Moonlight Serenade 1984
Music-Performance
77252 71 mins C B, V P
Tex Beneke, Marion Hutton, Johnny Desmond, hosted by Van Johnson
The original Glenn Miller singers reunite for this tribute concert that is devoted to Miller's big band hits, including "In the Mood," "Long Ago and Far Away" and "Kalamazoo." Filmed at the Glenn Island Casino. In VHS stereo.
Silverlight Productions — *Magnum Entertainment*

Glitter Dome, The 1984
Drama
80810 90 mins C B, V R, P
James Garner, John Lithgow, Margot Kidder, Colleen Dewhurst, directed by Stuart Margolin
Two policemaen discover the sleazier side of Hollywood when they investigate the murder of a pornographer. Based upon the novel by Joseph Wambaugh. Available in VHS and Beta HiFi.
HBO — *THORN EMI/HBO Video*

Gloria 1980
Drama
52751 123 mins C B, V, LV P
Gena Rowlands, John Adames, Buck Henry, directed by John Cassavetes
A fast-shooting, independent woman fights off the mob in order to protect a young boy.
MPAA:PG
Sam Shaw; Columbia — *RCA/Columbia Pictures Home Video*

Glorifying the American Girl 1929
Musical
01614 80 mins B/W B, V P
Mary Eaton, Dan Healey, Eddie Cantor, Rudy Vallee, directed by Millard Webb
Musical romp with Eddie Cantor and other Ziegfeld stars.
Paramount; Florenz Ziegfeld — *Budget Video; Discount Video Tapes; Video Yesteryear; Classic Video Cinema Collector's Club*

Glory at Sea 1952
War-Drama
66378 100 mins B/W B, V P
Trevor Howard, Richard Attenborough, Sonny Tufts, James Donald, Joan Rice, Bernard Lee
A tough officer takes command of an old U.S. destroyer which has been given to England in the early days of World War II. Original title: "The Gift Horse."
Molton — *Movie Buff Video*

Glory Boys, The 1984
Adventure
80293 110 mins C B, V P
Rod Steiger, Anthony Perkins, Gary Brown, Aaron Harris
A secret agent is hired to protect an Isreali scientist who is marked for assassination by the PLO and IRA.
Independent — *Prism*

Glove, The 1978
Adventure
65290 93 mins C B, V P
John Saxon, Rosey Grier, Joan Blondell
An ex-cop turned bounty hunter has his toughest assignment ever: bring in a 6'5", 250 pound ex-con.
MPAA:R
Julian Roffman — *Media Home Entertainment*

Gnome—Mobile, The 1967
Fantasy/Adventure
76812 84 mins C B, V R, P
Walter Brennan, Richard Deacon, Ed Wynn, Karen Dotrice, Matthew Garber
A lumber baron and his two grandchildren attempt to reunite a pair of forest gnomes with a lost gnome colony.
Buena Vista; Walt Disney Productions — *Walt Disney Home Video*

Go Bears! A Look to the 80's 1980
Football
50079 24 mins C B, V, FO R, P
Chicago Bears
Highlights of the 1979 Chicago Bears' football season.
NFL Films — *NFL Films Video*

Go for It 1976
Sports
59674 90 mins C B, V P
A potpourri of sports action, including surfing, skiing, hang-gliding, kayaking and mountain climbing.
MPAA:PG
Paul Rapp; Richard Rosenthal — *Media Home Entertainment*

Go! Go! Go! World 1964
Documentary
47647 85 mins C B, V, FO P
A "round the world" tour in the tradition of "Mondo Cane," showing the strange and bizarre activities of humankind: mud wrestlers, a Japanese pachinko parlor, Indian snake charmers and a Chinese baby exchange, among others.
Italy — *Video Yesteryear*

Go, Johnny Go! 1959
Musical
76802 75 mins B/W B, V P
Jimmy Clanten, Eddie Cochran, Jackie Wilson, Ritchie Valens
Rock promoter Alan Freed tries to find the mystery contestant who has unknowingly won his talent search contest.
Hal Roach Jr; Alan Freed — *Music Media*

Go Tell the Spartans 1978
War-Drama
45047 114 mins C B, V, LV, CED P
Burt Lancaster, Craig Wasson
In Viet Nam, 1964, a hard-boiled major is ordered to establish a garrison at Muc Wa with a platoon of burnt-out Americans and Vietnamese mercenaries.
MPAA:R
Spartan; Mar Vista — *Vestron Video; Time Life Video*

Go West 1940
Comedy
58293 82 mins B/W B, V P
The Marx Brothers, John Carroll, Diana Lewis
The brothers Marx help in the making and unmaking of the Old West.
MGM — *MGM/UA Home Video*

Godfather 1902-1959—The Complete Epic, The 1981
Drama
58876 368 mins C B, V R, P
Marlon Brando, Al Pacino, Robert Duvall, James Caan, Richard Castellano, Diane Keaton, Robert DeNiro, John Cazale, Lee Strasberg, Talia Shire, directed by Francis Ford Coppola
The complete Godfather saga, Francis Ford Coppola's epic work concerning the lives of a New York crime family. Both original "Godfather" films have been reedited into a chronological framework of the Corleone family history, with much previously discarded footage restored.
Paramount; Zoetrope — *Paramount Home Video*

Godfather, The 1972
Drama
38595 171 mins C B, V, LV R, P
Marlon Brando, Al Pacino, James Caan, Robert Duvall, Talia Shire, Diane Keaton, directed by Francis Ford Coppola
Based on the novel by Mario Puzo, this is the epic portrayal of the Corleone family's rise to the top of the criminal world.
Academy Awards '72: Best Picture; Best Actor (Brando); Best Screenplay (Puzo and Coppola). MPAA:R
Paramount — *Paramount Home Video; RCA VideoDiscs*

Godfather Part II, The 1974
Drama
38596 200 mins C B, V, LV R, P
Al Pacino, Robert De Niro, Robert Duvall, Talia Shire, Diane Keaton, directed by Francis Ford Coppola
Two generations of the Corleone family, fictional Mafia chieftains, are portrayed in this sequel to the "Godfather." The story of young Don Vito (De Niro) is intercut with the rise of his son, Michael (Pacino) to leadership of the family.
Academy Awards '74: Best Picture; Best Supporting Actor (De Niro); Best Director; Best Screenplay. MPAA:R
Paramount — *Paramount Home Video; RCA VideoDiscs*

God's Little Acre 1958
Drama
55318 110 mins B/W B, V P
Robert Ryan, Tina Louise, Michael Landon, Buddy Hackett, Vic Morrow, Jack Lord, Aldo Ray, directed by Anthony Mann
A man convinced that buried treasure is on his farm ruins his land to get at the gold.
Sidney Harmon — *King of Video; VCII; World Video Pictures*

Godsend, The 1979
Horror
69286 93 mins C B, V P
Cyd Hayman, Malcolm Stoddard, Angela Pleasence, Patrick Barr
A little girl is adopted, and she turns her new family's life into a nightmare.
MPAA:R
Cannon Group — *Vestron Video*

Godunov: The World to Dance In 1984
Dance/Documentary
70169 60 mins C B, V P
Alexander Godunov
This documentary features scenes of Godunov dancing and discussions with the ballet star about his defection from Russia, his life in the United States, and his termination from the American Ballet Theatre.
Kultur; Peter Rosen Associates; Metromedia — *Kultur*

Godzilla 1955
Horror
63423 80 mins B/W B, V, LV, CED P
Raymond Burr, Takashi Shimura
The radioactive monster Godzilla attacks Tokyo and terrifies the world.
Japanese — *Vestron Video*

Godzilla vs. Monster Zero **1970**
Science fiction/Horror
64020 93 mins C B, V R, P
Nick Adams
Godzilla, Monster Zero and Rodan are out to destroy the earth, but a heroic space pilot tries to stop them.
MPAA:G
Benedict Pictures Corp — *Paramount Home Video*

Godzilla vs. Mothra **1964**
Horror
64508 90 mins C B, V R, P
Akira Takarada, Yuriko Hoshi, Hiroshi Koizumi
Mighty Mothra is called in to save the populace from Godzilla, who is on a rampage.
Toho Company; American International — *Paramount Home Video*

Goin' All the Way **1982**
Drama
63088 85 mins C B, V P
Deborah Van Rhyn, Dan Waldman
Seventeen-year-old Monica decides that she has to prove her love to her boyfriend, Artie, by going all the way.
Four Rivers and Clark Film — *Monterey Home Video*

Goin' South **1978**
Western
38618 109 mins C B, V, LV R, P
Jack Nicholson, Mary Steenburgen, John Belushi, directed by Jack Nicholson
An outlaw is saved from being hanged by a young woman who agrees to marry and take charge of him.
MPAA:PG
Paramount — *Paramount Home Video*

Going Ape! **1981**
Comedy
53933 88 mins C B, V R, P
Tony Danza, Jessica Walter, Danny DeVito, Art Metrano, Rick Hurst
A young man inherits a bunch of orangutans. If the apes are treated well, a legacy of $5 million will follow.
MPAA:PG
Robert L Rosen — *Paramount Home Video*

Going Berserk **1983**
Satire
66331 85 mins C B, V, LV, CED P
John Candy, Joe Flaherty, Eugene Levy, Paul Dooley, directed by David Steinberg
The stars of SCTV's television comedy troupe are featured in this off-the-wall comedy which lampoons everything from religious cults to kung fu movies to "Father Knows Best."
MPAA:R
Universal — *MCA Home Video*

Going, Going, Gone **1985**
Baseball
81131 25 mins C B, V P
Reggie Jackson
"Mr. October" offers homerun hitting tips with some help from the University of Miami baseball team in this presentation.
Panasonic Film Library — *Major League Baseball Productions*

Going Hollywood **1983**
Film-History/Documentary
79333 75 mins C B, V P
Narrated by Robert Preston
A documentary that examines the stars and films of the great depression of the 1930's. In Beta Hi-Fi and VHS Stereo.
MPAA:G
Julian and Beverly Schlossberg — *Monterey Home Video*

Going in Style **1979**
Comedy
44760 90 mins C B, V R, P
George Burns, Art Carney, Lee Strasberg, directed by Martin Brest.
Three elderly gentlemen decide to liven up their lives by pulling a daylight bank stick-up.
MPAA:PG
Warner Bros — *Warner Home Video*

Going My Way **1944**
Musical-Drama
53398 126 mins B/W B, V P
Bing Crosby, Barry Fitzgerald, Rise Stevens, Frank McHugh, directed by Leo McCarey
A priest assigned to a down-trodden parish works to help the neighborhood's people. Songs include "Going My Way," "Ave Maria," "Swinging on a Star," and "The Day After Forever."
Academy Awards '44: Best Picture; Best Actor (Crosby); Best Supporting Actor (Fitzgerald); Best Director (McCarey).
Paramount; Leo McCarey — *MCA Home Video*

Going Places **1974**
Drama
63967 117 mins C B, V P
Gerard Depardieu, Patrick Dewaere, Jeanne Moreau, Miou-Miou, Isabelle Huppert
A pair of amiable, uninhibited bandits roam the French countryside doing as they please. Dubbed in English.
MPAA:R
Almi-Cinema 5 — *RCA/Columbia Pictures Home Video*

 (For explanation of codes, see USE GUIDE and KEY)

Gold Diggers of 1933 1933
Musical
64785 96 mins B/W CED P
Joan Blondell, Ruby Keeler, Dick Powell, Ginger Rogers
Showgirls help a songwriter save his show in this Busby Berkeley musical. Includes the number, "We're in the Money."
Warner Bros. — *RCA VideoDiscs*

Gold of the Amazon Women 1979
Adventure/Drama
80039 94 mins C B, V P
Bo Svenson, Anita Ekberg, Bond Gideon, Donald Pleasence, directed by Mark Lester
When two explorers set out to find gold, they stumble onto a society of man-hungry women.
Mi-Ka Productions; NBC Entertainment — *Embassy Home Entertainment*

Gold Raiders 1984
Adventure
78344 106 mins C B, V P
Robert Ginty, Sarah Langenfeld, William Steven
A team of secret agents are sent to Laos to find a plane carrying two hundred million dollars worth of gold.
P Chalong — *Media Home Entertainment*

Gold Rush, The 1925
Comedy
58614 85 mins B/W B, V, 3/4U R, P
Charlie Chaplin, Mack Swain, Tom Murray, Georgia Hale
Chaplin's tale of the Little Tramp's misplaced love in the days of the Klondike.
United Artists — *Cable Films; Video Yesteryear; Discount Video Tapes; Sheik Video; Budget Video; Western Film & Video Inc; Blackhawk Films; Classic Video Cinema Collector's Club*

Gold Rush, The 1925
Comedy
44192 60 mins B/W B, V P
Charlie Chaplin, Mack Swain
Chaplin's classic comic masterpiece about the hardships of life on the Alaskan frontier. Abridged.
Spectre Films — *Prism; Kartes Productions; Playhouse Video; See Hear Industries*

Gold Rush, The/Payday 1925
Comedy
48405 92 mins B/W B, V P
Charlie Chaplin, Georgia Hale, Mack Swain
Chaplin drifts along the Arctic tundra, searching for gold and love in "The Gold Rush." In "Payday," he goes out drinking with his buddies.
United Artists — *CBS/Fox Video*

Golddiggers of 1933 1933
Musical
73982 98 mins B/W B, V P
Joan Blondell, Dick Powell, Ruby Keeler, Ginger Rogers, directed by Mervyn LeRoy
A young man has problems when he wants to marry a show girl in this Busby Berkeley choreographed musical that features the song "We're In The Money."
Warner Bros — *Key Video*

Golden Age of Comedy, The 1958
Comedy
55593 78 mins B/W B, V P
Ben Turpin, Harry Langdon, Will Rogers, Jean Harlow, Carole Lombard, Laurel and Hardy, Keystone Kops
The great comedians of silent cinema are seen in clips from some of their funniest films.
Robert Youngson — *VidAmerica*

Golden Boy 1939
Drama
68261 101 mins B/W B, V P
William Holden, Adolphe Menjou, Barbara Stanwyck, Lee J. Cobb
A young man gives up being a great concert violinist and becomes a prizefighter.
William Perlberg; Columbia — *RCA/Columbia Pictures Home Video*

Golden Earring: Live from the Twilight Zone 1984
Music-Performance/Music video
80372 60 mins C B, V P
This is a concert featuring Dutch rockers Golden Earring plus their music video of "Twilight Zone". Available in VHS Dolby Hi-Fi Stereo and Beta Hi-Fi Stereo.
PMV Productions — *RCA/Columbia Pictures Home Video*

Golden Exterminator 1980
Martial arts
69279 80 mins C B, V P
Raymond Chan, James Park, Julia Song, Elliot Ku
Conservative members of the TAI gang battle a powerful group of slave traders and murderers. Mandarin dialogue, English subtitles.
CH
IFD Films & Arts — *Silverline Video*

Golden Lady 1979
Adventure
66283 90 mins C B, V P
Christina World, Suzanne Danielle, June Chadwick

A beautiful woman leads her entourage in a deadly game of international intrigue.
UG Prods — *Monterey Home Video*

Golden Moments **1960**
Baseball
49554 25 mins B/W B, V P
A collection of memorable moments in baseball history from 1905-1960, recalling a half-century of stars from Home Run Baker to Ted Williams.
Lew Fonseca — *Major League Baseball Productions*

Golden Rendezvous **1977**
Suspense
64891 120 mins C B, V P
Richard Harris, David Janssen, John Carradine, Burgess Meredith
A tale of treachery aboard a "gambler's paradise" luxury liner.
Film Trust-Milton Okun Prods; Golden Rendezvous Prods — *Vestron Video*

Golden Seal, The **1983**
Drama
65434 94 mins C B, V, LV, CED P
Steve Railsback, Michael Beck, Penelope Milford, Torguil Campbell
This is the tale of a small boy's innocence put in direct conflict with the failed dreams, pride and ordinary greed of adults.
Samuel Goldwyn Jr — *Embassy Home Entertainment*

Golden Sun **198?**
Martial arts
73958 90 mins C B, V P
Lei Hsiao Lung, Chen Pei Ling, Ou-Yang Chung
A young boxer sets out to find out the truth about Bruce Lee's death in this martial arts film.
Independent — *Unicorn Video*

Golden Tales & Legends—Vol. I **1985**
Fairy tales
77238 60 mins C B, V P
A collection of fairy tales featuring stories written by the Brothers Grimm and Hans Christian Anderson.
Maljack Productions — *MPI Home Video*

Golden Triangle, The **198?**
War-Drama/Adventure
70368 90 mins C B, V P
Lo Lieh, Sambat Metanen, Tien Nee, Tien Fong
It's a battle of the drug pushers set in the mountains surrounded by Laos, Thailand, and Burma where rival gangs fight for control of 70% of the world's opium crop.
Foreign — *Video City Productions*

Golden Voyage of Sinbad, The **1973**
Adventure/Fantasy
Closed Captioned
63445 105 mins C B, V P
John Phillip Law, Caroline Munro, Tom Baker
In the mysterious ancient land of Lemuria, Sinbad and his crew encounter a six-armed sword-brandishing statue, a one-eyed centaur and a griffin.
MPAA:G
Columbia; Charles H Schneer and Ray Harryhausen — *RCA/Columbia Pictures Home Video*

Goldengirl **1979**
Drama
55579 107 mins C B, V P
Susan Anton, James Coburn, Curt Jurgens, Robert Culp
A mad neo-Nazi doctor tries to produce a superwoman—specially fed, exercised, and emotionally conditioned since childhood to run in the Olympics.
MPAA:PG
Avco Embassy — *Embassy Home Entertainment*

Goldenrod **1977**
Drama
80893 100 mins C B, V P
A successful rodeo champion is forced to reevaluate his life when he sustains a crippling accident in the ring.
Talent Associates; Film Funding Ltd of Canada — *Prism*

Goldfinger **1964**
Adventure
52602 108 mins C B, V, LV P
Sean Connery, Honor Blackman, Gert Frobe, Shirley Eaton
James Bond, Agent 007, attempts to prevent an international gold smuggler from robbing Fort Knox.
United Artists — *CBS/Fox Video; RCA VideoDiscs*

Goldie Gold and Action Jack **1981**
Cartoons
80642 40 mins C B, V P
Animated
Futuristic reporter Goldie Gold and intern Action Jack team up to pursue stories with the help of computerized gadgetry.
Hanna-Barbera — *Worldvision Home Video*

Goldilocks and the Three Bears 1983
Fairy tales
Closed Captioned
69321 60 mins C B, V, LV, CED P
Tatum O'Neal, Alex Karras, Brandis Kemp, Donovan Scott, Hoyt Axton, John Lithgow, Carole King
This entry from "Faerie Tale Theatre" tells the story of Goldilocks, who wanders through the woods and finds the home of three bears.
Shelley Duvall — *CBS/Fox Video*

Goldwing 1984
Cartoons
70615 60 mins C B, V P
Animated
A powerful bionic super-hero stars in this adventure cartoon.
Videocraft International Ltd. — *Prism*

Goldy: The Last of the Golden Bears 1984
Drama/Adventure
76775 91 mins C B, V, CED P
An orphaned child and a lonely prospector risk their lives to save a Golden Bear from a circus owner.
Nu Image Films — *Vestron Video*

Golem, The 1920
Film-History
49069 70 mins B/W B, V P
Directed by Paul Wegener
A huge clay figure is given life by a rabbi in hopes of saving the Jews in the ghetto of medieval Prague. Silent.
German — *Sheik Video; International Historic Films; Video Yesteryear; Classic Video Cinema Collector's Club; Discount Video Tapes*

Golf 1978
Golf
44925 30 mins C B, V P
Fitness specialist Ann Dugan demonstrates exercises for golfers to help develop suppleness in hips and shoulders and strength in the back, forearm, and wrist. From the "Sports Conditioning" series.
Health N Action — *RCA/Columbia Pictures Home Video*

Golf Like a Pro with Billy Casper 1985
Golf
81600 51 mins C B, V P
All-time golf great Billy Casper demonstrates basic techniques that will help to improve your game.
Morris Video — *Morris Video*

Golf My Way 1983
Golf
66276 128 mins C B, V P
Jack Nicklaus
Step-by-step instruction on every element of the game, highlighted in super-slow-motion.
JN Productions — *Worldvision Home Video*

Golf My Way with Jack Nicklaus 1984
Golf
66579 120 mins C B, V P
Champion golfer Jack Nicklaus demonstrates step-by-step lessons on every element of golf for beginners or seasoned players. Crucial points are highlighted in super slow motion to highlight every detail
Worldvision — *Worldvision Home Video*

Goliath and the Barbarians 1960
Adventure
81505 86 mins C B, V P
Steve Reeves, Bruce Cabot
Goliath and his men go after the barbarians who are terrorizing and ravaging the Northern Italian countryside during the fall of the Roman Empire.
American International — *MGM/UA Home Video*

Gondoliers, The 19??
Opera/Comedy
65491 112 mins C B, V P
Keith Michell
A new version of Gilbert and Sullivan's opera. This is an entertaining lampoon against class bigotry.
Parsons and Whittemore Lyddon Ltd — *CBS/Fox Video*

Gone Are the Dayes 1984
Comedy
80049 90 mins C B, V R, P
Harvey Korman, Susan Anspach, Robert Hogan
A government agent is assigned to protect a family who are witnesses to an underworld shooting.
Walt Disney Productions — *Walt Disney Home Video*

Gone in 60 Seconds 198?
Adventure
79220 97 mins C B, V P
H.B. Halicki, Marion Busia, George Cole, James McIntyre, Jerry Daugirda
A car thief who works for an insurance adjustment firm gets double crossed by his boss, and the police are on his tail.
Independent — *Media Home Entertainment*

Gone With the West 1972
Western
80421 92 mins C B, V P
James Caan, Stefanie Powers, Sammy Davis Jr., Aldo Ray
Little Moon and Jud McGraw seek revenge upon the man who stole their cattle.
Virginia Lively Stone — *Unicorn Video*

Gone With the Wind 1939
Drama
80439 231 mins C B, V, LV, CED P
Clark Gable, Vivien Leigh, Leslie Howard, Olivia de Havilland, Hattie McDaniel, Butterfly McQueen, directed by Victor Fleming
A selfish southern girl pines away for the man she loves during the Civil War. One of the best-loved motion pictures from Hollywood's golden age which is filled with memorable characterizations.
Academy Awards '39: Best Picture; Best Actress (Leigh); Best Supporting Actress (McDaniel).
MGM; David O. Selznick — *MGM/UA Home Video; RCA VideoDiscs*

Gonzo Presents Muppet Weird Stuff 1985
Variety
Closed Captioned
81545 55 mins C B, V P
Gonzo, Kermit the Frog, John Cleese, Julie Andrews, Vincent Price, Madeline Kahn
Gonzo catches a cannonball and wrestles a brick blindfolded on a guided tour of his mansion.
Henson Associates — *Playhouse Video*

Good Book 1, The 1981
Religion
70711 60 mins C B, V P
Robert Morse, Marcia Lewis, music by Carol Weiss and Gene Casey, directed by Dan Smith
This tape features two fun musical stories from the Bible; "The Parable of the Sower and the Seed," and "The Story of David and Goliath."
Skylark Prods. Ltd. — *Kid Time Video*

Good Earth, The 1937
Drama
59361 138 mins B/W B, V P
Paul Muni, Luise Rainer, Charley Grapewin, Keye Luke, Walter Connolly, directed by Sidney Franklin
Pearl S. Buck's classic recreating the story of greed which ruined the lives of a simple farming couple in China.
Academy Awards '37: Best Actress (Rainer); Best Cinematography (Karl Freund).
MGM — *MGM/UA Home Video*

Good Guys Wear Black 1978
Adventure
31657 96 mins C B, V, LV, CED P
Chuck Norris, Anne Archer, James Franciscus
A mild-mannered professor keeps his former life as leader of a Vietnam commando unit under wraps until he discovers that he's number one on the C.I.A. hit list. He decides to use all his commando skills to stay alive and get to the only man who can stop the C.I.A.
MPAA:PG
Mar Vista — *Vestron Video; Time Life Video*

Good Neighbor Sam 1964
Comedy
77241 130 mins C B, V P
Jack Lemmon, Romy Schneider, Dorothy Provine, Mike Connors, Edward G. Robinson
A married advertising executive agrees to pose as a friend's husband in order for her to collect a multi-million dollar inheritance.
Columbia; David Swift — *RCA/Columbia Pictures Home Video*

Good Sam 1948
Comedy-Drama
69316 78 mins B/W B, V P
Gary Cooper, Ann Sheridan, Ray Collins, Edmund Lowe, Joan Lorring, directed by Leo McCarey
An incurable "Good Samaritan" finds himself in one jam after another as he tries too hard to help people.
RKO Radio; Rainbow Pictures — *Republic Pictures Home Video*

Good, the Bad and the Ugly, The 1968
Western
58481 161 mins C B, V, LV, CED P
Clint Eastwood, Eli Wallach, Lee Van Cleef, directed by Sergio Leone
A drifter, a Mexican outlaw, and a sadist are all out to get a cash box which was stolen and put in an unmarked grave during the Civil War.
United Artists; Alberto Grimaldi — *CBS/Fox Video; RCA VideoDiscs*

Goodbye Columbus 1969
Comedy/Drama
55541 105 mins C B, V, LV R, P
Richard Benjamin, Ali McGraw, Jack Klugman, Nan Martin, directed by Larry Pierce
Philip Roth's novel about a young Jewish librarian who has an affair with the spoiled daughter of a nouveau riche family.
MPAA:R
Paramount; Stanley Jaffe — *Paramount Home Video; RCA VideoDiscs*

(For explanation of codes, see USE GUIDE and KEY)

Goodbye Cruel World 1982
Comedy
81319 90 mins C B, V P
Dick Shawn, Cynthia Sikes, Chuck Mitchell
A suicidal television anchorman decides to spend life's last day filming the relatives who drove him to the brink.
MPAA:R
Sharp Films — *Lightning Video*

Goodbye Emmanuelle 1979
Drama
63347 92 mins C B, V R, P
Sylvia Kristel
This film follows the further adventures of Emmanuelle in her quest for sexual freedom and the excitement of forbidden pleasures.
MPAA:R
Miramax Films — *THORN EMI/HBO Video*

Goodbye Girl, The 1977
Comedy
58872 110 mins C B, V, LV, CED P
Richard Dreyfuss, Marsha Mason, Quinn Cummings, Barbara Rhoades, Marilyn Sokol, directed by Herbert Ross
Neil Simon's story of an over-the-hill Broadway chorus girl with a precocious nine-year-old daughter who shares her apartment with a young actor.
Academy Awards '77: Best Actor (Dreyfuss).
MPAA:PG
Warner Bros; MGM — *MGM/UA Home Video*

Goodbye Norma Jean 1975
Drama
47797 95 mins C B, V R, P
Misty Rowe, Terrence Locke, Patch Mackenzie
A detailed recreation of Marilyn Monroe's early years in Hollywood.
MPAA:R
A Sterling Gold Ltd; Larry Buchanan — *THORN EMI/HBO Video*

Goodbye People, The 1983
Comedy-Drama
64988 90 mins C B, V P
Judd Hirsch, Martin Balsam, Pamela Reed
An elderly man decides to reopen his Coney Island beachfront hot dog stand that folded 22 years earlier. Two people help him realize his impossible dream.
Unknown — *Embassy Home Entertainment*

Goodbye Pork Pie 1981
Adventure
69547 105 mins C B, V P
Tony Barry, Kelly Johnson
With the police on their trail, two young men speed on a 1000-mile journey in a small, brand-new, yellow, stolen car.
MPAA:R
Pork Pie Productions — *Embassy Home Entertainment*

Goodyear Jazz Concert with Bobby Hackett 1961
Music-Performance
46341 24 mins C B, V, FO P
Bobby Hackett, Urbie Green, Bob Wilbur, Dave McKenna, Nabil Totah, Morey Feld
A studio performance by Bobby Hackett's Sextet. The musical program consists of "Deed I Do," "Sentimental Blues," "The Saints," "Bill Bailey," "Struttin' with Some Barbecue," and "Swing That Music."
Mike Bryan, Goodyear — *Video Yesteryear*

Goodyear Jazz Concert with Duke Ellington 1962
Music-Performance
42955 27 mins C B, V, FO P
Duke Ellington and the Band start with "Take the A Train" and run through five other all-time Ellington hits.
Goodyear — *Video Yesteryear*

Goodyear Jazz Concert with Eddie Condon 1961
Music-Performance
46342 28 mins C B, V, FO P
Wild Bill Davison, Cutty Cutshall, Peanuts Hucko, Johnny Varo, Joe Williams, Eddie Condon, Buzzy Drootin
A studio concert by Eddie Condon and friends. The songs performed are "Royal Garden Blues," "Blue and Brokenhearted," "Big Ben Blues," "Stealin' Apples," "Little Ben Blues," and "Muskrat Ramble."
Mike Bryan, Goodyear — *Video Yesteryear*

Goodyear Jazz Concert with Louis Armstrong 1961
Music-Performance
46340 27 mins C B, V, FO P
Louis Armstrong, Trummy Young, Joe Darensbourg, Billy Kyle, Billy Cronk, Danny Barcelona, Jewell Brown
A studio performance by Louis Armstrong's All Stars. Tunes include "When It's Sleepy Time Down South," "C'est si Bon," "Someday You'll Be Sorry," "Jerry," "Nobody Knows de Trouble I've Seen," and "When the Saints Go Marching In."
Mike Bryan, Goodyear — *Video Yesteryear*

Goodyear TV Playhouse: "Marty" 1953
Drama
47483 51 mins B/W B, V, FO P
Rod Steiger, Nancy Marchand, Betsy Palmer, Nehemiah Persoff
One of the best-remembered television dramas of all time, later expanded into an Academy

Award-winning feature film. Rod Steiger portrays a lonely Bronx butcher who thinks he has finally found the girl for him. Written by Paddy Chayefsky and originally telecast on May 24, 1953. Opening credits and commercials are missing.
NBC — *Video Yesteryear*

Goodyear TV Playhouse: "The Gene Austin Story" **1957**
Musical-Drama/Biographical
47484 51 mins B/W B, V, FO P
George Grizzard, Edward Andrews, Jerome Cowan, Phyllis Newman, Gene Austin
A musical biography of 1920's pop singer Gene Austin, featuring the voice of Gene Austin dubbing for George Grizzard. Songs include "My Blue Heaven," "Ramona" and "My Melancholy Baby." Written by Ernest Kinoy.
NBC — *Video Yesteryear*

Goofy Over Sports **194?**
Cartoons
58627 46 mins C B, V R, P
Animated
Goofy stars in this compilation of sports cartoons from the Disney archives: "How to Play Football" (1944), "Double Dribble" (1946), "Art of Skiing" (1941), "How to Swim" (1942), "Art of Self Defense" (1941), and, "How to Ride a Horse" (a segment from the 1941 feature, 'The Reluctant Dragon').
Walt Disney Productions — *Walt Disney Home Video*

Gorath **1967**
Science fiction
80832 77 mins C B, V R, P
The world's top scientists are racing to stop a giant meteor from destroying the Earth.
Tono/Brenco Pictures — *Video Gems*

Gorgo **1961**
Science fiction/Drama
80953 78 mins C B, V P
Bill Travers, William Sylvester, Vincent Winter, Bruce Seton
The parent of a sea monster comes to save her offspring from being put on display in a London circus.
MGM — *United Home Video*

Gorilla **1956**
Adventure/Documentary
47638 79 mins C B, V, FO P
The story of a white hunter and a black native hunter in Africa searching for a killer gorilla.
Swedish — *Video Yesteryear*

Gorilla, The **1939**
Comedy
00400 67 mins B/W B, V P
Ritz Brothers, Anita Louise, Patsy Kelly, Lionel Atwill
Ritz Brothers are hired to protect a country gentlemen receiving strange notes.
20th Century-Fox; Darryl F Zanuck — *Budget Video; Discount Video Tapes; Video Connection; Video Yesteryear; Classic Video Cinema Collector's Club; Kartes Productions; Classic Video Cinema Collector's Club; See Hear Industries*

Gospel **1982**
Music-Performance
65449 92 mins C B, V P
The Mighty Clouds of Joy, Twinkie Clark and the Clark Sisters, Walter Hawkins and the Hawkins Family
A rousing musical theatrical tribute to the leading exponents of Gospel singing. In stereo VHS and Beta Hi-Fi.
Golden Door Productions — *Monterey Home Video*

Gotta Dance, Gotta Sing **1984**
Musical/Documentary
75287 53 mins C B, V P
Fred Astaire, Ginger Rogers, Shirley Temple, Carmen Miranda, Betty Grable
This is a compilation of memorable dance routines from great Hollywood films. In Beta Hi-Fi and VHS Dolby stereo.
RKO Home Video — *RKO HomeVideo*

Grace Jones—One Man Show **1982**
Music-Performance
63422 60 mins C B, V P
Grace Jones
In a concert recorded live in New York and at London's Drury Lane Theatre, Grace Jones performs such hits as "Warm Leatherette," "Walking in the Rain" and "Feel Up."
Island Pictures — *Vestron Video*

Graduate, The **1967**
Comedy-Drama
08365 106 mins C B, V, LV, CED P
Anne Bancroft, Dustin Hoffman, Katharine Ross, directed by Mike Nichols
A young man graduates with honors, meets and has an affair with one of his parents' friends, and is urged to date her daughter. He falls in love with the daughter.
Academy Awards '67: Best Director (Nichols); Film Daily Poll 10 Best Pictures of Year '67.
Avco Embassy — *Embassy Home Entertainment; RCA VideoDiscs*

Graduation Day **197?**
Horror
58960 90 mins C B, V P

Christopher George, Patch McKenzie, E. Danny Murphy
A chiller about the systematic murder of members of a high school track team.
David Baughn;Herb Freed — *RCA/Columbia Pictures Home Video; RCA VideoDiscs*

Graham Parker **1982**
Music-Performance
75922 60 mins C B, V P
This program presents Graham Parker performing some of his greatest hits.
New Music Inc — *Sony Corporation of America*

Grand Canyon Trail **1948**
Western
64387 68 mins B/W B, V, 3/4U P
Roy Rogers, Andy Devine, Charles Coleman
A cowboy's best friend invests his money in a wildcat gold mine.
Republic — *Nostalgia Merchant; Discount Video Tapes*

Grand Hotel **1932**
Drama
80621 115 mins B/W B, V, LV P
Greta Garbo, John Barrymore, Joan Crawford, Lewis Stone, Wallace Beery, Lionel Barrymore, directed by Edmund Goulding
The resident's lives at Berlin's Grand Hotel became intertwined over a twenty-four-hour period.
Academy Awards '32: Best Picture.
MGM; Irving Thalberg — *MGM/UA Home Video*

Grand Illusion **1937**
Film-Avant-garde
11400 111 mins B/W B, V P
Jean Gabin, Erich von Stroheim, Pierre Fresnay, directed by Jean Renoir
A classic anti-World War I presentation, in which French prisoners attempt to escape from their German captor. French with English subtitles.
FR
Continental — *CBS/Fox Video; Video Yesteryear; Sheik Video; Cable Films; Budget Video; Western Film & Video Inc; Cinema Concepts; Classic Video Cinema Collector's Club*

Grand Theft Auto **1977**
Adventure
51990 89 mins C B, V R, P
Ron Howard, Nancy Morgan, Marion Ross, Barry Cahill, Clint Howard
A young couple elope to Las Vegas. The bride's father, totally against the marriage, offers a reward for her return.
MPAA:PG
New World Pictures — *Warner Home Video*

Grandizer **1982**
Cartoons/Science fiction
59329 101 mins C B, V P
Animated
A tale of star civilizations, evil invaders and the quest of one man to protect his adopted homeland, the planet Earth.
EL, SP
Toei Animation; Terry Production — *Family Home Entertainment*

Grapes of Wrath, The **1940**
Drama
08553 129 mins B/W B, V P
Henry Fonda, Dorris Bowdon, Charley Grapewin, Jane Darwell, John Carradine, directed by John Ford
Epic story of the Okie migration to California during the depression. From John Steinbeck's great novel.
20th Century Fox; Darryl F Zanuck — *CBS/Fox Video*

Grass Is Greener, The **1961**
Comedy
65457 105 mins C B, V P
Cary Grant, Deborah Kerr, Jean Simmons, Robert Mitchum
An American millionaire invades part of an impoverished Earl's mansion and falls in love with the lady of the house. The earl is willing to go to any lengths to keep his wife, even a duel with pistols.
Universal — *Republic Pictures Home Video*

Grateful Dead — Dead Ahead, The **1980**
Music-Performance
59851 90 mins C B, V R, P
An historic documentary is presented based on a week long marathon of shows given by the Grateful Dead at Radio City Music Hall.
Stanley Sherman Organization; Grateful Dead Productions — *Warner Home Video; Pioneer Artists*

Grateful Dead in Concert, The **1977**
Music-Performance/Documentary
47046 120 mins C CED P
The Grateful Dead, directed by Jerry Garcia and Leon Gast
A concert by this popular rock group, with 20 songs including "Truckin'," "Casey Jones," and "Sugar Magnolia." The songs are interspersed with backstage shots, interviews with fans, and other scenes. Filmed at the Winterland in San Francisco.
Eddie Washington — *RCA VideoDiscs*

Grateful Dead Movie, The **1977**
Music-Performance/Documentary
81596 131 mins C B, V P

Directed by Jerry Garcia
This rockumentary looks at the lives and the music of the acid rock band The Grateful Dead. Available in VHS Stereo and Beta Hi-Fi.
Eddie Washington — *Monterey Home Video*

Grease **1978**
Musical
38932 110 mins C B, V, LV R, P
John Travolta, Olivia Newton-John, Stockard Channing, Eve Arden, Sha-Na-Na
Film version of the hit Broadway musical about high school life in the 1950's. Songs include "You're the One That I Love," "We Go Together," and "Summer Nights."
MPAA:PG
Paramount — *Paramount Home Video; RCA VideoDiscs*

Grease 2 **1982**
Musical
63426 114 mins C B, V, LV R, P
Maxwell Caulfield, Michelle Pfeiffer, Adrian Zmed, Lorna Luft, Didi Conn, Eve Arden, Sid Caesar, Tab Hunter
The saga of the T-Birds, the Pink Ladies and young love at Rydell High continues.
MPAA:PG
Paramount — *Paramount Home Video; RCA VideoDiscs*

Greased Lightning **1977**
Drama
53513 96 mins C B, V R, P
Richard Pryor, Pam Grier, Beau Bridges, Cleavon Little, Vincent Gardenia
The story of the first black auto racing champion, Wendell Scott, who had to overcome racial prejudice to achieve his success.
MPAA:PG
Warner Bros — *Warner Home Video*

Greaser's Palace **1972**
Comedy/Western
65321 ? mins C B, V P
Albert Henderson, Allan Arbus
Seaweedhead Greaser, owner of the town's saloon, faces his arch nemesis.
Cyma Rubin — *RCA/Columbia Pictures Home Video*

Great Adventure, The **1982**
Adventure
65691 90 mins C B, V P
Jack Palance, Joan Collins, Fred Romer
In the severe environment of the gold rush days on the rugged Yukon Territory, a touching tale unfolds of a young orpham boy and his eternal bond of friendship with a great northern dog.
MPAA:PG
Unknown — *Media Home Entertainment*

Great American Diet and Nutrition Test, The **1981**
Nutrition
57548 60 mins C B, V P
Hosted by Dr. Frank Field, Betty Furness
Viewers can test their knowledge on food additives, labeling, nutrition, obesity, vitamins, and diets.
NBC; Don Luftig — *Karl/Lorimar Home Video*

Great Bank Hoax, The **1978**
Comedy
Closed Captioned
80711 89 mins C B, V R, P
Richard Basehart, Ned Beatty, Burgess Meredith, Michael Murphy, Paul Sand, Arthur Godfrey
Three bank managers decide to rob their own bank to cover up the fact that all the assets have been embezzled.
MPAA:PG
Warner Bros. — *Warner Home Video*

Great Bear Scare, The **1984**
Cartoons
73369 60 mins C B, V P
Animated
The bears of Bearbank send Ted E. and Patti Bear to Monster Mountain to find out if Dracula is going to invade the town on Halloween.
Dimenmark International — *Family Home Entertainment*

Great British Striptease **1981**
Variety
60413 60 mins C B, V P
Sixteen of England's most fetching young women are featured performing the "Great British Striptease."
Kent Waldwin — *Monterey Home Video*

Great Caruso, The **1951**
Musical
53937 113 mins C B, V, CED P
Mario Lanza, Ann Blyth, Dorothy Kirsten
The story of Caruso's rise to operatic fame, from his childhood in Naples, Italy, to his collapse on the stage of the Metropolitan Opera House.
Academy Awards '51: Best Sound Recording; Film Daily Poll '51: Ten Best Pictures.
MGM — *MGM/UA Home Video*

Great Chase, The **1963**
Comedy/Film-History
80038 79 mins B/W B, V P
Buster Keaton, Lillian Gish, Pearl White, Noah Beery, narrated by Frank Gallop
A historical anthology of the funniest and most suspenseful classic movie chases.
Continental; Harvey Cort — *Embassy Home Entertainment*

 (For explanation of codes, see USE GUIDE and KEY)

Great Cities: London, Rome, Dublin, Athens 1980
Cities and towns/Europe
59640 100 mins C CED P
Hosted by Anthony Burgess, John Huston, Melina Mercouri, Jonathan Miller
The history and beauty of four magnificent cities is shown through the eyes of four very special residents of each city.
Learning Corp of America; John McGreevey; Neilsen Fearns Intl — *RCA VideoDiscs*

Great Dictator, The 1940
Comedy/Satire
04805 128 mins B/W B, V P
Charlie Chaplin, Paulette Goddard, Jack Oakie, Billy Gilbert, Reginald Gardner, Henry Daniell
Chaplin's first dialogue film turned to political satire. His ratings as Adenoid Hynkel brought the newreels and radio speeches of Hitler into their perspective.
rbc Films — *CBS/Fox Video; RCA VideoDiscs*

Great Escape, The 1963
Drama
44940 170 mins C B, V P
Steve McQueen, James Garner, Richard Attenborough, Charles Bronson, James Coburn
American, British, and Canadian prisoners in a German P.O.W. camp join in a single mass break for freedom. Based on the novel by Paul Brickhill.
United Artists — *CBS/Fox Video; RCA VideoDiscs*

Great Expectations 1983
Drama
Closed Captioned
73045 72 mins C B, V P
Based upon the Dickens classic about a young boy's rise from a humble childhood to find fortune and happiness.
Burbank Films — *Vestron Video*

Great Expectations 1978
Cartoons/Literature-English
75621 72 mins C B, V P
Animated
This animated version of Charles Dickens' classic is about a boy's meeting with an escaped convict.
WBTV Canada — *Children's Video Library*

Great Expectations/The Man with the Funny Hat 1983
Football
66219 45 mins C B, V, FO P
Highlights from the Dallas Cowboys' 1982-83 and a profile of Head Coach Tom Landry.
NFL Films — *NFL Films Video*

Great Figures in History: John F. Kennedy 1980
Presidency-US/Documentary
56757 105 mins C B, V, CED P
John F. Kennedy, hosted by Harry Reasoner
This program traces JFK through his Presidential years and assassination, and includes an interview with Rose Kennedy. Some scenes are in black-and-white.
CBS News — *CBS/Fox Video*

Great Gabbo, The 1929
Drama
08739 82 mins B/W B, V P
Erich von Stroheim, Betty Compson, Don Douglas, Margie Kane, directed by Erich von Stroheim
A ventriloquist who can only express himself through his dummy.
Sono Art; World Wide — *Movie Buff Video; Sheik Video; Discount Video Tapes; Cable Films; Video Yesteryear*

Great Gatsby, The 1974
Drama
10973 151 mins C B, V, LV R, P
Robert Redford, Mia Farrow, Bruce Dern, Karen Black, Sam Waterston, directed by Jack Clayton
Adaptation of F. Scott Fitzgerald's novel of the idle rich in the 1920's and one man's devotion to a flirtatious waif. Screenplay by Francis Ford Coppola.
Academy Awards '74: Best Song Score, Original or Adaptation; Best Achievement in Costume Design. MPAA:PG
Paramount; David Merrick — *Paramount Home Video; RCA VideoDiscs*

Great Gundown, The 1984
Drama
75672 90 mins C B, V P
An outlaw in New Mexico leaves his gang to return to his family and becomes a fugitive from both sides.
Satori Entertainment Corp. — *VidAmerica*

Great Guns 1941
Comedy
81548 74 mins B/W B, V P
Stan Laurel, Oliver Hardy, Sheila Ryan, Dick Nelson, directed by Montague Banks
Stan and Ollie enlist in the army to protect a spoiled millionaire's son but wind up being targets at target practice instead. Available in VHS and Beta Hi-Fi.
20th Century Fox — *Playhouse Video*

Great Guy 1936
Drama
08747 50 mins B/W B, V, 3/4U P
James Cagney, Mae Clarke, Ed Brophy
Food inspector wipes out graft in his town.

Grand Natl — *Prism; Cable Films; Video Connection; Discount Video Tapes; Classic Video Cinema Collector's Club*

Great Leaders 197?
Bible
35372 105 mins C B, V P
Ivo Garrani, Fernando Rey, Giorgio Ceridni
The inspiring stories of two Old Testament heroes, Gideon and Samson, are dramatized in this beautifully constructed film.
Sunn Classic — *United Home Video*

Great Locomotive Chase, The 1956
Adventure
66054 85 mins C B, V R, P
Fess Parker, Jeffrey Hunter
Based on a curious episode that unfolded during the Civil War, this film tells the tale of Yankee raiders who commandeered a locomotive deep in the heart of Confederate territory.
Walt Disney Productions — *Walt Disney Home Video; RCA VideoDiscs*

Great Love Experiment, The 1984
Drama
80805 52 mins C B, V P
Tracy Pollan, Esai Morales, Kelly Wolf, Scott Benderer
Everyone in a high school learns a valuable lesson about beauty and friendship when four popular students try to change the personality of an awkward classmate.
Scholastic Productions Inc. — *Scholastic Lorimar*

Great Moments in Baseball 197?
Baseball
45031 30 mins C B, V P
Babe Ruth, Lou Gehrig, Willie Mays, Yogi Berra, Joe DiMaggio, Joe Jackson
Highlights of the many stars and happenings that have made baseball the most spectacular sport of the past century.
Major League Baseball — *RCA/Columbia Pictures Home Video*

Great Movie Stunts and The Making of Raiders of the Lost Ark 1981
Filmmaking/Adventure
59857 107 mins C B, V, LV R, P
Harrison Ford
Two TV specials: "Movie Stunts" demonstrates how major action sequences were designed and executed, and "Making of Raiders" captures the cast and crew as they tackle the many problems created in filming the spectacular scenes.

Paramount — *Paramount Home Video; RCA VideoDiscs*

Great Muppet Caper, The 1981
Comedy
58826 95 mins C B, V, LV P
Charles Grodin, Diana Rigg, John Cleese, Robert Morley, Peter Ustinov, Jack Warden, directed by Jim Henson
A group of hapless reporters (Kermit, Fozzie Bear, and Gonzo) travel to London to follow up on a major jewel robbery.
MPAA:G
Universal; AFD; David Lazer — *CBS/Fox Video; RCA VideoDiscs*

Great Race, The 1965
Comedy
69797 147 mins C B, V R, P
Jack Lemmon, Tony Curtis, Natalie Wood, Peter Falk, Keenan Wynn, directed by Blake Edwards
A dastardly villain, a noble hero and a spirited suffragette are among the competitors in an uproarious New York-to-Paris auto race circa 1908, complete with pie fights, saloon brawls, and a confrontation with a feisty polar bear.
Warner Bros — *Warner Home Video*

Great Ride, A 1978
Adventure
78894 90 mins C B, V P
Perry Lang, Michael Macrae, Michael Sullivan
The state police are after two dirt bikers who are riding through areas where bike riding is illegal.
Hooker-Hulette Productions — *Monterey Home Video*

Great Riviera Bank Robbery, The 1979
Suspense/Drama
77421 98 mins C B, V P
Ian McShane, Warren Clarke, Stephen Greif
A genius executes a bank robbery on the French Riviera netting fifteen million dollars.
Jack Gill — *MPI Home Video*

Great St. Trinian's Train Robbery, The 1966
Comedy
63348 90 mins C B, V R, P
Frankie Howerd, Reg Varney, Desmond Walter Ellis
The perpetrators of the Great Train Robbery attempt to stash the loot at a remote school attended by a band of avaricious adolescent girls, with hilarious results.
British Lion — *THORN EMI/HBO Video*

Great Santini, The 1980
Drama
52710 118 mins C B, V R, P

Robert Duvall, Blythe Danner, Michael O'Keefe, Julie Ann Haddock, Lisa Jane Persky
The "Great Santini" is Lt. Col. Bull Meechum, a Marine pilot who treats his family as if they were a company of marines, abusing them in the name of discipline, as they struggle to show him their love.
MPAA:PG
Orion Pictures — *Warner Home Video; RCA VideoDiscs*

Great Scout and Cathouse Thursday, The **1976**
Comedy/Western
64358 96 mins C B, V, CED P
Lee Marvin, Oliver Reed, Robert Culp, Elizabeth Ashley, Kay Lenz
Three gold prospectors strike it rich, but one of them runs off with the money.
MPAA:PG
American International — *Vestron Video*

Great Skycopter Rescue, The **1982**
Adventure
80500 96 mins C B, V P
William Marshall, Aldo Ray, Russell Johnson, directed by Lawrence Foldes
Ruthless businessmen hire a motorcycle gang to terrorize the inhabitants of an oil-rich town, in an attempt to scare them away. A local teenage flying enthusiast organizes his friends into an attack force to fight back.
Star Cinema Productions Group III — *MGM/UA Home Video*

Great Smokey Roadblock, The **1976**
Adventure
65484 84 mins C B, V P
Henry Fonda, Eileen Brennan, Susan Sarandon, John Byner
While in the hospital, a sixty-year-old truck driver's rig is repossessed by the finance company. Deciding that it's time to make one last perfect cross country run, he escapes from the hospital, steals his truck and heads off into the night.
MPAA:PG
Allen R Bodoh — *Media Home Entertainment*

Great Space Coaster, The **1981**
Variety
80363 59 mins C B, V P
Join Gary Gnu, Goriddle and their friends as they explore the sights and sounds of America.
Sunbow Productions — *MGM/UA Home Video*

Great Teams/Great Years Volume One **1981**
Football
50653 48 mins C B, V, FO R, P
New York Jets, Buffalo Bills
This program highlights the accomplishments of the 1968 New York Jets, who, led by Joe Namath, pulled a stunning Super Bowl upset over the Baltimore Colts; and the 1973 Buffalo Bills, who set the NFL 14-game rushing record. O. J. Simpson's 2003 individual yards broke Jim Brown's record.
NFL Films — *NFL Films Video*

Great Texas Dynamite Chase, The **1976**
Comedy
52704 90 mins C B, V R, P
Claudia Jennings, Johnny Crawford, Jocelyn Jones
Two sexy young women drive across Texas with a carload of dynamite. They leave a trail of empty banks with the cops constantly on their trail.
MPAA:R
New World Pictures; David Irving — *Warner Home Video*

Great Waldo Pepper, The **1975**
Adventure
11584 107 mins C B, V P
Robert Redford, Susan Sarandon, Margot Kidder, Bo Svenson, directed by George Roy Hill
After the death of several people as a result of a wing-walking routine, a barnstorming pilot is permanently grounded. He finds he can't adjust to an "earth-bound" life and begins flying again under an assumed name.
MPAA:PG
Universal — *MCA Home Video*

Great White Death **1981**
Documentary
80794 88 mins C B, V R, P
Glenn Ford
Join Glenn Ford as he searches for the Great White Shark in a real life underwater adventure.
MPAA:PG
Jean Lebel — *Video Gems*

Greatest, The **1977**
Biographical/Drama
78880 100 mins C B, V P
Muhammad Ali, Robert Duvall, Ernest Borgnine, James Earl Jones, directed by Tom Gries
The filmed autobiography of the fighter who could float like a butterfly and sting like a bee, Muhammad Ali. In Beta Hi-Fi.
MPAA:PG
John Marshall; Columbia Pictures — *RCA/Columbia Pictures Home Video*

Greatest Adventure, The 1982
Space exploration/Documentary
59958 54 mins C B, V, LV, CED P
Narrated by Orson Welles, Alan Shepard, Gene Cernon, John Glenn, Tom Wolfe
An account of America's race for the moon, from the first orbital flight to Neil Armstrong's landing.
Video Associates — *Vestron Video;*

Greatest Comeback Ever, The 1978
Baseball
29355 58 mins C B, V P
Narrated by Phil Rizzuto and Bucky Dent
This program features the key moments that made the Yankees' struggle for the championship the greatest comeback ever.
Unknown — *VidAmerica*

Greatest Fights of the 70's 1981
Boxing
58868 116 mins C CED P
Muhammad Ali, Joe Frazier, George Foreman, Roberto Duran
Champions of the ring are seen in some of their most unforgettable confrontations.
Big Fights Inc — *CBS/Fox Video*

Greatest Game Ever Played, The 1984
Football
70270 55 mins C B, V, FO P
Frank Gifford, Sam Huff, John Unitas, Gino Marchetti
This film highlights the Baltimore Colts' sudden death overtime victory over the New York Giants in the 1958 NFL Championship Game.
NFL Films — *NFL Films Video*

Greatest Heroes of the Bible 1979
Religion
44944 95 mins C B, V P
This program contains two Bible stories. First, an enactment of how the Ten Commandments were handed down to us. Second, the story of Sampson, who lost his extraordinary power and then, with a great effort of will and spirit, regained it.
Sunn Classic Pictures — *VidAmerica*

Greatest Legends of Basketball 1978
Basketball
08372 60 mins C B, V P
Jerry West, Oscar Robertson, Elgin Baylor, John Wooden
Enjoy the highlights of the careers of basketball greats.
Viacom International — *CBS/Fox Video*

Greatest Show on Earth, The 1952
Drama
53789 153 mins C B, V, LV R, P
Betty Hutton, Cornel Wilde, James Stewart, Charlton Heston, Dorothy Lamour, directed by Cecil B. DeMille
Big top drama focusing on the lives and loves of circus performers.
Academy Award '52: Best Picture.
Paramount; Cecil B DeMille; Henry Wilcoxon — *Paramount Home Video; RCA VideoDiscs*

Greatest Story Ever Told, The 1956
Drama
Closed Captioned
65505 196 mins C B, V P
Max Von Sydow, Charlton Heston, Sidney Poitier, Claude Rains, Jose Ferrer, Telly Savalas, Angela Lansbury, Dorothy McGuire
Christ's journey from Galilee to Golgotha and the world of saints, sinners and believers that appear along the way are seen in this epic.
United Artists — *CBS/Fox Video*

Greek Street 1930
Musical
08672 51 mins B/W B, V, 3/4U P
Sari Maritzia, Arthur Ahmbling, Martin Lewis, directed by Sinclair Hill
The owner of small cafe in London discovers a poor girl singing in the street for food. He takes her in and spotlights her songs in his cafe.
Unknown — *Video Yesteryear*

Greek Tycoon, The 1978
Drama
62877 106 mins C B, V P
Anthony Quinn, Jacqueline Bisset, James Franciscus, Raf Vallone, Edward Albert
The widow of an American president marries a billionaire shipping magnate.
MPAA:R
Universal — *MCA Home Video*

Green Archer, The 1940
Mystery
57354 283 mins B/W B, V, FO P
Victor Jory, Iris Meredith
Fifteen episodes of the famed serial, featuring a spooked castle, complete with secret passages and tunnels, trap-doors, mistaken identity, and the mysterious masked figure, the Green Archer.
Columbia — *Video Yesteryear; Video Connection; Discount Video Tapes*

(For explanation of codes, see USE GUIDE and KEY)

Green Berets, The **1968**
War-Drama
38953 135 mins C B, V R, P
John Wayne, David Janssen, Jim Hutton, Aldo Rey, George Takei, Raymond St. Jacques
John Wayne stars as a Special Forces colonel, leading his troops against the enemy in this war drama of the Vietnam conflict.
Warner Bros — *Warner Home Video; RCA VideoDiscs*

Green Eyes **1980**
Drama
75461 97 mins C B, V P
Paul Winfield
A Vietnam veteran returns to Saigon and finds the girl who bore his baby.
King Features — *U.S.A. Home Video*

Green Mountain Railroading on the Rutland & When Steam Was King **1952**
Trains
66339 20 mins C B, V P, T
These two short films feature scenes of the Bennington and Rutland Railway, Central Vermont's Bellows Falls—Burlington Line and footage of steam-powered trains and locomotives from all over the country. Some sequences in black and white.
Carl Dudley — *Blackhawk Films*

Green Pastures, The **1936**
Comedy
81069 93 mins C B, V P
Rex Ingram, Oscar Polk, Eddie Anderson, George Reed, Abraham Graves, Myrtle Anderson
This is an adaptation of the Marc Connelly play about the black concept of heaven. Available in VHS and Beta Hi-Fi.
Warner Bros. — *Key Video*

Green Room, The **1978**
Drama
58235 90 mins C B, V R, P
Francois Truffaut, Nathalie Baye, Jean Daste, directed by Francois Truffaut
Truffaut's haunting tale of a man who erects a secret shrine to the dead, including his young bride. Based on Henry James, "Altar of the Dead." Subtitled.
MPAA:PG FR
Les Films du Carrosse — *Warner Home Video*

Greenstone, The **1980**
Fantasy/Adventure
70730 48 mins C B, V P
Narrated by Orson Welles
The green stone is a glowing rock in the forbidden forest that transports a young boy into an exciting new world.
Orson Welles — *Active Home Video*

Grendel, Grendel, Grendel **1982**
Fantasy
65653 90 mins C B, V P
Animated, voices by Peter Ustinov, Arthur Dignam, Julie McKenna, Keith Michell
An utterly urbane dragon wants to be friends, but for some reason people are just terrified of Grendel. It's true, he bites a head off once in a while, but nobody's perfect! An ingenious retelling of Beowulf.
Satori Entertainment — *Family Home Entertainment*

Grey Fox, The **1983**
Drama/Western
65115 92 mins C B, V P
Richard Farnsworth, Jackie Burroughs, Wayne Robson
A gentlemanly old stagecoach robber tries to pick up his life after thirty years in prison. Unable to resist another heist, he hides out in British Columbia where he meets an attractive suffragette.
MPAA:PG
Zoetrope Studios — *Media Home Entertainment*

Greystoke: The Legend of Tarzan, Lord of the Apes **1984**
Adventure
78142 130 mins C B, V, LV, CED R, P
Ralph Richardson, Ian Holm, Christopher Lambert, James Fox, Ian Charleson
The story of the seventh Earl of Greystoke from his birth in Africa, through his upbringing by a mystified band of apes, to his homecoming in the Scottish highlands.
Warner Home Video — *Warner Home Video*

Grim Reaper **198?**
Horror
78668 90 mins C B, V P
Tisa Farrrow, George Eastman
A woman on vacation meets up with a man who has his own ideas about population control.
Independent — *Monterey Home Video*

Grit of the Girl Telegrapher, The/In the Switch Tower **1915**
Drama
65769 47 mins B/W B, V P, T
Anna Q. Nilsson, Hal Clements, Walter Edwards, Frank Borzage

A pair of silent railroad dramas, which feature thrilling chase sequences, nefarious schemers and virginal heroines. Silent with piano scores by Jon Mirsalis.
Kalem — *Blackhawk Films*

Grizzly **1976**
Horror
59670 92 mins C B, V P
Christopher George, Andrew Prine, Richard Jaeckel
The largest carnivorous ground beast in the world goes on a killing spree. Also titled: "Killer Grizzly."
MPAA:PG
David Sheldon; Harvey Flaxman — *Media Home Entertainment*

Groove Tube, The **1972**
Satire
03563 75 mins C B, V P
Chevy Chase, Richard Belzer
A series of skits that spoof television.
MPAA:R
Ken Shapiro — *Media Home Entertainment*

Groovie Goolies Volume I **1971**
Cartoons
78351 57 mins C B, V P
Animated
Drac, Frankie, Wolfy and all the residents of Horrible Hall conjure up adventures in this animated collection of episodes from the television series.
Filmation Studios — *Embassy Home Entertainment*

Group Marriage **1983**
Comedy
65724 90 mins C B, V P
Claudia Jennings, Zack Taylor, Victoria Vetri
Six young professionals fall into a marriage of communal convenience and rapidly discover the many advantages and drawbacks of their thoroughly modern group marriage.
MPAA:R
Charles S Swartz — *United Home Video; Continental Video*

Grover Washington, Jr. in Concert **1982**
Music-Performance
59875 53 mins C B, V P
The lush, soulful music of Grover Washington, Jr. is captured in one of his rare public performances along with musicians Eric Gale, Richard Tee, and Steve Gadd. Songs include "Just the Two of Us," "Winelight," and "Come Morning." In stereo.
Bruce Buschel; Gary Delfiner — *Warner Home Video; Pioneer Artists; MGM/UA Home Video (disc only)*

Growing Pains **1982**
Horror
81039 60 mins C B, V P
Gary Bond, Barbara Keilermann, Norman Beaton
A young couple discover that their newly adopted son possesses extraordinary powers.
Hammer Films — *Thriller Video*

Grudge Fights **197?**
Boxing
07877 60 mins C B, V P
The biggest grudge battles in boxing history are highlighted, including Ali-Frazier, Louis-Schmeling, and Dempsey-Tunney.
Big Fights Inc — *VidAmerica*

Guardian, The **1984**
Drama
Closed Captioned
77407 102 mins C B, V P
Martin Sheen, Louis Gossett Jr.
The residents of a chic New York apartment building hire a security expert to aid them in combatting their crime problem.
MPAA:R
HBO — *Vestron Video*

Guardian of the Abyss **1982**
Horror
81038 60 mins C B, V P
Ray Lonnen, Rosalyn Landor, Paul Darrow, Barbara Ewing
A young couple who buy an antique mirror get more then they bargained for when they discover that it is the threshold to devil worship.
Hammer Films — *Thriller Video*

Guess Who Reunion, The **1983**
Music-Performance
65684 118 mins C B, V P
Before a live audience in Toronto, the original Guess Who perform the hits that made them world-wide superstars. Included are performances of "Shakin' All Over," "These Eyes," and "American Woman."
David Wolinsky; Bill Ballard; Dusty Cohl; Michael Cole; Anthony Eaton — *Music Media*

Guest in the House **1944**
Suspense
66379 121 mins B/W B, V P
Anne Baxter, Ralph Bellamy, Ruth Warrick, Marie McDonald, Margaret Hamilton
A seemingly friendly young woman is invited to stay with a family and brings hatred and distrust to them.
Hunt Stomberg; United Artists — *Movie Buff Video*

(For explanation of codes, see USE GUIDE and KEY)

Guide to Making Love, A 1983
Sexuality
65342 57 mins C B, V P
Bryce Britton, Rona Lee Cohen, R.N., M.N.
This program is a guide to sexual awareness; created to help couples fully realize and express their sexuality. It explains how couples can learn to achieve sexual harmony and overcome their inhibitions.
Guide Productions — *Vestron Video*

Gulag 1985
Drama
80324 130 mins C B, V P
David Keith, Malcolm McDowell
An American sportscaster is sentenced to ten years of hard labor in a Soviet prison.
HBO — *Prism*

Gulliver's Travels 1939
Fantasy/Cartoons
03588 77 mins C B, V, 3/4U P
Animated
Animated version of Jonathan Swift's classic about the adventures of Gulliver, an English sailor.
Paramount — *Hal Roach Studios; Nostalgia Merchant; Media Home Entertainment; Republic Pictures Home Video; Video Yesteryear; Sheik Video; Cable Films; King of Video; VCII; Video Connection; Budget Video; Discount Video Tapes; Western Film & Video Inc; Vestron Video (disc only); Kartes Productions; Classic Video Cinema Collector's Club*

Gulliver's Travels 1977
Adventure
54558 80 mins C B, V P
Richard Harris, Catherine Schell
In this partially animated adventure the entire land of Liliput has been constructed in miniature. Cartoon and real life mix in a 3-dimensional story of Dr. Lemuel Gulliver and his discovery of the small people in the East Indies.
MPAA:G
EMI — *United Home Video*

Gulliver's Travels 1979
Cartoons
79243 52 mins C B, V P
Animated
An animated version of the Swift Satire about a sailor whose voyage takes him to an unusual island.
Hanna-Barbera Productions — *Worldvision Home Video*

Gumball Rally, The 1976
Comedy
78624 107 mins C B, V P
Michael Sarrazin, Gary Busey, Raul Julia
An unusual assortment of people converge upon New York for a cross country car race to Long Beach, California.
MPAA:PG
Warner Bros; First Artists — *Warner Home Video*

Gumby Adventure, A 1956
Cartoons
64196 50 mins C CED P
Animated
Travel with Gumby and his pal Pokey as they meet their friends and rivals, the Blockheads.
EL, SP
Clokey Productions — *Family Home Entertainment*

Gumby Adventure Volume 1, A 1956
Cartoons
59324 50 mins C B, V P
Animated
Includes "Witty Witch," "Hot Rod Granny," "In a Fix," "King for a Day," "The Groobee," "Gopher Trouble," "Rain for Roo," "Chicken Feed," and "The Zoops."
EL, SP
Clokey Productions — *Family Home Entertainment*

Gumby Adventure Volume 2, A 1956
Cartoons
59325 50 mins C B, V P
Animated
Includes "The Magic Wand," "Mirrorland," "Robot Rumpus," "Moon Trip," "Trapped on the Moon," "Gumby on the Moon," "The Eggs and Trixie," "Eager Beavers," and "The Magic Show."
EL, SP
Clokey Productions — *Family Home Entertainment*

Gumby Adventure Volume 3, A 1956
Cartoons
64200 60 mins C B, V P
Animated
This volume includes "Baker's Tour," "Gumby Concerto," "The Black Knight," "Toying Around," "The Blockheads," "Gumby Racer," "Toy Crazy," "Sad King Ott's Daughter," and "The Reluctant Gargoyles."
EL, SP
Clokey Productions — *Family Home Entertainment*

Gumby Adventure Volume 4, A 1956
Cartoons
64201 60 mins C B, V P

Animated
This volume includes "The Kachinas," "The Glob," "School for Squares," "Goo for Pokey," "The Golden Iguana," "A Grobee Fight," "Hidden Valley," "Tricky Ball," and "Ricochet Pete."
EL, SP
Clokey Productions — *Family Home Entertainment*

Gumby Adventure Volume 5, A **1956**
Cartoons
64202 60 mins C B, V P
Animated
Includes "Gumby Business," "How Not to Trap Lions," "Lion Drive," "Odd Balls," "Toy Fun," "Train Trouble," "Toy Capers," "Even Steven," "The Ferris Wheel Mystery," and "Lion Around."
EL, SP
Clokey Productions — *Family Home Entertainment*

Gumby Celebration, Volume 10, A **1956**
Cartoons
70654 60 mins C B, V P
Animated
This volume includes "Egg Troubles," "In The Dough," "In the Morning," "Super Spray," "Rodeo King," "Northland Follies," "Pickles Problem," "Piano-Rolling Blues" and "All Broken-Up." Available in Hi-Fi stereo.
EL, SP
Clokey Productions — *Family Home Entertainment*

Gumby for President Volume 9 **1984**
Comedy
73370 60 mins C B, V P
Animated
Gumby, Pokey and his friends are out on the campaign trail with ten new adventures.
Clokey Productions — *Family Home Entertainment*

Gumby Summer, A **1984**
Fantasy
72451 30 mins C B, V P
Runaway robots, malicious blockheads and riled Indians give Gumby and Pokey trouble in the fantasy world of clay animation.
Clokey Productions — *Family Home Entertainment*

Gumby's Holiday Special **1956**
Holidays
65162 60 mins C B, V P
Animated
Gumby and Pokey celebrate Thanksgiving and Christmas in eight adventures that revolve around the holiday seasons, including "Pilgrims on the Rocks," "Son of Liberty," "Pokey's Price," "The Golden Gosling" and "Pigeon in a Plum Tree."
Clokey Productions — *Family Home Entertainment*

Gumby's Incredible Journey **1956**
Fantasy
66181 60 mins C B, V P
Animated
Ten exciting adventures of Gumby and his claymates.
Clokey Productions — *Family Home Entertainment*

Gun Riders **1969**
Western
58606 98 mins C B, V P, T
Scott Brady, Jim Davis, John Carradine
A gunman must seek out and stop a murderer of innocent people.
Independent Intl — *Blackhawk Films*

Gun Smugglers/Hot Lead **1951**
Western
81030 120 mins B/W B, V P
Tim Holt, Richard Martin, Martha Hyer
A western double feature: Tim Holt and his sidekick Chito must recover a shipment of stolen guns in "Gun Smugglers", and the duo gallup into action against a gang of train robbers in "Hot Lead".
RKO — *RKO HomeVideo*

Gunfight at the O.K. Corral **1957**
Western
38622 122 mins C B, V, LV R, P
Burt Lancaster, Kirk Douglas, Rhonda Fleming, Jo Van Fleet, directed by John Sturges
The story of Wyatt Earp and Doc Holliday who joined forces in Dodge City to rid the town of the criminal Clanton gang is portrayed definitively in this western classic.
Paramount — *Paramount Home Video; RCA VideoDiscs*

Gung Ho **1943**
War-Drama
08775 88 mins B/W B, V, 3/4U P
Randolph Scott, Noah Beery Jr., Alan Curtis, Grace McDonald
Marine raiders, in new outfit, train for invasion during World War II.
Universal; Walter Wanger — *Hal Roach Studios; Video Yesteryear; Budget Video; International Historic Films; Sheik Video; Cable Films; VCII; Video Connection; Discount Video Tapes; Cinema Concepts; Kartes Productions;*

Republic Pictures Home Video; Classic Video Cinema Collector's Club; See Hear Industries

---

Gunga Din 1939
Adventure
00257 117 mins B/W B, V, 3/4U P
Cary Grant, Douglas Fairbanks Jr., Joan Fontaine
Based on Kipling's adventure book, this story features three soldier comrades battling savages.
RKO; George Seaton — *Nostalgia Merchant; VidAmerica; King of Video; Blackhawk Films*

Gunplay 1951
Western
64406 61 mins B/W B, V, 3/4U P
Tim Holt, Joan Dixon, Richard Martin
Two cowboys befriend a boy whose father has been killed and search for the murderer.
RKO — *Nostalgia Merchant*

Guns of Fury 1945
Western
14661 60 mins B/W B, V P
Duncan Renaldo
Cisco and Pancho solve the troubles of a small boy in this wild western.
United Artists — *United Home Video; Video Connection; Discount Video Tapes*

Guns of Navarone, The 1961
Adventure
13253 159 mins C B, V P
Gregory Peck, David Niven, Anthony Quinn, Stanley Baker, Anthony Quayle, directed by J. Lee Thompson
British Intelligence in the Middle East sends six men to Navarone to destroy guns manned by the Germans.
Filmdom's Famous Five '61: Best Actor (Peck); Best Supporting Actor (Quinn).
Columbia; Carl Foreman — *RCA/Columbia Pictures Home Video; RCA VideoDiscs*

Gus 1976
Comedy
55568 96 mins C CED R, P
Ed Asner, Don Knotts, Gary Grimes, Tim Conway, Dick Van Patten, Ronnie Schell, Bob Krane, Tom Bosley, directed by Vincent McEveety
A mule with the ability to kick long field goals saves a professional football team from oblivion.
MPAA:G
Walt Disney — *RCA VideoDiscs*

Gus 1976
Comedy
70671 96 mins C B, V R, P
Edward Asner, Don Knotts, Gary Grimes, Tim Conway
The California Atoms own the worst record in the league until they begin to pull victories out of their field goal kicking mule of a mascot, Gus. The competition then plots a donkeynapping.
MPAA:G
Walt Disney Productions — *Walt Disney Home Video*

Guys and Dolls 1955
Musical
53663 149 mins C B, V, CED P
Marlon Brando, Jean Simmons, Frank Sinatra, Vivian Blaine, Stubby Kaye, Sheldon Leonard, directed by Joseph L. Mankiewicz
A New York gangster takes a bet that he can romance a Salvation Army lady. Frank Loesser's score includes "Luck Be a Lady," "If I were a Bell," "Sit Down You're Rocking the Boat."
Samuel Goldwyn — *CBS/Fox Video*

Gymnastics with National Championship Coach Paul Ziert 1985
Gymnastics/Physical fitness
81597 55 mins C B, V P
2 pgms
Gymnastics coach Paul Ziert describes a series of exercises that will aid gymnasts in improving their flexibility.
1.Developmental Gymnastics: Class III & IV Compulsory Exercises for Men 2.Developmental Gymnastics: Class III & IV Compulsory Exercises for Women
Morris Video — *Morris Video*

Gypsy 1962
Musical
74205 149 mins C B, V R, P
Rosalind Russell, Natalie Wood, Karl Malden
This is the life story of America's most famous striptease queen, Gypsy Rose Lee. Rosalind Russell gives a memorable performance as the infamous Gypsy.
Mervyn Le Roy — *Warner Home Video*

H

Hail 1972
Satire
76660 85 mins C B, V P
Richard B. Shull, Dick O'Neil, Phil Foster, Joseph Sirola, Dan Resin
A biting satire of what-might-have-been if certain key cabinet members had their way.
MPAA:PG

Fred Levinson Productions — *Monterey Home Video*

Hair 1979
Musical
37529 118 mins C B, V, CED P
Treat Williams, John Savage, Beverly D'Angelo
Film version of the 1960's Broadway musical about the carefree life of the flower children and the shadow of the Vietnam War that hangs over them.
MPAA:R
United Artists — *CBS/Fox Video; RCA VideoDiscs*

Hal Roach Comedy Classics Volume I 193?
Comedy
59154 80 mins B/W B, V, 3/4U P
Stan Laurel, Oliver Hardy, Harry Langdon, Charley Chase
Films include: "Hoosegow" (1930), with Laurel and Hardy; "The Head Guy" (1930), with Harry Langdon; "High Gear" (1931), with the Boyfriends and "On the wrong Trek" (1936), with Laurel and Hardy and Charley Chase.
Hal Roach — *Nostalgia Merchant*

Half-Shot at Sunrise 1930
Comedy
56907 78 mins B/W B, V, FO P
Wheeler and Woolsey, Dorothy Lee
Madcap vaudeville comedians play AWOL soldiers loose in 1918 Paris. Continuous one-liners, sight gags, and slapstick nonsense.
RKO — *Video Yesteryear; Cable Films; Discount Video Tapes; Classic Video Cinema Collector's Club; See Hear Industries*

Hall of Famers 1960
Baseball
49551 60 mins B/W B, V P
Three twenty-minute segments which highlight the careers of members of baseball's Hall of Fame who were elected before 1960.
Major League Baseball — *Major League Baseball Productions*

Hallmark Hall of Fame, The 1954
Drama
78099 103 mins B/W B, V, FO P
Maurice Evans, Dame Judith Anderson, House Jameson, Richard Waring, Guy Sorel
A first-rate mounting of great tragedy, "Macbeth," with Maurice Evans in the title role.
NBC — *Video Yesteryear*

Hallmark Theater (Sometimes She's Sunday) 1952
Drama
42970 26 mins B/W B, V, FO P
Adult fare about a Portuguese-American fisherman whose daughter becomes engaged to a typical American boy.
NBC — *Video Yesteryear*

Halloween 1978
Horror
42908 85 mins C B, V, LV P
Jamie Lee Curtis, Nancy Loomis, P.J. Soles, directed by John Carpenter
John Carpenter's horror classic has been acclaimed "the most successful independent motion picture of all time." A deranged youth returns to his hometown after fifteen years in an asylum with murderous intent.
MPAA:R EL, SP
Debra Hill — *Media Home Entertainment*

Halloween II 1981
Horror
47418 92 mins C B, V, LV, CED P
Jamie Lee Curtis, Donald Pleasance
Picking up precisely where "Halloween" left off, the sequel begins with the escape of vicious killer Shape, who continues to murder and terrorize the community of Haddonfield, Illinois. VHS in stereo.
MPAA:R
Universal — *MCA Home Video*

Halloween III: The Season of the Witch 1982
Horror
60586 98 mins C B, V, CED P
Tom Atkins, Stacey Nelkin, Dan O'Herlihy, Ralph Strait, directed by Tommy Lee Wallace
A mad warlock threatens to subject 50 million children to a Halloween they'll never forget, in this sequel produced by John Carpenter.
MPAA:R
Universal; John Carpenter — *MCA Home Video*

Hambone and Hillie 1984
Comedy/Adventure
79707 97 mins C B, V R, P
Lillian Gish, Timothy Bottoms, Candy Clark, OJ Simpson, Robert Walker, Jack Carter
An elderly woman makes a three thousand mile trek across the United States to search for her lost dog.
MPAA:PG
New World Pictures; Sandy Howard — *THORN EMI/HBO Video*

 (For explanation of codes, see USE GUIDE and KEY)

Hamlet **1948**
Drama
44362 142 mins B/W CED P
Sir Laurence Olivier, Jean Simmons, Stanley Holloway, Eileen Herlie, directed by Sir Laurence Olivier
Shakespeare's most famous tragedy about a young prince plagued by murder and madness. Academy Awards '48: Best Production; Best Actor (Olivier); Best Art Design, Black and White; Best Costume Design, Black and White.
Universal, J Arthur Rank — *RCA VideoDiscs*

Hammer Into Anvil **1968**
Adventure/Fantasy
70588 52 mins C B, V P
Patrick McGoohan, Patrick Cargill, Victor Madden, directed by Pat Jackson.
In this fourteenth episode of "The Prisoner" TV series, the Prisoner is having big problems with his Number 2. When push comes to shove, the Prisoner blows his Number 2 out.
Associated TV Corp. — *MPI Home Video*

Hammett **1982**
Mystery
69023 97 mins C B, V R, P
This mystery thriller plunges real-life writer and detective Dashiell Hammett into the world of his fictional characters.
MPAA:PG
Zoetrope Studios — *Warner Home Video*

Hand, The **1981**
Horror
58236 105 mins C B, V R, P
Michael Caine, Andrea Marcovicci, Annie McEnroe
A gifted cartoonist's hand is severed in an accident. Soon a hand is on the loose seeking out victims to satisfy an obsessive revenge.
MPAA:R
Orion Pictures — *Warner Home Video*

Hang 'Em High **1967**
Western
62777 114 mins C B, V P
Clint Eastwood, Inger Stevens, Ed Begley, Pat Hingle, James MacArthur
A cowboy is saved from a lynching and vows to hunt down the gang that nearly killed him.
United Artists — *CBS/Fox Video; RCA VideoDiscs*

Hangar 18 **1980**
Science fiction/Adventure
47685 97 mins C B, V P
Darren McGavin, Robert Vaughn, Garry Collins, Joseph Campanella, James Hampton, Tom Hallick, Pamela Bellwood
A space drama about two astronauts who witness an unexpected disaster in orbit.
MPAA:PG
Sunn Classic; Charles E Sellier Jr — *Worldvision Home Video*

Hanky Panky **1982**
Comedy
Closed Captioned
62810 103 mins C B, V P
Gene Wilder, Gilda Radner, Richard Widmark, Kathleen Quinlan, directed by Sidney Poitier
A comic thriller in the Hitchcock vein, in which Gene Wilder and Gilda Radner become involved in a search for top-secret plans.
MPAA:PG
Columbia — *RCA/Columbia Pictures Home Video; RCA VideoDiscs*

Hanna K **1983**
Drama
65512 111 mins C B, V P
Jill Clayburgh, Gabriel Byrne, Jean Yanne, Muhamad Bakri, David Clennon, Oded Kotler
The gripping story of divided passions set in the tumultuous state of Israel.
MPAA:R
Universal — *MCA Home Video*

Hanover Street **1979**
Drama
63442 109 mins C B, V P
Harrison Ford, Lesley-Anne Down, Christopher Plummer, Alec McCowan
An American bomber pilot and a British nurse fall in love in war-torn Europe, but another man is in love with the nurse as well.
MPAA:PG
Columbia; Paul N Lazarus II — *RCA/Columbia Pictures Home Video*

Hans Brinker **1969**
Musical
80156 103 mins C B, V R, P
Eleanor Parker, Richard Basehart, Cyril Ritchard
Young Hans Brinker and his sister participate in an iceskating race, hoping to win a pair of silver skates.
MMM Productions — *Warner Home Video*

Hansel and Gretel **1954**
Fairy tales
59048 82 mins C B, V P
Voices of Anna Russell, Mildred Dunnock
This famed Grimms fairy tale tells the story of the woodcutter's children who venture into the forest and are caught in the clutches of a wicked old witch. Puppet animation.
EL, SP
Hansel and Gretel Co — *Media Home Entertainment; RCA VideoDiscs*

Hansel and Gretel 1984
Fairy tales
Closed Captioned
73143 60 mins C B, V, CED P
Ricky Schroeder, Joan Collins, Paul Dooley, Bridgette Anderson, James Frawley
From "Faerie Tale Theatre" comes the story of two young children who get more than they bargained for when they eat a gingerbread house.
Shelley Duvall — *CBS/Fox Video*

Happiest Millionaire, The 1967
Musical
65634 144 mins C B, V R, P
Fred MacMurray, Tommy Steele, Greer Garson, Geraldine Page, Lesley Ann Warren, John Davidson
A newly immigrated lad finds a job as butler to a household that features pet alligators in the conservatory and a Bible-and-boxing school in the stables. In stereo VHS and Beta Hi-Fi.
Buena Vista — *Walt Disney Home Video*

Happy Birthday to Me 1981
Horror
58497 108 mins C B, V, LV P
Melissa Sue Anderson, Glenn Ford, directed by J. Lee Thompson
Several elite seniors at an exclusive private school mysteriously disappear—one by one.
MPAA:R
Columbia; John Dunning — *RCA/Columbia Pictures Home Video*

Happy Hooker Goes Hollywood, The 1980
Comedy
52761 86 mins C B, V, LV P
Martine Beswicke
The third film inspired by Xaviera Hollander's memoirs, in which the fun-loving Xaviera comes to Hollywood with the intention of making a movie based on her book, but soon meets up with a series of scheming, would-be producers.
MPAA:R
Golan Globus Productions; Alan Roberts — *MCA Home Video*

Happy Hooker Goes to Washington, The 1977
Comedy
55220 89 mins C B, V, CED P
Joey Heatherton, George Hamilton
The further adventures of the world's most famous madam find Xaviera Hollander the target of a U.S. Senate investigation.
MPAA:R
Cannon Releasing — *Vestron Video*

Hardcore 1979
Drama
47433 106 mins C B, V P
George C. Scott, Season Hubley, Peter Boyle, directed by Paul Schrader
A midwestern businessman travels to California to find his runaway daughter, who has become a prostitute and pornographic film star.
MPAA:R
Columbia — *RCA/Columbia Pictures Home Video*

Hard Country 1981
Drama
53352 101 mins C CED P
Jan-Michael Vincent, Kim Basinger, Michael Parks, Tanya Tucker
A young woman decides to break away from her boyfriend and her small Texas town, causing him to re-evaluate his life.
MPAA:PG
ITC; Martin Starger — *CBS/Fox Video*

Hard Day's Night, A 1964
Musical
69037 90 mins B/W B, V, LV, CED P
John Lennon, Paul McCartney, George Harrison, Ringo Starr
This program depicts, with good-natured honesty and fun, the Beatles' lighthearted message to youth.
Walter Shenson — *MPI Home Video*

Hard Times 1975
Drama
64236 92 mins C B, V P
Charles Bronson, James Coburn, Jill Ireland, Strother Martin
A Depression-era drifter becomes a bare knuckle street fighter, and a gambler decides to promote him for big stakes.
MPAA:PG
Columbia — *RCA/Columbia Pictures Home Video*

Hard to Hold 1984
Musical-Drama
72931 93 mins C B, V, LV, CED P
Rick Springfield, Patti Hansen, Janet Eiber
Rockin' Rick's film debut where he falls in love with a children's counselor after an automobile accident. Rick sings "Love Somebody" with music by Peter Gabriel.
MPAA:PG
D Constantine Conte — *MCA Home Video*

Hard Way, The 1980
Drama
81060 88 mins C B, V P
Patrick McGoohan, Lee Van Cleef, Donal McCann, Edna O'Brien
A world weary assassin is pressured by his boss to perform one last assignment. A surprise awaits him if he accepts.

Jack Gill — *Trans World Entertainment*

Hardbodies 1984
Comedy
Closed Captioned
70186 88 mins C B, V P
Grant Cramer, Teal Roberts, directed by Mark Griffiths
Three middle-aged men hit the beaches of Southern California in search of luscious young girls. In VHS Hi-Fi and Beta Hi-Fi.
MPAA:R
Columbia Pictures — *RCA/Columbia Pictures Home Video*

Harder They Come, The 1972
Musical-Drama
47048 93 mins C B, V R, P
Jimmy Cliff, Janet Barkley, Carl Bradshaw
A poor Jamaican youth becomes a success with a hit reggae record, but finds his fame is short-lived.
MPAA:R
New World Pictures — *THORN EMI/HBO Video; RCA VideoDiscs*

Harder They Fall, The 1956
Drama
21288 109 mins B/W B, V P
Humphrey Bogart, Rod Steiger, Jan Sterling
An unemployed reporter promotes a fighter for the syndicate, while doing an expose on the fight racket. Based on Budd Schulberg's novel.
Columbia — *RCA/Columbia Pictures Home Video*

Hardhat and Legs 1980
Comedy
81154 96 mins C B, V P
Sharon Gless, Kevin Dobson, Ray Serra, Elva Josephson, Bobby Short, directed by Lee Phillips
Comic complications arise when a New York construction worker falls in love with the woman who's teaching the modern sexuality course he's enrolled in.
Syzygy Productions — *Lightning Video*

Hardware Wars and Other Film Farces 1981
Science fiction/Satire
47397 48 mins C B, V R, P
A collection of four award-winning spoofs of big-budget film epics, featuring "Hardware Wars," "Porklips Now," "Bambi Meets Godzilla" and "Closet Cases of the Nerd Kind." Some black-and-white segments.
MPAA:G
Ernie Fosselius et al — *Warner Home Video*

Harlan County, U.S.A. 1976
Miners and mining/Documentary
44778 103 mins C B, V P
Directed by Barbara Kopple
The emotions of 180 coal mining families are seen up close in this classic documentary about their struggle to win a United Mine Workers contract in Kentucky.
Academy Award '76: Best Documentary.
Cinema 5 — *RCA/Columbia Pictures Home Video*

Harlem Rides the Range 1939
Western/Musical
66380 60 mins B/W B, V P
Herb Jeffries, Clarens Brooks, Spencer Williams
A singing cowboy foils the attempt by some bad guys to steal the deed to his sweetheart's radium mine. This all-black musical western hybrid stars popular singer Herb Jeffries, known here as "The Bronze Buckaroo."
Sack Amusement Enterprises — *Movie Buff Video*

Harold and Maude 1971
Comedy
38588 91 mins C B, V, LV R, P
Ruth Gordon, Bud Cort, directed by Hal Ashby
A classic cult film starring an unlikely pair: a rich, jaded 20-year old man and a wacky 80-year-old woman, who go off on a series of wild adventures.
MPAA:PG
Paramount — *Paramount Home Video; RCA VideoDiscs*

Harold Lloyd's Comedy Classics 1919
Comedy
69554 47 mins B/W B, V, FO P
Harold Lloyd, Snub Pollard, Bebe Daniels
Four early Harold Lloyd shorts from 1916-1919 are combined on this tape: "The Chef," "The Cinema Director," "Two Gun Gussie" and "I'm On My Way." Silent with musical score.
Pathe — *Video Yesteryear*

Harper 1966
Mystery
69024 119 mins C B, V R, P
Paul Newman
Paul Newman stars in this action-charged 1966 private-eye mystery.
Warner Bros — *Warner Home Video*

Harper Valley P.T.A. 1978
Comedy
66095 93 mins C B, V, CED P
Barbara Eden, Nanette Fabray, Louis Nye, Pat Paulsen, Ronny Cox
A tale of what happened when "my momma socked it to the Harper Valley P.T.A."
MPAA:PG

April Fool Productions — *Vestron Video*

Harrad Experiment, The 1973
Drama
06006 95 mins C B, V P
James Whitmore, Tippi Hedron, Don Johnson
An experiment in co-ed living in New England, Ivy League-type university. Based on Robert H. Rimmer's novel.
MPAA:R
Cinerama; Dennis Stevens and Cinema Arts Prod — *Wizard Video*

Harry and Son 1984
Drama
73031 117 mins C B, V, LV, CED P
Paul Newman, Robby Benson, Joanne Woodward, Ellen Barkin
A widowed construction worker faces the problems of raising his son.
MPAA:PG
Orion — *Vestron Video*

Harry and Walter Go to New York 1976
Comedy
21289 120 mins C B, V P
James Caan, Elliot Gould, Michael Caine, Diane Keaton
Two vaudeville performers are hired by a crooked British entrepreneur for a wild crime scheme.
MPAA:PG
Columbia — *RCA/Columbia Pictures Home Video*

Harry Chapin:The Final Concert 1981
Music-Performance
58867 89 mins C B, V, CED P
Harry Chapin
Taped live at Hamilton Place in Hamilton, Canada, this concert features the warm, energetic style which earned the singer-songwriter legions of devoted fans. Songs include, "Taxi," "Sequel," and "Cat's in the Cradle."
GRM Productions Inc. — *CBS/Fox Video*

Harry Owens and His Royal Hawaiians 1958
Music-Performance
78089 59 mins B/W B, V, FO P
This program presents a Hawaiian festival of music and dancing with Harry Owens and his band.
NBC — *Video Yesteryear*

Harry Tracy 1983
Drama
65343 111 mins C B, V P
Bruce Dern, Gordon Lightfoot, Helen Shaver
This is the tale of the legendary outlaw whose escapades made him both a wanted criminal and an exalted folk hero.
MPAA:PG
Cid and Marty Krofft; Albert Penzer — *Vestron Video*

Harum Scarum 1965
Musical-Drama
80152 95 mins C B, V P
Elvis Presley, Mary Ann Mobley, Fran Jeffries
A movie star travelling through the Middle East becomes involved in an attempted assassination.
Metro Goldwyn Mayer — *MGM/UA Home Video*

Hash House Fraud, A/The Sultan's Wife 191?
Comedy
59406 33 mins B/W B, V P, T
Louise Fazenda, Hugh Fay, Chester Conklin, The Keystone Cops, Gloria Swanson, Bobby Vernon
"A Hash House Fraud" (1915) features a frenetic Keystone chase. "The Sultan's Wife" (1917) concerns a woman who attracts the unwanted attention of a sultan.
Mack Sennett — *Blackhawk Films*

Hatari 1962
Adventure
64938 158 mins C B, V, LV R, P
John Wayne, Elsa Martinelli, Red Buttons, Hardy Kruger, directed by Howard Hawks
A team of professional big game hunters have an exciting time capturing wild beasts to send to zoos.
Paramount — *Paramount Home Video*

Hatfields and the McCoys, The 1975
Drama
80486 90 mins C B, V P
Jack Palance, Steve Forrest, Richard Hatch, Karen Lamm
A retelling of the most famous feud in American history, the legendary mountain war between the Hatfields and the McCoys.
Charles Fries Productions — *Worldvision Home Video*

Haunted Castle, The (Schloss Vogelod) 1921
Film-History
51397 56 mins B/W B, V, FO P
Arnold Korff, Lulu Keyser-Korf
The first German mystery film. Silent, with English subtitles.

FW Murnau — *Video Yesteryear; Discount Video Tapes; Classic Video Cinema Collector's Club*

Haunted Ranch **1943**
Western
38983 56 mins B/W B, V, FO P
The Range Busters (John "Dusty" King, David Sharpe, Max "Alibi" Terhune)
Reno Red has been murdered and a shipment of gold bullion is missing. A gang on the lookout for the gold tries to convince people that Red's ranch is haunted by his ghost.
Monogram — *Discount Video Tapes; Video Yesteryear; Blackhawk Films*

Haunted Strangler, The **1958**
Horror
59661 78 mins B/W B, V P
Boris Karloff, Elizabeth Allan
The story of a social reformer who discovers that he was once a notorious murderer. The realization causes him to become re-transformed into the killer.
John Croydon — *Media Home Entertainment*

Haunting of Julia, The **1981**
Horror
59046 96 mins C B, V P
Mia Farrow, Keir Dullea, Tom Conti
Peter Straub wrote this tale of revenge and remorse set in a London house reverberating with the guilty apprehension of a woman who succumbs to the ghost of a long dead child.
MPAA:R
Peter Fetterman — *Media Home Entertainment*

Haunts **1976**
Horror
78345 97 mins C B, V P
Cameron Mitchell, Aldo Ray, Mai Britt$mp2
A tormented woman has difficulty distinguishing between fantasy and reality in this horror film.
MPAA:PG
Burt Weissbourd — *Media Home Entertainment*

Have I Got a Story For You **1984**
Puppets
75534 60 mins C B, V P
Shari Lewis
Favorite children's stories are told by Shari Lewis and her puppets, including the delectable Lambchop.
MGM UA — *MGM/UA Home Video*

Having A Wonderful Time **1938**
Comedy
73689 70 mins B/W B, V P
Lucille Ball, Ginger Rogers, Douglas Fairbanks Jr, Red Skelton
A city girl goes to the mountains for a vacation and finds true love there.
RKO; Pandro S Berman — *RKO HomeVideo*

Having It All **1982**
Comedy
80634 92 mins C B, V P
Dyan Cannon, Barry Newman, Hart Bochner, Sylvia Sidney, Melanie Chartoff
A beautiful fashion designer tries to maintain her bi-coastal lifestyle and the two husbands that go along with it. Available in Beta Hi-Fi and VHS Stereo.
Hill/Mandeker Prods. — *U.S.A. Home Video*

Having Wonderful Time **1938**
Comedy
79682 71 mins B/W B, V P
Ginger Rogers, Lucille Ball, Eve Arden, Red Skelton, Douglas Faribanks Jr
A young girl tries to find culture on her summer vacation at a Catskills resort.
RKO — *RKO HomeVideo*

Hawaii **1966**
Drama
58827 161 mins C B, V, CED P
Max von Sydow, Julie Andrews, Richard Harris, Carroll O'Connor, Gene Hackman, directed by George Roy Hill
James Michener's novel about a New England farm boy who decides in 1820 that the Lord has commanded him to the island of Hawaii for the purpose of "Christianizing" the natives. Filmed on location.
EL, SP
United Artists; Walter Mirisch — *CBS/Fox Video*

Hawk the Slayer **1981**
Fantasy/Adventure
80635 90 mins C B, V P
Jack Palance, John Terry, Harry Andrews, Cheryl Campbell, Patrick Magee, Roy Kennear, Annette Crosbie
Two brothers fought a battle to the death in an imaginary land a long time ago. Available in Beta Hi-Fi and VHS Stereo.
Jack Gill; Chips Prods. — *U.S.A. Home Video*

Hawmps! **1976**
Comedy
49624 98 mins C B, V P
James Hampton, Christopher Connelly, Slim Pickens, Denver Pyle, directed by Joe Camp
A Civil War lieutenant trains his men to use camels. When the soldiers and animals begin to grow fond of each other, Congress orders the camels to be set free. The bad news turns into a happy ending.
MPAA:G

Mulberry Square Prods; Joe Camp — *Vestron Video*

He Kills Night After Night After Night 1970
Horror
77455 88 mins C B, V P
Jack May, Linda Marlowe, Justine Lord
The British police are baffled as they seek the man who has been killing woman after woman in the style of Jack the Ripper.
Dudley Birch Films — *Monterey Home Video*

He Knows You're Alone 1980
Horror
64567 94 mins C B, V, CED P
Don Scardino, Elizabeth Kemp, Tom Rolfing
A psychotic killer terrorizes young girls in his search for a suitable "bride."
MPAA:R
MGM/UA — *MGM/UA Home Video*

He-Man and the Masters of the Universe 198?
Science fiction/Cartoons
65011 91 mins C B, V P
Animated
He-Man, who lives on the planet Eternia, battles the evil force Skeletor and his band of villains. Based on the Mattel toys.
Filmation — *RCA/Columbia Pictures Home Video; RCA VideoDiscs*

He-Man and the Masters of the Universe, Vol. 5 1983
Cartoons/Adventure
66352 50 mins C B, V P
Animated
The He-Man saga continues with two more episodes featuring the treacherous Skeletor plotting more evil deeds in his efforts to gain control of Castle Greyskull.
Filmation — *RCA/Columbia Pictures Home Video*

He-Man and the Masters of the Universe, Volume VI 1984
Adventure
76027 60 mins C B, V P
Animated
Volume VI of this series features He-Man and Teela once again battling the forces of evil in two thrilling episodes.
Filmation Presentation — *RCA/Columbia Pictures Home Video*

He-Man and the Masters of the Universe-Volume VIII 1984
Adventure/Cartoons
Closed Captioned
70188 45 mins C B, V P
Animated
Two new episodes pit He-Man against the forces of evil: "Daimer the Demon" and "The Dragon's Gift." In Beta Hi-Fi.
Filmation — *RCA/Columbia Pictures Home Video*

He-Man and the Masters of the Universe, Volume X 1985
Cartoons/Adventure
77246 45 mins C B, V P
Animated
He-Man and his friends continue their on-going battle against Skeletor in two new adventures: "Disappearing Act" and "Evil-Lyn's Plot".
Filmation — *RCA/Columbia Pictures Home Video*

He-Man and the Masters of the Universe Volume XI 1985
Cartoons/Adventure
Closed Captioned
70567 45 mins C B, V P
Animated
These two episodes show the Man of He and his cohorts battling the forces of evil and nastiness in "The House of Shokoti." Available in Beta Hi-Fi.
Filmation — *RCA/Columbia Pictures Home Video*

He-Man and the Masters of the Universe: The Greatest Adventures of All 1983
Cartoons
65318 60 mins C B, V P
Animated
He-Man and his friends continue their battles against the evil forces of Skeletor.
Lou Scheimer — *RCA/Columbia Pictures Home Video*

He-Man and the Masters of the Universe Volume IX 1984
Adventure/Cartoons
Closed Captioned
80370 45 mins C B, V P
Animated
He-Man and the Masters of the Universe struggle for control of Eternia in two new adventures.

Filmation — *RCA/Columbia Pictures Home Video*

He Walked by Night **1948**
Mystery
08598 80 mins B/W B, V P
Richard Basehart, Scott Brady, Roy Roberts, Jack Webb, directed by Alfred M. Werker
Los Angeles homicide investigators track down a cop killer; from the files of the Los Angeles police.
Eagle Lion; Bryan Foy Productions — *Movie Buff Video; Video Yesteryear; Discount Video Tapes*

He Who Walks Alone **1978**
Drama
70714 74 mins C B, V P
Louis Gossett Jr., Clu Gulager, Mary Alice, James McEacheon, Barton Heyman, Barry Brown, Lonny Chapman, directed by Jerrold Freedman.
This telefilm documents the life of Thomas E. Gilmore, who became the South's first elected black sheriff in the 1960's.
EMI, NBC — *VCL Home Video*

Headless Horseman, The/Will Rogers **1922**
Comedy
10108 52 mins B/W B, V P, T
Will Rogers, directed by Edward Venturini
Will Rogers plays Ichabod Crane in Washington Irving's "Legend of Sleepy Hollow." Second half of program follows Roger's career from early vaudeville days to Ziegfeld.
Hodkinson — *Blackhawk Films*

Health 'n Action Exercise Programs **1978**
Physical fitness
47506 30 mins C B, V P
Ann Dugan 12 pgms
This series offers a diverse program of physical conditioning. Series A, "Get Fit Stay Fit," and series B, "Super Exercises," are 60 minutes each. Series C, "Sports Conditioning," consists of four 30-minute segments. Series D, "Rehabilitation and Injury," is comprised of six 30-minute programs.
1.Get Fit Stay Fit 2.Super Exercises 3.Sports Conditioning (Jog/Run, Golf, Tennis/Racquet Sports, Ski) 4.Rehabilitation and Injury (Prenatal, Postnatal, Hysterectomy, Mastectomy, Knee, Back)
Health n Action — *RCA/Columbia Pictures Home Video*

Hear O Israel **19??**
Middle East/Religion
38987 71 mins C B, V, FO P
Three classic short films about the land of Israel and the Jewish faith: "Hear O Israel," "The Changing Land," and "My Holiday in Israel." The first two have dialogue in English, the last is in Hebrew with no subtitles.
Unknown — *Video Yesteryear*

Hearse, The **1980**
Horror
59672 97 mins C B, V P
Trish Van Devere, Joseph Cotten
While fighting to maintain her sanity, a vacationing schoolteacher finds her life threatened by a sinister black hearse.
MPAA:PG
Mark Tenser — *Media Home Entertainment*

Heart Is a Lonely Hunter, The **1968**
Drama
Closed Captioned
77267 124 mins C B, V P
Sondra Locke, Alan Arkin, Chuck McCann, Stacy Keach, directed by Robert Ellis Miller
A deaf mute moves in with a Southern family to become closer to his only friend.
New York Film Critics Award '68: Best Actor (Arkin).
Warner Bros — *Warner Home Video*

Heart Like a Wheel **1983**
Drama
Closed Captioned
65499 113 mins C B, V P
Bonnie Bedelia, Beau Bridges, Bill McKinney, Leo Rossi
The true story of premier drag racer Shirley Muldowney, who had to break not only speed records but sexual barriers as well and contend with the reluctance of racing officials to license her.
MPAA:PG
20th Century Fox — *CBS/Fox Video*

Heart of the Golden West **1942**
Western
14373 54 mins B/W B, V, FO P
Roy Rogers, Sons of the Pioneers
Roy protects ranchers of Cherokee City from unjust shipping charges.
Republic — *Video Yesteryear; Video Connection; Cable Films*

Heart of the Rio Grande **1942**
Western
58604 70 mins B/W B, V P, T
Gene Autry, Smiley Burnette, Fay McKenzie, Edith Fellows, Joseph Stauch Jr
A spoiled young rich girl tries to trick her father into coming to her "rescue" at a western dude ranch.
Republic — *Blackhawk Films; Video Connection*

Heart of the Rockies 1937
Western
15441 54 mins B/W B, V P
Bob Livingston, Ray Corrigan, Max Terhune
Three Mesquiteers stop mountain family's rustling and illegal game trappers.
Republic — *Video Connection; Nostalgia Merchant*

Heart of the Stag 1984
Drama
80460 94 mins C B, V, LV P
Bruno Lawrence, Mary Regan, Terence Cooper
On an isolated sheep ranch in the New Zealand outback, a father and daughter suffer the repercussions of an incestuous relationship when she becomes enamoured of a hired hand.
MPAA:R
New World Pictures — *New World Video*

Heartaches 1982
Comedy
64040 90 mins C B, V, LV, CED P
Margot Kidder, Annie Potts, Robert Carradine, Winston Rekert
Two young women, one of them pregnant, decide to chuck everything and run off to Toronto. Once there, they get jobs in a mattress factory and rent an apartment together.
Canadian Film Development Corp — *Vestron Video*

Heartbeat 1946
Romance
16073 101 mins B/W B, V P
Ginger Rogers, Jean-Pierre Aumont, Basil Rathbone
Romance between a lady pickpocket and an overly polished diplomat with a yen for dancing.
RKO — *Movie Buff Video*

Heartbeat 1980
Drama
52714 109 mins C B, V R, P
Nick Nolte, John Heard, Sissy Spacek, Anne Dusenberry, directed by John Byrum
The story of Jack Kerouac (author of "On the Road"), his friend and inspiration Neal Casady, and the woman they shared, Carolyn Casady, based on her memoirs.
MPAA:R
Orion Pictures — *Warner Home Video*

Heartbeat City 1984
Music video
78628 48 mins C B, V P
The Cars
This is a compilation of conceptual music video by The Cars from their albums "Heartbeat City" "Panorama" and "Shake It Up" with clips directed by Andy Warhol and Timothy Hutton among others.
Elektra Entertainment — *Warner Home Video*

Heartbeeps 1981
Science fiction/Comedy
47419 79 mins C B, V P
Andy Kaufman, Bernadette Peters
In 1995, two domestic robot servants fall in love and run off together.
MPAA:PG
Universal — *MCA Home Video*

Heartbreak Kid, The 1972
Comedy
37412 106 mins C B, V P
Charles Grodin, Cybill Shepard, Eddie Albert, Jeannie Berlin
A glib, romantic dreamer becomes disillusioned with love and his marriage in this comedy by Neil Simon.
MPAA:PG
20th Century Fox — *Media Home Entertainment*

Heartbreakers 1984
Drama
77173 98 mins C B, V, CED P
Peter Coyote, Nick Mancuso, Carole Laure, Max Gail, Kathryn Harrold, directed by Bobby Roth
Two male best friends find themselves in the throes of drastic changes in their careers and romantic encounters. Tangerine Dream performs the musical score.
MPAA:R
Orion Pictures; Jethro Films — *Vestron Video*

Heartland 1981
Drama
47303 95 mins C B, V R, P
Conchata Ferrell, Rip Torn
Set in 1910, this film chronicles the story of one woman's life on the Wyoming Frontier, the hazards she faces, and her courage and spirit.
MPAA:PG
Michael Hausman; Beth Ferris — *THORN EMI/HBO Video*

Hearts and Minds 1974
Documentary/Vietnam War
55546 112 mins C B, V, LV R, P
Directed by Peter Davis
Gripping documentary about America's misguided involvement in Vietnam.
Academy Awards '74: Best Documentary (Schneider, Davis). MPAA:R
Touchstone; Bert Schneider; Audjeff — *Embassy Home Entertainment; Paramount Home Video*

Heart's Desire 1937
Musical-Drama
52210 79 mins B/W B, V, FO P
Richard Tauber, Lenora Corbett

Opera great Richard Tauber stars in this tale of an unknown Viennese singer who falls in love with an English girl.
Gaumont British — *Video Yesteryear*

Heat **1972**
Comedy-Drama
59050 101 mins C B, V P
Joe Dallasandro, Sylvia Miles, Andy Warhol, directed by Paul Morrissey
Andy Warhol's characters meet in Hollywood, in seedy motels and spacious mansions, and reveal themselves in all their desperate loneliness.
MPAA:R
Levitt Pickman — *Media Home Entertainment*

Heat and Dust **1982**
Drama
65519 130 mins C B, V P
Julie Christie, Greta Scacchi, Shashi Kapoor, Christopher Cazenove, Nickolas Grace
A young bride joins her husband at his post in India and is inexorably drawn to the country and its Prince of State. Years later her great niece journeys to modern day India in search of the truth about her scandalous and mysterious relative.
MPAA:R
Universal Classic — *MCA Home Video*

Heat of Desire **1984**
Drama
80383 90 mins C B, V P
Clio Goldsmith, Patrick Dewaere, Jeanne Moreau
A philosophy professor abandons everything for a woman he barely knows and is conned by her "relatives." With English subtitles.
MPAA:R FR
Triumph Films — *RCA/Columbia Pictures Home Video*

Heathcliff, Volume 1 **1984**
Cartoons
Closed Captioned
81433 45 mins C B, V P
Animated, voice of Mel Blanc
That rascally cat Heathcliff and his friends Cats and Company are making all kinds of mischief in this collection of four episodes from the series.
LBS; DIC — *RCA/Columbia Pictures Home Video*

Heathcliff and Marmaduke **1983**
Cartoons
66574 60 mins C B, V P
Animated
A program of animated adventures with the hapless dog Marmaduke matching wits with Heathcliff, the cat, his constant nemesis.
Ruby Spears — *Worldvision Home Video*

Heatwave **1983**
Drama
73021 92 mins C B, V R, P
Judy Davis, Richard Moir
Local residents oppose a multi-million dollar residential complex in Australia
MPAA:R
Hilary Linstead — *THORN EMI/HBO Video*

Heaven Can Wait **1978**
Fantasy
38933 100 mins C B, V, LV R, P
Warren Beatty, Julie Christie, Charles Grodin, Dyan Cannon, James Mason, Jack Warden
Remake of 1941's "Here Comes Mr. Jordan," about a football player who is mistakenly summoned to heaven before his time, and returns to earth in another man's body.
MPAA:PG
Paramount — *Paramount Home Video; RCA VideoDiscs*

Heaven Help Us **1985**
Comedy
80809 102 mins C B, V R, P
Donald Sutherland, John Heard, Wallace Shawn, Kevin Dillon, Andrew McCarthy, directed by Michael Dinner
Three mischievous boys find themselves continually in trouble with the priests running their Catholic high school during the mid-60's. Available in VHS and Beta HiFi.
MPAA:R
Tri Star Pictures — *THORN EMI/HBO Video*

Heavens Above **1963**
Comedy
29796 113 mins B/W B, V R, P
Peter Sellers, Cecil Parker, Isabel Jeans, Eric Sykes, Ian Carmichael
A sharp, biting satire on British clergy life. Sellers, a quiet, down-to-earth reverend, is appointed to a parish in a snooty neighborhood.
British Lion — *THORN EMI/HBO Video*

Heaven's Gate **1980**
Western
66449 220 mins C B, V, CED P
Kris Krisofferson, Christopher Walken, Isabelle Huppert, Jeff Bridges, John Hurt, directed by Michael Cimino
The original, uncut version of Michael Cimino's epic story about Wyoming's Johnson County cattle wars of the 1890's. Beta Hi-Fi and VHS stereo.
MPAA:R
United Artists — *MGM/UA Home Video*

(For explanation of codes, see USE GUIDE and KEY)

Heavy Petting 1983
Comedy
64979 90 mins C B, V P
A hilarious compilation of "love scene" footage from feature films of the silent era to the sixties, newsreels, news reports, educational films, old TV shows, and home movies.
Unknown — *Embassy Home Entertainment*

Heavy Traffic 1973
Comedy
59852 76 mins C B, V R, P
Animated
Ralph Bakshi's animated fantasy portrait of the hard-edged underside of city life, as a young cartoonist draws the people, the places and the paranoia of his environment.
MPAA:X
American International — *Warner Home Video*

Heckle y Jeckle 195?
Cartoons
48408 90 mins C B, V P
Animated
The talking magpies get in and out of mischief. Available in Spanish only.
SP
Terrytoons — *CBS/Fox Video*

Heidi 1937
Drama
22205 88 mins B/W B, V P
Shirley Temple, Jean Hersholt, Helen Westley
Johanna Spyri's classic tale puts Shirley Temple in the hands of a mean governess and the loving arms of her Swiss grandfather.
20th Century Fox — *CBS/Fox Video*

Heidi 1968
Drama
29433 100 mins C CED P
Maximilian Schell, Jean Simmons, Michael Redgrave
Based on Johanna Spyri's classic story of an orphan girl living with her grandfather in the Alps who is taken by her aunt to the city to be a playmate for a family's crippled daughter.
NBC — *RCA VideoDiscs*

Heidi 1979
Cartoons
77301 93 mins C B, V P
Animated
An orphan girl's optimism brings new life to the residents of a village in the Swiss Alps.
Vertlalen/Guzman Productions — *Pacific Arts Video*

Heidi 1967
Drama
76769 100 mins C B, V, CED P
Maximillian Schell, Jennifer Edwards, Michael Redgrave, Jean Simmons
This adaptation of the classic Johanna Spyri novel tells the story of an orphaned girl who goes to the Swiss Alps to live with her grandfather.
NBC — *Vestron Video*

Heidi's Song 19??
Cartoons/Musical
69591 90 mins C B, V P
Animated, voices of Lorne Greene, Sammy Davis Jr, Margery Gray
The classic tale of Heidi and her grandfather is enhanced by 16 original songs, dance sequences, and full animation.
Hanna Barbera — *Worldvision Home Video*

Heifetz and Piatigorsky 1981
Music-Performance
57251 78 mins B/W B, V P
Jascha Heifetz, Gregor Piatigorsky
Three presentations are featured on one cassette. First, Jascha Heifetz, the incomparable violinist and his accompanist, Emanuel Bay, give an impromptu recital at Pomona College. In a varied program, he plays Mendelsohn's "Sweet Remembrance," Brahm's "Sonatensatz," and "Hungarian Dance No. 7," Gluck's "Melodie," Prokofiev's "March" from "Love for Three Oranges," Wieniawsky's "Polonaise," and Dinicu-Heifetz's "Hora Stacatto." The second presentation features the great cellist Gregor Piatigorsky in a brilliant concert including Bach's "Bouree No. 1" and "Bouree No. 2" from "C-Major Suite," Chopin's "Slow Movement from Cello Sonata," Prokofiev's "Masques" from "Romeo and Juliet," Anton Rubinstein's "Romance," Tschaikowsky's "Waltz," and Schubert-Piatigorsky's "Introduction, Theme and Variations." The tape concludes with "The Portrait of an Artist," a look at the home and practice life of Jascha Heifetz. The varied program consists of Vitali's "Chaconne," Bach's "Prelude E-Major," Debussy's "Girl with the Flaxen Hair," Wieniawsky's "Scherzo Tarantella," and Paganini's "24th Caprice."
Kultur — *Kultur*

Heiress, The 1949
Drama
70554 115 mins B/W B, V P
Olivia De Havilland, Montgomery Clift, Ralph Richardson, directed by William Wyler
Based on the Henry James play "Washington Square," this film stars Olivia De Haviland as a wealthy and bitter woman pursued by the fortune-seeking bum (Clift) who left her waiting by the altar years earlier. In Hi-fi Mono on all formats.
Academy Awards '49: Best Actress (De Havilland); Best Costumes; Best Art Director; Best Film Score.

William Wyler; Paramount — *MCA Home Video*

Helen Keller: Separate Views 1982
Handicapped/Women
58560 91 mins C B, V P
Narrated by Martha Graham and President Eisenhower
A trio of upbeat films dealing with different views of the handicapped, including the "Helen Keller Story" and "One Eyed Men Are Kings," which offers a serio-comic look at blindness.
Academy Awards '74: Best Live Action Short ("Kings").
Mastervision et al — *Mastervision*

Hell Night 1981
Horror
59044 100 mins C B, V P
Linda Blair, Vincent Van Patten, Kevin Brophy
Three young people must spend the night in a mysterious mansion as part of their initiation into Alpha Signa Rho fraternity.
MPAA:R EL, SP
Compass International Pictures — *Media Home Entertainment*

Hell on Frisco Bay 1955
Drama
11771 93 mins C B, V P
Alan Ladd, Edward G. Robinson, Joanne Dru
Ex-waterfront cop, falsely imprisoned for manslaughter, sets out to clear his name.
Warner Bros — *United Home Video*

Hell River 1975
War-Drama
66241 100 mins C B, V R, P
Rod Taylor, Adam West
In 1941 Yugoslavia, Yugoslav partisans and Nazis battle it out at a place called Hell River.
Nobel Productions — *Video City Productions*

Hell to Eternity 1960
Biographical
80836 132 mins B/W B, V P
Jeffrey Hunter, Sessue Hayakawa, David Janssen, Vic Damone, Patricia Owens, directed by Phil Karlson
This true story of how World War II hero Guy Gabaldon managed to persuade 2,000 Japanese soldiers to surrender is available in VHS and Beta Hi Fi.
Allied Artists; Atlantic Pictures — *Key Video*

Hell Train 1980
Horror
77399 90 mins C B, V P
A group of desperate female prisoners are out to murder Nazi courtesans who sent them to concentration camps.

Independent — *Wizard Video*

Hellcats of the Navy 1957
War-Drama
58956 82 mins B/W B, V P
Ronald Reagan, Nancy Davis (Reagan), Arthur Franz
The true saga of the World War II mission to sever the vital link between mainland Asia and Japan. This was the only film that Ronald and Nancy Reagan appeared in together.
Columbia — *RCA/Columbia Pictures Home Video*

Hellfighters 1968
Drama
77215 121 mins C B, V P
John Wayne, Katherine Ross, Jim Hutton, directed by Andrew V. McLaglen
A group of Texas oil well fighters experience troubles between themselves and the women they love.
MPAA:G
Universal Pictures; Robert Arthur — *MCA Home Video*

Hellfire 1984
Ethics/Religion
73913 27 mins C B, V, 3/4U, FO R, P
A television evangelist believes his interpretation of the Bible is the key to salvation.
Mirage Productions Marcus Viscidi — *Republic Pictures Home Video*

Hellfire 1948
Western
80844 90 mins B/W B, V P
William Elliott, Marie Windsor, Forrest Tucker, Jim Davis
A gambler promises to build a church and follow the precepts of the Bible after a minister sacrifices his life for him.
Republic Pictures — *Republic Pictures Home Video*

Hello, Dolly! 1969
Musical
08424 146 mins C B, V, LV P
Barbra Streisand, Walter Matthau, Michael Crawford, Louis Armstrong, directed by Gene Kelly
Widow Dolly Levi, while matchmaking for her friends, sets her mind on a Yankee merchant. Based on the stage musical adapted from Thornton Wilder's play "Matchmaker'.
Academy Awards '69: Best Score of a Musical Picture; Best Art Direction; Best Sound.
MPAA:G EL, SP
20th Century Fox; Ernest Leham — *CBS/Fox Video*

Hellriders 1984
Adventure
81041 90 mins C B, V P
Adam West, Tina Louise
A motorcycle gang rides into a small town and subject its residents to a reign of terror.
MPAA:R
Renee Harman — *Trans World Entertainment*

Hells Angels Forever 1983
Adventure
65367 93 mins C B, V P
The Hells Angels, Willie Nelson, Jerry Garcia, Johnny Paycheck, Bo Diddley
"Hells Angels Forever" is a revealing ride into the world of honor, violence, and undying passion for motorcycles on the road.
MPAA:R
Richard Chase; Sandy Alexander; Leon Gast — *Media Home Entertainment*

Hells Angels on Wheels 1967
Drama
78667 95 mins C B, V P
Jack Nicholson, Adam Roarke, Sabrina Scharf, directed by Richard Rush
A gas station attendant joins up with the Angels for a cross country trip.
US Films — *Monterey Home Video*

Hell's Angels '69 1969
Adventure
65483 97 mins C B, V P
Tom Stern, Jeremy Slate, Conny Van Dyke
Two wealthy brothers plot a deadly game by infiltrating the ranks of the Hell's Angels.
MPAA:PG
Tom Stern — *Media Home Entertainment*

Hell's House 1932
Drama
08766 72 mins B/W B, V, 3/4U P
Bette Davis, Pat O'Brien, Junior Dirken, directed by Howard Higgin
Following the death of his mother, a young boy goes to city to live with relatives and becomes involved with a bootlegger.
Bennie F Ziedman Prod — *VCII; Video Yesteryear*

Hellstrom Chronicle, The 1971
Documentary/Insects
63966 90 mins C B, V P
A powerful documentary about man's impending struggle against insects.
Academy Awards '71: Best Documentary Feature. MPAA:G
Almi-Cinema 5 — *RCA/Columbia Pictures Home Video*

Help Yourself to Better Color TV 197?
Television
44991 30 mins C B, V P, T
Through the use of the indian-head test pattern and the color bar chart you can determine brightness, focus, contrast, tint, and color line-up with the help of this program.
AM Available
Unknown — *Blackhawk Films*

Helter Skelter 1976
Drama
80142 194 mins C CED P
Steve Railshark, Nancy Wolfe, George DiCenzo
The harrowing story of the murder of Sharon Tate and four others in her home at the hands of Charles Manson and his family.
Lorimar — *CBS/Fox Video*

He-Man and the Masters of the Universe, Volume XII 1985
Adventure/Cartoons
Closed Captioned
81434 45 mins C B, V P
Animated
He-Man and the Masters of the Universe struggle to maintain peace of Eternia in this collection of two episodes from the series.
Filmation — *RCA/Columbia Pictures Home Video*

Henry Fonda: The Man and His Movies 1984
Biographical/Documentary
78663 60 mins C B, V P
Narrated by Arthur Hill
This documentary features highlights from Henry Fonda's stage, screen and television appearances that spanned more than fifty years.
RKO — *RKO HomeVideo*

Henry Ford's America 1977
Automobiles
21251 57 mins C B, V, FO P
A look at the history of the automobile, the dynastic Ford talent that created it, and the business empire that rules it.
National Film Board of Canada — *Video Yesteryear*

Henry V 1945
Drama
44363 137 mins C B, V P
Laurence Olivier, Robert Newton, Leslie Banks, Leo Genn
The first movie version of Shakepeare's great drama, with brilliant dialogue and color.
J Arthur Rank — *Sheik Video; RCA VideoDiscs*

Hepburn and Tracy 1984
Biographical/Documentary
78657 45 mins C B, V P
Katherine Hepburn, Spencer Tracy
The finest moments from the film careers of Katherine Hepburn and Spencer Tracy, as a team and on their own. Some sequences in black and white.
RKO — *RKO HomeVideo*

Herbie Goes Bananas 1980
Comedy
79230 93 mins C B, V R, P
Cloris Leachman, Charles Martin Smith, Harvey Korman
While Herbie the VW is racing in a race in Rio de Janeiro, he is bothered by the syndicate, a pickpocket and a raging bull.
MPAA:G
Walt Disney Productions — *Walt Disney Home Video*

Herbie Goes to Monte Carlo 1977
Comedy
79229 104 mins C B, V R, P
Dean Jones, Don Knotts, Julie Sommars
While participating in a Paris to Monte Carlo race, Herbie the VW takes a detour and falls in love with a Lancia.
MPAA:G
Walt Disney Productions — *Walt Disney Home Video*

Herbie Hancock and the Rockit Band 1984
Music-Performance
65756 70 mins C B, V, CED P
Filmed live at the Hammersmith Odeon and Camden Hall in London, England, this program takes the home viewer through a multi-media presentation of break dancing, scratch music, robots and an explosive light show. In VHS Hi-Fi and Beta Hi-Fi.
CBS Records — *CBS/Fox Video*

Herbie Rides Again 1974
Comedy
59063 88 mins C B, V R, P
Helen Hayes, Ken Berry, Stephanie Powers, John McIntire, Keenan Wynn, directed by Robert Stevenson
In this "Love Bug" sequel, Herbie comes to the aid of an elderly woman who is trying to stop a ruthless tycoon from raising a skyscraper on her property.
MPAA:G
Walt Disney Productions — *Walt Disney Home Video; RCA VideoDiscs*

Hercules 1983
Adventure
Closed Captioned
66446 100 mins C B, V P
Lou Ferrigno, Sybil Danning, William Berger, Brad Harris, Ingrid Anderson
Legendary muscleman Hercules fights against the evil King Minos for his own survival and the love of Cassiopeia, a rival king's daughter.
MPAA:PG
Cannon Films — *MGM/UA Home Video*

Hercules 1959
Adventure
66268 107 mins C B, V, CED P
Steve Reeves, directed by Pietro Frandisci
The mythological demigod teams up with Jason and the Argonauts in search of the Golden Fleece.
MPAA:G
Oscar Film Galatea; Warner Bros; Embassy — *Embassy Home Entertainment*

Hercules Goes Bananas 197?
Comedy
66109 75 mins C B, V P
Arnold Schwarzenegger
Schwarzenegger plays Hercules in this hilarious comedy.
Arbor Weisberg — *Unicorn Video*

Hercules Unchained 1959
Adventure
64969 101 mins C B, V, CED P
Steve Reeves, Sylva Koscina, Primo Carnera
In this sequel to "Hercules," the superhero must use all his strength to save the city of Thebes and the woman he loves from the giant Antaeus.
Lux/Galatea — *Embassy Home Entertainment*

Herculoids, The 196?
Cartoons/Adventure
66275 60 mins C B, V P
Animated
Zandor, Tara, Dorno and the towering man of stone, Igoo, encounter adventures on a wild, semi-primitive planet.
Hanna Barbera — *Worldvision Home Video*

Herculoids, Vol II, The 1967
Cartoons/Adventure
77160 60 mins C B, V P
Animated
A team of futuristic animals attempt to save a king and his planetary community from alien invaders.
Hanna-Barbera — *Worldvision Home Video*

Here Comes Mr. Jordan 1941
Fantasy
21290 94 mins B/W B, V P

Robert Montgomery, Claude Rains, James Gleason, Evelyn Keyes
A young prizefighter, killed in a plane crash because of a mix-up in heaven, returns to life in the body of a murdered millionaire.
Academy Awards '41: Best Original Story; Best Screenplay.
Columbia — *RCA/Columbia Pictures Home Video*

Here Comes the Grump **1985**
Cartoons
70680 60 mins C B, V P
Animated
Princess Dawn, Terry, and their dog, Bip, survive through this program by avoiding the clumsily humorous wrath of the Grump and his mischievous magical dragon.
Embassy Entertainment — *Embassy Home Entertainment*

Here Comes Trouble **1948**
Comedy
66114 54 mins C B, V P
William Tracy
A newspaperman returns from war to get his old job back.
Fred Guiol — *Unicorn Video*

Here It Is, Burlesque **1979**
Variety
44917 88 mins C B, V, CED P
Ann Corio, Morey Amsterdam
Male and female striptease, baggy-pants comedians, exotic dancers and classic comedy sketches in this tribute to the living art, burlesque.
HBO; Michael Brandman — *Vestron Video*

Here We Go Again! **1942**
Comedy
64535 76 mins B/W B, V R, P
Fibber McGee and Molly, Edgar Bergen, Charlie McCarthy, Mortimer Snerd, Ray Noble and his Orchestra
Fibber McGee and Molly are planning their 20th anniversary celebration, but no one wants to come. Based on the popular NBC radio series.
RKO — *Blackhawk Films*

Heritage of the Bible, The **1982**
Bible
60380 111 mins C CED P
A recreation of Biblical history: "The Law and the Prophets" features inspired images of Raphael, Michelangelo, and others; "The Inheritance" uses famous archeological sites of Biblical times to recount stories of the Old Testament.
NBC Enterprises — *RCA VideoDiscs*

Heritage to Glory **1985**
Documentary/History-US
70683 45 mins C B, V P
Narrated by Ken Howard, directed by Fred Warshofsky
Part of the "In Defense of Freedom" series, this program looks at the history of the United States Marine Corps.
A.B. Marian — *MPI Home Video*

Hero High Volume 1 **1981**
Cartoons
74084 44 mins C B, V P
Animated
This fun-filled animated feature introduces you to future superheros and their ill-fated attempts to master their special powers.
Lou Scheimer; Norm Prescott — *Embassy Home Entertainment*

Heroes in the Ming Dynasty **1984**
Martial arts
72959 90 mins C B, V P
A martial arts period film set in the Ming Dynasty.
Foreign — *Unicorn Video*

Heroes of the Hills **1938**
Western
64422 54 mins B/W B, V, 3/4U P
Bob Livingston, Ray Corrigan, Max Terhune
The Three Mesquiteers back up a plan that would allow trusted prisoners to work for neighboring ranchers.
Republic — *Nostalgia Merchant*

Hester Street **1975**
Drama
79312 89 mins B/W B, V P
Carol Kane, Doris Roberts, Steven Keats, Mel Howard, directed by Joan Micklin Silver
When a young Jewish immigrant meets her husband in New York City at the turn of the century, she finds out her husband has dispensed with his Old World ways.
TimeLife Productions — *Vestron Video*

Hey Abbott! **1978**
Comedy/Film-History
59862 76 mins B/W B, V P
Bud Abbott, Lou Costello, Phil Silvers, Steve Allen, Joe Besser, narrated by Milton Berle
A compilation of A and C routines from their classic TV series. Sketches include "Who's on First," "Oyster Stew," "Floogle Street" and "The Birthday Party."
Ziv International — *VidAmerica*

Hey Cinderella! **1970**
Fairy tales/Comedy
47348 58 mins C B, V, LV R, P

The Muppets
The Muppets present their version of the classic fairy tale, in which Cinderella arrives at the ball in a coach pulled by a purple beast named Splurge and driven by Kermit the singing frog.
Henson Associates — *Muppet Home Video*

Hey Good Lookin' **1982**
Satire
63121 77 mins C B, V R, P
Animated, directed by Ralph Bakshi
Ralph Bakshi's irreverent look back at growing up in the 1950's bears the trademark qualities that distinguish his other adult animated features, "Fritz the Cat" and "Heavy Traffic."
Warner Bros — *Warner Home Video*

Hey There, It's Yogi Bear **1964**
Cartoons
77155 98 mins C B, V P
Animated, voices of Daws Butler, James Darren, Mel Blanc, H. Pat O'Malley, Julie Bennett
When Yogi Bear comes out of winter hiberation to search for food his travels take him to the Chizzling Brothers Circus.
Hanna-Barbera — *Worldvision Home Video*

Hide in Plain Sight **1980**
Suspense
53350 96 mins C B, V P
James Caan, Jill Eikenberry, Robert Viharo, directed by James Caan
A distraught blue-collar worker searches for his children who disappeared when his ex-wife and her mobster husband were given new identities by federal agents.
MPAA:PG
Robert Christiansen; Rick Rosenberg; MGM — *MGM/UA Home Video*

Hideous Sun Demon **1959**
Horror
36920 74 mins B/W B, V, 3/4U P
Robert Clarke, Patricia Manning, Nan Peterson
A physicist exposed to radiation must stay out of sunlight or he will turn into a scaly, lizard-like creature. Includes previews of coming attractions from classic science fiction films.
Clark King Entprs, Bob Clark — *Nostalgia Merchant*

High Anxiety **1977**
Comedy
52739 92 mins C B, V, CED P
Mel Brooks, Madeline Kahn, Cloris Leachman, Harvey Korman, Ron Carey, Howard Morris, Dick Van Patten, directed by Mel Brooks
An anxiety-prone psychiatrist arrives at a sanitorium to take up his official duties as the new head, and is immediately caught up in a twisted murder mystery. Brooks' "homage" to Hitchcock.
MPAA:PG
Twentieth Century Fox; Mel Brooks — *CBS/Fox Video*

High Ballin' **1978**
Drama/Adventure
69289 100 mins C B, V P
Peter Fonda, Jerry Reed, Helen Shaver
Three angry independents are set to take on the most vicious gang of hijackers ever to run the highways.
MPAA:PG
American International — *Vestron Video*

High Command **1938**
Drama
47467 84 mins B/W B, V, FO P
Lionel Atwill, Lucie Mannheim, James Mason
To save his daughter from an ugly scandal, the British general of a Colonial African outpost traps a blackmailer's killer.
Fanfare — *Video Yesteryear; Movie Buff Video; Discount Video Tapes*

High Country, The **1981**
Drama
62863 101 mins C B, V, CED P
Timothy Bottoms, Linda Purl, George Sims, Jim Lawrence, Bill Berry
Two misfits on the run from society learn mutual trust as they travel through the mountain country of Alberta, Canada.
MPAA:PG
Crown International — *Vestron Video*

High Crime **1973**
Crime-Drama
57064 91 mins C B, V, 3/4U P
James Whitmore, Franco Nero, Fernando Rey
A "French Connection"-style suspense story about the heroin trade, featuring high-speed chases and a police commissioner obsessed with capturing the criminals.
Ambassador Releasing — *Nostalgia Merchant*

High Crime **1973**
Suspense
81191 100 mins C B, V P
James Whitmore, Franco Nero, Fernando Rey
An intrepid police commissioner and his chief of detectives attempt to stop the flow of drug traffic into Italy.
MPAA:R
Ambassador Releasing Inc. — *Media Home Entertainment*

High Grass Circus **1976**
Circus
21258 57 mins C B, V, FO P
A tour of the Royal Brother Circus, the only tent circus in Canada.

National Film Board of Canada — *Video Yesteryear*

High Green **1983**
Trains
78170 22 mins C B, V P, T
A fascinating story of how a freight train is made up and gives keen insight into being an engineer in one of today's giant locomotives.
Blackhawk Films — *Blackhawk Films*

High Ice **1980**
Drama
69285 97 mins C B, V P
David Janssen, Tony Musante
A forest ranger and a lieutenant colonel are involved in a clash of wills over a rescue mission high in the snow-capped Washington state peaks.
ESJ Productions — *Vestron Video*

High Noon **1952**
Western
00259 85 mins B/W B, V P
Gary Cooper, Grace Kelly, Lloyd Bridges
Newly-married town marshal must choose between love and his duty to an ungrateful town.
Academy Awards '52: Best Actor (Cooper); Best Music Scoring (Dimitri Tiomkin); Best Song (High Noon).
United Artists; Stanley Kramer — *Republic Pictures Home Video; RCA VideoDiscs*

High Noon, Part II: The Return of Will Kane **1980**
Western
72453 100 mins C B, V P
Lee Majors, David Carradine
Will Kane returns to Hadleyville with his wife to find the town controlled by a sadistic marshall. This is a sequel to the 1952 film.
Charles Fries Productions; Ed Montage Prod — *U.S.A. Home Video*

High Plains Drifter **1973**
Western
59037 105 mins C B, V P
Clint Eastwood, directed by Clint Eastwood
A stranger is hired to protect a community against the imminent return of three gunmen sent to jail a year before.
MPAA:R
Universal; The Malpaso Co — *MCA Home Video*

High Risk **1976**
Adventure
60442 74 mins C B, V P
James Coburn, Lindsay Wagner, James Brolin, Anthony Quinn
Four Americans battle foreign armies, unscrupulous gunrunners and jungle bandits in a harrowing attempt to steal five million dollars.
Unknown — *Embassy Home Entertainment*

High Risk **1976**
Adventure
65422 74 mins C B, V P
James Brolin, Anthony Quinn, Lindsay Wagner, James Coburn, Ernest Borgnine
An action-adventure of four Americans who battle foreign armies, unscrupulous gunrunners, and jungle bandits in a harrowing attempt to steal five million dollars from an expatriate American living in the peaceful splendor of his Columbian villa.
MPAA:R
MGM — *Embassy Home Entertainment*

High Road to China **1983**
Adventure
66126 107 mins C B, V, LV, CED R, P
Bess Armstrong, Tom Selleck, Jack Weston, Robert Morley
A hard-drinking 1920's air ace is recruited by a young heiress to find her father.
MPAA:PG
City Films — *Warner Home Video*

High Rolling in a Hot Corvette **1977**
Adventure
76772 82 mins C B, V P
Joseph Bottoms, Greg Taylor
Two carnival workers leave their jobs and hit the road searching for adventure and excitement.
MPAA:PG
Martin Films — *Vestron Video*

High School Confidential **1958**
Drama
65458 85 mins B/W B, V P
Russ Tamblin, Mamie Van Doren
A tough-talking gang leader comes in contact with a drug ring and its leader. His dealings put him in constant danger.
MGM — *Republic Pictures Home Video*

High Sierra **1941**
Drama
64706 96 mins B/W B, V, CED P
Humphrey Bogart, Ida Lupino, Arthur Kennedy, Joan Leslie, Cornel Wilde, Alan Curtis, directed by Raoul Walsh
Bogart is Roy "Mad Dog" Earl, an aging gangster who hides out from the police in the High Sierras. Screenplay by John Huston and W.R. Burnett, whose novel this movie is based on.
Warner Bros — *CBS/Fox Video; RCA VideoDiscs*

 (For explanation of codes, see USE GUIDE and KEY)

High Society 1956
Musical/Comedy
80618 107 mins C B, V, LV P
Frank Sinatra, Bing Crosby, Grace Kelly, Louis Armstrong, Celeste Holm, directed by Charles Walters
A wealthy man attempts to win back his ex-wife who's about to be remarried. The Cole Porter score includes: "True Love," "Well Did You Evah," "Now You Has Jazz," "Mind If I Make Love to You" and "High Society Calypso."
MGM — *MGM/UA Home Video*

High Velocity 1976
Adventure
45048 105 mins C B, V P
Ben Gazzara, Paul Winfield
An action-packed adventure of two mercenaries involved in the challenge of a lifetime.
MPAA:PG
Takashi Ohashi — *Media Home Entertainment*

Higher and Higher 1943
Musical
10049 90 mins B/W B, V P, T
Frank Sinatra, Leon Errol, Michele Morgan, Jack Haley, Victor Borge, Mary McGuire
Bankrupt aristocrat conspires with servants to regain his fortune. Tries to marry his daughter into money.
RKO — *Blackhawk Films*

Highest Honor, The 1984
Drama
80044 99 mins C B, V P
John Howard, Atsuo Nakamura
The true story of a friendship between an Australian army officer and a Japanese security officer during World War II.
MPAA:R
Lee Robinson — *Embassy Home Entertainment*

Highpoint 1984
Comedy/Adventure
80043 91 mins C B, V P
Richard Harris, Christopher Plummer, Beverly D'Angelo
When an unemployed man becomes the chauffeur of a wealthy family, he finds himself in the middle of a mysterious murder.
MPAA:PG
Daniel M Fine — *Embassy Home Entertainment*

Hillbilly Bears 198?
Cartoons
78070 51 mins C B, V P
Animated
This program presents the most laughable family of bears in their exciting adventures.
Worldvision Home Video Inc — *Worldvision Home Video*

Hillbillys in a Haunted House 1967
Horror/Musical
59654 88 mins C B, V P
Ferlin Husky, Joi Lansing, Don Bowman, John Carradine, Lon Chaney, Basil Rathbone, directed by Jean Yarbrough
Two country and western singers enroute to the Nashville jamboree encounter a group of foreign spies "haunting" a house.
Bernard Woolner — *United Home Video*

Hills Have Eyes, The 1977
Adventure
59080 83 mins C B, V P
Susan Lanier, Robert Houston, Martin Speer, Dee Wallace, Russ Grieve, John Steadman, James Whitworth
A desperate family battles for survival and vengeance against a brutal band of belligerent terrorists.
MPAA:R
Peter Locke — *HarmonyVision*

Hills of Utah, The 1951
Western
65771 70 mins B/W B, V P, T
Gene Autry, Pat Buttram, Denver Pyle
Gene finds himself in the middle of a feud between the local mine operator and a group of cattlemen, while searching for his father's murderer.
Columbia — *Blackhawk Films*

Hindenburg, The 1975
Adventure/Suspense
47850 125 mins C B, V P
George C. Scott, Anne Bancroft, William Atherton, Roy Thinnes, Gig Young, Burgess Meredith, directed by Robert Wise
Intrigue and suspense highlight this fictionalized account of the historic disaster.
MPAA:PG
Universal — *MCA Home Video*

Hinkler: The Lone Eagle 1985
Biographical/Documentary
70373 50 mins B/W B, V R, P
Bert Hinkler
This tape follows the life story of the innovative aviator Bert Hinkler. The pilot's life achievements, and the events surrounding his mysterious death are presented in this provocative film.
Nagat Enterprises — *Video City Productions*

Hips, Hips, Hooray 1934
Comedy/Musical
54113 68 mins B/W B, V P, T

Wheeler and Woolsey, Ruth Etting, Thelma Todd, Dorothy lee
Two supposed "hot shot" salesmen are hired by a cosmetic company to sell flavored lipstick. "Hot shot" salesmen they are not, but funny they are.
RKO — *Blackhawk Films*

His Girl Friday **1940**
Comedy
08728 92 mins B/W B, V P
Cary Grant, Rosalind Russell, Ralph Bellamy, Gene Lockhart, directed by Howard Hawks
Reporter helps condemned man escape. Based on hit play "Front Page."
Columbia — *Hal Roach Studios; Prism; Movie Buff Video; Budget Video; Video Yesteryear; VCII; Cinema Concepts; Discount Video Tapes; Video Dimensions; Sheik Video; Cable Films; Video Connection; Western Film & Video Inc; Phoenix Films & Video; Kartes Productions; Classic Video Cinema Collector's Club; See Hear Industries*

His Kind of Woman **1951**
Drama
57137 120 mins B/W B, V P
Robert Mitchum, Jane Russell, Vincent Price, Tim Holt, Charles McGraw
A fall guy, being used to bring a racketeer back to the U.S. from Mexico, discovers the plan and tries to halt it.
RKO — *King of Video*

His Name Was King **196?**
Western
81518 90 mins C B, V P
Klaus Kinski, Anne Puskin
A man goes of the gang who murdered his brother and raped his young wife in the old west.
Foreign — *All Seasons Entertainment*

His Royal Slyness/Haunted Spooks **1920**
Comedy
56912 52 mins B/W B, V, FO P
Harold Lloyd
Two Harold Lloyd shorts. "His Royal Slyness" (1919) offers Harold impersonating the king of a small kingdom, while in "Haunted Spooks" (1920), Harold gets suckered into living in a haunted mansion. Both films include music score.
Hal Roach — *Video Yesteryear; Blackhawk Films*

Historical Yesterdays **197?**
History-US/Documentary
52456 ? mins B/W B, V P
Narrated by Lowell Thomas 4 pgms
Lowell Thomas hosts this series of documentaries about America in the twentieth century. Each program covers the events of one decade. Programs are available individually and were originally telecast by PBS under the series title, "Lowell Thomas Remembers."
1.The Roaring Twenties 2.The New Deal—The Thirties 3.The War Years—The Forties 4.The Fabulous Fifties
Unknown — *Blackhawk Films*

History Disquiz, The **1983**
History-Modern
64547 60 mins C LV P
Hosted by Steve Allen
This challenging game tests players' knowledge of 20th century events. More than 1500 questions are built around 50 film clips from the Hearst Time Capsule Library.
King Features Entertainment — *Optical Programming Associates*

History Is Made at Night **1937**
Drama/Romance
50930 97 mins B/W B, V, 3/4U R, P
Charles Boyer, Jean Arthur, Leo Carrillo, Colin Clive
A jealous husband forces his wife to seek divorce. On an Atlantic cruise, she finds true love and heartbreak.
AM Available
United Artists — *Lightning Video*

History of Aviation, The **19??**
Aeronautics
65646 120 mins B/W B, V R, P
This program gives a glimpse into aviation's past with authentic documentary footage.
Unknown — *Video City Productions*

History of Flight, The **1985**
History-US/Aeronautics
70708 30 mins C B, V P
Narrated by Burgess Meredith
This tape traces the history of aviation from the Wright Brothers, through Lindbergh and into the Space Age.
NASA — *Kid Time Video*

History of Pro Football, The **1983**
Football/Documentary
65015 87 mins C B, V, FO P
Rare footage and interviews with NFL personalities highlight this comprehensive program on the NFL's landmark events and its greatest players.
NFL Films — *NFL Films Video*

History of the Apollo Program **1985**
Space exploration
70575 45 mins C B, V P

 (For explanation of codes, see USE GUIDE and KEY)

This program outlines the history of NASA's moon exploration program.
Century Video Corp.; Finley Holiday — *Kid Time Video*

History of the World: Part I 1981
Comedy
52699 90 mins C B, V, LV P
Mel Brooks, Dom DeLuise, Madeline Kahn, Harvey Korman, Cloris Leachman, Ron Carey, Howard Morris, Sid Caesar, Jackie Mason
Mel Brooks' wildly satiric vision of human evolution, from the Dawn of Man to the French Revolution.
MPAA:R
Brooksfilms Ltd — *CBS/Fox Video; RCA VideoDiscs*

Hit, The 1985
Comedy-Drama
70382 105 mins C B, V P
John Hart, Terence Stamp, Laura Del Sol, Tim Roth, Fernando Rey, directed by Stephen Frears
A feisty young hooker gets mixed-up with two strong-armed hired killers as they escort an unusual stool-pigeon from his exile in Spain to their angry mob bosses.
Island Alive — *Embassy Home Entertainment*

Hit and Run 1982
Drama
69041 96 mins C B, V R, P
David Marks, a Manhattan cab driver, is haunted by recurring flashbacks of a freak hit-and-run accident in which his wife was struck down on a city street.
Charles Braverman — *THORN EMI/HBO Video*

Hit Lady 1974
Suspense
80306 74 mins C B, V P
Yvette Mimieux, Dack Rambo, Clu Gulager, Keenan Wynn
An elegant cultured woman becomes a hit lady for the syndicate.
Spelling/Goldberg Productions — *Prism*

Hitler 1962
Biographical
80835 103 mins B/W B, V P
Richard Basehart, Maria Emo, Cordula Trantow
This is the true story of the infamous Nazi dictators' rise to power and his historic downfall. Available in VHS and Beta Hi Fi.
Allied Artists — *Key Video*

Hitler: A Career 1984
/Biographical
78666 120 mins B/W B, V P
How the career of Adolph Hitler changed the world is presented in this documentary.
RKO — *RKO HomeVideo*

Hitler: The Last Ten Days 1973
Drama
68249 106 mins C B, V R, P
Based on an eyewitness account, the story of Hitler's last days in an underground bunker gives insight to his madness.
MPAA:PG
World Film Services Ltd; Tomorrow Entertainment — *Paramount Home Video*

Hitler's Henchmen 1984
World War II
78146 60 mins C B, V P
This film takes a powerful look at the inhumanity of war and the graphic reality of Nazi death camps during World War II.
MPI — *MPI Home Video*

H.M.S. Pinafore 1982
Opera
72447 90 mins C LV P
The opera is captured in a live performance.
Judith DePaul — *Pioneer Video Imports*

Hobbit, The 1978
Fantasy
00239 78 mins C B, V P
Narrated by Orson Bean, John Huston, and others
Based on Tolkien's Middle Earth fantasy, this tale illustrates the Hobbit's battle against the evil forces of dragons and goblins.
Rankin Bass — *Sony Corporation of America; RCA VideoDiscs*

Hobson's Choice 1954
Comedy
63321 102 mins B/W B, V R, P
Charles Laughton, John Mills, Brenda de Banzie, directed by David Leon
A prosperous businessman in the 1890's tries to keep his daughter from marrying, but the strong-willed daughter has other ideas.
British Lion — *THORN EMI/HBO Video*

Hold 'Em Jail 1932
Comedy
59408 65 mins B/W B, V P, T
Wheeler and Woolsey, Edgar Kennedy
Wheeler and Woolsey get involved in a prison football game.
RKO — *Blackhawk Films*

Hold That Ghost 1941
Comedy
63360 86 mins B/W B, V P

Bud Abbott, Lou Costello, Joan Davis, Richard Carlson, Mischa Auer, the Andrews Sisters, Ted Lewis and his Band
Abbott and Costello inherit an abandoned roadhouse where the illicit loot of its former owner, a "rubbed out" mobster, is supposedly hidden.
Universal — *MCA Home Video*

Holiday Inn **1942**
Musical
53399 101 mins B/W B, V P
Bing Crosby, Fred Astaire, Marjorie Reynolds, Walter Abel, Virginia Dale
A song and dance man decides to turn a Connecticut farm into an inn, open only on holidays. Songs include: "Happy Holiday," "Be Careful It's My Heart," and "White Christmas."
Academy Award '42: Best Song ("White Christmas").
Paramount; Mark Sandrich — *MCA Home Video*

Hollywood Boulevard **1976**
Comedy/Filmmaking
64840 93 mins C B, V R, P
Candice Rialson, Mary Woronov, Rita George, Jeffrey Kramer, Dick Miller, Paul Bartel, directed by Joe Dante and Allan Arkush
This behind-the-scenes glimpse of shoestring-budget moviemaking offers comical sex, violence, sight gags, one-liners, comedy bits, and mock-documentary footage. Commander Cody and His Lost Planet Airmen are featured.
MPAA:R
New World Pictures — *Warner Home Video*

Hollywood Goes to War **1954**
Documentary/Film-History
58651 41 mins B/W B, V, FO P
Bob Hope, Bing Crosby, Frank Sinatra, Betty Grable, Harpo Marx, Jimmy Durante, Eddie Cantor, Red Skelton, Abbott and Costello, Dinah Shore, Dorothy Lamour, Carmen Miranda
Five shorts produced for the entertainment of G.I.'s overseas or for home front bond drives: "The All-Star Bond Rally" features Bob Hope, Fibber McGee and Molly, Bing Crosby, Harry James and his Orchestra, Sinatra, Grable, Harpo Marx, and the Talking Pin-Ups; "Hollywood Canteen Overseas Special" features Dinah Shore, Eddie Cantor, Jimmy Durante, and Red Skelton; "Mail Call (Strictly G.I.)" is a filmed "Mail Call" radio program with Don Wilson announcing guests Dorothy Lamour, Cass Daley, and Abbott and Costello doing 'Who's on First'; "G.I. Movie Weekly—Sing with the Stars" features Carmen Miranda and her fruit-basket hat, a Portuguese 'follow-the-bouncing-ball' sing-along, Richard Lane, and Mel Blanc's voice; and "Invaders in Greasepaint," the story of 'Four Jills in a Jeep'—the North African USO tour by Martha Raye, Carol Landis, Mitzi Mayfair, and Kay Francis. Also includes newsreel footage of the girls touring, plus their memorable rendition of the wartime classic tune 'Snafu,' which was banned from the airwaves for its racy lyrics.
Office of War Information; Army Pictorial Service; Army-Navy Screen Magazine — *Video Yesteryear*

Hollywood High **1977**
Comedy/Exploitation
70363 81 mins C B, V P
Marcy Albrecht, Sherry Hardin, Rae Sperling, Susanne Kevin Mead
Four attractive teen couples converge on the mansion of an eccentric silent-film star for an unusual vacation experience.
MPAA:R
Lone Star Pictures — *Vestron Video*

Hollywood High Part II **1981**
Comedy
80705 86 mins C B, V P
April May, Donna Lynn, Camille Warner
Local police continue to curtail the adventures of three comely high school students who live for boys, beer and beaches.
MPAA:R
Lone Star Pictures — *Vestron Video*

Hollywood Hot Tubs **1984**
Comedy
76766 103 mins C B, V, CED P
Edy Williams, Donna McDaniel, Michael Andrew, Katt Shea
A teenager picks up some extra cash and a lot of fun as he repairs the hot tubs of the rich and famous.
MPAA:R
Seymour Borde and Associates — *Vestron Video*

Hollywood Man **1976**
Drama
66282 90 mins C B, V P
William Smith
The story of a Hollywood actor and his crew in a desperate fight against all odds to complete their independent film.
MPAA:R
Olympic Films — *Monterey Home Video*

Hollywood on Parade **1934**
Variety
52463 59 mins B/W B, V, FO P
Fredric March, Ginger Rogers, Jean Harlow, Jeanette MacDonald, Maurice Chevalier, Mary Pickford, Jackie Cooper
A collection of several "Hollywood on Parade" shorts produced by Paramount Studios between 1932 and 1934. Nearly every big star of the era is featured singing, dancing, or taking part in bizarre sketches.

Paramount — *Video Yesteryear; Discount Video Tapes*

Hollywood Out-Takes & Rare Footage **1985**
Outtakes and bloopers
77374 84 mins B/W B, V P
Joan Crawford, Marilyn Monroe, James Dean, W.C. Fields, Humphrey Bogart.
A collection of celebrity bloopers and blunders featuring gaffes from Humphrey Bogart, W.C. Fields, and James Dean.
RCA/Columbia Pictures Home Video — *RCA/Columbia Pictures Home Video*

Hollywood Outtakes and Rare Footage **1983**
Outtakes and bloopers/Film-History
66382 85 mins C B, V P
Marilyn Monroe, James Dean, Joan Crawford, Judy Garland, Humphrey Bogart, Ronald Reagan, Bette Davis, Vivien Leigh, Carole Lombard and others
A collection of rare and unusual film clips and excerpts that feature dozens of Hollywood stars in screen tests, promotional shorts, home movies, outtakes, TV appearances and World War II propaganda shorts. Some segments in black and white.
Manhattan Movietime — *Movie Buff Video*

Hollywood Palace **1968**
Variety
56906 55 mins B/W B, V, FO P
Victor Borge, Steve Allen, Jayne Meadows, King Family, Dino Desi and Billy, Mitchell Ayres Orchestra, Scots Guards
A program from the popular comedy-variety show, complete with commercials for Playtex, Bayer, Johnson's Wax, Kool, and Tegrin.
ABC — *Video Yesteryear*

Hollywood Palace, The **1967**
Variety
12841 52 mins B/W B, V, FO P
Vicki Carr, The Temptations, Mac Ronee, Jimmy Dean, Van Johnson, hosted by Jimmy Durante
Hollywood TV variety show highlighted by Durante and Johnson in a crazy "song writing team" sketch.
ABC — *Video Yesteryear*

Hollywood Palace Farewell Show, The **1970**
Variety
38989 52 mins B/W B, V, FO P
Ella Fitzgerald, Fred Astaire, Ethel Merman, Nat King Cole, Judy Garland, hosted by Bing Crosby
The last program in the series; a retrospective of great moments and performers who appeared on the "Hollywood Palace." Featuring, in addition to those named above, Jimmy Durante, Sammy Davis, Jr., Martha Raye, Herb Alpert, Ray Bolger, Gene Kelly, Bette Davis, Buster Keaton, Gloria Swanson, Imogene Coca, Groucho Marx, George Burns, and others.
ABC — *Video Yesteryear; Video Dimensions*

Hollywood Revels **1947**
Variety
78091 58 mins B/W B, V, FO P
Bill Rose, Hillary Dawn, Peggy Bond, Pat Dorsey, Aleen Dupree, Mickey Lotus Wing
A burlesque show including Can-Can dancers, singers and comedians are included in this film.
Unknown — *Video Yesteryear*

Hollywood Strangler, The **1982**
Horror
70724 72 mins C B, V P
Pierre Agostino, Carolyn Brandt, Forrest Duke, Chuck Alford
A string of strangulations leads to a shocking climax where in a murderous fashion photographer meets a homicidal fashion model.
Ray Steckler Prods. — *Active Home Video*

Hollywood Without Makeup **1965**
Film-History
04789 51 mins C B, V P
Home movie footage taken over the years by Ken Murray includes candid shots of over 100 stars of the film world.
Filmaster — *Budget Video; Video Yesteryear; Discount Video Tapes; Video Connection*

Hollywood's Greatest Trailers **194?**
Movie and TV trailers
64418 60 mins B/W B, V, 3/4U P
Theatrical previews from an assortment of classic films, including "Citizen Kane," "Top Hat," "It's a Wonderful Life," "Fort Apache" and many others. Some are in color.
RKO et al — *Nostalgia Merchant*

Holocaust **1978**
Drama
60387 475 mins C B, V P
Meryl Streep, James Woods
The war years of 1935 to 1945 are relived in this account of the Nazi atrocities, focusing on the Weiss family, destroyed by the monstrous crimes, and the Dorf family, Germans who thrived under the Nazi regime.
Titus Productions — *Worldvision Home Video; RCA VideoDiscs*

Holocaust: Susan Sontag **1982**
World War II/Religion
59557 58 mins C B, V P
Writer Susan Sontag explores the meaning of Hitler's genocide in this retrospective of the Holocaust.

Unknown — *Mastervision*

Holt of the Secret Service 1942
Adventure/Serials
64425 225 mins B/W B, V, 3/4U P
Jack Holt
A secret service agent runs afoul of saboteurs and fifth-columnists in this fifteen-episode serial.
Columbia — *Nostalgia Merchant; Discount Video Tapes*

Holy Koran, The 1982
Islam/Middle East
59555 60 mins C B, V P
This program shows why Islam is such a force in the world today. Islam's contributions to world science and culture are examined.
Unknown — *Mastervision*

Holy Land and Holy City 1982
Religion/Christianity
59556 58 mins C B, V P
A look at the Holy Land at Christmas, and an artist's chronicle of the activities of the Holy City, the Vatican in Rome, over the four year period of the Vatican Council during the reign of Pope John XXIII.
Unknown — *Mastervision*

Hombre 1967
Western
08434 111 mins C B, V P
Paul Newman, Fredric March, Richard Boone, Diane Cilento, Cameron Mitchell, Barbara Rush, Martin Balsam
A white man, raised by Apaches, is forced to a showdown. He has to help save the lives of people he loathes.
EL, SP
20th Century Fox; Martin Ritt; Irving Ravetch — *CBS/Fox Video*

Home Free All 1984
Drama
76778 92 mins C B, V P
Allan Nicholls, Roland Caccavo, Maura Ellyn, Shelley Wyant, Lucille Rivim
Two reacquainted childhood friends attempt to reconcile their frustrated ambitions with the realities of life.
Almi Films — *Vestron Video*

Home of the Brave 1949
War-Drama
81422 86 mins B/W B, V P
Lloyd Bridges, James Edwards, Frank Lovejoy, Jeff Corey, directed by Mark Robson
A black soldier goes insane after the racist remarks and treatment he receives from his white cohorts during a top secret mission in the South Pacific.
United Artists — *Republic Pictures Home Video*

Home Sweet Home 1914
Drama
58644 62 mins B/W B, V, FO P
Lillian Gish, Dorothy Gish, Henry Walthall, Mae Marsh, Blanche Sweet, Donald Crisp, Robert Haron, directed by D. W. Griffith
Suggested by the life of John Howard Payne, actor, poet, dramatist, critic, and world-wanderer, who wrote the title song amid the bitterness of his sad life. Silent with musical score.
Reliance Majestic Release — *Video Yesteryear; Classic Video Cinema Collector's Club*

Homebodies 1974
Suspense/Drama
80391 96 mins C B, V P
Ruth McDevitt, Linda Marsh, William Hansen, Peter Brocco, Frances Fuller
Six mild mannered senior citizens resort to violence and murder in order to prevent their brownstone from being torn down.
MPAA:PG
Marshal Backlar — *Embassy Home Entertainment*

Homesteaders of Paradise Valley 1947
Western
14353 54 mins B/W B, V P
Allan Lane, Bobby Blake
Hume brothers oppose Red Ryder and a group of settlers building a dam in Paradise Valley.
Republic — *Video Connection; Cable Films; Nostalgia Merchant*

Homework 1982
Drama
63843 90 mins C B, V, LV P
Joan Collins, Michael Morgan, Betty Thomas, Shell Kepler, Wings Hauser
A young man's after-school lessons with a teacher are definitely not part of the curriculum.
MPAA:R
Jensen Farley — *MCA Home Video*

Honey 1981
Drama
65352 89 mins C B, V P
Clio Goldsmith, Fernando Rey, Catherine Spaak
An attractive writer pays an unusual visit to the home of a distinguished publisher. Brandishing a pistol, she demands that he read aloud from her manuscript. As he reads, a unique fantasy unfolds, a dreamlike erotic tale.
Toni De Carlo — *Vestron Video*

Honey Boy **1982**
Drama
80636 96 mins C B, V P
Erik Estrada, Morgan Fairchild, Hector Elizondo, Yvonne Wilder, James McEachin
A young middleweight boxing contender finds the price of fame when he falls in love with his press agent: Available in Beta Hi-Fi and VHS Stereo.
Estrada Prods. — *U.S.A. Home Video*

Honeysuckle Rose **1980**
Musical-Drama
54807 119 mins C B, V, LV R, P
Willie Nelson, Dyan Cannon, Amy Irving, Slim Pickens, Joey Floyd, Charles Levin, Priscilla Pointer, directed by Jerry Schatzberg
A road-touring country-Western singer whose life is a series of one night stands, falls in love with an adoring young guitar player who has just joined his band. This nearly costs him his marriage when his wife, who waits patiently for him at home, decides she's had enough.
MPAA:PG
Warner Bros — *Warner Home Video*

Honky Tonk Freeway **1981**
Comedy
47304 107 mins C B, V R, P
Teri Garr, Howard Hesseman, Beau Bridges, directed by John Schlesinger
An odd assortment of people become involved in a small town Mayor's scheme to turn a dying hamlet into a tourist wonderland.
MPAA:PG
Universal — *THORN EMI/HBO Video*

Honkytonk Man **1982**
Drama
60562 123 mins C B, V R, P
Clint Eastwood, Kyle Eastwood, John McIntire, Alexa Kenin, directed by Clint Eastwood
Set during the Depression, this film spins the tale of a country singer who helps his nephew through the rites of passage.
MPAA:PG
Warner Bros — *Warner Home Video*

Honor Among Thieves **1982**
Drama
78896 93 mins C B, V P
Charles Bronson, Alain Delon
Two men from different walks of life are bound together by a crime they committed years before.
Gibro Films — *Monterey Home Video*

Honor Thy Father **1973**
Drama
73560 97 mins C B, V P
Raf Vallone, Richard Castellano, Brenda Vaccaro, Joe Bologna
The everyday life of a Mafia family as seen through the eyes of Bill Bonanno, the son of mob chieftan Joe Bonanno which was adapted from the book by Gay Talese.
CBS — *Prism*

Hoodoo Ann **1916**
Film-History
50633 27 mins B/W B, V P, T
Mae Marsh, Robert Harron
The story of Hoodoo Ann, from her days in the orphanage to her happy marriage. Silent.
Triangle — *Blackhawk Films*

Hooker **1983**
Documentary/Prostitution
80931 79 mins C B, V P
This documentary takes a revealing look at the private moments and public times of prostitutes.
Dave Bell Associates — *Vestron Video*

Hooper **1978**
Comedy
38950 90 mins C B, V R, P
Burt Reynolds, Jan-Michael Vincent, Robert Klein, directed by Hal Needham
A behind-the-scenes look at the world of movie stuntmen. Burt Reynolds is a top stuntman who becomes involved in a rivalry with an up-and-coming young man out to surpass him.
MPAA:PG
Warner Bros — *Warner Home Video; RCA VideoDiscs*

Hoppity Goes to Town **1941**
Cartoons/Fantasy
64544 78 mins C B, V P
Animated
This full-length animated feature from the Max Fleischer studios tells the story of the inhabitants of Bugville, who live in a weed patch in New York City. Songs by Frank Loesser and Hoagy Carmichael. Original title: "Mr. Bug Goes to Town."
Paramount; Max Fleischer — *Republic Pictures Home Video; Classic Video Cinema Collector's Club*

Hopscotch **1980**
Comedy
55580 107 mins C B, V, CED P
Glenda Jackson, Walter Matthau, Ned Beatty, Sam Waterston
A C.I.A. agent drops out when his overly zealous chief demotes him to a desk job. When he writes a book designed to expose the dirty deeds he leads his boss and KGB pal on a merry chase.
MPAA:R
Avco Embassy — *Embassy Home Entertainment*

Horowitz in London 1982
Music-Performance
60570 116 mins C LV P
In June 1982, Vladimir Horowitz returned to London for the first time in over 30 years for a performance including Chopin, Scarlatti Sonatas, Schumann's "Scenes from Childhood," and Rachmaninoff. In stereo.
John Vernon; Peter Gelb — *Pioneer Artists; RCA VideoDiscs*

Horowitz in London 1982
Music-Performance
75898 116 mins C B, V P
Vladimir Horowitz
This program presents a rare recital by one of the greatest pianists today, playing in London for Prince Charles at a benefit.
Columbia Artists — *Sony Corporation of America*

Horrible Double Feature 192?
Horror
10135 56 mins B/W B, V P, T
John Barrymore, Lon Chaney
Package includes John Barrymore in "Dr. Jekyll and Mr. Hyde" (1920). Also features "Hunchback of Notre Dame." Both films are condensed. From the "History of the Motion Picture" series.
Universal et al — *Blackhawk Films*

Horror Express 1973
Horror
08588 95 mins C B, V P
Christopher Lee, Peter Cushing, Telly Savalas, directed by Gene Martin
A creature from Prehistoric times, which has been removed from its tomb, is transported on the Trans-Siberian railroad. Passengers discover strange things happening.
MPAA:R
Scotia Intl; Bernard Gordon — *Prism; Media Home Entertainment; Budget Video; VCII; Sheik Video; King of Video; Video Connection*

Horror Hospital 1973
Horror
48475 91 mins C B, V P
Michael Gough, Robin Askwith, Vanessa Shaw
Patients are turned into zombies by a mad doctor in this hospital where no anesthesia is used. Those who try to escape are taken care of by the doctor's guards.
MPAA:R
Richard Gordon Productions — *United Home Video*

Horror of Frankenstein 1970
Satire/Horror
63349 93 mins C B, V R, P
Ralph Bates, Kate O'Mara
This spoof of the standard Frankenstein story features a philandering Baron whose interest in a very weird branch of science creates some shocking up-to-date innovations in the conventional plot.
Levitt-Pickman — *THORN EMI/HBO Video*

Horror Planet 1982
Science fiction/Horror
65718 93 mins C B, V P
Robin Clarke
An alien creature needs a chance to breed before escaping to spread its horror. When a group of explorers disturb it, the years of waiting are over, and the unlucky mother-to-be will never be the same.
MPAA:R
Richard Gordon; David Speechley — *Embassy Home Entertainment*

Horse Soldiers, The 1959
Adventure/Drama
59643 119 mins C CED P
John Wayne, William Holden, Constance Towers, directed by John Ford
Union Army cavalry officers travel deep into Confederate territory, squaring off against the southern army, and each other, along the way.
United Artists — *RCA VideoDiscs*

Horse Soldiers, The 1959
Western
72895 119 mins C B, V P
John Wayne, William Holden
An 1863 Union cavalry officer is sent 300 miles into Confederate territory to destroy a railroad junction.
United Artists — *CBS/Fox Video*

Hospital, The 1971
Drama
65497 101 mins C CED P
George C. Scott, Diana Rigg, Barnard Hughes, Nancy Marchand, Richard Dysart
A city hospital is beset by weird mishaps, and it transpires that a killer is on the loose.
United Artists — *CBS/Fox Video*

Hospital Massacre 1981
Horror
65108 89 mins C B, V, CED P
Barbi Benton, Jon Van Ness
A psychopathic killer who wants to play doctor with a young woman in the hospital repeatedly demonstrates his brutal bedside manner.
MPAA:R
Cannon Films — *MGM/UA Home Video*

Hostage Tower, The 1980
Drama
65711 97 mins C B, V P

 (For explanation of codes, see USE GUIDE and KEY)

Peter Fonda, Maud Adams, Britt Ekland, Billy Dee Williams
A group of internatioal crime figures capture a VIP, hold her hostage in the Eiffel Tower and demand $30 million in ransom.
MPAA:PG
Burt Nodella — *Embassy Home Entertainment*

Hostages **1979**
Suspense/Drama
80129 93 mins C B, V P
Stuart Whitman, Marisa Mell
A gang of criminals kidnap a family on vacation at a Caribbean island.
Excel Telemedia International — *King of Video*

Hot Lead and Cold Feet **1978**
Western/Comedy
77529 89 mins C B, V R, P
Jim Dale, Don Knotts, Karen Valentine
Twin brothers compete in a train race where the winner will take ownership of a small western town.
MPAA:G
Walt Disney Productions — *Walt Disney Home Video*

Hot Rock, The **1970**
Comedy
08466 97 mins C B, V P
Robert Redford, George Segal, Ron Leibman, Zero Mostel, Paul Sand, directed by Peter Yates
Four incredible goofs try to steal the world's hottest diamond.
MPAA:PG SP
20th Century Fox; Hal Landers and Bobby Roberts — *CBS/Fox Video*

Hot Rock Videos Volume 2 **1985**
Music video
81206 30 mins C B, V P
Rodney Dangerfield, Lou Reed, Meat Loaf
More conceptual music videos for viewing enjoyment. Available in VHS and Beta Hi Fi Stereo.
RCA Video Productions — *RCA/Columbia Pictures Home Video*

Hot Rock Videos Volume I **1984**
Music video
80368 28 mins C B, V P
A collection of music videos from performers such as Eurythmics and The Kinks. Available in VHS Hi-Fi Dolby Stereo and Beta Hi-Fi Stereo.
RCA Video Productions — *RCA/Columbia Pictures Home Video*

Hot Shorts **1984**
Comedy
70561 73 mins B/W B, V P
Phil Austin, Peter Bergman, Phil Proctor
The Firesign Theatre turn their satiric wit on Sataday matinee cliff hanger serials. While familiar characters cross the screen the re-recorded stereo soundtrack features hilarious new dialogue, sound effects, and music.
Bud Groskopf — *RCA/Columbia Pictures Home Video*

Hot Stuff **1980**
Comedy
51570 91 mins C B, V P
Dom Deluise, Jerry Reed, Suzanne Pleshette, Ossie Davis, directed by Dom Deluise
Officers on a burglary task force decide the best way to obtain convictions is to go into the fencing business themselves.
MPAA:PG
Columbia Pictures — *RCA/Columbia Pictures Home Video*

Hot Summer Night.. With Donna, A **1984**
Music-Performance
76028 60 mins C B, V P
Donna Summer gives an electrifying performance of her hits at a concert held at California's Pacific Amphitheater. Songs include "She Works Hard For the Money," "Bad Girls" and "Hot Stuff."
Christine Smith — *RCA/Columbia Pictures Home Video*

Hot T-Shirts **1979**
Comedy
47681 86 mins C B, V P
Ray Holland, Stephanie Lawlor, Pauline Rose, Corinne Alphen
A small town bar owner needs a boost for business, finding the answer in wet T-shirt contests.
MPAA:R
Cannon Films — *MCA Home Video*

Hot Times **1974**
Drama
65452 80 mins C B, V P
Henry Cory
A high school boy, after striking out with the high school girls, decides to go to New York and have the time of his life!
MPAA:R
Extraordinary Films — *Monterey Home Video*

Hotel New Hampshire, The **1984**
Comedy-Drama
73037 110 mins C B, V, CED P
Jodie Foster, Rob Lowe, Beau Bridges, Nastassia Kinski
This is an adaptation of John Irving's novel about a family's adventures in New Hampshire, Vienna and New York City.

MPAA:R
Orion — *Vestron Video*

Hothead (Coup de Tete) **1978**
Comedy
66016 90 mins C B, V P
Patrick Dewaere, directed by Jean-Jacques Annaud
A talented soccer player's quick temper causes him to be cut from his team, lose his job and even be banned from the local bar.
Gaumont SFP — *RCA/Columbia Pictures Home Video*

Hound of the Baskervilles, The **1959**
Mystery
47146 86 mins C B, V, CED P
Peter Cushing, Christopher Lee, Andre Morell
Sherlock Holmes solves the mystery of a supernatural hound threatening the life of a Dartmoor baronet.
EL, SP
United Artists; Hammer — *CBS/Fox Video*

Houndcats, The **1981**
Cartoons
75625 43 mins C B, V P
Animated 2 pgms
This program consists of two animated stories, starring the Houndcats.
1. The Misbehavin' Raven Mission 2. The Double Dealing Diamond Mission
DePatie Freleng — *Trans World Entertainment*

Houndcats Volume 3, The **1972**
Cartoons
76941 44 mins C B, V P
Animated
That zany band of trouble shooters, the Houndcats solve two mysteries with humorous results.
De Patie-Freleng Enterprises — *Trans World Entertainment*

Houndcats Volume 4, The **1985**
Cartoons
70389 43 mins C B, V P
Animated 2 pgms
This program features two more rollicking adventures starring the Hound cats.
1. The Who's Who That's Who Mission; 2. The Outta Sight Blight Mission.
DePatie Freleng — *Trans World Entertainment*

House Across the Bay, The **1940**
Drama
66634 88 mins B/W B, V P
George Raft, Walter Pidgeon, Joan Bennett, Lloyd Nolan
An ex-con discovers that his wife was having an affair during his imprisonment.
Walter Wanger Productions — *Monterey Home Video*

House Across the Bay, The **1940**
Drama
78897 88 mins B/W B, V P
George Raft, Joan Bennett, Walter Pidgeon, Lloyd Nolan, directed by Archie Mayo
A woman has her mobster husband arrested for tax evasion to protect him from his enemies.
Walter Wanger — *Monterey Home Video*

House by the Cemetery **1983**
Horror
70152 84 mins C B, V P
When a family moves into a house close to a cemetery, strange things start to happen to them.
MPAA:R
Almi Pictures — *Vestron Video*

House Calls **1978**
Comedy
47420 105 mins C B, V, LV P
Walter Matthau, Glenda Jackson, Art Carney, Richard Benjamin, Candice Azzara
A widowed surgeon turns into a swinging bachelor until he meets a stuffy English divorcee.
MPAA:PG
Universal — *MCA Home Video*

House of Lurking Death, The **1984**
Mystery
80448 60 mins C B, V P
James Warwick, Francesca Annis
Detectives Tommy and Tuppence find a box of chocolates laced with arsenic at the home of Lois Hargreaves, and the mad old maid is the prime suspect. Based on the Agatha Christie story.
London Weekend Television — *Pacific Arts Video*

House of Seven Corpses, The **1973**
Horror
58546 90 mins C B, V R, P
John Carradine, John Ireland, Faith Domergue
On the site of a lonely country estate, a motion picture company arrives planning to film a make-believe occult thriller.
MPAA:PG
Philip Yordan — *World Video Pictures; Video Gems; Budget Video; King of Video*

House of Shadows 1983
Horror
63387 90 mins C B, V P
John Gavin, Yvonne DeCarlo
A 20-year-old murder comes back to haunt the victim's friends in this suspenseful tale of mystery and terror.
Intercontinental Releasing — *Media Home Entertainment*

House of Wax 1953
Horror
78137 88 mins C B, V R, P
Charles Bronson, Vincent Price
The story of a deranged sculptor whose sinister wax museum showcases creations that were once alive.
Warner Home Video — *Warner Home Video*

House on Chelouche Street, The 1973
Drama
66135 111 mins C B, V, FO P
A well thought-out story of life in Tel Aviv under the rule of the British, before the creation of the country of Israel.
Israel — *Video Yesteryear*

House on Garibaldi Street, The 1979
Suspense/Crime-Drama
72454 100 mins C B, V P
Topol, Nick Mancuso
This is Isser Harel's account of the capture of Adolph Eichmann.
Charles Fries Production — *U.S.A. Home Video*

House on Sorority Row, The 1983
Horror
64898 90 mins C B, V, LV, CED P
The harrowing story of what happens when seven senior sisters have a last fling and get back at their housemother at the same time.
Artists Releasing Corp — *Vestron Video*

House That Bled to Death, The 1981
Horror
77443 60 mins C B, V P
Nicholas Ball, Rachel Davies, Brian Croucher, Pat Maynard, Emma Ridley
Strange things happen to a family when they move into a run down house where a murder occurred years before.
Hammer House of Horror — *Thriller Video*

House That Vanished, The 1973
Horror/Mystery
50728 84 mins C B, V P
Andrea Allan, Karl Lanchbury, directed by Joseph Larraz
A mysterious house provides horror, screams, and death for most of those who challenge it.
MPAA:R
Diana Daubeney — *Media Home Entertainment*

House Where Evil Dwells, The 1982
Horror
80859 88 mins C B, V P
Edward Albert, Susan George, Doug McClure
An American family is subjected to a reign of terror then they move into an old Japanese house possessed by three deadly samurai ghosts.
MPAA:R
Commercial Credit Services Holdings Ltd. — *MGM/UA Home Video*

Houston Astros: Team Highlights 1984
Baseball
81140 30 mins C B, V P
J.R. Richard, Phil Garner, Joe Niekro, Nolan Ryan, Ray Knight, Joe Sambito 4 pgms
Here are some selected highlights from the Houston Astros 1980's seasons.
1.1981: The Orange Force 2.1982: The First Generation 3.1983: Fighting Back 4.1984: Pulling Together
Major League Baseball — *Major League Baseball Productions*

How Funny Can Sex Be? 1976
Comedy
66078 97 mins C B, V P
Giancarlo Giannini, Laura Antonelli, Dulio Del Prete
Eight ribald sketches about loveItalian style.
MPAA:R
Howard Mahler Films — *CBS/Fox Video*

How I Won the War 1967
Comedy/Satire
78634 111 mins C B, V P
John Lennon, Michael Crawford, Michael Hordern, directed by Richard Lester
An inept officer must lead his battalion out of England into the Egyptian desert to conquer a cricket field.
MPAA:PG
Petersham Films Limited — *MGM/UA Home Video*

How Tennis Pros Win 1985
Tennis
81602 57 mins C B, V P
Trish Bostrom demonstrates basic techniques that will improve your tennis game.
Morris Video — *Monterey Home Video*

How the Animals Discovered Christmas 1956
Christmas/Cartoons
56153 13 mins C B, V P, T
Animated
A delightful tale about the animals of Cozy Valley and how they discover the spirit of Christmas.
AM Available
Coronet Films — *Blackhawk Films*

How to Avoid Being Cheated at Cards 1980
Games
53781 60 mins C B, V P
Card expert Buddy Farnan demonstrates ways to avoid being cheated at cards, all the tricks-of-the-trade impossible to detect, unless you know how they are done.
Unknown — *Essex Video; Video Tape Network*

How to Beat Home Video Games Volume I 1982
Video/Games
63365 60 mins C B, V P
Narrated by Philip M. Wiswell
"Volume I: The best Games" features strategies for high scoring on such Atari VCS games as "Space Invaders," "Asteroids," "Chopper Command" and "Frogger."
Vestron Video — *Vestron Video*

How to Beat Home Video Games Volume II 1982
Video/Games
63366 60 mins C B, V P
Narrated by Philip M. Wiswell
"Volume II: The Hot New Games" features strategies for beating 20 of the newest games for the Atari VCS, including "MegaMania," "Demons to Diamonds," "Pitfall" and "Riddle of the Sphynx."
Vestron Video — *Vestron Video*

How to Beat Home Video Games Volume III 1982
Video/Games
63367 60 mins C B, V P
Narrated by Philip M. Wiswell
"Volume III: Arcade Quality for the Home" previews new arcade quality game systems such as ColecoVision, Vectrex and Atari 5200, and demonstrates how to score high on games for these systems, including "Cosmic Chasm," "Donkey Kong," "Zaxxon" and "Galaxian."
Vestron Video — *Vestron Video*

How to Beat the High Cost of Living 1980
Comedy
64890 105 mins C B, V, CED P
Jessica Lange, Susan St. James, Jane Curtin, Richard Benjamin
Three women execute a crazy, comic shopping mall heist.
MPAA:PG
Filmways — *Vestron Video*

How to Break Up a Happy Divorce 1976
Comedy
80640 74 mins C B, V P
Barbara Eden, Hal Linden, Peter Bonerz, Marcia Rodd, directed by Jerry Paris
A divorced woman starts a vigorous campaign to win her ex-husband back by dating another man to make him jealous.
Charles Fries Prods. — *Worldvision Home Video*

How to Kill 400 Duponts 1965
Comedy/Drama
70370 98 mins C B, V R, P
Terry Thomas, Johnny Dorelli, Margaret Lee
In this film, a womanizing-thieving-master of disguises outwits an inspector as he plots 400 murders.
Foreign — *Video City Productions*

How to Marry a Millionaire 1953
Comedy
08552 96 mins C B, V P
Lauren Bacall, Marilyn Monroe, Betty Grable, William Powell, David Wayne, Cameron Mitchell
Three models pool their money and rent a lavish apartment to wage campaign to trap millionaire husbands.
20th Century Fox; Nunnally Johnson — *CBS/Fox Video*

How to Stuff a Wild Bikini 1965
Comedy
66130 90 mins C B, V R, P
Annette Funicello, Dwayne Hickman, Buster Keaton, Harvey Lembeck, Mickey Rooney
A young man in the Navy asks a local witchdoctor to keep on eye on his girl.
American Intl Pictures — *Warner Home Video*

How to Watch Pro Football 1981
Football
57776 53 mins C B, V P

Tom Landry, Marv Levy, John McKay, Chuck Noll, Sam Rutigliano, Don Shula, Dick Vermeil
A step-by-step guide designed to enhance every fan's enjoyment of the game. Seven top coaches take the viewer through everything from zone defense pass coverage to offensive strategy at the goal line. The two-sided interactive disc offers the same program content utilizing the unique technology of the interactive disc.
Optical Programming Associates — *MCA Home Video; Optical Programming Associates*

How to Win in Blackjack **1981**
Games
53780 90 mins C B, V P
Ken Uston, professional blackjack player, demonstrates his "card-counting" method, in which he keeps track of the cards so well that he can determine if the remaining cards will tip the odds in his favor.
Ken Uston — *Uston Institute of Blackjack*

Howard Jones: Like to Get to Know You Well **1984**
Music video
80155 58 mins C B, V R, P
Howard Jones performs his infectious brand of dance rock in this concert taped in England.
Stagefright Productions; Limelight Films — *Warner Home Video*

Howdy Doody **195?**
Comedy
59086 49 mins B/W B, V, FO P
Buffalo Bob Smith
Clarabell and Buffalo Bob show movies of Clarabell's recent trip. Princess Summerfall Winterspring and Zippy the Chimp, Flubadub, Dilly Dally, Inspector John, Mr. Bluster, and others also appear. Two complete shows.
NBC — *Video Yesteryear; Discount Video Tapes*

Howling, The **1981**
Horror
59340 91 mins C B, V, LV, CED P
Dee Wallace, Patrick MacNee, Dennis Dugan, Kevin McCarthy
A pretty television reporter takes a rest at a clinic inhabited by loonies, and located near woods inhabited by werewolves.
MPAA:R
Michael Finell;Jack Conrad — *Embassy Home Entertainment; RCA VideoDiscs*

H.R. Pufnstuf, Vol II **1969**
Adventure
80778 46 mins C B, V P
Billie Hayes, Jack Wild
This volume features two more episodes from the popular children's series.
Sid and Marty Krofft — *Embassy Home Entertainment*

H.R. Pufnstuf, Volume I **1969**
Adventure
76789 46 mins C B, V P
Billie Hayes, Jack Wild, Joan Gerber, Felix Silla, Jerry Landon
The Mayor of Magic Island H.R. Pufnstuf and his friend Jimmy battle the evil Witchiepoo and her bumbling henchmen as they struggle to find the Secret Path of Escape.
Sid and Marty Krofft — *Embassy Home Entertainment*

Huberman Festival, The **1984**
Music-Performance
65852 45 mins C B, V P
This program is a remarkable concert series for violin and orchestra performed by the Israeli Philharmonic and the world's seven most famous violinists.
Pacific Arts Video Records — *Pacific Arts Video*

Huckleberry Finn **1978**
Adventure
29235 97 mins C B, V, CED P
Kurt Ida, Don Manahan, Forrest Tucker
Based on the classic story by Mark Twain of the adventures of a Missouri boy and a runaway slave.
Sunn Classic Pictures — *VidAmerica*

Huckleberry Finn **1975**
Adventure
55535 78 mins C B, V, CED P
Ron Howard, Jack Elam, Merle Haggard, Donny Most
Television version of the Mark Twain classic about a boy and a runaway slave who take off together on a raft down the Mississippi.
ABC Pictures International — *CBS/Fox Video*

Huckleberry Finn **1974**
Musical
Closed Captioned
81560 118 mins C B, V P
Jeff East, Paul Winfield, Harvey Korman
This is the musical version of the Mark Twain story about the adventures a young boy and a runaway slave encounter along the Mississippi River. Available in VHS and Beta Hi-Fi.
United Artists — *Playhouse Video*

Huckleberry Finn **1981**
Cartoons
81321 72 mins C B, V P
Animated

This is a version of the classic Mark Twain novel about the adventures a young boy and a runaway slave encounter as they travel down the Mississippi River.
New Hope Productions — *Lightning Video*

Hud 1963
Drama
10952 112 mins B/W B, V, LV P
Paul Newman, Melvyn Douglas, Patricia Neal, Brandon DeWilde
Hard-driving, hard-drinking, woman-chasing young man, whose life is a revolt against the principles of his father, is the idol of his teenage nephew.
Academy Awards '63: Best Actress (Neal); Best Supporting Actor (Douglas); Best Cinematography.
Paramount — *Paramount Home Video; RCA VideoDiscs*

Hughes and Harlow: Angels in Hell 1977
Biographical/Drama
81396 94 mins C B, V P
Lindsay Bloom, Victor Holchak, Davis McLean
This is the story of the romance that occurred between Howard Hughes and Jean Harlow during the filming of "Hell's Angels" in 1930.
MPAA:R
Key Pictures — *Monterey Home Video*

Hughes Flying Boat, The 1980
Documentary/Aeronautics
57431 11 mins C B, V P, T
A look at Howard Hughes' legendary aircraft, "The Spruce Goose," hidden from public view for over thirty years, and the mystery hangar on Terminal Island. This program includes live commentary by Hughes from the cockpit during flight.
Bruce Frenzinger — *Blackhawk Films*

Hughie 1984
Drama
75288 53 mins C B, V P
This is a tape of the Broadway play about a hotel night clerk who develops friendships with the residents that come in during the night. In Beta Hi-Fi and VHS Dolby stereo.
RKO Home Video — *RKO HomeVideo*

Hugo the Hippo 1976
Cartoons
08483 90 mins C B, V P
Animated, voices of Paul Lynde, Burl Ives, Robert Morley, Marie and Jimmy Osmond
A forlorn baby hippo struggles to survive in the human jungle of old Zanzibar.
MPAA:G
20th Century Fox — *CBS/Fox Video*

Hulkamania 1985
Sports
81392 60 mins C B, V P
Hulk Hagan, The Iron Sheik, Big John Studd
The World Wrestling Federation's Heavyweight Champion talks about some of his favorite matches plus offers his workout and nutrition secrets.
Evart Enterprises — *Coliseum Video*

Hullabaloo 1965
Music-Performance
47480 45 mins B/W B, V, FO P
Gene Pitney, Junior Walker and the All-Stars, Leslie Uggams, hosted by Dean Jones
A March 23, 1965 episode of the popular rock 'n' roll variety show, featuring top hits by the artists of the day.
NBC — *Video Yesteryear*

Hullabaloo 1965
Music-Performance
58263 47 mins B/W B, V, FO P
David McCallum, Beau Brummels, Brenda Lee, Animals, Peter and Gordon, Michael Landon, Paul Revere and Raiders, Byrds, Chad Stewart, Jackie De Shannon
Two programs from the mid-Sixties Teenage rock 'n' roll show complete with mini-skirts. David McCallum appears as Illya Kuryakin, Chad drops Jeremy, and the Byrds transcend the proceedings with a performance of "The Times They Are A-Changin."
NBC — *Video Yesteryear*

Human Experiments 1979
Horror
53327 82 mins C B, V P
Linda Haynes, Jackie Coogan, Aldo Ray
A psychiatrist in a women's prison conducts a group of experiments in which he destroys the "criminal instinct" in the inmates through brute fear.
MPAA:R
Summer Brown; Gregory Goodell — *VidAmerica*

Human Monster, The 1939
Horror
72948 73 mins B/W B, V P
Bela Lugosi
A mad doctor played by Bela Lugosi is using his house as a front for some strange experiments.
Monogram — *United Home Video; Kartes Productions*

Human Vapour, The 1968
Science fiction
80824 81 mins C B, V R, P
A normal human being has the ability to vaporize himself at will and use it to terrorize Tokyo.

Tohol Brenco Pictures — *Video Gems*

Humanoids from the Deep 1980
Horror
54809 81 mins C B, V R, P
A horror tale wherein strange creatures rise from the depths of the ocean and attack mankind.
MPAA:R
New World Pictures — *Warner Home Video*

Humans: Happy Hour, The 1984
Music
65850 40 mins C B, V P
This program represents a pioneering step into the next wave of long-form music video with the Humans' songs fitting into the overall plot.
Pacific Arts Video Records — *Pacific Arts Video*

Humongous 1982
Horror
63374 93 mins C B, V P
Janet Julian, David Wallace, Janet Baldwin
A deranged giant must kill to survive.
MPAA:R
Embassy Pictures — *Embassy Home Entertainment*

Hunchback of Notre Dame, The 1923
Drama
07278 90 mins B/W B, V P, T
Lon Chaney, Patsy Ruth Miller, Norman Kerry, Ernest Torrance
The first film version of Victor Hugo's novel about the tortured hunchback bellringer of Notre Dame Cathedral. Silent.
Universal — *Blackhawk Films; Video Yesteryear; Budget Video; Classic Video Cinema Collector's Club; Kartes Productions*

Hunchback of Notre Dame, The 1939
Drama
00309 117 mins B/W B, V, 3/4U P
Charles Laughton, Maureen O'Hara, Edmund O'Brien
Victor Hugo's classic tale of the tortured hunchback bellringer of Notre Dame.
RKO — *Nostalgia Merchant; VidAmerica; King of Video; Blackhawk Films; Sheik Video; Cable Films; Video Connection; RCA VideoDiscs*

Hunger, The 1983
Horror
65220 100 mins C B, V, CED P
Catherine Deneuve, David Bowie, Susan Sarandon, Cliff de Young, directed by Tony Scott
A 2000-year-old vampire finds that her current lover is aging fast and therefore sets out to find some "new blood" to replace him.
MPAA:R
MGM UA — *MGM/UA Home Video*

Hungry i Reunion 1981
Comedy-Performance/Music-Performance
59930 90 mins C B, V P
Bill Cosby, Phyllis Diller, Ronnie Schell, Bill Dana, Mort Sahl, Irwin Corey, Jackie Vernon, Jonathan Winters, Kingston Trio, Limelighters, Lenny Bruce
A reunion of stars who made the "Hungry i" San Francisco's favorite nightclub of the 50's and 60's. Includes rare footage of Lenny Bruce in performance.
Tom Cohen — *Pacific Arts Video*

Hunt the Man Down 1950
Mystery
73695 68 mins B/W B, V P
Gig Young, Lynn Roberts, Gerald Mohr
A public defender must solve a killing for which an innocent man is charged.
RKO — *RKO HomeVideo*

Hunt the Man Down/Smashing the Rackets 1951
Mystery/Drama
79321 137 mins B/W B, V P
Gig Young, Lynne Roberts, Chester Morris, Frances Mercer
A double feature: In """Hunt the Man Down" a public defender tries to clear a captured fugitive's name, and in """Smashing the Rackets" a special prosecutor takes on the gangsters who have corrupted a big city.
RKO — *RKO HomeVideo*

Hunted! 1979
Drama
80795 90 mins C B, V R, P
A young Jewish boy teams up with a resistance fighter to find his mother in Nazi Germany during World War II.
German — *Video Gems*

Hunter, The 1980
Drama/Adventure
54671 97 mins C B, V, LV R, P
Steve McQueen, Eli Wallach, Kathryn Harrold, LeVar Burton, directed by Buzz Kulik
An action-drama based on the real life adventures of Ralph (Papa) Thorson, a modern day bounty hunter who makes his living by finding fugitives who have jumped bail.
MPAA:PG
Paramount — *Paramount Home Video*

Hunter 1977
Suspense
81122 120 mins C B, V P
James Franciscus, Linda Evans, Broderick Crawford
An attorney falsely accused of a crime sets out to even the score with the mysterious millionaire who set him up. Pilot for the series.
Lorimar Productions — *Karl/Lorimar Home Video*

Hunters of the Golden Cobra 1982
Adventure/War-Drama
80925 95 mins C B, V P
David Warbeck, Almanta Suska, Alan Collins, John Steiner
Two American soldiers plot to recover the priceless golden cobra from the Japanese general who stole the prized relic during the last days of World War II.
MPAA:R
World Northal — *Vestron Video*

Hurray for Betty Boop 1980
Cartoons
78141 81 mins C B, V R, P
Animated
An animated feature presents Betty Boop as she gets herself into the true spirit on an election year by running for President.
Warner Home Video — *Warner Home Video*

Hurricane 1979
Drama
63430 119 mins C B, V R, P
Mia Farrow, Jason Robards, Trevor Howard, Max Von Sydow
A hurricane wreaks havoc in a tropical paradise.
Paramount; Dino DeLaurentiis — *Paramount Home Video*

Hurricane Express 1932
Adventure/Serials
58633 223 mins B/W B, V P
John Wayne, Joseph Girard
Twelve episodes of the vintage serial, in which the Duke pits his courage against an unknown, powerful individual out to sabotage a railroad.
Mascot — *Video Connection; Video Yesteryear; Cable Films; Discount Video Tapes*

Hurry, Charlie, Hurry 1941
Comedy
73699 65 mins B/W B, V P
Leon Errol
A husband gets in trouble aided by his Indian friends.
RKO — *RKO HomeVideo*

Hussy 1980
Drama
66604 95 mins C B, V, LV P
Helen Mirren, John Shea
An unlikely pair of lovers find themselves enmeshed within an underworld conspiracy.
MPAA:R
World Northal — *Vestron Video*

Hustle 1975
Mystery
38934 120 mins C B, V R, P
Burt Reynolds, Catherine Deneuve, directed by Robert Aldrich
Burt Reynolds plays a detective investigating a young girl's supposed suicide who becomes romantically entangled with a high-priced call girl.
MPAA:R
Paramount — *Paramount Home Video*

Hustler Squad 1976
War-Drama
64297 98 mins C B, V P
John Ericson, Karen Ericson, Lynda Sinclaire, Nory Wright
A U.S. Army major and a Philippine guerrilla leader stage a major operation to help rid the Philippines of Japanese Occupation forces: they have four combat-trained prostitutes infiltrate a brothel patronized by top Japanese officers.
MPAA:R
Crown International Pictures — *United Home Video*

Hustling 1975
Drama
65665 96 mins C B, V P
Jill Clayburgh, Lee Remick
A reporter writing a series of articles on prostitution in New York City takes an incisive look at their unusual and sometimes brutal world.
Lillian Gallo — *Worldvision Home Video*

Hymn of the Nations 1944
Music-Performance
11235 25 mins B/W B, V, FO P
Jan Peerce, Arturo Toscanini and the NBC Symphony, the Westminster Choir
This wartime short features a rare filmed appearance by Arturo Toscanini, conducting two Verdi works: the overture to "La Forza del Destino" and "Hymn of the Nations."
Office of War Information — *Video Yesteryear; Blackhawk Films*

Hypnovision Stop Smoking Video Programming 1983
Smoking
69927 22 mins C B, V P

Through a number of positive subliminal messages, this program helps viewers to be more relaxed in their daily life without cigarettes, learn to take "one day at a time" to reduce anxiety, and substitute new positive behaviors for old, poor habits.
Self Improvement Video — *Self Improvement Video*

Hypnovision Stress Reduction 1985
Stress
81595 20 mins C B, V P
This program aids viewers in reducing stress in their daily lives.
Self Improvement Video — *Self Improvement Video*

Hypnovision Weight Loss Video Programming 1983
Physical fitness
69928 22 mins C B, V P
To help the viewer lose weight, this program uses a number of positive subliminal messages to deeply relax and then permantly change poor eating habits of the overeater.
Self Improvement Video — *Self Improvement Video*

Hysterectomy (Rehabilitation and Injury) 1978
Physical fitness
52757 30 mins C B, V P
Hosted by Ann Dugan
Exercises for women who have had a hysterectomy, including both specific-area and total-body movements to gradually improve muscle tone. Part of the "Rehabilitation and Injury" series.
Health 'N Action — *RCA/Columbia Pictures Home Video*

Hysteria 1964
Drama/Romance
79213 85 mins B/W B, V P
Robert Webber, Susan Lloyd, Maurice Denham, directed by Freddie Francis
When an American becomes involved in an accident and has amnesia, a mysterious benefactor pays all his bills and gives the man a house to live in.
MPAA:PG
Hammer Film Productions — *MGM/UA Home Video*

Hysterical 1983
Comedy
65389 86 mins C B, V P
The Hudson Brothers
This is a comedy about a haunted lighthouse occupied by the vengeful spirit of a spurned woman.
MPAA:PG
Gene Levy — *Embassy Home Entertainment*

I

I Am a Dancer 1972
Dance/Biographical
58460 90 mins C B, V R, P
Rudolph Nureyev, Margo Fonteyn, Carla Fracci, Lynn Seymour, Deanne Bergsma
Nureyev is seen as a pupil in ballet class, exhibiting the sweat and dedication needed.
Evdoros Demetriou — *THORN EMI/HBO Video*

I Am a Fugitive from a Chain Gang 1932
Drama
65065 90 mins B/W B, V P
Paul Muni, Glenda Farrell, Helen Vinson, Preston Foster, directed by Mervyn LeRoy
An innocent man is convicted and sentenced to a Georgia chain gang, where he is brutalized and degraded. Based on a true story.
Warner Bros — *Key Video; RCA VideoDiscs*

I Am the Cheese 1983
Suspense
80046 95 mins C B, V P
Robert Macnaughton, Hope Lange, Don Murray, Robert Wagner, Sudie Bond
When a boy undergoes psychiatric treatment in an institution, he finds out the truth about the death of his parents.
Almi Films — *Vestron Video*

I Confess 1953
Mystery/Drama
80080 95 mins B/W B, V R, P
Montgomery Clift, Anne Baxter, Karl Malden, Brian Aherne, directed by Alfred Hitchcock
When a priest hears the confession of a murder, the circumstances seem to point to him as the prime suspect.
Warner Bros. — *Warner Home Video*

I Cover the Waterfront 1933
Drama
11234 70 mins B/W B, V, FO P
Claudette Colbert, Ben Lyon, Ernest Torrance, Hobart Cavanaugh
A reporter exposes a fisherman who brings Chinese aliens into the country on his boat, or kills them when authorities are after him.
Edward Small Prods — *Video Yesteryear; Movie Buff Video; Budget Video; Video*

Connection; Discount Video Tapes; Western Film & Video Inc; Kartes Productions; Classic Video Cinema Collector's Club

---

I Crave the Waves 1983
Sports-Water/Documentary
66620 90 mins C B, V P
Bobby Owens, Lynne Boyer, Allen Sarlo, Becky Benson
A lighthearted tour around the world to some of the most exciting surf spots in California, Hawaii, Brazil and South Africa. Twenty of the world's top surfers are seen in action and at play. An additional California skateboarding short, "Four-Wheel-Drive," is also included.
MPAA:PG
Robert Rey Walker — *U.S.A. Home Video*

I Dismember Mama 1974
Horror
79851 81 mins C B, V R, P
Zooey Hall, Joanne Moore Jordan, Greg Mullauey, Marlene Tracy
A young man sick of his overbearing mother decides to hack her up into little pieces.
Independent — *Video Gems*

I Do! I Do! 1984
Musical
69923 116 mins C B, V P
Lee Remick, Hal Linden
This Los Angeles production of the Broadway musical covers 50 years of a marriage, beginning just before the turn of the century. In VHS Dolby stereo and Beta Hi-Fi.
Bonnie Burns — *RKO HomeVideo*

I Heard the Owl Call My Name 1973
Drama
75491 74 mins C B, V P
Tom Courtenay, Dean Jagger
An Anglican priest meets with mystical Indian tribesmen of Northwest America.
Tomorrow Entertainment — *Prism*

I Like to Hurt People 1984
Sports
81215 80 mins C B, V, LV P
The Sheik, Andre the Giant, Abdullah the Butcher, Ox Baker, Heather Feather, Dusty Rhodes
Wrestling superstars Andre the Giant, Heather Feather and Dusty Rhodes team up to overthrow the disgusting king of the ring, The Sheik. Not for young children or the squeamish.
Ruthless Video — *New World Video*

I Love All of You 1983
Drama/Romance
77454 103 mins C B, V P
Catherine Deneuve, Jean-Louis Trintignant, Gerard Depardieu, Serge Gainsbourg, directed by Claude Berri
An independent career woman finds it hard to stay with just one man. Available in Beta Hi-Fi and VHS Stereo.
Renn Productions — *Monterey Home Video*

I Love You 1982
Satire
60569 104 mins C B, V, CED P
Sonia Braga, Paulo Cesar Pereio, directed by Arnaldo Jabor
A man down on his luck mistakenly assumes a woman he meets is a hooker. She plays along, only to find that they are becoming emotionally involved.
MPAA:R
Atlantic Releasing Corp; Brazil — *MGM/UA Home Video*

I Love You, Alice B. Toklas 1968
Comedy
58237 93 mins C B, V R, P
Peter Sellers, Jo Van Fleet, Leigh Taylor-Young, directed by Hy Averback
A straight, uptight lawyer decides to join the peace and love generation. Screenplay by Paul Mazursky.
Warner Bros — *Warner Home Video*

I Married a Monster from Outer Space 1958
Horror/Science fiction
60213 78 mins B/W B, V R, P
Tom Tryon, Gloria Talbott
The vintage thriller about a race of monster-like aliens from another planet who try to conquer earth.
Gene Fowler Jr — *Paramount Home Video*

I Married a Witch 1942
Comedy
50936 77 mins B/W B, V R, P
Veronica Lake, Fredric March, Susan Hayward, Broderick Crawford, directed by Rene Clair
An enchantress released from the beyond gets romantic with a man running for governor.
AM Available
United Artists — *Lightning Video*

I Married Joan 1955
Comedy
58640 50 mins B/W B, V, FO P
Joan Davis, Jim Backus
Two episodes of this vintage sitcom: "Joan's Testimonial Luncheon," in which Joan thinks the girls in the bridge club don't like her when they plan a surprise luncheon; and "The St. Bernards," in which the Stevens' end up with three unwanted canines.

(For explanation of codes, see USE GUIDE and KEY)

NBC — *Video Yesteryear*

I Married Joan 1954
Comedy
63783 105 mins B/W B, V, 3/4U P
Joan Davis, Jim Backus, Beverly Wills
Four episodes from the popular TV series, with Joan Davis getting into mischief and mayhem: "Joan Sees Stars," "Joan the Matchmaker," "Joan Throws a Wedding" and "Joan's Surprise for Brad."
NBC — *Shokus Video*

I Never Promised You a Rose Garden 1977
Drama
58238 90 mins C B, V R, P
Kathleen Quinlan, Bibi Anderson, Sylvia Sidney, Diane Varsi
A disturbed 16-year-old girl spirals down into madness and despair while a hospital psychiatrist struggles to bring her back to life.
MPAA:R
Imorah Productions — *Warner Home Video*

I Ought to Be in Pictures 1982
Comedy
63397 107 mins C B, V, CED P
Walter Matthau, Ann-Margret, Dinah Manoff, Lance Guest
An estranged father and daughter come to terms in this Neil Simon comedy.
MPAA:PG
20th Century Fox — *CBS/Fox Video*

I Remember Mama 1948
Drama
07871 134 mins B/W B, V P, T
Irene Dunne, Barbara Bel Geddes, directed by George Stevens
A Norwegian family's life at the turn of the century is recreated.
RKO — *Blackhawk Films; Nostalgia Merchant*

I Sent a Letter to My Love 1981
Drama
63335 102 mins C B, V R, P
Simone Signoret, Jean Rochefort, Delphine Seyrig
An aging spinster, faced with the lonely prospect of the death of her crippled brother, places a personal ad for a companion in a local newspaper, using a different name. Unknown to her, the brother is the one who answers it.
Atlantic Releasing — *THORN EMI/HBO Video*

I Spit on Your Grave 1980
Horror
52853 98 mins C B, V P
Camille Keaton, Aaron Tabor, Richard Pace, Anthony Nichols
A woman is ravaged by a group of four men but gets her revenge against them with extreme violence.
MPAA:R
Jerry Gross — *Wizard Video; Vestron Video (disc only)*

I, the Jury 197?
Suspense
66075 100 mins C B, V, CED P
Armand Assante, Barbara Carrera
A remake of the 1953 Mike Hammer mystery as the famed PI investigates the murder of his best friend.
MPAA:R
20th Century Fox — *CBS/Fox Video*

I Walked with a Zombie 1943
Horror
00316 69 mins B/W B, V, 3/4U P
Frances Dee, Tom Conway, James Ellison
Suspense thriller about a nurse's experience with a zombie on a remote tropical isle.
RKO — *Nostalgia Merchant*

I Wanna Be a Beauty Queen 1979
Variety
80727 90 mins C B, V P
Divine, Little Nell, Andrew Logan
America's favorite drag queen Divine hosts the "Alternative Miss World" pagent featuring all sorts of bizarre contestants.
Richard Gayer — *Active Home Video*

I Will Fight No More Forever 1975
Drama
09106 74 mins C B, V R, P
James Whitmore, Ned Romero, Sam Elliott
Recounts the epic story of the legendary Chief Joseph who led the Nez Perce tribe on an historic 1,600-mile trek in 1877.
Stan Margulies — *Video Gems*

I Wonder Who's Killing Her Now? 1976
Comedy
80244 87 mins C B, V P
Bob Dishy, Joanna Barnes, Bill Dana, Steve Franken
A husband takes a large insurance policy on his wife and then intends to kill her to collect the premium.
Dennis F. Stevens — *U.S.A. Home Video*

I Wouldn't Leave Tereza for Any Other Girl 1976
Romance
70265 77 mins C B, V R, P
This zoo director brings home a chimpanzee. The chimp develops a friendship with the

director's son that brings both family and friends to a better understanding of love.
MPAA:G
Londonderry — *Video Gems*

Ice Castles 1979
Drama
44843 110 mins C B, V, CED P
Robby Benson, Lynn-Holly Johnson
A young figure skater's Olympic dreams are dimmed by an accident, but her boyfriend gives her the strength, encouragement, and love necessary to perform a small miracle.
MPAA:PG
John Kemeny — *RCA/Columbia Pictures Home Video*

Ice Pirates, The 1984
Science fiction/Comedy
73364 93 mins C B, V P
Robert Urich, Mary Crosby
A group of pirates steal frozen blocks of ice to fill the needs of a thirsty galaxy.
MPAA:PG
MGM UA Entertainment Co — *MGM/UA Home Video*

Ice Station Zebra 1968
Adventure
80628 150 mins C B, V P
Rock Hudson, Ernest Borgnine, Patrick McGoohan, Jim Brown, Lloyd Nolan, Tony Bill, directed by John Sturges
A nuclear submarine crew races Soviet seamen to find a piece of film from a Russian satellite hidden under a polar ice cap. Music by Michel Legrand. Available in VHS and Beta Hi-Fi.
MPAA:G
MGM — *MGM/UA Home Video*

Iceman 1984
Drama
73184 101 mins C B, V, LV, CED P
Timothy Hutton, Lindsay Crouse, directed by Fred Schepisi
Timothy Hutton and Lindsay Crouse star as a pair of scientists who find a frozen prehistoric man in a glacier and try to bring him back to life.
MPAA:PG
Patrick Palmer; Norman Jewision — *MCA Home Video*

If... 1969
Drama
64026 111 mins C B, V R, P
Malcolm McDowell, David Wood, Christine Noonan, Richard Warwick
Three unruly seniors at a British boarding school refuse to conform.
MPAA:R
Paramount — *Paramount Home Video*

If Things Were Different 1979
Drama
77152 96 mins C B, V P
Suzzane Pleshette, Tony Roberts, Arte Johnson, Chuck McCann, Don Murray
A woman must struggle to hold her family together after her husband is hospitalized with a nervous breakdown.
Bob Banner Associates — *Worldvision Home Video*

If You Could See What I Hear 1982
Comedy-Drama
64032 103 mins C B, V, LV, CED P
Marc Singer, R. H. Thomson, Sarah Torgov, Shari Belafonte Harper
The true-life story of blind singer-musician Tom Sullivan covers his life from college days to marriage. His refusal to acknowledge his limitations led to many incidents, some hilarious, some tragic.
MPAA:PG
Jensen Farley Pictures; Cypress Grove Productions — *Vestron Video*

If You Knew Susie 1948
Musical
29485 90 mins B/W B, V P, T
Eddie Cantor, Joan Davis, Allyn Joslyn, Charles Dingle
Two retired vaudeville actors living in a New England town are not accepted socially, that is until a letter from George Washington establishes them as descendants of a colonial patriot. They travel to Washington to claim $7,000,000,000 from the government.
RKO, Eddie Cantor — *Blackhawk Films*

Ill Met by Moonlight 1959
War-Drama
62866 104 mins B/W B, V P
Dirk Bogarde, Marius Goring, David Oxley, Cyril Cusack
During the German occupation of Crete, a group of British agents attempt to capture a Nazi general.
Rank; Lopert Films — *Embassy Home Entertainment*

I'm All Right Jack 1959
Comedy
33958 101 mins B/W B, V R, P
Peter Sellers, Ian Carmichael, Terry-Thomas
A shop steward is caught between two sides in a crooked financial scam in this satire on labor-management relations.
British Lion — *THORN EMI/HBO Video*

(For explanation of codes, see USE GUIDE and KEY)

I'm Dancing as Fast as I Can 1982
Drama
64027 107 mins C B, V, LV R, P
Jill Clayburgh, Nicol Williamson, Geraldine Page
A successful television producer becomes hopelessly dependent on tranquilizers.
MPAA:R
Paramount — *Paramount Home Video*

I'm on My Way/The Non-Stop Kid 191?
Comedy
59990 30 mins B/W B, V P, T
Harold Lloyd, Snub Pollard, Bebe Daniels
A Harold Lloyd double feature. Two classic shorts: "I'm on My Way" (1919), in which Harold's dreams of an idyllic marriage are shattered, and "The Non-Stop Kid" (1918), in which Harold must contend with a rival for the affection of his beloved. Silent.
Hal Roach — *Blackhawk Films*

Image of Bruce Lee, The 197?
Martial arts/Adventure
53944 88 mins C B, V P
Bruce Li, Chang Wu Lang, Chang Lei, Dana
Martial arts fight scenes prevail in this story about a jeweler who is swindled out of $1 million worth of diamonds.
MPAA:G
Alex Gouw — *Media Home Entertainment*

Imagine That! Great Moments in History, 2 1985
History
70709 60 mins C B, V P
Pat Morita, Arte Johnson, Scatman Crothers
Toby the Turtle and his puppet friends meet Paul Revere, Teddy Roosevelt and Beethoven in this series of adventures.
Century Video Corp. — *Kid Time Video*

Imagine That! Great Moments in History 1985
History
70574 60 mins C B, V P
Jim Backus, Arte Johnson, Pat Morita
This series of programs uses puppetry to introduce youngsters to historical figures. The stories told are designed to show kids how to improve social skills.
Century Video Corp. — *Kid Time Video*

Immortal Bachelor, The 1980
Comedy
80934 94 mins C B, V P
Giancarlo Giannini, Monica Vitti, Claudia Cardinale, Vittorio Gassman
This film tells the bawdy tale of a cleaning woman who murders her philandering husband.
MPAA:PG
S.J. International Pictures — *VidAmerica*

Immortal Battalion 1944
War-Drama
57355 89 mins B/W B, V, FO P
David Niven, Stanley Holloway, Reginald Tate, Peter Ustinov, directed by Carol Reed
The story of how newly-recruited civilians are molded into a hardened batallion of fighting men.
J Arthur Rank; 20th Century Fox — *Hal Roach Studios; Video Yesteryear; Discount Video Tapes*

Impact 1949
Drama
58545 83 mins B/W B, V, 3/4U P
Brian Donlevy, Ella Raines, directed by Arthur Lubin
A woman and her lover plan the murder of her rich industrialist husband, but the plan backfires and he survives.
United Artists — *Movie Buff Video; Hal Roach Studios; Discount Video Tapes*

Improper Channels 1982
Comedy
63361 91 mins C B, V, LV, CED P
Alan Arkin, Mariette Hartley
A man launches an all-out attack on the world of computers.
MPAA:PG
Alfred Pariser; Maury Ravinsky — *Vestron Video*

Impulse 1984
Drama
76763 95 mins C B, V, CED P
Tim Matheson, Meg Tilly, Hume Cronyn, John Karlen, Claude Earl Jones
The residents of a small town start to act very strangely when toxic waste turns up in their milk.
MPAA:R
Tim Zinnemann; Twentieth Century Fox — *Vestron Video*

In Cold Blood 1967
Drama
13257 133 mins B/W B, V P
Robert Blake, Scott Wilson, John Forsythe, directed by Richard Brooks
Truman Capote's factual novel provided the basis for this hard-hitting film about two misfit ex-cons who murdered a Kansas family in 1959.
Columbia — *RCA/Columbia Pictures Home Video*

In-Laws, The 1979
Comedy
38949 103 mins C B, V R, P
Peter Falk, Alan Arkin, directed by Arthur Hiller

A wild comedy with Peter Falk as a CIA agent and Alan Arkin as a dentist who becomes involved in Falk's crazy adventures.
MPAA:PG
Warner Bros — *Warner Home Video; RCA VideoDiscs*

In Love With An Older Woman **1982**
Comedy/Romance
72455 100 mins C B, V P
John Ritter, Karen Carlson
This movie shows the social difficulties that arise when a man dates an outgoing woman who is fifteen years his senior.
Poundridge Prods Ltd; Charles Fries Prods — *U.S.A. Home Video*

In Name Only **1939**
Drama
10053 102 mins B/W B, V P, T
Carole Lombard, Cary Grant, Kay Francis
Heartless woman marries for wealth and prestige and holds her husband to loveless marriage.
RKO; John Cromwell — *Blackhawk Films; RKO HomeVideo*

In Old California **1942**
Western
66312 89 mins B/W B, V P
John Wayne, Patsy Kelly, Binnie Barnes, Albert Dekker
A young Boston pharmacist searches for success in the California gold rush.
Republic — *Republic Pictures Home Video*

In Old New Mexico **1945**
Western
11264 60 mins B/W B, V P
Duncan Renaldo, Martin Garralaga, Gwen Kenyon, Pedro de Cordoba
The Cisco Kid and Pancho reveal the murderer of an old woman—a mysterious doctor who was after an inheritance.
United Artists — *United Home Video; Video Yesteryear*

In Old Santa Fe **1934**
Western
11785 60 mins B/W B, V P
Ken Maynard
Action western starring Ken Maynard—veteran of the plains.
Mascot — *Video Connection; Discount Video Tapes; Video Yesteryear; Sheik Video*

In Praise of Older Women **1978**
Comedy
09096 110 mins C B, V, LV, CED P
Karen Black, Tom Berenger, Susan Strasberg, Helen Shaver
A Hungarian "boy," 12-years-old, is corrupted by World War II. Based on a novel by Stephen Vizinczey.
Astral Films; Astral Bellevue Pathe and RSL Prod — *Embassy Home Entertainment; RCA VideoDiscs*

In Search of Anna **1979**
Drama
79345 90 mins C B, V P
Judy Morris, Richard Morris
When a convict is released from jail, he searches for the girl he left behind.
Australian — *Active Home Video*

In Search of Historic Jesus **1979**
Speculation/Religion
48476 91 mins C B, V P
John Rubenstein, John Anderson, narrated by Brad Crandall
The story attempts to pull together a careful tabulation of data about Jesus Christ, who was hardly known to the historians of his time.
MPAA:PG
Schick Sunn Classic — *United Home Video*

In Search of Noah's Ark **1976**
Bible/Documentary
35373 95 mins C B, V P
Narrated by Brad Crandell
This documentary covers research and information gathered during the last 5,000 years concerning the story of Noah and the universal flood.
Sunn Classic — *United Home Video*

In Search of the Castaways **1962**
Adventure
66318 98 mins C B, V R, P
Hayley Mills, Maurice Chevalier, George Sanders, Wilfrid Hyde-White
A teenage girl and her younger brother search for their father, a ship's captain who was reportedly lost at sea years earlier. Based on a story by Jules Verne.
Buena Vista — *Walt Disney Home Video*

In the Days of the Thundering Herd & The Law and the Outlaw **1914**
Western
77368 76 mins B/W B, V P, T
Tom Mix, Myrtle Stedman, directed by Tom Mix
2 pgms
In the first feature pony express rider sacrifices his job to accompany his sweetheart on a westward trek to meet her father. In the second

show, a fugitive falls in love with a rancher's daughter and risks recognition.
Selig Polyscope — *Blackhawk Films*

In the Heat of the Night **1967**
Drama
37525 109 mins C CED P
Sidney Poitier, Rod Steiger, Warren Oates, Lee Grant, directed by Norman Jewison
A wealthy industrialist in a small Mississippi town is murdered. A black man is accused, but when it is discovered that he is a homicide expert, he is asked to help solve the murder, despite resentment of the part of the town's chief of police.
Academy Awards '67: Best Picture; Best Actor (Steiger); Best Screenplay; Best Film Editing; Best Sound.
United Artists, Walter Mirisch — *CBS/Fox Video; RCA VideoDiscs*

In Which We Serve **1942**
War-Drama
59833 114 mins B/W B, V P
Noel Coward, John Mills, Bernard Miles, directed by Noel Coward
The spirit of the British Navy in World War II is captured in this classic about the sinking of the destroyer HMS Torrin during the Battle of Crete.
Noel Coward — *Embassy Home Entertainment*

Incoming Freshmen **1979**
Comedy
47851 84 mins C B, V P
Ashley Vaughn, Leslie Blalock, Richard Harriman, Jim Overbey
A young innocent girl discovers sex when she enrolls in a liberal co-ed institution.
MPAA:R
Cannon Films — *MCA Home Video*

Incredible Agent of Stingray, The **1980**
Science fiction
74425 93 mins C B, V P
Animated
Captain Troy Tempest and the Stingray crew take an underwater voyage to rescue a beautiful woman kept prisoner in Titanica.
ITC Entertainment — *Family Home Entertainment*

Incredible Detectives, The **1979**
Adventure/Cartoons
80643 23 mins C B, V P
Animated
A dog, a cat and a crow team up to search for a boy who has been kidnapped by a trio of hoods.
Ruby-Spears — *Worldvision Home Video*

Incredible Hulk, The **1977**
Adventure/Science fiction
58631 100 mins C B, V P
Bill Bixby, Susan Sullivan, Lou Ferrigno, Jack Colvin
A scientist achieves superhuman strength after he is exposed to a massive dose of gamma rays. The pilot for the television series.
Universal TV — *MCA Home Video*

Incredible Hulk, Volume I, The **1985**
Cartoons
77162 70 mins C B, V P
Animated
The secret origin of the Hulk is told in this collection of three episodes from the animated series.
Marvel Productions — *Prism*

Incredible Hulk, Volume II, The **1985**
Cartoons
70598 70 mins C B, V P

Animated
In this trio of cartoons from the TV series, the great green man battles gigantic mice, spiders and lizards; the huge and hungry Gammatron monster; and his arch-nemesis Dr. Octopus.
Marvel Productions — *Prism*

Incredible Journey, The 1963
Adventure/Animals
72795 80 mins C B, V P
A labrador retriever, bull terrier and Siamese cat mistake their caretakers intentions when he leaves for a hunting trip, believing he will never return. The three set out on a 250 mile adventure-filled trek across Canada's rugged terrain.
Walt Disney Productions; Buena Vista — *Walt Disney Home Video*

Incredible Journey of Dr. Meg Laurel, The 1979
Drama
80385 143 mins C B, V P
Lindsay Wagner, Jane Wyman, Dorothy McGuire, James Woods, Gary Lockwood
A young doctor leaves her Boston family to bring modern medicine to the Appalachian mountain people during the 1930's.
Paul Radin — *RCA/Columbia Pictures Home Video*

Incredible Master Beggars 1982
Martial arts
64945 88 mins C B, V R, P
Tan Tao Liang, Ku Feng, Han Kuo Tsai, Li Tang Ming, Li Hai Sheng, Lui I Fan, Pan Yao Kun
Against all odds, the Beggars challenge the Great Iron Master, using "Tam Leg" tactics versus the "Iron Cloth" fighting style.
MPAA:R
L and T Films Corp Ltd — *Video Gems*

Incredible Rocky Mountain Race, The 1977
Comedy
81515 97 mins C B, V P
Christopher Connelly, Forrest Tucker, Larry Storch, Mike Mazurki
Young Mark Twain and his rival enter in a grudge match from Missouri to California where the winner gets five rare Indian relics.
Sunn Classic — *Sagebrush Productions*

Incredible Rocky Mountain Race, The 1977
Adventure/Comedy
65761 97 mins C B, V P
Christopher Connelly, Forrest Tucker, Larry Storch, Mike Mazurki
The townspeople of St. Joseph, fed up with Mark Twain's destructive feud with a neighbor, devise a shrewd scheme to rid the town of the troublemakers.
Robert Stabler — *United Home Video*

Incredible Shrinking Woman, The 1981
Comedy
55548 88 mins C B, V, LV P
Lily Tomlin, Charles Grodin, Ned Beatty, Henry Gibson
A model homemaker and perfect mother and wife discovers that she is shrinking due to a unique blood condition that is effected by the chemicals found in her household products.
MPAA:PG
Universal; Hank Moonjean — *MCA Home Video*

Incubus, The 1982
Horror
63969 90 mins C B, V, LV, CED P
John Cassavetes, Kerrie Keane, Helen Hughes, Erin Flannery, John Ireland
A doctor and his teenaged daughter settle in a quiet New England community, only to encounter the incubus, a terrifying, supernatural demon.
MPAA:R
Artists Releasing Corp; Mark Boyman — *Vestron Video*

Independence 1976
History-US
70586 30 mins C B, V P
Eli Wallach, Anne Jackson, Pat Hingle, Patrick O'Neal, directed by John Huston, narrated by E.G. Marshall
This program dramaticaly recreates the debates, concerns, and events that led up to the U.S. Declaration of Independence in 1776.
Joyce and Lloyd Ritter — *MPI Home Video*

Independence Day 1983
Drama
68234 110 mins C B, V R, P
Kathleen Quinlan, David Keith
Kathleen Quinlan stars as a small town photographer who falls in love with a racing car enthusiast.
MPAA:R
Warner Brothers — *Warner Home Video*

Indiscreet 1958
Comedy
66464 100 mins C B, V P
Cary Grant, Ingrid Bergman, Phyllis Calvert, directed by Stanley Donen
An American diplomat in London falls in love with an actress but protects himself by saying he is married.

Grandon; Stanley Donen — *Republic Pictures Home Video*

Indiscretion of an American Wife 1954
Romance
65410 63 mins C B, V P
Jennifer Jones, Montgomery Clift
Set almost entirely in Rome's famous Terminal Station, the romance centers arount an ill-fated couple facing a turning point in their lives. They have only hours to decide whether they can have a future together, or whether Jones will go back to the United States and rejoin her husband.
Columbia — *CBS/Fox Video; Discount Video Tapes*

Informer, The 1935
Drama
00262 91 mins B/W B, V, 3/4U P
Victor McLaglen, directed by John Ford
Tells of a hard-drinking man who informs on a buddy to collect a reward during the Irish Rebellion.
Academy Award '35: Best Actor (McLaglen); N.Y. Film Critics '35: Best Film amd Director.
RKO; John Ford — *Nostalgia Merchant; King of Video*

Infra-Man 1976
Science fiction
80286 89 mins C B, V P
Infra-man is a bionic warrior who must destroy the Demon Princess and her army of prehistoric monsters in order to save the galaxy.
MPAA:PG
Joseph Brenner Associates — *Prism*

Inherit the Wind 1960
Drama
64562 127 mins B/W B, V, CED P
Spencer Tracy, Fredric March, Florence Eldridge, Gene Kelly, Dick York, directed by Stanley Kramer
A courtroom drama based on the 1925 Scopes "Monkey Trial," where a schoolteacher was indicted for teaching Darwin's Theory of Evolution to his students.
United Artists; Stanley Kramer — *CBS/Fox Video; RCA VideoDiscs*

Inheritance, The 1947
Suspense
66383 103 mins B/W B, V P
Jean Simmons, Katina Paxinou, Derrick de Marney, Derek Bond
The guardian of a young heiress plots to murder his mistress for her inheritance. Original title: "Uncle Silas."
Two Cities — *Movie Buff Video; Discount Video Tapes*

Inheritance, The 1976
Drama
52953 121 mins C B, V P
Anthony Quinn, Fabio Testi, Dominique Sanda
A poor woman who hungers for fortune marries into a wealthy family. After becoming the sole heiress, the family unites against her.
MPAA:R
Titanus; Gianni Hecht Lucari — *VidAmerica*

Inheritors, The 1985
Drama
81451 89 mins C B, V P
Nikolas Vogel, Roger Schauer, Klaus Novak, Johanna Tomek, directed by Walter Bannert
A young German boy becomes involved in with a neo-Nazi group as his home life deteriorates in 1938. Available in German with English subtitles or dubbed into English.
GE
Island Alive — *Embassy Home Entertainment*

Initiation, The 1984
Horror
80051 97 mins C B, V R, P
Vera Miles, Clu Gulager, James Read, Daphne Zuniga
There are plenty of surprises in store for a group of sorority pledges as they break into a department store to steal a security guard's uniform
MPAA:R
New World Pictures — *THORN EMI/HBO Video*

Initiation of Sarah, The 1978
Suspense/Mystery
79171 100 mins C B, V P
Kay Lenz, Robert Hays, Shelley Winters, Kathryn Crosby, Morgan Fairchild, Tony Bill
A college freshman joins a strange sorority after every other one on campus has rejected her.
Stonehenge/Charles Fries Productions — *Worldvision Home Video*

Inn of the Sixth Happiness, The 1958
Drama
66068 158 mins C B, V, CED P
Ingrid Bergman, Curt Jurgens, Robert Donat
The life of Gladys Aylward, an English servant girl who becomes a missionary in 1930's China, provides the basis of this story.
20th Century Fox — *CBS/Fox Video*

Innocent, The 1978
Drama
39077 115 mins C B, V, CED P
Laura Antonelli, Jennifer O'Neill, Giancarlo Giannini, directed by Luchino Visconti
Visconti's last film is the story of a husband who is drawn between the love of his faithful wife and his mistress, in turn-of-the-century Rome.

Filmed on location in Italy; English language version.
MPAA:R
Italy — *Vestron Video*

Inside Hitchcock 1984
Film/History
70584 55 mins C B, V P
Narrated by Cliff Robertson
This documentary reveals much about one of America's best loved film makers. Scenes from his movies and his last interview enliven this informative program.
Richard Schickel — *MPI Home Video*

Inside Moves 1980
Drama
55457 113 mins C B, V P
John Savage, Diana Scarwid, David Morse, directed by Richard Donner
A look at handicapped citizens trying to make it in everyday life, focusing on the relationship between an insecure, failed suicide and a volatile man who is only a knee operation away from a dreamed-about basketball career.
MPAA:PG
Goodmark Productions — *CBS/Fox Video*

Inside Out 1975
Adventure
76854 98 mins C B, V R, P
Telly Savalas, Robert Culp, James Mason, Aldo Ray, Doris Kunstmann
An ex-GI, a jewel thief and a German POW camp commandant band together to find a stolen shipment of Nazi gold from behind the Iron curtain.
MPAA:PG
Kettledrum Productions, Warner Bros. — *Warner Home Video*

Inside the Lines 1930
Drama
66136 73 mins B/W B, V, FO P
Betty Compson, Montagu Love, Mischa Auer, Ralph Forbes
A World War I tale of espionage and counter-espionage.
RKO — *Video Yesteryear*

Inspector Gadget, Volume II 1984
Cartoons
78374 90 mins C B, V P
Animated, the voice of Don Adams
Inspector Gadget goes to South Africa to find diamonds, but winds up fighting off ghosts and his nemesis, Dr. Claw. Available in Beta hi-fi and VHS stereo.
DIC Ent./Field Communications Corp. — *Family Home Entertainment*

Inspector Gadget, Volume III 1985
Cartoons
70653 90 mins C B, V P
Animated, The voice of Don Adams
The battle for the safety of the world rages on between the clever Inspector Gadget and that vile no-goodnik, Dr. Claw. Available in Hi-Fi Stereo.
DIC Ent./Field Communications Corp — *Family Home Entertainment*

Inspector Gaget, Volume 1 1984
Cartoons
74079 90 mins C B, V P
Animated, the voice of Don Adams
Comedian Don Adams lends his voice to the impeccable Inspector Gaget who along with his trusted companions, Penny and Brain, go up against the evil Dr. Claw.
Dic Enterprises — *Family Home Entertainment*

Inspector General, The 1949
Comedy
59663 97 mins C B, V P
Danny Kaye, Walter Slezak, Barbara Bates, Elsa Lanchester
A classic Danny Kaye vehicle of mistaken identities with the master comic portraying a carnival medicine man who is mistaken by the villagers for their feared Inspector General.
Warner Bros — *Prism; Media Home Entertainment; Budget Video; Video Yesteryear; Sheik Video; Cable Films; Discount Video Tapes; King of Video; Video Connection; Hal Roach Studios; Kartes Productions; Classic Video Cinema Collector's Club; See Hear Industries*

Installing a Lockset 1984
Home improvement
77263 30 mins C B, V P
Carpenter George Giangrante demonstrates the basics of installing almost any lockset.
You Can Do It Videos — *You Can Do It Videos*

Installing a Pre-Hung Door 1984
Home improvement
77262 30 mins C B, V P
This is a step by step demonstration of how to successfully install a pre-hung door.
You Can Do It Videos — *You Can Do It Videos*

Installing a Suspended Ceiling 1984
Home improvement
Closed Captioned
77264 30 mins C B, V P
A step by step demonstration of how to install a suspended ceiling.

(For explanation of codes, see USE GUIDE and KEY)

You Can Do It Videos — *You Can Do It Videos*

Installing Insulation and Sheetrock **1984**
Home improvement
Closed Captioned
77260 30 mins C B, V P
The procedures for installing insulation and sheetrock are demonstrated by carpenter George Giangrante.
You Can Do It Videos — *You Can Do It Videos*

Intermezzo **1939**
Drama/Romance
69385 70 mins B/W B, V, CED P
Ingrid Bergman, Leslie Howard
A married violinist falls in love with his protege, but while on a concert tour of Europe together, his longing for the family he left behind overshadows their happiness.
Selznick — *CBS/Fox Video*

International Crime **1937**
Mystery
73550 72 mins B/W B, V P
Rod La Rogue
This film is an adventure of the Radio hero The Shadow as he solves another touch crime.
Grand National — *Admit One Video*

International Velvet **1978**
Drama
66452 126 mins C B, V P
Tatum O'Neal, Anthony Hopkins, Christopher Plummer
In this sequel to "National Velvet," a young orphan overcomes all obstacles and becomes an internationally renowned horsewoman.
MPAA:PG
Byron Forbes Productions — *MGM/UA Home Video*

Intimate Moments **1982**
Drama
66044 82 mins C B, V P
Alexandra Stewart, Dirke Altevogt
Madame Claude runs an exclusive call-girl operation catering to the upper echelons of power in France, when she discovers that a newspaper is investigating her business.
MPAA:R
Claire Duval — *Embassy Home Entertainment*

Into the Night **1985**
Comedy/Adventure
Closed Captioned
80848 115 mins C B, V P
Jeff Goldblum, Michelle Pfeiffer, David Bowie, Carl Perkins, Richard Farnsworth, Dan Aykroyd, Paul Mazursky, Roger Vadim, Jim Henson, Paul Bartel, directed by John Landis
An insomniac aerospace engineer has plenty to keep him awake when a mysterious woman suddenly drops onto the hood of his car. B.B. King sings the title song. Available in VHS and Beta Hi Fi.
MPAA:R
Geroge Folsey Jr.; Ron Koslow — *MCA Home Video*

Intolerance **1916**
Film-History
33548 120 mins B/W B, V P
Lillian Gish, Mae Marsh, Constance Tallmadge, Bessie Love, Elmer Clifton, directed by D.W. Griffith
D. W. Griffith's most expansive effort, which contains four separate stories detailing mankind's intolerance through the centuries. Original color-tinted and toned print, with music score.
D W Griffith — *Glenn Video Vistas; Video Yesteryear; Budget Video; Sheik Video; Blackhawk Films; Discount Video Tapes; Western Film & Video Inc*

Intruder, The **1977**
Drama
77009 98 mins C B, V P
Jean-Louis Trintignent, Mireille Darc, Adolfo Celi
A man and his stepson are terrorized by a stranger in a panel truck as they travel from Rome to Paris.
Viaduc Productions S.A. — *VidAmerica*

Intruder Within, The **1981**
Horror
78397 91 mins C B, V P
Chad Everett, Joseph Bottoms, Jennifer Warren
Members of an offshore oil drilling crew stumble across a strange life form found during a search for oil deposits in Antarctica.
Flo Productions — *Trans World Entertainment*

Invaders from Mars **1953**
Science fiction
37400 78 mins C B, V P
Helena Carter, Arthur Franz, Jimmy Hunt, Leif Erickson, directed by William Cameron Menzies
A twelve-year-old boy witnesses the landing of a strange spacecraft, and he and his father set out to investigate. The father becomes possessed by alien entities who threaten to overtake the entire world. Includes previews of coming attractions from classic science fiction films.
20th Century Fox — *Nostalgia Merchant*

Invasion of the Blood Farmers **1984**
Horror
80475 86 mins C B, V P
Norman Kelley, Tanna Hunter, Bruce Detrick, Jack Neubeck, Paul Craig Jennings

Members of an ancient Druid cult murder young women in their search for a rare blood type to keep their queen alive.
Regal Video — *Regal Video*

Invasion of the Body Snatchers **1956**
Science fiction
55472 80 mins B/W B, V P
Kevin McCarthy, Dana Wynter, Carolyn Jones, King Donovan, directed by Don Siegel
The classic about the invasion of Southern California by seeds of giant plant pods which exude blank human forms that drain the emotional life of people and threaten to destroy the world.
Walter Wanger; Allied Artists — *Republic Pictures Home Video; RCA VideoDiscs*

Invasion of the Body Snatchers **1978**
Science fiction/Horror
66451 115 mins C B, V, CED P
Donald Sutherland, Brooke Adams, Veronica Cartwright, Leonard Nimoy, Jeff Goldblum, Kevin McCarthy, Don Siegel
A remake of the 1956 sci-fi classic—this time, the "pod people" are infesting San Francisco, with only a small group of people aware of the invasion. Beta Hi-Fi and VHS stereo.
MPAA:PG
United Artists — *MGM/UA Home Video*

Invasion of the Body Stealers **1983**
Science fiction
75462 93 mins C B, V P
Beings from another planet are stealing earthlings to revitalize their civilization.
King Features — *U.S.A. Home Video*

Invasion of the Flesh Hunters **1984**
Horror
70154 90 mins C B, V P
John Saxon
A group of tortured Vietnam veterans returns home carrying a cannibalistic curse on them.
Almi Pictures — *Vestron Video*

Invasion of the Girl Snatchers **1973**
Science fiction
77203 90 mins C B, V P
Elizabeth Rush, Ele Grigsby
Aliens from another planet subdue young earth girls and force them to undergo bizarre acts that rob them of their souls.
Lee Jones — *United Home Video*

Invincible Armor **197?**
Martial arts
70758 92 mins C B, V P
The wrong man is accused of murder when an ambitious minister of justice unleashes a sinister plot.
Foreign — *Trans World Entertainment*

Invincible from Hell, The **1981**
Martial arts
69280 80 mins C B, V P
Master Lee, Johnny Kin, Robert Ann, Linda Han
Japanese gangsters terrorize a small town near Shanghai until one man gets the townspeople to fight back. Mandarin dialogue, English subtitles.
CH
IFD Films & Arts — *Silverline Video*

Invincible, The **1980**
Adventure/Martial arts
56927 93 mins C B, V R, P
Bruce Li, Chen Sing, Ho Chung Dao
A martial arts student must find and correct another student who has turned bad.
MPAA:R
Fourseas Films — *Video Gems*

Invisible Dead, The **1985**
Horror
81034 90 mins C B, V P
Howard Vernon, Britt Carva
A courageous doctor must save a beautiful woman being held captive by an invisible man.
MPAA:R
Empire Entertainment — *Wizard Video*

Invisible Ghost, The **1941**
Horror
05520 70 mins B/W B, V, 3/4U R, P
Bela Lugosi, Polly Ann Young
A man carries out a series of grisly stranglings while under hypnosis by his insane wife.
Monogram — *Movie Buff Video; Sheik Video; Cable Films; Video Yesteryear; Discount Video Tapes*

Invisible Strangler **1984**
Drama
80144 85 mins C B, V P
Elke Sommer, Robert Foxworth, Stefanie Powers
A woman risks her life to catch a psychotic killer whose seriesof murders has left the police baffled.
MPAA:PG
Independent — *Trans World Entertainment*

Invitation au Voyage **1983**
Drama
65317 ? mins C B, V P
Laurent Malet, Nina Scott, Aurore Clement, Mario Adorf

This program follows the journey of a twin who refuses to accept the death of his sister, a rock singer. Subtitled in English.
MPAA:R
Claude Nedjar — *RCA/Columbia Pictures Home Video*

Invitation to a Gunfighter **1964**
Drama
65498 92 mins C CED P
Yul Brynner, George Segal, Janice Rule, Pat Hingle
A small-town tyrant hires a smooth gunfighter to keep down the farmers he has cheated.
United Artists — *CBS/Fox Video*

Invitation to a Wedding **1983**
Comedy
80924 89 mins C B, V P
John Gielgud, Ralph Richardson, Paul Nickolaus, Elizabeth Shepherd, directed by Joseph Brooks
When the best friend of a bridegroom falls in love with the bride, he stops at nothing to stop the wedding.
MPAA:PG
Chancery Lane Music Corp. — *Vestron Video*

Invitation to Paris **1960**
Variety/France
58652 51 mins B/W B, V, FO P
Maurice Chevalier, Les Djinns, Patachou, Fernandel, Les Compagnons de La Chanson, Jean Sablon, George Ulmer, Line Renaud
A French musical revue, set in the streets of Paris, which features the girls of the French Can-Can revue.
A Parisian — *Video Yesteryear*

Invitation to the Dance **1957**
Musical
60400 93 mins C B, V, CED P
Gene Kelly, Igor Youskevitch, Tomara Toumanova
Three classic dance sequences, "Circus," "Ring Around the Rosy" and "Sinbad the Sailor," based on music by Rimsky-Korsakov.
MGM; Arthur Freed — *MGM/UA Home Video*

Iphigenia **1979**
Drama
60343 100 mins C B, V P
Irene Papas, Costa Kazakos, Tatiana Papamoskou
Based on the classic Greek tragedy by Euripides, this story concerns the Greek leader, Agamemnon, and his lovely daughter, Iphigenia.
Almi Cinema 5 Film — *RCA/Columbia Pictures Home Video*

Irishman, The **1978**
Drama
65477 90 mins C B, V P
Bryan Brown
The tale of a proud North Queensland family and their struggles to stay together.
Anthony Buckley — *Vestron Video*

Irma La Douce **1963**
Comedy
58843 146 mins C CED P
Jack Lemmon, Shirley MacLaine, Herschel Bernardi, directed by Billy Wilder
A gendarme pulls a one-man raid on a back-street Parisian joint and falls in love with one of the ladies he arrests.
EL, SP
United Artists — *CBS/Fox Video*

Iron Bodies **1985**
Physical fitness
70733 60 mins C B, V P
Several well-developed men and women discuss the mental and physical sacrifices they've made in order to swell and harden their flesh.
West Coast Iron Bodies — *Active Home Video*

Iron Dragon Strikes Back, The **1984**
Martial arts
76946 90 mins C B, V P
Bruce Li
One man seeks out the men who murdered his martial arts instructor.
Foreign — *Trans World Entertainment*

Iron Maiden **1983**
Music-Performance
75903 18 mins C B, V P
This program presents the heavy metal group Iron Maiden performing songs such as "Run to the Hills," "The Trooper" and "Flight of Icarus."
EMI Records Ltd — *Sony Corporation of America*

Iron Mask, The **1929**
Adventure
08729 87 mins B/W B, V, 3/4U P
Douglas Fairbanks, Sr., Nigel de Brulier, Marguerite de la Motte, directed by Allan Dwan
Based on Alexandre Dumas' "Three Musketeers" and "The Man in the Iron Mask', the fearless d'Artagnan rights the wrongs in France. (Part talkie.)
United Artists — *Blackhawk Films; Cable Films; Discount Video Tapes; Classic Video Cinema Collector's Club*

Ironmaster **1983**
Fantasy
80895 98 mins C B, V P

George Eastman, Pamela Field
When a primitive tribesman is exiled from his tribe, he discovers a mysteriously power-filled iron staff on a mountainside.
American National Enterprises — *Prism*

Irreconcilable Differences 1984
Comedy
79667 112 mins C B, V, LV, CED P
Ryan O'Neal, Shelley Long, Drew Barrymore, Sam Wanamaker, directed by Charles Shyer
A ten-year-old girl sues her parents for divorce on the grounds of "irreconcilable differneces."
MPAA:PG
Warner Bros — *Vestron Video*

Isabel's Choice 1981
Drama/Romance
75456 96 mins C B, V P
Jean Stapleton, Richard Kiley, Peter Coyote
A middle-aged executive secretary must choose between romance and success.
King Features — *U.S.A. Home Video*

Isla Encantada, La (Enchanted Island) 1984
Drama
72962 90 mins C B, V P
The new adventures of Robinson Crusoe and Man Friday, as they pursue wild beasts and cannibals and fight off pirates.
Foreign — *Unicorn Video*

Island, The 1980
Adventure
48633 113 mins C B, V P
Christopher F. Bean
A New York reporter embarks on a Bermuda triangle investigation, only to meet with the murderous descendants of seventeenth-century pirates on a deserted island.
MPAA:R
Universal, Richard D Zanuck, David Brown — *MCA Home Video*

Island, The 1961
Drama
53724 96 mins B/W B, V, 3/4U P
Directed by Kaneto Shindo
One of Japan's best directors turns his talents to the existence of a family, the sole inhabitants of a small island. No dialogue.
Japan — *International Historic Films; Video Yesteryear; Budget Video; Discount Video Tapes*

Island at the Top of the World, The 1974
Adventure
63191 89 mins C B, V R, P
David Hartman, Donald Sinden, Jacques Marin, Mako, David Gwillim
A rich Englishman, an American archeologist, a French aeronaut and an Eskimo guide travel to the Arctic in 1908 aboard the airship Hyperion on a rescue mission.
Walt Disney Productions — *Walt Disney Home Video*

Island Claw 1980
Horror
80703 91 mins C B, V P
Barry Nelson, Robert Lansing
A group of marine biologists experimenting on a tropical island discover the "Island Claw", who evolved as the result of toxic waste seeping into the ocean.
Video Media — *Vestron Video*

Island Magic 1981
Sports-Water
52769 72 mins C B, V P
This program, shot on location in Hawaii, takes you through a dramatic tour of all of Hawaii's best surfing spots.
John Hitchcock — *Karl/Lorimar Home Video*

Island of Adventure 1981
Adventure
72887 85 mins C B, V P
Four children explore an island and find a gang of criminals inhabitating it.
Unknown — *Embassy Home Entertainment*

Island of Dr. Moreau, The 1977
Science fiction
53514 98 mins C B, V R, P
Burt Lancaster, Michael York, Barbara Carrera, Richard Basehart
The story of a scientist who has isolated himself on a Pacific island in order to continue his chromosome research, which has developed to the point where he can transform animals into semi-humans. Based on the H. G. Wells novel.
MPAA:PG
American International Pictures — *Warner Home Video; Vestron Video (disc only)*

Island of Nevawuz, The 1980
Fantasy
65708 50 mins C B, V P
A beautiful island is in trouble when J.B. Trumphorn decides to make lots of money by building factories and refineries on it. Will the Island of Nevawuz end up a polluted mess?
Paul Williams — *Embassy Home Entertainment*

Island of the Blue Dolphins 1964
Drama/Adventure
81440 99 mins C B, V P

Celia Kaye, Larry Domasin, Ann Daniel, George Kennedy
This is the true story of how a young Indian girl learned to survive alone on a desert island. Available in VHS and Beta Hi-Fi.
Universal; Robert B. Radnitz — *MCA Home Video*

Island of the Lost **1968**
Science fiction
80182 92 mins C B, V P
Richard Greene, Luke Halpin
An anthopologist's family must fight for survival when they become shipwrecked on a mysterious island.
Metro Goldwyn Mayer — *Republic Pictures Home Video*

Islands in the Stream **1977**
Drama
38609 110 mins C B, V R, P
George C. Scott, David Hemmings, Claire Bloom, Susan Tyrrell
Ernest Hemingway's last novel provides the basis for this story of an American artist living with his sons on the island of Bimini shortly before the outbreak of World War II.
MPAA:PG
Paramount — *Paramount Home Video*

Israel Folk Dance Festival **1981**
Dance
81570 60 mins C B, V P
This is a compilation highlighting the best performances of Israeli folkloric dance groups.
Troex Ltd. — *Kultur*

It **1927**
Drama
54109 71 mins B/W B, V P, T
Clara Bow, Gary Cooper, Antonio Moreno
To have "It" the possessor must have that strange magnetism which attracts both sexes. A female department store worker is out to land the store owner but isn't doing well, until she goes on his yachting trip and with "It" wins her man.
Unknown — *Blackhawk Films*

It Came from Hollywood **1982**
Documentary/Science fiction
64502 87 mins C B, V, LV R, P
Narrated by Dan Aykroyd, Cheech and Chong, John Candy and Gilda Radner
A compilation of scenes from "B" horror and science fiction films of the 1950's, highlighting the funny side of these classic schlocky movies. Some sequences are in black and white.
MPAA:PG
Paramount — *Paramount Home Video; RCA VideoDiscs*

It Don't Come Easy: 1978 New York Yankees **1978**
Baseball
33846 45 mins C B, V P
New York Yankees
Highlights of the turbulent but terrific season which saw manager Billy Martin fired and replaced by Bob Lemon is mid-season. The Yankees fell to fourteen games behind the Boston Red Sox in July, only to respond with the most memorable comeback in baseball history. They beat the Red Sox in a one-game playoff, whipped the Kansas City Royals in four games, then quickly dropped two games to the Los Angeles Dodgers in the World Series before sweeping the next four games and capturing their second straight title. Thurman Munson, Reggie Jackson, Bucky Dent and others led the way.
Major League Baseball — *Major League Baseball Productions*

It Happened at the World's Fair **1963**
Musical
80150 105 mins C B, V P
Elvis Presley, Joan O'Brien, Gary Lockwood, Kurt Russell
Two bush pilots escort a Chinese girl through the Seattle World's Fair.
Metro Goldwyn Mayer — *MGM/UA Home Video*

It Happened in New Orleans **1936**
Musical-Drama
11240 86 mins B/W B, V, FO P
Bobby Breen, Mae Robson, Alan Mowbray, Benita Hume
A charming portrayal of levee life in post-Civil War New Orleans.
RKO — *Video Yesteryear; Sheik Video*

It Happened One Night **1934**
Comedy
Closed Captioned
80366 105 mins B/W B, V P
Clark Gable, Claudette Colbert, Roscoe Karns, Walter Connolly, directed by Frank Capra
A runaway heiress falls in love with a newspaperman on a cross country bus trip.
Academy Awards '34: Best Picture; Best Actor (Gable); Best Actress (Colbert); Best Director (Capra)
Columbia Pictures; Frank Capra — *RCA/Columbia Pictures Home Video*

It Lives Again **1978**
Horror
78140 91 mins C B, V R, P
A hellspaun baby meets up with two other monster infants and goes on a murderous rampage.

Larry Cohen — *Warner Home Video*

It Should Happen to You **1953**
Comedy
65700 87 mins B/W B, V P
Judy Holliday, Jack Lemmon, Peter Lawford
An aspiring model, unable to find steady work, rents a large billboard in New York to attract attention. In Beta Hi-Fi.
Fred Kohlmar — *RCA/Columbia Pictures Home Video*

Italian Straw Hat, The **1927**
Romance
48748 72 mins B/W B, V P
Directed by Rene Clair
A Mack Sennett-styled chase farce in which a straw hat must be replaced to save a woman's virtue. Silent with English subtitles and musical score.
French — *Sheik Video; Video Yesteryear; Classic Video Cinema Collector's Club*

It's a Mad, Mad, Mad, Mad World **1963**
Comedy
47145 192 mins C B, V, CED P
Spencer Tracy, Sid Caesar, Milton Berle, Ethel Merman, Jonathan Winters, Jimmy Durante, Buddy Hackett, Mickey Rooney, Phil Silvers, Dick Shawn, Edie Adams, Dorothy Provine, Buster Keaton?The Three Stooges?Jack Benny?Jerry Lewis?directed by Stanley Kramer
A motley collection of people are overcome with greed and take off in all manner of conveyances after a hidden stash of money. No shtick is overlooked along the way.
United Artists; Stanley Kramer — *CBS/Fox Video; RCA VideoDiscs*

It's a Wonderful Life **1946**
Drama
44796 125 mins B/W B, V, 3/4U P
James Stewart, Donna Reed, Lionel Barrymore, directed by Frank Capra
A sentimental classic about a man who has worked hard all his life, but feels he is a failure and tries to commit suicide. A guardian angel comes to show him his mistake.
Liberty Films; RKO — *Prism; Nostalgia Merchant; Republic Pictures Home Video; Media Home Entertainment; Sheik Video; Cable Films; VCII; Video Connection; Video Yesteryear; Budget Video; Discount Video Tapes; Western Film & Video Inc; Cinema Concepts; Hal Roach Studios; Kartes Productions; Classic Video Cinema Collector's Club*

It's Alive **1974**
Horror
78139 91 mins C B, V R, P
An everyday Los Angeles couple gives birth to a hideous humanoid whose escape and murderous rampage causes citywide terror.
Larry Cohen — *Warner Home Video*

It's an Adventure, Charlie Brown **1983**
Cartoons
76846 50 mins C B, V P
Animated
This is a collection of six vignettes featuring Charlie Brown and the whole Peanuts gang.
Lee Mendelson; Bill Melendez — *Snoopy's Home Video Library*

It's Flashbeagle, Charlie Brown/She's a Good Skate, Charlie Brown **1984**
Cartoons
76848 50 mins C B, V P
Animated
A Peanuts double header: In "It's Flashbeagle Charlie Brown" Snoopy infects the Peanuts gang with dance fever and in "She's a Good Skate Charlie Brown" Snoopy trains Peppermint Patty to become a figure skating champion.
Lee Mendelson; Bill Melendez — *Snoopy's Home Video Library*

It's Good to Be Alive **1974**
Drama/Biographical
80307 100 mins C B, V P
Paul Winfield, Ruby Dee, Lou Gossett, directed by Michael Landon
The true story of how Brooklyn Dodgers' catcher Roy Campanella learned how to face life after an automobile accident had made him a quadraplegic.
Charles Fries Productions — *Prism*

It's in the Bag **1945**
Comedy
44794 87 mins B/W B, V, 3/4U P
Fred Allen, Jack Benny, William Bendix, Binnie Barnes, Robert Benchley, directed by Richard Wallace
A shiftless flea circus owner sells chairs he has inherited, not knowing that a fortune is hidden in one of them.
United Artists — *Nostalgia Merchant; Spotlite Video*

It's Magic, Charlie Brown! **1981**
Cartoons
75609 25 mins C B, V P
Animated
Snoopy as "The Great Houdini" makes Charlie Brown disappear and can't make him reappear.
Lee Mendelson Bill Melendez Productions — *Snoopy's Home Video Library*

 (For explanation of codes, see USE GUIDE and KEY)

It's My Turn 1980
Comedy-Drama
52749 91 mins C B, V, LV P
Jill Clayburgh, Michael Douglas, Charles Grodin, directed by Claudia Weill
A mathematics professor has her life upset when she falls in love with a retired baseball player, causing her to question her relationship with her live-in boyfriend.
MPAA:R
Rastar; Martin Elfand — *RCA/Columbia Pictures Home Video*

It's News to Me 1954
Game show
78090 30 mins B/W B, V, FO P
This program presents a panel who describe a current news story and then contestants decide whether the panel is telling the truth.
CBS; Goodson Todman — *Video Yesteryear*

It's the Easter Beagle, Charlie Brown/It was a short summer, Charlie Brown 1974
Cartoons/Holidays
76850 50 mins C B, V P
Animated
A collection of two Peanuts specials: The whole Peanuts gang are anxiously awaiting the coming of the Easter Beagle in "It's the Easter Beagle Charlie Brown" and Charlie Brown remembers all about summer camp in "It Was a Short Summer Charlie Brown."
Lee Mendelson; Bill Melendez — *Snoopy's Home Video Library*

It's the Great Pumpkin, Charlie Brown 1966
Cartoons
70740 77 mins C B, V P
Animated
In addition to Linus' telling of the "Great Pumpkin" legend, this three episode collection includes "What a Nightmare Charlie Brown," and "It Was A Short Summer, Charlie Brown."
Mendelson and Melendez in assoc. with United Features Synd. — *Snoopy's Home Video Library*

It's the Great Pumpkin, Charlie Brown/What a Nightmare, Charlie Brown 1978
Cartoons/Holidays
76849 50 mins C B, V P
Animated
Here are two Peanuts Halloween specials: In "It's the Great Pumpkin, Charlie Brown," Linus waits up all Halloween night to await the arrival of the Great Pumpkin and in "What a Nightmare, Charlie Brown" Snoopy has a nightmare after pigging out on dog food.
Lee Mendelson; Bill Melendez — *Snoopy's Home Video Library*

It's Your First Kiss Charlie Brown 1977
Cartoons
80276 26 mins C B, V P
Animated
Charlie Brown joins the school football team to win over the little redhaired girl.
Lee Mendelson; Bill Melendez — *Snoopy's Home Video Library*

It's Your Funeral 1968
Suspense/Fantasy
77416 52 mins C B, V P
Patrick McGoohan, Annette Andre, Derren Nesbitt
The Prisoner must foil an assassination attempt in the Village. An episode from "The Prisoner" series.
ITC Productions — *MPI Home Video*

Itzhak Perlman 1982
Music-Performance
64208 45 mins C B, V R, P
Itzhak Perlman, Carlo Maria Giulini and the Philharmonic Orchestra
Violinist Itzhak Perlman is featured in this performance of Beethoven's Concerto in D for Violin. In stereo.
EMI Music — *THORN EMI/HBO Video; Pioneer Artists*

Ivan the Terrible—Part I 1943
Drama
08702 96 mins B/W B, V, 3/4U P
Nikolai Cherkasov, Ludmila Tselikovskaya, Serafina Birman, directed by Sergei Eisenstein
Ivan, Grand Duke of Russia, is crowned as the first Czar of Russia. His struggles to preserve his country are the main concerns of this first half of Eisenstein's masterwork. Russian dialogue with English subtitles.
Russian — *Budget Video; International Historic Films; Sheik Video; Video Yesteryear; Western Film & Video Inc; Discount Video Tapes*

Ivan the Terrible—Part II 1946
Drama
08703 84 mins B/W B, V, 3/4U P
Nikolai Cherkassov, Serafima Birman, Piotr Kadochnikev, directed by Sergei Eisenstein
The landed gentry of Russia conspire to dethrone Ivan in the second part of this classic epic. Russian dialogue with English subtitles; contains color sequences.
RU
Russian; Janus Films — *Budget Video; International Historic Films; Sheik Video; Video Yesteryear; Western Film & Video Inc; Discount Video Tapes*

Ivanhoe 1953
Adventure
58706 106 mins C B, V P
Robert Taylor, Elizabeth Taylor, Joan Fontaine, George Sanders
Sir Walter Scott's classic novel of chivalric romance and courtly intrigue among the knights of medieval England.
Film Daily Poll '53: Ten Best of Year.
MGM — *MGM/UA Home Video*

J

J. Geils Band 1984
Music-Performance
75904 16 mins C B, V P
This program presents the J. Geils Band performing their hits "Freeze Frame," "Centerfold," "Love Stinks" and "Angel in Blue."
EMI Records — *Sony Corporation of America*

Jabberwalk 1979
Comedy
66237 110 mins C B, V R, P
A "Mondo Cane" American-style. A reckless and funny view of the bizarre in U.S. life.
MPAA:R
Intl Talent; Romano Vanderbis — *Video City Productions*

Jabberwocky 1977
Comedy
63961 104 mins C B, V P
Michael Palin, Max Wall, Deborah Fallender, directed by Terry Gilliam
Chaos prevails in the medieval cartoon kingdom of King Bruno the Questionable, who rules with cruelty, stupidity, lust and dust.
MPAA:PG
Almi-Cinema 5 — *RCA/Columbia Pictures Home Video*

Jack and the Beanstalk 1952
Comedy
11795 78 mins C B, V P
Bud Abbott, Lou Costello, Buddy Baer
While baby-sitting, Lou falls asleep and dreams he's Jack in the classic fairy tale.
Warner Bros — *United Home Video; Discount Video Tapes; See Hear Industries*

Jack and the Beanstalk 1967
Cartoons/Fairy tales
47689 51 mins C B, V P
Gene Kelly
Live action blends with animation in this telling of the classic story about a boy and his magic beans. Music by Sammy Cahn and Jimmy Van Heusen.
Hanna Barbera — *Worldvision Home Video*

Jack and the Beanstalk 1976
Musical/Fairy tales
64578 80 mins C B, V P
Animated, written and directed by Peter J. Solmo
An animated musical version of the familiar story of Jack, the young boy who climbs a magic beanstalk up into the clouds, where he meets a fearsome giant.
Sheridan View Properties Associates — *RCA/Columbia Pictures Home Video*

Jack and the Beanstalk 1983
Fairy tales
Closed Captioned
69325 60 mins C B, V, LV, CED P
Dennis Christopher, Katherine Helmond, Elliot Gould, Jean Stapleton
From the "Faerie Tale Theatre," this is the classic tale of Jack, who sells his family's cow for 5 magic beans, then climbs the huge beanstalk that sprouts from them and encounters an unfriendly giant.
Shelly Duvall — *CBS/Fox Video*

Jack Benny 196?
Variety
59312 110 mins B/W B, V, 3/4U P
Jack Benny, Bob Hope, George Burns, Bing Crosby, Walt Disney, Martin and Lewis, Elke Sommer, The Beach Boys, Rochester, Don Wilson
Three complete Benny shows spanning the period from 1953 to 1965. Sketches include a spoof of Hope's "Road" movies, and a Mary Poppins take-off.
CBS; NBC — *Shokus Video*

Jack Benny, II 1953
Comedy
66486 120 mins B/W B, V P
Jack Benny, Mary Livingston, Rochester, Don Wilson, Kirk Douglas, Dick Powell, Humphrey Bogart, Ronald Reagan
This tape contains three 1953 episodes of "The Jack Benny Show" plus Jack's dramatic appearance on "The General Electric Theater." Original commercials and network I.D.'s included.
CBS — *Shokus Video*

Jack Benny III 1957
Comedy
77195 120 mins B/W B, V P
Jack Benny, Mel Blanc, Fred Allen, Johnny Ray, Jayne Mansfield, Don Wilson

A collection of four vintage Benny shows (circa 1952-1957) that features Jack trying to get Liberace to appear on his show and he has to pay Johnny Ray $10,000 for an appearance.
CBS — *Shokus Video*

Jack Benny Program, The 1959
Comedy
58641 30 mins B/W B, V, FO P
Jack Benny, Ernie Kovacs, Don Wilson
Ernie shows Jack his collection of moustaches, and Jack and Ernie play jailbirds in a prison of the future as Killer Kovacs and Benny the Louse. Sponsored by Lucky Strike.
CBS — *Video Yesteryear*

Jack Benny Program, The 1958
Comedy
65337 60 mins B/W B, V P
Jack Benny, Don Wilson, Mel Blanc
Two shows, "The Christmas Show" and "The Railroad Station," are shown in complete form with Mr. Benny at his best.
J and M Productions — *MCA Home Video*

Jack Benny Show, The 1958
Comedy
42976 25 mins B/W B, V, FO P
Jack Benny, Dennis Day, Audrey Meadows
The cast does a parody of the "The Honeymooners" with Dennis playing Ed Norton and Jack playing Ralph Kramden (with the help of a pillow under his shirt).
CBS — *Video Yesteryear*

Jack La Lanne Way, The 1985
Physical fitness
70539 60 mins C B, V P
Jack La Lanne, Elaine La Lanne
Jack offers an exercise program for all ages to tone, firm-up, and strengthen the body. The two thirty-minute presentations follow La Lannes time-proven scientific approach to fitness.
Bookshelf — *Bookshelf Video*

Jack London Story 1943
Adventure
16074 93 mins B/W B, V P
Michael O'Shea, Susan Hayward, Virginia Mayo, Frank Craven
Biographical treatment of the famous author's life.
United Artists; Samuel Bronston — *Movie Buff Video*

Jack Nicklaus Sports Clinic 1977
Golf
37418 18 mins C B, V P
Jack Nicklaus
Golf pro Jack Nicklaus demonstrates proper golf techniques.
Sports Concepts — *CBS/Fox Video*

Jack O'Lantern 198?
Cartoons
79198 30 mins C B, V P
Animated
The good hearted goblin with the help of two children defeats Zelda the Witch and her husband Sir Archibald.
Rankin Bass Studios — *Prism*

Jack the Ripper 1980
Drama
65379 82 mins C B, V P
Klaus Kinski
The inimitable Kinski assumes the role of the most heinous criminal of modern history—Jack the Ripper.
MPAA:R
Cine Showcase — *Vestron Video*

Jackson County Jail 1976
Drama
51986 85 mins C B, V R, P
Yvette Mimieux, Tommy Lee Jones, Robert Carradine
While driving cross-country a young woman is robbed, imprisoned, and raped by a deputy, whom she kills. Faced with a murder charge she flees, with the law in hot pursuit.
MPAA:R
New World Pictures — *Warner Home Video*

Jacob: The Man Who Fought with God 197?
Bible
35371 118 mins C B, V P
Jacob's struggle to receive his father's blessing and inheritance rights is depicted, as well as his marriage to Rachel and the return of his brother Esau. From the "Bible" series.
Sunn Classic — *United Home Video*

Jacob Two—Two Meets the Hooded Fang 19??
Adventure
69611 90 mins C B, V P
Alex Karras
Based on the children's book by Mordecai Richler, this is the story of a young boy who meets the dreaded Hooded Fang, warden of the prison "from which no brat returns."
MPAA:G
John Flaxman — *Children's Video Library*

Jailbait 1954
Drama
73545 80 mins B/W B, V P
Lyle Talbot, Steve Reeves, directed by Ed Wood

This is one of Ed Wood's earlier films, about a group of small time crooks who are always in trouble with the law.
Howco Films — *Admit One Video*

Jailhouse Rock 1957
Musical-Drama
44643 96 mins B/W B, V, CED P
Elvis Presley, Judy Tyler, Vaughn Taylor, Dean Jones, Mickey Shaughnessy, directed by Richard Thorpe
While in jail for manslaughter, a teenager learns to play the guitar. After his release, he slowly develops into a top recording star. Songs include "Jailhouse Rock," "Treat Me Nice," "Baby, I Don't Care" and "Young and Beautiful."
MGM — *MGM/UA Home Video*

Jam Video Snap! The 1983
Music-Performance/Music video
77527 47 mins C B, V P
Paul Weller, Bruce Foxworth
This compilation of film and video clips from "The Jam's" late 70's/early 80's career includes many of the songs that won them a large European following and critical acclaim on both sides of the Atlantic.
Polygram Music Video — *Music Media*

Jamaica Inn 1939
Drama
58615 98 mins B/W B, V P
Charles Laughton, Maureen O'Hara, Leslie Banks, Robert Newton, directed by Alfred Hitchcock
In old Cornwall, an orphan girl becomes involved with smugglers.
Paramount — *Movie Buff Video; Cable Films; Discount Video Tapes*

James Bond 007—Coming Attractions 1977
Adventure
38977 32 mins C B, V, FO P
Sean Connery, Roger Moore, George Lazenby
A collection of promotional trailers from all ten James Bond films produced between 1962 and 1977, beginning with "Dr. No" and concluding with "The Spy Who Loved Me."
United Artists — *Video Yesteryear*

James Brown Live in Concert 1979
Music-Performance
56745 48 mins C B, V P
James Brown
James Brown and his band perform such hits as "Boogie Wonderland," and "Georgia," and takes the audience through the best of jazz, rock, and blues fusion. Taped before a capacity audience at the Summer Festival in Toronto, Canada.
Network Talent Intl — *Media Home Entertainment*

James Dean Story, The 1957
Drama/Biographical
65470 57 mins B/W B, V P
An intimate portrait of James Dean presented by Robert Altman. The program includes never before seen outtakes from "East of Eden" and rare footage from the Hollywood premiere of "Giant" and the infamous Highway Public Safety message Dean made for television.
Warner Brothers — *Pacific Arts Video*

James Dean: The First American Teenager 1976
Biographical/Film-History
59861 83 mins C B, V P
James Dean, Elizabeth Taylor, Sammy Davis Jr., Rock Hudson, Sal Mineo, Natalie Wood, Julie Harris, Jack Larson, Nicholas Ray
A look at the life and legend of the charismatic filmstar, with comments by those who knew him best and scenes from his films. (Some black and white footage.)
MPAA:PG
Ziv Intl; Goodtime Enterprises — *VidAmerica*

James Taylor in Concert 1979
Music-Performance
48861 90 mins C B, V, LV, CED P
James Taylor's first video concert features live performances of "Sweet Baby James," "Carolina on My Mind," "Steam Roller," "Whenever I See Your Smiling Face," "Up on the Roof," and "Handy Man."
CBS — *CBS/Fox Video*

Jane Doe 1983
Suspense/Drama
77383 96 mins C B, V P
Karen Valentine, William Devane, Eva Marie Saint, Stephen Miller, Jackson Davies
An amnesiac assault victim lies in a hospital bed under an assumed name trying to recall details of the crime to prevent the assailant from finishing the job. Available in VHS Stereo and Beta Hi-Fi.
ITC Productions — *U.S.A. Home Video*

Jane Fonda Challenge 1983
Physical fitness
Closed Captioned
65547 90 mins C B, V P
Included in the offering are fast paced warm-up, exercise, balance and stretching sections, plus an exciting 20-minute choreographed aerobic routine that can be performed separately by those with too few hours in a day.
Karl Video; RCA — *Karl/Lorimar Home Video*

 (For explanation of codes, see USE GUIDE and KEY)

Jane Fonda's Workout 1982
Physical fitness
59073 90 mins C B, V P
Jane Fonda
An exercise program designed for both beginners and intermediate exercise buffs.
Karl Video; RCA — *Karl/Lorimar Home Video; RCA VideoDiscs*

Jane Fonda's Workout for Pregnancy, Birth and Recovery 1983
Physical fitness/Pregnancy
65116 60 mins C B, V P
Jane Fonda
Jane Fonda supervises a complete fitness program for pregnant women from conception to recovery.
Stuart Karl — *Karl/Lorimar Home Video; RCA VideoDiscs*

Japanese Connection 1982
Martial arts
64947 96 mins C B, V R, P
Li Chao, Yang Wei, Wu Ming-Tsai
Warring crime chiefs fight furiously with deadly kung-fu action.
Foreign — *Video Gems*

Jason and the Argonauts 1963
Fantasy
44179 104 mins C B, V P
Todd Armstrong, Nancy Kovack, Gary Raymond, Laurence Naismith, Michael Gwynn
Jason, son of King of Thessaly, sails on the Argo to the land of Colchis, where the Golden Fleece is guarded by a seven-headed hydra.
Columbia; Morningside; World Wide Productions — *RCA/Columbia Pictures Home Video; RCA VideoDiscs*

Jaws 3 1983
Suspense
69538 97 mins C B, V, LV, CED P
Dennis Quaid, Bess Armstrong, Louis Gossett Jr.
In a deluxe amusement park, a great white shark escapes from its tank and proceeds to cause terror and chaos.
MPAA:PG
Universal — *MCA Home Video*

Jaws 1975
Suspense
11590 124 mins C B, V, LV, CED P
Roy Scheider, Robert Shaw, Richard Dreyfuss, Lorraine Gary, directed by Steven Speilberg
A 25-foot long Great White Shark attacks and terrorizes residents of a Long Island beach town. Three men set out on a boat to kill it at any cost. Based on the novel by Peter Benchley.
MPAA:PG
Universal, Richard Zanuck — *MCA Home Video; RCA VideoDiscs*

Jaws II 1978
Suspense
11591 116 mins C B, V, CED P
Roy Scheider, Lorraine Gary, Murray Hamilton, directed by Jeannot Szwarc
The sequel to "Jaws'. It's been four years since the maneating shark plagued the resort town of Amity. Suddenly a second shark stalks the waters and the terror returns.
MPAA:PG
Universal; Richard Zanuck; David Brown — *MCA Home Video*

Jaws of the Dragon 1976
Adventure/Martial arts
51089 96 mins C B, V R, P
James Nam, Johnny Taylor, Kenny Nam
The story of two rival gangs in the Far East.
MPAA:R
Robert Jeffery — *Video Gems*

Jayne Mansfield Story, The 1980
Biographical/Drama
79329 97 mins C B, V P
Loni Anderson, Arnold Schwarzenegger, Ray Buktenica, Kathleen Lloyd
This is the lifestory of Jayne Mansfield from her rise to Hollywood stardom to her tragic demise. In Beta Hi-Fi and VHS Stereo.
Alan Landsburg Productions — *U.S.A. Home Video*

Jazz and Jive 193?
Music
13645 60 mins B/W B, V P, T
Duke Ellington, Major Bowes, Dewey Brown
Duke Ellington provides early jazz background in "Black and Tan," his first movie. Dance numbers accompany Dewey Brown in "Toot the Trumpet," followed by Major Bowes in "Radio Revels."
Paramount et al — *Blackhawk Films*

Jazzball 1957
Variety/Music
81109 60 mins B/W B, V P
Duke Ellington, Louis Armstrong, Artie Shaw, Cab Calloway, Gene Krupa, Peggy Lee, Buddy Rich, Betty Hutton
A compilation of songs and performances by the great jazz stars of the 30's and 40's taken from various movie shorts and features.
NTA; Hal Roach — *Spotlite Video*

Jazz in America 1981
Music-Performance
60443 90 mins C B, V P
Dizzy Gillespie, Max Roach, Gerry Mulligan, Pepper Adams, Candido
An historical tribute to bebop by way of two concerts performed at Lincoln Center by Dizzy Gillespie and his Dream Band.
Gary Keys — *Embassy Home Entertainment; RCA VideoDiscs*

Jazz in America 1981
Music-Performance
65423 60 mins C B, V P
Gerry Mulligan, Billy Hart, Frank Luther, Harold Danko
With continuity and structure, this program shows contemporary jazz in an entertaining manner with "respect" for the music and performances.
Dick Reed; Paul Rosen — *Embassy Home Entertainment*

Jazz Singer, The 1980
Musical-Drama
53934 110 mins C B, V, LV R, P
Neil Diamond, Laurence Olivier, Lucie Arnaz, Catlin Adams, Franklyn Ajaye, directed by Richard Fleischer
Another remake of the 1927 classic about a Jewish boy who rebels against his father and family tradition to become a popular entertainer.
MPAA:PG
Paramount; Jerry Leider — *Paramount Home Video; RCA VideoDiscs*

Jazz Singer, The 1927
Musical-Drama
55581 88 mins B/W CED P
Al Jolson, Mary McAvoy, Warner Oland, William Demarest, directed by Alan Crosland
A Jewish cantor's son breaks with his family to become a singer of popular music. This film is of historical importance as the first successful part-talkie. Jolson's songs include "Toot Toot Tootsie," "Blue Skies," and "My Mammy."
Warner Bros; Vitaphone — *CBS/Fox Video*

Jazzercise 1982
Physical fitness
59132 ? mins C LV P
Judi Sheppard Missett
An exercise program requiring total participation from the viewer, which allows the participant to proceed at his own pace. A one-sided interactive disc.
AM Available
Art Ulene — *Optical Programming Associates*

Jazzercise 1982
Physical fitness
63166 60 mins C B, V P
Judi Sheppard Missett
Total physical fitness is the goal of this "jazz dance" exercise program, designed for all ages and stages of health. VHS is in stereo, has the music programmed on one track and the instructions on the other. This tape is a completely different production from the disc of the same name.
Jazzercise/Feeling Fine Productions — *MCA Home Video*

JD and the Salt Flat Kid 1978
Comedy
74085 90 mins C B, V P
Singer JD tears up the road to Nashville with quick cars, speeding romance and fast times.
MPAA:PG
Jesse Turner; Tommy Amato — *Embassy Home Entertainment*

Jefferson Starship 1984
Music-Performance
76037 60 mins C B, V P
Jefferson Starship delivers both recent hits, as well as some of their classic Jefferson Airplane numbers: "White Rabbit," "Somebody to Love," and "Winds of Change."
Norman Stangl; Ian McDougall — *RCA/Columbia Pictures Home Video*

Jekyll and Hyde...Together Again 1982
Comedy
64503 87 mins C B, V R, P
Mark Blankfield, Bess Armstrong, Krista Errickson
A New Wave comic version of the classic story of Dr. Jekyll and Mr. Hyde, with a serious young surgeon who turns into a drug-crazed punk rocker after sniffing a mysterious powder.
MPAA:R
Paramount — *Paramount Home Video*

Jeremiah Johnson 1972
Drama/Adventure
58239 108 mins C B, V, LV R, P
Robert Redford, Will Geer, directed by Sydney Pollack
The story of a man who turns his back on civilization, circa 1850, and learns a new code of survival in a brutal land of isolated mountains and hostile Indians.
MPAA:PG
Warner Bros; Sanford Productions — *Warner Home Video; RCA VideoDiscs*

Jerk, The 1979
Comedy
42938 94 mins C B, V, LV P
Steve Martin, Bernadette Peters, Catlin Adams directed by Carl Reiner
A jerk, not a bum, tells his rags-toriches-to-rags story in comedic flashbacks. Martin's ridiculous

misadventures pay tribute to Jerry Lewis movies of the late sixties.
MPAA:R
David V Picker and William E McEuen — *MCA Home Video; RCA VideoDiscs*

Jerry Lewis Show, The 1967
Variety
42967 50 mins C B, V, FO P
Jerry Lewis, Sonny and Cher, Baja Marimba Band
Jerry plays a bumbling oaf trying to make the swinging singles scene, while Sonny and Cher sing and the Baja Marimba Band plays.
NBC — *Video Yesteryear*

Jerry Lewis Show, The 1968
Variety
38992 50 mins B/W B, V, FO P
Jerry Lewis, Helen Traubel, Lionel Hampton, Gary and Ronnie Lewis, Joey Faye
A program from Jerry Lewis' variety series, featuring some typical comedy routines from Jerry and musical performances by Gary Lewis, Helen Traubel, and Lionel Hampton.
NBC — *Video Yesteryear*

Jesse James at Bay 1941
Western
14223 54 mins B/W B, V P
Roy Rogers, Gabby Hayes
Exciting saga of the notorious Jesse James and his fight against the railroads.
Republic — *Video Connection; Cable Films; Video Yesteryear; Discount Video Tapes; Nostalgia Merchant*

Jesse Owens Story, The 1984
Drama
75931 200 mins C B, V R, P
Dorian Harewood, Debbi Morgan, George Stanford Brown, Le Var Burton
The moving story of the four-time Olympic Gold medal winner's triumphs and misfortunes.
Harold Gast — *Paramount Home Video*

Jesse Rae 1980
Music-Performance
75917 10 mins C B, V P
This program presents the music of the award winning Scottish video artist Jesse Rae.
Scotland Video — *Sony Corporation of America*

Jesse Rae: Rusha/D.E.S.I.R.E. 1980
Music/Video
66159 13 mins C B, V P
Music combines with video art in these two music concept pieces. In stereo.
Scotland Video — *Sony Corporation of America*

Jessi's Girls 1983
Drama
65450 86 mins C B, V P
Sondra Currie, Regina Carrol, Jennifer Bishop
In retaliation for the murder of her husband, an angry young woman frees three female prisoners, and they embark on a bloody course of revenge. Together, they track down the killers, and one by one, they fight to even the score.
MPAA:R
Manson International — *Monterey Home Video*

Jesus 1979
Drama/Religion
47379 117 mins C B, V R, P
Brian Deacon
The Biblical story of Jesus Christ is dramatized in this family-oriented film, which was made on location in the Holy Land.
MPAA:G
The Genesis Project — *Warner Home Video*

Jesus Christ Superstar 1973
Musical-Drama
11592 108 mins C B, V, LV P
Ted Neeley, Carl Anderson, Yvonne Elliman, directed by Norman Jewison
A rock opera that portrays, in music, the last seven days in the life of Christ.
MPAA:G
Universal; Norman Jewison, Robert Stigwood — *MCA Home Video*

Jesus of Nazareth 1977
Drama/Biographical
48403 371 mins C B, V P
Robert Powell, Anne Bancroft, Ernest Borgnine, Claudia Cardinale, James Mason, Laurence Olivier, Anthony Quinn
An all-star cast portrays the life of Jesus Christ.
ATV Ltd; RAI Productions — *CBS/Fox Video; RCA VideoDiscs*

Jethro Tull—Slipstream 1981
Music-Performance
58881 60 mins C B, V P
Jethro Tull
This legendary English rock'n'roll group presents ten songs in this program conceived for video. Concert footage is combined with animation and special effects. The band members appear in a number of guises, with Ian Anderson adopting such roles as Aqualung and Dracula.
Chrysalis Records — *Chrysalis Visual Programming; RCA VideoDiscs; Pacific Arts Video*

Jezebel 1938
Drama
64456 104 mins B/W B, V, CED P
Bette Davis, George Brent, Henry Fonda, Fay Bainter, directed by William Wyler
A willful Southern belle loses her boyfriend through her selfish and spiteful nature. When he becomes ill, she realizes her cruelty and rushes to nurse him back to health.
Academy Awards '38: Best Actress (Davis); Best Supporting Actress (Bainter).
Warner Bros — *CBS/Fox Video; RCA VideoDiscs*

J.F.K. 1964
Presidency-US/Documentary
69305 60 mins B/W B, V P
Narrated by Cliff Robertson
This documentary chronicles the life and turbulent times of America's most beloved President.
Art Lieberman — *Media Home Entertainment*

Jig Saw 1978
Adventure
65302 97 mins C B, V P
Angie Dickinson, Lino Ventura
A father searches for his "dead" son, repeatedly risking his own life to stop the criminals from completing the deadly task.
Les Films Ariane; Lafferty; Harwood and Partners Ltd — *U.S.A. Home Video*

Jigsaw Man, The 1984
Suspense
81179 90 mins C B, V P
Michael Caine, Laurence Olivier, Susan George, Robert Powell, David Kelly, directed by Terence Young
A British-Russian double agent is sent back to England to retrieve a list of Soviet agents which he hid there many years ago. Available in Hi-Fi sound for both formats.
MPAA:PG
United Film Distribution — *THORN EMI/HBO Video*

Jim Fixx on Running 1980
Running
55560 60 mins C B, V P
The nation's most prominent authority on running discusses physical and psychological aspects of running, diet, clothes, measuring improvement, and other topics of interest to running enthusiasts.
Lee Bobker — *RCA/Columbia Pictures Home Video; MCA Home Video*

Jimi Hendrix 1973
Documentary/Music-Performance
79550 102 mins C B, V R, P
This documentary about the guitar playing legend features interviews with Eric Clapton and Pete Townsend along with concert footage from Jimi's appearances at the Woodstock and Isle of Wight festivals.
MPAA:R
Warner Bros — *Warner Home Video*

Jimi Plays Berkeley 1973
Music-Performance
72220 55 mins C B, V P
The master guitarist Jimi Hendrix electrifies a Berkeley audience.
Independent — *Vestron Video*

Jimi Plays Berkeley 197?
Music-Performance
71292 55 mins C B, V P
"Jimi Hendrix Live" views the musical intensity of this man at the peak of his career. Performances by Hendrix include "Purple Haze," "Hey Joe," and "Wild Thang."
Unknown — *HarmonyVision*

Jimmy the Kid 1982
Comedy
69676 95 mins C B, V R, P
Gary Coleman, Ruth Gordon, Dee Wallace, Paul Le Mat, Don Adams
A young boy becomes the unlikely target for an improbable gang of would-be crooks on a crazy, "fool-proof" crime caper.
Zephyr Films — *THORN EMI/HBO Video*

Jinxed 1982
Comedy
64569 104 mins C B, V, CED P
Bette Midler, Ken Wahl, Rip Torn, directed by Don Siegel
A Las Vegas nightclub singer tries to convince a gullible blackjack dealer to murder her crooked boyfriend, but the plan backfires when the gangster electrocutes himself while taking a shower.
MPAA:R
United Artists — *MGM/UA Home Video*

Jive Junction 1943
Musical
69559 62 mins B/W B, V, FO P
Dickie Moore, Tina Thayer, Gerra Young
A group of patriotic teenagers convert a barn into a canteen for servicemen and name it "Jive Junction."
Producers Releasing Corp — *Video Yesteryear*

Jivin' in Bebop 1946
Music-Performance
57762 60 mins B/W B, V P
Dizzy Gillespie and His Orchestra, Helen Humes, R Sneed
A compilation of all-black music from the 1940's, featuring singers and dancers of the period known as "jive."

WD Alexander — *Budget Video; Video Yesteryear; Discount Video Tapes*

Joan of Arc **1948**
Drama
58736 100 mins C B, V P
Ingrid Bergman, Jose Ferrer, John Ireland, Leif Ericson, directed by Victor Fleming
The life of Joan of Arc, based on the play by Maxwell Anderson.
Academy Awards '48: Best Cinematography, Color; Best Costume Design.
Sierra Pictures — *VidAmerica; MGM/UA Home Video (disc only)*

Joe **1970**
Comedy-Drama
59305 107 mins C B, V P
Peter Boyle, Susan Sarandon, Dennis Patrick, directed by John Avildsen
An odd friendship grows between a businessman and a blue-collar worker as they search together for the executive's runaway daughter. Thrust into the midst of the counter-culture, they react with an orgy of violence.
MPAA:R
Cannon; David Gil — *Vestron Video*

Joe Cocker—Live from Tokyo **1983**
Music-Performance
78956 60 mins C B, V P
A performance of the rock and blues singer in concert taped in Tokyo, Japan.
Japanese — *Trans World Entertainment*

Joe Gibbs' Washington Redskins: Two Years to the Title **1983**
Football
66217 45 mins C B, V, FO P
Team highlight of the 1981-82 and 1982-83 seasons for the Washington Redskins
NFL Films — *NFL Films Video*

Joe Kidd **1972**
Western
47421 88 mins C B, V P
Clint Eastwood, Robert Duvall, John Saxon, Don Stroud, directed by John Sturges
A land war breaks out in New Mexico between Mexican natives and American land barons.
MPAA:PG
Universal — *MCA Home Video*

Joe Louis Story, The **1953**
Biographical/Drama
66384 88 mins B/W B, V P
Coley Wallace, Paul Stewart, Hilda Simms
The story of Joe Louis' rise to fame as Boxing's Heavyweight Champion of the world.
United Artists — *Movie Buff Video*

Joe Piscopo **1984**
Comedy-Performance
73577 60 mins C B, V P
Joe Piscopo, Eddie Murphy
Joe does some of his best impressions from Frank Sinatra to Jerry Lewis and some memorable improvisations from Saturday Night Live in this one hour special.
HBO — *Vestron Video*

Jog/Run **1978**
Running
44924 30 mins C B, V P
Ann Dugan demonstrates warm-up exercises for joggers to help them stay "loose" and strengthen leg, foot, and ankle muscles used for running. From the "Sports Conditioning" series.
Health N Action — *RCA/Columbia Pictures Home Video*

John Cougar Mellencamp—Ain't That America **1985**
Music video
80780 58 mins C B, V P
Singer/song writer John Cougar Mellencamp rocks out such favorits as "Jack and Diane," "Pink Houses" and "Hurts So Good" in this collection of conceptual music videos. Available in VHS and Beta Hi-Fi Stereo.
Polygram Music Video — *RCA/Columbia Pictures Home Video*

John Curry's Ice Dancing **1980**
Dance
47380 75 mins C B, V R, P
John Curry, Peggy Fleming, Jo-Jo Starbuck
This production combines the artistry of classical ballet with championship figure skating. Musical selections choreographed by John Curry, Peter Martins, Twyla Tharp and others.
WCI — *Warner Home Video; RCA VideoDiscs*

John Lennon: Interview with a Legend **1981**
Music/Interview
52671 60 mins C B, V P
John Lennon, Tom Snyder
A television interview with John Lennon, made with Tom Snyder on the "Tomorrow Show," originally aired April 28, 1975. Lennon discusses what it was like to be a Beatle, how he dealt with worldwide popularity, the breakup of the group, and his life in New York during the post-Beatle era.
NBC — *Karl/Lorimar Home Video*

John McEnroe Story: The Rites of Passage, The 1981
Tennis
51750 90 mins C B, V P
John McEnroe
This program documents the rise to stardom of John McEnroe, the brash youngster from New York, who most tennis experts reluctantly agree is the best tennis player on tour. His 1981 Wimbledon victory over Bjorn Borg is included, as are his classic matches with Jimmy Connors.
Michael Mattei — *Karl/Lorimar Home Video*

John Waite—No Brakes Live 1985
Music-Performance
81204 50 mins C B, V P
John Waite performs such hits as "Change," "Missing You" and "Teurs" in this concert video. Available in Hi-Fi Stereo for both formats.
EMI Music Video — *RCA/Columbia Pictures Home Video*

Johnny Angel 1945
Mystery
10064 79 mins B/W B, V P, T
George Raft, Claire Tervor, Signe Hasso, Lowell Gilmore, Hoagy Carmichael
Merchant Marine captain unravels mystery of his father's murder.
RKO — *RKO HomeVideo; Blackhawk Films*

Johnny Appleseed/Paul Bunyan 198?
Cartoons
78903 60 mins C B, V P
Animated
This animated double feature retells the legends of the lives of Johnny Appleseed and Paul Bunyan.
Rankin-Bass Productions — *Prism*

Johnny Belinda 1982
Drama
73533 95 mins C B, V P
Rosanna Arquette, Richard Thomas, Dennis Quard, Candy Clark
A VISTA worker teaches a blind girl sign language and opens a whole new world for her. Available in Beta Hi-Fi and VHS stereo.
Dick Berg; Stonehenge Productions — *U.S.A. Home Video*

Johnny Carson 197?
Comedy
33698 60 mins C B, V, 3/4U P
Johnny Carson, Don Rickles, Pearl Bailey, Joey Heatherton, Ed McMahon
Highlights of the fabulous career of "The Tonight Show," starring Johnny Carson. The program shows material not seen in "The Tonight Show" anniversary programs.
NBC — *Shokus Video*

Johnny Dangerously 1984
Comedy
Closed Captioned
70657 90 mins C B, V P
Michael Keaton, Joe Piscopo, Danny De Vito, Maureen Stapleton, Marilu Henner, Peter Boyle, Griffin Dunne, Glynnis O'Connor, Dom De Louise, Richard Dimitri, div. by A. Heckerling
This send-up of gangster films follows Mr. Dangerously's efforts to go straight. Competitive crooks would rather see him killed than law-abiding, and his mother requires more and more expensive operations. Crime pays in Hi-Fi stereo on all formats.
MPAA:PG13
20 Century Fox — *CBS/Fox Video*

Jonny Firecloud 1979
Drama
80897 94 mins C B, V P
Ralph Meeker, Frank De Kova, Sacheen Little Feather, David Canary, Christina Hart
A modern Indian goes on the warpath when the persecution of his people reawakens his sense of identity.
American National Enterprises — *Prism*

Johnny Got His Gun 1971
Drama
59671 111 mins C B, V P
Timothy Bottoms, Jason Robards, Donald Sutherland, Diane Varsi, Kathy Field
Dalton Trumbo's story of a young war victim who realizes that his arms and legs have been amputated.
MPAA:R
Bruce Campbell — *Media Home Entertainment*

Johnny Guitar 1953
Western
00298 110 mins C B, V P
Joan Crawford, Ernest Borgnine, Sterling Hayden
Tough saloon owner finds her wealth can't buy everything—not even love.
Republic — *Republic Pictures Home Video*

Johnny Mathis' Twenty-Fifth Anniversary Concert 1983
Music-Performance
72335 90 mins C B, V P
Celebrated singer Johnny Mathis performs his hit songs to mark his 25th year in show business. Guest star Denise Williams joins Mathis.
Music America Live Productions — *Prism*

Johnny Nobody 1961
Drama
77232 88 mins B/W B, V P
William Bendix, Aldo Ray, Nigel Patrick, Yvonne Mitchell
A mysterious stranger murders a writer who has been taunting the residents of a quaint Irish town.
Medallion Pictures — *Monterey Home Video*

Johnny Tiger 1966
Drama
81017 100 mins C B, V P
Robert Taylor, Geraldine Brooks, Chad Everett, Brenda, Scott
A teacher has his hands full when he arrives at the Seminole Reservation in Florida to instruct the Indian children.
Universal Pictures — *Spotlite Video*

Johnny Tremain and the Sons of Liberty 1958
Adventure/Drama
66053 85 mins C B, V R, P
Luanna Patten, Richard Beymer
The story of the gallant American patriots who participated in the Boston Tea Party.
Walt Disney Productions — *Walt Disney Home Video*

Johnny Winter Live 1984
Music-Performance
76643 45 mins C B, V P
This program presents the best young, white blues artists of the '60's in a live concert appearance.
Concert Productions International — *Music Media*

Johnny Woodchuck's Adventures 1978
Cartoons
47862 60 mins C B, V P
Animated
Little Johnny Woodchuck is more precocious than his well-behaved brothers. One day, he leaves home and family behind and sets out on an adventure. Available in both English and Spanish versions.
EL, SP
ZIV Intl — *Family Home Entertainment*

Jokes My Folks Never Told Me 1977
Comedy
76794 82 mins C B, V P
Sandy Johnson, Mariwin Roberts
This film consists of a series of blackouts and sketches featuring a bevy of beautiful women.
Steven A. Vail; Ted Woolery — *Embassy Home Entertainment*

Jonathan Livingston Seagull 1973
Fantasy
63431 114 mins C B, V R, P
James Franciscus, Juliet Mills, Music by Neil Diamond
Based on the bestselling novella by Richard Bach, this film quietly envisions a world of love, understanding, achievement, hope and individuality.
Paramount — *Paramount Home Video*

Jonathan Winters Show, The 1957
Comedy/Variety
47475 29 mins B/W B, V, FO P
Jonathan Winters, Jeri Southern, Betty Johnson, the Eddie Sefranski Orchestra
Two complete 15-minute shows from Jonathan Winters' first network TV series, featuring several impromptu sketches by the host about fishing and General Custer. Original commercials included.
NBC — *Video Yesteryear*

Joni Mitchell: Shadows and Light 1980
Music-Performance
53858 60 mins C B, V P
Joni Mitchell
Singer/songwriter Joni Mitchell performs her unique blend of folk, jazz and rock 'n' roll music.
CFJ Enterprises — *Warner Home Video; Pioneer Artists; RCA VideoDiscs*

Joseph Andrews 1977
Drama
10987 98 mins C B, V R, P
Ann-Margret, Peter Firth, Jim Dale, Michael Hordern, Beryl Reid, directed by Tony Richardson
This adaptation of a 1742 Henry Fielding novel chronicles the rise of Joseph Andrews from servant to personal footman (and fancy) of Lady Booby.
MPAA:R
Paramount; Neil Hartley — *Paramount Home Video*

Josepha 1982
Drama
64909 114 mins C B, V P
Miou-Miou, Claude Brasseur, Bruno Cremer
A husband and wife, both actors, are forced to re-examine their relationship when the wife finds a new love while on a film location. In French with English subtitles.
MPAA:R
Albina Productions-Mondex Films-TFI Films — *RCA/Columbia Pictures Home Video*

Josie and the Pussycats in Outer Space, Vol. II 1972
Cartoons
77159 58 mins C B, V P
Animated, voices of Casey Kasem, Don Messick, Janet Waldo
An all girl rock group Josie and the Pussycats along with their traveling entourage become involved in a series of cosmic adventures after getting trapped in a NASA space capsule.
Hanna-Barbera — *Worldvision Home Video*

Josie and the Pussycats in Outer Space 197?
Cartoons
47690 58 mins C B, V P
Animated
Three episodes of the all-girl rock group launching their music into the far corners of the galaxy.
Hanna Barbera — *Worldvision Home Video*

Jour Se Leve, Le 1939
Drama
08686 85 mins B/W B, V, 3/4U P
Jean Gabin, Jules Berry, Arletty, directed by Marcel Carve
A distorted and maddening love affair causes a tormented man to commit murder. French with English subtitles.
FR
Sigma Prod — *Budget Video; Sheik Video; Video Yesteryear*

Journey 1977
Adventure
45007 87 mins C B, V P
Genevieve Bujold, John Vernon
A violent story of a girl who is rescued from the Sagueney River and falls in love with her rescuer. Choosing to remain in the remote pioneer community of this "hero," she brings everyone bad luck and misery.
MPAA:PG
First American Films — *United Home Video*

Journey Back to Oz 1980
Fantasy/Cartoons
65105 88 mins C B, V P
Animated, voices of Liza Minnelli, Ethel Merman, Danny Thomas, Milton Berle, Mickey Rooney, Mel Blanc, Margaret Hamilton
Dorothy and Toto return to the magical land of Oz just in time to help Scarecrow, Lion and Tin Man fend off an invasion of magic green elephants created by the Wicked Witch Mombi.
Filmation Associates — *MGM/UA Home Video*

Journey Back to Oz 1971
Fantasy
69583 90 mins C B, V P
Animated, voices of Liza Minnelli, Ethel Merman, Milton Berle, Mickey Rooney, Danny Thomas
This animated special features Dorothy and Toto returning to visit their friends in the magical land of Oz.
Filmation — *Family Home Entertainment*

Journey—Frontiers and Beyond 1983
Music-Performance
76650 98 mins C B, V P
Platinum rock group Journey is profiled on and behind the stage. Includes "Wheel in the Sky," "Stone in Love," "After the Fall" and "Escape."
Music Media — *Music Media*

Journey Into Fear 1942
Suspense
64369 71 mins B/W B, V, 3/4U P
Joseph Cotten, Dolores del Rio, Orson Welles, Agnes Moorehead, directed by Norman Foster and Orson Welles
An American armaments expert is smuggled out of Istanbul with Axis agents close behind who are determined to kill their enemy.
RKO — *RKO HomeVideo; Nostalgia Merchant*

Journey to the Center of the Earth 1959
Science fiction
Closed Captioned
81513 129 mins C B, V P
James Mason, Pat Boone, Arlene Dahl, Diane Baker, Thayer David
A scientist and student undergo a hazardous journey to find the center of the earth and along the way they find the lost city of Atlantis. Based upon the Jules Verne novel. Available in VHS and Beta Hi-Fi.
20th Century Fox — *Playhouse Video*

Journey to the Center of Time 1967
Science fiction
81565 83 mins C B, V P
Lyle Waggoner, Scott Brady, Gigi Perreau, Anthony Eisley
A scientist and his crew are hurled into a time trap when a giant reactor explodes.
Harold Goldman — *Academy Home Entertainment*

Joy House 1964
Suspense/Drama
81394 98 mins B/W B, V P
Jane Fonda, Alain Delon, Lola Albright, directed by Rene Clement
An American woman befriends a handsome French playboy when her husband sends gangsters to kill him. Available in VHS Stereo and Beta Hi-Fi.

 (For explanation of codes, see USE GUIDE and KEY)

MGM — *Monterey Home Video*

Joy of Natural Childbirth, The **1984**
Childbirth
80411 59 mins C B, V P
Join Lorenzo Lamas and his wife Michele as they discuss natural childbirth with John and Nancy Ritter and Kenny and Marianne Rogers. Available in Beta and VHS Stereo.
Ted Mather; Peter Henton — *MCA Home Video*

Joy of Relaxation, The **1983**
Physical fitness
64548 ? mins C LV P
This fully participative program is designed to help people manage everyday tension. The exercises are derived from clinically-tested relaxation techniques such a yoga, breathing, progressive relaxation, autogenics, visualization and meditation. Questionnaires are included.
Feeling Fine Productions — *Optical Programming Associates*

Joy of Sex **1984**
Comedy
80063 93 mins C B, V R, P
Colleen Camp, Christopher Lloyd, Ernie Hudson, Michelle Meyrink, directed by Martha Coolidge
An undercover narcotics agent is sent to Richard M. Nixon High School to investigate the school's extracurricular activities.
MPAA:R
Frank Konigsberg; Paramount — *Paramount Home Video*

Joy of Stocks: The Forbes Guide to the Stock Market, The **1983**
Finance
72463 104 mins C B, V P
This introductory video to the stock market is divided into ten instructional segments.
MGM UA — *MGM/UA Home Video*

Joy Ride to Nowhere **1978**
Adventure
81519 86 mins C B, V P
Leslie Ackerman, Sandy Serrano, Mel Welles, Ron Ross, Speed Stearns
Two young women steal a Cadillac with two million dollars in the trunk and ride away with the owner hot on their tail.
MPAA:PG
Affiliated Film Distributors — *All Seasons Entertainment*

Joy Sticks **1983**
Comedy
65350 88 mins C B, V P
Joe Don Baker
Something outrageously hilarious, very sexy and thoroughly entertaining is going on at the local video arcade!
MPAA:R
Greydon Clark — *Vestron Video*

Juarez **1939**
Biographical/Drama
73977 122 mins B/W B, V P
Paul Muni, John Garfield, Bette Davis, Claude Rains, Gale Sondergaard, directed by William Dieterle
A revolutionary leader overthrows the Mexican government and then becomes President of the country.
Warner Bros — *Key Video*

Jubilee **1978**
Musical/Drama
73149 103 mins C B, V P
Adam Ant, Toyah Willcox, Jenny Runacre, Little Nell
Adam Ant stars as a punk who takes over Buckingham Palace and turns it into a recording studio. Music by Eno, Adam and the Ants, and Siouxsie and the Banshees.
Megalovision — *VCL Home Video*

Jubilee U.S.A. **1960**
Music-Performance
47649 58 mins B/W B, V, FO P
Red Foley, Slim Wilson, Harold and Jimmy, Betty Patterson, Buddy Childre, The Harmonettes, The Pitch-Hikers, Bill Ring
Two episodes of this variety/country and western music show, complete with ABC's promos for their western series ("Maverick," "Colt 45," "The Lawman").
ABC — *Video Yesteryear*

Jud **1971**
Drama
70601 80 mins C B, V P
Joseph Kaufmann, Bonnie Bittner, Robert Deman, Claudia Jennings
Society's refusal to understand the young soldier returning from the Vietnam conflict leads him to violence and tragedy.
MPAA:PG
Unknown — *Prism*

Judas Priest Live **1984**
Music-Performance/Music video
76801 83 mins C B, V P
Rob Halford, Glenn Tipton, K.K. Downing
The high powered heavy metal frenzy of Judas Priest is captured in this concert video.
Geoffrey Thomas — *Music Media*

Judge Priest 1934
Comedy-Drama
08864 80 mins B/W B, V, 3/4U P
Will Rogers
Comedy-drama set in the old South.
Fox Film Corp — *Prism; Budget Video; Discount Video Tapes; Cable Films; Western Film & Video Inc; Classic Video Cinema Collector's Club; United Home Video; Kartes Productions; See Hear Industries*

Judgment at Nuremburg 1961
Drama
69380 178 mins B/W B, V P
Spencer Tracy, Burt Lancaster, Marlene Dietrich, Richard Widmark, Judy Garland, Montgomery Clift, Maximilian Schell, directed by Stanley Kramer
This film centers on the post-WWII trial of four Nazi officials accused of war crimes.
Academy Awards '61: Best Actor (Schell); Best Screenplay.
United Artists; Stanley Kramer — *CBS/Fox Video*

Judy and Her Guests 1963
Music-Performance
15370 60 mins B/W B, V, FO P
Judy Garland, Phil Silvers, Robert Goulet
Judy and her guests perform "I Happen to Like New York," "Get Happy," "Almost Like Being in Love," and other hits.
CBS — *Video Yesteryear*

Judy Garland Show, The 1964
Music-Performance
57172 55 mins B/W B, V P
Judy Garland, the Bobby Cole Trio, Mort Lindsey Orchestra
Judy Garland is featured in a concert show from her television series, originally broadcast March 22, 1964. Songs include "Sail Away," "Comes Once in a Lifetime," "Joey, Joey," "Poor Butterfly" and "As Long as He Needs Me."
CBS — *King of Video; Electric Video*

Judy Garland Christmas Show 1963
Variety
57173 50 mins B/W B, V P
Judy Garland, Liza Minnelli, Lorna Luft, Joey Luft, Jack Jones, Mel Torme
A holiday special from Judy Garland's mid-sixties television series, featuring the whole gang joining in on Christmas standards. Songs include "Have Yourself a Merry Little Christmas," "Sleigh Ride," "Winter Wonderland," "The Christmas Song," "What Child Is This," "Over the Rainbow," and others.
CBS — *King of Video*

Judy Garland (General Electric Theatre) 1956
Variety/Music-Performance
80759 30 mins B/W B, V P
Hosted by Ronald Reagan, Judy Garland, Nelson Riddle
A vintage kinescope featuring Judy with Nelson Riddle and his orchestra performing "I Feel A Song Coming On," etc., and her closing theme song "I Will Come Back."
CBS — *Video Yesteryear*

Judy Garland in Concert: Volume One 1964
Music-Performance
79317 60 mins B/W B, V P
Judy Garland
This is Judy's one-woman show originally broadcast in 1964 where she sings "That's Entertainment," "Over The Rainbow" and "Swing Low, Sweet Chariot." Available in stereo in both formats.
CBS — *RKO HomeVideo*

Judy Garland in Concert: Volume Two 1964
Music-Performance
79318 60 mins B/W B, V P
Judy Garland
This is a special one woman show Judy performed in 1964 where she sings "The Man That Got Away" and "Once in a Lifetime." Available in stereo in both formats.
CBS — *RKO HomeVideo*

Judy, Judy, Judy 1949
Music
15371 60 mins C B, V, FO P
Judy Garland
Outakes of the unreleased Garland version of "Annie Get Yor Gun," and footage from a February 1962 concert. (Some segments in black and white.)
MGM et al — *Video Yesteryear*

Juggernaut 1937
Drama/Mystery
46349 64 mins B/W B, V, FO P
Boris Karloff, Mona Goya, Arthur Margetson
A young woman hires a sinister doctor to murder her wealthy husband. The doctor, who happens to be insane, does away with the husband and then goes on a poisoning spree.
British, Grand National — *Video Yesteryear*

Julia 1977
Drama
44931 118 mins C B, V, CED P
Jane Fonda, Vanessa Redgrave, Jason Robards
Story of a writer who becomes involved in the holocaust of World War II when her friend, Julia, asks her to smuggle money into Berlin.

MPAA:PG
20th Century Fox — *CBS/Fox Video*

Julia **1976**
Drama
58552 83 mins C B, V R, P
Sylvia Kristel
"Emmanuelle's" Sylvia Kristel stars as a young woman coming of age in a sophisticated society.
MPAA:R
Cine Media Intl — *Video Gems*

Julia Child—The French Chef, Vol. I **197?**
Cookery
56890 120 mins C CED P
Julia Child
Julia Child prepares four wonderful creations in her entertaining style: roasted chicken, lasagna a la Francaise, strawberry souffle, and mousse au chocolat.
WGBH Boston — *RCA VideoDiscs*

July Group, The **197?**
Drama
81062 75 mins C B, V P
Nicholas Campbell, Calvin Butler, Maury Chaykin
A Quaker family's peaceful existence is threatened when kidnappers invade their home and hold them for ransom.
CBC — *Trans World Entertainment*

Jungle Book, The **1942**
Adventure
29360 105 mins C B, V P
Sabu, Joseph Calleia, Rosemary de Camp, Ralph Byrd
A lavish version of Rudyard Kipling's stories about Mowgli, the boy who was raised by wolves in the jungles of India. Musical score by Miklos Rosza.
United Artists; Alexander Korda — *Movie Buff Video; Budget Video; Video Connection; VCII; Cinema Concepts; Sheik Video; Cable Films; Video Yesteryear; Discount Video Tapes; Western Film & Video Inc; Nostalgia Merchant; Media Home Entertainment*

Jungle Heat **1984**
Adventure
75627 93 mins C B, V P
Peter Fonda, Deborah Raffin
Anthropoid mutants feed on living flesh and blood.
MPAA:PG
Unknown — *Trans World Entertainment*

Junior G-Men **1940**
Adventure/Serials
08873 237 mins B/W B, V, 3/4U P
Billy Halop, Huntz Hall
The Dead End Kids fight Fifth Columnists who are trying to sabotage America's war effort. Twelve episodes.
Universal — *Video Connection; Video Yesteryear*

Junior G-Men of the Air **1942**
Adventure/Serials
64385 215 mins B/W B, V, 3/4U P
The Dead End Kids
The Dead End Kids become teenage flyboys in this twelve-episode serial adventure.
Universal — *Nostalgia Merchant*

Junkman, The **1982**
Adventure
66614 97 mins C B, V P
H. B. Halicki, Christopher Stone, Susan Shaw, Hoyt Axton, Lynda Day George, Freddy Cannon and the Belmonts
A moviemaker whose new film is about to be premiered is being chased by a mysterious killer. The ultimate car chase film, this production used and destroyed over 150 automobiles.
MPAA:R
H B Halicki International — *Trans World Entertainment*

Jupiter Menace, The **1982**
Speculation
64211 84 mins C B, V R, P
George Kennedy
An examination of speculative theories dealing with the inevitable end of the world. Kennedy predicts a continuing cycle of unnatural occurrences and disasters which will culminate with the tilting of the earth's axis in the year 2000.
Jupiter Menace Ltd — *THORN EMI/HBO Video*

Just Tell Me What You Want **1980**
Comedy
52700 112 mins C B, V R, P
Alan King, Ali McGraw, Myrna Loy, Keenan Wynn, Tony Roberts, directed by Sidney Lumet
A wealthy married man's mistress wants to take over the operation of a failing movie studio he has acquired.
MPAA:R
Jay Presson Allan; Sidney Lumet; Warner Bros — *Warner Home Video*

Just the Way You Are **1984**
Comedy
81503 96 mins C B, V P
Kristy McNichol, Robert Carradine, Kaki Hunter, Michael Ontkean, directed by Edouard Molinaro

An attractive musician struggles to overcome a physical handicap and winds up falling in love while on vacation in the French Alps.
MPAA:PG
MGM/UA — *MGM/UA Home Video*

Just Win, Baby/NFL 83 **1984**
Football
72937 46 mins C B, V, FO P
Los Angeles Raiders
Highlights from Los Angeles Raiders 1983 season and "NFL 83."
NFL Films — *NFL Films Video*

Justice **1955**
Crime-Drama
66137 26 mins B/W B, V, FO P
William Prince, Jack Klugman, Biff McGuire, Jack Warden
A crusading attorney tries to keep a waterfront kangaroo court from applying its harsh justice to an admitted killer. A TV crime-drama also titled "Flight from Fear."
NBC — *Video Yesteryear*

Justin Morgan Had a Horse **1981**
Drama
47410 91 mins C B, V P
Don Murray, Lana Wood, Gary Crosby
The true story of a colonial school teacher in post-Revolutionary War Vermont who developed the Morgan horse, the first and most versatile American breed.
Walt Disney — *Walt Disney Home Video*

K

Kagemusha **1980**
Adventure
55458 160 mins C B, V P
Directed by Akira Kurosawa
A thief is rescued from the gallows because of his striking resemblance to a warlord in 16th Century Japan, but, unfortunately for him, he is required to pose as the ambitious lord when the lord is fatally wounded. In Japanese with English subtitles.
Cannes Film Festival '80: Co-winner of Grand Prize. MPAA:PG JA
Twentieth Century Fox — *CBS/Fox Video*

Kajagoogoo **1983**
Music-Performance
75905 11 mins C B, V P
This program presents the new band Kajagoogoo performing their songs "Too Shy," "Ooh to Be An" and "Hang on Now."
EMI Records Ltd — *Sony Corporation of America*

Kamikaze '89 **1983**
Science fiction
66447 106 mins C B, V P
Rainer Werner Fassbinder, Gunther Kaufman, Boy Gobert, directed by Wolf Gremm
German director Fassbinder has the lead acting role in this offbeat story of a police lieutenant in Berlin, circa 1989, who investigates a puzzling series of bombings. Music by Tangerine Dream.
TeleCulture; Trio Film — *MGM/UA Home Video*

Kanako **19??**
Photography
60579 ? mins C LV P
Kanako Higuchi, one of Japan's most famous and adored actresses, is presented by renowned photographer Kishin Shinoyama in this series of nude photographs. Stereo.
Japan — *Pioneer Video Imports*

Kansas **1982**
Music-Performance
75920 87 mins C B, V P
This program presents a live concert by the rock group Kansas.
Radio & Records Inc; The Carr Company — *Sony Corporation of America*

Kansas City Royals: Team Highlights **1984**
Baseball
81141 30 mins C B, V P
George Brett, Amos Otis, Hal McRae, Frank White, Dan Quisenberry 7 pgms
This series examines the history of the Kansas City Royals and looksback at the best moments from the team's previous seasons.
1.1969: 1969 Kansas City Royals 2.1970: Our K.C. Royals and The A.L. 3.1971: A Bright New Era 4.1973: 1972 Review-1973 Preview 5.1980: One Step Claser 6.1982: Playing a Winning Hand 7.1984: Transition to a Title.
Major League Baseball — *Major League Baseball Productions*

Kansas Pacific **1953**
Western
80740 73 mins C B, V P
Sterling Hayden, Eve Miller, Barton MacLane, Reed Hadley, Douglas Hadley
A group of Confederate sympathizers try to stop the Kansas Pacific Railroad from reaching the West Coast in the 1860's.
Allied Artists — *Hal Roach Studios*

Karate Kid, The **1984**
Drama/Martial arts
80782 126 mins C B, V P

Ralph Macchio, Pat Morita, Randee Heller, Martin Kove, directed by John Avildsen
A teenaged boy finds out that Karate involves using more than your fists when a handyman agrees to teach him the Martial arts. Available in VHS and Beta Hi-Fi Stereo.
MPAA:PG
Jerry Weintraub; Columbia Pictures — *RCA/Columbia Pictures Home Video*

Kardiac Kids...Again **1981**
Football
50650 24 mins C B, V, FO R, P
Cleveland Browns
The 1980 Cleveland Browns football season was full of thrilling, last-minute, come-from-behind victories which propelled the Browns into the playoffs, where they met the Oakland Raiders in subzero weather. Quarterback Brian Sipe was named AFC Player of the Year.
NFL Films — *NFL Films Video*

Kashmiri Run **1969**
Adventure
65000 96 mins C B, V P
Pernell Roberts
A group of men race through the Himalayas for the Kashmiri border to avoid capture by Chinese Communists.
Sagittarius Productions — *U.S.A. Home Video*

Kate Bush, Live at Hammersmith **1979**
Music-Performance
65089 52 mins C B, V R, P
Kate Bush
Kate Bush displays her wide range of talents as a songwriter, singer, pianist and choreographer in this live concert show taped at London's Hammersmith Theater in May, 1979.
Kate Bush; London Films — *THORN EMI/HBO Video*

Kathy Smith's Ultimate Video Workout **1984**
Physical fitness
70568 60 mins C B, V P
Kathy Smith
This hour of exercise is for all levels ability with attention paid to flexibility, strength development, and cardio-respiratory fitness.
JCI Video — *JCI Video*

Katy Caterpillar **1983**
Cartoons
75612 85 mins C B, V P
Animated
Katy Caterpillar tells storybook tales.
Unknown — *Children's Video Library*

Kavik the Wolf Dog **1984**
Adventure
76653 99 mins C B, V P
Ronny Cox, Linda Sorensen, Andrew Ian McMillian, Chris Wiggins, John Ireland
A heartwarming story of a courageous dog's love and suffering to be with the boy he loves.
Stanly Chase — *Media Home Entertainment*

Keaton Special/Valentino Mystique **192?**
Film-History
10159 56 mins B/W B, V P, T
Buster Keaton, Rudolph Valentino
Film shows Buster Keaton in his peak years in excerpts from "College" and "Steamboat Bill Jr." Also recounts career of Rudolph Valentino using newsreels, home movies, and feature excerpts.
United Artists et al — *Blackhawk Films*

Keep, The **1983**
Horror
65762 96 mins C B, V, CED R, P
Scott Glenn, Alberta Watson, Jurgen Prochnow, Robert Prosky
At the height of the Nazi onslaught, several German soldiers unleash an unknown power from a medieval stone fortress which begins to overtake them all.
MPAA:R
Gene Kirkwood; Howard W. Koch — *Paramount Home Video*

Keep My Grave Open **1975**
Horror
47670 85 mins C B, V P
Camilla Carr, Gene Ross
A bizarre tale of murder, a strange house, and a sexually driven woman.
MPAA:R
S F Brownrigg — *Unicorn Video*

Keeper, The **1984**
Horror
66488 96 mins C B, V P
Christopher Lee, Tell Schreiber
The patients at Underwood Asylum suffer unspeakable horrors while under the care of the Keeper.
Trans World Entertainment — *Trans World Entertainment*

Kelly's Heroes **1970**
Suspense
68244 143 mins C B, V, CED P
Clint Eastwood, Donald Sutherland, Telly Savalas, Don Rickles, Carroll O'Connor
A group of men set out to rob a bank and almost win World War II. In stereo.
MPAA:PG
MGM — *MGM/UA Home Video*

Ken Murray's Shooting Stars **1985**
Outtakes and bloopers
76925 62 mins C B, V P
A collection of celebrity home movies featuring such stars as Gregory Peck and Jack Lemmon at ease.
Ken Murray — *MPI Home Video*

Ken Uston's Beat the House **1984**
Games
77230 120 mins C B, V P
Ken Uston describes his proven method for winning at blackjack.
Ken Uston — *Uston Institute of Blackjack*

Kennedys Don't Cry **1983**
Documentary
70182 100 mins C B, V P
Narrated by Cliff Robertson
A sensitive and detailed look at the triumphs and tragedies of the Kennedy clan. Rare footage and interviews trace the growth of Joseph P. Kennedy's children and their influence on American history. Some segments are in black and white.
Maljack Productions — *MPI Home Video*

Kennel Murder Case **1933**
Mystery
01713 73 mins B/W B, V P
William Powell, Mary Astor, Jack LaRue, directed by Michael Curtiz
Debonair detective Philo Vance suspects that a clearcut case of suicide is actually murder.
Warner Bros — *Budget Video; Discount Video Tapes; Nostalgia Merchant; Video Dimensions; Sheik Video; Cable Films; Video Yesteryear; Video Connection; Classic Video Cinema Collector's Club*

Kenny Loggins Alive **1981**
Music-Performance
59879 60 mins C B, V P
Pop artist Kenny Loggins performs "This Is It," "Angry Eyes," "I Believe in Love," "Celebrate Me Home," and other hits before a hometown crowd in Santa Barbara during the final performance of his 1981 tour. In stereo.
Kenny Loggins Productions — *CBS/Fox Video; Pioneer Artists; RCA VideoDiscs*

Kentuckian, The **1955**
Adventure/Western
68228 104 mins C B, V, CED P
Burt Lancaster, Walter Matthau, Diana Lynn, John McIntire, Dianne Foster
Burt Lancaster stars as a rugged frontiersman who leaves with his son to go to Texas. On their journey the two are harassed by fighting mountaineers.
Hecht-Lancaster Productions — *CBS/Fox Video*

Kentucky Blue Streak **1935**
Adventure
59373 61 mins B/W B, V, FO P
Eddie Nugent, Junior Coughlin, Patricia Scott, Ben Carter's Colored Octette
A young jockey is framed for murder while riding at an "illegal" racetrack. Later, almost eligible for parole, he escapes from jail to ride "Blue Streak", in the Kentucky Derbys
Puritan Pictures Corp. — *Video Yesteryear*

Kentucky Fried Movie **1977**
Comedy
66064 85 mins C B, V, LV P
Bill Bixby, Jerry Zucker, James Abrahams, David Zucker, Donald Sutherland
A zany potpouri of satire about movies, TV, commercials, and contemporary society.
MPAA:R
Robert K. Weiss — *Media Home Entertainment*

Kentucky Rifle **1955**
Western
81406 80 mins C B, V P
Chill Wills, Lance Fuller, Cathy Downs, Jess Barker, Sterling Holloway, Jeanne Cagney
A Comanche Indian tribe will let a group of stranded pioneers through their territory only if they agree to sell the Kentucky rifles aboard their wagon. Available in VHS Stereo and Beta Hi-Fi.
Howco Productions — *Monterey Home Video*

Kermit and Piggy Story, The **1985**
Variety
Closed Captioned
80744 57 mins C B, V P
Kermit the Frog, Miss Piggy, Cheryl Ladd, Tony Randall, Loretta Swit, Raquel Welch
This is the romantic story of how a barnyard pig rose from the chorus line to superstardom and finds the frog of her dreams along the way. Available in VHS and Beta Hi Fi.
Henson Associates — *Playhouse Video*

Kerouac **1984**
Documentary/Drama
70732 90 mins C B, V P
Lawrence Farlinghetti, Allan Ginsberg, William S. Burroughs, Steve Allen, Jack Kerouac
This docudrama frames the life of the beat poet Jack Kerouac with excerpts from his appearance on the Steve Allen Show in 1959. The film includes interviews with many of Kerouac's contemporaries.
John Antonelli — *Active Home Video*

 (For explanation of codes, see USE GUIDE and KEY)

Key Largo 1948
Drama
31662 101 mins B/W B, V P
Humphrey Bogart, Lauren Bacall, Claire Trevor, Edward G. Robinson, Lionel Barrymore, directed by John Houston
A gangster melodrama set in Key West, Florida, where a group of hoods take over a hotel, intimidating the proprietor. Based on a play by Maxwell Anderson.
Academy Awards '48: Best Supporting Actress (Claire Trevor).
Warner Bros, Jerry Wald — *CBS/Fox Video; RCA VideoDiscs*

Kid, The and The Idle Class 1921
Comedy
08399 90 mins B/W B, V P
Charlie Chaplin, Jackie Coogan, Edna Purviance, directed by Charlie Chaplin
The Little Tramp adopts a homeless orphan in "The Kid," Chaplin's first feature-length film. This tape also includes "The Idle Class" a rare Chaplin short.
Charlie Chaplin Productions; First National — *CBS/Fox Video; Playhouse Video*

Kid From Left Field, The 1984
Drama
78136 80 mins C B, V R, P
This program presents the story of the San Diego Padres' rise from last place to the World Series led by a ten year old boy.
Vestron — *Vestron Video*

Kid from Not-So-Big, The 1978
Drama
47381 87 mins C B, V R, P
Jennifer McAllister, Veronica Cartwright, Robert Viharo, Paul Tulley
A family film that tells the story of Jenny, a young girl left to carry on her grandfather's frontier-town newspaper. When two con men come to town, Jenny sets out to expose them.
Boomming Ltd — *Warner Home Video*

Kid 'n' Hollywood & Polly Tix in Washington 1933
Comedy
64918 20 mins B/W B, V P, T
Shirley Temple
These two "Baby Burlesks" shorts star a cast of toddlers, featuring the most famous moppet of all time, Shirley Temple, in her earliest screen appearances.
Educational Pictures — *Blackhawk Films*

Kid Sister, The 1945
Comedy
47502 56 mins B/W B, V, FO P
Roger Pryor, Judy Clark, Frank Jenks, Constance Worth
A young girl is determined to grab her sister's boyfriend for herself, and enlists the aid of a burglar to do it.
Producers Releasing Corp — *Video Yesteryear*

Kid with the Broken Halo, The 1981
Comedy
65441 96 mins C B, V P
Gary Coleman, Robert Guillame
A wisecracking 12-year-old angel is always in and out of trouble and always needs help from his teacher.
Satellite Productions — *U.S.A. Home Video*

Kid with the 200 I.Q. 1983
Comedy
80243 96 mins C B, V P
Gary Coleman, Robert Guillaume, Harriet Nelson, Dean Butler, Kari Michaelson
When a thirteen year old boy goes to college majoring in astronomy, he encounters problems with campus social life.
Guillaume—Margo Productions — *U.S.A. Home Video*

Kidco 1983
Comedy
Closed Captioned
81557 104 mins C B, V P
Scott Schwartz, Elizabeth Gorcey, Cinnamon Idles, Tristine Skyler
This is the true story of a money-making corporation headed and run by a group of children ranging in age from nine to sixteen. Available in VHS and Beta Hi-Fi.
MPAA:PG
20th Century Fox — *Playhouse Video*

Kidnap Syndicate, The 1976
Adventure/Drama
80935 105 mins C B, V P
James Mason, Valentina Cortese
Kidnappers swipe two boys, releasing one, the son of a wealthy industrialist who meets their ransom demands. When they kill the other boy, a mechanic's son, the father goes on a revengeful killing spree.
MPAA:R
SJ International — *VidAmerica*

Kidnapped 1960
Adventure
56876 94 mins C CED P
Peter Finch, James MacArthur, Peter O'Toole, directed by Robert Stevenson
The Robert Louis Stevenson classic about a boy who sets out to try to collect the inheritance which is rightfully his but is being withheld by his uncle.
Walt Disney — *RCA VideoDiscs*

Kidnapped 1960
Adventure
69318 94 mins C B, V R, P
Peter Finch, James MacArthur, Peter O'Toole
A young boy is sold by his wicked uncle as a slave, and is helped by an outlaw. Based on the Robert Louis Stevenson classic.
Buena Vista — *Walt Disney Home Video*

Kids Are Alright, The 1979
Music-Performance
59130 106 mins C B, V R, P
The Who, Ringo Starr, Keith Richard, Steve Martin, Tom Smothers, Rick Danko
A feature-length compilation of performances and interviews spanning the first fifteen years of the rock group, The Who. Includes rare footage from the "Rolling Stones Rock and Roll Circus" film. Songs include: "My Generation," "I can't Explain," "Young Man's Blues," "Won't Get Fooled Again," "Baba O' Reilly," and excerpts from "Tommy."
MPAA:PG
Tony Klinger; Bill Curbishley — *THORN EMI/HBO Video; RCA VideoDiscs*

Kid's Auto Race/Mabel's Married Life 191?
Comedy
66119 21 mins B/W B, V P, T
Charlie Chaplin, Mabel Normand, Mack Swain
"Kid's Auto Race" (1914), also known as "Kid Auto Races at Venice," concerns a kiddie-car contest; "Mabel's Married Life" (1915) is about flirtations in the park between married individuals. Piano and organ scores.
Keystone — *Blackhawk Films*

Kids from Candid Camera 1985
Comedy
77180 60 mins C B, V P
Hosted by Allen Funt
A collection of classic children's segments from episodes of "Candid Camera."
Allen Funt Productions — *Vestron Video*

Kids from Fame, The 1983
Music-Performance/Dance
65106 75 mins C B, V, CED P
Debbie Allen, Gene Anthony Ray, Lee Curreri, Erica Gimpel, Lori Singer, Carlo Imperato
The cast of the TV show "Fame" sings and dances in a live sold-out performance at London's Royal Albert Hall. VHS in stereo.
MGM/UA Home Entertainment Group — *MGM/UA Home Video*

Kids Incorporated: The Beginning 1985
Variety
80735 60 mins C B, V P
This is the story of how the kids from "Kids Inc" hired the musicians who appear on the popular television series.
Hal Roach Studios — *Hal Roach Studios*

Kill 1973
Suspense
79189 110 mins C B, V P
Jean Seberg, James Mason, Stephen Boyd, Curt Jurgens
The police and Interpol team up to smash an international spy ring.
Illya Salkind; Alexander Salkind — *U.S.A. Home Video*

Kill and Go Hide 1976
Horror
53149 95 mins C B, V P
A young girl visits her mother's grave nightly to communicate with and command the ghoul-like creatures that haunt the surrounding woods.
Valiant Intl Pictures — *Monterey Home Video*

Kill and Kill Again 197?
Martial arts/Drama
47315 100 mins C B, V P
James Ryan, Anneline Kriel, Stan Schmidt, Bill Flynn, Norman Robinson, Ken Gampu, John Ramsbottom
A martial arts champion attempts to rescue a kidnapped Nobel Prize-winning chemist who has developed a high-yield synthetic fuel.
Igo Kantor — *Media Home Entertainment*

Kill Castro 1980
Drama
66635 90 mins C B, V P
Stuart Whitman, Robert Vaughn, Caren Kaye
A Key West boat skipper is forced to carry a CIA agent to Cuba on a mission to assassinate Castro.
MPAA:R
No Frills Inc — *Monterey Home Video*

Kill or Be Killed 1980
Martial arts/Adventure
47852 90 mins C B, V P
James Ryan, Charlotte Michelle, Norman Combes
A martial arts champion is lured to a phony martial arts contest by a madman bent on revenge.
MPAA:PG
Ben Vlok — *Media Home Entertainment*

Kill Squad 1981
Martial arts/Adventure
59084 85 mins C B, V P
Jean Claude, Jeff Risk, Jerry Johnson, Bill Cambra, Cameron Mitchell

A squad of martial arts masters follow a trail of violence and bloodshed to a vengeful, deadly battle of skills.
MPAA:R
Michael Lee — *HarmonyVision*

Kill the Golden Goose **1979**
Suspense/Martial arts
54079 91 mins C B, V R, P
Brad Von Beltz, Ed Parker, Master Bong Soo Han
Two martial arts masters work on opposite sides of a government corruption and corporate influence peddling case.
MPAA:R
Skytrain Kim Films — *Video Gems*

Killer Bait **1949**
Suspense
66385 99 mins B/W B, V P
Lizabeth Scott, Don Defore, Arthur Kennedy, Dan Duryea
A money-obsessed woman gets involved with gangsters, blackmail and murder.
Universal — *Movie Buff Video*

Killer Bats (Devil Bat) **1942**
Horror
11673 70 mins B/W B, V, FO P
Bela Lugosi, Dave O'Brien
Monstrous, blood-sucking bats are trained to kill at the smell of perfume.
PRC — *Video Yesteryear; Video Connection; Cable Films; United Home Video; Kartes Productions*

Killer Diller **1948**
Musical
66386 70 mins B/W B, V P
Nat King Cole, Butterfly McQueen, Moms Mabley
A all-black musical revue, featuring Nat King Cole and his Trio.
Albert Sack Productions — *Movie Buff Video; Discount Video Tapes*

Killer Force **1975**
Adventure
66104 100 mins C B, V, CED P
Telly Savalas, Peter Fonda, Maud Adams
An adventure of international diamond smuggling.
MPAA:R
American International Pictures — *Vestron Video*

Killers from Space **1954**
Science fiction
76916 72 mins B/W B, V P
Peter Graves, Barbara Bestar, James Scay
Aliens from the Planet Unknown are terrorizing the residents of Southern California.
RKO — *United Home Video*

Killer's Moon **1984**
Horror
80490 90 mins C B, V P
Four sadistic psychopaths escape from a prison hospital and unleash their murderous rage on anyone who crosses their path.
VCL Communications — *VCL Home Video*

Killers, The **1964**
Drama/Suspense
56873 95 mins C B, V P
Ronald Reagan, Lee Marvin, Angie Dickinson, John Cassavetes
After two hired assassins kill a teacher, they look into his past and try to find leads to a $1,000,000 robbery. Based on Ernest Hemingway's story.
Universal — *MCA Home Video*

Killing Fields, The **1984**
Drama
81489 142 mins C B, V, LV R, P
Sam Waterston, Dr. Haing S. Ngor, Athol Fugard, John Malkovich, Craig T. Nelson, directed by Roland Jaffe
This is the true story of the friendship between N.Y. Times correspondent Sydney H. Schanberg and his assistant Dith Pran during the 1975 Khmer Rouge uprising in Cambodia.
Hi-Fi stereo for all formats
Academy Awards '84: Best Supporting Actor (Ngor)?Best Cinematography?Best Film Editing
MPAA:R
Warner Bros; Goldcrest — *Warner Home Video*

Killing Heat **1984**
Drama
80729 104 mins C B, V P
Karen Black, John Thaw, John Kani, John Moulder-Brown
An independent career woman living in South Africa decides to abandon her career to marry a struggling jungle farmer. Available in VHS and Beta Hi-Fi Stereo.
MPAA:R
Satori Entertainment — *Key Video*

Killing Hour, The **1984**
Drama/Suspense
Closed Captioned
70660 97 mins C B, V P
Elizabeth Kemp, Perry King, Norman Parker, Kenneth McMillan, directed by Armand Mastroianni
A psychic painter finds that the visions she paints come true in a string of grisly murders. This ability interests a TV reporter and a homicide detective. Available in Hi-Fi stereo.
MPAA:R

20 Century Fox — *CBS/Fox Video*

Killing of Angel Street, The 1983
Drama
65731 100 mins C B, V P
Liz Alexander, John Hargreaves
A courageous young woman unwittingly becomes the central character in an escalating nightmare about saving a community from corrupt politicians and organized crime.
MPAA:PG
Anthony Buckley — *VidAmerica*

Killing of President Kennedy, The 1983
Documentary/Presidency-US
69584 80 mins C B, V P
This documentary explores all of the conspiracy theories and the alleged cover-up by the Warren Commission.
Independent — *VidAmerica*

Killing of President Kennedy: New Revelations Twenty Years Later, The 1983
Documentary
72527 60 mins C B, V P
An in-depth look at new evidence that has surfaced and suggests President John Kennedy's assassination was carried out differently from government accounts.
Mark Hollo — *VidAmerica*

Killpoint 1984
Suspense
70148 89 mins C B, V, LV, CED P
Richard Roundtree, Leo Fong, Cameron Mitchell
A special task force is assembled to catch the criminals who robbed a National Guard armory for its weapons.
MPAA:R
Crown International Pictures — *Vestron Video*

Kim Carnes 1984
Music-Performance
75911 15 mins C B, V P
This program presents a performance by Kim Carnes singing her songs "Bette Davis Eyes," "Invisible Hands," "Voyeur" and others.
EMI America Records — *Sony Corporation of America*

Kind Hearts and Coronets 1949
Comedy
36934 101 mins B/W B, V R, P
Alec Guinness, Dennis Price, Valerie Hobson, Joan Greenwood, directed by Robert Hamer
Guinness plays eight different roles in this movie as the relatives of an ambitious young man who sets out to bump them off in an effort to attain the ducal crown, with hilarious results.
J Arthur Rank — *THORN EMI/HBO Video*

King and I, The 1956
Musical
08427 133 mins C B, V, LV P
Deborah Kerr, Yul Brynner, Rita Moreno, Martin Benson
From the musical play based on the biography "Anna and the King of Siam" by Margaret Landon.
Academy Awards '56: Best Actor (Brynner); Best Scoring Musical. EL, SP
20th Century Fox — *CBS/Fox Video*

King Arthur & the Knights of the Round Table Vol. 1 1981
Cartoons
59327 60 mins C B, V P
Animated
The tale of King Arthur is told beginning with his birth to the mighty sword Excalibur.
EL, SP
ZIV International — *Family Home Entertainment*

King Arthur & the Knights of the Round Table Vol. 2 1981
Cartoons
59328 60 mins C B, V P
Animated
The tales of King Arthur continue with the Knights of the Round Table, Camelot, Lady Guinevere and his adventures with Sir Lancelot.
EL, SP
ZIV International — *Family Home Entertainment*

King Arthur, the Young Warlord 197?
Adventure
59350 90 mins C B, V R, P
Oliver Tobias
The struggle that was the other side of Camelot—the campaign against the Saxon hordes.
MPAA:PG
Heritage Enterprises — *Video Gems*

King Boxers, The 1980
Adventure/Martial arts
56925 90 mins C B, V R, P
Yasuka Kurate, Johnny Nainam
Japan's top actor, Yasuka Kurate, stars in this tale of elephant hunts, warding off Triad Society gangs, and personal combat. Also stars Johnny Nainam, Thailand's fists and kicks boxing champion.
MPAA:R

(For explanation of codes, see USE GUIDE and KEY)

Fourseas Films — *Video Gems*

King Creole 1958
Musical-Drama
08383 115 mins B/W B, V P
Elvis Presley, Carolyn Jones, Walter Matthau, Dean Jagger, Dolores Hart, Vic Morrow
A teenager with a criminal record becomes a successful pop singer in New Orleans.
Paramount — *CBS/Fox Video; RCA VideoDiscs*

King David 1985
Drama
Closed Captioned
81508 114 mins C B, V R, P
Richard Gere, Alice Krige, Cherie Lunghi, Hurd Hatfield, directed by Bruce Beresford
This is the story of David, the legendary Biblical hero whose acts of bravery paved the way for him to become king of Israel.
MPAA:PG13
Paramount — *Paramount Home Video*

King in New York, A 1957
Satire
08423 105 mins B/W B, V P
Charlie Chaplin, Dawn Addams, Michael Chaplin, directed by Charlie Chaplin
Chaplin plays the deposed king of a European mini-monarchy who comes to the United States in hope of making a new life.
Charlie Chaplin Productions — *CBS/Fox Video*

King Kong 1933
Horror
00308 105 mins B/W B, V, 3/4U P
Fay Wray, Bruce Cabot, Robert Armstrong
The original film classic which tells the story of Kong, a giant ape captured in Africa and brought to New York as a sideshow attraction. He escapes from his captors and rampages through the city, ending up on top of the newly built Empire State Building.
RKO — *Nostalgia Merchant; VidAmerica; King of Video; RCA VideoDiscs*

King Kong 1977
Horror
38616 135 mins C B, V, LV R, P
Jeff Bridges, Charles Grodin, Jessica Lange
An updated remake of the 1933 movie classic, about a giant ape on the loose in New York City, climbing skyscrapers and generally wreaking havoc, with the climax taking place atop the World Trade Center.
MPAA:PG
Paramount — *Paramount Home Video; RCA VideoDiscs*

King of Comedy, The 1983
Comedy-Drama
68258 101 mins C B, V P
Robert De Niro, Jerry Lewis, Diahnne Abbott, Sandra Bernhard
Lewis portrays a late-night talk show host and De Niro his greatest fan. De Niro cannot get on the show so he decides to kidnap Lewis to force him to put him on.
MPAA:PG
20th Century Fox — *RCA/Columbia Pictures Home Video; RCA VideoDiscs*

King of Hearts 1966
Satire
53672 101 mins C B, V, CED P
Alan Bates, Genevieve Bujold, directed by Philippe de Broca
In World War I, a Scottish soldier finds a war-torn town occupied only by lunatics who have escaped from the asylum and who want to make him their king.
United Artists; Fildebroc; Montoro — *CBS/Fox Video*

King of Jazz, The 1930
Musical
68254 93 mins C B, V P
Paul Whiteman, John Boles, Jeanette Loff, Bing Crosby and the Rhythm Boys, directed by John Murray Anderson
A lavish revue built around the Paul Whiteman Orchestra with comedy sketches and songs by the stars on Universal Pictures' talent roster. Musical numbers include George Gershwin's "Rhapsody in Blue," "Happy Feet" and "It Happened in Monterey." Filmed in two-color Technicolor with a cartoon segment by Walter Lantz.
Academy Award '30: Best Interior Decoration
Universal — *MCA Home Video*

King of Kong Island 1978
Horror
35370 92 mins C B, V P
Brad Harris, Marc Lawrence
Intent on world domination, a group of mad scientists implant receptors in the brains of gorillas on Kong Island, and the monster apes run amok.
Independent — *United Home Video*

King of Kung-Fu 198?
Martial arts
64963 90 mins C B, V P
Bobby Baker, Nam Chun Pan, Lam Chun Chi
A martial arts adventure featuring plenty of kung-fu kicks.
Dragon Lady Productions — *Unicorn Video*

King of the Gypsies 1978
Drama
29767 112 mins C B, V R, P

Sterling Hayden, Eric Roberts, Susan Sarandon, Brooke Shields
A young man, scornful of his gypsy heritage, runs away from the tribe and tries to make a life of his own. He is summoned home to his grandfather's deathbed, where he is proclaimed the new king of the gypsies, a role he is unwilling to accept.
MPAA:R
Paramount — *Paramount Home Video*

King of the Hill **1974**
Baseball
21303 57 mins C B, V, FO P
The career of big league ballplayer Ferguson Jenkins is followed in this program, through his last two seasons with the Chicago Cubs.
National Film Board of Canada — *Video Yesteryear*

King of the Kongo **1929**
Adventure/Serials
57356 213 mins B/W B, V, FO P
Jacqueline Logan, Boris Karloff, Richard Tucker
A handsome young man is sent by the government to Nuhalla, deep in the jungle, to break up a gang of ivory thieves. A newly-discovered sound-silent serial.
Mascot — *Video Yesteryear*

King of the Mountain **1981**
Adventure
60444 92 mins C B, V P
Harry Hamlin, Dennis Hopper, Joseph Bottoms, Deborah Van Valkenburgh, Dan Haggerty
The "Old King" and the "New King" must square off in this tale of daredevil roadracers.
MPAA:PG
Polygram — *Embassy Home Entertainment*

King of the Rocketmen **1949**
Adventure/Serials
07335 156 mins B/W B, V, 3/4U P
Tris Coffin, Mae Clark, I. Stanford Jolley
Jeff King thwarts an attempt by traitors to steal government scientific secrets. Serial in twelve episodes. Later released as a feature titled "Lost Planet Airmen'.
Republic — *Nostalgia Merchant; Video Connection; Republic Pictures Home Video*

King of the Zombies **1941**
Horror
51443 67 mins B/W B, V, FO P
Joan Woodbury, Dick Purcell
A scientist creates his own zombies without souls, to be used as the evil tools of a foreign government.
Monogram — *Video Yesteryear; Discount Video Tapes*

King, Queen, Knave **1974**
Drama
65431 94 mins C B, V P
Gina Lollobrigida, David Niven, John Moulder Brown
A shy, awkward 19-year old boy, keenly aware that his interest in girls is not reciprocated, has to go live with his prosperous uncle and his much younger wife when his parents are killed.
Avco Embassy — *Embassy Home Entertainment*

King Rat **1965**
War-Drama
13258 134 mins B/W B, V P
George Segal, Tom Courtenay, James Fox, directed by Bryan Forbes
This drama, set in a World War II Japanese prisoner-of-war camp, focuses on the effect of captivity on the English, Australian and American prisoners.
Columbia; James Woolf — *RCA/Columbia Pictures Home Video*

King Solomon's Mines **1937**
Adventure
59834 80 mins B/W B, V P
Sir Cedric Hardwicke, Paul Robeson, Roland Young, directed by Robert Stevenson
The search for King Solomon's Mines leads a safari through the treacherous terrain of the desert, fending off sandstorms, Zulus, and a volcanic eruption.
Gaumont — *Embassy Home Entertainment*

Kingdom of the Spiders **1978**
Horror
51119 90 mins C B, V P
William Shatner, Tiffany Bolling, Woody Strode
A desert town is invaded by swarms of killer tarantulas, which begin to consume townspeople.
MPAA:PG
Dimension Pictures — *United Home Video*

Kingfisher Caper, The **1976**
Adventure
78346 90 mins C B, V P
Hayley Mills, David McCallum
A power struggle between a businessman, his brother, and a divorced sister is threatening to rip a family-owned diamond empire apart.
MPAA:PG
Ben Vlok — *Media Home Entertainment*

Kings, Queens, Jokers **193?**
Comedy
10112 60 mins B/W B, V P, T
Harold Lloyd, Marie Dressler, Polly Moran, Edward G. Robinson, Gary Cooper, Joan Crawford
Package includes a foolish lover and ghosts in "Haunted Spooks," an escaped convict in

"Dangerous Females," and a search for lost jewels in "Stolen Jools."
MGM et al — *Blackhawk Films*

Kinks: One for the Road, The 1980
Music-Performance
65478 60 mins C B, V P
A showcase for the Kinks' vast repertoire, including "Victoria," "Lola," "You Really Got Me," and many more. Also included is authentic footage of The Kinks on British and American television shows. In stereo VHS and Beta Hi-Fi.
Independent — *Vestron Video*

Kipperbang 1982
Drama/Romance
65110 85 mins C B, V, CED P
John Albasiny, Abigail Cruttenden, directed by Michael Apted
During the summer of 1948, a 13-year-old boy wishes he could kiss the girl of his dreams, and he finally gets his big break in a school play.
MPAA:PG
David Puttnam; Enigma Television Ltd — *MGM/UA Home Video*

Kismet 1955
Musical
47399 113 mins C B, V P
Howard Keel, Ann Blyth, Dolores Gray, Vic Damone, directed by Vincente Minnelli
An Arabian Nights extravaganza about a Baghdad street poet who manages to infiltrate himself into the Wazir's harem. The music was adapted from Borodin by Robert Wright and George Forrest, producing such standards as "Baubles, Bangles and Beads," "Stranger in Paradise" and "And This Is My Beloved."
MGM — *MGM/UA Home Video*

Kiss—Animalize Live Uncensored 1985
Music-Performance
77460 90 mins C B, V P
Gene Simmons, Eric Carr, Paul Stanley, Vinnie Vincent
Those heavy metal mongers Kiss perform all their full-throttled headbanging hits in this live concert video. Available in VHS and Beta Hi Fi Stereo.
Music Vision — *RCA/Columbia Pictures Home Video*

Kiss Daddy Goodbye 1981
Horror
81395 81 mins C B, V P
Fabian Forte, Marilyn Burns, Jon Cedar
A widower keeps his two children isolated in order to protect their secret telekinetic. Available in VHS Stereo and Beta Hi-Fi.
MPAA:R
Contel — *Monterey Home Video*

Kiss Me Goodbye 1982
Comedy/Fantasy
66073 101 mins C B, V, CED P
Sally Field, James Caan, Jeff Bridges, Paul Dooley, Mildred Natwick
A woman must choose between her new fiance or the returned ghost of her late husband.
MPAA:PG
20th Century Fox — *CBS/Fox Video*

Kiss of the Tarantula 1975
Science fiction/Horror
65454 85 mins C B, V P
Eric Mason
The story of a young girl and her pet spiders as they spin a deadly web of terror.
MPAA:PG
Cinevu Productions — *Monterey Home Video*

Kit Carson 1940
Western
64376 97 mins B/W B, V, 3/4U P
John Hall, Dana Andrews, Ward Bond, Lynn Bari
Frontiersman Kit Carson leads a wagon train to California, fighting off marauding Indians all the way.
Edward Small — *Nostalgia Merchant*

Kitty: A Return to Auschwitz 1981
World War II/Judaism
47564 90 mins C B, V R, P
Kitty Hart spent her teenage years at the Auschwitz concentration camp and survived. Thirty-four years later, she returned to the camp with her grown son to walk over the land and recall the past.
CBC — *THORN EMI/HBO Video*

Kitty and the Bagman 1983
Comedy
72872 95 mins C B, V P
A comedy about two rival madams who ruled Australia in the 1920's.
MPAA:R
Anthony Buckley — *Embassy Home Entertainment*

Kitty Foyle 1940
Drama
07882 107 mins B/W B, V P
Ginger Rogers
From the novel by Christopher Morley, Ms. Rogers symbolizes the white-collar working girl whose involvement with a married man presents her with both romantic and social conflicts.
Academy Awards '40; Best Actress (Rogers).

RKO — *VidAmerica; Nostalgia Merchant; Blackhawk Films*

Klute 1971
Drama
54116 114 mins C B, V, LV R, P
Jane Fonda, Donald Sutherland, Charles Cioffi, Roy Scheider, directed by Alan J. Pakula
A small town policeman comes to New York in search of a missing friend and gets involved with a would-be actress, call-girl who is trying to break out of her surroundings.
Academy Awards '71: Best Actress (Fonda). MPAA:R
Warner Bros — *Warner Home Video; RCA VideoDiscs*

Knack—Live at Carnegie Hall, The 1982
Music-Performance
47812 ? mins C LV P
The power pop quartet performs "My Sharona," "Good Girls Don't," and other hits at their March 18, 1979 Carnegie Hall Concert. In stereo.
Unknown — *Pioneer Artists*

Knee (Rehabilitation and Injury) 1978
Physical fitness
52759 30 mins C B, V P
Hosted by Ann Dugan
Exercises for knee strengthening, relief of pain, and conditioning muscles and tissue to prevent further stress. Part of the "Rehabilitation and Injury" series.
Health 'N Action — *RCA/Columbia Pictures Home Video*

Knife in the Water 1962
Film-Avant-garde
11399 90 mins B/W B, V P
Leon Niemczyk, Jolanta Umecka, Zygmunt Malandowicz, directed by Roman Polanski
A journalist, his wife and a hitchhiker spend a day aboard a sailboat in this tension-filled, psychological drama. English subtitles.
Venice Film Festival: International Film Critics Award.
Kanawha Films Ltd — *CBS/Fox Video; Video Yesteryear; Budget Video; Western Film & Video Inc; Video Dimensions; Sheik Video*

Knightriders 1981
Adventure
66065 145 mins C B, V P
Ed Harris, Gary Lahti, Tom Savini, Amy Ingersoll
The story of a troup of motorcyclists who are members of a traveling Renaissance Fair.
MPAA:R
Richard Rubinstein — *Media Home Entertainment*

Knights of the Roundtable 1954
Drama
81497 106 mins C B, V P
Robert Taylor, Ava Gardner, Mel Ferrer, Anne Crawford, directed by Richard Thorpe
This is the story of the romantic triangle between King Arthur, Sir Lancelot and Guinevere during the civil wars of sixth century England.
MGM — *MGM/UA Home Video*

Knock on Any Door 1949
Drama
44840 100 mins B/W B, V P
Humphrey Bogart, John Derek, George Macready
A young hoodlum from the slums is tried for murdering a cop. He is defended by a prominent attorney who has known him from childhood.
Columbia — *RCA/Columbia Pictures Home Video*

Knockout, The/Dough and Dynamite 1914
Comedy
59369 54 mins B/W B, V, FO P
Charlie Chaplin, Roscoe 'Fatty" Arbuckle, Mabel Normand, Keystone Cops
Two Chaplin shorts: "The Knockout" (1914), in which Charlie referees a big fight; "Dough and Dynamite" (1914), in which a labor dispute at a bake shop leaves Charlie in charge when the regular baker walks out.
Keystone — *Video Yesteryear*

Kooky Classics 1984
Music-Performance
80620 54 mins C B, V P
Shari Lewis, Lamb Chop, Hush Puppy
Shari Lewis leads her friends Lamb Chop and Hush Puppy on a wacky tour through the world of music accompanied by a symphony orchestra.
Shari Lewis Enterprises — *MGM/UA Home Video*

Koroshi 1967
Suspense
81528 100 mins C B, V P
Patrick McGoohan, Kenneth Griffith, Yoko Tani, directed by Michael Truman and Peter Yates
Secret Agent John Drake is dispatched to Hong Kong to disband a secret society who are killing off international political figures.
Sidney Cole — *MPI Home Video*

Kovacs on the Corner 1952
Comedy
39003 30 mins B/W B, V, FO P
Ernie Kovacs, Edie Adams, the Dave Appell Trio
A program from Ernie Kovacs' first television series, originating in Philadelphia. Creative video

comedy by the first master of the genre, and a song or two from Edie Adams.
NBC — *Video Yesteryear*

Koyaanisqatsi 1983
Film-Avant-garde
65471 87 mins C B, V, LV P
A totally unconventional program that takes an intense look at modern life. Without dialogue or narration, it brings what are traditionally considered background elements—landscapes and cityscapes-up front, producing a unique view of the superstructure and mechanics of our daily lives.
Godfrey Reggio — *Pacific Arts Video*

Kraft Music Hall 1959
Variety
42966 25 mins B/W B, V, FO P
Milton Berle, Yvonne DeCarlo, The Trio Cotters
Aired March 25, 1959, this program offers a monologue by Uncle Miltie, a song by Yvonne DeCarlo, and the acrobatic Trio Cotters tossing a young lady around the stage.
NBC — *Video Yesteryear*

Kraft Music Hall Presents "Alan King Stops the Press" 1969
Variety
56904 55 mins B/W B, V, FO P
Alan King, Paul Lynde, Barbara Feldon
A comedy-variety show spoofing the newspaper industry. Paul Lynde interviews star quarterback Boyd Blowhard, the food editor reviews the cuisine at the Last Chance Diner, and a look behind the scenes at the Advice to the Lovelorn column.
NBC — *Video Yesteryear*

Kraft Music Hall, The 1969
Music/Variety
52459 60 mins B/W B, V, FO P
Eddy Arnold, the Lettermen, Judy Carne, Tom Seaver
A program from this popular TV series hosted by Eddy Arnold, who sings "You're Just Too Good to Be True" and "Love Is Blue."
NBC — *Video Yesteryear*

Kraft Television Theater 1951
Drama
47639 60 mins B/W B, V, FO P
Olive Deering, Mark Roberts, E. G. Marshall, George Reeves, Ed Herlihy
"Kelly" by Eric Hatch, the story of an average Kansas gas pump jockey who remembers the girl he knew in France during the war, and is surprised to find her in the U.S.A.
NBC — *Video Yesteryear*

Kramer vs. Kramer 1979
Drama
58498 105 mins C B, V, LV P
Dustin Hoffman, Meryl Streep, Jane Alexander, Justin Henry, Howard Duff, directed by Robert Benton
A woman abandons her husband and young son, leaving them to struggle and make a new life for themselves. Eventually she returns to fight for custody. Based on the novel by Avery Corman.
Academy Awards '79: Best Picture; Best Actor (Hoffman); Best Supporting Actress (Streep); Best Director (Benton); Best Screenplay Adaptation (Benton). MPAA:PG
Columbia; Stanley Jaffe — *RCA/Columbia Pictures Home Video; RCA VideoDiscs*

Kriemhilde's Revenge 1924
Drama/Film-History
64304 95 mins B/W B, V P, T
Paul Richter, Margareta Schoen, directed by Fritz Lang
The concluding part of Fritz Lang's massive version of the Nibelungenlied, which was the basis of Richard Wagner's Ring operas. Silent with organ score.
UFA — *Blackhawk Films; Classic Video Cinema Collector's Club*

Krokus: The Video Blitz 1984
Music video
80504 60 mins C B, V P
The Swiss band Krokus performs hit songs such as "Our Love" and "Ballroom Blitz."
Callner Shapiro — *RCA/Columbia Pictures Home Video; Pioneer Artists*

Kronos 1957
Science fiction
44356 78 mins B/W B, V, 3/4U P
Jeff Morrow, Barbara Lawrence, John Emery
A giant robot from space drains the Earth of all its energy resources. Includes preview of coming attractions from classic science fiction films.
Lippert; 20th Century Fox — *Nostalgia Merchant*

Krull 1983
Adventure
65460 ? mins C B, V, CED P
Ken Marshall, Lysette Anthony, Freddie Jones, Francesca Annis
In a fantasy adventure, set in a world peopled by creatures of myth and magic, a prince embarks on a quest to find the magical Glaive and then rescues his young bride. In stereo VHS and Beta Hi-Fi.
MPAA:PG
Ted Mann; Ron Silverman — *RCA/Columbia Pictures Home Video*

Kung Fu **1972**
Martial arts/Adventure
78625 75 mins C B, V P
Keith Carradine, David Carradine, Barry Sullivan, Keye Luke
A fugitive martial arts master roams across the Old West fighting injustice in this film that served as a pilot for the television series.
Warner Bros — *Warner Home Video*

Kung-Fu Commandos **1980**
Martial arts/Adventure
59347 90 mins C B, V R, P
John Lui, Shangkuan Lung
Five masters must face a warlord's army to rescue a captured agent.
MPAA:R
Unifilm International — *Video Gems*

Kung Fu For Sale **1981**
Martial arts
70701 95 mins C B, V P
Chong Hua
A young kung fu enthusiast, along with his mentor, fights for the respect of his family.
Master Arts — *Master Arts Video*

Kung Fu Kids **1984**
Martial arts
80145 85 mins C B, V P
A group of abandoned orphans become Kung-fu street performers to earn money.
Independent — *Trans World Entertainment*

Kung Fu Warrior, The **198?**
Martial arts
81049 91 mins C B, V P
Chang Lei, Kuan Hai Shan, Chan Lei
A vacationing young Kung fu enthusiast gets caught up in a bizarre chain of events that force him to fight for his life.
Foreign — *Trans World Entertainment*

Kwaidan **1964**
Horror/Suspense
65203 161 mins C B, V P
Directed by Masaki Kubayashi
A haunting, stylized quartet of supernatural stories, each with a suprise ending. Japanese dialogue with English subtitles.
JA
Bungei Production; Ninjin Club; Toho Company — *Video Yesteryear*

L

La Sylphide **1971**
Dance
58903 81 mins C B, V, 3/4U R, P
Ghislaine Thesmar, Michael Denard, the Paris Ballet Opera Company, conducted by Patrick Flynn, directed and choreographed by Pierre Lacotte
The Paris Opera Ballet's faithful adaptation of "the ballet that changed the course of ballet history," based on the 1832 production staged by Taglioni.
Kultur; Paris Ballet Opera Company — *Kultur*

Laboratory **1980**
Science fiction
80952 93 mins C B, V P
Camille Mitchell, Corinne Michaels, Garnett Smith
Things go awry when the earthling subjects of an alien experiment revolt against their captors.
Sandler Institutional Films — *United Home Video*

Ladies Night Out **1983**
Nightclub
65344 80 mins C B, V P
Peter Adonis Traveling Fantasy Show
"Ladies Night Out" is an all-male burlesque, featuring the highly acclaimed Peter Adonis Traveling Fantasy Show. In stereo.
Joanne Sobolewski; John J Burzichelli — *Vestron Video*

Lady Caroline Lamb **1973**
Drama
80325 123 mins C B, V P
Sarah Miles, Richard Chamberlain, Jon Finch, Laurence Olivier, John Mills
The wife of a member of Parliament has an affair with Lord Byron and brings about her own down fall.
Tomorrow Entertainment — *Prism*

Lady Chatterley's Lover **1981**
Drama
60592 107 mins C B, V, CED P
Sylvia Kristel, Nicholas Clay, Shane Briant, directed by Just Jaeckin
D.H. Lawrence's classic novel of an English lady who has an affair with the gamekeeper of her husband's estate is the basis of this film.
MPAA:R
Cine-Artist GmbH; London-Cannon Films Ltd and Producteurs Associes — *MGM/UA Home Video*

Lady Cocoa **1975**
Drama
72956 93 mins C B, V P
Lola Falana, Mean Joe Greene
A young woman gets released from jail for twenty-four hours and sets out for Las Vegas to find the man who framed her.
MPAA:R
Matt Cimber — *Unicorn Video*

Lady Eve, The **1941**
Comedy-Drama
73687 97 mins B/W B, V P
Barbara Stanwyck, Henry Fonda, Charles Coburn, directed by Preston Sturges
A beer tycoon comes out of the jungle and falls into the hands of a woman and her card shark father.
Paramount Pictures — *RKO HomeVideo*

Lady for a Night **1942**
Drama
66465 88 mins B/W B, V P
John Wayne, Joan Blondell, Ray Middleton
The lady owner of a gambling ship does her best to break into high society.
Republic — *Republic Pictures Home Video*

Lady from Louisiana, The **1942**
Drama
66313 84 mins B/W B, V P
John Wayne, Ona Munson, Dorothy Dandridge, Ray Middleton
A lawyer in old New Orleans out to rid the city of corruption falls in love with the daughter of a big-time gambler.
Republic — *Republic Pictures Home Video*

Lady From Shanghai, The **1948**
Mystery
80785 87 mins B/W B, V P
Orson Welles, Rita Hayworth, Everett Sloane, Glenn Anders, Gus Schilling, directed by Orson Welles
An adventurer becomes involved in a web of intrigue when a woman hires him to work on her husband's yacht. Available in Beta Hi Fi.
Richard Wilson; William Castle — *RCA/Columbia Pictures Home Video*

Lady Grey **1982**
Drama
80334 111 mins C B, V R, P
A poor farmer's daughter rises to the top of the country music charts.
E O Corporation — *THORN EMI/HBO Video*

Lady in Red **1979**
Drama
66103 90 mins C B, V, CED P
Pamela Sue Martin, Louise Fletcher, Robert Conrad
A story of America in the 30s, and the progress through the underworld of the woman who was Dillinger's last lover.
Julie Corman — *Vestron Video*

Lady of Burlesque **1943**
Mystery
12446 91 mins B/W B, V P
Barbara Stanwyck, Michael O'Shea, Janis Carter, Pinky Lee
Burlesque dancer is found dead, strangled with her own G-string. Based on Gypsy Rose Lee's "The G-String Murders."
United Artists; Stromberg — *Video Connection; Sheik Video; Cable Films; Video Yesteryear; Cinema Concepts; Kartes Productions*

Lady of the Evening **1979**
Comedy
80120 110 mins C B, V P
Sophia Loren, Marcello Mastroianni
A prostitute and a crook team up to seek revenge against the mob.
MPAA:PG
Italian — *King of Video*

Lady of the House **1978**
Drama
75496 100 mins C B, V P
Dyan Cannon, Susan Tyrell
A true story about a madame who rose from operator of a brothel to become a political force in San Francisco.
William Kayden Productions — *Prism*

Lady on the Bus **1978**
Drama
66605 102 mins C B, V, LV P
Sonia Braga
A sexually frustrated newlywed bride turns to other men for satisfaction.
MPAA:R
Atlantic Releasing — *Vestron Video*

Lady Scarface **1941**
Mystery
73691 66 mins B/W B, V P
Dennis O'Keefe, Frances Neal, Judith Anderson
A gunwoman is pursued and captured by a police officer.
RKO — *RKO HomeVideo*

Lady Sings the Blues **1972**
Musical
38612 144 mins C B, V, LV R, P
Diana Ross, Billy Dee Williams, Richard Pryor
Jazz singer Billie Holiday's autobiography becomes a musical drama covering her early career and problems with racism and drug addiction. Songs include "God Bless the Child" and "Lover Man."
MPAA:R
Paramount — *Paramount Home Video; RCA VideoDiscs*

Lady Takes a Chance **1943**
Comedy/Romance
65395 86 mins B/W B, V P
John Wayne, Jean Arthur
A romantic comedy about a New York working girl with matrimonial ideas and a rope-shy rodeo rider who yearns for the wide open spaces.

RKO — *VidAmerica*

Lady Vanishes, The 1938
Mystery
01743 99 mins B/W B, V P
Michael Redgrave, Paul Lukas, Margaret Lockwood, directed by Alfred Hitchcock
When a kindly old lady disappears from a fast-moving train, her young friend finds an imposter in her place.
Gaumont British — *Prism; Embassy Home Entertainment; Media Home Entertainment; Budget Video; Video Dimensions; Sheik Video; Cable Films; Video Connection; Discount Video Tapes; Western Film & Video Inc; Cinema Concepts; Spotlite Video; Hal Roach Studios; Classic Video Cinema Collector's Club*

Ladykillers, The 1955
Comedy
36940 87 mins C B, V R, P
Alec Guinness, Cecil Parker, Katie Johnson, Herbert Lom, Peter Sellers, directed by Alexander Mackendrick
A gang of bumbling bank robbers is foiled by a little old lady from whom they rent a room. Hilarious antics follow, especially on the part of Guinness, who plays the slightly demented-looking leader of the gang.
British Film Academy '55: Best Screenplay; Best Actress (Johnson).
Continental, J Arthur Rank — *THORN EMI/HBO Video*

Lamaze Method: Techniques for Childbirth Preparation, The 1984
Childbirth
65386 45 mins C B, V P
Patty Duke Astin introduces the 3 basic areas of the method: relaxation, breathing and expulsion techniques. ASPO-certified Lamaze instructor Marilyn Libresco leads an expectant couple through demonstrations.
Embassy Home Entertainment; Al Eicher — *Embassy Home Entertainment*

Land of the Lost, Volume 2 1974
Adventure
81449 46 mins C B, V P
A forest ranger and his two teenaged children find themselves in danger when a time warp transports them to a prehistoric world.
Sid and Marty Krofft — *Embassy Home Entertainment*

Land of the Lost, Volume I 1974
Science fiction/Adventure
76792 46 mins C B, V P
Wesley Eure, Ron Harper, Kathy Coleman, Spencer Milligan, Phillip Paley
A forest ranger and his two teenaged children become trapped in a time vortex while exploring the Colorado River.
Sid and Marty Krofft — *Embassy Home Entertainment*

Land of the Minotaur 1977
Horror
60348 88 mins C B, V P
Donald Pleasance, Peter Cushing, Luan Peters
A small village is the setting for horrifying ritual murders, demons and disappearances of young terrorists.
MPAA:PG
Frixos Constantine — *United Home Video*

Land That Time Forgot, The 1975
Science fiction
64889 90 mins C B, V P
Doug McClure, John McEnery, Susan Penhaligon
A WWI veteran, a beautiful woman, and their German enemies are stranded in a land of life outside time. Based on the novel by Edgar Rice Burroughs.
MPAA:PG
American International Pictures — *Vestron Video*

Language in Life 1982
Language arts/Science
59563 50 mins C B, V P
Human communications from a psychological standpoint, based on recent studies in language acquisition, are examined, as well as a survey of the basic units of speech.
McGraw Hill — *Mastervision*

Las Vegas Lady 1976
Drama
70609 90 mins C B, V P
Stella Stevens, Stuart Whitman, George De Cecenzo, directed by Noel Nosseck
Three shrewd casino hostesses plot a multimillion dollar heist in the nation's gambling capital.
MPAA:PG
Crown International, Zappala Prod. — *Prism*

Las Vegas Story, The 1952
Drama
57141 88 mins B/W B, V P
Victor Mature, Jane Russell, Vincent Price, Hoagy Carmichael
Gambling, colorful sights, and a murder provide the framework for this fictional, guided-tour of the city.
RKO — *King of Video*

Laserblast 1978
Science fiction
33888 87 mins C B, V P
Kim Milford, Cheryl Smith, Keenan Wynn, Roddy McDowall
A frustrated young man finds a powerful and deadly laser which was left near his home by aliens. Upon learning of its devastating capabilities, his personality changes and he seeks revenge against all who have taken advantage of him.
MPAA:PG
Charles Band — *Media Home Entertainment*

Lassie's Rescue Rangers 1982
Cartoons/Adventure
66005 60 mins C B, V P
Animated
The courageous collie saves the day in two spine-tingling adventures.
Filmation — *Family Home Entertainment*

Lassie's Rescue Rangers, Volume 2 1982
Cartoons/Adventure
69807 60 mins C B, V P
Animated
Three action-packed cartoon adventures feature Lassie as she joins forces with the courageous Rescue Rangers to help protect people and wildlife in the national forests.
Filmation — *Family Home Entertainment*

Lassie's Rescue Rangers, Volume 3 1985
Cartoons/Adventure
70359 60 mins C B, V P
Animated
This tape features further adventures of the king of collies as he leads the Rescue Rangers in the protection of Earth's beauty. The program comes in stereo on all formats.
Filmation — *Family Home Entertainment*

Lassiter 1984
Drama
72919 100 mins C B, V P
Tom Selleck, Lauren Hutton, Jane Seymour
Tom Selleck plays a jewel thief who is asked to steal diamonds for the FBI.
MPAA:R
Al Ruddy; Warner Bros — *Warner Home Video*

Last American Virgin, The 1982
Comedy
60567 92 mins C B, V, CED P
Lawrence Monoson, Diane Franklin, Steve Antin, Louisa Moritz
Three school buddies must deal with a plethora of problems in their search for girls who are willing. Music by Blondie, The Cars, The Police, The Waitresses, Devo, U2, Human League, Quincy Jones.
MPAA:R
Cannon Films Inc; Golan Globus Productions — *MGM/UA Home Video*

Last Challenge of the Dragon, The 1980
Adventure/Martial arts
56926 90 mins C B, V R, P
Bruce Lee
A son brings death to his family by humiliating the underworld martial arts king of the city.
MPAA:R
Goldig Film — *Video Gems*

Last Challenge of the Dragon 198?
Martial arts
64958 90 mins C B, V P
A martial arts adventure.
Dragon Lady Productions — *Unicorn Video*

Last Chase, The 1980
Adventure
47755 106 mins C B, V, CED P
Lee Majors, Burgess Meredith, Chris Makepeace
A famed race car driver becomes a vocal dissenter against the sterile society that has emerged, in this drama set in the near future.
MPAA:PG
Martyn Burke; Fran Rosati — *Vestron Video*

Last Cry for Help 1980
Suicide
52397 30 mins C B, V P

An alienated, depressed young girl attempts suicide. We see her experiences before the attempt and her emerging strength afterward as she learns to take control of her life.
AM Available
Learning Corp of America — *Unicorn Video*

Last Cry for Help, A 1979
Drama
79323 98 mins C B, V P
Linda Purl, Shirley Jones, Tony Lo Bianco, Murray Hamilton, Grant Goodeve
A psychiatrist helps out a seventeen-year-old girl who attempts suicide.
Myrt Hall Productions — *Unicorn Video*

Last Day of the War 1969
War-Drama
77380 95 mins C B, V P
George Maharis, Maria Perschy, James Philbrook
A U.S. Army platoon attempts to reach an Austrian spy before the Nazis kill him at the end of World War II. Available in Beta Hi-Fi and VHS Stereo.

MPAA:PG
Sagittarius Productions — *U.S.A. Home Video*

Last Days of Man on Earth 1973
Science fiction
65713 70 mins C B, V P
Jon Finch, Jenny Runacre, Hugh Griffith
In a deteriorating world, a search is on for a piece of microfilm which holds the formula for immortality.
MPAA:R
New World — *Embassy Home Entertainment*

Last Days of Pompeii, The 1935
Adventure
57142 96 mins B/W B, V P
Preston Foster, Basil Rathbone, Louis Calhern
A peace-loving blacksmith strives for wealth by becoming a gladiator.
RKO — *King of Video*

Last Detail, The 1974
Comedy-Drama
59603 104 mins C B, V P
Jack Nicholson, Randy Quaid, Otis Young, directed by Hal Ashby
A hard-boiled career petty officer commissioned to transfer a young sailor from one brig to another attempts to show the prisoner a good time.
MPAA:R
Columbia — *RCA/Columbia Pictures Home Video*

Last Fight, The 1982
Drama
78387 85 mins C B, V R, P
Willie Colon, Fred Williamson, Ruben Blades, Joe Spinell, Darlanne Fluegel.
A boxer risks his life and his girlfriend for one chance at the championship title.
MPAA:R
Jerry Masucci, Fred Williamson — *THORN EMI/HBO Video*

Last Flight of Noah's Ark, The 1980
Adventure/Drama
63192 97 mins C B, V R, P
Elliott Gould, Genevieve Bujold, Ricky Schroder, Vincent Gardenia, Tammy Lauren
This tale of adventure concerns a high-living pilot, a prim missionary and two stowaway orphans who must plot their way off a deserted island following the crash landing of their broken-down plane.
Walt Disney Productions — *Walt Disney Home Video*

Last Game, The 1980
Drama
80333 107 mins C B, V R, P
A college student is torn between his devotion to his blind father and going out for the college's football team.
E O Corporation — *THORN EMI/HBO Video*

Last Gun, the 1964
Western
81517 98 mins C B, V P
Cameron Mitchell
A legendary gunman on the verge of retirement has to save his town from a reign of terror before turning his gun in.
Foreign — *Sagebrush Productions*

Last Horror Film, The 1982
Horror
65692 87 mins C B, V P
Joe Spinell, Caroline Munro
A beautiful queen of horror films is followed to Cannes by her number one fan who, unbeknownst to her, is slowly murdering members of her entourage in a deluded and vain attempt to capture her attentions.
MPAA:R
David Winters; Judd Hamilton — *Media Home Entertainment*

Last House on the Left 1972
Horror/Exploitation
80685 82 mins C B, V, CED P
David Hess, Lucy Gratham, Sandra Cassel
Two girls are kidnapped from a rock concert by a gang of escaped convicts who subject them to a night of terror that they will never forget.
MPAA:R
Orion Pictures — *Vestron Video*

Last Hunter, The 1980
Drama
80686 97 mins C B, V P
Tisa Farrow, David Warbeck
A soldier fights for his life behind enemy lines during the Vietnam War.
MPAA:R
Worldwide Entertainment — *Vestron Video*

Last Married Couple in America, The 1980
Comedy
59683 103 mins C B, V P
George Segal, Natalie Wood, Richard Benjamin, Valerie Harper, Dom DeLuise
A couple fight to stay happily married amidst the rampant divorce epidemic engulfing their friends.
MPAA:R
Universal — *MCA Home Video*

(For explanation of codes, see USE GUIDE and KEY)

Last of Sheila, The 1973
Drama/Suspense
51963 118 mins C B, V R, P
Richard Benjamin, James Coburn, James Mason, Dyan Cannon, Joan Hackett, Raquel Welch
The yacht "Sheila" is the setting for a "Whodunit" parlor game to discover which of six people is a murderer.
MPAA:PG
Warner Bros — *Warner Home Video*

Last of the Mohicans 1932
Adventure/Serials
12541 156 mins B/W B, V P
Edwina Booth, Harry Carey, directed by Ford Beebe, B. Reaves Eason
Based on James Fenimore Cooper's novel of the Indian's life and death struggle during the French and Indian War. Twelve chapters, 13 minutes each.
Mascot — *Video Connection; Video Yesteryear; Discount Video Tapes*

Last of the Mohicans 1977
Adventure
57621 97 mins C B, V P
The classic novel by James Fenimore Cooper about the scout Hawkeye and his Mohican companions, Chingachgook and Uncas, comes to life in this film.
Schick Sunn — *United Home Video*

Last of the Mohicans, The 1936
Adventure
55351 91 mins B/W B, V, 3/4U P
Randolph Scott, Binnie Barnes, Bruce Cabot
James Fenimore Cooper's classic about the French and Indian War in colonial America.
Edward Small; United Artists — *Nostalgia Merchant; Blackhawk Films; Classic Video Cinema Collector's Club*

Last of the Pony Riders 1953
Western
64533 59 mins B/W B, V R, P
Gene Autry, Smiley Burnette, Kathleen Case
When the telegraph lines linking the East and West Coasts is completed, Gene and the other Pony Express riders find themselves out of a job. This was Autry's final feature film.
Columbia — *Blackhawk Films*

Last of the Red Hot Lovers 1972
Comedy
59424 98 mins C B, V, LV R, P
Alan Arkin, Paula Prentiss, Sally Kellerman, Renee Taylor, directed by Gene Saks
Neil Simon's Broadway hit about a middle-aged man who decides to have a fling and uses his mother's apartment to seduce three very strange women.
MPAA:PG
Paramount — *Paramount Home Video*

Last Plane Out 198?
Drama
80137 90 mins C B, V P
Jan Michael Vincent, Lloyd Batista, Julie Carmen, directed by David Nelson
A Texas journalist sent out on assignment to Nicaragua falls in love with a Sandanista rebel.
MPAA:R
Jack Cox Productions — *CBS/Fox Video*

Last Ride of the Dalton Gang, The 1979
Western
80157 146 mins C B, V R, P
Larry Wilcox, Jack Palance, Randy Quaid, Cliff Potts, Dale Roberston, Don Collier
This is a retelling of the wild adventures that made the Dalton gang legendary among outlaws.
Dan Curtis Productions — *Warner Home Video*

Last Starfighter, The 1984
Science fiction/Fantasy
79173 100 mins C B, V P
Lance Guest, Robert Preston, Barbara Bosson, Dan O'Herlihy, Catherine Mary Stewart
A young man who becomes an expert at a video game is recruited to fight in an inter-galactic war.
MPAA:PG
Gary Adelson; Lorimar; Universal — *MCA Home Video*

Last Summer 1969
Drama
70379 97 mins C B, V P
Barbara Hershey, Richard Thomas, Bruce Davidson, Cathy Burns, directed by Frank Perry
Three teenagers discover, love, sex and friendship on the white sands of Fire Island, N.Y. The summer vacation fantasy world they create shatters when a sweet but homely female teenager joins their groups.
MPAA:R
Allied Artists — *Key Video*

Last Tango in Paris 1973
Drama
13323 129 mins C B, V, LV P
Marlon Brando, Maria Schneider, Jean-Pierre Leaud, directed by Bernardo Bertolucci
Brando plays a middle-aged American who meets a French girl. Many revealing moments follow in their frantic, unlikely, and short-lived affair.
MPAA:X
United Artists — *CBS/Fox Video; RCA VideoDiscs*

Last Unicorn, The **1982**
Cartoons/Fairy tales
60583 95 mins C B, V, CED P
Animated, voices of Alan Arkin, Jeff Bridges, Tammy Grimes, Angela Lansbury, Mia Farrow, Robert Klein, Christopher Lee, Keenan Wynn
Peter Beagle's popular tale of a beautiful unicorn who goes in search of her lost, mythical "family." Music by Jimmy Webb.
MPAA:G
ITC Entertainment — *Playhouse Video*

Last Waltz, The **1978**
Music-Performance
73141 117 mins C B, V P
The Band, Bob Dylan, Joni Mitchell, Ringo Starr, Van Morrison, directed by Martin Scorsese
The Band's farewell 1976 concert on Thanksgiving Day was documented by Martin Scorsese and features performances by Bob Dylan, Eric Clapton and many other rock notables.
MPAA:PG
Robbie Robertson; Warner Bros — *CBS/Fox Video*

Last Waltz, The **1978**
Music-Performance
52603 117 mins C B, V P
The Band, Bob Dylan, Neil Young, Joni Mitchell, Van Morrison, Eric Clapton, Neil Diamond, Emmylon Harris, Muddy Waters, Ronnie Hawkins
Martin Scorcese filmed this rock documentary featuring the farewell performance of The Band, joined by a host of musical guests that they have been associated with over the years. Songs include: "Upon Cripple Creek," "Don't Do It," "The Night They Drove old Dixie Down," "Stage Fright" (The Band), "Helpless" (Young), "Coyote" (Mitchell), "Caravan" (Morrison), "Further On Up the Road" (Clapton), "Who Do You Love" (Hawkins), "Mannish Boy" (Waters), "Evangeline" (Harris), "Baby, Let Me Follow You Down" (Dylan).
MPAA:PG
Robbie Robertson, United Artists — *CBS/Fox Video; RCA VideoDiscs*

Last War, The **1968**
Science fiction
80799 79 mins C B, V R, P
Akiva Takarada, Yuriho Hoshi
A nuclear war between the United States and Russia triggers Armageddon.
Toho Films — *Video Gems*

Last Wave, The **1978**
Drama/Suspense
47382 103 mins C B, V R, P
Richard Chamberlain, Olivia Hamnett, Gulpilil, Frederick Parslow, directed by Peter Weir
An Australian attorney takes on a murder case involving an aborigine. He finds himself becoming distracted by apocalyptic visions concerning tidal waves and drownings that seem to foretell the future.
MPAA:PG
Australian; Peter Weir — *Warner Home Video*

Last Word, The **1980**
Comedy-Drama
69546 103 mins C B, V, CED P
Richard Harris, Karen Black, Martin Landau, Dennis Christopher
A man fights to protect his home, family and neighbors from a corrupt real estate deal involving shady politicians, angry policemen, and a beautiful television reporter.
MPAA:PG
Richard G Abramson; Michael Varhol — *Embassy Home Entertainment*

Late Show, The **1977**
Mystery/Comedy
51964 94 mins C B, V R, P
Art Carney, Lily Tomlin, Bill Macy, Eugene Roche, Joanna Cassidy, John Considine
A veteran private detective finds his world turned upside down when a former colleague arrives to visit nearly dead, and a woman whose cat is missing becomes his sidekick.
MPAA:PG
Warner Bros; Robert Altman — *Warner Home Video*

Laughfest **191?**
Comedy
10098 59 mins B/W B, V P, T
Ben Turpin, Barney Oldfield, Mabel Normand, Charlie Chaplin, Snub Pollard
Five classic slapstick shorts are included on this tape: "It's a Gift" (1923), with Snub Pollard, "Barney Oldfield's Race for a Life" (1913), "Kid Auto Races" and "Busy Day" (1914), both with Charlie Chaplin, and "Daredevil" (1923), starring Ben Turpin.
Mack Sennett et al — *Blackhawk Films*

Laughs for Sale **1963**
Comedy/Game show
78095 29 mins B/W B, V, FO P
Hal March, Cliff Arquette, Shecky Greene, Paul Winchell, Jerry Mahoney
A comedy game show with short skits and funny one-liners.
ABC — *Video Yesteryear*

Laura **1944**
Mystery/Crime-Drama
56463 85 mins B/W B, V P
Gene Tierney, Clifton Webb, Dana Andrews, Vincent Price, directed by Otto Preminger
A detective assigned to the murder investigation of the late Laura Hunt finds himself falling in love with her painted portrait.
Academy Awards '44: Best Cinematography.

Twentieth Century Fox — *CBS/Fox Video*

Laura **1979**
Drama/Romance
65433 95 mins C B, V P
Maud Adams, Dawn Dunlap
A journey through beauty, sensuality and innocence revolving around a 16 year old ballet dancer's first stirrings of sexuality.
MPAA:R
20th Century Fox — *Embassy Home Entertainment*

Laurel and Hardy Comedy Classics Volume I **1933**
Comedy
33910 84 mins B/W B, V, 3/4U P
Stan Laurel, Oliver Hardy, Mae Busch, May Wallace, Charlie Hall, Billy Gilbert
A collection of four classic comedy shorts starring Laurel and Hardy: "The Music Box," which won an Academy Award for Best Short Subject, "Country Hospital," "The Live Ghost," and "Twice Twos," all from 1932-33.
Hal Roach, MGM — *Nostalgia Merchant*

Laurel and Hardy Comedy Classics Volume II **1930**
Comedy
33911 75 mins B/W B, V, 3/4U P
Stan Laurel, Oliver Hardy, Billy Gilbert, Tiny Sandford, Anita Garvin
A collection of four Laurel and Hardy shorts from 1930 including "Blotto," "Towed in a Hole," "Brats," and "Hog Wild."
Hal Roach, MGM — *Nostalgia Merchant*

Laurel and Hardy Comedy Classics Volume III **1934**
Comedy
33912 75 mins B/W B, V, 3/4U P
Stan Laurel, Oliver Hardy, Billy Gilbert, Mae Busch, Tiny Sandford
Laurel and Hardy star in four separate comedy shorts, including "Oliver the 8th," "Busy Bodies," "Their First Mistake," and "Dirty Work," all from 1933-34.
Hal Roach, MGM — *Nostalgia Merchant*

Laurel and Hardy Comedy Classics Volume IV **1932**
Comedy
33913 75 mins B/W B, V, 3/4U P
Stan Laurel, Oliver Hardy, Jacqueline Wells, James Finlayson, Thelma Todd
Laurel and Hardy star in four of their comedy shorts from 1931-32. Included are "Another Fine Mess," "Come Clean," "Laughing Gravy," and "Any Old Part."
Hal Roach, MGM — *Nostalgia Merchant*

Laurel and Hardy Comedy Classics Volume V **1931**
Comedy
33914 84 mins B/W B, V, 3/4U P
Stan Laurel, Oliver Hardy, Edgar Kennedy, James Finlayson, Blanche Payson
Four classic comedy shorts starring Laurel and Hardy. Included are "Be Big," "The Perfect Day," "Night Owls," and "Help Mates," from 1929-31.
Hal Roach, MGM — *Nostalgia Merchant*

Laurel and Hardy Comedy Classics Volume VI **1935**
Comedy
33915 75 mins B/W B, V, 3/4U P
Stan Laurel, Oliver Hardy, Charlie Hall, Billy Gilbert, Ben Turpin, Mae Busch, James Finlayson
Laurel and Hardy comedy shorts are presented in this package: "Our Wife," "The Fixer Uppers," "Them Thar Hills," and "Tit for Tat," from 1932-35.
Hal Roach, MGM — *Nostalgia Merchant*

Laurel and Hardy Comedy Classics Volume VII **193?**
Comedy
47142 90 mins B/W B, V, 3/4U P
Stan Laurel, Oliver Hardy, Mae Busch, Daphne Pollard, James Finlayson
Four Laurel and Hardy two-reelers are combined on this tape: "Me and My Pal" (1933), "The Midnight Patrol" (1933), "Thicker than Water" (1935), and the classic "Below Zero" (1930).
Hal Roach; MGM — *Nostalgia Merchant*

Laurel and Hardy Comedy Classics Volume VIII **193?**
Comedy
59153 90 mins B/W B, V, 3/4U P
Stan Laurel, Oliver Hardy
This compilation of Laurel and Hardy shorts includes: "Men O' War" (1929), "Scram" (1932), "Laurel and Hardy Murder Case" (1930) and "One Good Turn" (1931).
Hal Roach — *Nostalgia Merchant*

Laurel and Hardy Comedy Classics Volume IX **193?**
Comedy
60422 100 mins B/W B, V, 3/4U P

Stan Laurel, Oliver Hardy
Includes the shorts; "Beau Hunks" (1931), "Chickens Come Home" (1931), "Going Bye-Bye" (1934), and "Berth Marks" (1929).
Hal Roach — *Nostalgia Merchant*

Laurel and Hardy Volume 1 196?
Cartoons
47655 59 mins C B, V P
Animated
Animated adventures of Laurel and Hardy.
EL, SP
Larry Harmon — *Unicorn Video*

Laurel and Hardy Volume 2 196?
Cartoons
47656 59 mins C B, V P
Animated
Animated short cartoons starring Laurel and Hardy.
EL, SP
Larry Harmon — *Unicorn Video*

Laurel and Hardy Volume 3 196?
Cartoons
47657 59 mins C B, V P
Animated
More animated adventures of Laurel and Hardy.
EL, SP
Larry Harmon — *Unicorn Video*

Laurel and Hardy Volume 4 196?
Cartoons
47658 59 mins C B, V P
Animated
Animated shorts starring cartoon characters of Laurel and Hardy.
EL, SP
Larry Harmon — *Unicorn Video*

Lavender Hill Mob, The 1951
Comedy
50942 78 mins B/W B, V R, P
Alec Guinness, Audrey Hepburn, Stanley Holloway
A prim and prissy bank clerk schemes to melt the bank's gold down and re-mold it into miniature Eiffel Tower paperweights.
Academy Award '52: Best Story and Screenplay (T.E.B. Clarke).
Universal; J Arthur Rank — *THORN EMI/HBO Video*

Law West of Tombstone 1938
Western
64415 73 mins B/W B, V, 3/4U P
Tim Holt, Harry Carey, Evelyn Brent
An ex-outlaw moves to a dangerous frontier town in order to clean things up.
RKO — *Nostalgia Merchant*

Lawless Frontier 1935
Western
58972 53 mins B/W B, V, 3/4U P
John Wayne, Gabby Hayes
In the early West, the Duke fights for law and order.
Monogram — *Sony Corporation of America; Cable Films; Video Connection; Discount Video Tapes; Spotlite Video*

Lawless Range 1935
Western
51637 56 mins B/W B, V P
John Wayne, Sheila Manners
John Wayne and the marshall's posse save the ranchers from trouble.
Republic — *Spotlite Video; Discount Video Tapes*

Lawless RAnge/The Man From Utah 1935
Western
81019 109 mins B/W B, V P
John Wayne, Sheila Manners, Gabby Hayes
This is an action packed western double feature: In "Lawless Range" the Duke and the marshall's aides save a ranch from falling into the wrong hands, and in "The Man From Utah" the Duke upholds law and order in the old West.
Monogram Pictures — *Spotlite Video*

Lawrence of Arabia 1962
Drama
68260 221 mins C B, V P
Peter O'Toole, Omar Sharif, Alec Guinness, Anthony Quinn
The true life story of T.E. Lawrence, the English officer who gained fame in the Middle East during World War I. In stereo.
Academy Awards '62: Best Picture, Best Director (Lean) Best Cinematography, Original Score (Maurice Jarre) MPAA:G
Sam Spiegel; Columbia — *RCA/Columbia Pictures Home Video; RCA VideoDiscs*

Lawrence Welk Show, The 1957
Television/Music
63625 60 mins B/W B, V, FO P
Lawrence Welk and his Orchestra, Alice Lon, The Lennon Sisters, Big Tiny Little Jr.
Originally telecast in March 1957, this show features Welk performing a rare accordion solo and dancing a polka with 10-year-old Peggy Lennon. Contains original commercials for the tail-finned 1957 Dodge.
ABC — *Video Yesteryear*

Lazarus Syndrome, The **1979**
Drama
65303 90 mins C B, V P
Lou Gossett Jr.
This is a hard-hitting film of a doctor's effort to expose illicit operating practices of the resident Chief of surgery.
Viacom Enterprises — *U.S.A. Home Video*

LCA Presents Family Entertainment Playhouse **197?**
Drama/Mystery
56883 120 mins C CED P
Geraldine Fitzgerald
Edgar Allan Poe's "The Gold Bug" pits an adventurous teenager against quicksand, a terrifying storm, and Captain Kidd's curse. "Rodeo Red" stars Geraldine Fitzgerald as a farm woman who teaches a runaway girl about facing her own problems.
Unknown — *RCA VideoDiscs*

Learn to Play for Beginners **1985**
Music
80476 120 mins C B, V R, P
Narrated by Richard Baker 12 pgms
This series is the first video instrumental method, offering an alternative or supplement to private lessons and self-instruction books. Music students will find all the basic instruction they need to know for each instrument.
1.Piano 2.Trumpet/Cornet 3.Clarinet 4.Saxophone 5.Tenor Saxophone 6.Trombone 7.Flute 8.Violin 9.Viola 10.Oboe 11.Bassoon 12.Tuba
Domestic Video Services Ltd — *The Willis Music Co*

Leather Boys, The **1966**
Drama
79107 103 mins C B, V P
Rita Tushingham, Dudley Sutton, Collin Campbell, directed by Sidney J. Furie
A teenaged girl marries a mechanic and then begins to cheat on him.
Allied Artists — *VidAmerica*

Leave 'Em Laughing **1981**
Biographical/Drama
80637 103 mins C B, V P
Mickey Rooney, Anne Jackson, Allen Goorwitz, Red Buttons, Elisha Cook, William Windom, directed by Jackie Cooper
This is the true story of a Chicago clown and his wife who cared for dozens of homeless children as he struggled from job to job. Available in Beta Hi-Fi and VHS Stereo.
Julian Fowles Prods; Charles Fries Prods. — *U.S.A. Home Video*

Leben von Adolf Hitler, Das (The Life of Adolf Hitler) **1961**
Documentary/World War II
47472 101 mins B/W B, V, FO P
Directed by Paul Rotha
A startling West German documentary feature on the life of Hitler, using much never-before-seen archival footage of Hitler's early life and rise to power. The full twelve-year span of the Third Reich is covered in painstaking detail.
West Germany — *Video Yesteryear*

Left Hand of God, The **1955**
Drama
73968 87 mins C B, V P
Humphrey Bogart, E.G. Marshall, Lee J. Cobb, Agnes Moorehead, directed by Edward Dmytryk
After a pilot escapes from a Chinese warlord, he disguises himself as a Catholic priest and takes refuge in a missionary hospital.
20th Century Fox — *Key Video*

Legacy of Horror **1978**
Horror/Suspense
70579 83 mins C B, V P
Elaine Boies, Chris Broderick, Marilee Troncone, Jeannie Cusik, directed by Andy Milligan
A weekend at the family's island mansion with two unfriendly siblings sounds bad enough, but when terror, death and a few family skeletons pop out of the closets, things go from bad to weird.
Ken Lane Films; Take One Film Group — *MPI Home Video*

Legend of Alfred Packer, The **1980**
Documentary/Drama
80214 87 mins C B, V P
Patrick Dray, Ron Haines, Bob Damon, Dave Ellingson
The true story of how a guide taking five men searching for gold in Colorado managed to be the sole survivor of a blizzard.
Mark Webb Productions — *Monterey Home Video*

Legend of Hiawatha, The **1982**
Cartoons
72452 35 mins C B, V P
Hiawatha must confront a demon who casts a plague on his people. This animated program is based on Henry Wadsworth Longfellow's poem.
Unknown — *Family Home Entertainment*

Legend of Sleepy Hollow, The **1949**
Cartoons/Adventure
59808 45 mins C B, V R, P
Narrated by Bing Crosby

The story of Ichabod Crane and the legendary ride of the headless horseman. Also includes two classic short cartoons, "Lonesome Ghosts" (1932) with Mickey Mouse and "Trick or Treat" (1952) with Donald Duck.
Walt Disney — *Walt Disney Home Video*

Legend of Sleepy Hollow, The 1979
Drama
37363 100 mins C B, V P
Washington Irving's classic tale of the Headless Horseman of Sleepy Hollow is brought to life on the screen.
Sunn Classic — *United Home Video*

Legend of the Lightning Bolt, The 1984
Football
79633 30 mins C B, V, FO P
This is a chronological history of the San Diego Chargers.
NFL Films — *NFL Films Video*

Legend of the Lone Ranger, The 1981
Western
47153 98 mins C B, V, CED P
Klinton Spilsbury, Michael Horse, Jason Robards
The origin of the fabled Lone Ranger and the story of his first meeting with his Indian companion, Tonto, are brought to life in this new version of the famous legend.
MPAA:PG
Universal; Walter Coblenz — *CBS/Fox Video*

Legend of the Northwest 1978
Adventure
51657 83 mins C B, V R, P
Denver Pyle
The loyalty of a dog is evidenced in the fierce revenge he has for the drunken hunter who shot and killed his master.
MPAA:G
GG Communications — *Video Gems*

Legend of the Northwest 1978
Adventure
80793 83 mins C B, V R, P
This is the story of Bearheart, a loyal dog who is out to avenge the death of his master.
G.G. Communications — *Video Gems*

Legend of the Werewolf 1975
Horror
58283 90 mins C B, V P
Peter Cushing, Hugh Griffith, Ron Moody
A child who once ran with the wolves has forgotten his past, except when the moon is full.
MPAA:R
Kevin Francis; Tyburn Studios — *VCL Home Video; Electric Video*

Legend of the Wolfwoman 1977
Horror
48328 84 mins C B, V P
Anne Borel, Fred Stafford
The beautiful Daniella assumes the personality of the legendary wolfwoman, leaving a trail of gruesome killings across the countryside.
MPAA:R
Dimension Pictures — *United Home Video; Continental Video*

Legend of Valentino, The 1983
Documentary/Biographical
74086 71 mins B/W B, V P
This is a biographical documentary of perhaps the world's greatest lover beginning with his immigration to America and ending at his unexpected, sudden death.
Wolper Productions — *Embassy Home Entertainment*

Legend of Young Robin Hood, The 197?
Drama
50963 60 mins C B, V R, P
The early life of the robber of the rich is depicted in this movie. He learns to use a longbow, and forms his convictions as he and other Saxons struggle at their integration into the Norman culture.
MPAA:G
Michael Christian Productions — *Video Gems*

Legendary Greats 1960
Baseball
49552 30 mins B/W B, V P
Men who left an everlasting mark on the game of baseball are profiled. Included are Hall of Famers Christy Mathewson, Babe Ruth, Ty Cobb, Connie Mack, and nine distinguished others.
Major League Baseball — *Major League Baseball Productions*

Legendary Personalities 193?
Film-History
10156 60 mins B/W B, V P, T
Package offers serious and light side of pre-40's years. Newsreel cameras film celebrities like Haile Selassie, George Bernard Shaw, and Sir Arthur Conan Doyle.
Unknown — *Blackhawk Films*

Legion of Missing Men, The 1937
War-Drama
59372 62 mins B/W B, V, FO P
Ralph Forbes, Ben Alexander, Hala Linda

 (For explanation of codes, see USE GUIDE and KEY)

Professional soldiers of fortune, the French Foreign Legion, fight the evil sheik Ahmed in the Sahara.
Unknown — *Video Yesteryear*

Legion of the Lawless **1940**
Western
64412 59 mins B/W B, V, 3/4U P
George O'Brien, Virginia Vale
A group of outlaws band together in order to spread terror and confusion among the populace.
RKO — *Nostalgia Merchant*

Lena Horne: The Lady and Her Music **1984**
Music-Performance
69922 134 mins C B, V P
Lena Horne's definitive Broadway performance of all the music she has been identified with during her career includes "Can't Help Lovin' That Man," "Stormy Weather," and "The Lady Is a Tramp." In VHS Dolby stereo and Beta Hi-Fi.
James Nederlander, Michael Frazier et al — *RKO HomeVideo*

Lenny Bruce **1967**
Comedy-Performance
10815 60 mins B/W B, V, FO P
Lenny Bruce
An uncensored San Francisco nightclub performance recording Bruce's off-beat, bewitching, and often unprecedented humor.
Filmmakers — *Video Yesteryear*

Lenny Bruce Performance Film, The **1968**
Comedy-Performance
58897 72 mins B/W B, V, CED P
Lenny Bruce
A videotape of one of Lenny Bruce's last nightclub appearances at Basin Street West in San Francisco. Also included is "Thank You Mask Man," a color cartoon parody of the Lone Ranger legend, with Lenny Bruce providing all the character voices.
Columbus Prods — *Vestron Video*

Leonor **1975**
Drama
37403 90 mins C B, V P
Liv Ullman
Liv Ullman demonstrates her versatility as an actress in this movie, in which she plays the mistress of the Devil.
France — *CBS/Fox Video*

Leopard in the Snow **1978**
Drama
72880 89 mins C B, V P
Keir Dullea, Susan Penhaligon, Kenneth More, Billie Whitelaw
The romance between a race car driver allegedly killed in a crash and a young woman is the premise of this film.
MPAA:PG
Harlequin Productions — *Embassy Home Entertainment*

Leopard Man, The **1943**
Horror
00314 66 mins B/W B, V, 3/4U P
Dennis O'Keefe, Margo, Rita Corday
An escaped leopard terrorizes a small town. After a search, the big cat is found dead, but the killings continue.
RKO — *Nostalgia Merchant*

Lepke **1975**
Drama
80442 110 mins C B, V R, P
Tony Curtis, Milton Berle, Gianni Russo, Vic Tayback, Michael Callan
The life and fast times of Louis "Lepke" Buchalter from his days in reform school to his days as head of Murder, Inc and his execution in 1944.
MPAA:R
Warner Bros; Menahem Golan — *Warner Home Video*

Let It Be **1970**
Musical
55586 80 mins C B, V, LV P
John Lennon, Paul McCartney, George Harrison, Ringo Starr, Billy Preston, Yoko Ono
A documentary look at a Beatles recording session, giving glimpses of the conflicts which led to the breakup.
United Artists — *CBS/Fox Video; RCA VideoDiscs*

Let the Balloon Go **1976**
Drama
64790 92 mins C B, V P
Robert Bettles, Sally Whiteman, Matthew Wilson, Terry McQuillan
Based on the international children's bestseller by Australian author Ivan Southall, the story is set in the year 1917 and centers around the plight of a slightly handicapped boy and his struggle to win respect.
MPAA:G
Film Australia — *MCA Home Video*

Let's Do It Again **1975**
Comedy
53515 112 mins C B, V R, P
Sidney Poitier, Bill Cosby, John Amos, Jimmie Walker, Ossie Davis, Denise Nicholas, Calvin Lockhart
An Atlanta milkman and his pal, a factory worker, bilk two big-time gamblers out of a large

sum of money in order to build a meeting hall for their fraternal lodge. A sequel to "Uptown Saturday Night."
MPAA:PG
Warner Bros; First Artists Film — *Warner Home Video*

Let's Break: A Visual Guide to Break Dancing 1984
Dance
70074 60 mins C B, V P
An instructional guide to breakdancing featuring New York City dancers showing off basic moves to the original music of Dennis McCarthy and Jim Cox.
Image Magnetic Associates Inc — *Warner Home Video*

Let's Dance with Arthur Murray 1980
Dance
56943 115 mins C B, V P
This instructional program features dance steps from the world-famous Arthur Murray technique, including basic ballroom etiquette, the waltz, the cha cha, the foxtrot, the samba, the rumba, and two types of disco.
Time-Life Video — *Vestron Video; Time Life Video*

Let's Go to the Zoo with Captain Kangaroo 1985
Animals
81534 58 mins C B, V P
Captain Kangaroo and Mr. Greenjeans visit some of America's greatest zoos such as Busch Gardens and the San Diego Zoo.
Jim Hirschfeld — *MPI Home Video*

Let's Go to the Zoo with Captain Kangaroo 1985
Children
70590 60 mins C B, V P
Bob Keeshan
Composed of short clips from the Captain's Library of shows, this program features segments introducing youngsters to many great zoo beasts.
Encyclopedia Britannica Educational Corporation — *MPI Home Video*

Let's Jazzercise 1983
Physical fitness/Dance
65206 57 mins C B, V P
Judi Sheppard Missett
This program includes a warm up aerobic activity and muscle toning and is completed by a cool down routine.
Priscilla Ulene; Judi Sheppard Missett — *MCA Home Video*

Let's Spend the Night Together 1983
Music-Performance
66040 94 mins C B, V, LV, CED P
Rolling Stones, directed by Hal Ashby
A chronicle of the Stones' 1981 American tour including 25 songs spanning their career. Stereo.
MPAA:PG
Ronald Schwary — *Embassy Home Entertainment*

Letter, The 1940
Drama/Suspense
73971 96 mins B/W B, V P
Bette Davis, Herbert Marshall, Gale Sondergaard, directed by William Wyler
A letter is used to blackmail a plantation owner's wife who seems to have murdered a man in self defense. Based on the play by Somerset Maugham.
Warner Bros — *Key Video*

Liana 1983
Drama
65383 110 mins C B, V P
Acclaimed screenwriter/director John Sayles wrote and directed this story of a woman's romantic involvement with another woman.
MPAA:R
Jeffrey Nelson — *Vestron Video*

Liar's Moon 1982
Drama
64877 106 mins C B, V, CED P
Matt Dillon
A local boy woos and weds the town's wealthiest young lady, only to be trapped in a family's intrigue.
MPAA:PG
Don P Behrns — *Vestron Video*

Liberace in Las Vegas 1980
Music-Performance
47377 84 mins C B, V R, P
Liberace, the Jimmy Mullander Orchestra, the Ballet Folklorico de Nacionale de Mexico
A musical extravaganza starring the multitalented Liberace and his special guests. Taped at the Las Vegas Hilton.
VC — *Warner Home Video*

Liberace Show Volumes 1 & 2, The 195?
Musical/Variety
60423 58 mins B/W B, V, 3/4U P
A camp classic, these two half-hour episodes of "Mr. Showmanship's" TV series feature some of the world's best-loved music.
NBC — *Nostalgia Merchant*

Liberation of L.B. Jones, The 1970
Drama
80373 101 mins C B, V P
Lee J. Cobb, Lola Falana, Anthony Zerbe, Roscoe Lee Browne, directed by William Wyler
A wealthy black undertaker wants a divorce from his wife who is having an affair with a white policeman.
MPAA:R
Columbia Pictures — *RCA/Columbia Pictures Home Video*

Lidsville, Volume I 1971
Adventure
76791 46 mins C B, V P
Charles Nelson Reilly, Billie Hayes, Butch Patrick
When a young boy falls into an enlarged magician's hat he lands in Lidsville, a village inhabited by living hats.
Sid and Marty Krofft — *Embassy Home Entertainment*

Life and Assassination of the Kingfish, The 1976
Biographical/Drama
81263 96 mins C B, V P
Edward Asner, Nicholas Pryor, Diane Kagan, Fred Cook, Gary Allen
This is the colorful life story of the Louisiana Governor and U.S. Senator, Huey P. Long.
Tomorrow Entertainment — *U.S.A. Home Video*

Life and Death of Colonel Blimp, The 1943
War-Drama
80933 115 mins C B, V P
Roger Livesey, Deborah Kerr, Anton Walbrook, Ursula Jeans, Albert Lieven, directed by Michael Powell
This film chronicles the life of a British soldier who survives three wars, falls in love with three women, and waltzes.
J. Arthur Rank — *VidAmerica*

Life and Times of Grizzly Adams, The 1974
Adventure
13007 93 mins C B, V P
Dan Haggerty, Denver Pyle, Don Shanks
This adventure film for the whole family is based on the rugged life of legendary frontiersman, Grizzly Adams.
MPAA:G
Sunn Classic — *United Home Video*

Life and Times of Judge Roy Bean, The 1972
Western/Comedy
68235 123 mins C B, V R, P
Paul Newman, Stacy Keach, Ava Gardner, Jacqueline Bisset, Anthony Perkins, Roddy McDowell, Victoria Principal, dir: by John Huston
Frontier justice and gallows humor abounds in this telling of the judge Roy Bean legend. The film is based on the life of the famed Texas hanging judge.
MPAA:PG
National General — *Warner Home Video*

Life Is a Circus, Charlie Brown! 1980
Cartoons
75607 30 mins C B, V P
Animated
Snoopy joins the traveling circus to be close to the dog of his dreams, Fifi, a French Poodle performer.
Bill Melendez — *Snoopy's Home Video Library*

Life Is Worth Living 1955
Religion
47481 71 mins B/W B, V, FO P
Bishop Fulton J. Sheen
Three programs from Bishop Sheen's long-running TV series, one of the most popular shows of the 1950's. The Bishop discussed religious matters, family life, read poetry and told jokes in an engagingly informal manner that was loved by audiences.
Dumont — *Video Yesteryear*

Life on Emile Zola, The 1937
Drama/Biographical
73976 117 mins B/W B, V P
Paul Muni, Gale Sondergaard, Gloria Holden
Writer Emile Zola invervenes in the case of Alfred Dreyfus who was sent to Devil's Island for a crime he did not commit.
Academy Awards '37: Best Picture; Best Screenplay.
Warner Bros — *Key Video*

Life of Oharu 1952
Drama
69561 136 mins B/W B, V, FO P
Kinuyo Tanaka, Toshiro Mifune, directed by Kenji Mizoguchi
Oharu, the beautiful daughter of a samurai who serves the Imperial Court, falls in love with a lower class servant. When they are caught together, the slave is executed and Oharu is banished from the kingdom. Japanese dialogue with English subtitles.
Japan — *Video Yesteryear*

Life with Father 1947
Comedy
11305 118 mins C B, V, FO P
William Powell, Irene Dunne, Elizabeth Taylor, Edmund Gwenn, Zasu Pitts
New York City of the 1880's is the delightful setting for this story of a stern but susceptible

father and his relationship with his knowing wife and four red-headed sons.
New York Film Critics Award '47: Best Male Performance (Powell).
Warner Bros; Robert Buckner — *Hal Roach Studios; Video Yesteryear; Budget Video; Video Connection; Sheik Video; Discount Video Tapes; Cinema Concepts; King of Video; See Hear Industries*

Lifeboat **1944**
Drama
Closed Captioned
80734 96 mins B/W B, V P
Tallulah Bankhead, John Hodiak, William Bendix, Canada Lee, Walter Slezak, Hume Cronyn, Henry Hull, Mary Anderson, directed by Alfred Hitchcock
When a freighter is sunk by a German U-boat, the eight survivors and the Nazi commander take refuge in a tiny lifeboat.
20th Century Fox — *Key Video*

Light at the Edge of the World, The **1971**
Adventure
72905 126 mins C B, V P
Kirk Douglas, Yul Brynner, Samantha Eggar
A lighthouse keeper near Cape Horn is tormented by a band of pirates.
MPAA:PG
Brynafilm; Triumfilm — *Media Home Entertainment*

Like a Mighty River... **1981**
Football
50648 24 mins C B, V, FO R, P
Dallas Cowboys
Danny White stepped into Roger Staubach's role as Cowboy quarterback drawing much praise. Although the defense was weak at times during the 1980 season, it toughened when it had to. The Cowboys, under the guidance of the ever-present Tom Landry, surged all the way to the NFC championship game, where they finally ran out of gas.
NFL Films — *NFL Films Video*

Likely Stories, Volume I **1981**
Comedy-Performance
80903 57 mins C B, V P
Richard Belzer, Christopher Guest, Rob Reiner, Marcia Strassman, David L. Lander, Michael McKean
A group of top comedians get together to tell their favorite jokes. Available in VHS Stereo and Beta Hi-Fi.
David Jablin — *U.S.A. Home Video*

Likely Stories, Volume II **1985**
Comedy-Performance
81256 59 mins C B, V P
Danny De Vito, John Rourke, Pee Wee Herman, Patrick MacNee, Rhea Perlman
This volume features Danny De Vito as a New Jersey politician and Pee Wee Herman satirizing a 1950's do's and dont's film. Available in VHS Stereo and Beta Hi-Fi.
David Jablin — *U.S.A. Home Video*

Li'l Abner **1940**
Musical
08730 78 mins C B, V P
Cranville Owen, Martha Driscoll, Buster Keaton
Al Capp's famed comic strip comes to life in this comedy, featuring all of the Dogpatch favorites.
RKO — *Discount Video Tapes; Sheik Video; Video Yesteryear; See Hear Industries*

Lili **1953**
Musical
66454 81 mins C B, V P
Leslie Caron, Jean-Pierre Aumont, Mel Ferrer, Kurt Kasznar, Zsa Zsa Gabor
A 16-year-old orphan joins a traveling carnival and falls in love with a crippled, embittered puppeteer. Leslie Caron sings the films's song hit, "Hi-Lili, Hi-Lo."
Academy Awards '53: Best Scoring of a Dramatic or Comedy Film (Bronislau Kaper).
MGM — *MGM/UA Home Video*

Lilies of the Field **1963**
Drama
70376 94 mins B/W B, V P
Sidney Poitier, Lilia Skala, Lisa Mann, Isa Crino, Stanley Adams, directed by Ralph Nelson
Five Eastern European refugee nuns enlist the aid of a free-spirited US Army veteran. The ex-GI, apprehensive throughout, is amusingly convinced to build a chapel and teach the sisters English.
Academy Award '63: Best Actor (Sidney Poitier).
U.A.; Rainbow Prods. — *Key Video*

Lilith **1964**
Drama
70562 114 mins B/W B, V P
Warren Beatty, Jean Seberg, Peter Fonda, Kim Hunter, directed by Robert Rossen
Beatty stars as a therapist who falls for one of the patients (Seberg) at the swank mental institution where he works. Available in Beta Hi-Fi.
Columbia — *RCA/Columbia Pictures Home Video*

Lily Tomlin Special: Volume I **1973**
Comedy/Variety
70180 45 mins C B, V P
Lily Tomlin, Richard Pryor
Lily's first award-winning television special features her entire repertoire of characters including Ernestine, the telephone operator,

five-year old Edith Ann, Mrs. Beasley, Suzie Sorority and the Shopping Bag Lady.
Emmy Awards '73: Best Special Program; Best Writing.
LIJA Productions — *Karl/Lorimar Home Video*

Limelight 1952
Drama
48406 144 mins B/W B, V P
Charles Chaplin, Claire Bloom, Buster Keaton, Nigel Bruce
A nearly washed-up music hall comedian is stimulated by a young ballerina to a final hour of glory.
Charles Chaplin — *CBS/Fox Video; Playhouse Video*

Limited Gold Edition II Cartoon Classics 1985
Cartoons
70559 50 mins C B, V P
Mickey Mouse, Donald Duck, Minnie Mouse, Pluto, Goofy, Jack Hannah, Jack Kinney.
7 pgms
Disney Studios compiled these collections from previously unreleased material and added interviews with the creators of some of these cartoons. Favorites and award winners highlight these limited edition specials.
1.Life with Mickey!; 2.From Pluto With Love; 3.An Officer and a Duck; 4.The World According to Goofy; 5.How the West Was Won: 1933-1960; 6.The Disney Dream Factory: 1933-1938; 7.Donald's Bee Pictures
Walt Disney Productions — *Walt Disney Home Video*

Lincoln Conspiracy, The 1977
Documentary
55596 87 mins C B, V P
This film uncovers startling new evidence, and concludes that high-level cabinet members conspired to assassinate President Lincoln.
MPAA:G
Sunn Classics — *VidAmerica*

Linda Ronstadt—Nelson Riddle "What's New" 1984
Music-Performance
72916 60 mins C B, V, LV, CED P
Linda Ronstadt performs great songs of the 1930s and '40s in concert with Nelson Riddle and His Orchestra.
Peter Asher — *Vestron Video*

Line, The 197?
Drama
79190 96 mins C B, V P
Russ Thacker, David Doyle
A group of soldiers mutiny against the Army because of the cruel treatment inflicted upon them during basic training.
MPAA:R
Robert J. Siegel; Virginia Largent — *U.S.A. Home Video*

Lion Has Wings, The 1940
War-Drama
81463 75 mins B/W B, V, LV P
Merle Oberon, Ralph Richardson, Flora Robson, June Duprez, directed by Michael Powell and Brian Desmond Hurst
This is the story of how Britain's Air Defense was set up to meet the challenge of Hitler's Luftwaffe during their "finest hours."
United Artist; Alexander Korda — *Embassy Home Entertainment*

Lion in Winter, The 1968
Drama
08367 134 mins C B, V, LV, CED P
Peter O'Toole, Katharine Hepburn, directed by Anthony Harvey
Katharine Hepburn portrays Eleanor of Aquitaine in this historical drama of twelfth-century English political history.
Academy Awards '68: Best Actress (Hepburn).
Avco Embassy — *Embassy Home Entertainment; RCA VideoDiscs*

Lion of the Desert 1979
Drama
65447 164 mins C B, V P
Anthony Quinn, Oliver Reed, Irene Papas, Rod Steiger, Raf Vallone, John Gielgud
This is the story of Omar Mukhtar, the great Libyan patriot whose twenty year long struggle to free his people from the yoke of Mussolini's Italian occupying forces became one of the most heroic sagas of the twentieth century.
MPAA:PG
Falcon International — *U.S.A. Home Video*

Lion, the Witch and the Wardrobe, The 1979
Fantasy/Cartoons
77187 100 mins C B, V, CED P
Animated
Four children stumble through an old wardrobe closet in an ancient country house and into the fantasy land of Narnia. Adapted from C.S. Lewis' "The Chronicles of Narnia."
Children's Television Workshop — *Vestron Video*

Lionel Hampton 1983
Music-Performance
75915 24 mins C B, V P
This program presents the jazz music of Lionel Hampton backed up by a 20-piece band.
digit recordings — *Sony Corporation of America*

Lipstick 1976
Drama
38935 88 mins C B, V, LV R, P
Margaux Hemingway, Anne Bancroft, Perry King, Chris Sarandon, Mariel Hemingway
A fashion model (Margaux Hemingway) seeks revenge on the man who brutally attacked and raped her.
MPAA:R
Paramount — *Paramount Home Video*

Liquid Sky 1983
Science fiction
65114 112 mins C B, V P
Anne Carlisle, Paula Sheppard, Bob Brady
An androgynous model living in Manhattan is the primary attraction for a UFO, which lands atop her penthouse in search of the chemical nourishment that her sexual encounters provide.
MPAA:R
Slava Tsukerman — *Media Home Entertainment*

List of Adrian Messenger, The 1963
Mystery
76806 98 mins B/W B, V P
Kirk Douglas, George C. Scott, Robert Mitchum, Dana Wynter, Burt Lancaster, Frank Sinatra, directed by John Huston
A crafty murderer resorts to a variety of disguises to eliminate potential heirs to a family fortune.
Kirk Douglas; Edward Lewis — *MCA Home Video*

Listen to Your Heart 1983
Drama
76046 90 mins C B, V P
Tim Matheson, Kate Jackson
In a contemporary love story, Tim Matheson and Kate Jackson find the strength of their relationship put to the test when they try to work together as well as love together.
CBS Motion Pictures for Television — *Key Video*

Lisztomania 1975
Fantasy
53516 105 mins C B, V R, P
Roger Daltry, Sara Kestelman, Paul Nicholas, Fiona Lewis, Ringo Starr, directed by Ken Russell
Ken Russell's vision of what it must have been like to be Franz Liszt and Richard Wagner, who are depicted as the first pop stars.
MPAA:R
Warner Bros — *Warner Home Video*

Little Annie Roonie 1925
Drama
10125 60 mins B/W B, V P, T
Mary Pickford, William Haines, Walter James, Gordon Griffith, Vola Vale, directed by William Beaudine
Tomboy policeman's daughter spends her time mothering her father and brother while getting into mischief with street punks. Tragedy ensues. (Silent).
Pickford — *Blackhawk Films*

Little Brown Burro, The 1979
Christmas/Cartoons
17270 23 mins C B, V, 3/4U R, P
Animated, narrated by Lorne Greene
Forlorn donkey realizes that by doing his best he can make his own kind of contribution.
AM Available EL, JA
Learning Corp of America — *Embassy Home Entertainment*

Little Caesar 1930
Crime-Drama
64457 80 mins B/W B, V, CED P
Edward G. Robinson, Douglas Fairbanks, Jr.
A small-time hood rises to become a gangland czar but his downfall is as rapid as his advancement. The role of Rico made Edward G. Robinson a star and also typecast him as a crook for all time.
Warner Bros — *CBS/Fox Video; RCA VideoDiscs*

Little Darlings 1980
Comedy
48511 95 mins C B, V, LV R, P
Tatum O'Neal, Kristy McNichol, directed by Ronald F. Maxwell
A summer camp full of fun, friendship, and rivalries is the setting for a race—between a pair of very opposite teenage girls—to lose their virginity.
MPAA:R
Stephen J. Friedman — *Paramount Home Video*

Little Dragons, The 1980
Martial arts
79343 90 mins C B, V P
Anne Sothern, Joe Spinell, Charles Lane
A grandfather and two young karate students rescue a family held captive by a backwoods gang.
Tony Bill — *Active Home Video*

Little Drummer Girl, The 1984
Suspense/Drama
Closed Captioned
76852 130 mins C B, V, LV R, P
Diane Keaton, Klaus Kinski, Yorgo Voyagis, Sami Frey, Michael Cristofer, directed by George Roy Hill
An actress sympathetic to the Palestinian cause is recruited by an Israeli counter intelligence agent to trap a fanatical terrorist leader.

MPAA:R
Robert L. Crawford; Warner Bros — *Warner Home Video*

Little Engine That Could, The **1963**
Literature
00692 10 mins C B, V P, T
Animated
The classic story about a little train engine that struggles to carry a load of children's toys over a mountain.
Coronet Films — *Blackhawk Films*

Little Girl Who Lives Down the Lane, The **1976**
Suspense
65345 90 mins C B, V P
Jodie Foster, Martin Sheen
A 13-year-old girl, when her father dies, is discovered to be keeping her mother's corpse in the cellar, and doesn't stop at more murders to keep her secret.
MPAA:PG
Harold Greenberg; Alfred Pariser — *Vestron Video*

Little House on the Prairie **1974**
Drama
53790 100 mins C CED P
Michael Landon, Karen Grassle, Melissa Gilbert, Melissa Sue Anderson, Lindsay Sidney Greenbush, Victor French
The original pilot movie for the popular TV series, in which Charles Ingalls uproots his young family for the plains of Kansas.
NBC — *RCA VideoDiscs*

Little House on the Prairie Volume I **1974**
Drama
80158 98 mins C B, V R, P
Michael Landon, Melissa Gilbert, Melissa Sue Anderson, directed by Michael Landon
This series pilot describes the strugglers of Laura Ingalls Wilder's family to survive in the American Wilderness.
Ed Friendly; Michael Landon Productions — *Warner Home Video*

Little House on the Prairie, Volume II **1979**
Drama
80159 98 mins C B, V R, P
Michael Landon, Karen Grassle, Melissa Gilbert, Melissa Sue Anderson, Dean Butler, Victor French
Two episodes from the series: In "The Craftsman" Albert Ingalls finds out about prejudice as a Jewish woodcarver's apprentice, and "The Collection" describes the transformation a con man undergoes when donning a priest's disguise.
Ed Friendly; Michael Landon Productions — *Warner Home Video*

Little House on the Prairie Volume III **1975**
Drama
80160 97 mins C B, V R, P
Michael Landon, Karen Grassle, Melissa Gilbert, Melissa Sue Anderson, Patricia Neal
A terminally ill widow asks Charles Ingalls to help her to find a home for her three children before she dies.
Emmy Award '75: Best Actress (Neal).
Ed Friendly; Michael Landon Productions — *Warner Home Video*

Little Johnny Jones **1980**
Musical
68236 92 mins C B, V R, P
George M. Cohan's classic musical in a 1980 revival. Songs include "Yankee Doodle Dandy" and "Give My Regards to Broadway."
Goodspeed Opera House — *Warner Home Video*

Little Kid's Dynamite All-Star Band, The **1982**
Musical
64955 90 mins C B, V R, P
Marty Brill, Jay Stuart, Willie De Jean, Mischa Bond, Bunky Butler
A children's rock group rehearses in a garage that has an antique brass mirror lying against a wall. The mirror has magical properties that allow two wacky musketeers to join the children in their adventures.
MPAA:G
Century Video — *Video Gems*

Little Laura and Big John **1973**
Adventure
13010 82 mins C B, V P
Fabian Forte, Karen Black
Follows the true-life exploits of the small-time Ashley Gang in turnof-the-century Florida.
Gold Key — *United Home Video*

Little Lord Fauntleroy **1980**
Drama
73534 98 mins C B, V P
Ricky Schroeder, Alec Guinness, directed by Jack Gold
A poor young boy growing up in New York City at the turn of the century suddenly discovers his aristocratic background. Available in Beta Hi-Fi and VHS stereo.
Norman Rosemont Productions — *U.S.A. Home Video*

Little Lulu 194?
Cartoons
56746 48 mins C B, V P
Animated
The popular comic book heroine gets into mischief with her pals, Tubby, Iggie, Wilbur and others. Includes "Little Angel" and "Operation Babysitting." Available in English and Spanish versions.
EL, SP
Paramount; Famous Studios — *Media Home Entertainment*

Little Match Girl, The 1984
Fairy tales/Musical
72882 54 mins C B, V P
A musical version of the Hans Christian Andersen classic.
Unknown — *Embassy Home Entertainment*

Little Men 1940
Drama
08615 86 mins B/W B, V, 3/4U P
Jack Oakie, Jimmy Lydon, Kay Francis, George Bancroft
A modern version of the famous classic juvenile story by Louisa May Alcott.
RKO — *Hal Roach Studios; Video Connection; Kartes Productions*

Little Mermaid, The 1981
Fantasy
72232 75 mins C B, V P
In this animated version of a Hans Christian Andersen fable a princess of the mermaids yearns to be human.
N W Russo — *Children's Video Library*

Little Mermaid, The 1984
Fairy tales
Closed Captioned
73576 60 mins C B, V, CED P
Pam Dawber, Treat Williams
From "Faerie Tale Theatre" comes the adaptation of the Hans Christian Andersen tale of a little mermaid who makes a big sacrifice to win the prince she loves.
Gaylord Productions; Platypus Productions — *CBS/Fox Video*

Little Mermaid, The 1978
Fairy tales/Cartoons
40728 71 mins C B, V R, P
Animated
An animated version of Hans Christian Andersen's tale about a little mermaid who rescues a prince whose boat has capsized. She immediately falls in love and wishes that she could become a human girl.
21st Century — *Video Gems*

Little Minister, The 1934
Romance/Drama
79319 101 mins B/W B, V P
Katharine Hepburn, John Beal, Alan Hale, Donald Crisp, directed by Richard Wallace
A filmed adaptation of the James Barrie novel about a free spirited gypsy who falls in love with a Scottish minister.
RKO; Pandros S. Berman — *RKO HomeVideo*

Little Miss Innocence 1982
Drama/Exploitation
70725 79 mins C B, V P
John Alderman, Sandra Dempsey, Judy Medford
A recording executive tries to survive the amorous advances of the two attractive female hitchikers that he drove home.
Activity Home — *Active Home Video*

Little Miss Marker 1980
Comedy
60589 112 mins C B, V P
Walter Matthau, Julie Andrews, Tony Curtis, Bob Newhart, Lee Grant, Sara Stimson
The often retold tale of Sorrowful Jones, a grouchy, stingy bookie who accepts a little girl as a security marker for a ten dollar bet.
MPAA:PG
Universal — *MCA Home Video*

Little Night Music, A 1977
Musical/Romance
69544 110 mins C B, V P
Elizabeth Taylor, Diana Rigg, Hermione Gingold, Len Cariou, Lesley Ann Down
Adapted from the Broadway play, this film centers around four ingeniously interwoven, contemporary love stories. Musical score by Stephen Sondheim.
MPAA:PG
New World Pictures — *Embassy Home Entertainment*

Little Orphan Annie 1932
Drama
10041 60 mins B/W B, V P, T
Mitzie Green, Edgar Kennedy, directed by John S. Robertson
Based on the comic strip, Annie is an orphan being cared for by a bum. He follows money making scheme, leaving her alone, but Annie finds newly orphaned boy in her travels.
RKO — *Blackhawk Films*

Little Prince, The 1984
Cartoons
78147 100 mins C B, V P
Animated 2 pgms
Two adventures which feature The Little Prince as he searches for and discovers great truths about faith, courage, friendship and caring.

Childrens Video Library — *Children's Video Library*

Little Prince—Next Stop, Planet Earth, The **1985**
Cartoons
76996 60 mins C B, V, CED P
Animated
A collection of two adventures featuring The Little Prince: in "Higher Than Eagles Fly," the Prince takes a balloon ride through the Andes mountains and in "The Chimney Sweep," a chimney sweep and his daughter are reunited.
Children's Video Library — *Children's Video Library*

Little Prince—Tales of the Sea, The **1983**
Cartoons
80978 49 mins C B, V P
Animated
In this volume, the Little Prince and a young Australian boy takea sea voyage, and befriend a Belgian sea captain who takes them on anexciting canal cruising journey.
Jambre Productions — *Children's Video Library*

Little Prince, The **1974**
Musical
38608 88 mins C B, V, LV R, P
Richard Kiley, Bob Fosse, Steven Warner, Gene Wilder, directed by Stanley Donen
Based on the story by Antoine de Saint-Exupery, this musical fable tells of a little prince from Asteroid B-612 who comes to visit the earth. Music and lyrics by Lerner and Loewe.
MPAA:G
Paramount — *Paramount Home Video*

Little Princess, The **1939**
Drama
05445 91 mins C B, V, 3/4U P
Shirley Temple, Richard Greene, Ian Hunter, Cesar Romero, Arthur Treacher, Anita Louise
The story of a little girl who doesn't believe that her missing Army Officer father is really dead.
Daryl Zanuck; 20th Century Fox — *Prism; Video Connection; VCII; World Video Pictures; Video Yesteryear; Sheik Video; Cable Films; Budget Video; Discount Video Tapes; Nostalgia Merchant; Media Home Entertainment; Hal Roach Studios; Classic Video Cinema Collector's Club; Kartes Productions; See Hear Industries*

Little Rascals, Book I, The **193?**
Comedy
66117 59 mins B/W B, V P, T
Farina Hoskins, Joe Cobb, Stymie Beard, Spanky McFarland, Scotty Beckett, Alfalfa Switzer, Mary Ann Jackson
Three "Our Gang" shorts: "Railroadin'" (1929), in which the gang takes off on a runaway train; "A Lad and a Lamp" (1932), wherein they find an Aladdin's lamp; "Beginner's Luck" (1935), in which Spanky wins a dress for a young actress.
Hal Roach — *Blackhawk Films*

Little Rascals, Book II, The **193?**
Comedy
64826 56 mins B/W B, V P, T
Stymie Beard, Wheezer Hutchins, Spanky McFarland, Alfalfa Switzer
A second package of "Our Gang" two-reelers: "Bear Shooters" (1930), in which the Gang goes hunting but runs into some bootleggers; "Forgotten Babies" (1933), has Spanky babysitting for the gang's brothers and sisters; and "Teacher's Beau" (1935), where the gang cooks up a scheme to chase their teacher's fiance away.
Hal Roach — *Blackhawk Films*

Little Rascals, Book III, The **1938**
Comedy
64917 54 mins B/W B, V P, T
Wheezer Hutchins, Dorothy De Borba, Stymie Beard, Spanky McFarland, Alfalfa Switzer, Darla Hood
Three more "Our Gang" two reelers are packaged on this tape: "Dogs Is Dogs"(1931), "Anniversary Trouble" (1935) and "Three Men in a Tub" (1938).
Hal Roach — *Blackhawk Films*

Little Rascals, Book IV, The **193?**
Comedy
65083 52 mins B/W B, V P, T
Wheezer, Stymie, Spanky, Alfalfa, Darla, Porky, Buckwheat
Another package of Our Gang favorites, including "Helping Grandma" (1931), "Little Papa" (1935) and "Bear Facts" (1938).
Hal Roach — *Blackhawk Films*

Little Rascals, Book V, The **193?**
Comedy
65084 49 mins B/W B, V P, T
Breezy Brisbane, Stymie, Spanky, Scotty, Alfalfa, Darla, Porky, Buckwheat
The comic adventures of the Little Rascals continue in this package of three original shorts: "Readin' and Writin'" (1932), "Sprucin' Up" (1935) and "Reunion in Rhythm" (1937).
Hal Roach — *Blackhawk Films*

Little Rascals, Book VI, The 193?
Comedy
65085 48 mins B/W B, V P, T
Stymie, Breezy, Spanky, Fidgets, Alfalfa, Darla, Porky, Buckwheat, Dorothy DeBorba, Billy Gilbert
Three more classic "Our Gang" comedy shorts are packaged on this tape: "Free Eats" (1932), "Arbor Day" (1936) and "Mail and Female" (1937).
Hal Roach — *Blackhawk Films*

Little Rascals, Book VII, The 193?
Comedy
65086 47 mins B/W B, V P, T
Spanky, Breezy, Dickie Moore, Stymie, Scotty, Alfalfa, Darla, Porky, Buckwheat
The "Our Gang" kids serve up another portion of comedy in these three shorts: "Hook and Ladder" (1932), "The Lucky Corner" (1936) and "Feed 'Em and Weep" (1938).
Hal Roach — *Blackhawk Films*

Little Rascals Book VIII, The 19??
Comedy
66305 42 mins B/W B, V P, T
Wheezer, Mary Ann Jackson, Spanky, Alfalfa, Buckwheat, Porky, Darla Hood
More fun and nuttiness with "Our Gang" in three original short comedies, "Bouncing Babies" (1929), "Two Too Young" (1936) and "The Awful Tooth" (1938).
Hal Roach — *Blackhawk Films*

Little Rascals Book IX, The 19??
Comedy
66306 48 mins B/W B, V P, T
Farina, Stymie, Spanky, Alfalfa, Buckwheat, Porky, Darla
The Little Rascals scamper into more mischief in these three original shorts: "Little Daddy" (1931), "Spooky Hooky" (1936) and "Hide and Shriek" (1938).
Hal Roach — *Blackhawk Films*

Little Rascals, Book X, The 19??
Comedy
66308 41 mins B/W B, V P, T
Jackie Cooper, Mary Ann Jackson, Spanky, Alfalfa, Buckwheat, Porky, Darla, Butch, Woim
The tenth compilation of original "Our Gang" comedies includes "The First Seven Years" (1929), "Bored of Education" (1936) and "Rushin' Ballet" (1937).
Academy Awards '36: Best Short Subject ("Bored of Education").
Hal Roach — *Blackhawk Films*

Little Rascals, Book XI, The 1938
Comedy
66340 42 mins B/W B, V P, T
Spanky McFarland, Alfalfa Switzer, Darla Hood, Porky, Buckwheat
The Little Rascals go dramatic in these three shorts, all with a "putting-on-a-show" theme: "Pay As You Exit" (1936), "Three Smart Boys" (1937) and "Our Gang Follies of 1938."
Hal Roach — *Blackhawk Films*

Little Rascals, Book XII, The 1937
Comedy
66341 53 mins B/W B, V P, T
Jackie Cooper, Farina Hoskins, Mary Ann Jackson, Spanky McFarland, Alfalfa Switzer, Darla Hood
The Little Rascals explore a haunted house, take a train ride and play football in these three original shorts: "Moan and Groan, Inc." (1929), "Choo-Choo!" (1932) and "The Pigskin Palooka" (1937).
Hal Roach — *Blackhawk Films*

Little Rascals, Book XIII, The 1937
Comedy
66442 48 mins B/W B, V P, T
Jackie Cooper, Farina, Wheezer, Chubby, Mary Ann, Spanky, Scotty, Alfalfa, Edgar Kennedy
The Our Gang kids return in three more original shorts: "Shivering Shakespeare" (1930), "The First Round-Up" (1934) and "Fishy Tales" (1937).
Hal Roach — *Blackhawk Films*

Little Rascals, Book XIV, The 193?
Comedy
65704 52 mins B/W B, V P, T
Wheezer, Mary Ann, Spanky, Porky, Alfalfa, Buckwheat, Darla
This package of shorts leads off with Our Gang's first talkie, "Small Talk" (1929), a three-reeler. The other two entries are "Little Sinner" (1935) and "Hearts Are Thumps" (1937).
Hal Roach — *Blackhawk Films*

Little Rascals, Book XV, The 193?
Comedy
65770 50 mins B/W B, V P, T
Edgar Kennedy, Tommy "Butch" Bond, Spanky McFarland, Scotty Beckett, Wheezer Hutchins
Those rascally imps return once again in three more original shorts: "When the Wind Blows" (1930), "For Pete's Sake" (1934) and "Glove Taps" (1937).
Hal Roach; MGM — *Blackhawk Films*

(For explanation of codes, see USE GUIDE and KEY)

Little Rascals, Book XVI, The 193?
Comedy
65768 50 mins B/W B, V P, T
Jackie Cooper, Chubby Chaney, Spanky McFarland, Alfalfa Switzer, Darla Hood, Wally Albright
More Little Rascals mayhem in these three original shorts: "Love Business" (1931), "Hi-Neighbor!" (1934) and "Came the Brawn" (1938).
Hal Roach; MGM — *Blackhawk Films*

Little Rascals, Book XVI, The 193?
Comedy
78169 50 mins B/W B, V P, T
Spanky, Stymie, Darla, Scotty, Chubby, Jackie, June Marlowe
This program presents three films of The Little Rascals getting into trouble and having their fun: "Love Business" (1931),"Hi-Neighbor!" (1934), and "Came the Brawn" (1937).
Hal Roach — *Blackhawk Films*

Little Rascals, Book XVIII, The 1929
Comedy
79855 41 mins B/W B, V P, T
Farina Hoskins, Wheezer Hutchins, Mary Ann Jackson, Joe Cobb
Here are two early "Our Gang" comedies from the silent era: "Saturday's Lesson" (1929) and "Wiggle Your Ears" (1929).
Hal Roach — *Blackhawk Films*

Little Rascals Christmas Special, The 1979
Christmas
65160 60 mins C B, V P
Animated, voices of Darla Hood, Matthew "Stymie" Beard
Spanky and the Little Rascals attempt to raise enough money to buy a winter coat for Spanky's mom and learn the true meaning of Christmas along the way.
King World Productions — *Family Home Entertainment*

Little Rascals Comedy Classics 1 193?
Comedy
65739 50 mins B/W B, V P
Spankie, Stymie, Alfalfa, Buckwheat
The Little Rascals romp again in this collection of original comedy two-reelers.
Hal Roach — *Republic Pictures Home Video*

Little Rascals On Parade, The 1937
Comedy
76829 60 mins B/W B, V P
Spanky McFarland, Alfalfa Switzer, Darla Hood
A collection of six vintage "Our Gang" shorts from the 30's: "FreeEats," "Arbor Day," "Mail and Female," "Hook and Ladder," "TheLucky Corner" and "Feed 'Em and Weep."
Hal Roach — *Republic Pictures Home Video*

Little Rascals, Book XIX, The 1936
Comedy
77366 55 mins B/W B, V P, A
Mary Ann Jackson, Jackie Cooper, Dickie Moore, Tommy Bond, Darla Hood, Stepin Fetchit
A collection of three "Our Gang" shorts: In "A Tough Winter," Stepin Fetchit helps the Gang clean up a mess; in "Mush and Milk," the cop treats the kinds of a boarding school to a day at an amusement park; and the Florydor perform in the "Our Gang Follies of 1936."
Hal Roach — *Blackhawk Films*

Little Red Riding Hood 1984
Fairy tales
Closed Captioned
73142 60 mins C B, V, CED P
Mary Steenburgen, Malcolm McDowell, directed by Graeme Clifford
From "Faerie Tale Theatre" comes the retelling of the story about a girl (Mary Steenburgen) off to give her grandmother a picnic basket only to get stopped by a wolf.
Shelley Duvall — *CBS/Fox Video*

Little River Band 1982
Music-Performance
47798 75 mins C B, V R, P
Selections from this Australian rock'n'roll band's six LP's, such as "It's a Long Way There," "Mistress of Mine," and "Just Say That You Love Me," are featured.
Capitol EMI Music — *THORN EMI/HBO Video; RCA VideoDiscs; Pioneer Artists*

Little Romance, A 1979
Drama
38942 105 mins C B, V R, P
Laurence Olivier, Diane Lane, Thelonious Bernard, Sally Kellerman, Broderick Crawford, directed by George Roy Hill
Two lonely, gifted children set out on a charming adventure that carries them across Europe to find love in Venice.
Academy Awards '79: Best Music Score (George Delrue) MPAA:PG
Orion Pictures — *Warner Home Video*

Little Sex, A 1982
Comedy
47849 94 mins C B, V P
Tim Matheson, Kate Capshaw, Edward Herrmann, Wallace Shaw

A young newlywed finds himself perpetually tempted by young women.
MPAA:R
Universal — *MCA Home Video*

Little Shop of Horrors **1960**
Horror
00408 70 mins B/W B, V P
Jackie Joseph, Jonathan Haze, Mel Welles, Jack Nicholson, directedby Roger Corman
Simple minded boy develops man-eating plant. Attempting to destroy it, he becomes its victim.
Filmgroup — *Prism; Budget Video; Movie Buff Video; Sheik Video; Video Connection; Video Yesteryear; Western Film & Video Inc; Discount Video Tapes; See Hear Industries*

Little Tough Guys **1938**
Drama
01717 84 mins B/W B, V, FO P
Helen Parrish, Billy Halop, Leo Georcy, Marjorie Main
When father goes to jail, the children must fend for themselves. Son gets involved in gang warfare plus reform school.
U I — *Video Yesteryear; Cable Films; Budget Video; Discount Video Tapes; Kartes Productions; See Hear Industries*

Little Women **1933**
Drama
58297 107 mins B/W B, V P
Katharine Hepburn, Joan Bennett, Paul Lukas, Edna May Oliver, Frances Dee, directed by George Cukor
Louisa May Alcott's Civil War story of the four March sisters, Jo, Beth, Amy, and Meg, who share their loves, their joys, and their sorrows. Academy Awards '33: Writing Adaptation (Victor Heerman, Sarah Y. Mason).
RKO — *MGM/UA Home Video*

Little Women **1983**
Cartoons/Literature
69535 60 mins C B, V, CED P
Animated
Louisa May Alcott's classic tale of four loving sisters who face the joys and hardships of life together comes to life in this animated program.
Toei Animation Productions — *Children's Video Library*

Littlest Warrior, The **1975**
Cartoons/Adventure
53139 70 mins C B, V P
Animated
Zooshio, the Littlest Warrior, is forced to leave his beloved forest and experiences many adventures before he is reunited with his family forever.
Ziv Intl — *Family Home Entertainment*

Live and Let Die **1973**
Adventure
64329 121 mins C LV P
Roger Moore, Jane Seymour, Yaphet Kotto
Agent 007 is out to thwart the villainous Dr. Kananga, a black mastermind who plans to control western powers with voodoo and hard drugs. Title song by Paul McCartney and Wings.
MPAA:PG
United Artists — *CBS/Fox Video; RCA VideoDiscs*

Live Infidelity: REO Speedwagon in Concert **1981**
Music-Performance
53410 90 mins C B, V, LV, CED P
A live performance by REO Speedwagon, featuring selections from their album, "Hi Infidelity."
MGM; CBS — *CBS/Fox Video*

Live Television **195?**
Drama
33696 110 mins B/W B, V, 3/4U P
Bob Cummings, Martin Balsam, Rip Torn, Ralph Edwards, Laurel and Hardy
Two classic examples from the live, pioneer days of television: "Playhouse 90: Bomber's Moon," and "This Is Your Life, Laurel and Hardy."
CBS, NBC — *Shokus Video*

Living Head, The **1963**
Adventure
56913 75 mins B/W B, V, FO P
Archeologists discover the ancient sepulcher of the great Aztec warrior, Acatl. Ignoring a curse, they steal his severed head and incur the fury of Xitsliapoli. Dubbed in English.
Mexican — *Video Yesteryear*

Living in Harmony **1968**
Suspense/Fantasy
77418 52 mins C B, V P
Patrick McGoohan, Alexis Kanne, David Bauer
The Prisoner mysteriously wakes up in an old western town called Harmony and defies the town's judge. This is an unaired episode from "The Prisoner" series.
ITC Productions — *MPI Home Video*

Living Language—French **1984**
Languages-Instruction
79184 60 mins C B, V P
A video course designed to instruct travelers on how to speak French.
Crown Video — *Karl/Lorimar Home Video*

Living Language—Spanish 1984
Languages-Instruction
79185 60 mins C B, V P
A video course designed to instruct travelers on how to speak Spanish
Crown Video — *Karl/Lorimar Home Video*

Liza in Concert 1981
Music-Performance
52670 60 mins C LV P
Liza Minnelli performs at the Theatre for the Performing Arts in New Orleans, featuring a New York medley: "Lullaby of Broadway," "I Guess the Lord Must Be in New York City," "Forty Second Street," "On Broadway," and "Theme from New York, New York." Also performed are "City Lights," "Arthur in the Afternoon," and "Cabaret."
Artel Home Video — *Pioneer Artists*

Loaded Guns 1975
Suspense/Drama
76799 90 mins C B, V P
Ursula Andress, Woody Strode
An airline stewardess who doubles as an intelligence counter-agent must totally immobilize a top drug trafficking ring.
Picturmedia — *Monterey Home Video*

Local Hero 1983
Adventure
65324 112 mins C B, V P
Peter Riegert, Denis Lawson, Fulton Mackay, Burt Lancaster
A Texas oil company sends an ace trouble-shooter to buy out a sleepy Scottish fishing village for a refinery and supertanker port, but both the oil men and the citizenry get more than they bargained for.
MPAA:PG
Puttnam — *Warner Home Video*

Lodger, The 1926
Suspense
47469 91 mins B/W B, V, FO P
Ivor Novello, Marie Ault, Arthur Chesney, Malcolm Keen, directed by Alfred Hitchcock
A mysterious lodger is thought to be a rampaging mass murderer of young women. This is the first Hitchcock film to explore themes and ideas that would become trademarks of his work.
Gainsborough — *Video Yesteryear; Video Dimensions; Festival Films; Classic Video Cinema Collector's Club; Discount Video Tapes*

Logan's Run 1976
Science fiction
58298 120 mins C B, V, CED P
Michael York, Richard Jordan, Jenny Agutter, Roscoe Lee Browne, Farrah Fawcett-Majors, Peter Ustinov
In the 23rd century, a hedonistic society exists in a huge bubble and takes it for granted that there is no life outside.
MGM — *MGM/UA Home Video*

Lolita 1962
Drama
53941 152 mins B/W B, V, CED P
James Mason, Shelley Winters, Peter Sellers, Sue Lyon, directed by Stanley Kubrick
Vladimir Nabokov's novel about a middle-aged professor's obsession with a teenage nymphet is the basis of this film.
MGM — *MGM/UA Home Video*

Lombardi 1980
Football
50088 48 mins C B, V, FO R, P
A tribute to Vince Lombardi and his legendary Green Bay Packers, 1960's "Team of the Decade."
NFL Films — *NFL Films Video*

London Medley and City of the Golden Gate 193?
Documentary/Cities and towns
79856 19 mins B/W B, V P, T
Movietone News visits London and San Francisco in this collection of newsreels.
Movietone News — *Blackhawk Films*

Lone Ranger, The 1980
Cartoons/Western
66003 60 mins C B, V P
Animated
Three tales of derring-do from the masked man and his faithful Indian sidekick.
Lone Ranger Television Inc — *Family Home Entertainment*

Lone Ranger, The 1956
Western
70754 87 mins C B, V P
Clayton Moore, Jay Silverheels, Lyle Bettger, Bonita Granville
Tonto and that strange masked man must prevent a war between ranchers and Indians.
Warner Bros.; Rather Corp. — *MGM/UA Home Video*

Lone Ranger, The 1938
Western/Serials
57357 234 mins B/W B, V, FO P
Western serial, extremely rare, about the masked man and his faithful Indian sidekick. From a long-sought print found in Mexico, this program is burdened by a noisy sound track, two completely missing chapters, an abridged episode #15, and containing Spanish subtitles.
Republic — *Video Yesteryear; Video Connection*

Lone Wolf, The 1972
Drama
65436 45 mins C B, V P
A boy learns kindness by befriending an old military dog which villagers think is mad and responsible for killing their sheep. After a brush with death, the boy convinces the villagers of the dog's good qualities and wins the admiration of his friends.
Columbia — *Embassy Home Entertainment*

Lone Wolf McQuade 1983
Western/Martial arts
64899 107 mins C B, V, LV P
Chuck Norris, Leon Isaac Kennedy, David Carradine, Barbara Carrera
Martial arts action abounds in this modern-day Western which pits a Texas Ranger against a band of mercenaries.
Orion Pictures — *Vestron Video; RCA VideoDiscs*

Loneliest Runner, The 1976
Drama
80161 74 mins C B, V R, P
Michael Landon, Lance Kerwin, DeAnn Mears, Brian Keith, directed by Michael Landon
A teenaged boy overcomes his bedwetting problem and becomes an Olympic track star.
NBC — *Warner Home Video*

Lonely Are the Brave 1962
Western/Drama
76805 107 mins B/W B, V P
Kirk Douglas, Walter Matthau, Gena Rowlands, Carroll O'Connor, George Kennedy, directed by David Miller
A maverick cowboy who escapes from jail heads for the mountains with the police hot on his trail.
Universal; Kirk Douglas; Edward Lewis — *MCA Home Video*

Lonely Boy/Satan's Choice 19??
Music/Documentary
65230 55 mins B/W B, V, FO P
This tape contains two cinema-verite documentaries from the National Film Board of Canada. "Lonely Boy" (1962) follows the early career of pop singer Paul Anka; and "Satan's Choice" (1966) provides an inside look at the members of a motorcycle gang.
National Film Board of Canada — *Video Yesteryear*

Lonely Guy, The 1984
Comedy
74091 91 mins C B, V, LV, CED P
Steve Martin, Charles Grodin, Judith Ivey, Steve Lawrence
This romantic comedy features Steve Martin as a jilted writer who writes a best-selling book about being a lonely guy and finds stardom does have its rewards.
MPAA:R
Universal — *MCA Home Video*

Lonely Hearts 1983
Romance/Comedy
65624 95 mins C B, V P
Wendy Hughes, Norman Kaye
This is a quiet story about a piano tuner, who at 50 finds himself alone after years of caring for his mother, and a sexually insecure spinster, whom he meets through a dating service.
MPAA:R
John B Murray — *Embassy Home Entertainment*

Lonely Lady, The 1983
Drama
66328 92 mins C B, V, LV, CED P
Pia Zadora, Lloyd Bochner, Bibi Besch, Joseph Cali
A young writer comes to Hollywood with dreams of success. She gets involved with the seamy side of moviemaking and is driven to a nervous breakdown.
MPAA:R
Universal — *MCA Home Video*

Lonely Wives 1931
Comedy
58728 86 mins B/W B, V P
Edward Everett Horton, Patsy Ruth Miller, Laura La Planta, Esther Ralston
A lawyer hires an entertainer to serve as his double because of his marital problems.
RKO — *Sheik Video; Video Yesteryear*

Loners, The 1972
Drama
80932 80 mins C B, V P
Dean Stockwell, Gloria Grahame, Scott Brady, Alex Dreier
Three teenagers run from the southwest police after they are accused of murdering a highway patrolman.
MPAA:R
Maple Leaf Productions — *VidAmerica*

Long Ago Tomorrow 1971
Drama
65703 90 mins C B, V P
Malcolm McDowell, Nanette Newman
A paralyzed athlete enters a church-run home rather than return to his family as the object of their pity.
MPAA:PG
Bruce Cohn Curtis — *RCA/Columbia Pictures Home Video*

Long Dark Hall, The 1951
Drama
66387 86 mins B/W B, V P
Rex Harrison, Lilli Palmer, Denis O'Dea
A chorus girl is murdered and her married lover is accused of the crime.
British Lion — *Movie Buff Video*

Long Day's Journey Into Night 1962
Drama
66473 174 mins B/W B, V P
Katharine Hepburn, Ralph Richardson, Jason Robards, Dean Stockwell
Eugene O'Neill's autobiographical drama deals with the life of his family, circa 1912, as his father and brother were forced to come to grips with his mother's drug addiction.
Landau Unger — *Republic Pictures Home Video*

Long Good Friday, The 1979
Crime-Drama
63331 109 mins C B, V R, P
Bob Hoskins, Helen Mirren, Dave King, Bryan Marshall, Derek Thompson, Eddie Constantine
Set in London's dockland, this is the story of an underworld king out to beat his rivals at their own game.
Hand Made Films; Barry Hanson — *THORN EMI/HBO Video*

Long John Silver 1955
Adventure
79852 106 mins C B, V R, P
Robert Newton, Connie Gilchrist, Kit Taylor, Rod Taylor
Long John Silver plans a return trip to Treasure Island with fresh clues to find the treasure.
TI Pictures — *Video Gems*

Long John Silver's Return to Treasure Island 1953
Adventure
70197 106 mins C B, V P
Robert Newton, Connie Gilcrest, Kit Taylor, Rod Taylor
Having returned to England from his sojourn to Treasure Island, famed pirate Long John Silver plans another search for the elusive treasure.
TI Pictures — *Hal Roach Studios; Discount Video Tapes*

Long Riders, The 1980
Western
78631 100 mins C B, V P
Stacy and James Keach, Randy and Dennis Quaid, David, Keith, and Robert Carradine, directed by Walter Hill
The Jesse James and Cole Younger gangs raid banks, trains, and stagecoaches in post Civil War Missouri.
MPAA:R
United Artists — *MGM/UA Home Video*

Long Shot 1981
Drama
73026 100 mins C B, V R, P
Two foosball enthusiasts work their way through local tournaments to make enough money to make it to the World Championships in Tahoe.
Unknown — *THORN EMI/HBO Video*

Long Voyage Home, The 1940
Adventure
80675 105 mins B/W B, V P
John Wayne, Thomas Mitchell, Ian Hunter, directed by John Ford
An adaptation of the Eugene O'Neill play about the lives of the crew members of a World War II cargo ship.
United Artists; John Ford — *Lightning Video*

Long Way Home, A 1981
Drama
78363 100 mins C B, V P
Timothy Hutton, Brenda Vaccaro, Rosanna Arquette
A young man attempts to reunite his brother and sister after they have been separated by the deaths of their parents.
Alan Landsburg Productions — *U.S.A. Home Video*

Longest Day, The 1962
War-Drama
08443 179 mins C B, V P
Richard Burton, Peter Lawford, Rod Steiger, John Wayne, Edmond O'Brien
The complete story of the D-Day landings at Normandy, as seen through the eyes of American, French, British and German participants.
EL, SP
20th Century Fox; Darryl F. Zanuck — *CBS/Fox Video*

Longest Yard, The 1974
Comedy
38589 121 mins C B, V, LV R, P
Burt Reynolds, Eddie Albert, directed by Robert Aldrich
A one-time pro football quarterback, now a prisoner, organizes his fellow convicts into a football team to play against the prison guards for a special game. Filmed on location at Georgia State Prison.
MPAA:R
Paramount — *Paramount Home Video; RCA VideoDiscs*

Look Back in Anger 1959
Drama
51965 99 mins B/W B, V R, P
Claire Bloom, Richard Burton, Mary Ure

Almost too late, a young man realizes how much he needs and wants his wife.
Gordon L.T. Scott — *Embassy Home Entertainment*

Look Back in Anger **1980**
Drama
80001 100 mins C B, V P
Malcolm McDowell, Lisa Barnes, Fran Brill, Raymond Hardie
A working-class man angered by society's hypocrisy lashes out at his upper-class wife, his mistress and the world.
Chuck Braverman/Don Boyd Prod. — *Warner Home Video*

Looker **1981**
Science fiction
47368 93 mins C B, V R, P
Albert Finney, James Coburn, Susan Dey, Leigh Taylor-Young
Stunning models are made even more beautiful by a plastic surgeon, but one by one they begin to die.
MPAA:PG
The Ladd Company; Howard Jeffrey — *Warner Home Video*

Lookin' to Get Out **1982**
Adventure/Comedy
65503 70 mins C B, V, CED P
Ann-Margret, Jon Voight, Burt Young
An ex-call girl living with her infant son in the owner's penthouse of a swank Las Vegas hotel spots the father of her child, and revenge is the only thing on her mind.
MPAA:R
Lorimar — *CBS/Fox Video*

Looking for Mr. Goodbar **1977**
Drama
38597 136 mins C B, V, LV R, P
Diane Keaton, Tuesday Weld, Richard Gere, directed by Richard Brooks
Diane Keaton portrays a young teacher who seeks escape from her claustrophobic existence by frequenting singles bars. Based on Judith Rossner's novel.
MPAA:R
Paramount — *Paramount Home Video; RCA VideoDiscs*

Looking Glass War, The **1969**
Horror
65468 108 mins C B, V P
Christopher Jones, Ralph Richardson, Pia Degermark, Anthony Hopkins
A Polish defector is sent behind the Iron Curtain on a final mission. Adapted from John Le Carre's best-selling spy novel. In Beta Hi-Fi.
MPAA:PG
John Box — *RCA/Columbia Pictures Home Video*

Looney Looney Looney Bugs Bunny Movie, The **1981**
Cartoons
47394 80 mins C B, V R, P
A feature-length compilation of classic Warner Brothers cartoons tied together with new animation. Cartoon stars featured include Bugs Bunny, Elmer Fudd, Porky Pig, Yosemite Sam, Duffy Duck and Foghorn Leghorn.
Warner Bros — *Warner Home Video; RCA VideoDiscs*

Looney Tunes and Merrie Melodies I **1933**
Comedy/Cartoons
38967 56 mins B/W B, V, FO P
Animated
A collection of eight Warner Brothers Vitaphone cartoons dating from 1931-33, most with jazzy musical accompaniments. Titles include "It's Got Me Again," "You Don't Know What You're Doin'," "Moonlight for Two," "Battling Bosko," "Red-Headed Baby," and "Freddy the Freshman."
Warner Bros — *Video Yesteryear*

Looney Tunes and Merrie Melodies II **194?**
Comedy/Cartoons
38969 51 mins B/W B, V, FO P
Animated
A second collection of seven Warner-Vitaphone cartoons from 1931-33, 1937, and 1941-43. Porky Pig, Daffy Duck, and Bugs Bunny are featured in the later World War II-oriented titles, "Scrap Happy Daffy" and Porky Pig's Feat." Earlier titles include "One More Time," "Smile, Darnya, Smile," and "Yodeling Yokels."
Warner Bros — *Video Yesteryear*

Looney Tunes and Merrie Melodies #3 **194?**
Cartoons
59367 60 mins C B, V, FO P
Cartoon classics from Warner Bros: "A Corny Concerto" (1943), with Porky and Bugs; "Foney Fables" (1942), a retelling of old fairy tales; "The Wacky Wabbit" (1942), featuring Bugs and Elmer Fudd; "Have You Got Any Castles" (1938); "Fifth Column Mouse" (1943); "To Duck or Not to Duck" (1943), with Elmer and Daffy; "The Early Worm Gets the Bird" (1940); and "Daffy the Commando (1943), with Daffy Duck.
Warner Bros — *Video Yesteryear*

Looney Tunes Video Show #1, The **195?**
Cartoons
62879 49 mins C B, V R, P
Animated

Seven Warner Brothers cartoon classics of the 1940's and 50's: Bugs Bunny and the Tasmanian Devil in "Devil May Hare," Sylvester in "Birds of a Father," "Daffy Duck and Porky Pig in "The Ducksters," the Road Runner and Wile E. Coyote in "Zipping Along," Sylvester and Tweety in "Room and Bird," Elmer Fudd in "Ant Pasted" and Speedy Gonzales in "Mexican Schmoes."
Warner Bros — *Warner Home Video*

Looney Tunes Video Show #2, The **195?**
Cartoons
62880 48 mins C B, V R, P
Animated
More Warner Brothers cartoon favorites: Daffy Duck in "Quackodile Tears," Porky Pig in "An Egg Scramble," Sylvester and Speedy Gonzales in "Cats and Bruises," Foghorn Leghorn in "All Fowled Up," Bugs Bunny and Yosemite Sam in "14 Carrot Rabbit," Professor Calvin Q. Calculus in "The Hole Idea" and Pepe Le Pew in "Two Scents Worth."
Warner Bros — *Warner Home Video*

Looney Tunes Video Show #3, The **195?**
Cartoons
62881 38 mins C B, V R, P
Animated
Seven more Warner Brothers cartoon shorts: Daffy Duck and Speedy Gonzales in "The Quacker Tracker," the Wolf and Sheepdog in "Double or Mutton," Claude Cat and Bulldog in "Feline Frameup," Bugs Bunny in "Eight Ball Bunny," Foghorn Leghorn in "A Featured Leghorn," Porky Pig and Sylvester in "Scaredy Cat" and Pepe Le Pew in "Louvre, Come Back to Me."
Warner Bros — *Warner Home Video*

Looney Tunes Video Show #4, The **195?**
Cartoons
62882 47 mins C B, V R, P
Animated
Another Warner Brothers cartoon assortment: Sylvester and Tweety in "Ain't She Tweet," Daffy Duck and Speedy Gonzales in "Astroduck," Bugs Bunny in "Backwoods Bunny," Pepe Le Pew in "Heaven Scent," Elmer Fudd in "Pests for Guests," Sylvester in "Lighthouse Mouse" and the Wolf and Sheepdog in "Don't Give Up the Sheep."
Warner Bros — *Warner Home Video*

Looney Tunes Video Show #5, The **195?**
Cartoons
62883 51 mins C B, V R, P
Animated
An additional package of Warner Brothers cartoons: Sylvester and Tweety in "Tugboat Granny," Daffy Duck in "Stork Naked," the Road Runner and Wile E. Coyote in "Fastest with the Mostest," Bugs Bunny in "Forward March Hare," Foghorn Leghorn in "Feather Dusted," Daffy Duck and Porky Pig in "China Jones" and Pepe Le Pew in "Odor of the Day."
Warner Bros — *Warner Home Video*

Looney Tunes Video Show #6, The **195?**
Cartoons
62884 49 mins C B, V R, P
Animated
More classic Warner Brothers cartoons: Foghorn Leghorn in "Feather Bluster," the Road Runner and Wile E. Coyote in "Lickety Splat," Bugs Bunny in "Bowery Bugs," Daffy Duck and Speedy Gonzales in "Daffy Rents," Porky Pig in "Dough for the Dodo," Sylvester and Elmer Fudd in "Heir Conditioned" and Pepe Le Pew in "Scent of the Matterhorn."
Warner Bros — *Warner Home Video*

Looney Tunes Video Show #7, The **195?**
Cartoons
62885 48 mins C B, V R, P
Animated
Seven additional Warner Brothers cartoon classics: Bugs Bunny in "A-Lad-In His Lamp," the Road Runner and Wile E. Coyote in "Beep Beep," Yosemite Sam in "Honey's Money," Foghorn Leghorn in "Weasel Stop," Daffy Duck and Elmer Fudd in "Don't Ax Me," Sylvester and Tweety in "Muzzle Tough" and Foghorn Leghorn in "The Egg-Cited Rooster."
Warner Bros — *Warner Home Video*

Loophole **1983**
Adventure
65353 105 mins C B, V P
Albert Finney, Martin Sheen, Susannah York
An out-of-work architect, hard pressed for money, joins forces with an elite team of expert criminals, in a scheme to make off with millions from the most established holding bank's vault.
David Korda; Julian Holloway — *Media Home Entertainment*

Lord Jim **1965**
Drama
13261 154 mins C B, V P
Peter O'Toole, James Mason, Curt Jurgens, Eli Wallach, Jack Hawkins, directed by Richard Brooks
A ship officer commits an act of cowardice that results in his dismissal and disgrace.
Columbia; Richard Brooks — *RCA/Columbia Pictures Home Video*

Lord of the Flies 1963
Drama
80121 91 mins B/W B, V P
James Aubrey, Tom Chapin, Hugh Edwards, directed by Peter Brook
When a group of English schoolboys are stranded on a desert island they turn into savages.
Lewis Allen — *King of Video*

Lord of the Rings 1978
Fantasy
58883 133 mins C B, V R, P
Animated
Ralph Bakshi's animated interpretation of Tolkien's classic tale of the hobbits, wizards, elves, and dwarfs who inhabit Middle Earth.
MPAA:PG
United Artists — *THORN EMI/HBO Video; RCA VideoDiscs*

Lords of Discipline, The 1983
Drama
66031 103 mins C B, V, LV R, P
David Keith, Robert Prosky, Barbara Babcock, Judge Reinhold
A military academy cadet is given the unenviable task of protecting a black freshman from racist factions at a southern school circa 1964.
MPAA:R
Paramount — *Paramount Home Video*

Lords of the New Church—Live from London, The 1985
Music-Performance
80781 60 mins C B, V P
The Lords of the New Church perform such new wave favorites as "Open Your Eyes," "Dance With Me" and "Live For Today" in this concert taped at London's Marquee Club. Available in VHS and Beta Hi Fi.
I.R.S. Video — *RCA/Columbia Pictures Home Video*

Loretta 1980
Music-Performance
45105 61 mins C B, V, LV P
Loretta Lynn
The queen of country music, Loretta Lynn, performs some of her best material, including "Coal Miner's Daughter," "Hey Loretta," "You're Looking at the Country," "Out of My Head and Back in Bed," "Wine, Women, and Song," "Naked in the Rain," and "Gospel Medley."
David Skepner — *MCA Home Video*

Los Angeles Dodgers: Team Highlights 1984
Baseball
81142 30 mins C B, V P
Tommy Lasorda, Fernando Velenzuela, Steve Garvey, Rick Monday, Greg Brock, Mike Marshall 6 pgms
The best and brightest moments from the L.A. Dodgers past seasons are featured in this presentation.
1.1976: Going On Twenty 2.1980: High Fivin' With The Dodgers 3.1981: The Tenth Player 4.1982: A Year at The Top 5.1983: Blending of the Blue 6.1984: Eye on the Future
Major League Baseball — *Major League Baseball Productions*

Los Angeles Rams 1984 Team Highlights 1985
Football
70547 70 mins C B, V, FO P
Eric Dickerson
The Rams winning the Wild Card Playoff berth became "A Family Tradition", and Eric Dickerson's record-setting 2,105 yards in rushing a family jewel. This tape features 47-minutes of highlights from the entire NFL's '84 season as well.
NFL Films — *NFL Films Video*

Losin' It 1982
Comedy
66047 104 mins C B, V, CED P
Tom Cruise, John Stockwell, Shelley Long
A shy young man travels to a Mexican border town to lose his virginity.
MPAA:R
Joel Michaels; Garth Drabinsby — *Embassy Home Entertainment*

Lost 1983
Adventure
80894 92 mins C B, V P
Sandra Dee, Don Stewart, Ken Curtis, Jack Elam, Sheila Newhouse
A young girl runs away into the wilderness because of the resentment she feels towards her new stepfather.
American National Enterprises — *Prism*

Lost and Found 1979
Comedy
63434 104 mins C B, V P
George Segal, Glenda Jackson, Maureen Stapleton, Hollis McLaren, John Cunningham, Paul Sorvino
An American professor of English and an English film production secretary fall in love on a skiing vacation.
MPAA:PG
Columbia; Melvin Frank — *RCA/Columbia Pictures Home Video*

Lost Empire, The 1983
Science fiction/Adventure
80670 86 mins C B, V P

 (For explanation of codes, see USE GUIDE and KEY)

Melanie Vincz, Raven De La Croix, Angela Aames, Paul Coufos
Three bountiful and powerful women team up to battle the evil Dr. Syn Do in order to save their empire.
MPAA:R
Jim Wynorski — *Lightning Video*

Lost Honor of Katharina Blum, The **1975**
Drama
69550 97 mins C B, V P
Angela Winkler, Mario Adorf, Dieter Lasar
Adapted from Heinrich Boll's Nobel Prize-winning novel, this film is about a woman who fights political and social injustice.
MPAA:R
New World Pictures — *Embassy Home Entertainment*

Lost in Space **1965**
Science fiction
14446 52 mins B/W B, V P
Guy Williams, June Lockhart, Jonathan Harris, Billy Mumy
The complete pilot episode of the series, in which the Robinson family becomes stranded somewhere in the universe.
Irwin Allen Prod — *Video Dimensions; Video Yesteryear*

Lost Jungle, The **1934**
Mystery/Serials
14262 156 mins B/W B, V P
Clyde Beatty, Cecelia Parker
Exciting animal treasure hunt; danger and mystery. Serial in 12 chapters, 13 minutes each.
Mascot — *Video Connection; Video Dimensions; Video Yesteryear; Discount Video Tapes*

Lost Moment, The **1947**
Drama
77480 89 mins B/W B, V P
Robert Cummings, Susan Hayward
A publisher travels to Italy to search for a valuable collection of love letters.
Walter Wanger — *Republic Pictures Home Video*

Lost Patrol, The **1934**
Adventure
10075 66 mins B/W B, V P, T
Victor McLaglen, Boris Karloff, Wallace Ford, Reginald Denny, Alan Hale
British soldiers lost in desert are shot down one by one by Arab marauders.
RKO — *Blackhawk Films; Nostalgia Merchant*

Lost Squadron **1932**
Adventure
57144 79 mins B/W B, V P
Richard Dix, Erich von Stroheim
A look at the dangers stuntmen go through in movie-making.
RKO — *King of Video*

Lost World, The **1925**
Drama
08855 62 mins B/W B, V, 3/4U P
Wallace Beery, Louis Stone, Bessie Love, Lloyd Hughes
A zoology professor leads a group on a South American expedition in search of the "lost world."
First National — *Video Yesteryear; Discount Video Tapes*

Lottery Bride, The **1930**
Drama
54111 85 mins B/W B, V P, T
Jeanette MacDonald, Joe E. Brown, Zasu Pitts, John Garrick, Carroll Nye
A young woman enters a dance marathon against the wishes of her boyfriend, to get funds to aid her criminal brother. When the police arrive at the contest in search for the brother, the woman aids in his escape. For this she is put in prison. It is not until a series of misunderstandings are cleared up that her and her boyfriend are reunited.
United Artists — *Blackhawk Films*

Louis Armstrong—Chicago Style **1975**
Biographical/Drama
79250 74 mins C B, V P
Ben Vereen, Red Buttons, Janet Mac Lachlan, Margaret Avery
How Louis Armstrong managed to fight the mob in the early 1930's and become a great jazz trompeter-vocalist.
Stonehenge/Charles Fries Productions — *Worldvision Home Video*

Louvre, The **1978**
Documentary/Museums
80162 53 mins C B, V R, P
Charles Boyer takes you on a trip through one of the world's great art museums.
NBC — *Warner Home Video*

Love Affair: The Eleanor and Lou Gehrig Story, A **1977**
Biographical/Drama
80639 96 mins C B, V P
Blythe Danner, Edward Herrmann, Patricia Neal, Ramon Bieri, Lainie Kazan, directed by Fiedler Cook
The true story of the love affair between baseball great Lou Gehrig and his wife Eleanor from his glory days as a New York Yankee, to his battle with an incurable disease.

Charles Fries Prods. — *Worldvision Home Video*

Love and Anarchy **1973**
Drama
63446 108 mins C B, V P
Giancarlo Giannini, Mariangela Melato, directed by Lina Wertmuller
An oppressed peasant vows to assassinate Mussolini after a close friend is murdered. Italian dialogue, English subtitles.
IT
Euro International Films
Technicolor — *RCA/Columbia Pictures Home Video*

Love and Bullets **1979**
Adventure
Closed Captioned
81065 95 mins C B, V P
Charles Bronson, Jill Ireland, Rod Steiger, Strother Martin, Bradford Dillman
An Arizona homicide detective is sent on a special assignment to Switzerland to bring a mobster's girlfriend back to the United States to testify against him in court. Available in VHS and Beta Hi-Fi.
MPAA:PG
Pancho Kohner — *Key Video*

Love and Death **1975**
Comedy
59336 89 mins C B, V P
Woody Allen, Diane Keaton, Georges Adel, Despo, Frank Adu, directed by Woody Allen
In 1812 Russia, a man condemned reviews the follies of his life. Woody Allen's satire on "War and Peace."
MPAA:PG
United Artists; Jack Rollins; Charles H Joffe — *CBS/Fox Video; RCA VideoDiscs*

Love and Faith **1978**
Drama
76889 154 mins C B, V P
Toshiro Mifune, Takashi Shimura, Yoshiko Nakana, directed by Kei Kumai
Two lovers are torn between their love for each other and their faiths during sixteenth century Japan with English subtitles.
JA
Toho — *Video Action*

Love at First Bite **1979**
Comedy
53517 96 mins C B, V R, P
George Hamilton, Susan Saint James, Richard Benjamin, Dick Shawn, Arte Johnson, Sherman Hemsley, Isabel Sanford
Dracula is forced to leave his Transylvanian home as the Rumanian government has designated his castle a training center for young gymnasts. Once in New York, the Count takes in the night life and falls in love with a woman whose boyfriend embarks on a campaign to warn the city of Dracula's presence.
MPAA:PG
American International — *Warner Home Video; RCA VideoDiscs; Vestron Video (disc only)*

Love Bug, The **1968**
Comedy
29736 110 mins C B, V, LV R, P
Dean Jones, Michele Lee, Hope Lange, Robert Reed, Bert Convy
A race car driver is followed home by a white Volkswagen which has a mind of its own.
MPAA:G
Walt Disney — *Walt Disney Home Video; RCA VideoDiscs*

Love Butcher, The **1982**
Horror
75586 84 mins C B, V P
Erik Stern, Kay Neer, Robin Sherwood
A crippled old gardener kills his female employers with his garden tools and cleans up neatly afterward.
MPAA:R
Desert Production — *Monterey Home Video*

Love Child **1982**
Drama
60563 97 mins C B, V R, P
Amy Madigan, Beau Bridges, MacKenzie Phillips, Albert Salmi, directed by Larry Peerce
The story of a young woman in prison who becomes pregnant and fights to have and keep her baby.
MPAA:R
Warner Bros — *Warner Home Video*

Love From a Stranger **1947**
Drama
81224 81 mins B/W B, V, LV P
Sylvia Sidney, John Hodiak, John Howard, Ann Richards
A young newlywed bride fears that the honeymoon is over when she suspects that her husband is a notorious killer and that she will be his next victim.
Eagle Lion — *New World Video*

Love Goddesses, The **1974**
Documentary/Women
65425 87 mins B/W B, V P
Marlene Dietrich, Greta Garbo, Jean Harlow, Gloria Swanson, Mae West, Betty Grable, Rita Hayworth, Elizabeth Taylor, Marilyn Monroe
A sixty-year treatment of woman on the screen reflecting with extraordinary accuracy the customs, manners and mores of the times.
Saul J Turell — *Embassy Home Entertainment*

Love Happy **1950**
Comedy
47992 85 mins B/W B, V P
The Marx Brothers, Vera-Ellen, Ilona Massey, Marion Hutton, Raymond Burr, Marilyn Monroe
A group of impoverished actors accidentally gain possession of valuable diamonds.
United Artists — *Republic Pictures Home Video*

Love in Germany, A **1984**
Drama
81213 110 mins C B, V P
Hanna Schygulla, Piotr Lysak, Elisabeth Trissenaar, directed by Andrzej Wajda
A tragic love affair develops between a German shopkeeper's wife and a Polish prisoner-of-war in a small German village during World War II.
MPAA:R GE
Triumph Films — *RCA/Columbia Pictures Home Video*

Love in the Afternoon **1957**
Comedy
80139 126 mins B/W CED P
Gary Cooper, Audrey Hepburn, John McGiver, Maurice Chevalier, directed by Billy Wilder
A Parisian private eye's daughter decides to investigate a philandering American millionaire and winds up falling in love with him.
Billy Wilder — *CBS/Fox Video*

Love Is a Many-Splendored Thing **1955**
Drama
08465 102 mins C CED P
William Holden, Jennifer Jones, Torin Thatcher, Isobel Elsom
Hong Kong in 1949. True story of a romance between lovely Eurasian doctor and an American war correspondent.
Academy Awards '55: Best Song, "Love Is a Many-Splendored Thing" (Sammy Fain, Paul Francis Webster).
20th Century Fox; Buddy Adler — *CBS/Fox Video*

Love Laughs at Andy Hardy **1946**
Comedy
49134 93 mins B/W B, V P
Sara Haden, Lina Romay, Bonita Granville, Fay Holden, Lewis Stone, Mickey Rooney
Andy Hardy, college boy, is in love and in trouble. Financial and romantic problems come to a head when Andy is paired with a six-foot tall blind date.
MGM — *Hal Roach Studios; Budget Video; Discount Video Tapes; VCII; Sound Video Unlimited; Classic Video Cinema Collector's Club*

Love Leads the Way **1984**
Biographical/Drama
76818 99 mins C B, V R, P
Timothy Bottoms, Eva Marie Saint, Arthur Hill, Susan Dey, Ralph Bellamy, Ernest Borgnine, Patricia Neal
This is the true story of how Morris Frank established the Seeing Eye dog movement in the 1930's.
Jimmy Hawkins; Walt Disney Productions — *Walt Disney Home Video*

Love Letters **1983**
Romance
79305 102 mins C B, V, CED P
Jamie Lee Curtis, James Keach
A young disc jockey falls under the spell of a box of love letters that her mother left behind.
MPAA:R
New Horizon Pictures — *Vestron Video*

Love Me Tender **1956**
Musical-Drama
64932 89 mins B/W CED P
Elvis Presley, Richard Egan, Debra Paget, Neville Brand, Mildred Dunnock, James Drury, Barry Coe
A Civil War-torn family is divided by in-fighting between two brothers who both seek the affections of the same women. Presley's first film.
20th Century Fox — *CBS/Fox Video*

Love on the Dole **1941**
Drama
78085 89 mins B/W B, V, FO P
Deborah Kerr, Clifford Evans, George Carney
In a gloomy industrial section of England during the early 30's a family struggles to survive and maintain dignity.
British National — *Video Yesteryear*

Love on the Run **1978**
Drama
58240 90 mins C B, V R, P
Jean-Pierre Leaud, Marie-France Pisier, Claude Jade, directed by Francois Truffaut
The further amorous adventures of Antoine Doinel, hero of "The 400 Blows," "Stolen Kisses," and "Bed and Board." This time out, the women from Doinel's past resurface to challenge his emotions.
MPAA:PG
Elsenoor Belleggin — *Warner Home Video*

Love Skills **1984**
Sexuality
80073 56 mins C B, V P
Five couples explore various sexual techniques from foreplay to sexual positions. Available in Beta Hi-Fi Stereo and VHS Dolby B Stereo.
MCA Home Video — *MCA Home Video*

Love Story 1970
Drama
38598 100 mins C B, V, LV R, P
Ryan O'Neal, Ali McGraw, Ray Milland, directed by Arthur Hiller
Ryan O'Neal and Ali McGraw achieved stardom in this popular adaption of Erich Segal's novel, with portrayals of a young couple who cross social barriers to marry.
Academy Awards '70: Best Original Score (Francis Lai). MPAA:PG
Paramount — *Paramount Home Video; RCA VideoDiscs*

Love Strange Love 1982
Drama
80930 97 mins C B, V P
Vera Fischer, Mauro Mendonca
A young boy develops a bizarre relationship with his mother who works in a luxurious bordello. Also available in an unedited 120-minute version.
Sharp Features — *Vestron Video*

Love Your Body 1983
Physical fitness
68524 60 mins C B, V P
Jayne Kennedy
Jayne Kennedy presents her own exercise program which will make you love your body.
Jeff Tuckman Prods; Chicago Teleprods; Jayne Kennedy Prod — *RCA/Columbia Pictures Home Video*

Loveless, The 1983
Drama
65693 85 mins C B, V P
Robert Gordon, Willem Dafoe, J. Don Ferguson
A menacing glance into the exploits of an outcast motorcycle gang. In the 50's, a group of bikers on their way to the Florida Cycle Races stop for lunch in a small-town diner. While repairs are being made on their motorcycles, they decide to take full advantage of their situation.
MPAA:R
G Nunes; A K Ho — *Media Home Entertainment*

Lovelines 1984
Comedy
Closed Captioned
80833 93 mins C B, V P
Greg Bradford, Michael Winslow, Mary Beth Evans, Tammy Taylor, Stacey Toten
Two rock singers from rival high schools meet and fail in love during a panty raid. Available in VHS and Beta Hi Fi Stereo.
MPAA:R
Tri Star Pictures — *Key Video*

Lovely . . . But Deadly 1982
Drama
77182 95 mins C B, V P
A young girl wages a war against the drug dealers in her school after her brother dies of an overdose.
MPAA:R
Elm Tree Productions — *Vestron Video*

Lovers and Liars 1981
Comedy/Romance
69548 93 mins C B, V, CED P
Goldie Hawn, Giancarlo Giannini
A romantic adventure in Rome turns into a series of comic disasters.
MPAA:R
Alberto Grimaldi — *Embassy Home Entertainment*

Loves And Times Of Scaramouche, The 1976
Comedy
76907 92 mins C B, V P
Michael Sarrazin, Ursula Andress, Aldo Maccione
An eighteenth century rogue becomes involved in a plot to assasinate Napoleon and winds up seducing Josephine in the process.
Federico Aicardi — *Embassy Home Entertainment*

Loves of a Blonde, The 1966
Comedy-Drama
73866 88 mins B/W B, V P
Directed by Milos Forman
A Czechoslovakian girl falls in love with a pianist when the reservist army comes to town. In Czechoslovakian with English subtitles and in Beta Hi-Fi.
Film Studio Barrandov — *RCA/Columbia Pictures Home Video*

Love's Savage Fury 1979
Drama
79197 100 mins C B, V P
Jennifer O'Neill, Perry King, Robert Reed, Raymond Burr, Connie Stevens, Ed Lauter
Two escapees from a Union prison camp seek out a hidden treasure that could determine the outcome of the Civil War.
Aaron Spelling Productions — *Prism*

Lovesick 1983
Comedy
66122 94 mins C B, V R, P
Dudley Moore, Elizabeth McGovern, Alec Guinness, John Huston, directed by Marshall Brickman
A New York psychiatrist falls in love with one of his patients.
MPAA:PG
Ladd Company — *Warner Home Video*

 (For explanation of codes, see USE GUIDE and KEY)

Loving Couples **1980**
Comedy
57229 120 mins C B, V, CED P
Shirley MacLaine, James Coburn, Susan Sarandon, Stephen Collins, Sally Kellerman, directed by Jack Smight
Two happily married couples meet each other after an automobile accident and two new couples emerge, only to collide hilariously at a weekend resort.
MPAA:PG
Time-Life Films — *Vestron Video; Time Life Video*

Loving You **1957**
Musical
47373 92 mins C B, V R, P
Elvis Presley, Wendell Corey, Lizabeth Scott, Dolores Hart
A small town boy with a musical style all his own becomes a big success. Features many early Elvis hits, including "Teddy Bear."
Hal B Wallis — *Warner Home Video*

Lucifer Complex, The **1978**
Science fiction
80657 91 mins C B, V P
Robert Vaughn, Merrie Lynn Ross, Keenan Wynn, Aldo Ray
Nazi doctors are cloning exact duplicates of such world leaders as the Pope and the President of the United States on a remote South American island in the year 1996.
Four Star Entertainment — *United Home Video*

Lucky Jim **1958**
Comedy
63327 91 mins B/W B, V R, P
Ian Carmichael, Terry-Thomas, Hugh Griffith
A junior lecturer in history at a small university tries to get himself in good graces with the head of his department, but is doomed from the start by doing the wrong things at the worst possible times.
Roy Boulting — *THORN EMI/HBO Video*

Lucky Luke: Daisy Town **1983**
Cartoons
66319 75 mins C B, V R, P
Animated
A full-length animated feature starrring Lucky Luke, the all-American cowboy who saves the little community of Daisy Town from the hot-headed Dalton Brothers gang. A wacky western spoof.
Dargaud Editeur — *Walt Disney Home Video*

Lucky Luke: The Ballad of the Daltons **1983**
Cartoons
66320 82 mins C B, V R, P
Animated
Easygoing cowboy hero Lucky Luke gets involved in a wild feud with the bumbling Dalton Brothers gang in this animated feature.
Dargaud Editeur — *Walt Disney Home Video*

Lucky Partners **1940**
Comedy
79681 101 mins B/W B, V P
Ronald Colman, Ginger Rogers, Jack Carson, directed by Lewis Milestone
When an artist and a woman share a winning lottery ticket, comic complications arise.
RKO — *RKO HomeVideo*

Lucky Texan **1934**
Western
15490 61 mins B/W B, V P
John Wayne
"Texas" John Wayne finds himself involved in a range war.
Monogram — *Sony Corporation of America; Video Connection; Video Dimensions; Cable Films; Video Yesteryear; Spotlite Video; Kartes Productions*

Lum and Abner **1949**
Television/Comedy
63626 29 mins B/W B, V, FO P
Chester Lauck, Norris Goff, Andy Devine, Zasu Pitts
This rare kinescope features an episode from the 1949 TV series "Lum and Abner," adapted from the duo's network radio show.
CBS — *Video Yesteryear*

Lunatics and Lovers **1976**
Comedy
47795 92 mins C B, V P
Marcello Mastroianni, Lino Toffalo
A bizarre nobleman meets a door-to-door musician who is in love with an imaginary woman.
MPAA:PG
Independent — *CBS/Fox Video*

Lunch Wagon **1981**
Comedy
59660 88 mins C B, V P
Pamela Bryant, Rosanne Katon
Two co-eds are given a restaurant to manage during summer vacation and wind up involved in a hilarious diamond chase and sex romp.
MPAA:R
Mark Bor — *Media Home Entertainment*

Lust for a Vampire **1970**
Horror
63322 92 mins C B, V R, P
Ralph Bates, Barbara Jefford, Suzanna Leigh
A deadly vampire preys on pupils and teachers alike when she enrolls at a British finishing school.

Hammer Films — *THORN EMI/HBO Video*

Lust in the Dust **1985**
Comedy/Western
81254 85 mins C B, V, LV P
Tab Hunter, Divine, Lainie Kazan, Geoffrey Lewis, Henry Silva, Cesar Romero, directed by Paul Bartel
A precious metal strike is made in the sleepy town of Chile Verde, New Mexico. Gold fever sweeps the west in this satirical oater.
MPAA:R
New World Pictures — *New World Video*

Lusty Men, The **1952**
Western
65157 113 mins B/W B, V P
Robert Mitchum, Susan Hayward, Arthur Kennedy, directed by Nicholas Ray
Two rival rodeo champions, both in love with the same woman, work the rodeo circuit until a tragic accident occurs.
RKO — *United Home Video*

Luv **1967**
Comedy
66012 95 mins C B, V P
Jack Lemmon, Peter Falk, Elaine May, directed by Clive Donner
A suicidal man is saved by a friend who takes him home. The would-be suicide finds new meaning by falling in love with his friend's wife.
MPAA:PG
Columbia — *RCA/Columbia Pictures Home Video*

Luv-Ya Blue! **1980**
Football
45128 24 mins C B, V, FO R, P
Houston Oilers
Highlights of the 1979 Houston Oilers football season.
NFL Films — *NFL Films Video*

Lydia **1941**
Drama
81462 98 mins B/W B, V, LV P
Merle Oberon, Joseph Cotten, Alan Marshall, George Reeves
An elderly lady gets to relive her romantic past when she has a reunion with four of her lost loves.
Alexander Korda — *Embassy Home Entertainment*

M

Ma Vlast (My Fatherland) **1982**
Music-Performance
47808 ? mins C LV P
The traditional performance of Smetana's "My Fatherland" which opened the 1981 Prague Spring International Music Festival performed by the Czech Philharmonic Orchestra (stereo).
Unknown — *Pioneer Video Imports*

Macabre Moments from The Phantom of the Opera **1925**
Horror
62872 34 mins B/W B, V P, T
Lon Chaney Sr., Norman Kerry, Mary Philbin
An edited version of this classic film, with story continuity maintained. Silent; includes color sequence.
Universal — *Blackhawk Films*

Macao **1952**
Drama
64374 81 mins B/W B, V, 3/4U P
Robert Mitchum, Jane Russell, William Bendix, Gloria Grahame
A wandering adventurer and a cafe singer cross paths with a wanted criminal in the exotic Far East.
RKO — *Nostalgia Merchant*

MacArthur **1977**
War-Drama
58426 144 mins C B, V P
Gregory Peck, Ivan Bonar, Ward Costello, Nicholas Coster, directed by Joseph Sargent
General Douglas MacArthur's life from Corregidor in 1942 to his dismissal a decade later in the midst of the Korean conflict.
MPAA:PG
Universal; Zanuck Brown Prods — *MCA Home Video*

Macbeth **1948**
Drama
66474 111 mins B/W B, V P
Orson Welles, Jeanette Nolan, Dan O'Herlihy, Roddy McDowall, Robert Coote, directed by Orson Welles
Shakespeare's classic tragedy is performed in this film with a celebrated lead performance by Orson Welles as the tragic king.
Republic — *Republic Pictures Home Video*

Mack, The **1973**
Drama
81475 110 mins C B, V P
Max Julien, Richard Pryor, Don Gordon, Roger E. Mosley, Carol Speed
The Mack is a pimp who comes out of retirement to reclaim a piece of the action in Oakland, California.
MPAA:R

Cinerama Releasing — *Embassy Home Entertainment*

MacKenna's Gold 1969
Western/Adventure
70192 128 mins C B, V P
Gregory Peck, Omar Sharif, Telly Savalas, Julie Newmar, Edward G. Robinson
A ragtag group of adventurers travel to Apache territory in search of a cache of gold that was rumored to have been buried there. In Beta Hi-Fi.
MPAA:PG
Columbia Pictures — *RCA/Columbia Pictures Home Video*

Mackintosh Man, The 1973
Adventure/Suspense
76855 100 mins C B, V R, P
Paul Newman, Dominique Sanda, James Mason, Ian Bannen, Nigel Patrick, directed by John Huston
A British intelligence agent is out to trap a Communist who has infiltrated the top ranks of the organization.
MPAA:PG
John Foreman; Warner Bros — *Warner Home Video*

Macon County Line 1974
Drama/Adventure
65390 89 mins C B, V P
Alan Vint, Jesse Vint, Cheryl Waters, Geoffrey Lewis, Joan Blackman, Max Baer
A series of deadly mistakes and misfortunes lead to a sudden turn around in the lives of 3 young people when they enter a small Georgia town and find themselves accused of brutally slaying the sheriff's wife.
MPAA:R
American International Pictures — *Embassy Home Entertainment*

Mad Bomber 1972
Suspense
12027 80 mins C B, V P
Vince Edwards, Chuck Connors, Neville Brand
Police search for a mad bomber who has terrorized the city.
Philip Yordan Prod; Official Films — *King of Video; World Video Pictures*

Mad Dog Morgan 1976
Biographical/Drama
77169 93 mins C B, V P
Dennis Hopper, David Gulpilil, directed by Philippe Mora
This is the true story of outlaw Dan "Mad Dog" Morgan who always kept one step ahead of the law.
MPAA:R
Jeremy Thomas — *THORN EMI/HBO Video*

Mad, Mad Monsters, The 1984
Cartoons
70614 60 mins C B, V P
Animated
The fun-loving creatures of the title aren't angry; they're merely loony.
Videocraft International Ltd. — *Prism*

Mad Max 1980
Adventure
66105 93 mins C B, V, LV, CED P
Mel Gibson
Set on the highways of the post-nuclear future, this film concerns rebel bikers who challenge the police who guard what is left of civilization.
MPAA:R
American International Pictures — *Vestron Video*

Mad Miss Manton, The 1938
Comedy/Mystery
73688 80 mins B/W B, V P
Barbara Stanwyck, Henry Fonda, Hattie McDaniel, Sam Levene
A society girl becomes a sleuth to solve a murder.
RKO — *RKO HomeVideo*

Mad Mission 3 1984
Satire
79710 81 mins C B, V R, P
Richard Kiel, Sam Kui, Karl Muka, Sylvia Chang, Tsuneharu Sugiyama
While on vacation in Paris, a Chinese man is recruited by James Bond to retrieve two jewels stolen from the English crown.
Cinema City Company — *THORN EMI/HBO Video*

Mad Monster Party 1968
Comedy
64975 94 mins C B, V, CED P
Animated, voices of Boris Karloff, Ethel Ennis, Phyllis Diller
Dr. Frankenstein is getting older and wants to retire from the responsibilities of being senior monster, so he calls a convention of creepy creatures to decide who should take his placethe Wolfman, Dracula, the Mummy, the Creature, It, the Invisible Man, or Dr. Jekyll and Mr. Hyde.
Avco-Embassy — *Embassy Home Entertainment*

Madame Bovary 1949
Romance/Drama
58871 114 mins B/W B, V P
Jennifer Jones, Van Heflin, Louis Jordan, James Mason, directed by Vincente Minnelli
Gustave Flaubert's classic novel concerning a woman's abandoned pursuit of love and the three men who loved her.

MGM; Pandro S Berman — *MGM/UA Home Video*

Madame Butterfly **1983**
Music-Performance
80328 135 mins C B, V R, P
Raina Kabalvanska, Nazareno Antinori, Elonora Jankovic
A performance of the Puccini opera about an American soldier and the Japanese woman he loves which was recorded at the Arena di Verona.
Covent Garden Video Productions — *THORN EMI/HBO Video*

Madame in Manhattan **1984**
Comedy-Performance/Puppets
78658 60 mins C B, V P
Wayland Flowers and Madame escort you through an unforgettable tour of the Big Apple.
RKO — *RKO HomeVideo*

Madame Rosa **1978**
Drama
59421 105 mins C B, V P
Simone Signoret, Claude Dauphin, directed by Molshe Mizrahi
The evocative portrayal of a survivor of both Nazi concentration camps and a life of prostitution.
Academy Awards '78: Best Foreign Film.
MPAA:PG
Raymond Danon; Roland Girard; Jean Bolvary; Libra Film Prod — *Vestron Video*

Madame X **1966**
Drama
70556 100 mins C B, V P
Lana Turner, John Forsythe, Ricardo Montalban, Burgess Meredith, Constance Bennett, Keir Dullea
Turner stars in one of the 6 remakes of the '29 film about a woman blackmailed into exile, out of the aristocracy she'd married into. After years of alcohol and degradation, she is put on trial for murder with her son assigned to defend her. In mono Hi Fi on all formats.
Universal — *MCA Home Video*

Made for Each Other **1939**
Drama
08677 100 mins B/W B, V, 3/4U P
Carole Lombard, James Stewart, Charles Coburn, Lucille Watson
A touching drama of young love and its disappointments; interfering mother-inlaw who wants to baby her married son and control the grandchild.
David O Selznick — *Movie Buff Video; Budget Video; VCII; Video Dimensions; Sheik Video; Cable Films; Video Connection; Video Yesteryear; Discount Video Tapes*

Made in Heaven **1952**
Comedy
80939 90 mins C B, V P
Petula Clark, David Tomlinson, Sonja Ziemann
A distrusting newlywed wife suspects that her husband is philandering about with the new maid they've just hired.
J. Arthur Rank — *VidAmerica*

Madhouse **1984**
Horror
72460 90 mins C B, V P
Trish Everly
A woman has bizarre recollections of her twin sister whom she finally meets in a hospital.
unknown — *VCL Home Video*

Madman **1982**
Horror
66186 89 mins C B, V R, P
Alexis Dubin, Tony Fish
A cocky young man, mocking a legend about an ax murderer, sets the wheels of terror in motion.
MPAA:R
Jensen Farley — *THORN EMI/HBO Video*

Madman **1979**
Adventure
76913 95 mins C B, V P
Sigourney Weaver, Michael Beck, F. Murray Abraham
This is the true story of Boris Abramovitch, a Russian-born Jew who led an incredible fight against Soviet oppression.
MPAA:PG
Alex Massis — *United Home Video*

Mafu Cage, The **1978**
Horror
77398 99 mins C B, V P
Carol Kane, Lee Grant
A rather strange woman puts her sisters' lover into a cage and subjects him to brutal torture.
Independent — *Wizard Video*

Magee and the Lady **1978**
Drama
81077 92 mins C B, V P
Tony Lo Bianco, Sally Kellerman
The crusty captain of a rusty ship must tame a spoiled debutante or lose his ship to a foreclosure firm.
MPAA:PG
Transatlantic Enterprises — *Academy Home Entertainment*

Magic **1978**
Drama
59835 106 mins C B, V, LV, CED P

 (For explanation of codes, see USE GUIDE and KEY)

Anthony Hopkins, Ann-Margret, Burgess Meredith, Ed Lauter, directed by Richard Attenborough
A ventriloquist and his dummy, an all-too-human counterpart, get involved with a beautiful but impressionable woman lost between the world of reality and the irresistible world of illusion.
MPAA:R
Joseph E Levine; Richard P Levine — *Embassy Home Entertainment*

Magic Adventure 198?
Cartoons
80719 82 mins C B, V P
Animated
A brother and his sister are in for the time of their lives when they meet the Wind Wizard who sends them on an unexpected journey.
Unknown — *All Seasons Entertainment*

Magic Christian, The 1970
Comedy
47988 88 mins C B, V P
Peter Sellers, Raquel Welch, Ringo Starr, Laurence Harvey, Richard Attenborough
The richest man in the world adopts a vagrant for his son, to prove that any man can be corrupted by money.
MPAA:PG
Grand Film; Commonwealth United — *Republic Pictures Home Video*

Magic Garden, The 1960
Comedy
11239 60 mins B/W B, V, FO P
Tommy Ramokgopa, directed by Donald Swanson
A thief loses his stolen money and it is found by honest people who put it to good use while the thief goes mad trying to locate it.
Donald Swanson — *Video Yesteryear; Sheik Video*

Magic of Doctor Snuggles, The 1985
Cartoons
76910 60 mins C B, V P
Animated
The kindly Doctor snuggles enters a balloon race to win prize money to help Granny Toots build a new cat hospital.
Kidpix — *Embassy Home Entertainment*

Magic Pony, The 1978
Adventure
40733 80 mins C B, V R, P
Voices of Jim Backus and Erin Moran
Ivan and his three brothers are sent to watch the fields and catch the culprit who has been destroying the wheat crop. The Magic Pony starts them on new adventures.
21st Century — *Video Gems; Vestron Video (disc only)*

Magic Pony, The 19??
Fantasy
69610 80 mins C B, V P
Animated, voices of Jim Backus and Erin Moran
With the help of a beautiful flying horse, a young man battles a greedy emperor to become the kind-hearted prince and live happily ever after with a beautiful princess and his Magic Pony.
MPAA:G
Samuel J Phillips — *Children's Video Library*

Magic Sword, The 1962
Adventure
38974 80 mins C B, V, FO P
Basil Rathbone, Estelle Winwood
A family-oriented adventure film about a young knight who sets out to rescue a beautiful princess who is being held captive by an evil sorcerer and his dragon.
United Artists — *Video Yesteryear; Sheik Video*

Magic Town 1947
Comedy-Drama
64539 103 mins B/W B, V P
Jane Wyman, James Stewart, Kent Smith, directed by William Wellman
An opinion pollster investigates a small town which exactly reflects the views of the entire nation, making his job a cinch.
RKO — *Republic Pictures Home Video*

Magical Mystery Tour 1967
Musical
53945 55 mins C B, V P
The Beatles, Victor Spinetti
On the road with an oddball assortment of people, the Beatles experience a strange assortment of incidents around the English countryside. Originally made for British television. Songs include: "The Fool on the Hill," "Blue Jay Way," "Your Mother Should Know," and the title tune.
Apple Films — *Media Home Entertainment; Western Film & Video Inc*

Magician, The 1959
Comedy-Drama
65626 101 mins B/W B, V, LV P
Max von Sydow, Gunnar Bjornstrand, directed by Ingmar Bergman
A wandering magician arrives in 19th century Stockholm with his troupe where they encounter considerable skepticism.
Janus Films — *Embassy Home Entertainment*

Magnavox Theater (The Three Musketeers) 1950
Drama
42969 53 mins B/W B, V, FO P
John Hubbard, Robert Clarke, Mel Archer, Marjorie Lord
This teleplay which remains true to the novel by Alexandre Dumas, was directed by Budd Boetticher and includes flashing swords and romance.
Hal Roach Jr — *Video Yesteryear*

Magnificent, The 1981
Martial arts
69277 80 mins C B, V P
Chen Sing, Carter Hwang, Casanova Wong, Bruce Lai, Doris Chen
After the 1911 Revolution, supporters of the deposed Ching government plot to overthrow the new government. Mandarin dialogue, English subtitles.
CH
IFD Films & Arts — *Silverline Video*

Magnificent Ambersons, The 1942
Drama
00261 88 mins B/W B, V, 3/4U P
Joseph Cotten, Agnes Moorehead, directed by Orson Welles
A turn-of-the century family clings to its genteel traditions during an era of rapid change. Orson Welles' second directorial effort.
RKO — *Nostalgia Merchant*

Magnificent Kick, The 1980
Adventure/Martial arts
60514 90 mins C B, V P
The story of a master Wong-Fai-Hung, inventor of the "Kick without Shadow," which was practiced by the late Bruce Lee.
Unknown — *Master Arts Video*

Magnificent Obsession 1954
Drama
70557 108 mins C B, V P
Jane Wyman, Rock Hudson, Barbara Rush, Agnes Moorehead, directed by Lloyd C. Douglas
A rich playboy accidently causes the death of a brain surgeon and blinds his wife. Guilty, the man devotes his life to the study of medicine and the restoration of the widow's eyesight. In Mono Hi-Fi on all formats.
Universal — *MCA Home Video*

Magnificent Seven, The 1960
Western
53791 126 mins C B, V, CED P
Yul Brenner, Steve McQueen, Robert Vaughn, James Coburn, Charles Bronson, Horst Buchholz, Eli Wallach, directed by John Sturges
Mexican villagers hire seven American gunmen to defend them against bandits.
United Artists; Walter Mirisch — *CBS/Fox Video; RCA VideoDiscs*

Magnifique, Le 1976
Comedy
11354 100 mins C B, V P
Jean-Paul Belmondo, Jacqueline Bisset
Belmondo is a master spy and novelist who mixes fantasy with reality when he chases women and solves cases.
CINE III — *Prism; Cinema Concepts*

Magnum Force 1973
Suspense/Crime-Drama
54796 124 mins C B, V R, P
Clint Eastwood, Hal Holbrook, Mitchell Ryan, David Soul, directed by Ted Post
A San Francisco homicide detective investigating a rash of gangster murders discovers that they are the work of a rookie police assassination squad whose members have been frustrated by red tape and civil liberties. A sequel to "Dirty Harry."
MPAA:R
Warner Bros, Robert Daly Prods — *Warner Home Video; RCA VideoDiscs*

Mahalia Jackson and Elizabeth Cotten: Two Remarkable Ladies 1974
Music/Documentary
58581 58 mins C B, V P
A close-up look at a pair of successful black women performers: "Mahalia Jackson," a filmed biography of the legendary singer, and "Freight Train," the courageous story of pioneer folksinger Elizabeth Cotten.
CBS — *Mastervision*

Mahler 1974
Biographical/Drama
80650 110 mins C B, V R, P
Robert Powell, Georgiana Hale, Richard Morant, Lee Montague, directed by Ken Russell
A dazzling look at the life, loves and music of composer Gustav Mahler.
MPAA:PG
Goodtimes Enterprises — *THORN EMI/HBO Video*

Mahogany 1976
Drama
59202 109 mins C B, V, LV R, P
Diana Ross, Billy Dee Williams, Jean Pierre Aumont
A world-famous high fashion model and designer gets a career boost when she daringly appears in a dress of her own creation at a Roman fashion show.
MPAA:R
Paramount — *Paramount Home Video; RCA VideoDiscs*

Main Event, The 1979
Comedy
37426 112 mins C B, V R, P
Barbra Streisand, Ryan O'Neal
A wisecracking young woman obtains the contract of a prize fighter who is about to retire. She becomes his manager and gets him back into the ring.
MPAA:PG
Warner Bros — *Warner Home Video; RCA VideoDiscs*

Main Street to Broadway 1953
Musical
76926 102 mins B/W B, V P
Tom Morton, Mary Murphy, Rex Harrision, Helen Hayes, Mary Martin, directed by Jay Garnett
A struggling young playwright attempts to launch his first play on the Broadway stage.
Lester Cowan — *MPI Home Video*

Major Dundee 1965
Adventure
76029 124 mins C B, V P
Charlton Heston, Richard Harris, James Coburn, Jim Hutton, directed by Sam Peckinpah
A union army officer with a hundred criminals volunteers from the prison he commands to chase a savage Indian leader through Mexico.
Jerry Bresler — *RCA/Columbia Pictures Home Video*

Make a Million 1935
Comedy
69557 66 mins B/W B, V, FO P
Charles Starrett, Pauline Brooks
An economics professor is fired from his post because of his radical theories about redistributing the country's wealth. To prove his point, he becomes a millionaire by advertising for money.
Monogram Pictures — *Video Yesteryear*

Make a Wish 1937
Drama
08671 80 mins B/W B, V, 3/4U P
Basil Rathbone, Leon Errol, Bobby Breen, Ralph Forbes
A noted composer goes stale in this colorful tale of backstage life. Music by Oscar Strauss.
RKO — *Sheik Video; Video Yesteryear*

Make Mine Mink 1960
Comedy
55343 100 mins B/W B, V P
Terry Thomas, Billie Whitelaw, Hattie Jacques
A madcap comedy about larceny, with a seasoned cast playing guests at an elegant but slightly run-down mansion. Bored, the group takes up a Robin Hood-like hobby of stealing from the rich and giving to the poor.
Continental — *Sheik Video; VidAmerica*

Make Room For Daddy I 1953
Comedy
77192 120 mins B/W B, V P
Danny Thomas, Jean Hagen, Rusty Hamer, Jesse White, Sherry Jackson
A collection of four early episodes from the series about the family life of a New York night club entertainer.
T & L Productions — *Shokus Video*

Make Room for Daddy II 1954
Comedy
77197 120 mins B/W B, V P
Danny Thomas, Jean Hagen, Rusty Hamer, Jesse White, Sherry Jackson
This is another volume of four episodes that chronicles the comedic foibles of the Williams family.
T&C Productions — *Shokus Video*

Making Love 1982
Drama
59630 112 mins C B, V, CED P
Kate Jackson, Harry Hamlin, Michael Ontkean, directed by Arthur Hiller
A love story concerning a young married couple whose seemingly-perfect world is shattered by the husband's homosexuality.
MPAA:R
Twentieth Century Fox — *CBS/Fox Video*

Making Michael Jackson's Thriller 1983
Music-Performance
65347 60 mins C B, V, LV, CED P
Michael Jackson
The program is a behind-the-scenes look at how an unprecendented music video was created. The program includes highlights of Jackson's highly acclaimed videos for "Billie Jean" and "Beat It," as well as the 10-minute video for the title song of the "Thriller" album. In stereo and Beta Hi-Fi.
John Landis — *Vestron Video*

Making of Star Wars, The/S.P.F.X. — The Empire Strikes Back 1980
Filmmaking/Science fiction
08478 100 mins C B, V, LV, CED P
Mark Hamill, Carrie Fisher, Harrison Ford, narrated by William Conrad
Behind-the-scenes look at the special effects of these two popular movies directed by George Lucas. The viewer will see how Luke's automobile is able to cruise above ground, how the droids, C-3PO and R2-D2 move around, and the workings of Yoda.
EL, SP

20th Century Fox; Gary Kurtz — *CBS/Fox Video*

Making of Superman, The **1979**
Filmmaking
75466 96 mins C B, V P
Christopher Reeve, Margot Kidder
A behind-the-scenes look at the making of "Superman-The Movie."
Salkind — *Family Home Entertainment*

Making of Superman—The Movie and Superman II, The **1984**
Science fiction/Filmmaking
66621 120 mins C B, V P
Christopher Reeve, Margot Kidder, Susannah York
These two hour-long documentaries chronicle the making of the Superman films, showing the construction of sets, special effects work and off-screen moments with the actors.
Dovemead Limited; Film Export; International Film Productions — *U.S.A. Home Video*

Making of Superman II, The **1981**
Filmmaking
75467 96 mins C B, V P
Christopher Reeve, Margot Kidder
A behind-the-scenes look at the making of "Superman II."
Salkind — *Family Home Entertainment*

Making of the Stooges, The **1985**
Comedy/Documentary
70386 47 mins B/W B, V P
Moe Howard, Larry Fine, Curly Howard, narrated by Steve Allen
This tape documents the 50-year history of the Three Stooges including rare footage of these slapstick stars.
Forest P. Gill, Mark S. Gillman — *Karl/Lorimar Home Video*

Making of 2:00 AM Paradise Cafe **1984**
Documentary/Music-Performance
80377 55 mins C B, V P
A behind the scenes documentary that details the recording of Barry Manilow's jazz influenced album "2:00 A.M. Paradise Cafe". Available in VHS Dolby Hi-Fi Stereo and Beta Hi-Fi.
Stiletto Ltd. Productions — *RCA/Columbia Pictures Home Video*

Making the Grade **1984**
Comedy
73365 105 mins C B, V P
A hoodlum poses as a preppy to settle some debts owed to the mob.
MPAA:PG
Cannon Films — *MGM/UA Home Video*

Malibu Beach **1978**
Comedy
48477 93 mins C B, V P
Kim Lankford, James Daughton
The California beach scene is the setting for this movie filled with bikini clad girls, tanned young men, and instant romances.
MPAA:R
Crown International — *United Home Video*

Malibu Express **1985**
Adventure/Mystery
81200 101 mins C B, V P
Darby Hinton, Sybil Danning, Art Metrano, Shelley Taylor Morgan, Niki Dantine, Barbara Edwards
A rich Texas millionaire gets his chance to become a private eye when a conscientious contessa asks him to stop and American corporation from selling computers to the Russians.
MPAA:R
The Sidaris Company — *MCA Home Video*

Malibu High **1979**
Drama
48480 92 mins C B, V P
Jill Lansing, Stuart Taylor
The accidental death of a young prostitute's client leads her to a new series of illegal activities of the "sex and hit" variety.
MPAA:R
Crown International — *United Home Video*

Malicious **1974**
Drama
44592 98 mins C B, V R, P
Laura Antonelli, Turi Ferro, Alessandro Momo, Tina Aumont, directed by Salvatore Samperi
A housekeeper hired for a widower and his three sons becomes the object of lusty affection of all four men. As Papa makes plans to court and marry her, his fourteen-year-old son plots to have her as a companion on his road to sensual maturity. Dubbed in English.
MPAA:R
Paramount, Silvio Clementelli — *Paramount Home Video*

Malta Story **1953**
War-Drama
62867 103 mins B/W B, V P
Alec Guinness, Jack Hawkins, Anthony Steel, Flora Robson
A British World War II flier becomes involved with the defense of Malta.
UA British; GFD — *Embassy Home Entertainment*

(For explanation of codes, see USE GUIDE and KEY)

Maltese Falcon, The 1941
Mystery
13594 101 mins B/W B, V P
Humphrey Bogart, Mary Astor, Sydney Greenstreet, Peter Lorre, directed by John Huston
After the death of his partner, detective Sam Spade finds himself enmeshed in the search for a priceless statuette.
National Board of Review Awards '41: Best Performances (Bogart and Astor).
Warner Brothers — *CBS/Fox Video; RCA VideoDiscs*

Mama (I Remember Mama) 195?
Comedy
59313 55 mins B/W B, V, 3/4U P
Peggy Wood, Dick Van Patten
This family comedy series set in San Francisco at the turn of the century includes two episodes: "Mama's Bad Day" (1950), in which Mama feels she's being taken for granted; and, "Mama's Nursery School" (1955), in which Mama becomes a substitute teacher. Includes original commercials.
CBS — *Shokus Video; Discount Video Tapes*

Mama (I Remember Mama) 1950
Drama
42977 29 mins B/W B, V, FO P
Peggy Wood, Judson Laire, Dick Van Patten, Rosemary Rice
Little Dagmar is entered in a spelling bee and Papa bets his life insurance money that she'll win.
CBS — *Video Yesteryear*

Mama (I Remember Mama) 1950
Comedy
39002 30 mins B/W B, V, FO P
Peggy Wood, Judson Laird, Rosemary Rice, Robin Morgan
A representative episode from the famous early TV series, "Madame Zodiac," in which Aunt Jenny has her fortune told with surprising results. Original commercials included.
CBS — *Video Yesteryear*

Mama (I Remember Mama) 1951
Comedy-Drama
47503 29 mins B/W B, V, FO P
Peggy Wood, Judson Laird, Robin Morgan, Rosemary Rice, Dick Van Patten, Ruth Gates
This episode of the popular TV series is titled "Mama's Bad Day." Family problems become more than Mama can bear, and she is conscience-stricken when she wishes she had never married.
CBS — *Video Yesteryear*

Mame 1974
Musical
74206 131 mins C B, V R, P
Lucille Ball, Beatrice Arthur
This is the story of Auntie Mame, who takes it on herself to teach a group of eccentrics how to live life to its fullest.
MPAA:PG
Robert Fryer; James Cresson — *Warner Home Video*

Man, a Woman, and a Bank, A 1979
Comedy
48404 100 mins C B, V P
Donald Sutherland, Brooke Adams, Paul Mazursky
Two con men plan to rob a bank by posing as workers during the bank's construction. An advertising agency woman snaps their picture for a billboard to show how nice the builders have been, then becomes romantically involved with one of the would-be thieves.
MPAA:PG
John B Bennett, Peter Samuelson — *Embassy Home Entertainment*

Man Against Crime Volume I 1956
Adventure
47640 60 mins B/W B, V, FO P
Frank Lovejoy
A gunless gumshoe travels the globe in search of crooks and intrigue. Vintage television.
NBC — *Video Yesteryear*

Man Against Crime Volume II 1956
Crime-Drama
47650 60 mins B/W B, V, FO P
Frank Lovejoy, Herschel Bernardi
Two episodes of the vintage TV series with Frank Lovejoy as detective Mike Barnett. In episode one, Mike is challenged to a duel by a nasty jai alai player who's been blackmailing his employer. In episode two, Mike gets involved with a Parisian narcotics ring.
NBC — *Video Yesteryear*

Man Alone, A 1955
Western
74485 96 mins C B, V P
Ray Milland, Raymond Burr
This is the story of a sheriff who defends a man falsely accused of robbing a stagecoach.
Republic — *Republic Pictures Home Video*

Man Called Horse, A 1970
Adventure
65495 114 mins C CED P

Stanford Howard
An English aristocrat is captured by Indians, lives with them and eventually becomes their leader.
Cinema Center — *CBS/Fox Video*

Man Called Horse, A **1969**
Western
Closed Captioned
81172 15t mins C B, V P
Richard Harris, Dame Judith Anderson, Jean Gascon
A British aristocrat, captured and tortured by the Sioux Indians in the Dakotas, later helps them fend off an attack by rival braves. Impressed, they offer to embrace him as a brother if he can endure the Sun Vow.
MPAA:PG
CBS Theatrical Films — *CBS/Fox Video*

Man Called Tiger **1981**
Martial arts
81473 97 mins C B, V P
A Chinese martial arts expert infiltrates a ruthless Japanese gang in order to find the man who murdered his father.
MPAA:R
World Northal Corporation — *Embassy Home Entertainment*

Man for All Seasons, A **1966**
Drama
Closed Captioned
21291 120 mins C B, V P
Paul Scofield, Robert Shaw, Orson Welles, Wendy Hiller, Susannah York, directed by Fred Zinneman
A biographical drama concerning sixteenth century Chancellor of England, Sir Thomas More, and his personal conflict with King Henry VIII.
Academy Awards '66: Best Picture; Best Actor (Scofield); Best Director (Zinneman).
Columbia — *RCA/Columbia Pictures Home Video; RCA VideoDiscs*

Man from Atlantis **1977**
Science fiction
66278 60 mins C B, V P
Patrick Duffy
Patrick Duffy stars as the water-breathing alien who emerges from his undersea home—the Lost City of Atlantis.
NBC — *Worldvision Home Video*

Man from Beyond **1922**
Adventure/Drama
59219 50 mins B/W B, V, 3/4U P
Harry Houdini, Arthur Maude
Frozen alive, a man returns 100 years later to try and find his lost love. Silent.
Houdini Picture Corp — *Video Yesteryear*

Man from Clover Grove, The **1978**
Comedy
56738 97 mins C B, V P
Ron Masak, Cheryl Miller, Jed Allan, Rose Marie
Hilarity takes over a town when a nutty boy inventor puts the sheriff in a spin.
EL, SP
Drew Cummings — *Media Home Entertainment*

Man from Music Mountain, The **1938**
Western
08788 54 mins B/W B, V, 3/4U P
Gene Autry, Smiley Burnette, Carol Hughes, Polly Jenkins
Worthless mining stock is sold in a desert mining town, but Gene and Smiley clear that up.
Republic — *Budget Video; Video Connection; Discount Video Tapes; Nostalgia Merchant*

Man from Snowy River, The **1982**
Adventure
65002 104 mins C B, V, CED P
Kirk Douglas, Tom Burlinson
Stunning cinematography highlights this heroic adventure story set in Australia in the 1880's, as a young man accepts the challenge of taming a herd of wild horses.
MPAA:PG
20th Century Fox — *CBS/Fox Video*

Man from Utah, The **1934**
Western
11268 55 mins B/W B, V, FO P
John Wayne, Gabby Hayes
The Duke tangles with the crooked sponsor of some rodeo events who has killed several of the participants.
Monogram — *Sony Corporation of America; Spotlite Video; Video Yesteryear; Video Connection; Cable Films; Discount Video Tapes*

Man in Grey, The **1945**
Romance
76639 116 mins B/W B, V P
James Mason, Margaret Lockwood, Stewart Granger, Phyllis Calvert
An intriguing story of a criss-cross love affair among 19th century English royalty.
Gainsborough — *VidAmerica*

Man in the Iron Mask, The **1939**
Adventure
55350 110 mins B/W B, V, 3/4U P
Louis Hayward, Alan Hale, Joan Bennett, directed by James Whale
Alexandre Dumas' classic novel provides the basis for this tale about the twin brother of King Louis XIV of France, who was kept prisoner with his face covered by a locked iron mask.

Edward Small; United Artists — *Nostalgia Merchant*

Man in the Santa Claus Suit, The **1979**
Fantasy/Comedy
79225 96 mins C B, V P
Fred Astaire, Gary Burghoff, John Byner, Nanette Fabray
A costume shop owner has an effect on three people who rent Santa Claus costumes from him.
Dick Clark Cinema Productions — *Media Home Entertainment*

Man in the White Suit, The **1951**
Comedy
45070 82 mins B/W B, V R, P
Alec Guinness, Joan Greenwood
A humble laboratory assistant in a textile mill invents a cloth that won't stain, tear, or wear-out and causes an industry-wide panic.
Universal, J Arthur Rank — *THORN EMI/HBO Video*

Man Inside, The **1976**
Drama
76640 96 mins C B, V P
James Franciscus, Stefanie Powers, Jacques Godin
An undercover agent infiltrates a powerful underworld narcotics ring and finds his honesty tested when $2 million is at stake.
CBC — *Trans World Entertainment*

Man of La Mancha **1972**
Musical
58839 121 mins C B, V, CED P
Peter O'Toole, Sophia Loren, James Coco, Harry Andrews, John Castle, Brian Blessed
Arrested by the Inquisition and thrown into prison, Miguel de Cervantes relates the story of Don Quixote. Based on the Broadway musical, with music by Mitch Leigh and lyrics by Joe Darion. Songs include "The Impossible Dream" and "Dulcinea."
MPAA:PG
United Artists — *CBS/Fox Video*

Man of the Frontier **1936**
Western
05580 60 mins B/W B, V, 3/4U P
Gene Autry, Smiley Burnette, Frances Grant
A vital irrigation project is being sabotaged, but Gene Autry exposes the culprits.
Republic — *Video Connection; Video Yesteryear; Discount Video Tapes*

Man on the Eiffel Tower, The **1948**
Crime-Drama
64342 82 mins B/W B, V P
Charles Laughton, Burgess Meredith, Franchot Tone, Patricia Roc, directed by Burgess Meredith
A mysterious crazed killer defies the police to discover his identity.
A & T — *Movie Buff Video; Classic Video Cinema Collector's Club; Cable Films; Discount Video Tapes*

Man on the Moon **1981**
Space exploration
58302 80 mins C B, V, CED P
Narrated by Walter Cronkite
This program traces the birth and development of the U.S. Space Program, leading to the Apollo 11 moon landing.
CBS News — *CBS/Fox Video*

Man They Could Not Hang, The **1939**
Horror
78966 70 mins B/W B, V P
Boris Karloff, Lorna Gray, Roger Pryor
When a doctor is hanged for a murder, his assistant brings the doctor back to life and he vows revenge against the jurors that sentenced him. In Beta Hi-Fi.
Columbia Pictures — *RCA/Columbia Pictures Home Video*

Man Who Fell to Earth, The **1976**
Science fiction
33703 118 mins C B, V P
David Bowie
A man from another planet ventures to earth and becomes a successful businessman. His ulterior motive for this visit is to come to the aid of his family on their ailing planet, at the expense of Earth.
MPAA:R
Cinema 5 — *RCA/Columbia Pictures Home Video*

Man Who Haunted Himself, The **1970**
Mystery/Suspense
63336 91 mins C B, V R, P
Roger Moore, Hildegarde Neil, Olga Georges-Picot
A man is possessed by a mysterious force that takes control of his ideal life and turns it into a nightmare.
Associated British Productions Ltd — *THORN EMI/HBO Video*

Man Who Knew Too Much, The 1956
Mystery/Drama
79678 120 mins C B, V P
James Stewart, Doris Day, Brenda De Banzie, Bernard Miles, directed by Alfred Hitchcock.
A doctor vacationing in Marrakech uncovers a murder plot and embroils his family in a frying pan of intrigue.
MPAA:PG
Alfred Hitchcock; Universal Classics — *MCA Home Video*

Man Who Knew Too Much, The 1934
Mystery
08745 87 mins C B, V P
Leslie Banks, Edna Best, Peter Lorre, Nova Pilbeam, directed by Alfred Hitchcock
Hitchcock's first international success — a British family man on vacation in Switzerland is told about an assassination plot by a dying agent.
Gaumont — *Media Home Entertainment; Prism; Active Home Video; Hal Roach Studios; VCII; Blackhawk Films; Video Yesteryear; Budget Video; Video Dimensions; Sheik Video; Cable Films; Video Connection; Discount Video Tapes; Western Film & Video Inc; Cinema Concepts; MCA Home Video; Spotlite Video; Kartes Productions; Classic Video Cinema Collector's Club*

Man Who Loved Cat Dancing, The 1973
Western
80148 127 mins C B, V P
Burt Reynolds, Sarah Miles, Jack Warden, Lee J Cobb, Jay Silverheels
A train robber falls in love with a woman he kidnaps after a heist.
MPAA:PG
Metro Goldwyn Mayer — *MGM/UA Home Video*

Man Who Loved Women, The 1983
Comedy
76030 118 mins C B, V P
Burt Reynolds, Julie Andrews, Kim Basinger, Marilu Henner, Cynthia Sikes, Jennifer Edwards, directed by Blake Edwards
Burt Reynolds stars in this hilarious comedy about a Los Angeles sculptor whose reputation as a playboy leads him to a midlife crisis.
MPAA:R
Blake Edwards; Tony Adams — *RCA/Columbia Pictures Home Video*

Man Who Loved Women, The 1977
Romance
44779 119 mins C B, V P
Charles Denner, Brigitte Fossey, Leslie Caron, directed by Francois Truffaut
An intelligent, sensitive bachelor worships all women. Trying to find the reasons for his obsession, he writes his memoirs and remembers all the women he has loved.
MPAA:R
Cinema 5 — *RCA/Columbia Pictures Home Video*

Man Who Shot Liberty Valance, The 1962
Western
33715 122 mins B/W B, V, LV R, P
James Stewart, John Wayne, Vera Miles, Lee Marvin, Edmond O'Brien, Andy Devine, Woody Strode, directed by John Ford
Liberty Valance terrorizes a small western town and is opposed by only two men, one of whom unknowingly is given credit for killing him and eventually becomes a U.S. senator.
Paramount — *Paramount Home Video; RCA VideoDiscs*

Man Who Would Be King, The 1975
Adventure
Closed Captioned
65500 129 mins C B, V, CED P
Sean Connery, Michael Caine
The two heroes are no ordinary jacks-of-trade. They have won honor fighting for the British Queen, yet found themselves adept at hustling strangers, blackmail, forging and assorted novel ways of earning money. Now that they've done it all, what else is left but to become kings?
MPAA:PG
Lorimar — *CBS/Fox Video*

Man with Bogart's Face, The 1980
Comedy
80731 106 mins C B, V P
Robert Sacchi, Misty Rowe, Sybil Danning, Franco Nero, Herbert Com, Victor Buono, Oivia Hussey
An actor who has undergone facial surgery to resemble Humphrey Bogart opens up his own private detective agency. Available in VHS and Beta Hi-Fi stereo.
MPAA:PG
Melvin Simon Prods. — *Key Video*

Man with the Golden Gun, The 1974
Adventure/Suspense
60582 125 mins C B, V, CED P

Roger Moore, Christopher Lee, Richard Loo, Britt Ekland, Maude Adams, Herve Villechaize, Clifton James
Roger Moore is the debonair secret agent 007 in this ninth James Bond flick, assigned to recover a small piece of equipment which can be utilized to harness the sun's energy.
MPAA:PG
United Artists — *CBS/Fox Video; RCA VideoDiscs*

Man with Two Brains, The 1983
Comedy
69310 91 mins C B, V, LV, CED R, P
Steve Martin, Kathleen Turner, David Warner, directed by Carl Reiner
A wacko brain surgeon marries a beautiful but coldhearted nymphomaniac but later falls in love with the brain of a young lady who has everything he desires—except a body.
MPAA:R
Aspen Society; William E McEuen and David Picker — *Warner Home Video*

Man Without a Star 1955
Western
76804 89 mins B/W B, V P
Kirk Douglas, Jeanne Crain, Claire Trevor, William Cambell, directed by King Vidor
A wandering cowboy helps the members of a ranch town fight off a ruthless cattle owner from taking over their land.
Universal; Aaron Rosenberg — *MCA Home Video*

Man, Woman and Child 1983
Drama
68248 100 mins C B, V R, P
Martin Sheen, Blythe Danner, Craig T. Nelson, David Hemmings
A typical American family is shocked when the child of an affair long ago appears at their door.
MPAA:PG
Paramount Pictures Corp — *Paramount Home Video*

Mandinga 1980
Drama
77391 100 mins C B, V P
Anthony Gizmond, Maria R. Ruizzi
Passions in the old south heat up when a cruel plantation owner becomes involved in a sadomasochistic relationship with an alluring slave girl.
MPAA:R
S.E.F.I. — *Wizard Video*

Mandingo 1975
Drama
44596 127 mins C B, V, LV R, P
James Mason, Susan George, Perry King, Richard Ward, Ken Norton, directed by Richard Fleischer
Based on the novel by Kyle Onstott, "Mandingo" portrays the brutal nature of slavery in the South. It deals with the tangled loves and hates of a family and their slaves. Heavyweight boxer Ken Norton makes his screen debut in the title role.
MPAA:R
Paramount, Dino De Laurentiis — *Paramount Home Video; RCA VideoDiscs*

Mango Tree, The 1977
Drama
79108 90 mins C B, V P
Geraldine Fitzgerald, Robert Helpmann, Christopher Pate
A young man comes of age in a small town during the 1920's.
Satori Films — *VidAmerica*

Manhattan 1979
Comedy
79688 96 mins B/W B, V, LV P
Woody Allen, Diane Keaton, Meryl Streep, Mariel Hemingway, Michael Murphy, directed by Woody Allen
A TV comedy writer has an affair with his best friend's wife and is also pursued by a seventeen year old girl.
MPAA:R
Jack Rollins; Charles H. Joffe — *MGM/UA Home Video*

Manhattan Transfer in Concert 1983
Music-Performance
60571 58 mins C LV P
The eclectic vocal group performs their mixture of pop, soul and jazz. Songs include "Operator," "Four Brothers," and "Gloria."
Ken Erhlich — *Pioneer Artists*

Manhunt 195?
Adventure
10035 25 mins B/W B, V P, T
Kirby Grant, Gloria Winters, Ewing Mitchell
Frightened young man flees to Mexico believing he killed a classmate. Sky King seeks to tell him the truth—his classmate is alive. From the TV series "Sky King."
CBS — *Blackhawk Films*

Manhunt 1985
Adventure
76859 93 mins C B, V P
Henry Silva, Mario Adorf, Woody Stode, Adolfo Celi
A man marked for execution by the mob launches his own assault on the organization's headquarters.

Independent — *Media Home Entertainment*

Manhunt in the African Jungle **1954**
Adventure/Serials
33952 240 mins B/W B, V, 3/4U P
Rod Cameron, Joan Marsh, Duncan Renaldo
An American undercover agent battles Nazi forces in Africa. A serial in fifteen episodes.
Republic — *Video Connection; Republic Pictures Home Video*

Maniac, The **1963**
Suspense
62807 86 mins B/W B, V P
Kerwin Mathews, Nadia Gray, Donald Houston, Liliane Brousse
An American artist living in France becomes involved with the daughter of a cafe owner, not suspecting that murder will follow.
Columbia — *RCA/Columbia Pictures Home Video*

Maniac **1981**
Horror
59042 91 mins C B, V P
Joe Spinell, Caroline Munro, Gail Lawrence
A psycho murderer slaughters and scalps his victims, adding the "trophies" to his collection. (This film carries a self-imposed equivalent X rating.)
Andrew Garroni — *Media Home Entertainment*

Maniac, The **1934**
Horror
08892 52 mins B/W B, V, 3/4U P
Bill Woods, Horace Carpenter
A mad doctor's assistant murders his boss, then impersonates him.
Dwain Esper — *Movie Buff Video; Admit One Video*

Manon Lescaut **1984**
Music-Performance
81177 135 mins C B, V R, P
Kirite Kanawa, Placido Domingo, Thomas Allen, conducted by Giuseppe Sinopoli
This is a performance of Puccini's opera about a pair of doomed lovers taped at London's Covent Garden. Available in VHS Hi-Fi and Beta Hi-Fi Stereo.
Gotz Friedrich — *THORN EMI/HBO Video*

Many Adventures of Winnie the Pooh, The **1976**
Cartoons
55565 74 mins C CED P
Animated
This collection of stories from A.A. Milne's children's classic includes "Winnie the Pooh and the Honey Tree," "Winnie the Pooh and the Blustery Day," and "Winnie the Pooh and Tigger Too."
MPAA:G
Walt Disney — *RCA VideoDiscs*

Many Happy Returns **1968**
Adventure/Fantasy
76920 50 mins C B, V P
Patrick McGoohan
The Prisoner escapes and works his way back to London attempting to solve the riddle of the Village. An episode from "The Prisoner" TV series.
ITC — *MPI Home Video*

Maps to Stars' Homes Video **1984**
Television/Theater
76016 60 mins C B, V P
A guided tour through Beverly Hills. See the mansions of your favorite movie and TV stars.
Shokus Video Productions — *Shokus Video*

Maria's Lovers **1984**
Drama
81057 103 mins C B, V P
Nastassja Kinski, John Savage, Robert Mitchum, Keith Carradine, Bud Cort, Vincent Spano, Anita Morris
The wife of an impotent World War Two veteran succumbs to the charms of a rakish lady killer.
MPAA:R
Cannon Films — *MGM/UA Home Video*

Marathon **1980**
Comedy-Drama
80242 100 mins C B, V P
Bob Newhart, Herb Edelman, Dick Gautier, Anita Gillette, directed by Jackie Cooper
When a married accountant enters the New York City Marathon, he ends up falling in love with a young woman.
Alan Landsburg Productions — *U.S.A. Home Video*

Marathon Man **1976**
Drama
38599 125 mins C B, V, LV R, P
Dustin Hoffman, Laurence Olivier, Marthe Keller, Roy Scheider, directed by John Schlesinger
Nightmarish thriller in which a marathon runner (Hoffman) becomes entangled in a plot involving a murderous Nazi fugitive (Olivier). Screenplay by William Goldman, based on his novel.
MPAA:R
Paramount — *Paramount Home Video; RCA VideoDiscs*

 (For explanation of codes, see USE GUIDE and KEY)

Marco 1973
Adventure
75494 109 mins C B, V P
Desi Arnaz Jr, Zero Mostel
This movie is a musical adventure of Marco Polo's life.
Tomorrow Entertainment — *Prism*

Marco Polo, Jr. 1972
Cartoons/Fantasy
69806 82 mins C B, V P
Animated, voice by Bobby Rydell
Marco Polo, Jr., the daring descendant of the legendary explorer, travels the world in search of his destiny in this song-filled, feature-length animated fantasy.
All and PAPI — *Family Home Entertainment*

Margin for Murder 1981
Mystery/Drama
80308 98 mins C B, V P
Kevin Dobson, Cindy Pickett, Donna Dixon, Charles Hallahan
Mike Hammer investigates a mysterious accident that killed his best friend.
Hamner Productions — *Prism*

Marianela 197?
Drama
52793 113 mins C B, V P
A disfigured peasant girl cares for a blind man, and the two fall in love. She doesn't tell him about her appearance until the day comes that he regains his sight. In Spanish.
SP
Luis Sanz — *Media Home Entertainment*

Marie Osmond: Exercises for Mothers-to-Be 1984
Physical fitness/Pregnancy
80498 60 mins C B, V P
Marie Osmond
Mom-to-be Marie Osmond demonstrates physical therapist Elizabeth Nobel's exercise program of gentle, no-strain toning movements. Marie also shows expectant women how to strengthen the essential childbirth muscles for an easier pregnancy and delivery.
MGM UA; 3 West Productions — *MGM/UA Home Video*

Marijuana—The Devils' Weed 1932
Exploitation
73555 56 mins B/W B, V P
This exploitation film tells the story of two sisters who get into a lot of trouble from smoking pot.
Independent — *Admit One Video*

Marilyn Monroe 1964
Documentary/Biographical
52770 30 mins C B, V P
Narrated by Mike Wallace
Marilyn Monroe's life from birth to death is documented. An actual television interview and news footage are included.
Fusco Entertainment — *Karl/Lorimar Home Video*

Marilyn Monroe, Life Story of America's Mystery Mistress 1963
Documentary/Biographical
76991 30 mins B/W B, V P
Narrated by Mike Wallace
The films and life of Maryilyn Monroe are remembered in this documentary.
Art Lieberman — *Karl/Lorimar Home Video*

Marjoe 1972
Documentary/Biographical
65099 88 mins C B, V P
Marjoe Gortner, directed by Howard Smith and Sarah Kernochan
This documentary follows the career of rock-style evangelist Marjoe Gortner, who spent 25 years of his life touring the country as a professional preacher.
Academy Awards '72: Best Documentary.
MPAA:PG
Cinema 10 — *RCA/Columbia Pictures Home Video*

Mark of Zorro, The 1920
Adventure
13738 91 mins B/W B, V P, T
Douglas Fairbanks, Marguerite De La Motte, Noah Beery, directed by Fred Niblo
Set to Gaylord Carter's score, Zorro, the famous Mexican Robin Hood, crusades for the rights of oppressed Mexicans.
United Artists — *Blackhawk Films; Discount Video Tapes; Sheik Video; Cable Films; Video Yesteryear; Western Film & Video Inc; Classic Video Cinema Collector's Club*

Mark Twain Classics 1982
Comedy
79676 90 mins C B, V P
Craig Wasson, Brooke Adams, Robert Lansing, Lance Kerwin 5 pgms
Five dramatizations of some of Mark Twain's best stories.
1.The Innocents Abroad 2.Life on the Mississippi 3.Pudd'nhead Wilson 4.The Mysterious Stranger 5.The Private History of a Campaign That Failed
The Great Amwell Company — *MCA Home Video*

Mark Twain's A Connecticut Yankee in King Arthur's Court **1978**
Comedy-Drama/Literature-American
58734 60 mins C B, V P
Richard Basehart, Roscoe Lee Brown, Paul Rudd
A man from Connecticut falls asleep and finds himself in King Arthur's Court.
WQED Pittsburgh — *Mastervision*

Marooned **1969**
Science fiction
66011 134 mins C B, V P
Gregory Peck, David Janssen, Richard Crenna, James Franciscus, Gene Hackman, Lee Grant, directed by John Sturges
Three astronauts are stranded in space after a retro-rocket misfires. In stereo.
MPAA:G
Columbia — *RCA/Columbia Pictures Home Video*

Marriage and Divorce Test, The **1981**
Marriage/Divorce
57550 60 mins C B, V P
Hosted by Dr. Frank Field
Viewers can test their knowledge of divorce and marriage, and then find out the answers from experts in the field.
NBC; Don Luftig — *Karl/Lorimar Home Video*

Marriage is Alive and Well **1980**
Comedy
81259 97 mins C B, V P
Joe Namath, Jack Albertson, Judd Hirsch, Melinda Dillon, Ingrid Wang, direcred by Russ Mayberry
A free-wheeling wedding photographer's unusual assignments provide him with an intimate perspective on marriage. Available in VHS stereo and Beta Hi-Fi.
Lorimar Prods. — *U.S.A. Home Video*

Martha Raye Show, The **1955**
Comedy/Variety
69576 60 mins B/W B, V, FO P
Martha Raye, Cesar Romero, David Burns, Rocky Graziano, Will Jordan
This episode from Martha Raye's popular TV series takes the form of an hour-long story musical, with Martha being groomed for the leading role in a new movie. Originally telecast on December 13, 1955.
NBC — *Video Yesteryear*

Martian Chronicles III: The Martians, The **1980**
Science fiction/Drama
79191 97 mins C B, V P
Rock Hudson, Darren McGavin, Gayle Hunnicutt, Bernie Casey
The United States space program sends the first manned space flight to Mars in this adaptation of Ray Bradbury's novel.
Stonehenge; Charles Fries Productions — *U.S.A. Home Video*

Martian Chronicles, Part II-The Settlers, The **1980**
Science fiction
75463 97 mins C B, V P
Rock Hudson, Bernadette Peters, Gayle Hunnicutt
The settlers are trying to make a new life on this strange world while the martians keep watchful eyes on them.
King Features — *U.S.A. Home Video*

Martian Chronicles, Volume I: The Expeditions, The **1980**
Science fiction
66618 100 mins C B, V P
Rock Hudson, Fritz Weaver, Roddy McDowall
The first segment of Ray Bradbury's story collection about the first American explorers to land on the planet Mars.
Charles Fries Productions — *U.S.A. Home Video*

Martin **1977**
Horror
65509 96 mins C B, V R, P
John Amplas, Lincoln Maazel, directed by George Romero
Martin is a charming young man, though slightly mad. He freely admits the need to drink blood. This contemporary vampire has found a new abhorrent means of killing his victims.
MPAA:R
Richard Rubinstein — *THORN EMI/HBO Video*

Martin Luther, His Life and Time **1924**
Christianity
42958 101 mins B/W B, V, FO P
This program traces the birth and youth of Luther and the great reformation within the church, examining both Luther the man and the church figure. Silent with musical score.
Lutheran Film Div — *Video Yesteryear*

Marty **1955**
Drama
37526 91 mins B/W B, V, CED P
Ernest Borgnine, Betsy Blair, Joe De Santis, Ester Minciotti, Jerry Paris, Karen Steele, directed by Delbert Mann
Ernest Borgnine's sensitive portrayal of Marty, a butcher from the Bronx, won him an Oscar. Marty is a painfully shy bachelor who feels trapped in a pointless life of family squabbles; when he finds love he also finds the strength to

(For explanation of codes, see USE GUIDE and KEY)

break out of what he feels is a meaningless existence.
Academy Awards '55: Best Production; Best Actor (Borgnine); Best Direction (Mann); Best Screenplay (Paddy Chayefsky).
United Artists — *CBS/Fox Video*

Marty/A Wind from the South **1953**
Drama
65013 118 mins B/W B, V P
Rod Steiger, Nancy Marchand, Julie Harris
Two classic original television dramas from the early 1950's are combined on this tape: Paddy Chayevsky's "Marty" with Rod Steiger as a lonely Bronx butcher; and James Costigan's "A Wind from the South," featuring Julie Harris as a romance-hungry Irish lass.
NBC; Fred Coe — *MGM/UA Home Video*

Marvelous Land of Oz, The **1982**
Musical/Fantasy
47422 104 mins C B, V P
The Children's Theater Company of Minneapolis
L. Frank Baum's sequel to "The Wonderful Wizard of Oz" picks up the story of the Scarecrow and Tin Woodman after Dorothy returns home to Kansas. This original musical production was taped live especially for video. VHS in stereo.
Television Theater Co — *MCA Home Video*

Marvelous stunts of Kung Fu **1983**
Martial arts
76942 86 mins C B, V P
Ling Yun, Wei Ping Line, Lung Fei
A beautiful woman, a fortune teller and a martial arts hero team up to seek vengeance against the evil empire.
Foreign — *Trans World Entertainment*

Marvin Mitchelson on Divorce **1984**
Divorce
72902 47 mins C B, V P
Marvin Mitchelson
The noted divorce lawyer discusses all aspects of divorce in a question and answer format.
Media Home Entertainment — *Media Home Entertainment*

Mary and Joseph **1979**
Drama
79193 147 mins C B, V P
Blanche Baker, Colleen Dewhurst, Lloyd Bochner, Stephen McHattie
How the lives of Mary and Joseph were affected by the arrival of Jesus Christ is portrayed in this dramatization.
Lorimar — *U.S.A. Home Video*

Mary Hartman, Mary Hartman Volume I **1976**
Comedy/Satire
78348 70 mins C B, V, LV P
Louise Lasser, Debralee Scott, Mary Kay Place, Greg Mullavey, Martin Mull
Here are three episodes from Norman Lear's satirical soap opera that evolves around the lives of the inhabitants of Fernwood, Ohio.
Embassy Television — *Embassy Home Entertainment*

Mary of Scotland **1936**
Drama
00263 123 mins B/W B, V, 3/4U P
Katharine Hepburn, Fredric March, directed by John Ford
The historical tragedy of Mary, Queen of Scots and her cousin, Queen Elizabeth I of England is enacted in this classic film.
RKO; Pandro S Berman — *Nostalgia Merchant; Blackhawk Films*

Mary Poppins **1964**
Musical
54464 140 mins C CED P
Julie Andrews, Dick Van Dyke, David Tomlinson, Glynis Johns, directed by Robert Stevenson
A magical English nanny arrives one day on the East Wind and takes over the household of a very proper London banker. She changes the lives of everyone, especially his two naughty children. From her they learn the wonders of life and how to make it enjoyable for themselves and others. Based on the novel by P. L. Travers.
Academy Awards '64: Best Actress (Andrews); Best Musical Score; Best Film Editing; Best Song ("Chim Chim Cher-ee").
Walt Disney — *RCA VideoDiscs*

Mary Tyler Moore Show, Vol. I, The **197?**
Comedy
52604 102 mins C CED P
Mary Tyler Moore, Ed Asner, Gavin McLeod, Ted Knight, Valerie Harper, Cloris Leachman
Four classic episodes from the memorable series which ran from 1970 to 1977: "Love Is All Around," the first episode, aired September 17, 1970; "The Final Show," the final episode, aired March 19, 1977; "Put on a Happy Face," aired February 24, 1973; and "Chuckles Bites the Dust," aired October 25, 1975. All four episodes won Emmys in various categories.
Emmy Awards: Outstanding Writing in a Comedy Series Single Episode '75-'76 ("Chuckles Bites the Dust"), '76-'77 ("The Final Show").
MTM Prods — *RCA VideoDiscs*

Mary White 1977
Drama/Biographical
81099 102 mins C B, V R, P
Ed Flanders, Kathleen Beller, Tim Matheson, Donald Moffatt, Fionnula Flanagan, directed by Jud Taylor
This is the true story of Mary White; the daughter of a newspaper editor who rejected her life of wealth and set out to find her own identity.
Emmy Awards '77: Outstanding Writing in a Special Program—Adaptation (Carol Ledner).
Radnitz/Mattel Productions — *Paramount Home Video*

Masada 1981
Drama
50652 131 mins C B, V P
Peter O'Toole, Peter Strauss, Barbara Carrera, Anthony Quayle, Giulia Pagano, David Warner, directed by Boris Sagal
Based on Ernest K. Gann's novel "The Antagonists," this dramatization recreates the first-century A.D. Roman siege of the fortress Masada, headquarters for a group of Jewish freedom fighters. This version is abridged from the original television presentation. Musical score by Jerry Goldsmith.
MCA TV; Arnon Milchan Prods — *MCA Home Video*

M*A*S*H 1970
Comedy
08464 116 mins C B, V, LV P
Donald Sutherland, Elliot Gould, Tom Skerritt, Sally Kellerman, JoAnn Pflug, Robert Duvall, directed by Robert Altman
A pair of surgeons at a Mobile Army Surgical Hospital in Korea create havoc with their late-night parties, and their practical jokes pulled on the nurses and other doctors.
MPAA:R
20th Century Fox; Aspen — *CBS/Fox Video*

M*A*S*H: Goodbye, Farewell and Amen 1983
Comedy-Drama
64303 120 mins C B, V, LV, CED P
Alan Alda, Mike Farrell, Harry Morgan, David Ogden Stiers, Loretta Swit, Jamie Farr, William Christopher
The final two-hour special episode of the TV series "M*A*S*H" follows Hawkeye, BJ, Col. Potter, Charles, Margaret, Klinger, Father Mulcahy and the rest of the men and women of the 4077th through the final days of the Korean War, the declaration of peace, the dismantling of the camp, and the fond and tearful farewells.
20th Century-Fox Television — *CBS/Fox Video*

Masked Marvel, The 1943
Adventure/Serials
07337 195 mins B/W B, V, 3/4U P
William Forrest, Louise Currie, Johnny Arthur
A serial in which the Masked Marvel saves America's war industries from sabotage. In twelve episodes.
Republic — *Video Connection; Republic Pictures Home Video*

Mass Appeal 1984
Drama
Closed Captioned
80849 99 mins C B, V P
Jack Lemmon, Zeljko Ivanek, CHarles Durning, Louise Latham, James Ray, Sharee Gregory
An adaptation of the Bill C. Davis play about the ideological debate between a young seminarian and a complacent but successful parish pastor.
MPAA:PG
Operation Cork Productions — *MCA Home Video*

Massacre at Fort Holman 1973
Adventure
58553 92 mins C B, V R, P
James Coburn, Telly Savalas, Bud Spencer
Seven condemned men are given a chance to live, if they can survive a suicide mission in the Southwest desert. Also known as "A Reason to Live, A Reason to Die."
MPAA:PG
Heritage Enterprises — *Video Gems*

Massacre At Fort Holman 1973
Western
80790 92 mins C B, V R, P
James Coburn, Telly Savalas, Bud Spencer
Two rival gangs fight for control of a Missouri fort in the early days of the Civil War.
MPAA:PG
Heritage Enterprises — *Video Gems*

Mastectomy (Rehabilitation and Injury) 1978
Physical fitness
52758 30 mins C B, V P
Hosted by Ann Dugan
Exercises for women who have had a mastectomy, including both specific-area and total-body movements to gradually improve muscle tone. Part of the "Rehabilitation and Injury" series.
Health 'N Action. — *RCA/Columbia Pictures Home Video*

Master Class 1985
Martial arts
81264 60 mins C B, V P
Sho Kosugi
The star of the "Ninja" movies demonstrates basic martial arts techniques in this

videocassette presentation. Available in VHS Stereo and Beta Hi-Fi.
Trans World Entertainment — *U.S.A. Home Video*

Master Cooking Course, The 1982
Cookery
59131 ? mins C LV P
Craig Claiborne, Pierre Franey
Two of the world's greatest cooking authorities offer a step-by-step guide to the techniques of gourmet cooking. Over 100 skills essential to the art of gourmet cooking are demonstrated. A participative program. A two-sided disc.
Optical Programming Associates — *Optical Programming Associates*

Master Cooking Course, The 1984
Cookery
77216 57 mins C B, V P
Master chefs Craig Claiborne and Pierre Franey offer a step by step guide to the techniques of gourmet cooking.
MCA Home Video — *MCA Home Video*

Master Mind 1973
Comedy
47676 86 mins C B, V P
Zero Mostel, Keiko Kishi, Brad Dillman, Herbert Berghof, Frankie Sakai
A renowned Japanese super sleuth attempts to solve the theft of a sophisticated midget android.
Malcolm Stewart — *Unicorn Video*

Master Ninja 2 1983
Martial arts/Adventure
81044 92 mins C B, V P
Sho Kosugi, Lee Van Cleef, Timothy Van Patten, David McCallum, Cotter Smith
The Master and his assistant Max travel across the United States to search for his long lost daughter in these two episodes from the series.
Viacom Productions — *Trans World Entertainment*

Master Ninja 3, The 1983
Martial arts/Adventure
81050 93 mins C B, V P
Sho Kasugi, Lee Van Cleef, Timothy Van Patten, Diana Muldaur, Mabel King
The Master and Max are back again in two new adventures: in "Fat Tuesday" the duo chop-sock a gun-running operation in New Orleans and in "Joggernaut" they help a mother and daughter get their produce to market.
Viacom Productions — *Trans World Entertainment*

Master Ninja 4, The 1983
Martial arts
81061 93 mins C B, V P
Lee Van Cleef, Timothy Van Patten, Sho Kosugi, George Maharis
The Master and Max travel to New York and Las Vegas seeking his long lost daughter in this collection of two episodes from "The Master" series.
Viacom Productions — *Trans World Entertainment*

Master of the House 1925
Drama
42956 118 mins B/W B, V, FO P
Directed by Carl Theodore Dreyer
Also known as "Thou Shalt Honour They Wife," this program is the story of a spoiled husband, a type extinct in this country but still in existence abraod. Silent with titles in English.
Unknown — *Video Yesteryear; Sheik Video*

Master of the World 1961
Horror
78138 95 mins C B, V R, P
A visionary tale of a fanatical 19th-century inventor who uses his wonderous flying fortress as an antiwar weapon.
Warner Home Video — *Warner Home Video*

Master Touch, The 1974
Mystery
80309 96 mins C B, V P
Kirk Douglas, Florinda Bolkan, Giuliano Gemma
When a legendary safe cracker is released from prison, he attempts one last heist at a Hamburg insurance company.
MPAA:PG
Warner Bros. — *Prism*

Matilda 1978
Comedy
64356 103 mins C B, V, CED P
Elliot Gould, Robert Mitchum, Harry Guardino, Clive Revill
An entrepreneur decides to manage a boxing kangaroo, which nearly succeeds in defeating the world heavyweight champion.
MPAA:PG
American International — *Vestron Video*

Matrimaniac, The 1916
Comedy
66138 48 mins B/W B, V, FO P
Douglas Fairbanks, Constance Talmadge
A man goes to great lengths to marry a woman against her father's wishes. Silent with music score.
Artcraft Paramount — *Video Yesteryear; Classic Video Cinema Collector's Club*

Matt the Gooseboy 1984
Cartoons/Folklore
74078 77 mins C B, V P
Animated
The animated feature is based on a Hungarian folktale about a boy who seeks vengeance on an evil landlord who steals his goose.
Pannpnia Films — *Family Home Entertainment*

Matter of Life and Death, A 19??
Drama
78364 98 mins C B, V P
Linda Lavin, Tyne Daly, Salome Jens, Ramon Bieri
A true story of a nurse who dedicated her life to treating the terminally ill with honesty and respect.
Big Deal Inc; Raven's Claw Productions — *U.S.A. Home Video*

Matter of Time, A 1976
Musical/Romance
64888 97 mins C B, V, CED P
Liza Minnelli, Ingrid Bergman, Charles Boyer, directed by Vincente Minnelli
A young woman relives the flamboyant past of an aging contessa.
MPAA:PG
American International Pictures — *Vestron Video*

Mausoleum 1983
Horror
66269 96 mins C B, V, CED P
Only one man can save a woman from eternal damnation.
MPAA:R
Jerry Zimmerman; Michael Franzese — *Embassy Home Entertainment*

Maverick Queen, The 1955
Western
74486 90 mins C B, V P
Barbara Stanwyck, Barry Sullivan
This is the story of a Pinkerton detective who infiltrates the "Wild Bunch" by becoming involved with a woman who knows them.
Republic — *Republic Pictures Home Video*

Max Dugan Returns 1983
Comedy-Drama
65329 98 mins C B, V, LV, CED P
Jason Robards, Marsha Mason, Donald Sutherland
An ex-con comes home from prison to visit his daughter, carrying a suitcase full of stolen money.
MPAA:PG
Herbert Ross — *CBS/Fox Video*

Max Maven's Mindgames 1984
Magic
70155 56 mins C B, V P
Magician Max Maven performs mindgames with the use of playing cards, signs and symbols and magic with money in such settings as Las Vegas, a tropical jungle, the moon and an operating room.
Mark Nelson and Bruce Seth Green — *MCA Home Video*

Max Roach 1981
Music-Performance
75899 19 mins C B, V P
This program presents the jazz music of Max Roach featuring the compositions "Six Bits Blues" and "Effie."
Jazz America Ltd — *Sony Corporation of America*

Mayerling 1937
Drama
11246 95 mins B/W B, V, FO P
Charles Boyer, Danielle Darrieux
Based on the tragic and hopeless affair between the Crown Prince Rudolph of Hapsburg and young Baroness Marie Vetsera.
FR
Nero Films — *Video Yesteryear; Sheik Video; Discount Video Tapes; Classic Video Cinema Collector's Club*

Maze 1984
Music-Performance
76674 20 mins C B, V P
This program presents a combination of jazz and mellow funk.
Capitol Records Inc — *Sony Corporation of America*

Maze Featuring Frankie Beverly 1982
Music-Performance
47813 ? mins C LV P
Maze, masters of mellow funk, perform their hits including "Joy and Pain," "Happy Feelin's," "Southern Girl," and "Feel That You're Feelin'." In stereo.
Unknown — *Pioneer Artists*

Maze Mania 1983
Games
64641 ? mins C LV P
This interactive videodisc combines the action of television with the fun of video games in a collection of maze games requiring the player to answer questions correctly in order to pass through a maze of live action visuals. Four complete games are included.
Optical Programming Associates — *Optical Programming Associates*

McCabe and Mrs. Miller **1971**
Western
51966 107 mins C B, V R, P
Warren Beatty, Julie Christie, William Devane, Keith Carradine, Shelley Duvall, directed by Robert Altman
A gambler and a madam operate a thriving brothel and gambling house in a frontier mining town.
Warner Bros — *Warner Home Video*

McQ **1974**
Crime-Drama
51961 116 mins C B, V R, P
John Wayne, Eddie Albert, Diana Muldaur, Clu Gulager
After several big dope dealers kill two police officers, a lieutenant resigns to track them down.
MPAA:PG
Warner Bros — *Warner Home Video*

McVicar **1980**
Drama
65604 90 mins C B, V P
Roger Daltrey, Adam Faith
A brutish and realistic depiction of crime and punishment based on the life of the professional John McVicar. In stereo VHS and Beta Hi-Fi.
MPAA:R
Bill Curbishley; Roy Baird; Roger Daltrey — *Vestron Video*

Mean Dog Blues **1978**
Drama
79675 108 mins C B, V P
George Kennedy, Kay Lenz, Scatman Crothers, Tina Louise, William Windom
A musician is convicted of hit and run driving after hitching a ride with an inebriated politician.
MPAA:PG
Bing Crosby Productions — *Vestron Video; Lightning Video*

Mean Johnny Barrows **1975**
Crime-Drama
47671 83 mins C B, V P
Fred Williamson, Roddy McDowell, Stuart Whitman, Luther Adler, Jenny Sherman, Elliot Gould
When Johnny Barrows returns to his home town after being dishonorably discharged from the Army he is offered a job as a gang hitman.
Fred Williamson — *Unicorn Video*

Mean Machine, The **1973**
Adventure
66196 89 mins C B, V P
Chris Mitchum, Barbara Bouchet, Arthur Kennedy
One man tries to get even with the mob.
MPAA:R
Tecisa Madrid — *Monterey Home Video*

Mean Season, The **1985**
Drama/Suspense
81176 106 mins C B, V R, P
Kurt Russell, Mariel Hemingway, Richard Jordan, Richard Masur, Andy Garcia, directed by Phillip Borsos
A Miami reporter hooks onto the story of his career when a mysterious man agrees to give him the grisly details of a series of murders he has committed. Available in Hi-Fi sound for both formats.
MPAA:R
Orion Pictures — *THORN EMI/HBO Video*

Mean Streets **1973**
Drama
Closed Captioned
80441 112 mins C B, V R, P
Robert DeNiro, Harvey Keitel, Amy Robinson, Richard Romanus, directed by Martin Scorsese
A New York City street punk who owes a loan shark a great deal of money, asks his buddy, a low echelon Mafioso, to act on his behalf.
MPAA:R
Jonathan Taplin; Warner Bros — *Warner Home Video*

Meatballs **1979**
Comedy
44915 92 mins C B, V R, P
Bill Murray, Harvey Atkin, Kate Lynch
The Activities Director at a summer camp who is supposed to organize fun for everyone prefers his own style of "fun."
MPAA:PG
Paramount — *Paramount Home Video; Vestron Video (disc only)*

Meatballs Part II **1984**
Comedy
Closed Captioned
80376 87 mins C B, V P
Pee Wee Herman, Kim Richards, Misty Rowe, Richard Mulligan, Hamiliton Camp
The future of Camp Sasquatch is in danger unless the camp's best fighter can beat Camp Patton's champ in a boxing match. Available in VHS and Beta Hi-Fi.
MPAA:PG
Tri Star Pictures — *RCA/Columbia Pictures Home Video*

Meatloaf in Concert **1977**
Music-Performance
73565 60 mins C B, V P
All the excitement of a Meatloaf live concert is captured here where Meatloaf performs "Bat Out of Hell" and "Dead Ringer for Love."
Robert Ellis; Mike Mansfield — *Prism*

(For explanation of codes, see USE GUIDE and KEY)

Mechanic, The 1972
Adventure
64901 100 mins C B, V P
Charles Bronson, Jan-Michael Vincent, Keenan Wynn, Jill Ireland, Linda Ridgeway
Bronson stars as Arthur Bishop, a wealthy professional killer for a powerful organization. He has innumerable ways to kill.
MPAA:PG
United Artists — *CBS/Fox Video*

Medium Cool 1969
Drama
66036 111 mins C B, V R, P
Robert Forster, Verna Bloom, Peter Bonerz, Marianna Hill, directed by Haskell Wexler
This commentary on life in the '60s focuses on a TV news cameraman and his growing apathy with the events around him.
MPAA:X
Paramount — *Paramount Home Video*

Meet Dr. Christian 1939
Drama
11765 72 mins B/W B, V P
Jean Hersholt, Robert Baldwin
The good old doctor settles some problems.
RKO; William Stephens — *Discount Video Tapes; Sheik Video; Video Yesteryear*

Meet John Doe 1941
Drama
54039 135 mins B/W B, V P
Gary Cooper, Barbara Stanwyck, Edward Arnold, James Gleason, directed by Frank Capra
An unemployed, down and out man is selected to represent the "typical American" because of his honesty. Unfortunately, he finds that he is being used to further the careers of corrupt politicians.
Warner Bros, Frank Capra — *Prism; Hal Roach Studios; Kartes Productions; Media Home Entertainment; Budget Video; Cinema Concepts; VCII; Sheik Video; Care Video Productions; Video Connection; Video Yesteryear; Discount Video Tapes; Western Film & Video Inc; Cinema Concepts; Classic Video Cinema Collector's Club*

Meet Marcel Marceau 1965
Mime
42974 52 mins C B, V, FO P
Marcel Marceau
The most famous contemporary pantomimist, Marcel Marceau himself does voice-over introductions of various skits including his popular character, "Bip," and special tributes to Harpo Marx, Buster Keaton, and Charlie Chaplin.
Unknown — *Video Yesteryear*

Meet Me in St. Louis 1944
Musical
44644 113 mins C B, V, CED P
Judy Garland, Margaret O'Brien, Mary Astor, Tom Drake, June Lockhart, Harry Davenport, directed by Vincente Minnelli
Wonderful music sets the mood for this charming tale of a family in St. Louis and the 1903 World's Fair. Judy Garland sings the title song "Trolley Song," along with "The Boy Next Door" and "Have Yourself a Merry Little Christmas."
MGM — *MGM/UA Home Video*

Meet Mr. Washington/Meet Mr. Lincoln 196?
Presidency-US
58811 79 mins C CED P
Two award-winning shows from the NBC series, "Project Twenty." "Meet Mr. Washington," tells the story of George Washington through his own words as well as letters and diaries of contemporaries and newspapers of the time. "Meet Mr. Lincoln," portrays Abe Lincoln as his contemporaries saw him.
NBC — *RCA VideoDiscs*

Meet the Navy 1946
Musical
66139 81 mins B/W B, V, FO P
Joan Pratt, Margaret Hurst, Lionel Murton
A post-war musical revue about a pianist and a dancer.
British — *Video Yesteryear*

Meet Your VCR 1982
Video
63997 48 mins C B, V P
Joan Lunden
This program was created to help the video consumer get the most out of his or her VCR by providing 10 easy lessons ranging from recording to maintenance.
3055 Corporation — *Karl/Lorimar Home Video*

Meeting at Midnight 1944
Mystery
54313 67 mins B/W B, V P
Sidney Toler, Joseph Crehan, Mantan Moreland, Frances Chan, directed by Phil Rosen
Charlie Chan is invited to a seance to solve a perplexing mystery. Chan discovers that they use mechanical figures and from there on solving the mystery is easy.
Monogram — *Hal Roach Studios; Video Connection; Video Yesteryear; Kartes Productions*

Megaforce 1982
Science fiction
63394 99 mins C B, V, CED P

Barry Bostwick, Persis Khambutta, Edward Mulhare, Henry Silva, Ralph Wilcox
This futuristic thriller follows the adventures of the military task force, Megaforce, on its mission to save a small democratic nation from attack.
MPAA:PG
20th Century Fox — *CBS/Fox Video*

Mein Kampf **1960**
Documentary/World War II
80393 117 mins C B, V P
The rise and fall of German fascism and its impact upon the world is examined in this documentary.
Tore Sjoberg — *Embassy Home Entertainment*

Mel Torme **1983**
Music-Performance
76665 53 mins C B, V P
A collection of hits from this legendary singer, composer, arranger and conductor. Includes: "New York State of Mind," "Born in the Night," "Down for Double" and many more.
One Pass Prod — *Sony Corporation of America*

Mel Torme and Della Reese in Concert **1981**
Music-Performance
55562 45 mins C LV P
Mel Torme, Della Reese, directed by Ron Brown
The two performers combine their talents in this concert recorded live at the Jubilee Auditorium in Edmonton, Canada. Stereo disc.
ITV — *MCA Home Video*

Mel Torme Special **1983**
Music-Performance
73986 53 mins C B, V P
"The Velvet Fog" sings some of his greatest hits from "Bluesette" to "New York State of Mind."
One Pass Prod — *Sony Corporation of America*

Melanie **1982**
Drama
65362 109 mins C B, V P
Glynnis O'Connor, Paul Sorvino, Burton Cummings
This gripping drama is the tale of one woman's extraordinary courage, determination, and optimism. Melanie refused to see herself as an unfit mother and emerged a winner in every way!
MPAA:PG
Richard Simpson; Peter Simpson — *Vestron Video*

Melody **1971**
Drama
60445 106 mins C B, V, CED P
Jack Wild, Mark Lester, Colin Barrie
A sensitive study of a special friendship which enables two adolescents to survive in a regimented and impersonal world. Features music by the Bee Gees.
MPAA:G
Levitt Pickman Films — *Embassy Home Entertainment*

Melody Master, The **1941**
Musical-Drama/Biographical
46346 80 mins B/W B, V, FO P
Alan Curtis, Ilona Massey, Binnie Barnes, Albert Basserman, Billy Gilbert, Sterling Holloway
A romanticized biography of composer Franz Schubert, chronicling his personal life and loves, along with performances of his compositions. Original title: New Wine.
United Artists — *Video Yesteryear; Discount Video Tapes; See Hear Industries*

Melody Ranch **1940**
Musical/Western
44812 84 mins C B, V P, T
Gene Autry, Jimmy Durante, George Hayes, Ann Miller
Gene returns to his home town as an honored guest.
Republic — *Blackhawk Films; Video Connection*

Melody Trail **1935**
Western/Musical
44808 60 mins B/W B, V P, T
Gene Autry, Smiley Burnette
Gene wins $1000 in a rodeo, loses the money to a gypsy, gets a job, falls for his employer's daughter ... and in the end captures both kidnapper and cattle rustlers.
Republic — *Blackhawk Films; Video Connection*

Melon Crazy **1985**
Comedy-Performance
81097 58 mins C B, V R, P
Comedian Gallagher describes his unusual fondness for watermelon in this concert performance.
Showtime — *Paramount Home Video*

Melvin and Howard **1980**
Comedy
55549 95 mins C B, V, LV P
Paul Le Mat, Jason Robards, Mary Steenburgen, Michael J. Pollard, Dabney Coleman, Elizabeth Cheshire, directed by Jonathan Demme
The story, according to Melvin Dummar, about the man who picked up Howard Hughes in the desert and then claimed to be heir to the Hughes fortune via the disputed Mormon will.

Academy Awards '80: Best Supporting Actress (Steenburgen); Best Original Screenplay (Bo Goldman). MPAA:R
Universal; Art Linson; Don Phillips — *MCA Home Video*

Memoirs of a Fairy Godmother 1982
Fairy tales
64952 90 mins C B, V R, P
Rosemary De Camp
The Godmother, an eccentric old lady, lives in the woods with her many pets. She enjoys telling stories and the film features animated versions of the tales of Cinderella, Snow White, Sleeping Beauty and many others.
MPAA:G
Century Video — *Video Gems*

Memorandum 1965
World War II
21395 59 mins B/W B, V, FO P
A Canadian Jew who survived the Holocaust in Europe returns to Germany to join a pilgrimage to the former concentration camp of Bergen-Belsen.
National Film Board of Canada — *Video Yesteryear*

Memory Lane Movies by Robert Youngson #1 195?
Documentary/Film-History
58647 62 mins B/W B, V, FO P
Five shorts compiled by film historian Robert Youngson from the Pathe archives: "The World of Kids" (1951), featuring an all-kid rodeo, kid golfers, etc.; "Animals Have All the Fun" (1952), a look at animal antics highlighted by a canine fashion show; "Batter Up" (1949), scenes of Babe Ruth, Lou Gehrig, Jimmy Fox, and Joltin' Joe included; "Those Exciting Days" (1955), chronicling the years before the First World War; and "This Was Yesterday" (1954), a look at America circa 1914.
Warner Bros — *Video Yesteryear*

Memory Lane Movies by Robert Youngson #2 195?
Documentary/Film-History
58648 61 mins B/W B, V, FO P
Five shorts compiled by film historian Robert Youngson from the Pathe archives: "I Never Forget a Face" (1956), including the 1920 Presidential campaign, the Scopes Monkey Trial, and other events of the day; "Horsehide Heroes" (1951), a look at the all-time greats, from Ted Williams to Ty Cobb; "Some of the Greatest" (1955), with scenes from the 1926 classic film 'Don Juan'; "The Swim Parade" (1949), featuring bathing beauties throughout the years; and "They Were Champions" (1955), featuring the greatest boxers of all time.
Warner Bros — *Video Yesteryear*

Memory Lane Movies by Robert Youngson #3 195?
Documentary/Film-History
58649 62 mins B/W B, V, FO P
Five shorts compiled by film historian Robert Youngson from the Pathe archives: "Gadgets Galore" (1955), a look at the early days of the automobile; "Faster and Faster" (1956), a potpourri of boat races; "Animals and Kids" (1956), featuring monkeys that play piano, etc; "It Happened to You" (1955), a scrapbook of World War I; and "Dare Devil Days" (1952), consisting of 'human flies' and the Like.
Warner Bros — *Video Yesteryear*

Memory Lane Movies by Robert Youngson #4 19??
Documentary/Film-History
58650 55 mins B/W B, V, FO P
Five shorts compiled by film historian Robert Youngson from the Pathe archives: "Blaze Buster" (1950), with spectacular scenes of early fires; "Lighter Than Air" (1951), a look at blimps, balloons and dirigibles; "When Sports Were King" (1954), a look at sports events of the 1920's; "I Remember When" (1954), featuring scenes of 'Little Old New York,' the Wright Bros., the 'Frisco Quake,' etc; "Coming of the Auto" (1953), a look at the early days of the motor car; and "Camera Hunting" (1954), a film biography of Thomas Edison.
Warner Bros — *Video Yesteryear*

Memory Lane Movies by Robert Youngson #5 195?
Documentary/Film-History
47470 62 mins B/W B, V, FO P
Six shorts compiled from Pathe newsreel footage by Robert Youngson: "This Mechanical Age" (1954), "Roaring Wheels" (1948), "Cavalcade of Girls" (1950), "They're Off!" (1949), "No Adults Allowed" (1953) and "Disaster Fighters" (1951).
Academy Awards '54: Best One-Reel Short Film ("This Mechanical Age").
Warner Bros — *Video Yesteryear*

Memory Lane Movies by Robert Youngson #6 195?
Documentary/Film-History
47471 62 mins B/W B, V, FO P
Six shorts compiled by Robert Youngson from Pathe newsreel footage: "Spills and Chills" (1949), "Fire, Wind and Flood" (1955), "A-Speed on the Deep" (1950), "Head Over Heels" (1953), "Too Much Speed" (1952) and "Say It with Spills" (1953).
Warner Bros — *Video Yesteryear*

Men, The 1950
Drama
64545 85 mins B/W B, V P

Marlon Brando, Teresa Wright, Everett Sloane, Jack Webb, directed by Fred Zinnemann
A paraplegic World War II veteran sinks into depression until his former girlfriend manages to bring him out of it. Marlon Brando's first film.
United Artists; Stanley Kramer — *Republic Pictures Home Video*

Men Are Not Gods **1937**
Drama
81464 90 mins B/W B, V, LV P
Rex Harrison, Miriam Hopkins, Gertrude Lawrence
The theatre nearly reflects real life when an actor playing Othello almost kills his wife during Desdemona's death scene.
Alexander Korda — *Embassy Home Entertainment*

Men at Work Live in San Francisco or Was It Berkeley? **1984**
Music-Performance/Music video
80133 58 mins C B, V P
Those eccentric rockers from the land down under perform their big hits in this program that combines live performance with music video.
CBS/Fox Video Music — *CBS/Fox Video*

Men in War **1957**
War-Drama
04000 104 mins B/W B, V P
Robert Ryan, Aldo Ray, Robert Keith, Philip Pine, Vic Morrow
Grim, suspenseful war film. 1950. American infantry platoon in Korea, surrounded by the enemy, fight for their objective. Based on Van Praag's novel.
UA; Security Prod — *King of Video; World Video Pictures*

Men of Destiny Volume I: World Political Figures **1979**
History-Modern/Documentary
29157 120 mins B/W B, V P
Narrated by Bob Considine
Presents authentic newsreels that capture the exact mood and drama of history. This program records the lives and momentous achievements of over 30 leaders in world history featuring Winston Churchill, Herbert Hoover, Mahatma Gandhi, Chrales De Gaulle, and many others.
Pathe News — *CBS/Fox Video*

Men of Destiny Volume II: Artists and Innovators **1979**
History-Modern/Documentary
29158 120 mins B/W B, V P
Narrated by Bob Considine
Presents authentic newsreels that capture the exact mood and drama of history. This volume features the achievements of over thirty world-renowned figures including Marie Curie, Thomas Edison, Albert Einstein, Jonas Salk, the Wright Brothers, and Charles Lindbergh.
Pathe News — *CBS/Fox Video*

Menudo—La Pelicula **1978**
Musical
80420 84 mins C B, V P
Menudo members Rene, Johnny, Xavier, Miguel, and Ricky sing ten songs in this musical. SP
Spanish — *Unicorn Video*

Mephisto **1981**
Drama
47753 140 mins C B, V P
Klaus Maria Brandauer, Krystyna Janda, directed by Istvan Szabo
The story of a provincial actor's climb to fame before and during the Nazi period.
Academy Awards '81: Best Foreign Language Film.
Manfred Durniok Productions — *THORN EMI/HBO Video*

Merry Christmas Mr. Lawrence **1983**
Drama
65513 124 mins C B, V P
David Bowie, Tom Conti, Ryuichi Sakamoto, Takeshi, Jack Thompson
A taut psychological World War II drama about clashing cultures and survival. In stereo VHS and Beta Hi-Fi.
MPAA:R
Universal — *MCA Home Video*

Merry Christmas to You **1980**
Christmas
54245 80 mins C B, V, 3/4U P
A collection of cartoons, singalongs, and Lone Ranger and Lassie adventures that all carry a Christmas theme.
Nostalgia Merchant — *Nostalgia Merchant*

Message, The **1977**
Drama
77384 176 mins C B, V P
Anthony Quinn, Irene Papas, Michael Ansara
This historical drama describes the conflict between Mohammad and the leaders of Mecca in the seventh century.
Satori Entertainment — *U.S.A. Home Video*

Messiah **1984**
Music-Performance
80054 145 mins C B, V R, P
Judith Nelson, Emma Kirkby, Paul Elliott, David Thomas
The choir of Westminister Abbey performs the 1754 Foundling Hospital version of George Handel's classic work.

BBC Television; National Video Corporation — *THORN EMI/HBO Video*

Metalstorm 1983
Adventure/Science fiction
65514 84 mins C B, V, LV, CED P
Jeffrey Byron, Mike Preston, Tim Thomerson, Kelly Preston, Richard Moll
It's the science fiction battle of the ages with giant cyclopses and intergalactic magicians on the desert planet of Lemuria. In stereo VHS and Beta Hi-Fi.
MPAA:PG
Universal — *MCA Home Video*

Meteor 1979
Science fiction
53518 107 mins C B, V R, P
Sean Connery, Natalie Wood, Karl Malden, Brian Keith, Martin Landau, Trevor Howard, Henry Fonda, Joseph Campanella
The U.S. and the Soviet Union both have an armed satellite orbiting in space, its fire power directed at an enemy nation. An American scientist calculates that only their combined weaponry can destroy the enemy.
MPAA:PG
American International — *Warner Home Video*

Metropolis 1926
Film-History
08705 120 mins B/W B, V, 3/4U P
Brigitte Helm, Alfred Abel, Gustav Froehlich, directed by Fritz Lang
Portrays a city of the future. (Silent, musical score added.)
UFA — *Budget Video; Video Yesteryear; Discount Video Tapes; International Historic Films; Sheik Video; Cable Films; Classic Video Cinema Collector's Club*

Metropolis 1926
Science fiction
81158 87 mins C B, V P
Brigitte Helm, Gustav Frihlich, Alfred Abel, directed by Fritz Lang
This is composer Giorgio Moroder's reconstructed version of the classic silent film about the confrontation that arises when a member of the elite class falls in love with a woman of the lower class. The digital soundtrack features music by Pat Benatar and Queen.
UFA; Giorgio Moroder Enterprises Ltd. — *Vestron Video*

Mexican Spitfire/Smartest Girl in Town, The 1940
Comedy
76845 125 mins B/W B, V P
Lupe Velez, Leon Errol, Donald Woods, Ann Southern, Gene Raymond
A comedy double feature: In "Mexican Spitfire" a man impersonates an English lord in order to save a contract for the spitfire's husband and in "The Smartest Girl in Town" a photographer's model mistakes a millionaire for a fellow magazine model.
RKO — *RKO HomeVideo*

Miami Dolphins 1984 Team Highlights 1985
Football
70548 70 mins C B, V, FO P
Dan Marino, Don Shula
Dan Marino's record-setting year paced the Dolphins to a 14-2 record and a Super Bowl showdown with the 49ers. This tape features 47-minutes of highlights from the '84 NFL season as well.
NFL Films — *NFL Films Video*

Michael Nesmith: Rio/Cruisin' 1981
Music/Video
66161 11 mins C B, V P
Two songs from the "Elephant Parts" video. In stereo.
Pacfic Arts Video — *Sony Corporation of America*

Mick Fleetwood-The Visitor 1981
Music-Performance
60383 106 mins C CED P
Fleetwood Mac's founder and drummer, Mick Fleetwood, travels to Ghana, Africa in a fascinating excursion combining rock music with traditional African sounds.
Colin Frewin — *RCA VideoDiscs*

Mickey 1917
Comedy
11247 80 mins B/W B, V, FO P
Mabel Normand, Lew Cody, Minta Durfee
A spoof on high society which contains a scene in which a squirrel scampers up the heroine's leg and is retrieved by the hero. (Silent.)
Mack Sennett — *Video Yesteryear; Sheik Video; Discount Video Tapes; Classic Video Cinema Collector's Club*

Mickey's Christmas Carol 1983
Cartoons
79174 60 mins C B, V R, P
Animated
Mickey Mouse returns along with all the other Disney characters in this adaptation of the Charles Dickens classic. Included in this video cassette is a documentary on how the featurette was made.

Walt Disney Productions — *Walt Disney Home Video*

Micki and Maude 1984
Comedy
Closed Captioned
80878 117 mins C B, V P
Dudley Moore, Amy Irving, Ann Reinking, Richard Mulligan, Wallace Shawn, Andre the Giant, directed by Blake Edwards
A TV reporter's wife enjoys a successful law career that leads to a judge's seat. Disappointed, her family-desiring husband meets, falls in love with, and then marries a young cellist. The bigamist then discovers that wife #1 is pregnant as well. He decides to maintain both marriages without informing either wife of the others existence. Fun ensues in Beta and VHS Hi-Fi.
MPAA:PG13
Columbia Pictures — *RCA/Columbia Pictures Home Video*

Mid Knight Rider 1984
Drama
66491 76 mins C B, V P
Michael Christian, Keenan Wynn
A penniless actor becomes a male prostitute at the service of bored, rich women. At an all-night orgy, he suddenly goes on a rampage, nearly killing one of his customers.
Trans World Entertainment — *Trans World Entertainment*

Midnight 1934
Mystery
12809 74 mins B/W B, V P
Humphrey Bogart, Sidney Fox, O.P. Hegge, Henry Hull
A jury foreman's daughter is romantically involved with a gangster who is interested in a particular case before it appears in court.
United International — *Blackhawk Films; Sheik Video; Cinema Concepts; Discount Video Tapes; Kartes Productions*

Midnight Cowboy 1969
Drama
60564 113 mins C B, V P
Dustin Hoffman, Jon Voight, Sylvia Miles, Brenda Vaccaro, John McGiver
James Leo Herlihy's novel about the relationship between a Texan and a pathetic derelict, set amidst seamy New York environs, is graphically depicted in this film.
MPAA:R
Jerome Hellman Prods; United Artists — *MGM/UA Home Video; RCA VideoDiscs*

Midnight Express 1978
Drama
35379 120 mins C B, V, LV P
Brad Davis, John Hurt, Randy Quaid, directed by Alan Parker
Harrowing tale of a young American who is arrested for drug smuggling in Turkey and undergoes mental and physical torture beyond belief in a Turkish prison.
MPAA:R
Columbia — *RCA/Columbia Pictures Home Video; RCA VideoDiscs*

Midnight Star in Concert 1984
Music-Performance
79187 60 mins C B, V P
The hot and funky sounds of Midnight Star are captured live in concert.
Gary Delfiner — *U.S.A. Home Video*

Midnite Spares 1985
Adventure
77402 90 mins C B, V P
Bruce Spence, Gia Carides, James Laurie
A young man's search for the men who kidnapped his father leads him into the world of car thieves and chop-shops.
Tom Burstall — *VCL Home Video*

Midsummer Night's Dream, A 1982
Literature-English
60201 120 mins C B, V R, P
Helen Mirren, Peter McEnery, Brian Clover
Shakespeare has created some of his most fanciful and unforgettable characters in this tale of devilish fairies, bewitched lovers and stolid workingmen-cum-actors.
BBC London; Time-Life Films — *Key Video; Time Life Video*

Midsummer Night's Sex Comedy, A 1982
Comedy
63108 88 mins C B, V R, P
Woody Allen, Mia Farrow, Mary Steenburgen, Tony Roberts, Julie Hagerty, directed by Woody Allen
Three turn-of-the-century couples spend an idyllic weekend in upstate New York. Music score by Felix Mendelssohn.
Orion Pictures; Robert Greenhut — *Warner Home Video*

Midway 1976
War-Drama
53394 132 mins C B, V P
Charlton Heston, Henry Fonda, James Coburn, Glenn Ford, Hal Holbrook, Robert Mitchum, Cliff Robertson, Robert Wagner
The epic WWII battle of Midway, the turning point in the war, is retold through Allied and Japanese viewpoints.
MPAA:PG

Universal; Walter Mirisch — *MCA Home Video (disc only)*

Mighty Joe Young 1949
Horror
00313 94 mins B/W B, V, 3/4U P
Terry Moore, Ben Johnson, Robert Armstrong
A young girl raises a giant ape in Africa, only to have it brought to New York, where it escapes.
Academy Awards '49: Best Special Effects.
RKO — *Nostalgia Merchant; King of Video*

Mighty Mouse in The Great Space Chase 1983
Cartoons
69529 88 mins C B, V, CED P
Animated
Mighty Mouse goes "up, up, and away" to save the day in his first full-length animated feature.
MPAA:G
Filmation Stuios — *Children's Video Library*

Mikado, The 1982
Music-Performance
66272 150 mins C B, V P
Gilbert & Sullivan's comic opera, a spoof of Victorian England "disguised" as a Japanese musical drama.
Unknown — *Embassy Home Entertainment*

Mike's Murder 1984
Drama
80077 110 mins C B, V R, P
Debra Winger, Mark Keyloun, Paul Winfield, Darrell Larson, directed by James Bridges
A woman tries to find out the truth about her lover's premature demise.
MPAA:R
The Ladd Company — *Warner Home Video*

Mildred Pierce 1945
Drama
59343 113 mins B/W LV P
Joan Crawford, Jack Carson, Zachary Scott, Eve Arden, Ann Blyth, directed by Michael Curtiz
A dowdy housewife leaves her husband, becomes the owner of a restaurant chain, and survives a murder case before true love comes her way.
Academy Awards '45: Best Actress (Crawford).
Warner Bros — *CBS/Fox Video; RCA VideoDiscs*

Milestones of the Century Volume I: The Great Wars 1979
History-Modern/Documentary
29155 120 mins B/W B, V P
Narrated by Ed Herlihy
This volume of "Milestones of the Century I" records over 30 momentous events in world history and features: FDR leading the nation; Europe ablaze—1914-1917; Hitler's Germany; Britain's Finest Hour; and the Korean Conflict.
Pathe News — *CBS/Fox Video*

Milestones of the Century Volume II: 20th Century—Turning Points 1979
History-Modern/Documentary
29156 120 mins B/W B, V P
Narrated by Ed Herlihy
This volume of great historic newsreels captures the exact mood and drama of history. Featured are: invention and industry, the era of flight, suffragettes and prohibition, the Russian Revolution, and the post-war world.
Pathe News — *CBS/Fox Video*

Militant Eagle 19??
Martial arts/Adventure
60512 90 mins C B, V P
Choi Yue, Lu Ping, Pai Ying
A fight of good vs. evil complete with nobles, warriors and villains who fight to the death.
Unknown — *Master Arts Video*

Milky Way, The 1936
Comedy
44972 89 mins B/W B, V P
Harold Lloyd, Adolphe Menjou, Verree Teasdale, Helen Mack, William Gargan
A milkman knocks out the world champion boxer. His prize is plenty of headaches and the women he loves.
Paramount — *Discount Video Tapes; Budget Video; Hal Roach Studios; See Hear Industries*

Million, Le 1930
Comedy
12448 85 mins B/W B, V P
Rene Lefebre, Annabelle, directed by Rene Clair
The promise of riches is the basis for the zany series of events as a mad hunt begins for a lost lottery ticket. French film, English subtitles.
FR
French — *Sheik Video; Video Yesteryear*

Milpitas Monster 1980
Horror
76914 80 mins C B, V P
Narrated by Paul Frees
A creature spawned in a Milpitas, California waste dump terrorizes the town residents.
MPAA:PG
Robert L. Burrill — *United Home Video*

Milton Berle Show, The 1966
Comedy/Variety
47476 59 mins B/W B, V, FO P
Milton Berle, Ben Blue, Roy Rogers, Dale Evans, the Dan Blocker Singers

This show, originally telecast December 2, 1966, was one of the last programs from Milton Berle's variety series. Featured are sketches, Vietnam and Christmas jokes and songs by Roy Rogers and Dale Evans. Original commercials included.
ABC — *Video Yesteryear*

Milton Berle Show, The **1963**
Comedy/Variety
47493 60 mins B/W B, V, FO P
Milton Berle, Janis Paige, Lena Horne, Laurence Harvey, Jack Benny, Kirk Douglas, Charlton Heston, Les Brown and his Orchestra
A typical Milton Berle variety program, highlighted by a biblical epic spoof, with Laurence Harvey as Spartacus, Jack Benny as Ben Hur and Milton as Cleopatra. Original commercials included.
NBC — *Video Yesteryear*

Milton Berle Show, The **1953**
Comedy
45017 120 mins B/W B, V, 3/4U P
Milton Berle, Jackie Cooper, Vic Damone, Peter Lawford, Carol Channing
Two complete (commercials included) Berle shows from 1953. Included are take-offs of "What's My Line" and "Dragnet" and Berle doing a soft-shoe routine with Lawford.
NBC — *Shokus Video*

Milwaukee Braves: Team Highlights **1962**
Baseball
81146 30 mins B/W B, V P
Warren Spahn 11 pgms
This series looks back at the many great moments from the Milwaukee Braves past seasons.
1.1953: The Milwaukee Story 2.1954: Milwaukee Braves '54 3.1955: Baseball with the Braves 4.1956: Braves Land 5.1957: Hail The Braves 6.1958: Pride of the Braves 7.1959: Fighting Braves of '59 8.1960: The Best of Baseball 9.1961: The Best of Baseball 10.1961: Big Moments with the Braves 11.1962: Around the League with the Braves
Major League Baseball — *Major League Baseball Productions*

Mini Musicals **1975**
Cartoons/Music
58588 75 mins C B, V R, P
Voices of Joni Mitchell, Jim Croce, Helen Reddy, Sonny and Cher
A collection of musical animated shorts, plus a special, added short—Stravinsky's "Petrouchka," conducted by the composer himself.
John Wilson — *Video Gems*

Minnesota Twins: Team Highlights **1984**
Baseball
81143 30 mins C B, V P
John Castino, Kent Hrbek, Ron Davis, Greg Gagne 7 pgms
The best and brightest moments from the Twins past seasons, along with a brief history of the team, are featured in this presentation.
1.1961: Pride of Upper Midwest 2.1970: Portrait of a Winner 3.1972:The Quilici Spirit 4.1979: A Team of Answers 5.1982: Building a New Tradition 6.1983: Climbing Toward The Top 7.1984: Finding Fame.
Major League Baseball — *Major League Baseball Productions*

Minor Miracle, A **1983**
Drama
72870 100 mins C B, V P
John Huston, Pele
This is the story of a group of people who get together to save an orphanage from the town planners.
MPAA:G
Unknown — *Embassy Home Entertainment*

Minsky's Follies **1983**
Comedy
75289 60 mins C B, V P
Phyllis Diller, Rip Taylor, Stubby Kaye
This is a recreation of an old time burlesque revue complete with strippers. In VHS Dolby stereo and Beta Hi-Fi.
RKO Home Video — *RKO HomeVideo*

Miracle of Lake Placid: Highlights of the 1980 Winter Olympics, The **1980**
Sports-Winter
39034 94 mins C CED P
Hosted by Jim McCay
A program of highlights from the 1980 Winter Olympics at Lake Placid, including excerpts of hockey games between the U.S. and Czechoslovakia, Russia, and Finland; all of Eric Heiden's five gold medal-winning speed races; the figure skating duel between Linda Fratianne and Anett Poetzch, and other events. All material was taken from ABC-TV coverage of the Games.
ABC — *RCA VideoDiscs; ABC Wide World of Learning*

Miracle of the Bells, The **1948**
Drama
69315 120 mins B/W B, V P
Fred MacMurray, Alida Valli, Frank Sinatra, Lee J. Cobb
A lovely, unknown actress rises to stardom overnight and falls in love with a cynical press agent who makes all her dreams come true.

Jesse L. Lasky Productions; RKO — *Republic Pictures Home Video*

Miracle on 34th Street **1947**
Drama
48598 94 mins B/W B, V P
Maureen O'Hara, John Payne, Edmund Gwenn, Natalie Wood, William Frawley
Macy's hires Kris Kringle as Santa Claus for its annual Thanksgiving Day parade. The situation snowballs as a daughter and mother learn to "believe."
20th Century Fox — *CBS/Fox Video*

Miracle Rider **1935**
Western/Serials
14625 195 mins B/W B, V P
Tom Mix, Joan Gale
Old West guns-and-hero tale. In fifteen chapters.
Mascot — *Video Connection; Video Yesteryear; Discount Video Tapes; Cable Films*

Miracle Worker, The **1979**
Drama/Biographical
47369 98 mins C B, V R, P
Patty Duke Astin, Melissa Gilbert
The story of blind, deaf and mute Helen Keller and her teacher, Annie Sullivan, whose patience and perseverance finally enables Helen to learn to communicate with the world.
Katz Gallin Productions; Halfpint Productions — *Warner Home Video*

Mirror Crack'd, The **1980**
Mystery
47305 105 mins C B, V, CED R, P
Elizabeth Taylor, Rock Hudson, Kim Novak, Tony Curtis
While filming a movie in the English countryside, an American actress is murdered, and Miss Marple must discover who the killer is. Based on the Agatha Christie novel.
MPAA:PG
Associated Film Dist; EMI Films Ltd — *THORN EMI/HBO Video*

Mirrors **1982**
Mystery
72449 83 mins C B, V P
The story of a women's dreams that result in horror and death in New Orleans.
John B Kelly Presentation; First American Films Release — *Monterey Home Video*

Mischief **1985**
Comedy
81412 97 mins C B, V P
Doug McKeon, Chris Nash, Kelly Preston, Catherine Mary Stewart
The high school class nerd and the new kid in town come of age during the 1950's as they go on the prowl looking for hot cuties to score with. Available in VHS and Beta Hi-Fi.
MPAA:R
20th Century Fox — *CBS/Fox Video*

Miserables, Les **1979**
Drama/Cartoons
69810 70 mins C B, V P
Animated
Victor Hugo's classic novel comes to life in this beautifully animated family feature.
Toei Animation Co Ltd — *Family Home Entertainment*

Misfits, The **1961**
Drama
59344 124 mins B/W CED P
Clark Gable, Marilyn Monroe, Montgomery Clift, Thelma Ritter, Eli Wallach, James Barton, Estelle Winwood, directed by John Huston
Arthur Miller wrote this parable involving a disillusioned divorcee and her relationship with three cowboys in the Nevada desert.
United Artists — *CBS/Fox Video; RCA VideoDiscs*

Miss All-American Beauty **1982**
Drama
75455 96 mins C B, V P
Diane Lane, Cloris Leachman, Brian Kerwin
An accomplished pianist enters a beauty pageant hoping to win a scholarship so that she can return to college.
King Features — *U.S.A. Home Video*

Miss Annie Rooney **1942**
Comedy-Drama
64367 86 mins B/W B, V, 3/4U P
Shirley Temple, Dickie Moore, William Gargan, Guy Kibbee, Peggy Ryan
Shirley Temple received her first screen kiss in this story of a poor Irish girl who falls in love with a wealthy young man.
Edward Small — *Nostalgia Merchant*

Miss Casino Comedy Show **1984**
Comedy
81520 60 mins C B, V P
Gary Owens and Ruth Buzzi are your judges as they look for the woman who will become Miss Las Vegas Casino.
All Seasons Entertainment — *All Seasons Entertainment*

Miss Nude America Contest, The **1980**
Variety
52862 78 mins C B, V P
The annual Miss Nude America Contest, presenting a group of unclad contestants being judged on physical attributes.

MPAA:R
Jim Blake; Jerry Gross Organization — *Wizard Video*

Miss Peach of the Kelly School **1980**
Cartoons
59364 115 mins C CED P
Animated
The students from the famed comic strip celebrate the opening of school, Thanksgiving, Valentine's Day, and the annual picnic.
Sheldon Riss — *Playhouse Video*

Miss Sadie Thompson **1954**
Drama
44841 91 mins C B, V P
Rita Hayworth, Jose Ferrer, Aldo Ray
Based on the novel "Rain" by Somerset Maugham, a promiscuous playgirl, a hypocritical minister, and a marine all clash on a Pacific island.
Columbia, Jerry Wald — *RCA/Columbia Pictures Home Video*

Missiles of October, The **1974**
Drama
15388 155 mins C B, V P
William Devane, Ralph Bellamy, Martin Sheen, Howard DaSilva
Story of the October 1962 Cuban Missile crisis, and how the White House dealt with the impending danger.
ABC; Herbert Brodkin; Robert Buzz Berger — *MPI Home Video*

Missing **1982**
Drama
59680 122 mins C B, V, LV, CED P
Jack Lemmon, Sissy Spacek, John Shea, Melanie Mayron, directed by Costa-Gavras
At the height of a military coup in a South American country, a young American writer disappears, causing the man's wife and father to embark on a frustrating search through government bureaucracy to discover what really happened to him.
MPAA:PG
Universal — *MCA Home Video*

Missing in Action **1984**
Adventure
80623 101 mins C B, V, LV P
Chuck Norris, M. Emmet Walsh
An army colonel returns to Vietnam to settle some old scores while on an MIA fact finding mission.
MPAA:R
Cannon Productions — *MGM/UA Home Video*

Missing in Action 2: The Beginning **1985**
Adventure/War-Drama
81501 96 mins C B, V P
Chuck Norris, Soon-Teck Oh, Cosie Costa, Steven Williams
An army colonel and his men are subjected to insidious torture when a sadistic Vietnamese colonel captures them during a mid-air rescue operation.
MPAA:R
Cannon Productions — *MGM/UA Home Video*

Mission Batangas **1969**
War-Drama/Adventure
80819 100 mins C B, V, LV P
Dennis Weaver, Vera Miles, Keith Larsen
An American pilot and a missionary nurse team up to steal the Philippine government's entire stock of gold bullion from the Japanese who captured it.
Diba Productions — *New World Video*

Mission Galactica: The Cylon Attack **1979**
Science fiction
58214 108 mins C B, V, LV P
Lorne Greene, Lloyd Bridges
The Battlestar Galactica is stranded in space without fuel and open to attack from the chrome-covered Cylons. Adama (Lorne Greene) is forced to stop Commander Cain's (Lloyd Bridges) efforts to launch an attack against the Cylons, while countering the attacks of the Cylon leader.
Universal TV — *MCA Home Video*

Mission Phantom **1979**
Adventure
77388 90 mins C B, V P
Andrew Ray, Ingrid Sholder, Peter Martel
A gang of intrepid spies on a covert mission in Russia plot to steal a cache of diamonds and help a woman to emigrate to the United States.
MPAA:R
James Reed — *Wizard Video*

Missionary, The **1982**
Comedy
66183 86 mins C B, V R, P
Michael Palin, Maggie Smith, Trevor Howard
A missionary tries to save the souls of a group of fallen women.
MPAA:R
Columbia — *THORN EMI/HBO Video*

Missouri Breaks, The **1976**
Western
58953 126 mins C B, V, CED P
Jack Nicholson, Marlon Brando, Randy Quaid, Kathleen Lloyd, Frederic Forrest, Harry Dean Stanton, directed by Arthur Penn

Thomas McGuane wrote the screenplay for this tale of Montana ranchers and rustlers fighting over land and livestock in the 1880's.
MPAA:PG
United Artists — *CBS/Fox Video*

Mrs. Brown, You've Got a Lovely Daughter **1968**
Musical
80149 95 mins C B, V P
Peter Noone, Stanley Holloway, Mona Washbourne
The Herman's Hermits gang inherit a dog and attempt to make a racer out of him.
MPAA:G
Metro Goldwyn Mayer — *MGM/UA Home Video*

Mrs. R's Daughter **1979**
Drama
80163 97 mins C B, V R, P
Cloris Leachman, Season Hubley, Donald Moffat, John McIntire, Ron Rifkin
An outraged mother will stop at nothing to bring her daughter's rapist to trial.
Dan Curtis Productions; NBC — *Warner Home Video*

Mr. & Mrs. Smith **1941**
Comedy
00287 95 mins B/W B, V, 3/4U P
Carole Lombard, Robert Montgomery, directed by Alfred Hitchcock
Madcap comedy of a married couple who discover their marriage isn't legal.
RKO — *Nostalgia Merchant*

Mr. Bill Looks Back Featuring Sluggo's Greatest Hits **1983**
Comedy
64927 31 mins C B, V P
Mr. Bill creator Walter Williams has filmed all new material never before televised to include with some previous footage.
Walter Williams — *Pacific Arts Video*

Mr. Blandings Builds His Dream House **1948**
Comedy
00266 93 mins B/W B, V, 3/4U P
Cary Grant, Myrna Loy
Domestic comedy revealing the difficulty a couple faces while trying to build their "dream house."
RKO — *Nostalgia Merchant*

Mr. Halpern and Mr. Johnson **1983**
Drama
65442 57 mins C B, V P
Laurence Olivier, Jackie Gleason
The provocative and compelling story of two strangers united by the death of a woman they both loved, and their revealing and surprising confrontation.
Edie and Ely Landau — *U.S.A. Home Video*

Mr. Hulot's Holiday **1953**
Comedy
12802 86 mins B/W B, V, FO P
Jacques Tati, Natalie Pascaud, Michelle Rolia
Jacques Tati's famous character Mr. Hulot, goes on vacationto a seaside resort, with slapstick results.
GDB International — *Embassy Home Entertainment; Video Yesteryear; Sheik Video; Video Dimensions; Budget Video; Discount Video Tapes; Western Film & Video Inc*

Mr. Klein **1975**
Drama
62815 123 mins C B, V P
Alain Delon, Jeanne Moreau, directed by Joseph Losey
In France during the Nazi occupation, a Catholic man searches for a Jew who has stolen his name and identity.
Quartet Films — *RCA/Columbia Pictures Home Video*

Mr. Lucky **1943**
Comedy
00286 99 mins B/W B, V, 3/4U P
Cary Grant, Laraine Day, Charles Bickford
Professional gambler tries to raise a new bankroll by fleecing a wealthy young lady, but falls in love instead.
RKO — *Nostalgia Merchant*

Mr. Magoo Cartoons **196?**
Comedy/Cartoons
64833 120 mins C CED P
Aminated, voice of Jim Backus
Sixteen classic cartoon selections are featured, including the well-known "Trouble Indemnity."
UPA — *RCA VideoDiscs*

Mister Magoo in Sherwood Forest **1964**
Cartoons/Comedy
64025 83 mins C B, V, LV R, P
Animated, voice of Jim Backus
As Friar Tuck, the nearsighted Mr. Magoo involves Robin Hood and his Merry Men in a series of zany adventures.
MPAA:G
UPA Pictures — *Paramount Home Video; RCA VideoDiscs*

Mr. Magoo in the King's Service **1966**
Cartoons
64939 92 mins C B, V R, P

Animated, voice of Jim Backus
Mr. Magoo is off on the King's business in this wacky full-length cartoon adventure.
UPA — *Paramount Home Video*

Mister Magoo... Man of Mystery 1983
Cartoons
65619 75 mins C B, V R, P
Animated, voice of Jim Backus
In this episode, Mr. Magoo plays four legendary literary and comic strip heroes: Dr. Watson, Dr. Frankenstein, the Count of Monte Cristo and Dick Tracey.
UPA Pictures — *Paramount Home Video*

Mister Magoo's Christmas Carol 1962
Cartoons/Christmas
64031 52 mins C B, V, LV R, P
Animated, voice of Jim Backus
Nearsighted Mr. Magoo, as Ebenezer Scrooge, receives Christmastime visits from three ghosts in this version of Dickens' classic tale.
MPAA:G
UPA Pictures — *Paramount Home Video*

Mr. Magoo's Storybook 1964
Fairy tales/Cartoons
64507 113 mins C B, V R, P
Animated, the voice of Jim Backus
Mr. Magoo acts all the parts in versions of three famous tales of literature: "Snow White and the Seven Dwarfs," "Don Quixote" and "A Midsummer Night's Dream."
UPA Pictures — *Paramount Home Video*

Mr. Majestyk 1974
Adventure
78630 103 mins C B, V P
Charles Bronson, Al Lettieri, Linda Cristal, directed by Richard Fleischer
When a Vietnam veteran's attempt to start his own business is thwarted by a Mafia hitman, he goes after him with a vengeance.
MPAA:PG
United Artists — *MGM/UA Home Video*

Mr. Mike's Mondo Video 1979
Comedy
66179 75 mins C B, V P
Michael O'Donoghue, Dan Aykroyd, Jane Curtin, Carrie Fisher, Teri Garr, Joan Haskett, Deborah Harry, Margot Kidder, Bill Murray, Loraine Newman, Gilda Radner, Julius LaRosa, Paul Schaeffer?Sid Vicious
A bizarre, outrageous comedy special declared too wild for television conceived by the Saturday Night Live alumnus Mr. Mike.
Lorne Michaels — *Pacific Arts Video*

Mr. Mom 1983
Comedy
Closed Captioned
65375 92 mins C B, V, LV, CED P
Michael Keaton, Teri Garr
A hard-working husband becomes a harried housewife and his wife turns into a high-powered executive.
MPAA:PG
Lynn Loring — *Vestron Video*

Mr. Moon's Magic Circus 1982
Circus
64954 90 mins C B, V R, P
Marcia Lewis, John Sarantos, Chuck Quinlan, Hank Adams, Marylin Magness, Mark Ganzel
A circus of musical fantasy for children that features original music, plenty of dancing, mishaps and circus fun.
Century Video — *Video Gems*

Mr. Moto's Last Warning 1939
Mystery
07077 71 mins B/W B, V P
Peter Lorre, George Sanders, Riccardo Cortez, Virginia Field
Conspirators, plotting to blow up the Suez Canal, are under the impression they have eliminated Mr. Moto.
20th Century Fox — *Discount Video Tapes; Cable Films; Video Connection; Video Yesteryear; Budget Video; Classic Video Cinema Collector's Club*

Mr. Peabody and the Mermaid 1948
Comedy
65737 89 mins B/W B, V P
William Powell, Ann Blythe
A middle-aged husband hooks a beautiful mermaid while fishing in the Caribbean and with time, falls in love with her.
Universal — *Republic Pictures Home Video*

Mr. Reeder in Room 13 1938
Suspense
47651 66 mins B/W B, V, FO P
Gibb McLaughlin
Based on the mystery stories created by Edgar Wallace, Mr. Reeder (a cultured English gentleman who fights crime) enlists the aid of a young man to get evidence on a gang of counterfeiters.
England — *Video Yesteryear*

Mister Roberts 1955
Comedy
38951 120 mins C B, V R, P
Henry Fonda, James Cagney, Jack Lemmon, William Powell, Betsy Palmer

The comic adventures of the crew of a navy cargo freighter in the South Pacific during World War II, adapted from the long running play. Academy Awards '55: Best Supporting Actor (Lemmon).
Warner Bros — *Warner Home Video; RCA VideoDiscs*

Mr. Robinson Crusoe 1932
Adventure
08856 76 mins B/W B, V P, T
Douglas Fairbanks Sr., William Farnum, Maria Alba
Rollicking adventure in the South Seas as man makes a bet that he can live on a desert island without being left any refinements of civilization.
United Artists — *Blackhawk Films; Sheik Video; Video Yesteryear; Classic Video Cinema Collector's Club; Kartes Productions*

Mr. Robinson Crusoe 1932
Adventure
81072 75 mins B/W B, V P
Douglas Fairbanks, William Farnum, Earle Brown, directed by Edward Sutherland
A man makes a bet that he can live alone on a desert island for a year.
United Artists — *MPI Home Video*

Mister Rogers Goes to School 1983
Education
64779 117 mins C CED P
Fred Rogers explores the questions children have about school, and helps prepare them for their first day. Includes two shows, one from 1979 and the other from 1983.
Family Communications — *RCA VideoDiscs*

Mr. Rogers—Helping Children Understand 1983
Ethics
64454 76 mins C CED P
Fred Rogers
Mr. Rogers hosts four informative programs for children ages 2-7. Includes "What Is Love?," "Pretendings" and "Death of a Goldfish."
Family Communications — *RCA VideoDiscs*

Mr. Rossi's Vacation 1983
Cartoons
77423 82 mins C B, V P
Animated, directed by Bruno Bozzetto
Mr. Rossi and his dog Harold go off in search of quiet on a let's get away-from-it-all vacation.
Italtoons Corp; Bruno Bozzetto Film — *Family Home Entertainment*

Mister Scarface 1978
Drama
79334 85 mins C B, V P
Jack Palance, Edmund Purdon, Al Cliver, Harry Bear
A young man searches for the man who murdered his father years earlier in a dark alley.
MPAA:R
PRO International — *Monterey Home Video; World Video Pictures*

Mr. Smith Goes to Washington 1939
Drama
21292 130 mins B/W B, V P
James Stewart, Jean Arthur, Edward Arnold, Claude Rains, directed by Frank Capra
An idealistic young statesman finds nothing but corruption when he takes his seat in the Senate. Academy Awards '39: Best Original Story; N.Y. Film Critics Award '39: Best Actor (Stewart).
Columbia — *RCA/Columbia Pictures Home Video*

Mr. Super Athletic Charm 194?
Adventure
10128 56 mins B/W B, V P, T
Douglas Fairbanks Sr.
Douglas Fairbanks portrays dashing swashbuckler in "Black Pirate" (1926) and "Thief of Bagdad" (1940) from the "History of Motion Picture" series.
United Artists — *Blackhawk Films*

Mr. Too Little 1979
Adventure
59071 90 mins C B, V R, P
Rosanno Brazzi
The traveling adventures of a circus poodle and his Bengal tiger buddy.
GG Communications — *Video Gems*

Mr. T's Be Somebody... Or Be Somebody's Fool 1984
Identity/Ethics
Closed Captioned
78892 60 mins C B, V P
Valerie Landsburg, New Edition
A variety program where Mr. T helps young people to gain confidence in themselves. In Beta and VHS Stereo.
Topper Carew; Henry Johnson — *MCA Home Video*

Mr. Wise Guy 1942
Comedy
00411 70 mins B/W B, V, 3/4U P
Leo Gorcey, Huntz Hall, East Side Kids
The East Side Kids break out of reform school to clear the brother of one of the Kids of a murder charge.
Prime TV — *Hal Roach Studios; Discount Video Tapes; See Hear Industries*

Mistress of the Apes 1979
Adventure
81400 88 mins C B, V P
Barbara Leigh, Garth Pillsbury, Walt Robin, Jenny Neumann
A group of scientists discover a tribe of near-men, who are the missing link in evolution on a jungle safari. Available in VHS Stereo and Beta Hi-Fi.
MPAA:R
Cineworld — *Monterey Home Video*

Mistress Pamela 1976
Drama
53146 95 mins C B, V P
Ann Michelle, Julian Barnes
When young Pamela goes to work in the household of handsome Lord Devonish, he sets about in his wild pursuit of her virginity.
MPAA:R
Intercontinental Releasing — *Monterey Home Video*

Misunderstood 1984
Drama
78629 92 mins C B, V P
Gene Hackman, Susan Anspach, Henry Thomas, Huckleberry Fox, directed by Jerry Schatzberg
A father and his two sons become closer to each other after their mother dies suddenly.
MPAA:PG
Keith Barish Productions; Accent Film's — *MGM/UA Home Video*

Moby Dick 1956
Adventure
Closed Captioned
65757 116 mins C B, V, CED P
Gregory Peck, Richard Basehart, Orson Welles, Leo Genn, Friedrich Ledebur, directed by John Huston
Herman Melville's high sea saga comes to life with Captain Ahab, obsessed with desire for revenge upon the great white whale, Moby Dick.
Warner Bros — *CBS/Fox Video*

Modern Problems 1981
Comedy
59426 93 mins C B, V, CED P
Chevy Chase, Patti D'Arbanville, Mary Kay Place, Brian Doyle-Murray, Neil Carter, Dabney Coleman
A man involved in a nuclear accident discovers he has acquired telekinetic powers, which he uses to turn the tables on his professional and romantic rivals.
MPAA:PG
Twentieth Century Fox — *CBS/Fox Video*

Modern Romance 1981
Comedy
58499 102 mins C B, V P
Albert Brooks, Kathryn Harrold, Bruno Kirby, George Kennedy, Bob Einstein, directed by Albert Brooks
The romantic misadventures of a neurotic film editor who continuously breaks up with his girlfriend and then attempts to win her back.
MPAA:R
Columbia; Andrew Scheinman — *RCA/Columbia Pictures Home Video*

Modern Times 1936
Comedy
08421 89 mins B/W B, V P
Charlie Chaplin, Paulette Goddard, Henry Bergman, Chester Conklin, directed by Charlie Chaplin
In his last silent film, Chaplin plays a factory workman who goes crazy from his repetitious job on an assembly line. Chaplin wrote the musical score which incorporates the tune "Smile," and also sings a gibberish song.
United Artists — *CBS/Fox Video; RCA VideoDiscs; Playhouse Video*

Mogambo 1954
Adventure
53351 116 mins C B, V P
Clark Gable, Ava Gardner, Grace Kelly, directed by John Ford
An American showgirl and a British archaeologist and his wife team up with a White hunter in Kenya, and set off on a gorilla hunt.
Sam Zimbalist; MGM — *MGM/UA Home Video*

Molly (The Goldbergs) 1955
Comedy
66140 27 mins B/W B, V, FO P
Gertrude Berg, Robert Harris, Arlene McQuade, Eli Mintz, Tom Taylor
In this episode of the long-running series, Molly is being menaced by two ex-cons.
Dumont — *Video Yesteryear*

Mommie Dearest 1981
Drama
58713 129 mins C B, V, LV R, P
Faye Dunaway, Diana Scarwid, Steve Forrest, Howard DaSilva, directed by Frank Perry
Faye Dunaway portrays Joan Crawford in this film version of Christina Crawford's memoirs, describing her mother as a neurotic tyrant who abused her children while presenting a glamourous screen image to the public.
MPAA:PG
Paramount; Frank Yablans — *Paramount Home Video; RCA VideoDiscs*

Mon Oncle 1958
Comedy
57338 87 mins C B, V P

Jacques Tati, Jean-Pierre Zola, Adrienne Serrantie, Alain Bacourt, directed by Jacques Tati
Droll, gangling Mr. Hulot aids his adoring nephew in war against his parents' modernized, push-button home. Subtitled in English.
Academy Award '58: Best Foreign Language Picture. FR
Continental Dist Co — *Budget Video; Discount Video Tapes; Video Yesteryear*

Money Hunt 1984
Mystery
76394 30 mins C B, V P
John Hillerman
$100,000 cash is secured in a safe deposit box; the first person who can solve the puzzle from the hints given in this program will claim the prize. Magnum P.I.'s John Hillerman is the host.
Rogers & Cowan Inc — *Karl/Lorimar Home Video*

Money Madness 1979
Music
37405 92 mins C B, V P
Eddie Money
Popular rock singer Eddie Money's rise to the top of the music business is chronicled in this program, in which he performs some of his songs.
New Line Cinema; Michael Mason — *CBS/Fox Video*

Monique 1970
Drama
64967 86 mins C CED P
Sibylla Kay, Joan Alcome, David Sumner
A menage a trois results when a couple hire a pretty French girl to help with their children.
Avco-Embassy — *Embassy Home Entertainment (disc only)*

Monique 1983
Suspense
81196 96 mins C B, V P
Florence Giorgetti, John Ferris
A sophisticated career woman is about to unleash a terrifying secret on her new husband.
Jacques Scandelari — *VCL Home Video*

Monkey Business 1931
Comedy
81199 77 mins B/W B, V P
The Marx Brothers, Thelma Todd, Ruth Hall, Harry Woods, directed by Norman Z. McLeod
Groucho, Harpo, Chico, and Zeppo stowaway aboard a luxury liner to hide from the authorities. While aboard the ship, the boys crash a society party and catch a few crooks in the process. Beta Hi-Fi Mono.
Paramount — *MCA Home Video*

Monsieur Verdoux 1947
Comedy
08406 123 mins B/W B, V P
Charlie Chaplin, Martha Raye, Isabella Elsom, Mady Corell, Allison Roddan, Robert Lewis
A prim and proper bank cashier marries and murders rich women in order to support his real wife.
Charles Chaplin — *CBS/Fox Video; Playhouse Video*

Monsignor 1982
Drama
60581 121 mins C B, V, CED P
Christopher Reeve, Fernando Rey, Genevieve Bujold, Jason Miller, directed by Frank Perry
An ambitious American priest becomes embroiled in the high stakes game of Vatican politics.
MPAA:R
Twentieth Century Fox — *CBS/Fox Video*

Monster a Go-Go! 1955
Science fiction
77200 70 mins B/W B, V P
Phil Morton, June Travis, directed by Herschell Gordon Lewis
A team of go-go dancers battle a ten-foot monster from outerspace.
Majestic International Pictures — *United Home Video*

Monster Club, The 1985
Horror
80477 104 mins C B, V P
Vincent Price, Donald Pleasance, John Carradine, Stuart Whitman, Britt Ekland, Simon Ward, directed by Roy Ward Baker
Vincent Price and John Carradine star in this music-horror compilation, featuring songs by Night, B.A. Robertson, The Pretty Things and The Viewers. Soundtrack music by John Williams, UB 40 and The Expressos. In Beta Hi-Fi and VHS stereo.
Milton Subotsky; ITC Film Distributors — *Thriller Video*

Monster from Green Hell 1958
Horror
09109 71 mins B/W B, V P
Jim Davis, Robert Griffin, Barbara Turner, Eduardo Cianelli
An experimental rocket containing radiation contaminated wasps crashes in Africa making giant killer wasps that are destroyed by a volcano.
DCA — *Mossman Williams Productions; Video Yesteryear*

Monster Walks, The 1932
Horror
12830 60 mins B/W B, V, FO P
Rex Lease, Vera Reynolds, Mischa Auer

A whodunit thriller complete with stormy nights, suspicious cripples, weird servants, and a screaming gorilla.
Mayfair — *Video Yesteryear; Sheik Video; Blackhawk Films*

Monsters, Madmen, Machines **1984**
Film-History/Science fiction
79684 57 mins C B, V P
Narrated by Gil Gerard
The eighty year history of science fiction films from "Metropolis" to "Star Wars" is presented in this retrospective.
RKO — *RKO HomeVideo*

Monsters on the March **1960**
Movie and TV trailers
42960 25 mins B/W B, V, FO P
This program consists of 14 movie trailers, including frightening coming attractions for movies such as the "The Return of the Fly," with Vincent Price, "Isle of the Dead" with Boris Karloff, "I Walked with a Zombie" with Frances Dee, and other, dating as far back as 1932 and up to 1960.
20th Century Fox et al — *Video Yesteryear*

Monte Walsh **1970**
Western
Closed Captioned
81173 100 mins C B, V P
Lee Marvin, Jack Palance, Jeanne Moreau, Jim Davis, Mitchell Ryan, directed by William A. Fraker
An aging cowboy sets out on one last adventure to avenge the death of his best friend. Hi-Fi sound for both formats.
MPAA:PG
CBS Theatrical Films — *CBS/Fox Video*

Montenegro **1981**
Drama
47799 97 mins C B, V R, P
Susan Anspach, Erland Josephson
The story of an American housewife living in Sweden who tires of her uncomplicated life as a wife and mother, and promptly flees her home and family in search of excitement.
Atlantic Releasing — *THORN EMI/HBO Video*

Montreal Expos: Team Highlights **1984**
Baseball
81144 30 mins C B, V P
Gary Carter, Tim Raines, Rusty Staub, Andre Dawson 7 pgms
This series provides a brief history of the Expos along with selected highlights of their past seasons.
1.1969: Expos 2.1979: Makin' It 3.1980: The Team of the '80's 4.1981: One Step Closer 5.1982: Year of the All-Stars 6. 1983: 15th Anniversary 7. 1984: Expos 1984.
Major League Baseball — *Major League Baseball Productions*

Monty Python and the Holy Grail **1975**
Comedy
63441 90 mins C B, V, LV P
John Cleese, Michael Palin, Eric Idle, Graham Chapman, Terry Jones, Terry Gilliam
The quest for the Holy Grail by King Arthur and his Knights of the Round Table is retold in the inimitable Python fashion.
MPAA:PG
Almi/Cinema V — *RCA/Columbia Pictures Home Video; RCA VideoDiscs*

Monty Python Live at the Hollywood Bowl **1982**
Comedy
64207 78 mins C B, V R, P
Eric Idle, Michael Palin, John Cleese, Terry Gillian, Terry Jones, Graham Chapman
A live concert performance by the madcap comedy troupe.
George Harrison; Handmade Films — *THORN EMI/HBO Video; RCA VideoDiscs*

Monty Python's Life of Brian **1979**
Comedy
37424 90 mins C B, V R, P
Eric Idle, Michael Palin, Graham Chapman, Terry Gilliam, John Cleese, Terry Jones
A typical Monty Python romp, this time through the Holy Land in the year 32 A.D. This is the hilarious story of Brian, a man who was born on the same night as Jesus Christ. Through a series of mishaps and misinterpretations, Brian is proclaimed the Messiah, a role he refuses to accept. Consequently, he spends most of his time running from the adoring multitudes, government officials, and several underground groups.
MPAA:R
Warner Bros — *Warner Home Video; RCA VideoDiscs*

Monty Python's The Meaning of Life **1983**
Comedy
65207 107 mins C B, V, LV, CED P
John Cleese, Michael Palin, Eric Idle, Graham Chapman, Terry Jones, Terry Gilliam
No aspect of life is to sacred for the probing Python crew. Religion, birth control, sex and death all get their respective dues. This program is in stereo on all formats.
Universal — *MCA Home Video*

Moon Is Blue, The 1953
Comedy
55467 100 mins B/W LV, CED P
William Holden, David Niven, directed by Otto Preminger
A young lady, armed with utter candor and good sense, sets out to bewilder a young man about town who doesn't believe marriage is for him.
Otto Preminger — *CBS/Fox Video*

Moon Madness 1983
Cartoons/Fantasy
77415 82 mins C B, V P
Animated
An astronomer takes a trip to the moon to find the selenites, proprietors of the fountain of youth.
Jean Image — *Vestron Video*

Moon of the Wolf 1972
Horror
69290 74 mins C B, V P
David Janssen, Barbara Rush, Bradford Dillman, John Beradino
A small town in bayou country is terrorized by a modern-day werewolf that rips its victims to shreds.
Filmways — *Worldvision Home Video*

Moonlight Sword and Jade Lion 197?
Martial arts
72176 94 mins C B, V P
Mao Yin, Wong Do
A Kung Fu action film taking place in ancient China.
Foreign — *Master Arts Video*

Moonlighting 1982
Drama
64795 97 mins C B, V, LV P
Jeremy Irons, Eugene Liponski, Jiri Stanislay, Eugeniusz Haczkiewicz, directed by Jerzy Skolimowski
This British/Polish film depicts four builders from Poland who travel to London to renovate a London residence. While in London, the Polish military imposes martial law, suspending the Gdansk agreement and outlawing Solidarity. Only one of the builders speaks English, and he decides not to tell the others what is happening back in Poland.
Cannes Film Festival '82: Best Screenplay.
MPAA:PG
Universal Classics — *MCA Home Video*

Moonraker 1979
Adventure
63549 126 mins C B, V P
Roger Moore, Lois Chiles, Richard Kiel, Michael Lonsdale, Corinne Clery
James Bond is aided by a female CIA agent, assaulted by a giant with jaws of steel and captured by Amazons when he sets out to protect the human race.
MPAA:PG
United Artists — *CBS/Fox Video; RCA VideoDiscs*

Moonshine County Express 1977
Adventure
51991 104 mins C B, V R, P
William Conrad, Susan Howard, Maureen McCormick, Claudia Jennings, John Saxon
Three daughters of a hillbilly moonshiner set out to avenge their father's senseless murder.
MPAA:PG
New World Pictures — *Warner Home Video*

Moonstone Gem, The 1983
Cartoons
65486 48 mins C B, V P
Animated
The Evil Baron threatens to steal the most precious gem of all—happiness—from King Gunther, Prince Jeremy and the Gunderlings.
Paul Fusco — *Media Home Entertainment*

More Candid Candid Camera 1983
Comedy
80690 60 mins C B, V, CED P
Allen Funt
Allen Funt presents this collection of uncensored "Candid Camera" classics that the censors would not allow on TV.
Allen Funt Productions — *Vestron Video*

More! Police Squad 1982
Comedy
81107 75 mins C B, V R, P
Leslie Nielsen, Alan North, Rex Hamilton, Peter Lupus
Join intrepid police captain Frank Drebin as he captures big city bad guys in this collection of the final three episodes from the series.
Paramount Pictures — *Paramount Home Video*

Morgan—A Suitable Case for Treatment 1966
Comedy
63324 93 mins B/W B, V R, P
Vanessa Redgrave, David Warner, Robert Stephens, Irene Handl
A schizophrenic artist refuses to recognize his wife's divorce. When she refuses to go back to him, he decides life is easier to cope with while dressed in a gorilla suit.
British Lion; Quintra — *THORN EMI/HBO Video*

Morning Glory 1933
Drama
29493 74 mins B/W B, V P, T

Katherine Hepburn, Douglas Fairbanks Jr., Adolphe Menjou
A small town girl takes her aspirations for a stage career very seriously.
Academy Awards '33: Best Actress (Hepburn).
RKO, Merian C Cooper — *RKO HomeVideo; Blackhawk Films*

Moron Movies **1985**
Comedy
76923 60 mins C B, V P
A collection of one-hundred-fifty short films that describe comedic uses for everyday products.
Len Cella — *MPI Home Video*

Mortuary **1981**
Suspense
65605 91 mins C B, V P
Christopher George, Lynda Day George
A young woman's nightmares come startlingly close to reality.
MPAA:R
Artists Releasing Corporation — *Vestron Video*

Moscow on the Hudson **1984**
Comedy
Closed Captioned
78874 115 mins C B, V P
Robin Williams, Maria Conchita Alonso, Cleavent Derricks, directed by Paul Mazursky
A Russian saxophone player defects at Bloomingdales in New York City while on tour with a Russian circus. In VHS and Beta Hi-Fi.
MPAA:R
Paul Mazursky; Columbia Pictures — *RCA/Columbia Pictures Home Video*

Moses **1976**
Drama/Religion
63393 141 mins C B, V P
Burt Lancaster, Anthony Quayle, Ingrid Thulin, Irene Papas, William Lancaster
Lancaster portrays the plight of Moses, who struggled to free his people from tyranny.
ITC Entertainment — *CBS/Fox Video*

Most Dangerous Game, The **1932**
Suspense
01677 78 mins B/W B, V P
Joel McCrea, Fay Wray, Leslie Banks, Robert Armstrong
A crazed big game hunter lures guests to his secluded island so he can hunt them down like animals.
RKO — *Media Home Entertainment; Budget Video; Discount Video Tapes; Video Dimensions; Sheik Video; Cable Films; Video Yesteryear; Video Connection; Western Film & Video Inc; Cinema Concepts; Kartes Productions; Classic Video Cinema Collector's Club; See Hear Industries*

Most Memorable Games of the Decade #1 **1980**
Football
50091 48 mins C B, V, FO R, P
Highlights from two of the longest overtime playoff games in NFL history: Miami 27, Kansas City 24, in 1971 and Oakland 37, Baltimore 31, in 1977.
NFL Films — *NFL Films Video*

Most Memorable Games of the Decade #2 **1980**
Football
50092 48 mins C B, V, FO R, P
Last second victories in two thrilling classics from 1974: AFC Playoff, Oakland 28, Miami 26; and the 24-23 Thanksgiving Day win by Dallas over Washington led by rookie quarterback Clint Longley.
NFL Films — *NFL Films Video*

Most Memorable Games of the Decade #3 **1980**
Football
50093 48 mins C B, V, FO R, P
Namath and Unitas combine for 872 passing yards in a 1972 regular season game: Jets 44, Colts 34. Plus, the last second victory in the 1976 AFC Playoff: Oakland 24, New England 21.
NFL Films — *NFL Films Video*

Motels, The **1984**
Music-Performance
75914 14 mins C B, V P
This program presents the Motels performing their latest hit songs.
Capital Records Inc — *Sony Corporation of America*

Mother Lode **1982**
Adventure
69283 101 mins C B, V P
Charlton Heston, Nick Mancuso
This action-adventure film tells of the conflict between two men, one driven by greed and the other by near madness, and the all-consuming lust for gold.
MPAA:PG
Agamemnon Films — *Vestron Video*

Mother's Day **1980**
Suspense
68224 98 mins C B, V P
Tiana Pierce, Nancy Hendrickson, Deborah Luee
Three former college roommates plan a reunion together in the wilderness. All was going well until they were dragged into an isolated house.

The terror begins. Two boys and their mother terrorize the girls.
United Film Distributors — *Media Home Entertainment*

MPAA:R
Martin Shafer; Andrew Sheinman — *RCA/Columbia Pictures Home Video*

Mothra **1962**
Horror
64915 101 mins C B, V P
Yumi Ito, Emi Ito
A giant moth wreaks havoc on Tokyo.
Tomoyuki Tanaka — *RCA/Columbia Pictures Home Video*

Motion Picture Camera, The **19??**
Filmmaking/Documentary
57432 32 mins C B, V P, T
From the Karl Malkames collection, we see the development of the movie camera.
Unknown — *Blackhawk Films*

Mount Rushmore, Four Faces on a Mountain **1985**
History-US/National parks and reserves
70707 21 mins C B, V P
Narrated by Burgess Meredith
This tape tells the story behind the granite likenesses of Washington, Lincoln, Jefferson and Teddy Roosevelt in Black Hills, North Dakota.
Century Video Corp. — *Kid Time Video*

Mountain Family Robinson **1979**
Adventure
66061 102 mins C B, V P
Robert Logan, Susan Damante Shaw, Heather Rattray, Ham Larsen
An urban family, seeking escape from the hassles of city life, moves to the Rockies.
MPAA:G
Arthur Dubs — *Media Home Entertainment*

Mountain Man **1976**
Drama
65725 96 mins C B, V P
Denver Pyle, Ken Berry, Cheryl Miller
A true story of one man's lonely, dangerous and inspired fight to save a part of the vanishing wilderness west of the Mississippi, a wilderness now regarded as one of the scenic wonders of the world.
Charles E Sellier Jr — *United Home Video*

Mountain Men, The **1980**
Adventure
58210 102 mins C B, V P
Charlton Heston, Brian Keith
A sweeping adventure drama set in the American West of the 1880's.

Mouse and His Child, The **1977**
Fantasy
65191 83 mins C B, V P
Animated, voices of Peter Ustinov, Cloris Leachman, Andy Devine
A gentle fantasy adventure about a toy wind-up mouse and his child who fall into the clutches of a villainous rat when they venture into the outside world.
Sanrio Film Distribution — *RCA/Columbia Pictures Home Video*

Mouse That Roared, The **1959**
Satire/Comedy
64914 83 mins C B, V P
Peter Sellers, Jean Seberg, Leo McKern
The Duchy of Grand Fenwick declares war on the United States. Peter Sellers is featured in three roles, as the Duchess, the Prime Minister, and a military leader.
Walter Shenson — *RCA/Columbia Pictures Home Video*

Mousercise **1985**
Physical fitness
76820 55 mins C B, V R, P
Kellyn and her Mousercisers perform a specially designed program of exercises for children and pre-teens, with special appearances from Mickey Mouse and other Disney characters.
Walt Disney Productions — *Walt Disney Home Video*

Movie, Movie **1978**
Comedy
56461 96 mins C CED P
George C. Scott, Trish Van Devere, Art Carney, Eli Wallach, Red Buttons, Barbara Harris, Ann Reinking, directed by Stanley Donen
A "double feature" movie, which simulates a typical 1930's moviegoing evening, with a newsreel, previews, a boxing drama (in black and white) and a Busby Berkeley-style musical.
MPAA:PG
Warner Bros, Lord Lew Grade — *RCA VideoDiscs*

Movie Museum I **1980**
Film-History
29731 600 mins B/W B, V P, T
Narrated by Paul Killiam
A fascinating and entertaining review of the first 25 years of the motion picture art form. The set comes on five cassettes and totals ten hours.
Unknown — *Blackhawk Films*

Movie Museum II **1980**
Film-History
29732 600 mins B/W B, V P, T
Narrated by Paul Killiam
A fascinating and entertaining review of the first 25 years of the motion picture art form. There are ten hours on five cassettes in the set.
Unknown — *Blackhawk Films*

Moving Out **1983**
Drama
77014 91 mins C B, V P
Vince Colosimo, Sally Cooper, Maurice Devincentis, Tibor Gyapjas
An adolescent migrant Italian boy finds it difficult to adjust to his new surroundings in Melbourne, Australia.
Pattinson Ballantyne Film Productions — *VidAmerica*

Moving Picture Boys in the Great War, The **1975**
Film-History/Documentary
10152 51 mins B/W B, V P, T
Movies had been invented and 1914-1918 found World War I being fought. Includes authentic films of the war taken from the archives of three different countries.
Blackhawk — *Blackhawk Films*

Moving Violation **1976**
Drama
70699 91 mins C B, V P
Eddie Albert, Kay Lenz, Stephen McHattie, Will Geer, Lonny Chapman, directed by Charles S. Dubin
Crooked cops chase two young men and a woman who've witnessed a murder. The sheriff did it. Hi-Fi stereo in both formats.
MPAA:PG
20th Century Fox; Roger and Julie Corman — *Key Video*

Mozart Story, The **1948**
Drama
11368 91 mins B/W B, V, FO P
Winnie Markus, Hans Holt
After Mozart's death, music minister to the Emperor, Antonio Solieri, reflects on how his jealousy and hatred of the musical genius held the great composer down during his brief life.
Unknown — *Video Yesteryear*

Mr. T **1983**
Cartoons
77157 50 mins C B, V P
Animated
Mr. T coaches an American teenage gymnastic team who travels throughout the world in search of adventure.
Ruby-Spears — *Worldvision Home Video*

Mr. Rossi's Dreams **1983**
Cartoons
80974 80 mins C B, V P
Animated, directed by Bruno Bozzetto
Mr. Rossi gets to act out his fantasies of being Tarzan, Sherlock Holmes and a famous movie star in this film.
Italtoons Corp; Bruno Bozzetto Film — *Family Home Entertainment*

Ms. 45 **1981**
Suspense
66198 82 mins C B, V P
Zoe Tamerlis, Steve Singer, Jack Thibeau
A "psycho" type thriller.
Navaron Films — *U.S.A. Home Video*

Muerte del Che Guevara, La **197?**
Drama
49748 92 mins C B, V P
Che Guevara leads a group of rebels to Bolivia, where they hope to start a revolution. They meet, in a climactic battle, with the loyal forces.
SP
Unknown — *Media Home Entertainment*

Muerto, El **19??**
Drama
66414 105 mins C B, V P
Thelma Biral, Juan Jose Camero, Francisco Rabal
In nineteenth century Buenos Aires, a young man flees his home after killing an enemy. Arriving in Montevideo, he becomes a member of a smuggling ring. Dialogue in Spanish.
SP
Spanish — *Media Home Entertainment*

Muppet Movie, The **1979**
Comedy
37421 94 mins C B, V, LV P
The Muppets, Edgar Bergen, Milton Berle, Mel Brooks, Madeline Kahn, Steve Martin
Kermit the Frog travels to Hollywood with his Muppet pals, planning to become a movie star when he gets there.
MPAA:G
Marble Arch — *CBS/Fox Video; RCA VideoDiscs*

Muppet Musicians of Bremen, The **1972**
Fairy tales/Comedy
47347 50 mins C B, V, LV R, P
The Muppets
Kermit the Frog narrates this story of a group of jazz-playing animals who want to escape from their masters and seek freedom and fame.
RLP Canada/Henson Associates — *Muppet Home Video*

Muppet Revue, The 1985
Variety
Closed Captioned
80743 56 mins C B, V P
Kermit the Frog, Fozzie Bear, Miss Piggy, Harry Belafonte, Linda Ronstadt, Paul Williams
Join Kermit the Frog and Fozzie Bear as they go down Muppet Memory Lane to remember some of the best moments from "The Muppet Show." Available in VHS and Beta Hi Fi.
Henson Associates — *Playhouse Video*

Muppet Treasures 1985
Variety
Closed Captioned
81546 55 mins C B, V P
Kermit the Frog, Fozzie Bear, Peter Sellers, Zero Mostel, Buddy Rich, Paul Simon, Ethel Merman
Kermit and Fozzie discover some unexpected treasures in the Muppet attic including cooking lessons with the Swedish Chef and episodes of "Pigs in Space" and "Veterinarian's Hospital".
Henson Associates — *Playhouse Video*

Muppets Take Manhattan, The 1984
Musical
Closed Captioned
80336 94 mins C B, V P
Kermit the Frog, Miss Piggy, Dabney Coleman, James Coco, Art Carney, directed by Frank Oz
The Muppets try to take their successful college musical to Broadway.
MPAA:G
David Lazer; Tri-Star Pictures — *CBS/Fox Video*

Murder at the Baskervilles 1937
Mystery
44813 67 mins B/W B, V P, T
Arthur Wonter, Ian Fleming, Lyn Harding
Sherlock Holmes is invited to visit Sir Henry Baskerville at his estate, but then finds that Baskerville's daughter's fiance is accused of stealing a race horse and murdering its keeper.
Unknown — *Blackhawk Films*

Murder by Death 1976
Comedy
44847 94 mins C B, V P
Peter Falk, Alec Guiness, David Niven, Maggie Smith, Peter Sellers, Eileen Brennan, Elsa Lanchester, Nancy Walker, Estelle Winwood
An eccentric millionaire invites the world's greatest detectives to dinner and offers one million dollars to the one who can solve the evening's murder.
MPAA:PG
Columbia, Ray Stark — *RCA/Columbia Pictures Home Video; RCA VideoDiscs*

Murder by Decree 1979
Mystery
41080 120 mins C B, V, CED P
Christopher Plummer, James Mason, Donald Sutherland, directed by Bob Clark
Christopher Plummer plays Sherlock Holmes as he finds his most challenging case when a group of anarchists, posing as local merchants, asks him and Dr. Watson for their help.
MPAA:PG
Avco Embassy — *Embassy Home Entertainment*

Murder By Phone 1982
Horror
65741 80 mins C B, V R, P
Richard Chamberlain, John Houseman
A deranged technician has turned his phone into an instrument of electronic death.
MPAA:R
Robert Cooper — *Warner Home Video*

Murder by Television 1935
Mystery
12829 55 mins B/W B, V, FO P
Bela Lugosi
A TV demonstration is the site of the murder of an electronics expert—a murder which takes place in full view of a room full of people.
Cameo — *Video Yesteryear; Discount Video Tapes*

Murder for Sale 1970
Drama
76654 90 mins C B, V P
John Gavin, Margaret Lee, Curt Jurgens
Secret Agent 117 stages an elaborate scam in order to infiltrate a ring of terrorists and criminals.
Marcello Danon — *Media Home Entertainment*

Murder in the Doll House 1979
Mystery
76891 92 mins C B, V P
Yusaku Matsuda, Hiroko Shino, Yoko Nosaki
A private detective must find out who is systematically killing off the family of Japanese toy executive. With English subtitles.
Toho — *Video Action*

Murder My Sweet 1944
Mystery
00264 95 mins B/W B, V, 3/4U P
Dick Powell, Claire Trevor
Private detective Philip Marlowe searches for an ex-convict's missing girl friend. Based on Raymond Chandler's novel "Farewell, My Lovely."
RKO — *Nostalgia Merchant; King of Video; Blackhawk Films*

 (For explanation of codes, see USE GUIDE and KEY)

Murder on Flight 502 1975
Drama
80310 97 mins C B, V P
Farrah Fawcett-Majors, Sonny Bono, Ralph Bellamy, Theodore Bikel, Dane Clark
A crisis arises on a 747 flight from New York to London when a letter is discovered that there is a murderer on board the plane.
Spelling/Goldberg Productions — *Prism*

Murder on the Orient Express 1974
Mystery
38600 128 mins C B, V, LV R, P
Albert Finney, Jacqueline Bisset, Ingrid Bergman, Lauren Bacall, Sean Connery, directed by Sidney Lumet
Agatha Christie's classic whodunit becomes an all-star film, with Albert Finney as Belgian master Sleuth Hercule Poirot, who eventually solves the murder puzzle aboard the famed Orient Express.
MPAA:G
Paramount — *Paramount Home Video; RCA VideoDiscs*

Murder: Ultimate Grounds for Divorce 1985
Mystery/Suspense
81120 90 mins C B, V P
Roger Daltrey, Toyah Wilcox, Leslie Ash, Terry Raven
A quiet weekend of camping turns into a night of horror for two couples when one of them plans an elaborate murder scheme.
Tim Purcell — *Karl/Lorimar Home Video*

Murderer's Row 1966
Mystery
44842 108 mins C B, V P
Dean Martin, Ann-Margret, Karl Malden, Beverly Adams
Daredevil bachelor and former counter-espionage agent Matt Helm is summoned from his life of leisure to insure the safety of an important scientist.
Columbia, Irving Allen — *RCA/Columbia Pictures Home Video*

Murderer's Wife 195?
Drama
65767 24 mins B/W B, V P, T
Audrey Totter, John Howard, June Kenny, Michael Chapin
A teacher at a private school seeks to prevent one of her students from making the same mistakes she did in her youth. An episode from the 1950's television drama series, "Fireside Theatre."
NBC — *Blackhawk Films*

Murph the Surf 1975
Drama/Biographical
81086 102 mins C B, V R, P
Robert Conrad, Don Stroud, Donna Mills, Luther Adler, directed by Marvin Chomsky
This is the true story of how two Miami playboys planned the jewel heist of the century and stole the Star of India sapphire.
MPAA:PG
American International Pictures — *Warner Home Video*

Murri Affair 1974
Mystery
80122 120 mins C B, V P
Catherine Deneuve
A woman from high society sets out to find her husband's killer.
French — *King of Video*

Muscle Motion 1983
Physical fitness
63895 92 mins C B, V P
This aerobic exercise workout is led by seven members of the Chippendales, an all-male revue cabaret for women only.
Nick De Noia; Satyr Corp — *Media Home Entertainment*

Muse Concert: No Nukes, The 1980
Music-Performance
58301 103 mins C B, V, CED P
Jackson Browne, Crosby Stills and Nash, James Taylor, Bruce Springsteen, Doobie Bros, Bonnie Raitt, Carly Simon, John Hall
A concert film of performances held at New York's Madison Square Garden for the benefit of the anti-nuclear power movement.
MPAA:PG
Warner Bros; MUSE Prods — *CBS/Fox Video*

M*U*S*H 1984
Cartoons
70611 60 mins C B, V P
Animated
Animals take the leading roles in this spoof of the popular TV series M*A*S*H.
International Videocraft Ltd. — *Prism*

Music of Melissa Manchester, The 1980
Music-Performance
59853 60 mins C B, V R, P
Manchester performs her greatest hits live in concert. Songs include "Don't Cry Out Loud," "Midnight Blue," and "Come in from the Rain."
Thanksgiving Whatever Inc — *Warner Home Video; Pioneer Artists; RCA VideoDiscs*

Music Shoppe, The 1982
Musical
64951 93 mins C B, V R, P
Gary Crosby, Nia Peeples, Benny Medina, Stephen Schwartz, David Jackson, Jesse White, Doug Kershaw, Gisele MacKenzie
Four teenagers form a rock band with the assistance of the local music store proprietor.
MPAA:G
Century Video — *Video Gems*

Music Video From "Streets of Fire" 1984
Music video
75020 30 mins C B, V P
This tape features three complete stereo music videos from the movie "Streets of Fire."
MCA Home Video — *MCA Home Video*

Musical Personalities No. 1 194?
Musical
11287 50 mins B/W B, V, FO P
Aunt Jemima, Dick Powell, Shirley Temple, Al Jolson, Lena Horne, Teddy Wilson
Four segments spanning three decades of music featuring some of the musical talent of the period from 1927 to 1943.
Educational et al — *Video Yesteryear*

Musicourt 1984
Music-Performance
78067 58 mins C B, V P
This program presents a superstar musical jam featuring Carlos Santana, Joe Cocker and others.
Pacific Arts Video Records — *Pacific Arts Video*

Mustang 197?
Drama
59551 70 mins C B, V P
Filmed entirely inside an actual house of prostitution, the Mustang Bridge Ranch, the largest legal brothel in the U.S., this film offers a portrait of the inner workings of a brothel.
Robert Guralnick — *Media Home Entertainment*

Mutant 1983
Horror
77406 100 mins C B, V, CED P
Wings Hauser, Bo Hopkins, Jennifer Warren, Lee Montgomery
The residents of a small town are terrorized by toxic waste mutants.
MPAA:R
Film Ventures International — *Vestron Video*

Mutiny on the Bounty 1962
Drama
56754 177 mins C B, V P
Marlon Brando, Trevor Howard, Richard Harris, directed by Lewis Milestone
Based on the novel by Charles Nordhoff and James Norman Hall, this account of the most famous mutiny in history aboard the Bounty in 1789 between Fletcher Christian and Captain Bligh is highlighted by lavish photography.
MGM, Aaron Rosenberg — *MGM/UA Home Video*

Mutiny on the Bounty 1935
Adventure
73367 132 mins B/W B, V P
Clark Gable, Charles Laughton, directed by Frank Lloyd
This is the 1935 version of the story of mean Captain Bligh, Fletcher Christian and the problems they have aboard the HMS Bounty.
Academy Award '36: Best Picture
MGM — *MGM/UA Home Video*

Mutiny on the Western Front: WW I 1981
Documentary/World War I
58576 60 mins C B, V P
An untold side of World War I, filmed on the actual locations in France and Germany, as 30,000 Anzac volunteers, suffering great casualties, mutiny against the callous and deluded Allied officers who lead them.
Australian — *Mastervision*

Mutal Respect 1977
Drama
81567 88 mins C B, V P
Lloyd Bridges, Beau Bridges
A dying wealthy man sets out to find the son he never knew.
MPAA:PG
Trans-Atlantic Enterprises — *Academy Home Entertainment*

My Best Girl 1927
Comedy
59652 78 mins B/W B, V P, T
Mary Pickford, Charles "Buddy" Rogers, directed by Sam Taylor
Mary attempts to bring her new sweetheart home for dinner, with disastrous results. A gentle satire on middle-American life in the 1920's. Organ score by Gaylord Carter.
Mary Pickford — *Blackhawk Films*

My Bloody Valentine 1981
Horror
55539 91 mins C B, V, LV R, P
Paul Kelman, Lori Hallier, directed by George Mihalka
A deranged killer stalks a town which has not celebrated Valentine's Day in twenty years—ever since a grisly killing took place.
MPAA:R

Paramount; John Dunning; Andre Link; Stephen Miller — *Paramount Home Video*

My Bodyguard 1980
Drama
55529 96 mins C B, V P
Chris Makepeace, Ruth Gordon, Matt Dillon, John Houseman, Martin Mull, directed by Tony Bill
An undersized high school student fends off attacking bullies by hiring a king-sized, withdrawn lad as his bodyguard. Their relationship, however, develops into true friendship.
MPAA:PG
Twentieth Century Fox; Don Devlin — *CBS/Fox Video*

My Brilliant Career 1980
Drama
56934 101 mins C B, V, CED P
Judy Davis
Sybylla's parents despair at her refusal to resign herself to a life of convention and drudgery, and attempts to "civilize" her fail. Sybylla knows that somehow she must be independent. Produced in Australia.
MPAA:G
Analysis Film Releasing Corp — *Vestron Video*

My Champion 1984
Drama
76021 101 mins C B, V P
Yoko Shimada, Chris Mitchum
A chance meeting propels Mike Gorman and Miki Tsuwa into a relationship based on the strong bond of love and athletic competition.
Yasuhiko Kawano — *Media Home Entertainment*

My Dinner with Andre 1981
Comedy-Drama
60328 110 mins C B, V, CED P
Andre Gregory, Wally Shawn, directed by Louis Malle
Two friends who haven't seen each other for a long time decide to catch up on each others' lives over dinner.
George W George; Beverly Karp — *Pacific Arts Video*

My Fair Lady 1964
Musical
49829 170 mins C B, V, CED P
Audrey Hepburn, Rex Harrison, Stanley Holloway, Wilfred Hyde White, Gladys Cooper, directed by George Cukor
A colorful production of Lerner and Loewe's musical version of "Pygmalion," about a Covent Garden flower girl who becomes a lady. Winner of 8 Academy Awards. Songs incude "On the Street Where You Live," "The Rain in Spain," and "I've Grown Accustomed to Her Face."
Academy Awards '64: Best Picture; Best Director (Cukor); Best Actor (Harrison); Best Color Cinematography.
Warner Bros — *CBS/Fox Video*

My Father's House 1975
Drama
77149 96 mins C B, V P
Cliff Robertson, Robert Preston, Eileen Brennan, Rosemary Forsyth
A magazine editor recalls his youth after he suffers a heart attack.
Filmways — *Worldvision Home Video*

My Father's Nurse 197?
Comedy-Drama
70375 97 mins C B, V R, P
While father convalesces upstairs, the family frolics about the house and plots his dispatch. When his new nurse secretly cures him, he takes to a wheelchair and mounts a comedic covert counter offensive.
Foreign — *Video City Productions*

My Favorite Brunette 1947
Comedy
12859 85 mins B/W B, V P
Bob Hope, Dorothy Lamour, Peter Lorre, Lon Chaney, Alan Ladd
A would-be private eye becomes involved with a murder, a spy caper, and a dangerous brunette.
Paramount — *Prism; Video Yesteryear; Budget Video; Sheik Video; Cable Films; VCII; Video Connection; Discount Video Tapes; Western Film & Video Inc; Cinema Concepts; Kartes Productions; See Hear Industries*

My Favorite Wife 1940
Comedy
64364 88 mins B/W B, V, 3/4U P
Irene Dunne, Cary Grant, Randolph Scott, Gail Patrick, directed by Garson Kanin
A lady explorer returns to civilization after being shipwrecked for seven years and finds that her husband is about to remarry.
RKO — *Nostalgia Merchant*

My Favorite Year 1982
Comedy
64565 92 mins C B, V, CED P
Peter O'Toole, Mark-Linn Baker, Joe Bologna, Jessica Harper, Lainie Kazan, directed by Richard Benjamin
A swashbuckling movie star who drinks too much is signed to make his television debut on a popular live variety show.
MPAA:PG
MGM/UA — *MGM/UA Home Video*

My Forbidden Past 1951
Drama
66334 81 mins B/W B, V, 3/4U P

Ava Gardner, Melvyn Douglas, Robert Mitchum
A New Orleans girl inherits a fortune and vows vengeance when the doctor she loves marries another.
RKO — *Nostalgia Merchant*

My Hero **1952**
Comedy
77196 100 mins B/W B, V P
Robert Cummings, Julie Bishop, John Litel
Here are four episodes from Cummings' first TV series, where he plays a real estate agent who's always in trouble with his boss and girlfriend.
Sharpe-Lewis Productions — *Shokus Video*

My Little Chickadee **1940**
Comedy
31595 91 mins B/W B, V P
W.C. Fields, Mae West, directed by Edward Cline
A classic comedy starring W.C. Fields and Mae West, striking sparks with each other on a trip out West.
Universal — *MCA Home Video; RCA VideoDiscs*

My Little Pony **1984**
Fairy tales
70196 30 mins C B, V P
Animated, Voices of Tony Randall and Sandy Duncan
The popular children's toy, My Little Pony, stars in this original made-for-video holiday production.
Hasbro Industries — *Children's Video Library*

My Man Godfrey **1936**
Comedy
00413 95 mins B/W B, V P
William Powell, Carole Lombard, Gail Patrick, directed by Gregory La Cava
A spoiled rich girl picks up a bum as part of a scavenger hunt and decides to keep him on as her butler.
Universal International; Gregory La Cava — *Prism; Media Home Entertainment; Movie Buff Video; Budget Video; Video Dimensions; Sheik Video; Cable Films; Video Connection; Video Yesteryear; Discount Video Tapes; Western Film & Video Inc; Hal Roach Studios; Kartes Productions; Classic Video Cinema Collector's Club; See Hear Industries*

My Side of the Mountain **1969**
Drama
81101 100 mins C B, V R, P
Teddy Eccles, Theodore Bikel
A thirteen-year-old boy decides to emulate his idol Henry David Thoreau and gives up his home and his family to live in the Canadian mountains.
MPAA:G
Paramount; Robert Radnitz — *Paramount Home Video*

My Therapist **1984**
Comedy-Drama
80267 81 mins C B, V P
Marilyn Chambers
A sex therapist's boyfriend cannot bear the thought of her having intercourse with other men as part of her work.
John Ward — *VCL Home Video*

My Therapist **1984**
Drama
80489 90 mins C B, V P
Marilyn Chambers
A therapist who works with men who have sexual problems finds out how to take her work home with her.
VCL Communications — *VCL Home Video*

My Tutor **1982**
Comedy
69028 97 mins C B, V, LV, CED P
Caren Kaye, Matt Lattanzi, Kevin McCarthy, Irene Golonka
A young woman is hired to tutor a young man in French. This film is a romantic comedy.
MPAA:R
Crown International — *MCA Home Video*

Mysterians, The **1958**
Science fiction
13023 85 mins C B, V P
Kenji Sahara
Race of gigantic scientific intellects attempts to conquer Earth. Dubbed in English from Japanese.
Exhibitor — *United Home Video*

Mysteries from Beyond Earth **1976**
Documentary/Speculation
55008 95 mins C B, V P
The bizarre world of psychic phenomena and the paranormal is explored in this compelling film. Among the many areas of investigation are UFO's, Kirlian Photography, psychic healing, and witchcraft.
Cine Vue — *United Home Video*

Mysterious Desperado **1949**
Western
76762 61 mins B/W B, V P
Tim Holt, Richard Martin
A young man, standing to inherit a large parcel of land, is framed.
RKO — *RKO HomeVideo*

(For explanation of codes, see USE GUIDE and KEY)

Mysterious Desperado/Rider From Tucson 1949
Western
80428 121 mins B/W B, V P
Tim Holt, Richard Martin
A western double feature: In "Mysterious Desperado" a young man is framed for a crime he did not commit in "Rider From Tucson" evil claim jumpers will resort to murder to gain control of a gold mine.
RKO — *RKO HomeVideo*

Mysterious Island 1961
Fantasy
Closed Captioned
21293 101 mins C B, V P
Herbert Lom, Michael Callan, Joan Greenwood
Some Confederate prison escapees, blown off course in an observation balloon, find the uncharted island of Captain Nemo. Based on Jules Verne's novel.
Columbia — *RCA/Columbia Pictures Home Video*

Mysterious Miniature World 1983
Documentary/Insects
63667 90 mins C B, V R, P
The earth's least visible inhabitants and its greatest survivors, the insects, are closely studied in this nature documentary.
Bill Burrud Productions — *Walt Disney Home Video*

Mysterious Two 1982
Science fiction
81265 97 mins C B, V P
John Forsythe, Priscilla Pointer, Vic Tayback, Noah Beery, Karen Werner
An extraterrestrial couple visit the Earth to search for disillusioned people who would like to join them for a trip to another galaxy. Available in VHS Stereo and Beta Hi-Fi.
Alan Landsburg Productions — *U.S.A. Home Video*

Mystery and Espionage 195?
Mystery/Suspense
53049 100 mins B/W B, V, 3/4U P
James Daly, Robert Alda, Preston Foster, John Howard
Four "camp" examples of what foreign intrigue, suspense, mystery, and general spying was all about on 1950's TV: "Overseas Adventure" (1953), starring James Daly as a newspaper correspondent in search of adventure; "Secret File, U.S.A." (1955), starring Robert Alda as the head of the cold war Army intelligence; "Waterfront" (1955), starring Preston Foster as Capt. John Herrick, commander of the tugboat Cheryl Ann; "Dr. Hudson's Secret Journal" (1956), starring John Howard as Center Hospital's top neurosurgeon.
NBC et al — *Shokus Video*

Mystery at Fire Island 1981
Mystery
80808 52 mins C B, V P
Frank Converse, Barbara Byrne, Beth Ehlers, Eric Gurry
A clever young girl and her cousin encounter some strange people as they try to find out why their fisherman friend mysteriously vanished.
Scholastic Productions Inc. — *Scholastic Lorimar*

Mystery Mansion 1983
Mystery
66601 95 mins C B, V P
Dallas McKennon, Greg Wynne, Jane Ferguson
A fortune in gold and a hundred-year-old mystery lead three children into an exciting treasure hunt.
Arthur R. Dubs — *Media Home Entertainment*

Mystery Mountain 1934
Western/Serials
08877 156 mins B/W B, V, 3/4U P
Ken Maynard, Gene Autry, Smiley Burnette
Twelve episodes depict the villain known as the "Rattler" attempting to stop the construction of a railroad over Mystery Mountain.
Mascot — *Video Connection; Cable Films; Video Yesteryear; Discount Video Tapes*

Mystery of the Mary Celeste, The 1937
Mystery
10629 64 mins B/W B, V P, T
Bela Lugosi, Shirley Grey, Edmund Willard
A tale of terror based on the bizarre case of the "Marie Celeste," an American ship found adrift and derelict on the Atlantic Ocean on December 5, 1872.
Guaranteed — *Blackhawk Films; Video Yesteryear; Sheik Video; Cable Films*

Mystery Squadron 1933
Adventure/Serials
10923 156 mins B/W B, V P
Bob Steele, Guinn Williams, J. Carroll Naish
Twelve chapters, 13 minutes each. Daredevil air action in flight against the masked pilots of the Black Ace.
Mascot — *Video Connection; Discount Video Tapes; Video Dimensions; Cable Films; Video Yesteryear*

MysteryDisc #1: Murder, Anyone? 1982
Mystery/Games
63402 ? mins C LV P

This interactive videodisc lets the viewer determine who murdered the millionaire. There are 16 variations with 16 possible solutions, and the viewer must hunt for clues and weigh the evidence in order to solve the mystery.
AM Available
VIDMAX — *VIDMAX; RCA VideoDiscs*

MysteryDisc #2: Many Roads to Murder **1983**
Mystery/Games
64860 ? mins C LV P
Set two years after "MysteryDisc #1," Detective Stew Cavanaugh assists an old college friend in solving a murder. Sixteen different plot lines and solutions are included for the viewer to investigate.
VIDMAX; Parallel Communications — *VIDMAX; RCA VideoDiscs*

N

Nabucco **1984**
Music-Performance
77171 132 mins C B, V R, P
Renato Bruson, Ghena Dimitrova, Dimiter Petkov
A performance of the Verdi opera about an oppressed people's yearning for freedom recorded at the Arena di Verona in Italy.
National Video Corporation Limited — *THORN EMI/HBO Video*

Nadia **1984**
Drama/Biographical
66612 100 mins C B, V P
Carrie Snodgress, Leslie Weiner, Johanna Carlo, Joe Bennett
This is the dramatized story of Nadia Comaneci, the young Romanian gymnast who won worldwide attention as a triple gold-medal winner in the 1976 Montreal Olympics.
Tribune Entertainment; Dave Bell Productions; Jadran Film — *U.S.A. Home Video*

Naked and the Dead, The **1958**
Drama
13027 131 mins C B, V P
Aldo Ray, Cliff Robertson, Joey Bishop
Based on Norman Mailer's novel of WW II men in war; their feelings, hates, desires, and courage.
Warner Bros; Paul Gregory — *United Home Video*

Naked Civil Servant, The **1980**
Drama
59704 80 mins C B, V R, P
John Hurt
The biography of Quentin Crisp, the witty homosexual who grew up in the 30's and 40's and lived through years of intolerance, ostracism and violence.
British Academy Awards '80: Best Actor (Hurt).
Euston Films; Thames Video — *THORN EMI/HBO Video*

Naked Eyes **1983**
Music-Performance
75906 14 mins C B, V P
This program presents the rock group Naked Eyes performing their hits "Always Something There to Remind Me," "Promises, Promises" and "When the Lights Go Out."
EMI America Records — *Sony Corporation of America*

Naked Face, The **1984**
Drama/Mystery
81055 105 mins C B, V P
Roger Moore, Rod Steiger, Elliott Gould, Art Carney, Anne Archer, directed by Bryan Forbes
Someone is stalking a psychiatrist, and police suspect that he murdered a patient and his secretary.
MPAA:R
Cannon Films — *MGM/UA Home Video*

Naked in the Sun **1957**
Western
80845 95 mins C B, V P
James Craig, Lita Milan, Barton MacLane
This is the true story of the events that led up to the war that the Osceola and Seminole Indians waged against a crooked slave trader.
Allied Artists — *Republic Pictures Home Video*

Naked Truth, The **1958**
Comedy
59836 92 mins C B, V P
Peter Sellers, Terry-Thomas, Shirley Eaton, Dennis Price
A greedy publisher tries to get rich quick by publishing a scandal magazine about the "lurid" lives of prominent citizens.
Mario Zampi — *Embassy Home Entertainment*

Nana **1955**
Drama
66388 118 mins C B, V P
Charles Boyer, Martine Carol
A French version of Emile Zola's novel about a dissolute courtesan who spends her life seducing the upper classes. English subtitles.
FR
Roitfield Productions — *Movie Buff Video*

Napoleon **1955**
Biographical/Drama
78967 123 mins C B, V P

Raymond Pellegrin, Orson Welles, Yves Montand, Eric von Stroheim, Jean Gabin, Jean Pierre Aumont
The life story of Napoleon from his days as a soldier in the French army to his exile to the Island of Elba.
Sacha Guitry — *MPI Home Video*

Nashville **1975**
Drama
38613 159 mins C B, V, LV R, P
Henry Gibson, Lily Tomlin, Ronee Blakley, Keith Carradine, directed by Robert Altman
The lives of twenty-four people during a five-day country music festival at the Grand Ole Opry are intertwined in this multi-level portrait of America at a particular time and place.
Academy Awards '75: Best Song (I'm Easy).
MPAA:R
Paramount — *Paramount Home Video; RCA VideoDiscs*

Nate and Hayes **1983**
Adventure
65616 100 mins C B, V, LV, CED R, P
Tommy Lee Jones, Michael O'Keefe, Max Phipps, Jenny Seagrove
Set during the mid-1800s in the South Pacific, the notorious real-life swashbuckler Captain "Bully" Hayes and young Reverend Nate pursue a cutthroat gang which has kidnapped Nate's wife.
MPAA:PG
Lloyd Phillips; Rob Whitehouse — *Paramount Home Video*

National Adultery **19??**
Comedy
65647 90 mins C B, V R, P
The eternal triangle is sketched in this comedy for adults only, starring 1981 Miss Spain.
Italian — *Video City Productions*

National Bodybuilding Championships 1984 **1985**
Physical fitness/Sports-Minor
77229 81 mins C B, V P
The nation's best bodybuilders compete for the bodybuilding champion's trophy taped at the New Orleans World's Fair.
American Sports Network — *American Sports Network*

National Gallery: Art Awareness Collection **19??**
Artists
14178 60 mins C LV P
A look at the great works in Washington, D.C.'s National Gallery of Art. A journey into the artistic genius of Rembrandt, Fragonard, Goya, Copley, Turner, Degas, Renoir, and a group of early American painters is included.
Unknown — *MCA Home Video*

National Gallery of Art, The **1984**
Arts/Museums
69837 ? mins C LV P
This linear program includes the story of the museum's beginnings and development and a comprehensive, detailed tour through one of the finest art collections in the world. The collection spans seven centuries—from Byzantine painters through Leonardo da Vinci and Rembrandt to Matisse and Calder.
Videodisc Publishing; VIDMAX — *Videodisc Publishing*

National Geographic: Great Whales/Sharks **1983**
Fishes/Animals
64778 120 mins C CED P
"Great Whales" (1978), an Emmy Award winning film, looks at whale anatomy, communication and migration. "Sharks" (1982) addresses man's fear and hatred of sharks while offering a look at the shark's vulnerability.
National Geographic Society — *RCA VideoDiscs*

National Geographic Society: The Incredible Machine/Mysteries of the Mind **197?**
Anatomy and physiology
64458 87 mins C CED P
"The Incredible Machine" (1975) offers a fascinating journey inside the human body. "Mysteries of the Mind" (1980) is a documentary which uses computer graphics and a synapse sculpture to examine the brain's structures. Both are multiple award-winning films, the latter having garnered two Emmy Awards.
National Geographic Society — *RCA VideoDiscs*

National Lampoon's Class Reunion **1982**
Comedy
66101 85 mins C B, V, LV, CED P
Shelley Smith, Gerrit Graham, Michael Lerner
A class reunion with some very wacky guests.
MPAA:R
20th Century Fox — *Vestron Video*

National Lampoon's Vacation **1983**
Comedy
65325 98 mins C B, V, LV, CED P
Chevy Chase, Beverly D'Angelo, Imogene Coca, Randy Quaid, Christie Brinkley

The Clark W. Griswold family of suburban Chicago embark on a westward cross-country vacation trip to remember, earmarked by a series of hysterical misadventures.
MPAA:R
Matty Simmons — *Warner Home Video*

Natural, The **1984**
Drama
Closed Captioned
80369 134 mins C B, V P
Robert Redford, Glenn Close, Robert Duvall, Kim Basinger, directed by Barry Levinson
An aging rookie outfielder who returns to the major leagues must battle with his past demons to lead his team to the World Series.
MPAA:PG
Tri Star Pictures — *RCA/Columbia Pictures Home Video*

Nazareth-Live! **1984**
Music-Performance
70223 58 mins C B, V P
The heavy-metal Scottish rockers perform their greatest hits in concert, including "Love Hurts," "Telegram," "Dressed to Kill," "Expect No Mercy," "Hearts Grown Cold" and others.
Irving Rappaport — *VCL Home Video*

Nazi Strike **1984**
World War II/Germany
76532 50 mins B/W B, V P
This program, put together with actual captured film, details Germany's conquests at the beginning of WW II.
Maljack Productions Inc — *MPI Home Video*

Nazi War Crime Trials **1945**
Documentary/World War II
47473 67 mins B/W B, V, FO P
A collection of seven American and Russian newsreel shorts that detail the Nuremberg Trials of Nazi war criminals. Featured are Goring, Van Pappen, Hess, Schact, Streicher and others. Includes grisly scenes of hangings and firing squad executions.
RKO Pathe News et al — *Video Yesteryear; Discount Video Tapes*

Nazis Strike, The / Schichlegruber Doing the Lambeth Walk **194?**
World War II/Documentary
47645 44 mins B/W B, V, FO P
Directed by Frank Capra, Anatole Litvak
"Nazis Strike" is a U.S. War Department film documentary showing America's entry into the war. Includes scenes from "Triumph of the Will." "Schichlegruber Doing the Lambeth Walk" is a satirical British film combining Nazi footage with popular music. Features the "Gestapo Hep-Cats."
US War Dept — *Video Yesteryear*

Nazis Strike, The **1943**
World War II/Documentary
50613 41 mins B/W B, V, 3/4U P
Directed by Frank Capra
Hope for peace is abandoned when the Nazis conquer Austria and Czechoslovakia, and invade Poland. Part of the "Why We Fight" series.
US War Department — *Western Film & Video Inc; Discount Video Tapes; MPI Home Video*

NBC Comedy Hour **1956**
Variety
38988 50 mins B/W B, V, FO P
Jonathan Winters, Guy Mitchell, Gretchen Wyler, Shecky Greene, hosted by Alan Young
Originally telecast in June 3, 1956, this special has a variety format with a "Watching All the Girls Go By" theme. Comedy from all, and songs by Gretchen Wyler.
NBC — *Video Yesteryear*

NBC Comedy Hour **1956**
Comedy/Variety
47498 60 mins B/W B, V, FO P
Groucho Marx, Jonathan Winters, Stan Freberg, Gale Storm, Ben Blue, Jack Albertson
An all-star variety show, featuring numerous top comics in a succession of sketches. Originally telecast on March 4, 1956.
NBC — *Video Yesteryear*

Nea **1978**
Drama
68264 101 mins C B, V P
Sam Frey, Ann Zacharias, Heinz Bennent
Nea is the story of turbulent erotic passion and a young girl's striving to get away from her father's home.
MPAA:R
Andre Genoves — *RCA/Columbia Pictures Home Video*

Neath Arizona Skies **1934**
Western
10944 54 mins B/W B, V P
John Wayne
This cowhand finds all the action he and his friends can handle under western skies.
Monogram — *Sony Corporation of America; Spotlite Video; Discount Video Tapes*

'Neath Arizona Skies/Paradise Canyon **1935**
Western
81020 109 mins B/W B, V P
John Wayne

Here is a double feature of two early John Wayne Westerns filled with lots of rumble tumble action.
Monogram Pictures — *Spotlite Video*

Negro Soldier 1944
World War II/Documentary
52320 40 mins B/W B, V, 3/4U P
Directed by Frank Capra
This wartime documentary focuses on the blacks' participation in World War II, and examines the important role played by the Negro in U.S. history.
US Office of War Information — *International Historic Films; Spotlite Video*

Neighbors 1981
Comedy
47431 90 mins C B, V, LV P
John Belushi, Dan Ackroyd, Kathryn Walker, Cathy Moriarty, directed by John Avildsen
A quiet, middle-class, suburban couple gets the shock of their lives when two loony people move next door.
MPAA:R
Columbia — *RCA/Columbia Pictures Home Video; RCA VideoDiscs*

Neil Diamond: Love at the Greek 1976
Music-Performance
65479 52 mins C B, V, LV, CED P
This stereo spectacular features the Grammy Award-winning star singing his greatest hits "Sweet Caroline," "Play Me," "Holly Holy," "I Am, I Said," "Song Sung Blue" and many more. In stereo VHS and Beta Hi-Fi.
Arch Angel TV — *Vestron Video*

Neil Sedaka in Concert 1981
Music-Performance
55558 54 mins C B, V, LV P
Neil Sedaka, directed by Gary Jones
From his 1960's hits ("Calendar Girl," "Oh Carol," and "Stairway to Heaven") to his 1970's comeback as a composer and performer of contemporary music, Sedaka's style and music are revealed in this concert recorded live at the Jubilee Auditorium in Edmonton, Canada.
Doug Hutton; Doug Holtby — *MCA Home Video*

Neil Sedaka in Concert 1984
Music-Performance
69921 60 mins C B, V P
Singer/songwriter/pianist Neil Sedaka performs his vast repertoire of hits in concert at the Forum in Ontario, Canada. In VHS Dolby stereo and Beta Hi-Fi.
Perry Rosemond — *RKO HomeVideo*

Nelvanamation 1980
Cartoons
54910 100 mins C B, V R, P
Animated
Four cosmic fantasies are featured in this program, including "Please Don't Eat the Planet," "A Cosmic Christmas," "The Devil and Daniel Mouse," and "Romie-O and Julie-8." The latter two are also available individually.
Nelvana Ltd — *Warner Home Video*

Nelvanamation II 1981
Cartoons
47386 50 mins C B, V R, P
Voices of Phil Silvers, Garrett Morris
A second anthology of fantasy cartoons for children of all ages, featuring "Take Me Out to the Ball Game," with music by Rick Danko, and "The Jack Rabbit Story" with music by John Sebastion.
Nelvana Ltd — *Warner Home Video*

Nest, The 1981
Drama
72875 109 mins C B, V P
This film is about the relationship between a widower and a young girl.
Unknown — *Embassy Home Entertainment*

Network 1976
Drama
44645 121 mins C B, V, LV, CED P
Faye Dunaway, Peter Finch, William Holden, Robert Duvall, Wesley Addy, Ned Beatty, Beatrice Straight, directed by Sidney Lumet
A satire of television and the men behind the networks.
Academy Awards '76: Best Actor (Finch); Best Actress (Dunaway); Best Supporting Actress (Straight); Best Screenplay Written Directly for the Screen (Chayefsky). MPAA:R
MGM — *MGM/UA Home Video*

Network Fall Preview Presentations 197?
Variety
33697 110 mins C B, V, 3/4U P
This program contains each of the three major network's presentations to its affiliates, spotlighting new shows to be seen in the autumn season. CBS's (1966) includes, "It's About Time," and "Run, Buddy, Run," NBC's (1969) highlights contain "The Bill Cosby Show," and "Then Came Bronson," and ABC's (1974) clips preview "Happy Days," amd "Marcus Welby, M.D." among others.
CBS et al — *Shokus Video*

Never a Dull Moment 1968
Comedy
70666 90 mins C B, V R, P

Dick Van Dyke, Edward G. Robinson, Dorothy Provine, Henry Silva, Joanna Moore, Tony Bill, Slim Pickens, Jack Elam, directed by Jerry Paris
Mobsters mistake an actor for an assassin in this gag filled adventure. They threaten the thespian into thievery, and trouble really starts when Ace, the actual assassin arrives.
MPAA:G
Walt Disney Productions/Ron Miller — *Walt Disney Home Video*

Never Cry Wolf 1984
Drama
75927 105 mins C B, V, LV, CED R, P
Charles Martin Smith, Brian Dennehy, Samson Jorah
The dramatic story of a young biologist's trek to the Artic region to study wolves.
Walt Disney — *Walt Disney Home Video*

Never Let Go 1960
Comedy-Drama
59837 91 mins C B, V P
Peter Sellers, Richard Todd, Elizabeth Sellars
A man unwittingly tracks down the mastermind of a gang of racketeers.
Peter de Sarigny — *Embassy Home Entertainment*

Never Love a Stranger 1958
Drama
76833 93 mins B/W B, V P
John Drew Barrymore, Steve McQueen, Lita Milan, Robert Bray
A young man who becomes a numbers runner for a mobster and ultimately winds up heading his own racket finds himself in conflict with his old boss and the District Attorney.
Allied Artists — *Republic Pictures Home Video*

Never On Sunday 1960
Comedy
81504 94 mins B/W B, V P
Melina Mercouri, Titos Vandis, Jules Dassin, Mitsos Liguisos, directed by Jules Dassin
An American intellectual tries to turn a Greek prostitute into a refined woman.
Academy Awards '60: Best Song "Never On Sunday."
Melafilm Prods. — *MGM/UA Home Video*

Never Say Never Again 1983
Suspense
69800 134 mins C B, V, LV, CED R, P
Sean Connery, Klaus Maria Brandauer, Max Von Sydow, Barbara Carrera
James Bond matches wits with a charming but sinister tycoon who is holding the world nuclear hostage as part of a diabolical plot by SPECTRE. In stereo on all formats.
MPAA:PG
Jack Schwartzman — *Warner Home Video*

Neverending Story, The 1984
Fantasy
Closed Captioned
79554 86 mins C B, V, LV R, P
Barret Oliver, Noah Hathaway, Gerald McRaney, Moses Gunn, directed by Wolfgang Petersen
A young boy helps a young warrior save a fantasy world from destruction. The music is composed by Klaus Doldinger and Giorgio Moroder. Available in Stereo VHS Hi-Fi and Beta Hi-Fi.
MPAA:PG
Warner Bros; Producers Sales Organization — *Warner Home Video*

New Adventures of Tarzan, The 1935
Adventure/Serials
08870 260 mins B/W B, V, 3/4U P
Herman Brix, Ula Holt, Frank Baker, Dale Walsh, Lewis Sargent
Twelve episodes, each 22 minutes long, depicts the adventures of Edgar Rice Burrough's tree-swinging character—Tarzan.
Burroughs and Tarzan — *Budget Video; Video Connection; Video Yesteryear; Discount Video Tapes*

New Adventures of Zorro, The 1981
Cartoons/Adventure
66004 60 mins C B, V P
Animated
Daring swordplay highlights these three tales of swashbuckling adventures.
Filmation — *Family Home Entertainment*

New Adventures of Zorro, Volume III, The 1985
Cartoons/Adventure
70358 60 mins C B, V P
Animated
This film features further swashbuckling heroism by the legendary Spanish-Californian swordsman. The program is available in stereo formats.
Filmation — *Family Home Entertainment*

New Centurions, The 1972
Drama
21294 109 mins C B, V P
George C. Scott, Stacy Keach, Jane Alexander
The film version of Joseph Wambaugh's novel about rookie cops on the Los Angeles Police Force.
MPAA:R
Columbia — *RCA/Columbia Pictures Home Video*

(For explanation of codes, see USE GUIDE and KEY)

New Deal—The Thirties, The 19??
History-US/Documentary
10148 ? mins B/W B, V P, T
Covers the Depression, Mahatma Ghandi, Thomas Edison, George Gershwin, Mt. Rushmore, Al Capone, FDR, John Dillinger, the Hindenberg, Lou Gehrig, and more.
Unknown — *Blackhawk Films*

New Kids, The 1985
Horror
Closed Captioned
81429 90 mins C B, V P
Shannon Presby, Lori Loughlin, James Spader, Eric Stoltz, directed by Sean S. Cunningham
An orphaned brother and sister find out the limitations of the good neighbor policy when a sadistic gang terrorizes them at their relatives' home in Florida. Available in VHS and Beta Hi Fi.
Columbia Pictures — *RCA/Columbia Pictures Home Video*

New Lion of Sonora, The 1970
Western
72891 120 mins C B, V P
Gilbert Roland, Leif Erickson
Two episodes of the "High Chaparral" TV series are herewith combined where Don Domingo (Gilbert Roland) returns to Arizona to head his family.
NBC — *Republic Pictures Home Video*

New Look 1981
Variety/Filmmaking
59843 44 mins C B, V, LV, CED P
Francis Ford Coppola, Bob Rafelson
An erotic men's video magazine including a centerfold, interviews with filmmaker Francis Ford Coppola and Bob Rafelson, and a series of vignettes.
Regie Cassette Video; Blay RCV — *Embassy Home Entertainment*

New Media Bible: The Story of Joseph, The 1976
Bible
64708 90 mins C CED P
This video dramatization of the Bible presents historically accurate settings and authentic details of the biblical stories of Joseph.
Genesis Project — *RCA VideoDiscs*

New Misadventures of Ichabod Crane, The 1981
Fantasy/Holidays
47254 25 mins C B, V, 3/4U, FO P
The headless horseman rides again, robbing coaches and scaring the townsfolk of Sleepy Hollow. Halloween fun begins when Ichabod comes to the rescue with his motley crew of friends.
AM Available
Coronet Films — *Embassy Home Entertainment*

New Speed Reading 1981
Education/Communication
52767 60 mins C B, V P
This complete speed reading course is divided into video chapters and allows the viewer to refer back and review the method and progress of speed reading. An instructional booklet with study schedules is included.
AM Available
Karl Video — *Karl/Lorimar Home Video*

New Three Stooges Cartoon Show, The 1984
Cartoons
72867 60 mins C B, V P
Animated
The first volume of this series features six cartoons from the series that features the voices of Moe Howard, Larry Fine and Joe de Rita.
Dick Brown, Normandy TV Three Production — *Embassy Home Entertainment*

New 3 Stooges Volume VII, The 1965
Cartoons
80770 30 mins C B, V P
Animated, Voices of Moe Howard, Larry Fine, Joe De Rita
Here is another volume of animated fun with The Three Stooges.
Cambria Studios — *Embassy Home Entertainment*

New Three Stooges, Volume V, The 1965
Cartoons
80396 30 mins C B, V P
Animated, voices of Moe Howard, Larry Fine, Joe De Rita
In this volume, The Stooges try such occupations as jet airplane racers and mailmen with the U.S. Postal Service.
Cambria Studios — *Embassy Home Entertainment*

New 3 Stooges Volume VI, The 1965
Cartoons
76911 30 mins C B, V P
Animated, voices of Moe Howard, Larry Fine, Joe deRita
This volume features the following four cartoons: "Stop Dragon Around," "Who's Lion,"

"To Kill a Clockingbird," and "Foul Weather Friend."
Dick Brown; Normandy TV Three Productions — *Embassy Home Entertainment*

New Three Stooges, Volume IV, The 1965
Cartoons
80041 30 mins C B, V P
Animated, voices of Moe Howard, Larry Fine, Joe DeRita
The three Stooges are at it again as they try out every job from movie stars to western heroes.
TV III Inc; Cambria Studios — *Embassy Home Entertainment*

New Video Aerobics, The 1982
Physical fitness
63364 57 mins C B, V, CED P
Leslie Lilien, Julie Lavin
This program instructs the home viewer in a complete and compact conditioning routine of aerobics. Contains a 40-minute advanced program and a 17-minute beginner's session.
Amstar Productions — *Vestron Video*

New York Giants 1984 Team Highlights 1985
Football
70549 70 mins C B, V, FO P
Phil Simms, Bill Parcells
The headlines read. "Giants Again!" as the hard-working New Yorkers finally regained their stature as NFL contenders. The tape features 47-Minutes of high-lights from the '84 NFL season as well
NFL Films — *NFL Films Video*

New York Mets: Team Highlights 1984
Baseball
81145 30 mins C B, V P
Gil Hodges, Casey Stengel, Tom Seaver, Rusty Staub, Darryl Strawberry, Dwight Gooden
11 pgms
You can catch the rising stars as this series looks back at the best moments from the Mets past seasons.
1.1963: Let's Go Mets 2.1969: Look Who's #1 3.1971: The Winning Way 4.1972: The Second Decade 5.1973: You Gotta Believe 6.1976: 15 Years of Fun 7.1980: Mets Magic 8.1981: Better All The Time 9.1982: Building a Fantastic Future 10.1983: We Can Make It Happen 11.1984: Don't Stop Us Now
Major League Baseball — *Major League Baseball Productions*

New York, New York 1977
Drama/Musical
63400 163 mins C B, V P
Robert De Niro, Liza Minnelli, directed by Martin Scorsese
A tragic romance evolves between a saxaphonist and an aspiring actress in this salute to the big band era.
MPAA:PG
United Artists — *CBS/Fox Video; RCA VideoDiscs*

New York Nights 1984
Drama
80665 104 mins C B, V P
Corinne Alphen, George Ayer, Bobbi Burns, Peter Matthey, Cynthia Lee
The lives of nine New Yorkers intertwine in a treacherous game of passion and seduction.
MPAA:R
International Talent Marketing — *Lightning Video*

New York-Yankees: Team Highlights 1984
Baseball
81147 30 mins C B, V P
Joe DiMaggio, Whitey Ford, Mickey Mantle, Billy Martin, Thurman Munson, Ron Guidry
7 pgms
This series chronicles the history of the Bronx Bombers from their humble beginnings to the present day.
1.Play Ball with the Yankees 2.Dynasty: The New York Yankees 3.50 Years of Yankee All-Stars 4.Home of Heroes 5.A New Era 6.1977: A Winning Tradition 7. 1978: It Don't Come Easy.
Major League Baseball — *Major League Baseball Productions*

New Zoo Revue 1984
Children/Variety
75928 60 mins C B, V P
This program presents the live children's programing package, The New Zoo Revue.
Family Home Entertainment — *Family Home Entertainment*

New Zoo Revue—Volume 2 1974
Variety
77424 60 mins C B, V P
In episode 1 Freddie the Frog tries to get everyone to listen to his poem, while Doug and Emmy try to convince Freddie that violence won't settle an argument in the second of these two episodes from the series.
Barbara Atlas; Douglas Momary — *Family Home Entertainment*

Newport Jazz Festival 1962
Music-Performance
55382 60 mins B/W B, V P
Duke Ellington, Count Basie, Roland Kirk
Jazz greats in concert at the famed jazz festival include Count Basie, Duke Ellington, Roland Kirk, Ruby Braff, Peewee Russell, Joe Williams,

Oscar Peterson Trio with Ray Brown, Lambert, Hendricks and Bavan, and others.
Unknown — *CBS/Fox Video; Discount Video Tapes*

News Front **1978**
Drama
73663 110 mins C B, V P
Bill Hunter, Wendy Hughes, John Ewart, Chris Hayward
The story of two brothers who worked in Australia's news media of the '50s and '60s is chronicled in this film. Some segments are in black and white.
David Elfick — *Embassy Home Entertainment*

Next of Kin **1985**
Horror
70250 90 mins C B, V P
Jackie Kerin, John Jarratt, Gerda Nicolson
A woman is plagued by nightmares after moving into her inherited estate. Suspense mounts as she discovers horrifying correlations between her mother's death and her situation.
VCL Communications — *VCL Home Video*

Next One, The **1984**
Science fiction
76771 105 mins C B, V P
Keir Dullea, Adrienne Barbeau, Jerenny Licht, Peter Hobbs
A mysterious visitor from another time winds up on an isolated Greek island as the result of a sinister magnetic storm.
Allstar Productions — *Vestron Video*

Next Victim **1971**
Horror
80828 87 mins C B, V R, P
George Hilton, Edwige French, Christina Airoldi, Ivan Rassimov
The unfaithful wife of an Austrian diplomat attempts to find out who has been slicing up beautiful jet-setters.
MPAA:PG
Laurie International — *Video Gems*

Next Year If All Goes Well **1983**
Comedy
77166 95 mins C B, V P
Isabelle Adjani, Thierry Lhermite
Two young lovers struggle to overcome their insecurities to establish a relationship.
FR
New World Pictures — *THORN EMI/HBO Video*

NFL '81 **1982**
Football
47716 47 mins C B, V, FO P
Highlights from the topsy-turvy 1981-82 NFL season, focusing on the great individual performances, the Playoffs, and the NFL's selections for the 1981-82 All-Pro Teams.
NFL Films — *NFL Films Video*

NFL '81 Official Season Yearbook **1982**
Football
47806 120 mins C CED P
Four half-hour segments: "NFL '81" - a season overview; "Superbowl XVI Highlights;" "A Very Special Team" - season highlights of the San Francisco 49'er's; "Stripes" - season highlights of the Cincy Bengals.
NFL Films — *RCA VideoDiscs*

NFL Follies Go Hollywood **1983**
Football
65155 23 mins C B, V, FO P
Football fumbles and goof-ups are integrated into a parody of movie genres in this entry from the "NFL Follies" series.
NFL Films — *NFL Films Video; Champions on Film and Video*

NFL SymFunny/Highlights of Super Bowl III **1980**
Football
56792 46 mins C B, V P
The antics of the NFL "ballet company" set to music by Beethoven, Bach, and "The Quarterback of Seville," plus Joe Namath's triumph against the Colts in the most incredible upset in Super Bowl history.
NFL Films — *VidAmerica*

NFL's Best Ever Coaches **1981**
Football
51702 46 mins C B, V, FO R, P
A profile of some of the most respected and successful coaches ever to pace the sidelines of an NFL stadium, including Paul Brown, Vince Lombardi, Don Shula, and Tom Landry.
NFL Films — *NFL Films Video*

NFL's Best Ever: The Professionals **1981**
Football
51703 46 mins C B, V, FO R, P
This program profiles some of the most determined, gutsy personalities ever to hit the NFL, who despite setbacks and long odds, struggled their way to success and recognition. It features Jim Plunkett, Jim Marshall, Bill Kilmer, Larry Brown, and Dick Vermeil.
NFL Films — *NFL Films Video*

NFL's Best Ever Quarterbacks **1981**
Football
51704 46 mins C B, V, FO R, P
The skillfully thrown passes and field leadership of former great quarterbacks Otto Graham, John Unitas, Roger Staubach, and Fran Tarkenton sparked their teams to success and provided a host of memories.
NFL Films — *NFL Films Video*

NFL's Best Ever Runners **1981**
Football
51705 46 mins C B, V, FO R, P
O. J. Simpson, Jim Brown, Hugh McElheny, and Walter Payton are some of the outstanding running backs who dart, slash, sweep, and fake their way through this program.
NFL Films — *NFL Films Video*

NFL's Best Ever Teams **1981**
Football
51706 46 mins C B, V, FO R, P
Throughout the NFL's history, there have been several teams who dominated their league for several years at a time: the Cleveland Browns of the 50's, the Green Bay Packers of the 60's, the Miami Dolphins of the early 70's, and Steelers, Cowboys, and Raiders of the middle and late 70's.
NFL Films — *NFL Films Video*

NFL's Inspirational Men and Moments, The **1980**
Football
50090 48 mins C B, V, FO R, P
Roger Staubach, O. J. Simpson, Fran Tarkenton, Joe Namath
A collection of short programs that reveal much about the inspirational aspects of pro football as well as the human side of a sport that's more than just a game.
NFL Films — *NFL Films Video*

Nicholas and Alexandra **1971**
Drama
69618 183 mins C B, V P
Michael Jayston, Janet Suzman, Tom Baker, Laurence Olivier, Michael Redgrave
This epic film chronicles the final years of Tsar Nicholas II and Empress Alexandra and their children from 1904 through their imprisonment and eventual execution under the new Lenin government.
MPAA:PG
Sam Spiegal — *RCA/Columbia Pictures Home Video*

Nicholas Nickleby **1947**
Drama
58885 103 mins B/W B, V R, P
Sir Cedric Hardwicke, Stanley Holloway, Derek Bond, Alfred Drayton, Sybil Thorndike, Sally Ann Howes
An ensemble cast is featured in this film adaptation of Charles Dickens' novel concerning an impoverished family dependent on a wealthy but villainous relative who sends young Nicholas into a series of wild adventures.
Ealing — *THORN EMI/HBO Video*

Nickel Mountain **1985**
Drama
81126 88 mins C B, V P
Michael Cole, Heather Langen Kamp, Ed Lauter, Brian Kerwin, Patrick Cassidy
A suicidal forty-year-old man finds a new reason to live when he falls in love with a pregnant sixteen-year-old girl who works at his diner.
Ziv International — *Karl/Lorimar Home Video*

Night and Day **1946**
Musical/Biographical
70380 128 mins B/W B, V P
Cary Grant, Eve Arden, Alexis Smith, Mary Martin, Monty Woolley, Dorothy Malone, Ginny Simms, Donald Woods.
This film presents the life of Cole Porter and features performances of many classic Porter tunes.
Warner Bros. — *Key Video*

Night and Fog **1955**
Documentary/World War II
02957 32 mins C B, V, FO P
Directed by Alain Resnais
A devastating documentary showing the gruesome atrocities of Hitler's Nazi purge against almost nine million innocent people.
Premier Prix dú Concourse de la Qualite.
Argos Films — *Video Yesteryear; International Historic Films; Films Inc; Anti Defamation League of Bnai Brith*

Night at the Opera, A **1935**
Comedy
39091 96 mins B/W B, V P
The Marx Brothers, Allan Jones, Kitty Carlisle, Sig Rumann, Margaret Dumont
The Marx Brothers get mixed up with grand opera in this finest of all their films. Allan Jones, as an opera singer on the rise, sings "Alone," and "Cosi Cosa."
MGM — *MGM/UA Home Video*

Night Before Christmas, The **1981**
Christmas
58946 30 mins C B, V P
Animated, Norman Luboff Choir
A heartwarming retelling of the charming "A Visit from St. Nicholas," animated, with holiday music.

AM Available
Bill Turnball; Playhouse Pictures — *Media Home Entertainment*

Night Creature 1979
Horror
79762 83 mins C B, V P
Donald Pleasance, Nancy Kwan
A writer is determined to kill the man-eating black leopard who nearly killed him once before.
MPAA:PG
Dimension Pictures — *United Home Video*

Night Crossing 1981
Drama/Adventure
59809 106 mins C B, V R, P
John Hurt, Jane Alexander, Glynnis O'Connor, Doug McKeon, Beau Bridges, directed by Delbert Mann
The fact-based story of two East German families who launch a daring escape to the West in a homemade hot air balloon.
MPAA:PG
Walt Disney Productions — *Walt Disney Home Video*

Night Gallery 1969
Fantasy/Drama
76808 95 mins C B, V P
Joan Crawford, Roddy McDowall, Tom Bosley, Barry Sullivan, Ossie Davis, Sam Jaffee, directed by Steven Spielberg, Boris Sagaland and Barry Shear
Rod Serling is your tour guide through an unusual art gallery consisting of portraits that reflect people's greed, desire and guilt. Pilot for the series that ran from 1969 to 1973.
Universal; William Sackheim — *MCA Home Video*

Night Games 1980
Drama
66051 100 mins C B, V, LV, CED P
Cindy Pickett, directed by Roger Vadim
A sexually unfulfilled woman experiences a passionate fantasy life.
MPAA:R
Raymond Chow — *Embassy Home Entertainment*

Night Has Eyes, The 1942
Mystery
66389 79 mins B/W B, V P
James Mason, Joyce Howard, Wilfred Lawson
A young teacher disappears on the Yorkshire moors at the same spot where her girl friend had vanished the previous year.
ABP — *Movie Buff Video; Discount Video Tapes*

Night Is My Future, The 1947
Drama
48857 89 mins B/W B, V, 3/4U P
Mai Zetterling, directed by Ingmar Bergman
A blind young man meets a girl who tries to bring him happiness.
Swedish — *Western Film & Video Inc; Video Yesteryear; Video Dimensions*

Night Moves 1975
Suspense/Mystery
51967 100 mins C B, V R, P
Gene Hackman, Susan Clark, Jennifer Warren
While tracking down a missing teenager, a Hollywood detective uncovers a bizarre smuggling ring.
MPAA:PG
Warner Bros — *Warner Home Video*

Night of the Assassin 1977
Drama/Suspense
70692 98 mins C B, V P
Klaus Kinski, Michael Craig, Eva Renzi, directed by Robert McMahon
A priest leaves his pulpit to practice terrorism in this intriguing film. He plans a surprise for a U.N. secretary visiting Greece that should put the U.S. and Greek governments in the palm of his hand.
Cinema Shares — *Lightning Video*

Night of the Bloody Apes 1978
Horror
79700 84 mins C B, V P
When a doctor transplants an ape's heart into his dying son's body, the results are deadly.
MPAA:R
William Calderon — *MPI Home Video*

Night of the Generals, The 1967
Drama
77376 148 mins C B, V P
Peter O'Toole, Omar Sharif, Tom Courtenay, Joanna Pettet, Donald Pleasance
A Nazi intelligence officer is pursuing three Nazi generals who may be involved in the brutal murder of a Warsaw prostitute.
MPAA:R
Columbia Pictures; Sam Spiegel — *RCA/Columbia Pictures Home Video*

Night of the Ghouls 1960
Horror
66336 75 mins B/W B, V, 3/4U P
Directed by Edward D. Wood
The last in Edward Wood's celebrated series of inept so-called horror films, begun with "Bride of the Monster" and "Plan 9 from Outer Space."
DCA — *Nostalgia Merchant*

Night of the Grizzly, The **1966**
Western/Adventure
81102 99 mins C B, V R, P
Clint Walker, Martha Hyer
An ex-lawman's peaceful life as a rancher is threatened when a killer grizzly bear goes on a murderous rampage terrorizing the residents of the Wyoming countryside.
Paramount — *Paramount Home Video*

Night of the Iguana, The **1964**
Drama
58296 125 mins B/W B, V P
Richard Burton, Deborah Kerr, Ava Gardner, Sue Lyon, directed by John Huston
A defrocked minister, acting as a guide to a group of women on a Mexican bus trip, affects the lives of three women. Based on Tennessee Williams' play.
MGM; Ray Stark — *MGM/UA Home Video*

Night of the Juggler **1980**
Suspense
47816 101 mins C B, V, 3/4U P
James Brolin, Cliff Gorman, Richard Castellano, Mandy Patinkin
A man encounters countless obstacles in trying to track down his daughter's kidnapper.
MPAA:R
Columbia — *Nostalgia Merchant; Media Home Entertainment*

Night of the Living Dead **1968**
Horror
01681 90 mins B/W B, V P
Judith O'Dea, Duane Jones, Russell Streiner, Karl Hardman
Space experiments set off high level of radiation that makes the newly-dead return to life. They march upon humanity devouring their flesh.
Continental; Streiner and Hardman — *Media Home Entertainment; Budget Video; VCII; Video Yesteryear; Nostalgia Merchant; Video Dimensions; Sheik Video; Cable Films; King of Video; Video Connection; Discount Video Tapes; Western Film & Video Inc; Vestron Video (disc only)*

Night of the Zombies **1983**
Horror
73040 101 mins C B, V P
The staff of a scientific research center are killed and then resurrected as cannibals who prey on the living.
Motion Picture Marketing — *Vestron Video*

Night Porter, The **1974**
Drama
59838 115 mins C B, V, LV, CED P
Dirk Bogarde, Charlotte Rampling, Philippe LeRoy, Gabriele Ferzetti
Max, a guilt-ridden ex-SS concentration camp officer, unexpectedly meets his former lover-victim.
Robert Gordon; Avco Embassy — *Embassy Home Entertainment*

Night Shift **1982**
Comedy
63122 106 mins C B, V, LV, CED R, P
Henry Winkler, Michael Keaton, Shelley Long
Two morgue attendants decide to spice up their late-night shift by running a call girl service on the side.
MPAA:R
The Ladd Company — *Warner Home Video*

Night Stage to Galveston **1952**
Western
65082 61 mins B/W B, V P, T
Gene Autry, Pat Buttram, Virginia Huston, Thurston Hall
Gene leads his Texas Rangers on a mission to uncover corruption in the Texas State Police during the turbulent post-Civil War days.
Columbia — *Blackhawk Films*

Night Terror **1976**
Drama
79249 73 mins C B, V P
Valerie Harper, Richard Romanus, Michael Tolan, Beatrice Manley
Everyone's after a woman who saw a highway partolman murdered on an expressway.
Charles Fries Productions — *Worldvision Home Video*

Night the Lights Went Out in Georgia, The **1981**
Drama
59335 112 mins C B, V P
Kristy McNichol, Dennis Quaid, Mark Hamill, Don Stroud
Based on the popular hit song, a brother and sister try to cash in on the country music scene in Nashville
MPAA:PG
Elliot Geisinger; Howard Kuperman; Ronald Saland; Howard Smith — *Embassy Home Entertainment; Trans World Entertainment*

Night Visitor, The **1970**
Suspense
51115 106 mins C B, V P
Max von Sydow, Liv Ullman, Trevor Howard, Per Oscarsson
A man whose convicted insanity is actually in doubt seeks violent vengeance on his tormentors.
MPAA:PG
Mel Ferrer — *United Home Video*

Night Warning 1982
Drama
69042 96 mins C B, V R, P
A portrayal of young love's perverted inner conflicts and sinister mystery.
Unknown — *THORN EMI/HBO Video*

Night with Lou Reed, A 1983
Music-Performance
65698 60 mins C B, V P
This is a visual record of the legendary rock star's sold-out engagement at The Bottom Line in New York featuring many of his greatest hits, including "Sweet Jane," "Walk on the Wild Side," "I'm Waiting for My Man," and "Rock 'n' Roll." In Beta Hi-Fi.
Bill Boggs; Richard Baker; RCA Video Productions Inc — *RCA/Columbia Pictures Home Video*

Nighthawks 1981
Suspense/Drama
55557 90 mins C B, V, LV, CED P
Sylvester Stallone, Billy Dee Williams, Rutger Hauer, Lindsay Wagner, directed by Bruce Malmuth
A New York City cop stalks Manhattan, hunting down an international terrorist on the loose, from disco, to subway, to an airborne tramway. Also available in a Spanish subtitled version.
MPAA:R
Universal; Martin Poll — *MCA Home Video*

Nightingale, The 1984
Fairy tales
Closed Captioned
73852 60 mins C B, V, LV, CED P
Mick Jagger, Barbara Hershey, Bud Cort, Mako, directed by Ivan Passer
From "Faerie Tale Theatre" comes the story of an Emperor who discovers the value of true friendship and loyalty from his palace kitchen maid who gives him a nightingale.
Gaylord Productions; Platypus Productions — *CBS/Fox Video*

Nightkill 1980
Drama/Suspense
63375 104 mins C B, V P
Jaclyn Smith, Mike Connors, James Franciscus, Robert Mitchum
A bored wife plots to do away with her wealthy, powerful husband with the aid of her attractive lover.
MPAA:R
Avco Embassy — *Embassy Home Entertainment*

Nightmare in Wax 1969
Horror
13028 95 mins C B, V P
Cameron Mitchell, Anne Helm
Famous actor, burned by wax, starts a wax museum and destroys all of his enemies.
Gold Key — *United Home Video*

Nightmare on Elm Street, A 1984
Horror
81091 92 mins C B, V P
John Saxon, Ronee Blakely, Heather Lagen Kamp, directed by Wes Craven
A teenaged girl decides to wage a battle against a man who is annihilating other teenagers in their dreams. This movie contains gratuitous violence which is not for the squeamish.
MPAA:R
New-Line Cinema — *Media Home Entertainment*

Nightmares 1983
Horror
66329 99 mins C B, V P
Christina Raines, Emilio Estevez, Moon Zappa, Lance Henriksen, Richard Masur, Veronica Cartwright
An anthology of four horrific tales in which common, everyday occurrences take on the ingredients of nightmare.
MPAA:PG
Universal — *MCA Home Video*

Nightwing 1979
Suspense
68263 103 mins C B, V, CED P
Nick Mancuso, David Warner, Kathryn Harrold
A suspense drama about three people who risk their lives to exterminate a colony of plague-carrying vampire bats.
MPAA:PG
Columbia — *RCA/Columbia Pictures Home Video*

Nine Ages of Nakedness 197?
Drama
59548 88 mins C B, V P
The story of a man whose ancestors have been plagued by a strange problem—beautiful, naked women who create carnal chaos.
George Harrison Marks — *Media Home Entertainment*

984—Prisoner of the Future 1984
Drama
76646 70 mins C B, V P
Don Francks, Stephen Markle and Gail Dahms
A shocking, futuristic tale of human self-destruction.
William I Macadam — *VCL Home Video*

Nine Lives of Fritz the Cat, The 1974
Comedy/Fantasy
64880 77 mins C CED P
Animated
The would-be cool cat of the 60's is fed up with his establishment life in the 70's, so he takes off into his other lives on a fantasy journey.
American International Pictures — *Vestron Video (disc only)*

---

9 to 5 1981
Comedy
49397 111 mins C B, V, LV, CED P
Jane Fonda, Lily Tomlin, Dolly Parton, Dabney Coleman
Three office secretaries rebel against their male chauvinistic boss, eventually raising office efficiency to a new all-time high.
MPAA:PG
20th Century Fox — *CBS/Fox Video*

1984 1984
Drama
80898 115 mins C B, V P
John Hurt, Richard Burton, Suzanna Hamilton, Cyril Cusack, directed by Michael Radford
This film is a faithful adaptation of the George Orwell novel about the grim consequences of life within a totalitarian society where inhabitants are under constant scrutiny of "Big Brother." Music by Eurythmics and Dominic Muldowney. Available in VHS Stereo and Beta Hi-Fi.
MPAA:R
Virgin Films; Umbrella-Rosenblum Films — *U.S.A. Home Video*

1984 Winter Olympics Highlights 1984
Sports-Winter
65625 60 mins C B, V P
Experience the excitement as more than 1200 of the best athletes from over 44 countries compete to bring home the gold at the XIV Winter Olympic Games held in Sarajevo, Yugoslavia.
ABC Sports; Curt Gowdy Jr — *Embassy Home Entertainment*

1981 NBA Playoffs and Championship Series: The Dynasty Renewed 1981
Basketball
53411 58 mins C B, V P
While the Celtics and 76ers tear up the Eastern Conference, the Lakers try to survive through Magic Johnson's Knee injury in the West. Once the long season ends, the playoffs provide plenty of upsets, drama, and classic basketball.
NBA — *CBS/Fox Video*

1958 NFL Championship Game 1984
Football
79635 47 mins C B, V, FO P
Highlights from the 1958 NFL championship games between the Baltimore Colts and the New York Giants.
NFL Films — *NFL Films Video*

1941 1979
Comedy
42939 120 mins C B, V, LV P
John Belushi, Dan Ackroyd, Ned Beatty, directed by Steven Spielberg
Spielberg has directed the most expensive comedy of all time with a budget exceeding 35 million dollars. His depiction of Los Angeles in the chaotic days after the bombing of Pearl Harbor combines elements of fantasy and black humor.
MPAA:PG
A Team Prods — *MCA Home Video*

1990: The Bronx Warriors 1983
Adventure
65368 86 mins C B, V P
Vic Morrow, Christopher Connelly, Fred Williamson
The controversial film that caused big waves in the big apple. "1990: The Bronx Warriors" is a brutal, heavy-metal journey into an urban hell.
MPAA:R
Fabrizio De Angelis — *Media Home Entertainment*

1978—The New York Yankees' Miracle Year 1978
Baseball
56879 100 mins C CED P
Highlights of the Yankees' 1978 season, their greatest comeback ever, including a tense game vs. the Red Sox, and memorable moments from their defeat of the Dodgers in the World Series.
Major League Baseball — *RCA VideoDiscs*

1979 World Series and All-Star Highlights 1979
Baseball
44845 55 mins C B, V P
The Pittsburgh Pirates come back from a three games to one deficit to defeat the Baltimore Orioles in seven games in the 1979 World Series. Willie Stargell's two-run homer in Game 7 puts the Pirates ahead to stay. In the 50th All-Star Game played that July, the National League continues to dominate the American League in a 7-6 victory.
Major League Baseball — *RCA/Columbia Pictures Home Video*

(For explanation of codes, see USE GUIDE and KEY)

1966 and 1967 NFL Championship Games 1984
Football
79636 52 mins C B, V, FO P
Highlights from two classic NFL championship confrontations between the Green Bay Packers and the Dallas Cowboys circa 1966 and 1967.
NFL Films — *NFL Films Video*

---

99 Women 1969
Drama
76827 90 mins C B, V P
Maria Schell, Herbert Lom, Mercedes McCambridge, Luciana Paluzzi
A sympathetic prison warden attempts to investigate conditions at a women's prison camp.
MPAA:X
Harry Alan Towers; Commonwealth — *Republic Pictures Home Video*

Ninja the Wonder Boy 1985
Cartoons
81103 92 mins C B, V R, P
Animated
This is the story of a young boy's magical and humorous journey towards becoming a master ninja.
Kidpix Inc. — *Paramount Home Video*

Ninja III: The Domination 1984
Martial arts
80627 92 mins C B, V P
Lucinda Dickey, Sho Kosugi
A Ninja master must exorcise the spirit of a deadly assassin out of a young woman. Available in VHS and Beta Hi-Fi.
MPAA:R
Cannon Films — *MGM/UA Home Video*

Ninotchka 1939
Comedy
80209 110 mins B/W B, V, LV P
Greta Garbo, Melvyn Douglas, Ina Claire, Bela Lugosi, directed by Ernest Lubitsch
A Russian agent comes to Paris and winds up falling in love with a playboy.
MGM — *MGM/UA Home Video*

No Drums, No Bugles 1971
Drama
80712 85 mins C B, V P
Martin Sheen, Davey Davison, Denine Terry, Rod McCarey
In 1862 a West Virginia farmer who is also a conscientious objector leaves his wife and baby daughter behind to live alone in a cave for three years rather than fight in the Civil War.
MPAA:G
Clyde Ware Prods — *All Seasons Entertainment*

No Effort: Subliminal Weight Loss Video 1984
Physical fitness
72945 20 mins C B, V P
Weight loss through subliminal suggestions is featured on this self-help tape.
Dick Sutphon — *United Home Video*

No Room to Run 1978
Drama
70646 101 mins C B, V P
Richard Benjamin, Paula Prentiss, Barry Sullivan
A concert promoter's life turns into a nightmare of deadly corporate intrigue when he arrives in Australia. Luckily, he finds time to fall in love.
Transatlantic Enterprises — *Academy Home Entertainment*

No Small Affair 1984
Comedy-Drama/Romance
Closed Captioned
77370 102 mins C B, V P
Jon Cryer, Demi Moore, George Wendt, Ann Wedgeworth, directed by Jerry Schatzberg
A sixteen-year-old aspiring photographer becomes romantically involved with a sultry twenty-two-year-old rock star. The musical score, by Rupert Holmes, is available in VHS Hi-Fi Stereo.
MPAA:R
Columbia Pictures; William Sackneim — *RCA/Columbia Pictures Home Video*

No Sweat 1984
Physical fitness
78905 60 mins C B, V P
L.A. Raiders' Lyle Alzado presents his own physical fitness regimen designed especially for men.
Karl Video — *Karl/Lorimar Home Video*

No Time For Sergeants 1958
Comedy
Closed Captioned
80709 119 mins B/W B, V R, P
Andy Griffith, Nick Adams, Murray Hamilton, Don Knotts, Jamie Farr, Myron McCormick, directed by Mervyn Le Roy
An adaptation of the Broadway play about the Air Force's unsuccessful attempts to indoctrinate a naive Georgia farm boy.
Warner Bros. — *Warner Home Video*

No Way Back 1976
Adventure
47668 92 mins C B, V P
Fred Williamson, Charles Woolf, Tracy Reed, Virginia Gregg, Don Cornelius, directed by Fred Williamson
Fred Williamson portrays Jesse Crowder, a man-for-hire expert with guns, fists, and martial arts in search of a woman's missing husband.

MPAA:R
Po Boy Productions — *Unicorn Video*

Nobody's Boy 1984
Cartoons
70751 80 mins C B, V P
Animated, voice of Jim Backus, directed by Jim Flocker
This tale of an 8-year-old boy's search for his mother's identity shows the power of mother/son love in overcoming their separation.
ATA Trading Corp. — *MPI Home Video*

Nobody's Perfekt 1979
Comedy
58957 95 mins C B, V P
Gabe Kaplan, Robert Klein, Alex Karras, Susan Clark
Three psychiatric patients decide to fight City Hall.
Mort Engelberg — *RCA/Columbia Pictures Home Video*

Nocturna 1979
Satire
55216 82 mins C B, V P
Yvonne DeCarlo, John Carradine
Hard times have fallen upon the house of Dracula and to help pay the taxes on the castle it has been converted to the Hotel Transylvania. In order to increase business and the blood supply at the hotel, Nocturna books a rock group to entertain the guests.
MPAA:R
Compass International Pictures — *Media Home Entertainment*

Noel's Fantastic Trip 1984
Cartoons
80788 69 mins C B, V P
Animated
Noel and his dog travel through outer space in a single prop airplane seeking adventure.
Turner Program Services;
Toei — *RCA/Columbia Pictures Home Video*

Nomugi Pass 1979
Drama
76890 154 mins C B, V P
Shinobu Otake, Micko Harada, Rentaro Mikuni, Takeo Jii
A young woman working in a silk mill must endure hardship and abuse during the early 1900's in Japan. With English subtitles.
JA
Toho — *Video Action*

None But The Lonely Heart 1944
Drama
00265 113 mins B/W B, V, 3/4U P
Cary Grant, Ethel Barrymore, Barry Fitzgerald
In the days before World War II, a Cockney drifter travels through England in search of spiritual fulfillment.
Academy Awards '44: Best Supporting Actress (Barrymore).
RKO — *Nostalgia Merchant; King of Video*

Norma Rae 1979
Drama
37411 114 mins C B, V, CED P
Sally Field, Ron Leibman, Beau Bridges
Sally Field portrays a textile worker who joins forces with a New York labor organizer to unionize a Southern mill.
Academy Awards '79: Best Actress (Field); Best Song ("It Goes Like It Goes"). MPAA:PG
20th Century Fox — *CBS/Fox Video*

Norman Conquests: Table Manners, The 1980
Comedy
59701 108 mins C B, V R, P
Tom Conti, Richard Briers, Penelope Keith
Part I of playwright Alan Ayckbourn's comic trilogy of love unfulfilled.
Thames Video — *THORN EMI/HBO Video*

Norman Conquests: Living Together, The 1980
Comedy
59702 93 mins C B, V R, P
Tom Conti
Part II concerns the happenings in the living room during Norman's disastrous weekend of unsuccessful seduction.
Thames Video — *THORN EMI/HBO Video*

Norman Conquests: Round and Round the Garden, The 1980
Comedy
59703 106 mins C B, V R, P
Tom Conti
Part III concerns Norman's furtive appearance in the garden, which suggests that the weekend is going to misfire.
Thames Video — *THORN EMI/HBO Video*

Norseman, The 1978
Drama
64361 90 mins C B, V, CED P
Lee Majors, Cornel Wilde, Mel Ferrer, Christopher Connelly
The leader of a band of Norsemen sets sail for the New World in search of his missing father.
MPAA:PG
American International — *Vestron Video*

North Avenue Irregulars, The 1979
Comedy
44295 99 mins C B, V R, P

Edward Herrmann, Barbara Harris, Susan Clark, Karen Valentine, Cloris Leachman, Ruth Buzzi
Playing a new minister in a small community, Edward Herrmann tries to halt the ripping-off of church funds by organized criminals. To do so, he organizes some female vigilantes from the parish, all of whom are daffy bumblers who seem incapable for the task.
MPAA:G
Walt Disney — *Walt Disney Home Video*

North by Northwest **1959**
Suspense
39088 136 mins C B, V, CED P
Cary Grant, Eva Marie Saint, James Mason, Leo G. Carroll, directed by Alfred Hitchcock
Quintessential Hitchcock—the tale of a self-assured Madison Avenue executive who inadvertently gets mixed up with international spies—contains the famous scene of Grant and Miss Saint dangling from the faces on Mount Rushmore.
MGM — *MGM/UA Home Video*

North Dallas Forty **1979**
Comedy-Drama
44593 117 mins C B, V, LV R, P
Nick Nolte, Mac Davis, Charles Durning, Bo Svenson, directed by Ted Kotcheff
An aging football player realizes that the game does not hold great illusions for him anymore. Through a woman he meets he is drawn away from the masculine violent world he is used to. This creates tension between him and the team's management. He must decide whether to submit to management or quit. Based on the novel by former Dallas Cowboy Peter Gent.
MPAA:R
Paramount, Frank Yablans — *Paramount Home Video; RCA VideoDiscs*

North Star, The **1943**
War-Drama
07037 82 mins B/W B, V P
Dana Andrews, Walter Huston, Anne Baxter, Farley Granger
Gripping war tale of Nazi over-running of eastern Russian city, with courageous villagers fighting back.
RKO — *Budget Video; Discount Video Tapes; Cable Films; Video Connection; Western Film & Video Inc; Classic Video Cinema Collector's Club; Kartes Productions; Republic Pictures Home Video; See Hear Industries*

Northern Pursuit **1943**
Adventure/Drama
73978 94 mins B/W B, V P
Errol Flynn, Helmut Dantine, Julie Bishop, directed by Raoul Walsh
A Canadian Mountie disguises himself to infiltrate a Nazi spy ring in this exciting adventure film.
Warner Bros — *Key Video*

Northwest Frontier **1959**
Adventure
59839 129 mins C B, V P
Lauren Bacall, Herbert Lom, Kennoth More, directed by J. Lee Thompson
A turn-of-the century adventure set in India about the courageous attempt to save the country from rebellion, and the infant prince from assassination.
Earl St John — *Embassy Home Entertainment*

Nosferatu **1922**
Horror
08704 63 mins B/W B, V, 3/4U P
Max vonSchreck, Alexander Cranach, Gustav vonWangenheim, directed by F. W. Murnau
First film version of Bram Stoker's novel "Dracula." (Silent, musical score added.)
Janus Films; German — *Blackhawk Films; Video Yesteryear; Sheik Video; Discount Video Tapes; Western Film & Video Inc; Classic Video Cinema Collector's Club*

Nostalgia World War II Video Library #1 **1945**
World War II/Propaganda
69573 46 mins B/W B, V, FO P
These three War Department shorts were all produced during the last year of World War II and served to exhort viewers to keep up the pace of war work and not slack off. Titles are "Battle Wreckage," "The War Speeds Up" and "It Can't Last."
US War Department — *Video Yesteryear*

Nostalgia World War II Video Library #2 **1942**
World War II
78086 60 mins B/W B, V, FO P
This program takes a look at the course of World War II and how people were inspired to work for the war effort. It includes "U.S. News Review Issues #2 and #5" and "The case of the Tremendous Trifle."
Office of War Information — *Video Yesteryear*

Nostalgia World War II Video Library #3 **1944**
World War II
78087 60 mins B/W B, V, FO P
This program presents informative documents and newsreels of World War II combat including "Film Communiques #3 and #4" and "U.S. Coast Guard Report #5."
Signal Corps.; U.S. Coast Guard — *Video Yesteryear*

Nostalgia World War II Video Library #5 1945
World War II
78109 53 mins B/W B, V, FO P
The shocking story of the aftermath of World War II is told from two fascinating and different perspectives in "Diary of a Sergeant" and "The Atom Strikes."
Army Pictorial Service Division — *Video Yesteryear*

Nostalgia World War II Video Library #4 1943
World War II
73644 61 mins B/W B, V, FO P
This collection of U.S. Hollywood and Government-produced dramatic short films from the World II era includes "A Letter from Bataan," "The Rear Gunner," "The Caissons Go Rolling Along," "I Don't Want to Change the Subject," "Keep 'Em Rolling," "The Marines' Hymn," "The U.S. Coast Guard Song, Semper Paratus, "Ten Years from Now," and "We've Got Another Bond to Buy."
US Government et al — *Video Yesteryear*

Nostalgia World War II Video Library #8 1944
World War II/Propaganda
80755 59 mins B/W B, V P
This volume of short films produced during World War II features "Life Line" (1943) and "Film Communique Issues Eight and Nine" as well as a "Private Snafu" cartoon.
U.S. Signal Corps; Warner Bros — *Video Yesteryear*

Not for Publication 1984
Satire
80811 87 mins C B, V R, P
Nancy Allen, David Naughton, Richard Paul, Alice Ghostley, Laurence Luckinbill, directed by Paul Bartel
A conflict of interest arises for a woman leading a double life as both a reporter for a trashy tabloid and an assistant to the Mayor of New York City. Available in VHS and Beta Hi Fi.
North Street Films — *THORN EMI/HBO Video*

Not Tonight Darling 1972
Drama
80792 70 mins C B, V R, P
Luan Peters, Vincent Ball, Jason Twelvetrees
A bored suburban housewife becomes involved with a fast-talking businessman who leads her into a web of deceit and blackmail.
MPAA:R
Donovan Winter — *Video Gems*

Nothing Personal 1980
Comedy/Romance
64887 96 mins C B, V, CED P
Donald Sutherland, Suzanne Somers
A tweedy college professor engages an eager young lawyer to take up his case.
MPAA:PG
American International Pictures; Filmways — *Vestron Video*

Nothing Sacred 1937
Comedy
08582 75 mins C B, V, 3/4U P
Fredric March, Carole Lombard, Walter Connolly, directed by William Wellman
A girl with a short time to live is given a gay time for two weeks, but it's all a publicity hoax. Based on James Street's novel.
David O Selznick — *Video Yesteryear; Discount Video Tapes; VCII; Cable Films; Video Connection; Budget Video; Classic Video Cinema Collector's Club*

Notorious 1946
Suspense/Drama
46213 101 mins B/W B, V, LV, CED P
Cary Grant, Ingrid Bergman, Claude Rains, Louis Calhern, Madame Konstantin, directed by Alfred Hitchcock.
A government agent and a girl whose father was convicted of treason undertake a dangerous mission to Brazil.
Selznick — *CBS/Fox Video*

Now and Forever 1982
Drama
65118 93 mins C B, V, LV, CED P
Cheryl Ladd, Robert Coleby
A young wife's life is shattered when her husband is wrongly accused and convicted of rape. After he is sent to prison, she begins drinking and taking drugs.
MPAA:R
Interplanetary Pictures — *MCA Home Video*

Now, Voyager 1942
Drama
58836 117 mins B/W CED P
Bette Davis, Gladys Cooper, Claude Rains, Paul Henreid, Bonita Granville
A lonely spinster is transformed into a vibrant young woman by her psychiatrist, and involves herself in an ill-fated affair with a suave continental.
Academy Awards '42: Best Scoring of a Comedy or Drama (Max Steiner).
Warner Bros — *RCA VideoDiscs*

Now You See It 1982
Magic/Games
59415 60 mins C B, V P
Magician Paul Daniels demonstrates a number of simple tricks and explains the secret of each.

Chrysalis; Peter Wagg — *Chrysalis Visual Programming*

Nowhere to Hide 1977
Adventure
65304 74 mins C B, V P
Lee Van Cleef
A United States Marshal is assigned to protect a mob hit-man scheduled to testify for the prosecution against his former chieftain.
VSC Enterprises — *U.S.A. Home Video*

Nudes in Limbo 1983
Arts
80852 53 mins C B, V P
This tape imaginatively explores the male and female anatomy in various abstract dimensions. Available in VHS and Beta Hi Fi Stereo.
Bruce Seth Green — *MCA Home Video*

Nudo Di Donna 1983
Comedy
80445 112 mins C B, V P
Nino Manfredi, Jean Pierre Cassel, George Wilson, Eleonora Giorgi, directed by Nino Manfredi
A man searches Venice to find a woman he saw in a nude photograph who looks like his estranged wife. With English subtitles.
IT
Horizon Films; Wonder Movies — *Pacific Arts Video*

Nuit de Varennes, La 1983
Comedy-Drama
69617 133 mins C B, V P
Marcello Mastroianni, Harvey Keitel, Jean-Louis Barrault, Hanna Schygulla, Jean-Claude Brialy
This historical romp is based on an actual chapter in French history when Louis XVI and Marie Antoinette fled from Paris to Varennes. In French with English subtitles.
MPAA:R
Renzo Rossellini; Opera Film; Gaumont FR3 — *RCA/Columbia Pictures Home Video*

Number Seventeen 1932
Mystery
01747 64 mins B/W B, V P
Leon M. Lion, Anne Grey, John Stuart, directed by Alfred Hitchcock
Female jewel thief has change of heart and helps detective foil an enemy gang's escape to France.
British — *Budget Video; Cable Films; Video Yesteryear; Western Film & Video Inc*

Nuremberg War Trials 194?
World War II
58602 11 mins B/W B, V P, T
An overview of Movietone news coverage of the historic trials of Nazi war criminals.
Movietone — *Blackhawk Films*

Nurse 1980
Drama
81266 100 mins C B, V P
Michael Learned, Robert Reed, Antonio Fargas, Tom Aldredge, directed by David Lowell Rich
A recently widowed woman resumes her career as a head nurse in a large urban hospital, after her son leaves for college. Available in VHS Stereo and Beta Hi-Fi.
Robert Halmi — *U.S.A. Home Video*

Nut House, The 1962
Comedy
80752 34 mins B/W B, V P
This is an unsold television pilot for a live comedy series that features a collection of skits and blackouts.
Jay Ward — *Video Yesteryear*

Nutcracker, The 1977
Dance
63115 78 mins C B, V, CED P
Mikhail Baryshnikov, Gelsey Kirkland
A lavish production of Tschaikovsky's famous ballet, choreographed and danced by Mikhail Baryshnikov. In stereo.
Jodav Productions; Kroyt-Brandt Productions — *MGM/UA Home Video*

Nutcracker, The 1982
Dance
60573 79 mins C LV P
American Ballet Theatre, Gelsey Kirkland, Alexander Minz, National Philharmonic
Tchaikovsky's Christmas ballet under the direction of Mikhail Baryshnikov comes alive in this presentation. Stereo.
Herman Krawitz; Yanna Kroyt Brandt — *Pioneer Artists*

Nutcracker Fantasy 1979
Fairy tales
65319 ? mins C B, V P
Animated, voices of Melissa Gilbert, Roddy McDowell, narrated by Michele Lee
An heroic mouse must rescue a beautiful sleeping princess from wicked mice. This delightful fairy tale is set to the music of Tchaikovsky.
MPAA:G
Walt DeFaria; Mark L Rosen; Arthur Tomioka — *RCA/Columbia Pictures Home Video*

Nutcracker, The 1978
Dance
44939 86 mins C B, V, CED P
Ekaterina Maximova, Vladimir Vasiliev, Nadia Pavlova and the Bolshoi Corps de Ballet, directed by Elena Maceret

Tchaikovsky's famous Christmastime ballet is performed by the Bolshoi Ballet.
MGM — *CBS/Fox Video*

Nutty Professor, The **1963**
Comedy
66411 107 mins C B, V R, P
Jerry Lewis, Stella Stevens, Howard Morris, Kathleen Freeman, directed by Jerry Lewis
A mild-mannered chemistry professor creates a potion that turns him into a suave, debonair, playboy-type with an irresistable attraction to women.
Paramount; Jerry Lewis — *Paramount Home Video*

Nyoka and the Tigerman **1942**
Adventure/Serials
44792 250 mins B/W B, V, 3/4U P
Kay Aldridge, Clayton Moore
The adventures of the jungle queen Nyoka and her rival Vultura in their search for the lost tablets of Hippocrates. In 15 episodes.
Republic — *Video Connection; Republic Pictures Home Video*

O

O Lucky Man **1973**
Drama
68237 115 mins C B, V R, P
Malcolm McDowell, Ralph Richardson, Rachel Roberts, Arthur Lowe, directed by Lindsay Anderson
A story of the rags-to-riches rise and fall of a modern-day man.
MPAA:R
Warner Bros — *Warner Home Video*

Oakland Athletics: Team Highlights **1983**
Baseball
81148 30 mins C B, V P
Rickey Henderson, Davey Lopes, Billy Martin
4 pgms
This series features selected highlights from the A's 1980-1983 seasons.
1.1980: Incredible But True. 2.1981: Only the Beginning 3.1982: Baseball: The A's Way 4.1983: Feelin' Stronger.
Major League Baseball — *Major League Baseball Productions*

Observations Under the Volcano **1984**
Filmmaking/Documentary
77302 82 mins C B, V P
John Huston, Albert Finney, Jacqueline Bissett
A documentary describing the filming of John Huston's movie "Under the Volcano".
Christian Blackwood — *Pacific Arts Video*

Obsession **1976**
Suspense
65098 98 mins C B, V P
Cliff Robertson, Genevieve Bujold, John Lithgow, directed by Brian DePalma
A rich, lonely businessman meets a mysterious young girl in Italy who is the mirror image of his late wife. Music by Bernard Herrmann.
MPAA:PG
Columbia Pictures — *RCA/Columbia Pictures Home Video*

Ocean's 11 **1960**
Comedy
63449 144 mins C B, V R, P
Frank Sinatra, Dean Martin, Sammy Davis Jr., Angie Dickenson, Peter Lawford, directed by Lewis Milestone
A gang of friends make plans to rob a Las Vegas casino. Part of the "A Night at the Movies" series, this tape simulates a 1960 movie evening, with a Bugs Bunny cartoon, "Person to Bunny," a newsreel and coming attractions for "The Sundowners" and "Sunrise at Campobello."
Warner Bros — *Warner Home Video*

Octagon, The **1980**
Martial arts/Suspense
64232 103 mins C B, V P
Chuck Norris, Karen Carlson, Lee Van Cleef, Kim Lankford
A retired martial arts champion becomes involved in perilous international intrigue.
MPAA:R
American Cinema Releasing — *Media Home Entertainment*

Octaman **1971**
Science fiction
70757 79 mins C B, V R, P
Kerwin Matthews, Pier Angeli, Harry Guardino, David Essex, Jeff Morrow, Norman Fields
A group of research scientists must find out who has been killing their colleagues who are researching a project in Mexico.
Filmers Guild — *Video Gems*

Octopussy **1983**
Adventure
65414 130 mins C B, V, LV, CED P
Roger Moore, Maud Adams, Louis Jourdan, Kristina Wayborn, Kabir Bedi
James Bond is sent on a mission to prevent a crazed Russian general from launching a nuclear attack against NATO forces in Europe.
MPAA:PG

Albert R Broccoli — *CBS/Fox Video*

Odd Angry Shot 1979
War-Drama
72227 90 mins C B, V P
A drama that ironically portrays the ravages of war in Australia.
Atlantic TV — *Vestron Video*

Odd Couple, The 1968
Comedy
38590 106 mins C B, V, LV R, P
Jack Lemmon, Walter Matthau, directed by Gene Saks
Neil Simon's long-running Broadway comedy about two divorced men who live together, but can't stand each other's habits. Basis for the recent TV series.
MPAA:G
Paramount — *Paramount Home Video; RCA VideoDiscs*

Odd Job, The 1978
Comedy
73034 100 mins C B, V P
Graham Chapman
A man unable to kill himself hires an "odd job" man to do it for him.
Atlantic Releasing — *Vestron Video*

Ode to Billy Joe 1976
Drama/Romance
51968 106 mins C B, V R, P
Robby Benson, Glynnis O'Connor, Joan Hotchkis, Sandy McPeak, James Best
The relationship of two star-crossed lovers ends in tragedy at the Tallahatchie Bridge.
MPAA:PG
Warner Bros — *Warner Home Video*

Odessa File, The 1974
Suspense/Drama
Closed Captioned
78881 128 mins C B, V P
Jon Voight, Mary Tamm, Maximilian Schell, directed by Ronald Neame
A journalist stumbles onto a diary of an SS Captain which leads him ultimately to ODESSA, a secret SS organization. The music is by Andrew Lloyd Weber. In Beta Hi-Fi.
MPAA:PG
John Woolf, Columbia Pictures — *RCA/Columbia Pictures Home Video*

Odyssey of the Pacific 1982
Adventure
60588 82 mins C B, V P
Mickey Rooney, Monique Mercure
While on a romp through the woods, a young Cambodian refugee and his siblings help an old railroad man rejuvenate a locomotive.
Cine Pacific Inc — *MCA Home Video*

Of Cooks and Kung-Fu 198?
Martial arts
64961 90 mins C B, V P
Jacky Chen, Chia Kai, Lee Kuen
A martial arts culinary adventure.
Dragon Lady Productions — *Unicorn Video*

Of Human Bondage 1935
Drama
11396 84 mins B/W B, V, FO P
Leslie Howard, Bette Davis
The first movie version of Somerset Maugham's classic novel in which a young medical student with a club foot falls in love with a promiscuous cockney waitress.
RKO — *Prism; Video Yesteryear; King of Video; Discount Video Tapes; Sheik Video; Cable Films; Video Connection; Budget Video; Western Film & Video Inc; Cinema Concepts; Hal Roach Studios; Kartes Productions; Classic Video Cinema Collector's Club*

Of Mice and Men 1981
Drama
80311 125 mins C B, V P
Robert Blake, Lew Ayres, Randy Qauid, Pat Hingle, Cassie Yates
An adaptation of the classic Steinbeck novel about the friendship between two southern itinerant ranch hands.
Mickey Productions; NBC Entertainment — *Prism*

Of The Dead 1979
Documentary/Death
81533 90 mins C B, V P
This documentary looks at such funeral practices as an on-camera cremation and embalming. Not for the very young or the squeamish.
Jean-Pol Ferbus; Dominique Garny — *MPI Home Video*

Of Unknown Origin 1983
Horror
69801 90 mins C B, V R, P
Peter Weller, Jennifer Dale, Lawrence Dane, Kenneth Welsh, Louis Del Grande, Shannon Tweed
A Manhattan brownstone is the battleground in a terror-tinged duel of survival between an upwardly mobile young executive and a destructive rodent intruder.
MPAA:R
Claude Heroux — *Warner Home Video*

Off the Wall 1982
Comedy
80698 86 mins C B, V P

Paul Sorvino, Rosanna Arquette, Patrick Cassidy, Billy Hufsey, Monte Markham, Mickey Gilley
Two hitchhikers attempt to escape from a southern maximum security prison camp after being framed for a crime that they did not commit.
MPAA:R
Jensen Farley Pictures — *Vestron Video*

Officer and a Gentleman, An **1982**
Drama
64022 126 mins C B, V, LV R, P
Richard Gere, Louis Gossett Jr., David Keith, Debra Winger, Robert Loggia, directed by Taylor Hackford
A young man enters Officer Candidate School to become a Navy pilot, and in 13 torturous weeks he learns the importance of discipline, love and friendship.
Academy Awards '82: Best Supporting Actor (Gossett) Best Song ("Up Where We Belong")
MPAA:R
Paramount; Lorimar — *Paramount Home Video; RCA VideoDiscs*

Oh Alfie **1975**
Comedy-Drama
65307 99 mins C B, V P
Joan Collins, Alan Price, Jill Townsend
In every man's life, there comes a time to settle down... but never when you're having as much fun as Alfie!
A D Associates Ltd — *Monterey Home Video*

Oh! Calcutta! **1972**
Musical
07863 105 mins C B, V P
Bill Macy, Mark Dempsey, Raina Barrett
Nudity and nuttiness are the theme for this zany erotic musical.
Bihar Film — *VidAmerica*

Oh, God **1977**
Comedy
38952 104 mins C B, V R, P
George Burns, John Denver, Paul Sorvino, directed by Carl Reiner
When God, in the person of George Burns, appoints a young supermarket assistant manager to spread his word, unexpected situations develop.
MPAA:PG
Warner Bros — *Warner Home Video; RCA VideoDiscs*

Oh God, Book II **1980**
Comedy
54806 94 mins C B, V R, P
George Burns, Suzanne Pleshette, David Birney, Louanne, John Louie, Howard Duff, directed by Gilbert Cates
God decides to enlist a child to remind people that He is still around. The young girl sets out to concoct a slogan which will make God a household name. She recruits her classmates to spread her "Think God" slogan via posters and graffiti. This leads to her suspension from school, and when she is seen talking to God (he is invisible to everyone but her) the child is sent to psychiatrists.
MPAA:PG
Warner Bros — *Warner Home Video*

Oh, God! You Devil **1984**
Comedy
Closed Captioned
77265 96 mins C B, V, LV R, P
George Burns, Ted Wass, Roxanne Hart, Ron Silver
God returns to earth to save a rock singer from selling his soul to the devil.
MPAA:PG
Warner Bros. — *Warner Home Video*

Oh, Heavenly Dog **1980**
Comedy
78887 104 mins C B, V P
Chevy Chase, Jane Seymour, Omar Sharif, directed by Joe Camp
A private eye returns from the dead as a dog to solve his own murder.
MPAA:PG
Mulbery Square Productions — *CBS/Fox Video*

O'Hara's Wife **1982**
Drama
64878 87 mins C B, V P
Ed Asner, Mariette Hartley, Jodie Foster
A loving wife continues to care for her family even after her untimely death.
Davis/Panzer — *Vestron Video*

Oklahoma! **1955**
Musical
56752 140 mins C B, V, CED P
Gordon MacRae, Shirley Jones, Rod Steiger, Gloria Grahame, Eddie Albert, Charlotte Greenwood, directed by Fred Zinnemann
Based on the Rodgers and Hammerstein Broadway hit, wherein a young cowboy's girl goes to a dance with a hired hand, realizes she loves the cowboy, and the hired hand threatens to kill them both. Songs include, "Oh, What a Beautiful Mornin," "The Surrey with the Fringe on Top," and "Oklahoma!" Dances choreographed by Agnes de Mille.
Academy Awards '55: Best Scoring Musical; Best Sound Recording.
Arthur Hornblow Jr, Magna Todd
AO — *CBS/Fox Video*

 (For explanation of codes, see USE GUIDE and KEY)

Olaf Weighorst: Painter of the American West **1978**
Artists
07344 54 mins C B, V, 3/4U P
Olaf Weighorst, John Wayne, Howard Hawks
Presents the life story and some of the works of renowned western painter Olaf Weighorst.
Olaf and Roy Weighorst — *Nostalgia Merchant*

Old Boyfriends **1979**
Drama
37420 103 mins C B, V, CED P
Talia Shire, Richard Jordan, John Belushi, Keith Carradine
A young woman searches for her true self through the lost loves of her past.
MPAA:R
Avco Embassy — *Embassy Home Entertainment*

Old Corral, The **1936**
Western
69572 54 mins B/W B, V, FO P
Gene Autry, Roy Rogers, Smiley Burnette, The Sons of the Pioneers
Sheriff Gene Autry romances a young woman who has come out West to escape a vicious Chicago mobster.
Republic — *Video Yesteryear; Kartes Productions; Sheik Video*

Old Curiosity Shop, The **1984**
Cartoons
81168 72 mins C B, V P
Animated
This is an adaptation of the classic Dickens story about a young girls and her grandfather who are evicted from their curiosity shop.
MPAA:G
Burbank Films — *Vestron Video*

Old Enough **1984**
Drama
81189 91 mins C B, V P
Sarah Boyd, Rainbow Harvest, Neill Barry, directed by Marisa Silver
An unusual friendship develops between two pre-pubescent teenagers as they explore New York City.
MPAA:PG
Dina Silver — *Media Home Entertainment*

Old Gun, The **1976**
Drama
81185 141 mins C B, V P
Philippe Noiret, Romy Schneider, Jean Bouise
A doctor seeks revenge against the Nazis who murdered his wife and child when they left Normandy in 1944.
Pierre Caro — *Media Home Entertainment*

Old Leather **1980**
Football
45122 30 mins C B, V, FO R, P
Narrated by John Facenda
A study of the men who gave life to pro football. Red Grange, Johnny Blood, George Halas and others are seen as they were in the beginning and as they are today.
NFL Films — *NFL Films Video*

Old Soldier, The **194?**
World War II
58603 11 mins B/W B, V P, T
General Douglas MacArthur
This compilation of Movietone newsreel footage offers scenes from the Battle of Manila, and a mini-documentary of MacArthur's life.
Movietone — *Blackhawk Films*

Old Yeller **1957**
Drama/Adventure
53797 83 mins C B, V, LV R, P
Dorothy McGuire, Fess Parker, Tommy Kirk, Kevin Corcoran, Jeff York, Beverly Washburn, Chuck Connors, directed by Robert Stevenson
A stray dog is befriended by a family of farmers in 1869 Texas. He saves the youngest boy's life, but sacrifices his in the process.
Walt Disney — *Walt Disney Home Video; RCA VideoDiscs*

Oliver and the Artful Dodger **1980**
Cartoons
79242 72 mins C B, V P
Animated
The Artful Dodger leads his gang from a London orphanage to search for Oliver Twists lost inheritance in this animated adaptation of the Charles Dickens novel.
Hanna-Barbera Productions — *Worldvision Home Video*

Oliver Twist **1922**
Drama
63983 77 mins B/W B, V P, T
Jackie Coogan, Lon Chaney, Gladys Brockwell, George Siegmann, Esther Ralston, directed by Frank Lloyd
This version of the Dickens classic is a vehicle for young Jackie Coogan. As orphan Oliver Twist, he is subjected to many frightening incidents before finding love and someone to care for him.
Sol Lesser — *Blackhawk Films; Classic Video Cinema Collector's Club*

Oliver Twist **1982**
Drama/Cartoons
Closed Captioned
73044 72 mins C B, V, CED P

Based upon the Dickens classic where young Oliver Twist is left in an orphanage to defend himself until he must join a criminal gang.
Burbank Films — *Vestron Video*

Oliver Twist **197?**
Cartoons/Literature-English
Closed Captioned
75620 72 mins C B, V P
Animated
This is an animated version of the classic tale by Charles Dickens.
WBTV Canada — *Children's Video Library*

Oliver's Story **1978**
Drama/Romance
81118 90 mins C B, V R, P
Ryan O'Neal, Candice Bergen, Ray Milland, Edward Binns, Nicola Pagetti, Charles Haid, directed by John Korty
In this sequel to "Love Story," Oliver Barrett finds true love once again when he falls for a recently divorced heiress to the Bonwit Teller retail chain.
MPAA:PG
Paramount; David V. Picker — *Paramount Home Video*

Olivia **1980**
Music-Performance
48540 60 mins C LV P
Olivia Newton-John, Andy Gibb, ABBA
Olivia hosts this musical television special, featuring such hits as "Hopelessly Devoted to You," "Have You Ever Been Mellow," and "Please Mr. Please." Olivia, Andy, and ABBA perform a medley of classic rock songs.
Unknown — *MCA Home Video*

Olivia in Concert **1983**
Music-Performance
64793 78 mins C B, V, LV, CED P
Directed by Brian Grant, music produced by John Farrar
Filmed during Olivia's first live shows in five years, the concert reflects the popular singer's transformation from a sweet, romantic songstress to a strong, aggressive charmer and entertainer. In stereo.
Olivia Newton-John; Christine Smith — *MCA Home Video*

Olivia—Physical **1981**
Music-Performance
59034 54 mins C B, V, LV, CED P
Olivia Newton-John
Olivia Newton-John performs favorites, modern funk, and earthy ballads in this video album. Songs include; "Magic," "Physical," "A Little More Love," "Make a Move On Me," and "Hopelessly Devoted." In stereo on VHS and Disc.
Scott Millaney — *MCA Home Video*

Olympia: Parts I and II **1936**
Sports/Documentary
20417 215 mins B/W B, V P
Directed by Leni Riefenstahl
Documentary coverage of the 1936 Olympics, held in Berlin. "Olympia" is said to be the finest existing record of the Olympic Games and their athletes. Part I and II are also available individually, as are two major sequences: the Marathon sequence and the Diving sequence.
Leni Riefenstahl — *Embassy Home Entertainment; Video Yesteryear; International Historic Films; Sheik Video; Western Film & Video Inc; Phoenix Films & Video*

Omen, The **1976**
Horror
41079 111 mins C B, V, LV, CED P
Gregory Peck, Lee Remick, Billie Whitelaw, David Warner, directed Richard Donner
"The Omen" is an effective horror piece on the coming of the "anti-Christ," personified in a young boy.
MPAA:R EL, SP
20th Century Fox — *CBS/Fox Video*

On a Clear Day You Can See Forever **1970**
Romance/Musical
65618 129 mins C B, V, LV, CED R, P
Barbra Streisand, Yves Montand, Bob Newhart, Jack Nicholson
A psychiatric hypnotist helps a girl to stop smoking, and finds that in trances she remembers previous incarnations.
Paramount Pictures — *Paramount Home Video*

On Any Sunday **1971**
Documentary/Motorcycles
80212 89 mins C B, V P
Steve McQueen, directed by Bruce Brown
This exhilarating documentary examines the sport of motorcycle racing with a focus on three men: Mert Lawwill, Malcolm Smith, and Steve McQueen.
MPAA:G
Cinema Five — *Monterey Home Video*

On Any Sunday II **1981**
Motorcycles
60410 89 mins C B, V P
Bruce Penhall, Kenny Roberts, Brad Lackey, Bob Hannah
World Champion motorcycle driver Bruce Penhall is among those profiled in this motorcyclist's cinematic delight, featuring high-powered cycles giving their all.

MPAA:PG
4 Way Motorsports — *Monterey Home Video*

On Approval 1944
Comedy
00415 80 mins B/W B, V P
Clive Brooks, Beatrice Lillie
Two couples spend a holiday on a deserted isle to test their love.
Sydney Box; British — *Budget Video; Sheik Video; Movie Buff Video; Classic Video Cinema Collector's Club*

On Broadway Tonight 1964
Variety
56910 52 mins B/W B, V, FO P
Hosted by Rudy Vallee, Robert Horton
A talent show featuring professional performers looking for the big break—singers, comedians, impressionists, and musicians.
CBS — *Video Yesteryear*

On Golden Pond 1981
Drama
59430 109 mins C B, V, LV P
Henry Fonda, Jane Fonda, Katharine Hepburn, Dabney Coleman, Doug McKeon, directed by Mark Rydell
The story of three generations coming to grips with life, mortality and their own emotional distance, set at a summer home in New England.
Academy Awards '81: Best Actor (Fonda); Best Actress (Hepburn); Best Screenplay Adaptation (Ernest Thompson). MPAA:PG
ITC; IPC Films — *CBS/Fox Video; RCA VideoDiscs*

On Her Majesty's Secret Service 1969
Adventure
64834 140 mins C CED P
George Lazenby, Diana Rigg, Telly Savalas
James Bond marries and he and his future wife must squelch deadly SPECTRE chief Blofeld who is about to unleash a lethal toxin.
MPAA:PG
United Artists — *RCA VideoDiscs*

On Her Majesty's Secret Service 1969
Adventure
65405 142 mins C B, V P
George Lazenby, Diana Rigg, Telly Savalas
In this sixth 007 cinematic adventure, James Bond is charged with no less a task than saving the human race from a deadly plague.
United Artists — *CBS/Fox Video*

On the Beach 1959
Drama/Science fiction
59337 133 mins B/W B, V, CED P
Gregory Peck, Anthony Perkins, Donna Anderson, Ava Gardner, Fred Astaire, directed by Stanley Kramer
Based on the novel by Nevil Shute. After most of the world has been destroyed by atomic waste, an American submarine sets out to investigate.
Stanley Kramer — *CBS/Fox Video*

On the Nickel 1980
Drama
79310 96 mins C B, V P
Ralph Waite, Donald Moffat, Hal Williams, Jack Kehoe, directed by Ralph Waite
An ex-alcoholic returns to Fifth Street in Los Angeles to save his friend from a life of despair. The musical score was composed by Tom Waits.
MPAA:R
Waite Productions — *Vestron Video*

On the Right Track 1981
Comedy
58852 98 mins C B, V P
Gary Coleman, Lisa Eilbacher
A young orphan living in Chicago's Union Station has the gift of being able to pick winning race horses.
MPAA:PG
20th Century Fox — *CBS/Fox Video*

On the Town 1949
Musical
47055 98 mins C B, V, CED P
Gene Kelly, Frank Sinatra, Vera Ellen, Ann Miller, Betty Garrett, directed by Gene Kelly and Stanley Donen
Three sailors find romance on a one-day leave in New York City. Based on the successful Broadway musical, with a score composed by Leonard Bernstein, Betty Comden, and Adolph Green. Additional songs by Roger Edens.
Academy Awards '49: Best Scoring, Musical (Roger Edens and Lennie Hayton).
MGM — *MGM/UA Home Video*

On the Waterfront 1954
Drama
Closed Captioned
73859 108 mins B/W B, V, CED P
Marlon Brando, Lee J. Cobb, Eva Marie Saint, Rod Steiger, directed by Elia Kazan
An ex-fighter gets a job working on the gang-ridden waterfront under a crooked gangster boss. This film is in Beta Hi-Fi.
Academy Awards '54: Best Picture; Best Actor, (Brando); Best Director (Kazan).
Sam Spiegel — *RCA/Columbia Pictures Home Video*

On Top of Old Smoky 1953
Western
66441 59 mins B/W B, V P, T

Gene Autry, Smiley Burnette, Gail Davis, Sheila Ryan
Singing ranger Gene is mistaken for a real Texas Ranger, who is a marked man.
Columbia — *Blackhawk Films*

Once in Paris **1984**
Drama
76022 100 mins C B, V P
Wayne Rogers, Gayle Hunnicutt, Jean Lenoir
A bittersweet romance that is at once subtle and believable, sophisticated and humorous about three people who meet in Paris.
MPAA:PG
Frank D Gilroy — *Embassy Home Entertainment*

Once Upon a Brothers Grimm **1977**
Fantasy
33583 102 mins C B, V P
Dean Jones, Paul Sand, Cleavon Little, Ruth Buzzi, Chita Rivera, Teri Garr
An original musical fantasy in which the Brothers Grimm meet a succession of their most famous storybook characters, including Hansel and Gretel, the Gingerbread Lady, Little Red Riding Hood, and Rumpelstiltskin.
Rothman-Wohl Productions; CBS — *United Home Video*

Once Upon a Honeymoon **1942**
Comedy
10039 115 mins B/W B, V P, T
Ginger Rogers, Cary Grant, Walter Slezak
American reporter predicts Hitler's movements by trailing Gestapo agents. Reporter and agents then attempt to outwit Germans.
RKO; Leo McCarey — *Blackhawk Films*

Once Upon a Scoundrel **1973**
Comedy
80891 90 mins C B, V P
Zero Mostel, Katy Jurado, Tito Vandis, Priscilla Garcia, A. Martinez, directed by George Schaeffer
A ruthless Mexican land baron arranges to have a young woman's fiancee thrown in jail so he can have her all to himself.
Carlyle Films — *Prism*

Once Upon a Time **1976**
Cartoons/Fantasy
50962 83 mins C B, V R, P
Animated
A pretty girl, her puppy, a charming prince, and a grinch combine for a magical, wondrous animated fantasy.
MPAA:G
N W Russo; G G Communications — *Video Gems*

Once Upon A Time **1968**
Fantasy/Adventure
70687 52 mins C B, V P
Patrick McGoohan, Leo McKern, Angelo Muscat
This second-to-last episode of "The Prisoner" finds Number 6 in the Embryo room locked into a deadly interrogation ritual with Number 2.
Associated TV Corp. — *MPI Home Video*

Once Upon a Time in America **1984**
Drama
Closed Captioned
80440 225 mins C B, V, LV R, P
Robert DeNiro, Treat Williams, James Woods, Elizabeth McGovern, Tuesday Weld, Burt Young
This is the uncut original version of director Sergio Leone's saga of five young men growing up in Brooklyn during the 20's who become powerful mob figures. Also available in a 143-minute version.
MPAA:R
Arom Milchan; The Ladd Company — *Warner Home Video*

Once Upon a Time in the West **1968**
Western
80520 165 mins C B, V, LV P
Henry Fonda, Claudia Cardinale, Jason Robards, Charles Bronson, directed by Sergio Leone
The uncut version of Sergio Leone's sprawling epic about a band of ruthless gunmen who set out to murder a mysterious woman.
MPAA:PG
Paramount — *Paramount Home Video*

One and Only, The **1978**
Comedy
58714 98 mins C B, V R, P
Henry Winkler, Kim Darby, Gene Saks, William Daniels, Harold Gould, Herve Villechaize, directed by Carl Reiner
An egotistical young man enters the world of professional wrestling.
MPAA:PG
Paramount; First Artists — *Paramount Home Video*

One and Only Genuine Original Family Band, The **1968**
Musical
55571 110 mins C B, V, LV R, P
Walter Brennan, Buddy Ebsen, Lesley Ann Warren, John Davidson, Kurt Russell, Wally Cox, Richard Deacon, Janet Blair
During the 1888 presidential campaigns of Grover Cleveland and Benjamin Harrison, old Grandpa Bower organizes his son, daughter-in-law, and eight grandchildren into a band, hoping to perform at the convention.
Walt Disney — *Walt Disney Home Video*

One Away **1980**
Drama
78669 83 mins C B, V P
A gypsy escapes from a South African prison and the police are in hot pursuit.
MPAA:PG
Silhouette Film Productions — *Monterey Home Video*

One Body Too Many **1944**
Comedy
01701 75 mins B/W B, V P
Jack Haley Sr., Jean Parker, Bela Lugosi, directed by Frank McDonald
Mystery spoof with wacky insurance salesman who's mistaken for a detective. Ends up in comedy of errors.
Paramount; Pine Thomas — *Budget Video; Hal Roach Studios; Discount Video Tapes; Video Connection*

One Dark Night **1982**
Horror
65748 94 mins C B, V R, P
Two high school girls plan an initiation rite for one of their friends who is determined to shed her "goody-goody" image.
MPAA:R
Michael Schroeder — *THORN EMI/HBO Video*

One Down Two to Go **1983**
Adventure
65355 84 mins C B, V P
Jim Brown, Fred Williamson, Jim Kelly, Richard Roundtree
When the mob is discovered to be rigging a championship karate bout, two dynamic expert fighters join in a climactic battle against the hoods.
MPAA:R
Fred Williamson — *Media Home Entertainment*

One-Eyed Jacks **1961**
Western
53935 141 mins C B, V R, P
Marlon Brando, Karl Malden, Katy Jurado, Elisha Cook, Slim Pickens, Ben Johnson, directed by Marlon Brando
Upon completing a prison term, an outlaw goes seeking an old friend who betrayed him, and finds he has become the sheriff.
Paramount — *Paramount Home Video*

One Flew Over the Cuckoo's Nest **1975**
Drama
58882 129 mins C B, V R, P
Jack Nicholson, Louise Fletcher, Brad Dourif, William Redfield, Scatman Crothers, directed by Milos Forman
Ken Kesey's novel about Randall P. McMurphy, the leader of a group ofinmates of a mental ward and his war against the repressive Nurse Ratched.
Academy Awards '75: Best Picture, Best Actor (Nicholson); Best Actress (Fletcher); Best Director (Forman); Best Screenplay Adaptation (Bo Goldman, Lawrence Hauben). MPAA:R
United Artists; Fantasy Films; Saul Zaentz; Michael Douglas — *THORN EMI/HBO Video; RCA VideoDiscs*

One Frightened Night **1935**
Mystery
66390 69 mins B/W B, V P
Mary Carlisle, Wallace Ford, Hedda Hopper, Charlie Grapewin
An eccentric millionaire informs his family members that he is leaving each of them one million dollars.
Mascot Pictures — *Movie Buff Video; Kartes Productions*

One from the Heart **1982**
Fantasy/Musical
68259 100 mins C B, V P
Teri Garr, Frederie Forrest, Natassia Kinski, Raul Julia, Laine Kazan, directed by Francis Ford Coppola
Two people somehow lost the romance in their lives and end up with other people only to realize that they miss each other. In stereo.
MPAA:R
Gray Frederickson; Fred Ross — *RCA/Columbia Pictures Home Video; RCA VideoDiscs*

125 Rooms of Comfort **1983**
Horror
76940 82 mins C B, V P
A mental patient has bizarre fantasies that create havoc among those who stand in his way.
Independent — *Trans World Entertainment*

100 Rifles **1969**
Western
29162 110 mins C B, V P
Jim Brown, Raquel Welch, Burt Reynolds, Fernando Lamas
An Indian bank robber and a black American lawman join up with a female Mexican revolutionary to help save the Mexican Indians from annihilation by a despotic military governor.
MPAA:R SP
20th Century Fox — *CBS/Fox Video*

One Man Jury **1978**
Crime-Drama
59813 95 mins C B, V P
Jack Palance, Christopher Mitchum, Joe Spinell, Pamela Shoop
An LAPD lieutenant, wearied by an ineffective justice system, becomes a one-man vigilante avenger.

MPAA:R
Theodor Bodnar; Steve Bono — *United Home Video*

One Million B. C. **1940**
Science fiction
44800 80 mins B/W B, V, 3/4U P
Victor Mature, Carole Landis, Lon Chaney Jr., directed by Hal Roach and Hal Roach Jr.
The saga of the struggle of primitive cavemen and their battle against dinosaurs and other monsters.
United Artists, Hal Roach — *Nostalgia Merchant*

One Night Stand **1977**
Horror
76933 90 mins C B, V P
Chapelle Jaffe, Brent Carver
A woman's chance encounter with a man in a singles bar leads to an evening of unexpected terror.
Independent — *Trans World Entertainment*

One Night Stand **1984**
Comedy-Drama
81453 94 mins C B, V P
Tyler Coppin, Cassandra Delaney, Jay Hackett
Four young people attempt to "amuse themselves" at the empty Sydney Opera House on the New Years Eve before World War III.
Hoyts Distribution; Astra Film Productions — *Embassy Home Entertainment*

One of Our Aircraft Is Missing **1941**
War-Drama
81423 103 mins B/W B, V P
Godfrey Tearle, Eric Portman, Hugh Williams, Pamela Brown, Googie Withers
The crew of a downed R.A.F. bomber struggles to escape Nazi capture while attempting to get back to England after the crash landing in Holland.
United Artists — *Republic Pictures Home Video*

One on One **1977**
Drama
51987 98 mins C B, V R, P
Robby Benson, Annette O'Toole, G.D. Spradlin, Gail Strickland
A high school basketball star from the country accepts an athletic scholarship to a big city university but is unprepared for the fierce competition he must face.
MPAA:PG
Warner Bros — *Warner Home Video*

One Rainy Afternoon **1936**
Comedy
11298 80 mins B/W B, V, FO P
Francis Lederer, Ida Lupino, Hugh Herbert, Roland Young, Donald Meek
A bit-player kisses the wrong girl in a Paris theater, causing a hilarious, massive uproar branding him as a notorious romantic "monster."
Pickford Lasky Productions — *Video Yesteryear; Sheik Video; Kartes Productions; Discount Video Tapes*

One Sings, the Other Doesn't **1977**
Drama
64913 105 mins C B, V P
Valerie Mairesse, Therese Liotard
This film follows the friendship of two young women over a period of 14 years, when each seeks to control her destiny and to find contentment. In French with English subtitles.
FR
Cine-Tamarus — *RCA/Columbia Pictures Home Video*

One Small Step for Man **1984**
Space exploration
72057 60 mins C B, V P
The Apollo series of lunar explorations is examined in this documentary, with an emphasis on the first manned moon landing.
NASA — *MPI Home Video*

One Step to Hell **1968**
Adventure
80035 90 mins C B, V P
Ty Hardin, Rossano Brazzi, Pier Angeli, George Sanders, Tab Hunter
A government police officer gives hot pursuit to a group of convicts who are running through the wilds of Africa.
NTA — *Republic Pictures Home Video*

One, The Only... Groucho, The **195?**
Comedy
79236 120 mins B/W B, V, 3/4U P
Groucho Marx
The original unedited pilot of Groucho's "You Bet Your Life" series from 1949, an episode from the series circa 1951, and his comeback series "Tell It to Groucho" make up this collection of kinescopes.
NBC et al — *Shokus Video*

1000 Mile Escort **1978**
Martial arts
70704 86 mins C B, V P
Pak Ying, Mai Suet
One man stands alone against the corruption of China's murderous South Sung Dynasty.
Master Arts — *Master Arts Video*

 (For explanation of codes, see USE GUIDE and KEY)

1001 Arabian Nights 1959
Fantasy/Cartoons
69620 76 mins C B, V P
Animated, voices of Jim Backus, Kathryn Grant, Hans Conreid, Herschel Bernardi
In this Arabian nightmare, the nearsighted Mr. Magoo is known as "Azziz" Magoo, lamp dealer and uncle of Aladdin.
Stephen Bosustow; UPA — *RCA/Columbia Pictures Home Video*

One Touch of Venus 1948
Musical
64546 82 mins B/W B, V P
Ava Gardner, Robert Walker, Eve Arden, Dick Haymes, Olga San Juan, Tom Conway
A young man impulsively kisses a marble statue of the goddess Venus, which comes to life. Based on the Broadway musical, with songs by Kurt Weill and Ogden Nash, including "Speak Low."
Universal — *Republic Pictures Home Video*

One Wild Moment 1978
Comedy
77371 88 mins C B, V P
Jean-Pierre Marielle, Victor Lanoux, directed by Claude Berri
Comic complications arise when a divorced man is seduced by his best friend's daughter while vacationing. The film is in French with English subtitles.
MPAA:R FR
Quartet/Films Incorporated — *RCA/Columbia Pictures Home Video*

Onion Field, The 1979
Drama
44979 126 mins C B, V, LV, CED P
John Savage, James Woods, Ronny Cox, Franklyn Seales
This true story concerns the murder of a policeman and the slow process of justice.
MPAA:R
Avco Embassy — *Embassy Home Entertainment*

Only Way, The 1970
War-Drama
65159 86 mins C B, V P
Jane Seymour, Martin Potter, Ben Christiansen
A semi-documentary account of the plight of the Jews in Denmark during the Nazi occupation. Despite German insistence, the Danes succeeded in saving most of their Jewish population from the concentration camps.
MPAA:G
UMC Pictures; Hemisphere -- Laterna — *United Home Video*

Only When I Laugh 1981
Comedy
58962 100 mins C B, V P
Marsha Mason, Kristy McNichol, James Coco, Joan Hackett, David Dukes
A poignant comedy about the relationship between a mother and her daughter, written by Neil Simon.
MPAA:R
Columbia — *RCA/Columbia Pictures Home Video*

Open City 1946
Drama
44973 103 mins B/W B, V P
Anna Magnani, Aldo Fabrizi, directed by Roberto Rossellini
A leader in the Italian underground resists Nazi control of the city. Italian dialogue with English subtitles.
Italy — *Discount Video Tapes; Video Yesteryear; Sheik Video; Budget Video; Western Film & Video Inc*

Opera Cameos 1955
Opera
47490 53 mins B/W B, V, FO P
Lucia Evangelista, Guilio Gari, Frank Valentino, Carlo Tomanelli, conducted by Giuseppe Bamboschek, hosted by John Ericson
A program from this 1950's TV series of operas, staged with full costumes and sets. Featured are highlights from Verdi's "La Traviata."
Dumont — *Video Yesteryear*

Operation Amsterdam 1960
War-Drama/Suspense
62865 103 mins B/W B, V P
Peter Finch, Eva Bartok, Tony Britton
The true story of a group of agents who went to Holland in 1940 to prevent a stock of industrial diamonds from falling into the hands of the Nazis.
20th Century Fox; Rank — *Embassy Home Entertainment*

Operation Petticoat 1959
Comedy
47995 120 mins C B, V P
Cary Grant, Tony Curtis, Joan O'Brien, Dina Merrill, Gene Evans, Arthur O'Connell
Determined to get his sub back in action, a commander bypasses regulations and uses "enterprising" methods to procure supplies.
Universal — *Republic Pictures Home Video*

Orca 1977
Adventure
10964 92 mins C B, V, LV R, P
Richard Harris, Charlotte Rampling, Bo Derek, Keenan Wynn, directed by Michael Anderson
A whale is out for revenge when a shark hunting seafarer captures and kills his pregnant mate.

MPAA:PG
Paramount; Dino De Laurentiis — *Paramount Home Video*

Ordeal of Dr. Mudd 1980
Drama
81267 143 mins C B, V P
Dennis Weaver, Arthur Hill, Susan Sullivan, Richard Dysart, directed by Paul Wendkos
This is the true story of Dr. Samuel Mudd, a Maryland physician who unwittingly aided John Wilkes Booth's escape by setting his broken leg. Available in VHS Stereo and Beta Hi-Fi.
B.S.R. Productions; Marble Arch Productions — *U.S.A. Home Video*

Order to Kill 1973
Drama
80123 110 mins C B, V P
Jose Ferrer, Helmut Berger
A gambling boss puts out a contract on a hit man.
Italian — *King of Video*

Ordinary People 1980
Drama
55205 125 mins C B, V, LV R, P
Mary Tyler Moore, Donald Sutherland, Timothy Hutton, Judd Hirsch, Elizabeth McGovern, directed by Robert Redford
An upper-middle class, Midwestern suburban family's life disintegrates in the wake of the emotional effects of one son's accidental death and the other son's emotional trauma.
Academy Awards '80: Best Picture; Best Director (Redford); Best Supporting Actor (Hutton); Best Screenplay Adaptation (Alvin Sargeant). MPAA:R
Wildwood Enterprises;
Paramount — *Paramount Home Video; RCA VideoDiscs*

Oriental Dreams 1982
Photography
47809 ? mins C LV P
A sensual portrait of five young women photographed with great sensitivity by Kenji Nagatomo, set to the music of Naoya Matsouka (stereo).
Unknown — *Pioneer Video Imports*

Origin of Life, The (Plus Scopes Trial Footage) 1982
Biology/Science
59559 60 mins C B, V P
A look at Darwinian theory and beginnings of life, plus rare Scopes Trial footage from the Rohauer Collection.
McGraw Hill — *Mastervision*

Original Amateur Hour, The 1954
Variety
47478 54 mins B/W B, V, FO P
Hosted by Ted Mack
Two programs from this popular series, originally telecast on May 22, 1954 and July 31, 1954. Performers include a trampoline bouncer, a Liberace imitator, the Penbrook Jug Band and New York Yankees pitcher Eddie Lopat.
NBC — *Video Yesteryear*

Original Amateur Hour, The 1953
Variety
47474 54 mins B/W B, V, FO P
Hosted by Ted Mack pgms
Two programs from this long-running series, originally telecast on August 15 and August 29, 1953. Featured contestants include a girl who spins a lariat while riding a unicycle, a ventriloquist, tap dancers and a lady who plays "Yankee Doodle" on sleigh bells.
NBC — *Video Yesteryear*

Original Amateur Hour, The 1954
Variety
47477 57 mins B/W B, V, FO P
Hosted by Ted Mack
Two programs from this series, originally telecast on October 3, 1953 and April 24, 1954. Contestants include a Johnny Ray impersonator, a man who plays Rachmaninoff on the banjo, a female barbershop quartet and a tap-dancing lady roller skater.
NBC — *Video Yesteryear*

Orphans of the Storm 1921
Drama
44990 127 mins B/W B, V P, T
Lillian Gish, Dorothy Gish, Monte Blue, Joseph Schildkraut, directed by D. W. Griffith
Two orphans marooned in Paris become separated by the turbulent maelstrom preceding the French Revolution. Silent.
United Artists — *Blackhawk Films; Classic Video Cinema Collector's Club*

Orpheus 1950
Film-Avant-garde
11398 95 mins B/W B, V, FO P
Jean Marais, Francois Perier, Maria Casares, directed by Jean Cocteau
Depicts the love of a poet for a princess who travels constantly from this world to the next. A legendary tale in a modern Parisian setting.
Andre Paulve Films du Palais Royal — *Video Yesteryear; Budget Video; Sheik Video; Western Film & Video Inc; Discount Video Tapes*

Oscar, The **1966**
Drama
66049 119 mins C B, V, CED P
Stephen Boyd, Elke Sommer, Jill St. John, Tony Bennett, Milton Berle, Eleanor Parker, Joseph Cotten, Edie Adams, Ernest Borgnine
The story of ego, greed and self-destruction in the film world of Hollywood.
MPAA:R
Joseph E Levine — *Embassy Home Entertainment*

Osterman Weekend, The **1983**
Suspense
65507 102 mins C B, V R, P
Burt Lancaster, Rutger Hauer, Craig Nelson, Dennis Hopper
A TV personality is looking forward to a reunion party with his closest friends. That is, until the CIA warns him that they are all Soviet agents. Suddenly, he and his family are caught in a nightmare of terror, deception, helplessness and violent death.
MPAA:R
Peter S Davis; William N Panzer — *THORN EMI/HBO Video*

Otello **1982**
Music-Performance/Opera
81485 135 mins C B, V R, P
Kiri Te Kanawa, Vladimir Atlantov, Piero Cappuccilli
This is a performance of the Verdi opera taped at the Arena di Verona in Rome.
National Video Corporation Ltd. — *THORN EMI/HBO Video*

Othello **1922**
Drama
47463 81 mins B/W B, V, FO P
Emil Jannings, Lya de Putti, Werner Krauss
A silent version of Shakespeare's tragedy, featuring Emil Jannings as the tragic Moor. Titles are in English; music score.
UFA — *Video Yesteryear; Discount Video Tapes; Classic Video Cinema Collector's Club*

Other Side of Midnight, The **1977**
Drama
80730 160 mins C B, V P
Susan Sarandon, Marie-France Pisier, John Beck, Raf Vallone, Clu Galgger, Sorrel Booke
A poor French girl who sleeps her way to fame and fortune becomes the mistress of a powerful shipping tycoon. Based upon the novel by Sidney Sheldon. Available in VHS and Beta Hi-Fi stereo.
MPAA:R
20th Century Fox — *Key Video*

Other Side of Nashville, The **1984**
Music-Performance/Documentary
66598 118 mins C B, V, LV, CED P
Johnny Cash, Kris Kristofferson, Bob Dylan, Kenny Rogers, Willie Nelson, Hank Williams, Jr, Emmylou Harris, Carl Perkins
Live performances, interviews and backstage footage combine to form a picture of the Nashville music scene. Over 40 songs are heard in renditions by country music's biggest stars. In stereo.
Geoffrey Menin; MGM UA — *MGM/UA Home Video*

Our Daily Bread **1934**
Drama
11394 74 mins B/W B, V, FO P
Tom Keene, Karen Morley, Barbara Pepper, directed by King Vidor
Desperate men and women from the Depression era come together and form a subsistence farm.
United Artists — *Video Yesteryear; Cable Films; Sheik Video; Budget Video; Discount Video Tapes; Western Film & Video Inc; Kartes Productions*

Our Finest Hour **1981**
Football
50647 24 mins C B, V, FO R, P
Oakland Raiders
When newly acquired quarterback Dan Pastorini was lost for the 1980 season with an injury, veteran Jim Plunkett calmly stepped in and made Raider fans forget the departed Ken Stabler. Plunkett's steadiness led the well-balanced Raiders to the Super Bowl championship, amidst owner Al Davis' battle with Oakland fans and commissioner Pete Rozelle, over Davis' attempt to move his team to Los Angeles.
NFL Films — *NFL Films Video*

Our Relations **1936**
Comedy
33905 65 mins B/W B, V, 3/4U P
Stan Laurel, Oliver Hardy, Alan Hale, Sidney Toler, James Finlayson, Daphne Pollard
Confusion reigns when Stan and Ollie meet their twin brothers, a pair of happy-go-lucky sailors whom the boys previously didn't know existed.
Hal Roach, MGM — *Nostalgia Merchant; Blackhawk Films*

Our Relations **1936**
Comedy
63987 95 mins B/W B, V P, T
Stan Laurel, Oliver Hardy, James Finlayson, Alan Hale, Daphne Pollard
Stan and Ollie's long-lost twin brothers come to town after being at sea for years, to the consternation of all concerned. This tape also

includes a 1935 Charley Chase short, "Southern Exposure."
Hal Roach; MGM — *Blackhawk Films*

Our Town 1940
Drama
08854 90 mins B/W B, V P
Martha Scott, William Holden, Thomas Mitchell, Fay Bainter, narrated by Frank Craven
Life, love, and death in a small New England town; based on the play by Thornton Wilder.
United Artists; Sol Lesser Prods — *Prism; Movie Buff Video; Budget Video; Video Yesteryear; Sheik Video; Cable Films; Video Connection; Discount Video Tapes; Western Film & Video Inc; Phoenix Films & Video; Kartes Productions; Classic Video Cinema Collector's Club*

Our Town 1977
Drama
56891 120 mins C B, V P
Ned Beatty, Sada Thompson, Ronny Cox, Glynnis O'Connor, Robby Benson, Hal Holbrook, John Houseman
This is the television version of Thornton Wilder's classic play about everyday life in Grovers Corners, a small New England town at the turn of the century.
Hartwest Productions; Saul Jaffe — *Mastervision; RCA VideoDiscs*

Out of Control 1985
Adventure
81251 78 mins C B, V, LV P
Betsy Russell, Martin Hewitt, Claudia Udy, Andrew J. Lederer
A fun-filled weekend trip turns into a deadly fight for survival when a teenager's plane crashes onto a deserted island.
MPAA:R
New World Pictures — *New World Video*

Out of the Blue 1982
Drama
65694 94 mins C B, V P
Dennis Hopper, Linda Manz, Raymond Burr
A frustrated teenager with a father in prison and a promiscuous and weak-willed mother runs away and quickly gets into trouble with the law. Her return home and her father's release from prison is anything than happy.
MPAA:R
Leonard Yakir, Gary Jules Jouvenat — *Media Home Entertainment*

Out of the Blue 1947
Comedy
81225 86 mins B/W B, V, LV P
George Brent, Virginia Mayo, Carole Landis, Turhan Bey
There's trouble in paradise for a married couple when a shady lady passes out in their apartment.
Eagle Lion — *New World Video*

Out of the Past 1947
Suspense
00290 97 mins B/W B, V, 3/4U P
Robert Mitchum, Kirk Douglas, Jane Greer
A cool and calculating private detective undermines a ruthless tycoon's empire.
RKO; Eagle Lion — *Nostalgia Merchant*

Out-Of-Towners, The 1970
Comedy
65733 98 mins C B, V R, P
Jack Lemmon, Sandy Dennis
Incredible mishaps occur when a middle-aged Ohio couple fly to New York City for the husband's job interview.
MPAA:G
Paramount; Jalem — *Paramount Home Video*

Outcast, The 1953
Western
80846 90 mins C B, V P
John Derek, Jim Davis, Joan Davis
A young man returns to Colorado attempting to obtain a ranch from his uncle which he believes is rightfully his.
Republic Pictures — *Republic Pictures Home Video*

Outland 1981
Science fiction
58242 109 mins C B, V, LV R, P
Sean Connery, Peter Boyle, Frances Sternhagen, James B. Sikking, directed by Peter Hyams
On Jupiter's volcanic moon, miners are suddenly plunging into insanity—and a lone federal marshal must uncover the secret that threatens everyone's survival.
MPAA:R
Outland Prods — *Warner Home Video; RCA VideoDiscs*

Outlaw, The 1943
Western
05538 95 mins B/W B, V P
Jane Russell, Jack Beutel, Walter Huston, Thomas Mitchell
A variation on the saga of Billy the Kid, wherein Billy and girlfriend Rio have a romantic interlude before the final showdown with Pat Garrett.
Howard Hughes — *Prism; Video Connection; King of Video; VCII; Discount Video Tapes; Video Yesteryear; Sheik Video; Cable Films; Classic Video Cinema Collector's Club; Hal Roach Studios; Kartes Productions; See Hear Industries*

Outlaw Blues 1977
Adventure/Drama
80959 101 mins C B, V P
Peter Fonda, Susan Saint James, John Crawford, Michael Lerner
An ex-convict becomes a national folk hero when he sets out to reclaim his stolen hit song about prison life.
MPAA:PG
Warner Bros. — *Warner Home Video*

Outlaw Josey Wales, The 1976
Western
58243 135 mins C B, V R, P
Clint Eastwood, Chief Dan George, Sondra Locke, directed by Clint Eastwood
A farmer becomes a one-man army to avenge the slaughter of his wife and child by Civil War renegades.
MPAA:PG
Warner Bros — *Warner Home Video*

Outlaws 1982
Music-Performance
75921 81 mins C B, V P
This program presents the Outlaws playing some of their superb compositions.
High Tide Management Inc — *Sony Corporation of America*

Outrageous 1977
Comedy
58963 100 mins C B, V P
Craig Russell, Hollis McLaren, Richard Easley, Allan Moyle
A comedy about the unlikely but touching relationship between a female impersonator and his schizophrenic girl friend.
MPAA:R
Herbert R Steinmann; Billy Baxter — *RCA/Columbia Pictures Home Video*

Outside the Law 1921
Crime-Drama
10121 77 mins B/W B, V P, T
Lon Chaney, Priscilla Dean
Lon Chaney plays dual roles of the underworld hood in "Black Mike Sylva," and a Chinese servant in "Ah Wing."
Universal — *Blackhawk Films; Classic Video Cinema Collector's Club*

Outsiders, The 1983
Drama
69025 91 mins C B, V, CED R, P
Matt Dillon
"The Outsiders" depicts the explosive conflict between rival gangs of poor and rich kids in the mid-1960's.
MPAA:PG
Zoetrope Studios — *Warner Home Video*

Outtakes I 197?
Outtakes and bloopers
33690 120 mins C B, V, 3/4U P
A large assortment of foul-ups, goofs, and laughs featuring stars and shows such as "Abbott and Costello," "Rowan and Martin," "Garry Moore," "The Tonight Show," "Star Trek," "The Twilight Zone," and "Cannon," in scenes that never made it to the television screen. Some black and white.
NBC et al — *Shokus Video*

Outtakes II 197?
Outtakes and bloopers
35528 120 mins C B, V, 3/4U P
Stars from popular TV shows including "Starksy and Hutch," "Three's Company," "The Newlywed Game" and "McHale's Navy" are seen messing up their lines and cracking up in these scenes that were edited from the finished programs. Some black and white segments are included.
ABC et al — *Shokus Video*

Outtakes III 1980
Outtakes and bloopers
45018 60 mins C B, V, 3/4U P
The casts of "WKRP," "MASH," "Mary Tyler Moore," and more blow lines, miss cues, and generally mess up.
CBS et al — *Shokus Video*

Outtakes IV 1980
Outtakes and bloopers
45020 120 mins C B, V, 3/4U P
The casts of "MASH," "Carol Burnett," "The Don Adams-Don Rickles Special," "Match Game," and more goof up, mess up and break up. Included are outtakes from 1950's commercials.
CBS et al — *Shokus Video*

Outtakes VI 1982
Outtakes and bloopers
47613 60 mins C B, V, 3/4U P
Boris Karloff, Bela Lugosi, The Marx Brothers, W. C. Fields, William Shatner, Leonard Nimoy, Jackie Cooper, Joe Garagiola
Another hour of flubs, goofs and breakdowns featuring favorite performers of movies and TV. There is no duplication between this program and any other Shokus "Outtake" tape. Some segments are in black and white.
NBC et al — *Shokus Video*

Outtakes VII 1983
Outtakes and bloopers
66462 60 mins B/W B, V, 3/4U P
Richard Simmons, Ted Knight, Alan Alda, Redd Foxx
More goofs and blunders from popular television shows are featured in this installment of the "Outtakes" series.

CBS et al — *Shokus Video*

Outtakes V 197?
Outtakes and bloopers
53053 60 mins C B, V, 3/4U P
Johnny Carson, Ed McMahon, Alan Alda, Mike Farrell, Harry Morgan, Jamie Farr, Bing Crosby, Jimmy Durante, Van Johnson
TV outtakes which also feature Sammy Davis Jr., Peter Lawford, Tony Randall, Alan Sherman, Martha Raye, Carol Burnett, Harvey Korman, Vicki Lawrence, Tim Conway, Bob Barker, Jim Lange, and others. Also included are outtakes from commercials, plus actual foreign commercials.
CBS et al — *Shokus Video*

Over the Brooklyn Bridge 1983
Comedy-Drama
80147 100 mins C B, V P
Elliott Gould, Sid Caesar, Shelley Winters, Margaux Hemingway, Carol Kane
A young Jewish man must give up his Catholic girlfriend in order to get the money he needs to buy a restaurant in Manhattan.
MPAA:R
Cannon Films — *MGM/UA Home Video*

Over the Edge 1979
Drama
52711 95 mins C B, V R, P
Michael Kramer, Matt Dillon, Pamela Ludwig, directed by Jonathan Kaplan
The music of Cheap Trick, The Cars, and The Ramones highlights this realistic tale of suburban youth on the rampage.
MPAA:PG
Orion Pictures — *Warner Home Video*

Owl and the Pussycat, The 1970
Comedy
44846 96 mins C B, V P
Barbra Streisand, George Segal, Robert Klein, directed by Herbert Ross
A hooker meets a bookstore clerk and, after some initial antagonism, they fall in love.
MPAA:R
Columbia, Ray Stark — *RCA/Columbia Pictures Home Video; RCA VideoDiscs*

Oxford Blues 1984
Drama
Closed Captioned
77463 98 mins C B, V P
Rob Lowe, Ally Sheedy, Amanda Pays, Gail Strickland
A Las Vegas valet goes to England's Oxford University in pursuit of the girl of his dreams. Available in VHS and Beta Hi Fi.
MPAA:PG13
MGM/United Artists — *CBS/Fox Video*

P

Pacific Inferno 1984
Adventure
80268 90 mins C B, V P
Jim Brown, Richard Jaeckel, Tim Brown, Wilma Reading
A true story of how the Japanese forced a group of World War II P.O.W.'s to recover 16 million dollars worth of silver from Manila Bay.
Jim Brown — *VCL Home Video*

Pack, The 1977
Horror
76856 99 mins C B, V R, P
Joe Don Baker, Hope Alexander-Willis, R.G. Armstrong, Richard B. Shull
The residents of a remote island are terrorized by a pack of wild dogs.
MPAA:R
Fred Weintraub; Paul Heller; Warner Bros. — *Warner Home Video*

Pack Up Your Troubles 1932
Comedy
33902 68 mins B/W B, V, 3/4U P
Stan Laurel, Oliver Hardy, James Finlayson, Jacquie Lyn
World War I veterans try to find the family of an orphaned little girl with humorous results.
Hal Roach, MGM — *Nostalgia Merchant*

Paddington Bear—Volume 1 1985
Cartoons
70670 50 mins C B, V R, P
Animated, narrated by Michael Hodern
Michael Bond's internationally famous creation gets into a variety of adventures after his adoption into the Brown family. This two-dimensional and stop action animation production includes 11 vignettes.
Walt Disney Productions — *Walt Disney Home Video*

Paddy Beaver 1984
Cartoons
78375 60 mins C B, V P
Animated
Paddy Beaver teaches the residents of the Green Forest how to depend upon each other in this animated feature.
Family Home Entertainment — *Family Home Entertainment*

Padre Padrone 1977
Drama
63436 90 mins C B, V P
Omero Antonutti, Saverio Marconi
This is the story of the personal rebellion of a Sardinian shepherd who was separated from

the world by his father until he was 20 years old. Italian dialogue, English subtitles.
Cannes Film Festival: Golden Palm Award. IT
Almi/Cinema V; Guiliani G. de Negri — *RCA/Columbia Pictures Home Video*

Pain in the A--, A **1977**
Comedy
80384 90 mins C B, V P
Lino Ventura, Jacques Brel, Caroline Cellier, directed by Edouard Molinaro
A hit man helps a suicidal shirt salesman solve his marital problems. With English subtitles.
MPAA:PG FR
Corwin-Mahler — *RCA/Columbia Pictures Home Video*

Paint Your Wagon **1970**
Musical
59860 164 mins C B, V, LV R, P
Lee Marvin, Clint Eastwood, Jean Seberg, Harve Presnell, directed by Joshua Logan
A western musical-comedy about a goldmining boom town, complete with a classic Lerner and Lowe score.
MPAA:PG
Paramount — *Paramount Home Video*

Painted Stallion, The **1937**
Western/Serials
08878 215 mins B/W B, V, 3/4U P
Ray 'Crash' Corrigan, Hoot Gibson
Twelve episodes, each running 18 minutes.
Republic — *Video Connection; Video Yesteryear; Nostalgia Merchant; Discount Video Tapes*

Paisan **1948**
Film-Avant-garde
06232 90 mins B/W B, V P
Maria Michi, Gar Moore, directed by Roberto Rossellini
Six stories of Allied soldiers encountering Italy's liberation during WWII. Italian film, English subtitles.
IT
J Burstyn; Italian — *Budget Video; Sheik Video; Cable Films; Video Yesteryear; Western Film & Video Inc; Discount Video Tapes*

Pajama Tops **1983**
Comedy
72456 120 mins C B, V P
Susan George, Robert Klein, Pia Zadora
This film was adapted, from the French farce, "Mou Mod."
Unknown — *U.S.A. Home Video*

Paleface, The **1948**
Comedy
80850 91 mins C B, V P
Jane Russell, Bob Hope, Robert Armstrong, Iris Adrian, Robert Watson, directed by Norman Z. McLeod
A cowardly dentist becomes a gunslinging hero when Calamity Jane starts aiming for him.
Available in VHS and BETA HI FI.
Academy Awards '48: Best Song "Buttons and Bows."
Paramount Pictures — *MCA Home Video*

Palm Beach **1979**
Drama
79344 90 mins C B, V P
Bryan Brown, Nat Young
The lives of several residents of an Australian town intertwine at a summer beach party.
Australian — *Active Home Video*

Palooka **1934**
Comedy-Drama
12858 94 mins B/W B, V, FO P
Jimmy Durante, Stuart Erwin, Lupe Velez
Based on the classic comic strip. Durante plays a fast-talking manager Knobby Walsh and sings his own classic, "Inka-Dinka-Doo."
Edward Small Prods — *Hal Roach Studios; Video Yesteryear; Cable Films; Sheik Video; Video Connection; Discount Video Tapes; Western Film & Video Inc; Kartes Productions; Classic Video Cinema Collector's Club; See Hear Industries*

Panama Lady **1939**
Romance
69588 65 mins B/W B, V P
Lucille Ball, Evelyn Brent
Lucille Ball stars as the sexy, sultry "Panama Lady" in this old-fashioned romance.
RKO — *VidAmerica*

Panama Lady **1939**
Drama
70050 65 mins B/W B, V P
Lucille Ball
A dance hall girl and oil prospector experience a series of mis-adventures before finding happiness out west.
RKO — *VidAmerica*

Pancho Villa **1972**
Adventure
70264 92 mins C B, V R, P
Telly Savalas, Clint Walker, Chuck Connors, Anne Francis
The tale of Mexican revolutionary Pancho Villa, and his invasion of Columbus, New Mexico, in 1916.
MPAA:PG
Scotia International — *Video Gems; World Video Pictures*

Panda and the Magic Serpent 1975
Cartoons/Fantasy
53140 78 mins C B, V P
Animated
An ancient Chinese legend tells of a boy who found a white snake his parents wouldn't let him keep. When he grows up, the snake turns into a beautiful maiden who saves his life.
Ziv Intl — *Family Home Entertainment*

Panda's Adventures 1984
Cartoons
76031 60 mins C B, V P
Animated
An animated tale of a Panda Prince, Lonlon, who is exiled from his Kingdom when he fails a test of courage. Through his adventures, he learns that true heroism and real courage come from the heart.
John Watkins; Simon Nuchtern — *RCA/Columbia Pictures Home Video*

Panic 1983
Horror
81531 90 mins C B, V P
David Warbeck, Janet Agren
A scientist terrorizes a small town when he becomes hideously deformed by one of his bacteria experiments.
Cinema Shares International — *MPI Home Video*

Panic in Echo Park 1977
Drama
66619 77 mins C B, V P
Dorian Harewood, Catlin Adams, Robin Gammell, Norman Barthold
A dedicated physician fights hospital authorities to trace the cause of an epidemic in a minority community.
Edgar J Scherick Associates — *U.S.A. Home Video*

Paper Chase, The 1973
Drama
08469 111 mins C B, V, CED P
Timothy Bottoms, Lindsay Wagner, John Houseman, Graham Beckel
Examines the repressive cloistered world of first-year students at Harvard Law School.
Academy Awards '73: Best Supporting Actor (Houseman). MPAA:PG
20th Century Fox — *CBS/Fox Video*

Paper Moon 1973
Comedy
38601 102 mins B/W B, V, LV R, P
Ryan O'Neal, Tatum O'Neal, Madeline Kahn, John Hillerman, directed by Peter Bogdanovich
Bright, winning story of a con man (Ryan O'Neal) who is left with a nine-year old orphan (Tatum O'Neal in her film debut) who proves to be a better crook. Set in depression-era Kansas, circa 1936.
Academy Awards '73: Best Supporting Actress (Tatum O'Neal). MPAA:PG
Paramount — *Paramount Home Video; RCA VideoDiscs*

Paper Tiger 1974
Adventure
80761 104 mins C B, V P
David Niven, Toshiro Mifune, Ando, Hardy Kruger directed by Ken Annakin
Niven plays an imaginative English tutor who fabricates fantastic yarns fictionalizing his past in order to impress his student, the son of the Japanese ambassador to a Southeast Asian country.
Joseph E. Levine — *Embassy Home Entertainment*

Papillon 1973
Drama
59308 150 mins C B, V, CED P
Steve McQueen, Dustin Hoffman, directed by Franklin Schaffner
The story of two convicts and their harrowing experiences on Devil's Island.
MPAA:PG
Robert Dorfmann — *CBS/Fox Video*

Paradise 1982
Romance
63368 100 mins C B, V, CED P
Phoebe Cates, Willie Aames, Richard Curnock, Tuvio Tavi
A young American boy and a beautiful English girl are the sole survivors of a caravan massacre in the Middle East during the 19th century. They discover a magnificent oasis and experience their sexual awakening.
MPAA:R
Robert Lantos; Stephen J. Ross — *Embassy Home Entertainment*

Paradise Canyon 1935
Western
54188 55 mins B/W B, V P
John Wayne
One of John Wayne's early action westerns.
Monogram — *Video Connection; Spotlite Video; Discount Video Tapes*

Paradise, Hawaiian Style 1966
Musical
08387 91 mins C B, V P
Elvis Presley, Suzanna Leigh, James Shigeta
Out-of-work pilot returns to Hawaii, where he and a buddy start a charter service with two helicopters.
EL, SP
Paramount; Hal Wallis — *CBS/Fox Video*

(For explanation of codes, see USE GUIDE and KEY)

Paradise in Harlem 1940
Drama
42951 83 mins B/W B, V, FO P
Frank Wilson, Mamie Smith, Edna Mae Harris
An all-black musical in which a cabaret performer witnesses a gangland murder, sees his sick wife die, and is pressured into leaving town by the mob.
Unknown — *Video Yesteryear; Sheik Video; Video Connection; Discount Video Tapes; See Hear Industries*

Parallax View, The 1974
Suspense
60331 102 mins C B, V R, P
Warren Beatty, Hume Cronyn, William Daniels, Paula Prentiss, directed by Alan J. Pakula
A reporter tries to disprove a report which stated that a presidential candidate's assassination was not a conspiracy.
MPAA:R
Paramount — *Paramount Home Video*

Paranoia 1969
Suspense
66475 94 mins C B, V P
Carroll Baker, Lou Castel, Colette Descombes
A beautiful jet-set widow is trapped in her own Italian villa by a young couple and slowly fed drugs as part of a murder plan.
MPAA:X
Commonwealth United — *Republic Pictures Home Video*

Parasite 1981
Horror/Science fiction
60431 85 mins C B, V P
Demi Moore, Robert Glaudini, James Davidson
In 1992, a doctor, a victim of the atomic age, is being eaten alive from the inside out.
MPAA:R
Irwin Yablans; Charles Band — *Wizard Video; Embassy Home Entertainment (disc only)*

Pardon Mon Affaire 1977
Comedy
65427 105 mins C B, V P
Jean Rochefort
The story of the complications that bedevil male-female relationships, here, there and everywhere.
MPAA:PG
First Artists — *Embassy Home Entertainment*

Pardon Mon Affaire 1977
Comedy
78638 107 mins C B, V, LV P
Jean Rochefort, Guy Bedos, Anny Duperey, directed by Yves Robert
When a middle-aged civil servant gets a look at a model in a garage, he decides it's time to cheat on his wife. This film has English subtitles.
MPAA:PG FR
First Artists — *Embassy Home Entertainment*

Pardon Us 1931
Comedy
59152 71 mins B/W B, V, 3/4U P
Stan Laurel, Oliver Hardy, June Marlowe
Two bootleggers find themselves in and out of prison.
Hal Roach;MGM — *Nostalgia Merchant*

Parent Trap, The 1961
Comedy
66321 127 mins C B, V, LV, CED R, P
Hayley Mills, Maureen O'Hara, Brian Keith, Charlie Ruggles, directed by David Swift
Hayley Mills plays a dual role in this heartwarming comedy as twin sisters who conspire to bring their divorced parents together again.
Buena Vista — *Walt Disney Home Video*

Paris Express 1953
Mystery/Drama
78968 82 mins C B, V P
Claude Rains, Herbert Lom, Felix Aylmer, Marius Goring, Marta Toren
When a man steals money from his employer, he boards the Paris Express to escape from the police.
Josef Shaftel; Raymond Struss — *MPI Home Video*

Paris Holiday 1957
Comedy
47664 100 mins C B, V P
Bob Hope, Fernandel, Anita Ekberg, Martha Hyer, Preston Sturges
An actor heading for Paris to find a noted author; latest screenplay finds mystery and romance.
United Artists — *Unicorn Video*

Paris, Texas 1984
Drama
Closed Captioned
81410 145 mins C B, V P
Nastassja Kinski, Harry Dean Stanton, Hunter Carson, Dean Stockwell, Aurore Clement, directed by Wim Wenders
An estranged father is picked up and taken to Los Angeles after he is found wandering around the Texas desert. After being reunited with his son, the two head back to Texas to win back his ex-wife's love. Ry Cooder's score can be heard in VHS and Beta Hi-Fi.
MPAA:PG
20th Century Fox — *CBS/Fox Video*

Parlor, Bedroom and Bath 1931
Comedy
57288 75 mins B/W B, V P
Buster Keaton, Charlotte Greenwood, Cliff Edwards
Buster Keaton stars in another one of his classic comedies from the Thirties.
Buster Keaton — *Video Yesteryear; Video Dimensions; Budget Video; Discount Video Tapes; Classic Video Cinema Collector's Club; See Hear Industries*

Partners 1982
Comedy
60332 92 mins C B, V R, P
Ryan O'Neal, John Hurt, Kenneth McMillan, Robyn Douglass, Jay Robinson, Rick Jason
A macho cop must go "undercover" with a gay cop to investigate the murder of a gay model.
MPAA:R
Paramount — *Paramount Home Video*

Party Animal, The 1983
Comedy
80669 78 mins C B, V P
Tim Carhart, Matthew Lausey, Robin Harlan
A college stud teaches a shy farm boy a thing or two about the carnal aspects of campus life.
MPAA:R
Alan C. Fox — *Lightning Video*

Party Games—For Adults Only 1984
Games
75019 130 mins C LV P
This tape features sixty good-natured sexy party games for adult parties.
Bosustow Entertainment Productions — *MCA Home Video*

Passage to Marseilles 1944
War-Drama
73980 110 mins B/W B, V P
Humphrey Bogart, Claude Rains, Sidney Greenstreet, Peter Lorre, Michele Morgan, directed by Michael Curtiz
Five convicts escape from Devil's Island to join up with the Free French forces fighting the Nazis during World War II.
Warner Bros — *Key Video*

Passante, La 1983
Drama
80451 106 mins C B, V P
Romy Schneider, Michel Piccoli, Helmut Griem, Gerard Klein
The lives of two women are brought together by a mysterious chain of events.
FR
Raymond Dannon — *Pacific Arts Video*

Passion of Joan of Arc 1928
Film-Avant-garde
11385 114 mins B/W B, V, FO P
Maria Falconeth, Eugena Sylvain, Maurice Schutz, directed by Carl Theodore Dreyer
A classic silent masterpiece and a notable cinema treatment of Joan of Arc.
Societe Generale de Films — *Video Yesteryear; Sheik Video; Western Film & Video Inc; Discount Video Tapes; Classic Video Cinema Collector's Club*

Passion of Love 1982
Drama/Romance
64355 117 mins C B, V, CED P
Laura Antonelli
Laura Antonelli is featured in this passionate, historical romance from filmmaker Ettore Scola. The film has won a special award at the Cannes Film Festival.
Franco Commipteri — *Vestron Video*

Pastures of Heaven 1951
Drama
66391 90 mins B/W B, V P
Buddy Ebsen, Thomas Mitchell, Lew Ayres, Tommy Rettig, John Steinbeck
A selection of dramatized stories by John Steinbeck, each introduced by the author.
Bryna Pictures — *Movie Buff Video*

Pat Benatar Hit Videos 1984
Music video
72929 60 mins C B, V P
Pat Benatar
A collection of Pat's videos from "Get Nervous" and "Live from Earth," this tape also includes a documentary on the making of "Love Is a Battlefield."
Rising Star Video Productions — *RCA/Columbia Pictures Home Video*

Pat Benatar in Concert 1985
Music-Performance
77461 72 mins C B, V P
Pat Benatar
Pat Benatar performs many of her big hits in this exciting concert video.
Music Vision — *RCA/Columbia Pictures Home Video*

Pat Garrett and Billy the Kid 1973
Western
72466 106 mins C B, V P
Kris Kristofferson, James Coburn, Bob Dylan
The story of the famous Southwestern outlaw who was tracked and killed by a man he once rode with. Sound track music by Bob Dylan.
MGM — *MGM/UA Home Video*

 (For explanation of codes, see USE GUIDE and KEY)

Country stars Jessica Lange as the courageous farmer Jewell Ivy—Touchstone Home Video

Paul Newman and Sally Field explore the power of the press in *Absence of Malice*—RCA/Columbia Pictures Home Video

Laurel and Hardy look part-private, part-potato in this scene from *Great Guns*—Playhouse Video

Burt Reynolds remains unimpressed by Dom DeLuise's rope tricks in *The End*—CBS/Fox Home Video

Gene Wilder shares a humorous thought with Gilda Radner in *Hanky Panky*—RCA/Columbia Pictures Home Video

Laurence Olivier and Vivien Leigh share chianti in *That Hamilton Woman*—Embassy Home Entertainment

Humphrey Bogart hears that they're serving fish again in this scene from *The Caine Mutiny*—RCA/Columbia Pictures Home Video

Madame X stars mysterious, bejeweled and bedazzled Lana Turner—MCA Home Video

A swashbuckling Bob Hope wants to hold the (Virginia) Mayo in *The Princess and the Pirate*—Embassy Home Entertainment

Michael Douglas and Kathleen Turner get chummy in *Romancing the Stone*—CBS/Fox Video

Maurice and Gregory Hines play the dancing Williams brothers in *The Cotton Club*—Embassy Home Entertainment

Grandview U.S.A.'s view is just grand for Jamie Lee Curtis and C. Thomas Howell—Key Video

The young Walter Brennan stars with Gary Cooper and Doris Davenport in *The Westerner*—Embassy Home Entertainment

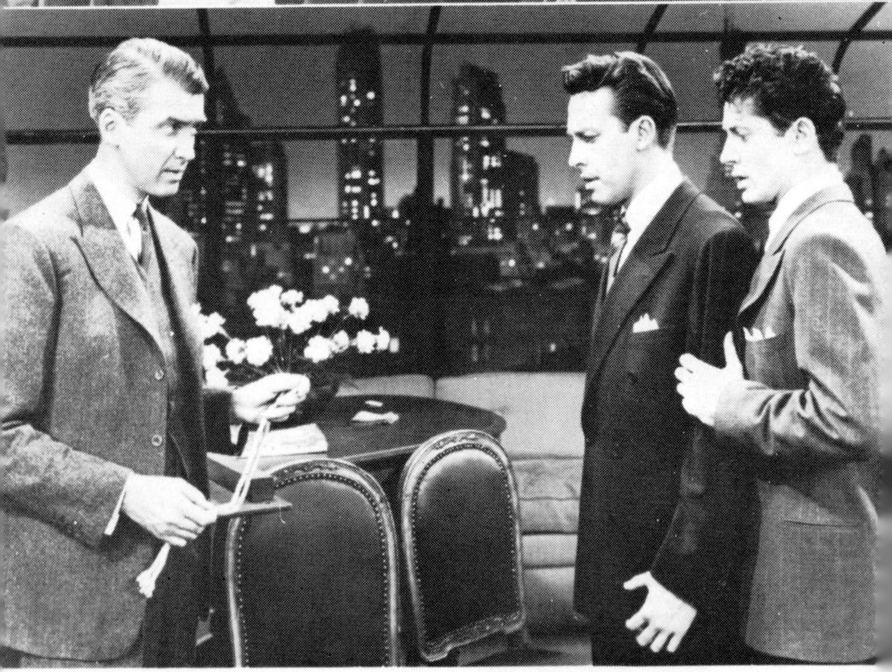

White, suburban punk Emilio Estevez is restrained by Richard Fornjoy in *Repo Man*—MCA Home Video

James Stewart lectures John Dall and Farley Granger on murder techniques in Hitchcock's *Rope*—MCA Home Video

Elvis Presley shares smiles with Debra Paget and Mildred Dunnock in *Love Me Tender*—Key Video

Quincy Jones leads the chorus in *We Are The World–The Video Event*–RCA/Columbia Pictures Home Video

In David Lean's *Summertime*, vacationing American Katharine Hepburn falls in love with a handsome Venetian merchant played by Rossano Brazzi—Embassy Home Entertainment

eff Goldblum and Michelle Pfeiffer star as unlikely adventurers in *Into the Night*—
'CA Home Video

'an-Michael Vincent and Joan Goodfellow discuss Captain Marvel and love in *Buster and*
'*illie*—RCA/Columbia Pictures Home Video

Gregory Peck has a fireside chat with Claude Jarman Jr. in *The Yearling*—MGM/UA Home Video

ichael Caine checks a barrel's pulse in this scene from *The Wrong Box*—RCA/Columbia ictures Home Video

What's a nice alien like you . . . Karen Allen and Jeff Bridges in *Starman*—RCA/Columbia Pictures Home Video

Harrison Ford plays a tough detective hunting renegade replicants in *Blade Runner*—Embassy Home Entertainment

Clint Eastwood spins the tunes that make your day in *Play Misty For Me* with Jessica Walter—MCA Home Video

Youngsters Robert Wagner and Joan Collins star in *Stopover Tokyo*—Key Video

Amy Irving explains the subtleties of Schubert to Dudley Moore in *Micki and Maude*—RCA/Columbia Pictures Home Video

Pinocchio meets Jiminy Cricket in this classic animated adventure—Walt Disney Home Vide

A courageous Mickey Mouse confronts the giant in *Mickey and the Beanstalk*, a segment c *Fun and Fancy Free*—Walt Disney Home Video

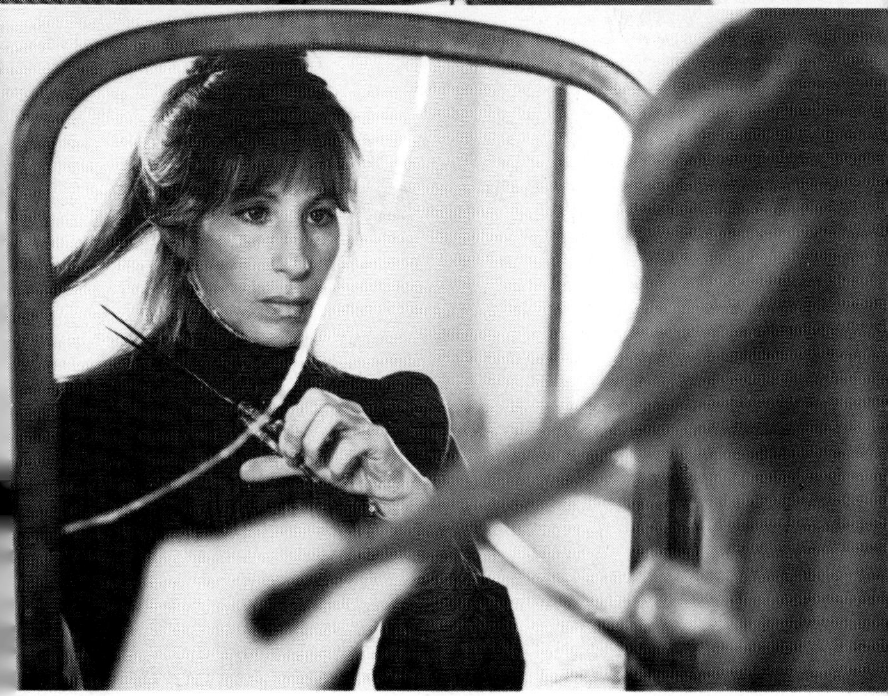

Manhattan star Woody Allen dictates a few thoughts into his tape recorder—MGM/UA Home Video

Barbra Streisand tries something completely different in *Yentl*—CBS/Fox Video

In *The Conquerer,* John Wayne plays Genghis Khan as an Oriental with Shakespearian mannerisms—MCA Home Video

Bill Murray amid the clutter as a gonzo journalist in *Where the Buffalo Roam*—MCA Home Video

Lily Tomlin gets smaller moment by moment in *The Incredible Shrinking Woman*—MCA Home Video

Ta-Daa . . . Robert Redford acknowledges the applause for his aerial stunts as *The Grea*
Waldo Pepper—MCA Home Video

Pat Travers in "Just Another Killer Day" **1984**
Music video
70190 30 mins C B, V P
This conceptual music video album features guitarist/vocalist Pat Travers performing "Killer," "Women on the Edge," "Hot Shot" and others.
PMV Presentations; Beth Broday — *RCA/Columbia Pictures Home Video*

Paternity **1981**
Comedy
58715 94 mins C B, V, LV R, P
Burt Reynolds, Beverly D'Angelo, Lauren Hutton, Norman Fell, Paul Dooley, Elizabeth Ashley, directed by David Steinberg
A middle-aged man sets out to find a woman to bear his child and then leave him alone.
MPAA:PG
Paramount — *Paramount Home Video; RCA VideoDiscs*

Paths of Glory **1957**
War-Drama
64905 86 mins B/W B, V, CED P
Kirk Douglas, George Macready, Ralph Meeker, Adolphe Menjou, Susanne Christian, directed by Stanley Kubrick
This adaptation of a novel by Humphrey Cobb examines the arrogance of generals and the senseless punishment of three soldiers in the French army during World War I.
United Artists — *CBS/Fox Video*

Patrick **1978**
Suspense
54537 115 mins C B, V P
Sir Robert Helpmann, Susan Penhaligon, Rod Mullinar
A coma patient suddenly develops strange powers and has a weird effect on the people he comes in contact with.
MPAA:PG
Vanguard/Monarch Release — *HarmonyVision*

Patsy, The **1964**
Comedy
80240 101 mins C B, V P
Jerry Lewis, Ina Balin, Keenan Wynn, Phil Harris, Peter Lorre, directed by Jerry Lewis
A group of Hollywood executives try to turn a bellhop into a comedy star.
Paramount — *U.S.A. Home Video*

Patton **1970**
War-Drama
08428 171 mins C B, V, LV P
George C. Scott, Karl Malden, Stephen Young, directed by Franklin J. Schaffner
George C. Scott portrays the brilliant and maniacal General Patton, whose leadership produced victory after victory in North Africa and Europe during World War II.
Academy Awards '70: Best Picture; Best Actor (Scott); Best Director (Shaffner). MPAA:PG
EL, SP
20th Century Fox — *CBS/Fox Video*

Paul Simon in Concert **1981**
Music-Performance
47376 60 mins C B, V R, P
Paul Simon
At a live concert in Philadelphia, Paul Simon performs some of his greatest old and new hits, including "Me and Julio," "Fifty Ways to Leave Your Lover," " One-Trick Pony," and "Sounds of Silence."
Michael Tannen; Phil Ramone; Peregrine Inc — *Warner Home Video; RCA VideoDiscs; Pioneer Artists*

Paul Simon Special, The **1977**
Music-Performance/Variety
66444 60 mins C B, V P
Paul Simon, Art Garfunkel, Chevy Chase, Lily Tomlin, Charles Grodin, The Jesse Dixon Singers
This 1977 TV special was produced by Lorne Michaels of "Saturday Night Live" and features appearances by a number of "SNL's" stars. Singer-songwriter Paul Simon performs eight of his songs, assisted on several by Art Garfunkel.
NBC; Lorne Michaels — *Pacific Arts Video*

Pavarotti **1984**
Opera/Music-Performance
66611 75 mins C B, V P
Luciano Pavarotti, Andrea Griminelli
Operatic tenor Luciano Pavarotti stars in this live concert taped in the Superstar Center of Las Vegas' Riviera Hotel. The program includes songs and arias by Verdi, Donizetti, Puccini and di Curtis.
Tibor Rudas Productions — *Trans World Entertainment*

Pavarotti in London **1982**
Music-Performance/Opera
64831 51 mins C B, V P
London's Royal Albert Hall was the setting for this concert which launched the Royal Philharmonic Orchestra's national fund appeal starring Pavarotti performing "Tosca," "Macbeth" and others. In stereo.
BBC; Polygram; Rodney Greenberg — *RCA/Columbia Pictures Home Video; Pioneer Artists; RCA VideoDiscs*

Pawnbroker, The **1965**
Drama
64540 100 mins B/W B, V P

Rod Steiger, Brock Peters, Geraldine Fitzgerald, directed by Sidney Lumet
A middle-aged Jewish pawnbroker in New York's Spanish Harlem finds that he cannot forget his terrible experiences in a Nazi concentration camp during World War II.
Commonwealth United — *Republic Pictures Home Video*

Payday **1972**
Musical-Drama
63333 98 mins C B, V R, P
Rip Torn, Ahna Capri, Michael C. Gwynne, Jeff Morris
Rip Torn stars as a declining country music star on tour in this portrayal of the seamy side of show business, from groupies to grimy motels.
Saul Zaentz Company — *THORN EMI/HBO Video*

Peacock Fan, The **1929**
Drama
59206 50 mins B/W B, V, 3/4U P
Lucian Preval
The Peacock Fan is protected by a deadly curse, with certain death to anyone who possesses it.
Chesterfield Motion Picture Corp — *Video Yesteryear*

Peck's Bad Boy **1921**
Comedy
60047 51 mins B/W B, V P, T
Jackie Coogan, Doris Day, Raymond Hatton, Wheeler Oakman, Lillian Leighton
Jackie and his friends let a circus lion loose and Jackie's father won't allow him to see the circus. He then decides to blackmail his father. A Blackhawk orchestral score has been added to this silent film.
First National — *Blackhawk Films; Classic Video Cinema Collector's Club*

Peck's Bad Boy with the Circus **1938**
Comedy
12812 67 mins B/W B, V, FO P
Tommy Kelly, Ann Gillis, Spanky MacFarland, Edgar Kennedy, Billy Gilbert
A troublesome youngster and his pals nearly wreck a circus and throw an obstacle race off course.
RKO — *Video Yesteryear*

Pedestrian, The **1974**
Drama
65391 97 mins C B, V P
Maximillian Schell
This is the story of a powerful industrialist and his secret. A human drama builds as a newspaper's investigation probes deep into the past to reveal the memory of events that time and fortune could not erase.
MPAA:PG
Cinerama Releasing — *Embassy Home Entertainment*

Peeping Tom **1963**
Horror/Drama
73552 88 mins C B, V P
Moira Shearer, Karl Boehm, directed by Michael Powell
A filmmaker kills women while filming the acts with a 16 millimeter camera. This is the original uncut version of the film.
Michael Powell — *Admit One Video*

Peerce, Anderson & Segovia **1981**
Music-Performance
57253 56 mins B/W B, V P
Jan Peerce, Marian Anderson, Andres Segovia
Three separate short films highlight performances by guitarist Andres Segovia, tenor Jan Peerce, assisted by Nadine Connor and contralto Marian Anderson.
Kultur — *Kultur*

Pele—The Master and His Method **1980**
Soccer
56453 60 mins C B, V P
Soccer star Pele gives tips on improving your play, and talks about the game.
Pepsico — *CBS/Fox Video; Champions on Film and Video*

Pendulum **1969**
Mystery/Drama
77242 106 mins C B, V P
George Peppard, Jean Seberg, Richard Kiley, Madeline Sherwood
A police captain sets out to clear himself of charges of murdering his wife and her lover.
MPAA:PG
Columbia Pictures; Stanley Niss — *RCA/Columbia Pictures Home Video*

Penitentiary **1979**
Drama
52861 99 mins C B, V P
Leon Isaacs, Jamaa Fanaka
A realistic story of a black fighter in prison.
MPAA:R
Jerry Gross — *Wizard Video*

Penitentiary II **1982**
Adventure
80362 108 mins C B, V P
Leon Issac Kennedy, Mr. T, Ernie Hudson, Glynn Turman
A welterweight fighter is after the man who murdered his girlfriend.
MPAA:R

Bob-Bea Productions — *MGM/UA Home Video*

Pennies from Heaven 1981
Musical
47776 107 mins C B, V, CED P
Steve Martin, Bernadette Peters, Christopher Walken, Jessica Harper, Vernel Bagneris, directed by Herbert Ross
An avante-garde reworking of 30's musicals involving a sheet music salesman accused of murder.
MPAA:R
MGM — *MGM/UA Home Video*

Penny Serenade 1936
Drama
11249 120 mins B/W B, V P
Cary Grant, Irene Dunne, Beulah Bondi, Edgar Buchanan
A young couple, having lost their baby, adopts a child, but their new found happiness is short-lived.
Columbia — *Spotlite Video; Video Yesteryear; Budget Video; Sheik Video; Cable Films; Video Connection; Discount Video Tapes; Prism; Republic Pictures Home Video; Hal Roach Studios; Kartes Productions; Classic Video Cinema Collector's Club*

Penthouse Video Volume One: The Girls of Penthouse 1985
Variety
76765 60 mins C B, V, LV, CED P
The first volume of this video magazine features of some of Penthouse's most popular centerfolds in intimate photo sessions.
Penthouse International — *Vestron Video*

People, The 1971
Drama
80312 74 mins C B, V P
Kim Darby, Dan O'Herlihy, Diane Varsi, William Shatner, directed by John Korty
A young teacher takes a job in a small town and finds out that her students have telepathic powers.
Metromedia Producers Corp. — *Prism*

People Are Funny 1946
Comedy
57364 94 mins B/W B, V, FO P
Jack Haley, Rudy Vallee, Ozzie Nelson, Art Linkletter, Helen Walker
Battling radio producers vie to land the big sponsor with an original radio idea. Comedy ensues when one of them comes up with a great idea—stolen from a local station.
Paramount — *Video Yesteryear*

People That Time Forgot, The 1977
Science fiction
66045 90 mins C B, V P
Edgar Rice Burroughs' novel about a rescue team that discovers a world of prehistoric monsters and tribes people provides the basis for this film.
MPAA:PG
John Dark — *Embassy Home Entertainment*

Pepper 1982
Adventure/Suspense
63362 88 mins C B, V P
International intrigue and super spying abound in this fast-paced, sexy adventure featuring Pepper, a female secret agent in the James Bond tradition.
Amero Brothers — *Vestron Video*

Pepper and His Wacky Taxi 196?
Comedy
66110 79 mins C B, V P
John Astin, Frank Sinatra Jr, Jackie Gayle, Alan Sherman
A father of four buys a '59 Cadillac and starts a cab company.
MPAA:G
Samuel S Dikel — *Unicorn Video*

Percy Faith and his Orchestra (The Best of Both Worlds) 1960
Music-Performance
12842 41 mins B/W B, V, FO P
Percy Faith and his Orchestra, Peter Nero
Percy Faith's 50-piece orchestra plays easy listening popular favorites.
BBC — *Video Yesteryear*

Perfect Crime, The 1978
Mystery/Adventure
80941 90 mins C B, V P
Joseph Cotten, Antony Steel, Janet Agreen
A Scotland Yard inspector must find out who has been killing off executives of a powerful world trust.
Ciat Productions — *VidAmerica*

Perfect Killer, The 1977
Drama
70595 85 mins C B, V P
Lee Van Cleef, Tita Barker, John Ireland, Robert Widmark
Van Cleef stars as a world weary Mafia hit-man who is doublecrossed bythis girl, set up by his best friend, and hunted by another hired assassin.
MPAA:R
JPT and Metheus Film Prods. — *Prism*

Perfect Strangers 1984
Drama/Suspense
70678 90 mins C B, V P
Anne Carlisle, Brad Rijn, John Woehrle, Matthew Stockley, Stephen Lack, directed by Larry Cohen
This Hitchcockian thriller develops around a murder and the child who witnesses it. The killer attempts to kidnap the young boy, but problems arise when he falls in love with the lad's mother.
MPAA:R
New Line Cinema — *Embassy Home Entertainment*

Performance 1970
Drama
58244 105 mins C B, V, LV R, P
James Fox, Mick Jagger, Anita Pallenberg, directed by Donald Cammell and Nicolas Roeg
The story of a hunted murderer who takes refuge with an outcast rock and roll star—and sees his sense of reality vanish in an orgiastic breakdown of barriers and roles.
MPAA:R
Warner Bros — *Warner Home Video*

Perfumed Handkerchief, The 1981
Music-Performance
81569 70 mins C B, V P
This is a performance of the Chinese comic opera that features commentary from Steve Allen and Jayne Meadows. Contains English subtitles.
CCTV — *Kultur*

Perils of Gwendoline, The 1984
Adventure/Comedy
77186 88 mins C B, V, CED P
Tawny Kitaen, Brent Huff, Zabou, directed by Just Jaeckin
A young woman leaves the convent to search for her long lost father.
MPAA:R
Samuel Goldwyn — *Vestron Video*

Perils of Pauline, The 1947
Musical
03825 96 mins B/W B, V P
Betty Hutton, John Lund, Billy DeWolfe, directed by George Marshall
A musical biography of Pearl White, the original queen of silent movie serials. Songs by Frank Loesser include "I Wish I Didn't Love You So," an Academy Award nominee.
Paramount; Sol C Siegel — *Prism; Hal Roach Studios; Budget Video; Video Yesteryear; Movie Buff Video; Discount Video Tapes; Sheik Video; Cable Films; Media Home Entertainment; VCII; Video Connection; Kartes Productions; See Hear Industries*

Perils of Penelope Pitstop, The 1984
Cartoons
66576 60 mins C B, V P
Animated
This compilation of cartoons stars lovely Penelope Pitstop, international race car driver, who has to ward off the advances of villainous Sylvester Sneekly while she drives.
Hanna Barbera — *Worldvision Home Video*

Perils of the Darkest Jungle 1944
Adventure/Serials
59149 180 mins B/W B, V, 3/4U P
Linda Sterling, Allan Lane
A white jungle goddess battles money-mad oil profiteers to prevent them from despoiling the jungle. Original title: "The Tiger Woman." A serial in twelve episodes, on two cassettes.
Republic — *Nostalgia Merchant*

Person to Person 1958
Interview
80758 30 mins B/W B, V P
Hosted by Edward R. Murrow
Edward R. Murrow electronically visits Groucho and Harpo Marx at their homes in California in this collection of two episodes from the series.
CBS — *Video Yesteryear*

Persona 1967
Drama
14440 83 mins C B, V, FO P
Bibi Andersson, Liv Ullmann, directed by Ingmar Bergman
A famous actress is stricken with psychosomatic dumbness and is placed under a nurse's care in an isolated house.
Svensk Filmindustri — *Video Yesteryear; Video Dimensions; Sheik Video; Budget Video*

Personal Best 1982
Drama
59854 124 mins C B, V R, P
Mariel Hemingway, Scott Glenn, Patrice Donnelly, directed by Robert Towne
Two woman athletes, Olympic runners, fall in love while competing against each other.
MPAA:R
Geffen Co; Warner Bros — *Warner Home Video*

Personals, The 1983
Comedy
80387 90 mins C B, V P
Bill Schoppert, Karen Landry
A recently divorced young man takes out a personal ad in a newspaper to find the woman of his dreams.
MPAA:PG
Patrick Wells — *Embassy Home Entertainment*

 (For explanation of codes, see USE GUIDE and KEY)

Pete Townsend **1982**
Music-Performance
76675 30 mins C B, V P
This program presents Pete Townsend performing his new hit songs.
Trinifold Ltd Warner Amex Satellite Entertainment Co — *Sony Corporation of America*

Peter Allen and the Rockettes **1981**
Music-Performance
58955 87 mins C B, V, CED P
Peter Allen, the Rockettes
Peter Allen — recorded live at his three-night, sell-out engagement, performing more than 20 songs, including: "Everything Old." "Flyaway," "Bicoastal," "You and Me," & "Don't Cry Out Loud" and " I Go to Rio." In Stereo.
20th Century Fox — *CBS/Fox Video; MCA Home Video (disc only)*

Peter and the Magic Egg **1983**
Cartoons
66182 60 mins C B, V P
Animated, voices by Ray Bolger
The story of Mama and Papa Doppler, in danger of losing their farm to greedy Tobias Tinwhiskers.
RLR Associates — *Family Home Entertainment; Coronet Films*

Peter Cottontail's Adventures **1978**
Cartoons
53141 70 mins C B, V P
Animated
Peter loves to play practical jokes until no one wants to be his friend anymore, teaching him the importance of his Green Forest friends, Johnny and Polly Woodchuck, Jimmy Skunk, Chatterer Chipmunk, Reddy and Granny Fox, and Sammy Bluejay.
Ziv Intl — *Family Home Entertainment*

Peter Grimes **1981**
Opera
59874 210 mins C LV P
Jon Vickers
The Royal Opera's production of Benjamin Britten's three-act opera set in a small English fishing town and concerning the inquest into the death of Grime's apprentice. In stereo.
Covent Garden Video — *Pioneer Artists*

Peter Lind Hayes Show, The **1957**
Variety
59087 51 mins B/W B, V, FO P
Peter Lind Hayes, Mary Healy, Jack Whiting, Genevieve, the Step Brothers, Zippy the chimp, Tony Marvin
A variety show set in Central Park with Peter and Mary singing, Peter miming, and Jack imitating famous mayors of New York.
CBS — *Video Yesteryear*

Peter Lundy and the Medicine Hat Stallion **1977**
Adventure/Western
80706 85 mins C B, V P
Leif Garrett, Mitchell Ryan, Bibi Besch, John Quade, Milo O'Shea
A teenaged Pony Express rider must outrun the Indians and battle the elements in order to carry mail from the Nebraska Territory to the West Coast.
Ed Friendly Prods. — *Vestron Video*

Peter-No-Tail **1983**
Fantasy/Cartoons
69537 82 mins C B, V, CED P
Animated, voices of Ken Berry, Dom DeLuise, Richard Kline, Tina Louise, Larry Storch, June Lockhart
A tail-less kitten wins the Cats Mastership and the heart of Molly Cream-Nose.
Stig Lasseby — *Children's Video Library*

Petrified Forest, The **1936**
Drama
64330 83 mins B/W B, V P
Bette Davis, Leslie Howard, Humphrey Bogart, Dick Foran, directed by Archie Mayo
Customers and employees at a diner in the Arizona desert are held captive by a group of thugs. Based on the play by Robert Sherwood.
Warner Bros — *Key Video; RCA VideoDiscs*

Phantasm **1977**
Horror
44980 90 mins C B, V, LV, CED P
Michael Baldwin, Bill Thornberry, Reggie Bannister, Kathy Lester
Two brothers discover the startling secret of the living dead when their friend is murdered.
MPAA:R
Avco Embassy — *Embassy Home Entertainment; RCA VideoDiscs*

Phantasm **1979**
Horror
80390 90 mins C B, V P
Michael Baldwin, Bill Thornbury, Kathy Lester
When two brothers try to find out who murdered their friend, it takes them to a mysterious house where some strange events occur.
MPAA:R
D. A. Coscarelli — *Embassy Home Entertainment*

Phantom Empire 1935
Western/Serials
38986 245 mins B/W B, V, FO P
Gene Autry, Frankie Darro, Betsy King Ross, Smiley Burnette
Gene faces the futuristic "Thunder Riders" from the subterranean city of Murania, which is located 20,000 feet beneath his ranch. A complete serial in twelve episodes.
Mascot — *Video Yesteryear; Video Connection; Sheik Video; Nostalgia Merchant; Discount Video Tapes*

Phantom Empire, The 1984
Music video
72928 60 mins C B, V P
Phantom Empire
The first of fifteen episodes of a rock video/cliffhanger serial inspired by the comics and pulps of the '40s.
Michael Uslan — *RCA/Columbia Pictures Home Video*

Phantom of the Opera 1925
Horror
10628 85 mins B/W B, V P, T
Lon Chaney Sr., Norman Kerry, Mary Philbin
An unknown entity terrorizes a Paris opera house. Silent with two-color Technicolor "Bal Masque" sequence.
Universal — *Blackhawk Films; Sheik Video; Video Yesteryear; Cable Films; Video Connection; Budget Video; Western Film & Video Inc; Discount Video Tapes; Cinema Concepts*

Phantom of the West 1931
Western
57366 166 mins B/W B, V, FO P
Tom Tyler
Ten-episode serial about a rancher who becomes "The Phantom of the West," in order to smoke out his father's killer.
Mascot — *Video Yesteryear; Video Connection; Discount Video Tapes*

Phantom Rancher, The 1939
Western
15484 61 mins B/W B, V P
Ken Maynard
This roaring melodrama finds Maynard donning a mask to find the real Phantom who is causing havoc.
Nat Saland — *United Home Video; Video Connection*

Phantom Tollbooth, The 1970
Adventure/Cartoons
63111 89 mins C B, V, CED P
Animated, directed by Chuck Jones
A young boy drives his car into a strange and enchanting fantasy land.
MPAA:G
MGM — *MGM/UA Home Video*

Phar Lap 1984
Adventure
Closed Captioned
80747 107 mins C B, V P
Ron Leibman, Tom Burlinson, Judy Morris, Celia De Burgh
This is the true story of how the horse Phar Lap rose from nowhere to win thirty-seven races within three years during the 1930's. Available in VHS and Beta Hi-Fi.
MPAA:PG
20th Century Fox — *Playhouse Video*

Pharmacist, The 1932
Comedy
62868 19 mins B/W B, V P, T
W.C. Fields, Grady Sutton
A typical day of frustration for druggist Fields, with grouchy customers and a robbery stick-up to top things off.
Mack Sennett — *Blackhawk Films*

Phase IV 1974
Science fiction
66033 83 mins C B, V R, P
Nigel Davenport, Michael Murphy, Lynne Frederick
A tale of killer ants retaliating against the humans attempting their extermination.
MPAA:PG
Paramount — *Paramount Home Video*

Phedre 1968
Drama
63617 93 mins C B, V, FO P
Marie Bell
Jean Racine's adaptation of the Greek legend involving Phedre, Theseus and Hippolyte is presented in French with English subtitles.
FR
French — *Video Yesteryear*

Phenomenal and the Treasure of Tutankamen 1977
Adventure
77395 90 mins C B, V P
The super hero Phenomenal and a clever thief race against time and each other to claim ownership of the Mask of Tutankamen.
MPAA:R
N.P. Films Ltda. — *Wizard Video*

Phil Collins 1983
Music-Performance
75910 17 mins C B, V P
This program presents Phil Collins singing his hit songs "In the Air Tonight," "Through These Walls" and others.

Philip Collins; Hit and Run Music — *Sony Corporation of America*

Phil Collins Live at Perkins Palace **1984**
Music-Performance
72181 60 mins C B, V R, P
The singer from Genesis performs many of the recent hits that have made him popular with audiences around the world.
DIR Broadcasting Inc — *THORN EMI/HBO Video*

Phil Silvers Special: Summer in New York **1960**
Comedy/Variety
52457 60 mins B/W B, V, FO P
Phil Silvers, Carol Lawrence, Carol Haney, Jack Gilford
A comedy special tribute to New York City, which includes sketches, songs, and two dance numbers by Broadway star Carol Haney. The cast of Silvers' "Sgt. Bilko" series makes a cameo appearance.
CBS — *Video Yesteryear*

Philadelphia Experiment, The **1984**
Science fiction
79219 101 mins C B, V R, P
Mitchell Pare, Nancy Allen, Di Cicco, directed by Stewart Raffill
Two World War Two sailors involved in a secret radar experiment in 1943 find themselves in 1984 by accident.
MPAA:PG
New World Pictures — *THORN EMI/HBO Video*

Philadelphia Phillies: Team Highlights **1984**
Baseball
81149 30 mins C B, V P
Pete Rose, Steve Carlton, Mike Schmidt, Joe Morgan, Juan Samuel, Glen Wilson
This series chronicles the one-hundred-year history of the Phillies along with selected highlights from past seasons.
1.Centennial: The First 100 Years 2.1980: The Team That Wouldn't Die 3.1981: Take It From the Top 4.1982: Rolling the Dice 5. 1983: Wheeze Did It 6.1984: Follow Us.
Major League Baseball — *Major League Baseball Productions*

Philadelphia Story, The **1940**
Comedy
47053 112 mins B/W B, V P
Katherine Hepburn, Cary Grant, James Stewart, Ruth Hussey, Roland Young, directed by George Cukor
A strong-willed Philadelphia girl finds the plans for her second marriage going awry when her first husband turns up. Based on the play by Philip Barry.
Academy Awards '40: Best Actor (Stewart); Best Screenplay (Donald Ogden Stewart).
MGM; Joseph L Mankiewicz — *MGM/UA Home Video*

Philco TV Playhouse: "Ernie Barger Is 50" **1953**
Drama
47485 60 mins B/W B, V, FO P
Ed Begley, Carmen Matthews, Howard St. John, directed by Delbert Mann
A live TV drama written by Tad Mosel. Ernie Barger is a middle class manufacturer who discovers that life has passed him by and no one needs him anymore.
NBC — *Video Yesteryear*

Phoenix, The **1978**
Adventure
76892 137 mins C B, V P
Tatsuya Nakadai, Tomisahoro Wakayama, Raoru Yumi, Reiko Ohara
An aging queen summons her marksman to find the Phoenix, a mythical bird that she believes will bring her eternal life. With English subtitles.
JA
Shin Nihon Eiga Co. — *Video Action*

Photonos **1982**
Music-Performance
66244 58 mins C B, V R, P
A video album by the Emmy-winning group Emerald Web. In stereo VHS.
Bob Kat Productions — *Video City Productions*

Piaf **1981**
Musical-Drama/Biographical
58703 115 mins C CED P
Jane Lapotaire
Jane Lapotaire portrays the legendary French singer Edith Piaf in this Broadway performance which won her a Tony Award for Best Actress.
MGM; CBS — *CBS/Fox Video*

Picture Music **1981**
Music-Performance
65377 60 mins C B, V P
A compilation of 14 of the hottest music videos, including top-ten hits by Kim Carnes, America, Steve Miller, J. Geils Band, Billy Squier and Thomas Dolby.
EMI Music — *Vestron Video; Pioneer Video Imports*

Picture of Dorian Gray, The **1945**
Drama
80857 111 mins B/W B, V P

Hurd Hatfield, George Sanders, Donna Reed, Angela Lansbury, Peter Lawford, Lowell Gilmore
An adaptation of the Oscar Wilde novel about a man who stays eternally young while his portrait ages through the years.
Academy Awards '45: Best Cinematography
MGM; Pandro S. Berman — *MGM/UA Home Video*

Piece of the Action, A **1977**
Comedy
80956 135 mins C B, V P
Sidney Poitier, Bill Cosby, James Earl Jones, Denise Nicholas, Hope Clarke, directed by Sidney Poitier
An ex-cop beats two con men at their own game when he convinces them to work for a Chicago community center. Music by Curtis Mayfield.
MPAA:PG
Warner Bros., First Artists Productions — *Warner Home Video*

Pieces **1983**
Horror
65606 90 mins C B, V P
Christopher George
A chain-saw wielding madman roams a college campus in search of human parts for a ghastly jigsaw puzzle.
MPAA:R
Spectacular Trading — *Vestron Video*

Pied Piper, The/Cinderella **1981**
Fairy tales
59706 70 mins C B, V R, P
Animated
A puppet animation version of the two classic fairy tales.
Mark Hall; Brian Cosgrove — *THORN EMI/HBO Video*

Pied Piper of Hamelin, The **1957**
Fairy tales
65291 90 mins C B, V P
Van Johnson, Claude Raines, Jim Backus, Kay Starr, Lori Nelson
This is the evergreen classic of the magical piper who claims an entire village and then disappears with the village children into a mountain when the townspeople fail to keep a promise.
Hal Stanley Productions Unlimited — *Media Home Entertainment*

Pied Piper of Hamelin, The **1984**
Fairy tales
Closed Captioned
73573 60 mins C B, V, CED P
Eric Idle
From "Faerie Tale Theatre" comes the story of a man who had a way with a magic flute and how it charmed the rats out of Hamelin.
Gaylord Productions; Platypus Productions — *CBS/Fox Video*

Pillow Talk **1959**
Comedy-Drama
69032 102 mins C B, V P
Rock Hudson, Doris Day, Tony Randall, Thelma Ritter
An interior decorator and a songwriter and notorious playboy share a party line telephone, but no other interests. In the process of disliking each other, they fall in love.
Universal International — *MCA Home Video*

Pimpernel Smith **1942**
Drama
66392 121 mins B/W B, V P
Leslie Howard, Mary Morris, Francis L. Sullivan, David Tomlinson
An absent-minded archeology professor travels into war-torn Europe to rescue refugees. Also titled: "Mr. V."
British National — *Movie Buff Video; Video Yesteryear*

Pinchcliffe Grand Prix, The **1981**
Comedy
59993 88 mins C B, V R, P
Animated
A master inventor designs the ultimate race car.
MPAA:G
Caprino Film Centre — *Video Gems*

Pink-A-Boo **1985**
Cartoons
80861 56 mins C B, V P
Animated
The rascally Pink Panther returns in this collection of nine classic cartoons.
Mirisch Geoffrey Productions — *MGM/UA Home Video*

Pink at First Sight **1984**
Cartoons
80361 49 mins C B, V P
Animated
The Pink Panther returns in a new collection of his funniest adventures.
Mirisch Geoffrey Productions — *MGM/UA Home Video*

Pink Flamingos **197**
Satire
64844 95 mins C B, V
Divine, David Lochary, Mink Stole, Edith Massey, directed by John Waters
Divine, the dainty 300-pound transvestite, faces the biggest challenge of his/her career when

he/she competes for the title of World's Filthiest Person.
MPAA:R
Saliva Films — *HarmonyVision*

Pink Floyd at Pompeii **1974**
Music-Performance
59079 90 mins C B, V P
Directed by Adrian Maben
The British rock group performs some of its most famous songs in this concert set at a ruined amphitheatre in Pompeii. Songs include "Echoes I & II," "Dark Side of the Moon," and "A Saucerful of Secrets." In stereo.
MPAA:G
April Fools — *HarmonyVision; RCA VideoDiscs; Vestron Video*

Pink Floyd The Wall **1982**
Musical-Drama
65221 95 mins C B, V P
Bob Geldof, directed by Alan Parker
Film version of Pink Floyd's 1979 LP, "The Wall." A surreal, impressionistic tour-de-force about a boy who grows up numb from society's pressures.
MPAA:R
MGM — *MGM/UA Home Video*

Pink Floyd's David Gilmour **1984**
Music video
72896 101 mins C B, V P
David Gilmour, Pete Townshend
This program contains the videos "After the Floyd," "Blue Light" and "All Lovers Are Deranged."
Pink Floyd — *CBS/Fox Video*

Pink Motel **1982**
Comedy
69394 90 mins C B, V R, P
Phyllis Diller, Slim Pickens
This is the story of several people and one hilarious night at a pink stucco motel which caters to couples.
MPAA:R
New Image; Wescom Productions — *THORN EMI/HBO Video*

Pink Panther, The **1964**
Comedy
55587 113 mins C B, V, LV P
Peter Sellers, David Niven, Robert Wagner, Claudia Cardinale
A priceless gem is sought by a wanted jewel thief whose accomplice is the wife of a French police inspector.
United Artists — *CBS/Fox Video; RCA VideoDiscs*

Pink Panther Strikes Again, The **1976**
Comedy
59628 103 mins C B, V, LV P
Peter Sellers, Herbert Lom, Lesley-Anne Down, Colin Blakely, Leonard Rossiter, directed by Blake Edwards
The fourth Panther film has Clouseau being hunted by Chief Inspector Dreyfus, who plans to rid the world of Clouseau once and for all.
MPAA:PG
United Artists — *CBS/Fox Video; RCA VideoDiscs*

Pinocchio **1976**
Musical
06061 76 mins C B, V P
Danny Kaye, Sandy Duncan
Classical story of Pinocchio in musical form.
Rothman and Wahl; Vidronics Company — *United Home Video*

Pinocchio **1968**
Fairy tales
47675 74 mins C B, V P
Collodi's classic tale of the little puppet boy and his adventures in becoming a real boy. Live action actors are combined with puppets from the Prague Marionette Theater.
Ron Merk — *Unicorn Video*

Pinocchio **1978**
Fantasy
56923 90 mins C B, V R, P
Animated
Another version of the classic story about a puppet who becomes a boy. This film adapted from the original 1882 manuscript.
GG Communications — *Video Gems*

Pinocchio **1984**
Fairy tales
Closed Captioned
73146 60 mins C B, V, CED P
Pee Wee Herman, James Coburn, Carl Reiner, Lainie Kazan
Pee Wee Herman is the puppet who wants to be a real little boy in this "Faerie Tale Theatre" adaptation of this childrens classic.
Shelley Duvall — *CBS/Fox Video*

Pinocchio in Outer Space **1964**
Cartoons/Fantasy
47436 71 mins C B, V P
Voices of Arnold Stang, Minerva Pious, Peter Lazer, Conrad Jameson
A new adventure featuring Pinocchio and his friends on a magical trip to Mars.
SFM Entertainment — *RCA/Columbia Pictures Home Video*

Pinwheel Songbook, The 1981
Variety
47383 57 mins C B, V R, P
Dale Engle, George James, Jim Jinkins, Arline Miyazaki, Betty Rozek
Entertainment for preschoolers, featuring songs, stories and characters from the award-winning TV series, "Pinwheel."
Warner Amex Satellite Entertainment Company — *Warner Home Video*

Pioneer Woman 1973
Western/Adventure
77151 74 mins C B, V P
Joanna Pettet, William Shatner, David Janssen, directed by Buzz Kulik
A family encounters hostility when they set up a frontier homestead in Nebraska in 1867.
Filmways — *Worldvision Home Video*

Pippi Goes on Board 1975
Adventure
29347 83 mins C B, V R, P
Inger Nilsson, directed by Olle Hellbom
Pippi's father arrives one day to take her sailing to Taka-Kuka, his island kingdom. She can't bear to leave her friends and jumps off the ship to return home. Based on the classic by Astrid Lindgren.
MPAA:G
N.W. Russo; GG Communications — *Video Gems*

Pippi in the South Seas 1974
Adventure
29236 99 mins C B, V R, P
Inger Nilsson, directed by Olle Hellbom
Pippi and her two friends decide to rescue her father, who is being held captive by a band of pirates. Based on the classic by Astrid Lindgren.
MPAA:G
N.W. Russo; GG Communications — *Video Gems*

Pippi Longstocking 1973
Comedy
50961 99 mins C B, V R, P
Inger Nillson
Mischievous Pippi creates havoc in her town through the antics of her pets, a monkey and a horse. Based on the children's book by Astrid Lindgren.
MPAA:G
N.W. Russo; GG Communications — *Video Gems*

Pippi on the Run 1974
Adventure
58586 99 mins C B, V R, P
The further adventures of Pippi, who, among other things, is "the strongest kid alive."
MPAA:G
N W Russo; GG Communications — *Video Gems*

Pippin 1981
Musical
53134 120 mins C B, V P
Ben Vereen, William Katt, Martha Raye, Chita Rivera
An original video production of Bob Fosse's Broadway smash featuring Ben Vereen recreating his original Tony-Award-winning role.
Sheehan Elkins Video Venture Ltd — *Family Home Entertainment; RCA VideoDiscs; Pioneer Artists*

Piranha 1978
Horror
64300 90 mins C B, V R, P
Bradford Dillman, Heather Menzies, Kevin McCarthy, Keenan Wynn
A rural Texas resort area is plagued by attacks from ferocious man-eating fish which a scientist created to be used as a secret weapon in the Vietnam War.
MPAA:R
New World Pictures — *Warner Home Video*

Piranha II: The Spawning 1982
Horror
78355 88 mins C B, V, LV P
A diving instructor and a biochemist seek to destroy mutations that are murdering tourists at a club.
MPAA:R
New World Pictures — *Embassy Home Entertainment*

Pirate, The 1948
Musical
58869 102 mins C B, V, CED P
Judy Garland, Gene Kelly, Walter Slezak, Gladys Cooper, George Zucco, Reginald Owen, the Nicholas Brothers, directed by Vincente Minnelli
A lonely girl on a remote Caribbean isle dreams of her romantic hero, the legendary pirate Black Macoco. To woo her, a traveling actor masquerades as the pirate. Music by Cole Porter, including "Be a Clown," "Mack the Black" and "You Can Do No Wrong."
MGM; Arthur Freed — *MGM/UA Home Video*

Pirate Movie, The 1982
Musical
60424 98 mins C B, V, CED P
Kristy McNichol, Christopher Atkins, Ted Hamilton
Gilbert and Sullivan's "The Pirates of Penzance" is combined with new pop songs in this tale of fantasy and romance.
MPAA:PG
Twentieth Century Fox — *CBS/Fox Video*

 (For explanation of codes, see USE GUIDE and KEY)

Pirates of Capri, The 1949
Adventure
66393 94 mins B/W B, V P
Louis Hayward, Binnie Barnes
Louis Hayward plays a dual role in this swashbuckler as a daring pirate and a mild-mannered clerk.
Italo English Coproductions — *Movie Buff Video*

Pirates of Penzance, The 1983
Musical/Comedy
64787 112 mins C B, V, LV, CED P
Kevin Kline, Angela Lansbury, Linda Ronstadt, Rex Smith, George Rose
This Gilbert and Sullivan musical comedy is the story of a band of fun-loving pirates and their young apprentice. An adaptation of the award-winning Broadway play. In stereo VHS and laser disc.
Universal — *MCA Home Video; CBS/Fox Video*

Pit, The 1981
Science fiction/Horror
65714 96 mins C B, V P
Sammy Snyders
A 12-year-old autistic boy gets his change for revenge against the people in his town who humiliate him when he stumbles on a huge hole in the forest, at the bottom of which are strange and deadly creatures.
MPAA:R
Bennett Fode — *Embassy Home Entertainment*

Pit and the Pendulum, The 1961
Horror
53519 80 mins C B, V R, P
Vincent Price, John Kerr, Barbara Steele, Luana Anders, directed by Roger Corman
A woman and her lover plan to drive her brother mad, and he responds by locking them in his torture chamber. Loosely based on the Poe story.
American International; Roger Corman — *Warner Home Video; Vestron Video (disc only)*

Pittsburgh Steelers 1984 Team Highlights 1985
Football
70552 70 mins C B, V, FO P
Surprise victories over the Broncos and Raiders made this year one of "A New Beginning" for the Steelmen. Forty-seven minutes of this tape offer a 1984 retrospective of the entire NFL.
NFL Films — *NFL Films Video*

Pittsburgh Steelers: The Championship Years 1982
Football
63162 96 mins C B, V, FO P
Pittsburgh Steelers
Highlights from the first four championship seasons of the 1970's team of the decade.
NFL Films — *NFL Films Video*

Pixote 1981
Drama
47432 127 mins C B, V P
Fernando Ramos Da Silva, Marilla Pera, Jorge Juliao, directed by Hector Babenco
Pixote is a ten-year-old street kid in Sao Paolo, Brazil. When he is sent to a juvenile detention center, he and his companions become hardened to criminal life. In Portuguese with English subtitles.
PR
Embrafilms — *RCA/Columbia Pictures Home Video*

Place Called Today, A 1971
Drama
60416 105 mins C B, V P
Lana Wood
A tale of big city politics where violence and fear in the streets is at the heart of the campaign.
Today Productions — *Monterey Home Video*

Place in the Sun, A 1951
Drama
55542 122 mins B/W B, V, LV R, P
Montgomery Cliff, Elizabeth Taylor, Shelley Winters, directed by George Stevens
A confused, ambitious factory worker in love with a wealthy debutante is threatened with a drab future by a simple working girl. Adapted from Theodore Dreiser's "An American Tragedy."
Academy Awards '51: Best Direction (Stevens); Best Screenplay (Michael Wilson, Harry Brown); Best Scoring (Franz Waxman).
Paramount; George Stevens — *Paramount Home Video; RCA VideoDiscs*

Places in the Heart 1984
Drama
Closed Captioned
80652 113 mins C B, V P
Sally Field, John Malkovich, Danny Glover, Ed Harris, Lindsay Crouse, Amy Madigan, directed by Robert Benton
A young Texas widow and her extended family band together to raise a successful cotton crop in order to save her farm during the Depression. Available in VHS and Beta Hi-Fi.
Academy Awards '84: Best Actress (Field)?Best Original Screenplay (Benton) MPAA:PG
Tri-Star Pictures — *CBS/Fox Video*

Plan 9 from Outer Space 1956
Science fiction/Horror
09112 78 mins B/W B, V, 3/4U P
Bela Lugosi, Tors Johnson, Lyle Talbot, Vampira
UFO's containing strange inhabitants from an unknown planet invade the earth. Includes previews of coming attractions from classic science fiction films.
Golden Turkey Awards for Worst Films of All Time: First Place.
DCA — *Nostalgia Merchant; Sheik Video; Video Yesteryear; Admit One Video*

Planet of the Apes 1968
Science fiction
29164 112 mins C B, V P
Charlton Heston, Roddy McDowall, Kim Hunter, directed by Franklin J. Schaffner
Four American astronauts are hurtled 2,000 years through time and space and crashland in the wilderness of a strange planet. They discover this world is dominated by apes.
EL, SP
20th Century Fox — *Playhouse Video*

Plastic Man 1982
Cartoons
65662 56 mins C B, V P
Animated
With his amazing ability to mold and stretch himself into any shape, Plastic Man stretches himself into new dimensions to play with Baby Plas.
Ruby Spears — *Worldvision Home Video*

Play It Again, Sam 1972
Comedy
38591 85 mins C B, V, LV R, P
Woody Allen, Diane Keaton, Tony Roberts, directed by Herbert Ross
Woody Allen's homage to "Casablanca," in which he plays a movie critic with the recurring hallucination of Humphrey Bogart offering him tips on how to make it with women. Bogart's advice comes in handy when Woody falls in love with his best friend's wife.
MPAA:PG
Paramount — *Paramount Home Video; RCA VideoDiscs*

Play Misty for Me 1971
Mystery/Drama
55551 102 mins C B, V, LV P
Clint Eastwood, Jessica Walter, Donna Mills, directed by Clint Eastwood
A disc jockey meets up with a psychotic fan and she becomes emotionally involved with him. Conflicts arise between the disc jockey's girlfriend and the obsessed fan, who becomes dangerously violent.
MPAA:R
Universal; Jennings Lang Malpaso Co — *MCA Home Video*

Playboy Jazz Festival, Volume 2, The 1984
Music-Performance
78876 90 mins C B, V P
Hosted by Bill Cosby
Some of the world's greatest jazz musicians from Dave Brubeck to Sarah Vaughn are gathered together in this concert taped at the Hollywood Bowl in California. In VHS Dolby Hi-Fi Stereo and Beta Hi-Fi Stereo.
Playboy Productions — *RCA/Columbia Pictures Home Video*

Playboy of the Western World, The 1962
Comedy
63319 96 mins C B, V R, P
Siobhan McKenna, Gary Raymond, directed by Brian Desmond Hurst
An innkeeper's daughter is infatuated with an upstart young playboy. Adapted from the classic play by John Millington Synge.
4 Provinces Films Ltd — *THORN EMI/HBO Video*

Playboy Playmate Workout 1984
Physical fitness
73856 60 mins C B, V, LV, CED P
Two Playboy Playmates take you on a fitness session that combines a workout with fantasies.
Playboy Productions — *CBS/Fox Video*

Playboy Video, Volume I 1982
Variety
63390 85 mins C B, V, LV, CED P
Barbara Carrera, John and Bo Derek, Lonny Chin, Shannon Tweed
This collector's edition contains interviews with John and Bo Derek and actress Barbara Carrera. Photo sessions with Shannon Tweed, 1982 Playmate of the year and Lonny Chin, the first video centerfold, are featured. Also includes a review of Playboy's history and a look at Paris' famed Crazy Horse saloon.
Playboy Enterprises — *CBS/Fox Video*

Playboy Video, Volume II 1983
Variety
64561 81 mins C B, V, LV, CED P
Dudley Moore, Sylvia Kristel, Lynda Wiesmeier, Candy Loving, Duran Duran
The second issue of this video magazine features interviews with Dudley Moore and Sylvia Kristel. Other segments include the "Playmate Playoffs," "Playmate of the Month"

and "Ribald Classics," as well as a look at New Wave rock band Duran Duran.
Playboy Enterprises — *CBS/Fox Video*

Playboy Video, Volume 3 **1983**
Variety
64907 85 mins C B, V, LV, CED P
Cheech and Chong, Marianne Gravatte, Craig Blankenhorn, Charlotte Kemp, Carol Doda
This volume features "Playboy's" 1983 Playmate of the Year, comedians Cheech Marin and Tommy Chong, "Sex in Public Places," December '82 Playmate of the Month, a Ribald Classic, the first topless dancer, and comedy capers.
Playboy Enterprises — *CBS/Fox Video*

Playboy Video, Volume 4 **1983**
Variety
65416 85 mins C B, V, LV, CED P
Willie Nelson, Marilyn Chambers, Barbara Edwards
The fourth volume of this series features Barbara Edwards, Playboy magazine's Miss September 1983, an interview with country music legend Willie Nelson, a tribute to 1980 Playmate of the Year Dorothy Stratten and a profile of x-rated movie star Marilyn Chambers.
Playboy Enterprises — *CBS/Fox Video*

Playboy Video Magazine—Volume 7 **1985**
Variety
Closed Captioned
80654 76 mins C B, V P
Joan Collins, Karen Velez, Pompeo Posar
This volume features an interview look at the 1985 Playmate of the Year Karen Velez and a portrait of renowned photographer Pompeo Posar. Available in VHS and Beta Hi Fi.
Playboy Enterprises — *CBS/Fox Video*

Playboy Video, Volume 5 **1984**
Variety
72189 75 mins C B, V P
"Playboy" magazine's 30th anniversary playmate, Morgan Fairchild and the "Playboy" candid camera are featured.
Playboy Enterprises — *CBS/Fox Video*

Playboy Video, Volume 6 **1984**
Variety
80132 67 mins C B, V P
This sixth volume features an intimate look at Tricia Lange, Miss June 1984 and an interview with G. Gordon Liddy and Timothy Leary. Available in VHS and Beta Hi-Fi.
Playboy Enterprises — *CBS/Fox Video*

Players **1979**
Drama
44594 120 mins C B, V R, P
Ali MacGraw, Dean-Paul Martin, Maximillian Schell, Pancho Gonzales, directed by Anthony Harvey
A young tennis hustler touring Mexico hooks up with a beautiful mysterious older woman. They seem to be from different worlds yet their love grows. She inspires him enough to enter Wimbledon. Several tennis pros appear, including Guillermo Vilas, John McEnroe, and Ilie Nastase.
MPAA:PG
Paramount, Robert Evans — *Paramount Home Video*

Playgirl on the Air **1985**
Variety
77382 60 mins C B, V P
Mark Harmon
This first volume of Playgirl's video-magazine features an interview with Mark Harmon and an intimate look at Chippendale's male burlesque stars.
Ira Ritter; Oak Media Corp. — *U.S.A. Home Video*

Playgirl's Hunkercise **1985**
Physical fitness
70742 120 mins C B, V P
Steve Ralleg, Jim Bolden
Hunky male centerfolds offer tips for developing strength, flexibility, muscle tone, and cardiovascular fitness in this exercise program.
Ritter/Greller Communications; Prism Entertainment — *Prism*

Playhouse 90 **1957**
Drama
80753 83 mins B/W B, V P
Mickey Rooney, Mel Torme, Kim Hunter, Edmond O'Brien, directed by John Frankenbeimer
This episode features a performance of Rod Serling's "The Comedian" which tells the story of a popular TV comedian who makes life miserable for his entourage as the rest of the country laughs at his jokes.
CBS — *Video Yesteryear*

Playmate Review **1983**
Variety
66072 90 mins C B, V, LV, CED P
Ten playmates from Playboy magazine, including 1982 Playmate of the Year Shannon Tweed, are featured in this candid pictorial.
Playboy Enterprises — *CBS/Fox Video*

Playmate Review #2 1984
Variety
Closed Captioned
70235 90 mins C B, V, CED P
Playmates from Playboy magazine are featured in this candid pictorial.
Playboy Enterprises — *CBS/Fox Video*

Playmate Review 3 1985
Variety
77467 59 mins C B, V P
This candid pictorial revue invites you to get up close and personal with six of Playboy's beautiful playmates including Barbara Edwards the 1984 Playmate of the Year.
Playboy Enterprises — *CBS/Fox Video*

Playtime 1967
Comedy
76793 108 mins C B, V P
Jacques Tati, Barbara Dennek, Jacqueline Lecomte, Jack Gautier, directed by Jarques Tati
Mr. Hulot is having a little difficulty keeping an appointment as everything and everybody gets in his way. With English subtitles.
FR
Specta Films — *Embassy Home Entertainment*

Playwrights '56: "The Battler" 1955
Drama
47486 60 mins B/W B, V, FO P
Paul Newman, Dewey Martin, Phyllis Kirk, directed by Arthur Penn
An early dramatic TV appearance by Paul Newman, as a young drifter who meets an interesting cross-section of people while hitchhiking around the country. Based on a story by Ernest Hemingway.
NBC — *Video Yesteryear*

Plaza Suite 1971
Comedy
65735 114 mins C B, V R, P
Walter Matthau, Maureen Stapleton, Barbara Harris, Lee Grant, Louise Sorel
Three sketches set in Suite 719 of New York City's Plaza Hotel, based on the play by Neil Simon.
MPAA:PG
Paramount — *Paramount Home Video*

Pleasure Palace 1980
Drama
80900 92 mins C B, V P
Omar Sharif, Victoria Principal, J.D. Cannon, Jose Ferrer, Hope Lange, Gerald O'Laughlin
A high rolling gambler plays a baccarat game for the ownership of a Las Vegas hotel casino as he vies for the affections of two beautiful women. Available in VHS Stereo and Beta Hi-Fi.
Norman Rosemont Productions — *U.S.A. Home Video*

Plow That Broke the Plains, The/The River 1937
History-US/Documentary
52319 60 mins B/W B, V P, T
Written and directed by Pare Lorentz
Two classic documentaries: "The Plow That Broke the Plains" deals with the New Deal efforts to improve the lot of Oklahoma "Dust Bowl" farmers. "The River" is a poetic history of the Mississippi River and its ecological balance.
US Information Service — *Blackhawk Films; Western Film & Video Inc; Classic Video Cinema Collector's Club; Discount Video Tapes*

Plumber, The 1979
Mystery/Suspense
80275 76 mins C B, V P
Judy Morris, Ivar Karts, Robert Coleby, directed by Peter Weir
A plumber who makes a house call extends his stay to torture a highly educated upper class woman.
Matt Carroll — *Media Home Entertainment*

Pocketful of Miracles 1961
Comedy/Drama
70377 136 mins C B, V P
Bette Davis, Glenn Ford, Peter Falk, Hope Lange, ArthurO'Connell, Ann-Margret, Thomas Mitchell, directed by Frank Capra
A poor, aging apple-seller wants her daughter to marry into a noble Spanish family. When the daughter returns from Spain with the family, the local riff-raff help Apple Annie to present herself as a woman of wealth and culture.
United Artists — *Key Video*

Poco 1977
Adventure
69531 88 mins C B, V, CED P
Chill Wills, Michelle Asburn, John Steadman
A dog named Poco gets separated from the girl who owns her in Yosemite National Park, and Poco tries to find her way home.
MPAA:G
Cinema Shares — *Children's Video Library*

Poco 1977
Drama
81161 88 mins C B, V P
Chill Wills, Michelle Ashburn, John Steadman
This is the story of Poco, a shaggy little dog who travels across the country to search for the young girl who owns him.
Cinema Shares International — *Vestron Video*

Pogo for President—"I Go Pogo" **1984**
Cartoons
70164 120 mins C B, V R, P
Animated, voices of Jonathan Winters, Vincent Price, Ruth Buzzi, Stan Freberg, Jimmy Breslin
Walt Kelly's Pogo Possum becomes an unlikely presidential candidate when Howland Owl proclaims him the winner of a presidential election.
MPAA:PG
Walt Disney Productions — *Walt Disney Home Video*

Point of Terror **1971**
Drama
80659 88 mins C B, V P
Peter Carpenter, Dyanne Thorne, Lory Hansen, Leslie Simms
A handsome rock singer seduces a record company executive's wife in order to further his career.
MPAA:R
Crown International Pictures — *United Home Video*

Police Academy **1984**
Comedy
79555 96 mins C B, V, LV, CED R, P
Steve Guttenberg, Kim Cattrall, Bubba Smith, George Gaynes, directed by Hugh Wilson
Faced with an ultimatum from the mayor, the Los Angeles Police Department seeks to recruit minorities for the force.
MPAA:R
The Ladd Company — *Warner Home Video*

Police Squad! Help Wanted **1982**
Comedy
80062 75 mins C B, V R, P
Leslie Nielsen, Alan North, Rex Hamilton, Peter Lupus
A collection of the first three episodes of the satirical police series about a detective and his captain fighting crime in the big city.
Paramount Pictures — *Paramount Home Video*

Police—The Synchronicity Concert, The **1984**
Music-Performance
78875 75 mins C B, V P
Stewart Copeland, Andy Summers, Sting, directed by Godley and Creme
The new wave group The Police perform their big hits in this concert taped from their "Synchronicity" tour. In VHS Dolby Stereo and Beta Hi-Fi.
A&M Records/I.R.S. Video Corp — *A & M Video; RCA/Columbia Pictures Home Video*

Policewomen **1974**
Crime-Drama
64295 99 mins C B, V P
Sondra Currie, Tony Young, Phil Hoover, Elizabeth Stuart, Jeanie Bell
A female undercover agent must stop a ring of gold smugglers.
MPAA:R
Crown International Pictures — *United Home Video*

Pollyanna **1960**
Comedy-Drama
59062 134 mins C B, V, LV, CED R, P
Hayley Mills, Jane Wyman, Richard Egan, Karl Malden, Nancy Olsen, Adolphe Menjou, Donald Crisp, Agnes Moorehead, Kevin Corcoran
A penniless American orphan comes to live with her aunt in the small town of Harrington, gradually changing the hearts of the entire community.
Academy Awards '60: Honorary Award for the most outstanding Juvenile Performance (Hayley Mills).
Walt Disney — *Walt Disney Home Video*

Pollyanna **1920**
Comedy-Drama
66304 60 mins B/W B, V P, T
Mary Pickford
A young orphan girl is adopted by her cold, embittered aunt and does her best to bring joy and gladness to all the new people she meets. Silent with music score.
Mary Pickford Company — *Blackhawk Films*

Poltergeist **1982**
Horror
47780 114 mins C B, V, CED P
Jobeth Williams, Craig T. Nelson, Beatrice Straight, Heather O'Rourke, Zelda Rubinstein, directed by Tobe Hooper
The presence of menacing spirits terrorizes a middle-class family, transporting the youngest member into a "world beyond."
MPAA:R
MGM; United Artists — *MGM/UA Home Video*

Pom-Pom Girls, The **1976**
Comedy
48481 90 mins C B, V P
Robert Carradine, Jennifer Ashley
High school seniors, intent on having one last fling before graduating, get involved in crazy antics, clumsy romances, and football rivalries.
MPAA:R
Crown International — *United Home Video*

Poochie **1984**
Cartoons
80976 30 mins C B, V P
Animated

Poochie is the pink pup with a heart of gold who travels to Cairo with his micro-chip sidekick Hermes to answer a young boy's distress call.
DIC Enterprises — *Children's Video Library*

Poor Little Rich Girl, The 1917
Comedy-Drama
66118 64 mins B/W B, V P, T
Mary Pickford
Mary Pickford received raves in this film, in which she portrayed Gwendolyn, one of her most tender child performances. Organ score.
Adolph Zukor — *Blackhawk Films*

Pop Always Pays 1940
Comedy
73698 67 mins B/W B, V P
Dennis O'Keefe, Leon Errol, Adele Pearce
A father gets in a jam when he has to make good on a bet with his daughter's boyfriend.
RKO — *RKO HomeVideo*

Pop Goes the Cork 1922
Comedy
59409 87 mins B/W B, V P, T
Max Linder
Three films by the man Chaplin referred to as his "professor," Max Linder: "Be My Wife," "Seven Years Bad Luck," and "The Three Must-Get-Theres." Linder was the foremost film comedian in early twentieth-century France, and made these three films during a stay in America.
Max Linder Productions — *Blackhawk Films*

Pope of Greenwich Village, The 1984
Drama
70392 122 mins C B, V P
Eric Roberts, Mickey Rourke, Daryl Hannah, Geraldine Page, Kenneth McMillan, Bert Young, directed by Stuart Rosenberg
A film about relationships, neighbors and friends set in New York's Greenwich Village, where the characters learn about the problems of self-deception, thieving and grandiose scheming.
MPAA:R
MGM/UA — *MGM/UA Home Video*

Popeye 1980
Comedy/Musical
55538 114 mins C B, V, LV R, P
Robin Williams, Shelley Duvall, Roy Walston, Paul Dooley, directed by Robert Altman
The cartoon sailor brought to life is on a search to find his long-lost father. Along the way, he meets Olive Oyl and adopts little Sweet Pea. Script by Jules Feiffer, music by Harry Nilsson.
MPAA:PG
Paramount; Robert Evans — *Paramount Home Video; RCA VideoDiscs*

Popeye and Friends in Outer Space 197?
Cartoons
65695 60 mins C B, V P
Animated
Popeye and Olive Oyl take their act into the ozone and beyond. As always, they get into big trouble with their arch enemy, Bluto. Luckily for Popeye and all concerned, cans of spinach are not as rare in outer space as Haley's Comet.
Paramount; Max Fleischer — *Media Home Entertainment*

Popeye and Friends in the South Seas 1961
Cartoons
81094 59 mins C B, V P
Animated, voice of Jack Mercer, Jackson Beck, Mae Questel, Arnold Stang
Join Popeye, Olive Oyl, Wimpy and Sweet Pea as they embark on a series of comedic adventures.
King Features — *Media Home Entertainment*

Popeye and Friends in the Wild West 1984
Cartoons
65370 60 mins C B, V P
Animated
The famous spinach eating sailor is back in ten gallon hat and spurs for uproarious western adventures. Also included in this cartoon collection are Krazy Kat, Beetle Bailey and Snuffy Smith.
Max Fleischer — *Media Home Entertainment*

Popeye the Sailor 193?
Cartoons
53800 54 mins C B, V, FO P
Animated
This cartoon package includes "Popeye Meets Aladdin and His Wonderful Lamp," "Popeye Meets Ali Baba and His 40 Thieves," and "Popeye the Sailor Meets Sinbad the Sailor."
Paramount; Max Fleischer — *Video Yesteryear; Western Film & Video Inc*

Popeye—Travelin' On About Travel 1984
Travel
76652 60 mins C B, V P
Animated
Popeye and Olive Oyl visit foreign and exotic lands in this hilarious program.
Media Home Entertainment — *Media Home Entertainment*

Poppies Are Also Flowers 1966
Adventure
59840 90 mins C B, V P
Senta Berger, Stephen Boyd, Yul Brynner, Angie Dickinson, Rita Hayworth, Trevor Howard,

Trini Lopez, E. G. Marshall, Eli Wallach, Omar Sharif
Also known as "The Poppy Is Also a Flower," this Ian Fleming thriller about the illegal world drug trade focuses on how the poppies converted into heroin are being channeled into the U.S.
Terence Young — *Embassy Home Entertainment*

Porky Pig's Screwball Comedies **1952**
Cartoons
81573 59 mins C B, V P
Animated, voice of Mel Blanc
This compilation of Porky Pig's classic cartoons includes "You Ought to Be in Pictures" "Boobs in the Woods" and "Wearing of the Grim".
Warner Bros. — *Warner Home Video*

Porky's **1982**
Comedy
64908 94 mins C B, V, LV, CED P
Dan Monahan, Wyatt Knight, Tony Ganios, Mark Herrier, Cyril O'Reilly, Roger Wilson
Set in south Florida in the early 1950's, this irreverent comedy follows the misadventures of six youths of Angel Beach High School. Their main interest is girls.
MPAA:R
Melvin Simon Productions; Astral Bellevue Pathe — *CBS/Fox Video*

Porky's II: The Next Day **1983**
Comedy
65492 100 mins C B, V P
Bill Wiley, Dan Monahan, Wyatt Knight, Cyril O'Reilly, Roger Wilson, Tony Ganious, Mark Herrier, Scott Colomby
The Angel Beach gang stir up their sleepy southern Florida town when they join forces to participate in the high school project, an innocent sounding tribute to Shakespeare. What starts out as a simple school project soon explodes into a townwide controversy... until our ingenious heroes strike back with an explosively comic scheme.
MPAA:R
Astral Bellevue Pathe Inc; 20th Century Fox Films — *CBS/Fox Video*

Port of Call **1948**
Drama/Romance
65628 100 mins B/W B, V P
Nine-Christine Jonsson, Bengt Elkund, directed by Ingmar Bergman
A direct, almost documentary telling of the love that grows between a seaman and a girl from reform school who has lost her self-respect.
Janus Films — *Embassy Home Entertainment*

Port of New York **1949**
Crime-Drama
47466 82 mins B/W B, V, FO P
Scott Brady, Yul Brynner, K. T. Stevens
A narcotics gang is smuggling large quantities of drugs into New York. A government agent poses as a gang member in order to infiltrate the mob and get the goods on them.
Eagle Lion — *Video Yesteryear; Movie Buff Video; Discount Video Tapes*

Portnoy's Complaint **1972**
Comedy-Drama
51969 101 mins C B, V R, P
Richard Benjamin, Karen Black, Lee Grant
The screen adaptation of Philip Roth's novel follows the frustrating experiences of a sexually obsessed young man as he relates them to his psychiatrist.
MPAA:R
Warner Bros — *Warner Home Video*

Portrait of a Showgirl **1982**
Drama
79195 100 mins C B, V P
Lesley Ann Warren, Rita Moreno, Tony Curtis, Dianne Kay, Howard Morris
An inexperienced showgirl learns the ropes of Las Vegas life from a veteran of the Vegas stages.
Hamner Prods — *Prism*

Portrait of a Stripper **1979**
Drama
80922 100 mins C B, V P
Lesley-Ann Warren, Edward Hermann, Vic Tayback, Sheree North, directed by John Alonzo
A widowed mother works part-time as a stripper to support her son. Trouble arises when her father-in-law attempts to prove that she is an unfit mother.
Moonlight Prods; Filmways — *Vestron Video*

Poseidon Adventure, The **1972**
Adventure
09094 117 mins C B, V, CED P
Gene Hackman, Ernest Borgnine, Shelley Winters, Red Buttons, Jack Albertson, Carol Lynley
The S.S. Poseidon, on her last voyage from New York to Athens, is capsized by a tidal wave on New Year's Eve.
Academy Awards '72: Best Song ("The Morning After"); Special Effects. MPAA:PG EL, SP
Twentieth Century-Fox; Irwin Allen — *CBS/Fox Video*

Possession **1981**
Horror
79308 97 mins C B, V P
Isabelle Adjani, Sam Neill, Heinz Bennent, Margit Carstensen, Shaun Lawtor

When A secret agent returns from a long mission, he notices that his wife has been acting very strangely.
MPAA:R
Limelight International Films — *Vestron Video*

Postman Always Rings Twice, The 1981
Drama
53555 122 mins C B, V, CED P
Jack Nicholson, Jessica Lange, John Colicos, Anjelica Huston, Michael Lerner, John P. Ryan, directed by Bob Rafelson
A luckless drifter becomes attracted to the unhappy wife of a middle-aged roadhouse owner, and the two attempt to kill the husband. Based on James M. Cain's novel.
MPAA:R
Bob Rafelson; Charles Mulvehill;
MGM — *CBS/Fox Video*

Postmark for Danger/Quicksand 1956
Mystery
76919 155 mins B/W B, V P
Terry Moore, Robert Beatty, Mickey Rooney, Jeanne Cagney, Peter Lorre
A "film noir" double feature: In "Postmark for Danger," a young actress returns from the dead to find a criminal and in "Quicksand" a mechanic becomes indebted to the mob when he borrows extra money for a date.
RKO; United Artists — *United Home Video*

Postnatal Exercise Program 1984
Physical fitness
81537 55 mins C B, V P
This is an exercise program designed for the unique conditions of the postnatal woman.
AM Available
American College of Obstsetricians nad Gynecologinsts — *Feeling Fine Programs*

Postnatal (Rehabilitation and Injury) 1978
Physical fitness
52756 30 mins C B, V P
Hosted by Ann Dugan
Reconditioning exercises after childbirth, including both specific-area and total-body movements to gradually improve muscle tone. Part of the "Rehabilitation and Injury" series.
Health 'N Action — *RCA/Columbia Pictures Home Video*

Pot O' Gold 1941
Musical
13045 87 mins B/W B, V P, T
Paulette Goddard, James Stewart, Horace Heidt Band
Girl's father, who hates dance bands, schedules Heidt on his radio quiz show.
United Artists — *Blackhawk Films; Movie Buff Video; Video Yesteryear; Sheik Video; Video Connection; Cable Films; Kartes Productions; Classic Video Cinema Collector's Club*

Pot Shots 1982
Documentary
66238 65 mins C B, V R, P
A candid look at the home-growing of marijuana.
Unknown — *Video City Productions*

Potemkin 1925
Film-History
08699 67 mins B/W B, V, 3/4U P
Alexander Antonov, Grigory Alexandrov, Vladimir Barsky, Mikhail Gomorov, directed by Sergei Eisentein
Recounts the heroic mutiny of Russian sailors in 1905.
Russian — *International Historic Films; Blackhawk Films; Sheik Video; Video Yesteryear; Budget Video; Western Film & Video Inc; Discount Video Tapes; Classic Video Cinema Collector's Club*

Powder Keg 1970
Adventure
77150 93 mins C B, V P
Rod Taylor, Dennis Cole, Michael Ansara, Fernando Lamas, Tisha Sterling
A railroad company hires a team of investigators to retrieve a hijacked train during the early 1900's.
Filmways — *Worldvision Home Video*

Powdersmoke Range 1935
Western
64414 71 mins B/W B, V, 3/4U P
Harry Carey, Hoot Gibson, Tom Tyler
A crooked frontier politician plots to steal valuable ranch property, until the law rides into town.
RKO — *Nostalgia Merchant*

Power, The 1981
Football
50651 24 mins C B, V, FO R, P
San Diego Chargers
The passing attack of Dan Fouts to John Jefferson, Kellen Winslow, and Charley Joiner was nearly unstoppable in 1980. Coach Don Coryell's 1980 Chargers travelled to the AFC Championship Game where they met the Oakland Raiders.
NFL Films — *NFL Films Video*

Power, The 1983
Horror
73032 87 mins C B, V P
As a small Aztec idol passes down from generation to generation the power of the idol becomes stronger.

 (For explanation of codes, see USE GUIDE and KEY)

MPAA:R
Film Ventures — *Vestron Video*

Power Dive 1941
Drama
66394 69 mins B/W B, V P
Richard Arlen, Jean Parker, Cliff Edwards
Test pilots from a large aviation company experience danger in the skies and romance on the ground.
Paramount — *Movie Buff Video*

Power Play 1978
Suspense
65012 95 mins C B, V, 3/4U P
Peter O'Toole, David Hemmings, Donald Pleasance
A young army colonel of a small European country joins forces with rebels to overthrow the government. After the coup, it is discovered that one of the rebels is a traitor.
Peter Cooper; Ronald I. Cohen — *Nostalgia Merchant; Media Home Entertainment*

Prairie Moon 1938
Western/Musical
44806 58 mins B/W B, V P, T
Gene Autry, Smiley Burnette
Gene becomes guardian of a gangster's sons and gets involved with cattle rustlers.
Republic — *Blackhawk Films; Video Connection*

Pray TV 1980
Satire
80680 92 mins C B, V P
Dabney Coleman
A sly con man turns a failing television station into a profitable one when the station starts to broadcast around-the-clock religious programming.
MPAA:PG
Orion Pictures — *Vestron Video*

Precious Pupp 198?
Cartoons
78071 51 mins C B, V P
Animated
This program presents the most charming dog alive with his owner in some wacky adventures.
Worldvision Home Video Inc — *Worldvision Home Video*

Predators of the Sea 1977
Documentary/Fishes
29166 93 mins C B, V R, P
An underwater program that reveals the fascinating world of the creatures of the deep. Highlights include a thrilling fight between an octopus and a deadly moray eel, a look at the seagoing crocodile, and deadly sharks in action.
Bill Burrud Productions — *Walt Disney Home Video*

Pregnancy Exercise Program 1984
Physical fitness
81538 51 mins C B, V P
This is an exercise program designed for pregnant women.
AM Available
American College of Obstetricians and Gynecologists — *Feeling Fine Programs*

Prelude to War 1942
World War II/Documentary
08907 53 mins B/W B, V P
Directed by Frank Capra
A compact look at the events of 1931-39; includes a series of contrasts between free societies and totalitarian governments. From the "Why We Fight" series.
Academy Awards '42: Best Documentary.
US War Department — *Budget Video; Western Film & Video Inc; Discount Video Tapes; MPI Home Video; National AudioVisual Center; Spotlite Video*

Premature Burial 1962
Horror
80929 81 mins C B, V P
Ray Milland, Richard Ney, Hazel Court, Heather Anger, directed by Roger Corman
A cataleptic Englishman's worst fears come true when he is buried alive by a mad doctor. Based upon the story by Edgar Allen Poe.
Santa Clara Productions — *Vestron Video*

Premiere Adventure of Super Ted, The 1984
Cartoons
80050 48 mins C B, V R, P
Animated
Super Ted and Spottyman travel around the world to battle the evil trio of Bulk, Skeleton, and Texas Pete.
Sirol Animation Limited — *Walt Disney Home Video*

Premiere of "A Star Is Born" 1954
Film-History
42959 30 mins B/W B, V, FO P
Doris Day, Judy Garland, Edward G. Robinson, James Dean, Elizabeth Taylor, Joan Crawford, Debbie Reynolds, Shelley Winters, Kim Novak, Lucille Ball, Desi Arnaz
From the lobby of the Pantages Theater in Hollywood, George Fisher, Jack Carson, George Jessel, and Larry Finley interview the brightest of Hollywood's stars of that era including Dean Martin, Hedda Hopper, Liberace (and his mother), Peggy Lee, Ray Bolger, and countless others.

Unknown — *Video Yesteryear*

Premonition, The 1975
Horror
66267 94 mins C B, V P
Sharon Farrel, Edward Bell, Danielle Brisebois
A parapsychologist searching for a missing child is drawn into a frightening maze of dream therapy and communication with the dead.
MPAA:PG
Robert Allen Schnitzer — *Embassy Home Entertainment*

Prenatal (Rehabilitation and Injury) 1978
Physical fitness/Pregnancy
52755 30 mins C B, V P
Hosted by Ann Dugan
Conditioning exercises for pregnant women including both specific-area and total body movements to gradually improve muscle tone. Part of the "Rehabilitation and Injury" series.
Health 'N Action — *RCA/Columbia Pictures Home Video*

Preppies 1982
Comedy
77414 83 mins C B, V P
Lynda Weismeyer, directed by Chuck Vincent
A war erupts when a preppie and his degenerate cousin fight over a fifty-million dollar inheritance.
Chuck Vincent — *Vestron Video*

Presenting Johnny Mathis 196?
Music-Performance
12822 46 mins B/W B, V, FO P
Johnny Mathis
Johnny Mathis in concert performing some of his best-known songs.
Unknown — *Video Yesteryear*

Pretty Baby 1978
Drama
38602 109 mins C B, V, LV R, P
Brooke Shields, Keith Carradine, Susan Sarandon, directed by Louis Malle
A photographer obsessed with the prostitutes in New Orleans red-light district, circa 1917, is bewitched by a twelve-year-old child prostitute. A sincere, humân study of a controversial subject.
MPAA:R
Paramount — *Paramount Home Video; RCA VideoDiscs*

Prevent Back Pain 1984
Back disorders/Physical fitness
81540 46 mins C B, V P
This is an exercise and relaxation program designed to help people with mild or chronic back pain.
AM Available
American Academy of Orthopaedic Surgeons — *Feeling Fine Programs*

Prey, The 1980
Horror
73025 80 mins C B, V R, P
Debbie Thurseon, Steve Bond
A predator is looking for a mate in the Colorado Rockies and kills five campers in the process.
MPAA:R
Unknown — *THORN EMI/HBO Video*

Pride and Passion 1984
Basketball
78354 58 mins C B, V P
Here are highlights from the 1984 NBA Playoffs and Championship Finals along with basketball bloopers in this program.
NBA — *Embassy Home Entertainment*

Pride and Prejudice 1940
Drama
59135 114 mins B/W B, V P
Greer Garson, Laurence Olivier, Edmund Gwenn, Edna May Oliver, Mary Boland, Maureen O'Sullivan, Ann Rutherford, Frieda Inescort
Jane Austen's classic novel of a proud and spirited English girl's fight against the prejudice of the man she loves.
MGM; Hunt Stromberg — *MGM/UA Home Video*

Pride and the Passion, The 1957
Drama
69382 132 mins C B, V, CED P
Cary Grant, Frank Sinatra, Sophia Loren, directed by Stanley Kramer
A small group of resistance fighters battling for Spanish independence in 1810 must smuggle a 6-ton cannon across the rugged terrain of Spain.
United Artists — *CBS/Fox Video*

Pride of Eagles Football 1980
Football
45129 24 mins C B, V, FO R, P
Philadelphia Eagles
Highlights of the 1979 Philadelphia Eagles football season.
NFL Films — *NFL Films Video*

Pride of the Yankees, The 1942
Biographical/Drama
65009 128 mins B/W B, V, LV, CED P
Gary Cooper, Teresa Wright, Babe Ruth

This is the classic story of baseball phenomenon Lou Gehrig who was stifled at the peak of his career by an incurable disease.
Samuel Goldwyn — *CBS/Fox Video*

Prime Cat **1972**
Drama
Closed Captioned
70695 86 mins C B, V P
Lee Marvin, Gene Hackman, Sissy Spacek, Angel Tompkins, Gregory Walcott, directed by Michael Ritchie
This film features drug trafficking, prostitution, extortion, loan sharking, fisticuffs and gangsters getting ground into mincemeat. Recorded with Hi-Fi sound.
CBS Theatrical Films — *Key Video*

Prime Cuts **1984**
Music-Performance
72190 45 mins C B, V P
A collection of rock videos featuring performances by Quiet Riot, Toto, Bonnie Tyler and other notables.
CBS Fox Video Music — *CBS/Fox Video*

Prime Cuts—Jazz & Beyond **1985**
Music-Performance/Video
70659 35 mins C B, V P
Miles Davis, Herbie Hancock, Chuck Mangione, Al DiMeola, Andreas Wollenweider, Hiroshima, Weather Report, Clark/Duke Project
This program compiles conceptual videos from some popular/jazz composers. The eight numbers come in Hi-Fi stereo on both formats, with digital mastering.
CBS Music Video Enterprises — *CBS/Fox Video*

Prime Cuts—Red Hots **1984**
Music video
80338 35 mins C B, V P
A collection of eight conceptual music videos from groups such as Wham! and REO Speedwagon.
CBS Music Video Enterprises — *CBS/Fox Video*

Prime Suspect **1982**
Drama
70257 96 mins C B, V P
Mike Farrell, Teri Garr, Veronica Cartwright, Lane Smith
The tranquil life of a happily married man is shattered when he becomes a suspect in a series of sex murders.
Tisch/Avnet TV — *U.S.A. Home Video*

Prince and the Pauper, The **1937**
Drama
64933 118 mins B/W CED P
Errol Flynn, Claude Rains, Alan Hale, Billy and Bobby Mauch
Young Edward VI changes places with a street urchin.
Warner Bros — *CBS/Fox Video*

Prince and the Pauper, The **1962**
Adventure
80356 93 mins C B, V R, P
Guy Williams, Laurence Naismith, Donald Houston, Jane Asher, Walter Hudd
A prince and a poor young boy swap their clothes and identities, thus causing a lot of confusion for their families.
Buena Vista — *Walt Disney Home Video*

Prince and the Pauper, The **1978**
Adventure
80274 113 mins C B, V P
Oliver Reed, Raquel Welch, Mark Lester, Ernest Borghine, directed by Richard Fleischer
When an English prince and a pauper discover that they have identical appearances, they decide to trade places with each other.
MPAA:PG
Warner Bros — *Media Home Entertainment*

Prince and the Showgirl, The **1957**
Comedy
47619 127 mins C B, V R, P
Laurence Olivier, Marilyn Monroe, Sybil Thorndike, directed by Laurence Olivier
An American showgirl in 1910 London is wooed by the Prince of Carpathia. Part of the "A Night at the Movies" series, this tape simulates a 1957 movie evening, with a Sylvester the Cat cartoon, "Greedy for Tweety," a newsreel and coming attractions for "Spirit of St. Louis."
Warner Bros — *Warner Home Video*

Prince Charming Revue, The **1983**
Music-Performance
65003 74 mins C B, V, CED P
England's New Wave rock group, Adam and the Ants, performs its hit singles in an elaborately staged show including a hand-painted pirate ship and castle backdrops. In stereo.
CBS — *CBS/Fox Video*

Prince Jack **1983**
Drama/Biographical
81416 100 mins C B, V P
Lloyd Nolan, Dana Andrews, Robert Guillaume, Cameron Mitchell

This film looks at the turbulent political career of President John F. Kennedy.
Jim Milio — *VCL Home Video*

Prince of Central Park, The 1975
Drama
77387 75 mins C B, V P
Ruth Gordon, T.J. Hargrave, Lisa Richard, Mark Vahanian
A runaway brother and sister learn a lesson from an elderly widow they meet in Central Park.
Lorimar Productions — *U.S.A. Home Video*

Prince of the City 1981
Drama
51994 167 mins C B, V, LV R, P
Treat Williams, Jerry Orbach, Richard Foronjy, Don Billett, Kenny Marino, directed by Sidney Lumet
An undercover cop is pressured into becoming an informant in an FBI investigation of corruption among police officers.
MPAA:R
Orion Pictures — *Warner Home Video; RCA VideoDiscs*

Princess and the Call Girl, The 1984
Adventure
81397 90 mins C B, V P
Carol Levy, Shannah Hall, Victor Bevine, directed by Radley Metzger
A call girl asks her lookalike roomate to take her place in Monaco for a lavishly erotic weekend. Available in VHS Stereo and Beta Hi-Fi.
Radley Metzger — *Monterey Home Video*

Princess and the Pea, The 1984
Fairy tales
Closed Captioned
73853 60 mins C B, V, LV, CED P
Liza Minnelli, Tom Conti, Pat McCormick, Beatrice Straight, directed by Tony Bill
From "Faerie Tale Theatre" comes the story of a princess who tries to prove that she's a blueblood by feeling the bump of a tiny pea under the thickness of twenty mattresses.
Gaylord Productions; Platypus Productions — *CBS/Fox Video*

Princess and the Pirate, The 1944
Comedy
80948 94 mins C B, V P
Bob Hope, Walter Slezak, Walter Brennan, Virginia Mayo, Victor McLagen, Bing Crosby
A hammy vaudevillian performer falls in love with a beautiful princess when they are captured by buccaneers on the Spanish Main.
Samuel Goldwyn — *Embassy Home Entertainment*

Principles of Paneling 1984
Home improvement
Closed Captioned
77261 30 mins C B, V P
This is a step-by-step demonstration of how to panel a room.
You Can Do It Videos — *You Can Do It Videos*

Prison de Mujeres 198?
Drama
80494 97 mins C B, V P
Carmen Montejo, Hilda Aguirre, Zully Keith, Susana Kamini
The shocking life of women who are imprisoned in a Spanish prison is depicted in this film which takes place in turn-of-the-century Spain. Dialogue in Spanish.
SP
Spanish — *Unicorn Video*

Prisoner, The 1968
Fantasy/Adventure
79701 120 mins C B, V P
Patrick McGoohan, Angelo Muscat, Leo McKern, Peter Wyngarde 17 pgms
One of the most ambitious television series ever produced. Patrick McGoohan stars as "Number 6", a prisoner in a surreal village supervised by a mayoral "Number 2." Plots revolve around "Number 2's" efforts to find out why he is imprisoned, identify number 1, escape from the village.
Associated TV Corp — *MPI Home Video*

Prisoner of Second Avenue, The 1974
Comedy-Drama
52707 105 mins C B, V R, P
Jack Lemmon, Anne Bancroft, Gene Saks, Elizabeth Wilson, directed by Melvin Frank
A New Yorker in his late forties faces the future, without a job or any confidence in his ability, with the help of his understanding wife. Based on the Broadway play by Neil Simon.
MPAA:PG
Warner Bros — *Warner Home Video*

Prisoner of Zenda, The 1952
Adventure
47400 101 mins C B, V P
Stewart Granger, Deborah Kerr, Louis Calhern, James Mason
A wanderer who closely resembles the king of a small European country becomes involved in a murder plot. Based on the novel by Anthony Hope.
MGM — *MGM/UA Home Video*

Prisoner of Zenda, The 1979
Comedy
69033 108 mins C B, V P
Peter Sellers, Jeremy Kemp, Lynne Frederick, Lionel Jeffries, Elke Sommer
Peter Sellers stars in the double role of Prince Rudolph of Ruritania and Syd, the cockney cab driver who doubles for Rudolph when the Prince is imprisoned by his jealous brother Michael.
Universal — *MCA Home Video*

Prisoners of the Lost Universe 1984
Science fiction
70224 94 mins C B, V P
Richard Hatch, Kay Lenz, John Saxon
Unwittingly transported to a hostile alternate universe by a renegade scientist, two terrified humans search desperately for the hidden Dimensional Door that is their only hope of escape.
John Hardy; Denis Johnson Jr — *VCL Home Video*

Pritikin Promise, The 1984
Physical fitness
76649 90 mins C B, V P
Hosted by Lorne Greene
This program tells how the Pritikin Promise assures you that you will be on your way to a longer, healthier life in just 28 days.
Robert Katz — *Media Home Entertainment*

Pritikin Promise Home Exercise Program, The 1984
Physical fitness
76651 60 mins C B, V P
Hosted by Lorne Greene
Follow world triathalon champion Dave Scott and the Pritikin Exercise team through a series of three exercise levels.
Robert Katz — *Media Home Entertainment*

Private Benjamin 1980
Comedy
58245 110 mins C B, V, LV R, P
Goldie Hawn, Eileen Brennan, Albert Brooks, Robert Webber, Barbara Barrie, Mary Kay Place, directed by Howard Zieff
A pampered, spoiled, upper-middle-class princess rebounds from a bad marriage by joining the army.
MPAA:R
Warner Bros — *Warner Home Video; RCA VideoDiscs*

Private Buckaroo 1942
Musical
07229 65 mins B/W B, V, FO P
The Andrews Sisters, Harry James and his Orchestra, Joe E. Lewis, Dick Foran
War-time entertainment in which Harry James and his Orchestra get drafted.
Universal — *Video Yesteryear; Cable Films; Budget Video; Discount Video Tapes; Kartes Productions; See Hear Industries*

Private Eyes, The 1980
Comedy
57231 91 mins C B, V, LV, CED P
Don Knotts, Tim Conway, Trisha Noble, Bernard Fox
Two bungling sleuths are engaged to investigate two deaths and are led on a merry chase through secret passages, past exploding bombs, and finally to a meeting with a ghostly adversary.
Lang Elliot; Wanda Dell; TriStar Pictures — *Vestron Video; Time Life Video*

Private Hell 36 1954
Mystery/Drama
81016 81 mins B/W B, V P
Ida Lupino, Howard Duff, Steve Cocharan, directed by Don Siegel
Two detectives turn greedy after they recover some stolen money from a robbery.
Filmmakers — *Spotlite Video*

Private Lessons 1981
Comedy
59677 83 mins C B, V, LV, CED P
Eric Brown, Sylvia Kristel, Howard Hesseman
A teenage boy is left alone for the summer in the care of an alluring maid and a scheming chauffer.
MPAA:R
Barry and Enright — *MCA Home Video*

Private Life of Don Juan 1934
Adventure
11250 97 mins B/W B, V, FO P
Douglas Fairbanks Sr., Merle Oberon, directed by Alexander Korda
Tired of his romantic reputation, Don Juan still finds his life complicated by an imposter using his identity.
United Artists — *Video Yesteryear; Movie Buff Video; Discount Video Tapes; Sheik Video; Cable Films; Budget Video; Western Film & Video Inc; Kartes Productions; See Hear Industries*

Private Life of Henry VIII, The 1933
Drama
08693 97 mins B/W B, V P
Charles Laughton, Elsa Lanchester, Robert Dunat, Merle Oberon, directed by Alexander Korda
The life and loves of infamous English King Henry VIII are lustily portrayed in this film, a tour de force for Charles Laughton.

Academy Awards '33: Best Actor (Laughton); Film Daily Poll Ten Best Pictures of the Year '33.
UA; Alexander Korda — *VCII; Blackhawk Films; Sheik Video; Cable Films; Video Connection; Video Yesteryear; Budget Video; Discount Video Tapes; Western Film & Video Inc; Cinema Concepts*

Private Lives of Elizabeth and Essex, The **1939**
Drama
73970 106 mins C B, V P
Bette Davis, Errol Flynn, Vincent Price, Nanette Fabray, Olivia de Havilland, directed by Michael Curtiz
The aging Queen Elizabeth of England must make a choice between her crown or the love of the Second Earl of Essex.
Warner Bros — *Key Video*

Private Passions **1985**
Drama
80322 86 mins C B, V P
Sybil Danning
A sultry stepmother gives her teenaged American cousin a lesson in love during his European vacation.
Independent — *Prism*

Private Popsicle **1982**
Comedy
68242 111 mins C B, V, CED P
Zachi Noy, Jonathan Segall, Yftach Katzur
A hilarious sex comedy starring Europe's popular Popsicle team. Dubbed in English.
MPAA:R
Noah Films — *MGM/UA Home Video*

Private School **1983**
Drama
65338 82 mins C B, V, LV, CED P
Phoebe Cates, Sylvia Kristel, Ray Walston
Two high school girls from the exclusive Cherryvale Academy for Women compete for the affections of a young man from nearby Freemount Academy for Men, while Cherryvale's headmistress is trying to raise funds to build a new wing.
MPAA:R
Universal — *MCA Home Video*

Privates on Parade **1984**
Comedy
80647 107 mins C B, V R, P
John Cleese, Denis Quilley, Simon Jones, Joe Melia, Nicola Pagett
This film centers around the comic antics of an Army song and dance unit entertaining the troops in the Malayan jungle during the late 40's.
MPAA:R
Handmade Films — *THORN EMI/HBO Video*

Prize Fighter, The **1979**
Comedy
63384 99 mins C B, V P
Tim Conway, Don Knotts
Two fight managers unknowingly get involved with a powerful gangster, who convinces one of them to fight in a fixed championship match.
MPAA:PG
New World Pictures — *Media Home Entertainment*

Prizzi's Honor **1985**
Comedy-Drama
70737 130 mins C B, V P
Jack Nicholson, Kathleen Turner, Robert Loggia, John Randolph, William Hickey, Lee Richardson, directed by John Huston.
Black humor and subtlety rule in this gangster film. The love between two rival mob assassins conflicts with one's family loyalty, and leads to deception and intrigue.
MPAA:R
ABC Motion Pictures — *Vestron Video*

Pro-Karate Championships (1976-1981) **1981**
Martial arts
59570 60 mins C B, V P
Highlights of the 1981 Full Contact Matches conducted under the auspices of the U.S. Professional Karate Association.
Professional Karate Assn — *Mastervision*

Pro Wrestling Illustrated **1985**
Sports
77184 60 mins C B, V P
Gordon Solie hosts this look at the most memorable wrestling matches and its peerless champions.
Independent Media Marketing — *Vestron Video*

Problems, 1950's Style **195?**
Television/Interview
62692 120 mins B/W B, V, 3/4U P
Three TV panel discussion/interview programs from the 1950's: "Stand Up and Be Counted!" (1956), in which audience members and guests discuss their problems; "People in Conflict," where guests ask advice of the panel; and "The Verdict Is Yours," with an actual courtroom trial.
CBS et al — *Shokus Video*

Prodigal Boxer, The **1980**
Adventure/Martial arts
56931 90 mins C B, V R, P
The great Kung-fu masters from all over China assemble for a championship, but anyone can

 (For explanation of codes, see USE GUIDE and KEY)

participate if willing to die if defeated. A student of martial arts decides to risk his life for revenge.
MPAA:R
Fourseas Film Company — *Video Gems*

Producers, The 1968
Comedy
41081 88 mins C B, V P
Zero Mostel, Gene Wilder, Dick Shawn, Kenneth Mars, Estelle Winwood, directed by Mel Brooks
Two conniving producers embark upon a get-rich-quick scheme to produce a flop Broadway show, "Springtime for Hitler."
EL, JA
Avco Embassy — *Embassy Home Entertainment; RCA VideoDiscs*

Professional Killers I 1973
Martial arts
76895 87 mins C B, V P
Jiro Tamiya, Koji Takahashi
A trio of hired assassins wander about the countryside killing off people who corrupt the land during Japan's Feudal era.
Shochiku Co. — *Video Action*

Professional Planting (Horticulture) 1982
Gardening/Plants
59576 50 mins C B, V P
This program offers the amateur an inside look at plant propagation from seed to tissue culture and examines techniques used by specialists for planting and transplanting.
Brooklyn Botanical Gardens — *Mastervision*

Professional Techniques (Horticulture) 1982
Gardening/Plants
59577 50 mins C B, V P
This program presents a variety of skillful pruning techniques, examines the art of bonsai, and reveals the secrets of botanists who obtain natural dyes and colorings from plants and trees.
Brooklyn Botanical Gardens — *Mastervision*

Professionals, The 1966
Western
13270 117 mins C B, V P
Burt Lancaster, Lee Marvin, Claudia Cardinale, Jack Palance, Robert Ryan, directed by Richard Brooks
Two men are hired to rescue a railroad tycoon's daughter from her kidnapper, a Mexican cutthroat.
MPAA:PG
Columbia; Pax Enterprises — *RCA/Columbia Pictures Home Video*

Professor Hippie, El 1979
Drama
47859 95 mins C B, V P
A history teacher befriends a group of students, taking them to a far-off part of the country where adventures befall them. In Spanish.
SP
Nicolas Carreras; Luis Repetto — *Media Home Entertainment*

Prom Night 1980
Horror
48939 91 mins C B, V, LV P
Jamie Lee Curtis, Leslie Nielsen
A masked killer stalks four high school senior girls during their senior prom, as revenge for a murder which took place six years ago.
MPAA:R
Avco Embassy, Peter Simpson — *MCA Home Video*

Promises in the Dark 1979
Drama
52713 119 mins C B, V R, P
Marsha Mason, Ned Beatty, Kathleen Beller, Susan Clark, Paul Clemens
This drama focuses on the complex relationship between a woman doctor and her seventeen-year-old female patient terminally ill with cancer.
MPAA:PG
Orion Pictures — *Warner Home Video*

Prophecy 1979
Horror
44595 102 mins C B, V R, P
Talia Shire, Robert Foxworth, Armand Assante, Victoria Racimo, Richard Dysart, directed by John Frankenheimer
A doctor and his wife travel to Maine to research the effects of pollution caused by the lumber industry. They encounter several terrifying freaks of nature and a series of bizarre human deaths.
MPAA:PG
Paramount, Robert L. Rosen — *Paramount Home Video*

Protocol 1984
Comedy
Closed Captioned
80707 96 mins C B, V, LV R, P
Goldie Hawn, Chris Sarandon, Andre Gregory, Cliff De Young, Ed Begley Jr., Gail Strickland, directed by Herbert Ross
A series of comic accidents lead a Washington cocktail waitress into the U.S. State Department employ as a protocol official.
MPAA:PG
Warner Bros. — *Warner Home Video*

Proud Rebel, The 1958
Western/Drama
69551 99 mins C B, V P

Alan Ladd, Olivia De Havilland, Dean Jagger, directed by Michael Curtiz
After his wife's death, a proud, stubborn man goes searching for a doctor who can help his mute son.
Buena Vista; Samuel Goldwyn Jr — *Embassy Home Entertainment*

Providence **1976**
Drama
57230 104 mins C B, V P
John Gielgud, Dirk Bogarde, Ellen Burstyn, directed by Alain Resnais
A dying novelist plans one last novel—a haunting story about the people he knows and the horrors of death he envisages.
Cinema 5; Yves Gasser; Klaus Hellwig — *RCA/Columbia Pictures Home Video*

Prudential Family Playhouse, The **1950**
Drama
47641 53 mins B/W B, V, FO P
Ruth Chatterton, Walter Abel, Cliff Hall, Eva Marie Saint
Sinclair Lewis' "Dodsworth," the story of a wealthy American couple who travel from their small American town to Europe.
CBS — *Video Yesteryear*

Prudential Family Playhouse, The **1950**
Drama
69579 53 mins B/W B, V, FO P
Ruth Chatterton, Walter Abel, Cliff Hall, Eva Marie Saint
An early television adaptation of Sinclair Lewis' classic novel about middle-age disaffection between a wealthy American couple. Originally telecast on October 24, 1950.
CBS — *Video Yesteryear*

Psycho **1960**
Suspense
11598 109 mins B/W B, V, LV P
Anthony Perkins, Janet Leigh, Vera Miles, John Gavin, Martin Balsam, directed by Alfred Hitchcock
A young woman steals a fortune and encounters a young peculiar man and his mysterious mother.
Paramount Prods — *MCA Home Video; RCA VideoDiscs*

Psycho II **1983**
Suspense
65208 113 mins C B, V, LV, CED P
Anthony Perkins, Vera Miles, Meg Tilly, Robert Loggia
After 22 years, Norman Bates is back home at the old Bates Motel in anticipation of new customers.
Universal Oak — *MCA Home Video*

Psycho Sisters **1972**
Horror
80295 85 mins C B, V P
Susan Strasberg, Faith Domergue, Sydney Chaplin, Steve Mitchell
Two sisters become involved in the accidental murder of a man who was a husband to one woman and lover to the other.
MPAA:PG
World Wide Films — *Prism*

Psychomania **1973**
Horror
56737 89 mins C B, V P
George Sanders, Beryl Reid, Nicky Henson
A drama of the supernatural, the occult, and the violence which lies just beyond the conventions of society for a group of motorcyclists.
MPAA:R
Del Tenney — *Media Home Entertainment; Sheik Video*

PT 109 **1963**
War-Drama
63452 159 mins C B, V R, P
Cliff Robertson, Ty Hardin, Robert Blake, Robert Culp
The World War II exploits of Lieutenant J.G. John F. Kennedy in the South Pacific. Part of the "A Night at the Movies" series, this tape simulates a 1963 movie evening, with a Foghorn Leghorn cartoon, "Banty Raids," a newsreel on the JFK assassination and coming attractions for "Critic's Choice" and "Four for Texas."
Warner Bros — *Warner Home Video*

Puberty Blues **1981**
Drama
81437 86 mins C B, V P
Neil Schofield, Jad Capelja, directed by Bruce Beresford
Two Australian girls become part of the local surfing scene in order to be accepted by the "in crowd" at their high school. Available in VHS and Beta Hi-Fi.
MPAA:R
Limelight Productions — *MCA Home Video*

Public Enemy **1931**
Crime-Drama
59427 85 mins B/W B, V P
James Cagney, Edward Woods, Leslie Fenton, Joan Blondell, Mae Clarke, Jean Harlow, directed by William Wellman
Two slum boys begin as bootleggers, and get in over their heads.

Warner Bros — *CBS/Fox Video; RCA VideoDiscs*

Puff the Magic Dragon 1978
Cartoons
80185 45 mins C B, V P
Animated, voice of Burgess Meredith
An animated adaptation of the Peter Yarrow song about little Jackie Paper and his friend Puff, The Magic Dragon.
The My Company — *Children's Video Library*

Puff the Magic Dragon in the Land of Lies 1979
Cartoons/Fantasy
79715 24 mins C B, V P, DL
Animated, voice of Burgess Meredith
Puff the Magic Dragon teaches a little girl the difference between fantasy and telling a lie.
Peter Yarrow; Romeo Muller — *Children's Video Library*

Puma Man 1980
Science fiction
81081 100 mins C B, V P
Donald Pleasance, Walter George Alton, Sydne Rome
Puma Man is a super hero who must stop the evil Dr. Kobras from using an ancient mask in his attempt to become ruler of the world.
Cinema Shares International — *Prism*

Pump It 1983
Physical fitness
66270 55 mins C B, V P
Hosted by Dr. David Engel
A body-building program focusing on specific parts of the body.
Al Eicher — *Embassy Home Entertainment*

Pumping Iron 1977
Documentary/Physical fitness
39086 85 mins C B, V P
Arnold Schwarzenegger, Mike Katz, Franco Columbu, Lou Ferrigno, directed by George Butler
A widely acclaimed documentary look at the sport of bodybuilding, following the behind-the-scenes action surrounding the competition for the Mr. Olympia title. The grueling training ritual and the constant striving for perfection are all explored.
MPAA:PG
Cinema 5 — *RCA/Columbia Pictures Home Video; RCA VideoDiscs*

Pumping Iron II: The Women 1985
Documentary/Physical fitness
81159 107 mins C B, V P
Lori Bowen, Bev Francis, Rachel McLish, Carla Dunlap, Lydia Cheng, directed by George Butler
This sequel to "Pumping Iron" takes an in-depth look at the world of female body building. The documentary also follows the ladies to a competition held at Caesar's Palace in Las Vegas.
Cinecom International Films — *Vestron Video*

Puppet Playhouse Presents Howdy Doody 195?
Variety
38995 60 mins B/W B, V, FO P
Buffalo Bob Smith, Clarabell the Clown, Chief Thundercloud 2 pgms
Two complete programs from September 13, 1948, and August 2, 1959, featuring the Peanut Gallery and all the familiar Howdy Doody characters and routines Commercials included.
NBC — *Video Yesteryear*

Purlie Victorious 1963
Comedy
58579 93 mins C B, V P
Ossie Davis, Ruby Dee, Godfrey Cambridge, Alan Alda
The award-winning Broadway hit, a comedy which takes a look at racial integration.
Hammer Bros — *Mastervision*

Purple Hearts 1984
War-Drama
73014 115 mins C B, V P
Cheryl Ladd, Ken Wahl, directed by Sidney Furie
Ken Wahl stars as a Navy doctor who falls in love with nurse Cheryl Ladd against the backdrop of the Vietnam war.
MPAA:R
Sidney Furie; Warner Bros — *Warner Home Video*

Purple Rain 1984
Musical-Drama
Closed Captioned
79549 113 mins C B, V, LV R, P
Prince, Apollonia Kotero, Morris Day, Clarence Williams III, directed by Albert Magnoli
A quasi-autobiographical video showcase for the multi talented pop-star Prince. The film tells of his struggle for love, attention, acceptance, and popular artistic recognition in Minneapolis.
Academy Awards '84: Best Original Song Score (Prince, John L. Nelson, and The Revolution)
MPAA:R
Warner Bros — *Warner Home Video*

Purple Rose of Cairo, The 1985
Comedy-Drama/Fantasy
80920 82 mins B/W B, V, CED P
Mia Farrow, Jeff Daniels, Danny Aiello, Dianne Weist, Van Johnson, Zoe Caldwell, John Wood, Edward Herrmann, Milo O'Shea, directed by Woody Allen
jThe dreams of a desperate Depression era waitress come true when her favorite film

character steps out of the screen and asks her to show him what real life is like.
MPAA:PG
Orion Pictures; Jack Rollins and Charles H. Joffe — *Vestron Video*

Purple Taxi, The **1977**
Drama
60342 93 mins C B, V P
Fred Astaire, Charlotte Rampling, Peter Ustinov
A romantic drama revolving around several wealthy foreigners who have taken refuge in beautiful southern Ireland.
CPH; BLD — *RCA/Columbia Pictures Home Video*

Pursuit of D. B. Cooper, The **1981**
Drama
47423 100 mins C B, V P
Robert Duvall, Treat Williams, Kathryn Harrold
This film recreates an actual hijacking that took place on Thanksgiving eve, 1971, when J. R. Meade (alias D. B. Cooper) bailed out of a 727 with $200,000 of the airline's money. He was never heard from again.
MPAA:PG
Universal — *MCA Home Video*

Puss in Boots **1982**
Fairy tales
63169 89 mins C B, V P
Garry Q. Lewis, Jason McLean, Carl Beck, Nancy Wagner
The Children's Theater Company of Minneapolis present a jazzed-up, New Orleans-style version of the "Puss in Boots" tale. VHS is in stereo.
Television Theater Company — *MCA Home Video*

Puss 'n' Boots Travels Around the World **1983**
Cartoons
66346 60 mins C B, V P
Animated
An all-new magical cartoon featuring the hero, Pussty, who is challenged by the villainous Rumblehog to complete a trip around the world in 80 days, while Rumblehog tries to thwart him at every turn. In Beta Hi-Fi.
MPAA:G
John Watkins; Simo Nuchtern — *RCA/Columbia Pictures Home Video*

Puss 'N' Boots **1984**
Fairy tales
Closed Captioned
73574 60 mins C B, V, CED P
Ben Vereen, Gregory Hines
From "Faerie Tale Theatre" comes the story of a cat who makes a serf a rich landowning nobleman.
Gaylord Productions; Platypus Productions — *CBS/Fox Video*

Putney Swope **1969**
Comedy
44780 84 mins B/W B, V P
Arnold Johnson, Laura Greene, Stanley Gottlieb, directed by Robert Downey
A mild mannered token black is mistakenly elected chairman of the board of the advertising firm he works for. He turns the straight-laced corporation into the wide open "Truth and Soul, Inc."
MPAA:R
Cinema 5 — *RCA/Columbia Pictures Home Video*

Q

Q—The Winged Serpent **1983**
Horror
68253 92 mins C B, V P
Michael Moriarty, Candy Clark, David Carradine, Richard Roundtree
Two city policemen and a petty crook are trying to track down the perpetrator of a bizarre series of slayings.
MPAA:R
Larco — *MCA Home Video*

QB VII **1974**
Drama
47784 313 mins C B, V P
Anthony Hopkins, Ben Gazzara, Lee Remick, Leslie Caron, Juliet Mills, John Gielgud, Anthony Quayle
A knighted physician brings a suit for libel against a novelist for implicating him of war crimes in a best-selling novel. Adapted from the novel by Leon Uris. Available only as a three-cassette set.
Emmy Awards '74: Best Supporting Actor, Single Performance, Comedy or Drama Special (Quayle); Best Supporting Actress, Single Performance, Comedy or Drama Special (Mills); Music Composition; Graphic Design and Title Sequence; Film Editing; Film Sound Editing.
Douglas S Cramer — *RCA/Columbia Pictures Home Video*

Quackser Fortune Has a Cousin in the Bronx **1970**
Drama/Comedy
51114 88 mins C B, V P
Gene Wilder, Margot Kidder
An Irish fertilizer salesman meets an exchange student from the U.S., who finds herself

attracted to this unlearned, but not unknowing, man.
MPAA:R
John H Cunningham; Mel Howard — *United Home Video*

Quadrophenia **1979**
Musical-Drama
65066 115 mins C B, V P
Phil Daniels, Mark Wingett, Philip Davis, Leslie Ash, Sting
Pete Townshend's rock opera about an alienated youth circa 1963 in Britain's rock scene who suffers from a 4-way split personality. Music by the Who.
MPAA:R
World Northal — *RCA/Columbia Pictures Home Video; RCA VideoDiscs*

Quartet **1981**
Drama
66125 101 mins C B, V R, P
Isabelle Adjani, Alan Bates, Maggie Smith, directed by James Ivory
Jean Rhys' novel concerning a young wife drawn into the social and emotional trap of a domineering English couple is the basis of this film.
Cannes Film Festival '81: Best Actress (Adjani).
MPAA:R
New World Pictures — *Warner Home Video*

Quatermass Conclusion, The **1979**
Science fiction
81483 105 mins C B, V R, P
John Mills, Simon MacCorkindale, Barbara Kellerman, Margaret Tyzack
An elderly British scientist comes out of retirement to stop an immobilizing death ray from outer space from destroying Earth.
Euston Film Productions — *THORN EMI/HBO Video*

Queen—Greatest Flix **1981**
Music
58724 60 mins C B, V R, P
A compilation of original video promos made to accompany the hit records which propelled the rock group Queen on their way to worldwide success. Songs include "Bohemian Rhapsody," "We Will Rock You," "Another One Bites the Dust," "Flash," "Killer Queen," "We Are the Champions," "Crazy Little Thing Called Love."
EMI Music — *THORN EMI/HBO Video; Pioneer Artists; RCA VideoDiscs*

Queen of Diamonds **198?**
Adventure
78670 90 mins C B, V P
Claudia Cardinale, Stanley Baker, Henri Charriere
A woman pulls off the biggest diamond robbery of all time.
Independent — *Monterey Home Video*

Queen of the Stardust Ballroom **1975**
Drama
52401 98 mins C B, V P
Maureen Stapleton, Charles Durning
A lonely widow goes to a local dance hall, where she meets a man and begins an unconventional late love.
AM Available
Robert Christiansen, Rick Rosenberg Prods — *Video Gems*

Queen The Works **1984**
Music video
76963 17 mins C B, V, LV P
Heavy metal rockers Queen performs in four conceptual music videos from "The Works" album.
Capitol — *Sony Corporation of America*

Querelle **1983**
Drama
65188 106 mins C B, V P
Brad Davis, Jeanne Moreau, Franco Nero, directed by Rainer Werner Fassbinder
Fassbinder's last film explores the seamy underworld of the French port of Brest, where Querelle, a handsome sailor, finds himself involved in a bewildering environment of drug smuggling and homosexuality. Dubbed in English.
MPAA:R
Triumph Films — *RCA/Columbia Pictures Home Video*

Quest for Fire **1982**
Adventure
62775 75 mins C B, V, LV, CED P
Everett McGill, Ron Perlman, Nameer El-Kadi, Rae Dawn Chong, directed by Jean-Jacques Annaud
A group of primitive men in the distant past fight rival tribes for the possession of fire.
MPAA:R
20th Century Fox — *CBS/Fox Video*

Question of Love, A **1978**
Drama
65305 90 mins C B, V P
Gena Rowlands, Jane Alexander
An admitted homosexual living in a lesbian relationship struggles to retain custody of her son from her ex-husband.
Viacom Enterprises — *U.S.A. Home Video*

Quick Dog Training with Barbara Woodhouse 1982
Pets
66271 90 mins C B, V P
A program on how to train your dog or pup.
Pillar Prods — *Embassy Home Entertainment*

Quiet Day In Belfast, A 1985
Drama
77359 92 mins C B, V P
Barry Foster, Margot Kidder
Northern Irish patriots and British soldiers clash in an Irish betting parlor.
Foreign — *Media Home Entertainment*

Quiet Man, The 1952
Comedy-Drama
55511 129 mins C B, V P
John Wayne, Maureen O'Hara, Barry Fitzgerald, Victor McLaglen, Ward Bond, Mildred Natwick, directed by John Ford
An archetypal John Ford comedy, an Irish village version of "Taming of the Shrew," the tamer being an ex-boxer retired to the land of his fathers and in need of a wife.
Academy Awards '52: Best Director (Ford); Best Color Cinematography (Winton Hoch, Archie Stout).
Republic; Argosy; John Ford; Merian C Cooper — *Republic Pictures Home Video; RCA VideoDiscs*

Quintet 1979
Science fiction/Drama
70697 118 mins C B, V P
Paul Newman, Bibi Andersson, Fernando Rey, Vittorio Gussman, David Langton, Nina Van Pallundt, Brigitte Fussey, directed by Robert Altman
The stakes in "Quintet," a form of backgammon, are high; you bet your life. But that's O.K.; this film is set during the planet's final ice age. Hi-Fi sound in both formats.
20th Century Fox — *Key Video*

Quiz Kids 1950
Game show
12851 30 mins B/W B, V, FO P
Fran Allison
Quizmistress Fran Allison asks the questions to a panel of five youngsters ranging in age from seven to fourteen.
CBS — *Video Yesteryear*

R

Rabid 1977
Horror
53520 90 mins C B, V R, P
Marilyn Chambers, Frank Moore, Joe Silver
A young girl undergoes a radical plastic surgery technique and develops a strange and unexplained lesion in her armpit—along with a craving for human blood.
MPAA:R
New World Pictures; Cinema Entertainment Enterprises — *Warner Home Video*

Raccoons and the Lost Star, The 1984
Cartoons
73705 49 mins C B, V P
Animated, narrated by Rich Little
The Raccoons must save the earth from Cyril Sneer in this animated adventure. With the purchase of this videocassette, a magic wand and a kite are included.
AM Available
Kevin Gillis — *Embassy Home Entertainment*

Raccoons' Big Surprise, The 1985
Cartoons
Closed Captioned
81455 30 mins C B, V P
Animated
The evil Cyril Sneer will stop at nothing to find out what the Raccoons' secret plans in the Evergeen Forest are.
Evergeen Marketing — *Embassy Home Entertainment*

Raccoons—Let's Dance, The 1984
Music video
66625 30 mins C B, V P
Animated, songs performed by Rita Coolidge, Leo Sayer, John Schneider, Dottie West
Melissa, Ralph and Bert Raccoon perform in six of their own original music videos, designed especially for children.
Evergreen Marketing — *Embassy Home Entertainment*

Raccoons on Ice 1982
Fantasy
63378 49 mins C B, V, LV P
Animated, narrated by Rich Little, music by Leo Sayer, Rita Coolidge and Rupert Holmes
Two cartoons featuring Ralph, Melissa and Bert Raccoon are contained on this cassette. In "Raccoons on Ice," they play a hockey game against the Brutish Bears. "Christmas Raccoons" finds them fighting to protect Evergreen Forest and their "raccoondominium" home.
Kevin Gillis; Sheldon S Wiseman — *Embassy Home Entertainment*

Race for Your Life, Charlie Brown **1977**
Comedy/Cartoons
38610 76 mins C B, V, LV R, P
Animated
Another in the popular series of "Peanuts" character films, featuring Charlie Brown, Snoopy, and all the gang spending an exciting summer in the American wilderness.
MPAA:G
Paramount — *Paramount Home Video; RCA VideoDiscs*

Rachel and the Stranger **1948**
Drama
66333 93 mins B/W B, V, 3/4U P
Loretta Young, Robert Mitchum, William Holden, Gary Gray
A God-fearing farmer declares his love for his wife when a handsome stranger nearly woos her away.
RKO — *Nostalgia Merchant*

Rachel, Rachel **1968**
Drama
77268 102 mins C B, V P
Joanne Woodward, James Olson, Estelle Parsons, directed by Paul Newman
A repressed, small town spinster schoolteacher gets one last chance at romance.
New York Film Critics & Golden Globe Awards '68: Best Actress (Woodward); Best Director (Newman). MPAA:R
Warner Bros.; Kayos Productions — *Warner Home Video*

Racket, The **1951**
Crime-Drama
64366 88 mins B/W B, V, 3/4U P
Robert Ryan, Robert Mitchum, Lizabeth Scott
A police captain attempts to break up the crime empire of a powerful racketeer.
RKO — *Nostalgia Merchant*

Racketeers of the Range **1939**
Western
64413 62 mins B/W B, V, 3/4U P
George O'Brien, Marjorie Reynolds
A cattleman fights a crooked attorney who wants to sell his client's stock to a large meat packing company.
RKO — *Nostalgia Merchant*

Radar Men from the Moon **1952**
Science fiction/Serials
07343 152 mins B/W B, V, 3/4U P
George Wallace, Aline Towne
Commando Cody protects the world from invaders from the moon. Serial in twelve episodes.
Republic — *Nostalgia Merchant; Video Connection; Discount Video Tapes; Republic Pictures Home Video*

Radio Ranch **1935**
Science fiction
07202 80 mins B/W B, V, FO P
Gene Autry, Frankie Darro, Betsy King Ross
Gene Autry and friends are up against an underground world that is complete with robots and death rays.
Mascot Pictures — *Video Yesteryear; Sheik Video; Discount Video Tapes*

Rafferty and the Gold Dust Twins **1975**
Comedy/Drama
Closed Captioned
80710 91 mins C B, V R, P
Alan Arkin, Sally Kellerman, MacKenzie Phillips, Charlie Martin Smith, directed by Dick Richards
Two women kidnap a motor vehicle inspector in Los Angeles and order him to drive to New Orleans at gunpoint.
MPAA:R
Warner Bros. — *Warner Home Video*

Rage **1981**
Drama
73536 98 mins C B, V P
David Soul, James Whitmore, Yaphet Kotto
A convicted rapist is sent to a therapy program to reform sex offenders. Available in Beta Hi-Fi and VHS stereo
Diane Silver Prods; Charles Fries Prods — *U.S.A. Home Video*

Rage of Paris, The **1938**
Comedy
00419 78 mins B/W B, V P
Danielle Darrieux, Douglas Fairbanks Jr., Mischa Auer
Ex-actress and head waiter pool their money to help a beautiful French girl catch a millionaire husband.
Universal; Buddy De Sylva — *Discount Video Tapes; Cable Films; King of Video; Budget Video; Movie Buff Video; Classic Video Cinema Collector's Club; Kartes Productions*

Raggedy Ann and Andy **1979**
Cartoons
78971 52 mins C B, V P
Animated, voices of June Foray, Daws Butler, directed by Chuck Jones
Two Raggedy Ann and Andy stories where they aid a boy who lost his Halloween pumpkin in ""The Pumpkin Who Couldn't Smile" and foil a plot to turn Santa's workshop into a factory in ""The Great Santa Claus Caper."
Chuck Jones — *MPI Home Video*

Raggedy Ann and Andy: A Musical Adventure 1977
Cartoons
59309 87 mins C B, V, CED P
Animated, directed by Richard Williams
The fun-filled exploits of America's favorite fictional doll, transformed into an enchanting animated musical, with sixteen songs by Joe Raposo.
MPAA:G
Lester Osterman — *Playhouse Video*

Raggedy Man 1981
Drama
59035 94 mins C B, V, LV P
Sissy Spacek, Eric Roberts, Sam Shepard, directed by Jack Fisk
A story of a woman raising two sons alone in a small Texas town during World War II, and the sailor who enters her lonely life.
MPAA:PG
Universal — *MCA Home Video*

Raging Bull 1980
Drama
53450 128 mins B/W B, V, LV P
Robert DeNiro, Cathy Moriarty, Joe Pesci, Frank Vincent, directed by Martin Scorcese
The story of Jake La Motta?the tough New York street kid who slugged his way to the world middle-weight boxing championship and then went on to lose everything, chronicling his ups and downs with women, his family, and the law. Academy Awards '80: Best Actor (DeNiro); Best Editing (Thelma Schoonmaker). MPAA:R
Irwin Winkler; Robert Chartoff; United Artists — *CBS/Fox Video; RCA VideoDiscs*

Ragtime 1981
Drama
59858 156 mins C B, V, LV R, P
James Cagney, Brad Dourif, Moses Gunn, Elizabeth McGovern, Ken McMillan, Pat O'Brien, Donald O'Connor, Mary Steenburgen, Howard E. Rollins, directed by Miles Forman
E. L. Doctorow's epic novel interweaving the lives and passions of a middle-class family against the scandals and events of America in transition circa 1906. Music composed by Randy Newman.
MPAA:PG
Dino De Laurentis; Paramount — *Paramount Home Video; RCA VideoDiscs*

Raid on Entebbe 1984
War-Drama
72184 113 mins C B, V R, P
Charles Bronson, Peter Finch
Dramatization of the Israeli rescue of passengers held hostage by terrorists at Uganda's Entebbe Airport.
MPAA:R
Edgar J Sherick Assocs; 20th Century Fox — *THORN EMI/HBO Video*

Raiders of Red Gap 1943
Western
43019 56 mins B/W B, V, FO P
Al "Fuzzy" St. John, Bob Livingston
A cattle company tries running homesteaders off their land to get control of it. The Lone Rider saves the day.
Producers Releasing Corp — *Video Yesteryear; Video Connection*

Raiders of the Lost Ark 1981
Adventure
Closed Captioned
69539 115 mins C B, V, LV, CED P
Harrison Ford, Karen Allen, Wolf Kahler, Paul Freeman, directed by Steven Spielbert
An adventurer and a feisty woman search for the Lost Ark of the Covenant, eluding Nazis, spies and others in the process.
MPAA:PG
Lucasfilm Ltd — *Paramount Home Video*

Railroaded 1947
Mystery
81226 72 mins B/W B, V, LV P
John Ireland, Sheila Ryan, Hugh Beaumont, directed by Anthony Mann
The police seek a wanton criminal who has taken a young boy hostage.
Eagle Lion — *New World Video; Discount Video Tapes*

Railroadin' 1941
Trains
60049 27 mins C B, V P, T
This story of America's railroad system begins with foot power, then animal, then the wheel, and finally progresses to a discussion of railroads. Includes shots of early locomotives up to 1941.
General Electric Company — *Blackhawk Films*

Rain 1932
Drama
08781 77 mins B/W B, V P
Joan Crawford, Walter Huston, William Gargan, Guy Kibbee
Somerset Maugham's tale of Puritanical minister's attempt to reclaim a "lost woman" on the island of Pago Pago.
United Artists — *United Home Video; Discount Video Tapes; VCII; Cable Films; Video Connection; Western Film & Video Inc*

Rain People, The 1969
Drama
69026 102 mins C B, V R, P

 (For explanation of codes, see USE GUIDE and KEY)

Shirley Knight, James Caan, Robert Duvall
In an effort to escape the responsibilities of her marriage and impending motherhood, a young woman sets out on a cross country trip. On her way she becomes involved with a football player who is retarded due to a sports injury.
MPAA:R
Warner Bros — *Warner Home Video*

Rainbow Brite **1984**
Cartoons
76995 45 mins C B, V, CED P
Animated
Rainbow Brite and the Color Kids attempt to brighten up the life of a little boy by sending him a special rainbow.
D.I.C. Productions — *Children's Video Library*

Rainbow Brite in Peril in the Pits **1983**
Cartoons
75611 30 mins C B, V P
Rainbow Brite must bring color to the world and battle Murky Dismal who is determined to drain all color.
Hallmark Properties — *Children's Video Library*

Rainbow Brite—Mighty Monstromork Menace **1983**
Cartoons
Closed Captioned
80977 48 mins C B, V, LV P
Animated
Murky Dismal invents the mighty monstromork which can drain all the color from the world and it is up to Rainbow Brite and her friends to stop him.
Hallmark Properties — *Children's Video Library*

Rainbow Goblins Story **1981**
Music-Performance
47297 52 mins C LV P
Masayoshi Takanaka
In a live concert at Budokan, Masayoshi Takanaka performs the music he composed to interpret a book called "Rainbow Goblins Story."
Yutaka Tanaka — *Pioneer Video Imports*

Rainbow: Live Between the Eyes **1984**
Music-Performance
76032 60 mins C B, V P
This music video features Rainbow's hit songs, including "Stone Cold," "Power" and "Smoke on the Water."
Aubrey Powell — *RCA/Columbia Pictures Home Video*

Rainbow Parade 2 **1936**
Cartoons
77364 21 mins C B, V P, T
Animated
A collection of three animated classics from Burt Gillette including "Molly Moo Cow and Robinson Crusoe," "Trolley Ahoy," and "Waifs Welcome."
RKO Radio Pictures — *Blackhawk Films*

Rainbow Parade, The **193?**
Cartoons
29484 50 mins C B, V P, T
Animated
Animator/director Burt Gillette's "Rainbow Parade" contains some of the most subtly textured color work to be found in animation. Features cartoon characters "Felix," "Molly Moo Cow," and "the Toonerville Folks."
Unknown — *Blackhawk Films*

Raise the Titanic **1980**
Drama/Adventure
56901 112 mins C B, V, LV, CED P
Jason Robards, Richard Jordan, Anne Archer
America's defense depends on the raising of the ship, discovered seventy years after it sank. This action drama chronicles the valiant efforts to lift it from its icy grave.
MPAA:PG
William Frye — *CBS/Fox Video*

Raisin in the Sun, A **1961**
Drama
60340 128 mins B/W B, V P
Sidney Poitier, Claudia McNeil, Ruby Dee, directed by Daniel Petrie
A sensitive drama of a black family's escape from their frustrating life in a crowded Chicago apartment.
Columbia — *RCA/Columbia Pictures Home Video*

Ramparts of Clay **1984**
Drama
72926 87 mins C B, V P
A young Tunisian girl wants to liberate herself from old customs other people. This film is in Arabic with subtitles.
MPAA:PG AB
Almi — *RCA/Columbia Pictures Home Video*

Rancho Notorious **1952**
Western
33592 89 mins C B, V P
Marlene Dietrich, Arthur Kennedy, Mel Ferrer, directed by Fritz Lang
Kennedy looks for the murderer of his sweetheart, and falls in love with Dietrich in the process. Tragic consequences follow.
RKO — *United Home Video*

Randy Newman Live at the Odeon 1985
Music-Performance
77459 57 mins C B, V P
Randy Newman, Ry Couder, Linda Ronstadt
Join Randy Newman, guitarist Ry Cooder and Linda Ronstadt as they perform such Newman standards as "Sail Away" "Short People" and "I Love LA" Available in VHS and Beta Hi Fi Stereo.
Music Vision — *RCA/Columbia Pictures Home Video*

Randy Rides Alone/Riders of Destiny 1935
Western
81021 106 mins B/W B, V P
John Wayne
This is an action-packed western double feature: in "Randy Rides Alone", a young man cleans up the territory single handedly and in "Riders of Destiny" the Texas Rangers are destined to ride to the rescue once more.
Monogram Pictures — *Spotlite Video*

Rangeland Racket 1941
Western
66145 60 mins B/W B, V, FO P
George Houston, Hillary Brooke, Al St. John
The Lone Rider (Houston) has been wrongly accused of a crime.
Unknown — *Video Yesteryear*

Rangers Take Over, The 1943
Western
51643 62 mins B/W B, V P
Dave O'Brien, James Newill
Gunlords are driven out by the Texas Rangers.
Producers Releasing Corp — *Video Yesteryear; Discount Video Tapes*

Ransom 1984
Drama
72910 90 mins C B, V P
Oliver Reed, Deborah Raffin
A group of wealthy citizens decide to take on an assassin who stalks a resort town.
Unknown — *Vestron Video*

Rape! A Crime of Violence 1982
Rape
60515 48 mins C B, V P
Awareness, precaution and defense of rape are exposed in this docudrama.
Bob Chaney — *Master Arts Video*

Rape of Love 1979
Drama
58500 117 mins C B, V P
Nathalie Nell, Alain Foures, directed by Yannick Bellon
One of the most chilling rape scenes on film opens this attempt at analyzing the emotional impact of such a crime on its victim. French with English subtitles.
FR
Films de L'Equinoxe — *RCA/Columbia Pictures Home Video*

Rappin' 1985
Musical
81502 92 mins C B, V P
Mario Van Peebles, Tasia Valenza, Harry Goz, Charles Flohe
An ex-con tries to save his little brother from a life of crime by landing him a contract with a record company. Available in VHS and Beta Hi-Fi.
MPAA:PG
Cannon Films — *MGM/UA Home Video*

Rapunzel 1983
Fairy tales
Closed Captioned
69323 60 mins C B, V, LV, CED P
Shelley Duvall, Gena Rowlands, Jeff Bridges
The classic tale of the beautiful young woman locked in a tall tower by a witch who is saved by the handsome prince who climbs her golden tresses is retold in this program from "Faerie Tale Theatre."
Shelley Duvall — *CBS/Fox Video*

Raquel: Total Beauty and Fitness 1984
Physical fitness
78395 90 mins C B, V R, P
Raquel Welch designed this program to keep men and women of all ages in top physical condition.
Thorn EMI — *THORN EMI/HBO Video*

Rare Breed, A 1981
Drama
65210 96 mins C B, V P
Forrest Tucker, George Kennedy
A young girl's filly is kidnapped en route to Europe for training, sparking a treacherous race against odds with time running out.
MPAA:PG
Carnoba Company — *U.S.A. Home Video*

Rascal Dazzle 1981
Comedy
74087 100 mins B/W B, V P
Narrated by Jerry Lewis
This is a montage-like tribute to that best-loved group of children, the Our Gang kids. Narrated by Jerry Lewis, this feature includes scenes with Spanky, Alfalfa, Darla and the rest of the gang.
Michael King; Bob King — *Embassy Home Entertainment*

Rascals, The 1981
Comedy-Drama
65392 93 mins C B, V P
This film depicts the coming of age of an irrepressible youth at a rural Catholic boys' school.
MPAA:R
Gilbert de Goldschmidt — *Embassy Home Entertainment*

Ratas del Asfalto 198?
Drama
77353 85 mins C B, V P
Ana Martin, Armando Silvestre
Two rival race car drivers battle in a fatal race.
SP
Foreign — *Unicorn Video*

Rattle of a Simple Man 1964
Comedy-Drama
63325 91 mins B/W B, V R, P
Harry H. Corbett, Diane Cilento, Michael Medwin, Thora Hird
A naive bachelor in London spends the night with a prostitute in order to win a bet.
Sydney Box — *THORN EMI/HBO Video*

Rattlers 1976
Suspense
77206 82 mins C B, V P
Sam Chew, Don Priest, Ron Gold
Chemically exposed snakes attack the inhabitants of the Mojave Desert area.
John McCauley — *U.S.A. Home Video*

Raven, The 1963
Horror
64886 86 mins C B, V R, P
Vincent Price, Boris Karloff, Peter Lorre, Jack Nicholson
A chilling tale of black magic based on the poem by Edgar Allan Poe.
American International Pictures — *Warner Home Video; Vestron Video (disc only)*

Ravishing Idiot, The 1964
Comedy
76798 99 mins B/W B, V P
Brigitte Bardot, Anthony Perkins, directed by Edouard Molinaro
An unemployed bank clerk becomes mixed up with Soviet spies through an unusual series of events.
Edouard Molinaro — *Monterey Home Video*

Raw Courage 1974
Drama
80664 90 mins C B, V, LV P
Ronny Cox, Art Hindle, Tim Maier, M. Emmett Walsh
A trio of marathon runners get more than they bargained for when they relax in New Mexico.
New World Pictures — *New World Video*

Raw Force 1981
Adventure/Martial arts
63385 90 mins C B, V P
Cameron Mitchell, Geoff Binney, John Dresden, John Locke, Ralph Lombardi
Three karate enthusiasts visit an island inhabited by a sect of cannibalistic monks who have the power to raise the dead.
MPAA:R
Ansor International Picture — *Media Home Entertainment*

Rawhide 1938
Western
10072 60 mins B/W B, V P, T
Lou Gehrig, Smith Ballew
Rancher's Protection Association forces landowners to knuckle under. Friction results.
20th Century Fox — *Blackhawk Films; Discount Video Tapes*

Razorback 1984
Horror
76853 95 mins C B, V R, P
Gregory Harrison, Bill Kerr, Arkie Whiteley, Judy Morris, Chris Haywood, directed by Russell Mulcahy
A young American travels to the Australian outback to search for his missing journalist wife.
MPAA:R
Hal McElroy; UAA Films Ltd — *Warner Home Video*

Razor's Edge, The 1984
Drama
Closed Captioned
77369 129 mins C B, V P
Bill Murray, Catherine Hicks, Theresa Russell, Denholm Elliott, directed by John Byrum
A free-spirited man embarks on a worldwide trek to find himself. Available in VHS Hi-Fi Dolby Stereo and Beta Hi-Fi Stereo. Based on the Somerset Maugham novel.
MPAA:PG13
Columbia Pictures — *RCA/Columbia Pictures Home Video*

Razor's Edge, The 1946
Drama
Closed Captioned
81066 146 mins B/W B, V P
Tyrone Power, Gene Tierney, Anne Baxter, Clifton Webb, Herbert Marshall, directed by Edmund Goulding
This is an adaptation of the Somerset Maugham novel about a rich young man who spends his time between World War I and World War II searching for essential truth. Available in VHS and Beta Hi-Fi.
Academy Awards '46: Best Supporting Actress (Baxter).

20th Century Fox; Darryl F. Zanuck — *Key Video*

RCA's All-Star Country Music Fair **1982**
Music-Performance
60388 82 mins C B, V P
Charlie Pride, Razzy Bailey, Sylvia, Earl Thomas Conley
A hoe-down recorded live at the 1982 Nashville Fan Fair, featuring a line-up of Nashville talent. In stereo.
RCA — *RCA/Columbia Pictures Home Video; RCA VideoDiscs*

Ready Steady Go **1983**
Music
65508 60 mins B/W B, V R, P
The Beatles, The Rolling Stones, The Who, The Animals, Gerry and the Pacemakers
The first in a series of classic rock video collectibles from the 1960's. This volume contains 16 of the '60's top hits which capture the magic and energy of this exciting rock era.
Dave Clark Production International; Picture Music International — *THORN EMI/HBO Video*

Ready Steady Go, Volume 2 **1985**
Music-Performance
80648 60 mins B/W B, V R, P
The Beatles, The Who, The Beach Boys, Marvin Gaye, Gene Pitney, Jerry Lee Lewis, The Rolling Stones
This second volume highlights more original performances from the classic British rock TV show of the sixties.
Dave Clark Production International; PMI — *THORN EMI/HBO Video*

Real Bruce Lee, The **1979**
Adventure/Martial arts
35390 108 mins C B, V R, P
Bruce Lee
This program contains actual early films of Bruce Lee, once feared lost but recently discovered in the Chinese film archives.
MPAA:R
Madison World Film Company — *Video Gems; Sun Video*

Real Life **1979**
Comedy/Satire
60212 99 mins C B, V R, P
Charles Grodin, Frances Lee McCain, Albert Brooks, directed by Albert Brooks
When a group of filmmakers moves into the home of a typical American family, they record an account of "real life" — Albert Brooks style.
MPAA:R
Penelope Spheers — *Paramount Home Video*

Rear Window **1954**
Drama/Suspense
66587 112 mins C B, V, LV, CED P
James Stewart, Grace Kelly, Thelma Ritter, Wendell Corey, Raymond Burr, directed by Alfred Hitchcock
A newspaper photographer with a broken leg passes the time while recuperating by observing his neighbors through the window. When he sees what he believes to be a murder committed, he decides to solve the crime himself.
Universal Classics — *MCA Home Video*

Rebecca **1940**
Drama
46214 130 mins B/W B, V P
Joan Fontaine, Laurence Olivier, Judith Anderson, George Sanders, C. Aubrey Smith, directed by Alfred Hitchcock.
Based on Daphne du Maurier's best selling novel about a young unsophisticated girl who marries a prominent country gentleman who is dominated by the memory of his first wife. Hitchcock's first American film.
Academy Awards '40: Best Picture; Best Cinematography.
Selznick — *CBS/Fox Video*

Rebecca of Sunnybrook Farm **1917**
Comedy-Drama
63981 77 mins B/W B, V P, T
Mary Pickford, Eugene O'Brien, Marjorie Daw
The original film version of the tale about an orphan who spreads sunshine and good cheer to all those around her. Silent with organ score by Gaylord Carter.
Artcraft Pictures — *Blackhawk Films*

Rebel Rousers **1969**
Drama
03573 81 mins C B, V P
Jack Nicholson, Cameron Mitchell, Diane Ladd, Bruce Dern
A violent motorcycle gang abuses women.
Paragon International Picture — *Media Home Entertainment; King of Video*

Rebel Without a Cause **1955**
Drama
38941 105 mins C B, V, LV R, P
James Dean, Natalie Wood, Sal Mineo, Jim Backus, directed by Nicholas Ray
James Dean's most remembered screen appearance, as a troubled teenager trying to find himself as his family settles in a new town.
Warner Bros — *Warner Home Video; RCA VideoDiscs*

Reborn 1984
Drama
72911 91 mins C B, V P
Dennnis Hopper, Michael Moriarty
A faith healer and a talent scout hire actors to be cured of fake ailments.
Unknown — *Vestron Video*

Reckless 1984
Adventure/Romance
75536 93 mins C B, V P
Aidan Quinn, Daryl Hannah
The passion and rebelliousness of a teenage couple upsets the small town they are trying to escape.
MPAA:R
MGM UA Entertainment
Company — *MGM/UA Home Video*

Recover From Back Pain 1984
Back disorders/Physical fitness
81539 49 mins C B, V P
This is an exercise program designed to help people who have severe back pains.
AM Available
American Academy of Orthopaedic
Surgeons — *Feeling Fine Programs*

Red Badge of Courage, The 1951
Drama
81496 69 mins B/W B, V P
Audie Murphy, Bill Mauldin, Douglas Dick, Royal Dano, directed by John Huston
This is an adaptation of the Stephen Crane novel about a young Union soldier who is determined to conquer his fears as he goes off to fight in the Civil War.
MGM — *MGM/UA Home Video*

Red Balloon, The 1956
Fantasy
65620 34 mins C B, V, CED P
Pascal Lamorisse, directed by Albert Lamorisse
This is the story of Pascal, a lonely French boy who befriends a wondrous red balloon which follows him everywhere.
Academy Awards '56: Best Original Screenplay.
FR
Films Montsouris; Lopert Films — *Embassy Home Entertainment; Video Yesteryear; Sheik Video; Western Film & Video Inc*

Red Balloon, The 1956
Fantasy
11251 34 mins C B, V, FO P
A child's "pet" balloon is destroyed by a gang, but a happy ending soon follows.
Academy Awards '56: Best Original Screenplay.
Albert Lamorisse — *Embassy Home Entertainment*

Red Baron, The 1984
Cartoons
70610 60 mins C B, V P
Animated
The aerial dogfights in this presentation take place between warring factions of real cartoon dogs.
Videocraft International Ltd. — *Prism*

Red Dawn 1984
Science fiction/Adventure
80495 114 mins C B, V, LV P
Patrick Swayze, C. Thomas Howell, Harry Dean Stanton, Powers Boothe, Ron O'Neal, directed by John Milius
A science fantasy of the future-that-might-be, as Russian invaders overrun America's heartland and take over the country. Eight small-town teenagers hide out in the rugged countryside and initiate guerrilla warfare. In VHS and Beta Hi-Fi Stereo.
MPAA:PG13
United Artists — *MGM/UA Home Video*

Red Flag: The Ultimate Game 1981
Adventure/Drama
80638 104 mins C B, V P
Barry Bostwick, Joan Van Ark, William Devane, George Coe, directed by Dan Taylor
This film shows a group of Air Force pilots who like to play intense war games in a small southwestern town. Available in Beta Hi-Fi and VHS Stereo.
Marble Arch Prods. — *U.S.A. Home Video*

Red Hot Rock 1985
Music-Performance/Music video
70384 60 mins C B, V P
Duran Duran, Queen, Dwight Twilley, O'Bryan, The Tubes
The Videos in this collection were deemed to risque for broadcast or cable TV, but are gathered here today for home enjoyment.
Picture Music International — *Vestron Video*

Red Nightmare 1953
Drama
39000 30 mins B/W B, V, FO P
Jack Webb, Jack Kelly, Jeanne Cooper, Peter Brown
This anti-communist propaganda film, produced for the Department of Defense by Warner Brothers, features the cast of "Dragnet." The story dramatizes the Red Menace, with communists conspiring to take over America, and shows what would happen to life in a small American town if the Commies took over. A typical Mc Carthy-era production.
Warner Bros — *Video Yesteryear*

Red Pony, The 1949
Drama
64541 89 mins C B, V P
Myrna Loy, Robert Mitchum, Peter Miles, Louis Calhern, Margaret Hamilton, Beau Bridges, directed by Louis Milestone
A young boy loses faith in his father when his pet pony dies. Based on a story by John Steinbeck, with musical score by Aaron Copland.
Republic — *Republic Pictures Home Video*

Red River 1948
Western
31665 125 mins B/W B, V P
John Wayne, Montgomery Clift, Walter Brennan, Joanne Dru, directed by Howard Hawks
The story of a cattle baron and the empire he builds.
United Artists — *Key Video; RCA VideoDiscs*

Red Shoes, The 1948
Drama
44365 133 mins C CED P
Moira Shearer, Anton Walbrook, Marius Goring, Robert Helpmann
A lovely ballerina is in a bitter struggle between career and marriage.
Academy Awards '48: Best Art Director, Color; Best Scoring, Drama (Brian Easdale).
Eagle Lion, J Arthur Rank — *RCA VideoDiscs*

Red Skelton's Funny Faces 1981
Comedy-Performance
81257 53 mins C B, V P
Red Skelton, Marcel Marceau
Red Skelton performs such classic routines as Freddie the Freeloader and the seagulls Heathcliff and Gertrude in this one man show. Available in VHS Stereo and Beta Hi-Fi.
Riff Markowitz — *U.S.A. Home Video*

Redd Foxx—Video in a Plain Brown Wrapper 1983
Comedy-Performance
66201 60 mins C B, V, LV, CED P
Foxx tackles all of his favorite subjectssex, marriage, death, crime and more sex.
Command Entertainment Marketing — *Vestron Video*

Redeemer, The 1977
Horror
35388 83 mins C B, V P
Christopher Flint, T.G. Finkbinder, Damien Knight
The Son of Satan sends invitations to a class reunion. In the style of "The Omen."
MPAA:R
Sheldon Tromberg — *United Home Video; Continental Video*

Redneck 1973
Drama
12041 92 mins C B, V P
Telly Savalas
A psychopathic killer and his partner take a teenage boy hostage.
Int'l Amusement Corp — *King of Video*

Reds 1981
Drama
63425 200 mins C B, V, LV R, P
Warren Beatty, Diane Keaton, Jack Nicholson, Maureen Stapleton, directed by Warren Beatty
"Reds" is the story of John Reed, a liberal American journalist who helped found the American Communist Party, documented the Bolshevik Revolution, and ultimately became the only American ever to be buried within the walls of the Kremlin.
Academy Awards '81: Best Supporting Actress (Stapleton); Best Direction; Best Cinematography. MPAA:PG
Paramount; Warren Beatty — *Paramount Home Video; RCA VideoDiscs*

Reefer Madness 1938
Exploitation
03565 67 mins B/W B, V P
Considered seriously at the time of its release, this low-budget depiction of the horrors of marijuana usage has become an underground comedy favorite. Overwrought acting and the lurid script contribute to the fun.
MPAA:PG
Dwain Esper Productions — *Media Home Entertainment; Budget Video; VCII; Select-a-Tape; Video Dimensions; Discount Video Tapes; Video Yesteryear; Sheik Video; Video Connection; Western Film & Video Inc; Vestron Video (disc only); Kartes Productions*

Reet, Petite and Gone 1947
Musical
08888 75 mins B/W B, V, 3/4U P
Louis Jordan and his Tympany Five, June Richmond
A story about a girl whose mother dies, leaving a will which a crooked lawyer alters.
Unknown — *Video Yesteryear; Discount Video Tapes*

Reflections in a Golden Eye 1967
Drama
80078 108 mins C B, V R, P
Elizabeth Taylor, Marlon Brando, Brian Keith, Julie Harris, directed by John Huston
There are all kinds of kinky activities going on at a Georgia army camp.

Warner Bros; Ray Stark — *Warner Home Video*

Reg'lar Fellers 1941
Comedy
66395 67 mins B/W B, V P
Alfalfa Switzer, Roscoe Ates, Sara Padden
The misadventures of a neighborhood gang of kids, based on the then-popular comic strip of the same name.
Producers Releasing Corporation — *Movie Buff Video*

Rehabilitation and Injury 1978
Health education
42781 30 mins C B, V P
Hosted by Ann Dugan 6 pgms
This series of cassettes covers aspects of rehabilitation and preventive medical care. See individual program listings.
1.Prenatal 2.Postnatal 3.Hysterectomy 4.Mastectomy 5.Knee 6.Back
Health 'N Action — *RCA/Columbia Pictures Home Video*

Rehearsal for Murder 1982
Mystery
70256 96 mins C B, V P
Robert Preston, Lynn Redgrave, Patrick MacNee, Jeff Goldblum, William Daniels, Lawrence Pressman
A successful playwright refuses to believe that his fiance, a film star, committed suicide on the eve of their wedding. The film follows his investigation into her death.
Levinson/Link Prods. in assoc. with Parpazian Prods — *U.S.A. Home Video*

Reil 1982
Western
72336 180 mins C B, V P
Arthur Hill, William Shatner
The pioneer days of Canada's western frontier days serve as the backdrop for this drama.
Canadian Broadcasting Corporation — *Prism*

Reincarnation of Peter Proud, The 1975
Suspense/Drama
79671 105 mins C B, V P
Michael Sarrazin, Jennifer O'Neill, Margot Kidder, Cornelia Sharpe
A college professor has nightmares about his previous life. Based on the novel by Max Ehrlich.
MPAA:R
Avco Embassy — *Vestron Video*

Reivers, The 1969
Comedy/Adventure
70381 107 mins C B, V P
Steve McQueen, Sharon Farrell, Will Geer, Michael Constantine, directed by Mark Rydell
Based on William Faulkner's last novel, this film shows the adventures of a young man's journey from the innocence of a small Mississippi town to the experiences of big city Memphis in 1905.
MPAA:PG
National General for Cinema Center — *Key Video*

Rembrandt 1936
Biographical/Drama
81466 86 mins B/W B, V, LV P
Charles Laughton, Elsa Lanchester, Gertrude Lawrence, Walter Hudd, directed by Alexander Korda
This film chronicles the life and times of the great Dutch painter, Rembrandt.
Alexander Korda — *Embassy Home Entertainment*

Renegade Monk 1982
Martial arts
64946 90 mins C B, V R, P
Lui Chung Liang, Hwang Hsing Shaw, Ko Shou Liang, Lang Shih Chia, Hsu Chung Hsing
An invincible warrior-monk dispenses his own brand of justicewith his fists.
MPAA:R
Foreign — *Video Gems*

Renegade Ranger, The/Scarlet River 1938
Western
81031 113 mins B/W B, V P
kRita Hayworth, Tim Holt, George O'Brien, Ray Whiltey, Tom Keene, Lon ChaneyJr., Myrna Loy, Bruce Cabot, Betty Furness
A western double feature: A Texas Ranger and his singing sidekick attempt to help out a woman accused of murder in the "The Renegade Ranger," and a cowboy tries to free his sweetheart from a band of cattle rustlers in "Scarlet River".
RKO — *RKO HomeVideo*

Repo Man 1983
Comedy
75016 92 mins C B, V P
Harry Dean Stanton, Emilie Estevez
This is a comedy about a young punk rocker who tries to win a '64 Chevy Malibu in a contest.
Universal — *MCA Home Video*

Reproduction of Life: Sex Education 1982
Reproduction/Sexuality
59565 53 mins C B, V P
The entire process from conception through prenatal development to birth itself is explained.
McGraw Hill — *Mastervision*

Resurrection of Zachary Wheeler, The 1972
Science fiction
33595 100 mins C B, V P
Angie Dickinson, Bradford Dillman, Leslie Nielson
A presidential candidate who narrowly escaped death in an auto crash is brought to a mysterious clinic. A reporter sneaks into the clinic and discovers the horrors of cloning.
MPAA:G
Gold Key — *United Home Video*

Retrievers, The 1982
Martial arts
77409 90 mins C B, V P
Max Thayer, Roselyn Royce
A young man and a former CIA agent team up to expose the unsavory practices of the organization.
Arista Films — *Vestron Video*

Return, The 1980
Science fiction
63323 90 mins C B, V R, P
Raymond Burr, Cybill Shepherd, Martin Landau, Jan-Michael Vincent
Two friends seek clues to the bizarre phenomena of the present in an extraterrestrial encounter they shared as children 25 years earlier.
Independent — *THORN EMI/HBO Video*

Return Engagement 1978
Drama/Romance
80672 76 mins C B, V P
Elizabeth Taylor, Joseph Bottoms, Peter Donat, James Ray, directed by Joseph Hardy
A lonely middle-aged ancient history professor falls in love with one of her students.
The Production Co. — *Lightning Video*

Return of a Man Called Horse, The 1976
Adventure
59429 125 mins C B, V, CED P
Richard Harris, Gail Sondergaard, Geoffrey Lewis, directed by Ervin Kershner
This sequel to "A Man Called Horse" tells the story of an English aristocrat who was captured and raised by Sioux Indians, and then returned to his native homeland.
United Artists — *CBS/Fox Video*

Return of Chandu, The 1934
Suspense
38979 61 mins B/W B, V, FO P
Bela Lugosi, Clara Kimball Young
Chandu the Magician fights to save the Princess Nadji from being sacrificed by a religious sect of cat worshippers. Story by Raymond Chandler.
Mascot — *Video Yesteryear; Sheik Video; Cable Films; Video Connection*

Return of Martin Guerre, The 1983
Mystery
65623 111 mins C B, V, LV P
Gerard Depardieu, Natalie Baye
A true, satisfyingly ingenious and provocative story, which revolves around Martin Guerre, who had disappeared as a young husband and resumed his marriage years later.
Societe Francaise de Production Cinematographique — *Embassy Home Entertainment*

Return of Martin Guerre, The 1982
Drama
80394 111 mins C B, V P
Gerard Depardieu, Nathalie Baye, directed by Daniel Vigne
A young man who mysteriously disappears from his wife returns several years later to resume his marriage. With English subtitles.
FR
Moustapha Akkad — *Embassy Home Entertainment*

Return of the Bad Men 1948
Western
10068 90 mins B/W B, V P, T
Randolph Scott, Robert Ryan, Anne Jeffreys, Gabby Hayes, Jason Robards, Jacqueline White
Man plans to stake claim in Oklahoma during land rush and finds romance.
RKO, Nat Holt — *RKO HomeVideo; Blackhawk Films; Nostalgia Merchant*

Return of the Dinosaurs 1983
Cartoons/Adventure
78398 82 mins C B, V P
Animated
When a comet almost collides with the Earth, the dinosaur patrol comes in to save the planet.
Independent — *Trans World Entertainment*

Return of the Dragon 1972
Adventure/Martial arts
55832 91 mins C B, V P
Bruce Lee, Nora Miao, Chuck Norris, directed by Bruce Lee
Lee's last picture concerns a Chinese restaurant in Rome which is menaced by gangsters who want to buy the property. On behalf of the owners, Lee duels an American karate champ in the Roman forum.
MPAA:R
Bryanston Pictures — *CBS/Fox Video; Video Gems*

Return of the Fly 1959
Science fiction
80733 78 mins B/W B, V P
Vincent Price, Brett Halsey, John Sutton, Dan Seymour
The son of the scientist who discovered how to move matter through space decides to continue his father's work, but does so against his uncle's wishes. Available in VHS and Beta Hi-Fi-Stereo.
20th Century Fox — *Key Video*

Return of the Man from U.N.C.L.E. 1983
Adventure
80143 96 mins C B, V P
Robert Vaughn, David McCallum, Patrick Macnee, Gayle Hunnicut, Geoffrey Lewis
Those dashing superagents Napoleon Solo and Illya Kuryakin come out of retirement to settle an old score with their nemesis THRUSH.
Michael Sloan Productions — *Trans World Entertainment*

Return of the Pink Panther, The 1975
Comedy
13595 113 mins C B, V, LV P
Peter Sellers, Christopher Plummer, Catherine Schell, directed by Blake Edwards
Inspector Clousseau is called upon to rescue the Pink Panther diamond stolen from a museum.
MPAA:G
United Artists; Blake Edwards — *CBS/Fox Video; RCA VideoDiscs*

Return of the Rams/NFL '83 1984
Football
75890 46 mins C B, V, FO P
This program presents scenes from the Los Angeles Rams' 1983 season.
NFL Films — *NFL Films Video*

Return of the Red Tiger 1981
Martial arts/Adventure
59416 82 mins C B, V P
Bruce Lee
Kung-Fu master Bruce Lee displays one of the foremost and exciting styles of kung-fu—the Tiger.
Unknown — *HarmonyVision*

Return of the Secaucus 7 1981
Comedy-Drama
60341 110 mins C B, V P
Mark Arnott, Gordon Clapp, Maggie Cousineau-Arndt, directed by John Sayles
A weekend reunion of seven friends who were activists during the turbulent '60's serves as the basis for this look at a group turning 30.
Libra Specialty Films — *RCA/Columbia Pictures Home Video*

Return of the Tall Blond Man With One Black Shoe 197?
Comedy
11356 84 mins C B, V P
Pierre Richard
A sequel to "The Tall Blond Man With One Black Shoe," whereby a "klutz" is mistakenly thought to be a master spy. French with English subtitles.
FR
Cinema 5 — *Prism; Cinema Concepts*

Return of the Tiger 1978
Adventure/Martial arts
50732 95 mins C B, V P
Bruce Li, Paul Smith, Chaing I, Angelea Mao, directed by Jimmy Shaw
The Hovver Night Club in Bangkok is used to cover up the operations of an international narcotic group headed by an American. A rival Chinese gang tries to dominate the drug market, and conflict ensues.
Jimmy Shaw — *Media Home Entertainment*

Return of the Zombies 1978
Horror
77389 95 mins C B, V P
Stan Cooper, Charles Quiney
A pack of zombies stalk the countryside craving for the flesh and innards of their creators.
MPAA:R
Prodimex — *Wizard Video*

Return to Boggy Creek 1977
Suspense
65330 87 mins C B, V, CED P
Dawn Wells
In a small fishing village, the townspeople learn from a photogrpaher that a "killer" beast whom they thought had disappeared has returned and is living in Boggy Creek. Some children follow the photographer into the swamp, despite hurricane warnings.
MPAA:PG
Bayou Productions — *CBS/Fox Video*

Return to Fantasy Island 1977
Drama
80313 100 mins C B, V P
Ricardo Montalban, Adrienne Barbeau, Pat Crowley, Laraine Day
Six people pay $50,000 each to spend a weekend on an island to live out their secret fantasies.
Spelling/Goldberg Productions — *Prism*

Return to Macon County 1975
Adventure
66097 90 mins C B, V, CED P

Nick Nolte, Don Johnson, Robin Mattson
A tale of three young, reckless youths on the loose.
American International Pictures — *Vestron Video*

Return to Oz 1984
Cartoons
70612 60 mins C B, V P
Animated
This sequel to L. Frank Baum's original "The Wizard of Oz" features an all new musical score.
Videocraft International Ltd. — *Prism*

Reuben, Reuben 1983
Comedy
Closed Captioned
78883 100 mins C B, V P
Tom Conti, Kelly McGillis, directed by Robert Ellis Miller
A drunken poet's life turns around when he falls in love with a beautiful young woman.
MPAA:R
Walter Shenson; Taft — *CBS/Fox Video*

Revenge 1972
Drama
59841 89 mins C B, V P
Joan Collins, James Booth, Ray Barrett, Ken Griffith
A thriller about the drive for revenge that ultimately destroys the family of a young girl who was brutally murdered.
Peter Rogers; George H Brown — *Embassy Home Entertainment*

Revenge of the Dead 1984
Horror
77219 100 mins C B, V P
A European archeological team discovers the existence of a powerful force that allows the dead to return to life.
Motion Picture Marketing — *Lightning Video*

Revenge of the Nerds 1984
Comedy
Closed Captioned
76927 89 mins C B, V P
Robert Carradine, Anthony Edwards, Ted McGinley, Julie Montgomery
A group of nerdish college freshmen revenge upon the fraternity that evicted them from their dorm.
MPAA:R
20th Century Fox — *CBS/Fox Video*

Revenge of the Ninja 1983
Adventure/Martial arts
65661 90 mins C B, V, CED P
Sho Kosugi
A Ninja hoping to escape his bloody past in Los Angeles gets mixed up with a drug trafficker, who turns out to be an American Ninja and his archfoe. The two polish off a slew of mobsters before their own inevitable showdown.
MPAA:R
Cannon Films — *MGM/UA Home Video*

Revenge of the Pink Panther 1978
Comedy
47804 99 mins C B, V, LV, CED P
Peter Sellers, Herbert Lom, Dyan Cannon, Robert Webber, directed by Blake Edwards
Inspector Clouseau tracks down an international drug ring which takes him around the world.
MPAA:PG
United Artists — *CBS/Fox Video; RCA VideoDiscs*

Revolt of Job, The 1984
Drama
75541 98 mins C B, V P
An elderly Jewish couple adopt an 8-year-old Gentile boy although it is illegal and against the beliefs of the orthodox community.
TeleCulture Inc — *MGM/UA Home Video*

Rhinestone 1984
Comedy
Closed Captioned
80337 111 mins C B, V P
Sylvester Stallone, Dolly Parton, Ron Liebman, directed by Bob Clark
A country singer must turn a cab driver into a singer in order to have a chance to sing at New York City's roughest country-western club, The Rhinestone.
MPAA:PG
Twentieth Century Fox — *CBS/Fox Video*

Rhythm and Blues 1 1983
Music-Performance
65225 57 mins C B, V P
Billy Eckstine, Ruth Brown, Billy Preston, Gloria Lynne, Sheer Delight, Gil Askey
Gospel roots are joyously evident in this program documenting the Rhythm and Blues movement from the farms to the cities.
Skylark Savoy Productions Ltd — *Video Gems*

Rhythmatist, The 1985
Music-Performance
81211 57 mins C B, V P
The Police's drummer Stuart Copeland discovers mystery and unusual music when he visits Africa. Available in VHS Dolby Hi-Fi Stereo and Beta Hi-Fi.
A&M Video — *RCA/Columbia Pictures Home Video*

Ribald Tales of Robin Hood, The 1980
Satire
55214 83 mins C B, V P
The Robin Hood legend is satirized in this comedy which concentrates on Prince John and his favorite pastimes: rape, pillage and plunder.
MPAA:R
Lima Productions — *Media Home Entertainment*

Rich and Famous 1981
Comedy-Drama
59311 117 mins C B, V, CED P
Jacqueline Bisset, Candice Bergen, David Selby, Hart Bochner, Matt Lattanzi, directed by George Cukor
The story of the 25-year friendship of two women, through college, marriage, and success.
MPAA:R
MGM — *MGM/UA Home Video*

Rich Little's Great Hollywood Trivia Game 1984
Game show
65601 60 mins C B, V P
The multi-talented impressionist brings his Hollywood repertoire together for the show biz trivia challenge of the year.
Vestron — *Vestron Video*

Richard Nixon—Checkers, Old Glory, Resignation 197?
Documentary/Presidency-US
57358 45 mins B/W B, V, FO P
Three historic broadcasts in the career of Richard Nixon: the "Checkers Speech" (1952) where Nixon defended himself against accusations of misusing campaign funds; "Old Glory" (1957), a short talk from New York's Chrysler Building in honor of flag day; and "Resignation" (1974), a kinescope of the TV pool feed from the Oval Room of the White House as Nixon announces he will leave office.
Unknown — *Video Yesteryear*

Richard Pryor: Here and Now 1983
Comedy-Performance
65697 75 mins C B, V, CED P
Richard Pryor
Filmed at the Saenger Theater in New Orleans, Pryor's sharp, witty commentaries are delivered with a unique piercing humor.
MPAA:R
Bob Parkinson; Andy Friendly — *RCA/Columbia Pictures Home Video*

Richard Pryor—Live and Smokin' 1971
Comedy-Performance
76777 47 mins C B, V, CED P
Richard Pryor displays his comedic talents in this 1971 performance where he does his classic "The Wino and the Junkie" routine.
Michael Blum Productions — *Vestron Video*

Richard Pryor Live in Concert 197?
Comedy-Performance
58898 78 mins C B, V P
Richard Pryor
Richard Pryor demonstrates his unique brand of humor before an enthusiastic audience.
Unknown — *Vestron Video; RCA VideoDiscs*

Richard Pryor Live on the Sunset Strip 1982
Comedy-Performance
63438 82 mins C B, V P
Richard Pryor
Filmed live at the Hollywood Palladium, this program captures Richard Pryor at his funniest, including his segment about "Pryor on fire."
MPAA:R
Columbia; Richard Pryor — *RCA/Columbia Pictures Home Video; RCA VideoDiscs*

Richard's Things 1980
Drama
69549 104 mins C B, V P
Liv Ullman, Amanda Redman
A man's wife and his girlfriend find love and comfort in each other after his death.
MPAA:R
Unknown — *Embassy Home Entertainment*

Richie Rich 1983
Cartoons
66575 60 mins C B, V P
Animated
Rich kid Richie Rich is featured in this compilation of exotic and comical adventures with his adolescent pals.
Hanna Barbera — *Worldvision Home Video*

Richie Rich 1980
Cartoons
79240 50 mins C B, V P
Animated
The world's wealthiest little boy, Richie Rich, and his girlfriend Gloria travel around the world to solve crimes.
Hanna-Barbera Productions — *Worldvision Home Video*

Rick Derringer 1982
Music-Performance
75909 58 mins C B, V P

This program presents Rick Derringer performing several of his monster hit songs at the Ritz night club in New York City.
Harrison Suggs Productions Inc — *Sony Corporation of America*

Rick Springfield Platinum Videos 1983
Music video
66632 30 mins C B, V P
This music video collection of Rick Springfield hits contains the following six songs: "Affair of the Heart," "Human Touch," "Souls," "Don't Talk to Strangers," "What Kind of Fool Am I" and "Jessie's Girl."
RCA Video Productions — *RCA/Columbia Pictures Home Video*

Riddle of the Sands 1984
Adventure
72533 99 mins C B, V P
Michael York, Jenny Agutter, Simon Mac Corkindale, directed by Tony Maylam
Two English yachtsmen in 1903 inadvertently stumble upon a German plot to invade England by sea.
Satori — *VidAmerica*

Ride in a Pink Car 1974
Drama
81078 83 mins C B, V P
Glen Corbett, Morgan Woodward, Ivy Jones
When a Vietnam Veteran returns home, he discovers that his welcoming committee is really a lynch mob.
MPAA:R
Clarion Pictures — *Academy Home Entertainment*

Ride in the Whirlwind 1967
Western
09005 83 mins C B, V P
Jack Nicholson, Cameron Mitchell, Millie Perkins, Katherine Squire
Three cowboys are mistaken for members of a gang by a posse.
Jack Nicholson; Monte Hellman — *Media Home Entertainment; Budget Video; Sheik Video; Video Yesteryear; Discount Video Tapes; Western Film & Video Inc*

Ride, Ranger, Ride 1936
Western
05586 56 mins B/W B, V, 3/4U P
Gene Autry, Smiley Burnette, Kaye Hughes, Max Terhune
Gene Autry joins the cavalry and foils a plot to start an Indian uprising.
Republic — *Nostalgia Merchant; Video Yesteryear*

Ride the Man Down 1953
Western
74487 90 mins C B, V P
Rod Cameron, Ella Raines
This is the story of a murderous land war between neighboring landowners.
Republic — *Republic Pictures Home Video*

Ride the Wind 1966
Western
72892 120 mins C B, V P
Lorne Greene, Dan Blocker
The "Bonanza" gang goes to the aid of the Pony Express.
NBC — *Republic Pictures Home Video*

Rider from Tucson 1950
Western
73702 60 mins B/W B, V P
Tim Holt, Richard Martin
A group of claim jumpers will stop at nothing to gain control of a gold mine.
RKO — *RKO HomeVideo*

Rider on the Rain 1970
Suspense
64973 115 mins C B, V P
Marlene Jobert, Charles Bronson, Jill Ireland
A young housewife is viciously raped by an escaped sex maniac. She kills him and disposes of his body, not knowing that he is being relentlessly pursued by a tough colonel.
Avco-Embassy — *Embassy Home Entertainment*

Riders of Destiny 1933
Western
15489 59 mins B/W B, V P
John Wayne
John Wayne leads a group of Rangers on the trail of justice.
Monogram — *Sony Corporation of America; Spotlite Video; Video Connection; Discount Video Tapes; Video Dimensions*

Riders of the Desert 1932
Western
11371 57 mins B/W B, V, FO P
Bob Steele
Plenty of hoofbeats through desert sands.
Worldwide — *Video Yesteryear; Video Connection*

Riders of the Range 1949
Western
73700 60 mins B/W B, V P
Tim Holt, Richard Martin
A cowboy rides into town just in time to save a girl's brother from gamblers.
RKO — *RKO HomeVideo*

(For explanation of codes, see USE GUIDE and KEY)

Riders of the Rockies 1937
Western
15457 60 mins B/W B, V P
Tex Ritter, Yakima Canutt, directed by Robert N. Bradbury
An honest cowboy turns rustler in order to trap a border gang.
Grand National — *United Home Video; Video Connection; Discount Video Tapes*

Riders of the Whistling Pines 1949
Western
64391 70 mins B/W B, V, 3/4U P
Gene Autry, Patricia White, Jimmy Lloyd
Gene solves a murder committed by a band of lumber thieves.
Gene Autry Productions; Columbia — *Nostalgia Merchant*

Ridin' on a Rainbow 1941
Western
54112 79 mins B/W B, V P, T
Gene Autry, Smiley Burnette
A has-been performer on a steamboat decides to rob a bank in the hopes of starting a new life for himself and his daughter. The money he robs had just been deposited by some cattlemen. One of the cattlemen joins the steamboat's crew, wins the daughter's heart, and gets to the father.
Republic — *Blackhawk Films; Video Connection*

Rififi 1954
Mystery
44160 115 mins B/W B, V P
Jean Servais, Carl Mohner, Robert Manuel, Jules Dassin, directed by Jules Dassin
A suspensful story of a successful jewel robbery in which the four thieves betray each other. French with English subtitles.
FR
UMPO; French — *Movie Buff Video; Video Yesteryear; Budget Video; Discount Video Tapes; Cable Films; Western Film & Video Inc*

Right of Way 1984
Drama
74110 102 mins C B, V P
Bette Davis, James Stewart, Melinda Dillon
A touching story of true love featuring two of the biggest stars to ever grace the silver screen. Stewart plays an elderly man who makes a suicide pact when he learns of his wife's terminal illness.
George Schaefer — *VCL Home Video*

Right Stuff, The 1983
Drama
Closed Captioned
74210 193 mins C B, V, LV R, P
Charles Frank, Scott Glenn, Ed Harris, Dennis Quaid, Sam Shephard
This program is based on the best-selling book by Tom Wolfe. It is the up-close and personal story of America's space program at its conception.
Academy Awards '83: Best Music Score; Best Film Editing; Best Sound; Best Sound Effect Editing. MPAA:PG
Irwin Winkler; Robert Chartoff — *Warner Home Video*

Right Stuff/NFL '83, The 1984
Football
72939 46 mins C B, V, FO P
Pittsburgh Steelers
Highlights from the Pittsburgh Steelers' 1983 season and "NFL 1983."
NFL Films — *NFL Films Video*

Rigoletto 1954
Opera
56916 90 mins C B, V, FO P
Aldo Silvani, Gerard Landry, Janet Vidor
Verdi's great opera concerning the intrigues in the court of the Duke of Mantua, and the clever plottings of Rigoletto—the hunchbacked court jester. Sung in Italian with dialogue dubbed in English.
Italy — *Video Yesteryear*

Rime of the Ancient Mariner 198?
Literature
47405 60 mins C B, V P
Narrated by Sir Michael Redgrave, directed by Raul De Silva
An adaptation of Samuel Taylor Coleridge's epic poem, set to images both real and animated; in two parts—Part I: The Life of Samuel Coleridge; Part II: The Rime of the Ancient Mariner.
International Film and Television Festival of New York: Gold Medal.
Kultur — *Kultur*

Ring of Death, The 1972
Mystery
80823 93 mins C B, V R, P
Franco Nero, Florinda Bolkan, Adolfo Celi
A tough cop investigating a routine case becomes a hunted man after someone kills the man he is following.
Mario Cecci Gori — *Video Gems*

Ringing Bell 1983
Fairy tales
65467 ? mins C B, V P
Animated
This is the story of a fluffly lamb whose mother is killed by a terrifying black wolf, leaving him alone and resolved to avenge her death. In Beta Hi-Fi.

Tsunemasa Hatano — *RCA/Columbia Pictures Home Video*

Ringo Rides West 1984
Cartoons
81074 55 mins C B, V P
Animated
This is the story of Ringo the cat who leads a courageous battle for truth and justice in the wild western frontier.
H. Lewis — *MPI Home Video*

Rink, The/The Immigrant 191?
Comedy
59368 56 mins B/W B, V, FO P
Charlie Chaplin, Mack Swain, Edna Purviance
Two Chaplin shorts: 'The Rink" (1916), in which Charlie defends his girlfriend's honor at a local roller skating rink; "The Immigrant" (1917), features Charlie as a newcomer to America.
Mutual — *Video Yesteryear*

Rio Bravo 1959
Western
58246 140 mins C B, V R, P
John Wayne, Dean Martin, Angie Dickinson, Rick Nelson, Walter Brennan, directed by Howard Hawks
The sheriff of a Texas border town takes a brutal murderer into custody—and faces a blockade of hired gunmen determined to keep his prisoner from being brought to justice.
Armada Productions — *Warner Home Video; RCA VideoDiscs*

Rio Grande 1950
Western
66466 105 mins B/W B, V P
John Wayne, Maureen O'Hara, Ben Jonson, Claude Jarman Jr., directed by John Ford
A U.S. Cavalry unit on the Mexican border conducts an unsuccessful campaign against marauding Indians.
Republic — *Republic Pictures Home Video*

Rio Lobo 1970
Western
54104 114 mins C B, V, CED P
John Wayne, Jorge Rivero, Jennifer O'Neill, Jack Elam, directed by Howard Hawks
After the Civil War, a Union Colonel goes to Rio Lobo to take revenge on two traitors. When he gets there he finds that one of the traitors is in a conspiracy with the town sheriff, trying to force a rancher to sign over all his land.
MPAA:G
National General Pictures, Cinema Center — *CBS/Fox Video*

Riot in Cell Block 11 1954
Drama
77481 80 mins B/W B, V P
Neville Brand, Leo Gordon, Emile Meyer, directed by Don Siegel
A convict leads four thousand prisoners in a riot at a maximum security penitentiary.
Allied Artists — *Republic Pictures Home Video*

Ripoff, The 1978
Adventure
79244 90 mins C B, V P
Lee Van Cleef, Karen Black, Edward Albert, Robert Alda
An aging jewel thief comes out of retirement to pull off a six million dollar jewelry heist.
Turi Vasile — *Worldvision Home Video*

Ripped Off 1974
Mystery
81157 72 mins C B, V P
Robert Blake, Ernest Borgnine, Catherine Spaak
A boxer framed for the murder of his manager sets out to clear his name by finding the killers.
MPAA:R
Ottavio Oppo. — *Lightning Video*

Rise and Fall of the Third Reich 1968
Documentary/History-Modern
68247 120 mins C B, V P
A pictorial record which tracks Adolph Hitler's path through the years between 1920 and 1945. Some segments are in black and white.
MGM — *MGM/UA Home Video*

Risky Business 1983
Comedy
65357 99 mins C B, V, LV, CED P
Tom Cruise, Rebecca de Mornay
A straight-arrow college-bound student encounters a street-smart call girl while his parents are out of town, resulting in a funny and harrowing week-long odyssey toward maturity. In VHS Dolby stereo/Beta Hi-fi.
MPAA:R
Steve Tisch Jon Avnet Production — *Warner Home Video*

Rita Hayworth: The Love Goddess 1983
Biographical/Drama
79330 97 mins C B, V P
Lynda Carter, Michael Lerner, Alejandro Rey, John Considine
A dramatization of Rita Hayworth's public and private life from 1934 to 1952. In Beta Hi-Fi and VHS Stereo.
Susskind Company — *U.S.A. Home Video*

Rituals 1979
Drama
60447 100 mins C B, V P

Hal Holbrook, Laurence Dane
A group of five calm, rational men suddenly turn desperate after a chain of nightmarish events.
Lawrence Dane; Day and Date Intl — *Embassy Home Entertainment*

Ritz, The **1976**
Comedy
Closed Captioned
80708 91 mins C B, V R, P
Rita Moreno, Jack Weston, Jerry Stiller, Kaye Ballard, Treat Williams, F. Murray Abraham, directed by Richard Lester
When a Cleveland sanitation man meets up with his wife's murderous brother at his father-in-law's funeral in New York, he hides out in an all-male bathhouse.
MPAA:R
Warner Bros. — *Warner Home Video*

Rivals of the Silver Fox **1980**
Martial arts
69281 80 mins C B, V P
Casanova Wong, Barry Lam, Chen Shao Peng, Lee Fat Yuen
Wang Fung seeks and finds his wife's murderer, but revenge is not easy. Mandarin dialogue, English subtitles.
CH
IFD Films & Arts — *Silverline Video*

River, The **1984**
Drama
70553 124 mins C B, V, LV P
Mel Gibson, Sissy Spacek, Scott Glenn, directed by Mark Rydell, written by Robert Dillon and Julian Barry
Tom and Mae Garvey fight floods, foreclosures, and government efforts to construct a hydroelectric plant in this third of '84's "back-to-the-farm" films. This tape features the beautiful photography of the film and stereo surround sound in all formats.
MPAA:PG13
Universal — *MCA Home Video*

River of Unrest **1937**
Drama
78107 69 mins B/W B, V, FO P
John Lodge, John Loder, Antoinette Cellier
Remarkable visual expressiveness and emotional power in a film about terrorism and open warfare during the Irish Rebellion.
Wardour — *Video Yesteryear*

River Rat, The **1984**
Drama
Closed Captioned
70357 93 mins C B, V, LV R, P
Tommy Lee Jones, Brian Dennehy, Martha Plimpton
The story of an ex-convict—wrongly imprisoned for thirteen years—who learns the value of love from his young daughter. The action takes place on the Mississippi River, where the reunited family faces many evil challenges.
MPAA:PG
Paramount Pictures Corp. — *Paramount Home Video*

Road Games **1981**
Suspense
60448 100 mins C B, V, CED P
Stacy Keach, Jamie Lee Curtis
A trucker is drawn into a web of intrigue surrounding a series of highway murders.
MPAA:PG
Avco Embassy; Richard Franklin — *Embassy Home Entertainment*

Road Runner vs. Wile E. Coyote: The Classic Chase **1963**
Cartoons
81574 54 mins C B, V R, P
Animated, directed by Chuck Jones
Wile E. Coyote engages in a battle of wits against the Road Runner in this collection of eight classic cartoons.
Warner Bros — *Warner Home Video*

Road to Bali **1953**
Comedy
47663 91 mins C B, V P
Bob Hope, Bing Crosby, Dorothy Lamour, Mervyn Vye, Ralph Moody, Jane Russell, Jerry Lewis, Dean Martin
Two vaudervillians performing in Australia are forced to hit the high seas due to a pair of matrimony-minded females.
Paramount — *Unicorn Video*

Road to Lebanon, The **1960**
Comedy
78104 50 mins B/W B, V, FO P
Danny Thomas, Bing Crosby, Bob Hope, Hugh Downs, Claudine Auger, Sheldon Leonard
This program presents an original musical comedy featuring many stars, spoofing the famous Hope-Crosby "Road" films.
NBC — *Video Yesteryear*

Road to Yesterday/The Yankee Clipper **1927**
Film-History
50640 56 mins B/W B, V P, T
William Boyd, Elinor Fair, Joseph Schildkraut, Jetta Boudal, Vera Reynolds
Four train passengers are transported back to previous lives in "The Road to Yesterday." "The Yankee Clipper races the British Lord of the Isles from China to New England to capture the tea trade. Both of these pictures are abridged versions. Silent.

Cecil B DeMille; Rupert Julian — *Blackhawk Films*

Road Warrior, The **1982**
Adventure
63453 95 mins C B, V, LV, CED R, P
Mel Gibson, directed by George Miller
There is only one man who can save the terrorized pilgrims who've barricaded themselves on the barren post WWIII plains of Australia. The Road Warrior - Mad Max. This action filled sequel to "Mad Max" features Gibson playing John Wayne in metal and leather. No kangaroos or koalas.
MPAA:R
Warner Bros; Kennedy Miller Productions — *Warner Home Video*

Road Warriors, The/NFL '82 **1983**
Football
66221 45 mins C B, V, FO P
Highlights of the N.Y. Jets 1982-83 season, plus an overview of the whole NFL season.
NFL Films — *NFL Films Video*

Roadhouse 66 **1984**
Drama
73660 90 mins C B, V R, P
When a preppie and a musician get stuck in an Arizona town for car repairs, the duo wind up in a drag race and fall in love. The soundtrack features music from Los Lobos, The Pretenders, and Dave Edmunds.
MPAA:R
Scott Rosenfelt; Mark Levinson — *Key Video*

Roaring Fire **1982**
Suspense/Martial arts
66025 95 mins C B, V R, P
Sonny Chiba
A martial arts thriller set against the backdrop of exotic Japan.
Shiteru Okada — *THORN EMI/HBO Video*

Roaring Twenties, The **1939**
Drama
64786 106 mins B/W B, V P
James Cagney, Humphrey Bogart, Jeffrey Lynn, Priscilla Lane
A WWI veteran returns to New York and becomes involved in bootlegging, builds up an empire and dies in a gang war.
Warner; Hal B. Wallis — *Key Video; RCA VideoDiscs*

Roaring Twenties, The **192?**
History-US/Documentary
10147 ? mins B/W B, V P, T
Newsreels picture Ku Klux Klan, the automobile era, the first total solar eclipse, the Charleston, Babe Ruth, Rudolph Valentino's death, Charles Lindbergh, and Black Tuesday when stock market crashed.
Unknown — *Blackhawk Films*

Rob McConnell **1983**
Music-Performance
75916 25 mins C B, V P
This program presents the jazz music of Rob McConnell featuring his hits "The Waltz I Blew for You" and "My Man Bill."
digit recordings — *Sony Corporation of America*

Robbers of the Sacred Mountain **1983**
Adventure
75489 95 mins C B, V P
Two adventurers seek meteorites in the jungles of Mexico.
Unknown — *Prism*

Robby the Rascal **1985**
Cartoons/Fantasy
81104 90 mins C B, V R, P
Animated
The evil Mr. Bullion devises a plan to steal a cybot, Robby the Rascal, from his inventor Dr. Rumplechips.
Kidpix Inc. — *Paramount Home Video*

Robe, The **1953**
Drama
08455 133 mins C B, V P
Richard Burton, Jean Simmons, Victor Mature, Michael Rennie
This moving religious picture follows the career of a drunken and dissolute Roman tribune, Marcellus, after he wins the robe of Christ in a dice game.
EL, SP
20th Century Fox — *CBS/Fox Video*

Robert et Robert **1979**
Comedy-Drama
47022 95 mins C B, V P
Charles Denner, Jacques Villeret, Jean-Claude Brialy
Two "ineligible" bachelors resort to a computerized matrimonial agency to find the girls of their dreams. French with English subtitles.
FR
Quartet Films — *RCA/Columbia Pictures Home Video*

Robert Klein: Child of the 50's, Man of the 80's **1984**
Comedy-Performance
80813 60 mins C B, V R, P
Robert Klein

The hilarious Robert Klein performs some of his classic routines in this concert taped at New York University in Manhattan's Greenwich Village.
HBO — *THORN EMI/HBO Video*

Roberto Clemente: A Touch of Royalty 1975
Baseball
33831 26 mins C B, V P
Roberto Clemente
The story of the near-legendary Pittsburgh Pirate outfielder and Hall of Famer is told through action footage of Clemente, on-iocation shooting in his native Puerto Rico, and interview with friends and family. His tragic death occurred on a mercy mission to aid Nicaraguan Refugees.
W and W Productions — *Major League Baseball Productions*

Robin and Marian 1976
Drama
65097 106 mins C B, V P
Sean Connery, Audrey Hepburn, Robert Shaw, Richard Harris, directed by Richard Lester
After a separation of twenty years, Robin Hood is reunited with Maid Marian, who is now a nun. Their dormant feelings for each other are reawakened as Robin spirits her to Sherwood Forest.
MPAA:PG
Columbia; Rastar — *RCA/Columbia Pictures Home Video*

Robin Hood 1973
Cartoons
Closed Captioned
79558 83 mins C B, V, LV, CED R, P
Animated, voices of Peter Ustinov, Terry Thomas, Phil Harris, Brian Bedford
A group of animals from Sherwood Forest act out their version of the Robin Hood legend.
Wolfgang Reitherman — *Walt Disney Home Video*

Robinhood of Texas 1947
Western/Musical
44807 71 mins B/W B, V P, T
Gene Autry, Cass County Boys
Gene and his friend help a sheriff round up a team of bank robbers and their loot while salvaging an almost defunct ranch and turning it into a fancy dude ranch.
Republic — *Blackhawk Films; Video Connection*

Robinhood of the Pecos 1941
Western
51640 56 mins B/W B, V P
Roy Rogers
A young, ex-Confederate soldier takes on northern post-war politicians and carpetbaggers.
Republic — *Discount Video Tapes; Video Yesteryear*

Robinson Crusoe 1936
Adventure
38978 34 mins B/W B, V, FO P
Narrated by "Uncle Don" Carney
A real oddity—this is a British silent film that was originally made in 1927. Ten years later, the film was re-edited, music and sound effects were added, along with a narration by children's radio personality "Uncle Don" Carney, which follows the plot of the famous adventure story.
Unknown — *Video Yesteryear*

Robinson Crusoe 1978
Cartoons
76972 86 mins C B, V P
Animated
An animated adaptation of the classic Defoe story about a man marooned on a small island.
Viacom — *Family Home Entertainment*

Robinson Crusoe and the Tiger 1972
Adventure
81448 109 mins C B, V P
Hugo Stiglitz, Ahui, directed by Rene Cardona, Jr.
A tiger tells the famous story of how Robinson Crusoe became stranded on a desert island.
MPAA:G
Avant Films — *Embassy Home Entertainment*

Robot Monster 1953
Science fiction
64921 58 mins B/W B, V P
George Nader, Claudia Barrett, directed by Phil Tucker
This ludicrous cheapie is considered to be one of the worst films of all time. Alien invaders (dressed in motheaten gorilla suits and diving helmets) attack mankind with a giant soap-bubble machine.
Astor — *Video Dimensions; Admit One Video*

Rock Adventure 1981
Music
47298 29 mins C LV P
Music by Baenzai and breathtaking visuals combine to express a mood of wild adventure.
Masaru Ohtaki; Tokyo Eizosha Company — *Pioneer Video Imports*

Rock Music with the Muppets 1985
Variety
Closed Captioned
80745 54 mins C B, V P
Kermit the Frog, Dr. Teeth, Floyd Pepper, Zoot, Alice Cooper, Debbie Harry, Paul Simon, Helen Reddy, Leo Sayer, Loretta Swit, Ben Vereen
The Muppets perform their own brand of rock and roll with their special musical guests. The songs featured include "Rock Around the Clock," "Call Me," "Rainbow Connection," and 'Disco Frog". Available in VHS and Beta Hi Fi.
Henson Associates — *Playhouse Video*

Rock 'n' Roll High School 1979
Musical
64299 94 mins C B, V P
P. J. Soles, Clint Howard, The Ramones
The music of the Ramones highlights this story of a high school out to thwart the principal at every turn.
MPAA:PG
New World Pictures — *Warner Home Video*

Rock, Rock, Rock 1956
Musical
59155 78 mins B/W B, V, 3/4U P
Chuck Berry, Fats Domino, Tuesday Weld, Frankie Lymon and the Teeangers
A young girl's father insists she earn enough money to buy a new gown for the Senior Prom. Classic musical numbers performed by a number of rock'n'roll pioneers.
DCA — *Nostalgia Merchant*

Rock, You Sinners 1957
Musical
59370 59 mins B/W B, V, FO P
Vintage rock 'n' roll from pre-Beatles England. A BBC DJ forced to play rock 'n' roll records gets the idea to put on a rock 'n' roll TV show.
England — *Video Yesteryear*

Rocketship 1936
Science fiction
81079 70 mins B/W B, V P
Buster Crabbe, Jean Rogers, Charles Middleton
Flash Gordon is out to save the earth from the clutches of Ming the Merciless. Edited from the popular serial.
Universal Pictures — *Prism*

Rocketship X-M—Special Edition 1950
Science fiction/Adventure
44357 77 mins B/W B, V, 3/4U P
Lloyd Bridges, Osa Massen, John Emery, Hugh O'Brien
A lunar mission goes awry and the crew lands on Mars. Contains newly photographed footage, a tinted sequence and previews of coming attractions from classic science fiction films.
Lippert — *Nostalgia Merchant*

Rockshow 1981
Music-Performance
58884 102 mins C B, V R, P
Paul McCartney and Wings
Paul and Wings perform 23 of their best songs before an audience of 67,000 fans at the King Dome in Seattle, Washington. Selections include "Jet," "Band on the Run," "Venus and Mars," "Maybe I'm Amazed," and "Yesterday."
MPL Communications — *THORN EMI/HBO Video; Pioneer Artists; RCA VideoDiscs*

Rocky 1976
Drama
37521 119 mins C B, V, LV, CED P
Sylvester Stallone, Talia Shire, Burgess Meredith, directed by John G. Avildsen
A young man from the slums of Philadelphia pursues his dream of becoming a boxing champion.
Academy Awards '76: Best Picture; Best Director (Avildsen); Best Achievement in Film Editing. MPAA:PG
United Artists — *CBS/Fox Video; RCA VideoDiscs*

Rocky II 1979
Drama
58810 119 mins C B, V, LV, CED P
Sylvester Stallone, Talia Shire, Burt Young, Burgess Meredith, Carl Weathers
This sequel to the box office smash finds Rocky frustrated by the commercialism which followed his match to Apollo, and soon considers a return bout.
MPAA:PG
United Artists; Irwin Winkler; Robert Chartoff — *CBS/Fox Video; RCA VideoDiscs*

Rocky III 1982
Drama
63395 100 mins C B, V, LV, CED P
Sylvester Stallone, Talia Shire, Burgess Meredith, Carl Weathers
The third in the "Rocky" trilogy finds heavyweight champ Rocky Balboa training with his former opponent Apollo Creed to prepare for a rematch with Clubber Lang.
MPAA:PG
United Artists — *CBS/Fox Video; RCA VideoDiscs*

Rocky Jones, Space Ranger: Blast Off 1953
Science fiction
11280 75 mins B/W B, V, FO P
Richard Crane, Scotty Beckett, Sally Mansfield, Maurice Cass

Rocky, his sidekick Winky, and Professor Newton travel through another space adventure in their ship, "The Orbit Jet."
Roland Reed — *Video Yesteryear*

Rocky Jones, Space Ranger: Pirates of Prah **1953**
Science fiction
11279 75 mins B/W B, V, FO P
Richard Crane, Scotty Beckett, Sally Mansfield, Maurice Cass
Rocky Jones, sidekick Winky, and Professor Newton confront space pirates in this episode.
Roland Reed — *Video Yesteryear*

Rocky Jones, Space Ranger: The Cold Sun **1953**
Science fiction
11278 75 mins B/W B, V, FO P
Richard Crane, Scotty Beckett, Sally Mansfield, Maurice Cass
An adventure in the series "Rocky Jones, Space Ranger," as Rocky, Winky, and Professor Newton travel through space.
Roland Reed — *Video Yesteryear*

Rocky Jones, Space Ranger: Trial of Rocky Jones **1953**
Science fiction
11281 75 mins B/W B, V, FO P
Richard Crane, Scotty Beckett, Sally Mansfield, Maurice Cass
Rocky Jones, trouble-shooter for the Office of Space Affairs, travels through the universe in his spaceship "The Orbit Jet" along with his pal Winky and Professor Newton.
Roland Reed — *Video Yesteryear*

Rocky King, Detective **1954**
Crime-Drama
47482 25 mins B/W B, V, FO P
Roscoe Karnes, Todd Karnes, Grace Carney, Jack Klugman
In the story "Return for Death," New York City Police detective Rocky King solves a murder in a mausoleum. An early, live cop show from TV's Golden Age.
Dumont — *Video Yesteryear*

Rod Stewart **1983**
Music-Performance
76671 16 mins C B, V P
This program presents Rod Stewart performing "Do Ya Think I'm Sexy," "Passion" and "Young Turks."
Embassy Hom ntertainment — *Sony Corporation of nerica*

Rod Stewart Live at the L.A. Forum **1980**
Music-Performance
54688 60 mins C B, V R, P
Rod Stewart
A look at highlights from Rod Stewart's 1979 appearance at the Forum. Songs include "Hot Legs," "Do Ya Think I'm Sexy," "Blondes Have More Fun," "Maggie May," and "You're in My Heart."
Warner Bros — *Warner Home Video; RCA VideoDiscs*

Rod Stewart: Tonight He's Yours **1982**
Music-Performance
60449 90 mins C B, V, LV, CED P
Rod Stewart, Tina Turner
Rod the Mod offers up 17 top hits from this concert taped at the L.A. Forum, including: "Do Ya Think I'm Sexy," "Maggie Mae" "You're in My Heart," and more.
Unknown — *Embassy Home Entertainment*

Rodan **1956**
Horror
63968 74 mins C B, V, LV, CED P
Kenji Sahara, Yumi Shirakawa
A gigantic prehistoric bird is disturbed from his slumber by H-bomb tests; he awakens to wreak havoc on civilization.
Toho Productions — *Vestron Video*

Rollerball **1975**
Science fiction
13596 123 mins C B, V, CED P
James Caan, John Houseman, Maud Adams, Moses Gunn, directed by Norman Jewison
In the year 2018 there is rollerball, a brutal sport combining the violence of all other sports.
MPAA:R
United Artists — *CBS/Fox Video*

Rolling Thunder **1977**
Drama
64360 99 mins C B, V, CED P
William Devane, Tommy Lee Jones, Linda Haynes
A Vietnam veteran returns home after eight years as a POW. Shortly afterward, his wife and son are murdered, causing him to seek revenge.
MPAA:R
American International — *Vestron Video*

Rollover **1981**
Drama
59855 118 mins C B, V R, P
Jane Fonda, Kris Kristofferson, Hume Cronyn, directed by Alan J. Pakula

A banker and board chairman get involved in the intrigue and danger of multi-million dollar world finance.
MPAA:R
Orion; Warner Bros. — *Warner Home Video*

Roman Holiday **1953**
Comedy/Romance
64782 118 mins B/W B, V P
Audrey Hepburn, Gregory Peck, Eddie Albert, directed by William Wyler
A princess on an official visit to Rome slips away without notice and falls in love with a newspaperman.
Academy Awards '53: Best Actress (Hepburn); Writing (Ian McLellan Hunter); Costume Design B&W (Edith Head).
Paramount; William Wyler — *Paramount Home Video; RCA VideoDiscs*

Roman Spring of Mrs. Stone, The **1961**
Drama
80443 104 mins C B, V R, P
Warren Beatty, Vivien Leigh, Lotte Lenya, Bessie Love, Jill St. John, directed by Jose Quintero
An actress comes to Rome seeking to revive her career but winds up falling in love with a gigolo.
Louis de Rochemont; Warner Bros. — *Warner Home Video*

Romance with a Double Bass **1974**
Comedy
79112 40 mins C B, V P
John Cleese, Connie Booth
When a musician and a princess take a skinny dip in the royal lake and get their clothes stolen, comic complications arise.
RPTA Video — *Pacific Arts Video*

Romancing the Stone **1984**
Adventure/Romance
Closed Captioned
73140 106 mins C B, V, CED P
Micheal Douglas, Kathleen Turner, Danny De Vito, directed by Robert Zemeckis
Kathleen Turner stars as a writer of romance novels who gets a chance to live out her story when she receives a phone call that her sister has been kidnapped in South America.
MPAA:PG
Micheal Douglas; 20th Century Fox — *CBS/Fox Video*

Romantic Comedy **1983**
Comedy
72897 102 mins C B, V P
Dudley Moore, Mary Steenburgen
A married man is in love with a single girl and when he becomes unhitched she marries another man.
MPAA:PG
Walter Mirisch; Morton Gottlieb — *CBS/Fox Video*

Romantic Englishwoman, The **1975**
Romance/Comedy
49925 117 mins C B, V R, P
Glenda Jackson, Michael Caine, Helmut Berger, directed by Joseph Losey
A married couple tests fidelity to its limits.
MPAA:R
New World — *Warner Home Video*

Romeo and Juliet **1968**
Drama
38603 138 mins C B, V, LV R, P
Olivia Hussey, Leonard Whiting, Michael York, directed by Franco Zeffirelli
A fresh, vital version of Shakespeare's classic romantic play, which won critical acclaim upon its release.
MPAA:PG
Paramount — *Paramount Home Video; RCA VideoDiscs*

Romeo and Juliet **1954**
Drama
59902 138 mins C B, V P
Laurence Harvey, Susan Shantall, Aldo Zollo, Sebastian Cabot, John Gielgud
Shakespeare's tale of young love, shot on Italian locations.
Rank; Verona — *Embassy Home Entertainment*

Romie-O and Julie-8 **1978**
Musical/Fantasy
54693 25 mins C B, V R, P
Animated
This musical fantasy tells of the special love between two young robots—an interpretation of the great love story, "Romeo and Juliet."
Original songs by John Sebastian.
Nelvana Productions — *Warner Home Video; Beacon Films*

Romper Room and Friends **1984**
Education
Closed Captioned
78884 45 mins C B, V P
4 pgms
Children learn about numbers, letters, words, movement, rhythm, and animals in the zoo in this series.
1.Numbers, Letters and Words 2.Go to the Zoo 3.Playful Projects 4.Movement and Rhythm
Romper Enterprises — *Playhouse Video*

 (For explanation of codes, see USE GUIDE and KEY)

Room Service 1938
Comedy
00256 78 mins B/W B, V, 3/4U P
The Marx Brothers, Lucille Ball, Ann Miller, Frank Albertson
A penniless theatrical producer connives to keep his hotel room until he can find a backer for his latest play.
RKO; Pandro S Berman — *Nostalgia Merchant; Blackhawk Films; VidAmerica*

Rooster Cogburn 1975
Western
58425 107 mins C B, V P
John Wayne, Katharine Hepburn, Richard Jordan, Anthony Zerbe, John McIntire
A Bible-thumping schoolmarm joins up with a hard-drinking, hard-fighting marshal in order to capture a gang of incompetent outlaws who killed her father.
MPAA:PG
Universal; Hal Wallis — *MCA Home Video*

Rootin' Tootin' Rhythm 1938
Western
11262 55 mins B/W B, V, FO P
Gene Autry
All's not quiet on the range, but Gene Autry comes along to sing things back to normal.
Republic — *Video Yesteryear; Discount Video Tapes*

Roots 1977
Drama
58247 90 mins C B, V R, P
Ed Asner, Lloyd Bridges, LeVar Burton, Chuck Connors, Lynda Day George, Lorne Greene, Burl Ives, O. J. Simpson, Cicely Tyson, Ben Vereen, Sandy Duncan 6 pgms
The complete version of Alex Haley's saga following a black man's search for his heritage, revealing an epic panorama of America's past. Available on six 90-minute tapes.
Wolper Pictures — *Warner Home Video*

Rope 1948
Drama
80413 81 mins C B, V, LV P
James Stewart, John Dall, Farley Granger, directed by Alfred Hitchcock
Two college students murder a friend for kicks and conceal the body in a truck which they will use as a buffet table for a dinner party. Hitchcock's first color film.
MPAA:PG
Sidney Bernstein, Alfred Hitchcock — *MCA Home Video*

Rose, The 1979
Musical
44932 134 mins C B, V, LV, CED P
Bette Midler, Alan Bates
A young, multitalented, and self-destructive rock star tries to come to grips with her love affairs, professional triumphs, and lonely restlessness.
MPAA:R
20th Century Fox — *CBS/Fox Video*

Rosebud Beach Hotel, The 1985
Comedy
80702 82 mins C B, V, CED P
Peter Scolari, Coleen Camp, Christopher Lee
A young man tries his hand at managing a run down hotel in order to please his demanding girlfriend.
MPAA:R
Alme Pictures — *Vestron Video*

Roseland 1977
Drama
64885 103 mins C B, V P
Christopher Walken, Geraldine Chaplin, Joan Copeland, Teresa Wright, Lou Jacobi
Three interlocking stories, set within New York's Roseland Ballroom, tell about lonely people who live to dance.
Cinema Shares International — *Vestron Video*

Rosemary's Baby 1968
Horror
55543 137 mins C B, V, LV R, P
Mia Farrrow, John Cassavettes, Ruth Gordon, Maurice Evans, Patsy Kelly, Elisha Cook, Charles Grodin, directed by Roman Polanski
After unwittingly becoming friendly with a coven of witches and warlocks, a young wife is impregnated by the Devil.
Academy Awards '68: Best Supporting Actress (Gordon). MPAA:R
Paramount; William Castle — *Paramount Home Video; RCA VideoDiscs*

Rostropovich 1982
Music-Performance
60576 65 mins C LV P
Mstislav Rostropovich, London Philharmonic Orchestra conducted by Carlo Maria Giulini
The great cellist performs Dvorak's "Cello Concerto" and Saint-Saens' "Cello Concerto No. 1." In stereo.
EMI Music Video — *Pioneer Artists*

Rough Cut 1980
Adventure
54672 111 mins C B, V, LV R, P
Burt Reynolds, Lesley-Anne Down, David Niven, Timothy West, Patrick Magee, directed by Donald Siegel
An American diamond thief living in London is pursued by a Scotland Yard detective who is about to retire and wants to finish his career in a blaze of glory.
MPAA:PG

Paramount — *Paramount Home Video*

Rough Riders of Cheyenne 1945
Western
64421 54 mins B/W B, V, 3/4U P
Sunset Carson, Peggy Stewart
Sunset ends the feud between the Carsons and the Sterlings.
Republic — *Nostalgia Merchant*

Roughnecks 1980
Drama
80314 240 mins C B, V P
Sam Melville, Cathy Lee Crosby, Vera Miles, Harry Morgan
A team of Texas oil drillers attempt to dig the deepest oil well in history.
Metromedia Producers Corp. — *Prism*

Round-Up Time in Texas 1937
Western
08895 54 mins B/W B, V, 3/4U P
Gene Autry, Smiley Burnette
Autry answers an urgent call for horses from South Africa's jungle-blocked diamond belt.
Republic — *Video Connection; Video Yesteryear; Discount Video Tapes*

Roustabout 1964
Musical-Drama
08384 101 mins C B, V P
Elvis Presley, Barbara Stanwyck, Joan Freeman, Leif Erickson, Sue Ann Langdon
A roving, reckless singer joins a carnival and romances the owner's daughter.
EL, SP
Paramount; Hal Wallis — *CBS/Fox Video*

Roxy Music: The High Road 1983
Music-Performance
65462 ? mins C B, V P
This concert film was recorded during Brian Ferry and Roxy Music's 1982 World Tour and features old standards such as "Avalon" and "Dance Away," plus many new songs. In stereo VHS and Beta Hi-Fi.
Robin Nash — *RCA/Columbia Pictures Home Video*

Roy Rogers and Dale Evans Show, The 1962
Television/Variety
63627 55 mins B/W B, V, FO P
Roy Rogers, Dale Evans, Cliff Arquette, The Sons of the Pioneers
A musical cross-country tour is provided in this show, first telecast on October 27, 1962. Original commercials for Tang and Dodge are included.
ABC — *Video Yesteryear*

Roy Rogers Show, The 1950
Western
77198 100 mins B/W B, V P
Roy Rogers, Carl Switzer, Dale Evans, Pat Brady
Roy, Dale, Trigger and Buttercup ride again to fight off the bad guys in this collection of four episodes from the series.
Roy Rogers Productions — *Shokus Video*

Royal Bed, The 1931
Romance
11252 74 mins B/W B, V, FO P
Lowell Sherman, Nance O'Neill, Mary Astor, Anthony Bushell, Gilbert Emery, Robert Emery
King Eric VIII is beset by many problems, the foremost being his wife, the Queen.
RKO — *Video Yesteryear*

Royal Wedding 1951
Musical
58873 100 mins C B, V, CED P
Fred Astaire, Jane Powell, Peter Lawford, Keenan Wynn, directed by Stanley Donen
A brother and sister dance team goes to London at the time of the royal wedding of Princess Elizabeth.
MGM — *MGM/UA Home Video (disc only); Discount Video Tapes*

Royal Wedding, The 1981
Documentary/Great Britain
58465 60 mins C B, V R, P
Highlights of the Royal Wedding of Prince Charles and Princess Diana, with all of the pageantry and splendor.
Thames TV — *THORN EMI/HBO Video*

R.S.V.P. 1984
Drama
77175 87 mins C B, V, LV, CED P
Harry Reems
A Hollywood party honoring a writer turns tragic when a body is found in the guest of honor's pool.
MPAA:R
Chuck Vincent Productions — *Vestron Video*

Rubber Rodeo 1984
Music-Performance
76666 18 mins C B, V P
This program presents the band with the unique punk-country sound. Songs included are: "Anywhere with You," "How the West Was Won," "The Theme from Rubber Rodeo" and many more.
Polygram Records Inc — *Sony Corporation of America*

Rubber Rodeo **1984**
Music-Performance
73987 18 mins C B, V P
The country punk band performs music from their debut album in four conceptual music videos.
Polygram Records — *Sony Corporation of America*

Rubik, The Amazing Cube, Volume II **1984**
Cartoons
77245 45 mins C B, V P
Animated
Rubik and his friends twist their way through two new animated adventures.
Ruby-Spears Enterprises — *RCA/Columbia Pictures Home Video*

Rubik, The Amazing Cube Vol. I **1984**
Cartoons
Closed Captioned
80378 45 mins C B, V P
Animated
Here are two episodes from the animated series based upon the popular puzzle.
Ruby-Spears Enterprises — *RCA/Columbia Pictures Home Video*

Ruby **1977**
Horror
35380 85 mins C B, V P
Piper Laurie
Horrifying tale of a young woman christened in blood and raised in sin, having a love affair with the supernatural.
MPAA:R
George Edwards — *United Home Video; Continental Video*

Ruby Gentry **1952**
Drama
65331 82 mins B/W B, V P
Charlton Heston, Jennifer Jones, Karl Malden
A girl from the wrong side of the tracks, cast aside by the man she loves, marries a wealthy businessman and sets out to destroy all those who snubbed her
David Selznick — *CBS/Fox Video*

Ruddigore **19??**
Opera/Comedy
65493 112 mins C B, V P
Vincent Price, Keith Michell, Sandra Dugdale
The Lords of Ruddigore have been bound for centuries by a terribly inconvenient curse; they must commit a crime every day or die a horribly painful death. When the Lord of Ruddigore passes his mantle on to the new heir, the young heir loses both his good reputation and his very proper fiancee. A new version of Gilbert and Sullivan's opera.
W L Leasing Limited — *CBS/Fox Video*

Rude Boy **1980**
Music-Performance
54105 60 mins C B, V P
The Clash, Ray Gange, directed by Jack Hazan and David Mingay
"Rude Bay" depicts the rise of The Clash, a top British rock band. Live concert footage features The Clash performing such hits as "White Riot" and "I Fought the Law." Included are rare films of early Clash shows.
Jack Hazan, David Mingay — *CBS/Fox Video*

Ruggles, The **1951**
Comedy
47642 24 mins B/W B, V, FO P
Charlie Ruggles, Erin O'Brien-Moore
Vintage TV sitcom with Charlie, his wife and children. In this episode, the Ruggles are presented with a pair of rabbits.
ABC — *Video Yesteryear*

Rules of the Game **1939**
Film-Avant-garde
06237 110 mins B/W B, V P
Marcel Dalio, Nora Gregor, Jean Renoir, directed by Jean Renoir
Renoir satirizes the social and sexual mores of the decadent French leisure class before WWII. French film, English subtitles.
FR
French — *Budget Video; International Historic Films; Sheik Video; Cable Films; Video Yesteryear; Western Film & Video Inc; Discount Video Tapes*

Ruling Class, The **1972**
Comedy/Satire
64983 154 mins C B, V, CED P
Peter O'Toole, Alastair Sim, Arthur Lowe
This irreverant comedy tells the story of the unbalanced 14th Earl of Gurney, who believes that he is Jesus Christ.
MPAA:PG
Avco-Embassy — *Embassy Home Entertainment*

Rumble Fish **1983**
Drama
65515 94 mins B/W B, V, LV, CED P
Matt Dillon, Mickey Rourke, Dennis Hopper, Diane Lane, Vincent Spano, Nicolas Case, directed by Francis Coppola
The story of two brothers whose relationship with themselves and their world leads to death for one and a new life for the other. In stereo VHS and Beta Hi-Fi.
MPAA:R
Universal — *MCA Home Video*

Rumor of War, A 1980
Drama
79188 105 mins C B, V P
Brad Davis, Keith Carradine, Stacy Keach, Brian Dennehy, Steve Forrest, Chris Mitchum
An adaptation of Philip Caputo's book about his transformation from college student to Vietnam veteran.
Stonehenge; Charles Fries Productions — *U.S.A. Home Video*

Rumpelstiltskin 1968
Fairy tales
47674 75 mins C B, V P
A beautiful young girl is tricked into promising her firstborn to a magic elf in return for his spinning straw into gold for her.
Ron Merk — *Unicorn Video*

Rumpelstiltskin 1984
Fairy tales
Closed Captioned
73144 60 mins C B, V, CED P
Ned Beatty, Shelley Duvall, Herve Villechaize, Paul Dooley
From "Faerie Tale Theatre" comes the story of a woman who can spin straw into gold (Shelley Duvall) and the strange man who saves her life (Herve Villechaize).
Shelley Duvall — *CBS/Fox Video*

Run, Angel, Run! 1969
Adventure
65728 90 mins C B, V P
William Smith, Valerie Starrett
An ex-biker is on the run from his former motorcycle gang.
MPAA:R
Fanfare — *VidAmerica*

Run for Life: An Olympic Fable 1979
Sports
72233 68 mins C B, V P
Animated
This animated feature concerns a young athlete running to restore support for his country's King in Ancient Greece.
Toei Animation — *Children's Video Library*

Run of the Arrow 1956
Western
13096 85 mins C B, V P
Rod Steiger, Brian Keith, Charles Bronson
An ex-Confederate soldier joins the Sioux nation, which is engaged in war against the white man.
Universal; RKO; Samuel Fuller — *United Home Video*

Run Silent, Run Deep 1958
War-Drama
68226 93 mins B/W B, V, CED P
Burt Lancaster, Clark Gable, Jack Warden, Don Rickles
A tense look at the realities of submarine warfare and underwater combat.
Jeffrey Productions — *CBS/Fox Video*

Run, Stranger, Run 1973
Suspense/Drama
73864 110 mins C B, V P
Ron Howard, Patricia Neal, Cloris Leachman, directed by Darren McGavin
A New England fishing village is disrupted by a series of murders committed by a young girl. Available in Beta Hi-Fi.
MPAA:PG
Darren McGavin; Cinema Five — *RCA/Columbia Pictures Home Video*

Runaway 1984
Science fiction/Adventure
Closed Captioned
81208 100 mins C B, V P
Tom Selleck, Cynthia Rhodes, Gene Simmons, Stan Shaw, Kirstie Alley, directed by Michael Crichton
A policeman and his assistant track down a group of killer robots wreaking havoc upon a metropolitan city. Available in VHS Dolby Hi-Fi Stereo and Beta Hi-Fi Stereo.
MPAA:PG13
Tri-Star Pictures — *RCA/Columbia Pictures Home Video*

Runaway Barge 1982
Adventure
75464 72 mins C B, V P
Nick Nolte, Tim Matheson, Jim Davis
An attempt is made to hijack a Mississippi River cargo.
King Features — *U.S.A. Home Video*

Runaway Truck 195?
Adventure
10033 25 mins B/W B, V P, T
Kirby Grant
Sky King takes to the air with novice pilot. Student pilot is then forced to make crucial decision. From the TV series "Sky King."
Unknown — *Blackhawk Films*

Runaways, The 1984
Suspense
80470 95 mins C B, V P
Steve Oliver, Sondra Currie, John Russell
A corrupt politician's wife falls in love with the man who saved her when she attempted suicide. The two try to escape her husband's wrathful vengeance.
Regal Video — *Regal Video*

Running Brave 1983
Drama
66322 90 mins C B, V, LV, CED R, P
Robbie Benson, Claudia Cron, Pat Hingle, Denis Lacroix
The true story of Billy Mills, a South Dakota Sioux Indian who became the only American in Olympic history to win the Gold Medal in the 10,000 meter run at the 1964 Tokyo Olympics.
Buena Vista; Englander Productions — *Walt Disney Home Video*

Running Hot 1983
Romance
73043 88 mins C B, V P
A hot romance develops between an escaped convict and the woman who wrote to him while he was in prison.
MPAA:R
Wescom — *Vestron Video*

Running Scared 1979
Drama
65091 92 mins C B, V R, P
Ken Wahl
Two young men, returning from military service as stowaways aboard an Army cargo plane, are caught by a paranoid intelligence agent and are thought to be spies.
MPAA:PG
EMI Films — *THORN EMI/HBO Video*

Running Wild 1973
Drama
76860 102 mins C B, V P
Lloyd Bridges, Dina Merrill, Pat Hingle, Gilbert Roland, Morgan Woodward
A freelance photographer becomes involved in a dispute to save a corral of wild mustang horses.
MPAA:G
Robert McCahon — *Media Home Entertainment*

Rush—Exit Stage Left 1981
Music-Performance
60384 60 mins C B, V P
This concert includes highlights from the group's two-hour stage show. Songs include "Limelight," "Xanadu," "The Trees," "Freewill" and "Closer to the Heart." In stereo.
Polygram Records; Moon Video Production — *RCA/Columbia Pictures Home Video; RCA VideoDiscs; Pioneer Artists*

Rush It 1977
Romance
79322 78 mins C B, V P
Tom Berenger, Jill Eikenberry
Two bike messengers who meet each other while working in New York City wind up falling in love.
Robbie Kenner — *Unicorn Video*

Russian Folk Song and Dance 1981
Music-Performance/Dance
57257 70 mins C B, V P
Narrated by Tony Randall
Four of Russia's great troupes perform their colorful native songs and dances: the Pyatnitsky Russian Folk and Dance Ensemble (primarily Ukranian), the Siberian-Omsk Folk Chorus (from Siberia and Northern Russia), the Uzbekistan Dance Ensemble (from Samarkand and Central Asia) and the Moldavia Folk Song and Dance Ensemble (from Southwest Russia).
Kultur — *Kultur*

Russians Are Coming, the Russians Are Coming, The 1966
Comedy
58837 126 mins C CED P
Alan Arkin, Carl Reiner, Theo Bikel, Eva Marie Saint, Brian Keith, Paul Ford, Jonathan Winters, Ben Blue, Tessie O'Shea, Doro Merande
A Russian sub accidentally runs aground off the New England coast causing havoc for the residents.
United Artists — *CBS/Fox Video; RCA VideoDiscs*

Rust Never Sleeps 1979
Music-Performance
31659 111 mins C B, V P
Neil Young
Neil Young performs all the songs that made him a star in this concert film. These include "I Am A Child" (Buffalo Springfield), "My, My, Hey, Hey" (Out of the Blue), "Comes a Time," "Sugar Mountain," "Cinnamon Girl," "Hurricane," "Thrasher," and many more.
LA Johnson — *Vestron Video; RCA VideoDiscs*

Rust Never Sleeps 1981
Music-Performance
72221 111 mins C B, V P
Neil Young's conceptual tour is captured in full swing, complete with four foot "roadeyes."
Independent — *Vestron Video*

Ruthless Four, The 1970
Western
81401 97 mins C B, V P
Van Heflin, Klaus Kinski, Gilbert Roland, George Hilton
Four prospectors combat the elements and each other in their attempt to retrieve a fortune in gold in the Nevada hills.
MGM — *Monterey Home Video*

Ryan's Daughter 1970
Drama/Romance
80624 194 mins C B, V P
Sarah Miles, Robert Mitchum, John Mills, Trevor Howard, Christopher Jones, directed by David Lean
A married Irish woman falls in love with a British major and is accused of betraying her country during the 1916 Irish Uprising. Music by Maurice Jarre. In Beta and VHS Hi-Fi.
Academy Awards '70: Best Supporting Actor (Mills); Best Cinematography. MPAA:PG
MGM — *MGM/UA Home Video*

S

Sabotage 1936
Suspense
13052 81 mins B/W B, V P
Oscar Homolka, directed by Alfred Hitchcock
Saboteur finds his world closing in on him when a bomb he made kills his young brother-in-law and his wife seeks secret revenge.
GB Prods — *Budget Video; Video Dimensions; Sheik Video; Cable Films; Video Yesteryear; Video Connection; Western Film & Video Inc; Discount Video Tapes; Classic Video Cinema Collector's Club; Kartes Productions; See Hear Industries*

Sabrina, Volume 1 1969
Cartoons
65622 23 mins C B, V P
Animated
What happens when a pretty teenage girl is also a witch? If it's Sabrina, you know you're in for plenty of amazing, amusing and action-packed adventures.
Filmation — *Embassy Home Entertainment*

Sabrina Volumes IV—VI 1969
Cartoons
78350 57 mins C B, V P
Animated
Sabrina, the teenage witch and the Archie gang get into all sorts of problems in this animated collection of episodes from the television series.
Filmation Studios — *Embassy Home Entertainment*

Sacco and Vanzetti 1971
Drama
51116 120 mins C B, V P
Milo O'Shea, Gian Maria Volonte, Cyril Cusak
An account of the flagrant miscarriage of justice subjected upon two Italian immigrants caught amidst witch-hunts and judicial negligence in the 1920's.
MPAA:PG
Unidis Largo Messico 6 Rome — *United Home Video*

Sacred Ground 1983
Drama
Closed Captioned
65501 100 mins C B, V, CED P
Tim McIntire, Jack Elam, Mindi Miller
A trapper and his pregnant wife unknowingly build shelter on the Paiute Indian's sacred burial ground. When the wife dies in childbirth, the pioneer is forced to kidnap a Paiute woman who has just buried her own deceased infant.
MPAA:PG
Pacific International — *CBS/Fox Video*

Sade: Diamond Life Video 1985
Music video
81175 30 mins C B, V P
This is a collection of four conceptual music videos from Sade's "Diamond Life" album. Available in digitally mastered Hi-Fi stereo for both formats.
CBS/Fox Video Music — *CBS/Fox Video*

Safari 3000 1982
Adventure
79212 91 mins C B, V P
Stockard Channing, David Carradine, Christopher Lee
A ""Playboy" writer is assigned to do a story on a three day, three thousand kilometer car race in Africa.
MPAA:PG
United Artists — *MGM/UA Home Video*

Saga of Death Valley 1939
Western
05533 56 mins B/W B, V P
Roy Rogers, Gabby Hayes, Donald Barry, Doris Day
Roy Rogers battles a band of outlaws and discovers that their leader is his own brother.
Republic — *Video Connection; Sheik Video; Cable Films; Nostalgia Merchant; Discount Video Tapes*

Sagebrush Trail 1933
Western
08845 63 mins B/W B, V, 3/4U P
John Wayne
Action on the plains as John Wayne rides into Indian trouble.
Monogram — *Sony Corporation of America; Video Connection; Cable Films; Discount Video Tapes; Spotlite Video*

Sahara 1943
War-Drama
58964 97 mins B/W B, V P
Humphrey Bogart, Dan Duryea, Bruce Bennett, Lloyd Bridges, Rex Ingram, J. Carrol Naish

An action story of desert battle and survival during World War II.
Columbia — *RCA/Columbia Pictures Home Video*

Sahara **1983**
Romance/Adventure
79207 111 mins C B, V P
Brooke Shields, John Rhys-Davies, Lambert Wilson, Sir John Mills, directed by Andrew McLaglen
An American heiress is kidnapped by Bedouin tribesmen while driving in an auto race through the Sahara. In Beta and VHS Hi-Fi.
MPAA:PG
Cannon Films — *MGM/UA Home Video*

Sailor Who Fell from Grace with the Sea, The **1976**
Drama
13663 105 mins C B, V P
Sarah Miles, Kris Kristofferson, Jonathan Kahn, Margo Cunningham, directed by Lewis John Carlino
A disillusioned sailor rejects the sea for the love of a young, sexually repressed widow.
MPAA:R
Avco Embassy; Martino Poll Production — *Embassy Home Entertainment; RCA VideoDiscs*

St. Helen's, Killer Volcano **1982**
Drama
64884 95 mins C B, V P
Art Carney, David Huffman, Cassie Yates
A young man and an old man develop a deep friendship amidst the devastation, fear, greed and panic surrounding the eruption of a volcano.
Michael Murphy — *Vestron Video*

Saint in London, The **1939**
Mystery
64380 72 mins B/W B, V, 3/4U P
George Sanders, Sally Grey
The Saint picks up a wounded man lying at the side of a country road and becomes involved in murder and intrigue.
RKO — *Nostalgia Merchant*

Saint in New York, The **1938**
Mystery
00297 71 mins B/W B, V P
Louis Hayward, Kay Sutton, Jack Carson
The Saint turns Robin Hood to help Civic Committee clean up a gang of desperados.
RKO — *Nostalgia Merchant*

St. Ives **1976**
Crime-Drama
72920 94 mins C B, V P
Charles Bronson, Jacqueline Bissett
A former police reporter goes undercover when he gets framed for a murder.
MPAA:PG
Warner Bros — *Warner Home Video*

Saint Jack **1979**
Drama
65384 112 mins C B, V P
Ben Gazzara
The story of a small-time pimp with big dreams working the pleasure palaces of late-night Singapore. Directed by Peter Bogdonovich.
MPAA:R
Peter Bogdonovich Productions — *Vestron Video*

Saint Strikes Back, The/Criminal Court **1946**
Suspense/Mystery
81025 127 mins B/W B, V P
George Sanders, Wendy Barrie, Barry Fitzgerald, Tom Conway, Steve Brodie
A suspense double feature: The Saint helps clear the name of the daughter of a San Francisco police commissioner in "The Saint Strikes Back," and a young lawyer becomes involved in murder in "Criminal Court".
RKO — *RKO HomeVideo*

Saint's Vacation The, The Narrow Margin **1952**
Mystery
76838 148 mins B/W B, V P
Hugh Sinclair, Sally Gray, Charles McGraw, Marie Windsor, Jacqueline White
A mystery, double feature: In "The Saint's Vacation," Simon Templar prevents a valuable secret from getting into the wrong hands and in "The Narrow Margin," strange things happen to a detective when he takes a train ride with a witness to Chicago.
RKO — *RKO HomeVideo*

Sakharov **1984**
Biographical/Drama
80321 120 mins C B, V P
The true story of the Russian physicist whose involvement in the dissident movement cannot be stopped by the Soviet government.
HBO — *Prism*

Salem's Lot: The Movie **1979**
Horror
69798 112 mins C B, V R, P
David Soul, James Mason, Lance Kerwin, Bonnie Bedelia, Lew Ayras, directed by Tobe Hooper
This film is based on Stephen King's novel about a sleepy New England village which is infiltrated by evil when a mysterious antiques dealer takes up residence in a forbidding hilltop house—and it becomes apparent that a vampire is on the loose.

Warner Bros — *Warner Home Video*

Sally of the Sawdust 1925
Comedy
10097 92 mins B/W B, V P, T
W. C. Fields, Carol Dempster, Alfred Lunt, directed by D. W. Griffith
W. C. Fields' first silent feature film where he portrays a carnival barker who adopts a young woman. Displays his talents at juggling, conning customers, and car chasing. Musical score.
United Artists — *Blackhawk Films*

Salute John Citizen 1942
War-Drama
69560 74 mins B/W B, V, FO P
Peggy Cummins, Stanley Holloway, Dinah Sheridan, Jimmy Hanley
The life of an average English family during the early days of World War II is depicted, focusing on the deprivation and horror of the Nazi blitzkrieg.
Gaumont — *Video Yesteryear*

Salute to Chuck Jones, A 1960
Cartoons
81579 56 mins C B, V R, P
Animated, voice of Mel Blanc, directed by Chuck Jones.
Here are a collection of eight Chuck Jones favorites including "Duck Dodgers in the 24 1/2th Century", "One Froggy Evening", "Rabbit Seasoning", and "Feed the Kitty".
Warner Bros. — *Warner Home Video*

Salute to Friz Freleng, A 1958
Cartoons
81578 57 mins C B, V R, P
Animated, voice of Mel Blanc, directed by Friz Freleng
This volume features several classic Friz Freleng cartoons including the Academy Award winners "Speedy Gonzales" ('55), "Birds Anonymous" ('57), and "Knighty Knight Bugs" ('58).
Warner Bros. — *Warner Home Video*

Salute to Mel Blanc, A 1958
Cartoons
81577 58 mins C B, V R, P
Animated, voice of Mel Blanc
This compilation pays tribute to the multi-talented Mel Blanc and features such memorable cartoons including "The Rabbit of Seville" "Little Boy Boo" "Robin Hood Daffy" and "Past Performances".
Warner Bros. — *Warner Home Video*

Same Time, Next Year 1978
Drama
31598 119 mins C B, V P
Ellen Burstyn, Alan Alda
A chance meeting between a traveling executive and a liberated housewife results in a sometimes sometimes tragic, always sentimental 25-year affair—but they meet only one day a year. Based on the Broadway play by Bernard Slade.
Universal — *MCA Home Video*

Sammy Bluejay 1983
Cartoons
65654 60 mins C B, V P
Animated
This program features two escapades—"Brainy Bluejay" and "Sammy's Revenge"—starring Sammy Bluejay, Peter Cottontail, and Reddy the Fox.
Ziv International — *Family Home Entertainment*

Samson and Delilah 1949
Drama
55544 128 mins C B, V, LV R, P
Victor Mature, Hedy Lamarr, Angela Lansbury, George Sanders, Henry Wilcoxon, Olive Deering, Fay Holden, directed by Cecil B. De Mille
The biblical story of Delilah, who after being rejected by Samson, cuts his hair and delivers him to his enemies.
Paramount; Cecil B De Mille — *Paramount Home Video*

Samson et Dalila 1981
Opera
59877 210 mins C LV P
The Royal Opera performs Camille Saint-Saens' first major opera, based in the biblical story of Samson, who sucumbs to the wiles of Dalila. In stereo.
Covent Garden Video — *Pioneer Artists*

Samurai Saga 1959
Adventure
76899 112 mins C B, V P
Toshiro Mifune, Yoko Tsukasa
Two samurais compete for the affections of a beautiful princess. With English subtitles.
JA
Toho — *Video Action*

San Francisco Blues Festival 1983
Music-Performance
76664 60 mins C B, V P
A blues celebration including "S.F. Bay Blues," "Louisiana Two Step," "What I Say" and many more.
Image Integration — *Sony Corporation of America*

San Francisco Blues Festival **1983**
Music-Performance
73985 60 mins C B, V P
Blues greats Clifton Chenier and Charles "Gatemouth" Brown perform in a concert taped at the San Francisco Blues Festival in 1983.
Image Intergration — *Sony Corporation of America*

San Francisco 49ers 1984 Team Highlights **1985**
Football
70543 46 mins C B, V, FO P
Joe Montana
The 49ers tallied a record 15 regular season victories and went on to win the Super Bowl by a stunning 22 points over the Miami Dolphins.
NFL Films — *NFL Films Video*

Sand Pebbles, The **1966**
Drama
08459 195 mins C B, V P
Steve McQueen, Richard Crenna, Richard Attenborough, Candice Bergen, Larry Gates
An American expatriate, transferred to a gunboat on the Yangtze River in 1926, falls in love with a missionary teacher.
EL, SP
20th Century Fox; Robert Wise — *CBS/Fox Video*

Sandahl Bergman's Body **1983**
Physical fitness/Dance
65215 60 mins C B, V P
A unique program combining fitness and the art of dance.
Cassini and Ray Productions — *Monterey Home Video*

Sanders of the River **1935**
Mystery
11369 80 mins B/W B, V, FO P
Paul Robeson, Leslie Banks, Robert Cochran
An officer of the river patrol causes rebellion among the natives when he tracks down those seeking to break the law.
Korda — *Video Yesteryear; Cable Films; Sheik Video; Video Connection; Kartes Productions*

Sanders of the River **1935**
Adventure
81468 97 mins B/W B, V, LV P
Paul Robeson, Leslie Banks, Robert Cochran, directed by Zoltan Korda
A tribal chief helps the British Commissioner of Affairs in Africa to thwart the evil intentions of a greedy king.
Alexander Korda — *Embassy Home Entertainment*

Sandpiper, The **1965**
Romance/Drama
80630 117 mins C B, V P
Elizabeth Taylor, Richard Burton, Charles Bronson, Eva Marie Saint, Morgan Mason, directed by Vincente Minnelli
A free-spirited artist falls in love with the married headmaster of her son's boarding school.
Academy Award '65: Best Song "The Shadow of Your Smile"
MGM;Venice Productions — *MGM/UA Home Video*

Sands of Iwo Jima **1949**
War-Drama
47057 109 mins B/W B, V P
John Wayne, Forrest Tucker, John Agar
A tough Marine sergeant trains a squad of rebellious recruits in New Zealand, and they later are responsible for the capture of Iwo Jima from the Japanese.
Republic — *Republic Pictures Home Video; RCA VideoDiscs*

Sanjuro **1962**
Drama
57340 96 mins B/W B, V P
Toshiro Mifune, Tatsuya Nakadai
Originally titled "Tsubaki Sanjuro." In mid-nineteenth century Japan, the chamberlain is suspected of fomenting political unrest. Subtitled in English.
JA
Toho — *Budget Video; Festival Films; Discount Video Tapes; Video Action*

Santa and the 3 Bears **1979**
Cartoons
78899 60 mins C B, V P
Animated
When a mother bear and her cubs discover the magic of Christmas in the forest, they decide to skip hibernating for the winter.
Tony Benedict Productions — *Prism*

Santa Claus Conquers the Martians **1964**
Fantasy/Comedy
80764 80 mins C B, V P
John Call, Pia Zadora, Leonard Hicks, Vincent Beck, Victor Stiles, Donna Conforti
A martian spaceship comes to Earth and kidnaps Santa Claus and two children. They take their captives to Mars, where Santa will work at an automated toy shop.
Jalor Prods. — *Embassy Home Entertainment*

Santa Fe Trail **1940**
Western
08782 110 mins B/W B, V, 3/4U P
Errol Flynn, Olivia de Havilland, Ronald Reagan, Van Heflin, Raymond Massey

Pre-Civil War historical fight for "bloody Kansas" with Jeb Stuart and George Custer beginning their military careers.
Warner Bros — *Prism; Nostalgia Merchant; Budget Video; VCII; Video Yesteryear; Sheik Video; Cable Films; Video Connection; Discount Video Tapes; Classic Video Cinema Collector's Club; Hal Roach Studios; Kartes Productions*

Santa Fe Uprising 1946
Western
64410 54 mins B/W B, V, 3/4U P
Allan "Rocky" Lane, Bobby Blake
Red Ryder has to save Little Beaver from kidnappers.
Republic — *Nostalgia Merchant*

Saps at Sea 1940
Comedy
33908 57 mins B/W B, V, 3/4U P
Stan Laurel, Oliver Hardy, James Finlayson, Ben Turpin, Rychard Cramer
A doctor advises Ollie to take a rest away from his job at a horn factory. He and Stan rent a boat, which they plan to keep tied to the dock until an escaped criminal happens by and uses the boys for his getaway.
Hal Roach, United Artists — *Nostalgia Merchant; Blackhawk Films*

Saps at Sea 1940
Comedy
63988 80 mins B/W B, V P, T
Stan Laurel, Oliver Hardy, Jimmy Finlayson, Ben Turpin, Rychard Kramer
Stan and Ollie are cast out to sea on the same boat with an escaped criminal. This tape also includes a 1934 Charley Chase short, "The Chases of Pimple Street."
Hal Roach; MGM — *Blackhawk Films*

Sarah and the Squirrel 1983
Cartoons
Closed Captioned
78888 74 mins C B, V P
Animated, voice of Mia Farrow
A young girl learns to survive in a forest after she becomes separated from her family during a war.
Satori — *Playhouse Video*

Sardinia Kidnapped 1975
Drama/Suspense
80505 95 mins C B, V P
Charlotte Rampling, Franco Nero, directed by Gianfranco Mingozzi
A beautiful girl is trapped in a clash between two powerful families while on vacation in Sardinia.
Silvio Clementelli — *Active Home Video*

Sasquatch 1976
Speculation
13101 94 mins C B, V P
Story of seven men who defied death in a primitive wilderness where no man had gone before. They lived to tell the tale of this legendary creature.
Gold Key — *United Home Video*

Satan's Blood 197?
Suspense/Horror
70744 85 mins C B, V P
Angel Aranda, Sandra Alberti
A young couple finds the interest rates at the devil's blood bank usorious.
Mogul Communications, Inc. — *All American Video*

Satan's Satellites 1958
Science fiction
73548 70 mins B/W B, V P
Judd Holdren, John Crawford, Leonard Nimoy, Ray Boyle
A rocket lands on earth with zombies that invade the planet.
Republic Pictures — *Admit One Video*

Satan's School for Girls 1973
Horror/Mystery
80315 74 mins C B, V P
Roy Thinnes, Kate Jackson, Jo Van Fleet, Lloyd Bochner, Pamela Franklin
When a young woman investigates the circumstances that caused her sister's suicide, it leads her to a satanic girl's academy.
Spelling/Goldberg Productions — *Prism*

Satellite Rescue in Space 1985
Space exploration
70705 30 mins C B, V P
This tape follows U.S. space shuttle astronauts on a satellite retrieval mission high above the Earth.
Century Video Corp./NASA — *Kid Time Video*

Saturday Night Fever 1977
Drama
38614 118 mins C B, V, LV R, P
John Travolta, Karen Gorney, Donna Pescow
A Brooklyn teenager who is king of the local disco begins to question his narrow view of life. Acclaimed for its disco dance sequences, with music by the Bee Gees.
MPAA:R
Paramount — *Paramount Home Video; RCA VideoDiscs*

Saturday Night Fever 1977
Drama
38958 118 mins C B, V R, P
John Travolta, Karen Gorney, Donna Pescow

A slightly edited version of the popular disco drama, with the sex-oriented scenes and some strong language toned down for PG audiences. Music by the Bee Gees.
MPAA:PG
Paramount — *Paramount Home Video*

Saturday Night Live: Eric Idle Vol I **1976**
Comedy/Variety
80171 64 mins C B, V R, P
John Belushi, Chevy Chase, Jane Curtin, Gilda Radner, Garrett Morris
Among the highlights from this 1976 episode are John Belushi's duet with Joe Cocker and special musical guests Stuff.
NBC; Lorne Michaels — *Warner Home Video*

Saturday Night Live: Buck Henry **1979**
Comedy/Variety
80176 120 mins C B, V R, P
Buck Henry, Bill Murray, Garrett Morris, Gilda Radner, Jane Curtin, John Belushi
Here are two vintage episodes from 1978 and 1979 that feature Buck Henry as guest host.
NBC; Lorne Michaels — *Warner Home Video*

Saturday Night Live: Carrie Fisher **1978**
Comedy
66131 67 mins C B, V R, P
Carrie Fisher, Not Ready For Prime Time Players
Carrie Fisher joins in a spoof of her Star Wars character in the sketch "New Kid on Earth," a beach party parody.
NBC — *Warner Home Video*

Saturday Night Live: Charles Grodin **1977**
Comedy/Variety
80173 67 mins C B, V R, P
Charles Grodin, John Belushi, Garrett Morris, Jane Curtin, Gilda Radner, Laraine Newman
Charles Grodin hosts this 1977 episode that features special musical guests Paul Simon and The Persuasions
NBC; Lorne Michaels — *Warner Home Video*

Saturday Night Live: Elliott Gould **1976**
Comedy/Variety
80170 67 mins C B, V R, P
John Belushi, Chevy Chase, Dan Aykroyd, Gilda Radner, Jane Curtin, Elliott Gould
The classic "Star Trek" spoof along with "The Killer Bees" sketch are just some of the highlights from this 1976 episode.
NBC; Lorne Michaels — *Warner Home Video*

Saturday Night Live: Eric Idle Vol. II **1979**
Comedy/Variety
80177 59 mins C B, V R, P
Eric Idle, Bill Murray, Garrett Morris, Gilda Radner, Jane Curtin, John Belushi
Monty Python's Eric Idle guest hosts this 1979 episode which features an appearance from Father Guido Sarducci.
NBC; Lorne Michaels — *Warner Home Video*

Saturday Night Live: Gary Busey **1979**
Comedy/Variety
80175 69 mins C B, V R, P
Gary Busey, Bill Murray, Gilda Radner, Jane Curtin, Garrett Morris
Among the highlights from this 1979 episode is a duet by Gregory Hines and Eubie Blake.
NBC; Lorne Michaels — *Warner Home Video*

Saturday Night Live: George Carlin **1975**
Comedy/Variety
80180 60 mins C B, V R, P
Chevy Chase, John Belushi, Jane Curtin, Michael O'Donoghue, Garrett Morris, George Carlin
This is the premiere episode of the long-running comedy series.
NBC; Lorne Michaels — *Warner Home Video*

Saturday Night Live: Lily Tomlin **1975**
Comedy/Variety
80169 67 mins C B, V R, P
Chevy Chase, John Belushi, Dan Aykroyd, Gilda Radner, Jane Curtin, Lily Tomlin, Laraine Newman
Lily Tomlin and her characters Ernestine, Sister Boogie Woman, and Edith Ann appear in this 1975 episode.
NBC; Lorne Michaels — *Warner Home Video*

Saturday Night Live: Madeline Kahn **1976**
Comedy/Variety
80167 68 mins C B, V R, P
Chevy Chase, Dan Aykroyd, Jane Curtin, John Belushi, Garrett Morris, Madeline Kahn
A spoof of "The Final Days" and Gilda Radner's impersonation of Barbara Walters are just some of the highlights from this 1976 episode.
NBC; Lorne Michaels — *Warner Home Video*

Saturday Night Live: Michael Palin **1979**
Comedy/Variety
80174 67 mins C B, V R, P
Bill Murray, John Belushi, Jane Curtin, Garrett Morris, Gilda Radner, Michael Palin

Month Python's Michael Palin hosts this 1979 episode that features special musical guests, The Doobie Brothers.
NBC; Lorne Michaels — *Warner Home Video*

Saturday Night Live: Peter Cook & Dudley Moore **1975**
Comedy/Variety
80166 67 mins C B, V R, P
Chevy Chase, Gilda Radner, Laraine Newman, Jane Curtin, John Belushi, The Muppets
Peter and Dudley reprise their classic "Derek and Clive" routine along with musical guest Neil Sedaka in this 1975 episode.
NBC; Lorne Michaels — *Warner Home Video*

Saturday Night Live: Ray Charles **1977**
Comedy/Variety
80168 62 mins C B, V R, P
John Belushi, Ray Charles, Dan Aykroyd, Bill Murray, Jane Curtin, Garrett Morris
The incomparable Ray Charles hosts this 1975 episode.
NBC; Lorne Michaels — *Warner Home Video*

Saturday Night Live: Richard Benjamin **1979**
Comedy/Variety
80165 64 mins C B, V R, P
Bill Murray, Gilda Radner, Garret Morris, Dan Aykroyd, Richard Benjamin
A spoof of "The China Syndrome" and Rickie Lee Jones singing "Chuck E's In Love" are some of the highlights from this 1979 show.
NBC; Lorne Michaels — *Warner Home Video*

Saturday Night Live: Robert Klein **1979**
Comedy/Variety
80178 108 mins C B, V R, P
Robert Klein, Bill Murray, John Belushi, Garrett Morris, Gilda Radner, Jane Curtin
Robert Klein guest hosts this 1979 episode that features special guest stars, The Muppets.
NBC; Lorne Michaels — *Warner Home Video*

Saturday Night Live: Rodney Dangerfield **1980**
Comedy/Variety
80164 68 mins C B, V R, P
Rodney Dangerfield, Bill Murrary, Don Novello, Harry Shearer
The comic who gets no respect hosts this episode that features musical guests the J. Geils Band.
NBC; Lorne Michaels — *Warner Home Video*

Saturday Night Live: Sissy Spacek **1977**
Comedy/Variety
80172 68 mins C B, V R, P
Sissy Spacek, Dan Aykroyd, Jane Curtin, Gilda Radner, Garrett Morris, John Belushi
Among the highlights from this 1977 show are Sissy Spacek portraying Amy Carter in a "Carter Call In" sketch and the "Gidget's Disease" commercial parody.
NBC; Lorne Michaels — *Warner Home Video*

Saturday Night Live: Steve Martin 2 **1978**
Comedy
66132 110 mins C B, V R, P
Steve Martin, Not Ready for Prime Time Players
One of the "wild and crazy guy's" hilarious SNL appearances.
NBC — *Warner Home Video*

Saturday Night Live, Vol. II **197?**
Comedy/Variety
60376 115 mins C CED P
Steve Martin, Richard Pryor, John Belushi, Chevy Chase, Bill Murray, Gilda Radner
Two Saturday Night Live programs with the original cast; Richard Pryor is host for a show telecast on December 13, 1975 and Steve Martin appears on an episode with an airdate of April 12, 1978.
NBC Enterprises; Lorne Michaels — *RCA VideoDiscs*

Saturday Night Live, Vol. I **1975**
Comedy/Variety
53792 112 mins C CED P
George Carlin, Steve Martin, John Belushi, Chevy Chase, Jane Curtin, Gilda Radner, Laraine Newman, Dan Ackroyd
The premiere telecast of October 11, 1975, hosted by George Carlin, which featured the Weekend Update, The Bees, The Muppets, Andy Kaufman, a film by Albert Brooks, musical guest Billy Preston, and a commercial for "New Dad." The other episode is the 29th original telecast from October 23, 1976, representing Steve Martin's first appearance as host. Sketches included "Jeopardy 1999," a spoof of the Mary Tyler Moore Show, Chevy's Weekend Update and his milk commercial, and a skit about beatniks. (11 minutes have been edited from the premiere show, and 5 minutes from the Martin show, of music and film segments).
NBC Enterprises; Lorne Michaels — *RCA VideoDiscs*

Saturday Night Live with Richard Pryor **1975**
Comedy/Variety
47621 65 mins C B, V R, P

Richard Pryor, Gil Scott-Heron, John Belushi, Dan Ackroyd, Gilda Radner, Laraine Newman, Jane Curtin, Chevy Chase
Richard Pryor appears in a samurai bellhop sketch, a spoof of "The Exorcist," and undergoes a peculiar personnel interview in this "SNL" episode. Other highlights include two songs by Gil Scott-Heron and a film by Albert Brooks.
NBC Enterprises; Lorne Michaels — *Warner Home Video*

Saturday Night Live with Steve Martin **1978**
Comedy/Variety
47622 65 mins C B, V R, P
Steve Martin, John Belushi, Dan Ackroyd, Laraine Newman, Gilda Radner, Bill Murray, Garrett Morris, Jane Curtin
Highlights from this 1978 show include the Czechoslovakian brothers, Steve Martin singing "King Tut," an appearance by the Blues Brothers and Steve and Gilda dancing frenetically to "Dancing in the Dark."
NBC Enterprises; Lorne Michaels — *Warner Home Video*

Saturday Serials **195?**
Adventure
53050 50 mins B/W B, V, 3/4U P
Richard Greene, Buster Crabbe, Al "Fuzzy" Knight
Two classic 1950's adventure shows: "The Adventures of Robin Hood" (1955), a British-made series staring Richard Greene as a man who robbed the rich and gave to the poor; and "Captain Gallant of the Foreign Legion" (1955), starring Buster Crabbe and Al "Fuzzy" Knight.
NBC et al — *Shokus Video*

Saturn 3 **1980**
Science fiction
41497 88 mins C B, V, LV P
Farrah Fawcett, Kirk Douglas
Two research scientists create a futuristic Garden of Eden in an isolated sector of our solar system, but love story turns to horror story when a killer robot arrives.
MPAA:R EL, SP
Associated Film Distribution Corp — *CBS/Fox Video*

Saul and David **197?**
Bible
35374 120 mins C B, V P
A beautifully filmed story of David's life with King Saul, the battle with Goliath, and the tragic end of Saul. From the "Bible" series.
Sunn Classic — *United Home Video*

Savage Attraction **1984**
Drama
72869 93 mins C B, V P
The true story of a sixteen year old who was debauched across three continents.
MPAA:R
Unknown — *Embassy Home Entertainment*

Savage Streets **1983**
Drama
77411 93 mins C B, V, CED P
Linda Blair, John Vernon, Sal Landi, Robert Dryer
A rowdy group of high school girls are in for a load of trouble when they play a trick on a Hollywood street gang.
MPAA:R
Ginso Investment Corp. — *Vestron Video*

Savages **1975**
Drama
80316 74 mins C B, V P
Andy Griffith, Sam Bottoms, Noah Beery
A hunter and his guide play a deadly cat and mouse game in the desert.
Spelling/Goldburg Productions — *Prism*

Savannah Smiles **1982**
Drama
66046 104 mins C B, V, LV, CED P
Bridgette Andersen, Mark Miller, Donovan Scott
A six-year old runaway befriends two escaped convicts.
MPAA:PG
Clark Paylow — *Embassy Home Entertainment*

Save the Tiger **1973**
Drama
58716 100 mins C B, V, LV R, P
Jack Lemmon, Jack Gilford, Laurie Heineman, Patricia Smith, Norman Burton, directed by John Avildsen
A middle-aged man, faced with a failing business, struggles with his conscience and changing American values.
Academy Awards '73: Best Actor (Lemmon).
MPAA:R
Paramount; Steve Shagan — *Paramount Home Video*

Saviors, Saints, and Sinners **1981**
Football
50645 50 mins C B, V, FO R, P
A summary of the 1980 NFL season, including a look at the All-Pro selections.
NFL Films — *NFL Films Video*

Sawdust and Tinsel **1953**
Drama
78637 85 mins B/W B, V, LV P
Harriet Andersson, Ake Gronberg, directed by Ingmar Bergman

A circus owner decides to leave his mistress when the circus arrives in the town where his wife and child live. This film has English subtitles.
SW
Janus Films — *Embassy Home Entertainment*

Say Amen, Somebody **1980**
Documentary/Music
66445 100 mins C B, V P
Willie May Ford Smith, Thomas A. Dorsey, Sallie Martin, Delois Barrett Cambell
A documentary look at the joyful world of gospel music. Two old-timers, Thomas A. Dorsey, the "Father of Gospel Music" and Sallie Martin, also known as Mother Smith, talk and sing about the gospel heritage as they experienced it.
UnitedArtists Classics; GTN Productions — *Pacific Arts Video*

Sayonara **1957**
Drama
69379 147 mins C B, V, CED P
Marlon Brando, James Garner, Ricardo Montalban, Patricia Owens, Red Buttons, Miyoshi Umeki
Based on the novel by James A. Michener, this is the story of American servicemen on leave in Japan during the Korean War, and the Japanese women that some have fallen in love with.
Academy Awards'57: Best Supporting Actor (Buttons); Best Supporting Actress (Umeki); Best Art Direction; Best Sound.
Warner Bros — *CBS/Fox Video*

Scandalous **1984**
Comedy/Mystery
66606 93 mins C B, V, LV, CED P
Robert Hays, John Gielgud, Jim Dale, Pamela Stephenson
A bumbling American TV reporter becomes involved with a gang of British con artists.
MPAA:PG
Orion — *Vestron Video*

Scanners **1981**
Horror
59339 102 mins C B, V, CED P
Stephen Lack, Jennifer O'Neill, Patrick McGoohan, Lawrence Dane
"Scanners" are telepaths who can will people to explode. One scanner in particular harbors Hitlerian aspirations for his band of psychic gangsters.
MPAA:R
Filmplan International — *Embassy Home Entertainment*

Scarecrow **1973**
Drama
58248 112 mins C B, V R, P
Gene Hackman, Al Pacino, Ann Wedgeworth, Eileen Brennan, directed by Jerry Schatzberg
The tragicomic tale of two born losers adrift on the road.
MPAA:R
Warner Bros — *Warner Home Video*

Scared to Death **1947**
Mystery
01684 70 mins C B, V P, T
Bela Lugosi, George Zucco, Joyce Compton, directed by Walt Mattox
Woman dies of fright when shown death mask of man she framed.
Screen Guild; Robert L Lippert — *Mossman Williams Productions; Sheik Video; King of Video; Video Connection; Video Yesteryear; Admit One Video*

Scarface **1932**
Drama
31599 94 mins B/W B, V P
Paul Muni, Ann Dvorak
A small-time crook builds himself up to a hot shot ganster, who eventually is double crossed by his mob.
United Artists — *MCA Home Video*

Scarface **1932**
Crime-Drama
66588 90 mins B/W B, V P
Paul Muni, Ann Dvorak, George Raft, Boris Karloff, directed by Howard Hawks
The brutal story of the life and death of a Chicago gangster is portrayed in this hard-hitting movie classic.
Howard Hughes; Universal — *MCA Home Video*

Scarface **1983**
Crime-Drama
66589 170 mins C B, V, LV, CED P
Al Pacino, Steven Bauer, Michelle Pfeiffer, Robert Loggia, directed by Brian De Palma
A remake of the 1932 classic film, with Al Pacino as a Cuban refugee who works his way up to becoming a major figure in Miami's crime scene. In stereo.
MPAA:R
Universal — *MCA Home Video*

Scarlet Pimpernel, The **1935**
Drama
08625 98 mins B/W B, V P
Leslie Howard, Merle Oberon, Raymond Massey, Anthony Bushell, John Gardner
"The Scarlet Pimpernel," supposed dandy of the English court, outwits the French Republicans during the Revolution.

United Artists; Alexander Korda; British — *Prism; Hal Roach Studios; Media Home Entertainment; Budget Video; Blackhawk Films; VCII; Sheik Video; Cable Films; Video Connection; Discount Video Tapes; Kartes Productions; Embassy Home Entertainment; Classic Video Cinema Collector's Club*

Scarlet Street **1945**
Mystery
01731 103 mins B/W B, V P
Edward G. Robinson, Joan Bennett, Dan Duryea, directed by Fritz Lang
Middle-aged cashier becomes an embezzler when he gets involved with a predatory, manipulating woman.
Universal — *Budget Video; Sheik Video; Cable Films; Video Connection; Video Yesteryear; Discount Video Tapes; Classic Video Cinema Collector's Club; Kartes Productions*

Scarred **1983**
Drama
71778 85 mins C B, V P
An unwed teenage mother becomes a prostitute to support her baby.
Rose-Marie Turko — *Vestron Video*

Scars of Dracula **1971**
Horror
63980 93 mins C B, V R, P
Christopher Lee, Jenny Hanley, Dennis Waterman, Wendy Hamilton
A young couple tangles with Dracula in their search for the man's missing brother.
MPAA:R
Hammer Productions — *THORN EMI/HBO Video*

Scavenger Hunt **1979**
Comedy
65409 117 mins C B, V P
Richard Benjamin, James Coco, Ruth Buzzi, Cloris Leachman, Cleavon Little, Roddy McDowall, Scatman Cruthers, Tony Randall, Robert Morley
The action begins when a deceased millionaire's will states that his 15 would-be heirs must compete in a scavenger hunt, and whoever collects all the items first wins the entire fortune.
MPAA:PG
Melvin Simon — *CBS/Fox Video*

Scenes from a Marriage **1973**
Drama
39080 168 mins C B, V P
Liv Ullmann, Erland Josephson, directed by Ingmar Bergman
Originally produced for Swedish television, this is an intimate chronicle of the disintegration of the "perfect" marraige.
Cinema 5 — *RCA/Columbia Pictures Home Video*

Schizo **1977**
Drama
06085 109 mins C B, V P
Lynne Rederick, John Layton
Devious intentions abound as a middleaged man is overcome by weird scenes and revelations. Much violent intensity.
MPAA:R
Pete Walker — *Media Home Entertainment*

Schizoid **1980**
Horror
55552 91 mins C B, V P
Klaus Kinski, Mariana Hill, directed by David Paulsen
An advice-to-the-lovelorn columnist receives a series of threatening letters causing her to wonder whether a psychiatrist is bumping off his own patients.
MPAA:R
Golan Globus Prod — *MCA Home Video*

Schizoid Man, The **1968**
Adventure/Fantasy
80418 50 mins C B, V P
Patrick McGoohan, Angelo Muscat, Colin Gordon, Alexis Kanner, Leo McKern
Number Two attempts to destroy The Prisoner's indentity through a new hypnotic technique.
Associated TV Corp — *MPI Home Video*

Schlock **1973**
Horror/Comedy
59056 78 mins C B, V P
Eliza Garrett, Saul Kahan, directed by John Landis
The classic story of beauty and the beast updated.
MPAA:PG
James C O'Rourke — *Wizard Video*

Scholastic Productions: As We Grow **1980**
Children/Identity
56885 70 mins C CED P
Twelve real-life episodes presenting early experiences in the lives of children at work and play. Produced by experts on children, this program will help children understand themselves and their world.
AM Available
Scholastic Inc — *RCA VideoDiscs*

School for Scandal **1965**
Satire
69581 100 mins B/W B, V P
Joan Plowright, Felix Aylmer

A British television adaptation of Richard Sheridan's play of the morals and manners of 18th century England.
BBC — *Video Yesteryear*

School for Sex 1969
Comedy
81404 81 mins C B, V P
Derek Aylward, Rose Alba, Hugh Latimer, Cathy Howard
A young man starts a school to teach young girls how to marry well and divest their husbands of their money.
Peter Walker — *Monterey Home Video*

Science Fiction Combo 196?
Science fiction
33700 125 mins C B, V, 3/4U P
Angela Cartwright, Billy Mumy, William Shatner, Leonard Nimoy
Three complete episodes from sci-fi TV series of the 1960's: "Lost in Space—The Reluctant Stowaway" (1965 pilot film), "The Twilight Zone—An Occurrence at Owl Creek Bridge" (1962), and "Star Trek—The Enemy Within" (1966). Only the "Star Trek" episode is in color.
CBS et al — *Shokus Video*

Scooby and Scrappy-Doo 1979
Cartoons
47692 60 mins C B, V P
Animated
Scooby and his energetic nephew pub, Scrappy-Doo, sniff out mysteries with their detective friends—Fred, Velma, Daphne and Shaggy. Three episodes.
Hanna Barbera — *Worldvision Home Video*

Scooby and Scrappy Doo, Vol III 1979
Cartoons
77161 60 mins C B, V P
Animated
Scooby and his nephew Scrappy Doo along with their friends Fred, Velma, Daphne and Shaggy set out to solve another mystery.
Hanna-Barbera — *Worldvision Home Video*

Scooby and Scrappy-Doo, Volume II 19??
Cartoons
69589 60 mins C B, V P
Animated
Scooby, Scrappy, Fred, Daphne, Velma and Shaggy get into more comical scrapes as they attempt to solve a mystery.
Hanna Barbera — *Worldvision Home Video*

Scooby Goes Hollywood 197?
Cartoons/Musical
47691 48 mins C B, V P
Animated
Everyone's favorite canine hits Hollywood in an attempt to be a star.
Hanna Barbera — *Worldvision Home Video*

Scrambled Feet 1983
Satire
75290 100 mins C B, V P
Madeline Kahn
This is an uninhibited satire of the world of show business. In Beta Hi-Fi and VHS Dolby stereo.
RKO Home Video — *RKO HomeVideo*

Scream Baby Scream 1984
Horror
80473 86 mins C B, V P
Ross Harris, Eugenie Wingate, Chris Martell, Suzanne Stuart, Larry Swanson
An unsuccessful artist switches from sculpting clay to carving young models' faces into hideous deformed creatures.
Regal Video — *Regal Video*

Scream Bloody Murder 197?
Suspense/Mystery
45051 90 mins C B, V P
Fred Holbert, Leigh Mitchell, Robert Knox, Suzette Hamilton
A young boy grinds his father to death with a tractor but mangles his own hand trying to jump off. After receiving a steel claw and being released from a mental institution he continues his murderous ways in and around his home town.
First American Films — *United Home Video*

Screams of a Winter Night 1979
Horror
35382 92 mins C B, V P
Ghostly tale of an evil monster from the lake and the terror he causes.
MPAA:PG
Richard H Wadsack, James L Wilson — *United Home Video*

Screwballs 1983
Comedy
65742 80 mins C B, V R, P
Peter Keleghan, Lynda Speciale
A freewheeling group of high school boys stirs up trouble for their snooty and virginal homecoming queen.
MPAA:R
Maurice Smith — *Warner Home Video*

Scrooge 1935
Fantasy
11397 61 mins B/W B, V, FO P
Seymour Hicks, Maurice Evans, Robert Cochran
A miser changes his ways after receiving visits from ghosts of Christmas past, present, and

 (For explanation of codes, see USE GUIDE and KEY)

future. Based on the classic novel "A Christmas Carol" by Charles Dickens.
Unknown — *Video Yesteryear; Blackhawk Films; Sheik Video; Discount Video Tapes*

Scrooge's Rock 'n' Roll Christmas **1983**
Musical/Christmas
75900 44 mins C B, V P
This program presents the Dickens story with Christmas carols sung by Three Dog Night, Rush and others.
Hitbound Records — *Sony Corporation of America*

Scrubbers **1982**
Drama
73024 93 mins C B, V R, P
Amanda York, Chrissie Cotterill
A young girl is sentenced to prison where she's forced to survive in a cruel and brutal environment.
MPAA:R
Don Boyd — *THORN EMI/HBO Video*

Scruffy **1980**
Cartoons
80644 72 mins C B, V P
Animated, voices of Alan Young, June Foray, Hans Conried, Nancy McKeon
An orphaned puppy encounters many dangerous adventures before finding true love.
Ruby-Spears — *Worldvision Home Video*

Scruggs **1970**
Music-Performance
37404 87 mins C B, V P
Earl Scruggs, Bob Dylan, Joan Baez, Doc Watson, The Byrds
A tribute to banjo virtuoso Earl Scruggs, featuring Scruggs in performance, along with Dylan, Baez, and others.
WNET New York — *CBS/Fox Video*

Scum **1979**
Drama
70604 96 mins C B, V P
Phil Daniels, Mick Ford, Ray Winstone, directed by Alan Clarke
Adapted from Roy Mintons acclaimed play, this British production looks at the struggle between three young men in a British Borstal (a prison for young convicts.)
GTO Films Ltd. — *Prism*

Sea Around Us, The **1952**
Documentary/Oceanography
10158 61 mins C B, V P, T
Narrated by Don Forbes
Science documentary of history and life of the ocean based on Rachel Carson's study.
Academy Award '52: Best Feature Documentary.
Irwin Allen; RKO — *Blackhawk Films; Nostalgia Merchant*

Sea Hawk, The **1940**
Adventure
73969 110 mins B/W B, V P
Errol Flynn, Claude Rains, Donald Crisp, Alan Hale, Flora Robson, Brenda Marshall, directed by Michael Curtiz
When an English pirate finds out that the Spanish are going to invade England with their Armada, he comes back to save the queen and his country.
Warner Bros — *Key Video*

Sea Lion, The **1921**
Drama
48712 50 mins B/W B, V, FO P
Hobart Basworth
A vicious sea captain, embittered by a past romance, becomes sadistic and intolerable, until the truth emerges. Silent.
Hobart Bosworth Prods — *Video Yesteryear*

Sea Prince and the Fire Child, The **1982**
Adventure/Cartoons
64910 70 mins C B, V P
Animated
This Japanese animated film follows two young lovers who set off on an adventure to escape the disapproval of their parents.
Tsunemasa Hatano — *RCA/Columbia Pictures Home Video*

Sea Shall Not Have Them, The **1955**
War-Drama/Adventure
81424 92 mins B/W B, V P
Michael Redgrave, Dick Bogarde, directed by Lewis Gilbert
A daring band of men rescue the four survivors of a Hudson aircraft crash in the North Sea.
United Artists — *Republic Pictures Home Video*

Sea Wolves, The **1981**
Adventure
53557 120 mins C B, V, CED P
Gregory Peck, Roger Moore, David Niven, Trevor Howard, Patrick Macnee, directed by Andrew V. McLaglen
A true WW II story about a commando-style operation undertaken by a group of middle-aged, boozing British businessmen in India in 1943.
MPAA:PG
Euan Lloyd; Lorimar — *CBS/Fox Video*

Sea World 1985
Oceanography
70577 45 mins C B, V P
This voyage into the briny deep will be of interest to children and parents alike.
Century Video Corp.; Finley Holiday — *Kid Time Video*

Seals and Crofts with Martin Mull Live 197?
Music-Performance
71289 30 mins C B, V P
In this film Seals and Crofts perform such hits as "Hummingbird," "Summer Breeze," and "The Eighth of January." Also includes Martin Mull, who also performs.
Independent — *Media Home Entertainment*

Search and Destroy 1978
Drama
64871 93 mins C B, V, CED P
Perry King, George Kennedy, Tisa Farrow
A deadly vendetta, born in the midst of battle in a Vietnamese jungle, is kept alive.
MPAA:PG
James Margellos — *Vestron Video*

Searchers, The 1956
Western
38954 119 mins C B, V, LV R, P
John Wayne, Jeffrey Hunter, Vera Miles, Natalie Wood, Ward Bond, directed by John Ford
John Wayne plays a Civil War veteran on the trail of a Comanche raiding party that kidnapped the daughter of one of his friends in this classic John Ford western.
Warner Bros — *Warner Home Video; RCA VideoDiscs*

Seasons for Assassins 1971
Suspense
65448 102 mins C B, V P
Joe Dallesandro, Martin Balsam
A gang of young ruthless hoodlums bring a wave of violence and terror upon the hapless citizens of Rome.
MPAA:R
Carlo Maietto — *U.S.A. Home Video*

Seattle Seahawks 1984 Team Highlights 1985
Football
70551 70 mins C B, V, FO P
The seahawk's intimidating defense and explosive offense helped them overccme adversity in a season characterized by some as "One From the Heart." The tape features 47-minutes of highlights from the '84 NFL season as well.
NFL Films — *NFL Films Video*

Second Chance 1953
Suspense/Drama
64370 82 mins C B, V, 3/4U P
Robert Mitchum, Linda Darnell, Jack Palance, directed by Rudolph Mate
A former prizefighter travels to South America where he protects a gangster's moll who is targeted for murder.
RKO — *Nostalgia Merchant*

Second Chorus 1940
Musical
01617 90 mins B/W B, V P
Fred Astaire, Paulette Goddard, Burgess Meredith, Artie Shaw, Directed by H.C. Potter
Rivalry of two trumpet players for a girl and a job with Artie Shaw Orchestra. Music, dance, and romance.
Paramount — *Budget Video; World Video Pictures; Sheik Video; Cable Films; VCII; Video Connection; Video Yesteryear; Discount Video Tapes; Cinema Concepts; Classic Video Cinema Collector's Club; Kartes Productions; See Hear Industries*

Second City Insanity 1981
Comedy
59076 60 mins C B, V P
Fred Willard, John Candy
The famed Second City improvisational troupe performs their unique brand of humor.
Toby Martin; Carol N Raskin — *Karl/Lorimar Home Video*

Second Coming of Suzanne, The 1980
Drama
56920 90 mins C B, V R, P
Sondra Locke, Richard Dreyfuss, Gene Barry
A beautiful woman encounters a Manson-like, hypnotic film director. Her role—to star in a Crucifixion. Set in 1969 San Francisco. A world premiere edition, winner at two international film festivals.
Michael Barry — *Video Gems*

Second Thoughts 1983
Comedy-Drama
65090 109 mins C B, V R, P
Lucie Arnaz, Craig Wasson, Ken Howard
A lady attorney becomes pregnant by one of her clients, an itinerant street musician. When she decides to get an abortion, he kidnaps her and tries to change her mind.
MPAA:PG
EMI Films; Universal — *THORN EMI/HBO Video*

Second Time Lucky 1984
Comedy/Fantasy
81124 98 mins C B, V P

Diane Franklin, Roger Wilson, Robert Morley, Jon Gadsby, Bill Ewens, directed by Michael Anderson
The devil makes a bet with God that if the world began all over again Adam and Eve would repeat their mistake they made in the Garden of Eden.
United International Pictures — *Karl/Lorimar Home Video*

Second Woman, The **1951**
Drama/Mystery
80741 91 mins B/W B, V P
Robert Young, Betsy Drake, John Sutton
A small town suspects that an architect is responsible for the death of his fiancee.
Cardinal Pictures — *Hal Roach Studios*

Secret Agent **1936**
Mystery
11317 83 mins B/W B, V, FO P
Madeleine Carroll, Peter Lorre, Robert Young, John Gielgud, Lilli Palmer
A British Intelligence agent has orders to eliminate an enemy agent and thinks he has succeeded. He later finds out that he killed an innocent tourist in Geneva.
Gaumont — *Video Yesteryear; Budget Video; Video Dimensions; Discount Video Tapes; Video Connection; Cable Films; Western Film & Video Inc; Hal Roach Studios; Kartes Productions; Classic Video Cinema Collector's Club*

Secret Agent #1 **1965**
Suspense
77419 50 mins B/W B, V P
Patrick McGoohan, Niall MacGinnes, Dawn Addams, directed by Don Chaffey
Secret agent John Drake is after the thief who stole top secret documents from an atomic laboratory. An episode from the "Secret Agent" series.
ITC Productions — *MPI Home Video*

Secret Beyond the Door **1948**
Mystery
70203 99 mins B/W B, V P
Joan Bennett, Michael Redgrove, Barbara O'Neill
A wealthy heiress marries a widower and soon discovers that he murdered his first wife.
Universal — *Republic Pictures Home Video*

Secret Fantasy **1981**
Drama
63383 88 mins C B, V P
Laura Antonelli
A musician overcomes his fears of inferiority as he makes his fantasies a reality by having other men admire his wife's beautiful body.
MPAA:R
Film Ventures — *Media Home Entertainment*

Secret Life of Adolph Hitler, The **1969**
World War II/Documentary
08910 52 mins B/W B, V, 3/4U P
Narrated by Westbrook Van Voorhis
A documentary on Adolph Hitler uses rare footage to portray the growth of the Third Reich.
Wolper — *Video Yesteryear; International Historic Films; Discount Video Tapes*

Secret Lives of Waldo Kitty Volume I, The **1975**
Cartoons
72886 48 mins C B, V P
Animated
A cartoon where Waldo Kitty imagines himself to be a variety of heroes such as Robin Cat and the Lone Kitty.
Filmation — *Embassy Home Entertainment*

Secret of NIMH, The **1982**
Fantasy
60565 83 mins C B, V, CED P
Animated, directed by Don Bluth, voices by Hermione Baddeley, John Carradine, Dom DeLuise, Elizabeth Hartman, Peter Strauss, Aldo Ray, Edie McClurg
Based on the story by Robert O'Brien, this animated tale produced by a staff of Disney-trained artists concerns a newly-widowed mouse with four wee ones to care for and protect against a series of dangers. Stereo.
MPAA:G
Mrs Brisby Ltd; MGM — *MGM/UA Home Video*

Secret of the Snake and Crane, The **197?**
Martial arts
72174 90 mins C B, V P
A resistance group relies on ancient fighting techniques to battle the rule of the Ching Dynasty in this Kung Fu action film.
Foreign — *Master Arts Video*

Secret of Yolanda, The **1982**
Drama
68246 90 mins C B, V P
Aviva Ger, Asher Zarfati, Shraga Harpaz
A steamy romance about a young deaf-mute whose guardian and riding instructor both fall for her.
MPAA:R
Noah Films — *MGM/UA Home Video*

Secret Policeman's Other Ball, The **1982**
Music-Performance/Comedy
63117 101 mins C B, V, CED P
John Cleese, Graham Chapman, Michael Palin, Terry Jones, Peter Townsend, Sting

A live concert by most of the Monty Python troupe and guest rock artists, staged for Amnesty International. In stereo.
MPAA:R
Amnesty International; Miramax Films — *MGM/UA Home Video*

Secret Squirrel 196?
Cartoons
47693 53 mins C B, V P
Animated
Eight episodes of adventure with the clever secret agent.
Hanna Barbera — *Worldvision Home Video*

Secret War of Harry Frigg, The 1968
Comedy
64559 123 mins C B, V P
Paul Newman, Sylva Koscina, Tom Bosley, Andrew Duggan
Private Harry Frigg, a nonconformist World War II G.I., is promoted to the rank of general as part of a scheme to help five Allied generals escape from the custody of the Germans.
MPAA:R
Universal — *MCA Home Video*

Secret World of Erotic Art, The 1985
Arts/History
70738 60 mins C B, V P
Peggy O'Brien, Tom Nolan
This documentation presents the history of erotic art from the middle ages to the 1900's, and concentrates on information rather than titillation.
Roberta Hagnes; Rick Houser — *Vestron Video*

Secret World of Reptiles, The 1977
Animals/Documentary
29170 94 mins C B, V R, P
A series that presents rare living relics of primeval times and traces the history of the reptile kingdom.
Bill Burrud Productions — *Walt Disney Home Video*

Secrets 1978
Drama
29225 85 mins C B, V P
Jacqueline Bisset
A beautiful, sensual, taken-for-granted wife has a brief afternoon of love with a charming stranger and leaves with a secret gift.
MPAA:R
Lone Star Pictures Intl — *Prism*

Secrets 1971
Drama
70606 81 mins C B, V P
Jacqueline Bisset, Robert Powell, Shirley Knight, Per Oscarsson
A long married couple finds that the answer to their marital doldrums may be in simultaneous extra matrital excursions.
Lone Star Pictures Intl. — *Prism*

Secrets of Women 1952
Comedy-Drama
65630 108 mins B/W B, V P
Anita Bjork, Karl Arne Homsten, Jarl Kulle, directed by Ingar Bergman
Three sisters-in-law tell about their affairs and marriages as they await their husbands at a lakeside resort.
Janus Films — *Embassy Home Entertainment*

Seducers, The 1980
Drama
56930 90 mins C B, V R, P
Sondra Locke, Colleen Camp, Seymour Cassel
A wealthy, middle-aged man unsuspectingly allows two young girls to use his telephone, and once inside, a night of bizarre mayhem and brutal murder begins.
MPAA:R
Peter Traynor, Larry Spiegel — *Video Gems*

Seduction, The 1982
Drama
59676 104 mins C B, V P
Morgan Fairchild, Michael Sarrazin, Vince Edwards, Andrew Stevens, Colleen Camp, Kevin Brophy
A superstar TV anchorwoman is harassed by a psychotic male admirer.
MPAA:R
Irwin Yablans; Bruce Cohn Curtis — *Media Home Entertainment; Embassy Home Entertainment (disc only)*

Seduction of Joe Tynan, The 1979
Drama
29735 107 mins C B, V, LV P
Alan Alda, Meryl Streep, Melvyn Douglas, directed by Alan Alda
Alan Alda wrote, directed, and starred in this movie about a senator who is torn between his political career and his personal life.
MPAA:R
Universal, Martin Bregman — *MCA Home Video*

Seduction of Mimi, The 1974
Film-Avant-garde
37402 92 mins C B, V P
Giancarlo Giannini, Mariangelo Melato, directed by Lina Wertmuller

A comic farce of politics and seduction about a Sicilian laborer's escapades with the Communists and the local Mafia.
MPAA:R
New Line Cinema — *CBS/Fox Video*

See It Now 1957
Documentary
78097 82 mins B/W B, V, FO P
Edward R. Murrow
An exploration of how automation is changing the way America works and how computers are revolutionizing industry.
CBS — *Video Yesteryear*

Seeds of Evil 1976
Horror
47666 80 mins C B, V P
Katherine Houghton, Joe Dallesandro, Rita Gam
A strange gardener grows flowers that can kill.
Chalmer Kirkbride — *Unicorn Video*

Seems Like Old Times 1980
Comedy
51571 102 mins C B, V, LV P
Goldie Hawn, Chevy Chase, Charles Grodin, Robert Guillaume, Harold Gould, directed by Jay Sandrich
A woman with a weakness for her ex-husband comes to his aid when two robbers force him to hold up a bank.
MPAA:PG
Columbia Pictures — *RCA/Columbia Pictures Home Video; RCA VideoDiscs*

Self Defense 1985
Martial arts
76990 60 mins C B, V P
A group of experts present a series of martial arts techniques which can help in dealing with impending acts of violence.
Karl Home Video — *Karl/Lorimar Home Video*

Self-Defense for Women 1985
Physical fitness
77420 60 mins C B, V P
A step by step demonstration of self-defense techniques for women.
Maljack Productions — *MPI Home Video*

Sell Out, The 1976
Adventure
76657 102 mins C B, V P
Richard Widmark, Oliver Reed, Gayle Hunnicutt, Sam Wanamaker
Oscar-winning actor Richard Widmark, and a highly-acclaimed cast star in a high-stakes game of tag, but no one's sure who "it" is.
MPAA:PG
Josef Shaftel — *Media Home Entertainment*

Selling Movies on Television 197?
Movie and TV trailers
42975 55 mins C B, V, FO P
Here are 67 TV commercials for some of the best and worst films ever released, featuring stars and scenes from such movies as "The Great Dictator," "The Glass Bottom Boat," and "Portnoy's Complaint."
CBS et al — *Video Yesteryear*

Semi-Tough 1977
Comedy
13313 107 mins C B, V, LV P
Burt Reynolds, Kris Kristofferson, Jill Clayburgh, directed by Michael Ritchie
Social satire involving a couple of pro-football buddies and the team owner's daughter.
MPAA:R
United Artists; David Merrick — *CBS/Fox Video; RCA VideoDiscs*

Senator Was Indiscreet, The 1947
Comedy
65736 81 mins B/W B, V P
William Powell, Ella Raines
A senator, seeking the Presidential nomination, tours the country making ridiculous and contradictory campaign promises.
Universal — *Republic Pictures Home Video*

Sender, The 1982
Horror
64504 92 mins C B, V, LV R, P
Kathryn Harrold, Zeljko Ivanek, Shirley Knight
A amnesiac young man is studied by a psychiatrist who discovers that her patient is a "sender," who can transmit his nightmares to other people. In stereo.
MPAA:R
Paramount — *Paramount Home Video*

Seniors 1978
Comedy
63363 87 mins C B, V, CED P
Dennis Quaid, Priscilla Barnes, Jeffrey Byron, Gary Imhoff
Fast-paced antics abound in this satire of students, sex and society.
MPAA:R
Cine Artists — *Vestron Video*

Senora Tentacion 1949
Musical-Drama
57360 82 mins B/W B, V, FO P
David Silva, Susana Guizar, Ninon Sevilla
Musical melodrama about a composer who fights to leave his mother, sister, and girlfriend in order to flee with Hortensia, a famous singer.
SP
Mexican — *Video Yesteryear*

Sensational Sixties 1980
Football
45124 30 mins C B, V, FO R, P
Narrated by John Facenda
The best players, plays, games, and moments from pro football's golden decade are captured in this memory-provoking program.
NFL Films — *NFL Films Video*

Sense of Loss, A 1972
Documentary/Great Britain
76038 135 mins B/W B, V P
This documentary deals with the on-going controversy in Northern Ireland, and the impact that it has on the day-to-day lives of the Irish.
Marcel Ophuls; Max Palevsky — *RCA/Columbia Pictures Home Video*

Sensual Man, The 1974
Comedy
68267 90 mins C B, V P
Giancarlo Giannini, Rossana Podesta, Lionel Stowder
A hot blooded Italian falls in love and gets married only to find out that his wife cannot consummate their marriage.
MPAA:R
Medusa Distribuzione — *RCA/Columbia Pictures Home Video*

Sensuous Caterer, The 1982
Comedy
64845 60 mins C B, V P
Marc Stevens
Stevens hosts a video Valentine's Day orgy and invites an uninhibited crowd of erotic stars and starlets to come and show their stuff.
A.O.E. Productions — *HarmonyVision*

Separacion Matrimonial 197?
Drama
52794 96 mins C B, V P
Jacqueline Andere, Ana Belen, Simon Andreu
A woman decides to forgive her husband and stop divorce proceedings when his outside love affair ends. Soon, however, he is up to his old tricks again. In Spanish.
SP
Luis Sanz — *Media Home Entertainment*

Separate Peace, A 1973
Drama
64028 104 mins C B, V R, P
John Heyl, Parker Stevenson, William Roerick
Based on the novel by John Knowles, this is the story of how responsibility for a crippling accident brings a young man face to face with his inner nature.
MPAA:PG
Paramount — *Paramount Home Video*

Separate Tables 1958
Drama
68231 98 mins B/W B, V, CED P
Burt Lancaster, Rita Hayworth, David Niven, Deborah Kerr
This film explores the separate yet connected dreams of people staying in the same hotel.
Clifton Productions — *CBS/Fox Video*

Separate Tables 1983
Drama
79210 50 mins C B, V P
Julie Christie, Alan Bates, Claire Bloom, Irene Worth, directed by John Schlesinger
An adaptation of Terence Rattigan's two one act plays about the lonely inhabitants of a hotel: """Table by the Window" and """Table Number Seven."
Edie and Ely Landau — *MGM/UA Home Video*

Separate Ways 1982
Drama
62864 92 mins C B, V, LV, CED P
Karen Black, Tony LoBianco, David Naughton
A middle-class couple find they must split up for a while to gain a new perspective of themselves and their marriage.
MPAA:R
Hickmar Productions — *Vestron Video*

Sergeant Pepper's Lonely Hearts Club Band 1978
Musical
14003 113 mins C B, V, LV P
Peter Frampton, the Bee Gees, Steve Martin, Aerosmith, Earth Wind and Fire, George Burns
The Beatles' famous story-in-song album is transferred to the screen starring some of the most popular rock n' roll singer-musicians of our time.
MPAA:PG
Universal; Robert Stigwood — *MCA Home Video*

Sergeant Sullivan Speaking 1953
Drama/Romance
77367 24 mins B/W B, V P, T
William Bendix, Joan Blondell, Sarah Selby
A romance develops between a widow and a police sergeant as the two search for the widow's lost sons. From the ABC-TV series "Return Engagement."
ABC — *Blackhawk Films*

Sergeant York 1941
Drama
58950 134 mins B/W B, V, CED P
Gary Cooper, Joan Leslie, Walter Brennan, Dickie Moore, Ward Bond, directed by Howard Hawks

(For explanation of codes, see USE GUIDE and KEY)

The story of the gentle, hillbilly farmer who becomes a hero of World War I.
Academy Awards '41: Best Actor (Cooper).
Warner Bros — *CBS/Fox Video; RCA VideoDiscs*

Serial 1980
Comedy
55540 92 mins C B, V, LV R, P
Martin Mull, Sally Kellerman, Tuesday Weld, Tom Smothers, Bill Macy, Barbara Rhoades, Christopher Lee
Cyra McFadden's novel about life in Marin County, California, spoofing open marriage, health foods, exercise, psychiatry, and cult religions comes to life in this film.
MPAA:R
Paramount; Sidney Beckerman — *Paramount Home Video*

Serial Previews # 1 194?
Movie and TV trailers/Serials
64417 60 mins B/W B, V, 3/4U P
An assortment of theatrical trailers from over thirty serials. Titles featured include "The Adventures of Red Ryder," "The Fighting Devil Dogs," "Superman," "The Spy Smasher," "The Adventures of Captain Marvel" and many others.
Republic et al — *Nostalgia Merchant*

Serpico 1974
Drama
29797 130 mins C B, V, LV R, P
Al Pacino, John Randolf, Jack Kehoe, Barbara Eda-Young
The story of Frank Serpico, a New York policeman who uncovered corruption in the police department.
MPAA:R
Dino De Laurentiis — *Paramount Home Video; RCA VideoDiscs*

Servant, The 1963
Drama
36933 112 mins B/W B, V R, P
Dirk Bogarde, James Fox, Sarah Miles, Wendy Craig, directed by Joseph Losey
British class hypocrisy is starkly portrayed in this story of a spoiled young gentleman's ruin by his socially inferior but crafty and ambitious manservant.
British Film Academy: Best Actor (Bogarde); Best Photography (Black and White); Most Promising Newcomer (Fox).
Springbok Prod, Landau Unger — *THORN EMI/HBO Video*

Sesenta Horas en el Cielo 1946
Comedy
57359 76 mins B/W B, V, FO P
Alady y Lepe
A comedy about two air cadets who gain fame by establishing a new record for duration in the air.
SP
Spain — *Video Yesteryear*

Sessions 1983
Drama
70717 96 mins C B, V P
Veronica Hamel, Jeffrey DeMunn, Jill Eikenberry, David Marshall Grant, George Coe, Henderson Forsythe, Deborah Hedwall
Mentally exhausted by her roles as a sister, single-parent, lover, exercise enthusiast, and high-priced prostitute, Leigh Churchill seeks professional counselling.
Thorn EMI in association with Sarabande Prods. — *VCL Home Video*

Set Up, The 1949
Drama
44986 72 mins B/W B, V P, T
Robert Ryan, Audrey Totter
The story of an average fighter who refuses to take a dive for a group of crooked gamblers, and fights to win.
Anglo Amalgamated Film — *Blackhawk Films; Nostalgia Merchant*

Seven Alone 1975
Adventure
44949 85 mins C B, V P
Dewey Martin, Aldo Ray, Anne Collins, Dean Smith, Stewart Peterson, directed by Earl Bellamy
Seven orphaned children, led by the oldest, a thirteen-year-old boy, undertake a treacherous 2000 mile journey from Missouri to Oregon. Based on the book "On to Oregon" by Monroe Morrow.
MPAA:G
Doty Dayton — *Children's Video Library*

Seven Beauties 1976
Comedy
44774 116 mins C B, V P
Giancarlo Giannini, Fernando Rey, Shirley Stoler, directed by Lina Wertmuller
The story of a dumb but likeable hood who shoots his sister's pimp to save his family's honor. He is caught and sent to an insane asylum. After volunteering for the Italian army, he finds himself in a Nazi concentration camp.
Cinema 5 — *RCA/Columbia Pictures Home Video*

---

7 Blows of the Dragon 1973
Adventure/Martial arts
54810 81 mins C B, V R, P
David Chiang
The Chinese novel, "All Men Are Brothers," is the basis for this spectacular martial arts epic.
MPAA:R

New World Pictures — *Warner Home Video*

Seven Brides for Seven Brothers 1954
Musical
58705 103 mins C B, V, CED P
Howard Keel, Jane Powell, Russ Tamblyn, Julie Newmar, Jeff Richards, Tommy Rall, Virginia Gibson, directed by Stanley Donen
When the eldest of seven brothers in the Oregon Territory brings home a wife, the other six sneak into town looking for brides.
Academy Awards '54: Best Scoring, Musical (Adloph Deutsch, Saul Chaplin).
MGM — *MGM/UA Home Video*

Seven Days Ashore/Hurry, Charlie, Hurry 1944
Comedy
76840 141 mins B/W B, V P
Gordon Oliver, Virginia Mayo, Dooley Wilson, Margaret Dumont, Leon Errol, Mildred Coles
A comedy double feature: In "Seven Days Ashore" three Merchant Marines on leave in San Francisco become romantically involved with three women and in "Hurry, Charlie, Hurry" a henpecked husband finds himself in a lot of trouble.
RKO — *RKO HomeVideo*

Seven Days in May 1964
Mystery/Drama
65617 120 mins B/W B, V, LV, CED R, P
Burt Lancaster, Kirk Douglas, Frederic March, Ava Gardner, John Houseman
An American general's aide discovers that his boss intends a military takeover because he considers the President's pacifism traitorous.
Seven Arts — *Paramount Home Video*

Seven Doors to Death 1944
Mystery
77201 70 mins B/W B, V P
Chick Chandler, June Clyde, George Meeker
Two strangers become meshed in a web of murder and intrigue.
PRC Pictures — *United Home Video*

Seven Miles from Alcatraz/Flight from Glory 1943
Drama
81027 127 mins B/W B, V P
James Craig, Bonita Granville, Chester Morris, Van Heflin, Onslow Stevens
A dramatic double feature: Two escaped convicts discover a hideout for Nazi spies in "Seven Miles From Alcatraz," and an evil man tries to recruit pilots to fly planes over the Andes Mountains in "Flight From Glory."
RKO — *RKO HomeVideo*

Seven-Per-Cent Solution, The 1976
Mystery
14002 113 mins C B, V P
Alan Arkin, Nicol Williamson, Laurence Olivier, Robert Duvall, Venessa Redgrave, Joel Grey, Samantha Eggar, directed by Herbert Ross
Sigmund Freud joins forces with Sherlock Holmes and Dr. Watson in the search for the real Professor Moriarity.
MPAA:PG
Universal; Herbert Ross Prod — *MCA Home Video*

Seven Samurai 1954
Adventure
29761 204 mins B/W B, V P
Takashi Shimura, Toshiro Mifune, Yoshio Inaba
A small Japanese farming village is beset by marauding bandits. Powerless to prevent these ongoing raids, the villagers hire seven professional soldiers. Japanese dialogue with English subtitles.
Academy Awards '55: Honorary Award. JA
Kingsley Intl, Toho Prod — *Embassy Home Entertainment; Budget Video; International Historic Films; Sheik Video; Discount Video Tapes; Video Action*

Seven-Ups, The 1973
Adventure
Closed Captioned
80655 109 mins C B, V P
Roy Scheider, Tony LoBianco, Larry Haines, Jerry Leon, directed by Phil D'Antoni
An elite group of New York City detectives seek to avenge the killing of a fellow squad member and bust criminals whose felonies are punishable by jail terms of seven-years or more.
Available in VHS and Beta Hi-Fi.
MPAA:PG
20th Century Fox — *CBS/Fox Video*

Seven Year Itch, The 1955
Comedy
08467 105 mins C B, V P
Marilyn Monroe, Tom Ewell, Evelyn Keyes, Sonny Tufts, Robert Strauss, Oscar Homolka
After a man sees his wife and son off to the country for the summer, he returns home to find that a lovely blonde has sublet the apartment above his.
20th Century Fox; Charles K Feldman and Billy Wilder — *CBS/Fox Video*

Seven Years Bad Luck 1920
Comedy
78106 67 mins B/W B, V, FO P
Max Linder
This is the famous movie in which a broken mirror brings a man proverbial bad luck for

 (For explanation of codes, see USE GUIDE and KEY)

seven years that seems to come all at once. Silent with music score.
Robertson Cole Distributing Corp — *Video Yesteryear*

1776 **1972**
Musical
64235 141 mins C B, V P
Howard da Silva, William Daniels, Ken Howard, Donald Madden, Blythe Danner
Based on the musical play, this is a light-hearted look at the signing of the Declaration of Independence. In simulated stereo.
MPAA:PG
Columbia — *RCA/Columbia Pictures Home Video*

7th Voyage of Sinbad, The **1958**
Fantasy
19083 89 mins C B, V, CED P
Kerwin Matthews, Kathryn Grant
Sinbad seeks to restore his fiancee from the midget size to which an evil magician has reduced her.
Columbia — *RCA/Columbia Pictures Home Video*

Severed Arm, The **1973**
Horror
58551 89 mins C B, V R, P
Deborah Waller, Paul Carr, David Cannon
Trapped in a cave, five men cut off the arm of a companion in order to ward off starvation.
Heritage Enterprises — *Video Gems*

Sex and Love Test, The **1981**
Sexuality
57549 60 mins C B, V P
Hosted by Dr. Frank Field
Viewers can test their knowledge on sexual problems, and find out the answers from psychiatrists and sex therapists.
International Film and TV Festival of New York: Silver Medal.
NBC; Don Luftig — *Karl/Lorimar Home Video*

Sex and the Office Girl **197?**
Drama
59552 76 mins C B, V P
An advertising agency turns into an after hours pleasure dome of erotic complications.
Filmco — *Media Home Entertainment*

Sex, Drugs and Rock-N-Roll **1984**
Drama
81426 90 mins C B, V P
Jeanne Silver, Sharon Kane, Tish Ambrose, Josey Duval
Several girls frequent a rock club looking for all the action they can get their hands on.
F.J. Lincoln — *Video Home Library*

Sex Machine, The **1976**
Drama
47750 80 mins C B, V P
Agostina Belli
Set in the year 2037, a scientist finds two of the world's greatest lovers and unites them so he can transform their reciprocating motion into electricity.
MPAA:R
Sylvio Clementelli — *Media Home Entertainment*

Sex Madness **1937**
Exploitation
05530 50 mins B/W B, V, FO P
A 1930's campy melodrama about the evils of lechery, lust, and passion.
Unknown — *Video Yesteryear; Budget Video; Video Dimensions; Sheik Video; Discount Video Tapes*

Sex Shop, Le **1973**
Satire
47781 92 mins C B, V P
Claude Berri, Juliet Berto
A man owns a shop where he sells exotic books and paraphernalia. When his relationship with his wife gets boring, they make use of the merchandise and adopt a swinging lifestyle.
MPAA:R
Pierre Grunstein — *RCA/Columbia Pictures Home Video*

Sex Through a Window **1972**
Drama
76780 81 mins C B, V P
A TV reporter becomes an obsessive voyeur after filing a report on high tech surveillance equipment.
MPAA:R
Mann Productions — *Vestron Video*

Sex with a Smile **1976**
Comedy
43072 100 mins C B, V R, P
Marty Feldman, Edvice Finich, Alex Marino, Enrico Monterrano, Giovanni Ralli
Five slapstick episodes by five different directors with lots of sexual satire pointed at religion and politics in Italy.
MPAA:R
Surrogate — *Video Gems*

Sextette **1978**
Musical/Comedy
59665 91 mins C B, V P
Mae West, Timothy Dalton, Ringo Starr, George Hamilton, Dom DeLuise, Tony Curtis, Alice Cooper, Keith Moon, George Raft, Rona Barrett

A lavish musical about an elderly star who is constantly interrupted by former spouses and well-wishers while on a honeymoon with her sixth husband.
MPAA:PG
Daniel Briggs; Robert Sullivan — *Media Home Entertainment*

Sexton Blake and the Hooded Terror **1953**
Mystery
12808 70 mins B/W B, V, FO P
Tod Slaughter, Greta Gynt
A British private detective is after "The Snake," a master criminal.
Unknown — *Video Yesteryear*

Sextoons **197?**
Cartoons
64846 90 mins C B, V P
Animated
This offers a collection of some of the world's greatest erotic animation.
Saliva Films — *HarmonyVision*

Shack Out On 101 **1955**
Drama
77249 80 mins B/W B, V P
Lee Marvin, Terry Moore, Keenan Wynn, Frank Lovejoy
A waitress in an isolated cafe on a busy highway notices suspicious activities among the cafe's clientele.
Allied Artists — *Spotlite Video*

Shadow of the Eagle **1932**
Mystery/Serials
12551 226 mins B/W B, V, FO P
John Wayne, Dorothy Gulliver, directed by Ford Beebe
Intrigue and mystery of carnival life. Twelve chapters, 13 minutes each.
Mascot — *Video Yesteryear; Video Connection; Discount Video Tapes*

Shadows **1922**
Drama
64354 70 mins B/W B, V P
Lon Chaney
A Chinese laundryman lives with a group of his countrymen in a New England seacoast village. All is peaceful until the local minister decides to convert the "heathen" Chinese. Silent with music score.
Preferred Pictures — *Classic Video Cinema Collector's Club; Blackhawk Films*

Shaft **1971**
Crime-Drama
60566 98 mins C B, V, CED P
Richard Roundtree
A black private eye finds himself at odds with a powerful racketeer.
MPAA:R
MGM — *MGM/UA Home Video*

Shaggy Dog, The **1959**
Comedy
58626 101 mins B/W B, V, LV R, P
Fred MacMurray, Jean Hagen, Tommy Kirk, Annette Funicello, Tim Considine, Kevin Corcoran, directed by Charles Barton
When young Wilby Daniels utters some magical words from the inscription of an ancient ring he turns into a shaggy dog causing havoc to family and neighbors.
MPAA:G
Walt Disney Productions — *Walt Disney Home Video; RCA VideoDiscs*

Shakespeare: Soul of an Age **1962**
Documentary
80179 51 mins C B, V R, P
Sir Michael Redgrave and Sir Ralph Richardson visit the historical sites of William Shakespeare's plays.
NBC — *Warner Home Video*

Shalako **1968**
Western
69384 113 mins C B, V P
Brigitte Bardot, Sean Connery
While on a hunting trip in New Mexico in the 1880's, a European countess is captured by an Apache, and a U.S. Army scout is sent to save her.
Cinerama Releasing — *CBS/Fox Video*

Shall We Dance **1937**
Musical
10051 116 mins B/W B, V P, T
Fred Astaire, Ginger Rogers, Edward Everett Horton
A famous ballet dancer marries a showgirl—or does he? The score by George and Ira Gershwin includes such memorable songs as "They All Laughed," "Let's Call the Whole Thing Off" and "They Can't Take That Away from Me."
RKO; Pandro S Berman — *Blackhawk Films; King of Video; Nostalgia Merchant*

Shamus **1973**
Comedy
21295 91 mins C B, V P
Burt Reynolds, Dyan Cannon
A detective hired to recover some missing diamonds becomes involved with the syndicate, a beautiful woman, and an army officer smuggling government surplus.
MPAA:PG

Columbia — *RCA/Columbia Pictures Home Video*

Shane 1953
Western
38619 117 mins C B, V, LV R, P
Alan Ladd, Jean Arthur, Van Heflin, Brandon de Wilde, Jack Palance, directed by George Stevens
A retired gunfighter, now drifter, comes to the assistance of a homestead family terrorized by a hired gunman. A classic of the Western film genre.
Academy Awards '53: Best Cinematography, Color.
Paramount — *Paramount Home Video; RCA VideoDiscs*

Shaolin Death Squad 1983
Martial arts
64564 90 mins C B, V P
A ruthless Japanese premier murders a statesman as the first step in his plan to become Emperor. The murdered man's daughter swears vengeance and enlists the Shaolin Death Squad to help.
MPAA:R
Satellite Consultants — *CBS/Fox Video*

Shaolin Traitor 1982
Martial arts
64944 99 mins C B, V R, P
Carter Wong, Shangkuan Ling-Feng, Lung Chun-Erh, Chang Yi, Lung Fei
Exotic weapons and dazzling martial-arts action are featured in this exciting tale of intrigue and mystery.
MPAA:R
L and T Films Corp Ltd — *Video Gems*

Shapeworks Plus 1985
Dance/Physical fitness
70719 100 mins C B, V P
Angela Hillemann
Ms. Hillemann, a ballet instructor at the University of Missouri, shows us a complete series of stretch and aerobic exercises designed to tone the entire body.
AM Available
To the Pointe: Hilleman Dancer's Studio — *To the Pointe Hillemann Dancers*

Shark! 1968
Drama
65686 92 mins C B, V P
Burt Reynolds, Barry Sullivan, Arthur Kennedy
An American gun smuggler stranded in a tiny seaport in the Middle East joins the crew of a marine biologist's boat, and soon discovers the boat's owner and his wife are trying to retrieve gold bullion that lies deep in shark-infested waters.
Excelsior — *Republic Pictures Home Video*

Shark Hunter 198?
Drama/Adventure
70596 95 mins C B, V P
Franco Nero, Jorge Luke, Mike Forrest
A shark hunter gets ensnared in the mobs nets of the Mexican coast as they race for a cache of sunken millions.
Unknown — *Prism*

Sharks' Treasure 1975
Adventure
81056 96 mins C B, V P
Cornel Wilde, Yaphet Kotto, John Neilson, David Canary, directed by Cornel Wilde
A band of escaped convicts commandeer a boat filled with gold.
MPAA:PG
United Artists; Cornel Wilde — *MGM/UA Home Video*

Sharky's Machine 1981
Adventure
59856 119 mins C B, V R, P
Burt Reynolds, Rachel Ward, Vittorio Gassman, Brian Keith, Charles Durning, Earl Holliman, directed by Burt Reynolds
A lively detective tale about an undercover cop hot on the trail of a crooked czar.
MPAA:R
Orion; Warner Bros — *Warner Home Video; RCA VideoDiscs*

Shattered 1972
Drama
65372 100 mins C B, V P
Peter Finch, Shelley Winters, Colin Blakely
Finch plays Harry, a man not only blamed for a failed marriage, but also held hostage in his home by his own paranoia and driven bouts of drinking. Slowly Harry's tenuous grip on sanity slips and at any moment his fragile and crumbling life may be shattered.
MPAA:R
Michael Klinger — *Media Home Entertainment*

Shazam 1981
Cartoons/Adventure
66007 60 mins C B, V P
Animated
Young Billy Batson says "shazam" and turns into the mighty Captain Marvel.
Filmation — *Family Home Entertainment*

Shazam!, Volume 2 1981
Cartoons/Adventure
69808 60 mins C B, V P
Animated
Three more adventures feature young Billy Batson, who transforms himself into the mighty Captain Marvel to fight dastardly villains.

Filmation — *Family Home Entertainment*

Shazam Volume III **1981**
Cartoons
79205 60 mins C B, V P
Animated
Captain Marvel and his family of super heroes fight off the bad guys in this collection of three animated adventures.
DC Comics; Filmation Associates — *Family Home Entertainment*

Shazzan **1983**
Cartoons
66577 60 mins C B, V P
Animated
Arabian nights adventures with Shazzan the genie are featured on this tape.
Hanna Barbera — *Worldvision Home Video*

Shazzan **198?**
Cartoons
78072 58 mins C B, V P
Animated
This program presents the adventures of the wonderful genie Shazzan and his masters.
Worldvision Home Video Inc — *Worldvision Home Video*

She **1925**
Adventure
47462 77 mins B/W B, V, FO P
Betty Blythe, Carlyle Blackwell, Mary Odette
H. Rider Haggard's famous story about the ageless Queen Ayesha, who renews her life force periodically by walking through a pillar of cold flame. Silent film with music score.
Reciprocity Films — *Video Yesteryear; Discount Video Tapes; Classic Video Cinema Collector's Club*

She Couldn't Say No **1952**
Comedy
10029 88 mins B/W B, V P, T
Robert Mitchum, Jean Simmons, Arthur Hunnicutt, Edgar Buchanan, Wallace Ford, directed by Lloyd Bacon
A wealthy heiress with good intentions plans to give her money away to those friends who had helped her when she was struggling. Things don't go quite as planned, however.
RKO — *Blackhawk Films*

She Waits **1971**
Drama/Suspense
80317 74 mins C B, V P
Dorothy McGuire, Patty Duke, David McCallum, directed by Delbert Mann
When a newly wed couple moves into an old house, the bride becomes possessed by the spirit of her husband's first wife.
Delbert Mann — *Prism*

She Wore a Yellow Ribbon **1949**
Western
00275 103 mins C B, V, 3/4U P
John Wayne, Joanne Dru, directed by John Ford
An undermanned cavalry outpost makes a desperate attempt to repel invading Indians. Academy Award '49: Best Cinematography, Color.
RKO; Argosy Pictures Corp — *Nostalgia Merchant; VidAmerica; King of Video*

Sheena **1984**
Adventure
Closed Captioned
77239 117 mins C B, V P
Tanya Roberts, Ted Wass, Donvan Scott, directed by John Guillermin
A television sportscaster aids a jungle queen in defending her kingdom from being overthrown by an evil prince. Available in VHS Hi-Fi Dolby Stereo and Beta Hi-Fi Stereo.
MPAA:PG
Columbia — *RCA/Columbia Pictures Home Video*

Sheena Easton **1983**
Music-Performance
75907 15 mins C B, V P
This program presents Sheena Easton performing her hit songs "Morning Train," "Machinery" and "Telefone."
EMI America Records — *Sony Corporation of America*

Sheena Easton: Act One **1983**
Music-Performance/Variety
73563 60 mins C B, V P
Sheena sings her hits "For Your Eyes Only," "Out Here on My Own" and "Wind Beneath My Wings" and Al Jarreau sings "Roof Garden" in this program that was originally broadcast on NBC.
Smith Hemion Productions — *Prism*

Sheena Easton—Live at the Palace, Hollywood **1982**
Music-Performance
66184 60 mins C B, V R, P
The Grammy Award winner sings "Modern Girl," "Morning Train," "For Your Eyes Only" and others.
Unknown — *THORN EMI/HBO Video; RCA VideoDiscs*

Sheer Madness **1984**
Drama
80855 105 mins C B, V P
Hanna Schgulla, Angela Winkler, directed by Margarethe Von Trotta
This film explores the intense friendship between a college professor and a troubled artist. With English subtitles.

GE
TeleCulture, Inc. — *MGM/UA Home Video*

Shell Shock **198?**
War-Drama
80131 90 mins C B, V P
Four GI's fight off the Germans and the longings for home during World War II.
Independent — *King of Video*

Shenandoah **1965**
Drama
53396 105 mins C B, V P
James Stewart, Doug McClure, Glenn Corbett, Patrick Wayne, Rosemary Forsythe, Katherine Ross
During the Civil War, a farmer tries to remain neutral but becomes involved when his only daughter becomes engaged to a Confederate soldier.
Universal — *MCA Home Video*

Sherlock Holmes and the Baskerville Curse **1984**
Mystery
65851 70 mins C B, V P
Animated, voice of Peter O'Toole
This production is an animated feature film with Peter O'Toole starring as the voice of Sherlock Holmes.
Pacific Arts Video Records — *Pacific Arts Video*

Sherlock Holmes and the Secret Weapon **1942**
Mystery
58893 68 mins B/W B, V, FO P
Basil Rathbone, Nigel Bruce, Lionel Atwill
Based on "The Dancing Men" by Sir Arthur Conan Doyle, Holmes battles Dr. Moriarty in order to save the British war effort.
Universal — *Prism; Kartes Productions; Video Yesteryear; Movie Buff Video; Admit One Video; Cable Films; Video Connection; Western Film & Video Inc; Budget Video; Discount Video Tapes*

Sherlock Holmes and the Sign of Four **1984**
Mystery
80444 48 mins C B, V P
Animated, voice of Peter O'Toole
Sherlock Holmes must find the man who murdered Bartholomew Sholto with a poison dart in the neck.
Eddy Graham — *Pacific Arts Video*

Sherlock Holmes and the Silver Blaze **1941**
Mystery
14295 67 mins B/W B, V P
Arthur Wontner, Ian Fleming, Lyn Harding
Sherlock Holmes mystery based on the Arthur Conan Doyle classic "The Silver Blaze."
Astor; British — *Mossman Williams Productions; Video Yesteryear*

Sherlock Holmes and the Woman in Green **1945**
Mystery
42927 67 mins B/W B, V P
Basil Rathbone, Nigel Bruce
Based on a character developed by Sir Arthur Conan Doyle, this mystery finds Holmes and Watson matching wits against the infamous Professor Moriarity.
Universal, Howard Benedict — *Movie Buff Video; Cable Films; Video Connection; Budget Video; Discount Video Tapes; Western Film & Video Inc; Classic Video Cinema Collector's Club*

Sherlock Holmes Double Feature **194?**
Mystery
55591 147 mins B/W B, V P
Basil Rathbone, Nigel Bruce
Two classic Sherlock Holmes features on one cassette: "The Adventures of Sherlock Holmes" (1939) and "Sherlock Holmes and the Voice of Terror" (1942).
Twentieth Century Fox; Universal — *CBS/Fox Video*

Sherlock Holmes Double Feature I **194?**
Mystery
64582 120 mins B/W B, V, 3/4U P
Basil Rathbone, Nigel Bruce
Paired in this double feature are "Sherlock Holmes and the Secret Weapon" and "The Woman in Green."
Universal — *Nostalgia Merchant*

Sherlock Holmes Double Feature II **1946**
Mystery
64583 120 mins B/W B, V, 3/4U P
Basil Rathbone, Nigel Bruce
This double feature contains "Dressed to Kill" and "Terror by Night."
Universal — *Nostalgia Merchant*

Sherlock Holmes I **1954**
Mystery
38997 54 mins B/W B, V, FO P
Ronald Howard, H. Marion Crawford 2 pgms
Two episodes from the English syndicated series bases on the exploits of master detective Sherlock Holmes: "The Case of the Impromptu Performance," and "The Case of the Exhumed Client."
British — *Video Yesteryear*

Sherlock Holmes II 1954
Mystery
38998 54 mins B/W B, V, FO P
Ronald Howard, H. Marion Crawford 2 pgms
Two more episodes from the syndicated British TV series of the 1950's: "The Case of the Baker Street Nursemaids" and "The Case of the Pennsylvania Gun."
British — *Video Yesteryear*

Sherlock's Rivals and Where's My Wife 1927
Adventure/Comedy
78082 53 mins B/W B, V, FO P
Milburn Morante, Monty Banks
This double feature includes a detective movie in which two used car dealers become amateur sleuths and a comedy in which a man has a hard time enjoying his weekend at a seashore resort.
BIP — *Video Yesteryear*

She's Dressed to Kill 1979
Suspense
66622 98 mins C B, V P
Eleanor Parker, Jessica Walter, John Rubenstein
A mysterious killer murders a group of fashion models one by one, in the incongruous setting of a secluded mountaintop resort.
Grant Case McGrath Enterprises; Barry Weitz Productions — *U.S.A. Home Video*

Shinbone Alley 1970
Musical/Cartoons
50960 83 mins C B, V R, P
Animated, voices of Carol Channing, Eddie Bracken, John Carradine, Alan Reed
An animated musical about Archy, a free-verse poet reincarnated as a cockroach, and Mehitabel, the alley cat with a zest for life. Based on the short stories by Don Marquis.
MPAA:G
Fine Arts Films — *Video Gems*

Shine on Harvest Moon 1938
Western
05534 60 mins B/W B, V, FO P
Roy Rogers, Mary Hart, Stanley Andrews
Roy Rogers brings a band of outlaws to justice and clears an old man suspected of being their accomplice.
Republic — *Video Yesteryear*

Shining, The 1980
Horror
58249 143 mins C B, V R, P
Jack Nicholson, Shelley Duvall, Scatman Crothers, Danny Lloyd, directed by Stanley Kubrick
Terror and violence overwhelms a family isolated and snowbound in a huge resort hotel with a history of violence. Based on the novel by Stephen King.
MPAA:R
Warner Bros — *Warner Home Video; RCA VideoDiscs*

Shmenges: The Last Polka, The 1984
Comedy/Satire
80693 54 mins C B, V P
John Candy, Eugene Levy, Rick Moranis, Robin Duke, Catherine O'Hara
Imitating the style of Martin Scorcese's '78 tribute to "The Band," this documentary looks at the life and career of the fictional polka kings, the Shmenges. Based upon the characters from the SCTV Network series.
Shmenges Productions — *Vestron Video*

Shock 1946
Mystery/Horror
53442 70 mins B/W B, V, FO P
Vincent Price, Lynn Bari, Frank Latimore, Anabel Shaw
A doctor is called upon to treat a woman and discovers that she saw him kill his wife.
AM Available
Twentieth Century Fox — *Video Yesteryear; Kartes Productions*

Shock Waves 1977
Horror
80294 84 mins C B, V P
Peter Cushing, Brooke Adams, John Carradine, Luke Halprin
A group of mutant zombie Nazi soldiers terrorize stranded tourists staying at a deserted motel on a small island.
Joseph Brenner Associates — *Prism*

Shogun 1980
Drama
54670 120 mins C B, V, LV R, P
Richard Chamberlain, Toshiro Mifune
A made for television feature that depicts the people, life-style, and traditions of Japan. A special 2-hour length version, based on the novel by James Clavell.
NBC — *Paramount Home Video; RCA VideoDiscs*

Shogun 1980
Drama
81098 550 mins C B, V R, P
Richard Chamberlain, Toshiro Mifune, Yoko Shimada, John Rhys-Davies, narrated by Orson Welles, directed by Jerry London
This is the complete version of the mini-series that chronicles the saga of how an English navigator became the first Shogun from the Western world. Adapted from the James Clavell novel.

Emmy Awards '80: Outstanding Dramatic Series.
Paramount; NBC Entertainment — *Paramount Home Video*

Shogun Assassin 1980
Adventure
55553 89 mins C B, V, LV P
Tomisaburo Wakayama
The story of a proud samurai named Lone Wolf who served his Shogun master well as the Official Decapitator, until the fateful day when the aging Shogun turned against him.
MPAA:R
Toho Company; Katsu Prod — *MCA Home Video*

Shogun's Ninja 1983
Martial arts/Suspense
64233 115 mins C B, V P
Henry Sanada, Sue Shiomi, Sonny Chiba
In 16th century Japan, an age-old rivalry between two ninja clans sparks a search for a dagger which will lead to one clan's hidden gold.
Toei Studios; Shigeru Okada — *Media Home Entertainment*

Shout for the Stars 1984
Football
79632 40 mins C B, V, FO P
A history of the Dallas Cowboys from their expansion team roots to their awesome teams of the 70's and 80's.
NFL Films — *NFL Films Video*

Shoot It Black, Shoot It Blue 1974
Crime-Drama
64212 93 mins C B, V R, P
Michael Moriarty
A rogue cop shoots a black purse snatcher and thinks he has gotten away with it. Unknown to him, however, a witness has filmed the incident and turns the evidence over to a lawyer.
Shoot It Company — *THORN EMI/HBO Video*

Shoot the Living, Pray for the Dead 1973
Western
80713 90 mins C B, V P
Klaus Kinski
While travelling through Mexico, the leader of a band of killers promises his guide half of a share in stolen gold if he can lead them to it.
Castor Film Productions — *All Seasons Entertainment*

Shoot the Moon 1982
Drama
47775 124 mins C B, V, CED P
Diane Keaton, Albert Finney, Karen Allen, Peter Weller, Dana Hill, Viveka Davis, Tracey Gold, Tina Yothers, directed by Alan Parker
An affluent California family experiences jealousy, anger and love following the breakup of the marriage.
MPAA:R
MGM — *MGM/UA Home Video*

Shoot the Sun Down 1974
Adventure
59812 102 mins C B, V P
Christopher Walken, Margot Kidder, Geoffrey Lewis
Four offbeat characters united in their lust for gold soon turn against each other.
MPAA:PG
David Leeds — *United Home Video*

Shooting, The 1966
Western
13629 82 mins C B, V P
Warren Oates, Millie Perkins, Jack Nicholson
A mysterious woman, bent on revenge, persuades a former bounty hunter and his partner to escort her across the desert, with tragic results.
Monte Hellman; Jack Nicholson — *Media Home Entertainment; Discount Video Tapes; King of Video; Sheik Video; Budget Video; Western Film & Video Inc*

Shooting Stars 1985
Crime-Drama
70736 96 mins C B, V P
Billy Dee Williams, Parker Stevenson, Efrem Zimbalist Jr., Edie Adams, directed by Richard Lang
Hawke and O'Keefe, two unemployed TV actors, take to the streets as crime fighting private investigators mirroring their on-screen personae.
Aaron Spelling and Douglas S. Kramer — *Active Home Video*

Shootist, The 1976
Western
38620 100 mins C B, V, LV R, P
John Wayne, Lauren Bacall, James Stewart, Ron Howard, directed by Don Siegel
John Wayne's last film appearance as an aging gunslinger afflicted with cancer, who seeks peace and solace in his final days, but finds himself involved in one final gun battle.
MPAA:PG
Paramount — *Paramount Home Video; RCA VideoDiscs*

Shop on Main Street, The 1965
Drama
78882 128 mins B/W B, V P
Ida Kaminska, Josef Kroner, Hana Slivkoua, directed by Jan Kadar and Elmar Klos

During the Second World War, a Nazi appointed "Aryan controller" befriends a Jewish widow who owns a button shop. This film is subtitled in English and available in Beta Hi-Fi.
Academy Awards '65: Best Foreign Language Film. CZ
Barrandov Film Studios — *RCA/Columbia Pictures Home Video*

Short Eyes **1979**
Drama
77220 100 mins C B, V P
Bruce Davidson, Miguel Pinero, Jose Perez, Shawn Elliott
When a child molester enters prison, the inmates act out their own form of revenge against him.
MPAA:R
Short Eyes Entertainment — *Lightning Video*

Short Films of D. W. Griffith, Vol. I, The **1912**
Film-History
47461 45 mins B/W B, V, FO P
Blanche Sweet, Mary Pickford, Charles West
Three early shorts made by the great director are on this tape: "The Battle," "The Female of the Species" and "The New York Hat." Silent with music score.
Biograph — *Video Yesteryear*

Shot in the Dark, A **1964**
Comedy
47151 101 mins C B, V, CED P
Peter Sellers, Elke Sommer, Herbert Lom, George Sanders, directed by Blake Edwards
The Second in the "Inspector Clouseau-Pink Panther" series of films. The bumbling Inspector Clouseau investigates the case of a parlormaid who is accused of murdering her lover.
EL, SP
United Artists; Walter Mirisch — *CBS/Fox Video; RCA VideoDiscs*

Shout, The **1978**
Horror
36189 87 mins C B, V P
Alan Bates, Susannah York, John Hurt, Tim Curry
A married couple becomes dominated by a malevolent seducer with aboriginal powers.
Cannes Film Festival '78: Jury Prize. MPAA:R
CPH; BLD — *RCA/Columbia Pictures Home Video*

Shout at the Devil **1976**
War-Drama
65378 128 mins C B, V P
Lee Marvin, Roger Moore, Barbara Parkins
A story based on an actual World War I incident involving the destruction of a German battleship on a river in Africa in 1913. Based on the novel by Wilbur Smith.
MPAA:PG
American International — *Vestron Video*

Show Boat **1951**
Musical-Drama
47054 115 mins C B, V P
Kathryn Grayson, Howard Keel, Ava Gardner, William Warfield, Joe E. Brown, Agnes Moorehead
The third movie version of Jerome Kern and Oscar Hammerstein II's 1927 musical play about the life and loves of a Mississippi riverboat theater troupe. The famous score includes "Old Man River," "Make Believe," "Can't Help Lovin' Dat Man," "Why Do I Love You," and "Bill."
MGM — *MGM/UA Home Video*

Show Business **1944**
Musical
44989 92 mins B/W B, V P, T
Eddie Cantor, Joan Davis
Romantic story of two show business teams: the boys are in burlesque and the girls are in vaudeville.
RKO — *Blackhawk Films*

Show Jumping World Cup **1981**
Sports-Minor
59567 75 mins C B, V P
The 1981 horse show-jumping competition for the Federation of Equestrians International World Cup.
Grand Prix Show Jumping — *Mastervision*

Showbiz Ballyhoo **1984**
Outtakes and bloopers
78359 90 mins C B, V P
How Hollywood filmmakers sparked audience excitement through publicity and promotion in the golden age of movies are shown in this program.
USA — *U.S.A. Home Video*

Showbiz Goes to War **1982**
Documentary/World War II
66623 90 mins C B, V P
Narrated by David Steinberg
The activities of Hollywood's biggest stars during World War II are the subject of this feature. Pin-up girls, USO shows, propaganda films, patriotic musicals and war bond drives are a few of the subjects seen along the way.
TAD Productions — *U.S.A. Home Video*

Showdown: Sugar Ray Leonard vs. Thomas Hearns, The **1981**
Boxing
59018 62 mins C CED P

The classic match between Sugar Ray Leonard and Tommy Hearns.
Main Event Prods — *RCA VideoDiscs*

Showtime at the Apollo 1955
Music-Performance
11277 75 mins B/W B, V, FO P
Lionel Hampton, Cab Calloway, Sarah Vaughn, The Four Tops, Herb Jeffries, Lulu Brown, Bill Bailey, Amos Vogel
Blues, jazz, and rock n' roll from the nostalgic 1950's; features some of the great black performers of the era.
Unknown — *Video Yesteryear*

Showtime at the Apollo 1955
Music-Performance
11276 75 mins B/W B, V, FO P
Duke Ellington, Dinah Washington, Nipsey Russell, Count Basie, Big Joe Turner, Nat 'King' Cole, Lionel Hampton
The Harlem Variety Revue features blues, jazz, and rock n' roll performances from great black artists of the 1950's.
Unknown — *Video Yesteryear*

Showtime at the Apollo 1954
Variety/Music-Performance
47643 79 mins B/W B, V, FO P
Hosted by Willie Bryant, Nipsy Russell, Mantan Moreland, Duke Ellington, Sarah Vaughn, Lionel Hampton, Nat King Cole Trio, Delta Rhythm Boys, Herb Jeffries, The Larks, Martha Davis and Spouse
Three syndicated rhythm and swing shows from the Apollo in New York City's Harlem: "Harlem Merry Go Round," "All-Star Revue," and "Showtime in Harlem."
Unknown — *Video Yesteryear*

Sicilian Connection, The 1974
Drama
80124 100 mins C B, V P
Ben Gazzara, Silvia Monti, Fausto Tozzi
A narcotics agent poses as a nightclub manager to bust open a drug smuggling organization.
Joseph Green Pictures — *King of Video*

Sid Caesar's Shape Up 1985
Physical fitness
80272 58 mins C B, V P
Sid Caesar demonstrates his own physical fitness program that saved his life.
Jim Gates — *Media Home Entertainment*

Sidney Sheldon's Bloodline 1979
Suspense
38929 116 mins C B, V R, P
Audrey Hepburn, Ben Gazzara, James Mason, directed by Terence Young
The popular best-selling novel transferred to film, starring Audrey Hepburn as a wealthy businesswoman who finds she is marked for death by persons unknown.
MPAA:R
Paramount — *Paramount Home Video*

Siegfried 1924
Drama
63993 100 mins B/W B, V P, T
Paul Richter, Margareta Schoen, directed by Fritz Lang
A massive extravaganza film, based on the legends of the Nibelungen. These same tales were also the basis of Richard Wagner's "Ring" cycle of operas. Silent with organ score.
UFA — *Blackhawk Films; Classic Video Cinema Collector's Club*

Sigmund and the Sea Monsters, Volume 2 1973
Adventure
81454 46 mins C B, V P
Johnny Whitaker, Billy Barty
Sigmund, the lovable sea monster, is in trouble again in this collection of two episodes from the series.
Sid and Marty Krofft — *Embassy Home Entertainment*

Sigmund and the Sea Monsters, Volume I 1973
Comedy
76790 46 mins C B, V P
Billy Barty, Johnny Whittaker, Mary Wickes, Rip Torn, Margaret Hamilton, Fran Ryan
Two young boys befriend a sea monster who's been disowned by his family for his inability to scare humans.
Sid and Marty Krofft — *Embassy Home Entertainment*

Sign of Zorro, The 1957
Adventure
59064 89 mins C B, V R, P
Guy Williams, Henry Calvin, Gene Sheldon, Romney Brent, Britt Lomond
The adventures of the masked swordsman as he champions the cause of the oppressed in early California. A full-length version of the popular late-50's Disney TV series.
Walt Disney Productions — *Walt Disney Home Video*

Silence of the North 1981
Drama
47424 94 mins C B, V P
Ellen Burstyn, Tom Skerrit
A true story about a widow with three children struggling to survive under rugged pioneer conditions on the Canadian frontier.
MPAA:PG

Universal — *MCA Home Video*

Silent Enemy, The 1930
Indians-North American/Documentary
12853 110 mins B/W B, V, FO P
An interesting documentary which tells the Ojibway Indian's way of life before the arrival of the white man. The title is a reference to hunger.
Unknown — *Video Yesteryear; Blackhawk Films; Classic Video Cinema Collector's Club*

Silent Laugh Makers No. 1 192?
Comedy
11283 50 mins B/W B, V, FO P
Charlie Chase, Stan Laurel, Oliver Hardy, Charlie Chaplin, Ben Turpin, Arthur Lake
A collection of four hilarious short movies from the silent picture era: "One Mama Man," "Lucky Dog," "His Night Out," and "Hop-a-Long."
Hal Roach — *Video Yesteryear*

Silent Laugh Makers No. 2 192?
Comedy
11284 50 mins B/W B, V, FO P
Charlie Chase, Oliver Hardy, Billy Bevan
Four short funny films of the silent era: "Fluttering Hearts," "Long Live the King," and "A Sea Dog Tale."
Hal Roach — *Video Yesteryear*

Silent Laugh Makers #3 192?
Comedy
66141 55 mins B/W B, V, FO P
Harry Langdon, Harold Lloyd, Bebe Daniels, Snub Pollard
Four comedy shorts: "Picking Peaches" (1924), directed by Frank Capra, Langdon's first for Mack Sennett; "All Tied Up" (1925), featuring "A Ton of Fun"—four rotund comedians; "Don't Shove" (1919), featuring Harold Lloyd wooing Bebe Daniels; "Some Baby" (1922), with Snub Pollard, written by Hal Roach.
Hal Roach et al — *Video Yesteryear*

Silent Madness 1984
Horror
81095 93 mins C B, V P
Belinda Montgomery, Viveca Lindfors, Sydney Lassick
A psychiatrist must stop a deranged killer from slaughtering helpless college coeds in a sorority house.
Gregory Earls — *Media Home Entertainment*

Silent Movie 1976
Comedy
81170 88 mins C B, V P
Mel Brooks, Marty Feldman, Dom DeLuise, Burt Reynolds, Anne Bancroft, James Caan, Liza Minnelli, Paul Newman, Sid Caesar, directed by Mel Brooks
A has been movie director is determined to make a comeback and save his studio from being taken over by a conglomerate. Hi-Fi Stereo in both formats.
MPAA:PG
20th Century Fox — *CBS/Fox Video*

Silent Movies—In Color 19??
Film-History
56915 52 mins C B, V, FO P
Five films produced in France between 1904 and 1914 in which color tints were added one frame at a time by hand. Films include: "The Nobleman's Dog," "Bob's Electric Theatre," "A Slave's Love," "A New Way of Traveling," and "The Life of Our Savior."
French — *Video Yesteryear*

Silent Partner, The 1978
Drama
45068 103 mins C B, V, LV, CED P
Elliot Gould, Christopher Plummer, Susannah York
A bank teller foils a robbery, but keeps some of the money for himself. Trouble ensues because the robber knows it and wants the money.
EMC Film Corp — *Vestron Video; Time Life Video*

Silent Rage 1982
Adventure/Martial arts
62811 100 mins C B, V P
Chuck Norris, Ron Silver, Steven Keats, Toni Kalem, Brian Libby
The sheriff of a small Texas town must destroy a murderous killer who has been made indestructible through genetic engineering.
MPAA:R
Columbia — *RCA/Columbia Pictures Home Video; RCA VideoDiscs*

Silent Rebellion 1982
Drama
81414 90 mins C B, V P
Telly Savalas, Keith Gordon, Michael Constantine, Yula Gavala
A Greek immigrant with his son return to his native land to be reunited with his mother and brother. The pair not only discover their heritage but also come to better understand each other as well.
David Horwatt — *VCL Home Video*

Silent Running 1971
Science fiction
53393 90 mins C B, V P
Bruce Dern, Cliff Potts, Ron Rifkin
Members of a space station crew in 2001 are space gardening to replenish a nuclear-devastated earth.

MPAA:G
Universal; Michel Gruskoff; Doug Trumbull — *MCA Home Video*

Silent Scream 1980
Horror
59669 87 mins C B, V P
Rebecca Balding, Cameron Mitchell, Avery Schreiber, Barbara Steele, Steve Doubet, Brad Reardon, Yvonne De Carlo
A gloomy old victorian mansion by the sea has a silent terror lurking within the walls.
MPAA:R
Jim Wheat; Ken Wheat — *Media Home Entertainment*

Silent Scream, The 1984
Horror
80479 60 mins C B, V P
Peter Cushing, Brian Cox, Elaine Donnelly
A former Nazi concentration camp commandant collects unusual animals and humans as a hobby. In Beta Hi-Fi and VHS stereo.
Hammer Films — *Thriller Video*

Silk Stockings 1957
Musical/Comedy
52747 117 mins C B, V P
Fred Astaire, Cyd Charisse, Janis Paige, Peter Lorre, George Tobias, directed by Rouben Mamoulian
A musical comedy adaptation of "Ninotchka," with Astaire as a charming American movie man, and Charisse as a Soviet official. Music and lyrics by Cole Porter highlight this film adapted from George S. Kaufman's hit Broadway play.
MGM; Arthur Freed — *MGM/UA Home Video*

Silkwood 1983
Drama
65720 131 mins C B, V, LV, CED P
Meryl Streep, Kurt Russell, Cher
A dramatization of the life of Karen Silkwood, the nuclear plant worker ad activist, who died in the 1974 under suspicious circumstances while investigating shoddy practices at ther plant.
MPAA:R
Mike Nichols; Michael Hausman — *Embassy Home Entertainment*

Silver Dream Racer 1983
Drama
79316 103 mins C B, V P
Beau Bridges, David Essex, Cristina Raines, Diane Keen
An up and coming English motorcycle racer wants to win the World Motorcycle Championship title away from an American biker.
MPAA:PG
Almi Films — *Vestron Video*

Silver Streak 1976
Comedy
41078 113 mins C B, V, CED P
Gene Wilder, Jill Clayburgh, Patrick McGoohan
Gene Wilder becomes involved with murder, intrigue, and a beautiful woman aboard a transcontinental express train.
MPAA:PG EL, SP
20th Century Fox — *CBS/Fox Video*

Silver Streak 1934
Drama
54115 72 mins B/W B, V P, T
Sally Blane, Charles Starett, Arthur Lake, Edgar Kennedy
The sickly son of a diesel train designer needs a iron lung pronto. A rival's super fast neato keen locomotive is the only hope for the boy. Murders, busted brides, runaway engines, and a crew that would rather walk enliven this race against time.
RKO — *Blackhawk Films*

Simon 1980
Comedy
52715 97 mins C B, V R, P
Alan Arkin, Madeline Kahn, directed by Marshall Brickman
A group of demented scientists brainwash a college professor into believing that his real mother is a Martian spaceship.
MPAA:PG
Orion Pictures — *Warner Home Video*

Simon & Garfunkel: The Concert in Central Park 1982
Music-Performance
47402 87 mins C B, V, LV, CED P
Paul Simon, Art Garfunkel
The September 1981 reunion concert by Simon and Garfunkel before 500,000 delirious fans in New York's Central Park is captured on this tape. Among the 20 selections performed are "April Come She Will," "Mrs. Robinson," "Scarborough Fair" and "The Sounds of Silence."
James Signorelli — *CBS/Fox Video*

Simple Story, A 1980
Drama
59383 110 mins C B, V P
Romy Schneider, Bruno Cremer, Claude Brasseur, directed by Claude Sautet
A woman faces her fortieth birthday with increasing uneasiness, though her life seems perfect from the outside.
Columbia — *RCA/Columbia Pictures Home Video*

Sin of Adam and Eve, The 1972
Drama
69804 72 mins C B, V P
Candy Wilson, George Rivers
This is the story of Adam and Eve in the Garden of Eden and their fall from grace.
MPAA:R
Michael Zachary — *United Home Video*

Sin of Harold Diddlebock, The 1947
Comedy
11312 95 mins B/W B, V, FO P
Harold Lloyd, Raymond Walburn, Edgar Kennedy, Franklin Pangborn
Harold Lloyd's last film which folows the life of the hero of Lloyd's classic silent picture, "The Freshman," in later years.
Preston Sturges — *Prism; Video Yesteryear; Budget Video; Discount Video Tapes; Glenn Video Vistas; Sheik Video; Cable Films; King of Video; Video Connection; Western Film & Video Inc; Classic Video Cinema Collector's Club; Hal Roach Studios; Kartes Productions; See Hear Industries*

Sinbad and the Eye of the Tiger 1977
Fantasy
21296 113 mins C B, V, LV P
Patrick Wayne, Jane Seymour, Taryn Power
The swashbuckling adventures of Sinbad the Sailor.
Columbia — *RCA/Columbia Pictures Home Video; RCA VideoDiscs*

Sinbad the Sailor 1947
Drama
00310 117 mins C B, V, 3/4U P
Douglas Fairbanks Jr., Maureen O'Hara, Anthony Quinn
Swashbuckler seeks a treasure island in this Arabian Nights film.
RKO; Stephen Ames — *Nostalgia Merchant; VidAmerica; King of Video*

Sing Along with Little Lulu 1983
Cartoons
66472 86 mins C B, V P
Animated
Little Lulu is herewith featured in a special collection of her popular cartoons.
Famous Studios — *Republic Pictures Home Video*

Sing Along with Mitch 1961
Music/Variety
52462 52 mins B/W B, V, FO P
Mitch Miller and the Sing Along Gang, Leslie Uggams, Diana Trask
This episode of the popular 60's series features Leslie Uggams in her first TV appearance. Mitch and the Sing Along Gang perform "Heart of My Heart," "Sweet Rosie O'Grady," "The Sidewalks of New York," and other songs.
NBC — *Video Yesteryear*

Sing Blue Silver 1984
Music video
80353 85 mins C B, V P
Simon Le Bon, Nick Rhodes, Andy Taylor, John Taylor
A behind the scenes look at Duran Duran's 1984 concert tour, where the band performs "Girls on Film" and "The Reflex."
EMI Music Video — *THORN EMI/HBO Video*

Sing Your Worries Away 1942
Musical/Comedy
45102 71 mins B/W B, V P, T
Buddy Ebsen, Bert Lahr, June Havoc
Two struggling songwriters and their girlfriends get entangled in a gaint swindle.
RKO — *Blackhawk Films*

Singer Presents Elvis (The 1968 Comeback Special) Outtakes 1968
Music-Performance/Outtakes and bloopers
47488 54 mins C B, V, FO P
Elvis Presley
Scenes and songs from Elvis' famous 1968 Singer special that were cut for being too sexy, too long, or because mistakes were made.
NBC — *Video Yesteryear*

Singer Presents "Elvis" (The 1968 Comeback Special) 1968
Music-Performance
47501 52 mins C B, V, FO P
Elvis Presley
The famous TV spectacular that brought Elvis back to performing in public. Songs featured include "Heartbreak Hotel," "Hound Dog" and "All Shook Up." Originally telecast on December 3, 1968.
NBC — *Video Yesteryear*

Singin' in the Rain 1952
Musical
39087 103 mins C B, V, CED P
Gene Kelly, Donald O'Connor, Jean Hagen, Debbie Reynolds, Rita Moreno, Cyd Charisse, directed by Gene Kelly and Stanley Donen
One of the all-time great movie musicals—an affectionate spoof of the turmoil that afflicted the motion picture industry in the late 1920's during the changeover from silent films to sound. Songs include the title tune, "Make 'Em Laugh," "All I Do Is Dream of You," and "You Are My Lucky Star." Music and lyrics by Arthur Freed and Nacio Herb Brown.
MGM — *MGM/UA Home Video*

Singing Buckaroo, The 1937
Western
78094 58 mins B/W B, V, FO P
Fred Scott, Victoria Vinton, Cliff Nazarro
Some bandits try to steal money from a pretty blonde and have to battle with a cowboy hero who rides to the damsel's rescue.
Republic — *Video Yesteryear*

Sinister Urge, The 1960
Drama
73553 82 mins B/W B, V P
Directed by Ed Wood
An early Ed Wood film about two policemen who are searching for the murderer of three call girls.
Edward Wood — *Admit One Video*

Sioux City Sue 1946
Western/Musical
44805 69 mins B/W B, V P, T
Gene Autry, Lynne Roberts, Sterling Holloway
Talent scouts are looking for a singing cowboy, find Gene, then trick him into being the voice of a talking donkey.
Republic — *Blackhawk Films; Video Connection*

Sir Arthur Conan Doyle 1927
Literature-English/Biographical
59411 11 mins B/W B, V P, T
An intimate portrait of the man who created Sherlock Holmes.
Unknown — *Blackhawk Films*

Sister Kenny 1946
Drama
10061 116 mins B/W B, V P, T
Rosalind Russell, Dean Jagger, Alexander Knox
Follows story of legendary nurse crusading for her treatment of infantile paralysis. Based on Elizabeth Kenny's novel, "And They Shall Walk."
RKO; Dudley Nichols — *Blackhawk Films*

Sisters 1973
Horror
53521 93 mins C B, V R, P
Margot Kidder, Charles Durning, directed by Brian DePalma
Siamese twins separated at birth are involved in a murder and the wrong one is arrested.
MPAA:R
American International; Edward R Pressman — *Warner Home Video*

Sisters of Death 1978
Suspense
48415 87 mins C B, V P
Arthur Franz, Claudia Jennings
Five women who once were members of a secret club are invited to a reunion at a remote castle in California. There they are trapped by an evil man on the edge of madness.
MPAA:PG
John B Kelly Presentations — *United Home Video*

Sitting Ducks 1980
Comedy
66066 88 mins C B, V P
Michael Emil, Zack Norman, directed by Henry Jaglom
Two friends involved in a scam attempt to outrun the moball the while swapping songs and confessions.
MPAA:R
Meira Attia Dor — *Media Home Entertainment*

---

600 Days to Cocos Island 1975
Adventure
66240 93 mins C B, V R, P
A story about a young couple who sell everything and sail away to adventure.
Gene Evans — *Video City Productions*

Six Pack 1982
Adventure
63396 108 mins C B, V, CED P
Kenny Rogers, Diane Lane, Erin Gray, Barry Corbin
Rogers stars as Brewster Baker, who returns to the stock car racing circuit with the help of six larcenous orphans adept at mechanics.
MPAA:PG
Kenny Loggins Productions — *CBS/Fox Video*

Six Shootin' Sheriff 1938
Western
11374 59 mins B/W B, V P
Ken Maynard
A member of a wild gang redeems himself and turns sheriff to make up for all his evil ways.
Worldwide — *United Home Video; Video Yesteryear; Video Connection; Sheik Video*

Six Weeks 1982
Comedy-Drama
68268 107 mins C B, V P
Dudley Moore, Mary Tyler Moore, Katherine Healy
Two opposite people are brought together by the illness of a little girl.
MPAA:PG
Peter Guber; Jon Peters — *RCA/Columbia Pictures Home Video; RCA VideoDiscs*

Sixteen Candles 1984
Comedy
73183 93 mins C B, V, CED P
Molly Ringwald, Paul Dooley, Anthony Michael Hall, directed by John Hughes
Molly Ringwald stars as a young girl who has just turned sweet sixteen and no one

remembers her birthday. Title song performed by The Stray Cats.
MPAA:PG
Hilton A Green; Universal — *MCA Home Video*

$64,000 Question **195?**
Game show
58636 29 mins B/W B, V, FO P
Hosted by Hal March
This episode of the classic show which ushered in the big-money quiz game features a Philippine-American lady lawyer who decides to keep her money, Virgil Earp (Wyatt's nephew) winning $32,000 in the Wild West category, and a Brooklyn woman winning $4,000 in the opera category. Sponsored by Revlon.
CBS — *Video Yesteryear*

Sizzle **1981**
Drama
79194 100 mins C B, V P
Loni Anderson, John Forsythe, Leslie Uggams, Roy Thinnes, Richard Lynch
When a nightclub singer's boyfriend is murdered by the mob, she stops at nothing to get revenge.
Aaron Spelling Productions — *Prism*

Skateboard Madness **198?**
Sports
75584 92 mins C B, V P
This program offers a tour of skating spots and performing skateboarding celebrities.
MPAA:PG
Unknown — *Monterey Home Video*

Ski **1978**
Sports-Winter
44923 30 mins C B, V P
Fitness expert Ann Dugan demonstrates exercises for skiers which show how to exert constant muscular effort to maintain body position, move with agility, and avoid injury. From the "Sports Conditioning" series.
Health N Action — *RCA/Columbia Pictures Home Video*

Ski Time **1984**
Sports-Winter
80425 102 mins C B, V P
A documentary that features exciting skiing competitions from New Zealand and France.
Warren Miller Enterprises — *Karl/Lorimar Home Video*

Skin Game **1971**
Comedy
80957 102 mins C B, V P
James Garner, Lou Gossett, Susan Clark, Ed Asner, Andrew Duggan, directed by Paul Bogart
A fast talking bunco-artist and his black partner travel throughout the pre-Civil War South while setting-up the ultimate con.
MPAA:PG
Warner Bros. — *Warner Home Video*

Skullduggery **1969**
Horror
77520 95 mins C B, V P
Thom Haverstock, Wendy Crewson, David Calderisi
A grop of medieval game players suffer through a night of unspeakable horror when a secret evil force spoils their good clean fun.
MPAA:PG
Peter Wittman; Ota Richter — *Media Home Entertainment*

Skyline **1984**
Comedy
77303 84 mins C B, V P
Antonio Resines, Beatriz Perez-Porro
A Spanish photographer comes to New York City to become a staff photographer on a magazine.
Fernando Colombo — *Pacific Arts Video*

Sky's The Limit, The **1943**
Comedy
43017 89 mins B/W B, V, FO P
Fred Astaire, Joan Leslie
A war hero spends his leave in New York City dressed in civilian clothes and falls in love.
RKO; David Hempstead — *Video Yesteryear; King of Video; Nostalgia Merchant*

Slap, The **1976**
Comedy
65721 103 mins C CED P
Isabelle Adjani, Lino Ventura
This program is meant to express the problems of adults and young people when they arrive at certain equinoxes in their lives.
MPAA:PG
Joseph Green — *Embassy Home Entertainment (disc only)*

Slap Shot **1977**
Comedy-Drama
14005 123 mins C B, V, LV P
Paul Newman, Michael Ontkean, Jennifer Warren, Lindsay Crouse, Strother Martin, directed by George Roy Hill
A satire of the world of professional hockey. An over-the-hill player-coach gathers an odd-ball mixture of has-beens and young players and reluctantly initiates using violence on the ice to make his team win.
MPAA:R
Universal; Robert J Wunsch; Stephen Friedman — *MCA Home Video*

Slapstick **193?**
Comedy
80466 76 mins B/W B, V P

Charlie Chaplin, Harold Lloyd, Charlie Chase, Buster Keaton, Ben Turpin, Stan Laurel
An anthology of great moments from Mack Sennett comedy shorts, featuring many great stars in some of their earliest film appearances.
Mack Sennett — *Spotlite Video*

Slapstick of Another Kind 1984
Comedy
66607 85 mins C B, V, LV P
Jerry Lewis, Madeline Kahn, Marty Feldman, Jim Backus
Jerry Lewis and Madeline Kahn play dual roles as an alien brother and sister and their adoptive Earth parents, who are being pursued by U.S. agents.
MPAA:PG
S Paul Company — *Vestron Video*

Slasher, The 1974
Mystery
77233 88 mins C B, V P
Farley Granger, Sylva Koscina, Susan Scott
A policeman must find the madman who has been killing off unfaithful married women.
Eugene Falorismot — *Monterey Home Video*

Slaughter in San Francisco 1981
Martial arts
81471 92 mins C B, V P
Chuck Norris, Don Wong
A Chinese-American cop leads a one-man fight against corruption in the San Francisco police department.
MPAA:R
World Northal Corporation — *Embassy Home Entertainment*

Slaughterhouse Five 1972
Science fiction/Folklore
62728 104 mins C B, V P
Michael Sacks, Ron Leibman, Valerie Perrine
A suburban optometrist comes unstuck in time and he experiences events during World War II, in the future on an alien planet and even his own death.
AM Available MPAA:R
Universal — *MCA Home Video*

Slave of Love, A 1978
Drama
80883 94 mins C B, V P
Elena Solovei, Rodion Nakhapetov, Alexander Kalyagin, directed by Nikita Mikhalkov
A beautiful young actress falls in love with her cameraman during the Russian Revolution. With English subtitles.
RU
Mosfilm Studio — *RCA/Columbia Pictures Home Video*

Slave of the Cannibal God 1979
Adventure
59300 86 mins C CED P
Stacy Keach, Ursula Andress, Claudio Cassinelli
A beautiful woman, searching for her missing husband in the jungles of New Guinea, hires a man bent on revenge against the human-eating cannibals as her guide.
MPAA:R
Dania Film — *Vestron Video*

Slavers 1977
Drama
66233 102 mins C B, V R, P
Trevor Howard, Britt Ekland, Ron Ely, Cameron Mitchell, Ray Milland
A tale of the African slave trade a la "Mandingo."
MPAA:R
Jurgen Goslav — *Video City Productions*

Slaves of Love 197?
Drama
59549 86 mins C B, V P
Two men, stranded on a desert island, discover it is inhabited by sex-starved females.
Dave Ackerman — *Media Home Entertainment*

Slayground 1984
Suspense
77165 85 mins C B, V P
Peter Coyote
A grieving father is out to get the man who accidentally murdered his daughter.
MPAA:R
Universal Pictures — *THORN EMI/HBO Video*

Sleepaway Camp 1983
Horror
76864 88 mins C B, V P
Mike Kellin, Jonathan Tiersten, Felissa Rose, Christopher Collet
A crazed killer hacks away at the inhabitants of a peaceful summer camp.
MPAA:R
Robert Hiltzik — *Media Home Entertainment*

Sleeper 1973
Comedy/Science fiction
64331 88 mins C B, V P
Woody Allen, Diane Keaton, John Beck, directed by Woody Allen
A New York schnook is frozen solid after a botched operation and revived two hundred years in the future, where he inadvertently gets mixed up with the political underground.
MPAA:PG
United Artists — *CBS/Fox Video; RCA VideoDiscs*

Sleeping Beauty 1983
Fairy tales
Closed Captioned
69322 60 mins C B, V, LV, CED P
Christopher Reeve, Bernadette Peters, Beverly D'Angelo
The classic tale of Sleeping Beauty and the handsome prince who wakens her is told by combining live action and animation. Part of "Faerie Tale Theatre."
Shelley Duvall — *CBS/Fox Video*

Sleeping Beauty 1982
Dance
76677 120 mins C B, V P
Fernando Bujones, Maryse Egasse, Berthica Prieto, Elba Rey, the Corps de Ballet and soloists of the Ballet del Teatro
This made-for-video production of the Tchaikovsky ballet was taped live at the Ballet del Teatro Municipal in Santiago, Chile and is a recreation of the 1939 Sadler's Wells staging.
Kultur — *Kultur*

Sleeping Beauty, The 1984
Dance
81178 135 mins C B, V R, P
Irina Kolpakova, Sergei Berezhnoi, conducted by Victor Fedotov
This is the Kirov Ballet's version of the classic Tchaikovsky ballet as choreographed by Marius Petipa. Available in VHS Hi-Fi and Beta Hi-Fi Stereo.
National Video Corporation Ltd. — *THORN EMI/HBO Video*

Sleeping Dogs 1982
Drama
65729 107 mins C B, V P
Sam Neill, Warren Oates
A man is caught between two powers: a repressive government and a violent resistance movement.
Roger Donaldson — *VidAmerica*

Sleeping Fist 198?
Martial arts
81063 85 mins C B, V P
Yuan Hsiao-Tien, Liang Chia-Yen
A young man learns the sleeping fist style of Kung fu in order to save the girl he loves from a ruthless gang of marauders.
Foreign — *Trans World Entertainment*

Sleuth 1972
Suspense/Mystery
37413 138 mins C B, V P
Sir Laurence Olivier, Michael Caine, Margo Channing, directed by Joseph L. Mankiewicz
A mystery novelist takes his work to the limits by playing diabolical and deadly tricks on his guest.
MPAA:PG
20th Century Fox — *Media Home Entertainment*

Slightly Honorable 1939
Mystery
08720 85 mins B/W B, V P
Pat O'Brien, Broderick Crawford, Edward Arnold, Eve Arden, directed by Tay Barnett
Crime in high society and police grafters, as a lawyer tangles with crooked politics.
United Artists; Walter Wanger — *Video Yesteryear; Movie Buff Video*

Slightly Pregnant Man, A 1979
Comedy
77010 92 mins C B, V P
Catherine Deneuve, Marcello Mastroianni
Comic complications abound as a construction worker becomes the world's first pregnant man.
S.J. International Pictures — *VidAmerica*

Slim and Trim Yoga with Billie Out of Pool 1983
Yoga/Physical fitness
76404 24 mins C B, V, 3/4U P
This entertaining and instructional program presents a system of exercises and meditation out of the pool.
Billie C Lange — *Billie C. Lange*

Slim and Trim Yoga with Billie In Pool 1983
Yoga/Physical fitness
76403 24 mins C B, V, 3/4U P
This entertaining and instructional program presents a system of exercises and meditation in the water.
Billie C Lange — *Billie C. Lange*

Slim Gourmet, The 1984
Cookery
72901 90 mins C B, V P
Barbara Gibbons, narrated by McLean Stevenson
Barbara Gibbons demonstrates the preparation of gourmet dishes that are low in calories.
Media Home Entertainment — *Media Home Entertainment*

Slime People 1963
Horror
58547 76 mins B/W B, V R, P
Robert Hutton, Les Tremayne, Robert Burton
Huge prehistoric monsters are let loose by an atomic explosion in Los Angeles.
Hansen Pictures — *Video Gems*

Slipstream 1972
Drama
76934 93 mins C B, V P

Julie Askew, Patti Oatman, Eli Rill
A young woman teaches an elusive disc-jockey a lesson about life and love.
Canadian — *Trans World Entertainment*

Slithis 1979
Science fiction
42911 86 mins C B, V P
This science fiction thriller has nature unleashing its revenge from the pollution of nuclear waste. Slithis was the killer they could not destroy.
Dick Davis — *Media Home Entertainment*

Slumber Party '57 1976
Comedy
55745 83 mins C B, V, LV P
At a slumber party, six girls get together and exchange stories of how they lost their virginity. Music by the Platters, Big Bopper, Jerry Lee Lewis, the Crewcuts, and Paul and Paula.
Unknown — *Vestron Video*

Slumber Party Massacre, The 1982
Horror
80773 84 mins C B, V P
Michele Michaels, Robin Stille, Andre Honore, Michael Villela
A psychotic killer wielding a large drill terrorizes a high school girls' slumber party.
MPAA:R
Santa Fe Productions — *Embassy Home Entertainment*

Small Change 1976
Comedy
54804 104 mins C B, V R, P
Geory Desmouceaux, Philippe Goldman, Jean-Francois Stevenin, Chantal Mercier, Francis Devlaeminck, directed by Francois Truffaut
"Small Change" captures the precious feeling of what it is like to be a child. It consists of a series of anecdotes, conversations, vignettes, and reflections—all spinning around the triumphs, frustrations, and intimate longings of a group of French children.
MPAA:PG
New World Pictures; Roger Corman — *Warner Home Video*

Small Town in Texas, A 1976
Drama
64359 96 mins C B, V, CED P
Timothy Bottoms, Susan George, Bo Hopkins
An ex-con returns home seeking revenge on the sheriff who framed him.
MPAA:PG
American International — *Vestron Video*

Smash Palace 1982
Drama
65363 100 mins C B, V P
Bruno Lawrence, Anna Jemison, Greer Robson, Keith Aberdein
Smash Palace is a compelling drama of a marriage jeopardized by a man's obsession with auto racing, and a women's need for love and affection.
Roger Donaldson — *Vestron Video*

Smash-Up 1947
Drama
05481 103 mins B/W B, V P
Susan Hayward, Lee Bowman, Marsha Hunt, Eddie Albert
A famous singer becomes an alcoholic, and her constant drunkenness drives her husband and child away.
United Artists — *Movie Buff Video; Discount Video Tapes*

Smashing of the Reich, The 1962
World War II
42962 84 mins B/W B, V, FO P
This program examines the fall of the German war machine with emphasis on air power.
Unknown — *Video Yesteryear; International Historic Films; Discount Video Tapes; Interurban Films*

Smithereens 1982
Drama
79221 90 mins C B, V P
Susan Berman, Brad Rinn, Richard Hell, directed by Susan Seidelman
A working-class girl leaves home and heads to New York City to become a rock and roll singer.
MPAA:R
New Line Cinema — *Media Home Entertainment*

Smokey and the Bandit 1977
Comedy
14008 96 mins C B, V, LV P
Burt Reynolds, Sally Field, Jackie Gleason, Jerry Reed, Mike Henry, directed by Hal Needham
A legendary truck driver and CB radio fanatic gives a lift to a female hitchhiker and sets off a crazy chain of events climaxing in a wild car chase.
MPAA:PG
Universal; Mort Engleberg — *MCA Home Video; RCA VideoDiscs*

Smokey and the Bandit II 1980
Comedy
48637 101 mins C B, V, LV, CED P
Burt Reynolds, Sally Field, Jackie Gleason, Jerry Reed, Mike Henry

The sequel to "Smokey and the Bandit." The Bandit is hired to transport a pregnant elephant from Miami to the Republican convention in Dallas. Sheriff Buford T. Justice and family are in hot pursuit.
MPAA:PG
Universal — *MCA Home Video*

Smokey and the Bandit Part 3 **1983**
Comedy/Adventure
66330 86 mins C B, V, LV, CED P
Jackie Gleason, Paul Williams, Jerry Reed, Pat McCormick
In this third installment of the "Smokey" saga, Sheriff Buford T. Justice is ready to retire when he is given the racing challenge of his life.
MPAA:PG
Universal — *MCA Home Video*

Smouldering Fires **1925**
Drama
65199 100 mins B/W B, V P
Pauline Frederick, Laura La Plante, Tully Marshall, directed by Clarence Brown
A tough businesswoman falls in love with an ambitious young employee, who is fifteen years younger than her. After they marry, problems arise in the form of the wife's attractive younger sister.
Universal Jewel — *Video Yesteryear*

Smurfs and the Magic Flute, The **1981**
Cartoons
65376 74 mins C B, V, LV, CED P
Animated
The Smurfs star in this musical tale about a flute with magical powers.
MPAA:G
Hanna Barbera Sepp International — *Children's Video Library*

Snake and Crane Arts of Shaolin **1980**
Martial arts
81524 93 mins C B, V P
There's plenty of action and battles going on in this martial arts film.
Alpha Film and Video — *All Seasons Entertainment*

Snake in the Monkey's Shadow **1982**
Martial arts/Suspense
75628 85 mins C B, V P
A martial arts expert demonstrates the deadliest fighting techniques.
MPAA:R
Ng See Yuen — *Trans World Entertainment*

Snoopy, Come Home **1972**
Cartoons
Closed Captioned
78886 80 mins C B, V P
Animated
Snoopy leaves his owner Charlie Brown to visit his former owner Lila in the hospital and returns with her to her apartment house.
Cinema Center Films — *Playhouse Video*

Snow Creature **1954**
Horror
76915 72 mins B/W B, V P
Paul Langton, Leslie Denison
When a troop of explorers bring back a snow creature from the Himalayas he escapes in the United States and wreaks havoc to the countryside.
United Artists — *United Home Video*

Snow Queen, The **1984**
Fairy tales
Closed Captioned
73570 60 mins C B, V, CED P
Melissa Gilbert, Lee Remick, Lance Kerwin
From "Fairy Tale Theatre" comes the adaptation of the Hans Christian Andersen tale about a boy and a girl who grow up together and are separated by evil spirits.
Gaylord Productions; Platypus Productions — *CBS/Fox Video*

Snow, The Movie **1983**
Comedy
65648 83 mins C B, V R, P
David Argue, Lance Curtis
Skiing, growing up, romance and good times is what it's all about in this film from 'down under.'
Snow Films Ltd — *Video City Productions*

Snow Treasure **1967**
Adventure
66624 96 mins C B, V P
James Franciscus, Ilona Rodgers, Paul Austad, Raoul Oyen
A group of children work to keep the Nazis from finding a cache of gold that is hidden in their Norwegian village. Filmed on location.
MPAA:PG
Sagittarius Productions — *U.S.A. Home Video*

Snow White and the Seven Dwarfs **1984**
Fairy tales
Closed Captioned
73855 60 mins C B, V, LV, CED P
Elizabeth McGovern, Rex Smith, Vincent Price, Vanessa Redgrave, directed by Peter Medak
From "Faerie Tale Theatre" comes the story of a princess who befriends seven little men to protect her from the jealous evil Queen.

(For explanation of codes, see USE GUIDE and KEY)

Gaylord Productions; Platypus Productions — *CBS/Fox Video*

Snow White and the Three Stooges 1961
Comedy
Closed Captioned
81554 108 mins C B, V P
Moe Howard, Curley Howard, Larry Fine, Carol Heiss, Patricia Medina, directed by Walter Lang
The Stooges fill in for the Seven Dwarfs when they go off prospecting in King Solomon's mines in this adaptation of the fairy tale. Available in VHS and Beta Hi-Fi.
20th Century Fox — *Playhouse Video*

Snow White Christmas 1980
Cartoons
78901 60 mins C B, V P
The wicked stepmother vows revenge against Queen Snow White, King Charming, and their daughter Young Snow White as she plans to open a Christmas Castle for the children of the kingdom.
Filmation — *Prism*

Snow White Live at Radio City Music Hall 1980
Variety
55569 90 mins C B, V R, P
Disney's film classic has been transformed into a stage show presented at New York City's Radio City Music Hall. The original music remains intact and a finale has been added.
Walt Disney — *Walt Disney Home Video*

Snowball Express 1972
Comedy
63125 120 mins C B, V R, P
Dean Jones, Nancy Olson, Harry Morgan, Keenan Wynn
When a New York City accountant inherits a hotel in the Rocky Mountains, he decides to move his family there. Upon arrival, they find that the place is falling apart.
MPAA:G
Walt Disney Productions — *Walt Disney Home Video*

Snowbeast 1977
Horror/Drama
81419 96 mins C B, V P
Bo Swenson, Yvette Mimieux, Sylvia Sidney, Clint Walker, Robert Logan
The residents of a ski resort are being terrorized by a half-human, half-animal beast who is leaving a path of dead bodies behind.
Douglas Cramer Prods. — *Worldvision Home Video*

Snowman, The 1982
Cartoons
76673 26 mins C B, V P
This program presents an animated story of a snowman who comes to life.
Snowman Enterprises LTD — *Sony Corporation of America*

So Fine 1981
Comedy
47395 91 mins C B, V R, P
Ryan O'Neal, Jack Warden, Mariangela Melato, Richard Kiel, directed by Andrew Bergman
Ryan O'Neal is a pants manufacturer who invents cellophane pants. Orders pour in for the new peekaboo style and zaniness ensues.
MPAA:R
Warner Bros; Mike Lobell — *Warner Home Video*

S.O.B. 1981
Comedy
53554 121 mins C B, V, CED P
Julie Andrews, William Holden, Richard Mulligan, Robert Preston, Shelley Winters, Robert Webber, Marisa Berenson, Robert Vaughn, Larry Hagman
Blake Edwards' bitter farce about Hollywood and the film industry wheelers and dealers who inhabit it. When a multi-million dollar picture bombs at the box office, the director turns suicidal, until he envisions reshooting it with a steamy, X-rated scene starring his wife, a star with a goody-two-shoes image.
MPAA:R
Blake Edwards; Tony Adams — *CBS/Fox Video*

Soft Cell 1983
Music-Performance
66022 55 mins C B, V R, P
"Tainted Love" and "Memorabilia" are two of the hits performed by this talented new band.
EMI Music — *THORN EMI/HBO Video*

Soggy Bottom U.S.A. 1984
Comedy
79196 90 mins C B, V P
Ben Johnson, Dub Taylor, Ann Wedgeworth, Lois Nettleton, Anthony Zerbe
A sheriff has his hands full trying to keep the law enforced in a small Southern town.
Independent — *Prism*

Soldier, The 1982
Drama
63370 90 mins C B, V, CED P
Ken Wahl, Klaus Kinski
The Russians are holding the world at ransom with a pile of stolen plutonium, and a soldier finds himself in the position to carry out an unauthorized and dangerous plan to preserve the balance of world power.

MPAA:R
Embassy — *Embassy Home Entertainment*

Soldier Blue 1970
Western
13665 109 mins C B, V, CED P
Candice Bergen, Peter Strauss, Donald Pleasance, Dana Elcar, directed by Ralph Nelson
A western adventure about a U.S. Calvary unit escorting gold across Cheyenne territory.
MPAA:R
Avco Embassy — *Embassy Home Entertainment*

Soldier of the Night 1984
Drama
81506 89 mins C B, V P
Two young people fall in love in the war torn area of Tel Aviv.
Cannon Productions — *MGM/UA Home Video*

Soldier's Story, A 1984
Drama
Closed Captioned
81207 101 mins C B, V P
Howard E. Rollins, Adolph Caesar, Denzel Washington, Patti La Belle, Wings Hauser, directed by Norman Jewison
This is an adaptation of the Charles Fuller play about a black army attorney who is sent to a southern army base to investigate the murder of an unpopular sergeant. The Herbie Hancock score can be heard VHS Dolby Hi-Fi Stereo and Beta Hi-Fi Stereo.
MPAA:PG
Columbia; Caldix Films Ltd. — *RCA/Columbia Pictures Home Video*

Soldier's Tale, The 1984
Cartoons/Music
73015 60 mins C B, V P
Animated, voices of Max Von Sydow and Andre Gregory
Igor Stravinskys' "The Soldier's Tale" is animated by New Yorker cartoonist R.O. Bleechman with the voices provided by Max Von Sydow and Andre Gregory.
MGM UA — *MGM/UA Home Video*

Sole Survivor 1984
Horror
80676 85 mins C B, V, CED P
Anita Skinner, Kurt Johnson, Caren Larkey
A group of zombies are searching for a beautiful advertising executive who was the sole survivor of a plane crash.
MPAA:R
International Film Marketing — *Vestron Video*

Solid Gold Five Day Workout, The 1984
Physical fitness
66412 100 mins C B, V, LV, CED R, P
The Solid Gold Dancers
A complete workout in five twenty-minute sessions that are designed to help develop specific and differentiated parts of the body every day. The dancers from the "Solid Gold" TV show demonstrate each exercise in an attractive setting.
Paramount Home Video — *Paramount Home Video*

Solo 1977
Romance
73039 90 mins C B, V P
This is the story of a young hitchhiker who enters the lives of a fire patrol pilot and his son.
MPAA:PG
Atlantic Releasing — *Vestron Video*

Solomon and Sheba 1959
Drama
81067 139 mins C B, V P
Yul Brynner, Gina Lollobrigida, Marisa Pavan, George Sanders, Alejandro Rey, directed by King Vidor
King Solomon's brother and the Egyptian Pharoah send the Queen of Sheba to Israel to seduce King Soloman. Available in VHS and Beta Hi-Fi.
United Artists; Ted Richmond — *Key Video*

Some Call It Loving 1973
Fantasy/Romance
72450 95 mins C B, V P
Zalman King, Richard Proyer, Tisa Farrow
James B. Harris' story is based on the classic tale of "Sleeping Beauty" brought up-to-date.
Pleasant Pastures — *Monterey Home Video*

Some Kind of Hero 1982
Comedy-Drama
60333 97 mins C B, V, LV R, P
Richard Pryor, Margot Kidder, Ray Sharkey, Ronny Cox, Lynne Moody, Olivia Cole
A Vietnam prisoner-of-war returns home to a changed world.
MPAA:R
Paramount — *Paramount Home Video; RCA VideoDiscs*

Some Like It Hot 1959
Comedy
29222 120 mins B/W B, V, LV P
Marilyn Monroe, Tony Curtis, Jack Lemmon, George Raft, Pat O'Brien, Nehemiah Persoff
Two unemployed musicians, witnesses to a Chicago murder, disguise themselves as girls and join an all-girl band headed for Miami to escape gangster's retaliation.

 (For explanation of codes, see USE GUIDE and KEY)

Academy Awards '59: Best Costume Design
EL, SP
United Artists — *CBS/Fox Video; RCA VideoDiscs*

Someday You'll Find Her Charlie Brown 1983
Cartoons
80277 26 mins C B, V P
Animated
Charlie Brown and Linus travel around the country to find a little girl that Charlie saw on television and fell in love with.
Lee Mendelson; Bill Melendez — *Snoopy's Home Video Library*

Someone I Touched 1975
Drama
81418 74 mins C B, V P
Cloris Leachman, James Olson, Glynnis O'Connor, Andy Robinson, Allyn Ann McLerie
A young woman, an expectant mother and her husband change their attitudes towards veneral disease when they are infected with it.
Dick Berg Prods; Charles Fries Prods. — *Worldvision Home Video*

Something Short of Paradise 1979
Comedy
77408 87 mins C B, V P
David Steinberg, Susan Sarandon, Jean-Pierre Aumont, Marilyn Sokol
The owner of a Manhattan movie theater has an on again-off again romance with a magazine writer.
MPAA:PG
Orion Pictures — *Vestron Video*

Something to Sing About 1936
Musical
08734 84 mins B/W B, V, 3/4U P
James Cagney, William Frawley, Evelyn Daw
Two-fisted bandleader in a musical melodrama about Hollywood studio life—the people and their problems.
Schertsinger; Meyers — *VCII; Sheik Video; Cable Films; Video Yesteryear*

Something Wicked This Way Comes 1983
Fantasy
65094 94 mins C B, V, CED R, P
Jason Robards, Jonathan Pryce, Diane Ladd, Pam Grier, Richard Davalos, James Stacy, directed by Jack Clayton
Two young boys discover the evil secret of a mysterious traveling carnival that visits their town. Based on the Ray Bradbury novel.
MPAA:PG
Buena Vista — *Walt Disney Home Video*

Sometimes a Great Notion 1971
Drama
62876 115 mins C B, V P
Paul Newman, Henry Fonda, Lee Remick, Richard Jaeckel, Michael Sarrazin, directed by Paul Newman
Trouble in a small Oregon town is caused by an independent family of lumberjacks. Based on the novel by Ken Kesey.
MPAA:PG
Universal — *MCA Home Video*

Somewhere in Time 1980
Fantasy/Romance
56871 103 mins C B, V, LV P
Christopher Reeve, Jane Seymour, Christopher Plummer, Teresa Wright, directed by Jeannot Szware
A playwright falls in love with a woman in an old portrait and, through self-hypnosis, goes back in time to discover what their relationship might have been.
MPAA:PG
Rastar, Stephen Deutsch — *MCA Home Video*

Son of Blob 1972
Horror/Science fiction
51087 87 mins C B, V R, P
Robert Walker, Godfrey Cambridge, Carol Lynley, Shelly Berman, Larry Hagman
When a scientist unknowingly brings home a piece of frozen blob from the North Pole, his wife accidentally revives the dormant grey mass. It begins a rampage of terror by digesting nearly everyone within its reach.
MPAA:PG
Jack H Harris — *Video Gems*

Son of Flubber 1984
Comedy
72793 96 mins C B, V P
Fred MacMurray, Nancy Olson, Tommy Kirk, Leon Ames, Joanna Moore
A sequel to "The Absent Minded Professor" which finds Fred MacMurray still toying with his prodigious invention, Flubber, now in the form of Flubbergas, which causes those who inhale it to float away.
Walt Disney Productions — *Walt Disney Home Video*

Son of Football Follies, The 1980
Football
45126 30 mins C B, V, FO R, P
Narrated by Mel Blanc
An updated version of "Football Follies," with Mel Blanc using his vast array of cartoon character voices to describe the bumblings on the football field.
NFL Films — *NFL Films Video; Champions on Film and Video*

Son of Football Follies/Highlights of Super Bowl XIV 1980
Football
56791 46 mins C B, V P
Gridiron goofs narrated by Bugs Bunny and Daffy Duck, plus highlights of the Rams and Steelers' Super Bowl XIV.
NFL Films — *VidAmerica*

Son of Godzilla 1966
Science fiction
09003 86 mins C B, V P
Tadao Takashima, Akiro Kubo, Berbay Maeda
Godzilla engages in exciting combat to protect his infant son.
Japanese — *Prism; Budget Video; Discount Video Tapes*

Son of Kong 1933
Horror
00312 70 mins B/W B, V, 3/4U P
Robert Armstrong, Helen Mack
King Kong's descendant is discovered on an island amidst prehistoric creatures.
RKO — *Nostalgia Merchant*

Son of Monsters on the March 1977
Movie and TV trailers
42961 27 mins C B, V, FO P
A sequel package to "Monsters on the March," this compilation offers trailers to ten horror and sci-fi classics, including "The Rocky Horror Picture Show," 'Planet of the Apes," "The Fearless Vampire Killers," "This Island Earth" and "I Was a Teenage Frankenstein."
20th Century Fox et al — *Video Yesteryear*

Son of Monte Cristo, The 1940
Adventure
08866 102 mins B/W B, V, 3/4U P
Louis Hayward, Joan Bennett, George Sanders, Florence Bates
A count's son meets a duchess whose country is threatened by renegades.
United Artists — *Sheik Video; Cable Films; Nostalgia Merchant; Discount Video Tapes; Video Connection; Video Yesteryear; Budget Video; Western Film & Video Inc; Movie Buff Video*

Son of Sinbad 1955
Adventure
15600 88 mins C B, V P
Dale Robertson, Sally Forrest, Vincent Price, Lili St. Cyr, Mari Blanchard
Sinbad, captured by Khalif of Bagdad, must bring him the secret of Greek fire to gain his freedom and free the city from the forces of mighty Tamarlane.
RKO; Howard Hughes — *United Home Video*

Son of the Sheik 1926
Romance
10116 62 mins B/W B, V P, T
Rudolph Valentino, Vilma Banky, Agnes Ayres, directed by George Fitzmaurice
In his last film, Valentino portrays a desert sheik whoabducts an unfaithful dancing girl.
First Natl — *Blackhawk Films; Sheik Video; Video Connection; Cable Films; Classic Video Cinema Collector's Club*

Son of Video Yesterbloop 1984
Comedy/Outtakes and bloopers
78105 54 mins C B, V, FO P
3 pgms
This program, partially in color, shows hilarious mishaps and general goofing around on sets in television and movie scenes from the 1930's to the 1970's.
1.Things You Never See In Pictures 2.Television Bloopers 3.Sports Snafus
Video Yesteryear — *Video Yesteryear*

Song of Freedom 1938
Drama
08885 70 mins B/W B, V, 3/4U P
Paul Robeson, Elizabeth Welch
The story of a black worker whose nonchalant singing is overheard by an opera impresario.
Treo — *Sheik Video; Video Yesteryear; Discount Video Tapes; Cable Films*

Song of Texas 1943
Western
08790 54 mins B/W B, V, 3/4U P
Roy Rogers, Harry Shannon, Pat Brady
Roy races Sam, once champion cowboy of the world, now drunkard.
Republic — *Video Yesteryear; Video Connection; Discount Video Tapes*

Song Remains the Same, The 1973
Music-Performance
79551 136 mins C B, V R, P
John Paul Jones, Jimmy Page, Robert Plant, John Bonham
All the excitement of Led Zeppelin's 1973 Madison Square Garden concert is captured in this film. Available in VHS Hi-Fi and Beta Hi-Fi Stereo.
MPAA:PG
Peter Grant; Warner Bros — *Warner Home Video*

Songwriter 1984
Musical-Drama
Closed Captioned
80783 94 mins C B, V P
Willie Nelson, Kris Kristofferson, Rip Torn, Melinda Dillon, Lesley Ann Warren, directed by Alan Rudolph

This is a high falutin' look at the lives and music of two popular country singers. Kristofferson and Nelson also wrote the musical score. Available in Beta and VHS Hi-Fi.
Tri-Star Pictures — *RCA/Columbia Pictures Home Video*

Sons of Katie Elder, The **1965**
Western/Drama
64024 122 mins C B, V R, P
John Wayne, Dean Martin, Earl Holliman, Michael Anderson Jr., Martha Hyer
Four brothers with diverse personalities return to their home town on the day their mother is buried.
Paramount — *Paramount Home Video; RCA VideoDiscs*

Sons of the Desert **1933**
Comedy
33904 69 mins B/W B, V, 3/4U P
Stan Laurel, Oliver Hardy, Mae Busch, Charley Chase
The boys try to fool their wives by pretending to go to Hawaii to cure Ollie of a bad cold, when in fact they are attending a convention in Chicago.
Hal Roach, MGM — *Nostalgia Merchant; Blackhawk Films*

Sons of the Desert **1933**
Comedy
63989 84 mins B/W B, V P, T
Stan Laurel, Oliver Hardy, Mae Busch, Charley Chase, Dorothy Christie
Stan and Ollie sneak away to a lodge convention in Chicago by telling their wives that they are going to Hawaii for Ollie's health. Also included on this tape is a 1935 Thelma Todd—Patsy Kelly short, "Top Flat."
Hal Roach; MGM — *Blackhawk Films*

Sophia Loren: Her Own Story **1980**
Drama/Biographical
58464 150 mins C B, V R, P
Sophia Loren, Armand Assante, Ed Flanders, John Gavin
The life story of Sophia Loren, from a spindly child growing up in working-class Naples, to a world-renowned movie star and beauty queen.
EMI TV Programs; Roger Gimbel — *THORN EMI/HBO Video*

Sophie's Choice **1982**
Drama
66070 157 mins C B, V, LV
Meryl Streep, Kevin Kline, Peter MacNicol, directed by Alan J. Pakula
An Auschwitz survivor settled in America struggles to forget the past.
Academy Awards '82: Best Actress (Streep).
MPAA:R
ITC Entertainment — *CBS/Fox Video; RCA VideoDiscs*

Sorceress **1982**
Drama
65749 83 mins C B, V R, P
Leigh Harris, Lynette Harris, Bob Nelson
The story of Traigon, a despotic ruler and devotee of the Black Arts, driven to become Master of the World.
MPAA:R
Jack Hill — *THORN EMI/HBO Video*

Sorrow and the Pity, The **1970**
World War II/Documentary
47021 265 mins B/W B, V P
Pierre Mendes-France, Louis Grave, Albert Speer
A documentary about anti-Semitism and the Nazi occupation of France during the Vichy regime in World War II.
Cinema 5 — *RCA/Columbia Pictures Home Video*

S.O.S. Titanic **1979**
Drama
58458 98 mins C B, V R, P
David Janssen, Cloris Leachman, Susan St. James, David Warner, Ian Holm, Helen Mirren
The story of the Titanic disaster, exactly as it happened. This film focuses on the courage that accompanied the tragedy and horror.
EMI — *THORN EMI/HBO Video*

Soul Experience, The **1984**
Music-Performance
73537 60 mins C B, V P
All the greats of rhythm and blues are represented on this program from Al Green to Bill Withers performing their great hits.
USA — *U.S.A. Home Video*

Soul Hustler **1976**
Drama
81405 81 mins C B, V P
Fabian, Casey Kasem, Larry Bishop, Nai Bonet
A con man becomes rich and famous when he becomes a tent show evangelist. Available in VHS Stereo and Beta Hi-Fi.
MPAA:PG
American Films Ltd. — *Monterey Home Video*

Sound of Love **1977**
Romance/Drama
76788 74 mins C B, V P
Celia De Burgh, John Jarratt
The mutual attraction between a deaf female hustler and a deaf race car driver leads to a deep relationship where they both learn about their own fears and desires.
Jane Scott — *Embassy Home Entertainment*

Sound of Music, The 1965
Musical-Drama
08363 174 mins C B, V, LV, CED P
Julie Andrews, Christopher Plummer, directed by Robert Wise
A true-life story of the Von Trapp family of Austria prior to World War II. Based on Rogers and Hammerstein play.
Academy Awards '65: Best Picture; Film Daily Poll 10 Best Pictures of Year '65.
20th Century Fox; Robert Wise — *CBS/Fox Video*

Sounder 1972
Drama
Closed Captioned
65734 105 mins C B, V R, P
Paul Winfield, Cicely Tyson, Kevin Hooks, Taj Mahal
The story of a Negro family of sharecroppers in rural Louisiana during the Depression.
MPAA:G
20th Century Fox — *Embassy Home Entertainment*

Soup for One 1982
Comedy
47802 84 mins C B, V P
Saul Rubinek, Marcia Strassman, Gerrit Graham
A hapless New Yorker searches for his "Dream Girl."
MPAA:R
Warner Bros — *Warner Home Video*

South of Pago Pago 1940
Adventure
64363 98 mins B/W B, V, 3/4U P
Victor McLaglen, Jon Hall, Frances Farmer, Gene Lockhart
The unsuspecting natives of a tropical isle are exploited by a gang of pirates who are searching for a seabed of rare pearls.
United Artists — *Nostalgia Merchant*

South of the Border 1939
Western
58605 70 mins B/W B, V P, T
Gene Autry, Smiley Burnette
Gene and Frog are sent to help investigate a threat to the Latin American country of "Palermo," (Also known as "South of Texas").
Republic — *Blackhawk Films; Video Connection*

South of the Rio Grande 1951
Western
72950 60 mins B/W B, V P
Duncan Renaldo
The Cisco Kid rides again as he comes to the aid of a rancher whose horses were stolen.
Eagle Lion — *United Home Video*

South Pacific 1958
Musical/Drama
55592 167 mins C B, V, CED P
Mitzi Gaynor, Rossano Brazzi, Ray Walston, France Nuyen
A young American Navy nurse and a Frenchman fall in love in World World II Hawaii. Based on Rodgers and Hammerstein's musical.
Academy Awards '58: Best Sound Recording.
Twentieth Century Fox — *CBS/Fox Video*

Southern Comfort 1981
Drama
65071 106 mins C B, V, CED P
Keith Carradine, Powers Boothe, Fred Ward, Franklyn Seales
A nine-man National Guard patrol on routine weekend maneuvers in Louisiana are marked for death by Cajun natives.
MPAA:R
20th Century Fox — *Embassy Home Entertainment*

Southerner, The 1945
Drama
11254 91 mins B/W B, V, FO P
Zachary Scott, Betty Field, directed by Jean Renoir
The story of how a poor Southern family struggles to make a living on the farm land.
United Artists — *Prism; Video Yesteryear; Movie Buff Video; Budget Video; VCII; Sheik Video; Video Connection; Western Film & Video Inc; Discount Video Tapes; Kartes Productions; Classic Video Cinema Collector's Club*

Soviet Army Chorus, Band, and Dance Ensemble 1981
Music-Performance
57256 70 mins C B, V P
This exciting music ensemble is seen on tour at various points in the USSR performing their spectacular blend of singing, dancing and acrobatics.
Kultur — *Kultur*

Soylent Green 1973
Science fiction
53940 95 mins C B, V, CED P
Charlton Heston, Leigh Taylor-Young, Chuck Connors, Joseph Cotten, Edward G. Robinson
In the 21st Century, a hard-boiled police detective investigates a murder and discovers what soylent green—the people's principal food—is made of.
MPAA:PG
MGM — *MGM/UA Home Video*

Space Angel Volume 1 1964
Science fiction/Cartoons
53150 50 mins C B, V P
Animated

A futuristic animated program for children.
EL, SP
TV Comics; Ziv Intl — *Family Home Entertainment*

Space Angel Volume 2 1964
Science fiction/Cartoons
53151 50 mins C B, V P
Animated
A futuristic animated program for children.
EL, SP
TV Comics; Ziv Intl — *Family Home Entertainment*

Space Ghost and Dino Boy 197?
Cartoons
66281 60 mins C B, V P
Animated
A ghostly cartoon character performs hilarious hijinx.
Hanna Barbera — *Worldvision Home Video*

Space Movie, The 1980
Space exploration/Documentary
54803 78 mins C B, V R, P
Directed by Tony Palmer
"The Space Movie" consists entirely of footage from NASA and the U.S. National Archives which tells the story of America's space effort (specifically the Apollo 11 moon flight). The footage, most of which has not been seen before, is mixed with music and a little narration, showing the beauty of space.
Virgin Films Ltd, British — *Warner Home Video*

Space Patrol 1955
Science fiction
59088 78 mins B/W B, V, FO P
Ed Kemmer, Lyn Osborn
The adventures of Buzz Corey, Commander in Chief of the Space Patrol, fighting interplanetary injustice.
ABC — *Video Yesteryear*

Space Patrol Volume 1 195?
Science fiction/Adventure
44339 120 mins B/W B, V, 3/4U P
Ed Kemmer, Lyn Osborn
Buzz Corey, Commander-in-Chief of the Space Patrol, tries to maintain interplanetary peace and protect the people of Earth's neighboring planets. These episodes from the early 1950's television series includes previews of coming attractions from classic science fiction films.
ABC — *Nostalgia Merchant*

Space Patrol Volume 2 195?
Science fiction
58584 90 mins B/W B, V, 3/4U P
Commander Buzz Corey maintains interplanetary peace in this early '50's TV series.
ABC — *Nostalgia Merchant; Video Dimensions*

Space Raiders 1983
Science fiction/Adventure
65743 84 mins C B, V R, P
Vince Edwards, David Mendenhall
A plucky 10-year-old blasts off into a futuristic world of intergalactic desperados, crafty alien mercenaries, starship battles and cliff-hanging dangers.
MPAA:PG
Roger Corman — *Warner Home Video*

Space Sentinels Volume 1 1977
Cartoons/Science fiction
72883 44 mins C B, V P
Animated
A cartoon features the Space Sentinels who are out to save the world from the evil space invaders.
Unknown — *Embassy Home Entertainment*

Space Shuttle Flights 1 thru 8 1985
Space exploration
70576 45 mins C B, V P
This production looks at the early shuttle flights and aims of the shuttle proram.
Century Video Corp.; Finley Holiday — *Kid Time Video*

Spaced Out 1980
Comedy
47800 85 mins C B, V R, P
A naughty sci-fi sex comedy that parodies everything from "Star Wars" to "2001."
MPAA:R
Miramax — *THORN EMI/HBO Video*

Spacehunter: Adventures in the Forbidden Zone 1983
Adventure
65315 90 mins C B, V P
Peter Strauss, Molly Ringwald, Michael Ironside, Ernie Hudson
Peter Strauss is the galactic bounty hunter who agrees to rescue 3 maidens from a plague-ridden planet. Available in VHS stereo and Beta Hi-Fi.
MPAA:PG
Don Carmody — *RCA/Columbia Pictures Home Video; RCA VideoDiscs*

Spaceketeers 1982
Cartoons/Science fiction
63118 100 mins C B, V P
Animated

An army of mutant invaders overrun a peaceful solar system. Spaceketeers to the rescue!
Toei Animation; Ginga Kikaku; Jim Terry Production Services — *Family Home Entertainment*

Spaceketeers Volume 1 1980
Science fiction/Cartoons
53163 46 mins C B, V P
Animated
Princess Aurora and Jesse Dart, with the help of a scientific wizard, risk everything to save the endangered galaxy.
EL, SP
Toei Animation; Ginga Kikaku; Jim Terry Prod — *Family Home Entertainment*

Spaceketeers Volume 2 1980
Science fiction/Cartoons
53164 46 mins C B, V P
Animated
Princess Aurora and Jesse Dart travel through space in search of their friend, Porkos, who is needed to stop blood-thirsty monsters from destroying the galaxy.
EL, SP
Toei Animation; Ginga Kikaku; Jim Terry Prod — *Family Home Entertainment*

Spaceketeers Volume 3 1980
Science fiction/Cartoons
64203 46 mins C B, V P
Animated
This third volume presents further adventures of Princess Aurora and her companion, Jesse Dart.
EL, SP
Toei Animation; Ginga Kikaku; Jim Jerry Prod — *Family Home Entertainment*

Spaceship 1983
Comedy
79307 80 mins C B, V P
Leslie Neilsen, Cindy Williams
A macho commander and a woman take the U.S.S. Spacecraft Vertigo on a voyage to search for interstellar life.
Almi Productions — *Vestron Video*

Sparkle 1976
Musical-Drama
79552 100 mins C B, V R, P
Irene Cara, Lonette McKee, Dwan Smith, directed by Sam O'Steen
This is the rags to riches saga of three sisters rise to the top of the music charts. Curtis Mayfield wrote the musical score.
MPAA:PG
Warner Bros — *Warner Home Video*

Sparrows 1926
Comedy-Drama
10124 75 mins B/W B, V P, T
Mary Pickford, Roy Stewart, Gustov von Seyffertitz, directed by William Beaudine
Set to William Perry's score, mother cares for her nine children on impoverished farm, warding off starvation and kidnappers. (Silent).
United Artists — *Blackhawk Films; Sheik Video; Discount Video Tapes; Video Yesteryear*

Spartacus 1960
Adventure
76803 185 mins C B, V P
Kirk Douglas, Laurence Olivier, Jean Simmons, Tony Curtis, Charles Laughton, Peter Ustinov, John Gavin, John Ireland, directed by Stanley Kubrick
A bold gladiator escapes from slavery with an army of slaves to challenge a power hungry Roman general.
Academy Awards '60: Best Supporting Actor (Ustinov); Best Art Direction; Best Cinematography.
Kirk Douglas; Edward Lewis — *MCA Home Video*

Spasms 1982
Horror
65511 92 mins C B, V R, P
Peter Fonda, Oliver Reed
The Demon Serpent, known as N'Gana Simbu, is the deadliest snake in the world. It strikes its victims, and the result is that the victim's bodies become hideously deformed and destroyed. With uncontrollable deady fury, the monstrous snake strikes continuously causing death and destruction.
MPAA:R
John C Pozhke; Maurice Smith — *THORN EMI/HBO Video*

Speaking of Animals 1983
Comedy
65313 60 mins C B, V P
In this hilarious film anthology, not only do the animals walk and talk like human beings, they also sing, dance and imitate the stars.
Jerry Fairbanks — *U.S.A. Home Video*

Speaking of Animals Vol. II 1984
Comedy
80245 60 mins C B, V P
Things are getting pretty funny in the zoo where our animal friends take on a variety of human personalities.
NTA — *U.S.A. Home Video*

Special Effects 1985
Horror
81452 103 mins C B, V P

 (For explanation of codes, see USE GUIDE and KEY)

Zoe Tamerlis, Eric Bogosian, Brad Rijn, Bill Oland, Richard Greene, directed by Larry Cohen
Fantasy and real life become dangerously intertwined when a film director wants to recreate an actress' murder for his next movie.
MPAA:R
New Line Cinema — *Embassy Home Entertainment*

Special Day, A 1977
Drama
58501 105 mins C B, V P
Sophia Loren, Marcello Mastroianni, directed by Ettore Scola
The day of a huge rally celebrating Hitler's visit to Rome in 1939 serves as the backdrop for an affair between a weary housewife and a radio announcer. Italian with English subtitles.
IT
Cinema 5; Carlo Ponti — *RCA/Columbia Pictures Home Video*

Special Delivery 1976
Adventure/Suspense
79672 99 mins C B, V P
Bo Svenson, Cybill Shephered, Vic Tayback, Jeff Goldblum
When three disabled Vietnam veterans rob a bank their plans go awry.
MPAA:PG
Bing Crosby Productions — *Vestron Video*

Special Valentine with Family Circus, A 1980
Cartoons/Holidays
75469 30 mins C B, V P
Animated
Cartoonist Bil Keane animates a special valentine program.
Cullen Kasden Productions Ltd — *Family Home Entertainment*

Specialist, The 1975
Drama
64298 93 mins C B, V P
Adam West, John Anderson, Ahna Capri
A lawyer is seduced by a beautiful "specialist" as part of a frame-up.
MPAA:R
Renaissance Productions — *United Home Video*

Spectacular Evening in Paris, A 1980
Nightclub
29238 106 mins C B, V P
This videotape presents the top night club acts from the top Parisienne clubs—Moulin Rouge, Madame Arthur, Lido, and Casino de Paris.
Harlan Kleiman — *VidAmerica*

Spectreman versus Hedron 196?
Science fiction
72186 60 mins C B, V P
Treacherous Dr. Gori unleashes the gas breathing Hedron on earth, while a young boy tries to revive Spectreman, the planet's last hope.
Fuji Studios — *King of Video*

Spectreman versus Zeron and Medron 196?
Science fiction
72187 60 mins C B, V P
Dr. Gori's greedy quest to conquer earth is escalated when he creates Zeron and Medron. Spectreman, having assumed the earth name, George, sets out to warn the Pollution Squad.
Fuji Studios — *King of Video*

Speed Kings? The/Love, Speed and Thrills 1915
Comedy
64534 19 mins B/W B, V R, P
Mabel Normand, Ford Sterling, Fatty Arbuckle, Mack Swain, Chester Conklin, The Keystone Cops
Two Mack Sennett comedy shorts are combined on this tape, both of which involve slapstick car chases.
Mack Sennett; Keystone — *Blackhawk Films*

Speed Learning 1983
Education
75901 30 mins C B, V P
This program shows ways to improve learning and comprehensive skills up to 300 percent.
Learn Inc — *Sony Corporation of America*

Speed Trap 1977
Adventure
76655 101 mins C B, V P
Tyne Daly, Joe Don Baker
Tyne Daly and Joe Don Baker team up to investigate a rash of mysterious car thefts in this exciting action drama.
Howard Pine; Fred Mintz — *Media Home Entertainment*

Speedway 1968
Musical
80151 100 mins C B, V P
Elvis Presley, Nancy Sinatra, Bill Bixby, Gale Gordon, William Schallert
A stock car driver finds himself being chased by an IRS agent during an important race.
Metro Goldwyn Mayer — *MGM/UA Home Video*

(For explanation of codes, see USE GUIDE and KEY)

Speedy Gonzales' Fast Funnies **1961**
Cartoons
81575 54 mins C B, V R, P
Animated, voice of Mel Blanc
The fastest mouse in all of Mexico zips around causing trouble for Sylvester and El Vulturo in this collection of eight classic cartoons that include "Cannery Woe" and "Tabasco Road".
Warner Bros — *Warner Home Video*

Spell, The **1977**
Drama
79245 86 mins C B, V P
Lee Grant, James Olson, Susan Myers, Barbara Bostock, Lelia Goldoni
An obese fifteen year old girl has the power to inflict illness and death upon the people she hates.
Charles Fries/Stone henge Productions — *Worldvision Home Video*

Spellbound **1945**
Drama
46215 111 mins B/W B, V, CED P
Ingrid Bergman, Gregory Peck, Leo G. Carroll, directed by Alfred Hitchcock
A young man suffering from amnesia and accused of murder, is helped by a female psychiatrist who loves him. One of Hitchcock's finest films of the 1940's, with a dream sequence designed by Salvador Dali.
Selznick — *CBS/Fox Video*

Spetters **1980**
Drama
65424 108 mins C B, V P
Rutger Hauer
The story revolves around four young people in Holland on a turbulent collision course with their dreams Tragic episodes force them to confront their strengths and weaknesses.
MPAA:R
Joop Van Der End — *Embassy Home Entertainment*

Sphinx **1980**
Suspense
58250 118 mins C B, V R, P
Lesley-Anne Downe, Frank Langella, John Gielgud, directed by Franklin J. Schaffner
A young woman stumbles on a secret hidden for centuries in the tomb of an Egyptian King.
MPAA:PG
Orion Pictures — *Warner Home Video*

Spider-Woman **1982**
Cartoons/Adventure
59039 100 mins C B, V P
A collection of Spider-Woman's most daring escapades.
Marvel Comics Group — *MCA Home Video*

Spiderman **1982**
Adventure
72337 90 mins C B, V P
Marvel Comics' superhero fights crime in the city in this live-action feature.
Charles Frief; Daniel R Goodman — *Prism*

Spies **1928**
Adventure
11253 90 mins B/W B, V, FO P
Gerda Maurus, Willy Fritsch, directed by Fritz Lang
A sly criminal poses as a famous banker to steal government information and create chaos in the world in this silent picture.
Janus Films — *Video Yesteryear; Blackhawk Films; Sheik Video; Classic Video Cinema Collector's Club; Discount Video Tapes*

Spinal Tap **1983**
Comedy/Musical
64980 90 mins C B, V, CED P
Rob Reiner, Christopher Guest, Michael McKean, Harry Shearer
An English heavy metal rock-and-roll band attempts a comeback tour of the U.S., only to fall into a series of misadventures caused by their totally inept tour planners.
MPAA:R
Embassy Pictures — *Embassy Home Entertainment*

Spirit of St. Louis, The **1957**
Biographical
74211 137 mins C B, V R, P
James Stewart
This is a biographical feature concerning the life of aviator Charles A. Lindbergh. Stewart stars as the pilot whose transatlantic flight made aviation history.
Leland Hayward — *Warner Home Video*

Spititual Kung Fu **1978**
Martial arts
81522 97 mins C B, V P
Jackie Chan
A young man masters the art of spiritual kung fu and uses it to take on a roving band of warriros.
Alpha Film and Video — *All Seasons Entertainment*

Splash **1984**
Fantasy
75635 109 mins C B, V, LV, CED R, P
Tom Hanks, Daryl Hannah, Eugene Levy, John Candy, directed by Ron Howard
A mermaid ventures into New York City in search of a man she has fallen for.
Brian Grazer Production — *Touchstone Home Video*

Splatter University **1984**
Horror
80678 78 mins C B, V P
Francine Forbes, Dick Biel, Cathy Lacommaro, Ric Randing, Dan Eaton
A deranged killer escapes from an asylum and begins to slaughter and mutilate comely coeds at a local college. Also available in a 79-minute uncensored version.
MPAA:R
Troma — *Vestron Video*

Splendor in the Grass **1961**
Drama
51970 124 mins C B, V R, P
Natalie Wood, Pat Hingle, Audrey Christie, Barbara Loden, Warren Beatty, Zohra Lampert, Sandy Dennis
A high school girl suffers an emotional collapse when the boy she loves stops seeing her. She attempts suicide, fails, and is committed to a mental institution for treatment.
Academy Awards '61: Best Original Story and Screenplay (William Inge).
Warner Bros;Elia Kazan — *Warner Home Video*

Split Enz **1982**
Music-Performance
75923 54 mins C B, V P
This program presents the group Split Enz performing some of their best songs.
Enz Productions Ltd — *Sony Corporation of America*

Split Image **1982**
Drama
66041 113 mins C B, V, CED P
Michael O'Keefe, Karen Allen, Peter Fonda, James Woods, directed by Ted Kotcheff
An all-American boy comes under the spell of a cult. His parents then hire a deprogrammer to bring the boy back to reality.
MPAA:R
Jeff Young — *Embassy Home Entertainment*

Split Second **1953**
Drama
73690 85 mins B/W B, V P
Jan Sterling, Alexis Smith, Stephen McNally, directed by Dick Powell
Two escaped prisoners hold hostages in a Nevada atomic bomb testing area.
RKO — *RKO HomeVideo*

Splitz **1984**
Comedy
80677 89 mins C B, V P
Robin Johnson, Pattielee, Shirley Stoler, Raymond Serra
An all-girl rock band agrees to help out a sorority house by participating in a series of sporting events.
MPAA:PG13
Film Ventures International — *Vestron Video*

Spoilers, The **1942**
Drama
65121 84 mins B/W B, V P
John Wayne, Randolph Scott, Marlene Dietrich, Margaret Lindsay
Two adventurers in the Yukon argue over land rights and the love of a saloon entertainer.
Universal — *MCA Home Video*

Spooks Run Wild **1941**
Comedy
12857 64 mins B/W B, V, FO P
The Bowery Boys, Bela Lugosi
Chills and laughs combine as the eerie Lugosi almost meets his match.
Monogram — *Video Yesteryear; Sheik Video; Discount Video Tapes; Admit One Video; Kartes Productions; See Hear Industries*

Sports Conditioning **1978**
Physical fitness/Sports
42780 30 mins C B, V P
Hosted by Ann Dugan 4 pgms
This series on tennis, golf, jogging, running, and skiing works toward improvement through conditioning.
1.Jog/Run 2.Golf 3.Tennis/Racquet Sports 4.Ski
Health N Action — *RCA/Columbia Pictures Home Video*

Spraggue **1984**
Mystery
70253 77 mins C B, V P
Michael Nouri, Glynis Johns, James Cromwell, Mark Herrier, Patrick O'Neal, Andrea Marcovicci
An amateur sleuth and his eccentric aunt set a trap for a doctor who specializes in causing heart attacks. Two beautiful women are caught in the murderous web.
M.F. Prods and Lorimar — *U.S.A. Home Video*

Spring Break **1983**
Comedy
65187 101 mins C B, V P
Perry Lang, David Knell, Steve Bassett, Paul Land, Jane Modean, Corinne Alphen
Two college students go to Fort Lauderdale on their spring vacation and have a wilder time that they bargained for.
MPAA:R
Columbia — *RCA/Columbia Pictures Home Video; RCA VideoDiscs*

Spring Fever **1981**
Comedy
72228 93 mins C B, V P
Susan Anton

Heartaches of the junior tennis circuit are brought to the screen in this sports comedy.
Tournament Productions — *Vestron Video*

Springhill 197?
Drama
81043 90 mins C B, V P
This is the true story of a mining disaster where seven miners were fighting to survive against the elements while buried 13,000 feet underground.
Foreign — *Trans World Entertainment*

Springtime in the Sierras 1947
Western
10709 54 mins B/W B, V, 3/4U R, P
Roy Rogers, Andy Devine
Roy Rogers and Andy Devine band together to fight a gang of poachers who prey on the wildlife of a game preserve.
Republic — *Cable Films; Discount Video Tapes; Video Yesteryear*

Spunky and Tadpole 196?
Cartoons
56749 48 mins C B, V P
Animated
Spunky and his faithful companion, Tadpole, get in and out of trouble and cliff-hanging adventures, spoofing some of the old classic films in the process. Available in English and Spanish versions.
EL, SP
Beverly Hills Film Corp — *Media Home Entertainment*

Spunky & Tadpole Volume 1 1960
Cartoons
80716 60 mins C B, V P
Animated, voices of Joan Gardner, Don Messick
This tape includes two episodes from the series "Lost in Outer Space" and "The Smugglers."
Beverly Film Corporation — *All Seasons Entertainment*

Spunky & Tadpole Volume 2 1960
Cartoons
80717 60 mins C B, V P
Animated, voices of Joan Gardner, Don Messick
Here are two more animated adventures from the series; "The Frozen Planet" and "The Secret of Cactus Corners."
Beverly Film Corporation — *All Seasons Entertainment*

Spunky & Tadpole Volume 3 1960
Cartoons
80721 60 mins C B, V P
Animated, voices of Joan Gardner, Don Messick
In this volume, Spunky and Tadpole become "Private Eyes"and take a "Moon Trip."
Beverly Film Corporation — *All Seasons Entertainment*

Spy in Black, The 1939
Adventure
11255 82 mins B/W B, V, FO P
Conrad Veidt, Valerie Hobson, Sebastian Shaw
A German submarine captain returns from duty at sea and is assigned to infiltrate one of the Orkney Islands and obtain confidential British information.
Korda — *Video Yesteryear; Discount Video Tapes*

Spy of Napoleon 1936
Drama
63618 77 mins B/W B, V, FO P
Richard Barthelmess, Dolly Hass, Francis I. Sullivan
During the Franco-Prussian War, Emperor Napoleon III recruits his illegitimate daughter to uncover traitors to the throne.
British — *Video Yesteryear*

Spy Smasher 1942
Mystery/Serials
33956 185 mins B/W B, V, 3/4U P
Kane Richmond, Marguerite Chapman
A serial of espionage and intrigue in twelve episodes.
Republic — *Nostalgia Merchant; Video Connection; Republic Pictures Home Video*

Spy Who Loved Me, The 1977
Adventure
60378 125 mins C B, V P
Roger Moore, Barbara Bach
James Bond must destroy a brilliant but savage villain and his henchman Jaws, in order to prevent them from using captured American and Russian atomic submarines in a plot to destroy the world.
MPAA:PG
United Artists — *CBS/Fox Video; RCA VideoDiscs*

Spyro Gyra 1980
Music-Performance
47396 56 mins C B, V R, P
Live performances of some of Spyro Gyra's well-known hits are interspersed with interviews with band members.
Hawk Productions — *Warner Home Video*

Squeeze Play 1979
Comedy
64214 92 mins C B, V R, P
A group of young women start a baseball team and challenge their boyfriends' team to a game.

 (For explanation of codes, see USE GUIDE and KEY)

It's a no-holds-barred competition featuring a sexy wet-T-shirt contest.
Troma Productions — *THORN EMI/HBO Video*

Squiddly Diddly 196?
Cartoons
69291 55 mins C B, V P
Animated
This tape is a compilation of "Squiddly Diddly" cartoons, about a star-struck squid hoping to break into show business.
Hanna-Barbera — *Worldvision Home Video*

Squirm 1976
Horror
64357 92 mins C B, V, LV, CED P
John Scardino, Patricia Pearcy, Jean Sullivan
A storm disrupts a highly charged power cable which electrifies ordinary worms into giant monsters.
MPAA:R
American International — *Vestron Video*

Squizzy Taylor 1984
Biographical/Drama
77011 82 mins C B, V P
Jacki Weaver, Alan Cassell, David Atkins
This is the true story of the rise and fall of Australian mob boss Squizzy Taylor.
Satori Entertainment — *VidAmerica*

S.S. Experiment 1980
Drama
77392 90 mins C B, V P
A sadistic Nazi S.S. officer forces female concentration camp prisoners to participate in a series of bizzare sexual experiments.
Foreign — *Wizard Video*

SS Girls 1978
War-Drama
58468 82 mins C B, V P
Gabriele Carrara, Marina Daunia, Vassilli Karis, Macha Magal, Thomas Rudy, Lucic Bogoljub Benny, Ivano Staccioli
After the attack of July 1944, Hitler does not trust the Wermacht and extends the power of the S.S. over Germany. General Berger entrusts Hans Schillemberg to recruit a specially chosen group of prostitutes who must test the fighting spirit and loyalty of the generals.
Topar Films — *Media Home Entertainment*

St. Louis Cardinals: Team Highlights 1984
Baseball
81151 30 mins C B, V P
Ozzie Smith, Lonnia Smith, Keith Hernandez, Whitey Herzog 4 pgms
This series features exciting selected highlights of the Cardinals 1981-1984 seasons.
1.1981: Red bird Revival 2.1982: A Season to Celebrate 3.1983: Get Excited 4. 1984: The Spirit Comes Alive
Major League Baseball — *Major League Baseball Productions*

Stacey! 198?
Drama
64948 87 mins C B, V R, P
Anne Randall, Marjorie Bennett, Anitra Ford, Alan Landers
Anne Randall, former Playboy Playmate, stars as Stacey Hansen, a beautiful private detective who finds herself involved in something more than just a friendly job of snooping.
MPAA:R
Unknown — *Video Gems*

Stacy's Knights 1983
Drama
65608 95 mins C B, V P
Andra Millian
A seemingly shy girl happens to have an uncanny knack for Blackjack. With the odds against her and an unlikely group of "knights" to aid her, she sets up an incredible "sting" operation.
MPAA:PG
Crown — *Vestron Video*

Stage Door 1937
Comedy-Drama
10054 92 mins B/W B, V P, T
Katharine Hepburn, Ginger Rogers, Lucille Ball, Eve Arden, Andrea Leeds, directed by Gregory La Cava
Based on Edna Ferber's play, set in theatrical boarding house, film follows ambitions of young aspiring actresses.
RKO; Pandro S Berman — *Blackhawk Films; Nostalgia Merchant*

Stagedoor Canteen 1943
Musical
08667 135 mins B/W B, V P
Tallulah Bankhead, Merle Oberon, Katharine Hepburn, Paul Muni, Ethel Waters, Johnny Weismuller
A simple love story of a soldier who falls for a canteen hostess. Dozens of top stars and band leaders.
UA; Sol Lesser; Frank Borzage — *Movie Buff Video; VCII; Sheik Video; Discount Video Tapes; Cable Films; Video Connection; Video Yesteryear*

Stage Fright 1983
Horror
72529 82 mins C B, V P

A bashful actress is transformed into a homicidal killer after a latent psychosis in her becomes active.
John Lamand; Colin Eggleston — *VidAmerica*

Stage Fright 1950
Mystery/Drama
80079 110 mins B/W B, V R, P
Jane Wyman, Marlene Dietrich, Alastar Sim, Dame Sybil Thorndike, directed by Alfred Hitchcock
A young woman will stop at nothing to clear her boyfriend who has been accused of murdering another woman's husband.
Warner Bros. — *Warner Home Video*

Stage Show with the Dorsey Brothers 1956
Variety
46345 28 mins B/W B, V, FO P
Tommy and Jimmy Dorsey and their Orchestra, Elvis Presley, Henny Youngman
A program from the Dorsey Brothers' television series featuring guest performers Elvis Presley and Henny Youngman. The original telecast date was March 17, 1956.
CBS — *Video Yesteryear*

Stagecoach 1939
Western
08599 100 mins B/W B, V P
John Wayne, Claire Trevor, Thomas Mitchell, George Bancroft, John Carradine, directed by John Ford
John Ford's western classic. Reactions of a group of people in a stagecoach under Indian attack.
Academy Awards '39: Best Supporting Actor (Thomas Mitchell); Best Scoring.
United Artists; Walter Wanger Productions — *Vestron Video; RCA VideoDiscs*

Stagecoach to Denver 1947
Western
10662 56 mins B/W B, V, 3/4U R, P
Allan Lane, Roy Barcroft, Bobby Blake
Red Ryder protects a friend's stagecoach line from outlaws.
Republic — *Cable Films; Video Connection; Discount Video Tapes; Nostalgia Merchant*

Stagestruck 1957
Drama
72946 95 mins B/W B, V P
Henry Fonda, Susan Strasberg, Christopher Plummer
A remake of 1933's "Morning Glory"; Susan Strasberg reprises the role made famous by Katharine Hepburn, as a determined, would-be actress.
RKO Radio Pictures — *United Home Video*

Stalag 17 1953
Adventure
29766 120 mins B/W B, V, LV R, P
William Holden, Don Taylor, Peter Graves, Otto Preminger, directed by Billy Wilder
World War II: American G.I.'s in German prison camp, thinking cynical sharp-tongued sergeant is a spy, beat him unmercifully. Based on the play by Donald Bevan and Edmund Trzcinski.
Academy Awards '53: Best Actor (Holden).
Paramount, Billy Wilder — *Paramount Home Video; RCA VideoDiscs*

Stand Easy 1952
Comedy
66396 71 mins B/W B, V P
Peter Sellers, Harry Secombe, Spike Milligan, Carole Carr
A comedy of errors about a group of Army misfits who save an atomic formula from spies.
Original title: "Down Among the Z Men."
EJ Fancey Productions — *Movie Buff Video*

Stand-In 1937
Comedy/Satire
50952 90 mins B/W B, V R, P
Humphrey Bogart, Leslie Howard, Joan Blondell, Alan Mowbray
A satire on Hollywood, in which a movie studio is saved from bankruptcy by a bookkeeping expert.
AM Available
United Artists — *Monterey Home Video*

Stand-In 1937
Comedy
66636 91 mins B/W B, V P
Humphrey Bogart, Joan Blondell, Leslie Howard, Alan Mowbray, Jack Carson
An efficiency expert is sent to save a Hollywood studio from bankruptcy.
United Artists; Walter Wanger — *Monterey Home Video*

Stanley 1972
Horror
17201 108 mins C B, V P
Chris Robinson, Alex Rocco, Susan Carroll
Vietnam vet uses a rattlesnake as his personal weapon of revenge against mankind.
MPAA:PG
Crown International Pictures — *United Home Video*

Star Ascending: The Dallas Cowboys 1965-69 1984
Football
79638 50 mins C B, V, FO P
Highlights from the Dallas Cowboys' early games circa 1965-1969.
NFL Films — *NFL Films Video*

(For explanation of codes, see USE GUIDE and KEY)

Star Bloopers **1979**
Outtakes and bloopers
63334 47 mins B/W B, V R, P
A collection of great movie moments that never made it to the screen, including missed cues, flubbed deliveries, malfunctioning props, and some rare Ronald Reagan footage.
Roy Self; John Gregory — *THORN EMI/HBO Video*

Star Chamber, The **1983**
Drama
65504 109 mins C B, V, CED P
Michael Douglas, Hal Holbrook
A conscientious judge who, seeing criminals freed on legal technicalities, comes to the conclusion that conventional law does not always reward the victims of crime, but often the criminals. Distressed by this, he turns to a friend and colleague for solace. His friend tells him of another type of justice that a group of judges have set up that is beyond conventional.
MPAA:R
20th Century Fox — *CBS/Fox Video*

Star Crash **1978**
Science fiction/Adventure
65712 92 mins C B, V, LV P
Caroline Munroe, Christopher Plummer, David Hasselhoff
A trio of adventurers square off against interstellar evil by using their wits and technological wizardry.
MPAA:PG
Nat and Patrick Wachsberger — *Embassy Home Entertainment*

Star 80 **1983**
Drama
65612 104 mins C B, V, LV, CED R, P
Mariel Hemingway, Eric Roberts, directed by Bob Fosse
The true show-business story of the stormy relationship of Playboy Playmate of the Year Dorothy Stratten and her manager-husband Paul Snider that ended in headline-making tragedy.
MPAA:R
Wolfgang Glattes; Kenneth Utt — *Warner Home Video*

Star Is Born, A **1954**
Musical-Drama
58251 150 mins C B, V R, P
Judy Garland, James Mason, Jack Carson, Charles Bickford, Tommy Noonan, directed by George Cukor
A young actress achieves Hollywood success and marries a famous leading man whose star wanes as hers shines brighter. Songs include "The Man That Got Away," and "Born in a Trunk."
Warner Bros — *Warner Home Video*

Star Is Born, A **1954**
Musical-Drama
66325 175 mins C B, V, LV, CED P
Judy Garland, James Mason, Jack Carson, Tommy Noonan, Charles Bickford, directed by George Cukor
This newly restored version of the 1954 classic reinstates over 20 minutes of long-missing footage, including three Garland musical numbers, "Here's What I'm Here For," "Shampoo Commercial" and "Lose That Long Face." In stereo.
MPAA:PG
Warner Bros; Transcona Enterprises — *Warner Home Video*

Star Is Born, A **1937**
Drama
11217 111 mins C B, V, FO P
Janet Gaynor, Fredric March, Adolphe Menjou, May Robson, Andy Devine, directed by William Wellman
A movie star declining in popularity marries a shy girl and helps her become a star. Her fame eclipses his and tragic consequences follow.
Academy Awards '37: Best Original Story; Special Academy Award to W. Howard Greene for color photography.
United Artists — *Prism; Video Yesteryear; Video Connection; VCII; Video Dimensions; Cable Films; King of Video; Budget Video; Western Film & Video Inc; Cinema Concepts; Classic Video Cinema Collector's Club; Kartes Productions*

Star Is Born, A **1976**
Musical
37425 140 mins C B, V R, P
Barbra Streisand, Kris Kristofferson, Paul Mazursky, Gary Busey, Oliver Clark
The tragic story of one rock star (Streisand) on her way to the top and another (Kristofferson) whose career is in decline. An updated version of the 1937 and 1955 movies.
Academy Awards '76: Best Song (Evergreen).
MPAA:R
Warner Bros — *Warner Home Video; RCA VideoDiscs*

Star of Midnight **1935**
Mystery
79680 90 mins B/W B, V P
Ginger Rogers, William Powell, Paul Kelly
A lawyer becomes involved in the disappearance of a woman and the murder of a columnist.
RKO — *RKO HomeVideo*

Star Packer 1934
Western
08829 53 mins B/W B, V, 3/4U P
John Wayne
"Duke" puts on a marshal's badge and cleans out the renegades.
Monogram — *Sony Corporation of America; Spotlite Video; Video Connection; Sheik Video; Cable Films; Discount Video Tapes; Kartes Productions*

Star-Spangled Cowboys 1982
Football
47710 23 mins C B, V, FO P
Team highlights of the 1981 Dallas Cowboys who recaptured the NFC Eastern Division Championship thanks to Tony Dorsett's 1,646 yards rushing.
NFL Films — *NFL Films Video*

Star Struck 1982
Musical/Comedy
65710 95 mins C B, V P
Jo Kennedy
An 18-year-old waitress dreams of becoming a new wave singer.
MPAA:PG
David Elfick; Richard Brennan — *Embassy Home Entertainment*

Star Trek I 1966
Science fiction
47615 100 mins C CED P
William Shatner, Leonard Nimoy, Jeffrey Hunter, Susan Oliver, DeForest Kelley
Star Trek's only two-part episode, "The Menagerie," incorporates the original 1964 pilot show as a flashback. Mr. Spock kidnaps the former captain of the Enterprise and returns to Talos IV, the scene of a mystery from years past.
NBC — *RCA VideoDiscs*

Star Trek: Arena 1967
Science fiction
70535 51 mins C B, V P
William Shatner, Leonard Nimoy, Carole Shelyne
Captain Kirk fights a duel to the death with a murderous alien commander.
Paramount; Gene Roddenberry — *Paramount Home Video*

Star Trek II 196?
Science fiction
56882 100 mins C CED P
William Shatner, Leonard Nimoy, DeForest Kelley, Joan Collins, Frank Gorshin
Two television episodes, "The City on the Edge of Forever," written by Harlan Ellison, and "Let That Be Your Last Battlefield."
NBC — *RCA VideoDiscs*

Star Trek: Balance of Terror 1966
Science fiction
70531 51 mins C B, V P
William Shatner, Leonard Nimoy, DeForest Kelly, Mark Lenard
The Enterprise plays a game of cat-and-mouse with a Romulan warship that has destroyed several Earth outposts.
Paramount; Gene Roddenberry — *Paramount Home Video*

Star Trek III 1967
Science fiction
59386 100 mins C CED P
William Shatner, Leonard Nimoy, DeForest Kelley, Nichelle Nichols, James Doohan, Walter Koenig
A double feature of two popular "Star Trek" episodes: "The Trouble with Tribbles" and "The Tholian Web."
NBC — *RCA VideoDiscs*

Star Trek III: The Search for Spock 1984
Science fiction
Closed Captioned
80508 105 mins C B, V, LV, CED P
William Shatner, Leonard Nimoy, DeForest Kelley, James Doohan, Nichelle Nichols, directed by Leonard Nimoy
Captain Kirk commandeers the USS Enterprise on a mission to the Genesis Planet to discover whether or not Mr. Spock still lives. In VHS and Beta Stereo Hi-Fi.
MPAA:PG
Paramount — *Paramount Home Video*

Star Trek: Charlie X 1966
Science fiction
80510 51 mins C B, V P
William Shatner, Leonard Nimoy, Grace Lee Whitney, Robert Walker, Jr., DeForest Kelley
A teenage boy who was spacedwrecked on an alien planet when young is rescued by the Enterprise. Upon meeting Yeoman Janice Rand, he begins to manifest strange powers.
Paramount; Gene Roddenbury — *Paramount Home Video*

Star Trek: Court Martial 1967
Science fiction
70537 51 mins C B, V P
William Shatner, Leonard Nimoy, Percy Rodriguez, Elisha Cook, Jr., Joan Marshall
Captain Kirk is accused of purposely sending a crewman to his death. Despite his denials, Kirk faces a court martial hearing.
Paramount; Gene Roddenberry — *Paramount Home Video*

Star Trek IV 1967
Science fiction
60386 100 mins C CED P
William Shatner, Leonard Nimoy, DeForest Kelley, Nichelle Nichols, Ricardo Montalban
Two "Star Trek" television episodes that provided the background for the recent feature films based on the series: "Space Seed" and "The Changeling."
NBC — *RCA VideoDiscs*

Star Trek: Dagger of the Mind 1966
Science fiction
80517 51 mins C B, V P
William Shatner, Leonard Nimoy, James Gregory, Morgan Woodward, Marianna Hill
On an inspection trip at a penal colony, Captain Kirk falls victim to a mind control machine invented by a crazed doctor.
Paramount; Gene Roddenbury — *Paramount Home Video*

Star Trek V 1967
Science fiction
64332 100 mins C CED P
William Shatner, Leonard Nimoy, DeForest Kelley, Nichelle Nichols, Mark Lenard
Two more well-liked episodes from the famous television series: "Mirror Mirror" and "Balance of Terror."
NBC — *RCA VideoDiscs*

Star Trek VI 1967
Science fiction
64784 100 mins C CED P
William Shatner, Leonard Nimoy, DeForest Kelley, Celia Lovsky, Mark Lenard, Jane Wyatt
Two more episodes in the popular TV series: "Amok Time" and "Journey to Babel."
NBC — *RCA VideoDiscs*

Star Trek: Miri 1966
Science fiction
80516 51 mins C B, V P
William Shatner, Leonard Nimoy, Grace Lee Whitney, Kim Darby, Michael J. Pollard
The Enterprise crew send a landing party down to a planet that is inhabited only by children.
Paramount; Gene Roddenbury — *Paramount Home Video*

Star Trek: Mudd's Women 1966
Science fiction
80514 51 mins C B, V P
William Shatner, Leonard Nimoy, Roger C. Carmel, Karen Steele
A galactic con man is picked up by the Enterprise, along with his three female traveling companions.
Paramount; Gene Roddenbury — *Paramount Home Video*

Star Trek: Shore Leave 1966
Science fiction
70532 51 mins C B, V P
William Shatner, Leonard Nimoy, DeForest Kelley
Captain Kirk allows the crew to take shore leave on an earthlike planet that proves to be full of unexplained phenomena.
Paramount; Gene Roddenberry — *Paramount Home Video*

Star Trek: Space Seed 1967
Science fiction
60211 50 mins C B, V R, P
William Shatner, Leonard Nimoy, DeForest Kelley, Nichelle Nichols, Ricardo Montalban
This is the classic TV episode which inspired the 1982 film "Star Trek II: The Wrath of Khan" where Khan, the leader of a race of supermen, tries to take over the Enterprise. Also included is a trailer for the feature film.
NBC — *Paramount Home Video*

Star Trek: The Conscience of the King 1966
Science fiction
70530 51 mins C B, V P
William Shatner, Leonard Nimoy, Arnold Moss, Barbara Anderson
Captain Kirk recognizes the leader of a traveling acting troupe as a convicted criminal and mass murderer.
NBC; Paramount; Gene Roddenberry — *Paramount Home Video*

Star Trek: The Corbomite Maneuver 1966
Science fiction
80518 51 mins C B, V P
William Shatner, Leonard Nimoy, DeForest Kelley, Clint Howard
The Enterprise plays cat and mouse with a massive alien starship that is controlled by a mysterious being.
Paramount; Gene Roddenbury — *Paramount Home Video*

Star Trek: The Enemy Within 1966
Science fiction
80513 51 mins C B, V P
William Shatner, Leonard Nimoy, DeForest Kelley
A malfunction in the transporter splits Captain Kirk in two—one good, the other evil.
Paramount; Gene Roddenbury — *Paramount Home Video*

Star Trek: The Galileo Seven 1967
Science fiction
70533 51 mins C B, V P

William Shatner, Leonard Nimoy, DeForest Kelley, James Doohan, Don Marshall
Mr. Spock is assigned to lead a landing party on Murasaki 312 and faces danger when his people are attacked by savages.
Paramount; Gene Roddenberry — *Paramount Home Video*

Star Trek: The Man Trap **1966**
Science fiction
80509 51 mins C B, V P
William Shatner, Leonard Nimoy, DeForest Kelley, Jeanne Bal, Alfred Ryder.
A salt vampire, the last remaining inhabitant of plante M-113, takes the form of Dr. McCoy's old girlfriend as a ruse to sneak aboard The Enterprise.
Paramount; Gene Roddenbury — *Paramount Home Video*

Star Trek: The Menagerie Parts I and II **1966**
Science fiction
70529 102 mins C B, V P
William Shatner, Leonard Nimoy, Jeffrey Hunter, Susan Oliver, Majel Barrett, Malachi Throne
Mr. Spock kidnaps the Enterprises's former captain and sets the ship on a course to the forbidden planet of Talos IV. This, Star Trek's only two-part episode, incorporates portions of the show's original 1964 pilot film.
Paramount; Gene Roddenberry — *Paramount Home Video*

Star Trek: The Motion Picture **1980**
Science fiction
48512 132 mins C CED P
William Shatner, Leonard Nimoy, DeForest Kelley, Stephen Collins, Persis Khambatta
The starship Enterprise must fight a mysterious alien invasion heading directly for Earth. With new equipment and a new mission, Captain Kirk orders the starship into Warp Drive to meet and conquer this destructive enemy.
MPAA:G
Gene Roddenberry — *RCA VideoDiscs*

Star Trek: The Motion Picture **1980**
Science fiction
64510 144 mins C B, V, LV R, P
William Shatner, Leonard Nimoy, DeForest Kelley, James Doohan, Stephen Collins, Persis Khambatta
The Enterprise fights a strange alien force that threatens Earth in this adaptation of the famous TV series. Twelve additional minutes of previously unseen footage have been added to this home video version of the theatrical feature. In stereo.
MPAA:G
Gene Roddenberry; Paramount — *Paramount Home Video*

Star Trek: The Naked Time **1966**
Science fiction
80512 51 mins C B, V P
William Shatner, Leonard Nimoy, DeForest Kelley, Bruce Hyde
The crew of the Enterprise becomes affected by an alien virus that releases all inhibitions.
Paramount; Gene Roddenbury — *Paramount Home Video*

Star Trek: The Return of the Archons **1967**
Science fiction
70538 51 mins C B, V P
William Shatner, Leonard Nimoy, DeForest Kelley, Torin Thatcher, George Takei
Kirk, Spock and McCoy beam down to a strange planet where the populace are held in mind control by a giant computer.
Paramount; Gene Roddenberry — *Paramount Home Video*

Star Trek: The Squire of Gothos **1967**
Science fiction
70534 51 mins C B, V P
William Shatner, Leonard Nimoy, Nichelle Nichols, William Campbell
The Enterprise crew runs into trouble when an irrational alien forces Captain Kirk to spar with him in a gothic castle.
Paramount; Gene Roddenberry — *Paramount Home Video*

Star Trek II: The Wrath of Khan **1982**
Science fiction
62784 113 mins C B, V, LV R, P
William Shatner, Leonard Nimoy, Ricardo Montalban, DeForest Kelley, directed by Nicholas Meyer
Admiral Kirk and the crew of the Enterprise are targeted for death by Khan, an old foe who blames Kirk for the death of his wife.
MPAA:PG
Paramount — *Paramount Home Video; RCA VideoDiscs*

Star Trek: Tomorrow Is Yesterday **1967**
Science fiction
70536 51 mins C B, V P
William Shatner, Leonard Nimoy, DeForest Kelley, James Doohan, Roger Perry
The Enterprise hits a black hole and is catapulted back through time to the 1960's.
Paramount; Gene Roddenberry — *Paramount Home Video*

Star Trek Volume 1 **1966**
Science fiction
44587 104 mins C B, V R, P
William Shatner, Leonard Nimoy, DeForest Kelley, Jeffrey Hunter, Susan Oliver
"The Menagerie," a two-part episode, tells the story of what happened to the former commander of the Enterprise, Captain Christopher Pike, and why Spock almost faced court martial.
NBC — *Paramount Home Video*

Star Trek Volume 2 **1967**
Science fiction
44584 104 mins C B, V R, P
William Shatner, Leonard Nimoy, DeForest Kelley, Jane Wyatt, Mark Lenard
In "Amok Time" Kirk authorizes an unscheduled voyage to Vulcan for Spock's marriage because although Vulcans are normally unemotional, when the time comes to marry they are compelled, under penalty of madness and death, to return to their home planet. Kirk becomes part of this ritual wedding ceremony. The second episode, "Journey to Babel," involves intrigue when the Enterprise is assigned the task of transporting delegates from many planets to the Babel Conference and Kirk suspects a spy on board. Among the delegates are Spock's parents, which presents the opportunity for reconciliation between Spock and his father.
NBC — *Paramount Home Video*

Star Trek Volume 3 **1968**
Science fiction
44583 104 mins C B, V R, P
William Shatner, Leonard Nimoy, DeForest Kelley, Nichelle Nichols
In the episode "Mirror, Mirror" a transporter malfunction throws the Enterprise crew into a parallel or mirror universe where command is asserted by force and advancement is achieved by assassination. The search for a missing Federation ship, the Defiant, leads the Enterprise into unchartered space in the episode "The Tholian Web." The ship appears on the viewing screen, but does not register on the sensors. It has suffered a power loss that also affects the Enterprise, causing weakness and insanity among the crew. When Kirk goes aboard the Defiant to investigate, he becomes stranded on the empty ship.
NBC — *Paramount Home Video*

Star Trek Volume 4 **196?**
Science fiction
44585 104 mins C B, V R, P
William Shatner, Leonard Nimoy, DeForest Kelley, Nichelle Nichols, James Doohan, George Takei
This program contains two episodes of the popular TV series Star Trek: "The Trouble with Tribbles ('67) and "Let That Be Your Last Battlefield" ('69). "The Trouble with Tribbles" speaks for itself. Tribbles—cute, fuzzy, seemingly harmless little creatures create problems for the crew of the Enterprise. In "Let That Be Your Last Battlefield" an age-old battle between two hostile alien powers engulfs the Enterprise.
NBC — *Paramount Home Video*

Star Trek Volume 5 **196?**
Science fiction
44586 104 mins C B, V R, P
William Shatner, Leonard Nimoy, DeForest Kelley, Joan Collins
This program contains two episodes from the popular TV series Star Trek. In "The Balance of Terror" ('66), Captain Kirk is about to perform a wedding for two crew members when the Romulans attack Outpost 4. This leads the Enterprise in pursuit of an attack ship, whose invisibility shield ultimately causes its own destruction. In "The City on the Edge of Forever," McCoy accidentally beams himself down to a strange planet, where he enters a time vortex and drastically changes history. Kirk and Spock must rescue him.
NBC — *Paramount Home Video*

Star Trek: What Are Little Girls Made Of? **1966**
Science fiction
80515 51 mins C B, V P
William Shatner, Leonard Nimoy, Majel Barrett:Michael Strong, Ted Cassidy, Sherry Jackson
Nurse Christine Chapel visits an old boyfriend whose scientific experiments with robots, have progressed farther than anyone had imagined.
Paramount; Gene Roddenbury — *Paramount Home Video*

Star Trek: Where No Man Has Gone Before **1966**
Science fiction
80511 51 mins C B, V P
William Shatner, Leonard Nimoy, Gary Lockwood, Sally Kellerman, George Takei
Two members of the Enterprise crew begin to develop unearthly psi powers after the ship is damaged by the energy barrier at the edge of the Milky Way galaxy. The second pilot for the series.
Paramount; Gene Roddenbury — *Paramount Home Video*

Star Wars **1977**
Science fiction/Adventure
47505 121 mins C B, V, LV, CED P
Mark Hamill, Carrie Fisher, Harrison Ford, Alec Guinness, Peter Cushing, David Prowse, directed by George Lucas
A long time ago in a galaxy far, far away, Rebel forces are engaged in a life-or-death struggle

with the tyrant leaders of the Galactic Empire. Musical score composed by John Williams. Academy Awards '77: Best Art Decoration; Set Decoration; Film Editing; Costume Design; Achievement in Sound; Visual Effects; Original Score. MPAA:PG EL, SP
20th Century Fox — *CBS/Fox Video*

Starflight One 1983
Adventure/Science fiction
81167 115 mins C B, V P
Ray Milland, Lee Majors, Hal Linden, Lauren Hutton, Robert Webber
A space shuttle is called upon to save the world's first hypersonic airliner trapped in an orbit above earth.
Orion Pictures — *Vestron Video*

Starman 1984
Science fiction/Romance
Closed Captioned
80877 115 mins C B, V P
Jeff Bridges, Karen Allen, Charles Martin Smith, Richard Jaeckel, directed by John Carpenter
An alien from an advanced civilization lands in Wisconsin. After meeting with ignorant hostility from the military, he clones himself into the form of a grieving young widow's recently expired husband. With the authorities in dogged pursuit, the wodow and the visitor travel to his redezvous spot in Arizona, falling in love as they go. Available in Dolby Hi Fi Stereo and Beta Hi Fi Stereo.
MPAA:PG
Columbia Pictures — *RCA/Columbia Pictures Home Video*

Starring the Barkleys 1973
Cartoons
81064 44 mins C B, V P
Animated
Here are two more episodes from the cartoon series where Arnie Barkley puts his paw in his mouth once again.
De Patie Freleng Productions — *Trans World Entertainment*

Stars Look Down, The 1939
Drama
07263 96 mins B/W B, V P
Michael Redgrave, Margaret Lockwood, Emlyn Williams
A mine owner forces miners to work in an unsafe mine in a Welsh town and disaster strikes. Based on the A. J. Cronin novel.
MGM; Carol Reed — *Budget Video; Cable Films; Discount Video Tapes; Video Yesteryear; Kartes Productions*

Stars of Jazz 1958
Music
21334 51 mins B/W B, V, FO P
Mel Torme, Andre Previn, Shelly Manne
Two programs from this series featuring jazz greats at their best.
ABC — *Video Yesteryear*

Stars on 45 1983
Music
65518 71 mins C B, V, LV, CED P
An elaborate live stage revue covering the past 30 years of pop music history. Featured are nostalgia tunes by Little Richard, Chuck Berry, Elvis, and the Beatles. Woodstock, Soul and Disco tunes are all highlighted in the show. In stereo VHS and Beta Hi-Fi.
MCA Pay Television — *MCA Home Video*

Stars on Parade/Boogie Woogie Dream 1946
Musical
11258 55 mins B/W B, V, FO P
Milton Wood, Jane Cooley, Francine Everett, Bob Howard, Eddie Smith, Phil Moore, Lena Horne, Teddy Wilson
A pair of all-black musicals which shows off a host of talent from the 1940's.
All American Pictures — *Video Yesteryear*

Start the Revolution Without Me 1970
Comedy
79556 91 mins C B, V R, P
Gene Wilder, Donald Sutherland, Orson Welles, Hugh Griffith, Billie Whitelaw, directed by Bud Yorkin
Two sets of identical twins who were separated at birth meet thirty years later on the eve of the French Revolution.
MPAA:PG
Norman Lear; Warner Bros. — *Warner Home Video*

Start to Finish the Grand Prix 1981
Automobiles-Racing
68245 89 mins C B, V, CED P
The highlights of the 1981 Grand Prix are presented in this film.
Formula One Constructors Association — *MGM/UA Home Video*

Starting Over 1979
Comedy-Drama
48513 105 mins C B, V, LV R, P
Burt Reynolds, Jill Clayburgh, Candice Bergen
His life racked by divorce, Phil Potter learns what it's like to be single, self-sufficient, and lonely once again. When a blind date grows into a serious affair, the romance is temporarily halted by his hang-up for his ex-wife.
MPAA:R
Alan J. Pakula — *Paramount Home Video; RCA VideoDiscs*

Starvengers **1982**
Cartoons/Science fiction
62425 105 mins C B, V P
Animated
When action and excitement meet futuristic technology, the result is the high-powered super-intelligence of the robot Starvenger.
EL, SP
Toei Animation; Terry Production — *Family Home Entertainment*

State of Siege **1973**
Drama
44781 119 mins C B, V P
Yves Montand, Renato Salvatori, O.E. Hasse
Unsettling American foreign policy results in the assasination of U.S. officials in South America.
Cinema 5 — *RCA/Columbia Pictures Home Video*

State of the Union **1948**
Comedy
31603 124 mins B/W B, V P
Spencer Tracy, Katherine Hepburn, Angela Lansbury, Van Johnson, directed by Frank Capra
A presidential candidate, backed by a millionairess, battles for integrity with his wife.
MGM — *MCA Home Video*

Stations West **1948**
Mystery
10070 92 mins B/W B, V P, T
Dick Powell, Jane Greer, Agnes Moorehead, Burl Ives, Tom Powers, Raymond Burr
Disguised Army officer is sent to uncover mystery of hijackers and murderers.
RKO — *RKO HomeVideo; Blackhawk Films*

Stay as You Are **1978**
Drama
47371 103 mins C B, V R, P
Marcello Mastroianni, Nastassia Kinski, Francisco Rabal, Monica Randal
A sensual, psychological drama about an older man who finds himself attracted to a young girl—who may be his daughter by a long-forgotten mistress.
Giovanni Bertolucci — *Warner Home Video*

Stay Hungry **1976**
Comedy-Drama
80135 102 mins C B, V P
Jeff Bridges, Sally Field, Arnold Sahwarzenegger, directed by Bob Rafeison
When a rich, disenchanted southerner buys a health spa, he finds new happiness when he falls in love with the spa's receptionist.
MPAA:R
United Artists — *CBS/Fox Video*

Staying Alive **1983**
Drama
Closed Captioned
65400 96 mins C B, V, LV, CED R, P
John Travolta, Cynthia Rhodes, Finola Hughes
A talented young dancer struggles to obtain a role in a professional Broadway musical. Along the way, he becomes intimately involved with two attractive young women. In stereo VHS and Beta Hi-Fi.
MPAA:PG
Paramount — *Paramount Home Video*

Steam and Diesel on the Bessemer and Lake Erie/ The Diesels Roar on the Pennsy **195?**
Trains
59991 24 mins B/W B, V P, T
"Steam and Diesel" shows the contrast between steam and diesel trains during the transitional period, the twilight years of the B. and L.E. "Diesels Roar" features the five "Geeps" rolling east and the westbound "Duquesne."
Fred McLeod — *Blackhawk Films*

Steamboat Bill, Jr. **1928**
Comedy
10095 72 mins B/W B, V P, T
Buster Keaton, Ernest Torrence, Marion Byron, Tom Lewis
Student returns to father's Mississippi river boat. After many misadventures, he marries daughter of his father's rival.
United Artists; Schenk Keaton Prod — *Blackhawk Films; Discount Video Tapes; Video Dimensions; Video Yesteryear; Classic Video Cinema Collector's Club; See Hear Industries*

Steel **1980**
Drama
66608 100 mins C B, V, LV P
Construction workers on a mammoth skyscraper face insurmountable odds and strong opposition to the completion of the building.
MPAA:R
World Northal — *Vestron Video*

Steel Cowboy **1978**
Drama
70715 100 mins C B, V P
James Brolin, Rip Torn, Jennifer Warren, Strother Martin, Melanie Griffith, Lou Frizzell, directed by Harvey Laidman
With his marriage, sanity and livelihood all on the line, an independent trucker agrees to haul a hot herd of stolen steer.

Roger Gimbel Prod. for EMI Television Programs — *VCL Home Video*

Steel Fisted Dragon 1982
Martial arts
78390 85 mins C B, V R, P
Steve Lee, Johnny Kong Kong, Peter Chan
A son seeks revenge on the gang who murdered his mother and burned her house to the ground.
MPAA:R
Independent — *THORN EMI/HBO Video*

Steel Town Tough/Steelers 50 Seasons 1983
Football
66218 45 mins C B, V, FO P
The Pittsburgh Steelers' 1982-83 season highlights plus a retrospective of their first 50 years.
NFL Films — *NFL Films Video*

Steinbeck's The Pearl 1948
Drama/Literature-American
58732 90 mins B/W B, V P
Pedro Armandez, Maria Marques
John Steinbeck's classic novel concerning two people who find a valuable pearl which disrupts their lives. (Original screenplay by Steinbeck).
RKO — *Mastervision*

Stella Dallas 1937
Drama
81445 106 mins B/W B, V, LV P
Barbara Stanwyck, Anne Shirley, John Boles, Alan Hale, Marjorie Main, directed by King Vidor
A lower class woman must learn to let go of the daughter she loves so that she may have a better life.
Samuel Goldwyn — *Embassy Home Entertainment*

Step Lively 1944
Musical/Comedy
64916 88 mins B/W B, V P, T
Frank Sinatra, Gloria De Haven, George Murphy, Walter Slezak, Adolphe Menjou, Anne Jeffreys
A young playwright tries to recover the money he loaned to a fast-talking Broadway producer and is forced to take the leading role in his play. This musical remake of "Room Service" was Frank Sinatra's first starring role.
RKO — *RKO HomeVideo; Blackhawk Films*

Steve Allen Plymouth Show, The 1960
Comedy/Variety
69580 60 mins B/W B, V, FO P
Steve Allen, Patrice Munsel, Jonathan Winters, Phil Harris, Don Knotts, Bill Dana, Les Brown Orchestra
This March, 1960 TV special features a large cast of comedians and singers performing comedy sketches, movie spoofs and musical numbers. All original Plymouth commercials are included.
NBC — *Video Yesteryear*

Steve Miller Band 1983
Music-Performance
69391 50 mins C B, V R, P
This music video showcases one of America's premier rock bands live in concert and includes the hits "Abracadabra," "Rock 'n Me" and "Fly Like an Eagle," among others.
EMI Music — *THORN EMI/HBO Video*

Stevie Nicks in Concert 1982
Music-Performance
60572 56 mins C B, V, CED P
The song siren of Fleetwood Mac performs "Sara," "Stop Draggin' My Heart Around," "Edge of Seventeen," and more in this March 1982 solo concert featuring a back-up band comprised of Roy Bittan, Bob Glaub, Bobby Hall, Russ Kunkel, Benmont Tench, Waddy Wachtel, Sharon Celani, and Lori Perry. Stereo.
Marty Callner — *CBS/Fox Video; Pioneer Artists*

Stick 1985
Suspense
Closed Captioned
81197 109 mins C B, V P
Burt Reynolds, Candice Bergen, George Segal, Charles Durning, Dar Robinson, directed by Burt Reynolds
Stick is an ex-con who wants to start a new life for himself in Miami. Based upon the Elmore Leonard novel. Available in Hi-Fi Stereo for both formats.
MPAA:R
Universal; Jennings Lang — *MCA Home Video*

Sticks of Death 1984
Martial arts
79875 90 mins C B, V P
When a man is left near death by gangsters, his grandfather teaches him the ancient martial art of the sticks of death.
Fred Farguar; Dr. Frank Schlercio — *VCL Home Video*

Stiletto 1969
Crime-Drama
08523 101 mins C B, V P
Alex Cord, Britt Ekland, Patrick O'Neal, Joseph Wiseman, Barbara McNair, Roy Scheider
A young man is rescued from a mob by a Mafia gang leader after raping a young girl. Based on a novel by Harold Robbins.

MPAA:R
Avco Embassy; Norman Rosemont — *Embassy Home Entertainment*

Still of the Night **1982**
Suspense
66067 91 mins C B, V, CED P
Meryl Streep, Roy Scheider, directed by Robert Benton
A Hitchcock-style thriller about a psychiatrist infatuated with a mysterious woman who may or may not be a killer.
MPAA:PG
United Artists — *CBS/Fox Video*

Still Smokin' **1983**
Comedy
64937 91 mins C B, V R, P
Cheech Marin, Tommy Chong
Cheech and Chong travel to Amsterdam to raise funds for a bankrupt film festival group by hosting a dope-a-thon.
MPAA:R
Paramount — *Paramount Home Video*

Sting, The **1973**
Comedy-Drama
14009 129 mins C B, V, LV P
Paul Newman, Robert Redford, Robert Shaw, Charles Durning, Eileen Brennan, directed by George Roy Hill
A pair of con-artists in Chicago of the 1930's set out to fleece a big time racketeer, pitting brain against brawn and pistol.
Academy Awards '73: Best Picture; Best Story and Screenplay; Best Art Direction; Best Set Decoration. MPAA:PG
Universal; Richard D Zanuck — *MCA Home Video; RCA VideoDiscs*

Sting II, The **1983**
Comedy
64794 102 mins C B, V, LV, CED P
Jackie Gleason, Mac Davis, Teri Garr, Karl Malden, Oliver Reed, directed by Jeremy Paul Kagan
A complicated comic plot concludes with the final con game involving a fixed boxing match where the stakes top a million dollars and where the payoff could be murder. A sequel to "The Sting."
MPAA:PG
Universal — *MCA Home Video*

Stir Crazy **1980**
Comedy
58435 104 mins C B, V, LV P
Richard Pryor, Gene Wilder, Nicholas Coster, Lee Purcell, directed by Sidney Poitier
Two down-on-their luck losers find themselves convicted of a robbery they didn't commit and sentenced to 120 years behind bars with a mean assortment of inmates.
MPAA:R
Columbia; Hannah Weinstein — *RCA/Columbia Pictures Home Video; RCA VideoDiscs*

Stolen Kisses **1969**
Drama
44775 90 mins C B, V P
Jean-Pierre Leaud, Delphine Seyrig, directed by Francois Truffaut
A continuation of the story of Antoine Doinel (first told in the picture "The 400 Blows") and his dishonorable discharge from the army, his initially awkward, but finally successful adventures with women.
Lopert Pictures — *RCA/Columbia Pictures Home Video*

Stomach Formula **1984**
Physical fitness
74076 49 mins C B, V P
This is the official Richard Simmons seven-minute a day workout of abdominal fitness.
Karl Home Video — *Karl/Lorimar Home Video*

Stone Boy, The **1984**
Drama
Closed Captioned
77465 93 mins C B, V P
Glenn Close, Robert Duvall, Jason Presson
A twelve-year-old boy accidentally kills his older brother on their family's Montana farm, causing much unpleasantness.
MPAA:PG
20th Century Fox — *CBS/Fox Video*

Stone Cold Dead **1980**
Mystery
69306 100 mins C B, V P
Richard Crenna, Paul Williams, Linda Sorensen, Belinda J. Montgomery
A sniper who selects only prostitutes as victims baits the police with photographs of the victims at the moment of their deaths.
MPAA:R
George Mendeluk; John Ryan — *Media Home Entertainment*

Stone Killer, The **1973**
Drama
76039 95 mins C B, V P
Charles Bronson, Martin Balsam, Norman Fell, Ralph Waite
Charles Bronson stars as a tough plainclothes cop in this action-packed drama set in the underworld of New York and Los Angeles.
MPAA:R
Michael Winner — *RCA/Columbia Pictures Home Video*

Stoner 1980
Martial arts/Adventure
59083 88 mins C B, V P
A martial arts adventure featuring a showdown between special agents and a depraved crime lord.
Unknown — *HarmonyVision*

Stop That Train 195?
Adventure
10036 25 mins B/W B, V P, T
Kirby Grant, Gloria Winters, Perry Kellman, Edward Foster, William Hale
Escaped convict plants explosives aboard train with railway president on it. With ten minutes to spare, Sky King tries to make a rescue. From the TV series "Sky King."
CBS — *Blackhawk Films*

Stopover Tokyo 1957
War-Drama
80834 100 mins C B, V P
Robert Wagner, Joan Collins, Edmund O'Brien, Ken Scott
An American intelligence agent uncovers a plot to assassinate the American High Commissioner while on leave in Japan. Available in VHS and Beta Hi Fi Stereo.
20th Century Fox — *Key Video*

Stories and Fables—Volume 1 1984
Fairy tales
66355 40 mins C B, V R, P
This first volume of children's fables contains live-action versions of "Simpleton Peter" and "The Well of the World's End."
Walt Disney — *Walt Disney Home Video*

Stories and Fables—Volume 2 1984
Fairy tales
66356 40 mins C B, V R, P
The tales of "The Soldier Who Didn't Wash" and "The Five Loaves" are included in this volume of children's fables.
Walt Disney — *Walt Disney Home Video*

Stories and Fables—Volume 3 1984
Fairy tales
66357 40 mins C B, V R, P
Live-action versions of "The Forbidden Door" and "Cap O'Rushes" are featured in this volume of children's tales for the whole family.
Walt Disney — *Walt Disney Home Video*

Stories and Fables, Volume 4 1984
Fantasy/Fairy tales
72788 50 mins C B, V P
A tale about a lazy young man who successfully masquerades as a man of the Cloth until he has an unforeseen encounter with the King.
Walt Disney Productions — *Walt Disney Home Video*

Stories and Fables, Volume 5 1984
Fairy tales
72789 50 mins C B, V P
Two amusing stories that children might learn something from.
Walt Disney Productions — *Walt Disney Home Video*

Stories and Fables, Volume 6 1984
Fairy tales
72790 50 mins C B, V P
Two enchanting stories, "The Foolish Brother," and "The Twelve Months" are included; the first features an inept bandit and the latter tells the tale of a lovely young girl driven to perform incredible feats by her contempt for stepmother and sisters.
Walt Disney Productions — *Walt Disney Home Video*

Stories and Fables, Volume 7 1984
Fairy tales
70166 40 mins C B, V R, P
Animated
The stories of "Clever Manka" and "The Russian and the Tartar" are included in this seventh volume of children's fairy tales
Walt Disney Productions — *Walt Disney Home Video*

Stories and Fables, Volume 8 1984
Fairy tales
70165 40 mins C B, V R, P
Animated
The stories of "The Straw Hat" and "Moses and the Lime Kiln" are included in this eighth volume of children's fairy tales.
Walt Disney Productions — *Walt Disney Home Video*

Stories and Fables, Volume 9 1985
Fairy tales
76814 50 mins C B, V R, P
This volume features the story of "Morwen of the Woodlands" who's a wise old monk who tries to cast a happiness spell over a young couple and the tale of "Nikorima," a warrior who must protect his village from an enemy tribe.
Walt Disney Productions — *Walt Disney Home Video*

Stories and Fables, Volume 10 1985
Fairy tales
76815 50 mins C B, V R, P
The stories of "The Widow's Lazy Daughter" and "Hinemoa" are told in this volume.
Walt Disney Productions — *Walt Disney Home Video*

Stories and Fables, Volume 11 1985
Fairy tales
76819 50 mins C B, V R, P
This volume features the story about "The Emperor and the Abbott", where a clever shepherd saves his friend The Abbott from embarrassment and the tale of "The Pedlar's Dream," where a peddler learns to follow his dreams.
Walt Disney Productions — *Walt Disney Home Video*

Stork Club, The 1945
Musical/Comedy
66397 98 mins B/W B, V P
Betty Hutton, Barry Fitzgerald, Don Defore, Robert Benchley, Bill Goodwin
A nightclub hat-check girl saves an elderly millionaire from drowning and he gets her a job in a show.
Paramount — *Movie Buff Video*

Storm Boy 1980
Ethics/Children
52420 90 mins C B, V R, P
An Australian boy learns about life from an adopted pelican, an Aborigine, and his own father in this adaptation of the story by Colin Thiele.
AM Available
South Australian Film Corp — *Embassy Home Entertainment*

Storm Over Wyoming 1950
Western
73701 60 mins B/W B, V P
Tim Holt, Richard Martin
A range war in Wyoming between sheepmen and cattlemen is due to a crooked sheep ranch foreman.
RKO — *RKO HomeVideo*

Story in the Temple Red Lily 197?
Martial arts
21770 88 mins C B, V P
Insurrectionists capture the Prince and Princess of the Sung Dynasty and only one man can save them in this Kung Fu bonanza.
Foreign — *Master Arts Video*

Story of Adele H., The 1975
Drama
58252 97 mins C B, V R, P
Isabelle Adjani, Bruce Robinson, directed by Francois Truffaut
The story of Adele Hugo, daughter of Victor Hugo, who threw her life away in self-destructive love.
MPAA:PG
Lês Films du Carosse — *Warner Home Video*

Story of O, The 1975
Drama
58809 97 mins C B, V P
Corinne Clery, Anthony Steel, directed by Just Jaeckin
The story of a young woman whose love for one man moves her to surrender herself to many men, in order to please him. Based on the classic novel by Pauline Reage.
MPAA:X
Allied Artists — *Independent United Distributors; MGM/UA Home Video (disc only)*

Story of the Silent Serials, The/Girls in Danger 19??
Film-History
29499 54 mins B/W B, V P, T
Gloria Swanson, Mae Marsh, Wallace Beery
These two selections capture the best of more than fourteen silent serials. Featured are Gloria Swanson tied to the railroad tracks by Wallace Beery, Mae Marsh threatened with death (or worse) in caveman times, and other classic cliffhanger situations. Narration and muscial score.
Unknown — *Blackhawk Films*

Story of Vernon and Irene Castle, The 1939
Musical
00274 93 mins B/W B, V, 3/4U P
Fred Astaire, Ginger Rogers
In this, their last film together, Astaire and Rogers portray two internationally successful ballroom dancers.
RKO — *Nostalgia Merchant*

Story of William S. Hart, The/The Sad Clowns 192?
Comedy
10102 50 mins B/W B, V P, T
William S. Hart, Charlie Chaplin, Buster Keaton, Harry Langdon
Featuring William S. Hart as a cowboy in "Hell's Hinges," and Chaplin in "Tumbleweeds," (1925). From "The History of the Motion Picture" series.
United Artists et al — *Blackhawk Films*

Storytime Classics 1983
Fairy tales
77183 78 mins C B, V P
A collection of popular faily tales narrated by Katherine Hepburn.
World of Stories Limited — *Vestron Video*

Storytime Classics: Rudyard Kipling's Just So Stories Vol. 1 1982
Fairy tales/Cartoons
80704 34 mins C B, V P
Animated
An animated adaptation of the Rudyard Kipling stories that explain "How the Camel Got His Hump" and "How the Elephant Got His Trunk".
Jouve Films — *Vestron Video*

Straight Time 1978
Drama
58253 114 mins C B, V R, P
Dustin Hoffman, Harry Dean Stanton, Gary Busey, Theresa Russell, M. Emmet Walsh, directed by Ulu Grosbard
An ex-convict hits the streets for the first time in six years and finds he is emotionally locked into a life of crime.
MPAA:R
Sweetwall Productions; First Artists Productions; Warner Bros — *Warner Home Video*

Strait Jacket 1964
Drama
64912 89 mins B/W B, V P
Joan Crawford, Leif Erickson, Diane Baker
After a woman is released from an insane asylum where she was sent 20 years earlier for killing her husband and his mistress, mysterious axe murders begin to occur in the neighborhood, and she is the prime suspect.
William Castle — *RCA/Columbia Pictures Home Video*

Strange And Deadly Occurence 1974
Drama
81417 74 mins C B, V P
Robert Stack, Vera Miles, L.Q. Jones, Herb Edelman
Strange things start to happen to a family when they move to a house in a remote area.
Worldvision; Alpine Productions, NBC — *Worldvision Home Video*

Strange Case of Dr. Jekyll and Mr. Hyde, The 1968
Horror
81037 128 mins C B, V P
Jack Palance, Leo Genn, Oscar Homolka, Billie Whitelaw, Denholm Elliott, directed by Charles Jarrot
This is an adaptation of the classic Robert Louis Stevenson book about a scientist who conducts experiments on himself to separate good from evil. Available in Beta Hi-Fi and VHS Stereo.
Dan Curtis Productions — *Thriller Video*

Strange Invaders 1983
Satire/Science fiction
65364 94 mins C B, V, LV P
Nancy Allen, Diana Scarwid, Louise Fletcher
The horrific and subtly humorous story of alien beings whose settlement in a small midwestern town is disturbed by a young professor determined to rescue his child from their clutches.
MPAA:PG
Walter Coblenz — *Vestron Video*

Strange Love of Martha Ivers, The 1946
Drama
66398 117 mins B/W B, V P
Barbara Stanwyck, Van Heflin, Kirk Douglas, Lisabeth Scott, Judith Anderson, directed by Lewis Milestone
An unscrupulous woman takes up with her old boyfriend, without bothering to keep the affair from her husband.
Paramount — *Movie Buff Video; Kartes Productions*

Strange Shadows in an Empty Room 1976
Mystery/Suspense
80700 97 mins C B, V P
Stuart Whitman, John Saxon, Martin Landau, Tisa Farrow, Carole Laure, Gayle Hunnicut
A veteran detective finds out some startling facts about his murdered sister during his investigation of the crime.
MPAA:R
American International Pictures — *Vestron Video*

Strangeness, The 198?
Horror
75626 90 mins C B, V P
Miners release a creature while searching for golden treasures.
unknown — *Trans World Entertainment*

Stranger, The 1946
Mystery
11318 85 mins B/W B, V, FO P
Edward G. Robinson, Loretta Young, Orson Welles, Richard Long, directed by Orson Welles
A government agent is assigned to the manhunt of a Nazi from Hitler's regime who has taken the new identity of a history professor about to marry the daughter of a Supreme Court Judge.
RKO — *Prism; Video Yesteryear; Movie Buff Video; Budget Video; VCII; Discount Video Tapes; Sheik Video; Cable Films; Kartes*

Productions; Classic Video Cinema Collector's Club

Stranger and the Gunfighter, The **1976**
Martial arts
Closed Captioned
73862 106 mins C B, V P
Lee Van Cleef, Lo Lieh
A western gunfighter and an Oriental master of martial arts team up to find a stolen Chinese fortune. Available in Beta Hi-Fi.
Carlo Ponti — *RCA/Columbia Pictures Home Video*

Stranger from Venus **1954**
Science fiction
44354 78 mins B/W B, V, 3/4U P
Patricia Neal, Helmet Dantine, Derek Bond
A frightening being from outerspace lands to warn Earth and pave the way for the arrival of a "mother ship." Includes previews of coming attractions from classic science fiction films.
Eros — *Nostalgia Merchant*

Stranger Is Watching, A **1982**
Horror
59847 92 mins C B, V, CED P
Rip Torn, Kate Mulgrew
A rapist-murderer holds the victim's 10-year-old daughter hostage, along with a New York TV anchorwoman.
MPAA:R
MGM — *MGM/UA Home Video*

Stranger on the Third Floor **1940**
Mystery
10065 64 mins B/W B, V P, T
Peter Lorre, John McGuire, Elisha Cook Jr.
Innocent man, released from prison, seeks his persecutors with a vengeance. Someone set him up, but who?
RKO — *Blackhawk Films; Nostalgia Merchant*

Stranger Who Cooks Like Me, The **1974**
Drama
77148 74 mins C B, V P
Meredith Baxter-Birney, Beau Bridges, Whitney Blake
An adopted girl and boy set out to find their real parents.
Filmways — *Worldvision Home Video*

Stranger's Gold **1971**
Western
80796 90 mins C B, V R, P
John Garko, Antonio Vilar, Daniela Giordano
A mysterious gunslinger eliminates corruption in a western mining town.
Phillip Yordan — *Video Gems*

Stranger's Kiss **1983**
Drama
72185 93 mins C B, V R, P
The director of a 1955 Hollywood movie encourages the two leads to have an off-screen romance to bring reality to his film. Conflict arises when the leading lady's boyfriend, the films financier, gets wind of the scheme.
MPAA:R
Douglas Dilge — *THORN EMI/HBO Video*

Strangers on a Train **1951**
Drama/Suspense
69309 101 mins B/W B, V R, P
Farley Granger, Robert Walker, Ruth Roman, Leo G. Carroll, directed by Alfred Hitchcock
A demented playboy entangles a tennis star in a bizarre scheme of "exchange murders."
Warner Bros — *Warner Home Video; RCA VideoDiscs*

Strangers: The Story of a Mother and Daughter **1979**
Drama
80674 88 mins C B, V P
Bette Davis, Gena Rowlands, Ford Rainey, Donald, Moffat, directed by Milton Katselas
A woman returns home to a New England fishing village after twenty years to settle the differences between herself and her mother.
Emmy Award '79: Outstanding Lead Actress in a Limited Series or Special (Davis)
Chris/Rose Prods. — *Lightning Video*

Straw Dogs **1972**
Drama
46200 114 mins C B, V, LV, CED P
Dustin Hoffman, Susan George, Peter Vaughan, T. P. McKenna, directed by Sam Peckinpah
An American mathematician, disturbed by the predominance of violence in American society, moves with his wife to an isolated Cornish village only to find a primitive savagery beneath the peaceful surface.
MPAA:R
ABC Pictures Corp. — *CBS/Fox Video*

Strawberry Shortcake in Big Apple City **1982**
Cartoons
60393 60 mins C B, V P
Animated
Strawberry Shortcake and her friends from Strawberryland meet new friends in Big Apple City.
EL, SP
Miller Rosen Productions — *Family Home Entertainment*

Strawberry Shortcake Meets the BerryKins 1983
Cartoons
80972 60 mins C B, V P
Animated
Strawberry Shortcake welcomes her new friends 'the BerryKins, who are responsible for the aromas of the fruits and flowers of strawberryland. Available in VHS Stereo and Beta Hi Fi.
Miller Rosen Productions — *Family Home Entertainment*

Strawberry Shortcake Pets on Parade 1982
Cartoons
65656 60 mins C B, V P
Animated
Strawberry Shortcake is named judge of a Pet Show and the first prize is a shiny new tricycle, and the Peculiar Purple Pieman of Porcupine Peak plots to swipe it. But Strawberry and her friends teach the Pieman a lesson he won't soon forget.
Miller Rosen Productions — *Family Home Entertainment*

Strawberry Shortcake's House-Warming Party 1983
Cartoons
69582 60 mins C B, V P
Animated
Strawberry Shortcake and her friends in Strawberryland have a house-warming party.
Miller Rosen Productions — *Family Home Entertainment*

Strawberry Statement, The 1970
Drama
80631 109 mins C B, V P
Kim Darby, Bruce Davidson, Bud Cort, James Coco, Kristina Holland, Bob Balaban, David Dukes
A campus radical convinces a college student to participate in the student strikes on campus during the 60's. The soundtrack features songs by Neil Young, Buffy Sainte-Marie.
MPAA:R
MGM — *MGM/UA Home Video*

Streamers 1983
War-Drama
66602 118 mins C B, V P
Matthew Modine, Michael Wright, Mitchell Lichenstein
Six young soldiers in a claustrophobic army barracks tensely await the orders that will send them to Vietnam. Based on the play by David Rabe.
MPAA:R
Robert Altman; Nick J. Mileti — *Media Home Entertainment*

Street Fighter, The 1975
Adventure/Martial arts
54106 85 mins C B, V, CED P
Sonny Chiba
Local hoodlum engages in fast-paced marital arts action.
MPAA:R
Unknown — *CBS/Fox Video*

Street Law 1979
Crime-Drama
65727 77 mins C B, V P
Franco Nero
A vivid and violent study of one man's frustrated ware on crime.
MPAA:R
Unknown — *VidAmerica*

Street Music 1981
Comedy/Romance
77176 88 mins C B, V, CED P
Larry Breeding, Elizabeth Daily, Ned Glass
A young couple residing in an old hotel organize a protest to save the building from being closed down.
Pacificon Productions — *Vestron Video*

Street People 1976
Drama
80679 92 mins C B, V P
Roger Moore, Stacy Keach, Ivo Gassani, Entore Manni
A Mafia godfather asks a lawyer and a race car driver to find out who smuggled a three-million dollar shipment of heroin inside of an Italian crucifix.
MPAA:R
American International Pictures — *Vestron Video*

Streetcar Named Desire, A 1951
Drama
Closed Captioned
58949 122 mins B/W B, V P
Vivien Leigh, Marlon Brando, Kim Hunter, Karl Malden, directed by Elia Kazan
Powerful film version of Tennessee Williams' play about a repressed southern widow who is abused and driven mad by her brutal brother-in-law.
Academy Awards '51: Best Actress (Leigh); Best Supporting Actress (Hunter); Best Supporting Actor (Malden).
Charles K Feldman; Elia Kazan — *CBS/Fox Video; Warner Home Video; RCA VideoDiscs*

Streets of Fire 1984
Musical-Drama/Fantasy
Closed Captioned
79679 93 mins C B, V, LV P
Michael Pare, Diane Lane, Rick Moranis, Amy Madigan, directed by Walter Hill

A soldier of fortune rescues a famous rock singer after she's kidnapped by a motorcycle gang.
Lawrence Gordon; Joel Silver — *MCA Home Video*

Strike Force 1984
Crime-Drama
70726 90 mins C B, V P
Robert Stack, Dorian Harewood, Herb Edelman
The jurors on an embezzlement case turn up bloody and headless around town, so a special criminal strike force is brought in to solve the murders.
Metromedia; Aaron Spelling/Douglas Cramer — *Active Home Video*

Strike Up The Band 1940
Musical/Comedy
80622 120 mins B/W B, V P
Judy Garland, Mickey Rooney, Paul Whiteman, William Tracy, June Preisser, directed by Busby Berkeley
A high school band turns to hot swing music and enters a national radio contest. Songs include "I Ain't Got Nobody," "Our Love Affair," "Drummer Boy" and "Do The Conga!"
Academy Awards '40: Best Sound Recording.
MGM; Arthur Freed — *MGM/UA Home Video*

Stripes 1981
Comedy
Closed Captioned
05938 105 mins C B, V P
Bill Murray, Harold Ramis, P. J. Soles, Warren Oates, John Candy, directed by Ivan Reitman
Two friends enlist in the Army to straighten out their lives.
MPAA:R
Columbia — *RCA/Columbia Pictures Home Video; RCA VideoDiscs*

Stripes 1982
Football
47709 23 mins C B, V, FO P
Team highlights of the '81 Bengals, who posted a 12-4 regular season record and won their first AFC Championship.
NFL Films — *NFL Films Video*

Stroker Ace 1983
Comedy
69308 96 mins C B, V, CED R, P
Burt Reynolds, Ned Beatty, Jim Nabors, Parker Stevenson, Loni Anderson
A flamboyant stock car driver tries to break an iron-clad promotional contract signed with a greedy fried-chicken magnate.
MPAA:PG
Warner Bros — *Warner Home Video*

Stromboli 1950
Drama
80661 81 mins B/W B, V P
Ingrid Bergman, Mario Vitale, Renzo Cesana, directed by Roberto Rossellini
An unhappy and homeless girl marries a poor Sicillian hoping to escape her plight, but finds herself imprisoned when the couple moves to a desert island.
RKO Radio Pictures — *United Home Video*

Strong Kids, Safe Kids 1984
Child abuse/Safety education
79180 42 mins C B, V, LV R, P
Animated
Henry Winkler, along with the Smurfs and The Flintstones, teaches parents and children the skills that are necessary to prevent sexual abuse.
Paramount; Fair Dinkum — *Paramount Home Video*

Struggle Through Death 197?
Martial arts
72175 93 mins C B, V P
Two young men escape the clutches of evil Ching Kue and attempt to free their fellow prisoners so they can overthrow the despot.
Foreign — *Master Arts Video*

Stryker 1983
Science fiction
69542 86 mins C B, V P
Steve Sandor, Andria Fabio
In the future, after a devastating war, bands of marauders fight each other for the scarcest resource—water.
MPAA:R
Cirio H Santiago — *Embassy Home Entertainment*

Stuck on You 1984
Comedy
78639 90 mins C B, V P
Irwin Corey
A couple engaged in a palimony suit takes their case to a judge to work out their differences.
MPAA:R
Troma Inc — *Embassy Home Entertainment*

Stuckey's Last Stand 1978
Comedy
80667 95 mins C B, V P
Whit Reichert, Tom Murray, Rich Casentino
A group of camp counselors prepare to take twenty-two children on a nature hike that they will never forget.
MPAA:PG
Lawrence G. Goldfarb — *Lightning Video*

Stud, The 1978
Drama
47801 90 mins C B, V R, P
Joan Collins, Oliver Tobias
The owner of a fashionable "after hours" dance spot hires a young, handsome stud to manage the club and attend to her personal needs.
MPAA:R
Brent Walker Film Productions — *THORN EMI/HBO Video*

Student Bodies 1981
Satire
58717 86 mins C B, V, LV R, P
Kristen Riter, Matthew Goldsby, Richard Brando, Joe Flood, directed by Mickey Rose
A spoof of high-school horror films a la "Halloween."
MPAA:R
Paramount — *Paramount Home Video*

Student Teachers, The 1977
Comedy
80774 79 mins C B, V P
Three attractive faculty members decide to spice up the campus life at Valley High.
Indepedent — *Embassy Home Entertainment*

Studio One: "The Defender" 1957
Drama
38124 104 mins B/W B, V, FO P
Steve McQueen, William Shatner, Ralph Bellamy, Martin Balsam
Courtroom melodrama originally televised live on the "Studio One" series in 1957.
CBS — *Video Yesteryear*

Study in Scarlet, A 1933
Mystery
48428 77 mins B/W B, V P
Reginald Owen, Alan Mowbray, Anna May Wong
Master sleuth Sherlock Holmes solves a series of complex murders with the aid of faithful companion Dr. Watson.
World Wide — *Budget Video; Cable Films; Video Yesteryear; Discount Video Tapes*

Stunt Man, The 1981
Drama/Satire
49398 129 mins C CED P
Peter O'Toole, Steve Railsback, Barbara Hershey, directed by Richard Bush
A satire on the world of moviemaking, in which an ex-Vietnam soldier-turned-stunt-man stages a battle of wits with a power-crazed movie director.
MPAA:R
20th Century Fox — *CBS/Fox Video*

Stunt Rock 1980
Adventure
66009 90 mins C B, V P
A feature film combining rock music, magic, and some of the most incredible stunts ever attempted.
MPAA:PG
Intertamar — *Monterey Home Video*

Stunts 1977
Adventure
66185 90 mins C B, V R, P
Robert Forster, Fiona Lewis
A film dealing with the thrilling and often horrifying lives of professional stuntmen.
New Line Cinema — *THORN EMI/HBO Video*

Style Council Far East and Far Out, The 1984
Music-Performance
78368 60 mins C B, V P
The unique sounds of The Style Council are captured in this concert taped in Japan.
Polygram Music Video Limited — *Music Media*

Styx—Caught in the Act 1984
Music-Performance
70187 87 mins C B, V P
Directed by Jerry Kramer
The rock group Styx is featured in a concert performance of some of their biggest hits, including "Too Much Time on My Hands," "Don't Let It End," "Best of Times," "Come Sail Away" and "Renegade. In Beta Hi-Fi Stereo and VHS Hi-Fi Dolby Stereo.
A & M Video — *A & M Video; RCA/Columbia Pictures Home Video*

Submission 1977
Drama
80284 107 mins C B, V P
Franco Nero, Lisa Gastoni
A pharmacist's sensuality is reawakened when she has a provacative affair with a clerk in her shop.
MPAA:R
Joseph Brenner Associates — *Prism*

Subterfuge 1968
Drama
65685 89 mins C B, V P
Joan Collins, Gene Barry, Richard Todd
When a special American security agent goes to England for a "vacation," his presence causes speculation and poses several serious questions for both British Intelligence and the underworld.
Commonwealth United TV — *Republic Pictures Home Video*

(For explanation of codes, see USE GUIDE and KEY)

Suburbia 1983
Drama
79313 99 mins C B, V P
Directed by Penelope Speeris
When a group of punk rockers move into a condemned suburban development, they become the targets of a viglante group.
MPAA:R
New Horizon Pictures — *Vestron Video*

Sudden Death 1977
Adventure
59041 84 mins C B, V P
Robert Conrad, Felton Perry
Two professional violence merchants put themselves up for hire.
Topar Films — *Media Home Entertainment*

Sudden Impact 1983
Crime-Drama/Adventure
Closed Captioned
65613 117 mins C B, V, LV, CED R, P
Clint Eastwood, Sondra Locke
"Dirty Harry" Callahan tracks down a revenge-obsessed murderess at the same time that local mobsters come gunning for him.
MPAA:R
Clint Eastwood; Warner Brothers — *Warner Home Video*

Suddenly Last Summer 1959
Drama
65701 114 mins B/W B, V, CED P
Katharine Hepburn, Elizabeth Taylor, Montgomery Cliff
A psychiatrist tries to solve the mystery behind a young girl's mental breakdown. Based on the play by Tennessee Williams.
Sam Spiegel — *RCA/Columbia Pictures Home Video*

Sugar Cookies 1977
Drama
52952 89 mins C B, V P
Lynn Lowry, Monique Van Vooren
An erotic horror story in which young women are the pawns as a satanic satyr and an impassioned lesbian play out a bizarre game of vengeance, love, and death.
MPAA:R
Lloyd Kaufman — *VidAmerica*

Sugar Ray Robinson—Pound for Pound 1982
Boxing
58735 120 mins C B, V P
Sugar Ray Robinson, Jake LaMotta, Bobo Olsen, Randy Turpin, Carmen Basilio
The career of legendary boxer Sugar Ray Robinson is highlighted, from his earliest amateur bouts through his memorable retirement at Madison Square Garden. Some sequences are in black and white.
Big Fights Inc — *VidAmerica*

Sugarland Express, The 1974
Drama
65119 109 mins C B, V P
Goldie Hawn, Ben Johnson, Michael Sacks, William Atherton, directed by Steven Spielberg
To save her son from adoption, a young woman helps her husband break out of prison. In their flight to freedom, they hijack a police car, holding the policeman hostage.
MPAA:PG
Universal — *MCA Home Video*

Summer Camp 1978
Comedy
59659 85 mins C B, V P
John C. McLaughlin, Matt Michaels, Colleen O'Neil
A ten year reunion at a summer camp turns into a bizarre weekend of co-ed football, midnight panty-raids, coupling couples and a wild disco party.
MPAA:R
Mark Borde — *Media Home Entertainment*

Summer Heat 1973
Drama
55594 71 mins C B, V P
Bob Garry, Nicole Avril, Pat Pascal
A no-holds-barred tour through the steamy world of the rich, the restless, and the young, when a young man spends his summer with his hypnotic aunt.
MPAA:X
World Wide Films Corp — *VidAmerica*

Summer in St. Tropez, A 1981
Drama
59698 60 mins C B, V R, P
Photographer David Hamilton's erotic and lyrical study of a household of girls in their first stages of womanhood living outside of society in the south of France.
Ken Kamura — *THORN EMI/HBO Video*

Summer Lovers 1982
Drama
63372 98 mins C B, V, LV, CED P
Peter Gallagher, Daryl Hannah, Valerie Quennessen
Three young people meet on the exotic Greek island of Santorini one summer to explore life and love.
MPAA:R
Filmways — *Embassy Home Entertainment*

Summer Magic 1963
Drama
76824 116 mins C B, V R, P
Hayley Mills, Burl Ives, Dorothy McGuire, Deborah Walley, Una Merkel, Eddie Hodges
A young girl plots to resettle her family in a tiny New England village after financial disaster strikes the household.
Walt Disney Productions — *Walt Disney Home Video*

Summer of Fear 1978
Horror
66017 94 mins C B, V R, P
Linda Blair
A happy young woman must overcome the evil forces brought on when her cousin comes to live with her.
Max A Keller; Micheline H Keller — *THORN EMI/HBO Video*

Summer of '42 1971
Drama
54117 102 mins C B, V R, P
Jennifer O'Neill, Gary Grimes, Jerry Houser, Oliver Conant, directed by Richard Mulligan
A touching story about a 15-year-old boy's coming of sexual age during his summer vacation on an island off New England. While his two friends are fumbling with girls their own age, he falls in love with a beautiful older woman.
Academy Award '71: Best Musical Score.
MPAA:R
Warner Bros, Mulligan Roth — *Warner Home Video; RCA VideoDiscs*

Summer of Secrets 1985
Horror
77007 100 mins C B, V P
A young couple get more than they bargained for when they make love in a demented doctor's beach house.
MPAA:PG
Australian — *VidAmerica*

Summer School 1977
Comedy
80724 80 mins C B, V P
John McLaughlin, Steve Rose, Phoebe Schmidt
A teenaged boy's girlfriend will stop at nothing to prevent him from going out with the pretty new girl in town.
MPAA:R
Colleen Meeker — *Active Home Video*

Summer Solstice 1981
Drama
59696 75 mins C B, V R, P
Henry Fonda, Myrna Loy, Lindsey Crouse, Stephen Collins
An aging couple visits the beach where they first met. There they recapture many of the good and difficult times from the past.
Bruce Marson; Stephen Schlow — *THORN EMI/HBO Video*

Summerdog 1979
Adventure
29237 90 mins C B, V R, P
James Congdon, Elizabeth Eisenman
The Norman family rescues an abandoned little dog named Hobo from a raccoon trap while they're vacationing in the mountains. In return Hobo saves them from one danger after another.
MPAA:G
GG Communications — *Video Gems*

Summer's Children 1984
Mystery/Suspense
76945 90 mins C B, V P
Tom Haoff, Paully Jardine, Kate Lynch
A man who suffers from amnesia during a car crash becomes the target of a mysterious killer.
Independent — *Trans World Entertainment*

Summertime 1955
Drama/Romance
81447 98 mins C B, V P
Katherine Hepburn, Rossano Brazzi, Darren Mc Gavin, directed by David Lean
A spinster secretary meets and falls in love with a married man while on vacation in Venice.
United Artists; Ilya Lopert — *Embassy Home Entertainment*

Sunburn 1979
Comedy
38936 110 mins C B, V R, P
Farrah Fawcett-Majors, Charles Grodin, Joan Collins
Action-packed comedy-mystery of an investigation into the violent death of an aging Acapulco industrialist.
MPAA:PG
Paramount — *Paramount Home Video*

Sundance and the Kid 1976
Western
66195 84 mins C B, V P
John Wade, Karen Blake
Two brothers try to collect an inheritance against all odds.
MPAA:PG
Film Ventures International — *Monterey Home Video*

Sunday Bloody Sunday 1971
Drama
70247 110 mins C B, V P
Glenda Jackson, Peter Finch, and Murray Head, directed by John Schlesinger

A bisexual love triangle between a designer, a doctor, and an executive. Sensitive treatment of controversial subject with attention to sociological details.
MPAA:R
United Artists; Vectia — *Key Video*

Sunday Too Far Away 1974
Drama
80776 100 mins C B, V P
The rivalries between Australian sheep shearers and graziers leads to an ugly strike.
Gil Brealey; Matt Carroll — *Embassy Home Entertainment*

Sundown 1941
War-Drama
11395 91 mins B/W B, V, FO P
Gene Tierney, Bruce Cabot, George Sanders, Harry Carey, Sir Cedric Hardwicke
A Eurasian girl helps the British uncover a Nazi plot in the African desert with her camel caravan.
United Artists; Walter Wanger — *Video Yesteryear; Movie Buff Video; Discount Video Tapes; Kartes Productions*

Sunningdale Mystery, The 1985
Mystery/Drama
70662 60 mins C B, V P
James Warwick, Francesca Annis
In this chapter of the "Partners in Crime" series, the Beresfords use their keen minds to prove the innocence of an accused murderess.
Unknown — *Pacific Arts Video*

Sunrise at Campobello 1960
Biographical/Drama
77269 143 mins C B, V P
Ralph Bellamy, Greer Garson, Hume Cronyn, Jean Hagen, directed by Vincent J. Donehue
An adaptation of the Tony award winning play that chronicles Franklin D. Roosevelt's battle to conquer polio and ultimately receive the Democratic presidental nomination in 1924.
Warner Bros — *Warner Home Video*

Sunset Boulevard 1950
Drama
38605 110 mins B/W B, V R, P
Gloria Swanson, William Holden, Erich von Stroheim, Nancy Olsen, directed by Billy Wilder
Famed tale of Norma Desmond, aging silent film queen, who, refusing to accept the fact that stardom has ended for her, hires a young screenwriter to help engineer her movie comeback.
Academy Awards '50: Best Story and Screenplay (Wilder, Charles Brackett, D.M. Marshman); Best Music Score (Franz Waxman).
Paramount — *Paramount Home Video; RCA VideoDiscs*

Sunset on the Desert 1942
Western
78093 53 mins B/W B, V, FO P
Roy Rogers, George Hayes, Trigger, Lynne Carver
A man returns to his hometown after ten years' absence in order to help his father's old partner.
Republic — *Video Yesteryear*

Sunset Serenade 1942
Western
05548 60 mins B/W B, V, 3/4U P
Roy Rogers, Trigger, Gabby Hayes, Helen Parrish
Roy Rogers outwits a murderous duo who plans to eliminate the new heir to a ranch.
Republic — *Nostalgia Merchant*

Sunshine Boys, The 1975
Comedy
54103 109 mins C B, V, CED P
George Burns, Walter Matthau, Richard Benjamin, Lee Meredith, Carol Arthur, directed by Herbert Ross
After a long separation, two veteran vaudeville partners, who have shared a hate-love relationship for decades, reunite to renew their friendship and their feud.
Academy Awards '75: Best Supporting Actor (Burns). MPAA:PG
MGM; Ray Stark — *MGM/UA Home Video*

Sunspot Vacations for Winter 1985
Travel
80468 90 mins C B, V P
Hosted by David Earle
This program helps travelers to select a vacation spot by exploring the diverse and unique attributes of many famous resort areas, including Hawaii, Mexico, the Bahamas, the Dominican Republic, Barbados, Puerto Rico, St. Maarten and St. Vincent
Videotakes — *Videotakes*

Super Bowl I 1980
Football
45108 30 mins C B, V, FO R, P
Narrated by John Facenda, Green Bay Packers, Oakland Raiders
Vince Lombardi's mighty Packers subdue Hank Stram's Chiefs in the first meeting between AFL and NFL Champions. Veteran quarterback Bart Starr and aging receiver Max McGee spark the Packers as they pull away in the second half of the 1967 game.
NFL Films — *NFL Films Video*

Super Bowl II **1980**
Football
45109 30 mins C B, V, FO R, P
Narrated by John Facenda, Green Bay Packers, Oakland Raiders
The Packers romp to their second straight Super Bowl triumph, 33-14, in Vince Lombardi's last game as Packer head coach, played in 1968.
NFL Films — *NFL Films Video*

Super Bowl III **1980**
Football
45110 30 mins C B, V, FO R, P
Narrated by John Facenda, New York Jets, Baltimore Colts
1969: Joe Namath, the flashy young Jet's quarterback, guarantees a victory for his side and produces. Namath connects with receiver George Sauer and Don Maynard in key situations. The Jets' secondary intercepts four passes from Earl Morrow and John Unitas. Matt Snell's seven-yard touchdown run and Jim Turner's three field goals give the Jets a 16-7 victory in one of the greatest upsets in sports history.
NFL Films — *NFL Films Video*

Super Bowl Chronicles **1984**
Football
75889 23 mins C B, V, FO P
This program features an elaborate production of highlights from the Super Bowls of the past 18 years.
NFL Films — *NFL Films Video*

Super Bowl IV **1980**
Football
45111 30 mins C B, V, FO R, P
Narrated by John Facenda, Kansas City Chiefs, Minnesota Vikings
1970: Coach Hank Stram's "Offense of the 70's," led by quarterback Len Dawson and flanker Otis Taylor, confuses the Viking defense. The Chief's defensive crew stifles quarterback Joe Kapp and the Viking offense. It adds up to a 23-7 victory for Kansas City.
NFL Films — *NFL Films Video*

Super Bowl V **1980**
Football
45112 30 mins C B, V, FO R, P
Narrated by John Facenda, Baltimore Colts, Dallas Cowboys
1971: A game "highlighted" by bobbles, mistakes, and a questionable ruling on a Baltimore touchdown pass, is brought to a heart-stopping climax when the Colt's Jim O'Brien boots a 33-yard field goal with just six seconds to play, giving the ecstatic Baltimore team a 16-13 win.
NFL Films — *NFL Films Video*

Super Bowl VI **1980**
Football
45113 30 mins C B, V, FO R, P
Narrated by John Facenda, Dallas Cowboys, Miami Dolphins
1972: Dallas' "Doomsday Defense" shuts down the aerial game of Miami quarterback Bob Griese and the running of fullback Larry Csonka. Coach Tom Landry's team finally wins "the big one," 24-3. Roger Staubach and Duane Thomas lead the Cowboy attack.
NFL Films — *NFL Films Video*

Super Bowl VII **1980**
Football
45114 30 mins C B, V, FO R, P
Narrated by John Facenda, Miami Dolphins, Washington Redskins
1973: The Dolphins cap a perfect 17-0 season as the "No-Name Defense" holds the Redskin offense scoreless in a 14-7 triumph.
NFL Films — *NFL Films Video*

Super Bowl VIII **1980**
Football
45115 30 mins C B, V, FO R, P
Narrated by John Facenda, Miami Dolphins, Minnesota Vikings
The Dolphins cruise to their second straight championship as Larry Csonka runs all over the Vikings' "Purple People Eaters," and the Dolphin defense contains Vikes' quarterback Fran Tarkenton, in this 1974 game.
NFL Films — *NFL Films Video*

Super Bowl IX **1980**
Football
45116 30 mins C B, V, FO R, P
Narrated by John Facenda, Pittsburgh Steelers, Minnesota Vikings
The Steelers, led by Terry Bradshaw, Franco Harris, and the "Steel Curtain" defense dominate this game and the Vikings are disappointed for the third time in three Super Bowl tries (1975).
NFL Films — *NFL Films Video*

Super Bowl X **1980**
Football
45117 30 mins C B, V, FO R, P
Narrated by John Facenda, Pittsburgh Steelers, Dallas Cowboys
1976: Terry Bradshaw and Lynn Swan team up to lead the Steelers over the Cowboys 21-17 and capture their second consecutive Super Bowl Championship. A late rally by Roger Staubach and his Dallas mates falls short.
NFL Films — *NFL Films Video*

Super Bowl XI **1980**
Football
45118 30 mins C B, V, FO R, P

(For explanation of codes, see USE GUIDE and KEY)

Narrated by John Facenda, Oakland Raiders, Minnesota Vikings
1977: Quarterback Ken Stabler leads the Raiders over the Vikings 32-14 as Minnesota once again fails to win their fourth Super Bowl effort.
NFL Films — *NFL Films Video*

Super Bowl XII **1980**
Football
45119 30 mins C B, V, FO R, P
Narrated by John Facenda, Dallas Cowboys, Denver Broncos
1978: The awesome Dallas pass rush forces Denver quarterback Craig Morton into numerous interceptions. The Cowboy's offense sputters at times, but capitalizes on enough breaks for a 27-13 victory.
NFL Films — *NFL Films Video*

Super Bowl XIII **1980**
Football
45120 30 mins C B, V, FO R, P
Narrated by John Facenda, Pittsburgh Steelers, Dallas Cowboys
In the first Super Bowl offensive explosion by both teams, the Cowboys rally from eighteen points behind with Roger Staubach at the helm. Fortunately for the Steelers, Terry Bradshaw has put enough points on the board already, and Pittsburgh has their third championship, by a 35-31 score, in the 1979 game.
NFL Films — *NFL Films Video*

Super Bowl XIV **1980**
Football
45121 30 mins C B, V, FO R, P
Narrated by John Facenda, Pittsburgh Steelers, Los Angeles Rams
1980: The World Champion Steelers were supposed to be too much for the supposed bunch of glamour boys from Los Angeles, who were making their first-ever Super Bowl appearance after years of frustration. The Rams proved to be more than worthy opponent however, and even outplayed the Steelers for three quarters until some late heroics by Terry Bradshaw and John Stallworth saved them from embarrassment.
NFL Films — *NFL Films Video*

Super Bowl XV **1981**
Football
50646 24 mins C B, V, FO R, P
Narrated by John Facenda, Oakland Raiders, Philadelphia Eagles
The Oakland Raiders, a non-playoff team the previous year, are led by quarterback Jim Plunkett and a nasty defense to a 27-10 Super Bowl victory over the NFC's best, the Philadelphia Eagles.
NFL Films — *NFL Films Video*

Super Bowl XVI **1982**
Football
47717 23 mins C B, V, FO P
A look at how the San Francisco 49ers fought for a 26-21 victory over the Cincy Bengals in Super Bowl XVI.
NFL Films — *NFL Films Video*

Super Bowl XVII **1983**
Football
69043 23 mins C B, V, FO P
This program contains the highlights of Super Bowl XVII, played between the Washington Redskins and the Miami Dolphins.
NFL Films — *NFL Films Video*

SuperBowl XVIII **1984**
Football
70271 23 mins C B, V, FO P
Los Angeles Raiders, Washington Redskins
Marcus Allen runs for a record 74-yard touchdown in the filmed highlights of the most lopsided Super Bowl to date.
NFL Films — *NFL Films Video*

Super Bowl XIX Highlights **1985**
Football
70542 23 mins C B, V, FO P
Joe Montana, Dan Marino
After their systematic 38-16 demolition of the powerful Dolphins, observers dubbed the 49ers the "Masters of the Game."
NFL Films — *NFL Films Video*

Super Colt 38 **196?**
Western
77354 88 mins C B, V P
Jeffrey Hunter, Rosa Maria Vazquez, Pedro Armendariz
One man must decide another man's fate, and defend the honor of the woman they both love.
Foreign — *Unicorn Video*

Super Colt 38 **1966**
Western
80493 88 mins C B, V P
Jeffrey Hunter, Rosa Maria Vasquez, Pedro Armendariz
Two former friends become bitter enemies as they vie for the love of the same woman. Dialogue in Spanish.
SP
Spanish — *Unicorn Video*

Super Exercises **1978**
Physical fitness
42779 60 mins C B, V P
Ann Dugan
This series of two 30-minute programs on one tape is intended for those concerned with gaining greater strength and endurance.

Health N Action — *RCA/Columbia Pictures Home Video*

Super Fuzz 1981
Comedy
65067 97 mins C B, V P
Terence Hill, Joanne Dru
A rookie policeman develops super powers after being exposed accidentally to radiation. Somewhat ineptly, he uses his abilities to combat crime.
MPAA:PG
Avco Embassy — *Embassy Home Entertainment*

Super Memories of the Super Bowls 1981
Football
51701 46 mins C B, V, LV P
This program contains highlights of the first fifteen NFL Super Bowls. Great performances by such memorable athletes as Bart Starr, Joe Namath, Franco Harris and Roger Staubach are captured.
NFL Films — *NFL Films Video*

Super Seventies, The 1980
Football
50087 48 mins C B, V, LV R, P
The decade's most memorable moments of thrilling runs and catches, exhilarating wins and crushing defeats.
NFL Films — *NFL Films Video*

Super Stars of the Super Bowls 1984
Football
79637 50 mins C B, V, FO P
The outstanding players of the Super Bowls past and present are remembered in this film.
NFL Films — *NFL Films Video*

Super Ted III: The Adventures Continue 1985
Cartoons
77531 49 mins C B, V R, P
Animated, voices of Roy Kinnear and Victor Spinetti
Super Ted and Spottyman team up to fight crime in this collection of six animated adventures.
Siriol Animation Ltd. — *Walt Disney Home Video*

Superboy 1966
Cartoons/Fantasy
81089 60 mins C B, V R, P
Animated
Join Superboy and his dog Krypto as they fight crime in this collection of eight animated adventures.
Filmation — *Warner Home Video*

Superchick 1971
Adventure
33614 94 mins C B, V P
Joyce Jillson, Louis Quinn, Thomas Reardon
An unassuming airline stewardess becomes a sexy, leggy blonde in between flights.
MPAA:R
Unknown — *United Home Video*

Superfly 1972
Drama
53522 98 mins C B, V R, P
Ron O'Neal, Carl Lee, Sheila Frazier, directed by Gordon Parks
A Harlem dope pusher gets involved with gangs and the police as he seeks to earn enough money with one last deal to be able to retire.
MPAA:R
Warner Bros — *Warner Home Video*

Supergirl 1984
Adventure/Fantasy
77204 114 mins C B, V P
Helen Slater, Faye Dunaway, Peter Cook, Mia Farrow, Brenda Vaccaro, directed by Jeannot Szwarc
Superman's cousin Kara leaves her native planet of Krypton to come to Earth to recover The Omegahedron Stone.
MPAA:PG
Tri-Star Pictures — *U.S.A. Home Video*

Supergirl: The Making of the Movie 1984
Filmmaking/Documentary
77381 60 mins C B, V P
Faye Dunaway, Helen Slater, Peter O'Toole
A behind the scenes look at the making of the "Supergirl" film. Available in Beta Hi-Fi and VHS Stereo.
Ilya Salkind — *U.S.A. Home Video*

Superman 194?
Cartoons
53806 59 mins C B, V P
Animated
This cartoon package features seven cartoon shorts released between 1941 and 1943. Included are "Superman #1," "Magnetic Telescope," "Japoteurs," "Bulleteers," "Jungle Drums," "Mechanical Monsters," and "The Mummy Strikes."
Paramount; Max Fleischer — *Media Home Entertainment*

Superman 1966
Cartoons/Fantasy
81090 60 mins C B, V R, P
Animated, voices of Bud Collyer, Joan Alexander, Jackson Beck

Join Superman as he foils crime in Metropolis in this collection of seven animated adventures.
Filmation — *Warner Home Video*

Superman III **1983**
Adventure
65358 125 mins C B, V, LV, CED P
Christopher Reeve, Richard Pryor, Jackie Cooper, Marc McClure, Annette O'Toole, Annie Ross, Pamela Stephenson, Robert Vaughn, Margot Kidder
This time the Man of Steel faces the awesome power of a criminally insane super-computer genius, who has been hoodwinked by a sinister tycoon seeking global dominance. In VHS Dolby Stereo/Beta Hi-fi.
MPAA:PG
Pierre Spengler — *Warner Home Video*

Superman Cartoons **194?**
Cartoons/Adventure
59055 75 mins C B, V P
A collection of rare animated Superman cartoons released from 1941 to 1943. Cartoons include: "Superman (First Episode)," "The Bulleteers," "The Magnetic Telescope," "The Japoteurs," "The Mechanical Monsters," "Volcano," "Terror on the Midway," "The Mummy Strikes," "Jungle Drums."
Max Fleischer; Paramount — *Wizard Video*

Superman-The Cartoons **1942**
Cartoons
73538 89 mins C B, V P
Animated, voices of Bud Collyer and Joan Alexander
Eight of the comic book hero's adventures from 1942 are featured along with a 1953 black and white short called "Stamp Day for Superman," starring the cast of the TV show.
Fleischer Studios; Famous Studios — *Admit One Video*

Superman—The Movie **1978**
Adventure
38938 144 mins C B, V, LV R, P
Christopher Reeve, Margot Kidder, Marlon Brando, Gene Hackman, Glenn Ford, directed by Richard Donner
A lavish retelling of the Superman legend, from his birth and flight from his home planet Krypton, to his becoming Earth's protector from the villain, Lex Luthor.
MPAA:PG
Warner Bros — *Warner Home Video; RCA VideoDiscs*

Superman II **1980**
Adventure
58254 127 mins C B, V, LV R, P
Christopher Reeve, Margot Kidder, Gene Hackman, Ned Beatty, Jackie Cooper, Terence Stamp, Valerie Perrine, E. G. Marshall, directed by Richard Lester
The sequel to "the movie" about the Man of Steel. This time, he has his hands full with three super-powered villains and a love-stricken Lois Lane.
MPAA:PG
Film Export; Warner Bros — *Warner Home Video; RCA VideoDiscs*

Superstition **1982**
Horror
81317 85 mins C B, V P
James Houghton, Albert Salmi, Lynn Carlin
A reverend and his family move into a vacant house near Black Poind despite warnings from the townspeople.
Almi Pictures — *Lightning Video*

Support Your Local Sheriff **1969**
Western/Comedy
80141 92 mins C CED P
James Garner, Joan Hackett, Walter Brennan, Bruce Dern, Jack Elam, Harry Morgan
When a stranger stumbles into a gold rush town, he winds up becomming the town's sheriff.
Cherokee Productions — *CBS/Fox Video*

Surabaya Conspiracy **1975**
Adventure/Drama
79337 90 mins C B, V P
Michael Rennie, Richard Jaeckel, Barbara Bouchet
Mystery and intrigue surround a search for gold in Africa.
PM Films — *Monterey Home Video*

Sure Thing, The **1985**
Comedy
81478 94 mins C B, V, LV P
John Cusack, Daphne Zuniga, Nicolette Sheridan, Viveca Lindfors, Boyd Gaines, directed by Rob Reiner
A horny college student discovers that casual sex with a California blonde isn't such a "sure thing" when he develops an attraction to a fellow classmate.
MPAA:PG13
Embassy; Monument Pictures — *Embassy Home Entertainment*

Surf II **1984**
Comedy
80125 91 mins C B, V P
Cleavon Little, Lyle Waggoner, Ruth Buzzi, Carol Wayne, Terry Kiser
A group of surfers are getting sick from drinking tainted soda pop.
MPAA:R
International Film Marketing — *King of Video; Media Home Entertainment*

Surfacing 1984
Drama
79892 90 mins C B, V P
Joseph Bottoms, Kathleen Beller, R.H. Thompson, Margaret Dragu
A girl braves the hostile Northern Wilderness to search for her missing father.
Beryl Fox; Philips Hobel — *VCL Home Video*

Surfing Beach Party 1984
Music-Performance
76644 56 mins C B, V P
This program recaptures the beach-blanket fun of the '50s and '60s California rock 'n' roll. Feature songs include "Surfin' Safari," "Fun, Fun, Fun," "Barbara Anne" and many more.
Music Media — *Music Media*

Survival Anglia's World of Wildlife, Vol. I 197?
Wildlife/Documentary
47060 90 mins C CED P
Narrated by Glen Campbell and David Niven
Two award-winning documentaries are featured in this package. "The Incredible Flight of the Snow Geese" follows the migration of these beautiful birds from the Canadian Arctic to the Texas plains. "Leopard of the Wild" follows the story of a man's involvement with an orphaned leopard cub.
SA Ltd — *RCA VideoDiscs*

Survival Anglia's World of Wildlife, Vol. 2 198?
Wildlife/Documentary
64455 104 mins C CED P
Hosted by Peter Ustinov and David Niven
Ustinov narrates the story of the Australian kangaroo, and Niven hosts an in-depth look at the annual breeding of penguins at the Falkland Islands.
SA Ltd — *RCA VideoDiscs*

Survival Run 1980
Adventure
66287 90 mins C B, V P
Peter Graves, Ray Milland, Vincent Van Patten
Six young teenagers are stranded in the desert.
MPAA:R
Lance Hool — *Media Home Entertainment*

Survivors, The 1983
Comedy
69616 102 mins C B, V P
Robin Williams, Walter Matthau, Jerry Reed
Two unemployed men find themselves the target of an out-of-work hit man, whom they disarm in a robbery attempt. One of the men takes off for survivalist camp, hotly pursued by the other, and then by the hit man.
MPAA:R
Bill Sackheim; Columbia — *RCA/Columbia Pictures Home Video; RCA VideoDiscs*

Susan Slept Here 1954
Comedy
13128 98 mins C B, V P
Dick Powell, Debbie Reynolds
Hollywood script writer is given protective custody of vagrant girl over Christmas vacation.
RKO — *United Home Video*

Suspense 1953
Suspense
80754 54 mins B/W B, V P
Walter Matthau, Jayne Meadows, Franchot Tone, Romney Brent
A collection of two episodes from the series: In "F.O.B. Vienna; in "All Hallows Eve" a man who murders his pawnbroker is plagued by a guilty conscience.
CBS — *Video Yesteryear*

Suspicion 1941
Suspense
00258 99 mins B/W B, V, 3/4U P
Cary Grant, Joan Fontaine, Cedric Hardwicke
Alfred Hitchcock's thriller about a woman who gradually realizes she is married to a killer.
Academy Award '41: Best Actress (Fontaine); '42 Film Daily Poll Ten Best Films of Year.
RKO — *Nostalgia Merchant*

Suzanne 1980
Drama
72229 102 mins C B, V P
A woman is torn between a need for adventure and a conviction for peace.
Guardian Trust Company — *Vestron Video*

Svengali 1931
Drama
54114 76 mins B/W B, V P, T
John Barrymore, Marion Marsh
Maestro Svengali enchants lovely maidens by using the magical powers embodied within his evil stare. Once he has them under his powers, he uses them to advance his musical career.
Warner Bros — *Blackhawk Films; Sheik Video; Cable Films; Video Connection; Video Yesteryear; Western Film & Video Inc; Discount Video Tapes; Movie Buff Video; Movie Buff Video; Classic Video Cinema Collector's Club; Kartes Productions*

Swamp Thing 1982
Mystery/Adventure
63376 91 mins C B, V, LV, CED P
Adriene Barbeau, Louis Jourdan
Done in "comic-book" format, this is the story of a group of scientists performing a top secret

experiment in a rural swamp and their nemesis, the lunatic Arcane.
MPAA:PG
Benjamin Melnicker; Michael Oslan — *Embassy Home Entertainment*

Swan Lake **1982**
Dance
47814 ? mins C LV P
Natalia Makarova, Anthony Dowell
The Royal Ballet performs "Swan Lake," recorded at the Royal Opera House Covent Garden, July 28, 1980. In stereo.
Unknown — *Pioneer Artists*

Swan Lake **1981**
Dance
57254 82 mins C B, V P
The Kirov Ballet, the Leningrad Philharmonic, directed by Konstantin Sergeyev
Tchaikovsky's complete "Swan Lake" ballet is performed by the Kirov Ballet troupe featuring Yelena Yevteyeva, John Markovsky and Valeri Panov. This interpretation is based on the celebrated Petipal Ivanov productions.
Kultur — *Kultur*

Swan Lake **1982**
Cartoons/Adventure
59667 75 mins C B, V P
Animated
The prince searches for a future bride to be queen when he becomes king. The swan which bears the golden crown possesses magical powers that hold the key.
Toei Company — *Media Home Entertainment*

Swap, The **1980**
Drama
64872 90 mins C B, V, CED P
Robert De Niro, Jennifer Warren
A man embarks on a desperate hunt for the killer of his young brother.
Christopher Dewey — *Vestron Video*

Swarm, The **1978**
Horror
53523 116 mins C B, V R, P
Michael Caine, Katharine Ross, Richard Widmark, Lee Grant, Richard Chamberlain, Olivia de Havilland, Henry Fonda, Fred MacMurray, Patty Duke Astin
A scientist must contend with a swarm of killer bees after the discovery of dead personnel on a government base.
MPAA:PG
Warner Bros; Irwin Allen — *Warner Home Video*

Sweater Girls **1980**
Comedy
79390 90 mins C B, V P
A female gang comes into a small town and decides to whoop it up with their boyfriends during their visit.
MPAA:R
Saturn International Pictures — *World Premiere*

Sweeney Todd—The Demon Barber of Fleet Street **1984**
Musical
69920 139 mins C B, V P
Angela Lansbury, George Hearn, directed by Harold Prince
This is a filmed performance of the Broadway musical by Stephen Sondheim. In VHS Dolby stereo and Beta Hi-Fi.
Richard Barr, Charles Woodward et al — *RKO HomeVideo*

Sweet 16 **1981**
Horror
64873 90 mins C B, V P
Susan Strasberg, Bo Hopkins
Sixteen-year-old Melissa is beautiful, mysterious, and promiscuous, but she can't understand why all her boyfriends end up dead.
MPAA:R
Jim Sotos; Martin Perfit — *Vestron Video*

Sweet Sweetback's Baadasssss Song **1971**
Drama
63416 97 mins C B, V P
Melvin Van Peebles, Simon Chuckster
A black pimp kills two policemen who had been beating a black militant. He uses his street-wise survival skills to elude his pursuers and escape to Mexico.
Cinemation — *Sun Video; Magnum Entertainment*

Sweet William **1979**
Drama
70605 88 mins C B, V P
Sam Waterston, Jenny Agutter, Anna Massey, Arthur Lowe
A philandering and seemingly irresistible young man finds that one sensitive woman hasn't the patience or time for his escapades.
Kendon Films — *Prism*

Swept Away **1975**
Drama
44782 116 mins C B, V P
Giancarlo Giannini
A rich and beautiful Milanese capitalist woman is shipwrecked on a desolate island with a swarthy Sicilian deckhand, who also happens to be a dedicated communist.
Cinema 5 — *RCA/Columbia Pictures Home Video; RCA VideoDiscs*

Swim Baby Swim 1984
Sports-Water/Infants
76393 60 mins C B, V P
Esther Williams
A step-by-step instructional guide to infant water safety presented by Esther Williams, former movie star, and Olympic-caliber professional swimmer.
Rogers & Cowan Inc — *Karl/Lorimar Home Video*

Swing High, Swing Low 1937
Comedy
08666 95 mins B/W B, V, 3/4U P
Carole Lombard, Fred MacMurray, Charles Butter- worth, Dorothy Lamour, directed by Mitchell Leisen
A struggling trumpet player becomes a hit in the jazz world and marries the girl he loves.
Paramount — *Budget Video; Discount Video Tapes; Video Yesteryear; Cable Films; Video Connection; Cinema Concepts*

Swing It, Sailor! 1937
Comedy
65202 61 mins B/W B, V P
Wallace Ford, Ray Mayer, Isabel Jewell, Mary Treen
Two zany sailors have a series of comic adventures while on shore leave.
Grand National Films — *Video Yesteryear*

Swing Shift 1984
Comedy-Drama
73011 100 mins C B, LV, CED P
Goldie Hawn, Kurt Russell, Ed Harris, directed by Jonathan Demme
Goldie Hawn stars as a woman who takes a job at an aircraft plant to help make ends meet after her husband goes off to war. A loving reminiscence of the American home front during World War II.
MPAA:PG
Jerry Bick; Warner Bros — *Warner Home Video*

Swing Time 1936
Musical
00273 103 mins B/W B, V, 3/4U P
Fred Astaire, Ginger Rogers, Helen Broderick, Betty Furness, Eric Blore
Fred plays a dancer who can't resist gambling, until he meets Ginger. The score by Jerome Kern and Dorothy Fields includes "Pick Yourself Up," "Never Gonna Dance," "The Waltz in Swing-time" and "A Fine Romance."
Academy Awards '36: Best Song (The Way You Look Tonight).
RKO; Pandro S Berman — *Nostalgia Merchant; RCA VideoDiscs*

Swingin' Singin' Years, The 1960
Music-Performance
21335 52 mins B/W B, V, FO P
Woody Herman, Charlie Barnet, Stan Kenton, Louis Jordan, Vaughn Monroe, Jo Stafford, hosted by Ronald Reagan
Famous bands and singers appear "live" from all over the U.S. in a program designed to recapture the era of "big band remotes." Reagan acts as host and announcer for the various orchestras.
ABC — *Video Yesteryear*

Swinging Cheerleaders, The 1974
Comedy
60414 90 mins C B, V P
Rainbeaux Smith, Colleen Camp, Jo Johnston
A group of amorous cheerleaders turn on the entire campus.
MPAA:PG
The Swinging Cheerleaders — *Monterey Home Video*

Swinging Ski Girls 197?
Drama
59554 85 mins C B, V P
Cindy Wilton, Dick Cassidy
A group of swinging, free-loving university co-eds spend a wild weekend at a ski lodge.
Robert Marsden — *Media Home Entertainment*

Swinging Sorority Girls 197?
Drama
59553 73 mins C B, V P
Susie Carlson, Anne Marlie
An intimate glimpse behind the closed doors of a sorority house during a wild homecoming weekend.
Robert Marsden — *Media Home Entertainment*

Swiss Conspiracy, The 1977
Suspense
44911 92 mins C B, V P
David Janssen, Senta Berger
Against the opulent background of the world's richest financial capital and playground of the wealthy, one man battles to stop a daring and sophisticated blackmail caper.
MPAA:PG
SJ International Pictures — *United Home Video*

Swiss Family Robinson, The 1960
Adventure/Drama
47408 126 mins C B, V, LV R, P
John Mills, Dorothy McGuire, James MacArthur, Tommy Kirk, Janet Munro, Sessue Hayakawa

A Swiss family, travelling to New Guinea, is blown off course and shipwrecked on a deserted tropical island. Forced to remain, they create a new life for themselves. Based on the novel by Johann Wyss.
Walt Disney — *Walt Disney Home Video; RCA VideoDiscs*

Swiss Miss **1938**
Comedy
33907 72 mins B/W B, V, 3/4U P
Stan Laurel, Oliver Hardy, Walter Woolf King, Della Lind, Eric Blore
Stan and Ollie are mousetrap salesmen who visit Switzerland and become involved with an egotistical songwriter and his wife.
Hal Roach, MGM — *Nostalgia Merchant; Blackhawk Films*

Swiss Miss **1938**
Comedy
63990 97 mins B/W B, V P, T
Stan Laurel, Oliver Hardy, Della Lind, Walter Woolf King, Eric Blore
Stan and Ollie are mousetrap salesmen on the job in Switzerland. Also included on this tape is a 1935 Thelma Todd-Patsy Kelly short, "Hot Money."
Hal Roach; MGM — *Blackhawk Films*

Switchblade Sisters **1975**
Adventure
63087 90 mins C B, V P
Robbie Lee, Joanne Nail
A crime gang of female ex-cons attack and kill at the slightest provocation.
Switchblade Sisters Productions — *Monterey Home Video*

Sword and the Sorcerer, The **1982**
Fantasy
62780 100 mins C B, V, LV P
Lee Horsely, Kathleen Beller, George Maharis, Simon MacCorkindale
A young prince finds his kingdom destroyed by an evil usurper and a powerful magician.
MPAA:R
Group I — *MCA Home Video*

Sword of Fury I **1973**
Adventure
76897 90 mins C B, V P
Hideki Takahashi, Jiro Tamiya
This film demonstrates how Musashi Miyamoto became Japan's greatest samurai. With Engish subtitles.
JA
Shochiku Co. — *Video Action*

Sword of Fury II **1973**
Adventure
76898 77 mins C B, V P
Hideki Takahashi, Jiro Tamiya
Two samurai fight to the death to determine who will become the premier swordsman of all Japan. With English subtitles.
JA
Shochiku Co. — *Video Action*

Sword of the Valiant **1983**
Fantasy
80856 102 mins C B, V P
Sean Connery, Miles O'Keefe, Trevor Howard, Lila Kedrova, John Rhys-Davies, Peter Cushing
The Green Knight arrives in Camelot to challenge Gawain.
MPAA:PG
Cannon Films — *MGM/UA Home Video*

Swordsman with an Umbrella **1978**
Martial arts
70703 85 mins C B, V P
Jiang Ming, Yu Er
Two tough swashbuckling ladies strive vengefully upon raping gangsters.
Master Arts — *Master Arts Video*

Sybil **1976**
Drama
59363 122 mins C B, V, CED P
Sally Field, Joanne Woodward, Brad Davis, Martine Bartlett, Jane Hoffman, directed by Daniel Petrie
The factually-based story of a woman who developed 16 distinct personalities, and the supportive psychiatrist who helped her put the pieces of her ego together.
Emmy Awards '77: Outstanding Special (Drama); Outstanding Lead Actress in a Drama Special (Sally Field); Outstanding Writing in a Special (Stewart Stern).
Lorimar — *CBS/Fox Video*

Sylvester **1985**
Drama
Closed Captioned
81427 104 mins C B, V P
Melissa Gilbert, Richard Farnsworth, Michael Schoeffling, Constance Towers
A sixteen-year-old girl and a cranky stockyard boss team up to train a battered horse named Sylvester for the National Equestrian trials. Available in VHS Dolby Hi-Fi Stereo and Beta Hi-Fi Stereo.
MPAA:PG
Columbia; Martin Jurow — *RCA/Columbia Pictures Home Video*

Sylvester and Tweety's Crazy Capers **1961**
Cartoons
81576 54 mins C B, V R, P
Animated, voice of Mel Blanc, directed by Friz Freleng
Sylvester keeps on the tail of Tweety Pie in this collection of eight classic cartoons that include "Tweet and Lovely", "Tree for Two" and "Hyde and Go Tweet".
Warner Bros — *Warner Home Video*

Sympathy for the Devil **1970**
Music
29175 110 mins C B, V P
Mick Jagger, The Rolling Stones
A program with sequences of pop political cartoons dealing with injustice and democracy. In this provocative show the Rolling Stones capture all the passionate defiance and thirst for justice of the revolutionary 60's.
Viacom International — *CBS/Fox Video*

Symphony of Living **1935**
Drama
78084 73 mins B/W B, V, FO P
A heart warming drama about a man's bitter betrayal by his own family and his incredible hardships and tragedies.
Invincible Pictures — *Video Yesteryear*

T

T-Men **1947**
Crime-Drama
64382 96 mins B/W B, V, 3/4U P
Dennis O'Keefe, June Lockhart, Wallace Ford
Two agents of the Treasury Department infiltrate themselves into a counterfeiting gang.
Eagle-Lion; Edward Small — *Nostalgia Merchant*

Table for Five **1983**
Drama
65001 120 mins C B, V, CED P
John Voight, Millie Perkins, Richard Crenna, Robbie Kiger, Roxana Zal, Son Hoang Bui, Marie Christine Barrault
A divorced father takes his children on a Mediterranean cruise and while sailing, he learns that his ex-wife has died. The father and his ex-wife's husband struggle over who should raise the children.
MPAA:PG
CBS Theatrical Films — *CBS/Fox Video*

Table Settings **1984**
Comedy
78656 90 mins C B, V P
Robert Klein, Stockard Channing, Dinah Manoff, Eileen Heckhard
A taped performance of James Lapines' comedy about the lives of three generations of a Jewish Family.
Showtime — *RKO HomeVideo*

Tag: The Assassination Game **1982**
Mystery/Drama
80772 92 mins C B, V P
Robert Carradine, Linda Hamilton, Michael Winslow, Kristine DeBell, Perry Lang
A college student writing an article for his school newspaper about a tag game uncovers some evil doings on campus.
MPAA:PG
New World Pictures — *Embassy Home Entertainment*

Takanaka World **1981**
Music-Performance
47296 40 mins C B, V P
Masayoshi Takanaka
As Masayoshi Takanaka performs his greatest hits, vivid visuals bring alive his daydreams.
Takeshi Shimizu; Hidenori Thea — *Paramount Home Video; Pioneer Video Imports*

Take a Good Look with Ernie Kovacs **1960**
Game show
42965 30 mins B/W B, V, FO P
Ernie Kovacs, Cesar Romero, Edie Adams, Carl Reiner
Zany skits abound as panelists attempt to guess the secret which the mystery guest is concealing.
ABC — *Video Yesteryear*

Take Down **1979**
Comedy
73955 96 mins C B, V P
Lorenzo Lamas, Kathleen Lloyd, Maureen McCormack, Edward Herrmann
Twelve members of a high school wrestling team have to get back into shape in time for a big wrestling match.
Buena Vista — *Unicorn Video*

Take It Big **1944**
Musical
78113 75 mins B/W B, V, FO P
Jack Haley, Harriet Hillard, Mary Beth Hughes, Airline Judge, Nils T. Granlund, Fuzzy Knight, Ozzie Nelson and his Orchestra
A pleasant musical about a band leader who is in love with a singer, though she is nuts about an impoverished actor who inherits a dude ranch.
Paramount — *Video Yesteryear*

 (For explanation of codes, see USE GUIDE and KEY)

Take It to the Limit **1980**
Motorcycles
66200 90 mins C B, V P
The best of motorcycle racing and champions is shown. In stereo.
Peter Starr — *U.S.A. Home Video*

Take the Money and Run **1969**
Comedy
46187 85 mins C B, V, LV, CED P
Woody Allen, Janet Margolin, Marcel Hillaire, directed by Woody Allen
A young man unsuccessfully tries to rob a bank and from that point on is unable to stay out of jail long enough to turn his new career into a profitable one.
MPAA:PG
Palomar Pictures International — *CBS/Fox Video*

Take This Job and Shove It **1981**
Comedy
58833 100 mins C B, V, CED P
Robert Hays, Art Carney, Barbara Hershey, David Keith, Martin Mull, Eddie Albert, Penelope Milford
A hot-shot efficiency expert is determined to streamline the Pickett Brewing Company, a Dubuque, Iowa brewery. He upsets the lives of his closest friends in the process, before realizing that his priorities in life are scrambled.
MPAA:G
Avco Embassy — *Embassy Home Entertainment*

Takin' It Off **1984**
Comedy
76768 90 mins C B, V P
Kitten Natividad, Adam Hadum, Ashley St. John, Angelique Pettyjohn
An exotic dancer's agent advises her to trim down her well endowed figure in order to become a serious actress.
Hanson and Gervasoni — *Vestron Video*

Taking My Turn **1984**
Musical
80452 87 mins C B, V P
A taped performance of the off Broadway musical revue about growing old gracefully.
Sonny Fox — *Pacific Arts Video*

Taking of Pelham One Two Three, The **1974**
Suspense
66077 102 mins C B, V, CED P
Robert Shaw, Walter Matthau, Martin Balsam, Hector Elizondo, James Broderick, directed by Joseph Sargent
A hijack team seizes a New York City subway car and holds the 17 passengers for ransom.
MPAA:R
United Artists — *CBS/Fox Video*

Tale of the Frog Prince, The **1983**
Fairy tales
Closed Captioned
69324 60 mins C B, V, LV, CED P
Robin Williams, Teri Garr, narrated by Eric Idle
This is the story of a special friendship between a frog turned prince by a witch's spell and the self-centered princess who saves him with a kiss. From Shelley Duvall's "Faerie Tale Theatre."
Shelley Duvall — *CBS/Fox Video*

Tale of Two Cities, A **1935**
Drama
58295 128 mins B/W B, V P
Ronald Colman, Elizabeth Allen, Edna May Oliver, Donald Woods, Basil Rathbone, directed by Jack Conway
Dickens' classic set during the French Revolution, about two men who bear a remarkable resemblance to each other, both in love with the same girl.
Film Daily Poll Ten Best Pictures of the Year '35.
MGM; David O Selznick — *MGM/UA Home Video*

Tale of Two Cities, A **1958**
Adventure
59903 117 mins B/W B, V, 3/4U P
Dirk Bogarde, Dorothy Tutin, Christopher Lee, Donald Pleasence, Ian Bannen
Dickens' classic about a lawyer who sacrifices himself to save another man from the guillotine.
Rank — *Embassy Home Entertainment*

Tale of Two Cities, A **1984**
Cartoons/Drama
80681 72 mins C B, V P
Animated
This is an adaptation of the Dickens classic about a man who sacrifices his own life for that of his friend to insure the happiness of the woman they both loved.
Burbank Films — *Vestron Video*

Tale of Two Critters, A **1977**
Adventure
59065 48 mins C B, V R, P
A young raccoon and a playful bear cub develop a rare friendship growing up in the wilds.
Walt Disney Productions — *Walt Disney Home Video*

Tales from Muppetland **197?**
Comedy
53793 102 mins C CED P

This two-sided disc contains two programs featuring the lovable Muppets: "Muppet Musicians of Bremen" (1972) and "Emmet Otter's Jug Band Christmas" (1977).
Henson Associates — *RCA VideoDiscs*

Tales from Muppetland II 1971
Comedy/Fairy tales
60382 108 mins C CED P
Two enchanting Muppet variations on classic fairy tales: "Hey, Cinderella" and "The Frog Prince."
Henson Associates — *RCA VideoDiscs*

Tales from the Crypt 1972
Horror
80318 92 mins C B, V P
Sir Ralph Richardson, Joan Collins, Peter Cushing, Ian Hendry, directed by Freddie Francis
A collection of five scary stories from the classic EC comics that bear the movie's title.
MPAA:PG
Metromedia Producers Corporation — *Prism*

Tales of Deputy Dawg—Volumes II & III 196?
Cartoons
29176 90 mins C B, V P
Animated
Two programs featuring Terrytoons' Deputy Dawg. Both available individually.
Viacom International — *CBS/Fox Video*

Tales of Hoffmann, The 1981
Opera
53400 210 mins C LV P
Introduction by John Gielgud, Placido Domingo
The Royal Opera's performance of Offenbach's "Tales of Hoffmann," produced by John Schlesinger.
Covent Garden Video Prods Ltd — *Pioneer Artists; RCA VideoDiscs*

Tales of Ordinary Madness 1983
Drama
79311 107 mins C B, V P
Ben Gazzara, Ornella Muti, Susan Tyrell, Tanya Lopert, directed by Marco Ferrari
A poet tries to devour life with a furious gulp and meets some unusual characters in his travels.
Fred Baker Productions — *Vestron Video*

Tales of Terror 1962
Horror
53524 88 mins C B, V R, P
Vincent Price, Peter Lorre, Basil Rathbone, directed by Roger Corman
Three tales of terror: "Morella," "The Black Cat," and "The Case of M. Valdemar." Based on stories by Edgar Allen Poe.
American International — *Warner Home Video*

Tales of Tomorrow Volume 1 195?
Science fiction
44338 120 mins B/W B, V, 3/4U P
Lon Chaney Jr., Bruce Cabot, Leslie Nielsen, Thomas Mitchell
Four episodes from the early 1950's television series focusing on the supernatural. Includes "Frankenstein," "Dune Roller," "Appointment on Mars," and "Crystal Egg." Includes previews of coming attractions from classic science fiction films.
ABC; George F. Foley Jr. — *Nostalgia Merchant*

Tales of Tomorrow, Volume 2 195?
Science fiction
58583 90 mins B/W B, V, 3/4U P
Boris Karloff, Walter Abel, Edmon Ryan, Rod Steiger
Four episodes from the early 1950's TV series focusing on the supernatural. "Past Tense," "A Child is Crying," "Ice from Space," and "The Window."
ABC; George F Foley Jr — *Nostalgia Merchant*

Talk of the Town 1982
Football
47713 23 mins C B, V, FO P
Team highlights of the 1981 New York Jets, who had the top-ranked defense in the AFC, the NFL Defensive Player of the Year in Joe Klecko, and the NFL Comeback Player of the Year with Richard Todd.
NFL Films — *NFL Films Video*

Talk to Me 1982
Drama
Closed Captioned
81558 90 mins C B, V P
Austin Pendleton, Michael Murphy, Louise Fletcher, Briar Backer, Clifton James
A successful New York accountant checks into the Hollins Communication Institute to cure his stuttering and falls in love with a squirrel-hunting stuttering woman from Arkansas. Available in VHS and Beta Hi-Fi Stereo.
Hollis Communication Institution Prods. — *Playhouse Video*

Talking in Your Sleep 1984
Music/Video
65403 4 mins C B, V P
The Romantics
The video clip "Talking in Your Sleep" features The Romantics and a cast of 100 models dressed, as the song implies, in a variety of sleepwear from robes to negligees.
Bob Dyke — *CBS/Fox Video*

 (For explanation of codes, see USE GUIDE and KEY)

Tall Blond Man with One Black Shoe, The 1973
Mystery
07139 90 mins C B, V P
Pierre Richard, Bernard Blier, Jean Rochefort, directed by Yves Robert
Decoy agent is completely unaware that he is the center of a plot by a French intelligence director to booby-trap an overly ambitious assistant. Dubbed in English.
MPAA:PG
Cinema 5 — *RCA/Columbia Pictures Home Video*

Tall in the Saddle 1944
Western
00278 79 mins B/W B, V, 3/4U P
John Wayne, Ella Raines
Portrayal of a tough, woman-hating cowboy working for a spinster and her attractive niece.
RKO; Robert Fellows — *Nostalgia Merchant*

Taming of the Shrew, The 1981
Comedy
66273 152 mins C B, V P
Directed by Peter Dews
Shakespeare's comedy about Petruchio's attempt to tame his fiery, free-spirited wife.
Unknown — *Embassy Home Entertainment*

Taming of the Shrew, The 1929
Drama
66354 66 mins B/W B, V P
Mary Pickford, Douglas Fairbanks, Edwin Maxwell, Joseph Cawthorn, directed by Sam Taylor
This early talkie version of Shakespeare's play is the only film that co-stars America's most popular acting couple of the 1920's. The film was re-edited in 1966, with some cleaning up of the soundtrack and a musical score added as well.
Pickford Corp; Elton Corp; United Artists — *Blackhawk Films*

Taming of the Shrew, The 1967
Comedy
21297 122 mins C B, V P
Elizabeth Taylor, Richard Burton, Michael York
A lavish screen version of the classic Shakespearean comedy.
Columbia — *RCA/Columbia Pictures Home Video; RCA VideoDiscs*

Tank 1983
Drama
75017 113 mins C B, V, LV, CED P
James Garner, Shirley Jones, G.D. Spradlin
This is the unusual story of an Army officer who takes on a small town sheriff with the aid of a World War II Sherman tank.
MPAA:PG
Irwin Yablans — *MCA Home Video*

Taps 1981
Drama
47398 126 mins C B, V, CED P
Timothy Hutton, George C. Scott, Ronny Cox
When a military school is threatened with closure, the students take over and start a siege. The situation snowballs with misunderstandings until the National Guard is called in.
MPAA:PG
20th Century Fox — *CBS/Fox Video*

Tarantulas: The Deadly Cargo 1977
Suspense
77205 95 mins C B, V P
Claude Akins, Charles Frank, Deborah Winters, Bert Remsen
A horde of deadly tarantulas spread terror and death through a small southwestern town.
Alan Landsburg Productions — *U.S.A. Home Video*

Target Eagle 1984
Adventure
72461 100 mins C B, V P
Terrorists land on the Mediterranean coast and a mercenary and a young woman attempt to halt them with only their wits and courage.
Unknown — *VCL Home Video*

Target for Today, The 8th Air Force Story 1943
World War II/Documentary
70371 85 mins B/W B, V P
This program chronicles a day in the life of WW II's largest bomber squadron. The film goes from the planning session to the heart of Germany for a major air strike.
United States Signal Corps of the Army — *Video City Productions*

Target for Tonight 1941
World War II/Documentary
23228 50 mins B/W B, V, FO P
An English documentary about a bombing raid on Germany during World War II.
Crown Film Unit — *Video Yesteryear; International Historic Films*

Targets 1969
Drama
60214 90 mins C B, V R, P
Boris Karloff, James Brown, Tim O'Kelly, directed by Peter Bogdanovich
Bogdanovich's directorial debut concerns an aging horror film star who confronts and disarms a mad sniper at a drive-in movie.
MPAA:PG

Peter Bogdanovich — *Paramount Home Video*

Tarka the Otter **198?**
Adventure
81048 91 mins C B, V P
Narrated by Peter Ustinov
This is the story of Tarka the Otter who encounters many dangers as he pursues his favorite eel meals.
Independent — *Trans World Entertainment*

Taro, The Dragon Boy **1985**
Cartoons
77373 75 mins C B, V P
Animated
A young boy searches for his mother who has been turned into a dragon
Turner Program Services;
Toei — *RCA/Columbia Pictures Home Video*

Tarzan and the Trappers **1958**
Adventure
11260 74 mins B/W B, V, FO P
Gordon Scott, Eve Brent, Ricky Sorenson, Maurice Marsac, Cheetah
Tarzan frees animals from trappers and prevents them from robbing the riches of a lost city.
RKO — *Video Yesteryear*

Tarzan of the Apes **1917**
Adventure
07279 63 mins B/W B, V, FO P
Elmo Lincoln, Enid Markey
The first screen version of the adventures of Tarzan. Silent.
First National — *Video Yesteryear; Sheik Video; Western Film & Video Inc; Cable Films*

Tarzan, the Ape Man **1932**
Adventure
55209 104 mins B/W B, V P
Johnny Weissmuller, Maureen O'Sullivan, directed by W. S. Van Dyke
The first Tarzan movie, featuring the characters created by Edgar Rice Burroughs.
MGM — *MGM/UA Home Video*

Tarzan, the Ape Man **1981**
Adventure
59310 112 mins C B, V, LV, CED R
Bo Derek, Richard Harris, directed by John Derek
Edgar Rice Burroughs' classic remade with the focus on Jane, as she explores the African jungles, learning about life and love from the Ape Man.
MPAA:R
Svengali Prods — *MGM/UA Home Video*

Tarzan's Revenge **1938**
Adventure
05446 70 mins B/W B, V, 3/4U R, P
Glenn Morris, Eleanor Holm, Hedda Hopper
Tarzan saves a safari of white travellers from vicious warriors.
20th Century Fox — *Budget Video; Video Yesteryear; Kartes Productions*

Tattoo **1981**
Drama
58849 103 mins C B, V, CED P
Bruce Dern, Maud Adams, Leonard Frey, Rikke Borge, John Getz
A model becomes the object of obsession for a tattoo artist who uses bodies as his canvas.
MPAA:R
20th Century Fox — *CBS/Fox Video*

Tax Tapes **1985**
Finance
70385 60 mins C B, V P
These tapes should help end the confusion surrounding viewer's preparation of federal income tax forms. The programs explain the tax laws and documents in clear, jargon-free terms. The short form program runs 30 minutes.
1.Long form; 2.Short form
RKO Home Video — *RKO HomeVideo*

Taxi Driver **1976**
Drama
47785 112 mins C B, V P
Robert DeNiro, Cybill Shepherd, Peter Boyle, Jodie Foster, directed by Martin Scorcese
A psychotic New York City cab driver goes on a violent rampage in an effort to rid the city of undesirables.
MPAA:R
Michael and Julia Phillips — *RCA/Columbia Pictures Home Video; RCA VideoDiscs*

Tchaikovsky Competition: Violin & Piano **1985**
Music-Performance
76967 90 mins C B, V P
Violinist Viktoria Mullova and pianist Peter Donahoe play their winning selections from the Tchaikovsky Competition taped in the Soviet Union.
Johnson Films; Hammer Films — *Mastervision*

Teachers **1984**
Comedy
Closed Captioned
77462 106 mins C B, V P
Nick Nolte, Jo Beth Williams, Lee Grant, Judd Hirsch, Ralph Macchio, Richard Mulligan, directed by Arthur Hiller
A lawsuit is brought against a high school for awarding a diploma to an illeterate student. Available in VHS and Beta Hi Fi.

MPAA:R
MGM/United Artist — *CBS/Fox Video*

Team of the 80's/NFL '82 **1983**
Football
66222 45 mins C B, V, FO P
Highlights of the San Diego Chargers' 1982-83 season along with an overview of the whole NFL Season.
NFL Films — *NFL Films Video*

Team on a Tightrope **1980**
Football
45127 24 mins C B, V, FO R, P
Dallas Cowboys
Highlights of the 1979 Dallas Cowboys football season.
NFL Films — *NFL Films Video*

Team That Battled Back, The **1980**
Football
50654 24 mins C B, V, FO R, P
New York Jets
The 1979 New York Jets weren't given much of a chance to be respectable. The coaching staff's indecision over whether Matt Robinson or Richard Todd should start at quarterback further complicated matters. Todd gradually settled into the role, behind an offensive line which was chiefly responsible for New York's leading the NFL in rushing yardage. The Jets finished with a surprising 8-8 record.
NFL Films — *NFL Films Video*

Team Together/NFL '83, A **1984**
Football
72935 46 mins C B, V, FO P
Denver Broncos
Highlights from the 1983 season of the Denver Broncos plus "NFL 83."
NFL Films — *NFL Films Video*

Teddy at the Throttle **1916**
Film-History
50631 20 mins B/W B, V P, T
Bobby Vernon, Gloria Swanson, Wallace Beery, Teddy (the Dog), directed by Clarence Badger
Teddy the Great Dane must rescue Gloria Swanson from a villain who has tied up her boyfriend. Silent.
Unknown — *Blackhawk Films*

Teddy at the Throttle/Speeding Along **1917**
Comedy
78120 54 mins B/W B, V, FO P
Gloria Swanson, Wallace Beery, Bobby Vernon, Keystone Teddy
A silent comedy about stealing fortunes from innocent heroines and a silent comedy about racing cars in a farm area.
Mack Sennett — *Video Yesteryear*

Teddy Pendergrass Live in London **1982**
Music-Performance
63399 75 mins C B, V P
Teddy Pendergrass
Filmed at England's Hammersmith Odeon in February 1982, this concert features the singer's most popular tunes, including "Close the Door," "If You Don't Know Me By Now," "Bad Luck," and "Wake Up Everybody."
Home Video Premiere
Productions — *CBS/Fox Video*

Teenage Zombies **1960**
Horror
69569 71 mins B/W B, V, FO P
Don Sullivan, Katherine Victor
A lady mad scientist kidnaps teenagers and uses her secret chemical formula to turn them into zombies, as the harbinger of her plan to enslave the world.
Governor — *Video Yesteryear*

Telefon **1977**
Suspense
75537 102 mins C B, V P
Charles Bronson, Lee Remick
The Soviets have a secret plan to destroy key U.S. military targets. The plan is so secret that the Soviet agents don't even know they will trigger the destruction.
MPAA:PG
MGM — *MGM/UA Home Video*

Telephone Book, The **1971**
Comedy
64968 88 mins C CED P
Sarah Kennedy, Norman Rose, Barry Morse
A young woman falls in love with the world's greatest obscene phone caller.
Rosebud Releasing — *Embassy Home Entertainment (disc only)*

Telescope—Interview with Harry Richman **1965**
Interview
46348 25 mins B/W B, V, FO P
Harry Richman
Vaudeville and nightclub star Harry Richman discusses his 50-year career in this candid interview.
CBC — *Video Yesteryear*

Television's Golden Age of Comedy **195?**
Comedy
11275 75 mins B/W B, V, FO P

Groucho Marx, Amos and Andy, Bob Hope, Dean Martin, Jerry Lewis, Jack Benny
"You Bet Your Life," with Groucho Marx, Amos and Andy's "Rare Coin," and an episode of "The Jack Benny Show" are featured in this vintage package of television comedy.
CBS et al — *Video Yesteryear*

Tell Them Willie Boy Is Here **1969**
Western
64791 98 mins C B, V P
Robert Redford, Katherine Ross, Robert Blake, Susan Clark, Barry Sullivan, directed by Abraham Polonsky
This western classic is based on the true story of a Paiute Indian, Willie Boy (Blake), and his white bride (Ross), who become the objects of the last great western manhunt after he kills her father in a "Marriage by Capture" on white man's territory. Sheriff Cooper (Redford) leads the manhunt.
MPAA:PG
Universal — *MCA Home Video*

Tempest **1928**
Drama
64318 105 mins B/W B, V P, T
John Barrymore, Louis Wolheim
A Russian peasant soldier rises through the ranks to become an officer, only to be undone by his love for the daughter of his commanding officer. Silent with musical score.
United Artists — *Blackhawk Films; Classic Video Cinema Collector's Club*

Tempest **1982**
Drama
64573 140 mins C B, V P
John Cassavetes, Gena Rowlands, Susan Sarandon, Vittorio Gassman, RaulJulia, directed by Paul Mazursky
A New York architect, fed up with city living, chucks it all and brings his daughter with him to live on a barren Greek island. VHS in stereo.
MPAA:PG
Columbia — *RCA/Columbia Pictures Home Video; RCA VideoDiscs*

Tempest, The **1985**
Drama
70650 126 mins C B, V P
Efrem Zimbalist, William H. Basset, Ted Sorrel, Kay E. Kuter, Edward Edwards, Nicholas Hammond, Ron Palillo, directed by William Woodman
Shakespeare's "Tempest" is a storm sent by a wise magician to bring Naple's royal family to Caliban, the desolate island where he remains in exile. This presentation uses American actors and accents set against an artist's recreation of England's Globe Theatre stage. This is a two-cassette package.
Paganiniana Publications — *Kultur*

Tempest, The/The Eagle **1927**
Film-History
50641 56 mins B/W B, V P, T
John Barrymore, Camilla Horn, Rudolph Valentino, Louise Dressler
A Russian soldier is betrayed and humiliated by the woman he loves in "The Tempest." In "The Eagle," an outcast guardsman becomes the Russian version of Robin Hood.
United Artists — *Blackhawk Films*

Tempter, The **1978**
Horror
80766 96 mins C B, V P
Mel Ferrer, Arthur Kennedy, Alida Valli, Anita Strindberg
A psychiatrist discovers through hypnosis that the daughter of an Italian nobleman has inherited the curse of an ancestress who was burned at the stake as a witch.
MPAA:R
Edmundo Amati — *Embassy Home Entertainment*

"10" **1979**
Comedy
37423 123 mins C B, V, LV R, P
Dudley Moore, Julie Andrews, Bo Derek, directed by Blake Edwards
A successful songwriter who has everything he could want out of life somehow feels that his life is incomplete. He searches for something more—and finds it in the person of Bo Derek, the woman of his dreams, whom he rates as the ultimate on the popular girl-watching scale. He pursues her, determined to overcome any obstacles—with unpredictable results. Music by Henry Mancini; also features Ravel's "Bolero."
MPAA:R EL, SP
Orion Pictures, Warner Brothers — *Warner Home Video; RCA VideoDiscs*

Ten Brothers of Shao-lin **198?**
Martial arts
64957 90 mins C B, V P
Chia Ling, Wang Tao, Chang Yi
A martial arts adventure from the days of warlords and warriors.
Dragon Lady Productions — *Unicorn Video*

10CC **1985**
Music-Performance
77400 60 mins C B, V P
Kevin Godley, Lol Creme
The rock band 10CC perform their hits "The Things We Do For Love" and "Wall Street Shuffle" in this concert taped at London's Hammersmith Odeon.
Bruce Gowers — *VCL Home Video*

Ten Commandments, The 1956
Drama
38611 219 mins C B, V, LV R, P
Charlton Heston, Yul Brynner, Anne Baxter, Yvonne DeCarlo, directed by Cecil B. DeMille
Lavish Biblical epic that tells the life story of Moses (Charlton Heston) who turned his back on a privileged life to lead his people to freedom.
Academy Awards '56: Best Special Effects.
Paramount — *Paramount Home Video; RCA VideoDiscs*

Ten Days that Shook the World 1927
Drama
08698 104 mins B/W B, V, 3/4U P
Directed by Sergei Eisenstein and Grigori Alexandrov
This Russian epic details the events which culminated in the Russian Revolution of October 1917, using the actual locations and many actual participants.
Amkino; Russian — *Video Yesteryear; International Historic Films; Sheik Video; Western Film & Video Inc; Classic Video Cinema Collector's Club; Phoenix Films & Video*

Ten from Your Show of Shows 1973
Variety
44799 92 mins B/W B, V P, T
Sid Caesar, Imogene Coca, Carl Reiner, Howard Morris
A compilation of vintage comedy routines from the famous variety series of the 50's, "Your Show of Shows." Sketches include a takeoff on "This Is Your Life," and some movie spoofs.
Walter Reade — *Media Home Entertainment; Sheik Video*

Ten Little Indians 1975
Mystery
64965 98 mins C B, V P
Herbert Lom, Richard Attenborough, Oliver Reed, Elke Sommer
Ten people are gathered in an isolated inn under mysterious circumstances. One by one they are murdered, each according to a verse from a children's nursery rhyme. Based on the novel and stage play by Agatha Christie.
Avco-Embassy — *Embassy Home Entertainment*

---

10 Magnificent Killers 1977
Martial arts
76937 97 mins C B, V P
Ten martial arts masters set to rid the Japanese countryside of evil feudal war lords.
Foreign — *Trans World Entertainment*

Tenant, The 1976
Horror
68251 126 mins C B, V R, P
Roman Polanski, Isabelle Adjani, Melvyn Douglas, Jo Van Fleet, Bernard Fresson, Shelley Winters
A disturbing film about an apartment tenant whose neighbors' actions drive him to insanity.
MPAA:R
Marianne Productions — *Paramount Home Video*

Tender Mercies 1983
Drama
65087 93 mins C B, V, CED R, P
Robert Duvall, Tess Harper, Betty Buckley, directed by Bruce Beresford
A down-and-out country-and-western singer finds his life redeemed by the love of a good woman.
Academy Awards '83: Best Actor (Duvall) Best Original Screenplay (Horton Foote) MPAA:PG
Universal — *THORN EMI/HBO Video*

Tender Warrior, The 1975
Adventure
66243 85 mins C B, V R, P
Dan Haggerty
A beautifully photographed animal adventure.
MPAA:G
William Thompson Productions — *Video City Productions*

Tendres Cousines 1983
Comedy
65602 90 mins C B, V P
This comedy follows the exploits of two cousins coming of age in the French countryside. Along with the rest of their relatives and friends, they become entwined in a web of unrequited love and intricate relationships.
MPAA:R
Crown — *Vestron Video*

Tennis/Racquet Sports 1978
Tennis
44926 30 mins C B, V P
Exercise specialist Ann Dugan performs exercises for tennis, squash, handball, and racquetball players to use to help mobilize the body for aggressive play. From the "Sports Conditioning" series.
Health N Action — *RCA/Columbia Pictures Home Video*

Tentacles 1977
Horror
64883 90 mins C B, V, CED P
John Huston, Shelley Winters, Bo Hopkins, Henry Fonda
A giant octopus wreaks havoc and terror.
MPAA:PG

American International Pictures — *Vestron Video*

10th Victim, The 1965
Drama/Science fiction
65432 92 mins C B, V P
Ursula Andress, Marcello Mastroianni
A futuristic thriller about a society where violence is channeled into legalized murder hunts. A beautiful TV actress is the hunter and the 10th victim will bring her all the material things she desires.
Avco-Embassy — *Embassy Home Entertainment*

Terminal Island 1977
Mystery
79764 88 mins C B, V P
Phyllis Davis, Tom Selleck, Don Marshall, Ena Hartman, Marta Kristen
Two groups of male prisoners on a penal colony find themselves fighting over the colony's only female inhabitants.
MPAA:R
Dimension Pictures — *United Home Video*

Terminator, The 1984
Science fiction
80646 108 mins C B, V R, P
Arnold Schwarzenegger, Michael Biehn, Linda Hamilton, Paul Winfield, directed by James Cameron
The Terminator is a futuristic cyborg sent to present day earth to kill the woman who will conceive the child destined become the arch enemy of the earth's future rulers.
MPAA:R
Gale Ann Hurd — *THORN EMI/HBO Video*

Terms of Endearment 1983
Drama
75807 129 mins C B, V R, P
Shirley MacLaine, Jack Nicholson, Debra Winger, directed James L. Brooks
This story follows the relationship between a young woman and her mother, over a thirty year period.
Academy Awards '83: Best Picture; Best Actress (MacLaine); Best Supporting Actor (Nicholson); Best Director (Brooks); Best Screenplay (Brooks). MPAA:PG
Paramount — *Paramount Home Video*

Terror 1979
Horror
48502 86 mins C B, V P
John Nolan, Carolyn Courage, James Aubrey
Supernatural forces and the shocking effect their mysterious powers have on the life of a young girl are depicted in this shocking tale.
MPAA:R
Crystal Film Production — *United Home Video; Video City Productions*

Terror, The 1963
Horror
59664 81 mins C B, V P
Jack Nicholson, Boris Karloff
A lieutenant in Napoleon's army finds himself trapped by a mad baron's fear of the unknown.
Roger Corman — *Prism; Media Home Entertainment; Budget Video; Discount Video Tapes; Cinema Concepts; World Video Pictures; Hal Roach Studios*

Terror by Night 1946
Mystery
42928 60 mins B/W B, V P
Basil Rathbone, Nigel Bruce
Based on a character developed by Sir Arthur Conan Doyle, Holmes and Watson solve two murders and thwart an attempted jewel theft on a train.
Universal, Howard Benedict — *Movie Buff Video; Video Connection; Video Yesteryear; Budget Video; Cable Films; Western Film & Video Inc; Discount Video Tapes; Classic Video Cinema Collector's Club*

Terror by Night/Meeting at Midnight 194?
Mystery
44856 122 mins B/W B, V, 3/4U P
Basil Rathbone, Nigel Bruce, Sidney Toler
In "Terror by Night" (1946), Sherlock Holmes and Dr. Watson board a train to protect a fabulous diamond. In "Meeting at Midnight" (1944), Charlie Chan becomes involved in magic and murder.
Universal, Monogram — *Nostalgia Merchant*

Terror in the Aisles 1984
Horror/Movie and TV trailers
76807 84 mins C B, V P
Donald Pleasence and Nancy Allen take you on a terrifying journey through some of the scariest moments in horror film history.
MPAA:R
Universal; Stephen J. Netburn; Andrew J. Kuehn — *MCA Home Video*

Terror in the Swamp 1985
Horror
76959 89 mins C B, V, LV P
Billy Holliday
A swamp creature is terrorizing the residents of a small town.
MPAA:PG
New World Pictures — *New World Video*

 (For explanation of codes, see USE GUIDE and KEY)

Terror in the Wax Museum **1973**
Horror
79674 94 mins C B, V P
Ray Milland, Broderick Crawford, Elsa Lanchester, Maurice Evans, John Carradine
The owner of a wax museum is killed while mulling over selling the museum to an American.
MPAA:PG
Bing Crosby Productions — *Lightning Video*

Terror of Tiny Town **1933**
Western/Musical
14349 65 mins B/W B, V P
Jed Buell's Midgets, directed by Sam Newfield
Terror erupts in a small midwestern town. All-midget cast.
Columbia — *Video Connection; Discount Video Tapes; Budget Video; Admit One Video*

Terror on the 40th Floor **1974**
Suspense/Drama
80319 98 mins C B, V P
John Forstyhe, Anjanette Comer, Don Meredith, Joseph Campanella
Seven people make an attempt to escape from the fortieth floor of an enflamed skyscraper.
Metromedia Producers Corporation — *Prism*

Terror on Tour **1983**
Horror
64234 90 mins C B, V P
Dave Galluzzo, Richard Styles, Rick Pemberton
The Clowns, a rock group on their way up, center their stage performance around sadistic, mutilating theatrics. When real murders begin, they become prime suspects.
Rick Whitfield — *Media Home Entertainment*

Terror Out of the Sky **1978**
Suspense
77209 100 mins C B, V P
Ephraim Zimbalist Jr, Dan Haggerty, Tovah Feldshuh, Lonny Chapman
A beekeeper and his assistant must track down three killer queen bees who kill off a schoolbus full of children in New Orleans.
Allen Landsburg Productions — *U.S.A. Home Video*

Terrorism: The Russian Connection **1985**
Documentary
76964 60 mins C B, V P
This documentary focuses on the recruitment and training techniques of the P.L.O. and other terrorist groups.
Canadian Broadcasting Company — *Mastervision*

Terry Bears Volume II **196?**
Cartoons
29177 90 mins C B, V P
Animated
A cartoon feature with "Terry Bears."
Viacom International — *CBS/Fox Video*

Terry Fox Story, The **1983**
Drama
65349 96 mins C B, V, CED P
Robert Duvall, Chris Makepiece, Eric Fryer
In the spring of 1980, a brave young man who had lost his right leg to cancer dipped his artificial limb into the Atlantic Ocean and set off on a "Marathon of Hope" across Canada. He ran 3,000 miles before he collapsed in Ontario.
Michael A Levine; Gurston Rosenfeld — *Vestron Video*

Terrytoons Salutes the Olympics **1979**
Sports/Cartoons
72234 60 mins C B, V P
Animated
An animated salute to the Olympics featuring the Terrytoon all stars, including Deputy Dawg.
Viacom — *Children's Video Library*

Terrytoons: The Good Guys Hour **1985**
Cartoons
80975 53 mins C B, V P
Animated
Here is a collection of classic Terrytoons cartoons that feature such favorites as Mighty Mouse, the mighty Heroes, Deputy Dawig and James Hound.
Terrytoons — *Children's Video Library*

Terrytoons, Vol. I, Featuring Mighty Mouse **196?**
Cartoons
56884 100 mins C CED P
Animated
Nineteen complete cartoons featuring Mighty Mouse, Heckle and Jeckle, Deputy Dawg, Little Roquefort, and others.
Terrytoons — *RCA VideoDiscs*

Tess **1980**
Drama
52748 170 mins C B, V, LV P
Nastassia Kinski, Peter Firth, Leigh Lawson, John Collin, directed by Roman Polanski
Thomas Hardy's novel "Tess of the d'Urbervilles," concerning a young woman who is a victim of both circumstance and a rigid Victorian society, tortured by guilt for the wrongs she feels she has committed, is the basis for this movie.

Academy Awards '80: Best Cinematography; Best Art Direction; Best Costume Design.
MPAA:PG
Claude Beri; Renn Productions; Burrill Productions — *RCA/Columbia Pictures Home Video; RCA VideoDiscs*

Testament 1983
Drama
Closed Captioned
65763 90 mins C B, V, CED R, P
Jane Alexander, William Devane, Ross Harris, Roxana Zal
Following a massive nuclear attack, a mother and her children struggle to survive against the backdrop of death, disease and destruction.
MPAA:PG
Lynne Littman — *Paramount Home Video*

Tex 1982
Drama
60557 103 mins C B, V, LV R, P
Matt Dillon, Jim Metzler, Meg Tilly, Bill McKinney, Frances Lee McCain, Ben Johnson, Emilio Estevez
The poignant and moving story of a teenager coming of age in a small Texas town. Based on the novel by S.E. Hinton.
MPAA:PG
Walt Disney Productions — *Walt Disney Home Video*

Texaco Star Theater 1951
Variety/Comedy
58264 60 mins B/W B, V, FO P
Milton Berle, Danny Thomas, Fran Warren, Sid Stone, Frank Galop, Alan Roth and his Orchestra
Originally broadcast on May 29, 1951, Uncle Miltie presides over the hilarity. Guests include Carlos Ramirez and his Senoritas, novelty dancers Harold and Lola, Beatrice Kraft and her Oriental dancers, 15-year-old violinist Michael Rabin, and singer Vivian Dellachiesa. Sketches include "The Chandeliers," a comic troupe of acrobats, and "United Nations of Show Business."
NBC — *Video Yesteryear*

Texas Chainsaw Massacre, The 1974
Horror
59058 86 mins C CED, LV P
Marilyn Burns, Paul A Partain, Edwin Neal, directed by Tobe Hooper
An idyllic summer afternoon drive becomes a nightmare for two young people pursued by a chainsaw-wielding maniac.
MPAA:R
Tobe Hooper; New Line Cinema — *Media Home Entertainment; Vestron Video (disc only)*

Texas Lady 1956
Western
80847 86 mins C B, V P
Claudette Colbert, Barry Sullivan
When a woman wins $50,000 gambling, she buys a Texas newspaper on the stipulation that she can edit it.
RKO — *Republic Pictures Home Video*

Texas Lightning 1981
Adventure
66063 93 mins C B, V P
Cameron Mitchell, Channing Mitchell, Maureen McCormick, Peter Jason
A truck driver is intent on showing his shy son the fine points of life.
MPAA:R
Jim Sotos — *Media Home Entertainment*

Texas Terror 1940
Western
29440 50 mins B/W B, V P
John Wayne, Gabby Hayes
John Wayne plays a cowboy who mistakenly believes he has shot his friend. He becomes a ranch foreman and saves the ranch from horse theives, finally discovering who really shot his friend.
Monogram — *Sheik Video; Video Dimensions; Sony Corporation of America*

Texas to Bataan 1942
Western
11263 56 mins B/W B, V, FO P
Range Busters
The Range Busters ship horses to the Philippines and encounter enemy spies.
Monogram — *Video Yesteryear*

Texersize 1984
Physical fitness
65706 37 mins C B, V P
Irlene Mandrell
This program exercises all major muscle groups and gives a complete cardio-vascular workout.
Panda Productions; Haghland Productions — *Embassy Home Entertainment*

Thank God It's Friday 1978
Comedy/Musical
63965 100 mins C B, V P
Valerie Landsburg, Terri Nunn, Chick Vennera
A dance contest at a Hollywood disco, where the participants are caught up in the glamor and glitter of disco nightlife, is the focal point of this film. Music by Donna Summer and The Commodores.
Academy Awards '78: Best Song ("Last Dance"). MPAA:PG
Casablanca Productions; Columbia Pictures — *RCA/Columbia Pictures Home Video*

 (For explanation of codes, see USE GUIDE and KEY)

Thank You Mr. President 1984
Documentary/Presidency-US
79169 55 mins C B, V P
Narrated by E.G. Marshall
The wit and humor of John F. Kennedy are captured in this documentary that features excerpts of his press conferences.
D. J. Mendelsohn Productions — *Worldvision Home Video*

That Championship Feeling 1984
Basketball
73857 60 mins C B, V P
Here are highlights from the 1983 NBA Playoffs and World Championship Series featuring the Philadelphia '76ers.
NBA — *CBS/Fox Video*

That Championship Season 1982
Drama
66116 110 mins C B, V, CED P
Martin Sheen, Bruce Dern, Stacy Keach, Robert Mitchum, Paul Sorvino
Long-dormant animosities surface at the reunion of a championship basketball team.
MPAA:R
Cannon — *MGM/UA Home Video*

That Cold Day in the Park 1969
Drama
66469 91 mins C B, V P
Sandy Dennis, Michael Burns, Suzanne Benton, directed by Robert Altman
A disturbed spinster entices a homeless young man into her apartment and makes him a prisoner.
MPAA:R
Commonwealth United; Robert Altman — *Republic Pictures Home Video*

That Darn Cat 1965
Comedy
76823 115 mins C B, V R, P
Hayley Mills, Dean Jones, Dorothy Provine, Neville Brand, Elsa Lanchester, Frank Goishin
A Siamese cat becomes an agent for the F.B.I. and helps to unravel a kidnapping-robbery.
MPAA:G
Buena Vista; Walt Disney Productions — *Walt Disney Home Video*

That Hamilton Woman 1941
Biographical/Drama
81469 125 mins B/W B, V, LV P
Laurence Olivier, Vivien Leigh, Gladys Cooper, Alan Mowbray, directed by Alexander Korda
This is the story of the tragic love affair between the British naval hero Lord Nelson and Lady Hamilton.
Alexander Korda — *Embassy Home Entertainment*

That Sinking Feeling 1979
Comedy
76795 82 mins C B, V P
Robert Buchanan, John Hughes, Billy Greenlees, Alan Love, directed by Bill Forsyth
A group of bored teenagers decide to steal ninety sinks from a plumber's warehouse.
MPAA:PG
Samuel Goldwyn Company — *Embassy Home Entertainment*

That Touch of Mink 1962
Comedy/Romance
65456 99 mins C B, V P
Cary Grant, Doris Day
In New York City, a young naive girl finds herself involved with a business tycoon. On a trip to Bermuda, both parties get an education as they play their game of "cat and mouse."
Universal — *Republic Pictures Home Video*

That Uncertain Feeling 1941
Comedy
05460 86 mins B/W B, V, FO P
Merle Oberon, Melvyn Douglas, Burgess Meredith, Alan Mowbray, Eve Arden
A husband and wife develop marital problems when the wife gets the hiccups.
Ernst Lubitsch; United Artists — *Video Yesteryear; Discount Video Tapes; Budget Video; Classic Video Cinema Collector's Club; See Hear Industries*

That Was Rock (The TAMI/TNT Show) 1964
Music-Performance
65481 90 mins B/W B, V P
Chuck Berry, James Brown, Ray Charles, Bo Diddley, Marvin Gaye, Gerry & The Pacemakers, Lesley Gore, Jan & Dean, Smokey Robinson & the Miracles, The Ronettes, The Rolling Stones, The Supremes, Ike & Tina Turner
The TAMI/TNT shows were the greatest dance concerts ever, and now they are together in one rock and roll, thythm and blues extravaganza. In stereo VHS and Beta Hi-Fi.
Lee Savin; Phil Spector — *Music Media*

That'll Be the Day 1973
Musical
63320 86 mins C B, V R, P
Ringo Starr, Keith Moon, David Essex, Rosemary Leach
Set in the early rock 'n' roll era of the 1950's, this is the story of a wayward young man and his aspirations to musical superstardom.
David Puttnam; Sanford Lieberson — *THORN EMI/HBO Video*

That's Dancing! 1985
Musical/Dance
81054 104 mins C B, V, LV P
Fred Astaire, Ginger Rogers, Ruby Keeler, Cyd Charisse, Gene Kelly, Liza Minnelli, Sammy Davis, Jr., Mikhail Baryshnikov, Ray Bolger, directed by Jack Haley, Jr.
This anthology features same of film's finest moments in dance from classical ballet to break-dancing. Available in VHS and Beta Hi-Fi stereo.
MGM — *MGM/UA Home Video*

That's Entertainment 1974
Musical
44646 132 mins C B, V, LV, CED P
Judy Garland, Fred Astaire, Frank Sinatra, Gene Kelly, Esther Williams, Bing Crosby, directed by Jack Haley Jr.
A compilation of scenes from the classic MGM musicals beginning with "The Broadway Melody" (1929) and ending with "Gigi" (1958).
MPAA:G
MGM — *MGM/UA Home Video*

That's Entertainment, Part II 1976
Musical
58291 133 mins C B, V P
Fred Astaire, Gene Kelly, John Barrymore, Lionel Barrymore, Jack Benny, Judy Garland, Maurice Chevalier, Bing Crosby, Jimmy Durante, Clark Gable, Jean Harlow, Elizabeth Taylor, Robert Taylor
A cavalcade of great musical and comedy sequences from MGM movies of the past. Also stars Jeanette MacDonald, Nelson Eddy, the Marx Bros., Laurel and Hardy, Jack Buchanan, Ann Miller, Mickey Rooney, Louis Armstrong, Oscar Levant, Cyd Charisse.
MPAA:G
MGM — *MGM/UA Home Video*

That's Singing 1984
Musical/Variety
81121 111 mins C B, V P
Hosted by Tom Bosley, Nell Carter, Barry Bostwick, Robert Morse, Debbie Reynolds, Diahann Carroll, Chita Rivera, Ethel Merman, Ray Walston
This is a tribute to the the American musical theatre featuring performances of memorable songs from twenty Broadway shows.
Iris Merlis — *Karl/Lorimar Home Video*

That's the Way of the World 1975
Drama
80904 97 mins C B, V P
Harvey Keitel, Ed Nelson, Bert Parks, Cynthia Bostick, Earth, Wind and Fire
A young record producer finds himself swept up in a web of payola when the Mafia forces him to promote a mediocre group. Music by Earth, Wind and Fire. Available in VHS stereo and Beta Hi-Fi.
MPAA:PG
United Artists — *U.S.A. Home Video*

The Master Ninja 1978
Martial arts
70388 93 mins C B, V P
Lee Van Cleef, Sho Kosugi, Timothy Van Patten
In this first program of the series, our hero deserts the Japanese secret order of the "Ninja" to search for his missing daughter. Van Cleef plays the AWOL American hunted by an assassin specializing in Ninja dispatch.
Nigel Watts/Viacom — *Trans World Entertainment*

Theatre of Death 1967
Horror
13141 90 mins C B, V P
Christopher Lee, Julian Glover
Paris police are baffled by a series of mysterious murders, each bearing a trace of vampirism.
Associated British Productions Ltd — *United Home Video*

Them! 1954
Horror/Science fiction
76857 93 mins B/W B, V R, P
James Whitmore, Edmund Gwenn, Fess Parker, James Arness, Onslow Stevens, directed by Gordon Dougles
A group of mutated giant ants wreak havoc on a southwestern town.
David Weisbart; Warner Bros — *Warner Home Video*

There's a Girl in My Soup 1970
Comedy
65316 95 mins C B, V P
Peter Sellers, Goldie Hawn
Sellers is a gourmet who moonlights as a self-styled Casanova, and Goldie is the young girl who takes refuge at his London love nest when she is ejected by her boyfriend from their flat.
M J Frankovich; John Boulting — *RCA/Columbia Pictures Home Video*

There's a Meetin' Here Tonight 1981
Music-Performance
53859 117 mins C LV P
The Limelighters, Glen Yarborough, Kingston Trio
Performances by folk immortals The Limelighters, Glenn Yarborough, and the Kingston Trio.
Intl Teleview Inc; Bill Williams; Susan Shore — *Pioneer Artists*

There's Naked Bodies On My T.V.! 197?
Satire/Comedy
59550 79 mins C B, V P
A sexy spoof of TV shows, "Happy Daze," "Bernie Milner," and "Don't Come Back Kotler."
CHK Productions — *Media Home Entertainment*

There's No Business Like Show Business 1954
Musical
37416 117 mins C B, V, CED P
Ethel Merman, Donald O'Connor, Marilyn Monroe, Dan Dailey, Johnny Ray, Mitzi Gaynor
A top husband and wife vaudevillian act return to the stage with their three children, who are now also in the act. Includes 24 songs by Irving Berlin.
20th Century Fox — *CBS/Fox Video*

Therese and Isabellee 1968
Drama
81408 102 mins C B, V P
Essy Persson, Anna Gael, Barbara Laage, Anne Vernon, directed by Redley Metzger
This film recounts the torrid affair between two French schoolgirls, therese and Isabelle. Available in VHS Stereo and Beta Hi-Fi.
Radley Metzger — *Monterey Home Video*

These Girls Won't Talk 192?
Comedy
11286 50 mins B/W B, V, FO P
Colleen Moore, Carole Lombard, Betty Compson
Three female stars of early motion pictures are featured separately in: "Her Bridal Nightmare," "Campus Carmen," and "As Luck Would Have It."
Mack Sennett et al — *Video Yesteryear*

These Three 1936
Drama
81446 92 mins B/W B, V, LV P
Miriam Hopkins, Merle Oberon, Joel McCrea, Bonita Granville, directed by William Wyler
The lives of three people are irrevocably changed due to a malicious lie a teenaged girl tells about them. Based upon Lillian Hellman's "The Children's Hour."
Samuel Goldwyn — *Embassy Home Entertainment*

They All Laughed 1981
Comedy
59870 115 mins C B, V, LV, CED P
Ben Gazzara, John Ritter, Audrey Hepburn, Colleen Camp, Patti Hansen, Dorothy Stratten, directed by Peter Bogdonovich
A madcap private eye caper involving a team of detectives who are both following and being followed by a bevy of dazzling women.
MPAA:PG
PSO; Moon Pictures — *Vestron Video*

They Call Me Bruce 1982
Comedy/Martial arts
66091 88 mins C B, V, CED P
Johnny Yune, Margaux Hemingway
A bumbling Bruce Lee lookalike meets a karate-chopping Mafia moll in this farce.
Elliot Hong — *Vestron Video*

They Call Me Mr. Tibbs! 1970
Mystery
65008 108 mins C B, V, CED P
Sidney Poitier, Barbara McNair, Martin Landau, Juano Hernandez, Anthony Zerbe, Edward Asner, Norma Crane
Lieutenant Virgil Tibbs (Poitier) must track down a murder case which involves his friend, the Reverend Logan Sharpe (Landau). He is torn between his duty as a policeman, his concern for the reverend and the threat of turmoil in the town. Sequel to "In the Heat of the Night."
MPAA:PG
United Artists — *CBS/Fox Video*

They Call Me Trinity 1972
Western
08480 110 mins C B, V, CED P
Terence Hill, Bud Spencer, Farley Granger, Steffen Zacharias, directed by E. B. Clucher
Lazy drifter-gunslinger and his outlaw brother join forces with Mormon farmers to rout bullying outlaws.
MPAA:G
Avco Embassy; West Film Productions — *Embassy Home Entertainment*

They Came to Cordura 1959
Drama
64579 123 mins C B, V P
Gary Cooper, Rita Hayworth, Van Heflin, Tab Hunter, directed by Robert Rossen
In Mexico circa 1916, six American heroes are recalled to their headquarters in Cordura. On the way, they encounter hardships and unexpected danger.
Columbia — *RCA/Columbia Pictures Home Video*

They Died With There Boots On 1941
Adventure/Western
73979 141 mins B/W B, V P
Errol Flynn, Sidney Greenstreet, Anthony Quinn, Hattie McDaniel, directed by Raoul Walsh
The Battle of Little Big Horn where General Custer met his match in Sitting Bull is recreated in this film, starring Errol Flynn as the unlucky namesake of Custer's Last Stand.

Warner Bros — *Key Video*

They Drive by Night **1940**
Drama
64934 97 mins B/W CED P
Humphrey Bogart, Ann Sheridan, George Raft, Ida Lupino, Alan Hale, Gale Page, Roscoe Karns
A truck driver loses his brother in an accident and subsequently gets involved in a murder.
Warner Bros — *Key Video*

They Knew What They Wanted **1940**
Drama
76836 96 mins B/W B, V P
Charles Laughton, Carole Lombard, Harry Carey, Karl Malden, William Gargan, directed by Garson Kanin
An elderly Italian grape grower decides to marry a lonely waitress after a series of passionate correspondences.
RKO — *RKO HomeVideo*

They Made Me a Criminal **1939**
Drama
08762 92 mins B/W B, V, 3/4U P
John Garfield, Ann Sheridan, Claude Rains, Dead End Kids
A champion prizefighter, believing he murdered a man in a drunken brawl runs away. (Remake of "The Life of Jimmy Dolan.')
Warner Bros — *VCII; Video Dimensions; Sheik Video; Discount Video Tapes; Cable Films; Video Connection; Video Yesteryear; Sound Video Unlimited; Western Film & Video Inc; Cinema Concepts*

They Paid With Bullets: Chicago 1929 **197?**
Drama
80714 88 mins C B, V P
Peter Lee Lawrence, Ingrid Schoeller
This is the story of one man's rise to power, and eventual downfall as a Mafia consigliatore.
Guilio Diamante — *All Seasons Entertainment*

They Saved Hitler's Brain **1964**
Horror
13142 91 mins B/W B, V P
Walter Stocker, Audrey Caire
Fanatical survivors of the Nazi holocaust give eternal life to the brain of their leader in the last hours of the war.
Crown Intl Pictures — *United Home Video*

They Went That-a-Way & That-a-Way **1978**
Comedy
69552 96 mins C B, V P
Tim Conway, Richard Kiel
Two bumbling deputies pose as convicts in this madcap prison caper.
MPAA:PG
International Picture Show Company — *Embassy Home Entertainment*

They Were Cars **1973**
Language arts
05228 11 mins C B, V, 3/4U P
Especially designed for "Corrective" and "Remedial" reading programs to reinforce "basic reading skills" for primary and intermediate students.
Unknown — *Blackhawk Films; Video Connection; Budget Video; Discount Video Tapes; Hal Roach Studios; Kartes Productions*

They Won't Believe Me **1947**
Suspense
64377 95 mins B/W B, V, 3/4U P
Robert Young, Susan Hayward, Rita Johnson, Jane Greer
A man plots to kill his wife, but before he does, she commits suicide. He ends up on trial for her "murder."
RKO — *Nostalgia Merchant*

They're Playing with Fire **1984**
Suspense
79708 96 mins C B, V R, P
Sybil Danning, Eric Brown, Andrew Prine, Paul Clemens, K.T. Stevens
An English teacher seduces her student and gets him involved in a murder plot.
MPAA:R
New World Pictures; Hickmar Productions — *THORN EMI/HBO Video*

Thief **1981**
Crime-Drama
47152 126 mins C B, V, CED P
James Caan, Tuesday Weld, Willie Nelson, James Belushi, Robert Prosky
A big-time professional thief enjoys pulling off heists on his own, but is forced to work for a crime syndicate in an attempt to bring in more money for his family.
MPAA:R
United Artists — *CBS/Fox Video*

Thief **1971**
Suspense/Drama
81123 74 mins C B, V P
Richard Crenna, Angie Dickinson, Cameron Mitchell, Hurd Hatfield, Robert Webber, directed by William Graham
A successful businessman attempting to put his criminal past behind him, must find a quick way to get some money to pay off a gambling debt.
Metromedia — *Karl/Lorimar Home Video*

Thief of Bagdad, The 1924
Adventure
13175 143 mins B/W B, V P, T
Douglas Fairbanks, Anna May Wong
A fabulous Arabian Nights fantasy, with Fairbanks as a notorious thief who reforms for the love of a princess. Silent with original music score.
United Artists — *Blackhawk Films; Sheik Video; Western Film & Video Inc; Festival Films; Cable Films; Classic Video Cinema Collector's Club; Discount Video Tapes; Kartes Productions*

Thief of Baghdad 1961
Adventure/Fantasy
78641 89 mins C B, V P
Steve Reeves, Georgia Moll
A thief in love with a Sultan's daughter who has been poisoned seeks out the magical blue rose which is the antidote.
Joseph E. Levine; Embassy — *Embassy Home Entertainment*

Thief of Baghdad, The 1978
Fantasy
36182 101 mins C B, V R, P
Peter Ustinov, Roddy McDowall, Terrence Stamp, directed by Clive Donner
A fantasy-adventure about a genie, a prince, beautiful maidens, a happy-go-lucky thief, and magic.
MPAA:G
Palm Films Ltd — *Video Gems*

Thief of Hearts 1984
Drama/Romance
Closed Captioned
77445 100 mins C B, V, LV R, P
Steven Bauer, Barbara Williams, John Getz, George Wendt, Christine Ebersole directed by Douglas Day Stewart
When a thief steals a frustrated woman's diary, he pursues the woman to act out her sexual fantasies. Available in stereo in all formats.
MPAA:R
Paramount Pictures — *Paramount Home Video*

Thief Who Came to Dinner, The 1973
Comedy
80958 103 mins C B, V P
Ryan O'Neal, Jacqueline Bisset, Warren Oates, Jill Clayburgh, Ned Beatty, directed by Bud Yorkin
A computer analyst and a wealthy socialite team up to become jewel thieves and turn the tables on Houston's high society set.
MPAA:PG
Warner Bros. — *Warner Home Video*

Thighs and Whispers: The History of Lingerie 1982
Clothing and dress
59077 45 mins C B, V P
A brief history of lingerie, entertaining and informative.
Karl Video — *Karl/Lorimar Home Video*

Thin Thighs in 30 Day 1983
Physical fitness
66197 60 mins C B, V P
Wendy Stehling
How to have good looking legs is discussed and demonstrated.
WCP Video — *U.S.A. Home Video*

Thing, The 1951
Science fiction
44002 80 mins B/W B, V, 3/4U P
James Arness, Kenneth Tobey, Margaret Sheriden
Alien creature terrorizes an Arctic research team.
RKO; Howard Hawks — *Nostalgia Merchant; VidAmerica; King of Video; RCA VideoDiscs*

Thing, The 1982
Science fiction/Horror
62875 127 mins C B, V, LV, CED P
Kurt Russell, A. Wilford Brimely, T.K. Carter, directed by John Carpenter
A team of scientists at a remote Antarctic outpost discover a buried spaceship with an unwelcome alien survivor still alive. VHS in stereo. Also available subtitled in Spanish.
MPAA:R
Universal — *MCA Home Video*

Things Are Tough All Over 1982
Comedy
63433 87 mins C B, V P
Cheech Marin, Tommy Chong, Shelby Fiddis, Rikki Marin, Evelyn Guerrero, Rip Taylor
Cheech and Chong play dual roles as themselves and as two rich Arab brothers who hire Cheech and Chong to drive a car full of money from Chicago to Las Vegas.
MPAA:R
Columbia; Howard Brown — *RCA/Columbia Pictures Home Video; RCA VideoDiscs*

Things to Come 1936
Science fiction
12826 92 mins B/W B, V P
Raymond Massey, Ralph Richardson, Sir Cedric Hardwicke, directed by William Cameron Menzies
Based on the H. G. Wells story of a war lasting from 1940 to 2036 and how scientists aim to rebuild the world when peace is achieved.

London Films; Alexander Korda — *Prism; Media Home Entertainment; Movie Buff Video; Video Yesteryear; Budget Video; Sheik Video; Cable Films; Video Connection; Discount Video Tapes; Cinema Concepts; Hal Roach Studios; Kartes Productions; Classic Video Cinema Collector's Club*

Things We Did Last Summer, The **1978**
Comedy
78068 46 mins C B, V R, P
John Belushi, Dan Aykroyd, Bill Murray, Gilda Radner, Garrett Morris, Laraine Newman
Members of the original cast of "Saturday Night Live" are featured in this special program where they show how they spent their summer vacations.
NBC; Lorne Michaels — *Pacific Arts Video*

Think Dirty **1978**
Comedy
64577 93 mins C B, V P
Marty Feldman, Judy Cornwell, Shelley Berman
An advertising executive develops a series of sexy commercials at the same time that his wife is forming a "clean up TV" group.
MPAA:R
Quartet Films — *RCA/Columbia Pictures Home Video*

Third Man, The **1949**
Mystery
08595 105 mins B/W B, V P
Orson Wells, Joseph Cotton, Alida Valli, directed by Sir Carol Reed
An American writer arrives in Vienna to take job with an old friend whom he finds has been murdered. Based on Graham Greene's mystery.
Academy Awards '50: Best Cinematography.
Selznick Releasing Organization;
British — *Media Home Entertainment; Prism; Budget Video; VCII; Video Yesteryear; Video Dimensions; Sheik Video; Video Connection; Discount Video Tapes; Cable Films; Western Film & Video Inc; Cinema Concepts; Classic Video Cinema Collector's Club; Vestron Video (disc only); Hal Roach Studios*

Thirsty Dead **1977**
Horror
36928 90 mins C B, V P
John Considine, Jennifer Billingsley
A science fiction-horror film wherein corpses return to life.
Unknown — *King of Video*

---

38 Special Wild Eyed and Live **1984**
Music-Performance
80386 75 mins C B, V P
This is a concert featuring southern rockers 38 Special performing such hits as "Caught Up in You" and "Hold on Loosely."
AM Video — *A & M Video; RCA/Columbia Pictures Home Video*

35mm Motion Picture Projector, The **1956**
Film-History
54110 30 mins B/W B, V P, T
A look at a private collection of 35mm motion picture projectors that is the largest collection in existence anywhere.
Unknown — *Blackhawk Films*

---

30 Is a Dangerous Age, Cynthia **1968**
Comedy
76040 85 mins C B, V P
Dudley Moore, Suzy Kendall, Eddie Foy Jr
Dudley Moore stars as a night club pianist who has set himself a goal to get married and write a hit musical before he reaches thirty.
Walter Shenson — *RCA/Columbia Pictures Home Video*

---

39 Steps, The **1935**
Mystery
48695 81 mins B/W B, V P
Robert Donat, Madeleine Carroll, Godfrey Tearle, Lucie Mannheim, Peggy Ashcroft, directed by Alfred Hitchcock
A man becomes involved in a murder and an international spy ring. Classic Hitchcock suspense with many of his trademark directorial touches.
Gaumont — *Embassy Home Entertainment; VCII; Video Yesteryear; Video Dimensions; Sheik Video; Cable Films; Video Connection; Budget Video; Western Film & Video Inc; Discount Video Tapes; RCA VideoDiscs; Spotlite Video; Hal Roach Studios; Classic Video Cinema Collector's Club*

This Gun For Hire **1942**
Western
68255 81 mins B/W B, V P
Alan Ladd, Veronica Lake, Robert Preston, Laird Cregar
Ladd plays a paid gunman working within a criminal organization who is hired by German spies, is double crossed and ends up wanting revenge.
Paramount — *MCA Home Video*

This Is a Hijack **1975**
Adventure/Suspense
76661 90 mins C B, V P
Adam Roarke, Neville Brand, Jay Robinson, Lynn Borden, Dub Taylor
A story of a gambler who can't pay his debts and decides to make a deal to hijack his wealthy boss.

MPAA:PG
Fanfare Corp — *Monterey Home Video*

This Is Elvis **1981**
Biographical/Musical
68238 144 mins C B, V R, P
The life of Elvis is presented in this film. There are 42 minutes of footage that has never been seen before and more than three dozen songs.
MPAA:PG
David L Wolper — *Warner Home Video*

This Is Spinal Tap **1984**
Satire/Musical
78356 82 mins C B, V P
Michael McKean, Christopher Guest, Harry Shearer, Tony Hendra, Bruno Kirby, directed by Rob Reiner
A filmmaker wants to make a documentary about the career and music of the heavy metal band Spinal Tap. Included in this videocassette are Spinal Tap's music videos "Hell Hole" and "Heavy Metal Memories."
MPAA:R
Karen Murphy — *Embassy Home Entertainment*

This Is the Army **1943**
Musical-Drama
11316 105 mins C B, V, FO P
George Murphy, Joan Leslie, Ronald Reagan, Alan Hale, Kate Smith, and the men of the Armed Services
A robust tribute to the American soldier, containing the songs, "This is the Army, Mr. Jones," "I Left My Heart at the Stage Door Canteen," "Oh, How I Hate to Get Up in the Morning," and many more.
Academy Award '43: Best Scoring Musical.
Warner Bros — *Video Yesteryear; Discount Video Tapes; Sheik Video; Cable Films; Video Connection; Budget Video; Classic Video Cinema Collector's Club; See Hear Industries*

This Is Your Life: Laurel and Hardy **1954**
Interview
42972 30 mins B/W B, V, FO P
Ralph Edwards, Stan Laurel, Oliver Hardy
Stan and Ollie appear somewhat stunned as old girlfriends and assocaites from Hollywood appear, including Vivian Blaine and Leo McCarey.
NBC — *Video Yesteryear; Sheik Video*

This Island Earth **1955**
Science fiction
64789 86 mins C B, V P
Jeff Morrow, Faith Domergue, Rex Reason, directed by Joseph M. Newman
The planet Metaluna is in desperate need of uranium to power their defense against enemy invaders. A nuclear scientist and a nuclear fission expert are kidnapped to help out.
Universal — *MCA Home Video*

This Land Is Mine **1943**
Drama
76835 103 mins B/W B, V P
Charles Laughton, Maureen O'Hara, George Sanders, Walter Slezak, Una O'Connor, directed by Jean Renoir
A timid French schoolteacher gathers enough courage to defy the Nazis when they attempt to occupy his town.
Academy Award '43: Best Sound Recording.
RKO — *RKO HomeVideo*

Thomas Crown Affair, The **1968**
Drama/Adventure
55588 102 mins C B, V P
Steve McQueen, Faye Dunaway, Jack Weston
A multi-millionaire executes a daring daylight robbery of a bank and gets away with two million in cash.
Academy Awards '68: Best Song ("Windmills of Your Mind"). EL, SP
United Artists; Mirisch Corp — *CBS/Fox Video*

Thomas Dolby **1983**
Music-Performance
69393 58 mins C B, V R, P
This music video by the popular rock star includes such songs as "She Blinded Me with Science," "Europa" and "One of Our Submarines."
EMI Music — *THORN EMI/HBO Video; Pioneer Video Imports*

Thomas Dolby **1984**
Music-Performance
75913 16 mins C B, V P
This program presents the new British singer Thomas Dolby performing his hit songs.
EMI Records Ltd — *Sony Corporation of America*

Thompson Twins Live at Liverpool, The **1983**
Music-Performance
73020 60 mins C B, V R, P
Tom Bailey, Joe Leeway, Alannah Currie
The Thompson Twins, recorded concert at Liverpool's Royal Court, perform "Lies and Love on Your Side".
Unknown — *THORN EMI/HBO Video*

Thorn, The **1973**
Satire
77254 90 mins C B, V P
Bette Midler, John Bassberger
The Virgin Mary and Joseph try to raise Jesus Christ in the modern world.

MPAA:R
Peter Alexander — *Magnum Entertainment*

Thorpe's Gold **1984**
Documentary/Sports
72947 75 mins C B, V P
A documentary about Olympic star Jim Thorpe, multi-award winner in the 1912 Olympics. Some black-and-white segments.
VCI — *United Home Video*

Those Endearing Young Charms **1945**
Romance
10044 82 mins B/W B, V P, T
Robert Young, Laraine Day, Anne Jeffreys, Lawrence Tierney
Romance developes between young Air Corps mechanic and salesgirl. Complications arise when another man enters the scene.
RKO — *Blackhawk Films*

Those Krazy, Klassic, Kolor Kartoons, Volume I **1985**
Cartoons
81529 58 mins C B, V P
Animated
Here is a compilation of classic cartoons such as "Felix the Cat" and "Old Mother Hubbard" that the whole family can enjoy.
MPI; Academy Video — *MPI Home Video*

Those Lips, Those Eyes **1980**
Comedy-Drama
80625 106 mins C B, V P
Frank Langella, Thomas Hulce, Glynnis O'Connor, Jerry Stiller, Kevin McCarthy
A pre-med student takes a job as a prop boy in a summer stock company and winds up falling in love with the company's lead dancer.
MPAA:R
United Artists — *MGM/UA Home Video*

Those Magnificent Men in Their Flying Machines **1965**
Comedy
08461 138 mins C B, V P
Stuart Whitman, Sarah Miles, Robert Morley, Albert Sordi, James Fox, Gert Frobe
In 1910 a wealthy British newspaper publisher is persuaded to sponsor an air race from London to Paris. Contestants from all over the world come.
EL, SP
20th Century Fox — *CBS/Fox Video*

Those Wild Bloopers **1984**
Outtakes and bloopers
73549 65 mins B/W B, V P
All kinds of foulups and blunders from Bogart, Abbott and Costello and Bette Davis are in this program.
Admit One — *Admit One Video*

Thousand Clowns, A **1965**
Comedy-Drama
58838 118 mins B/W CED P
Jason Robards Jr., Barry Gordon, William Daniels, Barbara Harris, Gene Saks, Martin Balsam
A nonconformist writer resigns from his job as chief writer for an obnoxious kiddie show in order to enjoy life.
United Artists — *CBS/Fox Video*

Threat, The **1949**
Mystery
73694 66 mins B/W B, V P
Michael O'Shea, Virginia Grey, Charles McGraw
An escaped killer returns to settle the score with those who convicted him.
RKO — *RKO HomeVideo*

Three Avengers **1980**
Martial arts
81474 93 mins C B, V P
There's lots of trouble abounding when two kung fu masters and an American Chinese boy open a martial arts school.
MPAA:R
World Northal Corporation — *Embassy Home Entertainment*

Three Broadway Girls **1932**
Comedy
47774 78 mins B/W B, V, 3/4U R, P
Joan Blondell, Ina Claire, Madge Evans, David Manners, Lowell Sherman
Three gold-diggers go husband hunting.
United Artists — *Movie Buff Video; Cable Films; Kartes Productions*

Three Caballeros, The **1945**
Cartoons
59811 70 mins C B, V R, P
Animated
Donald Duck stars in this program of shorts about South America, full of music and variety. Stories include "Pablo the Penguin," "Little Gauchito," and adventures with Joe Carioca.
Walt Disney — *Walt Disney Home Video*

Three Cheers for the Redskins **1983**
Football
65016 53 mins C B, V, FO P
A colorful study of the Washington Redskins' 1971 season, their first with George Allen as head coach, following the death of Vince Lombardi.
NFL Films — *NFL Films Video*

 (For explanation of codes, see USE GUIDE and KEY)

Three Days of the Condor 1975
Drama
38604 118 mins C B, V, LV R, P
Robert Redford, Faye Dunaway, Cliff Robertson, Max Von Sydow, directed by Sydney Pollack
CIA researcher Redford finds himself on the run from unknown killers when he is left the only survivor of the mass murder of his office staff.
MPAA:R
Paramount — *Paramount Home Video; RCA VideoDiscs*

Three Faces West 1940
Western
66467 79 mins B/W B, V P
John Wayne, Charles Coburn, Sigrid Gurie, Sonny Bupp
A dust bowl community is helped by a Viennese doctor who left Europe to avoid Nazi capture.
Republic — *Republic Pictures Home Video*

Three Husbands 1950
Drama
66399 80 mins B/W B, V P
Emlyn Williams, Eve Arden, Howard Da Silva, Ruth Warrick, Billie Burke
Three husbands receive letters from a dead friend claiming that he had affairs with each of their wives.
United Artists — *Movie Buff Video*

Three in the Attic 1968
Comedy-Drama
65069 92 mins C B, V P
Christopher Jones, Yvette Mimieux, John Beck
A college student juggles three girlfriends at the same time. When the girls find out they are being two-timed, they lock their boyfriend in an attic and exhaust him with forced sexual escapades.
MPAA:R
American International Pictures — *Embassy Home Entertainment*

Three Little Pigs, The 1984
Fairy tales
Closed Captioned
73571 60 mins C B, V, CED P
Billy Crystal, Jeff Goldblum, Valerie Perrine
From "Faerie Tale Theatre" comes the story of three little pigs, the houses they lived in and the wolf that tries to do them in.
Gaylord Productions; Platypus Productions — *CBS/Fox Video*

Three Musketeers, The 1974
Adventure
59645 107 mins C CED P
Richard Chamberlain, Raquel Welch, Michael York, Oliver Reed, Faye Dunaway, Charlton Heston, Christopher Lee, directed by Richard Lester
Sword play, romance, and slapstick comedy abound in this exuberant big-budget version of the Alexandre Dumas classic.
MPAA:PG
Alexander Salkin — *RCA VideoDiscs*

Three Musketeers, The 1973
Cartoons
66581 47 mins C B, V P
Animated
An animated retelling of the Alexander Dumas classic about three swordsmen and their problems with Cardinal Richleau.
Unknown — *Worldvision Home Video*

Three Musketeers, The 1973
Adventure
65440 107 mins C B, V P
Richard Chamberlain, Raquel Welch, Faye Dunaway, Michael York
A tongue-in-cheek version of the Alexander Dumas classic.
MPAA:PG
Film Trust SA — *U.S.A. Home Video*

Three Musketeers, The 1976
Adventure/Cartoons
69528 74 mins C B, V, CED P
Animated
D'Artagnan and the fabled Musketeers engage in swashbuckling adventures in Paris and England.
Pendennis Films — *Children's Video Library*

Three Musketeers, The 1948
Adventure
81495 126 mins C B, V P
Lana Turner, Gene Kelly, June Allyson, Gig Young, Angela Landsbury, Vincent Price, directed by George Sidney
Those three musketeers who are all for one and one for all battle the evil Cardinal Richileu in this rollicking adaptation of the Dumas classic story.
MGM — *MGM/UA Home Video*

Three Musketeers, The 1933
Adventure/Serials
14629 156 mins B/W B, V P
John Wayne, Raymond Hatton
Modern adaptation of Dumas' classic puts the three friends in fast airplanes. In twelve chapters.
Mascot — *Video Connection; Video Dimensions; Video Yesteryear; Discount Video Tapes; Classic Video Cinema Collector's Club*

Three Penny Opera 1963
Musical
78083 100 mins C B, V, FO P

Curt Jurgens, Hildegarde Neff, Gert Frobe, June Ritchie, Lino Ventura, Sammy Davis Jr.
Mack the Knife presides over an exciting world of thieves, murderers, beggars, prostitutes and corrupt officials, in this film version of the famous Kurt Weill-Bertold Brecht operetta.
Embassy Pictures — *Video Yesteryear*

---

3 Reyes Magos, Los **198?**
Cartoons
77352 86 mins C B, V P
Animated
This is an animated retelling of the legend of the three wisemen who brought gifts to Jesus Christ on the Epiphany.
SP
Foreign — *Unicorn Video*

Three Stooges, The **1949**
Comedy
63098 60 mins B/W B, V P
Moe, Larry, Curly and Shemp
Three original shorts by the comedy trio, including: "Disorder in the Court" (1936—Curly), "Sing a Song of Six Pants" (1949—Shemp) and "Malice in the Palace" (1949—Shemp).
Columbia — *Admit One Video*

Three Stooges Comedy Capers Volume I **194?**
Comedy
60421 80 mins B/W B, V, 3/4U P
Moe Howard, Larry Fine, Curly Howard, Shemp Howard
This compilation includes: "Disorder in the Court" (1936), "Malice in the Palace" (1949), "Sing a Song of Six Pants" (1947), "The Brideless Groom" (1947).
Columbia Pictures — *Nostalgia Merchant*

Three Stooges Comedy Classics **193?**
Comedy
80463 79 mins B/W B, V P
Moe Howard, Larry Fine, Curly Howard, Shemp Howard, Ted Healy
The antics of the Stooges are featured in this collection of five original shorts, along with an early Ted Healy comedy that features all four Stooges.
Columbia — *Spotlite Video*

Three Stooges, Volume XI, The **1942**
Comedy
77244 60 mins B/W B, V P
Moe Howard, Curly Howard, Shemp Howard
This volume features "Boobs In Arms" where the boys become greeting card salesmen, in "Whats The Matador" the Stooges are being chased around a bullfighting ring by a jealous husband, and in "Mutts to You" the trio take home an abandoned baby.
Columbia — *RCA/Columbia Pictures Home Video*

Three Stooges, Volume XII, The **1942**
Comedy
Closed Captioned
80884 60 mins B/W B, V P
Curly Howard, Moe Howard, Larry Fine
Here are three more vintage Stooges shorts: In "Loco Boy Makes Good" the Stooges try to save an ailing hotel; in "Matri-Phony" the boys go back to ancient Erysipelas and incur the wrath of emperor Octopus Grabus; and in "Saved by the Belle" our heroes sell earthquake shock absorbers.
Screen Gems — *RCA/Columbia Pictures Home Video*

Three Stooges Meet Hercules, The **1961**
Comedy
69619 80 mins B/W B, V P
The Three Stooges, Vicki Trickett, Quinn Redeker
The Three Stooges are transported back to ancient Ithaca by a time machine with a young scientist and his girlfriend. When the girl is captured, they enlist the help of Hercules to rescue her.
Norman Maurer; Columbia — *RCA/Columbia Pictures Home Video*

Three Stooges Videodisc, Vol. 1, The **194?**
Comedy
60385 106 mins B/W CED P
Moe Howard, Larry Fine, Curly Howard, Christine McIntyre
Four classic Three Stooges two-reelers are on this disc: "Dizzy Pilots" (1943), "A Bird in the Head" (1946), "Three Missing Links" (1938) and "Micro-Phonies" (1945).
Columbia — *RCA VideoDiscs*

Three Stooges Volume I, The **194?**
Comedy
44844 60 mins B/W B, V P
Moe Howard, Larry Fine, Curly Howard
Three shorts featuring Curly, Moe and Larry are included in this package: "A Bird in the Head" (1946), "Dizzy Pilots" (1943), and "Three Sappy People" (1939).
Columbia — *RCA/Columbia Pictures Home Video*

Three Stooges Volume II, The **194?**
Comedy
58540 60 mins B/W B, V P
Moe Howard, Larry Fine, Curly Howard

 (For explanation of codes, see USE GUIDE and KEY)

The Three Stooges are seen in three shorts: "Uncivil Warriors" (1935), "Three Missing Links" (1938), and "Micro-Phonies" (1945).
Columbia — *RCA/Columbia Pictures Home Video*

Three Stooges Volume III, The **194?**
Comedy
52754 60 mins B/W B, V P
Moe Howard, Larry Fine, Curly Howard
Three comedy shorts: "Pop Goes the Easel" (1935), in which the Stooges run amuck in an art studio; "Calling All Curs" (1939), in which a prize pooch is stolen from the Stooges' dog hospital; and "An Ache in Every Stake" (1941), in which the Stooges, as icemen, are hired to prepare a fancy birthday dinner.
Columbia — *RCA/Columbia Pictures Home Video*

Three Stooges Volume IV, The **193?**
Comedy
58958 60 mins B/W B, V P
Moe Howard, Larry Fine, Curly Howard, Charley Chase, Walter Brennan
Three classic "Stooges" shorts: "Woman Haters" (1934), the story of three woman haters, with dialogue spoken in rhyme; "Three Little Beers" (1935), in which the boys decide to enter a golf tournanment sponsored by their beer company; and, "Tassels in the Air" (1938), in which the Stooges are hired as interior decorators.
Columbia — *RCA/Columbia Pictures Home Video*

Three Stooges Volume V, The **193?**
Comedy
Closed Captioned
62813 60 mins B/W B, V P
The Three Stooges
Another package of Three Stooges two-reelers, featuring the antics of Moe, Larry and Curly. The tape contains "Pardon My Scotch" (1935), "Disorder in the Court" (1936) and "Healthy, Wealthy and Dumb" (1938).
Columbia — *RCA/Columbia Pictures Home Video*

Three Stooges Volume VI, The **193?**
Comedy
64575 60 mins B/W B, V P
Moe Howard, Larry Fine, Curly Howard
The Three Stooges ride again in another package of three vintage two-reelers: "Violent Is the Word for Curly" (1938), "Punch Drunks" (1934) and "A-Plumbing We Will Go" (1940).
Columbia — *RCA/Columbia Pictures Home Video*

Three Stooges Volume VII, The **194?**
Comedy
65101 60 mins B/W B, V P
Moe Howard, Larry Fine, Curly Howard
Those mirthful Stooges are back again in another package of three original shorts: "Dutiful But Dumb" (1941), "Movie Maniacs" (1936) and "Oily to Bed, Oily to Rise" (1939).
Columbia — *RCA/Columbia Pictures Home Video*

Three Stooges, Volume VIII, The **1984**
Comedy
65702 60 mins B/W B, V P
Larry Fine, Moe Howard, Curly Howard
The Three Stooges entertain in three more short films—"Cash and Carry," "No Census, No Feeling," and "Some More of Samoa." An added attraction is a music video of "The Curly Shuffle."
Columbia — *RCA/Columbia Pictures Home Video*

Three Stooges Volume IX, The **193?**
Comedy
Closed Captioned
72923 60 mins B/W B, V P
Moe Howard, Larry Fine, Curly Howard
More of the classic shorts featuring Moe, Larry, and Curly.
Columbia — *RCA/Columbia Pictures Home Video*

Three Stooges, Volume X, The **1945**
Comedy
Closed Captioned
78877 60 mins B/W B, V P
Moe Howard, Larry Fine, Curly Howard
The Stooges are back again with three more classic shorts: "If a Body Meets a Body" (1945) "Spook Louder" (1943) and "Men in Black" (1934). In Beta and VHS Hi-Fi.
Screen Gems — *RCA/Columbia Pictures Home Video*

Three Tales of Love & Friendship **1984**
Fantasy
65722 118 mins C CED P
A compilation of children's programs including "The Red Balloon" (1956), "The Unicorn" (1972), and "The Lone Wolf" (1983). Each story centers on the magical powers of love and friendship that can make dreams come true.

Films Monsouris; Carol Reed; Jadren Film Zagreb — *Embassy Home Entertainment (disc only)*

3:10 to Yuma 1957
Western
77375 92 mins B/W B, V P
Glenn Ford, Van Heflin, Felicia Farr, directed by Delmer Daves
A common farmer successfully holds a dangerous killer at bay while waiting turn the outlaw over to the marshal arriving on the 3:10 train to Yuma.
Columbia Pictures — *RCA/Columbia Pictures Home Video*

Three Warriors 1977
Drama
63345 100 mins C B, V R, P
Charles White Eagle, Lois Red Elk, McKee "Kiko" Red Wing, Christopher Lloyd, Randy Quaid
A young Indian boy is forced to leave the city and return to the reservation, where his contempt for the traditions of his ancestors slowly turns to appreciation and love.
Saul Zaentz; Sy Gomberg — *THORN EMI/HBO Video*

Three Way Weekend 1981
Comedy
81566 78 mins C B, V P
Dan Diego, Jody Lee Olhava, Richard Blye
Two young girls set off on a back-packing trip through the mountains of Southern California to enjoy camping and romance.
MPAA:R
Alston/Zanitsch International Films — *Academy Home Entertainment*

Three Weird Sisters, The 1948
Drama
66400 100 mins B/W B, V P
Nova Pilbeam, Nancy Price, Mary Clare, Mary Merrall, Hugh Griffith
Three crippled sisters in a Welsh village plot to kill their wealthy half-brother and his secretary. Based on the novel by Charlotte Armstrong.
British National; Pathe — *Movie Buff Video*

Three Word Brand 1921
Western
52465 75 mins B/W B, V, FO P
William S. Hart, Jayne Navak, S. J. Bingham
William S. Hart plays three roles in this film, a homesteader who is killed by Indians and his twin sons, who are separated after their father's death and reunited many years later. Silent with musical score.
William S Hart Co — *Video Yesteryear; Classic Video Cinema Collector's Club*

Threepenny Opera, The 1931
Musical-Drama
52467 105 mins B/W B, V P
Lotte Lenya, Rudolph Forster, Carola Neher, directed by G. W. Pabst
The first film version of the Bertolt Brecht-Kurt Weill musical play about London lowlife in the 19th century. Lotte Lenya portrays her most famous character, prostitute Jenny Brown. Songs include "Mack the Knife."
UFA; Germany — *Video Dimensions; Video Classics; Cable Films; Discount Video Tapes; Embassy Home Entertainment*

Threshold 1983
Drama
65758 97 mins C B, V P
Donald Sutherland, Jeff Goldblum
The story of an internationally-acclaimed surgeon who is frustrated by his inability to save a dying 20-year-old woman born with a defective heart.
MPAA:PG
Jon Slan; Micheal Burns — *CBS/Fox Video*

Threshold: The Blue Angels Experience 1974
Aeronautics/Armed Forces-US
29751 89 mins C B, V, 3/4U P
Narrated by Leslie Nielsen
A true life adventure of six men and "a team" which they created. It is a photographic exploration of extraordinary feats accomplished by these F-14 Phantoms flyers.
MPAA:G
Paul Marlow — *Aero/Space Visuals Society*

Thumbelina 1984
Cartoons/Fairy tales
Closed Captioned
72924 45 mins C B, V P
Animated
An animated version of the Hans Christian Andersen fairy tale about a little girl who's only as tall as a thumb.
John Watkins and Simon Nuchtern — *RCA/Columbia Pictures Home Video*

Thumbelina 1984
Fairy tales
Closed Captioned
73854 60 mins C B, V, LV, CED P
Carrie Fisher, William Katt, Burgess Meredith, directed by Michael Lindsay-Hogg
From "Faerie Tale Theatre" comes the story of a tiny girl who gets kidnapped by a toad and a mole but meets the man of her dreams in the nick of time.
Gaylord Productions; Platypus Productions — *CBS/Fox Video*

Thundarr the Barbarian **1980**
Cartoons
65663 57 mins C B, V P
In this episode, Thundarr, Princess Ariel and Ookla the Mot fight sorcery and slavery.
Ruby Spears — *Worldvision Home Video*

Thundarr the Barbarian **1983**
Adventure/Cartoons
80645 40 mins C B, V P
Animated
Thundarr the Barbarian defends justice in the bizarre civilization that has emerged from the ashes of a destroyed earth.
Ruby-Spears — *Worldvision Home Video*

Thunder and Lightning **1977**
Adventure/Comedy
Closed Captioned
70700 94 mins C B, V P
David Carradine, Kate Jackson, directed by Corey Allen
A mismatched young couple chase a truckload of poisoned moonshine. Action packed chases ensue in Hi-Fi stereo.
MPAA:PG
20th Century Fox; Roger Corman — *Key Video*

Thunder Country **1974**
Adventure
80297 78 mins C B, V P
Mickey Rooney, Ted Cassidy, Chris Robinson
Federal agents and drug runners are after a group of four convicts who have just escaped from prison.
Joseph Brenner Associates — *Prism*

Thunder in the City **1937**
Comedy-Drama
08865 85 mins B/W B, V P
Edward G. Robinson, Nigel Bruce, Ralph Richardson
An American promoter descends on London with all the modern day advertising methods.
Columbia; Alexander Esway — *Movie Buff Video*

Thunder of Steam in the Blue Ridge, The **1958**
Trains
47820 20 mins B/W B, V P, T
Photographed in the mountainous area on the Norfolk and Western's mail line between Roanoke and Bedford, Virginia, this film shows the N and W's tough locomotives pulling and pushing on the mountain grades.
Unknown — *Blackhawk Films*

Thunderball **1965**
Adventure
64452 125 mins C B, V P
Sean Connery, Adolfo Celi, Claudine Auger
The fourth installment in Ian Fleming's James Bond series finds Bond on a mission to thwart SPECTRE, which has threatened to blow up Miami by atomic bomb if 100 million pounds of sterling ransom is not paid.
Academy Award '65: Special Visual Effects.
United Artists — *CBS/Fox Video; RCA VideoDiscs*

Thunderbirds 2086 **1984**
Cartoons
77236 50 mins C B, V P
Animated
An elite group of daredevil cadets fly throughout the galaxy to protect the world from disaster.
ITC Productions — *MPI Home Video*

Thunderbirds Are Go **1966**
Adventure/Puppets
68241 92 mins C B, V, CED P
The world's favorite electronic puppets, the Tracy brothers, launch through the uncharted worlds of adventure.
Associated Television Limited — *MGM/UA Home Video*

Thunderbirds in Outer Space **1981**
Cartoons
70655 92 mins C B, V P
Animated
These popular space-age marionettes save the day anytime someone is plunging into the sun or drifting aimlessly to their death in space.
Available in Hi-Fi stereo.
ITC Entertainment — *Family Home Entertainment*

Thunderbolt and Lightfoot **1974**
Drama
58847 115 mins C B, V, CED P
Clint Eastwood, Jeff Bridges, George Kennedy, Geoffrey Lewis, directed by Michael Cimino
A bank robber posing as a preacher is saved by a young stranger when his former partners come gunning for him.
MPAA:R
United Artists — *CBS/Fox Video; RCA VideoDiscs*

Thundering Mantis **1976**
Martial arts
76936 85 mins C B, V P
A martial arts student goes after the men who killed his Kung-Fu master.
Foreign — *Trans World Entertainment*

Thundering Mantis **1976**
Martial arts
78957 85 mins C B, V P

A rousing martial arts film with a shattering climax that features the thundering mantis style of Kung-fu.
Japanese — *Trans World Entertainment*

THX 1138 **1971**
Science fiction/Drama
51971 88 mins C B, V R, P
Robert Duvall, Donald Pleasance, Maggie McOmie, directed by George Lucas
In the dehumanized world of the future, a computer-matched couple discover love. Since emotion is outlawed, the woman is killed for the offense, but the man escapes and tries to fight the system.
MPAA:PG
Warner Bros;American Zoetrope — *Warner Home Video*

Tiara Tahiti **1962**
Adventure
59842 100 mins C B, V P
James Mason, John Mills, Claude Dauphin, Rosenda Monteros
Intrigue, double-cross, romance, and violence ensue when two old army acquaintances clash in Tahiti.
Earl St John — *Embassy Home Entertainment*

Ticket of Leave Man, The **1937**
Mystery
80757 71 mins B/W B, V P
Tod Slaughter, John Warwick, Marjorie Taylor
London's most dangerous killer fronts a charitable organization which he uses to cheat philanthropists out of their fortunes.
George King; MGM — *Video Yesteryear*

Ticket to Heaven **1981**
Drama
47779 109 mins C B, V, CED P
Nick Mancuso, Meg Foster, Kim Cattrail
A thriller dealing with cult religions in California. A school teacher gradually falls under the influence of a quasi-religious order.
Stalker Productions — *MGM/UA Home Video*

Tiffany Jones **1975**
Drama
81409 90 mins C B, V P
Anouska Hempel, Ray Brooks
Tiffany Jones is a secret agent who has a secret that presidents andrevolutionaries are willing to kill for. Available in VHS Stereo and Beta Hi-Fi.
MPAA:R
Peter Walker — *Monterey Home Video*

Tiger Town **1983**
Drama
65633 76 mins C B, V R, P
Roy Scheider, Justin Henry, Ron McLarty, Bethany Carpenter, Noah Moazezi
A baseball player, ending an illustrious career with the Detroit Tigers, sees his hopes of winning a pennant slipping away. On the other hand, a die-hard Tigers fan is convinced that a "true believer" can make anything happen.
Susan B Landau; Thompson Street Pictures — *Walt Disney Home Video*

Tiger's Claw **197?**
Martial arts/Adventure
47702 90 mins C B, V P
Chin Long
Shen roves the country honing his Kung Fu technique, obsessed by his fanatical desire to challenge Kuo, the best in China.
Kwong Ming Motion Picture Co — *Master Arts Video*

Tigers Don't Cry **1981**
Drama
81070 105 mins C B, V P
Anthony Quinn
An unusual friendship develops between a male nurse and the African dignitary that he kidnaps as they flee from the authorities.
Alan Girney — *MPI Home Video*

Tightrope **1984**
Suspense/Drama
80076 115 mins C B, V, CED R, P
Clint Eastwood, Genevieve Bujold, Dan Hedaya, Jennifer Beck, directed by Richard Tuggle
A police inspector must find out who is killing prostitutes in New Orleans' French Quarter.
MPAA:R
Clint Eastwood; Warner Bros — *Warner Home Video*

Till Marriage Do Us Part **1980**
Comedy
58899 97 mins C B, V, LV, CED P
Laura Antonelli, Alberto Lionello, Jean Rochefort
An innocent couple discover on their wedding night that they are really brother and sister.
Pio Angeletti; Adriano de Micheli — *Vestron Video*

Till the Clouds Roll By **1946**
Musical
01623 137 mins C B, V P
Judy Garland, Frank Sinatra, Van Heflin, Robert Walker, Directed by Richard Whorf
A musical biography of songwriter Jerome Kern, with an all-star cast performing a cavalcade of his great tunes.
MGM; Arthur Freed — *MGM/UA Home Video; Prism; Cable Films; See Hear Industries*

(For explanation of codes, see USE GUIDE and KEY)

Tillie's Punctured Romance **1914**
Comedy
08713 73 mins B/W B, V, 3/4U P
Charlie Chaplin, Marie Dressler
A silent comedy which established Chaplin and Dressler as comedians.
Paramount — *Blackhawk Films; Budget Video; Sheik Video; Video Yesteryear; Discount Video Tapes; Nostalgia Merchant*

Tim **1979**
Drama
65113 94 mins C B, V P
Mel Gibson, Piper Laurie, Peter Gwynne
This Australian film tells of the evolving relationship between a handsome, mentally retarded young man and an attractive businesswoman in her mid-40's.
Michael Pate; Satori Productions — *Media Home Entertainment*

Time After Time **1979**
Science fiction/Adventure
52701 112 mins C B, V R, P
Malcolm McDowell, David Warner, Mary Steenburgen, Patti D'Arbanville
H. G. Wells and Jack the Ripper leave London circa 1893 in Wells' famous time machine and arrive in San Francisco in 1979.
MPAA:PG
Orion Pictures; Warner Bros — *Warner Home Video*

Time Bandits **1981**
Fantasy
59389 110 mins C B, V, LV R, P
John Cleese, Sean Connery, Shelley Duvall, Katherine Helmond, Ian Holm, Michael Palin, Ralph Richardson, David Warner, Kenny Baker, directed by Terry Gilliam
An English youngster and a group of dwarves pass through time holes on assignment by the Maker to patch up part of his creation.
MPAA:PG
Handmade Films — *Paramount Home Video; RCA VideoDiscs*

Time Capsule: The Los Angeles Olympic Games/1932 **1984**
Sports/Documentary
66613 60 mins B/W B, V P
Directed by Bud Greenspan
The 1932 Los Angeles Olympic Games are the subject of this documentary which utilizes rare and never-before-seen action footage. Among the athletes seen participating are Mildred "Babe" Didrikson, Glenn Cunningham and swimmer Eleanor Holm.
Lorimar — *U.S.A. Home Video*

Time Fighters **1985**
Fantasy/Cartoons
80769 60 mins C B, V P
Animated
A time machine has the ability to travel at the speed of light from prehistoric times to the distant future. This is a great help to the Time fighters.
Kidpix — *Embassy Home Entertainment*

Time Machine **1978**
Science fiction/Adventure
45010 99 mins C B, V P
John Beck, Priscilla Barnes, Andrew Duggan
Based H.G. Wells' classic novel, this movie tells the story of a scientist who invents a machine that enables him to travel through time and undertakes a journey into the future, only to find a civilization dominated by a group of hideous people called Morlocks, the only survivors of a devastating war.
MPAA:G
Schick Sunn Classic — *United Home Video*

Time Machine, The **1960**
Science fiction/Adventure
63112 103 mins C B, V P
Rod Taylor, Yvette Mimieux, Alan Young, directed by George Pal
An English scientist of the year 1899 builds a conveyance that carries him far into the future, where he discovers the remnants of man's civilization. Based on H.G. Well's pioneering novel.
MGM — *MGM/UA Home Video*

Time to Die, A **1983**
Adventure
65354 89 mins C B, V P
Edward Albert Jr., Rex Harrison, Rod Taylor
A victim of heinous war crimes, obsessed with revenge, stalks his prey for a final confrontation.
MPAA:R
Charles Lee — *Media Home Entertainment*

Timefighters in the Land of Fantasy **1984**
Cartoons/Fantasy
81105 95 mins C B, V R, P
Animated
A team of time-travelers use their time machine to venture into the worlds of such classic fairytales as Cinderella and Jack and the Beanstalk.
Kidpix Inc. — *Paramount Home Video*

Timerider **1983**
Science fiction
64581 93 mins C B, V, CED P
Fred Ward, Belinda Bauer, Peter Coyote, Richard Masur

A motorcyclist riding through the California desert is accidentally thrown back in time to 1877, the result of a scientific experiment that went awry.
MPAA:PG
Jensen Farley Pictures — *Pacific Arts Video*

Times Square **1980**
Musical
58463 111 mins C B, V R, P
Tim Curry, Trini Alvarado, Robin Johnson, Peter Coffield, Anna Maria Horsford, directed by Alan Moyle
A 13-year-old girl learns about life on her own when she teams up with a defiant, anti-social child of the streets. A New Wave rock music score is featured.
MPAA:R
Robert Stigwood; Jacob Brackman — *THORN EMI/HBO Video*

Timex All-Star Comedy Show **1962**
Comedy
12849 45 mins B/W B, V, FO P
Johnny Carson, Carl Reiner, Mel Brooks, Dr. Joyce Brothers, Buddy Hackett, Kaye Stevens
Spoof on TV shows and other fun, featuring a comic cast.
ABC — *Video Yesteryear*

Timex All Star Jazz Show **1957**
Music-Performance
46344 62 mins B/W B, V, FO P
Louis Armstrong, Duke Ellington and his Orchestra, Bobby Hackett, Dizzy Gillespie, George Shearing
Jackie Gleason hosts this television special which features a compendium of great performances by many jazz stars.
Unknown — *Video Yesteryear*

Tin Drum, The **1979**
Drama
47370 141 mins C B, V R, P
Oskar Matzerath, a self-made dwarf, narrates this parable of modern society in violent transition. Subtitled.
Academy Awards '79: Best Foreign Language Film. GE
New World Pictures — *Warner Home Video*

Tin Man **1983**
Drama
65485 95 mins C B, V P
Timothy Bottoms, Deana Jurgens, Troy Donahue
A garage mechanic born totally deaf designs and builds a computer that can both hear and speak for him. His world is complicated when a young speech therapist introduces him to a world of new and wonderful sounds, but also to a world of unscrupulous and exploitive computer salesmen. Slowly he realizes that he must make the decisions that will mold his future.
John G Thomas — *Media Home Entertainment*

Tina Turner **1982**
Music-Performance
64209 55 mins C B, V R, P
Tina Turner
Tina Turner stomps and shouts her way through an exciting program of hits including "Proud Mary," "Honky-Tonk Woman," "Jumping Jack Flash" and others. In stereo.
EMI Music — *THORN EMI/HBO Video*

Tina Turner Private Dancer **1984**
Music video
76962 17 mins C B, V P
Sultry Tina Turner performs four songs from her "Private Dancer" album.
Capitol Records — *Sony Corporation of America*

Tina Turner—Queen of Rock and Roll **1984**
Music-Performance
72420 60 mins C B, V P
Tina Turner entertains at Harlem's Apollo Theatre, giving her typically enthralling performance.
Unknown — *VCL Home Video*

Tintorera...Tiger Shark **1978**
Adventure
66286 91 mins C B, V P
Susan George, Fiona Lewis, Jennifer Ashley
Three shark hunters attempt to discover why swimmers are disappearing.
MPAA:R
Gerald Green — *Media Home Entertainment*

Tip Top! with Suzy Prudden—Ages 3-6 **1982**
Physical fitness
62887 53 mins C B, V R, P
The first home video program series designed for young children; instructor Suzy Prudden leads her viewers through warmup activities and stimulating exercises set to contemporary music.
Warner Home Video; Warner Amex — *Warner Home Video*

Tip Top! with Suzy Prudden—Age 7 and Above **1982**
Physical fitness
62888 48 mins C B, V R, P
Suzy Prudden leads her video class of enthusiastic youngsters through a specially designed series of exercises for this specific age group.

Warner Home Video; Warner Amex — *Warner Home Video*

To All a Goodnight 1980
Horror
69307 90 mins C B, V P
Jennifer Runyon, Forrest Swanson, Linda Gentile, William Lover
Five young girls and their boyfriends are in for an exciting Christmas holiday until a mad Santa Claus puts a damper on things.
MPAA:R
Jay Rasumny — *Media Home Entertainment*

To Be or Not To Be 1942
Comedy
65365 102 mins B/W B, V P
Carole Lombard, Jack Benny, Robert Stack, directed by Ernst Lubitsch
Set in wartime Poland, Lombard and Benny are Maria and Josef Tura, the Barrymores of the Polish stage, who use the talents of their acting troupe against the Gestapo and manage to exit laughing.
United Artists — *Vestron Video*

To Be or Not to Be 1983
Comedy
Closed Captioned
72191 108 mins C B, V P
Mel Brooks, Anne Bancroft
Anne Bancroft and Mel Brooks are actors in Poland during WWII who plan to thwart the Nazis.
MPAA:PG
Warner Bros — *CBS/Fox Video*

To Catch a King 1984
Suspense
72338 90 mins C B, V P
Robert Wagner, Teri Garr
Adaptation of Jack Higgins' novel about a Nazi plan to kidnap the Duke of Windsor.
Home Box Office — *Prism*

To Catch a Thief 1955
Mystery
53936 97 mins C B, V, LV R, P
Cary Grant, Grace Kelly, Jessie Royce Landis, directed by Alfred Hitchcock
An ex-jewel thief falls for a wealthy American girl, who suspects him of his old thievery, when a similar rash of jewel thefts occur.
Paramount — *Paramount Home Video*

To Forget Venice 197?
Drama
63447 90 mins C B, V P
Erland Josephson, Mariangela Melato, David Pontremoli, Eleonora Giorgi, directed by Franco Brusati
This film portrays the sensitive relationships among four people, and their shared fears of growing older. Dubbed in English.
Rizzoli Film — *RCA/Columbia Pictures Home Video; Embassy Home Entertainment (disc only)*

To Joy 1950
Drama
78636 90 mins B/W B, V, LV P
This early Ingmar Bergman film deals with the problems and frustrations of the young in Swedish society. This film has English subtitles.
SW
Janus Films — *Embassy Home Entertainment*

To Kill a Clown 1972
Drama/Suspense
66285 82 mins C B, V P
Alan Alda, Blythe Danner, Heath Lamberts
A young couple who move to an isolated island find their lives filled with terror.
MPAA:R
Teddy B Sills — *Media Home Entertainment*

To Kill a Mockingbird 1962
Drama
14034 129 mins B/W B, V P
Gregory Peck, Brock Peters, Phillip Afford, Mary Badham
A southern lawyer, the town's most distinguished citizen, defends a black man accused of rape. This costs him many friendships but earns him the admiration of his two motherless children.
Academy Awards '62: Best Actor (Peck).
Universal; Brentwood Prod — *MCA Home Video*

To Kill a Stranger 1983
Suspense
81413 90 mins C B, V P
Donald Pleasence, Dean Stockwell, Angelica Maria
A woman discovers that the good samaritan policy has its drawbacks when the man who helps her out after an accident is a rapist and a murderer.
J. Lopez-Moctezuma — *VCL Home Video*

To Paris with Love 1955
Comedy
77008 75 mins C B, V P
Alec Guinness, Odile Versuis, Vernon Gray
A British father and his son fall in love with a shop girl and her boss while on vacation in Paris.
J. Arthur Rank — *VidAmerica*

To Race the Wind 1980
Biographical/Drama
73954 97 mins C B, V P

Steve Guttenberg, Lisa Eilbacher, Randy Quaid, Barbara Barrie
A blind man wants to be treated like a normal person as he struggles through Harvard Law School. Based upon Harold Krents' autobiography.
Walter Grauman Prods; Viacom — *Unicorn Video*

To Russia...with Elton **197?**
Music-Performance
47047 75 mins C B, V P
Narrated by Dudley Moore
Elton John's successful 1979 tour of the Soviet Union is captured in this concert documentary. Elton performs "Your Song," "Goodbye Yellow Brick Road," "Benny and the Jets," "Back in the USSR" and many other songs.
ITC Entertainment — *CBS/Fox Video; RCA VideoDiscs*

To See Such Fun **1981**
Comedy
59929 90 mins C B, V P
Peter Sellers, Marty Feldman, Benny Hill, Eric Idle, Alec Guinness, Margaret Rutherford, Dirk Bogarde, Spike Milligan
Hilarious excerpts from 80 years of the greatest British movie comedies.
Herbert Wilcox; Michael Grade — *Pacific Arts Video*

To Sir, With Love **1967**
Comedy-Drama
13294 105 mins C B, V P
Sidney Poitier, Lulu, Judy Geeson, Christian Roberts, Suzy Kendall, Faith Brook
Teacher in London's tough East End tosses books in the wastebasket and proceeds to teach his class about life.
Columbia; James Clavell — *RCA/Columbia Pictures Home Video*

To the Lighthouse **1983**
Drama
81563 115 mins C B, V P
Rosemary Harris, Michael Clough, Suzanne Bertish, Linsey Baxter
A proper British holiday turns into a summer of disillusionment in this adaptation of the Virginia Woolf novel.
Epic Pictures — *Epic Pictures*

Toast of New York, The **1937**
Drama
57166 109 mins B/W B, V P
Edward Arnold, Cary Grant, Frances Farmer, Jack Oakie, Donald Meek
Jim Fisk rises from a New England peddler to one of the first Wall Street giants of industry, in this story about the early years of the tycoon.
RKO; Edward Small — *King of Video*

Toast of the Town **1949**
Comedy
12838 51 mins B/W B, V, FO P
Hosted by Ed Sullivan
Genuine vaudeville complete with dancers, a ventriloquist, trick-shot golfers, and the "kooky" music of Fane and Foster. Also features the Ray Block Orchestra.
CBS — *Video Yesteryear*

Toast of the Town **1956**
Variety
66459 120 mins B/W B, V, 3/4U P
Ed Sullivan, Lucille Ball, Desi Arnaz, Vivian Vance, William Frawley, Orson Welles, The Ames Brothers
Two original Ed Sullivan TV programs, both featuring appearances by the cast of "I Love Lucy." The program of October 3, 1954 is a full one-hour tribute to "the Ricardos." The show of February 5, 1956 has Lucy and Desi promoting their latest picture, "Forever Darling," along with other guest stars. Original commercials and I.D.'s are included.
CBS — *Shokus Video*

Toby and the Koala Bear **1983**
Cartoons
Closed Captioned
78889 77 mins C B, V P
Animated
A little boy and a pet Koala bear leave a convict colony and befriend an Aborigine boy, who teaches the pair how to survive in the Australian woods.
Satori — *Playhouse Video*

Todd Rundgren Videosyncracy **1983**
Music-Performance
64928 12 mins C B, V P
Todd Rundgren performs three songs on this Video 45: "Hideaway," "Can We Still Be Friends" and "Time Heals."
Alchemedia Productions — *Sony Corporation of America*

Todos los Dias, Un Dia **1979**
Drama
66408 89 mins C B, V P
Julio Iglesias, Isa Lorenz, Carol Lynley
A world famous singer on an island vacation meets and falls in love with a beautiful young girl who is unaware of his fame.
Argentinismas — *Unicorn Video*

Toga Party **1979**
Comedy
78895 82 mins C B, V P
Bobby H. Charles, Mary Mitchell
A college fraternity house throws a wild toga party where what goes on usually comes off.

Funky Films Limited — *Monterey Home Video*

Together 1979
Romance/Drama
76904 91 mins C B, V P
Maximillian Schell, Jacqueline Bisset, Terence Stamp, Monica Guerritore
A divorced woman and a male chauvinist test the limits of their sexual liberation.
Lefco Productions — *Embassy Home Entertainment*

Tol'able David 1921
Drama
33634 79 mins B/W B, V P
Richard Barthelmess, Gladys Hulette, Ernest Torrance, directed by Henry King
A simple tale of mountain folk, done in the tradition of Mark Twain stories. The youngest son of a family yearns to be a mail driver. His community is troubled by the presence of three outlaws. Silent.
First National — *Festival Films; Video Yesteryear; Blackhawk Films; Sheik Video; Classic Video Cinema Collector's Club*

Tom and Jerry Cartoon Festival, Vol. I 195?
Cartoons
48860 60 mins C B, V, LV, CED P
Animated
The cat and mouse team fight their way through a cartoon festival including "The Flying Cat," "The Bodyguard," "The Little Orphan," "Jerry's Cousin," "Dr. Jekyll and Mr. Mouse," "Mouse Follies," "The Cat and the Mermouse," and "The Cat Concerto."
MGM — *MGM/UA Home Video*

Tom and Jerry Cartoon Festival, Vol. II 194?
Cartoons
59848 58 mins C B, V, CED P
A second compilation of the best of MGM's classic Tom and Jerry cartoon shorts, including "Mouse Trap," "Cat Napping," "Invisible Mouse," "Saturday Evening Puss," and more.
MGM — *MGM/UA Home Video*

Tom and Jerry Cartoon Festival, Vol. 3 19??
Cartoons
66453 59 mins C B, V, CED P
Animated
Another collection of Tom and Jerry favorites from the 1940's and 1950's including "The Hollywood Bowl," "Million Dollar Cat," "The Night Before Christmas" and "Two Little Indians."
MGM — *MGM/UA Home Video*

Tom & Jerry Cartoon Festival 1967
Cartoons
81053 58 mins C B, V P
Animated, directed by William Hanna and Joseph Barbera
This volume features seven more Tom and Jerry classics: "Johann Mouse," "Pet Peeve," "The Mouse From H.U.N.G.E.R," "The Zoat Cat," "Baby Butch," "Fraidy Cat," "The Dog House" and "Baby Puss."
Academy Awards '52: Best Short Subject (Cartoon) "Johann Mouse"
MGM; Fred Quimby — *MGM/UA Home Video*

Tom Brown's School Days 1940
Drama
08860 80 mins B/W B, V, 3/4U P
Cedric Hardwicke, Jimmy Lydon, Freddie Bartholomew
Depicts life among the boys in an English school during the Victorian era.
RKO — *Budget Video; Sheik Video; Cable Films; Discount Video Tapes; Video Yesteryear*

Tom Corbett, Space Cadet 1951
Science fiction
42968 30 mins B/W B, V, FO P
Frankie Thomas, Jack Grimes, Al Markhim
This popular space opera from the early days of television shows how one cadet who is the smallest in size becomes the biggest in courage and team cooperation.
ABC — *Video Yesteryear*

Tom Corbett, Space Cadet Volume 1 195?
Science fiction/Adventure
44312 90 mins B/W B, V, 3/4U P
Frankie Thomas, Jan Merlin
The adventures of Tom Corbett, a Space Cadet at the U.S. Space Academy, where men and women train to become agents to protect Earth and its neighbor planets.
ABC — *Nostalgia Merchant*

Tom Corbett, Space Cadet Volume 2 195?
Science fiction
58585 90 mins B/W B, V, 3/4U P
This early '50's TV series follows the adventures of Tom Corbett, a space cadet at the U.S. Space Academy.
ABC — *Nostalgia Merchant*

Tom, Dick, and Harry 1941
Comedy
10038 86 mins B/W B, V P, T
Ginger Rogers, George Murphy, Burgess Meredith, Allen Marshall, Phil Silvers

Dreamy girl is engaged to three men and unable to decide which to marry. It all depends on a kiss.
RKO — *Blackhawk Films*

Tom Edison, the Boy Who Lit Up the World **1980**
Adventure/Biographical
75617 49 mins C B, V P
This is the story of Tom Edison's life and how he changed the world.
VidAmerica — *Children's Video Library*

Tom Edison: The Making of an American Legend **19??**
Biographical/Inventions
69587 49 mins C B, V P
David Huffman
This is the story of young Thomas Edison, a telegraph operator who becomes one of history's greatest inventors.
Unknown — *VidAmerica*

Tom Horn **1980**
Western
54795 98 mins C B, V R, P
Steve McQueen, Linda Evans, Richard Farnsworth, Billy Green Bush, Slim Pickens, directed by William Wiard
The true story of an Old West gunman, Tom Horn, who at the age of 40 has already been a western railroad worker, stagecoach driver, U.S. Cavalry scout, silver miner, Teddy Roosevelt Rough Rider, and a Pinkerton Detective. Now he is invited by Wyoming ranchers to stop the cattle rustlers. He does that job well, and at the same time finds romance.
MPAA:R
Warner Bros — *Warner Home Video*

Tom Jones **1963**
Comedy
52738 129 mins C B, V, LV P
Albert Finney, Susannah York, Hugh Griffith, Dame Edith Evans, David Tomlinson, directed by Tony Richardson
A comedy based on Henry Fielding's novel about a rustic playboy's wild life in eighteenth-century London with brigands, beauties, and scoundrels.
Academy Awards '63: Best Picture; Best Director (Richardson); Best Screenplay (John Osborne); Best Original Score (John Addison).
EL, SP
Woodfall Prods; United Artists; Lopert Pictures — *CBS/Fox Video; RCA VideoDiscs*

Tom Jones Live in Las Vegas **1981**
Music-Performance
53137 60 mins C B, V P
Tom Jones
Superstar Tom Jones lights up a Vegas showroom performing "What's New Pussycat?," "She's a Lady," "Green Green Grass of Home," "It's Not Unusual," "Love Me Tonight," "Ladies' Night," "Working My Way Back to You," "Woman," "I'll Never Fall in Love Again," and others.
Jay Harvey Prods — *Family Home Entertainment*

Tom Sawyer **1973**
Musical
Closed Captioned
81559 99 mins C B, V P
Johnny Whitaker, Jeff East, Jodie Foster, Warren Oates, Celeste Holm
This is a musical version of the classic Mark Twain story about a young man's life on the Mississippi River during the 1840's. Available in VHS and Beta Hi-Fi.
United Artists — *Playhouse Video*

Tom Thumb **1958**
Fairy tales/Fantasy
73366 92 mins C B, V P
Russ Tamblyn, Peter Sellers, Terry-Thomas, directed by George Pal
The classic Grimm Brothers fairy tale about the small boy who saves the village treasury from the bad guys is brought to life in this film.
Academy Award 1958: Best Special Effects.
Galaxy Pictures — *MGM/UA Home Video*

Tomboy **1940**
Comedy
12813 70 mins B/W B, V, FO P
Jackie Moran, Marcia Mae Jones
A shy country boy and a not-so-shy city girl team up to catch crooks.
Monogram — *Video Yesteryear*

Tomboy **1985**
Drama
80927 91 mins C B, V P
Betsy Russell, Eric Douglas, Jerry Dinome, Kristi Somers, Toby Iland
A pretty teenaged female mechanic is determined to win the love and respect of a superstar auto racer.
MPAA:R
Crown International Pictures — *Vestron Video*

Tommy **1975**
Musical
58965 108 mins C B, V, LV P
Ann-Margret, Elton John, Oliver Reed, Tina Turner, Roger Daltrey, Eric Clapton, Keith Moon, directed by Ken Russell
Peter Townsend's rock-opera about the deaf, dumb, and blind boy who becomes a celebrity.
MPAA:PG

Robert Stigwood; Columbia — *RCA/Columbia Pictures Home Video; RCA VideoDiscs*

Tomorrow **1983**
Drama
65455 102 mins B/W B, V P
Robert Duvall
The powerful tale of the love of two lonely people of the earth, carrying them through the ordeals of pregnancy and birth and culminating in a baffling murder trial.
Gilbert Pearlman; Paul Roebling — *Monterey Home Video*

Tomorrow at Seven **1933**
Mystery/Suspense
63619 62 mins B/W B, V, FO P
Chester Morris, Vivienne Osborne, Frank McHugh
A mystery writer/amateur detective is determined to discover the identity of the Black Ace, a mysterious killer who always warns his intended victim, then leaves an ace of spades on the corpse as his calling card.
RKO — *Video Yesteryear*

Toni Basil—Word of Mouth **1981**
Music-Performance
66038 30 mins C B, V P
This video is Toni Basil's debut and as a purely visual artist she presents herself as an accomplished singer, dancer and choreographer. Includes "Mickey," "My Little Red Book," "Nobody," "Time After Time," "Be Stiff," "Space Girls," and "Problem."
Radical Choice — *Chrysalis Visual Programming*

Tonight for Sure **1961**
Film-Avant-garde
47644 66 mins B/W B, V, FO P
Directed by Francis Ford Coppola
Coppola's first film, produced as a student at UCLA. Two men ruminate on bad experiences with naked women. Nudity. Music by Carmen Coppola.
Francis Ford Coppola — *Video Yesteryear*

Tonight Show, The **1969**
Variety
42978 78 mins C B, V, FO P
Jerry Lewis, Ed McMahon, Doc Severinson and his Orchestra
Appearances by George Carlin, Jim Turner and his musical saw, Charlie Callis, the Smothers Brothers, and Mason Williams highlight this zany show aired March 25, 1969. Jerry Lewis hosts.
NBC — *Video Yesteryear*

Tonio Kroger **1965**
Drama
69565 92 mins B/W B, V, FO P
Jean-Claude Brialy, Nadja Tiller, Gert Frobe
A young writer travels through Europe in search of intellectual and sensual relationships and a home that will suit him. German dialogue with English subtitles.
Germany — *Video Yesteryear*

Tony Bennett Songbook, A **1981**
Music-Performance
60375 94 mins C CED P
This stereo program recorded live in New York features the exciting Tony Bennett in an intimate nightclub atmosphere singing "I Left My Heart in San Francisco," a Duke Ellington medley, and much more.
Dennis H. Paget — *RCA VideoDiscs*

Tony Powers **1981**
Music-Performance
75908 54 mins C B, V P
This program presents Tony Powers performing his songs "Don't Nobody Move," "Midnite Trampoline" and "Odyssey."
Tony Powers Music Inc — *Sony Corporation of America*

Too Hot to Handle **1980**
Drama
54799 88 mins C B, V R, P
Cheri Caffaro
A voluptuous lady contract killer fights against the mob with all the weapons at her disposal. Filmed on location in Manila.
New World; Roger Corman — *Warner Home Video*

Too Late the Hero **1970**
Drama/World War II
46205 133 mins C B, V P
Michael Caine, Cliff Robertson, Henry Fonda, directed by Robert Aldrich
A British combat patrol whose mission is to wipe out a Japanese communication site, finds a horde of enemy planes. The Japanese chase them through the jungle relaying messages via loud speakers that their lives will be spared only if they surrender.
MPAA:PG
Cinerama Release — *CBS/Fox Video*

Too Scared To Scream **1985**
Suspense
77412 104 mins C B, V P
Mike Connors, Anne Archer, Leon Isaac Kennedy, John Heard, Ian McShane, directed by Tony Lo Bianco
A policeman and an undercover agent team up to solve a bizarre series of murders at a Manhattan apartment house.

MPAA:R
Mike Connors; The Movie Store — *Vestron Video*

Toolbox Murders, The **1978**
Mystery
48358 93 mins C B, V P
Cameron Mitchell, Pamelyn Ferdin
An unknown psychotic murderer brutally claims victims one at a time, leaving a town on the verge of horror, and the police mystified.
MPAA:R
Cal Am Productions — *United Home Video*

Tootsie **1982**
Comedy
66443 110 mins C B, V P
Dustin Hoffman, Jessica Lange, Teri Garr, Dabney Coleman, Bill Murray, directed by Sydney Pollack
A desperate, unemployed actor dresses as a woman to land a starring role in a television soap opera.
Academy Awards '82: Best Supporting Actress (Lange) MPAA:PG
Columbia Pictures — *RCA/Columbia Pictures Home Video; RCA VideoDiscs*

Top Cat **196?**
Cartoons
47694 50 mins C B, V P
Animated voices of Arnold Stang, Allen Jenkins, Maurice Gosfield
Two episodes in which T.C. and his gang of street-wise cats drive Officer Dibble nuts.
Hanna Barbera — *Worldvision Home Video*

Top Cat, Volume II **1983**
Cartoons
66580 60 mins C B, V P
Animated
Top Cat, the feline wise guy, leads his gang of dimwitted stooges through their usual shenanigans in this collection of early 60's TV cartoons.
Hanna Barbera — *Worldvision Home Video*

Top Cat Volume 2 **1961**
Cartoons
79172 50 mins C B, V P
Animated, voices of Arnold Stang, Marvin Kaplan, Jean Vander Pyl
Top Cat and his gang of alley cats are trying to live the good life in New York City, but officer Dibble is making things difficult for them.
Hanna-Barbera — *Worldvision Home Video*

Top Hat **1935**
Musical
00270 97 mins B/W B, V, 3/4U P
Fred Astaire, Ginger Rogers, Erik Rhodes, Helen Broderick, Edward Everett Horton, Eric Blore
As usual, Ginger thinks Fred is someone he isn't. It takes the whole length of the film to straighten her out. Irving Berlin's score includes, "Top Hat," "Cheek to Cheek" and "The Piccolino."
RKO; Pandro S Berman — *Nostalgia Merchant; VidAmerica; King of Video*

Top Secret **1984**
Comedy
80061 90 mins C B, V R, P
Val Kilmen, Lucy Gutteridge, Omar Sharif, Peter Cushing, directed by Jim Abrahams
An American rock star touring through Europe becomes involved in a plot to reunite Germany during World War II.
MPAA:PG
Paramount Pictures; Jon Davidson — *Paramount Home Video*

Topaz **1969**
Drama/Suspense
80414 126 mins C B, V P
John Forsythe, Philippe Noiret, Karin Dor, Michael Piccoli, directed by Alfred Hitchcock
An American CIA agent and a French Intelligence agent combine forces to find information about Russian involvement in Cuba.
Universal; Alfred Hitchcock — *MCA Home Video*

Topkapi **1964**
Drama
65408 122 mins C B, V, CED P
Melina Mercouri, Maximilian Schell, Peter Ustinov, Robert Morley
Filmed in Istanbul, the movie centers around the famed Topkapi Palace Museum, an impregnable fortress filled with wealth and splendor which seems impossible to break in to.
United Artists — *CBS/Fox Video*

Topper **1937**
Comedy
44797 97 mins B/W B, V, 3/4U P
Cary Grant, Roland Young, Constance Bennett, Billie Burke, directed by Norman Z. McLeod
Based on the Thorne Smith novel this is the story of Marion and George Kirby, who after a car accident do not wish to be dead and become ghosts instead. They get involved in many ghostly escapades.
MGM, Hal Roach — *Nostalgia Merchant; Blackhawk Films*

Topper **1937**
Comedy
70739 97 mins C B, V P
Gary Grant, Roland Young, Constance Bennet, Billie Burke, directed by Norman Z. McLeod

 (For explanation of codes, see USE GUIDE and KEY)

Hal Roach Studios colorized this originally black and white classic using a new computer technique.
MGM, Hal Roach — *Hal Roach Studios*

Topper Returns **1941**
Comedy
08733 87 mins B/W B, V P
Roland Young, Joan Blondell, Dennis O'Keefe, Rochester, Carole Landis
Topper finds the murderer of a girl, with the help of his ghostly friends, the Kirbys.
United Artists; Hal Roach — *Prism; Movie Buff Video; Budget Video; Sheik Video; Cable Films; Video Yesteryear; Video Connection; Discount Video Tapes; Nostalgia Merchant; Kartes Productions; Classic Video Cinema Collector's Club; See Hear Industries*

Topper Takes a Trip **1939**
Comedy
64371 85 mins B/W B, V, 3/4U P
Constance Bennett, Roland Young, Billie Burke, Alan Mowbray, Franklin Pangborn
Cosmo Topper takes a trip to the Riviera, with the ghostly spirit of Marion Kirby in hot pursuit.
Hal Roach — *Nostalgia Merchant*

Tora! Tora! Tora! **1970**
War-Drama
08439 144 mins C B, V, LV P
Martin Balsam, Soh Yomamura, Joseph Cotten, E. G. Marshall, Jason Robards, directed by Richard Fleisher
The story of December 7, 1941 is retold from both Japanese and American viewpoints in this large-scale production.
MPAA:G
20th Century Fox; Elmo Williams — *CBS/Fox Video*

Torch, The **1950**
Drama
66401 83 mins B/W B, V P
Paulette Goddard, Gilbert Roland, Pedro Armendariz
A general falls for a daughter of nobility amidst the turbulent backdrop of the Mexican Revolution.
Eagle Lion — *Movie Buff Video*

Torchlight **1985**
Drama
80771 90 mins C B, V, LV P
Pamela Sue Martin, Steve Railsback, Ian McShane, Al Corley, Rita Taggart
A young couple's life slowly starts to crumble when a wealthy art dealer teaches them how to free base cocaine. Carly Simon sings "All the Love in the World."
MPAA:R
Torch Productions — *Embassy Home Entertainment*

Torn Between Two Lovers **1979**
Romance/Drama
78362 100 mins C B, V P
Lee Remick, George Peppard, Joseph Bologna, directed by Delbert Mann
A woman must decide between staying with her husband or starting a new relationship with an anarchist.
Alan Landsburg Productions — *U.S.A. Home Video*

Torn Curtain **1966**
Suspense
64558 125 mins C B, V P
Paul Newman, Julie Andrews, Lila Kedrova, David Opatoshu, directed by Alfred Hitchcock
An American scientist poses as a defector to East Germany in order to do some undercover work. Unfortunately, his fiancee follows him behind the Iron Curtain.
Universal — *MCA Home Video*

Torvill & Dean: Path to Perfection **1984**
Sports-Winter
66572 60 mins C B, V P
Olympic ice dancing gold medalists Torvill and Dean are featured in eight of their pre-Olympic performances, including 3 World Skating Championships.
Robert J. Brady Company — *THORN EMI/HBO Video*

Total Self-Defense **1981**
Safety education
52673 45 mins C B, V P
A woman instructor shows how women can protect themselves in situations such as purse snatching, rape, or other attack. In the second part, two third degree black belts in karate demonstrate "street or full-contact karate." This tape was designed as an interactive, instructional program.
Karl Video Corp — *Karl/Lorimar Home Video*

Totally Go-Go's **1982**
Music-Performance
59695 77 mins C B, V R, P
The chart-topping, all-girl rock band performs live in concert in Hollywood. Songs include "We Got the Beat," "Our Lips Are Sealed," and songs from their two hit albums.
IRS Records — *THORN EMI/HBO Video; RCA VideoDiscs*

Touch & Go **1980**
Adventure
77005 92 mins C B, V P

Wendy Hughes
Three beautiful women commit grand larceny in order to raise funds for underprivileged children.
MPAA:PG
John Pellatt — *VidAmerica*

Touch of Class, A **1973**
Comedy
08475 105 mins C B, V P
George Segal, Glenda Jackson, Paul Sorvino, Hildegard Neil, Cec Linder
American insurance adjustor initiates a love affair with an English divorcee.
Academy Awards '73: Best Actress (Jackson).
MPAA:PG
Avco Embassy — *CBS/Fox Video*

Touch of Love: Massage, The **1980**
Massage
48635 28 mins C B, V, LV P
A simple and beautiful way to experience pleasure through touch is presented.
Bruce Seth Green — *MCA Home Video*

Touch of Magic in Close-Up, A **1982**
Magic
59992 78 mins C B, V R, P
Siroco
The amazing Siroco, renowned master of "close-up" magic, mystifies, and then demonstrates the secrets behind many of the illusions.
MPAA:G
Pegicorn Video Corp — *Video Gems*

Touch of Satan, A **1974**
Horror
55317 90 mins C B, V P
Michael Berry, Emby Mallay, Lee Amber, Yvonne Wilson, directed by Don Henderson
Devil worshippers and evil satanic rites abound in this horror of the world beyond. (Original title "A Touch of Melissa.")
Dundee Prods — *King of Video*

Touched **1982**
Drama
65292 89 mins C B, V P
Robert Hays, Kathleen Beller, Ned Beatty
Two young people struggle to cope with the outside world. They struggle against all odds to gain new confidence after being released from a psychiatric hospital. It is a story of determination, hope, and most of all, love.
MPAA:R
Barclay Lottimer; Dirk Petersmann — *Media Home Entertainment*

Touched by Love **1984**
Drama
70193 95 mins C B, V P
Deborah Raffin, Diane Lane
The true story of a handicapped child who learns to power of love from her devoted teacher. In Beta Hi-Fi.
MPAA:PG
Columbia Pictures — *RCA/Columbia Pictures Home Video*

Tough Enough **19??**
Drama
65332 107 mins C B, V P
Dennis Quaid, Charlene Watkins
A country-western singer-songwriter decides to finance his fledgling career by entering amateur boxing matches and then finds himself rising to the top of amateur boxing.
MPAA:PG
Michael Leone; Andrew D T Pfeffer — *CBS/Fox Video*

Tough Guy **197?**
Martial arts/Adventure
47701 90 mins C B, V P
Chen Ying, Charlie Chiang
Two undercover policemen battle local gangsters in a bid to smash their crime ring.
Independent — *Master Arts Video*

Tourist Trap **1979**
Science fiction
42917 85 mins C B, V P
Chuck Connors
While traveling through the desert, a couple's car has a flat. A woman's voice lures the man into an abandoned gas station, where he discovers that the voice belongs to a mannequin.
MPAA:PG
J. Larry Carroll — *Media Home Entertainment*

Tower of Evil **1972**
Horror
48473 86 mins C B, V P
Bryant Haliday, Jill Haworth
Tourists and archaeologists visit an island where ancient Phoenician treasure is buried. Most of them are haunted by terror and grisly murder.
MPAA:R
Grenadier Films Ltd — *United Home Video*

Towering Inferno, The **1974**
Drama
29178 165 mins C B, V, CED P
Steve McQueen, Paul Newman, William Holden, Faye Dunaway, Fred Astaire
Irwin Allen's dramatic suspense story of a holocaust that engulfs the world's tallest skyscraper on the night of its glamorous and prestigious dedication ceremonies.

Academy Awards '74: Best Song ("We May Never Love Like this Again"). MPAA:PG
20th Century Fox — *CBS/Fox Video*

Town Called Hell, A **1972**
Suspense
12025 95 mins C B, V P
Robert Shaw, Stella Stevens, Martin Landau, Telly Savalas
Two men hold an entire town hostage while looking for "Aguila," the Mexican revolutionary. Greed, evil, and violence take over.
Philip Yordan; Official Films — *King of Video; World Video Pictures; Video Gems*

Town That Dreaded Sundown, The **1976**
Suspense
65138 90 mins C B, V R, P
Ben Johnson, Andrew Prine, Dawn Wells
A mad killer is on the loose in a small Arkansas town. Based on a true story, this famous murder spree remains an unsolved mystery.
MPAA:R
Charles B Pierce Productions — *Warner Home Video*

Toy, The **1982**
Comedy-Drama
66010 99 mins C B, V P
Richard Pryor, Jackie Gleason, Ned Beatty, Wilfred Hyde-White, directed by Richard Donner
A janitor finds himself the new "toy" of the son of a department store owner.
MPAA:PG
Columbia — *RCA/Columbia Pictures Home Video; RCA VideoDiscs*

Toy Soldiers **1984**
Drama/Adventure
80461 85 mins C B, V, LV P
Cleavon Little
A group of college students are held for ransom in a war-torn Central American country. When they escape, they join forces with a seasoned mercenary who leads them as a vigilante force.
MPAA:R
New World Pictures — *New World Video*

Tracks **1976**
Suspense
75585 90 mins C B, V P
Dennis Hopper, Dean Stockwell, Taryn Power, directed by Henry Jaglom
A disoriented soldier has paranoia and hallucinations on a long train ride.
MPAA:R
Rainbow Pictures — *Monterey Home Video*

Trading Places **1983**
Comedy
Closed Captioned
66409 106 mins C B, V, LV, CED R, P
Eddie Murphy, Dan Aykroyd, Jamie Lee Curtis, Ralph Bellamy, Don Ameche, directed by John Landis
Two elderly businessmen make a wager that basic intelligence is more important than heredity in creating a successful life, using their rich nephew and an unemployed street hustler as guinea pigs.
MPAA:R
Paramount; Aaron Russo — *Paramount Home Video*

Tragedy of Antony and Cleopatra, The **1985**
Drama
70649 190 mins C B, V P
Timothy Dalton, Lynn Redgrave, Nichelle Nichols, John Carradine, Barrie Ingham, Anthony Greary, Walter Koenig, dir. by Lawrence Carra
This presentation of Shakespeare's Roman Empire tragedy features American actors and accents set against an artist's reproduction of England's Globe Theater Stage. The program comes on two tapes.
Paganiniana Publications — *Kultur*

Tragedy of King Richard II, The **1982**
Drama
66149 180 mins C B, V P
David Birney, Paul Shenar
The first of Shakespeare's 28 plays to be released in this videocassette series is the historical play, "Richard II."
Bard Prods — *Kultur*

Tragedy of Macbeth, The **1985**
Drama
80402 150 mins C B, V P
Jeremy Brett, Piper Laurie, Simon MacCorkindale, Millie Perkins, BarryPrimus
A new adaptation of the Shakespearean tragedy about a Scottish general's zealous quest for power.
Unknown — *Kultur*

Trail Beyond, The **1934**
Western
81526 57 mins B/W B, V P
John Wayne, Noah Berry Jr.
A cowboy and his sidekick go on the trek to the northwest to find a girl and a gold mine.
Monogram Pictures — *Spotlite Video*

Trail Beyond, The **1934**
Western
10934 57 mins B/W B, V P

John Wayne
"Duke" hits the trail after robbers.
Monogram — *Sony Corporation of America; Discount Video Tapes*

Trail of the Pink Panther **1982**
Comedy
66074 97 mins C B, V, CED P
Peter Sellers, David Niven, Herbert Lom, Capucine, Burt Kwuok, directed by Blake Edwards
This sixth "Panther" vehicle concerns the disappearance of Inspector Clouseau.
MPAA:PG
United Artists — *CBS/Fox Video*

Trail Riders **1942**
Western
11267 55 mins B/W B, V, FO P
John King, David Sharpe, Max Terhune, Evelyn Finley, Forest Taylor, Charles King
The Range Busters set a trap to capture a gang of outlaws who killed the son of the town marshal during a bank robbery.
Monogram — *Video Yesteryear; Discount Video Tapes; Video Connection*

Trail Street **1947**
Western
10069 84 mins B/W B, V P, T
Randolph Scott, Robert Ryan, Anne Jeffreys, Gabby Hayes, Madge Meredith, Jason Robards
Traces story of men and women who began great wheat empire out of Kansas wilderness.
RKO; Nat Holt — *Blackhawk Films; Nostalgia Merchant*

Trailing Trouble **1937**
Western
11266 60 mins B/W B, V, FO P
Ken Maynard
A cowboy and a killer have several confrontations in between the cowboy's efforts to steer clear of the case of his own mistaken identity which marks him for treachery.
Grand National — *Video Yesteryear; Video Connection*

Train Killer, The **1983**
Suspense
80114 90 mins C B, V P
Michael Sarazin
A mad Hungarian is bent on destroying the Orient Express.
Wescom Productions — *Vestron Video*

Train Robbers, The **1973**
Western
74212 92 mins C B, V R, P
John Wayne, Ann-Margret, Rod Taylor, Ben Johnson, Christopher George
This is the story of a widow who employs the services of three cowboys to help her recover some stolen gold.
MPAA:PG
Michael Wayne; Batjac Productions — *Warner Home Video*

Traitor, The **1936**
Western
14219 57 mins B/W B, V P
Tim McCoy
Undercover man joins a gang of bandits.
Puritan — *United Home Video; Video Connection; Discount Video Tapes*

Traitors of the Blue Castle, The **1958**
Adventure
76902 100 mins C B, V P
Kanjuro Aroshi, Ryuzaburo Nakamura
Two samurai must preserve the honor of the Emperor in nineteenth century Japan.
Toho — *Video Action*

Tramp and A Woman, The **1915**
Comedy
38966 45 mins B/W B, V, FO P
Charlie Chaplin, Edna Purviance
Two shorts made for the Essanay Company in 1915 which offer the Little Tramp wooing Edna Purviance in typical Chaplin fashion. Silent with musical score.
Essanay — *Video Yesteryear*

Transformers: More than Meets the Eye, The **1985**
Cartoons/Adventure
70651 60 mins C B, V P
Animated
This presentation shows the popular TV characters finding that appearances can be deceiving. Available in Hi-Fi stereo.
Sunbow Productions/Marvel Productions — *Family Home Entertainment*

Transformers: The Ultimate Doom, The **1985**
Cartoons
70652 60 mins C B, V P
Animated
The popular TV characters discover that all preceding dooms pale when compared to their current dilemma. Available in Hi-Fi stereo.
Sunbow Productions/Marvel Productions — *Family Home Entertainment*

Trap Them and Kill Them **1984**
Horror
76943 90 mins C B, V P
Gabrielle Tinti, Susan Scott, Donald O'Brien

A group of Americans traveling through the Amazon jungle encounter aterrifying aborigine tribe.
Foreign — *Trans World Entertainment*

Trapeze 1956
Drama
68227 105 mins C B, V, CED P
Burt Lancaster, Tony Curtis, Gina Lollabrigida
The story of three people who want to perform the mid-air triple somersault, an almost impossible feat.
Susan Productions — *CBS/Fox Video*

Trapped 1949
Crime-Drama
66402 78 mins B/W B, V P
Lloyd Bridges, John Hoyt, Barbara Payton
Government agents let a criminal escape their custody so he can lead them to a gang of counterfeiters.
Eagle Lion — *Movie Buff Video*

Trauma 1985
Horror
81033 90 mins C B, V P
Fabio Testi, Arthur Kennedy
A policeman uncovers a bizarre connection between a girls' school and a villa which caters to the kinkier needs of rich men.
MPAA:R
Empire Entertainment — *Wizard Video*

Traviata, La 1983
Opera
65517 105 mins C B, V, LV, CED P
Teresa Stratas, Placido Domingo, Cornell MacNeil, Alan Monk, Axelle Gall, Pina Cei
A film version of Giuseppe Verdi's opera classic. In stereo VHS and Beta Hi-Fi.
MPAA:G
Universal Classics; Accent Films — *MCA Home Video*

Treasure 1984
Games
72907 60 mins C B, V, LV P
An actual treasure hunt is presented on this tape. Viewers are given clue questions which will lead to a jackpot of a half-million dollars which is hidden somewhere in the United States.
Renan Productions — *Vestron Video*

Treasure Island 1934
Adventure
56756 102 mins B/W B, V, CED P
Wallace Beery, Jackie Cooper, Lionel Barrymore, Nigel Bruce, directed by Victor Fleming
A stirring adaptation of Robert Louis Stevenson's pirate tale about Long John Silver and young Jim Hawkins, set in eighteenth-century England.
MGM, Hunt Stromberg — *MGM/UA Home Video*

Treasure Island 1950
Adventure
58625 87 mins C B, V, LV R, P
Bobby Driscoll, Robert Newton, Basil Sydney, directed by Byron Haskin
Robert Louis Stevenson's spine-tingling tale of pirates and buried treasure, in which young cabin boy Jim Hawkins matches wits with Long John Silver.
MPAA:G
Walt Disney Productions — *Walt Disney Home Video; RCA VideoDiscs*

Treasure of the Four Crowns 1982
Adventure/Suspense
65107 97 mins C B, V, CED P
Tony Anthony
An aging history professor hires a team of tough commandos to recover four legendary crowns containing the source of mystical powers. The crowns are being held under heavy guard by a crazed cult leader. VHS in stereo.
MPAA:PG
Cannon Films — *MGM/UA Home Video*

Treasure of the Sierra Madre, The 1948
Adventure
76041 124 mins B/W B, V P
Humphrey Bogart, Walter Huston
The fate that brings three soldier-of-fortune prospectors together during the days of the gold rush tempts them onward through many hardships for the sake of finding gold.
Warner Bros — *Key Video*

Treasure of the Sierra Madre, The 1948
Drama
44948 126 mins B/W CED P
Humphrey Bogart, Walter Huston, Tim Holt, Bruce Bennett, directed by John Huston
Greed and suspicion surround three prospectors in their search for gold.
Academy Awards '48: Best Supporting Actor (Huston); Best Director (Huston); Best Screenplay (Huston)
Warner Bros. — *Key Video; RCA VideoDiscs*

Treasure of the Yankee Zephyr 1983
Adventure
65480 97 mins C B, V P
Ken Wahl, George Peppard, Lesley Ann Warren

A trio join in the quest for a plane that has been missing for 40 years... with a cargo of $50 million.
MPAA:PG
Film Ventures — *Vestron Video*

Treasure Seekers, The 1979
Adventure
80496 88 mins C B, V P
Rod Taylor, Stuart Whitman, Elke Sommer, Keenan Wynn, Jeremy Kemp
Four rival divers set off on a perilous Caribbean expedition in search of the legendary treasure of Morgan the Pirate.
Stuart Whitman Inc — *MGM/UA Home Video*

Trenchcoat 1983
Comedy
66052 95 mins C B, V R, P
Margot Kidder, Robert Hays
A detective spoof in which an aspiring mystery writer travels to Malta where she is drawn into a real-life conspiracy.
Jerry Leider — *Walt Disney Home Video*

Trial of the Catonsville Nine, The 1972
Drama
65190 85 mins C B, V P
Ed Flanders, Douglass Watson, William Schallert, directed by Gordon Davidson
A riveting political drama that focuses on the trial of nine anti-war activists, including Father Daniel Berrigan, during the Vietnam War days of the late '60s.
MPAA:PG
Cinema 5 — *RCA/Columbia Pictures Home Video*

Tribute 1980
Drama
55744 123 mins C B, V, LV, CED P
Jack Lemmon, Robby Benson, Lee Remick, directed by Bob Clark
Bernard Slade's play, brought to the screen, about Scotty Templeton, a dying man determined to achieve a reconciliation with his son. The tense conflict between father and son plays out against Scotty's fight for life, weaving moments of high comedy into the drama.
MPAA:PG
Joel B Michaels; Garth H Drabinsky — *Vestron Video*

Tribute to Billie Holiday, A 1979
Music-Performance
42923 57 mins C B, V P
This tribute to Billie Holiday features the talents of Nina Simone, Maxine Weldon, Morganna King, Carmen McRae, and Esther Phillips. The orchestra was arranged and conducted by Ray Ellis with additional arranging by Tommy Newsom.
Jack Sidney III — *Media Home Entertainment*

Trick or Treats 1982
Horror
70153 90 mins C B, V P
Carrie Snodgrass, David Carradine
A strange twist of fate causes a young boy's pranks to backfire on Halloween night.
MPAA:R
Lone Star Pictures — *Vestron Video*

Trilogy of Terror 1975
Horror/Suspense
78145 78 mins C B, V P
Karen Black
Karen Black stars in three short horror tales from the pen of Richard Matheson, showing her versatility as she plays a tempting seductress, a mousy schoolteacher and the terrified victim of an African Zuni fetish doll.
MPI Home Video — *MPI Home Video*

Trinity Is Still My Name 1975
Western
08481 117 mins C B, V, CED P
Bud Spencer, Terrence Hill
Petty rustler brothers, unconcerned with danger or hopeless odds, endure mishaps and adventures as they try to right wrongs.
MPAA:G
Avco Embassy — *Embassy Home Entertainment*

Trip, The 1967
Fantasy
69288 85 mins C B, V P
Peter Fonda, Dennis Hopper, Susan Strasberg, Bruce Dern
Written by Jack Nicholson, this film is a psychedelic journey to the world of inner consciousness.
American International — *Vestron Video*

Triumphs of a Man Called Horse 1982
Western
73019 91 mins C B, V R, P
Richard Harris
An indian must save his people from prospectors in order to keep his title as Peace, Chief of the Yellow Hand Sioux.
MPAA:R
Cinema Center — *THORN EMI/HBO Video*

Trojan Women, The 1971
Drama
65211 105 mins C B, V P
Katharine Hepburn, Vanessa Redgrave
This program is strongly anti-war in its telling. All of the Trojan warriors and princes have been

killed and the Conquerors must divide the only remains of the war—the Trojan women and their children.
MPAA:G
Josef Shaftel Productions — *U.S.A. Home Video*

Tron **1982**
Science fiction
63128 96 mins C B, V, LV, CED R, P
Jeff Bridges, Bruce Boxleitner, David Warner, Cindy Morgan, Barnard Hughes, directed by Steven Lisberger
A video game designer is sucked into a computer and finds that he must dc battle with his own creations in order to survive.
MPAA:PG
Walt Disney Productions — *Walt Disney Home Video; RCA VideoDiscs*

Trouble in the Glen **1954**
Drama
76828 91 mins C B, V P
Orson Welles, Victor McLaughlin, Forrest Tucker, Margaret Lockwood
An American soldier becomes involved in a Scottish small town's dispute between the town residents and a laird over a closed road.
Republic Pictures — *Republic Pictures Home Video*

Trouble with Angels, The **1966**
Comedy
68266 112 mins C B, V P
Hayley Mills, June Harding, Rosalind Russell, Gypsy Rose Lee, Binnie Barnes, directed by Ida Lupino
Two young girls turn a convent upside down with their endless practical jokes.
Columbia — *RCA/Columbia Pictures Home Video*

Trouble with Father **195?**
Comedy
53092 50 mins B/W B, V, 3/4U P
Stu Erwin, June Erwin
Two episodes of the classic comedy series about a bumbling father whose every attempt to fix something, surprise someone, or raise his kids turned to disaster. Also titled "The Stu Erwin Show": "Yvette" (1954), in which Stu wants to surprise June with an unusual gift—a lifelike female mannequin; "What Paper Do You Read?" in which Stu enrolls in an evening class on government.
ABC — *Shokus Video*

Trouble with Harry, The **1955**
Mystery/Comedy
80075 90 mins C B, V P
John Forsythe, Shirley MacLaine, Edmund Gwenn, Jerry Mathers, directed by Alfred Hitchcock
When a little boy finds a dead body in a Vermont town, it causes all kinds of problems for the members of the community.
MPAA:PG
Alfred Hitchcock; Universal Classics — *MCA Home Video*

Truck Stop Women **1975**
Adventure
64882 88 mins C B, V, CED P
Claudia Jennings
Female truckers become involved in smuggling on the highway.
Mark Lester — *Vestron Video*

True Confessions **1981**
Drama
59849 110 mins C B, V, LV, CED P
Robert DeNiro, Robert Duvall, Ken McMillan, Charles Durning, Burgess Meredith, Louisa Moritz, directed by Ulu Grosbard
John Gregory Dunne's novel about two brothers, one a priest and the other a detective, who are pitted against each other in a tale of corruption in the Church, provides the basis for this film.
MPAA:R
United Artists — *MGM/UA Home Video*

True Game of Death, The **197?**
Martial arts/Adventure
47695 90 mins C B, V P
Bruce Lee, Shou Lung
A story of the circumstances behind the death of superstar Bruce Lee.
Ho Shin Motion Picture Co Ltd — *Master Arts Video*

True Glory, The **1945**
World War II/Documentary
50643 85 mins B/W B, V, FO P
Directed by Garson Kanin
An account of the teamwork between British and American troops in World II from the Normandy Invasion to the Allied Occupation of Germany.
Academy Award '45: Best Documentary Feature.
US War Dept; British Ministry of Information — *Video Yesteryear*

True Grit **1969**
Western
38621 128 mins C B, V, LV R, P
John Wayne, Glen Campbell, Kim Darby, Robert Duvall, directed by Henry Hathaway
John Wayne portrays U.S. Marshal Rooster Cogburn, who is hired by a young girl to find her

father's killer, in this popular film that won Wayne his only Oscar.
Academy Awards '69: Best Actor (Wayne).
MPAA:G
Paramount — *Paramount Home Video; RCA VideoDiscs*

True Heart Susie 1919
Film-History
11389 87 mins B/W B, V, FO P
Lillian Gish, Robert Harring, directed by D.W. Griffith
A simple, moving story about a girl who is in love with a man who marries a girl from the city. (Silent.)
Artcraft — *Video Yesteryear; Sheik Video; Discount Video Tapes; Classic Video Cinema Collector's Club*

Truite, La (The Trout) 1983
Drama
76033 80 mins C B, V P
Isabelle Huppert, Jean-Pierre Cassel, Daniel Olbrychski, Jeanne Moreau
A young woman leaves her family's trout farm to embark on a journey around the world.
MPAA:R
Yves Rousset-Rouard — *RCA/Columbia Pictures Home Video*

Truly Tasteless Jokes 1985
Comedy-Performance
80682 60 mins C B, V, CED P
Marsha Warfield, Denny Johnson, Andrew "Dice" Clay
This is a video version of the popular best-selling book featuring appearances by top comedians.
Alamance Company — *Vestron Video*

Truth About UFO's & ET's, The 1982
Speculation/Occult sciences
66030 90 mins C B, V P
Brad Steiger, the world's leading investigator of the psychic and extraterrestrial examines UFO's, ET's, impossible fossils, poltergeists and "Star People".
Atlan Productions — *United Home Video*

Tubby the Tuba 1977
Musical/Fantasy
69527 81 mins C B, V, CED P
Animated voices of Dick Van Dyke, Pearl Bailey, Jack Gilford, Hermione Gingold
Tubby the Tuba searches for a melody he can call his own. In stereo.
MPAA:G
Alexander Schure Productions — *Children's Video Library*

Tubes...Live at the Greek, The 1979
Music-Performance
65214 60 mins C B, V P
Rock 'n' roll's most outrageous group appear in a night of pure musical madness. In Beta Hi-Fi and stereo VHS.
The Tubes — *Monterey Home Video*

Tubes Video, The 1981
Music-Performance
58466 53 mins C B, V R, P
This program is built around songs on the Tubes LP, "The Completion Backward Principle" but also features new numbers and a few older hits.
EMI Music — *THORN EMI/HBO Video; Pioneer Artists; RCA VideoDiscs*

Tucker and the Horse Thief 1985
Adventure
80807 45 mins C B, V P
A girl dresses and lives like a boy for safety's sake during the California Gold Rush.
Scholastic Productions Inc. — *Scholastic Lorimar*

Tuff Turf 1985
Drama
81214 113 mins C B, V, LV P
James Spader, Kim Richards, Paul Mones, Matt Clark, Olivia Barash, Catya Sassoon
The new kid in a lower class section of Los Angeles engages the local toughs in a bitter turf dispute. Music by Jim Carroll, Lene Lovich, and Southside Johnny.
MPAA:R
New World Pictures — *New World Video*

Tulips 1981
Comedy/Romance
69543 91 mins C B, V, CED P
Gabe Kaplan, Bernadette Peters, Henry Gibson
A would-be suicide takes a contract out on himself, and then meets a woman who makes life worth living again. Together they attempt to evade the gangland hit man.
MPAA:PG
Astral Bellevue Pathe Bennettfilms Inc — *Embassy Home Entertainment*

Tulsa 1949
Western
03995 96 mins C B, V P
Susan Hayward, Robert Preston, Chill Wills
High spirited rancher's daughter begins crusade against oil drillers when her father is killed.
Eagle Lion; Walter Wanger — *Hal Roach Studios; Movie Buff Video; Nostalgia Merchant; Budget Video; Discount Video Tapes; Classic Video Cinema Collector's Club; Kartes Productions; See Hear Industries*

Tumbleweeds **1925**
Western
38980 114 mins B/W B, V, FO P
William S. Hart
This, William S. Hart's last western, is the story of the last great land rush in America, the opening of the Oklahoma Territory to homesteaders. The film is preceded by a sound prologue, made in 1939, in which Hart speaks for the only time on screen, to introduce the story. Silent, with musical score.
United Artists — *Video Yesteryear; Blackhawk Films*

Tunnel, The **1935**
Drama
66403 94 mins B/W B, V P
Richard Dix, Leslie Banks, Madge Evans, C. Aubrey Smith, George Arliss, Walter Huston
An American engineer battles the elements in an attempt to build an undersea transatlantic tunnel, linking the U.S. and Britain.
Gaumont British — *Movie Buff Video*

Tunnelvision **1976**
Satire
52866 75 mins C B, V P
Larraine Newman, Chevy Chase
A spoof of television comprised of irreverent sketches.
MPAA:R
Worldwide Film Corp — *HarmonyVision*

Turandot **1983**
Opera
65660 138 mins C B, V P
Set in Peking, Puccini's opera opens with the proclamation that Princess Turandot will become the bride of the royal suitor who can successfully answer 3 riddles. Unsuccessful suitors lose not only the hand of the princess, but their heads as well.
ORF Productions — *MGM/UA Home Video*

Turandot **1983**
Music-Performance/Opera
81486 135 mins C B, V R, P
Nicola Martinucci, Cecillia Gasdia, Ivo Vinco
The legend of Princess Turandot comes alive in this production of the Puccini opera taped at the Arena di Verona in Rome.
National Video Corporation Ltd. — *THORN EMI/HBO Video*

Turk 182! **1985**
Comedy-Drama
Closed Captioned
81411 96 mins C B, V P
Timothy Hutton, Robert Culp, Robert Urich, Kim Catrall, Peter Boyle, Darren McGavin, directed by Bob Clark
The angry brother of a disabled fireman takes on City Hall in order to win back the pension that he deserves. Available in VHS and Beta Hi-Fi.
MPAA:PG13
20th Century Fox — *CBS/Fox Video*

Turning Point, The **1979**
Drama
44933 119 mins C B, V, CED P
Shirley MacLaine, Anne Bancroft, Mikhail Baryshnikov, directed by Herbert Ross
A woman who gave up ballet for motherhood must come to terms with herself as her daughter's ballet career is launched.
MPAA:PG EL, SP
20th Century Fox — *CBS/Fox Video*

Tut: The Boy King **1977**
Archeology/Museums
02810 52 mins C B, V R, P
Narrated by Orson Welles
Welles' narration eloquently describes some of the treasures viewed by Howard Carter when he first opened the tomb of King Tut in 1922 in this exciting artistic experience.
George Foster Peabody Award; Christopher Award.
NBC — *Warner Home Video*

Tut: The Boy King/The Louvre **197?**
Museums/Archeology
47061 100 mins C CED P
Narrated by Orson Welles and Charles Boyer
Two popular documentary programs are combined in this package. "Tut" presents a tour of the marvelous treasures found in Tutankhamen's tomb. "The Louvre" offers an intimate view of the art masterpieces of this most famous of museums.
NBC — *RCA VideoDiscs*

TV Variety **195?**
Variety
59315 120 mins B/W B, V, 3/4U P
Arthur Godfrey, Ed Sullivan, Mickey Rooney, Jaye P. Morgan, Joey Forman, Joe E. Lewis, Spike Jones
Music, comedy, and dance from TV's "Golden Age": "Arthur Godfrey's Talent Scouts" (1954), a classic live episode; "The Ed Sullivan Show" (1957), season premiere for 1957; and "The Spike Jones Show" (1954), a musical half-hour featuring the entire City Slickers.
CBS;NBC — *Shokus Video*

TV Variety, II **195?**
Variety
47614 120 mins B/W B, V, 3/4U P
This tape contains three different vintage programs: "The Walter Winchell Show" (December 31, 1956), with guests Frankie Laine, Lisa Kirk, Jack Carter and Russ Tamblyn;

"Texaco Star Theater" (January 18, 1949) with Milton Berle and guests Tony Martin and Carmen Miranda; "Person to Person" with Edward R. Murrow interviewing Groucho Marx (1954) and Harpo Marx (1958). All programs include original commercials and network logos.
NBC — *Shokus Video*

TV Variety, Book VII 195?
Variety
79234 120 mins B/W B, V, 3/4U P
Spike Jones, Jack Benny, Lucille Ball, Desi Arnaz, Shirley MacLane, Van Johnson
Four Kinescopes of classic variety shows: "The Ed Wynn Show" (1950); "The Spike Jones Show" (1956); "The Jimmy Durante Show" (1954); and a half hour 1955 Easter Seals telethon hosted by Jack Benny.
NBC et al. — *Shokus Video*

TV Variety, Book VIII 195?
Variety
79235 115 mins B/W B, V, 3/4U P
Frank Sinatra, Dagmar, Bing Crosby, Jackie Gleason
Three rare kinescopes of variety shows: from 1952, the first "Honeymooners" sketch on "Toast of the Town," "The Frank Sinatra Show" from 1951, and "The Edsel Show" from 1957 featuring Sinatra and Crosby.
ABC et al — *Shokus Video*

TV Variety III 1950
Variety/Comedy
62690 120 mins B/W B, V, 3/4U P
Bob Hope, Marilyn Maxwell, Jack Carson, Hal March, Jack Gilford
Two complete kinescoped variety shows from 1950: "The Bob Hope Comedy Hour" and "4 Star Revue," hosted by Jack Carson. Original commercials and network I.D.'s are included.
NBC — *Shokus Video*

TV Variety, IV 1951
Variety
62691 60 mins B/W B, V, 3/4U P
Perry Como, Faye Emerson, Fred Waring, Frankie Laine, Patti Page, Frank Fontaine, Tommy Dorsey
Two fifteen-minute programs, "The Perry Como Show" and "The Faye Emerson Show" are combined with a half-hour "Frankie Laine Show," all from 1950 kinescopes.
CBS et al — *Shokus Video*

TV Variety, V 1956
Variety
66487 115 mins B/W B, V P
Four representative daytime variety shows of the mid-1950's are combined on this tape: "The Garry Moore Show," "Arthur Godfrey Time," "The Robert Q. Lewis Show" and "The Tennessee Ernie Ford Show." Original commercials and network I.D.'s are included.
CBS — *Shokus Video*

TV Variety, VI 1955
Comedy/Variety
76015 120 mins B/W B, V, 3/4U P
Two tv variety shows: "Dinner with the President," with Ethel Merman, Lucy and Desi, Eddie Fisher and many more; "The Perry Como Show," with Rosemary Clooney, Nat King Cole, Rin Tin Tin, and others.
CBS; NBC — *Shokus Video*

TV's Classic Guessing Games 1956
Game show
66460 120 mins B/W B, V, 3/4U P
Arlene Francis, Steve Allen, Dorothy Kilgallen, Deborah Kerr, Lucille Ball, Desi Arnaz, Bill Cullen, Fred Allen, Garry Moore
Four vintage game shows of the 1954-56 seasons are combined on this tape, including three episodes of "What's My Line" and one segment of "I've Got a Secret." Original commercials and network I.D.'s included.
CBS — *Shokus Video*

Twelve Angry Men 1957
Drama
64835 95 mins B/W B, V P
Henry Fonda, Martin Balsam, Lee J. Cobb, E.G. Marshall, Jack Klugman, Jack Warden, directed by Sidney Lumet
Based on a TV play by Reginald Rose, this is a classic drama of a deadlocked jury and one man who makes the others listen to reason.
United Artists — *Key Video; RCA VideoDiscs*

Twelve Chairs, The 1970
Comedy
65112 94 mins C B, V P
Mel Brooks, Dom DeLuise, Frank Langella, Ron Moody, directed by Mel Brooks
In 1927 Russia, a rich matron admits on her deathbed that she has hidden her jewels in the upholstery of one of twelve chairs. The chairs, however, are no longer in her home, and a madcap search begins for them.
MPAA:PG
Michael Hertzberg — *Media Home Entertainment*

Twelve O'Clock High 1949
War-Drama
29179 132 mins B/W B, V P
Gregory Peck, Hugh Marlowe, Gary Merrill, Millard Mitchell, Dean Jagger
An epic drama about the heroic 8th Air Force. Peck, as a bomber-group commander, is forced to drive his men to the breaking point in the fury of battle.

 (For explanation of codes, see USE GUIDE and KEY)

Academy Awards '49: Best Supporting Actor (Jagger)
20th Century Fox — *CBS/Fox Video*

Twelve Tasks of Asterix, The **1984**
Cartoons
73791 81 mins C B, V R, P
Animated
The gallant warrior Asterix matches brains and brawn with Caesar and the entire Roman Empire.
Productions Dargaud Films — *Walt Disney Home Video*

Twenty Questions **1952**
Game show
58637 30 mins B/W B, V, FO P
Hosted by Bill Slater
The "Mennen Mystery Voice" tells the viewing audience what secret object the panel has 20 questions to guess, in this vintage quiz show. Sponsored by Mennen.
Dumont — *Video Yesteryear*

27th Annual Academy Awards Presentations, The **1955**
Variety
47495 79 mins B/W B, V, FO P
Grace Kelly, Marlon Brando, Humphrey Bogart, Audrey Hepburn, Bing Crosby, William Holden, Bette Davis, hosted by Bob Hope and Thelma Ritter
Telecast on March 30, 1955, this program honored the Oscar winners of 1954 including Grace Kelly, Eva Marie Saint, Edmond O'Brien, Marlon Brando, Walt Disney, Elia Kazan and others. The nominated songs are performed by Johnny Desmond, Tony Martin, Rosemary Clooney, Peggy King and Dean Martin.
NBC — *Video Yesteryear*

20,000 Leagues Under the Sea **1973**
Cartoons
66583 47 mins C B, V P
Animated
An animated version of the Jules Verne classic about Captain Nemo and his submarine.
Hanna-Barbera — *Worldvision Home Video*

20,000 Leagues Under the Sea **1954**
Adventure
44303 127 mins C CED P
Kirk Douglas, James Mason, Peter Lorre
From a futuristic submarine, Captain Nemo wages war. Battleships and giant squid answer the challenge of Nemo's atomic powered death machine. This adaptation of the Jules Verne classic comes with VHS stereo or Beta Hi-Fi sound.
Academy Award '54: Special Effects. MPAA:G
Walt Disney Productions — *RCA VideoDiscs*

20,000 Leagues Under the Sea **1973**
Cartoons
78902 60 mins C B, V P
Animated
This is an animated version of the Jules Verne classic science fiction novel.
Hanna-Barbera — *Prism*

---

20 Years of World Series **1958**
Baseball
49553 40 mins B/W B, V P
A collection of highlights from among the most exciting of the World Series played between 1938 and 1957.
Lew Fonseca — *Major League Baseball Productions*

Twice a Woman **1979**
Drama
70599 90 mins C B, V P
Bibi Andersson, Anthony Perkins, Sandra Dumas
A man and woman divorce, and then both fall in love with the same provocative young woman.
William Howerd/MGS; Actueel Films — *Prism*

Twigs **1984**
Theater/Drama
78662 138 mins C B, V P
Cloris Leachman
A taped performance of George Furthis' Tony Award-winning drama about a mother and her three daughters who meet the day before Thanksgiving.
Showtime — *RKO HomeVideo*

Twilight People **1975**
Horror
79763 84 mins C B, V P
John Ashley, Pat Woodell, Pam Grier
When a mad scientist's creations turn on him for revenge, he runs for his life.
MPAA:PG
Dimension Pictures — *United Home Video*

Twilight Zone—The Movie **1983**
Horror
65359 101 mins C B, V, LV, CED P
Dan Aykroyd, Albert Brooks, Vic Morrow, Kathleen Quinlan, John Lithgow
Four short horrific tales are anthologized in this film as a tribute to Rod Serling and his popular TV series. Three of the episodes, "Kick the Can," "It's a Good Life" and "Nightmare at

20,000 Feet," are based on original "Twilight Zone" scripts.
MPAA:PG
Steven Spielberg; John Landis — *Warner Home Video*

Twist 1976
Drama
77385 106 mins C B, V P
Bruce Dern, Ann-Margret, Sydne Rome, Maria Schell, Charles Aznavour, directed by Claude Chabrol
A game of cat and mouse ensues when an American writer and his French wife suspect each other of infidelity.
Barnabe Productions; Gloria Films — *U.S.A. Home Video*

Twist of Fate 1984
Music-Performance
66504 19 mins C B, V, LV, CED P
Olivia Newton-John, John Travolta
Six of Olivia Newton-John's music videos are combined on this tape, including four songs from the movie "Two of a Kind;" the title tune, "Livin' in Desperate Times," "Take a Chance" and "Twist of Fate," plus "Heart Attack" and "Tied Up." Stereo in all formats.
MCA — *MCA Home Video*

Twisted Brain 1974
Horror
79757 89 mins C B, V P
Pat Cardi, John Niland
When an honor student becomes the unwilling subject of a biological experiment the result is something that is half man and half beast.
MPAA:R
Crown International — *United Home Video*

Twisted Cross, The 1956
World War II/Documentary
54835 53 mins B/W B, V R, P
Narrated by Alexander Scourby
The story of Adolph Hitler and the Nazi movement is recreated, tracing Hitler's lowly beginnings in 1923, to his days as conqueror of the European mainland, to his defeat and suicide.
NBC; Henry Salomon — *Warner Home Video*

Twisted Sister's Stay Hungry 1984
Music video
72876 120 mins C B, V P
Twisted Sister
A conceptual version of Twisted Sisters' album "Stay Hungry" with concert footage.
Unknown — *Embassy Home Entertainment; Pioneer Artists*

Two Assassins in the Dark 198?
Martial arts
64960 90 mins C B, V P
Wang Tao, Chang Yi, Lung Chun-Eng
A martial arts adventure about a pair of kung-fu killers.
Dragon Lady Productions — *Unicorn Video*

Two Best World Series Ever, The 1978
Baseball
13319 60 mins C B, V P
Cincinnati Reds, Boston Red Sox, New York Yankees, Los Angeles Dodgers
Best plays from the 1975 and 1978 World Series are contained in this program. In '75 Sparky Anderson's Reds prevail in seven games over the Red Sox in one of the most exciting and dramatic series ever. The Yankees come from two games behind in '78 to win their second consecutive championship in six games over the Dodgers.
Warner Qube — *VidAmerica*

Two Faces of Evil, The 1982
Horror
81040 60 mins C B, V P
Anna Calder-Marshall, Gary Raynmond, Pauline Delany, Philip Latham
A family's vacation turns into a night of unbearable terror when they pick up a sinister hitchhiker.
Hammer Films — *Thriller Video*

Two Graves to Kung-Fu 1982
Martial arts/Adventure
59994 95 mins C B, V R, P
Liu Chia-Yung, Shek Kin, Chen Hung-Lieh
A young kung-fu student is framed for murder. When the real murderers kill his teacher, he escapes from prison to seek revenge.
MPAA:R
L and T Films Corp Ltd — *Video Gems*

200 Motels 1971
Comedy/Musical
75538 99 mins C B, V P
Frank Zappa, Ringo Starr, The Mothers of Invention
A story of what happens to a rock group that has been on the road too long.
MPAA:R
Murakami Wolf Productions Inc — *MGM/UA Home Video*

Two Kennedys, The 1981
Drama
69038 118 mins C B, V P
This film deals extensively with the mystery surrounding the Kennedy family while making political connections with no holds barred.

Italy — *MPI Home Video*

Two Mules for Sister Sara **1970**
Western
47425 105 mins C B, V P
Clint Eastwood, Shirley MacLaine, directed by Don Siegel
An American mercenary in 19th century Mexico gets mixed up with a cigar-smoking nun. The two make plans to capture a French garrison.
MPAA:PG
Universal — *MCA Home Video*

Two Reelers—Comedy Classics I **1933**
Comedy
38971 54 mins B/W B, V, FO P
Edgar Kennedy, Harry Gribbon, Harry Sweet, Jack Norton, Maxine Jennings, Willie Best
This package includes a 1944 Edgar Kennedy short, "Feather Your Nest" (RKO), and two 1933 films, "How Comedies Are Born" and "Dog Blight."
RKO — *Video Yesteryear*

Two Reelers—Comedy Classics II **194?**
Comedy
38972 53 mins B/W B, V, FO P
Leon Errol, Dorothy Granger, Billy Gilbert, Edgar Kennedy
A second package of three vintage shorts: "Chicken Feed" (1939) with Billy Gilbert, "Twin Husbands" (1946) with Leon Errol, and Edgar Kennedy in "False Roomers" (1938).
RKO — *Video Yesteryear*

Two Reelers—Comedy Classics III **194?**
Comedy
38973 52 mins B/W B, V, FO P
Edgar Kennedy, Jed Prouty
More laughs, with two Edgar Kennedy shorts, "A Merchant of Menace" (1933), and "Social Terrors" (1946). Also, Jed Prouty is featured in "Coat Tales" (193).
RKO — *Video Yesteryear*

Two Reelers—Comedy Classics IV **1936**
Comedy
38970 56 mins B/W B, V, FO P
Bert Lahr, Gene Austin, June Brewster, Carol Tevis, Grady Sutton
"Bridal Bail" (1934), "No More West" (Educational-1934) with Bert Lahr singing and clowning, and "Bad Medicine" (1936) with crooner Gene Austin comprise this comedy package.
RKO — *Video Yesteryear*

Two Reelers—Comedy Classics #5 **19??**
Comedy
69556 55 mins B/W B, V, FO P
Leon Errol, the Ritz Brothers, Charlotte Greenwood
A compilation of three vintage comedy shorts by popular stars of the 1930's: "Dear Deer" (1942) with Leon Errol, "Hotel Anchovy" (1934) with the Ritz Brothers and "Love Your Neighbor" (1930) with Charlotte Greenwood.
Educational — *Video Yesteryear*

2001: A Space Odyssey **1968**
Science fiction
44639 141 mins C B, V, LV, CED P
Keir Dullea, Gary Lockwood, directed by Stanley Kubrick
A space voyage to Jupiter turns into chaos when a computer, HAL 9000, takes over, killing several astronauts. This space voyage traces the context of man's history; man vs. the machinery he made.
Academy Awards '68: Best Visual Effects.
MGM — *MGM/UA Home Video*

2010 **1984**
Science fiction
Closed Captioned
81059 116 mins C B, V, LV P
Roy Scheider, John Lithgow, Helen Mirren, Bob Balaban, Keir Dullea, Madolyn Smith, directed by Peter Hyams
In this sequel to "2001," the United States and Russia reluctantly team up to reclaim the "Discovery" spaceship before its decaying orbit around Jupiter brings it crashing down onto the planet's surface. Based upon the Arthur C. Clarke novel.
MPAA:PG
MGM; Peter Hyams — *MGM/UA Home Video*

2000 Year Old Man, The **1982**
Cartoons/Comedy
78347 25 mins C B, V P
Animated, the voices of Carl Reiner and Mel Brooks
This is the animated version of the Mel Brooks-Carl Reiner comedy classic routine, featuring the reminiscences of the bemused patriarch of the past, the 2000 Year Old Man.
MPAA:G
Leo Salkin — *Media Home Entertainment*

Two Tickets to Broadway **1951**
Comedy/Musical
57167 106 mins C B, V P
Tony Martin, Janet Leigh, Gloria DeHaven, Smith and Dale
A small-town singer and a crooner arrange a hoax to get themselves on Bob Crosby's TV show.

RKO; Howard Hughes — *King of Video*

Two-Way Stretch **1960**
Comedy
47306 84 mins B/W B, V R, P
Peter Sellers, Wilfrid Hyde-White, Liz Fraser, David Lodge
Three prison inmates in a progressive jail plan to break out, pull a diamond heist, and break back in, all in the same night.
Showcorporation; British — *THORN EMI/HBO Video*

Two Wondrous Tigers **1979**
Martial arts
70390 87 mins C B, V P
John Chang, directed by Wilson Tong
An awesome Kung-Fu gang terrorizes a small town until a local upstart out-chops the bullies.
Alex Gouw — *Trans World Entertainment*

Two Worlds of Jennie Logan, The **1981**
Fantasy
75465 99 mins C B, V P
Lindsay Wagner, Linda Gray, Marc Singer, John Darling
A Victorian mansion and antique dress take Jennie Logan back to the turn of the century where she finds romance, intrigue and murder.
King Features — *U.S.A. Home Video*

Tycoon **1947**
Drama
29469 120 mins C B, V P, T
John Wayne, Laraine Day, Sir Cedric Hardwicke
A young American railroad builder finds action and romance in Latin America.
RKO — *Blackhawk Films; Nostalgia Merchant; King of Video*

U

U2 Live at Red Rocks "Under A Blood Red Sky" **19??**
Music-Performance
72933 60 mins C B, V P
One of rock's hottest bands is featured, performing songs from their album "Under A Blood Red Sky," filmed in Denver, Colorado.
Steve Lilywhite — *MCA Home Video*

Ub Iwerks Cartoon Festival **193?**
Cartoons
29488 57 mins C B, V P, T
Animated
Seven delightful cartoons by one of the pioneering geniuses of animation. Includes: "The Brave Tin Soldier," "Happy Days," "Fiddlesticks," "Jack and the Beanstalk," "The Headless Horseman," and "The Little Red Hen."
Ub Iwerks — *Blackhawk Films*

Ub Iwerks Cartoonfest Two **193?**
Cartoons
29489 46 mins C B, V P, T
Animated
More cartoons from the pen of the immortal Iwerks. Six color masterpieces of such great tales as "Tom Thumb," "Jack Frost," "Aladdin and the Wonderful Lamp," "Ali Baba," "Sinbad," and "Spooks."
Ub Iwerks — *Blackhawk Films*

Ub Iwerks Cartoonfest Three **193?**
Cartoons
59989 30 mins C B, V P, T
Animated
A compilation of Iwerks classics: "Simple Simon" (1935), "Puss in Boots" (1934), "Dick Whittington's Cat" (1936), and "Don Quixote" (1934).
Celebrity Productions — *Blackhawk Films*

Ub Iwerks Cartoonfest Four **1935**
Cartoons
62874 30 mins C B, V P, T
Animated
Another collection of enjoyable cartoons from the pen of Ub Iwerks. Included are "The Valiant Tailor," "Mary's Little Lamb," "The Brementown Musicians" and "Balloonland," all from 1934-35.
Ub Iwerks — *Blackhawk Films*

UB Iwerks Cartoonfest Five **193?**
Cartoons
65705 23 mins C B, V P, T
Animated
Three more fabulous Cinecolor cartoons from the UB Iwerks studio are combined on this tape: "Queen of Hearts" (1934), "Old Mother Hubbard" (1935) and "Humpty Dumpty" (1935), all from the Comicolor Cartoons series.
Ub Iwerks; Celebrity Productions — *Blackhawk Films*

Ugetsu **1953**
Film-Avant-garde
06241 96 mins B/W B, V P
Machiko Kyo, Masayuki Mori, directed by Kenji Mizoguchi

This classic Japanese film concerns a sixteenth-century legend of of a potter and a farmer who travel in search of their dreams.
JA
Japanese — *Budget Video; Sheik Video; Western Film & Video Inc; Discount Video Tapes; Video Dimensions; Video Action*

Ultimate Fitness **1984**
Physical fitness
81536 60 mins C B, V P
Physical fitness expert Deborah Crocker demonstrates the Esquire aerobics program both men and women can do.
AM Available
Esquire Press — *Esquire Press*

Ultimate Swan Lake, The **1984**
Dance
70168 126 mins C B, V P
The Bolshoi Ballet starring Natalia Bessmertnova, Boris Akimov, Alexander Bogatyrev, hosted by Gene Kelly
This dynamic performance of the "Swan Lake" ballet featured choreography by Yuri Grigorovich of the world famous Bolshoi Ballet. In Dolby stereo.
Kultur International Films — *Kultur*

Ultimate Thrill, The **1974**
Adventure
59069 84 mins C B, V R, P
Britt Ekland, Barry Brown, Michael Blodgett
A successful man plays Russian Roulette for big stakes.
General Cinema; Centaur Films — *Video Gems*

Ultra Flash **1983**
Dance
65346 60 mins C B, V P
A fantasy that is performed to some of today's hottest dance music. In stereo
Niles Siegal Organization — *Vestron Video*

Ultraman II **1984**
Cartoons/Adventure
66489 84 mins C B, V P
Animated
In four new adventures, superhero Ultraman battles prehistoric monsters, killer beasts, an evil tornado and a sinister, life-threatening cloud, as he fights for peace on earth.
Tsuburaya Productions — *Trans World Entertainment*

Umbrellas of Cherbourg **1963**
Musical-Drama
65443 90 mins C B, V P
Catherine Deneuve, Nino Castelnuovo
As a universal statement of love, this tender story has become a timeless musical classic. Subtitled in English.
MPAA:G FR
Landau Unger — *U.S.A. Home Video*

Uncanny, The **1978**
Horror
47817 85 mins C B, V, 3/4U P
Peter Cushing, Ray Milland, Samantha Eggar, Donald Pleasence
A writer theorizes that a number of mysterious deaths were caused by a secret society of fatal felines.
Astral Films — *Media Home Entertainment; Nostalgia Merchant*

Uncle Sam Magoo **196?**
Cartoons/History-US
66037 60 mins C B, V R, P
Animated, voice of Jim Backus
Mr. Magoo provides a history lesson in his own inimitable style.
UPA — *Paramount Home Video*

Uncommon Valor **1983**
Drama
Closed Captioned
65732 105 mins C B, V R, P
Gene Hackman, Fred Ward, Reb Brown, Randall "Tex" Cobb, Robert Stack
After useless appeals to the government for information on his son who is listed as "missing in action" in Vietnam, Colonel Rhodes takes matters into his own hands.
MPAA:R
John Milius; Buzz Feitshans — *Paramount Home Video*

Under California Stars **1948**
Western
38981 71 mins C B, V, FO P
Roy Rogers, Andy Devine, Jane Frazee, the Sons of the Pioneers
A shady gang making a living rounding up wild horses decides they can make more money by capturing Roy Rogers' horse, Trigger.
Republic — *Video Yesteryear; Discount Video Tapes; VCII; Video Connection*

Under Capricorn **1949**
Mystery
07880 117 mins C B, V P
Directed by Alfred Hitchcock; Ingrid Bergman, Joseph Cotten, Michael Wilding
A dark tale of love and sensitivity, frustration and terror, headed by an all-star cast.
Warner Bros — *VidAmerica*

Under Fire **1983**
Drama
65600 128 mins C B, V, LV P

Gene Hackman, Nick Nolte, Joanna Cassidy
Three news correspondents chronicle the final days of the Samoza regime in Nicaragua.
MPAA:R
Orion Pictures — *Vestron Video*

Under the Rainbow **1981**
Comedy
51996 97 mins C B, V R, P
Chevy Chase, Carrie Fisher, Eve Arden, Joseph Maher, Robert Donner, Mako, Billy Barty
Undercurrents of foreign political intrigue add to the comic situations encountered by a talent scout and a secret service agent in and around a hotel inhabited by the midgets who have been signed to play the Munchkins in "The Wizard of Oz."
MPAA:PG
Orion Pictures — *Warner Home Video*

Under the Roofs of Paris (Sous les Toits de Paris) **1929**
Romance
12863 95 mins B/W B, V, FO P
Directed by Rene Clair
A tale of young lovers in a crowded tenement. Music and imaginative technique occupy this first French sound film. French with English subtitles.
FR
Tobis — *Video Yesteryear; Sheik Video; Cable Films; Discount Video Tapes*

Under the Volcano **1984**
Drama
77214 112 mins C B, V P
Albert Finney, Jacqueline Bisset, Anthony Andrews, directed by John Huston
A disparate alcoholic ex-British consulate mulls over his life in Mexico during "The Day of the Dead" ceremony in 1939.
Universal Pictures — *MCA Home Video*

Underground Aces **1980**
Comedy
80699 93 mins C B, V P
Dirk Benedict, Melanie Griffith, Frank Gorshin, Jerry Ohrbach, RobertHegyes, Audrey Landers
A group of parking lot attendants transform a shiek into an attendant in order to help him meet the girl of his dreams.
MPAA:PG
Orion Pictures — *Vestron Video*

Undersea Adventures of Captain Nemo Volume 1, The **1975**
Cartoons
53156 60 mins C B, V P
Animated
Captain Nemo and his crew of the submarine Nautilus take the viewer on a series of daring battles and rescues in this undersea adventure.
EL, SP
Rainbow Animation — *Family Home Entertainment*

Undersea Adventures of Captain Nemo Volume 2, The **1975**
Cartoons
64197 60 mins C B, V P
Animated
The Nautilus crew battles bloodthirsty sharks as they accidentally uncover a sunken treasure worth a fortune.
EL, SP
Rainbow Animation — *Family Home Entertainment*

Undersea Adventures of Captain Nemo Volume 3, The **1975**
Cartoons
64198 60 mins C B, V P
Animated
Captain Nemo's team encounters Killer Whales and a poisonous squid as it battles criminal whale poachers. Then the crew travels to the icy regions of the world to confront a ferocious polar bear and a deadly sea leopard.
EL, SP
Rainbow Animation — *Family Home Entertainment*

Undersea Adventures of Captain Nemo, Volume 4, The **1975**
Cartoons
70656 60 mins C B, V P
Animated
This presentation shows Captain Nemo and the Nautilus crew battling unsportsmanlike fishermen and the Loch Ness bomb. Available in Hi-Fi Stereo.
Rainbow Animation — *Family Home Entertainment*

Undersea Kingdom **1936**
Adventure/Serials
14630 136 mins B/W B, V P
Ray 'Crash' Corrigan
Adventure beneath the ocean floor. In twelve chapters of thirteen minutes; the first chapter runs twenty minutes.
Republic — *Video Connection; Video Dimensions; Discount Video Tapes; Nostalgia Merchant*

Undersea World of Jacques Cousteau Vol. I, The **1978**
Documentary/Adventure
47059 100 mins C CED P
Narrated by Rod Serling

Two of Cousteau's journeys on the Calypso are featured: "Sharks" and "The Singing Whale." Spectacular underwater footage is included.
Media Producers Corp — *RCA VideoDiscs*

Underwater 1955
Adventure
66332 99 mins C B, V, 3/4U P
Jane Russell, Richard Egan, Gilbert Roland
A team of skin divers face danger when they begin a search for underwater treasure.
RKO — *Nostalgia Merchant*

Unfaithfully Yours 1948
Comedy
72898 105 mins B/W B, V P
Rex Harrison, Linda Darnell
A conductor suspects his wife is cheating on him.
Preston Sturges; RKO — *CBS/Fox Video*

Unfaithfully Yours 1984
Comedy
72899 96 mins C B, V P
Dudley Moore, Nastassia Kinski, Armand Assante, Albert Brooks
A symphony conductor suspects his wife of fooling around with a musician; in retaliation, he plots an elaborate scheme to murder her. Based on the 1948 Preston Sturges film.
MPAA:PG
20th Century Fox — *CBS/Fox Video*

Unholy Wife, The 1957
Drama
79765 94 mins C B, V P
Rod Steiger, Diana Dors, Tom Tryon, Marie Windsor
A young woman plans to murder her wealthy husband, but her plan goes awry when she accidentally kills someone else.
RKO — *United Home Video*

Unicorn the Island of Magic 1984
Cartoons/Fantasy
80374 92 mins C B, V P
Animated
When Unico the magical unicorn comes down to earth, he learns a lesson from the Trojan Horse about love and courage.
Sanrio Productions — *RCA/Columbia Pictures Home Video*

Unicorn, The 1983
Drama
65435 29 mins C B, V P
Diana Dors, Celia Johnson
A small boy hears the legend that if one rubs the horn of a Unicorn his wishes will come true. Mistakenly he buys a one-horned goat and sets out to fulfill his dreams.
Janus Films — *Embassy Home Entertainment*

Unicorn Tales I 1980
Fairy tales
57573 90 mins C B, V P
Four stories for children, adapted from classic fairy tales, told in a modern way, with music. "The Magic Pony Ride" (based on the Ugly Duckling) is about a lonely little girl who meets a pony considered useless, and the two of them learn how to see and believe. In "The Stowaway" (based on Pinocchio), a young boy arrives in a new city and meets a lovable old man who leads him on the path to truth. "Carnival Circus" (based on Cinderella) concerns a young girl who fails at everything until she saves the circus and realizes that everyone has a special talent for something. In "The Maltese Unicorn" (based on The Boy Who Cried Wolf), a boy discovers that if he wants to be believed he must be a man of his word.
Viacom — *Playhouse Video*

Unicorn Tales II 1980
Fairy tales
57574 90 mins C B, V P
Four stories for children, adapted from classic fairy tales, told in a modern way, with music. In "Big Apple Birthday" (based on Alice in Wonderland), a girl who is bored by everything visits a new city and learns that there can be joy in every moment. "The Magnificent Major" (based on The Wizard of Oz) concerns a young girl who doesn't like to read. When she is transported to a land of non-readers, she is eager to return home so she can read. In "The Magic Hat" (based on The Emperor's New Clothes), a young boy moves to a new city, finding it difficult to make friends until he wears a magic hat. The magic of friendship, however, lasts longer than the "powers" of the hat. "Alex and the Wonderful 'Doo Wah' Lamp" (based on Aladdin and the Magic Lamp) concerns a boy who conjures up three genies from an old lamp, who promise to grant his every request. After being turned into several different people, however, he realizes he is happiest as himself.
Viacom — *Playhouse Video*

Union City 1981
Suspense/Drama
47434 82 mins C B, V P
Deborah Harry, Everett McGill, Dennis Lipscomb, Pat Benatar, directed by Mark Reichart
Deborah Harry of Blondie stars in this "new-wave" mystery about an accidental murderer who is on the run from the law.
MPAA:R
Cantina Blues Films; Kinesis Ltd — *RCA/Columbia Pictures Home Video*

Universe, The 1982
Astronomy/Science
59558 55 mins C B, V P
A comprehensive survey of what man knows today about our solar system and the seemingly infinite number of other systems and galaxies in all of universal space and time.
McGraw Hill — *Mastervision*

Universe, The 1985
Astronomy
70706 30 mins C B, V P
Narrated by William Shatner
Travelling sans U.S.S. Enterprise, Mr. Shatner takes a non-fictional look at our solar system and the stars beyond.
NASA — *Kid Time Video*

Unknown Comedy Show, The 1982
Comedy-Performance
80901 56 mins C B, V P
Murray Langston, Johnny Dark, James Marcel
The Unknown Comic, Murray Langston, performs some of his best stand-up routines in this taped concert. Available in VHS Stereo and Beta Hi-FI.
Bill Osco; Murray Langston — *U.S.A. Home Video*

Unknown Powers 1980
Drama/Occult sciences
33806 97 mins C B, V R, P
Samatha Eggar, Jack Palance, Will Geer, Roscoe Lee Brown
Science and drama are combined to examine ESP and Magic. Are they gifts or curses, and how are peoples lives affected by them?
MPAA:PG
International TV Films — *Video Gems*

Unmarried Woman, An 1978
Drama
44934 124 mins C B, V, CED P
Jill Clayburgh, Alan Bates
A woman must make a new life for herself after her husband suddenly divorces her after seventeen years of marriage.
MPAA:R
20th Century Fox — *CBS/Fox Video*

Unofficial Baseball Handbook, The 1985
Baseball
70759 30 mins C B, V P
This is a humorous and irreverent look inside the world of baseball featuring gaffes and bloopers from your favorite major-league stars and mascots.
Major League Baseball — *Major League Baseball Productions*

Unseen, The 1980
Horror
52951 91 mins C B, V P
Barbara Bach, Sydney Lassick, Stephen Furst
Three young women from a TV station are covering a story in a remote area of California. Before nightfall, two are horribly killed, leaving the third to come face to face with the terror.
Triune Films — *VidAmerica*

Unsinkable Molly Brown, The 1964
Musical
80619 128 mins C B, V P
Debbie Reynolds, Harve Presnell, Ed Begley, Martita Hunt, Hermione Baddeley, directed by Charles Walters
A spunky backwoods girl is determined to break into the upper crust of Denver's high society. The Meredith Wilson score features "He's My Friend" and "I'll Never Say No." Available in VHS and Beta Hi-Fi.
MGM — *MGM/UA Home Video*

Unsuitable Job for a Woman, An 1982
Mystery
77453 94 mins C B, V P
Billie Whitelaw, Paul Freeman, Pippa Guard
A young woman in charge of a detective agency becomes obsessed with the young man whose death she is investigating. Available in Beta Hi-Fi and VHS Stereo.
Boyd's Co Films Ltd. — *Monterey Home Video*

Until September 1984
Romance
80629 96 mins C B, V P
Karen Allen, Thierry Lhermitte, Christopher Cazenove, Johanna Pavlis, directed by Richard Marquand
An American tourist meets and falls in love with a married banker while stranded in a Parisian hotel.
MPAA:R
United Artists — *MGM/UA Home Video*

Up from the Depths 1979
Horror
69287 85 mins C B, V P
Sam Bottoms
Something from beneath the ocean is turning the paradise of Hawaii into a nightmare.
MPAA:R
New World Pictures — *Vestron Video*

Up In Smoke 1979
Comedy
48514 87 mins C B, V, LV R, P
Cheech Marin, Tommy Chong
A pair of free-spirited burn-outs team up for a tongue-in-cheek spoof of sex, drugs, and rock and roll.

(For explanation of codes, see USE GUIDE and KEY)

MPAA:R
Lou Adler, Lou Lombardo — *Paramount Home Video; RCA VideoDiscs*

Up Pompeii **1971**
Comedy
33642 90 mins C B, V P
Frankie Howard, Patrick Cargill
A sexy, hilarious story in which a servant accidentally gains possession of a scroll containing a plot against Emperor Nero. The conspirators try every means possible to recover the scroll.
MPAA:R
Ned Sherrin — *United Home Video*

Up the Creek **1984**
Comedy
70149 95 mins C B, V P
Tim Matheson, Stephen Furst, John Hillerman, James B. Sikking
Four college students enter a whitewater raft race to gain some respect for their school. The soundtrack features songs by Heart, Cheap Trick and The Beach Boys.
MPAA:R
Orion Pictures — *Vestron Video*

Up the Sandbox **1972**
Comedy-Drama
66326 98 mins C B, V P
Barbra Streisand, David Selby, Jane Hoffman, Barbara Rhodes
A bored housewife fantasizes about her life in order to avoid facing her mundane existence.
MPAA:R
Warner Bros — *Warner Home Video*

Uptown Saturday Night **1974**
Comedy
53525 104 mins C B, V R, P
Sidney Poitier, Bill Cosby, Harry Belafonte, Flip Wilson, Richard Pryor, Calvin Lockhart
Two working men attempt to recover a stolen lottery ticket from the black underworld after being ripped off at a gambling place.
MPAA:PG
Warner Bros — *Warner Home Video*

Urban Cowboy **1980**
Drama
54668 135 mins C B, V, LV R, P
John Travolta, Debra Winger, Scott Glenn, Madolyn Smith, Barry Corbin, directed by James Bridges
A young Texas farmer comes to Houston to work in a refinery and learns about life by hanging out at Gilley's, a roadhouse bar. Here he and his friends, dressed in their cowboy gear, drink, fight, and prove their manhood by riding a mechanical bull.
MPAA:PG
Paramount — *Paramount Home Video; RCA VideoDiscs*

URGH! A Music War **1981**
Music-Performance
77468 124 mins C B, V P
The Go Go's, The Cramps, XTC, Devo, The Police, Steel Pulse
Thirty-seven once familiar new wave bands from Devo to XTC got together for this historic concert. Available in Beta & VHS Hi-Fi.
Lorimar Productions — *CBS/Fox Video*

U. S. Men's Gymnastics Championship **1981**
Gymnastics
59568 60 mins C B, V P
The top male gymnasts in the U.S. compete for the 1981 titles.
CBS; Transworld Intl — *Mastervision*

U.S. Women's Gymnastics Championship **1981**
Gymnastics/Women
59569 60 mins C B, V P
The top female gymnasts in the U.S. compete for the 1981 titles.
CBS; Transworld Intl — *Mastervision*

Used Cars **1980**
Comedy
51573 113 mins C B, V P
Kurt Russell, Jack Warden, Deborah Harmon
A car dealer is desperate to put his jalopy shop competitors out of business. The owners go to great lengths to stay afloat.
MPAA:R
Columbia Pictures — *RCA/Columbia Pictures Home Video; RCA VideoDiscs*

Users, The **1978**
Drama
75495 125 mins C B, V P
Jaclyn Smith, Tony Curtis, John Forsythe, Red Buttons, George Hamilton
A small-town girl meets a faded film star and becomes involved in the movie business.
Aaron Spelling Productions — *Prism*

Utilities **1983**
Comedy
80695 94 mins C B, V, CED P
Robert Hays, Brooke Adams, John Marley, Ben Gordon, Helen Burns
A frustrated social worker enlists the help of his friends in his efforts to impress an attractive policewoman by taking on a large corporate utility.
MPAA:PG
New World Pictures — *Vestron Video*

Utopia Sampler, The 1983
Music-Performance
64929 11 mins C B, V P
Utopia, featuring Todd Rundgren, performs three songs on this Video 45: "Hammer in My Heart," "You Make Me Crazy" and "Feet Don't Fail Me Now."
Neo-Utopian Laboratories — *Sony Corporation of America*

V

Vagabond Lover 1929
Musical
07239 66 mins B/W B, V, FO P
Rudy Vallee, Sally Blane, Marie Dressler
The amusing tale of the loves, hopes, and dreams of an aspiring saxophone player.
RKO — *Video Yesteryear*

Valley Girl 1983
Comedy
69284 95 mins C B, V, LV, CED P
Nicolas Cage, Deborah Foreman
A typical "valley girl" shocks her peers when she falls for a leather-jacketed freak. Contains music by Men at Work, The Clash, Culture Club and others.
MPAA:R
Wayne Crawford and Andrew Lane — *Vestron Video*

Valley of Fire 1951
Western
63995 63 mins B/W B, V P, T
Gene Autry, Gail Davis, Pat Buttram
Gene is working hard cleaning up the town of Quartz Creek. He decides to import a caravan of brides for the men in town, but a local gambler kidnaps the wagon train.
Columbia — *Blackhawk Films*

Valley of Terror 1938
Western
10071 59 mins B/W B, V P, T
Kermit Maynard, Rocky the Horse
A James Oliver Curwood saga of the Old West.
Ambassador — *Blackhawk Films; Discount Video Tapes*

Vamping 1984
Mystery/Drama
73662 107 mins C B, V R, P
Patrick Duffy, Catherine Hyland
A desperate saxophonist robs a house and winds up in a mysterious menage a trois.
MPAA:R
Howard Kling; Stratton Rawson — *Key Video*

Vampire Bat, The 1932
Horror
47792 69 mins B/W B, V P
Lionel Atwill, Fay Wray, Melvyn Douglas
A vampire bat and its supernatural powers provide the basis of this suspense-horror story.
Majestic — *Movie Buff Video; Western Film & Video Inc*

Vampyr 1932
Film-Avant-garde
08594 66 mins B/W B, V, 3/4U P
Julian West, Sybille Schmitz, Harriet Gerard, directed by Carl H. Dreyer
Low-key, experimental approach by Dreyer makes for an eerie film. Music by Wolfgang Zeller. Little dialogue.
Germany — *Video Yesteryear; Budget Video; Sheik Video; Discount Video Tapes; Classic Video Cinema Collector's Club*

Van, The 1977
Comedy
48478 90 mins C B, V P
Stuart Gertz, Deborah White
A teenage boy buys a van in hopes it will attract girls—one in particular—to him.
MPAA:R
Crown International — *United Home Video*

Van Nuys Blvd. 1979
Comedy
48479 93 mins C B, V P
Bill Adler, Cynthia Wood
The popular boulevard is the scene where the cool southern California guys converge for cruising and girl watching.
MPAA:R
Crown International — *United Home Video*

Vanessa 1977
Drama
55253 90 mins C B, V P
The story of an innocent young girl's introduction to the erotic pleasures of the Orient.
MPAA:X
Intercontinental Releasing Corp — *VidAmerica*

Vanishing American 1926
Western
55815 114 mins B/W B, V P
Richard Dix, Noah Beery, directed by George B. Seitz
The mistreatment of the American Indian is depicted in this sweeping Western epic. Musical score.
Paramount — *Festival Films; Video Yesteryear*

Vanishing Point 1971
Drama
08458 98 mins C B, V P

Barry Newman, Cleavon Little, Gilda Texler, Dean Jagger
Ex-racer and former cop sets out to deliver a souped-up car. Taking pep pills along the way, he eludes police, meets up with a number of characters, and finally crashes into a roadblock.
MPAA:PG EL, SP
20th Century Fox; Cupid Productions — *CBS/Fox Video*

Vanishing Wilderness **1973**
Documentary/Animals
77519 90 mins C B, V P
This documentary looks at the wild animals roaming across North America.
MPAA:G
Pacific International Enterprises — *Media Home Entertainment*

Vanity Fair **1932**
Romance
29685 73 mins B/W B, V P
Myrna Loy, Conway Tearle
A modern-dress version of Thackeray's famous novel. Myrna Loy portrays Becky Sharpe, an amoral social climber.
Hollywood — *Movie Buff Video; Sheik Video*

Varan the Unbelievable **1961**
Horror
64296 70 mins B/W B, V P
Myron Healy, Tsuruko Kobayashi
A chemical experiment near a small island in the Japanese archipelago disturbs a prehistoric monster beneath the water. The awakened monster spreads terror on the island.
Jerry A. Baerwitz — *United Home Video*

Variety **1925**
Drama
48728 104 mins B/W B, V, FO P, T
Emil Jannings, Lya de Putti, Warwick Ward, directed by E. A. Dupont
An aging acrobat seduces a young girl. Later, he kills a man who is interested in the girl. Silent.
Oscar Werndorff, UFA — *Video Yesteryear; Sheik Video; Classic Video Cinema Collector's Club; Discount Video Tapes*

Vatican Conspiracy **1981**
Mystery/Suspense
81194 90 mins C B, V P
Terence Stamp
The members of the Vatican's College of Cardinals do everything in their power to discredit a newly appointed radical pontiff.
Fabian Arnaud; Enzo Gallo — *VCL Home Video*

Vault of Horror, The **1973**
Horror
54911 86 mins C B, V, 3/4U P
Terry-Thomas, Curt Jurgens, Glynis Johns, Dawn Addams, Daniel Massey, Tom Baker
A collection of five terrifying tales based on original stories from the E. C. comic books of the 1950's.
MPAA:R
Cinerama Releasing — *Nostalgia Merchant*

Vegas **1978**
Mystery/Drama
80320 74 mins C B, V P
Robert Urich, June Allyson, Tony Curtis, Will Sampson, Greg Morris
A private detective with Las Vegas showgirls as assistants solves the murder of a teenage runaway girl.
Aaron Spelling Productions — *Prism*

Velveteen Rabbit, The **1985**
Fairy tales
80602 27 mins C B, V P
Marie Osmond
This is a classic children's story of a toy rabbit that wants to be real. The Enchanted Musical Playhouse presents this program.
Nightstar/Centerpoint Production — *King of Video*

Vengance Valley **1951**
Western
80742 83 mins C B, V P
Burt Lancaster, Joanne Dru, Robert Walker, Sally Forrest, John Ireland, Hugh O'Brian
A ranch foreman's life is endangered when he attempts to conceal a terrible secret involving his weak foster brother.
MGM — *Hal Roach Studios*

Venom **1982**
Horror
64881 92 mins C B, V, CED P
Sterling Hayden, Klaus Kinski, Sarah Miles
A deadly black mamba is loose in an elegant townhouse.
MPAA:R
Richard R. St. Johns — *Vestron Video*

Venus in Furs **1970**
Horror
76834 90 mins C B, V P
James Darren, Klaus Kinski, Barbara McNair, Dennis Price, Maria Rohm
A jazz musician working in Rio de Janeiro falls in love with a mysterious woman who resembles a murdered woman whose body he discovered months earlier.
MPAA:R
Harry Alan Towers; Commonwealth — *Republic Pictures Home Video*

Vera Cruz 1954
Adventure
65010 94 mins C B, V, CED P
Gary Cooper, Burt Lancaster, Denise Darcel
Two soldiers of fortune become involved in the Mexican War for independence.
United Artists — *CBS/Fox Video*

Verdict, The 1982
Drama
66071 122 mins C B, V, LV, CED P
Paul Newman, James Mason, Charlotte Rampling, Jack Warden, Milo O'Shea, directed by Sidney Lumet
A down-and-out lawyer takes on the system against impossible odds.
MPAA:R
20th Century Fox — *CBS/Fox Video*

Verdi's Rigoletto at Verona 1985
Music-Performance
76966 128 mins C B, V P
A performance of the Verdi opera about a deformed court jester taped in Verona, Italy: Available in VHS and Beta Hi-Fi.
Poly Video — *Mastervision*

Vertigo 1958
Suspense
75018 126 mins C B, V, LV, CED P
James Stewart, Kim Novak, Barbara Bel Geddes, Tom Helmore, directed by Alfred Hitchcock
This is the classic Hitchcock tale of obsession, fear and murder. A private detective is hired to follow a mysterious woman, whom he gradually falls in love with. Music by Bernard Herrmann.
MPAA:PG
Alfred Hitchcock; Paramount — *MCA Home Video*

Very Private Affair, A 1962
Drama
63113 95 mins C B, V P
Marcello Mastroianni, Brigitte Bardot
A movie star finds that she has no privacy from the hordes of fans and newspaper people. The glare of publicity helps to destroy her relationship with a married director.
MGM — *MGM/UA Home Video*

Very Special Christmas, A/Sleeping Beauty 1982
Fairy tales/Christmas
64956 52 mins C B, V P
Animated
A young boy saves Santa from trouble in "A Very Special Christmas." "Sleeping Beauty" is a new version of the classic fairy tale. Both of these animated films are combined on this tape.
Ron Merk — *Unicorn Video*

Very Special Team, A 1982
Football
47715 23 mins C B, V, FO P
Team highlights of the 1981 San Francisco 49ers, who came out of nowhere to win the NFC Championship.
NFL Films — *NFL Films Video*

Vez en la Vida, Una 1949
Musical-Drama
47464 75 mins B/W B, V, FO P
Libertad Lamarque, Luis Aldas, Raimundo Pastore
A young farm girl travels to the big city, where she becomes a nightclub dancer and gets involved with a shady character. Spanish dialogue.
SP
Argentina — *Video Yesteryear*

Viaje Fantastico En Groso 1984
Adventure
72961 108 mins C B, V P
Let go of your imagination and launch into a thrilling adventure and fantasy in this adult-oriented drama.
SP
Foreign — *Unicorn Video*

Vic Braden's Tennis for the Future, Volume 1 1981
Tennis
63428 120 mins C B, V R, P
The first volume of the series covers four tennis fundamentals: forehand, backhand, serve and volley. From Braden's successful PBS program, "Tennis for the Future."
WGBH Education Foundation — *Paramount Home Video*

Vic Braden's Tennis for the Future, Volume 2 1981
Tennis
64500 120 mins C B, V R, P
This segment covers the approach shot (spin and service return), the overhead shot, lob and drop shots, and conditioning.
WGBH Education Foundation — *Paramount Home Video*

Vic Braden's Tennis for the Future, Volume 3 1981
Tennis
68250 120 mins C B, V R, P
This program is rich in useful, hands-on information and demonstrations of technique.
WGBH Education Foundation — *Paramount Home Video*

 (For explanation of codes, see USE GUIDE and KEY)

Vic 'n' Sade 1957
Comedy
47491 15 mins B/W B, V, FO P
Bernadine Flynn, Art Van Harvey, Eddie Gillilan
A TV adaptation of one of radio's most popular programs, featuring the original cast performing in a bare studio setting.
WNBQ Chicago — *Video Yesteryear*

Vice Squad 1982
Drama
63666 97 mins C B, V, LV, CED P
Wings Hauser, Season Hubley, Gary Swanson
A violent and twisted killer-pimp goes on a murderous rampage, and a hooker helps a vice squad plainclothesman trap him.
MPAA:R
Sandy Howard; Frank Capra Jr — *Embassy Home Entertainment*

Victims Fightback 1984
Documentary
70729 55 mins C B, V P
Narrated by Lawrence Pressman
This tape graphically depicts the plight of crime victims, and makes a case for retaliation. It also shows how counselling has helped some victims.
HBO — *Active Home Video*

Victor/Victoria 1982
Comedy
47778 133 mins C B, V, CED P
Julie Andrews, James Garner, Robert Preston, Lesley Ann Warren, Alex Karvas, directedd by Blake Edwards
A down-on-her-luck actress in Depression era Paris impersonates a man impersonating a woman in order to be a show biz success.
MPAA:PG
MGM — *MGM/UA Home Video*

Victory 1981
Drama
53553 120 mins C B, V, CED P
Sylvester Stallone, Michael Caine, Max von Sydow, Pele, Carole Laure, Bobby Moore, directed by John Huston
A soccer match between WW II American prisoners of war and a German team is set up so that the players can escape through the sewer tunnels of Paris.
MPAA:PG
Freddie Fields — *CBS/Fox Video*

Victory at Sea 1960
World War II/Documentary
29437 98 mins B/W B, V R, P
Narrated by Alexander Scourby
This is a condensation of the classic television series which portrayed the exploits of the U.S. Navy during World War II. Its impressive musical score was composed by Richard Rodgers.
NBC — *Warner Home Video; Embassy Home Entertainment; RCA VideoDiscs*

Victory at Sea, Volume I 1952
World War II/Documentary
79692 30 mins B/W B, V P
Narrated by Alexander Scourby
The events which led up to Europe's involvement in World War II are the subject of this award winning series.
NBC — *Embassy Home Entertainment*

Victory at Sea, Volume II 1952
World War II/Documentary
79693 30 mins B/W B, V P
Narrated by Alexander Scourby
A stirring account of the events that led up to America's military involvement in World War Two, Pearl Harbor.
NBC — *Embassy Home Entertainment*

Victory at Sea, Volume III 1952
World War II/Documentary
79694 30 mins B/W B, V P
Narrated by Alexander Scourby
The great anti-submarine battles of World War Two are examined.
NBC — *Embassy Home Entertainment*

Victory at Sea, Volume IV 1952
World War II/Documentary
79695 30 mins B/W B, V P
Narrated by Alexander Scourby
The victories of Japan's military and the Battle of Midway are remembered.
NBC — *Embassy Home Entertainment*

Victory at Sea, Volume V 1952
World War II/Documentary
79696 30 mins B/W B, V P
Narrated by Alexander Scourby
The exciting World War II naval battles fought in the Mediterranean are remembered in this documentary.
NBC — *Embassy Home Entertainment*

Victory at Sea, Volume VI 1952
World War II/Documentary
79697 30 mins B/W B, V P
Narrated by Alexander Scourby
The decisive World War II battle of Guadalcanal is remembered by the men who fought in it.
NBC — *Embassy Home Entertainment*

Victory at Sea, Volume VII 1952
World War II/Documentary
76783 30 mins B/W B, V P

Narrated by Leonard Graves, music by Richard Rodgers
The daring naval maneuvers which led to the United States' conquest of the Mediterranean during 1940-1942 is examined.
NBC — *Embassy Home Entertainment*

Victory at Sea, Volume IX **1952**
World War II/Documentary
76784 30 mins B/W B, V P
Narrated by Leonard Graves, music by Richard Rodgers
The naval invasion of North Africa during 1942-1943 is discussed in this volume.
NBC — *Embassy Home Entertainment*

Victory at Sea, Volume VIII **1952**
World War II/Documentary
76782 30 mins B/W B, V P
Narrated by Leonard Graves, music by Richard Rodgers
This volume details the naval battles which led to the struggle for the Solomon Islands.
NBC — *Embassy Home Entertainment*

Victory at Sea, Volume X **1952**
World War II/Documentary
76785 30 mins B/W B, V P
Narrated by Leonard Graves, music by Richard Rodgers
The exciting naval battles that were fought in the South Atlantic during World War II are remembered in this volume.
NBC — *Embassy Home Entertainment*

Victory at Sea, Volume XI **1952**
World War II/Documentary
76786 30 mins B/W B, V P
Narrated by Leonard Graves, music by Richard Rodgers
This volume examines the naval battles that were fought in the Northern Battle Theater during World War II.
NBC — *Embassy Home Entertainment*

Victory at Sea, Volume XII **1952**
World War II/Documentary
76787 30 mins B/W B, V P
Narrated by Leonard Graves, music by Richard Rodgers
The United States naval carriers which led to the conquest of Micronesia is the subject of this volume of the award-winning series.
NBC — *Embassy Home Entertainment*

Vida Sigue Igual, La **19??**
Drama
66413 102 mins C B, V P
Julio Iglesias, Jean Harrington
A famous singer turned soccer player is severely injured in an auto accident. His life and career depend on whether he will ever walk again. Dialogue in Spanish.
SP
Spanish — *Media Home Entertainment*

Vida Sigue Igual, La **197?**
Drama
52796 102 mins C B, V P
Jean Harrington, Charo Lopez
An up-and-coming law student and soccer player becomes paralyzed in an auto accident and must contend with a change of attitude from his friends and lover.
SP
Star Films; Filmayer Produccion — *Media Home Entertainment*

Video a Go-Go Volume 1 **1985**
Music video
81205 30 mins C B, V P
Kool and the Gang, Animotion, Stephanie Mills, Bananarama, the Bar-Kuys
Here is a collection of conceptual music-videos for your dancing and listening pleasure. Available in Hi-Fi Stereo for both formats.
Polygram Music Video — *RCA/Columbia Pictures Home Video*

Video Aerobics **1979**
Physical fitness
59306 57 mins C B, V P
Instructors Susie Murphy and Leslie Lilian demonstrate a complete conditioning routine which includes aerobic exercises for all areas of the body. Contains both a 17-minute beginners program and a challenging 40-minute advanced session.
Amstar Productions — *Vestron Video*

Video Dictionary of Classical Ballet, The **1983**
Dance
76676 270 mins C B, V, 3/4U P
Merrill Ashley, Denise Jackson, Kevin MacKenzie, Georgina Parkinson
An index to over 800 ballet steps. All steps are clearly written and numbered on the tape and correspondingly indicated in the accompanying booklet, enabling the viewer to find any step with ease. On four cassettes.
AM Available
Kultur — *Kultur*

Video Dictionary of Classical Ballet, The **1984**
Dance
66609 270 mins C B, V, 3/4U P
Merrill Ashley, Kevin MacKenzie, Denise Jackson, Georgina Parkinson

Three of the most outstanding principal dancers of leading American ballet companies demonstrate the complete language of ballet in this program. More than 800 variations in international Russian, French and Cecchetti styles are illustrated to piano accompaniment, with many movements shown in slow motion with multiple camera angles.
AM Available
First Ballet Inc — *Kultur; Trans Media Communications Network*

Video Rewind—The Rolling Stones Great Video Hits 1984
Music video
79849 60 mins C B, V, LV, CED P
Mick Jagger, Charlie Watts, Ron Wood, Keith Richards, Bill Wynman
A collection of twelve uncensored music videos from those bad boys of rock and roll—The Rolling Stones.
Promotone BV — *Vestron Video*

Video System Test Tape, The 1982
Video
73543 10 mins C B, V P
This program shows how to test your TV and VCR systems
Admit One — *Admit One Video*

Video Trivialities 1984
Games/Video
79348 720 mins C B, V R, P
A trivia game that comes complete with a board and video tapes that feature thousands of questions and answers.
AM Available
Mark Walbridge — *Video Trivialities*

Video Vixens 1984
Comedy
76781 85 mins C B, V P
A television executive shakes up a permissive society by producing the most erotic awards show ever seen on television.
Troma Films — *Vestron Video*

Video Yesterbloop 197?
Outtakes and bloopers
57363 81 mins C B, V, FO P
A few sections in black and white. A collection of bloopers from TV, including "Steve Allen Show," "All My Children," "The Price Is Right," "Happy Days," "Mork and Mindy," and "One Day at a Time." Quality is not perfect. Contains some nudity and strong language.
ABC et al — *Video Yesteryear*

Videocycle 1984
Physical fitness/Bicycling
70362 60 mins C B, V P
These tapes permit stationary bikers to enjoy beautiful scenery, music, coaching and even on-screen compionship without moving from their monitor.
1.Yellowstone Park I 2.Grand Teton Park
Cycle Vision Tours — *Cycle Vision Tours*

Videocycle 1984
Physical fitness
80482 60 mins C B, V, 3/4U P
2 pgms
An exercise program with three self-paced workouts designed specifically for indoor cycling. Spectacular scenery and music, pulse checks, trial maps and a tour coach all add to the exercies experience.
1.Grand Teton Tour 2.Yellowstone Tour I
AM Available
Cycle Vision Tours — *Cycle Vision Tours*

Videodrome 1983
Science fiction/Horror
64788 87 mins C B, V, LV P
Deborah Harry, James Woods, directed by David Cronenberg
This film dramatizes what it would be like if television took over the world. Stars Deborah Harry, lead singer of the rock group Blondie. Special effects by Rick Baker ("An American Werewolf in London").
Universal — *MCA Home Video*

VIDI's Video Greetings 1985
Holidays
80481 4 mins C B, V P
Animated 13 pgms
A series of video greeting cards, which are designed for various holidays and special events, such as birthdays and St. Valentine's Day.
1.The Twelve Days 2.Good King Wenceslas 3.Twas the Night Before Christmas—2010 4.The Nativity 5.An Old-Fashioned Christmas 6.The Hannukah Story and Dreidel Game 7.Peace on Earth 8.Surprise Party Birthday 9.Party Games 10.Astrology Birthdays 11.Music Vidi-O Birthday 12.Alphabet Soup 13.The Many Victories of Cupid 14.Personalized Vidis
Videograf — *Videograf*

Vie Continue, La 1982
Drama
64241 93 mins C B, V P
Annie Giradot, Jean-Pierre Cassel, Michel Aumont, directed by Moshe Mizrahi
A woman suddenly finds herself alone after 20 years, following the death of her husband. Dubbed in English.
Cineproduction/SFPC — *RCA/Columbia Pictures Home Video*

Vietnam: Chronicle of a War 1981
Vietnam War/Documentary
52746 88 mins C B, V P
Narrated by Walter Cronkite, Dan Rather, Morley Safer, Charles Collingwood, Charles Kuralt, Mike Wallace, Eric Sevareid
Drawing upon the resources of the CBS News Archives, this CBS News Collectors Series program presents a retrospective portrait of American military involvement as witnessed by on-the-scene correspondents and camera crews. Some portions are in black-and-white.
CBS News — *CBS/Fox Video*

Vietnam: In the Year of the Pig 1968
Documentary/Vietnam War
81530 103 mins B/W B, V P
Directed by Emile de Antonio
This documentary examines the horror and bloodshed of the war in southeast Asia.
Emile de Antonio — *MPI Home Video*

Vietnam: Remember 1968
Documentary/Vietnam War
79699 60 mins C B, V P
A documentary that recalls some of the fierce battles of the Vietnam War.
Maljack Productions — *MPI Home Video*

Vietnam: The Ten Thousand Day War 1980
Vietnam War/Documentary
81444 49 mins C B, V, LV P
Narrated by Richard Basehart 13 pgms
This series examines the emotional and physical impact of the Vietnam War on the men who fought in it.
1.Vietnam 2.Dien Bien Phu 3.Days of Decision 4.Uneasy Allies 5.The Trial 6.Firepower 7.Siege 8.Frontline America 9.Soldiering On 10.The Village War 11.Peace 12.Surrender 13.The Unsung Soldiers
Michael Maclear — *Embassy Home Entertainment*

Vigilante 1983
Drama
64900 91 mins C B, V P
Robert Forster
A frustrated ex-cop, tired of seeing criminals returned to the street, joins a vigilante squad dedicated to law and order.
Artists Releasing Corp — *Vestron Video*

Vigilantes Are Coming, The 19??
Adventure/Serials
12560 230 mins B/W B, V P
Bob Livingston, Kay Hughes, Quinn 'Big Boy' Williams, directed by Mack V. Wright, Ray Taylor
"The Eagle" sets out to revenge his family and upsets the plot of a would-be dictator to establish an empire in California. In twelve chapters—first is 32 minutes, each additional chapter is 18 minutes.
Republic — *Video Connection; Nostalgia Merchant; Discount Video Tapes*

Vigilantes of Boom Town 1946
Western
08898 54 mins B/W B, V, 3/4U P
Allan 'Rocky' Lane, Bobby Blake
Senator's daughter thinks prize fighting is a disgrace.
Republic — *Video Connection; Nostalgia Merchant*

Vikings, The 1958
Adventure
80860 116 mins C B, V P
Kirk Douglas, Ernest Borgnine, Janet Leigh, Tony Curtis, directed by Richard Fleischer
A Viking king and his son kidnap a Welsh princess and hold her for ransom.
United Artists — *MGM/UA Home Video*

Village of the Damned 1960
Science fiction
64572 78 mins B/W B, V, CED P
George Sanders, Barbara Shelley, Martin Stephens, Laurence Naismith
A group of unusual children in a small English village are found to be the vanguard of an alien invasion.
MGM — *MGM/UA Home Video*

Village of the Giants 1965
Science fiction/Comedy
80762 82 mins C B, V P
Ron Howard, Johnny Crawford, Tommy Kirk, Beau Bridges, Freddy Cannon, Beau Brummels
A group of beer-guzzling teenagers become giants after eating a mysterious substance invented by a twelve-year-old genius.
Bert I. Gordon — *Embassy Home Entertainment*

Villain Still Pursued Her, The 1941
Comedy
08731 67 mins B/W B, V, 3/4U P
Anita Louise, Alan Mowbray, Buster Keaton, Hugh Herbert
Old-fashioned melodrama; poor hero and rich villain vie for the sweet heroine.
RKO — *Movie Buff Video; Video Yesteryear*

Vintage Commercials 1980
Advertising/Comedy
29733 60 mins C B, V, 3/4U P

 (For explanation of codes, see USE GUIDE and KEY)

Dick Van Dyke, Mary Tyler Moore, Ernie Kovacs, Andy Griffith, Danny Thomas, Lucille Ball
A package of commercials from the 1950's and 1960's, all featuring top TV celebrities such as The Monkees, Lucille Ball and Desi Arnaz, Ozzie and Harriet, and the Flintstones, selling everything from cigarettes to orange juice. Some segments in black and white.
CBS et al — *Shokus Video*

Vintage Commercials, II 1982
Advertising/Comedy
47612 60 mins C B, V, 3/4U P
Buster Keaton, The Three Stooges, Lucille Ball, Desi Arnaz, Jack Benny, Steve Allen, Jay North, Ernie Kovacs
An hour of classic television commercials from the 50's, 60's and early 70's. A number of spots featuring celebrities are included, pitching for such products as Skippy Peanut Butter, Ipana, Westinghouse, Alka Seltzer, Bosco, Quik, Seven-Up and Kool-Aid. Some segments are in black and white.
CBS et al — *Shokus Video*

Vintage Commercials, III 1983
Advertising/Documentary
66461 60 mins B/W B, V, 3/4U P
Lucille Ball, Desi Arnaz, Hillary Brooke, Andy Devine, Dwayne Hickman
Another hour of classic TV commercials, mostly from the 1950's, is featured with many celebrity spokespersons. Also on this tape is a newsreel highlighting the beginnings of commercial television broadcasting at the 1939 New York World's Fair.
CBS et al — *Shokus Video*

Vintage Sitcoms 195?
Comedy
53048 100 mins B/W B, V, 3/4U P
Jackie Gleason, Gale Storm, Charles Farrell, George Burns, Gracie Allen, Jackie Cooper
Four top situation comedies from the 1940's and 1950's: "The Life of Riley" (1949), starring Jackie Gleason as Chester A. Riley; "My Little Margie" (1952), starring Gale Storm and Charles Farrell as daughter and father; "The Burns and Allen Show" (1952), a classic episode involving Gracie's party plans; "The People's Choice" (1955), starring Jackie Cooper and his dog "Cleo."
NBC; CBS — *Shokus Video*

Violent Ones, The 1968
Drama
80467 96 mins C B, V P
Fernando Lamas, David Carradine
Three men who are suspected of raping a young girl are threatened with lynching by an angry mob of townspeople.
Harold Goldman — *Spotlite Video*

Violent Years, The 1952
Drama
73554 80 mins B/W B, V P
An all girl gang go out and attack lonely service station attendants and couples parked in lovers' lanes.
Independent — *Admit One Video*

Virgin Witch, The 1975
Horror
80292 89 mins C B, V P
Vicki and Ann Michelle, Patricia Haines, Neil Hallett, James Chase
Two sisters are trapped in a deserted mansion where a witches coven intends to use the sisters as virgin sacrifices.
MPAA:R
Joseph Brenner Associates — *Prism*

Virus 1982
Drama/Science fiction
65369 102 mins C B, V P
George Kennedy, Glenn Ford, Robert Vaughn, Chuck Connors, Olivia Hussey
"Virus" is a revealing look at both man's genius for self-destruction and his super-human determination to carry on life and hope in a destroyed world.
MPAA:PG
Haruki Kadokawa — *Media Home Entertainment*

Visions of Diana Ross, The 1985
Music video
80779 30 mins C B, V P
Diana Ross, Julio Iglesias
The sizzling sounds of Diana Ross come alive in this collection of six conceptual music videos. This tape features an extended version of "Swept Away" and "Missing You." Available in VHS and Beta Hi-Fi Stereo.
RCA Video Productions — *RCA/Columbia Pictures Home Video*

Visions of Faith 1955
Religion/Music
59090 70 mins B/W B, V, FO P
Saint Luke's Choristers
A collection of hymns with visuals showing "God's handiwork." Hymns include: "Father of Mercies," "I Wonder As I Wander," "Jesus My Lord, My God, My All," " The Hallelujah Chorus," "O Divine Redemmer," and others.
USA — *Video Yesteryear*

Visiting Hours 1982
Suspense
63392 101 mins C B, V, CED P
Lee Grant, William Shatner, Linda Purl, Michael Ironside
An outspoken television journalist delivers a controversial editorial on women's rights. She is

consequently brutally attacked by an angered viewer.
MPAA:R
20th Century Fox — *CBS/Fox Video*

Visitor From the Grave 1981
Horror
77444 60 mins C B, V P
Simon MacCorkindale, Kathryn-Leigh Scott, Gareth Thomas, Mia Nadasi
When an American heiress and her boyfriend dispose of a dead man's body, his spirit comes back to haunt them.
Hammer House of Horror — *Thriller Video*

Viva Knievel 1977
Adventure
78626 106 mins C B, V P
Evel Knievel, Gene Kelly, Lauren Hutton, Red Buttons, Leslie Nielsen, Cameron Mitchell
Crooks plan to sabotage Knievel's daredevil jump in Mexico and then smuggle cocaine back into the States in his coffin.
MPAA:PG
Warner Bros — *Warner Home Video*

Viva Las Vegas 1963
Musical
59137 85 mins C B, V, CED P
Elvis Presley, Ann-Margret, William Demarest, Jack Carter, Cesare Danova, Nicky Blair, directed by George Sidney
A sports car enthusiast and his friend go to Las Vegas for the Grand Prix where they both fall for a swimming instructor.
MGM — *MGM/UA Home Video*

Viva Max 1969
Comedy
47994 93 mins C B, V P
Peter Ustinov, Jonathan Winters, John Astin, Pamela Tiffin, Keenan Wynn, directed by Jerry Paris
A modern-day Mexican general and his men fake their way across the Alamo.
Montmorency Prods — *Republic Pictures Home Video*

Viva Zapata! 1952
Drama/Biographical
70378 112 mins B/W B, V P
Marlon Brando, Anthony Quinn, Jean Peters, Margo, Arnold Moss, directed by Elia Kazan
This film shows the life of Mexican revolutionary Emiliano Zapata, from his leading the peasant revolt in the early 1900's, to his eventual corruption by power and greed.
20th Century Fox — *Key Video*

Vivacious Lady 1938
Comedy
00289 90 mins B/W B, V, 3/4U P, T
Ginger Rogers, James Stewart, James Ellison
Romantic comedy about a young college professor who marries a chorus girl.
RKO; Pandro S Berman — *Blackhawk Films; Nostalgia Merchant*

Voice from the Screen, The 1926
Film-History/Technology
58659 34 mins B/W B, V, FO P
An address by Edward B. Craft, Executive Vice President of Bell Telephone Laboratories, presented before the New York Electrical Society, in which he discusses the "new Vitaphone Sound-Film system." An original demonstration of the first commercially viable method of adding sound to motion pictures.
Vitaphone — *Video Yesteryear*

Volcano 1976
Drama/Biographical
65465 ? mins C B, V P
Narrated by Donald Britlain and Richard Burton
A painful but extraordinary portrait of writer Malcolm Lowry, author of "Under the Volcano," which explores his battle with alcohol and the guilt that followed the success of this novel. In Beta Hi-Fi.
Almi Release — *RCA/Columbia Pictures Home Video*

Voltron, Defender of the Universe: Castle of Lions 1985
Cartoons
70721 83 mins C B, V P
Animated
Voltron, the ancient robot hero, joins with the castle lions and space explorers to save this galaxy on part of his overall universe protection plan. Recorded in Beta and VHS Hi-Fi stereo.
World Events Prods. — *Sony Corporation of America*

Von Ryan's Express 1965
War-Drama
08426 117 mins C B, V P
Frank Sinatra, Trevor Howard, Brad Dexter, Edward Mulhare, directed by Mark Robson
American Air Force Colonel leads a group of prisoners of war in taking control of a freight train.
EL, SP
20th Century Fox; Saul David — *CBS/Fox Video*

Voyage en Ballon 1959
Adventure
74088 82 mins C B, V P
This is the delightful story of a young boy who stowsaway on his grandfather's hot air balloon.
Film Sonor; Film Montsouris — *Embassy Home Entertainment*

Voyage of the Damned **1977**
Drama/World War II
46150 134 mins C B, V P
Faye Dunaway, Max von Sydow, Oskar Werner, Malcolm McDowell, Orson Welles, James Mason, Lee Grant, Katherine Ross, Ben Gazzara
The story of one of the most tragic incidents of World War II: the flight of 937 German-Jewish refugees bound for Cuba aboard the Hamburg-Amerika liner S.S. St. Louis. Based on Gordon Thomas' and Max Morgan-Witts' novel of the same title.
MPAA:G
Robert Fryer, Avco Embassy — *CBS/Fox Video*

Voyage to the Bottom of the Sea **1961**
Science fiction/Adventure
Closed Captioned
80748 106 mins C B, V P
Walter Pidgeon, Joan Fontaine, Barbara Eden, Peter Lorre, Robert Sterling, Michael Ansara, Frankie Avalon, directed by Irwin Allen
The crew of an atomic submarine must destroy a deadly radiation belt which has set the polar ice cap ablaze.
20th Century Fox — *Playhouse Video*

Voyager from the Unknown **1983**
Science fiction/Adventure
81438 91 mins C B, V P
Jon-Erik Hexum, Meeno Peluce, Ed Begley Jr., Faye Grant, Fionula Flanagan
A "time cop" and an orphan travel through time to set the course of history straight. Here are two episodes from the "Voyagers!" series. Available in VHS and Beta Hi-Fi.
Universal; James D. Parriott; Scholastic Prods. — *MCA Home Video*

W

W **1974**
Suspense/Drama
81156 95 mins C B, V P
Twiggy, Dirk Benedict, Eugene Roche, Michael Conrad, directed by Richard Quine
A woman and a private detective must find the cause of three near-fatal accidents. A single letter "W" is found at the scene of the crimes.
MPAA:PG
Mel Ferrer; Bing Crosby Productions — *Lightning Video*

Wackiest Wagon Train in the West, The **1977**
Western/Comedy
53942 86 mins C B, V R, P
Bob Denver, Forrest Tucker, Jeannine Riley
A hapless wagon master is saddled with a dummy assistant as they guide a party of five characters across the West.
MPAA:G
Topar Films — *Media Home Entertainment*

Wacko **1983**
Comedy
65219 84 mins C B, V P
Stella Stevens, George Kennedy, Joe Don Baker
A group of nymphets and tough guys get caught up in a wild Halloween-pumpkin-lawnmower murder.
MPAA:PG
Michael R Starita — *Vestron Video*

Wacky and Packy **1975**
Cartoons
73562 70 mins C B, V P
Animated
A caveman and his pachyderm run amok in the modern world causing trouble wherever the pair travel.
Filmation Studios — *Prism*

Wacky World of Mother Goose, The **1967**
Cartoons
08521 81 mins C B, V, CED P
Animated, voice of Margaret Rutherford
All the familiar Mother Goose characters brought together in a delightful tale of secret agents and sinister surprises.
Avco Embassy; Arthur Rankin, Jr. — *Embassy Home Entertainment*

Wages of Fear **1955**
Drama
06243 138 mins B/W B, V P
Yves Montand, Charles Vanel, Peter Van Eyck, directed by Henri-Georges Clouzot
Realistic drama of disastrous oil well explosion in Central America. French film, dubbed in English.
Hal Roach Dist; DCA — *Movie Buff Video; Budget Video; Video Yesteryear; Western Film & Video Inc; Discount Video Tapes*

Wagonmaster **1950**
Western
00291 85 mins B/W B, V, 3/4U P
Ben Johnson, Joanne Dru, directed by John Ford
Roving cowboys join a group of Mormons in their trek across the western frontier.
RKO — *Nostalgia Merchant*

Wait Until Dark 1967
Suspense
58255 105 mins C B, V R, P
Audrey Hepburn, Alan Arkin, Richard Crenna, Efrem Zimbalist Jr., Jack Weston
A photographer unwittingly smuggles a drug-filled doll into New York, and his blind wife, alone in their apartment, is terrorized by murderous crooks in search of it.
Warner Bros — *Warner Home Video*

Waitress 1981
Comedy
63357 85 mins C B, V R, P
Jim Harris, Carol Drake, Carol Bever
Three beautiful girls are waitresses in a crazy restaurant where the chef gets drunk, the kitchen explodes, and the customers riot.
Troma Productions — *THORN EMI/HBO Video*

Wake of the Red Witch, The 1948
Adventure
59091 106 mins B/W B, V P
John Wayne, Gail Russell, Gig Young
This South Sea saga pits an adventurous sea captain against a shipping magnate with a fortune of pearls and a beautiful woman at stake.
Republic — *Republic Pictures Home Video*

Wake Up the Echoes 1982
Football
63165 52 mins C B, V, FO P
George Gipp, Knute Rockne, Frank Leahy, Ara Parseghian, Joe Theisman, Joe Montana, Jim Crowley
Highlights from 60 years of Notre Dame Football history are on this tape, from rare footage shot in 1913 to 1966's "Game of the Century" against Michigan State. Some sequences are in black and white.
NFL Films — *NFL Films Video*

Walking Tall 1973
Drama
79668 126 mins C B, V P
Joe Don Baker, Elizabeth Hartman, Noah Beery, directed by Phil Karlson
A Tennessee sheriff takes a stand against syndicate-run gambling and loses his wife in the process.
MPAA:R
Bing Crosby Productions — *Lightning Video*

Walking Tall—Part II 1975
Drama
79669 109 mins C B, V P
Bo Svenson, Noah Beery, Angel Tompkins, Richard Jaeckel, directed by Earl Bellamy
Tennessee Sheriff Buford Pusser attempts to find the man who killed his wife.
MPAA:PG
Bing Crosby Productions — *Vestron Video*

Walking Tall—The Final Chapter 1977
Drama
79670 112 mins C B, V P
Bo Svenson, Forrest Tucker, Leif Garrett, Morgan Woodward
A dramatization of the final months in the life of Tennessee sheriff Buford Pusser.
MPAA:PG
Bing Crosby Productions — *Lightning Video*

Walt Disney Christmas, A 1982
Cartoons/Christmas
53798 45 mins C B, V R, P
Animated
Six classic cartoons with a wintry theme are combined for this program: "Pluto's Christmas Tree" (1952), "On Ice," "Donald's Snowball Fight;" two Silly Symphonies from 1932-33: "Santa's Workshop" and "The Night Before Christmas" and an excerpt from the 1948 feature "Melody Time," entitled "Once Upon a Wintertime."
Walt Disney Prods — *Walt Disney Home Video*

Waltz Across Texas 1983
Drama
65382 100 mins C B, V P
The story of a young couple whose mutual dislike for each other turns romantic as they are joined in a quest to discover oil in west Texas.
Martin Jurow — *Vestron Video*

Waltz of the Toreadors 1962
Comedy
50956 105 mins C B, V R, P
Peter Sellers, Dany Robin, Margaret Leighton, Cyril Cusack
A retired general tries to make up for lost time in an affair with a French woman that has been carried on platonically for seventeen years.
AM Available
Independent Artists — *VidAmerica*

Wanderers, The 1979
Drama
52712 113 mins C B, V R, P
Ken Wahl, John Friedrich, Karen Allen, Linda Manz, directed by Philip Kaufman
Richard Price's novel about youth gangs coming of age in the Bronx in 1963. The "Wanderers" are a non-violent gang about to graduate high school, prowling the Bronx with the feeling that something is slipping away from them.
MPAA:R
Orion Pictures — *Warner Home Video*

(For explanation of codes, see USE GUIDE and KEY)

Wanted: Babysitter 1975
Mystery
79340 90 mins C B, V P
Robert Vaughn, Vic Morrow, Maria Scheider, Sydne Rome
A young student accidentally becomes involved in a plot to kidnap the child she is babysitting.
Independent — *Active Home Video*

Wanton Countess, The 1955
Drama
70372 125 mins C B, V R, P
Alida Valli, Farley Granger, directed by Luchino Visconti
Set in 1866 as the Austrians prepare for war with Italy, this film shows a countess falling in love with a charming but scoundrelly Austrian lieutenant.
Fleetwood Films — *Video City Productions*

War and Peace 1956
Drama
77448 208 mins C B, V, LV R, P
Audrey Hepburn, Mel Ferrer, Henry Fonda, Anita Ekberg, directed by King Vidor
An adaptation of the Tolstoy novel about three families caught up in Russia's Napoleonic Wars from 1805 to 1812. Nino Rota wrote the score.
Paramount Pictures — *Paramount Home Video*

War Chronicles—Volume 1 1985
World War II/Documentary
70677 120 mins C B, V P
Narrated by Patrick O'Neal, directed by Don Horan
This epic series looks at both the European and Japanese Theaters, and pays special attention to the individual turning points of the War. Actual film footage from the War, interviews with participants, and combat paintings by Mort Kuntsler combine to give viewers a thorough understanding of these historic events.
Lou Reda Productions/Mort Zimmerman — *U.S.A. Home Video*

War Comes to America 1945
World War II/Documentary
50617 67 mins B/W B, V, 3/4U, FO P
Directed by Frank Capra
An overview of American heritage, emphasizing the events which forced us to fight for survival. Frank Capra's philosophy paints a loving portrait of the American. Part of the "Why We Fight" series, contained on two cassettes.
US War Department — *Western Film & Video Inc; Budget Video; Discount Video Tapes; MPI Home Video; National AudioVisual Center*

War Games 1983
Drama
Closed Captioned
65415 110 mins C B, V, LV, CED P
Mathew Broderick, Dabney Coleman, John Wood, Ally Sheedy
An extremely bright young man, thinking that he's sneaking an advance look at a new line of video games, breaks into the country's Norod missile-defense system and challenges it to a game of global thermonuclear warfare.
MPAA:PG
Harold Schneider — *CBS/Fox Video; RCA VideoDiscs*

War In Space, The 1977
Science fiction
76893 91 mins C B, V P
Kent Saku Marita, Yuko Asano, Ryo Ikebe
Powerful U.N. Space Bureau Starships and UFO's band together to battle alien invaders among the volcanoes and deserts of Venus.
Toho — *Video Action*

War in the Sky 1982
World War II/Documentary
59356 90 mins C B, V R, P
Directed by William Wyler, Lloyd Bridges, James Stewart, narrated by Peter Lawford
Director William Wyler's account of the Army Air Corps in action. Extraordinary footage of the Thunderbolt, the P47 Fighter, and the B17 Bomber.
US Office of War Information — *Video Gems*

War Lover, The 1962
War-Drama
81212 105 mins B/W B, V P
Steve McQueen, Robert Wagner, Shirley Anne Field, Bill Edwards
A daredevil flying captain and his pilot find themselves vying for the affections of the same woman during World War II in England.
Columbia; Arthur Hornblow, Jr. — *RCA/Columbia Pictures Home Video*

War of the Wildcats 1943
Western
59093 102 mins B/W B, V P
John Wayne, Martha Scott, Albert Dekker
Western action with the Duke as a tough oil wildcatter battling a powerful land baron.
Republic — *Republic Pictures Home Video*

War of the Worlds, The 1953
Science fiction
38617 85 mins C B, V, LV R, P
Gene Barry, Ann Robinson, Les Tremayne
H.G. Wells' classic novel of the invasion of Earth by Martians, updated to 1950's California, with spectacular special effects depicting the

destruction caused by the Martian war machines.
Academy Awards '53: Special Effects.
Paramount — *Paramount Home Video; RCA VideoDiscs*

War Wagon, The 1967
Western
65122 101 mins C B, V P
John Wayne, Kirk Douglas, Howard Keel, Robert Walker Jr., Keenan Wynn, Bruce Dern, directed by Burt Kennedy
Two cowboys and an Indian plot to ambush the gold-laden armored stagecoach of a ruthless cattle baron.
Universal — *MCA Home Video*

War Years—The Forties, The 194?
World War II/Documentary
10149 ? mins B/W B, V P, T
Film covers Hitler, Stalin, Churchill, MacArthur, the Battle of the Bulge, Nuremberg war trials, and Harry Truman.
Unknown — *Blackhawk Films*

Warlock Moon 1975
Horror
66107 75 mins C B, V P
Laurie Walters, Joe Spano
A young woman is lured to a secluded spa and falls prey to a coven of witches.
EL, SP
Cintel Prod — *Unicorn Video*

Warlords of the 21st Century 1982
Science fiction/Adventure
65075 91 mins C B, V, CED P
Michael Beck, Annie McEnroe, James Wainwright
A gang of bandits who speed around the galaxy in an indestructible battle cruiser are challenged by a fearless space lawman.
Lloyd Phillips; Rob Whitehouse — *Embassy Home Entertainment*

Warner Brothers Cartoons 195?
Cartoons
53801 54 mins C B, V, FO P
Animated
Included in this collection are "The Wabbit Who Came to Supper" (1942), "A Tale of Two Kitties" (1948), "Case of the Missing Hare" (1942), "Hamateur Night" (1938), "Wackiki Wabbit" (1953), "Daffy Duck and the Dinosaur" (1939), and "Fresh Hare" (1942).
Warner Bros — *Video Yesteryear*

Warning, The 1980
Drama
81184 101 mins C B, V P
Martin Balsam, Guiliano Gemma
An honest police commissioner and his chief must carry out an investigation into the ties between the mob and the police department.
Mario Cacchi Gori — *Media Home Entertainment*

Warren Miller's Sailing Film Festival 1984
Boating
80886 72 mins C B, V P
Director Warren Miller travels around the world to capture such sailing events as world cup yachting in the Atlantic and wind surfing in California for this festive film.
Warren Miller — *Karl/Lorimar Home Video*

Warren Zevon 1982
Music-Performance
75924 68 mins C B, V P
This program presents Warren Zevon performing his hit songs in concert.
Front Line — *Sony Corporation of America*

Warrior and the Sorceress, The 1984
Fantasy
77174 81 mins C B, V, LV, CED P
David Carradine, Luke Askew, Maria Socas
A warrior offers his services to rival factions who are fighting for control of a water well in an impoverished village.
MPAA:R
Roger Corman; New Horizons — *Vestron Video*

Warrior of the Lost World 1984
Science fiction
80812 90 mins C B, V R, P
Robert Ginty, Persis Khambatta, Donald Pleasence
A warrior must destroy the evil Omega Force who tyrannically rule the world in the distant future. Available in VHS and Beta Hi Fi.
Roberto Bessi; Frank E. Hildebrand — *THORN EMI/HBO Video*

Warriors of the Wasteland 1983
Drama
65750 92 mins C B, V R, P
Fred Williamson
In the year 2019 when the world has been devastated by a nuclear war, the few survivors try to reach a distant land which emits radio signals indicating the presence of human life but are hindered by attacks from the fierce Templars, led by a self-styled priest called One.
MPAA:R

 (For explanation of codes, see USE GUIDE and KEY)

Fabrizio De Angelis — *THORN EMI/HBO Video*

Warriors, The 1979
Drama
38937 94 mins C B, V, LV R, P
Michael Beck, James Remer, Deborah Van Valkenburgh
A contemporary action story about a war between New York City street gangs that rages from Coney Island to the Bronx.
MPAA:R
Paramount — *Paramount Home Video*

Washington Affair, The 1977
Drama
66048 90 mins C B, V, CED P
Tom Selleck, Carol Lynley, Barry Sullivan
A tale of intrigue and blackmail in the nation's capital.
MPAA:PG
Walter G O'Conner — *Embassy Home Entertainment*

Washington Redskins 1984 Highlights 1985
Football
70550 70 mins C B, V, FO P
Art Monk
The Skins returned as "Winners and Still Champions" in '84 with two victories over the cowboys and a division clinching 29-27 thriller over the cards. The tape features 47-minutes of highlights from the '84 NFL season as well.
NFL Films — *NFL Films Video*

Washington Square 1959
Variety
69578 59 mins B/W B, V, FO P
Ray Bolger, Vera-Ellen, Jose Greco, Richard Haydn, Kay Armen
This musical variety show is set against the backdrop of New York's Greenwich village, featuring song, dance and comedy. Originally telecast in May, 1959.
NBC — *Video Yesteryear*

Watch Me When I Kill 1981
Drama/Suspense
65751 95 mins C B, V R, P
Richard Stewart, Sylvia Kramer
A young nightclub dancer stops by a drugstore seconds after the owner was killed. She doesn't see the killer's face, but his rasping voice remains to torment her.
MPAA:R
Herman Cohen — *THORN EMI/HBO Video*

Watch Mr. Wizard 195?
Science/Television
52461 30 mins B/W B, V, FO P
Don Herbert (Mr. Wizard)
This popular children's science show of the 1950's and 60's demonstrated interesting scientific experiments for young people to do. In this episode, Mr. Wizard tells his young assistant how to make bombs.
NBC — *Video Yesteryear*

Watch on the Rhine 1943
Drama
73972 113 mins B/W B, V P
Bette Davis, Paul Lukas, Donald Woods, Beulah Bondi, Geraldine Fitzgerald
A couple of German anti-Nazi underground leaders escape from the madness of socialist Germany. Adapted from the play by Lillian Hellman.
Warner Bros — *Key Video*

Watch Out, Crimson Bat! 1969
Martial arts
76896 87 mins C B, V P
Yoko Matsuyama, Goro Ibuki
A blind swordswoman must deliver a sack containing a valuable secret which can win a war.
Shochiku Co. — *Video Action*

Watched 1973
Suspense
73035 95 mins C B, V P
Stacy Keach
A former U.S. attorney has a nervous breakdown and kills a narcotics agent.
Palmyra Films — *Vestron Video*

Watcher in the Woods, The 1981
Suspense/Science fiction
59319 83 mins C B, V P
Bette Davis, Carroll Baker, David McCallum, directed by John Hough
When a family moves to an English country house, their children encounter something frightening in the woods.
MPAA:PG
Walt Disney Prods — *Walt Disney Home Video*

Water Babies, The 1979
Musical
80777 93 mins C B, V P
James Mason, Billie Whitelaw, David Tomlinson, Paul Luty, Sammantha Coates
When a twelve-year-old chimney sweep's apprentice is wrongly accused of stealing silver, the boy and his dog fall into a pond and become animated cartoons.
Ariadne Films — *Embassy Home Entertainment*

Watermelon Man 1970
Comedy
80882 97 mins C B, V P

Godfrey Cambridge, Estelle Parsons, Howard Caine, directed by Melvin Van Peebles
The tables are turned for a bigoted white man when he wakes up one morning and to discover he has become black.
MPAA:R
Columbia Pictures — *RCA/Columbia Pictures Home Video*

Watership Down **1978**
Fantasy
53526 92 mins C B, V R, P
Animated, directed by Martin Rosen
Richard Adam's allegorical novel about how a group of rabbits escape fear and overcome oppression while searching for a new and better home is the basis for this animated film.
MPAA:PG
Nepenthe Productions — *Warner Home Video; RCA VideoDiscs*

Wavelength **1983**
Drama
65393 87 mins C B, V P
Robert Carradine
A rock star living in the Hollywood Hills with his girlfriend stumbles on an ultrasecret government project involving aliens from outerspace recovered from a recent unidentified flying object crash site. The FBI, CIA, NASA and the Army Intelligence combine all their resources to find and destroy them.
MPAA:PG
James Rosenfield — *Embassy Home Entertainment*

Way Down East **1920**
Drama/Film-History
08710 119 mins B/W B, V P
Lillian Gish, Richard Barthelmess, Lowell Sherman, Creighton Hale, directed by D. W. Griffith
The story of a country girl who is tricked into a fake marriage by a scheming playboy. The final sequence is in color, and this tape includes the original Griffith-approved musical score.
United Artists — *Glenn Video Vistas; Sheik Video; Video Yesteryear; Western Film & Video Inc; Discount Video Tapes*

Way He Was, The **1976**
Comedy
80187 87 mins C B, V P
Steve Friedman, Al Lewis, Merrie Lynn Ross, Doodles Weaver
A satrical re-enactment of the events that led up to the Watergate burglary and the cover up that followed.
MPAA:R
Goldenwest Releasing — *United Home Video*

Way He Was, The **1976**
Satire
79760 87 mins C B, V P
Steve Friedman, Al Lewis, Doodles Weaver
A satrical look at the Watergate break-in and the cover-up that followed it.
Goldenwest Releasing — *United Home Video*

Way Out West **1937**
Comedy
33906 65 mins B/W B, V, 3/4U P
Stan Laurel, Oliver Hardy, Sharon Lynne, James Finlayson, Rosina Lawrence
The boys travel westward to deliver a mine deed to the daughter of a recently departed friend. A crooked saloonkeeper tries to swindle them.
Hal Roach, MGM — *Nostalgia Merchant; Blackhawk Films*

Way Out West **1937**
Comedy
63991 87 mins B/W B, V P, T
Stan Laurel, Oliver Hardy, Rosina Lawrence, Jimmy Finlayson, Sharon Lynne
The boys travel out West to deliver the deed to a gold mine to the daughter of their late prospector friend. Also included on this tape is a 1932 Thelma Todd—ZaSu Pitts short, "Red Noses."
Hal Roach; MGM — *Blackhawk Films*

Way They Were, The **1984**
Football
79634 23 mins C B, V, FO P
Profiles of the New York Jets stars past and present along with highlights of the team's 1968 championship season.
NFL Films — *NFL Films Video*

Way We Were, The **1973**
Drama/Romance
63963 118 mins C B, V P
Barbra Streisand, Robert Redford, Bradford Dillman, Viveca Lindfors, Herb Edelman
Set during the 1940's, this is the story of the attraction of two totally opposite people, the love that binds them together, and the differences that tear them apart.
Academy Awards '73: Best Song ("The Way We Were"); Best Music Score. MPAA:PG
Columbia Pictures; Ray Stark — *RCA/Columbia Pictures Home Video; RCA VideoDiscs*

Wayne Murder Case **1938**
Mystery
78114 61 mins B/W B, V, FO P
June Clyde, Regis Toomey, Jason Robards Sr.
A fast-moving, cleverly constructed murder mystery, wherein a rich old man dies just as he is about to sign a new will. Though no one was standing near him, a knife is found embedded in his back.

Tiffany — *Video Yesteryear*

Wayne Newton at the London Palladium **1983**
Music-Performance
66448 63 mins C B, V P
Wayne Newton, The Jive Sisters, Don Vincent and his Orchestra
Wayne Newton performs a show-stopping program for his legions of fans at the London Palladium. Songs include such pop masterpieces as "Danke Schoen," "Jambalaya," "The Impossible Dream," "I Made It Through The Rain" and others. VHS in stereo.
ITC Productions — *MGM/UA Home Video*

W. C. Fields Festival **1933**
Comedy
00428 60 mins B/W B, V P
W.C. Fields
Included are "The Golf Specialist," "The Dentist," and "The Fatal Glass of Beer."
Mack Sennett — *Prism; Budget Video; Discount Video Tapes; Sheik Video; Sound Video Unlimited; See Hear Industries*

We All Loved Each Other So Much **1977**
Comedy
63435 124 mins C B, V P
Vittorio Gassman, Nino Manfredi, Stefano Satta Flores, Stefania Sandrelli
From the end of World War II through the next 30 years, this sensitive comedy follows the lives of three friends who have all loved the same woman. Italian dialogue, English subtitles.
IT
Almi/Cinema V; Pio Angeletti and Adriano de Micheli — *RCA/Columbia Pictures Home Video*

We Are the World—The Video Event **1985**
Music video/Documentary
80880 30 mins C B, V P
Diana Ross, Michael Jackson, Lionel Ritchie, Billy Joel, Ray Charles, Stevie Wonder, Bruce Springsteen, Willie Nelson, Bob Dylan, Quincy Jones, narrated by Jane Fonda
This is a look at the recording of the USA for Africa's "We Are the World." This Beta and VHS Hi Fi Stereo program includes a complete video clip of the song.
Ken Kragen; Ken Yates — *RCA/Columbia Pictures Home Video*

We Dive at Dawn **1943**
War-Drama
64372 98 mins B/W B, V, 3/4U P
John Mills, Eric Portman, directed by Anthony Asquith
A British submarine is disabled in the Baltic sea by enemy gunfire and the crewmen desperately seek help.
J. Arthur Rank; GFD; Gainsborough — *Nostalgia Merchant*

We of the Never Never **1982**
Drama
65100 136 mins C B, V P
Angela Punch McGregor, Arthur Dignam, Tony Barry, directed by Igor Auzins
A city-bred Australian woman marries a cattle rancher and moves from civilized Melbourne to the barren outback of the Northern Territory.
Triumph Films — *RCA/Columbia Pictures Home Video*

Weather in the Streets **1984**
Drama/Romance
81562 108 mins C B, V P
Michael York, Joanna Lumley, Lisa Eichhorn, Isabel Dean, Norman Pitt
A young woman enters into an ill-fated love affair after spending a few moments with an aristocratic married man.
MPAA:PG
Alan Shallcross — *Epic Pictures*

Weber and Fields, Al Jolson, and This Is America **19??**
Music/Variety
57365 29 mins B/W B, V, FO P
This tape contains three priceless programs. "Weber and Fields" (1930), the dynamic vaudeville duo, are seen performing their classic "Oyster" routine. "A Jolson's Screen Test" (1948) is the rarest Jolson on film. "This Is America" (1943), narrated by Dwight West, is a wartime tour along the Great White Way subtitled "Broadway Dim Out."
Unknown — *Video Yesteryear*

Wedding Party, The **1969**
Comedy
63418 90 mins C B, V P
Jill Clayburgh, Robert DeNiro, directed by Brian DePalma
An apprehensive groom is overwhelmed by his too-eager bride and her inquisitive relatives at a prenuptial celebration.
Ajay Films — *VidAmerica*

Wedding Rehearsal **1932**
Comedy
81470 84 mins B/W B, V, LV P
Merle Oberon, Roland Young, John Loder, Wendy Barrier, Maurice Evans, directed by Alexander Korda
A Guards officer thwarts his grandmother's plans to marry him off by finding suitors for all the young ladies offered to him.

Alexander Korda — *Embassy Home Entertainment*

Weekend of Shadows 1977
Drama
80392 94 mins C B, V P
John Waters, Melissa Jaffer, Graeme Blundell
A police sergeant leads a group of townspeople in a search for the man who murdered a farmer's wife.
Tom Jeffrey; Matt Carroll — *Embassy Home Entertainment*

Weekend Pass 1984
Comedy
73041 92 mins C B, V, CED P
Three rookie sailors who have just completed basic training are out on a weekend pass determined to forget everything they have learned.
MPAA:R
Marylin J Tenser Crown International — *Vestron Video*

Weight Watchers Magazine Guide to a Healthy Lifestyle 1985
Nutrition/Physical fitness
Closed Captioned
80921 60 mins C B, V, CED P
Lynn Redgrave hosts this program that features fitness and diet tips from the Weight Watchers program.
Weight Watchers Magazine — *Vestron Video*

Welcome to Blood City 1977
Drama
80671 96 mins C B, V P
Jack Palance, Keir Dullea, Samantha Eggar, Barry Morse
An anonymous totalitarian organization kidnaps a man and transports him electronically to a fantasy western town where the person who murders the most people becomes the town's "kill master"
EMI; Len Herberman Prods — *Lightning Video*

Welcome to L.A. 1977
Drama/Satire
Closed Captioned
72193 106 mins C B, V P
Sissy Spacek, Sally Kellerman, Keith Carradine
Robert Altman's satire of life in Southern California has become a cult favorite over the years.
MPAA:R
Lions Gate Films — *CBS/Fox Video*

Welcome to Pooh Corner, Volume I 1984
Fantasy
72791 111 mins C B, V P
A series of made-for-video episodes involving Winnie the Pooh's misadventures in the Hundred Acre Wood. The live-action series features all Pooh's cronies, Tigger, Christopher Robin and Eeyore.
Walt Disney Productions — *Walt Disney Home Video*

Welcome to Pooh Corner—Volume 4 1985
Cartoons/Adventure
70669 111 mins C B, V R, P
Animated
Pooh and his pals from the Hundred Acre Wood star in several new episodes, including: "Hello, Hello There," "The Old Swimming Hole," "Practice Makes Perfect" and "Pooh Makes a Trade."
Walt Disney Productions — *Walt Disney Home Video*

Welcome to Pooh Corner—Volume 2 1984
Cartoons
79227 115 mins C B, V R, P
Animated
Winnie the Pooh and the gang from the Hundred Acre Wood learn how to create a safe, accident free environment.
Walt Disney Productions — *Walt Disney Home Video*

Welcome to Pooh Corner—Volume 3 1985
Fantasy
76822 111 mins C B, V R, P
Winnie the Pooh and his friends of the Hundred Acre Wood are back in this new volume where Piglet discovers that everyone is special in their own way and Roo pretends to have a great adventure.
Walt Disney Productions — *Walt Disney Home Video*

Went the Day Well? 1942
War-Drama
66404 96 mins B/W B, V P
Leslie Banks, Elizabeth Allan, Frank Lawton, Basil Sydney
English villagers fight back when a squad of German paratroopers attempt a takeover in their town.
Ealing — *Movie Buff Video*

We're No Angels 1955
Comedy-Drama
65401 103 mins C B, V R, P
Humphrey Bogart, Aldo Ray, Joan Bennett, Peter Ustinov, Basil Rathbone, Leo G. Carroll
Three escapees from Devil's Island hide out with the family of a kindly French storekeeper.
Paramount — *Paramount Home Video*

Werewolf of Washington **1979**
Horror
65308 90 mins C B, V P
Dean Stockwell, Biff Maguire, Clifton James
As the full moon hovers over Washington, terror lies waiting in the corridors of power.
Millco Productions — *Monterey Home Video*

West-Bound Limited, The **1923**
Drama
78115 70 mins B/W B, V, FO P
Johnny Harron, Ella Hall, Claire McDowell
A romantic adventurer rescues the girl from certain death as a train is about to hit her, and the two fall in love. Silent with music score.
FBO — *Video Yesteryear*

West of the Divide **1934**
Western
15487 60 mins B/W B, V P
John Wayne
The Duke heads out west ready for action.
Monogram — *Sony Corporation of America; Video Connection; Discount Video Tapes; Video Dimensions; Sheik Video; Cable Films; Spotlite Video; Kartes Productions*

West Side Story **1961**
Musical
37522 151 mins C B, V, LV, CED P
Natalie Wood, Richard Beymer, Russ Tamblyn, Rita Moreno, George Chakiris, directed by Robert Wise and Jerome Robbins
Gang rivalry on New York's West Side erupts in a ground-breaking musical that won ten Academy Awards. The Jets and the Sharks fight for their own turf and Tony and Maria fight for their own love. Amid the frenetic and brilliant choreography by Jerome Robbins, who directed the original Broadway show, and the high caliber score by Leonard Bernstein and Stephin Sondheim, there is the bittersweet message that tragedy breeds friendship.
Academy Awards '61: Best Picture; Best Supporting Actor (Chakiris); Best Direction (Wise/Robbins); Best Supporting Actress (Moreno); Best Cinematography: Color; Best Scoring Musical; Best Film Editing; Best Costume Design: Color; Best Art Direction: Color; Best Sound Recording. EL, SP
United Artists; Robert Wise — *CBS/Fox Video; RCA VideoDiscs*

Western Double Feature #1 **194?**
Western
07314 120 mins B/W B, V, 3/4U P
Wild Bill Elliot, Sunset Carson
Double feature; in "Calling Wild Bill Elliot" (1943), Wild Bill comes to the aid of homesteaders; in "Santa Fe Saddlemates" (1945), Sunset Carson breaks up a diamond smuggling ring.
Republic — *Nostalgia Merchant*

Western Double Feature #2 **19??**
Western
07316 120 mins B/W B, V, 3/4U P
John Wayne, Monte Hale
Double feature; in "Night Riders" (1939), John Wayne battles injustice; in "Home on the Range" (1946, color), Monte Hale protects a wild animal refuge.
Republic — *Nostalgia Merchant*

Western Double Feature #3 **1950**
Western
07318 134 mins C B, V, 3/4U P
Roy Rogers, Dale Evans, Rex Allen
In "Twilight in the Sierras" (1950), Roy catches a gang of crooks. "Under Mexicali Stars" (1950), features Rex as a cowboy who uncovers a counterfeiting ring.
Republic — *Nostalgia Merchant*

Western Double Feature #4 **194?**
Western
07320 120 mins B/W B, V, 3/4U P
Roy Rogers, Dale Evans, Trigger, Gabby Hayes, Allan 'Rocky' Lane
Double feature; in "Don't Fence Me In" (1945), Roy Rogers helps out a woman reporter; in "Sheriff of Wichita" (1948), a frontier investigator solves a crime.
Republic — *Nostalgia Merchant*

Western Double Feature #5 **19??**
Western
07322 108 mins B/W B, V, 3/4U P
Gene Autry, Roy Rogers, Smiley Burnette, Sons of the Pioneers
"The Big Show" (1937), features songs, action, and horses. "Home in Oklahoma" (1946), has Roy tracking down a murderer.
Republic — *Nostalgia Merchant*

Western Double Feature #6 **1950**
Western
07324 120 mins C B, V, 3/4U P
Roy Rogers, Dale Evans, Trigger, Bob Livingston, Bob Steele
Double feature; "Trigger Jr'. (1950) is the story of Trigger's colt; "Gangs of Sonora" (1941, black and white) deals with a fight to save a small frontier newspaper.
Republic — *Nostalgia Merchant*

(For explanation of codes, see USE GUIDE and KEY)

Western Double Feature #7 1945
Western
07326 120 mins B/W B, V, 3/4U P
Wild Bill Elliott, Buster Crabbe
Double feature; "Phantom of the Plains" deals with a plan to save a woman from a gigolo; "Prairie Rustlers" tells of the problems of a man who is the identical double of Billy the Kid.
Republic; PRC — *Nostalgia Merchant*

Western Double Feature #8 194?
Western
07328 121 mins B/W B, V, 3/4U P
Roy Rogers, Monte Hale, John Carradine
Ranchers waiting to get right-of-way through oil land run into an ambitious resort owner in "Silver Spurs" (1943). "Out California Way" (1946), features Monte as a young cowboy looking for work in Hollywood.
Republic — *Nostalgia Merchant*

Western Double Feature #9 194?
Western
07330 120 mins B/W B, V, 3/4U P
Lash LaRue, Don 'Red' Barry, Noah Beery
Double feature; in "Cheyenne Takes Over" (1947), Lash LaRue battles outlaws; in "Tulsa Kid" (1940), a young man must face a gunfighter.
Eagle Lion; Republic — *Nostalgia Merchant*

Western Double Feature #10 19??
Western
07332 120 mins C B, V, 3/4U P
Roy Rogers, Dale Evans, Trigger
Double feature; in "Bells of Coronado" (1950), Roy Rogers must solve a murder and uranium ore theft; in "King of the Cowboys" (1943, black and white), Roy Rogers investigates a band of saboteurs.
Republic — *Nostalgia Merchant*

Western Double Feature #11 1950
Western
33916 121 mins B/W B, V, 3/4U P
Roy Rogers, Penny Edwards, Gordon Jones, Riders of the Purple Sage, Gabby Hayes
Roy and Trigger act as modern day Robin Hoods to end crooked dealing in the West; Roy hides behind a a smile and a song to capture murderers of a deputy and a ranch owner.
Republic — *Nostalgia Merchant*

Western Double Feature #12 1944
Western
33917 108 mins B/W B, V, 3/4U P
Bob Livingston, Wild Bill Elliot, Bobby Blake, Duncan Renaldo
Red Ryder learns of a plot to scare ranchers into selling out before an oil strike is discovered; the Three Mesquiteers are sent to the Caribbean as U.S. envoys to sell Army horses.
Republic;Producers Releasing Corp — *Nostalgia Merchant*

Western Double Feature #13 194?
Western
33919 108 mins B/W B, V, 3/4U P
Red Ryder, Three Mesquiteers, Bobby Blake
Red Ryder foils outlaws trying to swindle the Duchess' stage line in a small isolated town in "Wagon Wheels Westward" (1945). "Rocky Mountain Rangers" (1940), features the Three Mesquiteers pursuing the deadly Barton Gang.
Republic — *Nostalgia Merchant*

Western Double Feature #14 1952
Western
33921 123 mins B/W B, V, 3/4U P
Tim Holt, Jack Holt, Nan Leslie, Noreen Nash
Outlaws, good guys and romance on the old frontier. Amateur Robin Hoods steal back money wrongfully taken.
RKO — *Nostalgia Merchant*

Western Double Feature #15 1950
Western
33923 122 mins B/W B, V, 3/4U P
Roy Rogers, Trigger, Penny Edwards, Don "Red" Barry, Lynn Merrick
Roy Rogers breaks up a cattle rustling ring; the good guys try to bring law and order to a vast Wyoming territory plagued by a crooked political boss.
Republic — *Nostalgia Merchant*

Western Double Feature #16 1946
Western
33925 108 mins B/W B, V, 3/4U P
Gene Autry, Smiley Burnette, Roy Rogers, Gabby Hayes
Autry is sent to quell a revolution in Mexico; Roy Rogers' horse Lady and Gabby Hayes' horse Golden Sovereign are the focal points of the second part of this double feature.
Republic — *Nostalgia Merchant*

Western Double Feature #17 194?
Western
44855 121 mins C B, V, 3/4U P
Roy Rogers, Sunset Carson
This double feature stars Roy Rogers in "The Golden Stallion" ('49). Roy battles diamond smugglers who use wild horses to transport the

 (For explanation of codes, see USE GUIDE and KEY)

goods. The second feature, "The Cherokee Flash" ('45), starring Sunset Carson, deals with a respectable citizen's outlaw past catching up to him.
Republic — *Nostalgia Merchant*

Western Double Feature #18 194?
Western
33927 108 mins B/W B, V, 3/4U P
Roy Rogers, Andy Devine, Dale Evans
A Roy Rogers double feature: In "Eyes of Texas" (1948), a westerner turns his ranch into a camp for war-orphaned boys. In "Helldorado" (1946), Roy travels to Las Vegas.
Republic — *Nostalgia Merchant*

Western Double Feature #19 19??
Western
33929 108 mins B/W B, V, 3/4U P
Roy Rogers, Gene Autry
"Night Time in Nevada" (1948), has Roy bringing a ruthless murderer to justice. "The Old Corral" (1937), features a clash between gangsters in limousines and deputies on horseback.
Republic — *Nostalgia Merchant*

Western Double Feature #20 1945
Western
33931 108 mins B/W B, V, 3/4U P
Roy Rogers, Dale Evans, Pat Brady, Trigger
Roy helps a young woman foil a plot by crooks to swindle her inheritance. Roy appears in his first starring role (1938) and fights an outlaw gang.
Republic — *Nostalgia Merchant*

Western Double Feature #21 194?
Western
33933 121 mins C B, V, 3/4U P
Roy Rogers, Red Ryder, Dale Evans, Bobby Blake
Roy battles crooks in "Susanna Pass" (1949). In "Sheriff of Las Vegas" (1944), Red must find the murderer of Judge Blackwell.
Republic — *Nostalgia Merchant*

Western Double Feature #22 194?
Western
33935 108 mins B/W B, V, 3/4U P
Roy Rogers
A Roy Rogers double feature: In "Under California Stars" (1948), Roy rounds up a gang of wild horse rustlers. In "San Fernando Valley" (1944), Roy brings law and order to the valley.
Republic, Monogram — *Nostalgia Merchant*

Western Double Feature #23 19??
Western
59146 122 mins B/W B, V, 3/4U P
Roy Rogers, Dale Evans
In "Spoilers of the Plains" (1951), Roy finds cattle rustlers and sets out to capture the spoilers. "Lights of Old Santa Fe" (1947), features Roy as a cowboy who rescues a beautiful rodeo owner from bankruptcy.
Republic — *Nostalgia Merchant*

Western Double Feature #24 194?
Western
59147 122 mins C B, V, 3/4U P
Roy Rogers, Dale Evans, Eddie Dean
In "Cowboy and the Senorita" (1944), Roy solves the mystery of a missing girl. "Colorado Serenade" (1946), is a musical western in Cinecolor starring Eddie Dean.
Republic;Producers Releasing Corp — *Nostalgia Merchant*

Western Double Feature #25 19??
Western
59148 122 mins B/W B, V, 3/4U P
Roy Rogers, Dale Evans, Andy Devine, Sons of the Pioneers
In "Pals of the Golden West" (1951), Roy discovers how valuable Trigger is. "Springtime in the Sierras" (1947), features Roy raising and selling thoroughbreds.
Republic — *Nostalgia Merchant*

Westerner, The 1940
Western
80949 100 mins B/W B, V P
Gary Cooper, Walter Brennan, Doris Davenport, Dana Andrews, directed by William Wyler
A cowboy strolls into a western Texas border town and becomes involved in a land war with the legendary Judge Roy Bean.
Academy Awards '40: Best Supporting Actor (Brennan).
Samuel Goldwyn — *Embassy Home Entertainment*

Westinghouse Studio One: Hold Back the Night 1952
War-Drama
21332 60 mins B/W B, V, FO P
John Forsythe
A Korean war drama from one of the most famous series of early television.
CBS — *Video Yesteryear*

Westinghouse Studio One: "Little Men, Big World" 1952
Crime-Drama
47500 60 mins B/W B, V, FO P
Jack Palance, Shepperd Strudwick, Ray Walston
An original TV drama by Reginald Rose about small town racketeers being menaced by a big city mob. Originally telecast on October 13, 1952.
CBS — *Video Yesteryear*

Westinghouse Studio One (Summer Theatre) 1952
Drama
66144 56 mins B/W B, V, FO P
Kevin McCarthy, Frances Starr, Katharine Bard
A live TV dramatization of "Jane Eyre" by Charlotte Bronte.
CBS — *Video Yesteryear*

Westinghouse Summer Theater 1951
Drama
78100 59 mins B/W B, V, FO P
Richard Purdy, Martin Brooks, Maria Riva, Robert Harris, Betty Furness
A touching story about a meek bank accountant with a strange secret and a beautiful wife.
CBS — *Video Yesteryear*

Westworld 1973
Science fiction
59362 90 mins C B, V, CED P
Yul Brynner, Richard Benjamin, James Brolin, directed by Michael Crichton
Michael Crichton wrote this story of an adult vacation resort of the future which offers the opportunity to live in various fantasy worlds serviced by lifelike robots. When an electrical malfunction occurs, the robots begin to go berserk.
MPAA:PG
MGM — *MGM/UA Home Video*

Whale of a Tale, A 1976
Drama
80658 90 mins C B, V P
William Shatner, Marty Allen, Abby Dalton, Andy Devine, Nancy O'Conner
A young boy trains a killer whale to appear in the big show in the main tank, at "Marine land."
MPAA:G
Independent — *United Home Video*

What Ever Happened to Baby Jane? 1962
Suspense
65139 132 mins B/W B, V R, P
Bette Davis, Joan Crawford, Victor Buono, Anna Lee, B.D. Merrill, directed by Robert Aldrich
Two sisters, one a demented former childhood star and the other a crippled ex-screen actress, live together in an uneasy truce until events drive one of them over the brink of madness.
Seven Arts; Warner Bros — *Warner Home Video*

What Price Hollywood 1932
Comedy
10059 88 mins B/W B, V P, T
Constance Bennett, Lowel Sherman, Neil Hamilton, directed by George Cukor
Aspiring young starlet decides to crash film world by using a director.
RKO; Selznick — *Blackhawk Films*

What the Peeper Saw 1972
Horror
60349 97 mins C B, V P
Britt Ekland, Mark Lester, Hardy Kruger, Lilli Palmer
A wealthy author's wife's comfortable life turns into a terrifying nightmare when her young stepson starts exhibiting strange behavior.
Joseph E Levine; Avco Embassy — *United Home Video*

What Would Your Mother Say? 1981
Variety
64847 83 mins C B, V P
Bill Margold, Tiffany Clark, Maria Tortuga, Kevin Gibson, Tamara Webb, Mike Ranger, Monique Monge
A hidden camera takes you inside actual casting sessions with over 40 of Hollywood's erotic stars and starlets who didn't know they were being filmed.
Real Peephole Production — *HarmonyVision*

Whatever Happened to Aunt Alice? 1969
Mystery/Drama
46197 101 mins C B, V P
Geraldine Page, Ruth Gordon, Rosemary Forsyth, Robert Fuller, Mildred Dunnock, directed by Lee H. Katzin
A woman murdered her husband to inherit his estate only to discover it is worthless. Meanwhile, she must continue killing for her protection until she learns that her husband's stamp collection was worth $100,000.
MPAA:PG
Robert Aldrich — *CBS/Fox Video*

What's New Pussycat? 1965
Comedy
58853 108 mins C B, V, CED P
Peter Sellers, Peter O'Toole, Romy Schneider, Paula Prentiss, Woody Allen, Ursula Andress, Capucine
A young engaged man is reluctant to give up the girls who love him and seeks the aid of a

married psychiatrist who turns out to have problems of his own.
United Artists — *CBS/Fox Video*

What's Up Doc? 1972
Comedy
52708 94 mins C B, V R, P
Barbra Streisand, Ryan O'Neal, Kenneth Mars, Austin Pendleton, directed by Peter Bogdanovich
An eccentric woman and an equally eccentric professor become involved in a chase to recover four identical flight bags containing top secret documents, a wealthy woman's jewels, the professor's musical rocks, and the girl's clothing. Bogdanovich's homage to screwball comedies of the thirties.
MPAA:G
Warner Bros; Saticoy Productions — *Warner Home Video; RCA VideoDiscs*

What's Up Tiger Lily? 1966
Comedy
08579 90 mins C B, V, LV, CED P
Woody Allen, Tatsuya Mihashi, Mie Hana
This legitimate Japanese spy movie was re-edited by Woody Allen, who also added a new dialogue track, with laughable results. Music by the Lovin' Spoonful.
Henry G Saperstein Entprs — *Vestron Video; Cable Films*

Wheel of Fortune 1942
Drama
66468 83 mins B/W B, V P
John Wayne, Frances Dee, Edward Ellis
A shrewd country lawyer is forced to expose his girlfriend's father as a crooked gambler.
Republic — *Republic Pictures Home Video*

When a Stranger Calls 1979
Suspense
52753 97 mins C B, V, LV, CED P
Carol Kane, Charles Durning, Colleen Dewhurst, Rachel Roberts
A babysitter is terrorized by threatening phone calls and soon realizes that the calls are coming from within the house.
MPAA:R
Columbia; Doug Chapin; Steve Feke — *RCA/Columbia Pictures Home Video*

When Eagles Fly 197?
Drama
80424 120 mins C B, V P
Jennifer Dale, Robin Ward
A young woman who works at a major metropolitan hospital is seeking revenge against the man who loves her.
Independent — *Unicorn Video*

When Knights Were Bold 1936
Comedy
78112 55 mins B/W B, V, FO P
Fay Wray, Jack Buchanan, Martita Hunt
An Englishman residing in India inherits a castle in his native land. Returning home, he is knocked unconscious by a falling suit of armor while trying to impress a young lady and dreams himself back to medieval days.
Capitol — *Video Yesteryear*

When Lightning Strikes 1934
Adventure
65200 51 mins B/W B, V P
Francis X. Bushman, Lightning the Wonder Dog
Lightning, the Wonder Dog prevents the owner of a rival lumber company from stealing his master's land, utilizing his talents of running, swimming, barking and smoking cigars.
Regal Productions — *Video Yesteryear*

When the Line Goes Through 1971
Drama
80720 90 mins C B, V P
Martin Sheen, Davey Davidson, Beverly Washburn
The lives of two pretty blond sistes change after a drifter arrives in their small West Virginia town.
JPD — *All Seasons Entertainment*

When the North Wind Blows 1974
Adventure
45013 113 mins C B, V P
Henry Brandon, Herbert Nelson, Dan Haggerty
An old, lone trapper hunts for and later befriends the majestic snow tiger of Siberia in the Alaskan wilderness.
MPAA:G
Sunn Classic Pictures — *United Home Video*

When Worlds Collide 1951
Science fiction
55545 82 mins C B, V, LV R, P
Richard Derr, Barbara Rush, Larry Keating, Peter Hanson, directed by Rudolph Mate
Another planet is found to be rushing inevitably towards earth, but before the collision a few people escape in a spaceship.
Academy Awards '51: Best Special Effects.
Paramount; George Pal — *Paramount Home Video*

When's Your Birthday? 1937
Comedy
56905 77 mins B/W B, V, FO P
Joe E. Brown, Marian Marsh, Edgar Kennedy
Joe E. Brown stars in this comedy about a prize-fighter who studies the stars to secure success in the ring.

RKO — *Video Yesteryear*

Where the Boys Are 1960
Comedy
72467 99 mins C B, V P
George Hamilton, Jim Hutton, Yvette Mimieux, Connie Francis, Paula Prentiss, Dolores Hart
Four college girls go to Fort Lauderdale and meet men they are conveniently compatible with during spring break.
MGM — *MGM/UA Home Video*

Where the Buffalo Roam 1980
Comedy
72932 98 mins C B, V P
Bill Murray, Peter Boyle
One of Bill's early starring roles as the legendary "gonzo" journalist Dr. Hunter S. Thompson.
MPAA:R
Art Linson — *MCA Home Video*

Where the Red Fern Grows 1974
Drama
79314 97 mins C B, V P
James Whitmore, Beverly Garland, Jack Ging, Lonny Chapman
Two Redbone hounds teach a young boy a lesson about responsibility and growing up.
MPAA:G
Lyman Dayton Productions — *Vestron Video*

Where the Toys Come From 1984
Fantasy
79228 68 mins C B, V R, P
Two toys try to discover their roots in a journey that takes them around the world.
Walt Disney Productions — *Walt Disney Home Video*

Where Time Began 1977
Science fiction/Adventure
65716 87 mins C B, V P
The discovery of a strange manuscript of a scientist's journey to the center of the earth leads to the decision to recreate the dangerous mission. Based on the Jules Verne classic novel, "Journey to the Center of the Earth."
MPAA:G
International Picture Show — *Embassy Home Entertainment*

Where's Poppa? 1970
Comedy
65334 84 mins C B, V P
George Segal, Ruth Gordon, Trish Van Devere
A Jewish lawyer's aged mother constantly harms his love life, and he considers various means of getting rid of her.
United Artists — *Key Video*

Which Way Is Up? 1977
Comedy
14013 94 mins C B, V P
Richard Pryor, Lonette McKee, Margaret Avery, Morgan Woodward, Marilyn Coleman, directed by Michael Schultz
The story of an orange picker who accidentally becomes a union hero. He leaves his wife and family at home while he seeks work in Los Angeles. There he finds himself a new woman, starts a new family, and sells out to the capitalists.
MPAA:R
Universal; Steve Krantz Prod — *MCA Home Video*

Whisky Galore 1948
Comedy
50957 81 mins B/W , B, V R, P
Basil Radford, Joan Greenwood, Gordon Jackson, James Robertson Justice
A whiskey-less Scottish island gets a lift when a ship carrying 50,000 cases of spirits becomes wrecked off their coast. A full-scale rescue operation and evasion of the British government ensues.
Ealing Studios — *THORN EMI/HBO Video*

Whispering Shadow 1933
Mystery/Serials
12555 156 mins B/W B, V P
Bela Lugosi, Robert Warwick, directed by Al Herman, Colbert Clark
Serial starring the master criminal known as the "faceless whisperer." Twelve chapters, 13 minutes each.
Mascot — *Video Connection; Video Yesteryear*

Whistle Down the Wind 1962
Drama
78640 98 mins B/W B, V P
Hayley Mills, Bernard Lee, Alan Bates, directed by Richard Attenborough
Three children find a murderer hiding in a barn and believe that he is Jesus Christ.
Pathe — *Embassy Home Entertainment*

Whistle Stop 1946
Drama
66405 84 mins B/W B, V P
George Raft, Ava Gardner, Victor McLaglen
A small-town girl divides her flirtatious attentions between an erratic playboy and a villainous night club owner.
United Artists — *Movie Buff Video; Discount Video Tapes*

White Dawn, The 1975
Drama
64029 110 mins C B, V R, P
Warren Oates, Timothy Bottoms, Lou Gossett
Three sailors, separated from their ship during a hunt, struggle to survive in the Arctic wasteland.
MPAA:R
Paramount — *Paramount Home Video*

White Fire 1984
Suspense
76944 90 mins C B, V P
Robert Ginty, Fred Williamson
Two jewel thieves will stop at nothing to own White Fire, a two hundred carat diamond.
Trans World Entertainment — *Trans World Entertainment*

White Heat 1949
Drama
29233 114 mins B/W B, V, CED P
James Cagney, Virginia Mayo, Edmond O'Brien
A ruthless gangster has a mother complex, but to all others around him, he's a heartless killer. One of Cagney's best roles.
Warner Bros — *CBS/Fox Video; RCA VideoDiscs*

White Legion 1936
Drama
78111 81 mins B/W B, V, FO P
Jan Keith, Tala Birell, Snub Pollard
Workers and engineers push their way through steaming jungles and reeking swamps while building the Panama Canal. Many fall victim to yellow fever, relying on dedicated doctors—the "white legion"—to complete the project.
Grand National Films — *Video Yesteryear*

White Lightning 1973
Adventure
58828 101 mins C CED P
Burt Reynolds, Ned Beatty, Bo Hopkins, Jennifer Billingsley, Louise Latham
An adventure drama of murder, revenge, and moonshine in the new South.
MPAA:PG
United Artists; Levy Gardner Lavin Productions — *CBS/Fox Video; RCA VideoDiscs*

White Line Fever 1975
Adventure
64911 89 mins C B, V P
Jan-Michael Vincent, Kay Lenz
A young trucker's search for a happy life with his childhood sweetheart is complicated by a corrupt group in control of the long-haul trucking business.
MPAA:PG
John Kemeny — *RCA/Columbia Pictures Home Video*

White Mane 1952
Drama
65621 38 mins B/W B, V P
Alain Emery, Frank Silvera
The poignant, poetic story of a proud and fierce white stallion that continually alludes attempts to be captured by ranchers, only to be "tamed" by the love of a small boy.
William Snyder — *Embassy Home Entertainment*

White Music 1981
Music
47299 35 mins C LV P
A fantasy ski adventure set in the south of France provides a visual interpretation of the background rock music composed by Talizman.
Masaru Ohtaki — *Pioneer Video Imports*

White Rose, The 1983
War-Drama
65222 108 mins C B, V P
Lena Stolze, Wulf Kessler, Oliver Siebert, Ulrich Tucker, directed by Michael Verhoeven
A group of dissident students in Munich, circa 1942, put their lives in danger by distributing anti-Nazi propaganda. In German with English subtitles.
GE
TeleCulture Films — *MGM/UA Home Video*

White-Water Sam 1978
Adventure
66637 87 mins C B, V P
Keith Larsen
White-Water Sam and his Siberian Husky, Sybar, embark on an exciting trip through the uncharted wilds of the Great Northwest.
MPAA:G
Keith Larsen — *Monterey Home Video*

White Zombie, The 1932
Horror
08586 73 mins B/W B, V P
Bela Lugosi, Madge Bellamy, John Harron, directed by Victor Halperin
Corpses return to life in this classic horror film. Zombies rob graves and take bodies to sugar mill where zombies work around the clock for mad White Zombie.
United Artists — *Mossman Williams Productions; Cable Films; Video Connection; Video Yesteryear; Budget Video; Discount Video Tapes; Western Film & Video Inc; Admit One Video*

Who Has Seen the Wind? 1977
Drama
72884 102 mins C B, V P
Jose Ferrer, Brian Painchaud, Charmion King
A young boy must learn how to grow up during the Depression.

Astral Films; Souris River Films — *Embassy Home Entertainment*

Who Is The Black Dahlia? **1975**
Mystery/Drama
79247 96 mins C B, V P
Efrem Zimbalist Jr., Lucie Arnaz, Ronny Cox, Macdonald Carey, Linden Chiles
A detective tries to figure out who murdered a twenty two year old girl nicknamed "The Black Dahlia" back in 1947.
Douglas S. Cramer Company — *Worldvision Home Video*

Who Killed Doc Robbin? **1948**
Mystery
08718 50 mins C B, V, FO P
Larry Olsen, Don Castle, by Bernard Carr
A group of youngsters try to clear their friend, Dan, the town handyman, when the sinister Dr. Robbins is murdered.
United Artists — *Video Yesteryear; Budget Video; Sheik Video; Discount Video Tapes*

Who Killed Mary What's 'Er Name? **1971**
Adventure
59352 90 mins C B, V R, P
Red Buttons, Sylvia Miles, Conrad Bain, Ron Carey, Alice Playten, Sam Waterson
An ex-fighter tracks a playgirl's killer through street gangs and bizarre cults.
MPAA:PG
Heritage Enterprises — *Video Gems*

Who Rocks America—1982 American Tour, The **1983**
Music-Performance
64334 118 mins C B, V, CED P
The rock group's final concert of their North American tour at the Maple Leaf Gardens in Toronto, Canada on December 17, 1982 includes such songs as "Pinball Wizard," "Who's Next," and "Tommy." In stereo on VHS format.
Jack Calmes — *CBS/Fox Video*

Who Slew Auntie Roo? **1971**
Mystery/Suspense
80687 90 mins C B, V P
Shelley Winters, Sir Ralph Richardson, Mark Lester, Lionel Jeffries, Hugh Griffith, directed by Curtis Harrington
An elderly widow gets a surprise from two unexpected guests at her annual Christmas celebration for orphans.
MPAA:PG
Orion Pictures — *Vestron Video*

Who'll Stop the Rain? **1978**
Drama
76043 126 mins C B, V P
Nick Nolte, Tuesday Weld, Michael Moriarty
Nolte plays a temperamental Vietnam veteran who is enlisted in a smuggling scheme to transport a large amount of heroin from Vietnam into California.
MPAA:R
United Artists — *Key Video*

Wholly Moses! **1980**
Comedy
51572 125 mins C B, V, LV P
The son of a slave in biblical times becomes convinced his mission is to lead the chosen, instead of his brother-in-law, Moses.
MPAA:PG
Columbia Pictures; Freddie Fields — *RCA/Columbia Pictures Home Video; RCA VideoDiscs*

Whoops Apocalypse **1983**
Comedy
65336 137 mins C B, V P
John Cleese, John Barron, Richard Griffiths, Peter Jones, Bruce Montague, Barry Morse
This program is a version of the British hit television series. It is a biting account of events leading up to World War III, full of rapid fire wit, one liners, and manic energy.
Humphrey Barclay — *Pacific Arts Video*

Who's Afraid of Virginia Woolf? **1966**
Drama
58256 127 mins B/W B, V R, P
Richard Burton, Elizabeth Taylor, George Segal, Sandy Dennis, directed by Mike Nichols
A night-long journey into the private hell of an embittered, embattled marriage. Adapted from Edward Albee's classic modern play.
Academy Awards '66: Best Actress (Taylor), Supporting Actress (Dennis), Best Cinematography—Black and White (Haskell Wexler).
Warner Bros — *Warner Home Video*

Who's Minding the Mint? **1967**
Comedy
70563 97 mins C B, V P
Jim Hutton, Dorothy Provine, Milton Berle, Joey Bishop, Bob Denver, Walter Brennan, directed by Howard Morris
A money checker at the U.S. Mint must replace 50,000 dollars he lost or face prison. He enlists a team of counterfeitors to infiltrate the Mint over the weekend and replace the lost cash. Available on Beta Hi-Fi.
Columbia — *RCA/Columbia Pictures Home Video*

 (For explanation of codes, see USE GUIDE and KEY)

Who's Out There?—A Search for Extraterrestrial Life 198?
Space exploration/Science fiction
72058 60 mins C B, V P
Orson Welles narrates this informative and entertaining film that speculates on whether life exists beyond our solar system.
NASA — *MPI Home Video*

Whose Life Is It Anyway? 1981
Drama
59366 118 mins C B, V, CED P
Richard Dreyfuss, John Cassavetes, Christine lahti, Bob Balaban, Kenneth McMillan, Kaki Hunter, Thomas Carter, directed by John Badham
A talented sculptor is paralyzed in an auto accident and decides not to live anymore. What follows is his struggle, both legally and morally, to convince the hospital authorities to let him die.
MPAA:R
MGM — *MGM/UA Home Video*

Why Do I Call You Sexy? 1983
Cosmetology
66176 90 mins C B, V P
Famed hairstylist and makeover artist of the Stars, Jose Eber, offers tips to women on hair and makeup.
Karl Video — *Karl/Lorimar Home Video*

Why Shoot the Teacher 1979
Drama
65394 101 mins C B, V P
Bud Cort, Samantha Eggar
An amusingly told story of life on the prairies at the height of the Great Depression. It's an account of one man's first collision with reality.
Laurence Hertzog — *Embassy Home Entertainment*

Wicker Man, The 1975
Mystery
56739 103 mins C B, V P
Edward Woodward, Britt Ekland, Diane Cilento, Ingrid Pitt, Christopher Lee
The disappearance of a young girl leads to the terrible secret of the Wicker Man.
Peter Snell — *Media Home Entertainment*

Widow's Nest 1977
Suspense
77258 90 mins C B, V P
Patricia Neal, Susan Oliver, Lila Kedrova, Valentina Cortese
Three widowed sisters live in a bizarre fantasy world when they lock themselves in a dingy mansion.
Navarro Prods. — *Magnum Entertainment*

Wifemistress 1979
Drama
39031 101 mins C B, V P
Marcello Mastroianni, Laura Antonelli, directed by Marco Vicario
Set in the early 1900's, this is the story of an invalid wife who resents her neglectful husband. When he goes into hiding because of a murder he didn't commit, the wife begins to drift into a world of her fantasies. Italian dialogue, English subtitles.
MPAA:R IT
Franco Cristaldi, Quartet Films — *RCA/Columbia Pictures Home Video; CBS/Fox Video (disc only)*

Wilbur and Orville: The First to Fly 1979
Adventure/Aeronautics
75619 47 mins C B, V P
This is the story of the Wright Brothers' early unsuccessful attempts at flying.
VidAmerica — *Children's Video Library*

Wild and Woolly 1917
Western/Comedy
69555 61 mins B/W B, V, FO P
Douglas Fairbanks Sr.
The son of a New York railroad tycoon travels out West on business expecting to find himself on the rugged frontier. Silent with musical score.
Artcraft — *Video Yesteryear; Classic Video Cinema Collector's Club*

Wild Blue Yonder, The 1985
Documentary/History-US
70684 45 mins C B, V P
Narrated by Ken Howard, directed by Fred Warshofsky
Part of the "In Defense of Freedom" series, this program traces the history of the United States Air Force.
A.B. Marian — *MPI Home Video*

Wild Bunch, The 1969
Western
38955 127 mins C B, V, LV R, P
William Holden, Ernest Borgnine, Robert Ryan, directed by Sam Peckinpah
A brutal, bloody western about a group of losers in the dying days of the lawless frontier, fighting and killing those in their path.
MPAA:R
Warner Bros — *Warner Home Video; RCA VideoDiscs*

Wild Geese, The 1978
Adventure
65407 132 mins C B, V, CED P
Richard Burton, Roger Moore, Richard Harris
The adventure begins when a veteran band of mercenaries land deep inside Africa to rescue the imprisoned leader of an emerging African

nation. Their mission meets an unexpected turn when the soldiers are betrayed by those who helped finance their trip!
MPAA:R
Allied Artists — *CBS/Fox Video*

Wild Gypsies 1969
Adventure
81216 85 mins C B, V, LV P
Todd Grange, Gayle Clark, Laurel Welcome
A band of gypsies seek revenge against a renegade member who attacked a fellow gypsy and murdered his former lover.
Manson International Pictures — *New World Video*

Wild Horse 1931
Western
43018 68 mins B/W B, V, FO P
Hoot Gibson, Stepin Fetchit
A pair of bronco busters sign up to work at a rodeo ranch and take charge when trouble strikes.
Allied — *Video Yesteryear*

Wild Horse Canyon 1925
Western
58265 68 mins B/W B, V, FO P
Yakima Canutt, Edward Cecil, Helene Rosson, Jay Talbet
Yakima Canutt, the man credited with creating the profession of stunt man, stars in this tale about a lady rancher who requires saving from her evil foreman. The climactic stampede scene gives Yakima a chance to demonstrate a high dive off a cliff and a somersault onto his horse. Silent, with musical score.
Unknown — *Video Yesteryear; Discount Video Tapes*

Wild Horses 1984
Western
75671 90 mins C B, V P
A rugged 1970's cowboy is determined to make a living by capturing and selling wild horses, but is plagued by hunters.
Satori Entertainment Corp. — *VidAmerica*

Wild in the Country 1961
Drama
64935 114 mins C B, V, CED P
Elvis Presley, Hope Lange, Tuesday Weld, Millie Perkins, John Ireland, Gary Lockwood
A woman psychiatrist and a social worker rehabilitate a delinquent rural boy.
20th Century Fox — *CBS/Fox Video*

Wild Life, The 1984
Comedy
Closed Captioned
80412 96 mins C B, V P
Christopher Penn, Rick Moranis, Hart Bochner, Eric Stoltz, Jenny Wright, Lea Thompson
A recent high school graduate takes on a wild and crazy wrestler as his roommate in a swinging singles apartment complex. Available in VHS and Beta Hi Fi Stereo.
MPAA:R
Art.Linson; Cameron Crowe — *MCA Home Video*

Wild Orchids 1929
Drama
80211 103 mins B/W B, V P
Greta Garbo, Lewis Stone, Nils Asther
A husband suspects his wife of infidelity while they take a business cruise to Java. One of Garbo's eartliest silent films.
MGM — *MGM/UA Home Video*

Wild Party, The 1974
Drama
65429 90 mins C B, V P
Raquel Welch, James Coco, Perry King, David Dukes
It's 1929, a year of much frivolity in Hollywood; and drinking, dancing, maneuvering and almost every sort of romance are the rule of the night at silent-film comic Jolly Grimm's sumptuous, star-studded party.
MPAA:R
United Artists — *Embassy Home Entertainment*

Wild Ride, The 1960
Drama
38975 59 mins B/W B, V, FO P
Jack Nicholson, Georgianna Carter
Jack Nicholson, in an early starring role, portrays a rebellious punk of the beat generation who hotrods his way into trouble and tragedy.
Filmgroup — *Video Yesteryear; Discount Video Tapes*

Wild Rides 1982
Documentary
66327 27 mins C B, V P
Matt Dillon
Teen heartthrob Matt Dillon takes viewers on a tour of America's most exciting roller coasters. The soundtrack features music by The Who, Steely Dan, Steve Miller, The Cars and Jimi Hendrix. In stereo.
Klein & Video Programs — *Warner Home Video*

Wild Strawberries 1959
Drama
60426 90 mins B/W B, V P
Victor Sjostrom, Bibi Anderson, Ingrid Thulin, Max von Sydow, Gunnar Bjornstrand, directed by Ingmar Bergman

 (For explanation of codes, see USE GUIDE and KEY)

Bergman's classic of fantasy, dreams and nightmares concerning an aging professor who must come to terms with his faults and become reconciled to the idea of approaching death.
A B Svensk; Janus Films — *CBS/Fox Video; Cable Films*

Wild Swans, The 198?
Cartoons/Fairy tales
73865 62 mins C B, V P
Animated
A young girl must save her six brothers who have been turned into swans by an evil witch.
John Watkins; Simon Nuchtern — *RCA/Columbia Pictures Home Video*

Wild Times 1979
Western
73561 200 mins C B, V P
Sam Elliott, Trish Stewart, Ben Johnson, Dennis Hopper, Pat Hingle
This movie is based upon Brian Garfield's novel about Hugh Cardiff, a hero who lived his life to the hilt.
Rattlesnake Prods; Golden Circle — *Prism*

Wild Wheels 1975
Drama
81614 81 mins C B, V P
Casey Kasem, Dovie Beams, Terry Stafford, Robert Dix
A group of dune buggy enthusiasts seek revenge against a gang of motorcyclists who have ravaged a small California beach town.
MPAA:PG
American Films Ltd. — *Video Gems*

Wild, Wild World of Jayne Mansfield 1968
Documentary
52733 120 mins C B, V P
The life and times of Jayne Mansfield is explored in this unique program. Jayne's world wide examination of sexual mores is traced, from prostitution, nudist colonies, and the racy strip clubs of Europe, to the transvestite and topless bars of America.
Southeastern Pictures — *Movie Buff Video; Vintage Video; Discount Video Tapes*

Wilderness Family Part 2 1977
Adventure
63381 104 mins C B, V P
Robert Logan, Susan D. Shaw
The further adventures of the Robinson family, who left civilization for the freedom of the wilderness, are portrayed.
MPAA:G
Pacific International Enterprises — *Media Home Entertainment*

Will: G. Gordon Liddy 1982
Biographical/Drama
79331 97 mins C B, V P
Robert Conrad, Kathy Cannon, Gary Bayer, Peter Ratray
A dramatization of Liddy's autobiography of how the former FBI agent became involved in the breakin at the Democratic Headquarters at the Watergate Hotel. In Beta Hi-Fi and VHS Stereo.
A. Shane Company — *U.S.A. Home Video*

Will of a People, The 1946
Spain/Documentary
12852 55 mins C B, V, FO P
A well done story of the Spanish revolution and the rise to power of Generalissimo Franco, told in footage from Spanish archives.
Unknown — *Video Yesteryear; International Historic Films*

Will Rogers: Champion of the People 1979
Biographical
57787 49 mins C B, V, 3/4U P
Robert Hays
The early years of Will Rogers, during which he fought for law and order in his Oklahoma hometown, are chronicled.
AM Available
Schick Sunn — *United Home Video*

Willie Nelson and Family In Concert 1984
Music video
Closed Captioned
72893 89 mins C B, V, CED P
Willie Nelson
Willie Nelson performs such hits as "On the Road Again" "Georgiaon My Mind."
Unknown — *CBS/Fox Video*

Willy McBean and His Magic Machine 1959
Fantasy/Puppets
81082 94 mins C B, V P
Animated
A little boy and his monkey must foil an evil professor's plan to travel back through time and change the course of history, everyday.
Magna Pictures — *Prism*

Willy Wonka and the Chocolate Factory 1971
Musical/Fantasy
79557 100 mins C B, V R, P
Gene Wilder, Denise Nickerson, Leonard Stone, Dodo Denney, directed by Mel Stuart
A poor young boy wins a tour of Willy Wonka's Chocolate Factory, a place filled with many surprises.

David L Wolper — *Warner Home Video*

Wilma 1977
Biographical/Drama
73863 100 mins C B, V P
Cicely Tyson, Shirley Jo Finney
The true story of a young woman who overcame polio to win three gold medals in the 1960 Olympics. Available in Beta Hi-Fi.
Cappy Productions — *RCA/Columbia Pictures Home Video*

Win, Place, or Steal 1972
Comedy
73036 88 mins C B, V P
McLean Stevenson, Alex Karras, Dean Stockwell
Three men are willing to do anything except work.
MPAA:PG
Omega — *Vestron Video*

Wind in the Willows, The 1982
Cartoons
63189 47 mins C B, V R, P
Animated, narrated by Basil Rathbone, the voice of Eric Blore
"The Wind in the Willows," originally a part of the 1950 feature "Ichabod and Mr. Toad," is the tale of J. Thaddeus Toad, who has a strange mania for fast cars. Also on this tape are two Disney cartoons with similar automotive themes, "Motor Mania" with Goofy, and "Trailer Horn" with Donald Duck and Chip 'n' Dale.
Walt Disney Productions — *Walt Disney Home Video; Vestron Video*

Wind in the Willows, The 1983
Cartoons/Literature-American
75622 97 mins C B, V P
Animated
This animated film is based on Kenneth Grahame's famous tale.
Rankin Bass — *Children's Video Library*

Wind in the Willows 1984
Fairy tales
80817 78 mins C B, V R, P
Animated
This is an adaptation of the Kenneth Grahame story about how Ratty, Badger and Mole try to save Toad Hall from destruction by the weasels. Available in VHS and Beta Hi Fi.
Mark Hall; Brian Cosgrove — *THORN EMI/HBO Video*

Windom's Way 1957
Romance
75674 90 mins B/W B, V P
Peter Finch, Mary Ure
Based on a novel by James Ramsey Ullman, this is a tale of abiding love.

Rank Film Distributors — *VidAmerica*

Window, The 1949
Suspense
64365 73 mins B/W B, V, 3/4U P
Bobby Driscoll, Barbara Hale, Arthur Kennedy, Ruth Roman
A little boy has a reputation for telling lies, so no one believes him when he says he witnessed a murder... except the killer.
RKO — *Nostalgia Merchant*

Winds of Change 1979
Folklore/Cartoons
65102 90 mins C B, V P
Animated, voice of Peter Ustinov
A magical retelling of five ancient Greek myths which features a disco-rock musical score. Written by Norman Corwin.
Sanrio Film Distribution — *RCA/Columbia Pictures Home Video*

Winds of Kitty Hawk 19??
Aeronautics/Biographical
72457 90 mins C B, V P
Michael Moriarty
The struggles and ultimate triumphs of Orville and Wilbur Wright are dramatized in this E.W. Swackhamer film.
Lawrence Schiller — *U.S.A. Home Video*

Windwalker 1981
Drama
69378 108 mins C B, V P
Trevor Howard
An aged Indian chief shares the extraordinary memories of his life with his grandchildren. Native American dialect and English subtitles are used throughout the film.
Pacific International Pictures — *CBS/Fox Video*

Windy City 1984
Drama
Closed Captioned
77464 103 mins C B, V P
John Shea, Kate Capshaw, Josh Mostel
A group of seven childhood friends must come to terms with the harsh realities of their failed ambitions when they reunite for a weekend in Chicago.
MPAA:R
CBS Theatrical Films — *CBS/Fox Video*

Wings 1927
Adventure
80398 136 mins B/W B, V, LV, CED P
Clara Bow, Buddy Rogers, Richard Arlen, Gary Cooper, directed by William Wellman

 (For explanation of codes, see USE GUIDE and KEY)

Here is the silent film classic about two men who go off to join the Air Force during World War I. Available in VHS and Beta Hi-Fi.
Academy Awards '27: Best Picture
Paramount Pictures — *Paramount Home Video*

Winners of the West **1940**
Western/Serials
14266 169 mins B/W B, V P
Anne Nagel, Dick Foran, James Craig
A landowner schemes to prevent a railroad from running through his property. The railroad's chief engineer leads the good guys in an attempt to prevent sabotage. A serial in thirteen chapters.
Universal — *Video Connection; Nostalgia Merchant; Video Yesteryear*

Winnie the Pooh and Friends **1984**
Cartoons
79179 46 mins C B, V R, P
Animated
Winnie the Pooh and his friends from the Hundred Acre Wood are trying to arrange for a birthday party for Eeyore.
Walt Disney Productions — *Walt Disney Home Video*

Winning **1969**
Drama
64560 123 mins C B, V P
Paul Newman, Joanne Woodward, Robert Wagner, Richard Thomas
A race car driver will let nothing stand in the way of his winning the Indianapolis 500, including his wife.
MPAA:PG
Universal — *MCA Home Video*

Winning Edge, The—John McEnroe/Ivan Lendl—Private Lessons with the Pros **1985**
Tennis
81164 45 mins C B, V P
Stars John McEnroe and Ivan Lendl give a step-by-step demonstration of basic tennis maneuvers.
Video Tennis Productions — *Vestron Video*

Winning of the West **1953**
Western
62873 57 mins B/W B, V P, T
Gene Autry, Smiley Burnette
Ranger Gene vows to protect a crusading publisher from unscrupulous crooks.
Columbia — *Blackhawk Films*

Winning Tradition: 1977 New York Yankees, A **1977**
Baseball
33828 32 mins C B, V P
Thurman Munson, Ron Guidry, Graig Nettles, Reggie Jackson, Mickey Rivers
Highlights of the Yankees 1977 season in which they came from behind to beat the Kansas City Royals in the ninth inning of the fifth and final American League Championship game, then went on to defeat the Los Angeles Dodgers in a six-game World Series.
Major League Baseball — *Major League Baseball Productions*

Winslow Boy, The **1948**
Drama
63326 112 mins B/W B, V R, P
Robert Donat, Cedric Hardwicke, Margaret Leighton, Frank Lawton, directed by Anthony Asquith
This film fictionalizes the events of a famous Edwardian court case, in which a cadet at the Royal Naval College was wrongly accused of theft and expelled. His father fought it through the courts to a satisfactory conclusion.
British Lion — *THORN EMI/HBO Video; Movie Buff Video*

Winsome Witch **196?**
Cartoons
69293 55 mins C B, V P
Animated
This tape is a compilation of "Winsome Witch" cartoons, in which a good-natured witch helps people in distress.
Hanna-Barbera — *Worldvision Home Video*

Winter Kills **1979**
Drama
37408 97 mins C B, V P
Jeff Bridges, John Huston, Anthony Perkins
The investigation of the fifteen-year-old assassination of a President results in numerous plots and counter-plots, intrigues and assumed identities.
MPAA:R
Avco Embassy — *CBS/Fox Video*

Winter Light **1962**
Drama
65629 80 mins B/W B, V P
Max von Sydow, Gunnar Bjornstrand, Ingrid Thulin, directed by Ingmar Bergman
"Winter Light" examines a day in the life of a tormented, widowed pastor who has lost his faith in God and searches for the spiritual guidance he is unable to give to his congregation.
Janus Films — *Embassy Home Entertainment*

Winter of Our Dreams 1983
Drama
65444 89 mins C B, V P
Judy Davis, Bryan Brown
A lonely prostitute becomes romantically involved with a married bookshop owner. Her love turns into a burning obsession until she is forced to free herself from her old dependencies and begin a new life.
Satori Entertainment Corp — *U.S.A. Home Video*

Winter Training 1982
Aeronautics
47787 45 mins C B, V, 3/4U P
This edited version of "Threshold: The Blue Angels Experience" contains the most spectacular highlights of the performance by the Navy's famed precision aerobatics demonstration team.
Paul Marlow — *Aero/Space Visuals Society*

Wishmaker, The 1985
Fairy tales
81613 54 mins C B, V P
A young man squanders the three wishes granted to him for helping a strange old woman and her timid daughter.
Video Gems — *Video Gems*

Witch Who Came from the Sea, The 1976
Horror
72957 98 mins C B, V P
Millie Perkins, Loni Chapman, Vanessa Brown
A witch terrorizes the ships at sea in this adult drama.
MPAA:R
Matt Cimber — *Unicorn Video*

Witches' Brew 1979
Comedy
64977 98 mins C B, V, CED P
Teri Garr, Richard Benjamin, Lana Turner
Three young women try to use their undeveloped skills in witchcraft and black magic to help their husbands get a prestigious position at a university, with calamitous yet hilarious results.
MPAA:PG
Merritt-White Ltd — *Embassy Home Entertainment*

Witching Time 1984
Horror
80480 60 mins C B, V P
Jon Finch, Prunella Gee, Patrica Quinn, Ian McCulloch
A young composer is visited by a 17th-Century witch while his wife is away from home. When the wife returns, both women fight to possess him. In Beta Hi-Fi and VHS Stereo.
Hammer Films — *Thriller Video*

With Buffalo Bill on the U.P. Trail 1925
Western
69571 74 mins B/W B, V, FO P
Roy Stewart, Cullen Landis, Kathryn McGuire
Young Buffalo Bill Cody, wagon train scout, leads his caravan of settlers Westward through danger and uncharted land.
Independent — *Video Yesteryear*

With Six You Get Eggroll 1968
Comedy
80138 95 mins C B, V P
Doris Day, Brian Keith, Pat Carroll, Alice Ghostley, directed by Howard Morris
A widow with three sons and a widower with a daughter decide to tie the knot despite their children's hatred for one another.
National General — *Playhouse Video; CBS/Fox Video*

Without a Trace 1983
Drama
69374 119 mins C B, V, CED P
Kate Nelligan, Judd Hirsch
A mother becomes frantic when her 6-year-old son disappears, and a detective steps in to help.
MPAA:PG
Stanley Jaffe — *CBS/Fox Video*

Without Reservations 1946
Comedy
13196 101 mins B/W B, V P
Claudette Colbert, John Wayne
Hollywood-bound novelist encounters a Marine flyer and his pal aboard a train.
RKO; Mervyn LeRoy — *United Home Video; Video Connection*

Witness for the Prosecution 1957
Mystery/Drama
64563 114 mins B/W B, V, CED P
Charles Laughton, Tyrone Power, Marlene Dietrich, Elsa Lanchester, directed by Billy Wilder
An unemployed man is accused of murdering a wealthy widow whom he befriended. What starts out as a straightforward court case becomes increasingly complicated in this adaptation of an Agatha Christie stage play.
United Artists — *CBS/Fox Video*

Wiz, The 1978
Musical/Fantasy
48639 133 mins C B, V, LV P
Diana Ross, Michael Jackson, Nipsey Russell, Ted Ross, Mabel King, Thelma Carpenter
A version of the long-time favorite "The Wizard of Oz," based on the Broadway musical. It is

reset in a fantasy version of New York City, centering on a young black woman searching for her identity.
MPAA:G
Universal — *MCA Home Video*

Wizard of Mars, The 1964
Science fiction
80183 81 mins C B, V P
John Carradine, Roger Gentry
Four astronauts encounter alien terrors and an evil wizard when their spaceship crash lands on Mars.
NTA — *Republic Pictures Home Video*

Wizard of Oz, The 1982
Fantasy
65402 78 mins C B, V R, P
Animated
The animated version of the classic film "The Wizard of Oz" is ideally suited for young children. Featured are the voices of Lorne Greene and Aileen Quinn. In stereo VHS and Beta Hi-Fi.
Paramount — *Paramount Home Video*

Wizard of Oz, The 1939
Musical/Fantasy
44640 101 mins C B, V, LV, CED P
Judy Garland, Ray Bolger, Frank Morgan, Bert Lahr, Jack Haley, directed by Victor Fleming
A Kansas farm girl dreams she and her dog are somewhere over the rainbow, in the wonderful land of Oz. On her adventure to find the "Great Oz" she is joined by the Scarecrow, the Tin Man, and the Cowardly Lion. Based on the book by Frank L. Baum.
Academy Awards '39: Best Original Music Score (Stothart); Best Song: "Over the Rainbow" (Harburg and Arlen).
MGM — *MGM/UA Home Video*

Wok Before You Run 1984
Cookery
73703 60 mins C B, V P
This program explains how to use a wok in cooking and even comes with a wok when you purchase the videocassette.
AM Available
Steven Yan — *Embassy Home Entertainment*

Wolf Lake 1979
Drama
75488 90 mins C B, V P
Rod Steiger, David Hoffman
A World War II veteran and a Vietnam army deserter have a clash ofpersonalities.
Unknown — *Prism*

Wolfen 1981
Horror
58257 115 mins C B, V R, P
Albert Finney, Gregory Hines, Tom Noonan, directed by Michael Wadleigh
A thriller which spins a tale of myth and menace as creatures from the darkness live among us.
MPAA:R
Orion Pictures — *Warner Home Video*

Wolfman 1982
Horror
63354 91 mins C B, V R, P
Earl Owensby, Kristina Reynolds
In 1910, a young man learns that his family is heir to the curse of the Werewolf.
UG Productions — *THORN EMI/HBO Video*

Woman Called Golda, A 1982
Biographical/Drama
63429 ? mins C B, V R, P
Ingrid Bergman, Leonard Nimoy
Ingrid Bergman portrays the fiery Golda Meir, one of the most powerful women and one of the most important political figures of the 20th century.
Emmy Awards '82: Best Actress (Bergman); Film Editing.
Paramount TV — *Paramount Home Video*

Woman in Grey 1919
Adventure
57433 ? mins B/W B, V P, T
Arline Pretty, Henry Sell
A man and a woman battle wits when they attempt to locate and unravel the Army Code while staying one jump ahead of J. Haviland Hunter, a suave villain after the same fortune. Silent.
Unknown — *Blackhawk Films*

Woman in Red, The 1984
Comedy
80401 87 mins C B, V, LV, CED P
Gene Wilder, Charles Grodin, Kelly Le Brock, Gilda Radner, Judithlvey, directed by Gene Wilder
A married advertising executive searches the streets of San Francisco for a beautiful woman he saw in an underground garage.
Academy Awards '84: Best Song ("I Just Called to Say I Love You") MPAA:PG13
Victor Drai; Orion Pictures — *Vestron Video*

Woman in the Dunes 1964
Drama
33443 127 mins B/W B, V P
Directed by Hiroshi Teshigahara
A man and a woman are trapped in a shack at the bottom of a sand pit among isolated dunes. Based on the highly acclaimed novel by Kobe Abe. In Japanese with English subtitles.

JA
Unknown — *Sheik Video; Western Film & Video Inc; Budget Video; Video Action*

Woman in the Moon **1929**
Science fiction
07285 115 mins B/W B, V, 3/4U P
Klaus Pohl, Willie Fritsch, Gustav von Wagenheim, Gerda Maurus, directed by Fritz Lang.
An incongruous mixture of people embark upon a trip to the moon and discover water, an area with atmosphere, and gold. (Silent with musical soundtrack).
UFA — *International Historic Films; Video Yesteryear; Festival Films*

Woman of Paris, A/Sunnyside **1923**
Comedy/Drama
81551 111 mins B/W B, V P
Charlie Chaplin, Adolphe Menjou, Edna Purviance, directed by Charlie Chaplin
This double feature highlights the talents of Charlie Chaplin. "A Woman of Paris" is the tragic story of a country girl who winds up a kept woman and an overworked hotel handyman almost loses his girlfriend and his job in "Sunnyside."
United Artists — *Playhouse Video*

Woman of the Town, The **1943**
Western
66406 90 mins B/W B, V P
Claire Trevor, Albert Dekker, Barry Sullivan
The story of frontier marshal Bat Masterson and Dora Hall, the dance hall girl he loved.
United Artists — *Movie Buff Video; Independent United Distributors*

Woman of the Year **1942**
Comedy
58704 114 mins B/W B, V P
Spencer Tracy, Katharine Hepburn, directed by George Stevens
The first of the classic Tracy/Hepburn films concerns the rocky marriage of a political columnist and a sportswriter.
Academy Awards '42: Best Original Screenplay (Ring Lardner, Jr.). Film Daily Poll '42: Ten Best of Year.
MGM — *MGM/UA Home Video*

Woman Rebels, A **1936**
Drama
10055 88 mins B/W B, V P, T
Katharine Hepburn, Herbert Marshall, Elizabeth Allan, Donald Crisp, Van Heflin
Courageous Victorian woman challenges establishment with radical positions on womens' rights.
RKO; Pandro S Berman — *Blackhawk Films*

Women, The **1939**
Comedy-Drama
77379 133 mins B/W B, V, LV P
Norma Shearer, Joan Crawford, Rosalind Russell, Joan Fontaine, Paulette Goddard, Ruth Hussey, Marjorie Main, directed by George Cukor
An adaptation of the Clare Boothe Luce play about a group of women who destroy their best friends' reputations at various social gatherings. Includes a Technicolor fashion show sequence.
MGM — *MGM/UA Home Video*

Women in Love **1970**
Drama
58840 129 mins C B, V, CED P
Glenda Jackson, Jennie Linden, Alan Bates, Oliver Reed, Eleanor Bron
D. H. Lawrence's novel about two girls having their first sexual encounters in the Midlands during the 1920's provides the basis for this film.
Academy Awards '70:; Best Actress (Jackson). MPAA:R
United Artists — *CBS/Fox Video*

Women's Track and Field **1985**
Track athletics
81598 50 mins C B, V P
8 pgms
Coach Ken Foreman demonstrates the basic mechanical techniques for various women's track and field events.
1.Talent Search 2.Javelin 3.Long Jump 4.High Jump 5.Discus/Shot Put 6.Sprints, Hurdles & Relays 7.Middle Distance Running 8.Conditioning
Morris Video — *Morris Video*

Wonderful World of Puss 'N Boots, The **1970**
Adventure
63380 80 mins C B, V P
Animated
This is an animated version of the classic children's adventure tale of a clever, brave cat.
MPAA:G
Toei Company — *Media Home Entertainment; Vestron Video*

Woodstock **1970**
Musical
38957 180 mins C B, V R, P
Canned Heat, Richie Havens, The Who, Joan Baez, Country Joe and the Fish, Jimi Hendrix, Santana, Crosby Stills and Nash
A chronicle of the great 1969 Woodstock rock concert, celebrating the music and lifestyle of the late sixties. Classic performances by a great number of popular rock performers and groups. Available on two tapes, labeled "Woodstock I" and "Woodstock II," each running 90 minutes.

Academy Awards '70: Best Feature Documentary. MPAA:R
Wadleigh Maurice Ltd; Bob Maurice — *Warner Home Video; RCA VideoDiscs*

Woody Woodpecker and His Friends, Volume I 1982
Cartoons
62781 80 mins C B, V, LV, CED P
Animated
Ten favorite 1940-1955 Walter Lantz "cartunes" were chosen for this tape: "Knock Knock," "Bandmaster," "Ski for Two," "Hot Noon," "The Legend of Rockabye Point," "Wet Blanket Policy," "To Catch a Woodpecker," "Musical Moments from Chopin," "Bats in the Belfry" and "Crazy Mixed-Up Pup."
Walter Lantz — *MCA Home Video*

Woody Woodpecker and His Friends, Volume III 1984
Cartoons
79677 55 mins C B, V P
Animated
A collection of eight classic cartoons featuring Woody, Andy Panda, and Chilly Willy circa 1940-1944.
Walter Lantz; Universal — *MCA Home Video*

Woody Woodpecker and His Friends, Volume II 1983
Cartoons
65339 59 mins C B, V P
Animated
A compilation of 8 classic cartoons from 1941 through 1954 selected by Woody's creator, Walter Lantz. Woody Woodpecker, Andy Panda and Wally Walrus are featured.
Walter Lantz Productions; Universal — *MCA Home Video*

Word, The 1978
Drama
78361 400 mins C B, V P
David Janssen, James Whitmore, Eddie Albert, John Huston, Florinda Bolkan
When a public relations executive is hired to promote a new Bible, he stumbles across treachery and murder.
Stonehenge Prods; Charles Fries Prods — *U.S.A. Home Video*

Work/Police 1916
Comedy
58656 54 mins B/W B, V, FO P
Charlie Chaplin, Billy Armstrong, Charles Insley, Marta Golden, Edna Purviance, directed by Charlie Chaplin
Two Chaplin two-reelers: "Work (The Paper Hanger)" (1915), in which Charlie is hired to repaper a house; and "Police" (1916), in which Charlie plays an ex-con who is released into the cruel world. Silent with music score.
Essanay — *Video Yesteryear*

Working Girls 1975
Drama
79766 80 mins C B, V P
Sarah Kennedy, Laurie Rose, Mark Thomas
Three girls who share an apartment in Los Angeles are willing to do anything for money. MPAA:R
Independent — *United Home Video*

Working Stiffs 1979
Comedy
81108 75 mins C B, V R, P
Jim Belushi, Michael Keaton, Val Bisoglio, Allan Arbus, Lorna Patterson
This is a collection of the first three episodes from the series about two brothers who seek to climb the corporate ladder while working as janitors in their uncle's office building.
Paramount TV — *Paramount Home Video*

World According to Garp, The 1982
Comedy
63123 136 mins C B, V, CED R, P
Robin Williams, Mary Beth Hurt, John Lithgow, directed by George Roy Hill
This film version of John Irving's popular novel chronicles the life of T.S. Garp, a bizarre everyman beset by the destructive forces of modern society.
MPAA:R
Warner Bros — *Warner Home Video*

World at War 1943
World War II
50618 44 mins B/W B, V, 3/4U P
Directed by Samuel Spewack
The events from 1931-1941 which led to the U.S. involvement in World War II are documented by newsreels and enemy film footage.
Office of War Information — *International Historic Films; Spotlite Video*

World at War, The 1980
World War II/Documentary
59699 104 mins B/W B, V R, P
Narrated by Sir Laurence Olivier
The highly acclaimed documentary about World War II told through newsreel footage, containing remarkable interviews with statesmen, military leaders, and the men and women who fought it.
Thames Video — *THORN EMI/HBO Video*

World at War, The 1980
World War II/Documentary
69628 52 mins B/W B, V R, P

Narrated by Sir Laurence Olivier 26 pgms
This 26-volume series depicts, through actual film footage, all of the horror and heroism of World War II in great historical detail. Each program is available separately.
1.A New Germany 1933-39 2.Distant War 1939-40 3.France Falls—May-June 1940 4.Alone—Britain—May 1940-June 1941 5.Barbarossa—June-December 1941 6.Banzai—Japan Strikes 7.On Our Way—America Enters the War 8.Desert—The War in North Africa 9.Stalingrad 10.Wolfpack 11.Red Star 12.Whirlwind 13.Tough Old Gut 14.It's a Lovely Day Tomorrow 15.Home Fires 16.Inside the Reich—Germany 1940-44 17.Morning 18.Occupation 19.Pincers 20.Genocide 21.Nemesis 22.Japan 1941-45 23.The Island to Island War 24.The Bomb 25.Reckoning 26.Remember
Jeremy Isaacs; Thames Television — *THORN EMI/HBO Video*

World of Apu, The 1959
Drama
55810 103 mins B/W B, V P
Directed by Satyajit Ray
The concluding part of Ray's highly acclaimed "Apu Trilogy" covering Apu's manhood. In Bengali dialogue with English subtitles.
India — *Festival Films; Budget Video; Video Yesteryear*

World of dBase, The 1984
Electronic data processing
70189 75 mins C B, V P
An instructional guide to the use of the dBase database management computer software program, featuring the advancements of the dBase III system. In Beta Hi-Fi.
Software Video Productions — *RCA/Columbia Pictures Home Video*

World of Hans Christian Andersen, The 1985
Cartoons/Adventure
70566 73 mins C B, V P
Animated
Hans relates the delightful yarns that gave him his start in the story telling business.
Turner Program Services, Inc. — *RCA/Columbia Pictures Home Video*

World of Martial Arts, The 1982
Martial arts
59685 60 mins C B, V P
Narrated by John Saxon, Chuck Norris, Al Thomas
This program offers a basic training in budojujutsu, a combination of techniques from seven different martial arts.
Universal — *MCA Home Video; Optical Programming Associates*

World Series, 1943 1943
Baseball
33864 ? mins B/W B, V P
New York Yankees, St. Louis Cardinals
Both teams incorporate new faces to replace stars serving in the war. The Yankees avenge their previous year's defeat by the Cardinals by winning this World Series four games to one. Spud Chandler pitches two victories for manager Joe McCarthy's Bronx Bombers.
Lou Fonseca — *Major League Baseball Productions*

World Series, 1944 1944
Baseball
33863 ? mins B/W B, V P
St. Louis Cardinals, St Louis Browns
In the first and only series played between two St. Louis teams, the Cardinals prevail in six games, led by shortstop Marty Marion and pitchers Max Lanier and Ted Wilks. First baseman George McQuinn bats .438 for the Browns.
Lou Fonseca — *Major League Baseball Productions*

World Series, 1945 1945
Baseball
33862 ? mins B/W B, V P
Detroit Tigers, Chicago Cubs
Tiger stars recently returned from military service, pitcher Virgil Trucks and slugger Hank Greenberg, lead the Detroit club to a four games to three victory over the Cubs.
Lou Fonseca — *Major League Baseball Productions*

World Series, 1946 1946
Baseball
33861 ? mins B/W B, V P
St. Louis Cardinals, Boston Red Sox
Enos Slaughter scores all the way from first base on Harry Walker's single to score the winning run for the Cardinals in game seven. Harry Breechen recorded three victories for St. Louis against the likes of Red Sox sluggers Ted Williams, Dom DiMaggio, and Rudy York.
Lou Fonseca — *Major League Baseball Productions*

World Series, 1947 1947
Baseball
33860 ? mins B/W B, V P
New York Yankees, Brooklyn Dodgers
Al Gionfriddo's leaping catch of Joe DiMaggio's long drive sends the Yankees and Dodgers into a seventh game showdown. Yankee outfielder Tommy Henrich drives in the winning run and Joe Page hurls five scoreless innings to preserve the victory.
Lou Fonseca — *Major League Baseball Productions*

World Series, 1948 **1948**
Baseball
33859 ? mins B/W B, V P
Cleveland Indians, Boston Braves
Behind the pitching of Bob Lemon and Gene Bearden and the solid fielding of Ken Keltner, Joe Gordon, and Lou Boudreau, the Indians outlast Warren Spahn, Johnny Sain and the rest of the Braves, who were headed for Milwaukee in a few years, in six games.
Lou Fonseca — *Major League Baseball Productions*

World Series, 1949 **1949**
Baseball
33858 ? mins B/W B, V P
New York Yankees, Brooklyn Dodgers
Allie Reynolds and Preacher Roe trade 1-0 victories in the first two games, then the Yankees win the next three with Joe Page, Gerry Coleman, and Johnny Mize in starring roles.
Lou Fonseca — *Major League Baseball Productions*

World Series, 1950 **1950**
Baseball
33848 ? mins B/W B, V P
New York Yankees, Philadelphia Phillies
The "Whiz Kids" of Philadelphia surprise the National League in winning the pennant, but the Yankees, in the midst of five consecutive World Championship seasons, make easy picking of the Phillies in four straight games.
Lou Fonseca — *Major League Baseball Productions*

World Series, 1951 **1951**
Baseball
33852 ? mins B/W B, V P
New York Yankees, New York Giants
The Giants enter the series coming off their emotional playoff victory over the Dodgers which featured Bobby Thompson's "Shot Heard 'Round the World" in the ninth inning of the final game. They run out of miracles against the Yankees however, as Eddie Lopat and Allie Reynolds lead a solid pitching staff to a six-game victory for the Yankees in Joe DiMaggio's final season and Mickey Mantle's first.
Lou Fonseca — *Major League Baseball Productions*

World Series, 1952 **1952**
Baseball
33857 ? mins B/W B, V P
New York Yankees, Brooklyn Dodgers
Vic Raschi and Allie Reynolds win two games apiece for the Yankees and Billy Martin makes a diving catch of Jackie Robinson's pop-up to save the seventh and deciding game for the New Yorkers. Pee Wee Reese and Duke Snider each batted .345 to lead the Dodger effort.
Lou Fonseca — *Major League Baseball Productions*

World Series, 1953 **1953**
Baseball
33856 ? mins B/W B, V P
New York Yankees, Brooklyn Dodgers
Yankee second baseman Billy Martin bats .500 and drives in the winning run in the final game as the Yankees defeat the Dodgers four games to two, capturing their unprecedented fifth consecutive World Series title.
Lou Fonseca — *Major League Baseball Productions*

World Series, 1954 **1954**
Baseball
33849 ? mins B/W B, V P
New York Giants, Cleveland Indians
The Indians won a record 111 games during the regular season, but did not win their next game until the following year. The Giants, sparked by Willie Mays' famous catch of Vic Wertz deep line drive, went on to defeat player-manager Lou Boudreau's Cleveland team in four straight games.
Lou Fonseca — *Major League Baseball Productions*

World Series, 1955 **1955**
Baseball
33850 ? mins B/W B, V P
Brooklyn Dodgers, New York Yankees
It's a dream come true for the bums from Brooklyn. For the first time in six tries the Dodgers beat their cross-town rivals, the hated Yankees, in the World series. Johnny Padres notches three of the Brooklyn wins, including a 2-0 masterpiece in game seven at Yankee Stadium. Sandy Amoros' catch of Yogi Berra's long fly ball thwarted an important Yankee rally and was the key defensive play of the series.
Lou Fonseca — *Major League Baseball Productions*

World Series, 1956 **1956**
Baseball
33855 ? mins B/W B, V P
New York Yankees, Brooklyn Dodgers
The Dodgers came from behind to win each of the first two games, but the Yankees captured the next three contests, including Don Larsen's perfect game in game five at Yankee Stadium. Jackie Robinson's tenth inning hit gave the Dodgers a 1-0 victory in game six to tie the series. The Yankees won easily in the seventh game to give manager Casey Stengel his sixth world championship.
Lou Fonseca — *Major League Baseball Productions*

World Series, 1957 **1957**
Baseball
33851 ? mins B/W B, V P
Milwaukee Braves, New York Yankees
The Braves, led by the hitting of Hank Aaron, Eddie Mathews, and Joe Adcock, surprise Casey Stengel's World Champion Yankees in seven games. Righthander Lew Burdette is the hero, pitching three of the Braves' victories.
Lou Fonseca — *Major League Baseball Productions*

World Series, 1958 **1958**
Baseball
48143 ? mins C B, V P
New York Yankees, Milwaukee Braves
The Yankees avenge their previous year's defeat by the Braves by rallying from a three games to one deficit to defeat Eddie Mathews, Hank Aaron and the hard-hitting Braves in seven games. Mickey Mantle and Whitey Ford spark the Yankee comeback.
Lou Fonseca — *Major League Baseball Productions*

World Series, 1959 **1959**
Baseball
33854 ? mins B/W B, V P
Los Angeles Dodgers, Chicago White Sox
After the White Sox captured the opening game 11-0, the Dodgers, with fine relief pitching by Larry Sherry and steady hitting by Gil Hodges, beat Chicago in six games. Their old Brooklyn fans saw a collection of familiar faces and few new kids playing on a team that now belonged to the West Coast.
Lou Fonseca — *Major League Baseball Productions*

World Series, 1960 **1960**
Baseball
33826 ? mins B/W B, V P
New York Yankees, Pittsburgh Pirates
Bill Mazeroski's leadoff home run off Ralph Terry in the bottom of the ninth in game seven at Forbes Field gives the Pirates a 10-9 victory and wins the World Series over the Yankees, four games to three.
Lou Fonseca — *Major League Baseball Productions*

World Series, 1961 **1961**
Baseball
33853 ? mins B/W B, V P
New York Yankees, Cincinnati Reds
This was the year Roger Maris and Mickey Mantle combined for 115 home runs. Although neither had a very good World Series, Elston Howard, Bobby Richardson, and several reserve players led the Yankees to a four games to one victory over Fred Hutchinson's Reds. Whitey Ford's two pitching victories gave him four straight series wins.
Lou Fonseca — *Major League Baseball Productions*

World Series, 1962 **1962**
Baseball
33824 ? mins C B, V P
New York Yankees, San Francisco Giants
In a series frequently interrupted by rain delays, the Yankees outlast the Giants four games to three. With the Yankees leading by a run with two out in the bottom of the ninth in game seven, the Giants load the bases and big Willie McCovey steps to the plate. His scorching line drive is driven right into the glove of Yankee second baseman Bobby Richardson, for the final out.
Lou Fonseca — *Major League Baseball Productions*

World Series, 1963 **1963**
Baseball
33823 ? mins C B, V P
Los Angeles Dodgers, New York Yankees
Sandy Koufax breaks Carl Erskine's World Series strikeout record, fanning fifteen while the Dodgers are en route to a four game sweep over the defending champion Yankees.
Lou Fonseca — *Major League Baseball Productions*

World Series, 1964 **1964**
Baseball
33822 ? mins C B, V P
St. Louis Cardinals, New York Yankees
Young Yankee pitchers Jim Bouton and Mel Stottlemyre are impressive, but Bob Gibson is even better for the Cardinals. A grand slam home run by Ken Boyer is the big hit in this series, won by the Cardinals four games to three. The great Mickey Mantle, in what is to be his last World Series, adds to his record status for the October Classic.
Lou Fonseca — *Major League Baseball Productions*

World Series, 1965 **1965**
Baseball
33821 ? mins C B, V P
Los Angeles Dodgers, Minnesota Twins
Sandy Koufax and Don Drysdale stymie the big Minnesota bats of Harmon Killebrew and Bob Allison long enough for the Dodgers to squeak by the Twins in seven games. "Sweet" Lou Johnson swings a hot bat for the Dodgers.
Lou Fonseca — *Major League Baseball Productions*

World Series, 1966 **1966**
Baseball
33820 ? mins C B, V P
Baltimore Orioles, Los Angeles Dodgers
Dave McNally, Jim Palmer, Steve Barber, and Wally Bunker, with relief help from Moe

Drabowsky, send the Dodgers down in four straight. Sandy Koufax and Don Drysdale pitch well for the Dodgers, but the Robinsons, Frank and Brooks, provide timely hitting for the Orioles.
Lou Fonseca — *Major League Baseball Productions*

World Series, 1967 **1967**
Baseball
33819 ? mins C B, V P
St. Louis Cardinals, Boston Red Sox
The Red Sox, ninth place finishers the previous year, are led to the series by Carl Yastrzemski, Tony Conigliaro, and Ken Harrelson. Boston ace Jim Lonborg flirts with a no-hitter in one game, but the St. Louis bats finally quell the Sox in seven games, led by Lou Brock, Orlando Cepeda, and Tim McCarver, and the pitching of Bob Gibson.
Lou Fonseca — *Major League Baseball Productions*

World Series, 1968 **19??**
Baseball
33818 ? mins C B, V P
Detroit Tigers, St. Louis Cardinals
The Tigers stage a comeback to beat the Cardinals in seven games after falling behind three games to one. Mickey Lolich tosses three of the Tiger victories and Mickey Stanley, normally a centerfielder, stars at shortstop. Bob Gibson wins two games for the Cardinals, setting a series game strikeout record in the process.
Lou Fonseca — *Major League Baseball Productions*

World Series, 1969 **1969**
Baseball
33817 40 mins C B, V P
New York Mets, Baltimore Orioles
The Miracle Mets stun the world by taking four straight from the mighty Orioles after losing the opening game. Outstanding defensive plays by Tommie Agee and Ron Swoboda stymie Baltimore rallies. Jerry Koosman wins two games, and MVP Donn Clendenon and utility infielder Al Weis pace the Mets' hitting attack.
W and W Prods — *Major League Baseball Productions*

World Series, 1970 **1970**
Baseball
33816 40 mins C B, V P
Baltimore Orioles, Cincinnati Reds
Brooks Robinson's incredible fielding and .429 batting average help the Orioles to a four games to one victory over the Reds. Baltimore's pitching staff silences the Big Red Machine sluggers like Johnny Bench and Lee May.
W and W Prods — *Major League Baseball Productions*

World Series, 1971 **1971**
Baseball
33815 40 mins C B, V P
Pittsburgh Pirates, Baltimore Orioles
The sensational hitting of Roberto Clemente and two clutch pitching wins by Steve Blass lead the Pirates to a seven-game triumph over the defending champion Orioles. This series featured the first night game in World Series history.
W and W Productions — *Major League Baseball Productions*

World Series, 1972 **1972**
Baseball
33814 40 mins C B, V P
Oakland A's, Cincinnati Reds
The A's win a seven-game thriller without their star outfielder Reggie Jackson, who is lost to an injury. Gene Tenace provides the home run heroics, and MVP left fielder Joe Rudi makes a remarkable catch that many consider as the turning point of the series.
W and W Prods — *Major League Baseball Productions*

World Series, 1973 **1973**
Baseball
33813 40 mins C B, V P
Oakland A's, New York Mets
The Oakland A's win their second consecutive title, in seven games. The talented Mets pitching staff holds the powerful A's in check, but Bert Campaneris and Reggie Jackson belt home runs in the final game to finally subdue the gallant New Yorkers.
W and W Prods — *Major League Baseball Productions*

World Series, 1974 **1974**
Baseball
33812 26 mins C B, V P
Oakland A's, Los Angeles Dodgers
The A's win their third straight world championship in a tightly contested, five game series in which four games were decided by 3-2 scores. The fielding of second baseman Dick Green and relief pitching of series MVP Rollie Fingers makes the difference for the A's.
W and W Prods — *Major League Baseball Productions*

World Series, 1975 **1975**
Baseball
33811 35 mins C B, V P
Cincinnati Reds, Boston Red Sox
In one of the most memorable and exciting World Series ever played, the Reds take a three games to two lead after five games. Carlton Fisk's dramatic 12th inning homer evens the series in game six. The Red Sox take an early lead in the final game, but series MVP Pete Rose and Joe Morgan lead a Cincinnati

comeback to give the Reds their first World Championship in 35 years.
Major League Baseball — *Major League Baseball Productions*

World Series, 1976 **1976**
Baseball
33810 30 mins C B, V P
Cincinnati Reds, New York Yankees
The Reds demolish the Yankees in four straight, led by MVP catcher Johnny Bench. Yankee catcher Thurman Munson performs gallantly, batting .529 for the series. Reds' manager Sparky Anderson is "miked" throughout, giving the viewer a rare glimpse at a manager's feelings during pressure-filled games.
Major League Baseball — *Major League Baseball Productions*

World Series, 1977 **1977**
Baseball
33809 30 mins C B, V P
New York Yankees, Los Angles Dodgers
Yankee slugger Reggie Jackson grabs the spotlight by belting five homers in the series, won by New York 4 games to 2. Jackson's heroics include three consecutive home runs in the final game. Yankee pitcher Mike Torrez goes undefeated in his two starts. This program also captures the antics of Dodger manager Tom Lasorda and sets the mannerisms of baseball players to ballet music.
Major League Baseball — *Major League Baseball Productions*

World Series, 1978 **1978**
Baseball
33808 31 mins C B, V P
New York Yankees, Los Angeles Dodgers
The Yankees beat the Dodgers in six games for the second year in a row. Yankee shortstop Bucky Dent wins the series MVP award while Graig Nettles, Reggie Jackson, Thurman Munson, and rookie Brian Doyle lead the champs at bat and on the field. Ron Cey and Davey Lopes excel for the Dodgers. The victory caps a memorable season for New York, one in which they came from 14 games out of first place in July to eventually win a one-game playoff with the Boston Red Sox for the American League East Championship.
Major League Baseball — *Major League Baseball Productions*

World Series, 1979 **1979**
Baseball
33847 31 mins C B, V P
Pittsburgh Pirates, Baltimore Orioles
Oriole Manager Earl Weaver is hailed as a genius after expertly maneuvering his Birds to a 3-1 lead after four games. Baltimore never won another game in the series though, as MVP Willie "Pops" Stargell and the Pirate relief pitchers rose to the occasion and dominated the remainder of the series. Stargell's two-run homer off Scott McGregor in game seven moved the Pirate ahead to stay.
Major League Baseball — *Major League Baseball Productions*

World Series, 1980 **1980**
Baseball
49548 30 mins C B, V P
Philadelphia Phillies, Kansas City Royals
The clutch hitting of Mike Schmidt and Pete Rose, and the heart-stopping relief provided by Tug McGraw leads the Phillies to a six-game victory over the Royals. George Brett, Willie Aikens, and Amos Otis try to carry the Royals back after falling behind two games to none, but their impressive efforts are not enough to overcome the Phillies.
MAJ — *Major League Baseball Productions; RCA VideoDiscs*

World Series, 1981 **1981**
Baseball
59377 30 mins C B, V P
New York Yankees, Los Angeles Dodgers
The Yankees fall apart after winning the first two games. The series begins to turn in Los Angeles when rookie pitchers Fernando Valenzuela and Dave Righetti meet, with the Dodgers' Valenzuela emerging victorious. Timely hitting by Ron Cey, Steve Yeager, Jay Johnstone and Pedro Guerrero carries the Dodgers to a six-game victory over the faltering Yankees.
Major League Baseball Productions — *Major League Baseball Productions*

World Series, 1982 **1982**
Baseball
64659 45 mins C B, V P
St. Louis Cardinels, Milwaukee Brewers
Willie McGee, Bruce Sutter, and MVP Darrell Porter lead the NL champion Cardinals to victories in games 6 and 7 as the Redbirds defeat the Milwaukee Brewers 4 games to 3. The big bats of Milwaukee's Robin Yount and Cecil Cooper could not overcome the loss of their injured ballpen ace, Rollie Fingers.
Major League Baseball — *Major League Baseball Productions*

World Series, 1984: The Sounds of the Series **1984**
Baseball
81128 36 mins C B, V P
Detroit Tigers, San Diego Padres
Here are the exciting highlights from the 1984 World Series where Sparky Anderson's Tigers mauled Dick Williams' Padres to become the world champions.
Major League Baseball — *Major League Baseball Productions*

 (For explanation of codes, see USE GUIDE and KEY)

World Series, 1983: 1983 World Series 1983
Baseball
81127 36 mins C B, V P
Baltimore Orioles, Philadelphia Phillies
Here are highlights of the 1983 fall classic from which the Baltimore Orioles emerged as the world champions.
Major League Baseball — *Major League Baseball Productions*

World War II: The European Theatre 194?
World War II/Documentary
44984 55 mins B/W B, V P, T
In this footage from the Fox/Movietone newsreel vaults, six separate subjects are covered: "Battle of the Atlantic," "Battle of Britain," "War in the Desert," "Liberation of Paris," "Fall of Hitler's Nazis," and "1945: Year of Triumph."
Movietone — *Blackhawk Films*

World War II: The Pacific Theatre 194?
World War II/Documentary
29471 55 mins B/W B, V P, T
A compilation taken from actual newsreel footage of World War II. The show begins with the authentic scenes of Pearl Harbor and closes with a final surrender of Japan in 1945.
Movietone — *Blackhawk Films*

World War II Video Series—Attack: The Battle of New Britain 1945
World War II/Documentary
66361 50 mins B/W B, V, 3/4U P
A filmed record of the invasion of New Britain in the South Pacific theater of war.
Office of War Information — *Nostalgia Merchant*

World War II Video Series—Something for Our Boys 1945
World War II/Documentary
66362 50 mins B/W B, V, 3/4U P
Judy Garland, Bob Hope, Carmen Miranda and others
A selection of shorts featuring many Hollywood and radio stars performing overseas for the pleasure of Allied troops during 1943-1945.
Office of War Information — *Nostalgia Merchant*

World War II Video Series—The Stillwell Road 1945
Documentary/World War II
66337 50 mins B/W B, V, 3/4U P
The story of the China-Burma-India campaign during World War II, with authentic documentary footage of jungle battles and aerial combat.
US Army — *Nostalgia Merchant*

World War II Video Series—Tried by Fire! 19??
World War II/Documentary
66360 50 mins B/W B, V, 3/4U P
The combat history of World War II's 84th Infantry Division, from its activities early in the war through the Battle of the Bulge, is chronicled.
Office of War Information — *Nostalgia Merchant*

World's Greatest Photography Course, The 1983
Photography
66000 90 mins C B, V P
A step-by-step course designed for people who want to learn how to take great 35mm pictures.
Video Corporation of America — *VidAmerica*

Worth the Wait! 1981
Baseball
55597 59 mins C B, V P
Highlights of the 1980 World Series between the Kansas City Royals and the Philadelphia Phillies, and the 1980 All-Star Game in which the National League stars defeated the American League stars in the Summer Classic.
Major League Baseball — *VidAmerica*

Wrestling Queen 1975
Sports/Circus
70735 79 mins C B, V P
Vivian Vachon, Black Jack Mulligan, Andre the Giant, Killer Kowalski, Mad Dog and Killer Vachon
This tape presents twelve wrestlers wrestling all out.
MPAA:PG
Vachon Video — *Active Home Video*

Wrestling's Bloopers, Bleeps and Bodyslams 1985
Sports/Outtakes and bloopers
81393 60 mins C B, V P
Captain Lou Albano, Vince McMahon, Freddy Blassie, Ivan Putsky, Paul "The Butcher" Vachon
Catch your favorite wrestling stars off guard as they commit many gaffes and goofs in this edited collection of outtakes from the "Tuesday Night Titans" program
Evart Enterprises — *Coliseum Video*

Wright Brothers: Masters of the Sky, The 19??
Biographical/Aeronautics
69586 47 mins C B, V P

Two young daredevils defy traditional thought, fix their eyes and hopes on the sky, and overcome a steady stream of failures to provide man with the means to fly.
Unknown — *VidAmerica*

Wrong Box, The **1966**
Comedy
80382 105 mins C B, V P
Peter Sellers, Dudley Moore, Peter Cook, Michael Caine, Ralph Richardson, Gerald Sim
Two elderly Victorian brothers try to kill each other to collect on a Fortune.
Columbia Pictures — *RCA/Columbia Pictures Home Video*

Wrong Is Right **1982**
Adventure/Comedy
60339 117 mins C B, V P
Sean Connery, Katherine Ross, Robert Conrad, George Grizzard, Henry Silva, directed by Richard Brooks
A black comedy revolving around international terrorism, news reporting and the CIA.
MPAA:R
Columbia — *RCA/Columbia Pictures Home Video*

Wrong Man, The **1956**
Suspense
47618 126 mins B/W B, V R, P
Henry Fonda, Vera Miles, Anthony Quayle, directed by Alfred Hitchcock
A musician is accused of a robbery that he did not commit. Part of the "A Night at the Movies" series, this tape simulates a 1956 movie evening, with a color Bugs Bunny cartoon, "A Star Is Bored," a newsreel and coming attractions for "Toward the Unknown."
Warner Bros — *Warner Home Video*

Wuthering Heights **1939**
Drama/Romance
81476 104 mins B/W B, V, LV P
Laurence Olivier, Merle Oberon, David Niven, Donald Crisp, Geraldine Fitzgerald, directed by William Wyler
This is the story of the doomed romance between a young aristocratic girl and the boy who works in her father's stable. Based on the classic Emily Bronte novel.
Samuel Goldwyn — *Embassy Home Entertainment*

X

X -- The Man with X-Ray Eyes **1963**
Science fiction
65140 79 mins C B, V R, P
Ray Milland, Diana Van Der Vlis, Harold J. Stone, directed by Roger Corman
A scientist uses himself as a guinea pig to test a new serum on his eyes that will enable him to see through things. Though a success, the effect continues to strengthen, driving the scientist to the brink of madness.
American International — *Warner Home Video*

Xanadu **1980**
Musical/Fantasy
48640 96 mins C B, V, LV P
Olivia Newton-John, Michael Beck, Gene Kelly
A beautiful muse comes down to earth and meets an artist and a nightclub owner. She helps the two of them fulfill their dreams, as they collaborate on a roller-disco venture.
MPAA:PG
Universal — *MCA Home Video*

X-Tro **1983**
Science fiction/Horror
65088 80 mins C B, V, CED R, P
Philip Sayer, Bernice Stegers, Danny Brainin, Simon Nash, Maryam D'Abo
A man who was mysteriously kidnapped by aliens returns to his family three years later. Infected by alien spores, he transmits the ghastly sickness by biting his wife and son.
MPAA:R
New Line Cinema — *THORN EMI/HBO Video*

Y

Y&T Live at the San Francisco Civic **1985**
Music-Performance
81525 60 mins C B, V P
Y&T perform their own brand of headbanging heavy metal in this concert taped at the San Francisco Civic Center.
A&M Video — *A & M Video; RCA/Columbia Pictures Home Video*

Yakuzza, The **1975**
Adventure
78627 112 mins C B, V P
Robert Mitchum, Richard Jordan, Takakura Ken, Brian Keith, directed by Sydney Pollack
An ex G.I. returns to Japan to help an old army buddy find his kidnapped daughter.
MPAA:R
Warner Bros — *Warner Home Video*

(For explanation of codes, see USE GUIDE and KEY)

Yankee Clipper **1927**
Adventure
10118 51 mins B/W B, V P, T
William Boyd, Elinor Fair, directed by Rupert Julian.
Deceit, treachery, and romance are combined in this depiction of fierce race from China to New England between the Yankee Clipper, and the English ship, Lord of the Isles.
PDC — *Blackhawk Films; Classic Video Cinema Collector's Club*

Yankee Doodle **198?**
Cartoons
79199 30 mins C B, V P
Animated
A blacksmith and two Militiamen help Paul Revere to complete his midnight ride.
Rankin Bass Studios — *Prism*

Yankee Doodle Cricket **1976**
Language arts
00232 26 mins C B, V, 3/4U, FO P
Patriotic animals compose "Yankee Doodle Dandy," help Thomas Jefferson write The Declaration, and assist Paul Revere.
AM Available
Chuck Jones Entp — *The Center for Humanities; Family Home Entertainment*

Yankee Doodle Dandy **1942**
Musical-Drama
13317 126 mins B/W B, V, LV P
James Cagney, Joan Leslie, Walter Huston, Richard Whorf, directed by Michael Curtiz
Nostalgic view of the Golden Era of show business and the man who made it glitter—George M. Cohan. His early days, triumphs, songs, musicals, and romances.
Academy Awards '42: Best Actor (Cagney); Best Sound Recording; Best Musical Scores.
Warner Bros — *CBS/Fox Video; RCA VideoDiscs*

Yankee Doodle in Berlin **1919**
Comedy
64305 60 mins B/W B, V P, T
Ford Sterling, Ben Turpin, Marie Prevost, Bothwell Browne
A spoof of World War I dramas with the hero dressing up as a woman and seducing the Kaiser into giving up his war plans. Typical Sennett slapstick with a music and effects score added to the silent film.
Mack Sennett — *Blackhawk Films*

Year of Living Dangerously, The **1982**
Adventure
Closed Captioned
64940 114 mins C B, V, CED P
Mel Gibson, Sigourney Weaver, Linda Hunt, directed by Peter Weir
An Australian journalist covering a political story in Indonesia, circa 1965, becomes involved with a British attache at the height of the bloody fighting and rioting in Jakarta during the coup against President Sukarno.
Academy Awards '83: Best Supporting Actress (Hunt) MPAA:PG
MGM/UA — *MGM/UA Home Video*

Yearling, The **1946**
Drama
81494 128 mins C B, V P
Gregory Peck, Jane Wyman, Calude Jarman Jr., Chill Wills, directed by Clarence Brown
This is an adaptation of the Marjorie Kinnan Rawlings novel about a young boy's love for a yearling fawn.
Academy Awards '46: Best Cinematography?Best Art Direction?Best Interior Direction
MGM — *MGM/UA Home Video*

Yellow Hair and the Fortress of Gold **1984**
Exploitation
70690 102 mins C B, V P
Laurene Landon, Ken Robertson, directed by Matt Cimber
This film follows the adventures of an Indian Princess in her quest for the elk horn containing the man that will lead her to the fortress of gold.
MPAA:R
Crown — *Lightning Video*

Yellow Rose of Texas, The **1944**
Western
10684 55 mins B/W B, V P
Roy Rogers, Dale Evans
Roy Rogers works as an undercover insurance agent to clear the name of an old man falsely accused of a stagecoach robbery.
Republic — *Video Connection; Sheik Video; Cable Films; Video Yesteryear; Discount Video Tapes*

Yellowbeard **1983**
Comedy
65348 97 mins C B, V, LV P
Marty Feldman, Cheech and Chong, Madeline Kahn, Peter Boyle, James Mason, Graham Chapman, John Cleese
This is the saga of the infamous priate, whose 15 years in prison have done little to squelch his appetitie for larceny, lechery and lunacy.
MPAA:PG
Carter De Haven — *Vestron Video*

Yellowstone **1936**
Mystery
66407 65 mins B/W B, V P

Andy Devine, Ralph Morgan, Judith Barrett
An ex-con is murdered at Yellowstone National Park, at the site of a hidden cache of money.
Universal — *Movie Buff Video; Discount Video Tapes*

Yentl 1983
Musical-Drama
70236 134 mins C B, V, CED P
Barbra Streisand, Mandy Patinkin, Amy Irving, Nehemiah Persoff, directed by Barbra Streisand
A young woman must disguise herself as a man in order to enter the forbidden world of knowledge.
United Artists — *CBS/Fox Video*

Yeomen of the Guard, The 19??
Opera/Comedy
65494 112 mins C B, V P
Joel Grey, Elizabeth Gale, David Hillman, Claire Powell, Alfred Marks
A colonel, condemned to death in the Tower of London on false charges of sorcery, is helped to escape by a family loyal to him. In order to save his own life, he masks his true identity and takes his place among the yeomen of the guard, beginning the series of misadventures—some humorous, some tragic—that make "Yeomen of the Guard" one of Gilbert and Sullivan's most beloved musicals.
Moving Pictures Company Ltd — *CBS/Fox Video*

Yes, Giorgio 1982
Musical/Comedy
60399 111 mins C B, V, CED P
Luciano Pavarotti, Kathryn Harrold
An opera star falls in love with his female doctor. Songs include "If We Were in Love," "I Left My Heart in San Francisco," and arias by Verdi, Donizetti and Puccini. VHS in stereo.
MPAA:PG
MGM — *MGM/UA Home Video*

Yessongs 1973
Music-Performance
80186 70 mins C B, V P
Steve Howe, Rick Wakeman, Jon Anderson, Chris Squire, Alan White
The exciting progressive rock sounds of Yes are captured in this 1973 concert.
Vistar International Productions — *VidAmerica*

Yes You Can Microwave 1984
Cookery
70569 53 mins C B, V P
Donovan Jon Fandre
This program offers viewers a short basic course in microwave cooking.
AM Available
JCI Video — *JCI Video*

Yesterday Machine 196?
Science fiction
66239 85 mins B/W B, V R, P
Tim Holt
A "camp" sci-fi film combining Nazis and rock 'n' roll.
Russ Marker — *Video City Productions*

Yoga for Pregnancy 1984
Yoga/Pregnancy
79346 60 mins C B, V, 3/4U P
Integral Hatha Yoga instructor Georgina Clarke teaches a specially designed system of yoga exercises for the expectant mother.
LDR International — *LDR International*

Yoga Moves with Alan Finger 1983
Yoga/Physical fitness
65311 60 mins C B, V, LV, CED P
This is a complete introductory program to more than 26 yoga positions which help to tone and strengthen the body and to develop flexibility.
Lynda Guber — *MCA Home Video*

Yogi's First Christmas 1980
Cartoons
69590 100 mins C B, V P
Animated
Yogi Bear joins his friends for a musical celebration of Christmas at the Jellystone Lodge.
Hanna Barbera — *Worldvision Home Video*

Yojimbo 1962
Film-Avant-garde
06244 138 mins B/W B, V P
Toshiro Mifuen, Eijiro Tono, Suuzu Yamda, directed by Akira Kurosawa
19th century town is scene for political uprisings. Professional killer comes, and battling political sides bid for his services. Japanese film, English subtitles.
JA
Japan — *Budget Video; International Historic Films; Sheik Video; Cable Films; Video Yesteryear; Discount Video Tapes; Video Action*

Yoko Ono Then and Now 1984
Music-Performance/Interview
78367 56 mins C B, V P
Yoko Ono looks back on her life before and after John Lennon along with songs performed by both John and Yoko.
Barbara Graustark — *Music Media*

Yol 1982
Drama
66348 111 mins C B, V P
Tarik Akan, Serif Sezer, directed by Serif Goren

Five Turkish prisoners are granted temporary leave to visit their families in this bittersweet Turkish-made feature.
Cannes Film Festival '82: Palme d'Or for Best Picture. MPAA:PG
Triumph Films; Edi Hubschmid — *RCA/Columbia Pictures Home Video*

Yor, the Hunter from the Future 1983
Fantasy/Adventure
69615 88 mins C B, V P
Reb Brown
Lost in a time warp where the past and the future mysteriously collide, Yor sets out on a search for his real identity, with his only clue a golden medallion around his neck.
MPAA:PG
Michele Marsala — *RCA/Columbia Pictures Home Video; RCA VideoDiscs*

You and Me, Kid—Volume 3 1985
Language arts
77534 111 mins C B, V R, P
Sonny Melendrez, Gallagher, Ruby Keeler, Patrick Wayne, Lynn Redgrave.
Host Sonny Melendrez and his special guests lead children through various games, songs and exercises that the whole family can enjoy.
Walt Disney Productions — *Walt Disney Home Video*

You and Me, Kid Volume I 1983
Family/Parents
72798 111 mins C B, V P
Four complete half-hour programs encourage parents and children to participate in the viewing of "You and Me, Kid" together.
Walt Disney Productions — *Walt Disney Home Video*

You and Me, Kid Volume 2 1985
Family/Children
80354 111 mins C B, V R, P
A collection of four episodes from The Disney Channel series that features activities that children and parents can do together.
Walt Disney Productions — *Walt Disney Home Video*

You Bet Your Life 195?
Game show
33694 120 mins B/W B, V, 3/4U P
Four top episodes from the hit quiz show starring Groucho Marx and his flunkie, George Fenneman. Guest stars Harry Ruby and William Peter Blatty appear in two of the shows.
NBC — *Shokus Video*

You Can Do It 1984
Magic
80154 60 mins C B, V P
Shari Lewis aided by Charley Horse and Lamb Chop, shows children how to perform magic tricks
MGM/UA Home Video — *MGM/UA Home Video*

You Can Win: Negotiating For Power, Love and Money 1983
Psychology
81439 55 mins C B, V P
Dr. Tessa Albert Warschaw
Secrets for getting what you want from your boss, your kids and your mate are revealed.
Available in Stereo Hi Fi for both formats.
MCA Home Video — *MCA Home Video*

You Can't Take It With You 1984
Comedy
80116 116 mins C B, V P
Colleen Dewhurst, James Coco, Jason Robards, directed by Ellis Raab
A taped performance of the Rodgers and Hart comedy about the strange pasttimes of the Sycamore family.
Ellen M Krass Productions — *Vestron Video*

You Light Up My Life 1977
Drama
21298 90 mins C B, V P
Didi Conn, Michael Zaslow, Melanie Mayron
The story of a young girl trying to break into the music business and establish herself.
Academy Awards '79: Best Song ("You Light Up My Life").
Columbia — *RCA/Columbia Pictures Home Video*

You Only Live Once 1937
Drama
50959 86 mins B/W B, V R, P
Henry Fonda, Sylvia Sidney, Ward Bond, directed by Fritz Lang
An ill-fated young couple are separated when he is put in prison. He shoots his way out and the two begin a harrowing run from the law.
AM Available
United Artists — *Monterey Home Video*

You Only Live Once 1937
Drama
66638 86 mins B/W B, V P
Sylvia Sidney, Henry Fonda
An escaped convict and his girlfriend attempt to cross the border into Canada while remaining one step ahead of the police.
Walter Wanger — *Monterey Home Video*

You Only Live Twice 1967
Adventure
59639 115 mins C B, V, CED P
Sean Connery, Donald Pleasence, Karin Dor, directed by Lewis Gilbert
Agent 007 battles Blofeld, the despicable head of Spectre, in this thriller set in Japan.
United Artists; Albert Broccoli — *CBS/Fox Video; RCA VideoDiscs*

You Were Never Lovelier 1942
Musical/Comedy
80381 98 mins B/W B, V P
Fred Astaire, Rita Hayworth, Xavier Cugat, Adolphe Menjou, directed by William A. Seiter
An Argentinian hotel tycoon creates a mysterious admirer to get his daughter interested in marriage. The musical score is by Jerome Kern and Johnny Mercer.
Columbia Pictures — *RCA/Columbia Pictures Home Video*

You'll Never Get Rich 1941
Musical
64580 88 mins B/W B, V P
Fred Astaire, Rita Hayworth, Robert Benchley
A Broadway dance director is drafted into the Army, where his romantic troubles cause him to wind up in the guardhouse more than once. Songs by Cole Porter include "Since I Kissed My Baby Goodnight" and "The Astairable Rag."
Columbia — *RCA/Columbia Pictures Home Video*

Young and Free 1978
Drama
65453 87 mins C B, V P
Erik Larsen
Following the death of his parents, a young boy must learn to face the perils of an unchartered wilderness alone, and ultimately must choose between returning to civilization, or remain with his beloved wife and life in the wild.
Keith Larson — *Monterey Home Video*

Young and Innocent 1937
Mystery
01752 80 mins B/W B, V P
Derrick De Marney, Nova Pilbeam, Percy Marmont, directed by Alfred Hitchcock
Based on Josephine Tey's novel, Chief Constable's daughter helps fugitive prove he didn't strangle film star.
Gaumont; British — *Budget Video; Video Dimensions; Sheik Video; Cable Films; Video Connection; Video Yesteryear; Western Film & Video Inc; Kartes Productions; Classic Video Cinema Collector's Club*

Young and Willing 1942
Comedy
66639 84 mins B/W B, V P
William Holden, Susan Hayward, Eddie Bracken, Robert Benchley, Martha O'Driscoll
A group of struggling actors get hold of a terrific play and try various schemes to get it produced.
United Artists — *Monterey Home Video*

Young and Willing 1942
Comedy
78898 84 mins B/W B, V P
William Holden, Susan Hayward, Eddie Bracken, Robert Benchley
A group of struggling actors living in a boarding house try to get a producer interested in their play.
Paramount Pictures — *Monterey Home Video*

Young Aphrodities 1966
Drama
72873 87 mins B/W B, V P
A tale of two teenagers who find each other's passions in an underdeveloped country.
Unknown — *Embassy Home Entertainment*

Young at Heart 1954
Musical-Drama
47993 117 mins C B, V P
Frank Sinatra, Doris Day, Gig Young, Ethel Barrymore, Dorothy Malone, Robert Keith, Elizabeth Fraser, Alan Hale Sr
Fanny Hurst's lighthearted tale of a cynical hard-luck musician who finds happiness when he falls for a small-town girl. A remake of the 1938 "Four Daughters." Songs include the title tune, "You, My Love" and "Just One of Those Things."
Warner Bros — *Republic Pictures Home Video*

Young Bing Crosby 193?
Musical
12824 39 mins B/W B, V, FO P
Bing Crosby
Bing Crosby stars in short, delightful musical comedies by Mack Sennett made before Crosby entered feature-length musical comedy: "Crooner's Holiday," "Blue of the Night," and "Bing, Bing, Bing."
Mack Sennett — *Video Yesteryear*

Young Caruso, The 1951
Musical-Drama/Biographical
52464 78 mins B/W B, V, FO P
Gina Lollobrigida, Ermanno Randi, the voice of Mario Del Monaco
A dramatic biography of legendary tenor Enrico Caruso following his life from childhood poverty in Naples to the beginning of his rise to fame. Dubbed in English.
Italian Films Export — *Video Yesteryear*

Young Doctors in Love 1982
Comedy
63420 95 mins C B, V, LV, CED P
Dabney Coleman, Sean Young, Michael McKean
This spoof of medical soap operas features a chaotic scenario at City Hospital, where the young men and women on the staff have better things to do than attend to their patients.
MPAA:R
ABC Motion Pictures — *Vestron Video*

Young Frankenstein 1974
Comedy
55576 108 mins B/W B, V, LV, CED P
Peter Boyle, Gene Wilder, Marty Feldman, Madeleine Kahn, Cloris Leachman, Gene Hackman, directed by Mel Brooks
Young Frederic Frankenstein, a brain surgeon, goes back to Transylvania and learns the secrets of his grandfather's notebooks.
MPAA:PG
Twentieth Century Fox — *CBS/Fox Video*

Young Love, First Love 1979
Drama
80902 96 mins C B, V P
Valerie Bertinelli, Timothy Hutton, Arlen Dean Snyder, Fionnuala Flanagan
Two teenagers suffering from love must choose between conforming to the traditional values that they were raised with or to the liberal attitudes of their peers. Available in VHS Stereo and Beta Hi-Fi.
Lorimar Productions — *U.S.A. Home Video*

Young Philadelphians, The 1959
Drama
63448 150 mins B/W B, V R, P
Paul Newman, Barbara Rush, Alexis Smith, Billie Burke, Brian Keith
An ambitious young lawyer works hard at making an impression on the snobbish Philadelphia upper crust. Part of the "A Night at the Movies" series, this tape simulates a 1959 movie evening, with a Bugs Bunny Cartoon, "People Are Bunny," a newsreel and coming attractions for "The Nun's Story" and "The Hanging Tree."
Warner Bros — *Warner Home Video*

Young, the Old, and the Bold, Try and Catch the Wind, The 1980
Football
50094 48 mins C B, V, FO R, P
A fascinating feature on sling-shot armed quarterbacks and sticky-fingered receivers of the 1960's including John Brodie, Roman Gabriel, Sonny Jurgenson, Charlie Taylor, Bob Hayes, and Paul Warfield in their prime.
NFL Films — *NFL Films Video*

Young Tiger, The 1980
Adventure/Martial arts
56921 102 mins C B, V R, P
Jackie Chan
A ninety-minute movie never before seen in the U.S. featuring an expert in martial arts who is accused of murder. Also included is a twelve-minute documentary featuring Jackie Chan, kung-fu sensation, demonstrating his skills.
MPAA:R
Fourseas Film Company — *Video Gems*

Young Warriors, The 1983
Adventure/Drama
78633 104 mins C B, V P
Ernest Borgnine, James Van Patten, Richard Roundtree
A group of college fraternity brothers become vigilantes to avenge the death of a woman killed by a street gang.
MPAA:R
Cannon Films — *MGM/UA Home Video*

Your Financial Survival 1983
Finance
73557 58 mins C B, V P
This program advises you on various aspects of finance such as borrowing money and savings plans
Admit One — *Admit One Video*

Your Hit Parade 1957
Television/Music
57362 30 mins B/W B, V, FO P
Snooky Lanson, Gisele MacKenzie, Russell Arms, Dorothy Collins, Raymond Scott, Andre Baruch
Broadcast on March 2, 1957, this long-running series performed the top songs of the week, chronicling the taste of Americans in popular music from 1950 to 1959.
NBC — *Video Yesteryear*

Your Hit Parade 1952
Variety
66142 23 mins B/W B, V, FO P
Dorothy Collins, Eileen Wilson, Snooky Lanson, Russell Arms, Andre Baruch
For the week of June 14, 1952, Snooky sings the No. 1 tune, "Kiss of Fire." Also, "Extras" by the Hit Parade singers and dancers and other hits of the day.
NBC — *Video Yesteryear*

Your Show of Shows 1950
Variety
11273 25 mins B/W B, V, FO P

Hosted by Melvyn Douglas, Sid Caesar, Imogene Coca, Marguerite Piazza, Jack Russell, Billy Williams Quartet
Comedy, song, and some technical difficulties highlight this entry in the famous series.
NBC — *Video Yesteryear*

Your Show of Shows 1950
Variety
11272 25 mins B/W B, V, FO P
Hosted by Marsha Hunt, Sid Caesar, Imogene Coca, Marguerite Piazza, Bill Hayes, Jack Russell
A vintage edition of the legendary variety program.
NBC — *Video Yesteryear*

Your Ticket Is No Longer Valid 1984
Drama
72912 96 mins C B, V P
Richard Harris, George Peppard
When Richard Harris becomes impotent, he hires a hit woman to kill him.
MPAA:R
Unknown — *Vestron Video*

You're a Big Boy Now 1966
Comedy
69027 96 mins C B, V R, P
Elizabeth Hartman, Geraldine Page, Peter Kastner, Julie Harris, Rip Torn, Michael Dunn, Tony Bill, Karen Black
Virginal young man working in New York Public Library, is told by his father to move out of his house and grow up. Moving out, he soon becomes involved with a man-hating actress and a discotheque dancer.
Warner Bros — *Warner Home Video*

You're Not Elected Charlie Brown 1972
Cartoons
79265 25 mins C B, V P
Animated
Charlie Brown and Linus are running against each other for the office of student body president.
Lee Mendelson-Bill Melendez Productions — *Snoopy's Home Video Library*

You're the Greatest, Charlie Brown! 1979
Cartoons
75608 30 mins C B, V P
Animated
Peppermint Patty coaches Charlie Brown in the decathalon event for the school's track team.
Lee Mendelson Bill Melendez Productions — *Snoopy's Home Video Library*

You've Got to Have Heart 1977
Comedy
80279 98 mins C B, V P
Carroll Baker, Edwige French
A young bridegroom's life gets complicated after he does not sexually satisfy his bride on their wedding night.
MPAA:R
Joseph Brenner Associates — *Prism*

Yum-Yum Girls 1978
Adventure
55554 89 mins C B, V, LV P
Judy Landers, Tanya Roberts, Barbara Tully, Michelle Daw
Naive and innocent Melody Pearson comes to New York to fulfill her dreams of a modeling career and soon learns the nitty-gritty of the modeling world.
MPAA:R
Canon Releasing — *MCA Home Video*

Z

Z 1969
Suspense
44783 128 mins C B, V P
Yves Montand, Irene Papas
A man known as "Z" leads the growing opposition party. He is struck down by a speeding truck before hundreds of onlookers. A trial follows, but seven witnesses vanish.
Academy Award '69: Best Foreign Film.
Cinema 5 — *RCA/Columbia Pictures Home Video; RCA VideoDiscs*

Zabriskie Point 1970
Drama
72468 111 mins C B, V P
Two loners epitomize the counter-culture as they wander the ominous desert terrain.
MPAA:R
Metro Goldwyn Mayer — *MGM/UA Home Video*

Zapped 1982
Comedy
63373 98 mins C B, V, LV, CED P
Scott Baio, Willie Aames, Felice Schachter, Heather Thomas, Scatman Crothers
One of the more unassuming boys in a group of teenagers possesses special magical powers.
MPAA:R EL, JA
Embassy Pictures — *Embassy Home Entertainment*

 (For explanation of codes, see USE GUIDE and KEY)

Zebra Force **1976**
Crime-Drama
76656 81 mins C B, V P
Mike Lane, Richard X. Slattery, Rockne Tarkington, Glenn Wilder, Anthony Caruso
A group of army veterans embark on a personal battle against organized crime, utilizing their military training with deadly precision.
MPAA:R
Joe Tronatore; Larry Price — *Media Home Entertainment*

Zelig **1983**
Comedy
65614 79 mins B/W B, V, LV, CED R, P
Woody Allen, Mia Farrow, Susan Sontag, Saul Bellow, Bricktop, Irving Howe, directed by Woody Allen
Woody Allen's spoof of documentary films stars him as Leonard Zelig, the famous "Chameleon Man" of the 1920's, whose personalisty was so vague that he would take on the characteristics of whomever he was in contact with. Filmed in black-and-white, the movie simulates the "look" of vintage newsreels, complete with stentorian narration.
MPAA:PG
Robert Greenhut — *Warner Home Video*

Zero for Conduct **1933**
Comedy
12856 49 mins B/W B, V, FO P
Directed by Jean Vigo
A fantasy-filled rebellion against authority set in a boys' school. French with English subtitles.
FR
Gaumont, Franco Film — *Video Yesteryear; Sheik Video; Budget Video; Western Film & Video Inc; Discount Video Tapes*

Zero to Sixty **1978**
Comedy-Drama
65073 96 mins C B, V, CED P
Darren McGavin, Sylvia Miles, Denise Nickerson
A newly divorced man finds that his car has been repossessed for nonpayment. Seeking out the manager of the finance company, he gets a job as a repossession agent of high-priced, unpaid-for cars.
MPAA:PG
Katherine Browne — *Embassy Home Entertainment*

Ziegfeld Follies **1946**
Musical
64571 109 mins C B, V, CED P
Fred Astaire, Judy Garland, Gene Kelly, Red Skelton, Fannie Brice, Lena Horne, Lucille Ball, Esther Williams, directed by Vincente Minelli
A lavish revue of musical numbers and comedy sketches featuring many MGM stars of the World War II era. Highlights include Fred Astaire and Gene Kelly's only duet, "The Babbitt and the Bromide," Lena Horne singing "Love," Judy Garland as "Madame Cremation" and a Fred Astaire-Lucille Bremer ballet set to "Limehouse Blues."
MGM — *MGM/UA Home Video*

Zig Zag Triumph of Stream **197?**
Documentary
50634 24 mins C B, V P, T
Narrated by Jack Kelso
A tribute to the more than 120 years of history of the steam engine in Australia.
Unknown — *Blackhawk Films*

Ziggy Stardust and the Spiders from Mars **1972**
Music-Performance
73861 90 mins C B, V P
David Bowie as Ziggy Stardust performs in a 1972 "farewell" concert that was filmed by D.A. Pennabaker.
Mainman Productions; Pennabaker Associates — *RCA/Columbia Pictures Home Video*

Ziggy's Gift **1983**
Cartoons
70195 30 mins C B, V P
Animated, music by Harry Nilsson
Ziggy, the lovable cartoon character created by Tom Wilson, is featured in this made-for-video Christmas program.
Lena Tabori — *Vestron Video*

Zis Boom Bah **1942**
Musical/Comedy
66143 61 mins B/W B, V, FO P
Peter Lind Hayes, Mary Healey, Grace Hayes, Huntz Hall, Benny Rubin
A college throws a variety show to save itself.
Monogram — *Video Yesteryear*

Zoltan... Hound of Dracula **1977**
Horror
66024 85 mins C B, V R, P
Michael Pataki, Reggie Nalder, Jose Ferrer
The vampire's canine companion carries on the Dracula family reputation.
Albert Band; Frank Perilli — *THORN EMI/HBO Video*

Zombie **1980**
Horror
52860 93 mins C B, V P
Tisa Farrow, Ian McCulloch
A reporter and a missing scientist's daughter go to the island of Matool to find the scientist, and encounter a mysterious doctor and hundreds of man-eating zombies.
MPAA:R EL, SP

Jerry Gross; Ugo Tucci — *Wizard Video; Vestron Video (disc only)*

Zombie Lake 1985
Horror
81036 90 mins C B, V P
Howard Vernon, Nadine Pascal
A group of zombie Nazi soldiers prey upon anyone who dares to swim in their Zombie Lake.
MPAA:R
Empire Entertainment — *Wizard Video*

Zoom the White Dolphin 1974
Cartoons
76912 94 mins C B, V P
Animated
A family living on a tropical island befriends a dolphin family.
Embassy — *Embassy Home Entertainment*

Zorba, the Greek 1964
Drama
55527 142 mins B/W B, V P
Anthony Quinn, Alan Bates, Irene Papas, Lila Kedrova
A British writer and a Greek opportunist on Crete take lodgings with an aging courtesan. The writer is attracted to a woman who is stoned by the villagers when they find he has spent the night with her. Based on a novel by Nicolai Kazantzakis.
Academy Awards '64: Best Supporting Actress (Kedrova); Best Cinematography; Best Art Direction.
Twentieth Century Fox — *CBS/Fox Video*

Zorro Rides Again 1937
Adventure/Serials
12559 217 mins B/W B, V P
John Carroll, Helen Christian, Noah Beery, directed by William Witney, John English
Zorro risks his life to outwit enemy agents endeavoring to secure ancestor's property. In twelve chapters, the first runs 30 minutes, the rest 17.
Republic — *Video Connection; Nostalgia Merchant; Discount Video Tapes*

Zorro, the Gay Blade 1981
Comedy
58850 96 mins C B, V, CED P
George Hamilton, Lauren Hutton, Brenda Vaccaro, Ron Leibman
Hamilton portrays the swashbuckling crusader and his long-lost brother, Bunny Wigglesworth, in this spoof of the Zorro legend.
MPAA:PG
20th Century Fox — *CBS/Fox Video*

Zorro's Black Whip 1944
Western/Serials
07342 168 mins B/W B, V P
Linda Stirling, George Lewis
A young girl dons the mask of her murdered brother to fight outlaws in the old West. Serial in twelve episodes.
Republic — *Nostalgia Merchant; Video Connection; Budget Video; Discount Video Tapes; Video Yesteryear*

Zorro's Fighting Legion 1939
Adventure/Serials
12558 215 mins B/W B, V P
Reed Hadley, Sheila Darcy, directed by William Witney, John English
Zorro forms a legion to help the president of Mexico fight a band of outlaws endeavoring to steal gold shipments. A serial in 12 chapters.
Republic — *Video Connection; Video Dimensions; Cable Films; Nostalgia Merchant; Budget Video; Discount Video Tapes*

SUBJECT CATEGORY INDEX

Captain Caution
Captain Harlock
Captain Scarlett
Castaway Cowboy, The
Chain Gang Killings, The
Challenge, The
Challenge, The
Challenge to Be Free
Chandu on the Magic Island
Change of Mind
Charlie and the Talking Buzzard
Chinese Connection, The
Chinese Web, The
Circle of Iron
Clash of the Titans
Claws
Cloak and Dagger
Clones of Bruce Lee, The
Comic Book Kids 2, The
Conan the Barbarian
Conan the Destroyer
Conqueror, The
Conquest
Convoy
Corrupt Ones, The
Corsican Brothers, The
Corsican Brothers, The
Count of Monte Cristo, The
Count of Monte Cristo, The
Countryman
Courage of Rin Tin Tin, The
Crack Shadow Boxers
Cross Creek
Cry of the Black Wolves
Cry of the Innocent
Cuchillo ("Knife")
Dance of the Dead
Dangerous Holiday
Daring Game
Dark Crystal, The
Davy Crockett and the River Pirates
Davy Crockett, King of the Wild Frontier
Day of the Cobra, The
Day of the Dolphin, The
Dead Don't Die, The
Dead Wrong
Deadly and the Beautiful, The
Deadly Encounter
Death Hunt
Death Journey
Death Sport
Death Stalk
Death Wish II
Deathcheaters
Desert of the Tartars, The
Desperately Seeking Susan
Diamonds Are Forever
Diary of a Rebel
Dick Deadeye
Dick Tracy Double Feature #2
Do Not Forsake Me Oh My Darling
Dr. No
Dogs of War, The
Don Q., Son of Zorro
Don Winslow of the Navy
Double McGuffin, The
Down to the Sea in Ships
Dragnet
Dragonslayer
Driver, The
Drums
El Cid
Elephant Boy
Elmer
Empire Strikes Back, The
Enchanted Forest
Encounter with the Unknown
Enigma
Enter the Dragon
Enter the Ninja
Escape
Escape from New York
Escape from the Bronx
Escapadein Japan
Escape to Athena
Escape to the Sun
Every Which Way But Loose
Exit the Dragon, Enter the Tiger
Exterminator II
Exterminators of the Year 3000
Eye for an Eye, An
Fables of the Green Forest
Fabulous Adventures of Baron Munchausen, The
Fallout
Fantastic Balloon Voyage, The
Far Pavilions, The
Fast Company
Ferry to Hong Kong
Ffolkes
Fiction Makers, The
Fighting Black Kings
Fighting Life
Fire and Ice
Firecracker
Firefox
Fish Hawk
Fist
Fist of Fear—Touch of Death
Fist of Vengeance
Fists of Fury
Fists of Fury II
Five Came Back
Five Mile Creek—Volume 5
Five Mile Creek—Volume 6
Five Mile Creek, Volume 1
Five Mile Creek Volume 2
Five Mile Creek—Volume 3
Five Weeks in a Balloon
Flashpoint Africa
Fleshburn
Flight of the Eagle, The

Star Crash
Star Wars
Starflight One
Stoner
Stop That Train
Street Fighter, The
Stunt Rock
Stunts
Sudden Death
Sudden Impact
Summerdog
Superchick
Supergirl
Superman III
Superman Cartoons
Superman—The Movie
Superman II
Surabaya Conspiracy
Survival Run
Swamp Thing
Swan Lake
Swiss Family Robinson, The
Switchblade Sisters
Sword of Fury I
Sword of Fury II
Tale of Two Cities, A
Tale of Two Critters, A
Target Eagle
Tarka the Otter
Tarzan and the Trappers
Tarzan of the Apes
Tarzan, the Ape Man
Tarzan, the Ape Man
Tarzan's Revenge
Tender Warrior, The
Texas Lightning
They Died With There Boots On
Thief of Bagdad, The
Thief of Baghdad
This Is a Hijack
Thomas Crown Affair, The
Three Musketeers, The
Three Musketeers, The
Three Musketeers, The
Three Musketeers, The
Three Musketeers, The
Thundarr the Barbarian
Thunder and Lightning
Thunder Country
Thunderball
Thunderbirds Are Go
Tiara Tahiti
Tiger's Claw
Time After Time
Time Machine
Time Machine, The
Time to Die, A
Tintorera...Tiger Shark
Tom Corbett, Space Cadet Volume 1
Tom Edison, the Boy Who Lit Up the World
Touch & Go
Tough Guy
Toy Soldiers
Traitors of the Blue Castle, The
Transformers: More than Meets the Eye, The
Treasure Island
Treasure Island
Treasure of the Four Crowns
Treasure of the Sierra Madre, The
Treasure of the Yankee Zephyr
Treasure Seekers, The
Truck Stop Women
True Game of Death, The
Tucker and the Horse Thief
20,000 Leagues Under the Sea
Two Graves to Kung-Fu
Ultimate Thrill, The
Ultraman II
Undersea Kingdom
Undersea World of Jacques Cousteau Vol. I, The
Underwater
Vera Cruz
Viaje Fantastico En Groso
Vigilantes Are Coming, The
Vikings, The
Viva Knievel
Voyage en Ballon
Voyage to the Bottom of the Sea
Voyager from the Unknown
Wake of the Red Witch, The
Warlords of the 21st Century
Welcome to Pooh Corner—Volume 4
When Lightning Strikes
When the North Wind Blows
Where Time Began
White Lightning
White Line Fever
White-Water Sam
Who Killed Mary What's 'Er Name?
Wilbur and Orville: The First to Fly
Wild Geese, The
Wild Gypsies
Wilderness Family Part 2
Wings
Woman in Grey
Wonderful World of Puss 'N Boots, The
World of Hans Christian Andersen, The
Wrong Is Right
Yakuzza, The
Yankee Clipper
Year of Living Dangerously, The
Yor, the Hunter from the Future
You Only Live Twice
Young Tiger, The
Young Warriors, The
Yum-Yum Girls
Zorro Rides Again
Zorro's Fighting Legion

Advertising

Vintage Commercials

Aeronautics

Africa

Alcoholism

Anatomy and physiology

Animals

Archeology

Armed Forces-US

Artists

Arts

Astronomy

Automobiles

Automobiles-Racing

Back disorders

Baseball

Chicago White Sox: Team Highlights
Cincinnati Reds: Team Highlights
Cleveland Indians: Team Highlights
50 Years of Baseball Memories
Going, Going, Gone
Golden Moments
Great Moments in Baseball
Greatest Comeback Ever, The
Hall of Famers
Houston Astros: Team Highlights
It Don't Come Easy: 1978 New York Yankees
Kansas City Royals: Team Highlights
King of the Hill
Legendary Greats
Los Angeles Dodgers: Team Highlights
Milwaukee Braves: Team Highlights
Minnesota Twins: Team Highlights
Montreal Expos: Team Highlights
New York Mets: Team Highlights
New York-Yankees: Team Highlights
1978—The New York Yankees' Miracle Year
1979 World Series and All-Star Highlights
Oakland Athletics: Team Highlights
Philadelphia Phillies: Team Highlights
Roberto Clemente: A Touch of Royalty
St. Louis Cardinals: Team Highlights
20 Years of World Series
Two Best World Series Ever, The
Unofficial Baseball Handbook, The
Winning Tradition: 1977 New York Yankees, A
World Series, 1943
World Series, 1944
World Series, 1945
World Series, 1946
World Series, 1947
World Series, 1948
World Series, 1949
World Series, 1950
World Series, 1951
World Series, 1952
World Series, 1953
World Series, 1954
World Series, 1955
World Series, 1956
World Series, 1957
World Series, 1958
World Series, 1959
World Series, 1960
World Series, 1961
World Series, 1962
World Series, 1963
World Series, 1964
World Series, 1965
World Series, 1966
World Series, 1967
World Series, 1968
World Series, 1969
World Series, 1970
World Series, 1971
World Series, 1972
World Series, 1973
World Series, 1974
World Series, 1975
World Series, 1976
World Series, 1977
World Series, 1978
World Series, 1979
World Series, 1980
World Series, 1981
World Series, 1982
World Series, 1984: The Sounds of the Series
World Series, 1983: 1983 World Series
Worth the Wait!

Basketball

Basketball with Gail Goodrich
Fundamentals of Women's Basketball
Greatest Legends of Basketball
1981 NBA Playoffs and Championship Series: The Dynasty Renewed
Pride and Passion
That Championship Feeling

Bible

Great Leaders
Heritage of the Bible, The
In Search of Noah's Ark
Jacob: The Man Who Fought with God
New Media Bible: The Story of Joseph, The
Saul and David

Bicycling

Videocycle

Biographical

Abe Lincoln: Freedom Fighter
Alexander the Great
Amazing Howard Hughes, The
American Caesar
Amin: The Rise and Fall
Anne of the Thousand bays
Bethune
Big Mo
Bogie: The Last Hero
Born Again
Bruce Lee The Man/The Myth
Catholic Hour, The
Churchill and the Generals
Clarence Darrow
Conrack
Cross Creek
Damien: The Leper Priest
Danton
Dawn!
Dionne Quintuplets
Mussolini and I
Evel Knievel
Evening with Quentin Crisp, An
Executioner's Song, The

Biology

Boating

Boxing

Canada

Cartoons

Chemistry

Child abuse

Childbirth

Children

China

Christianity

Christmas

Circus

Cities and towns

Clothing and dress

Comedy

Young Doctors in Love
Young Frankenstein
You're a Big Boy Now
You've Got to Have Heart
Zapped
Zelig
Zero for Conduct
Zis Boom Bah
Zorro, the Gay Blade

Comedy-Drama

Apartment, The
Apprenticeship of Duddy Kravitz, The
Back Roads
Barney Oldfield's Race for a Life/Super-Hooper-Dyne Lizzies
Baron Muenchhausen
Benji
Big Chill, The
Billy Liar
Breach of Promise
Breakfast Club, The
Buck and the Preacher
Butterflies Are Free
Can She Bake a Cherry Pie?
Cannery Row
Casey's Shadow
Cheaper to Keep Her
Class of Miss MacMichael, The
Clean Slate (Coup de Torchon)
Clown, The
Coast to Coast
Cold Feet
Danny Boy
Devil's Eye
Diary of a Mad Housewife
Diner
Dinner at Eight
Doctor at Sea
Dog Day Afternoon
Eyes Right
Fireside Theatre: Sergeant Sullivan Speaking
For the Love of Benji
Four Friends
Fuzz
George
Gidget
Gin Game, The
Good Sam
Goodbye People, The
Graduate, The
Heat
Hit, The
Hotel New Hampshire, The
If You Could See What I Hear
It's My Turn
Joe
Judge Priest
King of Comedy, The
Lady Eve, The
Last Detail, The
Last Word, The
Loves of a Blonde, The
Magic Town
Magician, The
Mama (I Remember Mama)
Marathon
Mark Twain's A Connecticut Yankee in King Arthur's Court
M*A*S*H: Goodbye, Farewell and Amen
Max Dugan Returns
Miss Annie Rooney
My Dinner with Andre
My Father's Nurse
My Therapist
Never Let Go
No Small Affair
North Dallas Forty
Nuit de Varennes, La
Oh Alfie
One Night Stand
Over the Brooklyn Bridge
Palooka
Pillow Talk
Pollyanna
Pollyanna
Poor Little Rich Girl, The
Portnoy's Complaint
Prisoner of Second Avenue, The
Prizzi's Honor
Purple Rose of Cairo, The
Quiet Man, The
Rascals, The
Rattle of a Simple Man
Rebecca of Sunnybrook Farm
Return of the Secaucus 7
Rich and Famous
Robert et Robert
Second Thoughts
Secrets of Women
Six Weeks
Slap Shot
Some Kind of Hero
Sparrows
Stage Door
Starting Over
Stay Hungry
Sting, The
Swing Shift
Those Lips, Those Eyes
Thousand Clowns, A
Three in the Attic
Thunder in the City
To Sir, With Love
Toy, The
Turk 182!
Up the Sandbox
We're No Angels
Women, The
Zero to Sixty

Comedy-Performance

Best of the Big Laff-Off, The
Billy Connolly—Bites Yer Bum
Billy Crystal: A Comic's Line
Buddy Hackett: Live and Uncensored
Carlin at Carnegie
Carlin on Campus
Carrott Gets Rowdie
Comedy Tonight
David Steinberg in Concert
Dirty, Dirty Jokes
Don Rickles—Buy this Tape, You Hockey Puck
Evening with Professor Irwin Corey, An
Evening with Robin Williams, An
Father Guido Sarducci Goes to College
Franken and Davis at Stockton State
Franken and Davis Special, The
Gallagher—Stuck in the 60's
Gallagher—The Maddest
George Burns in Concert
Hungry i Reunion
Joe Piscopo
Lenny Bruce
Lenny Bruce Performance Film, The
Likely Stories, Volume I
Likely Stories, Volume II
Madame in Manhattan
Melon Crazy
Red Skelton's Funny Faces
Redd Foxx—Video in a Plain Brown Wrapper
Richard Pryor: Here and Now
Richard Pryor—Live and Smokin'
Richard Pryor Live in Concert
Richard Pryor Live on the Sunset Strip
Robert Klein: Child of the 50's, Man of the 80's
Truly Tasteless Jokes
Unknown Comedy Show, The

Communication

New Speed Reading

Cookery

Cooking for Compliments
Craig Claiborne's New York Times Video Cookbook
Flavors of China
Julia Child—The French Chef, Vol. I
Master Cooking Course, The
Master Cooking Course, The
Slim Gourmet, The
Wok Before You Run
Yes You Can Microwave

Cosmetology

Why Do I Call You Sexy?

Crime-Drama

Adventures of Ellery Queen, The
Black Marble, The
Blade
Brannigan
Con Artists, The
Corrupt
Cross Country
Dear Detective
Detour
Dick Tracy
Dick Tracy
Dick Tracy
Dick Tracy Double Feature # 1
Dick Tracy Meets Gruesome
Dick Tracy Returns
Dick Tracy Returns
Dick Tracy vs. Crime Inc.
Dick Tracy vs. Crime Inc.
Dick Tracy's G-Men
Dick Tracy's G-Men
Dillinger
Enforcer, The
Family, The
French Connection, The
Gangster Wars, The
Gangsters
Gauntlet, The
High Crime
House on Garibaldi Street, The
Justice
Laura
Little Caesar
Long Good Friday, The
Magnum Force
Man Against Crime Volume II
Man on the Eiffel Tower, The
McQ
Mean Johnny Barrows
One Man Jury
Outside the Law
Policewomen
Port of New York
Public Enemy
Racket, The
Rocky King, Detective
St. Ives
Scarface
Scarface
Shaft
Shoot It Black, Shoot It Blue
Shooting Stars
Stiletto
Street Law
Strike Force
Sudden Impact
T-Men
Thief
Trapped

Dance

Death

Disasters

Divorce

Documentary

Drama

Ecstasy
Eddie and the Cruisers
Eddie Macon's Run
Edie in Ciao! Manhattan
Edward and Mrs. Simpson
8 1/2
Electric Dreams
Electric Horseman, The
Eleni
Elephant Man, The
Elizabeth of Ladymead
Elmer
Elmer Gantry
Elusive Corporal, The
Emanuelle Around the World
Emanuelle in America
Emanuelle in Bangkok
Emanuelle the Queen
Emilienne
Emily
Emmanuelle
Emmanuelle Black and White
Emmanuelle in the Country
Emmanuelle, the Joys of a Woman
Enchanted Island
Endangered Species
Endless Love
Enigma
Entertaining Mr. Sloane
Entre Nous (Between Us)
Escape from Alcatraz
Escapadein Japan
Escort Girls
Esposa y Amante
Europeans, The
Evel Knievel
Every Man for Himself and God Against All
Evil Mind, The
Evil That Men Do, The
Executioner's Song, The
Executive Action
Exodus
Explosion
Eyes, The Mouth, The
Fabulous Dorseys, The
Face in the Crowd, A
Fail Safe
Fake Out
Fall of the House of Usher, The
Fall of the Roman Empire, The
Fallen Idol
Falling In Love
Fame Is the Spur
Family Life
Fanny
Fanny and Alexander
Fantasies
Fantasy in Blue
Fantasy Island
Far Cry From Home, A
Farewell to Arms, A
Fast Lane Fever
Fast Walking
Father
Father Figure
Fear
Feelin' Up
Fiend
55 Days at Peking
Fight for Your Life
Fighter, The
Final Assignment
Final Countdown, The
Fiona
Fire Over England
Firepower
Fires on the Plain
First Blood
First Born
First Deadly Sin, The
First Love
F.I.S.T.
Fitzcarraldo
Five Mile Creek—Volume 4
Flaming Star
Flight from Vienna
Flying Blind
Foolish Wives
For Ladies Only
For Love of Ivy
Force of Evil
Forced Landing
Ford Startime
Forever Emmanuelle
Formula, The
Fort Apache, The Bronx
Fountainhead, The
Four Deuces, The
Four Horsemen of the Apocalypse, The
Fourth Wish, The
Frances
Francis Gary Powers: The True Story of the U-Z Spy Incident
Francis Gary Powers: The True Story of the U-2 Spy Incident
Frantic
Freedom
French Connection II
French Lieutenant's Woman, The
French Postcards
French Quarter
French Woman, The
Friendly Persuasion
From the Life of the Marionettes
Front, The
Fugitive: The Final Episode, The
Full Hearts and Empty Pockets
Fyre
Gallipoli
Gambler, The
Gandhi
Garden of the Finzi-Continis, The

Drawing

Drug abuse

Education

Electronic data processing

Ethics

Europe

Exploitation

Fairy tales

Stories and Fables, Volume 6
Stories and Fables, Volume 7
Stories and Fables, Volume 8
Stories and Fables, Volume 9
Stories and Fables, Volume 10
Stories and Fables, Volume 11
Storytime Classics
Storytime Classics: Rudyard Kipling's Just So Stories Vol. 1
Tale of the Frog Prince, The
Tales from Muppetland II
Three Little Pigs, The
Thumbelina
Thumbelina
Tom Thumb
Unicorn Tales I
Unicorn Tales II
Velveteen Rabbit, The
Very Special Christmas, A/Sleeping Beauty
Wild Swans, The
Wind in the Willows
Wishmaker, The

Family

You and Me, Kid Volume I
You and Me, Kid Volume 2

Fantasy

Adventures of Babar, The
Adventures of Buckaroo Banzai, The
Alice in Wonderland
Alice in Wonderland
Alice's Adventures in Wonderland
Angel on My Shoulder
Aquaman
Ator the Fighting Eagle
B.C. Rock
Barbarella
Batman
Benji's Very Own Christmas Story
Best of Marvel Comics, The
Bishop's Wife, The
Butterfly Ball, The
Care Bears Battle the Freeze Machine, The
Change of Mind
Checkmate
Chitty Chitty Bang Bang
Clan of the Cave Bear, The
Comic Book Kids, The
Company of Wolves, The
Conan the Destroyer
Conquest
Curse of the Cat People
Daddy Long Legs
Dance of the Dead
Darby O'Gill and the Little People
Dark Crystal, The
Daydreamer, The
DeathStalker
Devil and Daniel Mouse, The
Devil and Max Devlin, The
Diary of Forbidden Dreams
Do Not Forsake Me Oh My Darling
Dorothy in the Land of Oz
Dot and Santa Claus
Dot and the Kangaroo
Dragonslayer
Dreamscape
Dunderklumpen
Dune
Dungeonmaster, The
Endgame
Escape to Witch Mountain
Excalibur
Fallout
Fantastic Animation Festival
Final Programme, The
Fire and Ice
Flight of Dragons
Fraggle Songs, Volume One
Freaky Friday
Free for All
Galaxy Express
General, The
Girl Who Was Death, The
Gnome—Mobile, The
Golden Voyage of Sinbad, The
Greenstone, The
Grendel, Grendel, Grendel
Gulliver's Travels
Gumby Summer, A
Gumby's Incredible Journey
Hammer Into Anvil
Hawk the Slayer
Heaven Can Wait
Here Comes Mr. Jordan
Hobbit, The
Hoppity Goes to Town
Ironmaster
Island of Nevawuz, The
It's Your Funeral
Jason and the Argonauts
Jonathan Livingston Seagull
Journey Back to Oz
Journey Back to Oz
Kiss Me Goodbye
Last Starfighter, The
Lion, the Witch and the Wardrobe, The
Lisztomania
Little Mermaid, The
Living in Harmony
Lord of the Rings
Magic Pony, The
Man in the Santa Claus Suit, The
Many Happy Returns
Marco Polo, Jr.
Marvelous Land of Oz, The
Moon Madness
Mouse and His Child, The
Mysterious Island

Neverending Story, The
New Misadventures of Ichabod Crane, The
Night Gallery
Nine Lives of Fritz the Cat, The
Once Upon a Brothers Grimm
Once Upon a Time
Once Upon A Time
One from the Heart
1001 Arabian Nights
Panda and the Magic Serpent
Peter-No-Tail
Pinocchio
Pinocchio in Outer Space
Prisoner, The
Puff the Magic Dragon in the Land of Lies
Purple Rose of Cairo, The
Raccoons on Ice
Red Balloon, The
Red Balloon, The
Robby the Rascal
Romie-O and Julie-8
Santa Claus Conquers the Martians
Schizoid Man, The
Scrooge
Second Time Lucky
Secret of NIMH, The
7th Voyage of Sinbad, The
Sinbad and the Eye of the Tiger
Some Call It Loving
Something Wicked This Way Comes
Somewhere in Time
Splash
Stories and Fables, Volume 4
Streets of Fire
Superboy
Supergirl
Superman
Sword and the Sorcerer, The
Sword of the Valiant
Thief of Baghdad
Thief of Baghdad, The
Three Tales of Love & Friendship
Time Bandits
Time Fighters
Timefighters in the Land of Fantasy
Tom Thumb
Trip, The
Tubby the Tuba
Two Worlds of Jennie Logan, The
Unicorn the Island of Magic
Warrior and the Sorceress, The
Watership Down
Welcome to Pooh Corner, Volume I
Welcome to Pooh Corner—Volume 3
Where the Toys Come From
Willy McBean and His Magic Machine
Willy Wonka and the Chocolate Factory
Wiz, The
Wizard of Oz, The
Wizard of Oz, The
Xanadu
Yor, the Hunter from the Future

Film

Academy Award Winners Animated Short Films
Best of the New York Erotic Film Festival Parts I & II
Breakin'
Inside Hitchcock

Film-Avant-garde

All Screwed Up
Atalante, L'
Avant Garde and Experimental Film Program No. 1
Avant-Garde #2
Bete Humaine, La
Blood of a Poet
Cabinet of Dr. Caligari
Electric Light Voyage
Eraserhead
Forbidden Zone
Grand Illusion
Knife in the Water
Koyaanisqatsi
Orpheus
Paisan
Passion of Joan of Arc
Rules of the Game
Seduction of Mimi, The
Tonight for Sure
Ugetsu
Vampyr
Yojimbo

Film-History

America at the Movies
America/The Fall of Babylon
Art and Science of Making Movies, The
Avenging Conscience, The
Battle at Elderbush Gulch, The/The Musketeers of Pig Alley
Birth of a Nation, The
Birth of a Nation
Blood and Sand/Son of the Sheik
Chaplin: A Character Is Born/Keaton: The Great Stone Face
Dracula/The Garden of Eden
D.W. Griffith: An American Genius
Earth
Eisenstein
Enchanted Studio, The/More from the Enchanted Studio
End of St. Petersburg, The
Favorite Black Exploitation Cartoons
Favorite Racists Cartoons
Film Firsts
From Broadway to Hollywood
General, The/Slapstick

Filmmaking

Finance

First aid

Fishes

Fishing

Folklore

Football

France

Gambling

Game show

Games

Gardening

Germany

Golf

Great Britain

Gymnastics

Handicapped

Health education

History

History-Modern

History-US

Holidays

Special Valentine with Family Circus, A
VIDI's Video Greetings

Home improvement

Constructing Stud Walls
Installing a Lockset
Installing a Pre-Hung Door
Installing a Suspended Ceiling
Installing Insulation and Sheetrock
Principles of Paneling

Horror

Abbott and Costello Meet Dr. Jekyll and Mr. Hyde
Abominable Dr. Phibes, The
Alien Dead
Alison's Birthday
Alone in the Dark
Alone in the Dark
American Werewolf in London, An
Amityville Horror, The
Amityville 3D
Amityville II: The Possession
And Now the Screaming Starts
Andy Warhol's Dracula
Andy Warhol's Frankenstein
Assault on Precinct 13
Astro Zombies, The
Asylum
Atom Age Vampire
Audrey Rose
Awakening, The
Basket Case
Beast, The
Beast Must Die, The
Beast Within, The
Because of the Cats
Bedlam
Before I Hang
Being, The
Bela Lugosi Meets a Brooklyn Gorilla
Beyond Evil
Beyond the Door
Beyond the Door II
Billy the Kid Versus Dracula
Birds, The
Black Cat, The/The Raven
Black Magic Terror
Black Room, The
Black Room, The
Blackenstein
Blacula
Blade of the Ripper
Blood and Black Lace
Blood Beach
Blood Couple
Blood Legacy
Blood Lust
Blood Mania
Blood of Dracula's Castle
Blood Voyage
Bloodbeat
Bloodsuckers
Bloodsucking Freaks
Blue Sunshine
Body Snatcher, The
Boogey Man, The
Brain, The
Brain That Wouldn't Die, The
Bride of Frankenstein
Bride of the Monster
Brides Wore Blood, The
Brood, The
Bug
Burning, The
Burnt Offerings
Campus Corpse, The
Captain Kronos: Vampire Hunter
Carpathian Eagle, The
Carrie
Castle of Evil
Castle of the Walking Dead
Cat People
Cat People
Cauldron of Blood
Chamber of Fear
Chamber of Horrors
Changeling, The
Children of the Corn
Children of the Full Moon
Company of Wolves, The
Confessional, The
Copperhead
Count Dracula
Count Yorga, Vampire
Crater Lake Monster, The
Crawling Eye, The
Crawling Hand, The
Crazed
Creature from Black Lake
Creeping Flesh, The
Creeping Terror
Creepshow
Crimson
Crocodile
Crucible of Terror
Cujo
Curtains
Dagora, the Space Monster
Damien—Omen II
Dark, The
Dark Places
Dawn of the Dead
Dawn of the Mummy
Day of Judgement
Day of the Animals
Dead and Buried
Deadly Blessing
Deadly Eyes
Deadly Games

Identity

Indians-North American

Infants

Insects

Interview

Fighting Black Kings
Fighting Life
Firecracker
Fist
Fist of Vengeance
Fists of Fury
Fists of Fury II
Force of One, A
Forced Vengeance
Game of Death
Golden Exterminator
Golden Sun
Heroes in the Ming Dynasty
Image of Bruce Lee, The
Incredible Master Beggars
Invincible Armor
Invincible from Hell, The
Invincible, The
Iron Dragon Strikes Back, The
Japanese Connection
Jaws of the Dragon
Karate Kid, The
Kill and Kill Again
Kill or Be Killed
Kill Squad
Kill the Golden Goose
King Boxers, The
King of Kung-Fu
Kung Fu
Kung-Fu Commandos
Kung Fu For Sale
Kung Fu Kids
Kung Fu Warrior, The
Last Challenge of the Dragon, The
Last Challenge of the Dragon
Little Dragons, The
Lone Wolf McQuade
Magnificent, The
Magnificent Kick, The
Man Called Tiger
Marvelous stunts of Kung Fu
Master Class
Master Ninja 2
Master Ninja 3, The
Master Ninja 4, The
Militant Eagle
Moonlight Sword and Jade Lion
Ninja III: The Domination
Octagon, The
Of Cooks and Kung-Fu
1000 Mile Escort
Pro-Karate Championships (1976-1981)
Prodigal Boxer, The
Professional Killers I
Raw Force
Real Bruce Lee, The
Renegade Monk
Retrievers, The
Return of the Dragon
Return of the Red Tiger
Return of the Tiger
Revenge of the Ninja
Rivals of the Silver Fox
Roaring Fire
Secret of the Snake and Crane, The
Self Defense
7 Blows of the Dragon
Shaolin Death Squad
Shaolin Traitor
Shogun's Ninja
Silent Rage
Slaughter in San Francisco
Sleeping Fist
Snake and Crane Arts of Shaolin
Snake in the Monkey's Shadow
Spititual Kung Fu
Steel Fisted Dragon
Sticks of Death
Stoner
Story in the Temple Red Lily
Stranger and the Gunfighter, The
Street Fighter, The
Struggle Through Death
Swordsman with an Umbrella
Ten Brothers of Shao-lin
10 Magnificent Killers
The Master Ninja
They Call Me Bruce
Three Avengers
Thundering Mantis
Thundering Mantis
Tiger's Claw
Tough Guy
True Game of Death, The
Two Assassins in the Dark
Two Graves to Kung-Fu
Two Wondrous Tigers
Watch Out, Crimson Bat!
World of Martial Arts, The
Young Tiger, The

Mass media

Behind Your Radio Dial

Massage

Touch of Love: Massage, The

Middle East

Hear O Israel
Holy Koran, The

Mime

Meet Marcel Marceau

Miners and mining

Harlan County, U.S.A.

Music-Performance

Musical

Alice in Wonderland
American in Paris, An
Annie
Babes in Arms
Babes in Toyland
Bal, Le
Band Wagon, The
Beach Party
Beat Street
Bells Are Ringing
Best Little Whorehouse in Texas, The
Bikini Beach
Black and Tan/St. Louis Blues
Blue Hawaii
Blues Brothers, The
Bohemian Girl, The
Breaking Glass
Breaking the Ice
Brigadoon
Bugsy Malone
Butterfly Ball, The
Bye, Bye, Birdie
Camelot
Can't Stop the Music
Carefree
Charlotte's Web
Chitty Chitty Bang Bang
Colgate Comedy Hour: "Let's Face It," The
Comic Book Kids, The
Copacabana
Dames
Damn Yankees
Damsel in Distress, A
Dixie Jamboree
Doctor Doolittle
Doll Face
Double Trouble
Duke Is Tops, The
Dynamite Chicken
Easy Come, Easy Go
Electric Boogalo, Breakin 2
Eubie!
Evergreen
Fabulous Dorseys, The
Fast Forward
Fiddler on the Roof
Fiesta
Finian's Rainbow
Flying Down To Rio
Follow the Fleet
Footlight Parade
42nd Street
Fred Astaire: Change Partners and Dance
Fred Astaire: Puttin' on His Top Hat
Fun and Fancy Free
Fun in Acapulco
Funny Face
Gaiety
Gay Divorcee, The
George White's Scandals
Get Crazy
G. I. Blues
Girls, Girls, Girls
Glorifying the American Girl
Go, Johnny Go!
Gold Diggers of 1933
Golddiggers of 1933
Gotta Dance, Gotta Sing
Grease
Grease 2
Great Caruso, The
Greek Street
Guys and Dolls
Gypsy
Hair
Hans Brinker
Happiest Millionaire, The
Hard Day's Night, A
Harlem Rides the Range
Heidi's Song
Hello, Dolly!
High Society
Higher and Higher
Hillbillys in a Haunted House
Hips, Hips, Hooray
Holiday Inn
Huckleberry Finn
I Do! I Do!
If You Knew Susie
Invitation to the Dance
It Happened at the World's Fair
Jack and the Beanstalk
Jive Junction
Jubilee
Killer Diller
King and I, The
King of Jazz, The
Kismet
Lady Sings the Blues
Let It Be
Liberace Show Volumes 1 & 2, The
Li'l Abner
Lili
Little Johnny Jones
Little Kid's Dynamite All-Star Band, The
Little Match Girl, The
Little Night Music, A
Little Prince, The
Loving You
Magical Mystery Tour
Main Street to Broadway
Mame
Man of La Mancha
Marvelous Land of Oz, The
Mary Poppins
Matter of Time, A
Meet Me in St. Louis
Meet the Navy
Melody Ranch
Melody Trail
Menudo—La Pelicula
Mrs. Brown, You've Got a Lovely Daughter

Muppets Take Manhattan, The
Music Shoppe, The
Musical Personalities No. 1
My Fair Lady
New York, New York
Night and Day
Oh! Calcutta!
Oklahoma!
On a Clear Day You Can See Forever
On the Town
One and Only Genuine Original Family Band, The
One from the Heart
One Touch of Venus
Paint Your Wagon
Paradise, Hawaiian Style
Pennies from Heaven
Perils of Pauline, The
Pinocchio
Pippin
Pirate, The
Pirate Movie, The
Pirates of Penzance, The
Popeye
Pot O' Gold
Prairie Moon
Private Buckaroo
Rappin'
Reet, Petite and Gone
Robinhood of Texas
Rock 'n' Roll High School
Rock, Rock, Rock
Rock, You Sinners
Romie-O and Julie-8
Rose, The
Royal Wedding
Scooby Goes Hollywood
Scrooge's Rock 'n' Roll Christmas
Second Chorus
Sergeant Pepper's Lonely Hearts Club Band
Seven Brides for Seven Brothers
1776
Sextette
Shall We Dance
Shinbone Alley
Show Business
Silk Stockings
Sing Your Worries Away
Singin' in the Rain
Sioux City Sue
Something to Sing About
South Pacific
Speedway
Spinal Tap
Stagedoor Canteen
Star Is Born, A
Star Struck
Stars on Parade/Boogie Woogie Dream
Step Lively
Stork Club, The
Story of Vernon and Irene Castle, The
Strike Up The Band
Sweeney Todd—The Demon Barber of Fleet Street
Swing Time
Take It Big
Taking My Turn
Terror of Tiny Town
Thank God It's Friday
That'll Be the Day
That's Dancing!
That's Entertainment
That's Entertainment, Part II
That's Singing
There's No Business Like Show Business
This Is Elvis
This Is Spinal Tap
Three Penny Opera
Till the Clouds Roll By
Times Square
Tom Sawyer
Tommy
Top Hat
Tubby the Tuba
200 Motels
Two Tickets to Broadway
Unsinkable Molly Brown, The
Vagabond Lover
Viva Las Vegas
Water Babies, The
West Side Story
Willy Wonka and the Chocolate Factory
Wiz, The
Wizard of Oz, The
Woodstock
Xanadu
Yes, Giorgio
You Were Never Lovelier
You'll Never Get Rich
Young Bing Crosby
Ziegfeld Follies
Zis Boom Bah

Musical-Drama

All That Jazz
Body Rock
Bongo Man
Cabaret
Carnival Rock
Cotton Club, The
Cucaracha, La
Fame
Flashdance
Footloose
Frankie and Johnnie
Funny Girl
Going My Way
Goodyear TV Playhouse: "The Gene Austin Story"
Hard to Hold
Harder They Come, The

Mystery

Physical fitness

Physics

Plants

Pregnancy

Presidency-US

Prisons

Running

Safety education

Satire

Science

Science fiction

Serials

Sexuality

Smoking

Soccer

Space exploration

Spain

Speculation

Truth About UFO's & ET's, The

Sports

Best of the WWF, Vol. I, The
Bulls Eye Archery
Dreams of Gold
Dreams of Gold
Go for It
Hulkamania
I Like to Hurt People
Olympia: Parts I and II
Pro Wrestling Illustrated
Run for Life: An Olympic Fable
Skateboard Madness
Sports Conditioning
Terrytoons Salutes the Olympics
Thorpe's Gold
Time Capsule: The Los Angeles Olympic Games/1932
Wrestling Queen
Wrestling's Bloopers, Bleeps and Bodyslams

Sports-Minor

Arnold Schwarzenegger: Mr. Olympia (The Comeback)
National Bodybuilding Championships 1984
Show Jumping World Cup

Sports-Water

Adventures in Paradise
Endless Summer, The
I Crave the Waves
Island Magic
Swim Baby Swim

Sports-Winter

Alpine Ski School
Miracle of Lake Placid: Highlights of the 1980 Winter Olympics, The
1984 Winter Olympics Highlights
Ski
Ski Time
Torvill & Dean: Path to Perfection

Stress

Hypnovision Stress Reduction

Suicide

Last Cry for Help

Surgery

Nose Job

Suspense

Alice Sweet Alice
Anderson Tapes, The
Ants
Are You in the House Alone?
Avalanche
Baby, The
B.A.D. Cats
Baffled
Barcelona Kill, The
Big Sleep, The
Black Magic Terror
Blood on the Sun
Blood Simple
Blow Out
Body Double
Body Heat
Boston Strangler, The
Brannigan
Bushido Blade, The
Catamount Killing, The
Catch Me a Spy
Centerfold Girls, The
Chain Reaction, The
Checkmate
Children, The
Christina
Christine
Cloak and Dagger
Clown Murders, The
Cold Room, The
Coma
Confessional, The
Cornered
Cross Country
Cruise Into Terror
Cruise Missile
Curse of King Tut's Tomb, The
Custodio de Senoras
Dain Curse, The
Dangerous Summer, A
Dark Forces
Dark Room, The
Day of the Jackal, The
Dead Don't Die, The
Dead Easy
Dead of Night
Dead Zone, The
Deadline
Deadly Force
Deadly Game, The
Death Games
Death Machines
Death Rage
Death Sentence
Deathtrap
Deep, The
Deep Red: Hatchet Murders
Devil's Undead, The
Dial "M" for Murder

Technology

Television

Tennis

Theater

Track athletics

Trains

Travel

Variety

Playboy Video, Volume II
Playboy Video, Volume 3
Playboy Video, Volume 4
Playboy Video Magazine—Volume 7
Playboy Video, Volume 5
Playboy Video, Volume 6
Playgirl on the Air
Playmate Review
Playmate Review #2
Playmate Review 3
Puppet Playhouse Presents Howdy Doody
Rock Music with the Muppets
Roy Rogers and Dale Evans Show, The
Saturday Night Live: Eric Idle Vol I
Saturday Night Live: Buck Henry
Saturday Night Live: Charles Grodin
Saturday Night Live: Elliott Gould
Saturday Night Live: Eric Idle Vol. II
Saturday Night Live: Gary Busey
Saturday Night Live: George Carlin
Saturday Night Live: Lily Tomlin
Saturday Night Live: Madeline Kahn
Saturday Night Live: Michael Palin
Saturday Night Live: Peter Cook & Dudley Moore
Saturday Night Live: Ray Charles
Saturday Night Live: Richard Benjamin
Saturday Night Live: Robert Klein
Saturday Night Live: Rodney Dangerfield
Saturday Night Live: Sissy Spacek
Saturday Night Live, Vol. II
Saturday Night Live, Vol. I
Saturday Night Live with Richard Pryor
Saturday Night Live with Steve Martin
Sheena Easton: Act One
Showtime at the Apollo
Sing Along with Mitch
Snow White Live at Radio City Music Hall
Stage Show with the Dorsey Brothers
Steve Allen Plymouth Show, The
Ten from Your Show of Shows
Texaco Star Theater
That's Singing
Toast of the Town
Tonight Show, The
TV Variety
TV Variety, II
TV Variety, Book VII
TV Variety, Book VIII
TV Variety III
TV Variety, IV
TV Variety, V
TV Variety, VI
27th Annual Academy Awards Presentations, The
Washington Square
Weber and Fields, Al Jolson, and This Is America
What Would Your Mother Say?
Your Hit Parade
Your Show of Shows
Your Show of Shows

Video

CBS/FOX Guide to Home Videography, The
Duran Duran: Girls on Film/Hungry Like the Wolf
Electric Light Voyage
Evolutionary Spiral
How to Beat Home Video Games Volume I
How to Beat Home Video Games Volume II
How to Beat Home Video Games Volume III
Jesse Rae: Rusha/D.E.S.I.R.E.
Meet Your VCR
Michael Nesmith: Rio/Cruisin'
Prime Cuts—Jazz & Beyond
Talking in Your Sleep
Video System Test Tape, The
Video Trivialities

Vietnam War

Hearts and Minds
Vietnam: Chronicle of a War
Vietnam: In the Year of the Pig
Vietnam: Remember
Vietnam: The Ten Thousand Day War

Volcanoes

Eruption: St. Helens Explodes

War-Drama

Adventures of the Flying Cadets
Air Force
Another Time, Another Place
Back to Bataan
Battle Cry
Battle Hell
Battle of El Alamein, The
Battle of El Alamein, The
Battle of the Bulge, The
Battle of the Commandos
Battle of the Last Panzer, The
Beguiled, The
Berlin Express
Big Red One, The
Birth of a Nation, The
Boat, The
Boys in Company C, The
Brady's Escape
Breakthrough
Bridge Too Far, A
Colditz Story, The
Commandos
Cross of Iron
Cruel Sea, The
Dam Busters, The
Deep Six, The
Desert Fox, The
Dirty Dozen, The
Double Agents
Drums in the Deep South
Eagle Has Landed, The

Western

Wildlife

Women

World War I

World War II

Yoga

Videodisc Index

This index is divided into two sections: Capacitance Electronic Discs (CED) and Laser Optical Discs (LV). An alphabetical listing of titles available in both disc formats follows. Please refer to the alphabetical program listings in the main text of this *Guide* to find the disc source.

CAPACITANCE ELECTRONIC DISCS

Ben Hur
Benji
Best Defense
Best Friends
The Best Little Whorehouse in Texas
The Best of Popeye
The Best of 60 Minutes
The Best of Terrytoons
Betrayal
The Betsy
The Bette Midler Show
Big Bad Mama
Big Blue Marble
The Big Chill
The Big Fights, Volumes 1-3
Big Jake
The Big Red One
The Big Sleep
The Billion Dollar Hobo
Billy Jack
Billy Joel: Live from Long Island
Birdman of Alcatraz
The Birds
The Black Hole
The Black Marble
Black Orpheus
The Black Stallion
The Black Stallion Returns
Black Sunday
Blade Runner
Blame it on Rio
Blazing Saddles
Blondie: Eat to the Beat
Bloody Mama
Blow Out
Blue Hawaii
The Blue Lagoon
Blue Thunder
Blues Alive
The Blues Brothers
The Boat
Bob Welch & Friends
Bobby Jo and the Outlaw
Body and Soul
Body Heat
Bolero
Bonnie and Clyde
The Boogey Man
Born Free
Born Losers
The Bostonians
Boxcar Bertha
The Boy Who Left Home to Find Out About the Shivers
The Boys from Brazil
The Boys in the Band
The Boys of Summer
Brainstorm
Brannigan
Breaker Morant
Breakfast at Tiffany's
Breakheart Pass
Breakin'
Breaking Away
Breakout
Breathless
Brian's Song
The Bridge on the River Kwai
A Bridge Too Far
Brigadoon
Brimstone and Treacle
Broadway Danny Rose
Bronco Billy
Brubaker
Buddy Buddy
The Bugs Bunny/ Road Runner Movie
Bullitt
Bullwinkle & Rocky & Friends, Vol. 1
Bus Stop
Butch Cassidy and the Sundance Kid
Butterfly
Cabaret
Caddyshack
La Cage aux Folles
La Cage aux Folles II
California Suite
Caligula
Candid Candid Camera
The Candidate
Candleshoe
Cannery Row
The Cannonball Run
Capricorn One
Captain Blood
Carbon Copy
Caring for Your Newborn
Carlin at Carnegie
Carlin on Campus
Carnal Knowledge
Carny
Carole King: One to One
Carrie
The Cars: 1984-1985 —Live
Cartoon Classics Volume 1: Chip 'n' Dale Featuring Donald Duck
Cartoon Classics Volume 2: Pluto
Cartoon Classics Volume 3: Disney's Scary Tales
Cartoon Classics Volume 4: Sport Goofy
Casablanca
Cat Ballou
Cat on a Hot Tin Roof
Cat People
Catch-22
Caveman
CBS/Fox Guide to Complete Dog Care
The Challenge
The Champ
A Change of Seasons
The Changeling
The Charge of the Light Brigade
Chariots of Fire
A Charlie Brown Festival I-IV
The Charlie Daniels Band: The Saratoga Concert
Charlotte's Web
Charly
Chatterbox
Cheech & Chong's Nice Dreams
Children of the Corn
The China Syndrome
Chinatown
Chitty Chitty Bang Bang
The Christine McVie Concert
Chu Chu and the Philly Flash
The Cincinnati Kid
Cinderella

Citizen Kane
City Lights
Clarence Darrow
Clash of the Titans
Class of 1984
Class Reunion
Cleopatra
A Clockwork Orange
Close Encounters of the Third Kind (The Special Edition)
Coal Miner's Daughter
Cold River
The Collector
College Football Classics, Vol. I
Coma
Comancheros
Comedy Tonight
Coming Home
The Compleat Beatles
Complete Tennis from the Pros, Vol. 1: Strokes and Technique
Conan the Barbarian
The Count of Monte Cristo
The Country Girl
Cousin, Cousine
Crackers
Crazy Mama
Creepshow
Crosby, Stills & Nash: Daylight Again
Cross Creek
Cruising
Cujo
Cutter's Way
Daffy Duck's Movie: Fantastic Island
Damien—Omen II
The Dark Crystal
Dark Victory
David Copperfield
The Day After
A Day at the Races
The Day of the Dolphin
Days of Heaven
D.C. Cab
Dead and Buried
The Dead Zone
Deadly Blessing
Deadly Force
Deal of the Century
Death Hunt
Death on the Nile
Death Wish
Death Wish II
Deathstalker
The Deep
The Deer Hunter
Defiance
The Defiant Ones
Deliverance
The Desert of the Tartars
Dial "M" for Murder
Diamonds Are Forever
Diana Ross in Concert
The Diary of Anne Frank
Dillinger
Diner
The Dirty Dozen
Dirty Harry
Disney Cartoon Parade, Volumes 1-5
Diva
Divine Madness
Dr. Detroit
Doctor Doolittle
Dr. No
The Dr. Seuss Video Festival
Dr. Strangelove
Dr. Zhivago
Dog Day Afternoon
The Dogs of War
A Doll's House
Dolly in London
The Domino Principle
Don Kirshner's Rock Concert, Vol. 1
Don't Look Now
The Doobie Brothers Live
Dot and Santa Claus
Dot and the Bunny
Dot and the Kangaroo
Double Exposure
Dracula *(1931)*
Dragonslayer
Dressed to Kill *(1980)*
The Dresser
Duck Soup
Dumbo
Dunderklumpen
Duran Duran
Earth, Wind and Fire in Concert
The Earthling
East of Eden
Easy Money
Easy Rider
Eddie and the Cruisers
Eddie Macon's Run
Educating Rita
El Cid
El Dorado
The Electric Horseman
Electric Light Orchestra Live at Wembly
The Elephant Man
Elephant Parts
Elmer Gantry
Elton John: Visions
Elvis: Aloha from Hawaii
Elvis—His 1968 Comeback Special
Elvis on Tour
Emanuelle in America
Emanuelle in Bangkok
Emily
The Emperor's New Clothes
The End
Endangered Species
Endless Love
The Endless Summer
The Enforcer
Enter the Dragon
Enter the Ninja
The Entity
Eroticise
Escape from Alcatraz
Escape from New York
Escape to Athena
Escape to Witch Mountain
Eubie!
Eurythmics—Sweet Dreams (The Video Album
An Evening with Robin Williams
An Evening with the Royal Ballet
Every Which Way But Loose
Everything You Always Wanted to Know About Sex . . .

Evil Under the Sun
Evilspeak
Excalibur
The Exorcist
Exposed
The Exterminator
An Eye for an Eye
The Eyes of Laura Mars
Eyewitness
Faerie Tale Theatre
Fairy Tale Classics
The Falcon and the Snowman
Falling in Love Again
Fame
Family Entertainment Playhouse, Vol. 2
Fanny and Alexander
Fantastic Voyage
Farewell, My Lovely
Fast Times at Ridgemont High
Fear No Evil
Fiddler on the Roof
Final Assignment
The Final Conflict
The Final Countdown
Final Exam
Firebird 2015 AD
Firefox
The Firesign Theatre Presents Nick Danger in the Case of the Missing Yolk
The First Barry Manilow Special
First Blood
F.I.S.T.
A Fistful of Dollars
Five Mile Creek, Volume 1
Flaming Star
The Flamingo Kid
Flash Gordon
Flashdance
Fleetwood Mac
Fleetwood Mac in Concert—Mirage Tour 1982
The Flying Deuces
The Fog
Foolin' Around
Footloose
For a Few Dollars More
For Your Eyes Only
Forbidden Planet
Forced Vengeance
Foreplay
The Formula
Fort Apache, The Bronx
48 Hrs.
42nd Street
Foul Play
Four Friends
The Four Musketeers
The Four Seasons
Fraggle Songs, Volume 1
Frances
Frankenstein *(1931)*
The French Connection
The French Lieutenant's Woman
Friday the 13th
Friday the 13th Part II
Friendly Persuasion
Frogs
From Russia with Love
The Fugitive: The Final Episode
Fun in Acapulco
Funny Girl
A Funny Thing Happened on the Way to the Forum
Futureworld
Fuzz
Gallagher—Stuck in the 60's
Gallagher—The Maddest
Game of Death
Gandhi
Gas Pump Girls
The Gauntlet
Gentleman Jim
Get Crazy
The Getting of Wisdom
G.I. Blues
Gigi
Gilda
Gimme Shelter
Girl Groups: The Story of a Sound
Giselle
Go Tell the Spartans
The Godfather
The Godfather, Part II
Godzilla
Going Berserk
Gold Diggers of 1933
The Golden Seal
Goldfinger
Goldilocks
Goldy—The Last of the Golden Bears
Gone With the Wind
Good Guys Wear Black
The Good, the Bad and the Ugly
Goodbye, Columbus
The Goodbye Girl
Grace Jones: One Man Show
The Graduate
The Grateful Dead in Concert
Grease
Grease II
The Great Caruso
Great Cities: London, Rome, Dublin Athens
The Great Dictator
The Great Escape
Great Figures in History: John F. Kennedy
The Great Gatsby
The Great Locomotive Chase
Great Movie Stunts and The Making of Raiders of the Lost Ark
The Great Muppet Caper
The Great Santini
The Great Scout and Cathouse Thursday
The Great Space Coaster Supershow
The Great Train Robbery
The Greatest Adventure
Greatest Fights of the 70's
The Greatest Show on Earth
The Green Berets
Greystoke: The Legend of Tarzan, Lord of the Apes
Grover Washington, Jr. in Concert
Gulliver's Travels

A Gumby Adventure
Gunfight at the OK Corral
The Guns of Navarone
Gus
Guys and Dolls
Hair
Halloween II
Halloween III: The Season of the Witch
Hamlet
Hang 'em High
Hanky Panky
Hansel and Gretel
The Happy Hooker
The Happy Hooker Goes to Washington
Hard Country
A Hard Day's Night
Hard to Hold
The Harder They Come
Harold and Maude
Harper Valley PTA
Harry and Son
Harry Chapin: The Final Concert
Hawaii
He Knows You're Alone
He-Man and the Masters of the Universe
Heart Like a Wheel
Heartaches
Heaven Can Wait
Heaven's Gate
Heidi
Hello, Dolly!
Helter Skelter
Henry V
Herbie Hancock and the Rockit Band
Herbie Rides Again
Hercules
Hercules Unchained
Here It Is, Burlesque
The Heritage of the Bible
High Anxiety
The High Country
High Noon
High Road to China
High Sierra
History of the World: Part 1
The Hobbit
Hollywood Hot Tubs
Holocaust
Hooper
Hopscotch
Horowitz in London
The Horse Soldiers
The Hospital
Hospital Massacre
The Hotel New Hampshire
The Hound of the Baskervilles
The House on Sorority Row
How to Beat the High Cost of Living
The Howling
Huckleberry Finn
Hud
The Hunchback of Notre Dame *(1939)*
The Hunger
I Am a Fugitive from a Chain Gang
I Love You
I Ought to Be in Pictures
I Spit on Your Grave
I, the Jury
Iceman
if You Could See What I Hear
Improper Channels
Impulse
The In-Laws
In Praise of Older Women
In the Heat of the Night
The Incubus
Inherit the Wind
Inn of the Sixth Happiness
Intermezzo
Invasion of the Body Snatchers
Invitation to a Gunfighter
Invitation to the Dance
Irma La Douce
Irreconcilable Differences
The Island of Dr. Moreau
It Came from Hollywood
It's a Mad, Mad, Mad, Mad World
Jack and the Beanstalk
Jailhouse Rock
James Taylor in Concert
Jane Fonda's Workout
Jane Fonda's Workout for Pregnancy, Birth & Recovery
Jason and the Argonauts
Jaws
Jaws II
Jaws III
Jazz in America
The Jazz Singer *(1927)*
The Jazz Singer *(1980)*
Jeremiah Johnson
The Jerk
Jesus of Nazareth
Jethro Tull—Slipstream
Jezebel
Jinxed
Joan of Arc
Joe
John Curry's Ice Dancing
Juggernaut
Julia
Julia Child—The French Chef, Vol. 1
Junior Bonner
The Keep
Kelly's Heroes
Kenny Loggins Alive
The Kentuckian
Key Largo
Kidnapped
The Kids Are Alright
The Kids from Fame
Killer Force
King Creole
King Kong *(1932)*
King of Comedy
King of Hearts
Kipperbang
Kiss Me Goodbye
Klute
Kotch
Kramer vs. Kramer
Krull
Lady Chatterley's Lover
Lady Sings the Blues
The Last American Virgin

The Last Chase
Last House on the Left
Last Tango in Paris
The Last Unicorn
The Last Valley
The Last Waltz
The Last Word
Laura
Lawrence of Arabia
LCA Presents Family Entertainment Playhouse
The Legend of the Lone Ranger
Lenny
Let It Be
Let's Spend the Night Together
Liar's Moon
Linda Ronstadt with Nelson Riddle & His Orchestra "What's New"
The Lion in Winter
The Lion, the Witch and the Wardrobe
Little House on the Prairie
The Little Mermaid
The Little Prince—Next Stop, Planet Earth
Little Red Riding Hood
Little River Band Live Exposure
Little Women
Live and Let Die
Live Infidelity: REO Speedwagon in Concert
Logan's Run
Lolita
Lone Wolf McQuade
The Lonely Guy
The Lonely Lady
The Longest Day
The Longest Yard
Lookin' to Get Out
Looking for Mr. Goodbar
The Looney, Looney, Looney Bugs Bunny Movie
The Lord of the Rings
Lords of the Rings: Superstars and Superbouts
Losin' It
Love and Death
Love at First Bite
The Love Bug
Love in the Afternoon
Love is a Many-Splendored Thing
Love Letters
Love Me Tender
Love Story
Lovers and Liars
Mad Max
Mad Monster Party
Magic
The Magic Pony
The Magnificent Seven
Magnum Force
Mahogany
The Main Event
Making Love
Making Michael Jackson's Thriller
The Making of Star Wars . . .
The Maltese Falcon
A Man Called Horse
A Man for All Seasons
The Man from Snowy River
Man of La Mancha
Man on the Moon
The Man Who Loved Liberty Valance
The Man Who Would Be King
The Man with the Golden Gun
The Man with Two Brains
Mandingo
The Many Adventures of Winnie the Pooh
Marathon Man
Marty
Mary Poppins
The Mary Tyler Moore Show, Vol. 1
M*A*S*H
M*A*S*H: Goodbye, Farewell and Amen
Matilda
A Matter of Time
Mausoleum
Max Dugan Returns
Meatballs
Meet Me in St. Louis
Meet Mr. Washington/Meet Mr. Lincoln
Meet Your Animal Friends
Megaforce
Metalstorm
Mick Fleetwood—The Visitor
Midnight Cowboy
Midnight Express
Mighty Mouse in The Great Space Chase
Mildred Pierce
The Miracle of Lake Placid
The Mirror Crack'd
The Misfits
Miss Peach of the Kelly School
Missing
The Missouri Breaks
Mr. Magoo Cartoons
Mr. Magoo in Sherwood Forest
Mr. Mom
Mister Roberts
Mister Rogers Goes to School
Mister Rogers: Helping Children Understand
Moby Dick
Modern Problems
Modern Times
Mommie Dearest
Monique
Monsignor
Monty Python and the Holy Grail
Monty Python Live at the Hollywood Bowl
Monty Python's Life of Brian
Monty Python's The Meaning of Life
The Moon is Blue
Moonraker
More Candid Candid Camera
Movie, Movie
The Muppet Movie
Murder by Death
Murder by Decree
Murder on the Orient Express
The MUSE Concert: No Nukes

The Music of Melissa
Manchester
Mutant
My Dinner with Andre
My Fair Lady
My Favorite Year
My Little Chickadee
My Tutor
Mystery Disc #1:
Murder, Anyone?
Mystery Disc #2:
Many Roads to
Murder
The MUSE Concert:
No Nukes
The Music of Melissa
Manchester
Mutant
My Dinner with Andre
My Fair Lady
My Favorite Year
My Little Chickadee
My Tutor
Mystery Disc #1:
Murder, Anyone?
Mystery Disc #2:
Many Roads to
Murder
Nashville
Nate and Hayes
National Geographic
Presents: Great
Whales/Sharks
National Geographic
Society: The
Incredible Machine/
Mysteries of the
Mind
National Lampoon's
Vacation
Neighbors
Neil Diamond: Love
at the Greek
Network
Never Cry Wolf
Never Say Never
Again
The New Media
Bible: The
Story of Joseph
The New Video
Aerobics
New York, New York
The New York
Yankees' Miracle
Year: 1978
NFL '81 Official
Season Yearbook
Night Games
Night of the Living
Dead

The Night Porter
Night Shift
Nighthawks
Nightwing
The Nine Lives of
Fritz the Cat
9 to 5
Norma Rae
The Norseman
North by Northwest
North Dallas Forty
Nothing Personal
Notorious
Now and Forever
Now, Voyager
The Nutcracker
The Nutty Professor
Octopussy
The Odd Couple
An Officer and a
Gentleman
Oh! Calcutta!
Oh, God!
Oklahoma!
Old Boyfriends
Old Yeller
Olivia in Concert
Olivia—Physical
Oliver Twist
The Omen
On a Clear Day You
Can See Forever
On Golden Pond
On Her Majesty's
Secret Service
On the Beach
On the Town
On the Waterfront
One Flew Over the
Cuckoo's Nest
One from the Heart
The Onion Field
Ordinary People
The Oscar
The Other Side of
Nashville
Our Town
Outland
The Outsiders
The Owl and the
Pussycat
The Paper Chase
Paper Moon
Papillon
Paradise
Parasite
The Parent Trap
Paternity
Paths of Glory
Patton

Paul Simon in
Concert
Pavarotti in London
Pennies from Heaven
Penthouse Video,
Volume One: The
Girls of Penthouse
The Perils of
Gwendoline
Peter Allen and
the Rockettes
Peter-No-Tail
The Petrified Forest
Phantasm
The Phantom
Tollbooth
Piaf
The Pied Piper of
Hamelin
Pink Floyd at
Pompeii
The Pink Panther
The Pink Panther
Strikes Again
Pinocchio
Pippin
The Pirate
The Pirate Movie
The Pirates of
Penzance
The Pit and the
Pendulum
A Place in the Sun
Planet of the Apes
Play It Again, Sam
Playboy Playmate's
Workout
Playboy Video
Volumes 1-5
Playmate Review
Poco
Police Academy
Pollyanna
Poltergeist
Popeye
Porky's
The Poseidon
Adventure
The Postman Always
Rings Twice
Pretty Baby
The Pride and the
Passion
The Pride of the
Yankees
The Prince and the
Pauper
The Prince Charming
Revue
Prince of the City

Private Benjamin
The Private Eyes
Private Lessons
Private Popsicle
Private School
The Producers
Psycho
Psycho II
Public Enemy
Pumping Iron
The Purple Rose of Cairo
Purple Taxi
Puss 'N' Boots
Quadrophenia
Queen—Greatest Flix
Quest for Fire
Quick Dog Training with Barbara Woodhouse
The Quiet Man
Race for Your Life, Charlie Brown
Raggedy Ann and Andy: A Musical Adventure
Raging Bull
Ragtime
Raiders of the Lost Ark
Rainbow Brite II
Raise the Titanic
Rapunzel
The Raven
RCA's All-Star Country Music Fair
Rear Window
Rebel Without a Cause
The Red Balloon
Red River
The Red Shoes
Redd Foxx—Video in a Plain Brown Wrapper
Reds
Reefer Madness
The Return of a Man Called Horse
The Return of the Pink Panther
The Return of the Streetfighter
Return to Boggy Creek
Return to Macon County
Revenge of the Ninja
Revenge of the Pink Panther
Rich and Famous
Richard Pryor: Here and Now
Richard Pryor Live in Concert
Richard Pryor Live on Sunset Strip
Ring of Bright Water
Rio Bravo
Rio Lobo
Risky Business
Road Games
The Road Warrior
The Roaring Twenties
Robin Hood
Rockshow
Rocky
Rocky II
Rocky III
Rod Stewart Live at the L.A. Forum
Rod Stewart: Tonight He's Yours
Rodan
Rollerball
Rolling Thunder
Roman Holiday
Romancing the Stone
Romeo and Juliet
The Rose
Rosebud Beach Hotel
Rosemary's Baby
Royal Wedding *(with Fred Astaire*
R.S.V.P.
The Ruling Class
Rumble Fish
Rumpelstiltskin
Run Silent, Run Deep
Running Brave
Rush Exit...Stage Left
The Russians Are Coming, the Russians Are Coming
Rust Never Sleeps
Sacred Ground
The Sacred Music of Duke Ellington
The Sailor Who Fell from Grace with the Sea
Sands of Iwo Jima
Saturday Night Fever
Saturday Night Live, Vol.1
Saturday Night Live, Vol.2
Savage Streets
Savannah Smiles
Sayonara
Scandalous
Scanners
Scarface *(1982)*
Scholastic Productions: As We Grow
The Sea Wolves
Search and Destroy
The Searchers
The Secret of NIMH
The Secret Policeman's Other Ball
The Seduction
Seems Like Old Times
Semi-Tough
Seniors
Separate Tables
Separate Ways
Sergeant York
Serpico
Seven Brides for Seven Brothers
Seven Days in May
The Seven Year Itch
The 7th Voyage of Sinbad
Sex on the Run
Shadows and Light
Shaft
The Shaggy Dog
Shane
Sharky's Machine
Sheena Easton—Live at the Palace, Hollywood
The Shining
Shogun
Shoot the Moon
The Shootist
A Shot in the Dark
The Shout
The Showdown: Sugar Ray Leonard vs. Thomas Hearns
The Silent Partner
Silent Rage
Silkwood
Silver Streak
Simon & Garfunkel: The Concert in Central Park
A Simple Story
Sinbad and the Eye of the Tiger
Singin' in the Rain
Six Pack
Six Weeks
Sixteen Candles
The Slap
Slave of the Cannibal God
Sleeping Beauty

Tom and Jerry 1-3
Tom Jones
Tom Sawyer
Tommy
A Tony Bennett Songbook
Tootsie
Topkapi
Tora! Tora! Tora!
Totally Go-Go's
The Towering Inferno
The Toy
Trading Places
The Trail of the Pink Panther
Trapeze
La Traviata
Treasure
Treasure Island
Treasure of the Four Crowns
The Treasure of the Sierra Madre
Tribute
Trinity is Still My Name
Tron
Truck Stop Women
True Confessions
True Grit
Truly Tasteless Jokes
Tubby the Tuba
The Tubes Video
Tulips
The Turning Point
Tut: The Boy King/The Louvre
12 Angry Men
20,000 Leagues Under the Sea
Twilight Zone—The Movie
Two of a Kind
2001: A Space Odyssey
Uncommon Valor
The Undersea World of Jacques Cousteau, Vol.1
An Unmarried Woman
Up in Smoke
Urban Cowboy
Used Cars
Utilities
Utopia
Valley Girl
Venom
Vera Cruz
The Verdict
Vertigo
Vice Squad
Victor/Victoria
Victory
Victory at Sea
Video Rewind
Village of the Damned
Visiting Hours
Viva Las Vegas
The Wacky World of Mother Goose
War Games
The War of the Worlds
Warlords of the 21st Century
Warrior and the Sorceress
The Washington Affair
Wasn't That a Time!
Watership Down
The Way We Were
A Week at the Races
Weekend Pass
The Weight Watchers Guide to a Healthy Lifestyle
West Side Story
Westworld
What's New Pussycat?
What's Up, Doc?
What's Up Tiger Lily?
When a Stranger Calls
Where's Poppa?
White Heat
White Lightning
The Who Rocks America—1982 American Tour
Wholly Moses!
Who's Afraid of Opera? Vols.1-3
Whose Life Is It Anyway?
Wifemistress
The Wild Bunch
The Wild Geese
Wild in the Country
Wimbledon Tennis: 1979-1980
Wimbledon 1981/ Wimbledon: A Century of Greatness
Wings
Winter Kills
Witches' Brew
With Six You Get Eggroll
Without a Trace
Witness for the Prosecution
The Wizard of Oz
Women in Love
The Woman in Red
Woodstock
Woody Woodpecker and Friends, Volume 1
The World According to Garp
World Series 1980
X-Tro
Yankee Doodle Dandy
The Year of Living Dangerously
Yes, Giorgio
Yoga Moves with Alan Finger
Yor, the Hunter from the Future
You Only Live Twice
Young Doctors in Love
Young Frankenstein
Z
Zapped!
Zelig
Zero to Sixty
Ziegfeld Follies
Zombie
Zorro, the Gay Blade

LASER OPTICAL DISCS

Abba
Abba in Concert
ABC—Mantrap
Absence of Malice
The Absent-Minded Professor
The Adventures of Buckaroo Banzai
The Adventures of Eliza Fraser
The Adventures of Robin Hood
The Adventures of the Wilderness Family
Aerobicise: The Beautiful Workout
Aerobicise: The Beginning Workout
Aerobicise: The Ultimate Workout
The African Queen
Aida
Air Supply in Hawaii
Airplane!
Airplane II: The Sequel
Alice in Wonderland
Alien
All That Jazz

The Allman Brothers Band—Brothers of the Road
Altered States
Alvin Purple
Alvin Rides Again
America Live in Central Park
American Ballet Theatre/Don Quixote
American Graffiti
An American in Paris
An American Werewolf in London
The Amityville Horror
Amityville II: The Possession
Among the Cinders
The Anderson Tapes
And God Created Woman
And Justice for All
Angel of H.E.A.T.
Angelo My Love
Angels Die Hard
Animal House
The Annenberg
Anne Byrd's Cookery
Annie
Annie Hall
Any Which Way You Can
Apocalypse Now
April Wine
Armed Forces Workout
Arthur
Ashford & Simpson
Asia in Asia
Atlantic City
Autumn Sonata
Avenging Angel
The Bad News Bears
Badlands
Ball of Fire
The Ballad of Gregorio Cortez
Bananas
Bang the Drum Slowly
Barbarella
Barefoot in the Park
Barry Manilow Live at the Greek
Basic Karate and Self Defense
Battlestar Galactica
B.C. Holiday Happenings
The Beach Girls
The Beastmaster
Beatlemania—The Movie
Beat Street
Beauty and the Beast
Being There
Belly Dancing—You Can Do It!
Ben Hur
A Berenstain Bears Celebration
Bernadette Peters in Concert
Best Defense
Best Friends
The Best Little Whorehouse in Texas
The Best of Mary Hartman, Mary Hartman, Volume II
The Best Years of Our Lives
The Bette Midler Show
Between the Lines
The Big Chill
The Big Sleep
Billy Crystal: A Comic's Line
Billy Joel: Live from Long Island
Billy Squier Live in the Dark
Biology: Lesson 1, Respiration; Lesson 2, Climate and Life
Bio Sci Video Disc
Bite the Bullet
The Black Hole
The Black Stallion
The Black Stallion Returns
Blade Runner
Blame It on Rio
Blazing Saddles
Blow Out
Blue Hawaii
The Blue Lagoon
The Blues Brothers
Blue Thunder
The Boat
Bob Marley & the Wailers
Body Heat
Body Music
La Boheme
Bolero
Bon Voyage, Charlie Brown
Bonnie and Clyde
The Border
The Bostonians
The Bounty
The Boy Who Left Home to Find Out About the Shivers
The Boys from Brazil
Brainstorm
Brass Target
Breaker Morant
Breakfast at Tiffany's
Breakin'
Breathless
The Bridge of San Luis Rey
The Bridge on the River Kwai
Brigadoon
Broadway Danny Rose
Brubaker
Buck Rogers in the 25th Century
Bugsy Malone
Bury Me an Angel
Bustin' Loose
Butch Cassidy and the Sundance Kid
Butterfly
Cabaret
Cactus Flower
Caddyshack
La Cage Aux Folles
Caledonian Dreams
California Suite
Caligula
Camelot
The Cannonball Run
Capricorn One
Carbon Copy
Carlin at Carnegie
Carlin on Campus
Carnal Knowledge
Carole King—One to One
Carrie
The Cars: 1984-1985—Live
Cartoon Classics Volume 1: Chip 'n' Dale with Donald Duck
Cartoon Classics Volume 2: Pluto
Cartoon Classics Volume 3: Disney's Scary Tales
Cartoon Classics Volume 4: Sport Goofy
Cartoon Classics Volume 5: Disney's Best of 1931-1948

Casablanca
Cat on a Hot Tin Roof
Cat People (*1982*)
Catch-22
Catherine the Great
The Champ
Champions
The Changeling
Chapter Two
Chariots of Fire
The Charlie Daniels Band: The Saratoga Concert
Charlotte's Web
Charly
Cheech & Chong's Next Movie
Cheech & Chong's Nice Dreams
Cher: A Celebration at Caesar's
Chick Corea/Gary Burton Live in Tokyo
Children of the Corn
The China Syndrome
Chinatown
Chitty Chitty Bang Bang
Christine
Christine McVie Concert
A Christmas Story
The Cincinnati Kid
Cinderella
City Heat
Clash of the Titans
Class
Class of 1984
Claude Bolling: Concerto for Classic Guitar and Jazz Piano
A Clockwork Orange
Close Encounters of the Third Kind (The Special Edition)
Clouds Over Europe
Coal Miner's Daughter
Coast to Coast
Coma
Come Back to the 5 and Dime Jimmy Dean, Jimmy Dean
Coming Home
The Competition
The Compleat Beatles
Conan the Barbarian
Conan the Destroyer
Continental Divide
The Conversation
Cool Cats
Cool Hand Luke
The Cotton Club
Country
Crackers
The Creative Camera
Crimes of Passion
Crosby, Stills & Nash: Daylight Again
Cross Country
Cujo
Daffy Duck's Movie: Fantastic Island
Dark Waters
Daryl Hall and John Oates—Rock 'n Soul Live
Dave Mason Live at Perkins Palace
David Bowie
David Bowie-Serious Moonlight
Davy Crockett and the River Pirates
The Day After
A Day at the Races
Days of Heaven
D.C. Cab
Dead Men Don't Wear Plaid
The Dead Zone
Deal of the Century
Death Hunt
Death Watch
Death Wish
Death Wish II
The Deep
The Deer Hunter
Deliverance
Developing Your Financial Strategy
Diamonds Are Forever
Diana Ross in Concert
Diner
Dinner at Eight
The Dirt Band Tonite
The Dirty Dozen
Dirty Harry
Diva
Dr. Detroit
Dr. No
The Dr. Seuss Video Festival
Dr. Strangelove
Doctor Zhivago
Dodsworth
Dolly in London
Don't Look Now
Donovan's Reef
Downhill Racer
Dracula (1979)
Dragonslayer
Dressed to Kill (1981)
Drums
Dumbo
Dunderklumpen
Dune
Duran Duran
Dvorak's Slavic Dance
Earth, Wind and Fire in Concert
Easy Money
Easy Rider
Eddie and the Cruisers
Eddie Macon's Run
Educating Rita
El Cid
Electric Boogaloo, Breakin' 2
Electric Dreams
The Electric Horseman
Elephant Boy
The Elephant Man
Elephant Parts
Elton John in Central Park, New York
Elton John: Visions
Elvis on Tour
Emmanuelle
Emmanuelle, The Joys of a Woman
The Emperor's New Clothes
The Empire Strikes Back
Enchanted Forest
The End
Endless Love
The Endless Summer
Enigma
Enter the Dragon
Ernie Kovacs: Television's Original Genius
Eroticise
Escape from Alcatraz
Escape from New York
Escape to Witch Mountain
Eurythmics—Sweet Dreams (The Video Album)
The Eve
An Evening with Ray Charles
An Evening with Robin Williams

Everything You Always Wanted to Know About Sex . . .
The Exorcist
The Eyes of Laura Mars
The Fabulous Fleischer Folio, Volume One
Faerie Tale Theatre
Fail Safe
Falling in Love
Falstaff
Fame
The Fan
La Faniculla Del West
Fanny and Alexander
Fast Times at Ridgemont High
The Female Impersonator Pageant
Fiddler on the Roof
La Fille Mal Gardee
The Final Terror
Finian's Rainbow
Firefox
Firestarter
The First Barry Manilow Special
First Born
First Monday in October
The First National Kidisc
Five Mile Creek, Volume 1
Flash Gordon
Flashdance
Fleetwood Mac
The Fog
Football Follies
Footloose
For a Few Dollars More
For Your Eyes Only
Forbidden Planet
Force 10 from Navarone
Fort Apache, The Bronx
42nd St.
48 Hours
Foul Play
The Four Feathers
The Four Seasons
Fraggle Songs, Volume One
The French Connection
The French Lieutenant's Woman
Friday the 13th, Part 3
The Frog Prince
From Russia with Love
From the New World
Fun and Games
Funny Face
Funny Girl
A Funny Thing Happened on the Way to the Forum
Galaxina
Gallagher—Some Uncensored Evening
Gallagher—Stuck in the 60's
Gallagher—The Maddest
Gallipoli
The Gambler
Gandhi
Gardening at Home
Gas Pump Girls
Get Crazy
Ghost Story
Gigi
Gimme Shelter
Girl Groups
Girls of Rock and Roll
Give My Regards to Broad Street
Gloria
Go Tell the Spartans
The Godfather
The Godfather, Part II
Godzilla
Goin' South
Going Berserk
A Golden Decade of College Football
The Golden Seal
Goldfinger
Goldilocks and the Three Bears
Gone With the Wind
Good Guys Wear Black
The Good, the Bad and the Ugly
Goodbye, Columbus
The Goodbye Girl
Gorky Park
Grace Jones: One Man Show
The Graduate
Grand Hotel
Grateful Dead/ Dead Ahead, The
Grease
Grease 2
The Great Escape
The Great Gatsby
Great Movie Stunts and The Making of Raiders of the Lost Ark
The Great Muppet Caper
The Great Train Robbery
The Greatest Adventure
The Greatest Show on Earth
Greystoke: The Legend of Tarzan, Lord of the Apes
Grover Washington, Jr. in Concert
Gunfight at the OK Corral
The Guns of Navarone
Guys and Dolls
Hair
Halloween
Halloween II
Hanky Panky
Hansel and Gretel
Happy Birthday to Me
The Happy Hooker
The Happy Hooker Goes Hollywood
The Happy Hooker Goes to Washington
Hardcore
A Hard Day's Night
Hard Times
Hard to Hold
Harold and Maude
Harry and Son
Harry Chapin: The Final Concert
Hatari!
Heart of the Stag
Heartaches
Hearts and Minds
Heaven Can Wait
Hello, Dolly!
Herbie Hancock and the Rockit Band
He-Man and the Masters of the Universe
Hercules
Here It Is, Burlesque
Hey, Cinderella
Highest Honor
High Point
High Road to China
High Sierra
High Society
The History Disquiz
History of the World, Part I
H.M.S. Pinafore
Hocus Pocus, It's Magic
Homework
Honeysuckle Rose

Horowitz in London
Hostage Tower
Hotel New Hampshire
Hot Stuff
A Hot Summer Night with Donna
House Calls
House on Sorority Row
Hot to Watch Pro Football
The Howling
The Huberman Festival Vol. 1
Hud
The Hunger
The Hunter
Hussy
I Like to Hurt People
I Spit on Your Grave
Iceman
Ice Pirates
Idolmaker
If You Could See What I Hear
I'm Dancing as Fast as I Can
Improper Channels
Impulse
In Cold Blood
In Praise of Older Women
The Incredible Shrinking Woman
The Incubus
Infinity Factory
Invasion of the Body Snatchers
Iron Maiden
Irreconcilable Differences
Islands in the Stream
It Came from Hollywood
It's a Mad, Mad, Mad, Mad World
It's My Turn
It's 1984
Itzhak Perlman
Jack and the Beanstalk
James Taylor in Concert
Jam Introduction to Computer Literacy
Jason and the Argonauts
Jaws
Jaws III
The Jazz Singer (1980)
Jazzercise
Jefferson Starship
Jeremiah Johnson
The Jerk
Jesus Christ Superstar
J. Geils Band
Jim Fixx on Running
Joe
Joy of Family
The Joy of Relaxation
The Joy of Stocks
Judy Garland in Concert
The Jungle Book
Kajagoogoo
Kanako
Kelly's Heroes
Kenny Loggins Alive
Kentucky Fried Movie
Kevin Rowland/Dexy's Midnight Runners
Key Largo
Kids From Fame in Concert
Killing Point
Kim Carnes
The King of Comedy
The King and I
King Kong (1977)
Klute
The Knack—Live at Carnegie Hall
Koyaanisqatsi
Kramer vs. Kramer
Krull
Lady Chatterly's Lover
Lady on the Bus
Lady Sings the Blues
Lamaze
Lassiter
The Last Detail
Last of the Red Hot Lovers
Last Tango in Paris
Lawrence of Arabia
Lenny
The Lenny Bruce Performance Film
Let It Be
Let's Bowl
Let's Spend the Night Together
Linda Ronstadt with Nelson Riddle and His Orchestra—"What's New"
The Lion Has Wings
The Lion in Winter
Lipstick
Little Darlings
The Little Drummer Girl
The Little Foxes
The Little Mermaid
The Little Prince
Little Red Riding Hood
Little River Band Live Exposure
Live and Let Die
Live Infidelity: REO Speedway in Concert
Liza Minnelli in Concert
Logan's Run
Lone Wolf McQuade
The Lonely Guy
The Lonely Lady
The Longest Yard
Looking for Mr. Goodbar
The Lords of Discipline
Loretta
Losin' It
Love and Death
Love at First Bite
The Love Bug
Love From a Stranger
Love Story
Loverboy
Loving Couples
Lust in the Dust
Lydia
Ma Vlast (My Fatherland)
Mad Max
Magic
The Magic Pony
The Magician
The Magnificent Seven
Mahogany
Making Michael Jackson's Thriller
The Making of Star Wars/S.P.F.X.—The Empire Strikes Back
The Maltese Falcon
Mame
A Man For All Seasons
The Man Who Fell to Earth
The Man Who Loved Women
The Man Who Shot Liberty Valance
The Man With the Golden Gun
The Man with Two Brains
Mandingo
Manhattan
Manhattan Transfer in Concert
Manon
Manon Lescaut
The Many Adventures of Winnie the Pooh

Marathon Man
Mars and Beyond
Mary Poppins
M*A*S*H
M*A*S*H: Goodbye, Farewell and Amen
Mass Appeal
The Master Cooking Course
Max Dugan Returns
Maze Featuring Frankie Beverly
Maze Mania
Meatballs
Meet Me in St. Louis
Meet Your Animal Friends
La Melodie D'Amour
Mel Torme and Della Reese in Concert
Melvin and Howard
Men Are Not Gods
Metalstorm
Metropolitan Opera/Don Carlo
Metropolitan Opera/Lucia Di Lammermoor
Mickey Mouse and Donald Duck Cartoon Collection, Volume 1-3
Midnight Express
Mildred Pierce
A Minor Miracle
Missing
Missing in Action
Mission Batangas
Mission Galactica: The Cylon Attack
Mr. Magoo in Sherwood Forest
Mr. Magoo's Christmas Carol
Mr. Mom
Mommie Dearest
Monty Python and the Holy Grail
Monty Python's The Meaning of Life
The Moon Is Blue
Moonlighting
The Motels
The Mountain Men
The Muppet Movie
The Muppet Musicians of Bremen
Murder by Death
Murder on the Orient Express
Muscle Motion
The MUSE Concert: No Nukes
Music Is
The Music of Melissa Manchester
Mutiny on the Bounty
My Bloody Valentine
My Fair Lady
My Tutor
Mysterious Island
Mystery Disc #1: Murder Anyone?
Mystery Disc #2: Many Roads to Murder
Naked Eyes
Nashville
Nate and Hayes
National Gallery: Art Awareness Collection
The National Gallery of Art
National Lampoon's Class Reunion
National Lampoon's Vacation
Neighbors
Neil Diamond: Love at the Greek
Neil Sedaka in Concert
Network
Never Cry Wolf
The Neverending Story
Never Say Never Again
New Look
NFL SymFunny/ Legends of the Fall
Night Games
The Night Porter
Night Shift
Nighthawks
9 to 5
Ninotchka
1941
Norma Rae
North by Northwest
North Dallas Forty
Notorious
Now and Forever
The Nutcracker
Obsession
Octopussy
The Odd Couple
An Officer and a Gentleman
Oklahoma!
Oh God!, You Devil
Old Yeller
Olivia
Olivia in Concert
Olivia—Physical
The Omen
On a Clear Day You Can See Forever
On Golden Pond
On Her Majesty's Secret Service
Once Upon a Time in America
Once Upon a Time in the West
The One and Only Genuine Original Family Band
One From the Heart
One Night Stand—A Keyboard Event
The Onion Field
Only When I Laugh
Orca
Orchestra De Paul Mauriat
Ordinary People
Oriental Dreams
Otello
The Other Side of Nashville
Out of Control
Out of the Blue
Outland
Paint Your Wagon
Paper Moon
The Parent Trap
Party Games—For Adults Only
Passion of Love
Pastel Color
Paternity
Patton
Paul Simon in Concert
Pavarotti in London
Penthouse Video Volume One: The Girls of Penthouse
Performance
Peter Allen and the Rockettes
Peter Grimes
Pete's Dragon
Phantasm
Picture Music
The Pied Piper of Hamelin

The Pink Panther
The Pink Panther Strikes Again
Pinocchio
Pippin
The Pirates of Penzance
Pink Floyd: The Wall
The Pit and the Pendulum
A Place in the Sun
Play It Again, Sam
Play Misty for Me
Playboy Video, Volumes 1-4
Playmate Review
Police Academy
The Police—Synchronicity
Pollyanna
Popeye
Poltergeist
Porky's
Porky's 2—The Next Day
The Postman Always Rings Twice
Pretty Baby
The Pride of the Yankees
Prince of the City
The Princess and the Pirate
Private Benjamin
The Private Eyes
Private Lessons
Private School
Prom Night
Protocol
Psycho
Psycho II
Purple Rain
Puss 'N' Boots
Quadrophenia
Queen—Greatest Flix
Queen—The Works
Quest for Fire
Raccoon's Collection
Race for Your Life, Charlie Brown
Raggedy Man
Raging Bull
Ragtime
Raiders of the Lost Ark
Railroaded
Rainbow Brite—Mighty Monstromork Menace
Rainbow Brite, Vols. 1-2
Rainbow Goblins Story
Rainbow Live Between the Eyes
Raise the Titanic
Rapunzel
The Raven
Raw Courage
Rear Window
Rebel Without a Cause
Reckless
Red Dawn
Redd Foxx—Video in a Plain Brown Wrapper
Reds
Rembrandt
The Return of Martin Guerre
The Return of the Pink Panther
Revenge of the Pink Panther
Rich and Famous
Richard Pryor—Here and Now
Richard Pryor—Live and Smokin'
Richard Pryor—Live on the Sunset Strip
The Right Stuff
Risky Business
The River
The River Rat
The Road Warrior
Robin Hood
Rock Adventure
Rockshow
Rocky
Rocky II
Rocky III
Rod Stewart: Tonight He's Yours
Rodan
Romeo and Juliet
Rope
The Rose
Rosemary's Baby
Rostropovich
Rough Cut
Roxy Music—The High Road
R.S.V.P.
Rumble Fish
Rumpelstiltskin
Running Brave
Rush Exit . . Stage Left
The Sailor Who Fell from Grace with the Sea
Samson and Delilah
Samson et Dalila
Sanders of the River
Saturday Night Fever
Saturn 3
Savage Streets
Savannah Smiles
Save the Tiger
Scandalous
Scarface (1982)
The Secret of NIMH
The Secret Policeman's Other Ball
The Searchers
The Seduction of Joe Tynan
Seems Like Old Times
Semi-Tough
The Sender
Sgt. Pepper's Lonely Hearts Club Band
Serial
Serpico
Seven Days in May
Sex on the Run
Shadows and Light
The Shaggy Dog
Shane
Sheena Easton
Sheena Easton Live at the Palace, Hollywood
Shogun
Shogun Assassin
The Shootist
A Shot in the Dark
The Silent Partner
Silent Rage
Silkwood
Simon & Garfunkel: The Concert in Central Park
Sinbad and the Eye of the Tiger
Singin' in the Rain
Sixteen Candles
Slap Shot
Slapstick of Another Kind
Sleeper
Sleeping Beauty
Slumber Party '57
Smokey and the Bandit
Smokey and the Bandit II
Smokey and the Bandit Part 3
The Smurfs and the Magic Flute
The Snow Queen
A Soldier's Tale

The Solid Gold Five Day Workout
Some Kind of Hero
Some Like It Hot
Something Wicked This Way Comes
Somewhere in Time
Sonezaki Shinju
Son of Football Follies/Big Game America
Sophie's Choice
The Sound of Music
Sounder
Southern Comfort
South Pacific
Soylent Green
Space Disc 1-7
Space Hunter
Space Shuttle Mission Reports: STS 5, 6 & 7
Splash
Spring Break
The Spy Who Loved Me
Stalag 17
Star Crash
Stardust Memories
Star 80
A Star Is Born (*1954*)
Starstruck
Star Trek—The Motion Picture
Star Trek II: The Wrath of Khan
Star Trek III: The Search for Spock
Star Wars
Stars on 45
Starting Over
Staying Alive
Steel
Steve Miller Band Live
Stevie Nicks in Concert
Still of the Night
The Sting
The Sting II
Stir Crazy
The Story of O
Strange Invaders
Straw Dogs
Stray Cats
Streets of Fire
Strike Up the Band
Stripes
Strong Kids, Safe Kids
Student Bodies
Styx—Caught in the Act
Sudden Impact
Suddenly Last Summer
Summer Lovers
Super Memories of the Super Bowls
Super 70's
Superman—The Movie
Superman II
Superman III
The Sure Thing
The Survivors
Swamp Thing
Swan Lake
Swept Away
Swing Shift
Swiss Family Robinson
The Sword and the Sorcerer
Table for Five
Takanaka World
Take the Money and Run
The Tale of the Frog Prince
Tales of Hoffmann
Tank
Tarzan, the Ape Man (*1981*)
Taxi Driver
Teatro Alla Scala/Ernani
Tempest
"10"
The Ten Commandments
Ten to Midnight
Terms of Endearment
Terror in the Swamp
The Terry Fox Story
Tess
Testament
Tex
The Texas Chainsaw Massacre
That Hamilton Woman
That's Dancing
That's Entertainment
There's a Meetin' Here Tonight
These Three
They All Laughed
They Call Me Bruce
They Shoot Horses, Don't They?
Thief of Hearts
The Thing (*1981*)
Things Are Tough All Over
35mm Photography
This is Spinal Tap
Thomas Dolby
Three Days of the Condor
The Three Little Pigs
The Three Stooges
Thumbelina
Thunderball
Till Marriage Do Us Part
Time Bandits
The Time Machine
To Catch a Thief
Tom & Jerry Cartoon Festival, Vol. 1-2
Tom Jones
Tommy
Tootsie
Tora! Tora! Tora!
Torchlight
The Touch of Love: Massage
The Toy
Toy Soldiers
Trading Places
The Trail of the Pink Panther
La Traviata
Treasure
Treasure Island
The Treasure of Sierra Madre
Tribute
Tron
Tropical High Noon
True Confessions
True Grit
The Tubes Video
Tuff Turf
Twilight Zone—The Movie
Twisted Sister's Stay Hungry
Twist of Fate
2001: A Space Odyssey
2010
Uncommon Valor
Under Fire
Unfaithfully Yours
Up in Smoke
Up the Creek
Urban Cowboy
Used Cars
Valley Girl
The Velveteen Rabbit
The Verdict
Vertigo
Vice Squad
Victor/Victoria
Video Rewind
Videodrome

Vietnam: The Ten Thousand Day War
Vincent Van Gogh: A Portrait in Two Parts
War and Peace
War Games
The War of the Worlds
The Warrior and the Sorceress
The Warriors
Wave Length
The Way We Were
Wedding Rehearsal
Weekend Pass
We're All Devo
The Westerner
West Side Story
What's Up Tiger Lilly?
When a Stranger Calls
When Worlds Collide
White Music
The Who Rocks America: 1982 World Tour
Wholly Moses!
The Wild Bunch
Wild Gypsies
Wings
The Wiz
The Wizard of Oz
The Woman in Red
The Women
Woody Woodpecker and Friends
The World of Martial Arts
Wuthering Heights
Xanadu
Yankee Doodle Dandy
The Year of Living Dangerously
Yellowbeard
Yentl
Yeoman of the Guard
Yes Giorgio
Yoga Moves with Alan Finger
Yor: The Hunter From the Future
Young Doctors in Love
Young Frankenstein
You Only Live Twice
Yum-Yum Girls
Z
Zapped!
Zelig

Closed-Captioned Index

Following is an alphabetical list of home video programs currently available with closed captions. Distributors of the programs and the formats in which closed captioning is available are listed next to the title. Captioning of all programs is provided by The National Captioning Institute, Falls Church, Virginia.

Against All Odds (RCA/Columbia Pictures Home Video: B,V,CED)
Airforce (Key Video: B,V)
All The Right Moves (CBS/Fox Video: B,V,LV,CED)
American Dreamer (CBS/Fox Video: B,V)
Annie (RCA/Columbia Pictures Home Video: B,V)
Avenging Angel (New World Video: B,V,LV,CED)

Bachelor Party (CBS/Fox Video: B,V)
Battle for the Planet of the Apes (Playhouse Video: B,V)
B.C.: The First Thanksgiving (Embassy Home Entertainment: B,V)
Beany and Cecil, Volumes 4–8 (RCA/Columbia Pictures Home Video: B,V)
Beauty and the Beast (CBS/Fox Video: B,V,LV,CED)
Beneath the Planet of the Apes (Playhouse Video: B,V)
Best Defense (Paramount Home Video: B,V,LV,CED)
The Best of 60 Minutes (CBS/Fox Video: B,V)
The Big Chill (RCA/Columbia Pictures Home Video: B,V,LV,CED)
Bill Cosby, Himself (CBS/Fox Video: B,V)
Billy Budd (Key Video: B,V)
Birdy (RCA/Columbia Pictures Home Video: B,V,LV,CED)
Blue Thunder (RCA/Columbia Pictures Home Video: B,V)
Body Double (RCA/Columbia Pictures Home Video: B,V,LV,CED)
A Boy Named Charlie Brown (CBS/Fox Video: B,V)
The Boy Who Left Home to Find Out About the Shivers (CBS/Fox Video: B,V,LV,CED)
Breakheart Pass (Key Video: B,V)
Brian's Song (RCA/Columbia Pictures Home Video: B,V,CED)
Brother from Another Planet (Key Video: B,V)
Bubba Until It Hurts (Continental Video: B,V)
The Buddy System (Key Video: B,V)

The Caine Mutiny (RCA/Columbia Pictures Home Video: B,V)
Cannonball Run II (Warner Home Video: B,V,LV)
The Care Bears Battle the Freeze Machine (Family Home Entertainment: B,V)
The Care Bears Movie (Vestron Video: B,V)
Careful, He Might Hear You (CBS/Fox Video: B,V)
Cast a Giant Shadow (Key Video: B,V)

The Cat in the Hat and Dr. Seuss on the Loose (Playhouse Video: B,V)
Champions (Embassy Home Entertainment: B,V)
Chapter Two (RCA/Columbia Pictures Home Video: B,V)
Children's Songs and Stories (Playhouse Video: B,V)
The China Syndrome (RCA/Columbia Pictures Home Video: B,V)
Cinderella (CBS/Fox Video: B,V,LV,CED)
City Heat (Warner Home Video: B,V,LV)
The Class of Miss MacMichael (CBS/Fox Video: B,V)
Cloak and Dagger (MCA Home Video: B,V)
Close Encounters of the Third Kind: The Special Edition (RCA/Columbia Pictures Home Video: B,V)
Cold Feet (CBS/Fox Video: B,V)
The Complete Guide to Dog Care (CBS/Fox Video: B,V,CED)
Conan the Destroyer (MCA Home Video: B,V)
Conquest of the Planet of the Apes (Playhouse Video: B,V)
Constructing Stud Walls (You-Can-Do-It Videos: B,V)
The Cotton Club (Embassy Home Video: B,V,LV,CED)
Country Music With the Muppets (Playhouse Video: B,V)
Crimes of Passion (New World Video: B,V)
D.C. Cab (MCA Home Video: B,V)
David Copperfield (Vestron Video: B,V)
The Dead Zone (Paramount Home Video: B,V,LV,CED)
Dot and the Bunny (CBS/Fox Video: B,V,CED)
The Dresser (RCA/Columbia Pictures Home Video: B,V,LV,CED)
The Driver (CBS/Fox Video: B,V)
Dune (MCA Home Video: B,V)

Easy Money (Vestron Video: B,V)
Educating Rita (RCA/Columbia Pictures Home Video: B,V,LV,CED)
The Empire Strikes Back (CBS/Fox Video: B,V)
The Emperor's New Clothes (CBS/Fox Video: B,V,LV,CED)
Escape from the Planet of the Apes (Playhouse Video: B,V)
The Eyes of Laura Mars (RCA/Columbia Pictures Home Video: B,V,LV)
The Evil That Men Do (RCA/Columbia Pictures Home Video: B,V)

Faerie Tale Theatre (CBS/Fox Video: B,V,LV,CED)
Fail Safe (RCA/Columbia Pictures Home Video: B,V)
Fairy Tales Volumes II and III (Embassy Home Entertainment: B,V)
The Falcon and the Snowman (Vestron Video: B,V)
Falling in Love (Paramount Home Video: B,V,LV)
The Fantastic Adventures of Unico, Volume I (RCA/Columbia Pictures Home Video: B,V)
Fast Forward (RCA/Columbia Pictures Home Video: B,V)
Finders Keepers (Key Video: B,V)
Firestarter (MCA Home Video: B,V)
First Aid: The Video Kit (CBS/Fox Video: B,V)
First Born (Paramount Home Video: B,V,LV)
The Flamingo Kid (Vestron Video: B,V)
Flashdance (Paramount Home Video: B,V,LV,CED)
Flim-Flam Man (Playhouse Video: B,V)
Footloose (Paramount Home Video: B,V,LV,CED)
For a Few Dollars More (Key Video: B,V)

Foxes (Key Video: B,V)
French Connection II (CBS/Fox Video: B,V)
Friday the 13th-The Final Chapter (Paramount Home Video: B,V,LV,CED)
The Frog Prince (CBS/Fox Video: B,V,LV,CED)

Garbo Talks (CBS/Fox Video: B,V)
Giant (Warner Home Video: B,V,LV)
G.I. Joe: A Real American Hero (Family Home Entertainment: B,V)
G.I. Joe: A Real American Hero-The Revenge of the Cobra (Family Home Entertainment: B,V)
Give My Regards to Broad Street (CBS/Fox Video: B,V)
The Golden Voyage of Sinbad (RCA/Columbia Pictures Home Video: B,V)
Goldilocks (CBS/Fox Video: B,V)
Gone With the Wind (MGM/UA Home Video: B,V)
Gonzo's Weird Stuff (Playhouse Video: B,V)
The Graduate (Embassy Home Entertainment: B,V)
Grand Hotel (MGM/UA Home Video: B,V)
Grandview U.S.A. (Key Video: B,V)
Great Expectations (Vestron Video: B,V)
The Greatest Story Ever Told (CBS/Fox Video: B,V)
Green Ice (Key Video: B,V)
Greystoke: The Legend of Tarzan (Warner Home Video: B,V)

Hanky Panky (RCA/Columbia Pictures Home Video: B,V,CED)
Hansel and Gretel (CBS/Fox Video: B,V,LV,CED)
Hardbodies (RCA/Columbia Pictures Home Video: B,V,CED)
Hard to Hold (MCA Home Video: B,V,LV)
Harry and Tonto (Key Video: B,V)
The Heart is a Lonely Hunter (Warner Home Video: B,V,LV)
Heart Like a Wheel (CBS/Fox Video: B,V)
Heathcliff Volume 1 (RCA/Columbia Pictures Home Video: B,V)
Helter Skelter (Key Video: B,V)
He-Man and the Masters of the Universe, Volumes 7-12 (RCA/Columbia Pictures Home Video: B,V)
Hercules (MGM/UA Home Video: B,V,LV)
Horse Soldiers (CBS/Fox Video: B,V)
The Hospital (Key Video: B,V)
Hot Dog, The Movie (Key Video: B,V)
How-To Videos (You-Can-Do-It Videos: B,V)

Installing a Pre-Hung Door (You-Can-Do-It Videos: B,V)
Installing a Suspended Ceiling (You-Can-Do-It Videos: B,V)
Installing Insulation and Sheetrock (You-Can-Do-It Videos: B,V)
Installing Locksets (You-Can-Do-It Videos: B,V)
Into the Night (MCA Home Video: B,V)
Irreconcilable Differences (Vestron Video: B,V)
It Happened One Night (RCA/Columbia Pictures Home Video: B,V)

Jack and the Beanstalk (CBS-Fox Video: B,V,LV,CED)
Jane Fonda's Prime Time Workout (Karl/Lorimar Home Video: B,V)

Jane Fonda's Workout Challenge (Karl/Lorimar Home Video: B,V)
Jim Henson's Muppet Videos (Playhouse Video: B,V)
Johnny Dangerously (CBS/Fox Video: B,V)
Journey to the Center of the Earth (Playhouse Video: B,V)
Juggernaut (Key Video: B,V)
Karate Kid (RCA/Columbia Pictures Home Video: B,V,LV, CED)
The Kermit and Piggy Story (Playhouse Video: B,V)
The Killing Fields (Warner Home Video: B,V)
The Killing Hour (CBS/Fox Video: B,V)
King David (Paramount Home Video: B,V,LV)
Kings' Row (Key Video: B,V)
Kramer vs. Kramer (RCA/Columbia Pictures Home Video: B,V)

The Laughing Policeman (Key Video: B,V)
Lifeboat (Key Video: B,V)
Lilies of the Field (Key Video: B,V)
The Lion, the Witch and the Wardrobe (Vestron Video: B,V,CED)
Little Big Man (Key Video: B,V)
Little Red Riding Hood (CBS/Fox Video: B,V,LV,CED)
The Little Drummer Girl (Warner Home Video: B,V,LV)
The Lorax and the Hoober Bloob Highway (Playhouse Video: B,V)
Love and Bullets (Key Video: B,V)
Lovelines (Key Video: B,V)
Lust in the Dust (New World Video: B,V,LV,CED)

A Man Called Horse (CBS/Fox Video: B,V)
A Man For All Seasons (RCA/Columbia Home Pictures Video: B,V)
The Man Who Would Be King (CBS/Fox Video: B,V)
Max Maven's Mindgames (MCA Home Video: B,V)
Meatballs II (RCA/Columbia Pictures Home Video: B,V)
Men at Work Concert From San Francisco . . . Or Was It Berkeley? (CBS/Fox Video: B,V)
Mickey and Maude (RCA/Columbia Pictures Home Video: B,V,LV,CED)
Mischief (CBS/Fox Video: B,V)
Mrs. Soffel (MGM/UA Home Video: B,V)
Mr. Mom (Vestron Video: B,V)
Mr. T's Be Somebody . . . Or Be Somebody's Fool (MCA Home Video: B,V)
Monte Walsh (CBS/Fox Video: B,V)
Moscow on the Hudson (RCA/Columbia Pictures Home Video: B,V)
The Muppet Review (Playhouse Video: B,V)
The Muppets Take Manhattan (CBS/Fox Video: B,V)
Muppet Treasures (Playhouse Video: B,V)
Mysterious Island (RCA/Columbia Pictures Home Video: B,V,LV)

The Natural (RCA/Columbia Pictures Home Video: B,V,LV)
The Neverending Story (Warner Home Video: B,V,LV)
The New Kids (RCA/Columbia Pictures Home Video: B,V)
The New Three Stooges, Volumes 1–2 (Embassy Home Entertainment: B,V)
A Night in Heaven (Key Video: B,V)
The Nightingale (CBS/Fox Video: B,V,LV,CED)

Night of the Comet (CBS/Fox Video: B,V)
Night Patrol (New World Video: B,V)
The Night They Raided Minsky's (Key Video: B,V)
No Small Affair (RCA/Columbia Pictures Home Video: B,V)
No Sweat (Karl/Lorimar Home Video: B,V)

The Odessa File (RCA/Columbia Home Video: B,V)
Oh God! You Devil (Warner Home Video: B,V,LV)
Oh Heavenly Dog (CBS/Fox Video: B,V,LV)
The Old Curiosity Shop (Vestron Video: B,V)
Oliver Twist (Vestron Video: B,V)
On the Waterfront (RCA/Columbia Pictures Home Video: B,V,LV,CED)
Once Upon a Time in America (Warner Home Video: B,V,LV)
The Organization (Key Video: B,V)
Oxford Blues (CBS/Fox Video: B,V)

Paris Blues (Key Video: B,V)
Paris, Texas (CBS/Fox Video: B,V)
A Passage to India (RCA/Columbia Pictures Home Video: B,V)
Phar Lap (Playhouse Video: B,V)
Pink Floyd's David Gilmour (CBS/Fox Video: B,V)
Pinocchio (CBS/Fox Video: B,V,LV,CED)
Places in the Heart (CBS/Fox Video: B,V)
Planet of the Apes (Playhouse Video: B,V)
Playboy, Volume VII (CBS/Fox Video: B,V)
Playmate Review II and III (CBS/Fox Video: B,V)
Pocketful of Miracles (Key Video: B,V)
Police Academy (Warner Home Video: B,V)
Prime Cut (Key Video: B,V)
Prime Cuts II (CBS/Fox Video: B,V)
The Prince and the Pauper (Key Video: B,V)
The Princess and the Pea (CBS/Fox Video: B,V,LV,CED)
Principles of Paneling (You-Can-Do-It Videos: B,V)
Protocol (Warner Home Video: B,V,LV)
Purple Rain (Warner Home Video: B,V)
The Purple Rose of Cairo (Vestron Video: B,V)
Puss in Boots (CBS/Fox Video: B,V,LV,CED)

The Raccoons' Big Surprise (Embassy Home Video: B,V)
Racing With the Moon (Paramount Home Video: B,V,LV,CED)
Raiders of the Lost Ark (Paramount Home Video: B,V,LV,CED)
Rainbow Brite, Volume II (Vestron Video: B,V,LV)
Rapunzel (CBS/Fox Video: B,V,LV,CED)
The Razor's Edge (RCA/Columbia Pictures Home Video: B,V)
Reuben, Reuben (CBS/Fox Video: B,V)
Revenge of the Nerds (CBS/Fox Video: B,V)
Rhinestone (CBS/Fox Video: B,V)
The Right Stuff (Warner Home Video: B,V)
The River (MCA Home Video: B,V)
The River Rat (Paramount Home Video: B,V,LV)
Robin Hood (Walt Disney Home Video: B,V)
Robinson Crusoe and the Tiger (Embassy Home Video: B,V)
Rock Music with the Muppets (Playhouse Video: B,V)

Romancing the Stone (CBS/Fox Video: B,V,LV)
Romantic Comedy (CBS/Fox Video: B,V)
Romper Room, Volumes 1–4 (CBS/Fox Video: B,V)
Rubik the Amazing Cube, Volumes 1–2 (RCA/Columbia Pictures Home Video: B,V)
Rumplestilskin (CBS/Fox Video: B,V,LV,CED)
Runaway (RCA/Columbia Pictures Home Video: B,V,CED)

Sacred Ground (CBS/Fox Video: B,V)
The Scarlet and the Black (CBS/Fox Video: B,V)
Scrooge (CBS/Fox Video, B,V)
The Seven-Ups (CBS/Fox Video: B,V)
Sexcetera....The World According to Playboy (Key Video: B,V)
Sheena (RCA/Columbia Pictures Home Video: B,V)
Sleeping Beauty (CBS/Fox Video: B,V,LV,CED)
The Slugger's Wife (RCA/Columbia Pictures Home Video: B,V)
Snoopy Come Home (CBS/Fox Video: B,V)
The Snow Queen (CBS/Fox Video: B,V,LV,CED)
Snow White and the Seven Dwarves (CBS/Fox Video: B,V,LV,CED)
A Soldier's Story (RCA/Columbia Pictures Home Video: B,V,CED)
Songwriter (RCA/Columbia Pictures Home Video: B,V,LV,CED)
Sounder (Paramount Home Video: B,V,LV,CED)
Starman (RCA/Columbia Pictures Home Video: B,V,LV,CED)
Star Trek III: The Search for Spock (Paramount Home Video: B,V,LV,CED)
Staying Alive (Paramount Home Video: B,V)
Stick (MCA Home Video: B,V)
Stone Boy (CBS/Fox Video: B,V)
Strawberry Shortcake and the Baby Without a Name (Family Home Entertainment: B,V)
A Streetcar Named Desire (Warner Home Video: B,V)
Streets of Fire (MCA Home Video: B,V)
Stripes (RCA/Columbia Pictures Home Video: B,V)
Sudden Impact (Warner Home Video: B,V)
Support Your Local Sheriff (Key Video: B,V)
The Sure Thing (Embassy Home Video: B,V,LV)
Sylvester (RCA/Columbia Pictures Home Video: B,V)

A Tale of Two Cities (Vestron Video: B,V)
Tank (MCA Home Video: B,V,LV,CED)
Teachers (CBS/Fox Video: B,V)
Terms of Endearment (Paramount Home Video: B,V,LV,CED)
Testament (Paramount Home Video: B,V,LV,CED)
Thief of Hearts (Paramount Home Video: B,V,LV)
The Three Stooges, Volumes 5, 9-12 (RCA/Columbia Pictures Home Video: B,V)
Thumbelina (RCA/Columbia Pictures Home Video: B,V)
Thumbelina (CBS/Fox Video: B,V,LV,CED)
Thunder and Lightning (Key Video: B,V)
Tightrope (Warner Home Video: B,V,LV)
To Be or Not to Be (CBS/Fox Video: B,V,LV)
Tootsie (RCA/Columbia Pictures Home Video: B,V)
Trading Places (Paramount Home Video: B,V,LV,CED)
Tuff Turf (New World Video: B,V)

Turk 182 (CBS/Fox Video: B,V)
Twelve Angry Men (Key Video: B,V)
Two of a Kind (CBS/Fox Video: B,V,LV,CED)
2010 (MGM/UA Home Video: B,V,LV,CED)

Uncommon Valor (Paramount Home Video: B,V,LV,CED)
Unfaithfully Yours-*1984 version* (Parmount Home Video: B,V,LV)
Unico in the Island of Magic, Volume Two (RCA/Columbia Pictures Home Video: B,V)
Until September (MGM/UA Home Video: B,V)

Voyage to the Bottom of the Sea (Playhouse Video: B,V)

War Games (CBS/Fox Video: B,V)
We Are the World (RCA/Columbia Pictures Home Video: B,V)
Weight Watcher's Guide to a Healthy Lifestyle (Key Video: B,V)
Where's Poppa (Key Video: B,V)
Where the Boys Are-*1984 version* (Key Video: B,V)
Who Has Seen the Wind (Embassy Home Entertainment: B,V)
The Wild Life (MCA Home Video: B,V)
Willie Nelson and Family in Concert (CBS/Fox Video: B,V,CED)
Windy City (CBS/Fox Video: B,V)
Wombling Free (RCA/Columbia Pictures Home Video: B,V)
The World of Henry Orient (Key Video: B,V)

The Year of Living Dangerously (MGM/UA Home Video: B,V,LV,CED)
Yentl (CBS/Fox Video: B,V,CED)

Cast Index

This revised index includes complete videographies for over 280 actors, actresses, directors and other screen personalities.

To provide as thorough a reference section as possible, cameo appearances, soundtrack narrations and other peripheral involvements appear in the listings, where known.

Trivia pursuers will note some interesting credits included herein; for example, small parts played by current superstars Richard Dreyfuss (*The Graduate*) and Sylvester Stallone (*Bananas* and *The Prisoner of Second Avenue*) early in their careers. Also while Charles Laughton's role in *Mutiny on the Bounty* is an obvious inclusion, you might not be familiar with his role in *Early Elvis* as the substitute host of *The Ed Sullivan Show* on the night that Elvis made his first appearance.

This compilation reflects our efforts to list performers that readers are likely to look for while striving to keep the section down to a manageable length.

LOUIS ARMSTRONG

Best of Louis Armstrong, The
Goodyear Jazz Concert with Louis Armstrong
Hello, Dolly!
High Society
That's Entertainment, Part II
Timex All-Star Jazz Show
TV Variety, Book VIII

JEAN ARTHUR

Devil and Miss Jones, The
Lady Takes a Chance, The
Mr. Smith Goes to Washington
Shane

FRED ASTAIRE

Amazing Dobermans, The
Band Wagon, The
Carefree
Damsel In Distress
Easter Bunny Is Coming to Town, The
Finian's Rainbow
Flying Down to Rio
Follow the Fleet
Funny Face
Gay Divorcee, The
Ghost Story
Gotta Dance, Gotta Sing
Holiday Palace, The
Man in the Santa Claus Suit, The
On the Beach
Purple Taxi, The
Royal Wedding
Second Chorus
Shall We Dance
Silk Stockings
Sky's the Limit, The
Story of Vernon and Irene Castle, The
Swing Time
That's Dancing
That's Entertainment
That's Entertainment, Part II
Top Hat
Towering Inferno, The
You'll Never Get Rich
You Were Never Lovelier
Ziegfeld Follies

GENE AUTRY

Blue Canadian Rockies
Boots and Saddles
Call of the Canyon
Cow Town
Git Along, Little Dogies
Heart of the Rio Grande
Hills of Utah, The
Last of the Pony Riders
Man from Music Mountain, The
Man of the Frontier
Manhattan Merry-Go-Round
Melody Ranch
Melody Trail
Mystery Mountain
Night Stage to Galveston
Old Corral, The
On Top of Old Smoky
Phantom Empire
Prairie Moon
Radio Ranch
Ridin' on a Rainbow
Robinhood of Texas
Rootin' Tootin' Rhythm
Sioux City Sue
South of the Border
Valley of Fire
Western Double Feature #5, 16
Winning of the West

DAN AYKROYD

Blues Brothers, The
Doctor Detroit
Into the Night
Mr. Mike's Mondo Video
Neighbors
1941
Saturday Night Live
Trading Places
Twilight Zone—The Movie

LAUREN BACALL

Big Sleep, The
Dark Passage
Fan, The
How to Marry a Millionaire
Key Largo
Murder on the Orient Express
Northwest Frontier
Premiere of "A Star Is Born"
Shootist, The

LUCILLE BALL

Abbott and Costello in Hollywood
Affairs of Annabel, The
Annabel Takes a Tour
Bob Hope Chevy Show, The
Comedy and Kid Stuff
Five Came Back
Follow the Fleet
Girl, a Guy and a Gob, A
Great Gildersleeve, The
Having Wonderful Time
I Dream Too Much
Mame
Panama Lady
Premiere of "A Star Is Born"
Room Service
Stage Door
Toast of the Town
Top Hat
TV's Classic Guessing Games
TV Variety, Book VII
Vintage Commercials I–III

ANNE BANCROFT

Audience with Mel Brooks, An
Bell Jar, The
Elephant Man, The
Garbo Talks
Graduate, The
Hindenburg, The
Jesus of Nazareth
Lipstick
Prisoner of Second Avenue, The
Silent Movie
To Be or Not to Be
Turning Point, The

BRIGITTE BARDOT

Contempt
Doctor at Sea
Famous T and A
Ravishing Idiot, The
Shalako
Very Private Affair, A

JOHN BARRYMORE

Bulldog Drummond Double Feature
Dinner at Eight
Dr. Jekyll and Mr. Hyde
Horrible Double Feature
Svengali
Tempest, The/The Eagle
That's Entertainment, Part II

LIONEL BARRYMORE

America
Bells, The

Captains Courageous
David Copperfield
Dr. Kildare's Strange Case
It's a Wonderful Life
Key Largo
That's Entertainment, Part II
Treasure Island

ALAN BATES

King of Hearts
Quartet
Rose, The
Separate Tables
Shout, The
Unmarried Woman, An
Women in Love
Zorba the Greek

WARREN BEATTY

Bonnie and Clyde
Dollars
Heaven Can Wait
Lilith
McCabe and Mrs. Miller
Parallax View, The
Reds
Roman Spring of Mrs. Stone, The
Splendor in the Grass

MICHAEL BECK

Golden Seal, The
Holocaust
Madman
Megaforce
Warriors, The
Xanadu

JOHN BELUSHI

All You Need Is Cash
Animal House
Blues Brothers, The
Continental Divide
Goin' South
Neighbors
1941
Saturday Night Live
Things We Did Last Summer

RICHARD BENJAMIN

Catch-22
City Heat
Diary of a Mad Housewife
First Family
Goodbye Columbus
House Calls
How to Beat the High Cost of Living
Last Married Couple in America, The
Last of Sheila, The
Love at First Bite
My Favorite Year
No Room to Run
Portnoy's Complaint
Saturday Night Live: Richard Benjamin
Scavenger Hunt
Sunshine Boys, The
Westworld
Witches' Brew

JACK BENNY

Big Time, The
Comedy and Kid Stuff III
Hollywood Palace, The
It's a Mad, Mad, Mad, Mad World
It's in the Bag
Jack Benny
Jack Benny I-III
Jack Benny Program, The
Jack Benny Show, The
Jack Benny Visits Walt Disney
Milton Berle Spectacular, The
Take a Good Look/The Jack Benny Show
That's Entertainment, Part II
To Be or Not to Be
TV Variety, Book VII
Vintage Commercials II

CANDICE BERGEN

Bite the Bullet
Carnal Knowledge
Domino Principle, The
Gandhi
Rich and Famous
Sand Pebbles, The
Starting Over

INGMAR BERGMAN

After the Rehearsal
Brink of Life
Cries and Whispers
Devil's Eye
Fanny and Alexander
Magician, The
Night Is My Future, The
Persona
Port of Call
Scenes from a Marriage
Secrets of Women
Wild Strawberries
Winter Light

INGRID BERGMAN

Adam Had Four Sons
Arch of Triumph
Bells of St. Mary's, The
Cactus Flower
Casablanca
Fear
Gaslight
Hideaways, The
Indiscreet
Inn of the Sixth Happiness, The
Intermezzo
Joan of Arc
Matter of Time, A
Murder on the Orient Express
Notorious
Spellbound
Stromboli
Under Capricorn
Woman Called Golda, A

MILTON BERLE

Bloopers from "Star Trek" and "Laugh-in"
Broadway Danny Rose
Broadway Highlights
Cracking Up
Hey Abbott!
It's a Mad, Mad, Mad, Mad World
Journey Back to Oz
Kraft Music Hall, The
Lepke
Milton Berle Hour, The
Milton Berle Show, The
Muppet Movie, The
Oscar, The
Texaco Star Theatre
TV Variety, II

JACQUELINE BISSET

Airport
Bullitt
Class
Day for Night
Deep, The
Detective, The
Famous T and A
Greek Tycoon, The
Magnifique, Le
Murder on the Orient Express
Observations Under the Volcano
Rich and Famous
Secrets
St. Ives
Thief Who Came to Dinner, The
Together
Under the Volcano

KAREN BLACK

Bad Manners
Can She Bake a Cherry Pie?
Capricorn One
Chanel Solitaire
Come Back to the 5 and Dime Jimmy Dean, Jimmy Dean
Day of the Locust
Easy Rider
Family Plot
Great Gatsby, The
In Praise of Older Women
Killing Heat
Last Word, The
Little Laura and Big John
Nashville
Portnoy's Complaint
Ripoff, The
Separate Ways
Trilogy of Terror
You're a Big Boy Now

HUMPHREY BOGART

African Queen, The
Angels with Dirty Faces
Barefoot Contessa, The
Big Breakdowns, The
Big Sleep, The
Caine Mutiny, The
Casablanca
Coming Attractions
Dark Passage
Dark Victory
Harder They Fall, The
High Sierra
Hollywood Outtakes and Rare Footage
Jack Benny, II
Key Largo
Knock on Any Door
Left Hand of God, The
Maltese Falcon, The
Midnight
Passage to Marseilles
Petrified Forest, The
Presidential Blooper Reel
Roaring Twenties, The
Sahara
Stand-In
They Drive by Night
Treasure of the Sierra Madre, The
27th Annual Academy Awards
We're No Angels

MARLON BRANDO

Apocalypse Now
Burn!
Formula, The
Godfather, The
Godfather: The Complete Epic, The
Guys and Dolls
Last Tango in Paris
Men, The
Missouri Breaks, The
Mutiny on the Bounty
One-Eyed Jacks
On the Waterfront
Reflections in a Golden Eye
Sayonara
Streetcar Named Desire, A
Superman—The Movie
27th Annual Academy Awards
Viva Zapata!

BEAU BRIDGES

Dangerous Company
For Love of Ivy
Four Feathers
Greased Lightning
Heart Like A Wheel
Honky Tonk Freeway
Hotel New Hampshire, The
Love Child
Night Crossing
Norma Rae
Red Pony, The
Silver Dream Racer
Stranger Who Looks Like Me, The
Village of the Giants

JEFF BRIDGES

Cutter's Way
Heaven's Gate
Kiss Me Goodbye
King Kong
Last Unicorn, The
Rapunzel
Starman
Stay Hungry
Thunderbolt and Lightfoot
Tron
Winter Kills

LLOYD BRIDGES

Abilene Town
Airplane!
Airplane II: The Sequel
Bear Island
Crash of Flight 401, The
Daring Game
East of Eden
High Noon
Home of the Brave
Mission Galactica: The Cylon Attack
Roots
Running Wild
Sahara
Trapped
War in the Sky
White Tower, The

CHARLES BRONSON

Borderline
Breakheart Pass
Breakout
Cabo Blanco
Chino
Death Hunt
Death Wish
Death Wish II
Dirty Dozen, The
Drum Beat
Evil That Men Do, The
Family, The
Great Escape, The
Hard Times
Honor Among Thieves
Love and Bullets
Magnificent Seven, The
Mechanic, The
Once Upon a Time in the West
Raid on Entebbe
Rider on the Rain
Run of the Arrow
Sandpiper, The
St. Ives
Stone Killer, The
Telefon

MEL BROOKS

Audience with Mel Brooks, An
Blazing Saddles
Free to Be . . . You and Me
High Anxiety
History of the World: Part I, The
Muppet Movie, The
Producers, The
Silent Movie
Timex All-Star Comedy Show
To Be or Not to Be
Twelve Chairs, The
2000 Year Old Man, The
Young Frankenstein

GENEVIEVE BUJOLD

Anne of the Thousand Days
Caesar and Cleopatra
Choose Me

Coma
Earthquake
Final Assignment
Journey
King of Hearts
Last Flight of Noah's Ark, The
Monsignor
Murder by Decree
Obsession
Tightrope

CAROL BURNETT

Annie
Between Friends
Carol Burnett Show: Bloopers and Outtakes, The
Chu Chu and the Philly Flash
Four Seasons, The
Son of TV Bloopers

GEORGE BURNS

Big Time, The
Broadway Highlights
Comedy and Kid Stuff
Damsel in Distress
George Burns and Gracie Allen Show, The
George Burns in Concert
George Burns Twice
George Burns Show, The
Going in Style
Hollywood Palace, The
I Married Joan/The Burns and Allen Show
Jack Benny
Jack Benny Show, The
Oh, God!
Oh, God! Book II
Oh, God! You Devil
Sgt. Pepper's Lonely Hearts Club Band
Sunshine Boys, The
Vintage Sitcoms

ELLEN BURSTYN

Alice Doesn't Live Here Anymore
Exorcist, The
Providence
Same Time, Next Year
Silence of the North

RICHARD BURTON

Alexander the Great
Anne of the Thousand Days
Becket
Bluebeard
Breakthrough
Circle of Two
Cleopatra
Divorce His, Divorce Hers
Exorcist II: The Heretic
Longest Day, The
Look Back in Anger
Lovespell
Night of the Iguana, The
1984
Robe, The
Sandpiper, The
Taming of the Shrew, The
Tempest, The
Who's Afraid of Virginia Woolf?
Wild Geese, The

GARY BUSEY

Barbarosa
Big Wednesday
Carny
D.C. Cab
Foolin' Around
Saturday Night Live: Gary Busey
Star Is Born, A
Straight Time

JAMES CAAN

Bolero
Brian's Song
Bridge Too Far, A
Chapter Two
Comes a Horseman
Coming Attractions
Countdown
Death Valley Days, Volume II
Dorado, El
Freebie and the Bean
Gambler, The
Godfather, The
Godfather: The Complete Epic, The
Gone With the West
Harry and Walter Go to New York
Hide in Plain Sight
Kiss Me Goodbye
Rain People, The
Rollerball
Silent Movie
Thief

SID CAESAR

Admiral Broadway Revue, The
Barnaby and Me
Caesar's Hour
Dorothy in the Land of Oz
Fiendish Plot of Dr. Fu Manchu, The
Grease II
History of the World Part I, The
Hollywood Palace, The
It's a Mad, Mad, Mad, Mad World
Over the Brooklyn Bridge
Sid Caesar's Shape Up
Silent Movie
Your Show of Shows

JAMES CAGNEY

Angels with Dirty Faces
Big Breakdowns, The
Blood on the Sun
Bob Hope Chevy Show, The
Coming Attractions
Footlight Parade
Great Guy
Mister Roberts
Presidential Blooper Reel
Public Enemy, The
Ragtime
Roaring Twenties, The
Something to Sing About
White Heat
Yankee Doodle Dandy

MICHAEL CAINE

Beyond the Limit
Blame It on Rio
Bridge Too Far, A
California Suite
Deathtrap
Dressed to Kill
Eagle Has Landed, The
Hand, The
Harry and Walter Go to New York
Island, The
Jigsaw Man, The
Man Who Would Be King, The
Romantic Englishwoman, The
Sleuth
Swarm, The
Too Late the Hero
Victory
Wrong Box, The

DYAN CANNON

Author! Author!
Bob & Carol & Ted & Alice
Coast to Coast
Deathtrap
Heavaen Can Wait

Honeysuckle Rose
Lady of the House
Last of Sheila, The
Shamus

EDDIE CANTOR

Big Time, The
Colgate Comedy Hour, The
Hollywood Goes to War
If You Knew Susie
Show Business

FRANK CAPRA

Arsenic and Old Lace
Attack—The Battle of New Britain
It Happened One Night
It's a Wonderful Life
Meet John Doe
Mr. Smith Goes to Washington
Pocketful of Miracles
Prelude to War
Silent Laugh Makers #3
State of the Union
Under Nazi Guns/On to Tokyo

ART CARNEY

Better Late than Never
Cavalcade of Stars
Defiance
Emperor's New Clothes, The
Going in Style
House Calls
Late Show, The
Movie, Movie
Muppets Take Manhattan, The
Naked Face, The
St. Helens, Killer Volcano
Sunburn

LESLIE CARON

American in Paris, An
Fanny
Father Goose
Gigi
Lili
Man Who Loved Women, The
That's Entertainment

JOHN CARRADINE

Bees, The
Best of Sex and Violence, The
Big Foot
Billy the Kid Versus Dracula
Black Cat, The/The Raven
Bloody Legacy
Blood of Dracula's Castle
Bogey Man, The
Cain's Cutthroats
Captain Kidd
Captains Courageous
Daniel Boone
Death at Love House
Demon Rage
Everything You Always Wanted to Know About Sex
Five Came Back
Frankenstein's Island
Gallery of Horror
Golden Rendezvous
Grapes of Wrath, The
Greatest Heroes of the Bible
Gun Riders
House of Seven Corpses
Howling, The
Judgment of Solomon, The
Monster Club, The
Secret of NIMH, The
Shock Waves
Shootist, The
Silent Night, Bloody Night
Silver Spurs
Stagecoach
Ten Commandments, The
Terror in the Wax Museum
Tragedy of Antony and Cleopatra
Vampire Hookers
Wizard of Mars, The

ROBERT CARRADINE

Aloha Bobby and Rose
Big Red One, The
Coming Home
Just the Way You Are
Long Riders, The
Mean Streets
Orca
Revenge of the Nerds
Tag: The Assassination Game
Wavelength

CHARLIE CHAPLIN

America Between the Great Wars
Chaplin: Keystone Beginnings
Chaplin Mutuals, Vol. I–IV
Chaplin Revue, The
Charlie Chaplin Carnival
Charlie Chaplin Cavalcade
Charlie Chaplin Festival
Charlie Chaplin's Keystone Comedies
Circus, The/Day's Pleasure, A
City Lights
Flicker Flashbacks
Fun Factory/Clown Princes of Hollywood
Gold Rush, The
Great Dictator, The
Kid's Auto Race/Mabel's Married Life
King in New York, A
Knockout, The/Dough and Dynamite
Laughfest
Limelight
Modern Times
Monsieur Verdoux
Rink, The/The Immigrant
Slapstick
Tillie's Punctured Romance
Woman of Paris, A/Sunnyside
Work/Police

CYD CHARISSE

Band Wagon, The
Brigadoon
Silk Stockings
Singin' in the Rain
That's Entertainment
That's Entertainment, Part II
Ziegfeld Follies

CHEVY CHASE

Caddyshack
Deal of the Century
Ernie Kovacs: Television's Original Genius
Foul Play
Groove Tube, The
Modern Problems
Oh, Heavenly Dog
Saturday Night Live
Seems Like Old Times
Under the Rainbow

MAURICE CHEVALIER

Fanny
Gigi
In Search of the Castaways

Invitation to Paris
Love in the Afternoon
That's Entertainment

JULIE CHRISTIE

Billy Liar
Darling
Doctor Zhivago
Don't Look Now
Heat and Dust
Heaven Can Wait
McCabe and Mrs. Miller
Separate Tables

JILL CLAYBURGH

First Monday in October
Griffin and Phoenix
Hanna K.
Hustling
I'm Dancing as Fast as I Can
It's My Turn
Silver Streak
Starting Over
Unmarried Woman, An
Wedding Party, The

MONTGOMERY CLIFT

Heiress, The
I Confess
Indiscretion of an American Wife
Judgment at Nuremburg
Misfits, The
Place in the Sun, A
Red River
Suddenly Last Summer

JOAN COLLINS

Big Sleep, The
Bitch, The
Dark Places
Decameron Nights
Dynasty of Fear
Empire of Ants
Great Adventure, The
Hansel and Gretel
Homework
Oh Alfie
Playboy Video Magazine Vol. 7
Star Trek II
Star Trek Volume 5
Stopover Tokyo
Stud, The
Subterfuge
Sunburn
Tales From the Crypt

SEAN CONNERY

Anderson Tapes, The
Bridge Too Far, A
Darby O'Gill and the Little People
Diamonds Are Forever
Dr. No
Five Days One Summer
From Russia with Love
Goldfinger
James Bond 007—Coming Attractions
Longest Day, The
Man Who Would Be King, The
Meteor
Murder on the Orient Express
Never Say Never Again
Outland
Robin and Marian
Shalako
Sword of the Valiant
Thunderball
Wrong Is Right
You Only Live Twice

GARY COOPER

Along Came Jones
Ball of Fire
Farewell to Arms, A
Fighting Caravans
Fountainhead, The
Friendly Persuasion
Good Sam
High Noon
It
Leave 'Em Laughing
Love in the Afternoon
Meet John Doe
Pride of the Yankees
Sergeant York
They Came to Cordura
Vera Cruz
Westerner, The
Wings

FRANCIS FORD COPPOLA

Apocalypse Now
Conversation, The
Cotton Club, The
Dementia 13
Godfather, The
Godfather: The Complete Epic, The
New Look
One from the Heart
Rain People, The
Tonight for Sure
You're a Big Boy Now

JOAN CRAWFORD

Hollywood Outtakes and Rare Footage
Johnny Guitar
Mildred Pierce
Night Gallery
Premiere of "A Star Is Born"
Rain
Strait Jacket
What Ever Happened to Baby Jane?
Women, The

BING CROSBY

Bells of St. Mary's, The
Bing Crosby Festival
Bing Crosby Show, The
Country Girl, The
Going My Way
High Society
Holiday Inn
Hollywood Goes to War
Hollywood Palace, The
Jack Benny
King of Jazz, The
Legend of Sleepy Hollow, The
Outtakes II, V
Princess and the Pirate, The
Road to Bali, The
Road to Lebanon, The
That's Entertainment
That's Entertainment, Part II
TV Variety, Book VIII
Young Bing Crosby

TONY CURTIS

Boston Strangler, The
Brainwaves
Count of Monte Cristo, The
Defiant Ones, The
Great Race, The
Lepke
Little Miss Marker
Mirror Crack'd, The
Operation Petticoat
Portrait of a Showgirl
Premiere of "A Star Is Born"
Sex on the Run
Sextette
Some Like It Hot
Spartacus
Trapeze
Users, The
Vegas
Vikings, The

PETER CUSHING
Bloodsuckers
Dynasty of Fear
Ghoul, The
Shock Waves
Sword of the Valiant
Tales from the Crypt

BETTE DAVIS
All About Eve
Big Breakdowns, The
Dark Victory
Death on the Nile
Fashions of 1934
Hell House
Hollywood Outtakes and Rare Footage
Hollywood Palace, The
Jezebel
Juarez
Letter, The
Little Foxes, The
Now Voyager
Of Human Bondage
Petrified Forest, The
Pocketful of Miracles
Presidential Blooper Reel
Private Lives of Elizabeth and Essex, The
Right of Way
Strangers: The Story of a Mother and Daughter
27th Annual Academy Awards
Watch on the Rhine
Watcher in the Woods, The
What Ever Happened to Baby Jane?

DORIS DAY
Man Who Knew Too Much, The
Pillow Talk
That Touch of Mink
With Six You Get Eggroll
Young at Heart

JAMES DEAN
America at the Movies
East of Eden
Giant
Hollywood Outtakes and Rare Footage
James Dean: The First American Teenager
Premiere of "A Star Is Born"
Rebel Without a Cause

OLIVIA DE HAVILLAND
Adventures of Robin Hood, The
Captain Blood
Charge of the Light Brigade, The
Dark Mirror
Dodge City
Gone With the Wind
Heiress, The
Proud Rebel, The
Santa Fe Trail
Swarm, The

DOM DELUISE
Best Little Whorehouse in Texas, The
Cannonball Run, The
End, The
History of the World: Part I, The
Hot Stuff
Last Married Couple in America, The
Muppet Movie, The
Peter-No-Tail
Secret of NIMH, The
Twelve Chairs, The
Wholly Moses!

ROBERT DE NIRO
America at the Movies
Bang the Drum Slowly
Bloody Mama
Deer Hunter, The
Falling in Love
Godfather Part II, The
Godfather: The Complete Epic, The
King of Comedy
Mean Streets
New York, New York
Obsession
Once Upon a Time in America
Raging Bull
Scarface
Swap, The
Taxi Driver
True Confessions
Wedding Party, The

BRIAN DE PALMA
Blow Out
Body Double
Carrie
Dressed to Kill
Fury, The
Sisters
Wedding Party, The

BO DEREK
Bolero
Change of Seasons, A
Fantasies
Orca
Playboy Video, Volume 1
Tarzan, the Ape Man
"10"

BRUCE DERN
Black Sunday
Bloody Mama
Coming Home
Cowboys
Driver, The
Family Plot
Great Gatsby, The
Harry Tracy
Rebel Rousers
Silent Running
Support Your Local Sheriff
Tattoo
That Championship Season
Trip, The
Twist
War Wagon, The

MARLENE DIETRICH
Around the World in 80 Days
Black Fox
Blue Angel, The
Judgment at Nurem-burg
Love Goddesses, The
Piaf, the Woman
Rancho Notorious
Spoilers, The
Stage Fright
Witness for the Prose-cution

MATT DILLON
Flamingo Kid, The
Little Darlings
Outsiders, The
Over the Edge
Rumble Fish
Tex

KIRK DOUGLAS
Arrangement, The
Big Sky, The
Catch Me a Spy
Champion
Eddie Macon's Run
Final Countdown, The
Fury, The
Gunfight at the O.K. Corral

Hollywood Bloopers
Jack Benny, II
Light at the Edge of the World, The
List of Adrian Messenger, The
Lonely Are the Brave
Man from Snowy River, The
Man Without a Star
Master Touch, The
Milton Berle Spectacular, The
My Dear Secretary
Out of the Past
Paths of Glory
Saturn 3
Seven Days in May
Spartacus
Strange Love of Martha Ivers, The
20,000 Leagues Under the Sea
Vikings, The
War Wagon, The

MELVYN DOUGLAS

Annie Oakley
Being There
Billy Budd
Candidate, The
Captains Courageous
Death Squad
Ghost Story
Hud
I Never Sang for My Father
Lamp at Midnight
Mr. Blandings Builds His Dream House
My Forbidden Past
Ninotchka
Seducation of Joe Tynan, The
Tenant, The
That Uncertain Feeling
Your Show of Shows

MICHAEL DOUGLAS

China Syndrome, The
Coma
It's My Turn
Romancing the Stone
Star Chamber, The

RICHARD DREYFUSS

American Graffiti
Apprenticeship of Duddy Kravitz, The
Buddy System, The
Close Encounters of the Third Kind
Competition, The
Dillinger
Goodbye Girl, The
Graduate, The
Jaws
Second Coming of Suzanne, The

FAYE DUNAWAY

Arrangement, The
Bonnie and Clyde
Champ, The
Chinatown
Country Girl, The
Eyes of Laura Mars
First Deadly Sin, The
Four Musketeers, The
Mommie Dearest
Network
Supergirl
Supergirl: The Making of the Movie
Thomas Crown Affair, The
Three Days of the Condor
Three Musketeers, The
Towering Inferno, The
Voyage of the Damned

IRENE DUNNE

Ann Vickers
I Remember Mama
Life with Father
Penny Serenade

JIMMY DURANTE

Broadway Highlights
Hollywood Goes to War
Hollywood Palace, The
It's a Mad, Mad, Mad, Mad World
Melody Ranch
Outtakes V
Palooka
That's Entertainment
That's Entertainment, Part II

CHARLES DURNING

Best Little Whorehouse in Texas, The
Breakheart Pass
Die Laughing
Dog Day Afternoon
Final Countdown, The
Fury, The
Greek Tycoon, The
Harry and Walter Go to New York
North Dallas Forty
Sharky's Machine
Sisters
Starting Over
Sting, The
Tilt
True Confessions
When a Stranger Calls

ROBERT DUVALL

Apocalypse Now
Betsy, The
Breakout
Bullitt
Conversation, The
Countdown
Eagle Has Landed, The
Falling For the Stars
Godfather, The
Godfather Part II, the
Godfather: The Complete Epic, The
Greatest, The
Great Santini, The
Joe Kidd
Lady Ice
M*A*S*H
Natural, The
Pursuit of D.B. Cooper, The
Rain People, The
Seven-Per-Cent Solution, The
Stone Boy, The
Tender Mercies
Terry Fox Story, The
THX 1138
Tomorrow
True Confessions
True Grit

SHELLEY DUVALL

Annie Hall
Brewster McCloud
Faerie Tale Theatre
McCabe and Mrs. Miller
Nashville
Popeye
Rapunzel
Rumpelstiltskin
Shining, The

CLINT EASTWOOD

Any Which Way You Can
Beguiled, The
Bronco Billy
City Heat
Coogan's Bluff
Dirty Harry
Death Valley Days
Eiger Sanction, The
Enforcer, The
Escape from Alcatraz
Every Which Way But Loose

Firefox
Fistful of Dollars, A
For a Few Dollars More
Gauntlet, The
Good, the Bad and the Ugly, The
Hang 'Em High
High Plains Drifter
Honkytonk Man
Joe Kidd
Kelly's Heroes
Magnum Force
Outlaw Josey Wales, The
Paint Your Wagon
Play Misty for Me
Sudden Impact
Thunderbolt and Lightfoot
Tightrope

SAMANTHA EGGAR

Collector, The
Curtains
Demonoid
Doctor Doolittle
Exterminator, The
Light at the Edge of the World, The
Seven-Per-Cent Solution, The
Unknown Powers
Why Shoot the Teacher?

DUKE ELLINGTON

Black and Tan
Check and Double Check
Duke Ellington Story, The
Ella Fitzgerald in Concert
Goodyear Jazz Concert with Duke Ellington
Jazz and Jive
Sacred Music of Duke Ellington, The
Showtime at the Apollo
Timex All-Star Jazz Show

DOUGLAS FAIRBANKS SR.

Americano, The
Birth of a Legend
Black Pirate, The
Don Q., Son of Zorro
Matrimaniac, The
Mr. Robinson Crusoe
Mr. Super Athletic Charm
Private Life of Don Juan, The
Taming of the Shrew, The
Thief of Bagdad, The
Wild and Wooly

MIA FARROW

Avalanche
Broadway Danny Rose
Death on the Nile
Great Gatsby, The
Hurricane
Haunting of Julia, The
Last Unicorn, The
Midsummer Night's Sex Comedy, A
Purple Rose of Cairo, The
Rosemary's Baby
Sarah and the Squirrel
Supergirl
Zelig

FARRAH FAWCETT

Cannonball Run, The
Logan's Run
Murder in Texas
Saturn 3
Sunburn

SALLY FIELD

Absence of Malice
Back Roads
End, The
Hooper
Kiss Me Goodbye
Norma Rae
Places in the Heart
Smokey and the Bandit
Smokey and the Bandit II
Stay Hungry
Sybil

W.C. FIELDS

Bank Dick, The
Barber Shop, The
Best of W.C. Fields, The
David Copperfield
Dentist, The
Fatal Glass of Beer, The
Flask of Fields, A
Funny Guys and Gals of the Talkies
My Little Chickadee
Outtakes VI
Pharmacist, The
Sally of the Sawdust
W.C. Fields Festival

ALBERT FINNEY

Annie
Dresser, The
Duellists, The
Looker
Loophole
Murder on the Orient Express
Observations Under the Volcano
Shoot the Moon
Tom Jones
Under the Volcano
Wolfen

CARRIE FISHER

Empire Strikes Back, The
Garbo Talks
Making of Star Wars, The/S.P.F.X.—The Empire Strikes Back
Mr. Mike's Mondo Video
Saturday Night Live: Carrie Fisher
Star Wars
Thumbelina
Under the Rainbow

ERROL FLYNN

Adventures of Captain Fabian
Adventures of Robin Hood, The
Big Breakdowns, The
Big Surprise, The
Captain Blood
Charge of the Light Brigade, The
Dawn Patrol, The
Dodge City
Gentleman Jim
Northern Pursuit
Prince and the Pauper, The
Private Lives of Elizabeth and Essex, The
Santa Fe Trail
Sea Hawk, The
Son of Hollywood Bloopers

HENRY FONDA

Battle of the Bulge, The
Boston Strangler, The
Fail Safe
Fort Apache
Gideon's Trumpet
Grapes of Wrath, The
Great Smokey Roadblock, The
I Dream Too Much
Jezebel
Lady Eve, The
Longest Day, The
Mad Miss Manton, The
Meteor
Midway
Mister Roberts

Judy Garland Show, The
Judy, Judy, Judy
Meet Me in St. Louis
Pirate, The
Premiere of "A Star Is Born"
Star Is Born, A
Strike Up the Band
That's Entertainment
That's Entertainment, Part II
Till the Clouds Roll By
Wizard of Oz, The
World War II Video Series—Something for the Boys
Ziegfeld Follies

JAMES GARNER

Castaway Cowboy
Glitter Dome, The
Great Escape, The
Fan, The
Sayonara
Skin Game
Support Your Local Sheriff
Victor/Victoria

TERI GARR

Black Stallion Returns, The
Do It Debbie's Way
First Born
Mr. Mom
Prime Suspect
Tale of the Frog Prince, The
Tootsie
Young Frankenstein

RICHARD GERE

American Gigolo
Beyond the Limit
Bloodbrothers
Breathless
Cotton Club, The
Days of Heaven
King David
Looking for Mr. Goodbar
Officer and a Gentleman, An

MEL GIBSON

Attack Force Z
Gallipoli
Mad Max
River, The
Road Warrior, The
Tim
Year of Living Dangerously, The

LILLIAN GISH

Battle of Elderbush Gulch, The
Birth of a Nation
Broken Blossoms
Follow Me, Boys!
Great Chase, The
Hambone and Hillie
Home Sweet Home
Intolerance
Orphans of the Storm
True Heart Susie
Way Down East

JACKIE GLEASON

Cavalcade of Stars
Mr. Halpern and Mr. Johnson
Smokey and the Bandit I-III
Sting, The
Toy, The
TV Variety, Book VIII
Vintage Sitcoms

RUTH GORDON

Abe Lincoln in Illinois
Any Which Way You Can
Every Which Way But Loose
Harold and Maude
Jimmy the Kid
My Bodyguard
Rosemary's Baby
Where's Papa?

ELLIOT GOULD

Bob & Carol & Ted & Alice
Bridge Too Far, A
Capricorn One
Devil and Max Devlin, The
Dirty Tricks
Escape to Athena
Falling in Love Again
Harry and Walter Go to New York
Jack and the Beanstalk
Last Flight of Noah's Ark, The
M*A*S*H
Matilda
Mean Johnny Barrows
Muppet Movie, The
Naked Face, The
Over The Brooklyn Bridge
Saturday Night Live: Elliot Gould

BETTY GRABLE

Bob Hope Chevy Show II, The
Day the Bookies Wept, The
Follow the Fleet
Gay Divorcee, The
Gotta Sing, Gotta Dance
Hollywood Goes to War
How to Marry a Millionaire
Love Goddesses, The

CARY GRANT

Arsenic and Old Lace
Bachelor and the Bobby Soxer, The
Charade
Every Girl Should Be Married
Father Goose
Grass is Greener, The
Gunga Din
His Girl Friday
In Name Only
Indiscreet
Mr. Blandings Builds His Dream House
Mr. Lucky
My Favorite Wife
Night and Day
None But the Lonely Heart
North by Northwest
Notorious
Once Upon a Honeymoon
Operation Petticoat
Penny Serenade
Philadelphia Story, The
Pride and the Passion, The
Suspicion
That Touch of Mink
To Catch a Thief
Toast of New York
Topper

D.W. GRIFFITH

Abraham Lincoln
Avenging Conscience, The
Babylon Story from "Intolerance," The
Battle of Elderbush Gulch, The
Birth of a Nation
Broken Blossoms
Dream Street
D.W. Griffith: An American Genius
Film Firsts
Home Sweet Home
Intolerance
Movies' Story, The
Orphans of the Storm
Short Films of D.W. Griffith, Vol. I, The
True Heart Susie
Way Down East

CHARLES GRODIN

All Night Long
Great Muppet Caper, The
Heartbreak Kid, The
Heaven Can Wait
It's My Turn
King Kong
Paul Simon Special, The
Rosemary's Baby
Saturday Night Live: Charles Grodin
Seems Like Old Times
Sunburn
Woman in Red, The

ALEC GUINNESS

Bridge on the River Kwai, The
Brother Sun, Sister Moon
Captain's Paradise, The
Empire Strikes Back, The
Fall of the Roman Empire, The
Kind Hearts and Coronets
Ladykillers, The
Lavender Hill Mob, The
Lawrence of Arabia
Little Lord Fauntleroy
Lovesick
Making of Star Wars, The
Malta Story, The
Man in the White Suit, The
Murder by Death
Star Wars
To Paris With Love
To See Such Fun

GENE HACKMAN

All Night Long
America At The Movies
Bite The Bullet
Bonnie and Clyde
Bridge Too Far, A
Conversation, The
Domino Principle, The
Downhill Racer
French Connection, The
French Connection II
Hawaii
Marooned
Misunderstood
Night Moves
Prime Cut
Poseidon Adventure, The
Scarecrow
Superman—The Movie
Superman II
Uncommon Valor
Under Fire

GEORGE HAMILTON

Dead Don't Die, The
Evel Knievel
From Hell To Victory
Happy Hooker Goes To Washington, The
Love At First Bite
Once Is Not Enough
Zorro, the Gay Blade

JEAN HARLOW

Dinner at Eight
Love Goddesses, The
That's Entertainment

RICHARD HARRIS

Camelot
Golden Rendezvous
Hawaii
Highpoint
Last Word, The
Major Dundee
Mutiny On The Bounty
Return of a Man Called Horse, The
Robin and Marian
Tarzan, the Ape Man
Triumps of a Man Called Horse
Wild Geese, The
Your Ticket Is No Longer Valid

GOLDIE HAWN

Best Friends
Bloopers From "Star Trek" and "Laugh-In"
Cactus Flower
Dollars
Duchess and the Dirt-water Fox, The
Foul Play
Lovers and Liars
Outtakes I
Private Benjamin
Protocol
Seems Like Old Times
Sugarland Express, The
Swing Shift
There's a Girl In My Soup

HELEN HAYES

Airport
Candleshoe
Farewell To Arms, A
Herbie Rides Again
Main Street To Broadway
Stagedoor Canteen

RITA HAYWORTH

Circus World
Gilda
Lady From Shanghai
Love Goddesses, The
Miss Sadie Thompson
Poppies Are Also Flowers
Renegade Ranger, The/Scarlet Rider
Separate Tables
They Came to Cordura
Trouble in Texas
You'll Never Get Rich
You Were Never Lovelier

AUDREY HEPBURN

Breakfast At Tiffany's
Charade
Funny Face
Lavender Hill Mob, The
Love In The Afternoon
My Fair Lady
Robin and Marian
Roman Holiday
Sidney Sheldon's Bloodline
They All Laughed
27th Annual Academy Awards
Wait Until Dark
War and Peace

KATHARINE HEPBURN

Adam's Rib
African Queen, The
Alice Adams
Christopher Strong
Dragon Seed
Lion In The Winter, The
Little Minister, The
Little Women
Long Day's Journey Into Night
Mary Of Scotland
Morning Glory
On Golden Pond
Philadelphia Story, The
Rooster Cogburn
Stage Door
Stagedoor Canteen
State of the Union

Storytime Classics
Suddenly Last Summer
Summertime
Trojan Woman, The
Woman of the Year
Woman Rebels, A

CHARLTON HESTON

Antony and Cleopatra
Awakening, The
Beneath the Planet of the Apes
Ben Hur
Call of the Wild
El Cid
Earthquake
Elizabeth the Queen
55 Days at Peking
Four Musketeers, The
Greatest Show on Earth, The
Major Dundee
Midway
Mother Lode
Mountain Men, The
Planet of the Apes
Ruby Gentry
Son of Monsters on the March
Soylent Green
Ten Commandments, The
Three Musketeers, The

GREGORY HINES

Cotton Club, The
Deal of the Century
History of the World—Part I
Saturday Night Live: Gary Busey
Wolfen

ALFRED HITCHCOCK

Birds, The
Blackmail
Family Plot
Foreign Correspondent
Frenzy
I Confess
Lady Vanishes, The
Lifeboat
Lodger, The
Man Who Knew Too Much, The
Mr. and Mrs. Smith
Murder
North by Northwest
Notorious
Number Seventeen
Psycho
Rear Window
Rebecca
Rope
Sabotage
Secret Agent
Spellbound
Stage Fright
Strangers on a Train
Suspicion
Thirty-Nine Steps, The
To Catch a Thief
Topaz
Torn Curtain
Trouble With Harry, The
Under Capricorn
Vertigo
Wrong Man, The
Young and Innocent

DUSTIN HOFFMAN

Agatha
All the President's Men
Graduate, The
Kramer vs. Kramer
Marathon Man
Midnight Cowboy
Papillon
Straight Time
Straw Dogs
Tootsie

WILLIAM HOLDEN

Alvarez Kelly
Born Yesterday
Bridge on the River Kwai, The
Christmas Tree, The
Country Girl, The
Damien—Omen II
Earthling, The
Golden Boy
Horse Soldiers, The
Moon is Blue, The
Network
Our Town
Rachel and the Stranger
S.O.B.
Stalag 17
Sunset Boulevard
Towering Inferno, The
27th Annual Academy Awards
Wild Bunch, The
Young and Willing

JUDY HOLLIDAY

Adam's Rib
Bells Are Ringing
Born Yesterday
It Should Happen To You

BOB HOPE

Bing Crosby Show, The
Bloopers From "Star Trek" and "Laugh-In"
Bob Hope Chevy Show
Bob Hope Chevy Show I-III, The
Bobby Darin and Friends
Boy, Did I Get a Wrong Number
Comedy and Kid Stuff III
Hollywood at War
Hollywood Goes to War
Jack Benny
Jack Benny Show, The
Jack Benny Visits Walt Disney
Muppet Movie, The
My Favorite Brunette
Paleface, The
Paris Holiday
Princess and the Pirate, The
Road to Bali, The
Road to Lebanon, The
Television's Golden Age of Comedy
27th Annual Academy Awards
World War II Video Series—Something for Our Boys

LESLIE HOWARD

Big Breakdowns, The
Forty-Ninth Parallel, The
Gone With The Wind
Intermezzo
Of Human Bondage
Petrified Forest, The
Pimpernel Smith
Scarlet Pimpernel, The
Spitfire
Stand-In

ROCK HUDSON

Avalanche
Giant
Ice Station Zebra
Magnificent Obsession
Mirror Crack'd, The
Pillow Talk

WILLIAM HURT

Altered States
Big Chill, The
Body Heat
Eyewitness
Gorky Park

JOHN HUSTON

African Queen, The
American Caesar
Angela
Annie
Battle for the Planet of the Apes
Bible, The

Breakout
Chinatown
Great Cities: London, Rome, Dublin, Athens
Hobbit, The
Let There Be Light
List of Adrian Messenger, The
Lovesick
Maltese Falcon, The
Minor Miracle, A
Misfits, The
Moby Dick
Observations Under The Volcano
Prizzi's Honor
Red Badge of Courage, The
Reflections in a Golden Eye
Tentacles
Treasure of the Sierra Madre, The
Under the Volcano
Winter Kills

LAUREN HUTTON

American Gigolo
Gambler, The
Gator
Lassiter
Zorro, The Gay Blade

TIMOTHY HUTTON

Father Figure
Falcon and the Snowman, The
Long Way Home, The
Ordinary People
Taps
Turk 182
Young Love, First love

AMY IRVING

Carrie
Competition, The
Far Pavilions
Fury, The
Honeysuckle Rose
Micki and Maude
Yentl

AL JOLSON

Coming Attractions
Jazz Singer, The
Musical Personalities No. 1
Weber and Fields, Al Jolson and This Is America

JENNIFER JONES

Dick Tracy's G-Men
Madame Bovary
Towering Inferno, The

TOMMY LEE JONES

Amazing Howard Hughes, The
Back Roads
Betsy, The
Coal Miner's Daughter
Eyes of Laura Mars
Jackson County Jail
Nate and Hayes
Rolling Thunder

MADELINE KAHN

At Long Last Love
Blazing Saddles
City Heat
First Family
Gonzo Presents Muppet Weird Stuff
Hideaways, The
High Anxiety
History of the World: Part I, The
Muppet Movie, The
Paper Moon
Saturday Night Live: Madeline Kahn
Scrambled Feet
Simon
Slapstick of Another Kind
What's Up Doc?
Wholly Moses!
Yellowbeard
Young Frankenstein

BORIS KARLOFF

Abbott and Costelo Meet Dr. Jekyll and Mr. Hyde
Bedlam
Before I Hang
Big Breakdowns, The
Black Cat, The/The Raven
Black Room, The
Blind Man's Bluff
Body Snatcher, The
Chamber of Fear
Criminal Code, The
Daydreamer, The
Frankenstein
Haunted Strangler, The
Juggernaut
Lost Patrol, The
Man They Could Not Hang, The
Mr. Wong, Detective
Monsters on the March
Outtakes VI
Raven, The
Scarface
Tales of Tomorrow
Terror, The
You'll Find Out

BUSTER KEATON

Balloonatic, The/One Week
Blacksmith, The
Boom in the Moon
Buster Keaton Festival Vol. I
Buster Keaton Rides Again/The Railrodder
College
Ed Wynn Show, The
Fun Factory/Clown Princes of Hollywood
Funny Thing Happened on the Way to the Forum, A
General, The
Great Chase, The
Hollywood Palace, The
How To Stuff A Wild Bikini
It's a Mad Mad Mad Mad World
Keaton Special/ Valentino Mystique
Kovacs and Keaton
L'il Abner
Limelight
Parlour, Bedroom and Bath
Silent Laugh Makers
Slapstick
Steamboat Bill, Jr.
Sunset Boulevard

DIANE KEATON

Annie Hall
Godfather, The
Godfather Part II, The
Godfather: The Complete Epic, The
Harry and Walter Go to New York
Little Drummer Girl, The
Looking For Mr. Goodbar
Love and Death
Lovers and Other Strangers
Manhattan
Play It Again, Sam
Reds
Shoot The Moon
Sleeper

DAVID KEITH

Back Roads
Brubaker
Firestarter
Great Santini, The
Gulag
Independence Day
Lords of Discipline
Officer and a Gentleman, An
Rose, The
Take This Job and Shove It

GENE KELLY

American in Paris, An
Brigadoon
Forty Carats
Hello, Dolly!
Hollywood Palace, The
Inherit the Wind
Invitation to the Dance
Jack and the Beanstalk
On the Town
Pirate, The
Singin' in the Rain
That's Dancing
That's Entertainment
That's Entertainment Part II
Three Musketeers, The
Ultimate Swan Lake, The
Xanadu
Ziegfeld Follies

GRACE KELLY

Children of Theatre Street, The
Country Girl, The
Dial M For Murder
Fabulous Fifties, The
High Noon
High Society
Mogambo
Rear Window
To Catch a Thief
27th Annual Academy Awards

GEORGE KENNEDY

Airport
Bandolero
Bolero
Boston Strangler, The
Cahill: United States Marshall
Charade
Chattanooga Choo Choo
Cool Hand Luke
Death on the Nile
Dirty Dozen, The
Island of Blue Dolphins
Lonely Are the Brave
Shenandoah
Sons of Katie Elder
Strait Jacket
Thunderbolt and Lightfoot

DEBORAH KERR

America at the Movies
Arrangement, The
Grass is Greener, The
King and I, The
Life and Death of Colonel Blimp, The
Love on the Dole
Night of the Iguana, The
Prisoner of Zenda, The
Separate Tables
TV's Classic Guessing Games

MARGOT KIDDER

Amityville Horror, The
Glitter Dome, The
Heartaches
Making of Superman I and II, The
Mr. Mike's Mondo Video
Quackser Fortune Has a Cousin in the Bronx
Quiet Day in Belfast, A
Reincarnation of Peter Proud, The
Shoot The Sun Down
Sisters
Some Kind of Hero
Superman—The Movie
Superman II
Superman III
Trenchcoat

KLAUS KINSKI

Doctor Zhivago
For a Few Dollars More
Little Drummer Girl, The
His Name Was King
Night of the Assassin
Ruthless Four, The
Shoot the Living, Pray for the Dead
Soldier, The
Venus in Furs

NASTASSIA KINSKI

Boarding School
Exposed
For Your Love Only
Hotel New Hampshire, The
Maria's Lovers
Paris, Texas
Tess
Unfaithfully Yours

ERNIE KOVACS

Bell, Book and Candle
Ernie Kovacs: Television's Original Genius
Game Show Program II
Kovacs and Keaton
Kovacs on the Corner
Take a Good Look/The Jack Benny Show
Take a Good Look With Ernie Kovacs
Vintage Commercials, II

KRIS KRISTOFFERSON

Alice Doesn't Live Here Anymore
Blume in Love
Celebration, A
Convoy
Flashpoint
Heaven's Gate
Other Side of Nashville, The
Pat Garrett and Billy the Kid
Rollover
Sailor Who Fell from Grace With the Sea, The
Semi-Tough
Songwriter
Star Is Born, A

STANLEY KUBRICK

Clockwork Orange, A
Dr. Strangelove

Lolita
Paths of Glory
Shining, The
Spartacus
2001: A Space Odyssey

ALAN LADD

Boy on a Dolphin
Captain Caution
Deep Six, The
Drum Beat
Hell on Frisco Bay
Joan of Paris
My Favorite Brunette
Premiere of "A Star Is Born"
Proud Rebel, The
Shane
This Gun For Hire

BURT LANCASTER

Airport
America at the Movies
Apache
Atlantic City
Birdman of Alcatraz, The
Elmer Gantry
Executive Action
Go Tell The Spartans
Gunfight at the O.K. Corral
Island of Dr. Moreau, The
Jim Thorpe—All American
Judgment at Nuremburg
Kentuckian, The
List of Adrian Messenger, The
Moses
Osterman Weekend, The
Professionals, The
Run Silent, Run Deep
Separate Tables
Seven Days In May
Trapeze
Vengeance Valley
Vera Cruz

JESSICA LANGE

All That Jazz
Cat on a Hot Tin Roof
Country
Frances
How to Beat the High Cost of Living
King Kong

CHARLES LAUGHTON

Abbott and Costello Meet Captain Kidd
Arch of Triumph
Beachcomber, The
Captain Kidd
Colgate Comedy Hour IV, The
Early Elvis
Hobson's Choice
Hunchback of Notre Dame, The
Mutiny on the Bounty
Private Life of Henry VIII, The
Sidewalks of London
Spartacus
They Knew What They Wanted
This Land Is Mine
Tuttles of Tahiti, The
Witness for the Prosecution

LAUREL AND HARDY

Atoll K *(Utopia)*
Blockheads
Bohemian Girl, The
Bullfighters, The
Chump at Oxford, A
Flying Deuces, The
Fun Factory/Clown Princes of Hollywood
Great Guns
Hal Roach Comedy Classics
Laurel and Hardy Comedy Classics Volumes I-IX
Live Television
Movie Struck
Our Relations
Pack Up Your Troubles
Pardon Us
Saps at Sea
Silent Laugh Makers
Sons of the Desert
Swis Miss
That's Entertainment Part II
This Is Your Life: Laurel and Hardy
Way Out West

BRUCE LEE

Bruce Lee: The Man/The Myth
Chinese Connection, The
Enter the Dragon
Fist of Fear, Touch of Death
Fists of Fury
Game of Death, The
Real Bruce Lee, The
Return of the Dragon
True Game of Death, The

CHRISTOPHER LEE

Against All Odds
Albino
Bear Island
Boy Who Left Home to Find Out About the Shivers, The
Castle of the Walking Dead
Circle of Iron
Dark Places
Devil's Undead, The
Dracula and Son
End of the World
Eye for an Eye, An
Far Pavilions
Horror Express
Horror Hotel
Keeper, The
Last Unicorn, The
Longest Day, The
Man with the Golden Gun, The
Meatcleaver Massacre
1941
Rosebud Beach Hotel
Safari 3000
Scars of Dracula
Serial
Sons of Monsters of the March
Tale of Two Cities, A
Theatre of Death
Three Musketeers, The
Wicker Man, The

JANET LEIGH

Bye Bye Birdie
Premiere of "A Star Is Born"
Psycho
Two Tickets to Broadway

VIVIEN LEIGH

Caesar and Cleopatra
Fire Over England
Gone With the Wind
Hollywood Outtakes and Rare Footage
Roman Spring of Mrs. Stone, The
Sidewalks of London
Streetcar Named Desire, A
That Hamilton Woman

JACK LEMMON

Apartment, The
Bell, Book and Candle
Buddy Buddy
China Syndrome, The
Days of Wine and Roses, The
Ernie Kovacs: Television's Original Genius

Good Neighbor Sam
Great Race, The
Irma La Douce
It Should Happen to You
Kotch
Luv
Mass Appeal
Missing
Mister Roberts
Odd Couple, The
Out-of-Towners, The
Prisoner of Second Avenue, The
Save the Tiger
Some Like It Hot
Tribute

JERRY LEWIS

At War with the Army
Colgate Comedy Hour, The
Cracking Up
Dean Martin and Jerry Lewis Television Party
Don't Raise the Bridge, Lower the River
Errand Boy, The
It's a Mad, Mad, Mad, Mad World
Jack Benny
Jack Benny Show, The
Jerry Lewis Show, The
King of Comedy
Nutty Professor, The
Patsy, The
Rascal Dazzle
Road to Bali, The
Slapstick of Another Kind
Television's Golden Age of Comedy
Tonight Show, The
27th Annual Academy Awards

HAROLD LLOYD

Don't Shove/Two Gun Gussie
Fun Factory/Clown Princes of Hollywood
Funstuff
Harold Lloyd's Comedy Classics
His Royal Slyness/Haunted Spooks
Keystone Comedies, 1-8
Kings, Queens, Jokers
Silent Laugh Makers # 3
Sin of Harold Diddlebock, The
This Is Your Life

SONDRA LOCKE

Any Which Way You Can
Bronco Billy
Every Which Way But Loose
Gauntlet, The
Heart Is a Lonely Hunter, The
Outlaw Josey Wales, The
Second Coming of Suzanne, The
Sudden Impact

CAROLE LOMBARD

Hollywood Outtakes and Rare Footage
In Name Only
Made for Each Other
My Man Godfrey
Mr. and Mrs. Smith
Nothing Sacred
Racketeer
Swing High, Swing Lcw
These Girls Won't Talk
They Knew What They Wanted
To Be or Not to Be

SOPHIA LOREN

Aida
Angela
Blood Feud
Chase, The
El Cid
Fall of the Roman Empire, The
Favorita, La
Firepower
Lady of the Evening
Man of La Mancha
Pride and the Passion, The
Sophia Loren: Her Own Story
Special Day, A

PETER LORRE

Algiers
Arsenic and Old Lace
Casablanca
Collectors Item: The Left Fist of David
Coming Attractions
Five Weeks in a Balloon
M
Maltese Falcon, The
Man Who Knew Too Much, The
Mr. Moto's Last Warning
Patsy, The
Postmark for Danger/Quicksand
Raven, The
Secret Agent
Silk Stockings
Stranger on the Third Floor
Tales of Terror
20,000 Leagues Under the Sea
You'll Find Out

MYRNA LOY

Ants
Bachelor and the Bobby Soxer, The
Best Years of Our Lives
End, The
Just Tell Me What You Want
Mr. Blandings Builds His Dream House
Red Pony, The
Renegade Ranger, The/Scarlet River
Summer Solstice

BELA LUGOSI

Bela Lugosi Meets a Brooklyn Gorilla
Black Cat, The/The Raven
Body Snatcher, The
Bowery at Midnight
Bride of the Monster
Chandu on the Magic Island
Devil Bat, The
Dracula
Ghosts on the Loose
Glen or Glenda
Hollywood on Parade
Human Monster, The
Invisible Ghost
Killer Bats
Monsters on the March
Murder by Television
Mystery of the Mary Celeste, The
Ninotchka
One Body Too Many
Outtakes VI
Plan Nine from Outer Space
Scared to Death
S.O.S. Coastguard
Spooks Run Wild
White Zombie
You'll Find Out

MALCOLM MCDOWELL

Blue Thunder
Britannia Hospital
Caligula
Cat People
Clockwork Orange, A

If . . .
Get Crazy
Gulag
Little Red Riding Hood
Long Ago Tomorrow
Look Back in Anger
Time After Time
Voyage of the Damned

ALI MACGRAW

Convoy
Getaway, The
Goodbye Columbus
Just Tell Me What You Want
Love Story
Players

SHIRLEY MACLAINE

All in a Night's Work
Apartment, The
Around the World in 80 Days
Being There
Change of Seasons, A
Irma La Douce
Loving Couples
Terms of Endearment
Trouble With Harry, The
Turning Point, The
TV Variety, Book VII

STEVE MCQUEEN

Baby, The Rain Must Fall
Blob, The
Bullitt
Cincinnati Kid, The
Getaway, The
Great Escape, The
Hunter, The
Magnificent Seven, The
Never Love a Stranger
On Any Sunday
Papillon
Reivers, The
Sand Pebbles, The
Thomas Crown Affair, The
Tom Horn
Towering Inferno, The
War Lover, The

DEAN MARTIN

Airport
All in a Night's Work
At War with the Army
Bandolero
Bells Are Ringing
Cannonball Run, The
Colgate Comedy Hour, The
Dean Martin and Jerry Lewis Television Party
Dean Martin Show, The
Hollywood Palace, The
Jack Benny Show, The
Murderer's Row
Ocean's 11
Premiere of "A Star Is Born"
Rio Bravo
Road to Bali, The
Sons of Katie Elder, The
Television's Golden Age of Comedy

STEVE MARTIN

All of Me
Dead Men Don't Wear Plaid
Funnier Side of Eastern Canada, The
Jerk, The
Kids Are Alright, The
Lonely Guy, The
Man with Two Brains, The
Pennies from Heaven
Saturday Night Live, Vol. II
Saturday Night Live: Steve Martin 2
Saturday Night Live with Steve Martin
Sgt. Pepper's Lonely Hearts Club Band

LEE MARVIN

Big Red One, The
Big Sleep, The
Cat Ballou
Death Hunt
Dirty Dozen, The
Donovan's Reef
Gorky Park
Great Scout and Cathouse Thursday, The
Killers, The
Man Who Shot Liberty Valance, The
Monte Walsh
Paint Your Wagon
Prime Cut
Professionals, The
Shack Out on 101
Shout at the Devil

THE MARX BROTHERS/ GROUCHO MARX

Animal Crackers
At the Circus
Copacabana
Day at the Races, A
Duck Soup
Funny Guys and Gals of the Talkies
Game Show Program
Girl in Every Port, A
Go West
Hollywood Goes to War
Hollywood Palace, The
Love Happy
Monkey Business
NBC Comedy Hour
Night at the Opera, A
Night in Casablanca, A
One, The Only . . . Groucho, The
Outtakes VI
Room Service
Stagedoor Canteen
Television's Golden Age of Comedy
That's Entertainment, Part II
TV Variety, II
Vintage Commercials
You Bet Your Life

JAMES MASON

Bad Man's River
Blue Max, The
Caught
Cross of Iron
Boys from Brazil, The
Dangerous Summer, A
Desert Fox, The
Evil Under the Sun
Fall of the House of Usher, The
Fall of the Roman Empire, The
Fire Over England
Heaven Can Wait
High Command
Inside Out
Jesus of Nazareth
Journey to the Center of the Earth
Kidnap Syndicate, The
Kill
Last of Shelia, The
Lolita
Mackintosh Man, The
Madame Bovary
Man in Grey, The
Mandingo
Night Has Eyes, The
North by Northwest
Prisoner of Zenda, The
Salem's Lot: The Movie
Sidney Sheldon's Bloodline
Star Is Born, A
Tiara Tahiti
20,000 Leagues Under the Sea
Verdict, The

Voyage of the Damned
Water Babies, The
Yellowbeard

MARSHA MASON

Audrey Rose
Blume in Love
Chapter Two
Goodbye Girl, The
Max Dugan Returns
Only When I Laugh
Promises in the Dark

WALTER MATTHAU

Bad News Bears, The
Buddy Buddy
Cactus Flower
California Suite
Casey's Shadow
Charade
Charley Varrick
Ensign Pulver
Face in the Crowd, A
Fail Safe
First Monday in October
Hello, Dolly!
Hopscotch
House Calls
I Ought to Be in Pictures
Kentuckian, The
King Creole
Kotch
Little Miss Marker
Lonely Are the Brave
Odd Couple, The
Plaza Suite
Sunburn
Sunshine Boys, The
Survivors, The
Suspense
Taking of Pelham One Two Three, The

VERA MILES

Back Street
Hell Fighters
Mission Batangas
Our Family Business
Psycho
Psycho II
Roughnecks, The
Strange and Deadly Occurrence, A

RAY MILLAND

Attic, The
Cruise Into Terror
Dead Don't Die, The
Escape to Witch Mountain
Lost Weekend, The
Love Story
Man Alone, A
Oliver's Story
Our Family Business
Premature Burial
Slavers
Starflight One
Terror in the Wax Museum
X—The Man with X-Ray Eyes

ANN MILLER

Melody Ranch
On the Town
Room Service
Stage Door
That's Entertainment
That's Entertainment, Part II

HAYLEY MILLS

Deadly Strangers
In Search of the Castaways
Kingfisher Caper, The
Parent Trap, The
Pollyanna
Summer Magic
That Darn Cat

LIZA MINNELLI

Arthur
Cabaret
Evening with Liza Minnelli, An
Journey Back to Oz
Liza in Concert
Matter of Time, A
New York, New York
Princess and the Pea, The
Silent Movie
That's Dancing
That's Entertainment

VINCENTE MINNELLI

American in Paris, An
Band Wagon, The
Bells Are Ringing
Brigadoon
Four Horsemen of the Apocalypse, The
Gigi
Kismet
Madame Bovary
Matter of Time, A
Meet Me in St. Louis
Pirate, The
Ziegfeld Follies

ROBERT MITCHUM

Amsterdam Kill, The
Big Sleep, The
Blood on the Moon
Breakthrough
Crossfire
El Dorado
Farewell, My Lovely
Grass Is Greener, The
Gung Ho
His Kind of Woman
List of Adrian Messenger, The
Locket, The
Longest Day, The
Lusty Men, The
Macao
Maria's Lovers
Matilda
Midway
My Forbidden Past
Nightkill
Out of the Past
Rachel and the Stranger
Racket, The
Red Pony, The
Ryan's Daughter
Second Chance
She Couldn't Say No
That Championship Season

MARILYN MONROE

All About Eve
Bus Stop
Clash by Night
Gentlemen Prefer Blondes
Hollywood Outtakes and Rare Footage
How to Marry a Millionaire
Love Goddesses, The
Love Happy
Marilyn Monroe
Marilyn Monroe, Life Story of America's Mistress
Misfits, The
Seven Year Itch, The
Some Like It Hot
There's No Business Like Show Business

MONTY PYTHON

All You Need Is Cash *(Idle)*
And Now For Something Completely Different
Gonzo Presents Muppet Weird Stuff *(Cleese)*
Great Muppet Caper, The *(Cleese)*
Jabberwocky *(Palin)*
Missionary, The *(Palin)*
Monty Python and he Holy Grail
Monty Python's Life of Brian

Monty Python's The Meaning of Life
Odd Job, The *(Chapman)*
Pied Piper of Hamelin, The *(Idle)*
Privates on Parade *(Cleese)*
Romance With a Double Bass *(Cleese)*
Secret Policeman's Other Ball, The *(Cleese)*
Tale of the Frog Prince, The *(Idle)*
To See Such Fun *(Idle)*
Whoops Apocalypse *(Cleese)*
Yellowbeard *(Chapman, Cleese)*

DUDLEY MOORE

Alice's Adventures in Wonderland
Arthur
Bedazzled
Best Defense
Derek and Clive Get the Horn
Foul Play
Lovesick
Micki and Maude
Playboy Video, Volume II
Romantic Comedy
Saturday Night Live: Peter Cook and Dudley Moore
Six Weeks
"10"
30 Is a Dangerous Age, Cynthia
Unfaithfully Yours
Wholly Moses!
Wrong Box, The

MARY TYLER MOORE

Change of Habit
Mary Tyler Moore Show, Vol. I, The
Ordinary People
Outtakes III
Six Weeks
Vintage Commercials

ROGER MOORE

Cannonball Run, The
Escape to Athena
Fiction Makers, The
For Your Eyes Only
James Bond 007—Coming Attractions
Live and Let Die
Man Who Haunted Himself, The
Man with the Golden Gun, The
Octopussy
Sea Wolves, The
Shout at the Devil
Wild Geese, The

ZERO MOSTEL

Foreplay
Front, The
Funny Thing Happened on the Way to the Forum, A
Hot Rock, The
Marco
Producers, The

EDDIE MURPHY

Best Defense
48 Hours
Saturday Night Live
Trading Places

BILL MURRAY

Caddyshack
Meatballs
Mr. Mike's Mondo Video
Razor's Edge, The
Saturday Night Live
Stripes
Things We Did Last Summer
Where The Buffalo Roam

PAUL NEWMAN

Absence of Malice
Buffalo Bill and the Indians
Butch Cassidy and the Sundance Kid
Cat on a Hot Tin Roof
Cool Hand Luke
Drowning Pool, The
Exodus
Fort Apache, the Bronx
Harper
Harry and Son
Hombre
Hud
Life and Times of Judge Roy Bean, The
Mackintosh Man, The
Playwrights '56: "The Battler"
Quintet
Rachel, Rachel
Secret War of Harry Frigg, The
Silent Movie
Slapshot
Sometimes a Great Notion
Sting, The
Torn Curtain
Towering Inferno, The
Verdict, The
Winning
Young Philadelphians, The

JACK NICHOLSON

Black Cat, The/The Raven
Border, The
Carnal Knowledge
Chinatown
Easy Rider
Goin' South
Last Detail, The
Little Shop of Horrors, The
Missouri Breaks, The
On a Clear Day You Can See Forever
One Flew Over the Cuckoo's Nest
Postman Always Rings Twice, The
Prizzi's Honor
Raven, The
Rebel Rousers
Reds
Ride in the Whirlwind
Shining, The
Shooting, The
Terms of Endearment
Terror, The
Wild Ride, The

DAVID NIVEN

Around the World in 80 Days
Bachelor Mother
Better Late Then Never
Candleshoe
Charge of the Light Brigade, The
Curse of the Pink Panther, The
Dawn Patrol, The
Death on the Nile
Dinner at the Ritz
Escape to Athena
Eternally Yours
55 Days at Peking
Guns of Navarone, The
Immortal Battalion
King, Queen, Knave
Moon Is Blue, The
Murder by Death
Paper Tiger, The
Pink Panther, The
Rough Cut
Sea Wolves
Separate Tables
Spitfire
Stairway to Heaven

Survival Anglia's World of Wildlife, Vol. 2
Trail of the Pink Panther, The
Wuthering Heigts

NICK NOLTE

Cannery Row
Death Sentence
Deep, The
48 Hours
Heartbeat
North Dallas Forty
Return to Macon County
Runaway Barge
Teachers
Under Fire
Who'll Stop the Rain

KIM NOVAK

Bell, Book and Candle
Mirror Crack'd, The
Premiere of "A Star Is Born"
Vertigo

MAUREEN O'HARA

At Sword's Point
Big Jake
Hunchback of Notre Dame, The
Magnificent Matador
Miracle on 34th Street
Parent Trap, The
Quiet Man, The
Rio Grande
Sinbad the Sailor
This Land Is Mine

LAURENCE OLIVIER

As You Like It
Betsy, The
Boys from Brazil, The
Bridge Too Far, A
Clash of the Titans
Clouds Over Europe
Dracula
Fire Over England
Forty-Ninth Parallel, The
Hamlet
Henry V
I Stand Condemned
Jesus of Nazareth
Jigsaw Man, The
Lady Caroline Lamb
Little Romance, A
Marathon Man
Mr. Halpern and Mr. Johnson
Nicholas and Alexandra
Pride and Prejudice
Rebecca
Romeo and Juliet
Seven-Per-Cent Solution, The
Sleuth
Spartacus
That Hamilton Woman
World at War, The
Wuthering Heights

RYAN O'NEAL

Barry Lyndon
Bridge Too Far, A
Driver, The
Irreconcilable Differences
Love Story
Main Event, The
Oliver's Story
Paper Moon
Partners
So Fine
Thief Who Came to Dinner, The
What's Up Doc?

TATUM O'NEAL

Bad News Bears, The
Circle of Two
Goldilocks and the Three Bears
International Velvet
Little Darlings
Paper Moon

PETER O'TOOLE

Becket
Bible, The
Caligula
Kidnapped
Lawrence of Arabia
Lion in Winter, The
Man of La Mancha
Masada
My Favorite Year
Night of the Generals, The
Power Play
Ruling Class, The
Sherlock Holmes and the Baskerville Curse
Sherlock Holmes and the Sign of Four
Stunt Man, The
Supergirl
Supergirl: The Making of the Movie
What's New Pussycat?

AL PACINO

America at the Movies
. . . And Justice for All
Author! Author!
Bobby Deerfield
Cruising
Dog Day Afternoon
Godfather, The
Godfather Part II, The
Godfather: The Complete Epic, The
Scarecrow
Scarface
Serpico

DOLLY PARTON

Best Little Whorehouse in Texas, The
Captain Kangaroo and His Friends
Dolly in London
9 to 5
Rhinestone

GREGORY PECK

Behold a Pale Horse
Boys from Brazil, The
Guns of Navarone, The
MacArthur
Marooned
Moby Dick
Omen, The
On the Beach
Roman Holiday
Sea Wolves
Spellbound
Twelve O'Clock High
Yearling, The

SEAN PENN

Bad Boys
Crackers
Falcon and the Snowman, The
Fast Times at Ridgemont High
Taps

ANTHONY PERKINS

Black Hole, The
Catch-22
Crimes of Passion
Friendly Persuasion
Glory Boys, The
Mahogany
Murder on the Orient Express
On the Beach
Psycho
Psycho II
Ravishing Idiot, The
Trial, The
Twice a Woman
Winter Kills

BERNADETTE PETERS
Annie
Heartbeeps
Jerk, The
Martian Chronicles, Part II
Pennies from Heaven
Sleeping Beauty
Tulips

MARY PICKFORD
Birth of a Legend, The
Hollywood on Parade
Little Annie Rooney
My Best Girl
Pollyanna
Poor Little Rich Girl
Rebecca of Sunnybrook Farm
Short Films of D.W. Griffith, The
Sparrows
Taming of the Shrew, The

SIDNEY POITIER
Bedford Incident, The
Buck and the Preacher
Defiant Ones, The
Fast Forward
For Love of Ivy
Greatest Story Ever Told, The
In the Heat of the Night
Let's Do It Again
Lilies of the Field
Piece of the Action, A
Raisin in the Sun, A
Stir Crazy
They Call Me Mr. Tibbs!
To Sir, with Love
Uptown Saturday Night

DICK POWELL
Big Breakdowns, The
Coming Attractions
Conqueror, The
42nd Street
Gold Diggers of 1933
Jack Benny, II
Murder My Sweet
Musical Personalities No. 1
Susan Slept Here

TYRONE POWER
Witness for the Prosecution

ELVIS PRESLEY
Aloha from Hawaii
Blue Hawaii
Change of Habit
Coming Attractions
Double Trouble
Early Elvis
Easy Come, Easy Go
Elvis Comeback Special
Elvis in Concert in Hawaii
Elvis in Concert in 1968
Elvis Live in '56
Elvis on Television
Elvis on Tour
Elvis—'68 Comeback Special
Flaming Star
Fun in Acapulco
G.I. Blues
Girls, Girls, Girls
Harum Scarum
It Happened at the World's Fair
Jailhouse Rock
King Creole
Love Me Tender
Loving You
Paradise Hawaiian Style
Roustabout
Singer Presents "Elvis"
Speedway
Stage Show
Tickle Me
Viva Las Vegas
Wild in the Country

ROBERT PRESTON
Blood on the Moon
Finnegan Begin Again
Going Hollywood
Last Starfighter, The
Mame
My Father's House
Semi-Tough
S.O.B.
Tulsa
Victor/Victoria

VINCENT PRICE
Abbott and Costello Meet Frankenstein
Abominable Dr. Phibes, The
Adventures of Captain Fabian
Alice Cooper: Welcome to My Nightmare
Black Cat, The/The Raven
Boy Who Left Home to Find Out About the Shivers, The
Butterfly Ball, The
Champagne for Caesar
Devil's Triangle
Fall of the House of Usher, The
Fly, The
Gonzo Presents Muppet Weird Stuff
Laura
Monster Club, The
Pit and the Pendulum, The
Private Lives of Elizabeth and Essex, The
Raven, The
Return of the Fly
Ruddigore
Shock
Snow White and the Seven Dwarves
Son of Sinbad
Tales of Terror
Ten Commandments, The
Three Musketeers, The

RICHARD PRYOR
Bingo Long Traveling All-Stars & Motor Kings, The
Blue Collar
Bustin' Loose
California Suite
Car Wash
Greased Lightning
Lady Sings the Blues
Muppet Movie, The
Outtakes II
Richard Pryor: Here and Now
Richard Pryor: Live and Smokin'
Richard Pryor Live in Concert
Richard Pryor Live on the Sunset Strip
Saturday Night Live, Vol. II
Silver Streak
Some Call It Loving
Some Kind of Hero
Stir Crazy
Superman III
Toy, The
Uptown Saturday Night
Which Way Is Up?
Wholly Moses!
Wiz, The

BASIL RATHBONE
Adventures of Robin Hood, The
Captain Blood

Court Jester, The
David Copperfield
Dawn Patrol, The
Dressed to Kill
Last Days of Pompeii, The
Magic Sword, The
Make a Wish
Sherlock Holmes and the Secret Weapon
Sherlock Holmes Double Features
Tale of Two Cities, A
Tales of Terror
Terror by Night/ Meeting at Midnight
Victoria Regina
We're No Angels
Wind in the Willows, The
Woman in Green, The

RONALD REAGAN

Bedtime for Bonzo
Dark Victory
Death Valley Days
Famous Generals
Fight for the Sky, The
Hellcats of the Navy
Hollywood Outtakes and Rare Footage
Jack Benny, II
Judy Garland (General Electric Theatre)
Killers, The
Outtakes II
Presidential Blooper Reel
Santa Fe Trail
Star Bloopers
Swingin' Singin' Years, The
Take I: Rescued from the Editor's Floor
This Is the Army

ROBERT REDFORD

All the President's Men
Barefoot in the Park
Bridge Too Far, A
Brubaker
Butch Cassidy and the Sundance Kid
Candidate, The
Downhill Racer
Electric Horseman, The
Great Gatsby, The
Great Waldo Pepper, The
Hot Rock, The
Jeremiah Johnson
Natural, The
Ordinary People
Sting, The
Tell Them Willie Boy Is Here
Three Days of the Condor
Way We Were, The

SIR MICHAEL REDGRAVE

Dam Busters, The
Dead of Night
Fame Is the Spur
Heidi
Kipps
Lady Vanishes, The
Nicholas and Alexandra
Rime of the Ancient Mariner
Sea Shall Not Have Them, The
Stars Look Down, The

VANESSA REDGRAVE

Agatha
Bear Island
Bostonians, The
Blow Up
Camelot
Julia
Man for All Seasons, A
Morgan—A Suitable Case for Treatment
Murder on the Orient Express
Snow White and the Seven Dwarves
Trojan Woman, The

CHRISTOPHER REEVE

Bostonians, The
Deathtrap
Making of Superman I and II
Monsignor
Sleeping Beauty
Somewhere in Time
Superman—The Movie
Superman II
Superman III

CARL REINER

All of Me
Caesar's Hour
Dead Men Don't Wear Plaid
End, The
Gidget Goes Hawaiian
It's a Mad, Mad, Mad, Mad World
Jerk, The
Man with Two Brains, The
Oh, God!
Oh, God! Book II
Pinocchio
Russians Are Coming, Russians Are Coming, The
Take a Good Look with Ernie Kovacs
Timex All-Star Comedy Show, The
2000-Year-Old Man, The

BURT REYNOLDS

At Long Last Love
Best Friends
Best Little Whorehouse in Texas, The
Cannonball Run, The
Cannonball Run II
City Heat
Deliverance
End, The
Everything You Always Wanted to Know About Sex
Fuzz
Gator
Hooper
Hustler
Longest Yard, The
Man Who Loved Cat Dancing, The
Man Who Loved Women, The
100 Rifles
Outtakes III
Paternity
Rough Cut
Semi-Tough
Shamus
Shark!
Sharkey's Machine
Silent Movie
Smokey and the Bandit
Smokey and the Bandit II
Starting Over
Stick
Stroker Ace
White Lightning

EDWARD G. ROBINSON

Big Breakdowns, The
Breakdowns of 1936 and 1937
Cincinnati Kid, The
Good Neighbor Sam
Hell on Frisco Bay
Key Largo
Little Caesar
Premiere of "A Star Is Born"
Presidential Blooper Reel
Red House, The

Scarlet Street
Soylent Green
Stranger, The
Ten Commandments, The

GINGER ROGERS

Bachelor Mother
Carefree
Far Frontier, The
Fifth Avenue Girl
Flying Down to Rio
Follow the Fleet
42nd Street
Gay Divorcee, The
Gold Diggers of 1933
Gotta Dance, Gotta Sing
Having A Wonderful Time
Hollywood on Parade
Kitty Foyle
Lucky Partners
Once Upon a Honeymoon
Shall We Dance
Stage Door
Star of Midnight
Story of Vernon and Irene Castle, The
Swing Time
That's Dancing
That's Entertainment
13th Guest, The
Tom, Dick and Harry
Top Hat
Vivacious Lady

ROY ROGERS

Billy the Kid Returns
Colorado
Dark Command
Disney's American Heroes
Frontier Pony Express
Grand Canyon Trail
Heart of the Golden West
Jesse James at Bay
Milton Berle Show, The
My Pal Trigger
Old Corral, The
Roy Rogers and Dale Evans Show, The
Saga of Death Valley
Shine on Harvest Moon
Song of Nevada
Song of Texas
Sunset Serenade
Under California Stars
Western Double Feature #3, 4, 6, 8, 10, 11, 15, 17-25
Yellow Rose of Texas

MICKEY ROONEY

Adventures of Huckleberry Finn, The
Babes in Arms
Bill
Black Stallion, The
Breakfast at Tiffany's
Captains Courageous
Care Bears Movie, The
Domino Principle, The
How to Stuff a Wild Bikini
It's a Mad, Mad, Mad, Mad World
Journey Back to Oz
Leave 'Em Laughing
Little Lord Fauntleroy
Love Laughs at Andy Hardy
Milton Berle Hour, The
Odyssey of the Pacific
Outtakes II, III
Playhouse 90
Postmark for Danger/ Quicksand
Strike Up the Band
That's Entertainment
That's Entertainment, Part II
Thunder Country
TV Variety

DIANA ROSS

Diana Ross in Concert
Free to Be . . . You and Me
Lady Sings the Blues
Mahogany
Wiz, The

KATHARINE ROSS

Betsy, The
Butch Cassidy and the Sundance Kid
Daddy's Deadly Darling
Final Countdown, The
Graduate, The
Hellfighters
Murder in Texas
Shenandoah
Swarm, The
Tell Them Willie Boy Is Here
Voyage of the Damned
Wrong Is Right

JANE RUSSELL

French Line, The
Gentlemen Prefer Blondes
His Kind of Woman
Las Vegas Story, The
Macao
Outlaw, The
Road to Bali, The
Underwater

SUSAN SARANDON

Atlantic City
Beauty and the Beast
Buddy System, The
Duce and I, The
Great Smokey Roadblock, The
Great Waldo Pepper, The
Hunger, The
Joe
King of the Gypsies
Other Side of Midnight
Pretty Baby
Something Short of Paradise
Tempest

JOHN SAVAGE

Deer Hunter, The
Inside Moves
Onion Field, The

TELLY SAVALAS

Battle of the Bulge
Beyond Reason
Birdman of Alcatraz
Capricorn One
Dirty Dozen, The
Escape to Athena
Greatest Story Ever Told
Inside Out
Kelly's Heroes
Killer Force
Massacre at Fort Hamilton
On Her Majesty's Secret Service
Silent Rebellion

ROY SCHEIDER

All That Jazz
Blue Thunder
French Connection, The
Jaws
Jaws II
Klute
Marathon Man
Still of the Night
Seven-Ups, The
Tiger Town
2010

MARTIN SCORSESE

Alice Doesn't Live Here Anymore
Boxcar Bertha

King of Comedy
Last Waltz, The
Mean Streets
New York, New York
Raging Bull

GEORGE C. SCOTT

Bible, The
Changeling, The
Dr. Strangelove
Flim-Flam Man, The
Formula, The
Hardcore
Hindenberg, The
Hospital, The
Islands in the Stream
List of Adrian Messenger, The
Movie Movie
New Centurions, The
Patton
Savage Is Loose, The
Taps

RANDOLPH SCOTT

Abilene Town
Captain Kidd
Follow the Fleet
Gung Ho
My Favorite Wife
Return of the Bad Men
Spoilers, The
Trail Street

GEORGE SEGAL

Black Bird, The
Blume in Love
Carbon Copy
Cold Room, The
Deadly Game, The
Duchess and the Dirtwater Fox, The
Fun with Dick and Jane
Hot Rock, The
Invitation to a Gunfighter
King Rat
Last Married Couple in America, The
Lost and Found
Owl and the Pussycat
Stick
Touch of Class, A
Where's Poppa?
Who's Afraid of Virginia Woolf?

TOM SELLECK

Bunco
Coma
High Road to China
Lassiter
Midway
Runaway
Sacketts, The

PETER SELLERS

After the Fox
Alice's Adventures in Wonderland
America at the Movies
Battle of the Sexes, The
Being There
Bobo, The
Dr. Strangelove
Down Among the Z-Men
Fiendish Plot of Dr. Fu Manchu, The
Ghost in the Noonday Sun
Great McGonagall, The
Heavens Above
I Love You, Alice B. Toklas
I'm All Right Jack
Ladykillers, The
Lolita
Magic Christian, The
Mouse That Roared, The
Muppet Treasures
Murder by Death
Naked Truth, The
Never Let Go
Pink Panther, The
Pink Panther Strikes Again, The
Prisoner of Zenda, The
Return of the Pink Panther, The
Shot in the Dark, A
Stand Easy
There's a Girl in My Soup
To See Such Fun
Tom Thumb
Trail of the Pink Panther, The
Two-Way Stretch
What's New Pussycat?
Woman Times Seven
Wrong Box, The

MARTIN SHEEN

Apocalypse Now
Badlands
Cassandra Crossing, The
Catch-22
Catholics
Dead Zone, The
Enigma
Final Countdown, The
Little Girl Who Lives Down the Lane, The
Loophole
Missiles of October, The
That Championship Season

BROOKE SHIELDS

Alice Sweet Alice
Blue Lagoon, The
Children's Songs and Stories with the Muppets
Endless Love
King of the Gypsies
Pretty Baby
Sahara
Tilt

TALIA SHIRE

Godfather, The
Godfather Part II, The
Godfather: The Complete Epic, The
Old Boyfriends
Prophecy
Rocky
Rocky II
Rocky III

FRANK SINATRA

Around the World in 80 Days
Bob Hope Chevy Show, II
Bulova Watch Time
Colgate Comedy Hour, The
Dean Martin Show, The
Devil at 4 O'Clock, The
First Deadly Sin, The
Guys and Dolls
Higher and Higher
High Society
Hollywood Goes to War
List of Adrian Messenger, The
Miracle of the Bells, The
Ocean's 11
On the Town
Pride and the Passion, The
Step Lively
That's Entertainment
That's Entertainment, Part II
Till the Clouds Roll By
TV Variety, Book VIII
Von Ryan's Express
Young at Heart

SISSY SPACEK

Badlands
Carrie
Coal Miner's Daughter
Ginger in the Morning

Heartbeat
Missing
Prime Cut
Raggedy Man
River, The
Saturday Night Live: Sissy Spacek
Welcome to L.A.

STEVEN SPIELBERG

Close Encounters of the Third Kind
Duel
Jaws
Night Gallery
1941
Poltergeist
Raiders of the Lost Ark
Sugarland Express, The

SYLVESTER STALLONE

Bananas
Death Race 2000
First Blood
F.I.S.T.
Nighthawks
Prisoner of Second Avenue
Rhinestone
Rocky
Rocky II
Rocky III
Victory

BARBARA STANWYCK

Annie Oakley
Bride Walks Out, The
Escape to Burma
Golden Boy
Lady Eve, The
Lady of Burlesque
Mad Miss Manton, The
Maverick Queen, The
Meet John Doe
Roustabout
Stella Dallas
Strange Love of Martha Ivers, The

MARY STEENBURGEN

Cross Creek
Goin' South
Little Red Riding Hood
Melvin and Howard
Midsummer Night's Sex Comedy, A
Old Boyfriends
Ragtime
Romantic Comedy
Time After Time

ROD STEIGER

Amityville Horror, The
Back from Eternity
Breakthrough
Chosen, The
Dr. Zhivago
F.I.S.T.
Glory Boys, The
Goodyear TV Playhouse: "Marty"
Harder They Fall, The
In the Heat of the Night
Jesus of Nazareth
Lion of the Desert
Longest Day, The
Love and Bullets
Marty
Nazis, The
Oklahoma!
On the Waterfront
Pawnbroker, The
Run of the Arrow
Tales of Tomorrow
27th Annual Academy Awards
Unholy Wife, The
Wolf Lake

JAMES STEWART

Bandolero
Bell, Book and Candle
Big Sleep, The
Greatest Show on Earth, The
It's a Wonderful Life
Made for Each Other
Magic Town
Man Who Knew Too Much, The
Man Who Shot Liberty Valance, The
Mr. Smith Goes to Washington
Philadelphia Story, The
Pot O'Gold
Rear Window
Right of Way
Rope
Shenandoah
Shootist, The
Spirit of St. Louis, The
That's Entertainment
Vertigo
Vivacious Lady
War in the Sky

MERYL STREEP

Deer Hunter, The
Falling in Love
French Lieutenant's Woman, The
Holocaust
In Our Hands
Kramer vs. Kramer
Manhattan
Seduction of Joe Tynan, The
Silkwood
Sophie's Choice
Still of the Night

BARBRA STREISAND

All Night Long
Coming Attractions
For Pete's Sake
Funny Girl
Hello Dolly!
Main Event, The
On a Clear Day You Can See Forever
Owl and the Pussycat, The
Star Is Born, A
Up the Sandbox
Way We Were, The
What's Up Doc?

DONALD SUTHERLAND

Animal House
Bear Island
Bethune
Crackers
Day of the Locust
Disappearance, The
Don't Look Now
Eagle Has Landed, The
Eye of the Needle
Gas
Heaven Help Us
Invasion of the Body Snatchers
Johnny Got His Gun
Kelly's Heroes
Kentucky Fried Movie
Klute
Lady Ice
M*A*S*H
Max Dugan Returns
Nothing Personal
Ordinary People
Start the Revolution Without Me
Threshold

GLORIA SWANSON

Hash House Fraud, A/ The Sultan's Wife
Hollywood Palace, The
Love Goddesses, The
Sunset Boulevard
Teddy at the Throttle

ELIZABETH TAYLOR

Between Friends
Cat on a Hot Tin Roof
Cleopatra
Divorce His, Divorce Hers
Driver's Seat, The

Father's Little Dividend
Giant
Ivanhoe
James Dean: The First American Teenager
Life with Father
Little Night Music, A
Love Goddesses, The
Mirror Crack'd, The
Place in the Sun, A
Premiere of "A Star Is Born"
Reflections in a Golden Eye
Return Engagement
Sandpiper, The
Suddenly, Last Summer
Taming of the Shrew, The
That's Entertainment
That's Entertainment, Part II
Who's Afraid of Virginia Woolf?
Winter Kills

SHIRLEY TEMPLE

Bachelor and the Bobby Soxer, The
Comedy Festival #3
From Broadway to Hollywood
Funny Guys and Gals of the Talkies
Funstuff
Get Happy
Good Old Days
Gotta Dance, Gotta Sing
Heidi
Kid 'n' Hollywood & Polly Tix in Washington
Little Princess, The
Miss Annie Rooney
Musical Personalities, No. 1
Shirley Temple Festival
Shirley Temple Storybook Theatre Vols. I-IV

THE THREE STOOGES

Classic Comedy Video Sampler
Comedy Festival #1
It's a Mad, Mad, Mad, Mad World
Making of the Stooges, The
New Three Stooges Vols. I-VII
Snow White and the Three Stooges
Stooges Shorts Festival
Three Stooges, The
Three Stooges Comedy Classics
Three Stooges Festival, The
Three Stooges Meet Hercules, The
Three Stooges Videodisc, Vol. I, The
Three Stooges Vols. I-XII
Vintage Commercials II

GENE TIERNEY

Laura
Sundown

LILY TOMLIN

All of Me
Incredible Shrinking Woman, The
Late Show, The
Nashville
9 to 5
Paul Simon Special, The
Saturday Night Live: Lily Tomlin

SPENCER TRACY

Adam's Rib
Captains Courageous
Devil at 4 O'Clock, The
Inherit the Wind
It's A Mad, Mad, Mad, Mad World
Judgment at Nuremburg
State of the Union
Woman of the Year

JOHN TRAVOLTA

Blow Out
Boy in the Plastic Bubble, The
Carrie
Grease
Saturday Night Fever
Staying Alive
Twist of Fate
Two of a Kind
Urban Cowboy

LIV ULLMAN

Bridge Too Far, A
Cries and Whispers
Forty Carats
Leonor
Persona
Richard's Things
Scenes from a Marriage

RUDOLPH VALENTINO

Blood and Sand
Eagle, The
Keaton Special/ Valentino Mystique
Roaring Twenties, The
Son of the Sheik
Tempest, The/The Eagle

DICK VAN DYKE

Bye Bye Birdie
Chitty Chitty Bang Bang
Country Girl, The
Mary Poppins
Outtakes I
Tubby the Tuba
Vintage Commercials

JON VOIGHT

Catch-22
Champ, The
Coming Home
Conrack
Deliverance
Lookin' to Get Out
Midnight Cowboy
Odessa File, The
Table for Five

ERICH VON STROHEIM

Blind Husbands
Foolish Wives
Grand Illusion
Great Gabbo, The
Lost Squadron
Napoleon
Sunset Boulevard

MAX VON SYDOW

Conan the Barbarian
Death Watch
Dreamscape
Dune
Exorcist, The
Exorcist II: The Heretic
Flight of the Eagle, The
Greatest Story Ever Told, The
Hawaii
Hurricane
Magician, The
Never Say Never Again
Night Visitor, The
Shame
Soldier's Tale, The
Three Days of the Condor
Wild Strawberries
Winter Light

CHRISTOPHER WALKEN

Annie Hall
Brainstorm
Dead Zone, The
Deer Hunter, The
Heaven's Gate
Pennies from Heaven

JOHN WAYNE

Allegheny Uprising
America at the Movies
Angel and the Badman
Back to Bataan
Big Jake
Brannigan
Cahill: United States Marshal
Chisum
Circus World
Comancheros, The
Conqueror, The
Cowboys, The
Dark Command
Dawn Rider/Frontier Horizon
Donovan's Reef
El Dorado
Fighting Seabees, The
Flying Leathernecks
Flying Tigers
Fort Apache
Green Berets, The
Hatari
Hellfighters
Horse Soldiers, The
In Old California
John Wayne Double Features I-II
Lady for a Night
Lady from Louisiana, The
Lady Takes a Chance, The
Lawless Range/The Man From Utah
Longest Day, The
Long Voyage Home, The
Lucky Texan
Man From Utah, The
Man Who Shot Liberty Valance, The
McQ
'Neath Arizona Skies/ Paradise Canyon
Quiet Man, The
Randy Rides Alone/ Riders of Destiny
Red River
Rio Bravo
Rio Grande
Rio Lobo
Rooster Cogburn
Sands of Iwo Jima
Searchers, The
Shadow of the Eagle
She Wore a Yellow Ribbon
Shootist, The
Sons of Katie Elder, The
Spoilers, The
Stagecoach
Tall in the Saddle
Three Faces West
Three Musketeers, The
Trail Beyond, The
Train Robbers, The
True Grit
Tycoon
Wake of the Red Witch, The
War of the Wildcats
War Wagon, The
Western Double Feature #2
Wheel of Fortune

SIGOURNEY WEAVER

Deal of the Century
Eyewitness
Madman
Year of Living Dangerously, The

RAQUEL WELCH

Bandolero
Bedazzled
Bluebeard
Fantastic Voyage
Four Musketeers, The
Fuzz
Kermit and Piggy Story, The
Last of Sheila, The
Magic Christian, The
100 Rifles
Prince and the Pauper, The
Raquel's Total Beauty and Fitness
Son of Monsters on the March
Three Musketeers, The
Wild Party, The

TUESDAY WELD

Author! Author!
Cincinnati Kid, The
Looking for Mr. Goodbar
Once Upon a Time in America
Rock, Rock, Rock
Serial
Thief
Who'll Stop the Rain
Wild in the Country

ORSON WELLES

America at the Movies
Battle of Austerlitz
Battle of Neretva
Black Magic
Bloopers from "Star Trek" and "Laugh-In"
Butterfly
Catch-22
Citizen Kane
Ferry to Hong Kong
Finest Hours, The
Greatest Adventure, The
Greenstone, The
In Our Hands
Journey Into Fear
King's Story, A
Lady From Shanghai, The
Last Sailors, The
Macbeth
Man for All Seasons, A
Mr. Arkadin
Moby Dick
Muppet Movie, The
Shogun
Start the Revolution Without Me
Stranger, The
Third Man, The
Toast of the Town
Trial, The
Trouble in the Glen
Tut: The Boy King
Voyage of the Damned
Who's Out There?
Witching, The

MAE WEST

Love Goddesses, The
My Little Chickadee
Sextette

BILLY WILDER

Apartment, The
Irma La Douce
Lost Weekend, The
Love in the Afternoon
Seven Year Itch, The
Some Like It Hot
Stalag 17
Sunset Boulevard
Witness for the Prosecution

GENE WILDER

Blazing Saddles
Bonnie and Clyde
Everything You Always Wanted to Know About Sex
Frisco Kid, The
Hanky Panky

Little Prince, The
Producers, The
Quackser Fortune Has A Cousin in the Bronx
Silver Streak
Start the Revolution Without Me
Stir Crazy
Willie Wonka and the Chocolate Factory
Woman in Red, The
Young Frankenstein

ROBIN WILLIAMS

Can I Do It . . . Till I Need Glasses?
Catch a Rising Star's 10th Anniversary
Comedy Tonight
Evening with Robin Williams, An
Moscow on the Hudson
Popeye
Survivors, The
Tale of the Frog Prince, The
World According to Garp, The

TREAT WILLIAMS

Eagle Has Landed, The
Flashpoint
Hair
Once Upon a Time In America
1941
Prince of the City
Pursuit of D.B. Cooper, The
Ritz, The

SHELLEY WINTERS

Bloody Mama
Blume in Love
Diary of Anne Frank, The
Double Life, A
Ellie
Elvis
Initiation of Sarah, The
King of the Gypsies
Lolita
Over the Brooklyn Bridge
Place in the Sun, A
Poseidon Adventure, The
Premiere of "A Star Is Born"
Shattered
S.O.B.
Tenant, The
Tentacles
Who Slew Auntie Roo?

NATALIE WOOD

Affair, The
Bob & Carol & Ted & Alice
Bob Hope Chevy Show II, The
Brainstorm
Candidate, The
Great Race, The
Gypsy
I'm a Stranger Here Myself
James Dean: The First American Teenager
Last Married Couple in America, The
Meteor
Miracle on 34th Street
Rebel Without a Cause
Searchers, The
Splendor in the Grass
West Side Story

JOANNE WOODWARD

Crisis at Central High
End, The
Harry and Son
Rachel, Rachel
Sybil
Winning

MICHAEL YORK

Accident
Brother Sun Sister Moon
Cabaret
Final Assignment
Four Musketeers, The
Island of Dr. Moreau, The
Logan's Run
Murder on the Orient Express
Riddle of the Sands
Romeo and Juliet
Taming of the Shrew, The
Three Musketeers, The
Weather in the Streets

Video Program Sources Index

Following is an alphabetical index of companies whose video programs are included in *The Guide*. The corporate name, address, and phone number(s) are listed for each. Most companies' programs may be purchased at a local retail or video specialty store. However, a consumer may have to contact the company directly when the program cannot be rented or purchased at a nearby store. Comments concerning videodisc availability are indicated where appropriate.

A & M VIDEO
1416 North LaBrea Avenue
Hollywood, CA 90028
213-469-2411

ACADEMY HOME ENTERTAINMENT
341 North Maple Drive
Suite 406B
Beverly Hills, CA 90210
213-858-1056
800-972-0001

ACTIVE HOME VIDEO
211 South Beverly Drive
Suite 100
Beverly Hills, CA 90212
213-274-8233
800-824-6109

ADMIT ONE VIDEO
311 Adelaide Street East
Toronto, Ontario
Canada, M5A IN2
416-863-9316

AERO/SPACE VISUALS SOCIETY
2500 Seattle Tower
Seattle, WA 98101
206-624-9090

ALL AMERICAN VIDEO
1124 Kings Road
Suite 203
Los Angeles, CA 90069
213-650-2122

ALL SEASONS ENTERTAINMENT
18121 Napa Street
Northridge,CA 91325
818-886-8680
800-423-5599

AMERICAN SPORTS NETWORK INC.
8926 Valley Boulevard
PO Box 386
Rosemead,CA 91770
818-572-4727

AMSTAR PRODUCTIONS
2020 Avenue of the Stars
Suite 240
Century City, CA 90067
213-556-1325

BILLIE C. LANGE
PO Box 386
Cullman, AL 35055
205-734-2993

BLACKHAWK FILMS
1235 West Fifth
Box 3990
Davenport, IA 52808
319-323-9736

BOOKSHELF VIDEO
301 West Dyer Road
Santa Ana, CA 92707
714-556-7918
714-957-0206

BUDGET VIDEO
1534 North Highland Avenue #108
Hollywood, CA 90028
213-466-2431

CABLE FILMS
Country Club Station
Box 7171
Kansas City, MO 64113
913-62-2804

CAPTAIN BIJOU
PO Box 87
Toney,AL 35773
205-852-0198

CBS/FOX VIDEO
1211 Avenue of the Americas
New York, NY 10036
212-819-3200
(Some programs available on LV and CED)

CHAMPIONS OF FILM AND VIDEO
745 State Circle
PO Box 1941
Ann Arbor, MI 48106
313-761-5175

CHILDREN'S VIDEO LIBRARY
1011 High Ridge Road
PO Box 4995
Stamford, CT 06907
203-968-0100

CHRYSALIS VISUAL PROGRAMMING INC
645 Madison Avenue
15th Floor
New York, NY 10022
212-758-3555

CLASSIC VIDEO CINEMA COLLECTOR'S CLUB INC
17240 East Goldwin
Southfield, MI 48075
313-552-1055

CLEVER CLEAVER PRODUCTIONS
4652 Cass Street
Suite 51
San Diego, CA 92109
619-488-2327
619-276-2126

COLISEUM VIDEO
430 West 54th Street
New York, NY 10019
212-489-8130

CYCLE VISION TOURS INC
1020 Green Valley Road, N.W.
Albuquerque, NM 87107
505-345-5217

DISCOUNT VIDEO TAPES INC
1117 North Hollywood Way
PO Box 7122
Burbank, CA 91510
213-843-3366

ELECTRIC VIDEO INC
1116 Edgewater Avenue
Ridgefield, NJ 07657
201-941-4404
800-654-7186

EMBASSY HOME ENTERTAINMENT
1901 Avenue of the Stars
Los Angeles,CA 90067
213-553-3600
(Some programs available on LV and CED)

EPIC PICTURES
1940 South Cotner Avenue
Los Angeles,CA 90025
213-273-8477

ESQUIRE PRESS
PO Box 648
Holmes, PA 19043

ESSEX VIDEO
8841 Wilbur Avenue
Northridge,CA 91324
213-993-5322
800-421-4150

FAMILY HOME ENTERTAINMENT
A Division of International Video Entertainment
7920 Alabama Avenue
Canoga Park,CA 91304-4991
818-888-3040
800-423-5558

FEELING FINE PROGRAMS
3575 Cahuenga Boulevard West
Suite 425
Los Angeles,CA 90068
213-850-6400

FESTIVAL FILMS
2841 Irving Avenue South
Minneapolis, MN 55408
612-870-4744

GLENN VIDEO VISTAS LTD
6924 Canby Avenue
Suite 103
Reseda,CA 91335
213-981-5506

HAL ROACH STUDIOS, INC
1600 North Fairfax Avenue
Hollywood,CA 90046
213-850-0525

HARMONY VISION
116 North Robertson Boulevard
Suite 610
Los Angeles, CA 90048
213-652-8844
(Harmony Vision titles are distributed by Vestron Video.)

IMAGE ENTERTAINMENT
6311 Romaine Street
Hollywood, CA 90038
213-468-8867

INDEPENDENT UNITED DISTRIBUTORS
430 West 54th Street
New York, NY 10019
212-582-6405
800-223-4057

INTERNATIONAL HISTORIC FILMS
PO Box 29035
Chicago, IL 60629
312-436-8051
(Some programs also available in PAL and SECAM.)

INTERURBAN FILMS
PO Box 60
Seal Beach,CA 90740
213-431-1473

IRS VIDEO
633 North La Brea
Los Angeles,CA 90036
213-931-9119

JCI VIDEO
5308 Derry Avenue
Suite P
Agoura Hills, CA 91301
800-223-7479

KARL HOME VIDEO
899 West 16th Street
Newport Beach,CA 92663
714-645-7053

KEY VIDEO
1298 Prospect Avenue
La Jolla,CA 92037
213-697-0544

KID TIME VIDEO
2340 Sawtelle
Boulevard
Los Angeles, CA 90064
213-452-9006

KING OF VIDEO
3529 South Valley
View Boulevard
Las Vegas, NV 89103
702-362-2520
800-634-6143

KULTUR
1340 Ocean Avenue
Sea Bright, NJ 07760
201-842-6693

LDR INTERNATIONAL
PO Box 291285
Hollywood CA 90027
213-382-4065

LIGHTNING VIDEO
1011 High Ridge Road
PO Box 4384
Stamford, CT 06907
203-322-8720
(Lightning Video titles are distributed by Vestron Video.)

MAGNUM ENTERTAINMENT
1940 South Cotner
Avenue
Los Angeles, CA 90025
213-479-0946

MAJOR LEAGUE BASEBALL PRODUCTIONS
1212 Avenue of the
Americas
New York, NY 10036
212-921-8100

MASTER ARTS VIDEO
11549 Amigo Avenue
Northridge, CA 91326
213-368-9220

MASTERVISION INC
969 Park Avenue
New York, NY 10028
212-879-0448

MCA HOME VIDEO
70 Universal City Plaza
Universal City, CA
91608
818-508-4000
(Some programs available on LV or CED)

MEDIA HOME ENTERTAINMENT INC
116 North Robertson
Boulevard
Suite 909
Los Angeles,CA 90048
213-855-1611
800-421-4509
(Some programs available on LV)

MGM/UA HOME VIDEO
1350 Avenue of the
Americas
New York, NY 10019
212-408-0600
(Some programs available on LV and ED)

MONTEREY HOME VIDEO
A division of
International Video
Entertaiment
7920 Alabama Avenue
Canoga Park, CA
91304-4991
818-888-3040
800-423-5558

MORRIS VIDEO
413 Avenue G, #1
Redondo Beach, CA
90277
800-621-0849 ext. 313

MOSSMAN WILLIAMS PRODUCTIONS
Box 7135
Kansas City, MO 64113
816-363-4352

MOVIE BUFF VIDEO
c/o Manhattan
Movietime
250 West 95th Street
New York, NY 10025
212-666-0331

MPI HOME VIDEO
15825 Rob Roy Drive
Oak Forest, IL 60452
312-687-7881
(Some programs available on LV or CED)

MUPPET HOME VIDEO
500 South Buena
Vista Street
Burbank, CA 91521
818-840-1859
(Muppet Home Video titles are distributed by Walt Disney.)

MUPPET MUSIC HOME VIDEO
500 South Buena
Vista Street
Burbank,CA 91521
818-840-1859
(Muppet Music Home Video titles are distributed by Walt Disney.)

MUSIC MEDIA
116 North Robertson
Boulevard
Suite 909
Los Angeles, CA 90048
213-855-1611
800-421-4509
(Music Media titles are distributed by Media Home Entertainment Inc.)

NEW WORLD VIDEO
1888 Century Park East
Fifth Floor
Los Angeles, CA 90067
213-201-0741

NFL FILMS VIDEO
330 Fellowship Road
Mt.Laurel, NJ 08054
609-778-1600
(Some programs available on LV)

NOSTALGIA MERCHANT
6255 Sunset Boulevard
Suite 1019
Hollywood, CA 90028
213-464-1406
800-421-4495
(Nostalgia Merchant titles are distributed by Media Home Entertainment Inc.)

OPTICAL PROGRAMMING ASSOCIATES
c/o MCA Home Video
70 Universal City Plaza
Universal City, CA 91608
213-508-4315
800-257-5209
(Consumer orders only)
(Programs available on LV)

PACIFIC ARTS VIDEO RECORDS
PO Box 22770
Carmel, CA 93922
408-624-4704
800-538-5856
(Some programs available on CED)

PARAMOUNT HOME VIDEO
5555 Melrose Avenue
Los Angeles, CA 90038
213-468-5000
(Some programs available on LV and CED)

PIONEER ARTISTS INC
200 West Grand Avenue
Montvale, NJ 07645
201-573-1122
(Programs available on LV)

PIONEER VIDEO IMPORTS
200 West Grand Avenue
Montvale, NJ 07645
201-573-1122
(Programs available on LV)

PLAYHOUSE VIDEO
1211 Avenue of the Americas
New York, NY 10036
212-819-3238

PRISM
1875 Century Park East
Suite 1010
Los Angeles, CA 90067
213-277-3207

RCA/COLUMBIA PICTURES HOME VIDEO
2901 W. Alameda Avenue
Burbank, CA 91505
818-954-4905
(Some programs available on LV or CED)

RCA VIDEODISCS
1133 Avenue of the Americas
New York, NY 10036
212-930-4700
(Programs available on CED)

REGAL VIDEO INC
PO Box 674
Bowling Green Station
New York, NY 10274
212-244-4270
(Some programs available in NTSC and PAL.)

REPUBLIC PICTURES HOME VIDEO
12636 Beatrice Street
Los Angeles, CA 90066
213-306-4040

RKO HOMEVIDEO
15840 Ventura Boulevard
Suite 303
Encino, CA 91436
818-906-1722

SAGEBRUSH PRODUCTIONS
1940 South Cotner Avenue
Los Angeles, CA 90025
213-479-0946

SCHOLASTIC LORIMAR
899 West 16th Street
Newport Beach, CA 92663
213-653-9570
714-645-7053
818-986-4464

SELECT-A-TAPE
8570 Holloway Drive
Los Angeles, CA 90069
213-652-6552
800-421-4465

SELF IMPROVEMENT VIDEO, INC
77 Ives Street
Suite 282
Providence, RI 02906
401-246-0810

SHEIK VIDEO CORPORATION
1823-25 Airline Highway
Metairie, LA 70001
504-833-9458
800-535-6005

SHOKUS VIDEO
PO Box 8434
Van Nuys, CA 91049
818-704-0400

SILVERLINE VIDEO
PO Box 247
Clayton,CA 94517
415-672-5011

SNOOPY'S HOME VIDEO LIBRARY
116 North Robertson Boulevard
Los Angeles, CA 90048
213-855-1611
800-421-4509
(Snoopy's Home Video Library titles are distributed by Media Home Entertainment.)

SONY CORPORATION OF AMERICA
Video Software Operations
9 West 57th Street
New York, NY 10019
212-371-5800

SOUND VIDEO UNLIMITED
7000 North Austin Avenue
Niles, IL 60648
312-561-2500
800-323-4243

SPORTSVIDEO
7920 Alabama Avenue
Canoga Park, CA 91304-4991
818-888-3040
(A division of International Video Entertainment.)

SPOTLITE VIDEO
12636 Beatrice Street
PO Box 66930
Los Angeles, CA 90066-0930
213-306-4040
(A division of Republic Pictures Home Video.)

THORN EMI/HOME BOX OFFICE VIDEO INC
1370 Avenue of the Americas
New York, NY 10019
212-977-8990
(Some programs available on CED)

THRILLER VIDEO
7920 Alabama Avenue
Canoga Park, CA 91304-4991
818-888-3040
(A division of International Video Entertainment.)

TO THE POINTE HILLEMANN DANCERS
10410 Metcalf Avenue
Overland Park, KS 66212
913-341-0799

TOUCHSTONE HOME VIDEO
500 South Buena Vista Street
Burbank, CA 91521
818-840-6056

TRANS WORLD ENTERTAINMENT
6430 Sunset Boulevard
Suite 501
Hollywood, CA 90028
213-461-0467
800-521-0107

TWILIGHT VIDEO
6430 Sunset Boulevard
Suite 501
Hollywood, CA 90028
213-461-0467
800-521-0107

UNICORN VIDEO
20822 Dearborn Street
Chatsworth, CA 91311
818-407-1333
800-528-4330

UNITED HOME VIDEO
6535 East Skelly Drive
Tulsa, OK 74145
918-622-6460
800-331-4077

USA HOME VIDEO
A Division of International Video Entertainment
7920 Alabama Avenue
Canoga Park, CA 91304-4991
818-888-3040
800-423-5558

USTON INSTITUTE OF BLACKJACK
2140 Taylor Street #1201
San Francisco, CA 94133
415-775-7358

VCII INC
7313 Varna Avenue
North Hollywood, CA 91605
213-764-0319
800-423-2587
(Programs available in NTSC and PAL.)

VESTRON VIDEO
1011 High Ridge Road
PO Box 4000
Stmford, CT 06907
203-968-0000
(Some programs available on LV and CED)

VICTORY VIDEO
PO Box 87
Toney, AL 35773
205-852-0918

VIDAMERICA INC
231 East 55th Street
New York, NY 10022
212-355-1600
(VidAmerica titles are distributed by Vestron Video; some programs available on CED)

VIDEO ACTION
708 West First Street
Los Angeles, CA 90012
213-617-3545

VIDEO CITY PRODUCTIONS
4266 Broadway
Oakland, CA 94611
415-428-0202

VIDEO CONNECTION
3123 Sylvania Avenue
Toledo, OH 43613
419-472-7727

VIDEO DIMENSIONS
110 East 23rd Street
Suite 603
New York, NY 10010
212-533-5999

VIDEO GEMS
731 North La Brea Avenue
PO Box 38188
Los Angeles, CA 90038
213-938-2385
800-421-3252

VIDEO HOME LIBRARY
75 Spring Street
New York, NY 10012
212-925-7744
800-221-5480

VIDEO TRIVIALITIES
303 West Colfax #775
Denver, CO 80204
800-835-2246 ext.39

VIDEO YESTERYEAR
Box C
Sandy Hook, CT 06482
203-426-2574
800-243-0987

VIDEODISC PUBLISHING INC
381 Park Avenue South
Suite 1601
New York, NY 10016
212-685-5522
(Programs available on LV)

VIDEOGRAF
144 West 27th Street
New York, NY 10001
212-242-7871

VIDEOTAKES
220 Shrewsbury Avenue
Red Bank, NJ 07701
201-747-2444

VIDMAX
36 East 4th Street
Suite 734
Cincinnati, OH 45202
513-421-3999
(Programs available on LV)

WALT DISNEY HOME VIDEO
500 South Buena Vista Street
Burbank, CA 91521
818-840-1859
800-423-2259
(Some programs available on LV and CED)

WARNER HOME VIDEO INC
4000 Warner Boulevard
Burbank, CA 91522
213-954-6000
(Some programs available on LV and CED)

WESTERN FILM & VIDEO INC
30941 Agoura Road
Suite 302
Westlake Village, CA 91361
213-889-7350

THE WILLIS MUSIC CO.
7380 Industrial Road
Florence, KY 41042
606-283-2050
800-354-9749

WIZARD VIDEO INC
948 North Fairfax Avenue
Los Angeles, CA 90046
213-859-0034
(Wizard Video distributed by Spectrum Video Distributors. Discs distributed by Vestron Video.)

WORLD PREMIERE
3125 West Burbank Boulevard
Burbank, CA 91505
818-843-0948
800-437-9063

WORLD VIDEO PICTURES INC
11669 Santa Monica Boulevard
Suite 106
Los Angeles, CA 90025
213-477-3088

WORLDVISION HOME VIDEO INC
660 Madison Avenue
New York, NY 10021
212-832-3838

YOU-CAN-DO-IT VIDEOS
PO Box 25060
Philadelphia, PA 19147
215-735-7741

Photo Copyrights

Photo section pictures courtesy of:

CBS/FOX VIDEO
The End, © 1978 United Artists Corporation
Romancing the Stone, © 1984 Twentieth Century Fox Film Corporation
Yentl, © 1983 Ladbroke Entertainments Limited

EMBASSY HOME ENTERTAINMENT
Blade Runner, © 1982 Warner Bros.
The Cotton Club, © 1984 Orion Pictures Corporation
The Princess and the Pirate, © 1944 Regent Pictures, Inc., renewed 1972
That Hamilton Woman, © 1941 Alexander Korda Films, Inc., renewed 1968
Summertime, © 1955 Lopert Films, Inc.
The Westerner, © 1940 Samuel Goldwyn, renewed 1967

KEY VIDEO
Grandview, U.S.A., © 1984 Warner Bros.
Love Me Tender, © 1956 Twentieth Century Fox Film Corp.
Stopover Tokyo, © 1957 Twentieth Century Fox Film Corp.

MCA HOME VIDEO
The Conqueror, © 1983 Universal City Studios, Inc.
The Great Waldo Pepper, © 1982 Universal Studios, Inc.
The Incredible Shrinking Woman, © 1980 Universal City Studios, Inc.
Into the Night, © 1985 MCA Videocassette, Inc.
Madame X, © 1985 MCA Videocassette, Inc.
Repo Man, © 1984 Universal City Studios, Inc.
Rope, © 1948 Transatlantic Pictures Corp., renewed 1975
Play Misty for Me, © 1982 Universal City Studios, Inc.
Where the Buffalo Roam, © 1984 Universal City Studios, Inc.

MGM/UA HOME VIDEO
Manhattan, © 1979 United Artists Corporation
The Yearling, © 1946 Loew's Incorporated, renewed 1973 Metro-Goldwyn-Mayer, Inc.

MUSIC VISION
We Are the World—The Video Event, © 1985 United Support of Artists for Africa

PLAYHOUSE VIDEO
Great Guns, © 1941 Twentieth Century Fox Corporation, renewed 1969

RCA/COLUMBIA PICTURES HOME VIDEO
Absence of Malice, © 1981 Columbia Pictures Industries, Inc.
Buster and Billie, © 1974 Columbia Pictures Home Video
The Caine Mutiny, © 1985 RCA/Columbia Pictures Home Video
Hanky Panky, © 1982 Columbia Pictures Industries, Inc.
Micki & Maude, © 1984 Columbia Pictures Industries, Inc.
Starman, © 1984 Columbia Pictures Industries, Inc.
The Wrong Box, © 1984 Columbia Pictures Industries, Inc.

TOUCHSTONE HOME VIDEO
Country, © 1984 Buena Vista Distribution Co., Inc.

WALT DISNEY HOME VIDEO
Fun and Fancy Free, © 1947 Walt Disney Productions, renewed 1974
Pinocchio, © 1940 Walt Disney Productions, renewed 1967

FRONT COVER CASSETTE BOXES COURTESY OF:

CBS/Fox Video
Embassy Home Entertainment
Karl/Lorimar Home Video
MCA Home Video
Media Home Entertainment
MGM/UA Home Video
Paramount Home Video
RCA/Columbia Pictures Home Video
RKO Home Video
Sony Corporation of America
Thorn EMI/HBO Video
Vestron Video
Walt Disney Home Video
Warner Home Video